Medicine, Ethics
and
the Law

Third Edition

For Denis, Alison, Jessica, Kate and James with all my love

Medicine, Ethics and the Law

Third Edition

by

DEIRDRE MADDEN

BCL, LLM, PhD, BL
Professor of Law, University College Cork

Bloomsbury Professional

Published by
Bloomsbury Professional
Maxwelton House
41–43 Boltro Road
Haywards Heath
West Sussex
RH16 1BJ

Bloomsbury Professional
The Fitzwilliam Business Centre
26 Upper Pembroke Street
Dublin 2

ISBN: 978 178043 915 0

© Bloomsbury Professional Limited 2016
Bloomsbury Professional, an imprint of Bloomsbury Publishing Plc

British Library Cataloguing-in-Publication Data
A catalogue record for this book is available from the British Library

Typeset by Marlex Editorial Services Ltd, Dublin, Ireland
Printed and bound in Great Britain by
CPI Group (UK) Ltd, Croydon, CR0 4YY

Preface

The relationship between medicine, ethics and the law continues to engage academic and public interest in Ireland as we continue to explore issues such as the importance of patient-centred care, respect for autonomy and human dignity, the protection of human rights, and the appropriate role of law in healthcare. Since the last edition of this book was published in 2011, there have been significant changes in Irish society through, for example, the enactment of the Children and Family Relationships Act, the passing of the Marriage Equality Referendum, and the introduction of the Assisted Decision-Making (Capacity) Act, which enshrine important policy decisions which were long overdue. Although parts of these Acts have not yet been commenced at the time of writing, it is anticipated that these changes will undoubtedly give the judiciary some interpretative challenges in the coming years.

The Irish courts have also examined many thorny issues in the last few years such as those relating to gestational surrogacy, the maintenance of life support in pregnancy and assisted suicide in cases which have sparked huge public debate and commentary. In some of these cases the Supreme Court has criticised the lack of legislative guidance clarifying what are essentially matters of public policy. Although these difficult issues will never receive unanimous consensus in any society, this does not exempt our elected representatives from their responsibility to act in the public interest by conducting informed debates and public consultations, listening to the experiences of those affected by these gaps in the law, and seeking to rectify these lacunae in a clear and comprehensive way rather than leaving these matters to be decided by the courts based on the facts of one individual case.

My hope in writing this book is to provide readers with a sense of the interplay between the three disciplines of medicine, ethics and law - the sometimes clear synergies between their underpinning philosophies on some matters and the often different disciplinary perspectives on others. I have aimed to provide a comprehensive and accessible description and analysis of the main legal and ethical issues in healthcare and the relationship between doctors and patients by examining relevant case law and legislative provisions in Ireland, legal principles in other jurisdictions, and useful academic contributions to the field. This book does not attempt to discuss every aspect of health care and choices have been made to keep the book to a (somewhat) reasonable size. It therefore does not deal with clinical negligence other than in relation to the topic of informed consent as there are excellent books already in existence which cover this topic in depth. Other topics such as organ donation, control of fertility and termination of pregnancy may be covered in future editions.

The process of researching and writing a book of this breadth is challenging yet hugely interesting and enjoyable. I am very grateful to my brilliant colleagues in the School of Law in University College Cork for their willingness to share their expertise in helping me to understand areas of law that touch on medical law such as constitutional law, family law, children's rights, freedom of information and data protection, human rights, mental health law and more. Any errors in understanding of these topics is mine alone.

I am also very appreciative of the knowledge and wisdom of colleagues in other disciplines such as ethics, philosophy, sociology, health economics and medicine, within my own university and elsewhere, which I am extremely fortunate to benefit from through participation in inter-disciplinary research projects and conferences. My understanding of and interest in medical law over many years has been shaped by my interactions with students, academic and professional colleagues as well as visits to many universities around the world. Over the course of my career I have also been privileged to be a member of a number of regulatory bodies, expert advisory boards and working groups on areas discussed in this book and have learned enormously from the expertise of colleagues on all of those groups.

I would like to express my sincere thanks to the staff at Bloomsbury Professional, in particular Sarah Sheehy, who has been a pleasure to work with. Her patience and support throughout the last few months have made this process much easier than it otherwise might have been.

On a personal note I continue to learn from my late parents Clare and Alf who taught me the value of hard work, integrity, and the importance of family and I miss them both every day. I am grateful as always to my partner Denis and my wonderful children Alison, Jessica, Kate and James for their love and support. Without them none of this would be worthwhile.

D.M.

July 2016

Contents

Chapter 1   Provision of Healthcare in Ireland

Chapter 2   Regulation of Medical Practice in Ireland

Chapter 3   Protection of Personal Health Information

Chapter 4   Assisted Reproduction

Chapter 5   Artificial Insemination and Egg Donation

Chapter 6   In Vitro Fertilisation

Chapter 7   Surrogacy

Chapter 8   Genetics

Chapter 9   Capacity and Assisted Decision-Making

Chapter 10   Consent and Refusal of Treatment

Chapter 11   Medical Treatment of Children and Minors

Table of Cases

B

F

G

H

N

O

P

Q

R

X

Y

Z

Table of Legislation

Bunreacht na hÉireann

United Kingdom

European Legislation

International Treaties and Conventions

Statutory Instruments

Other Jurisdictions

Chapter 1

Provision of Healthcare in Ireland

INTRODUCTION

[1.01] The government has been involved in the funding and allocation of healthcare resources in Ireland since the 19th century, with many of the principles upon which the present healthcare system is founded informed by that historical context. This chapter will examine the development of the role of the State in healthcare provision from the 19th century and the structure of the modern system. It will examine the legal rights of citizens to healthcare and whether such rights may be enforced against the State either under the provisions of the Constitution, or by virtue of international obligations. The involvement of the government in the decision-making process as it relates to allocation of healthcare resources at a national level is also examined.

THE ROLE OF THE STATE IN HEALTHCARE PROVISION

The historical context

[1.02] The role of the State in relation to free health provision in Ireland can be traced back to the 19th century when, through the Poor Relief (Ireland) Act 1851, the Poor Law bodies took over the dispensaries and provided free services for those who were unable to pay for them.[1] Until then:

> People did not expect the state to provide for more than a minimum level of medical care for the population. Government in these islands had not yet accepted a general responsibility for the health of the population, nor a duty to make medical facilities available to all at little or no cost to the patient…Only the medical care of the very poor and the control of infections associated with poverty were considered to warrant public intervention. These responsibilities were known to contemporaries as 'medical relief' and 'public health' respectively.[2]

[1.03] The provision of infirmaries for the care of the sick and diseased poor in each county was financed by public and charitable efforts. A dispensary service operated which divided the country into districts with medical officers and sometimes midwives to attend to the poor. These medical officers, whose recruitment and educational qualifications were assessed under criteria laid down by the Poor Law Commission, had to attend every sick person in the district possessing a ticket entitling them to attendance

---

[1] Report of the Expert Panel on Medical Need for Medical Card Eligibility (Sept 2014) p 11 accessible at
www.hse.ie/eng/services/publications/corporate/expertpanelmedicalneed.pdf.
[2] Barrington, *Health, Medicine & Politics in Ireland 1900–1970* (Institute of Public Administration, 1987) p 4

1

at home or at the dispensary. These officers were often the medical doctors for the workhouses and soon became responsible for other duties, such as vaccination and birth registration, leading to the emergence of the 'general' practitioner and calls for further development in the health service.[3] At the same time, these doctors were free to devote the time not spent on these duties to private practice. These private patients were normally seen at the doctor's house. 'It was taken for granted that private and public patients should be seen in separate premises, since 'respectable' people feared catching infections from the poor.'[4] This was the genesis of the divide between public and private healthcare provision in Ireland which remains the case today.

[1.04] The public health movement developed with the aim of preventing the spread of infectious disease in Ireland and Great Britain. Legislation was enacted to protect water supplies, appoint sanitary inspectors, destroy unsound food, isolate those suffering from infectious disease and supervise slaughterhouses. However, the apathy with which many local authorities approached their tasks, the poverty of the majority of Irish people and the opposition to increases in taxation with which to fund these improvements, made sure that progress was very slow in this context. At the turn of the 20th century few people worried about the State's role in ensuring access to high-quality healthcare because the limitations then placed on medicine's ability to conquer disease were such that hospitals remained places of last resort for those with untreatable illness, and for those with insufficient means to access even minimum medical care.[5]

[1.05] Pressure for reform of the system began to grow around the early 1900s as access to medical care began to be viewed as a social right of all citizens, mirrored by an increased role and responsibility for government. Health insurance was introduced in Britain in 1911 to give people some protection against medical costs and loss of income due to ill health and unemployment. Compulsory contributors to the scheme included most wage earners, whose contribution would be boosted by contributions from employers and the State. Others could join on a voluntary basis. This insurance was to entitle the contributor to free attendance by a medical practitioner and free medicines. The contributor would be entitled to maternity and sick benefits as well as disability and sanatorium benefits. The difficulty in the Irish context was its practical applicability here in very different social circumstances. Due to the intervention of many factors – socio-political issues, religious hierarchical opinion, the resistance of sections of the medical profession and the financial implications – insurance-based medical benefit was not introduced to Ireland, and the development of the health systems in Ireland and Britain thereafter continued along different paths.

[1.06] A national health insurance scheme for Ireland was again put forward in the 1930s, although with a different emphasis. Around this time, a more modern hospital service was put in place and the National Health Insurance Act 1941 was designed to extend hospital benefits rather than medical benefit. It suffered from problems relating

---

[3] Hensey, *The Health Services of Ireland* (2nd edn, Institute of Public Administration 1972) p 8.

[4] Barrington, *Health, Medicine & Politics in Ireland 1900–1970* (Institute of Public Administration, 1987) p 11.

[5] For a more detailed discussion of medicine and Irish society in the 20th century, see Barrington, *Health, Medicine & Politics in Ireland 1900–1970* (Institute of Public Administration, 1987).

to funding, extensions to the insured person's family, and applicability to those outside the system, such as the self-employed. The consequent lack of attention given to the dispensary service, together with the prevalence of tuberculosis, led to many problems in the early 1940s.

[1.07] Ironically, 'the Emergency' during World War II advanced the health service in a number of ways due to a widening of access to the service and a focus on strategic plans for the development of a comprehensive system. Deprivation and poverty during these years increased concentration on the control of infectious diseases and pressure for the establishment of a separate Department of Health, which was set in motion in 1944. The Department of Local Government and Public Health had, by the end of 1945, a strategy for the provision of a free health service and other short-term objectives such as the improved treatment of tuberculosis and other conditions, as well as the protection of the health of mothers and children. 'The challenge was to persuade the government and the medical profession to follow the road charted by the Department.'[6]

[1.08] The Public Health Bill was drafted in 1945 primarily to deal with infectious diseases (which proved controversial in its methodology), but also dealt with the provision of maternity services, and the compulsory medical inspection of school children. Although much opposition was voiced to the Bill's provision of powers of detention and inspection, on grounds of State interference with individual liberty and increasing control over citizens' lives, there was nonetheless a good deal of support for the aim of improvement of the health of mothers and children. However, due to the inevitable interference of personal political ambitions and rumblings within the medical profession about intervention in its practices, the sponsor of the Bill was forced to resign in 1946 when the Bill was at its final stage. Despite this setback, a separate Department of Health was set up in 1946, with the first Minister for Health appointed in 1947. Many of the provisions of the doomed 1945 Bill were restated with some amendments but the two most controversial issues remained the impact that a free mother-and-child health service would have on the medical profession, and the interference with family authority and privacy imposed by compulsory medical inspection in schools. The Catholic hierarchy was also extremely concerned at the direction of 'State medicine' and its interference with the Church's position on contraception, abortion and sex education. This led to an alliance between the Church and the medical profession in opposition to the provisions of the Act and the more wide-ranging ambitions for reform of the health services to which the government of the day seemed committed.

[1.09] When pressure was put on the subsequent Minister for Health, Dr Noel Browne, to introduce a mother-and-child scheme as provided for by the Act, much opposition came his way, both political and religious. Although the Minister was heavily committed to other issues, such as hospital building programmes and the eradication of tuberculosis, he was obliged to make good on the scheme set out in the Act. His proposals for the introduction of such a scheme emphasised that the services (which provided for children up to 16 years and maternity care for expectant mothers) would be free and voluntary. The Minister also wanted to introduce a medical card as a substitute for the dispensary tickets that entitled the holder to once-off care. These issues together

---

6   Barrington, *Health, Medicine & Politics in Ireland 1900–1970* (Institute of Public Administration, 1987) p 167.

with a hostile relationship with the medical profession led to vociferous opposition to the scheme both from the profession itself and the Catholic hierarchy that eventually caused the Minister to resign having failed to secure the support of his government colleagues for the introduction of his scheme. The influence of the Catholic Church on politics became clear when correspondence between the Church, the Minister and the Taoiseach was released to the press after the Minister's resignation.

[1.10] In the aftermath of this debacle the Government fell and the general election that followed concentrated on health issues as never before. The new Minister for Health tactically decided to introduce a weakened version of the mother-and-child scheme as part of a wider extension of health services enabled by the hospital building programme and other improvements brought about by his predecessor. Despite resistance to the idea of a free health service, an uneasy compromise was reached with the profession and the Church, and the Health Act 1953 became law. Section 14 of the Act required health authorities to introduce 'general medical services' for persons unable to acquire them for themselves or their dependants 'by their own industry or other lawful means.' Such services included a general practitioner medical and surgical service, medicines, ophthalmic, dental and aural treatment, and a range of associated medical equipment.

[1.11] The Act differentiated between three categories of people for the provision of health services[7]- those who were on the lowest incomes were eligible for all publicly provided healthcare services free of charge (35% of the population); middle-income earners who were eligible for public hospital services free or with a nominal charge, as well as mother and child services (50% of the population); and high income earners who were only eligible for free tuberculosis treatment. The first of these groups, ie those on the lowest incomes, had their names placed on the General Medical Services Register and were issued with a 'medical card' which replaced the former ticketing mechanism. These categories effectively remained in existence until 1991 with some minor alterations.

[1.12] The 1953 Act also gave each local authority discretion to provide some services to those who could not afford them on a case by case basis. In 1970 the Health Act introduced full and limited eligibility criteria, describing the first of the two categories described above. It also provided for a scheme to compensate persons of lower income for expenditure on prescribed drugs, and for those suffering from certain diseases, regardless of income. The dispensary system was replaced with a choice-of-doctor scheme which removed the stigma of the dispensary system, allowed all general practitioners to treat public patients and took control from the department over the organisation of general practice. Changes were made to health service administration with the setting up of eight regional health boards, and the profession became reconciled to working within a system that was publicly funded and centrally planned. Eligibility criteria were altered in the Health (Amendment) Act 1991 to provide for full eligibility for those on low incomes who were entitled to the medical card, and limited eligibility for the remainder of the population. Local health boards retained discretion to provide medical cards in cases of particular hardship. The Health (Amendment) Act 2005 introduced GP Visit Cards aimed at low income households that did not meet the criteria

---

[7] Considine and Dukelow, *Irish Social Policy: A Critical Introduction* (Gill and MacMillan 2009.)

4

for full eligibility to help with the costs of accessing GP provided health services.[8] Finally, the Health (Miscellaneous Provisions) Act in 2001 extended medical cards to all persons over 70 years of age, the eligibility and income threshold criteria for which was altered in 2009 and 2013. From 5 August 2015 everyone aged 70 or over, ordinarily resident in Ireland, is eligible for free GP care regardless of income. Free GP care was further extended to children under the age of 6 in 2015.

Private health insurance

[1.13] The foundation of the Voluntary Health Insurance (VHI) scheme in 1957 may have been motivated in part by a desire to provide private income for the medical profession who had, with the help of the Catholic Church as outlined above, opposed a comprehensive public health system such as existed in Britain. Private health insurance generally provides preferential access to healthcare at rates less than the full economic cost, the balance of the costs being provided by the State. The opening of the market to foreign competitors by the Health Insurance Act in 1994 led to the entry to the Irish market of other health insurers, all of whom are required to provide community rating, open access and lifetime cover to members. Health insurance companies must offer a minimum level of benefits to patients in respect of in-patient and out-patient treatment, maternity benefits, convalescence and psychiatric treatment. The minimum accommodation level is semi-private in a public hospital. Health insurance companies must accept anyone who wishes to join, subject to any applicable waiting periods before coverage takes effect, regardless of age, sex or health status.

[1.14] The Health Insurance Authority is the independent statutory regulator for the private health insurance market in Ireland. The Authority monitors the operation of health insurance businesses and advises the Minister for Health in this regard, including assessing the effect of any regulations or new legislation on consumers. The Authority aims to ensure that consumers are aware of their rights, that policies and publicity material describe coverage in a fair and comparable way and that community rating, open enrolment and lifetime coverage are protected and maintained. The Authority also reviews the appropriateness of the procedures used by insurers in their dealings with consumers. One of the Authority's functions relates to the operation of a Risk Equalisation Scheme which aims to equitably neutralise differences in insurers' costs that arise due to variations in the health status of their members.[9]

[1.15] In summary, the main factors that give Irish medical services their character are 'the legacy of the nineteenth century, the role of the state as the chief mediating force between the medical profession and the patient ... the aspiration for a health service comparable to Britain's and the limits set by the formidable alliance of the Catholic Church and the medical profession.'[10] These characteristics, also shaped by economic factors such as severe cutbacks on health spending in the 1980s followed by increased

---

[8] Medical cards are also given to sufferers of thalidomide, survivors of symphysiotomy, children in foster care, persons in receipt of medical cards who are returning to work (they may keep the card for three years) and persons participating in various government schemes.

[9] www.hia.ie/about-us.

[10] Barrington, *Health, Medicine & Politics in Ireland 1900–1970* (Institute of Public Administration, 1987) p 286.

availability of funding with the birth of the Celtic Tiger in the 1990s, have led to sharp criticism in recent years of the disparity in levels of services available to public and private patients, the growth of private health insurance and concerns over lengthy waiting lists for treatment.

THE CURRENT STRUCTURE OF THE IRISH HEALTH SERVICE

[1.16] 'The Irish healthcare system has developed in an ad hoc fashion over the last decades and is somewhat difficult to categorise as it is a mixed system of funding and provision structures. The system is an eclectic mix of elements of the private and national health service models... Services are delivered through a combination of private, public and voluntary organisations and the system has been criticised for being fragmented.'[11] The public system is predominantly tax-funded and is determined annually in negotiations between the Departments of Finance and Health. Funding is provided by the Department of Health to the Health Service Executive (HSE) as well as voluntary hospitals and other service delivery agencies in the voluntary sector.

[1.17] A further unique element of the Irish health system is the State's contract with hospital consultants which traditionally enabled them to operate as salaried employees in the public service and also charge 'fee for service' for private work. There was a re-negotiation of the consultants contract in 2008 under which new hospital consultants are now appointed under either a Category A contract, which allows them to work only in public hospitals, or on a Category B contract, which permits limited private practice in public hospitals. In practice, hospitals rely extensively on junior doctors, who have varying levels of competence and experience depending on their stage of education, to work long hours. 'While the system does result in adequate remuneration for individual junior doctors who work long hours, it does mean that there is a considerable overtime wages burden on the Irish taxpayer, which in terms of quality of patient outcomes does not always represent the best value for money.'[12] The European Working Time Directive has been a driving force in the move to increase the number and availability of consultants and to reduce the long working hours of junior doctors.

[1.18] In Ireland, those without private health insurance[13] are either covered by the General Medical Scheme (GMS) or rely on the public health system. Depending on whether an individual has a full medical card or a GP Visit card, the GMS provides free hospital and/or general practitioner care to holders of medical cards. In 2003 29% of the population had medical cards, and in 2014 this had risen to 40% reflecting the effect of the recession and high unemployment rates during that time. 'A unique element of Irish healthcare, and one that contrasts greatly with other countries, is the mix of private and public patients within publicly funded organisations receiving different standards of

---

[11] Brady and O'Donnell, 'The Structure of the Irish Health Service' in Brady (ed) *Leadership and management in the Irish Health Service* (Gill and MacMillan 2010) 5.

[12] Brady and O'Donnell, 'The Structure of the Irish Health Service' in Brady (ed) *Leadership and management in the Irish Health Service* (Gill and MacMillan 2010) 5 at 9.

[13] The numbers of those with private medical insurance has fluctuated in Ireland in recent years due to the impact of the economic recession on income levels. In 2014, 44% of the population paid for private health insurance, down from a high of 50.9% in 2008. See Annual Report of the Health Insurance Authority 2014, s 3.2.1, available at www.hia.ie.

care. Ireland does provide universal access to specialist services as hospital outpatient visits are free at point of service. However this service may be provided by a non-consultant hospital doctor in training and therefore the standard of care can differ considerably from that enjoyed by patients who are able to attend privately.'[14]

[1.19] The importance and value of medical cards to those who might otherwise not be in a financial position to access healthcare services is undeniable. This became the subject of considerable political and public controversy in 2013–14 when discretionary medical cards were withdrawn from individuals with certain medical conditions who were assessed as not meeting the criteria:

> Contributory factors included a long-established political and public level of dissatisfaction with the Medical Card system; its perceived complexity and operational inefficiencies; a general lack of understanding of the term 'discretionary' in the context of Medical Cards; inconsistency in the assessment for Medical Card eligibility; the evolution over the last 30-40 years of the Medical Card as a valuable asset to obtain and then retain; the inflated value of the Medical Card arising from the automatic entitlements to a range of non-medical benefits; and a lack of appreciation of predictable consequences arising from the 2011 centralisation of the administration of the GMS scheme to the Primary Care Reimbursement Scheme (PCRS).[15]

This led to the establishment of an Expert Panel to address the question of whether medical conditions could be listed in priority order as to their suitability for medical cards. The Expert Panel concluded that such a prioritisation exercise was neither feasible nor desirable as it risks inequity by diagnosis and fragmentation of services. It made a series of recommendations for improvement of the operation and governance of the medical card system.[16]

[1.20] Other health services provided by the State include mother-and-infant services during and immediately after birth, childhood vaccinations, free or subsidised care for those with Hepatitis C contracted from the use of blood products within Ireland, medication and appliances for patients with certain long-term illnesses. Since 1991 all persons, regardless of income, are entitled to free in-patient services in public hospitals and out-patient clinics. Patients who do not have medical cards must pay a nominal amount for in-patient hospital care. Non-medical card holders attending Accident and Emergency services must also pay a fee unless referred to A & E by their general practitioner. There is also a Drug Payment Scheme in operation which limits the maximum monthly payment by an individual or family for prescription medicines, with the remainder of the costs being paid by the State.[17]

[1.21] The Minister for Health is responsible for the development and operation of the health services in accordance with legislation and public policy. The Department, which was set up in 1947, supports the Minister in the formulation, development and evaluation of health policy. Its stated objectives include the strategic development of services; the encouragement of the highest standards of effectiveness, efficiency, equity,

---

[14] Brady and O'Donnell, note 11 at 7.
[15] Report of the Expert Panel on Medical Need for Medical Card Eligibility (Sept 2014) 5 available at www.hse.ie/eng/services/publications/corporate/expertpanelmedicalneed.pdf.
[16] Report of the Expert Panel on Medical Need for Medical Card Eligibility (Sept 2014).
[17] www.hse.ie/eng/services/list/1/schemes/drugspaymentscheme/.

quality and value for money in the health system; the improvement of accountability at all levels of the health services; the encouragement of a customer-service ethos in the health service; the optimisation of staff performance; and the representation of Irish interests in international forums relating to health issues.[18] The State's role in the provision of health services has therefore changed substantially in character from provider of services to the poor to overall regulation of safety and quality standards and an increase in management of targets and objectives within the health system.

[1.22] Health services in Ireland are provided by a number of different bodies, namely Health Service Executive (HSE), voluntary hospitals and agencies, specialist bodies, and bodies established under the Health (Corporate Bodies) Act 1961. Prior to the establishment of the HSE, local health boards had a statutory responsibility under the Health Act 1970 (as amended by the Health (Amendment) (No 3) Act 1996 to administer the services provided for in health legislation and by the Minister. Health boards existed to manage services across geographical areas and were based on population size, local planning and development advice. The Boards were made up of elected county councillors, health and other professionals and Ministerial nominees, who often represented user groups. The Boards' functions included resource allocation, co-operation with voluntary bodies providing services in the area and implementing government policy. Public hospitals, which include regional and county hospitals, and district, fever and orthopaedic hospitals, were managed by the Health Boards and funding was sought from the budget allocated to each board by the Department of Health. The Hospitals Board was also established by the 1970 Act to advise the Minister for Health in relation to the work of hospitals and to regulate the role, number and qualifications of consultants appointed to hospitals. The Health Board structure was abolished and replaced by the establishment of the HSE, which is discussed below.

[1.23] The voluntary health sector has long been recognised by the Department of Health as playing an integral role in the provision of health services in Ireland, through identification of community needs and development of appropriate responses. This sector is the major provider of services to those suffering from mental disabilities in the country. Voluntary hospitals, first instigated in the early 18th century to cater for the sick poor, are funded by the Department of Health but run by boards comprised of religious and lay members. Private hospitals and clinics also exist in the healthcare system, some of which are managed by religious orders; others are managed by commercial enterprises and largely financed by direct payment for services from patients or indirectly through health insurers and private investors. At the current time, such private enterprises exist without any State regulation, although it is intended that this will change with the introduction of licensing legislation in 2016–2017.

[1.24] Specialist bodies have also been established under specific Acts, such as the Food Safety Authority of Ireland and the Health Products Regulatory Authority. These bodies provide an advisory service to the Department of Health on a range of issues, such as food safety and the licensing of medicinal products for human use. Other bodies set up under the Health (Corporate Bodies) Act 1961 for the purpose of advising on health policy and the provision of health services on a national basis, include the Health Research Board (which promotes, commissions and conducts medical research); the

---

[18] *Statement of Strategy* (Department of Health 2015). Available at www.health.gov.ie.

Irish Blood Transfusion Service Board (which organises the national blood transfusion service); and the National Rehabilitation Board (which provides guidance, training, information and public awareness services for people with physical disabilities). There are a number of professional regulatory bodies such as the Medical Council, the Dental Council and the Nursing and Midwifery Board, which maintain a register of health practitioners, monitor standards of education and training and provide a disciplinary process to inquire into alleged unprofessional conduct and unfitness to practise. Professional regulation is discussed in detail in Chapter 2.

Reform of the health service

[1.25] The modern reform of the Irish health services began with the publication by the Department of Health in 1994 of the strategy document called *Shaping a Healthier Future: A Strategy for Effective Healthcare in the 1990s*. It was based on three principles: equity, quality and accountability. On equity, the strategy proposed that access to healthcare should be based on need rather than ability to pay. On quality, it recommended a more modern approach using audit as a tool to ensure the best outcomes. On accountability, it required service providers to take responsibility for achieving agreed objectives.[19] A new National Health Strategy, *Quality and Fairness: A Health System for You*, was published in 2001. Following its publication and the associated strategy for Primary Care, *Primary Care: A New Direction*, (2001) the 10-year Health Reform Programme was developed to implement the actions set out in the Strategy. This also added a fourth principle, namely 'people-centeredness', to the three principles set out in the earlier strategy document. In 2003, an independent Audit of Structures and Functions of the Health System, and the Commission on Financial Management and Controls in the Health Service were also published with broadly similar conclusions and recommendations for the system which provided the background for government decisions on the Health Service Reform Programme.

[1.26] The main findings and recommendations of these reports were, inter alia, that the multiplicity of health boards and specialist agencies operating in the public health sector had resulted in a complex and fragmented system. There was a need for rationalisation, standardisation and much improved coordination within the system, greater clarity of roles, accountability and responsibility, including the roles of the Department and the delivery system. As a consequence of these and other reports, the main elements of the Reform Programme focused on structural reform, legislation, modernisation and improvement coupled with increased investment and enhanced governance and accountability.

[1.27] The structural aspects of the reform programme led to rationalisation of health service agencies to reduce fragmentation, including abolition of the health board/health authority structure. This resulted in the establishment of the Health Service Executive (HSE) as a single national entity to manage the health services, as well as some restructuring of the Department of Health and the establishment of the Health Information and Quality Authority (HIQA). The HSE was established on 1 January 2005 under the Health Act 2004. HIQA was established on 15 May 2007 under the

---

[19] See generally O'Shea, *Clinical Directorates in the Irish Health Service* (Blackhall Publishing, 2009) Ch 4.

Health Act 2007. The Department of Health was restructured to take account of these changes, and now reflects its current core roles of national policy development and oversight of the operations of the State bodies under its aegis. This separation of policy and executive functions is in keeping with overall government policy at the time, which was to divest Ministers of executive functions and enable them to focus on policy and planning.

[1.28] The Health Service Executive has responsibility for the management and delivery of health and personal social services in the Republic of Ireland. Its objective, according to the Act, is 'to use the resources available to it in the most beneficial, effective and efficient manner to improve, promote and protect the health and welfare of the public.' It was given responsibility for the integration of the delivery of services and in so doing, it replaced the previous structure of the regional health boards, the Eastern Regional Health Authority and other agencies and organisations. The HSE is the largest organisation in the State, employing over 120,000 people. Its stated mission is to ensure uniform high-quality, safe services across the public system, efficient management of healthcare resources and accountability for their use.

[1.29] HIQA was established to underpin patient safety and quality in the new restructured health service. A core function of the Authority is to set standards on safety and quality of services and to monitor enforcement of these standards in an open and transparent way. Other functions of the Authority include: undertaking investigations into the safety, quality and standards of services where it is believed that there is a serious risk to the health or welfare of a person receiving services; carrying out reviews to ensure best outcomes/value for money for the resources available to the HSE; inspecting and registering designated residential care services for older people (eg nursing homes), for children and for people with disabilities; monitoring of foster care services, day facilities and children's detention centres; undertaking Health Technology Assessments to inform decision-making for safety and quality; adopting a central role in health information development and implementation of the recommendations set out in the National Health Information Strategy; evaluating information available on services provided by the HSE and other service providers and on the health and welfare of the population, identifying information deficiencies and advising the HSE and Minister accordingly.

[1.30] Part 9 of the Health Act 2004 also established a statutory complaints framework to help ensure a high standard of complaints management within the health service. This came into effect in 2007. Any person receiving public health or personal social services in Ireland may make a complaint about the actions or failures of the HSE, their service providers, or HSE contractors who provide services on behalf of the HSE. The HSE policy called *Your Service Your Say* provides a complaint service for issues concerning care, treatment or practice.[20] An appeal mechanism is provided to the Office of the Ombudsman which is mandated to investigate complaints about the administrative actions of government departments and the HSE.[21] The Health Act 2007 provided for protected disclosures or 'whistleblowing' safeguards. Under the Act, employees making protected disclosures in good faith and on reasonable grounds about issues of patient

---

[20] www.hse.ie.
[21] www.ombudsman.gov.ie/en/.

safety or patient welfare are protected from penalisation in the workplace and from civil liability.

[1.31] Other important pieces of legislation introduced to support the reform programme included the Health and Social Care Professionals Act 2005, the Pharmacy Act 2007 and the Medical Practitioners Act 2007. The Health and Social Care Professionals Act 2005 provides for a system of statutory registration for twelve health and social care professions to ensure that members of the public can be confident that health and social care professionals providing services are properly qualified, competent and fit to practise. There is an overarching Health and Social Care Professionals Council, with separate registration boards for each profession. The first Council was established on 26 March 2007. The Pharmacy Act 2007 reforms the regulation of pharmacy practice by setting new standards of governance, fitness to practise and registration for pharmacy. It also lifts restrictions on qualified EU pharmacists setting up practice in Ireland. The Medical Practitioners Act 2007 provides for an enhanced system of regulation of the medical profession in Ireland. Some of the important changes introduced by the Act (discussed in Chapter 2) include increased non-medical membership on the Medical Council, Fitness to Practise hearings to be held in public, and the statutory obligation on medical practitioners to maintain their professional competence throughout their careers by participation in competence assurance schemes which include peer review and clinical audit.

[1.32] The Clinical Indemnity Scheme (CIS) was established in 2002, following enactment of the National Treasury Management Agency (Amendment) Act in 2000, to rationalise pre-existing medical indemnity arrangements by transferring to the State, via the Health Service Executive (HSE), hospitals and other healthcare agencies, responsibility for managing clinical negligence claims and associated risks. Under the CIS, the State assumes full responsibility for the indemnification and management of all clinical negligence claims, including those which are birth-related. The CIS therefore manages all clinical negligence claims taken against healthcare enterprises, hospitals and clinical, nursing and allied healthcare practitioners covered by the scheme.[22]

Patient Safety and Quality Assurance

[1.33] In the years from 2002–2007 a number of investigations were carried out in Ireland following adverse clinical events. These events, in particular the Report of Judge Maureen Harding Clark SC following the inquiry into peripartum hysterectomy at Our Lady of Lourdes Hospital, Drogheda, 2006[23] and a number of reports into the management of breast cancer, caused significant public and political concern about the level of safety in Irish hospitals and other health services. The general findings from these reports highlighted a long list of failings, such as:

- lack of appropriately skilled senior personnel in acute care specialties;
- lack of senior clinical leadership within hospitals or on a national level;

---

[22] www.stateclaims.ie.
[23] *Report of the Lourdes Hospital Inquiry* (Dept of Health and Children, 2006), available at www.health.gov.ie.

- poor team working within hospitals and lack of integration of primary care professionals in the medical team;
- lack of protocols within hospital departments to deal with referrals between departments;
- insufficient communication with general practitioners following hospital discharge;
- poor communication processes with patients and their families following adverse events;
- lack of structured adverse event reporting, or monitoring systems;
- inconsistent system of root cause analysis of adverse events and complaints;
- poor management skills;
- deficits in staff knowledge of hospital policy;
- insufficient induction of healthcare staff;
- dysfunctional processes and interpersonal relationships and management structures within hospitals;
- lack of engagement and poor working relations between management and clinicians;
- poor communication and protocols within and between hospitals regarding transfer of patients;
- lack of clerical support for consultants with clinical leadership and educational roles;
- difficulties in relation to availability of medical records in emergency cases
- under-developed or absence of leadership of or responsibility for clinical governance programmes;
- lack of or failure to implement formal risk management policies;
- lack of clarity in relation to accountability and reporting relationships within hospitals;
- failure to develop or implement clinical audit processes, and;
- failure to participate in continuous professional development programmes.

[1.34] As a result of these failures in the health system, in January 2007 the Commission on Patient Safety and Quality Assurance was established to propose a system-wide response to these issues.[24] This was in keeping with increased international emphasis on patient safety and quality assurance. The Commission reported to the Minister for Health in 2008 with a series of recommendations in relation to the need for effective governance and leadership to ensure that the environment in which healthcare takes place is supportive of safe and good-quality care, greater accountability of institutions and their management for institutional performance, greater accountability in the different bodies that regulate clinical practice, a strengthened system of information on adverse clinical events and complaints and patient reporting to be formalised, thereby providing a stronger role for patients and carers in providing feedback on care received.

[1.35] The Report of the Commission, entitled *Building a Culture of Patient Safety*, was accepted by the Government in 2009 and an implementation process was put in place by the Department of Health in partnership with other relevant bodies such as the HSE,

---

24 Available at www.health.gov.ie.

HIQA, professional regulatory bodies and educators. It was acknowledged that full implementation of the report would require significant legislative action in relation to the introduction of licensing of all healthcare providers, structural changes in relation to governance and accountability mechanisms, professional changes in terms of clinical audit and adverse event reporting, and investment in information technology infrastructure to support patient safety initiatives such as a unique health identifier and an electronic health record. It will also require structural and organisational changes in healthcare providers, and legislative exemptions from Freedom of Information legislation for certain categories of information, such as adverse event reports and clinical audit.[25] Many of these changes have already occurred through the leadership of professional training bodies and regulatory authorities. Other changes, in particular the introduction of a licensing system for healthcare facilities, still await the introduction of legislation. The key objective of the licensing framework will be to improve patient safety by ensuring that healthcare providers do not operate below core standards that are applied in a consistent and systematic way. The proposed licensing framework will ensure mandatory standards and a legal structure through which HIQA can work with providers to ensure that these standards are met.

[1.36] A further document entitled Future Health, a Strategic Framework for Reform of the Health Service 2012–2015 was published by the Department of Health in 2012 setting out the reform agenda.[26] It acknowledges that the current system is unfair to patients; it fails to meet their needs fast enough and does not deliver value for money. The health system is facing major challenges in the years ahead including long waiting lists, reduced budgets, an ageing population, and an increase in chronic disease at a population level. The promises pledged in this plan include free access to healthcare for all based on need rather than income; no distinction between private and public patients; and universal primary care with GP care free at the point of use. The plan is based on four pillars namely: health and wellbeing, service reform, structural reform, and financial reform. The first step in the roll out of free GP care for all was announced by the Government in the budget in October 2013, with the introduction of free GP care for all children under six years of age regardless of the income of their parents. It was to be introduced in summer 2014, at a cost of about €37 million a year, but there were delays in getting the legislation passed and negotiating the new contract with GPs. It was finally introduced and became operational in July 2015.[27] As a further step in the direction of free universal access to GP care, it is planned that this will be extended to all children under the age of 11 years but no date has been given for this development.

LEGAL RIGHTS TO HEALTHCARE

The enforcement of human rights

[1.37] In the context of human rights and their enforcement generally, there is a distinction drawn between negative rights and positive rights. This distinction is seen particularly in international human rights law, where a significant emphasis is placed on

---

25 See further www.patientsafetyfirst.gov.ie/.

26 www.health.gov.ie.

27 Further details at www.hse.ie.

equality, autonomy and anti-discrimination. There is an awareness found in many bills of rights and political writings of the need to protect the individual against the power of the State. The rights given to citizens limit the State's power in certain respects, for example the right to privacy limits the State's power to interfere in the private lives of its citizens. These rights are often classified as 'negative' in the sense of non-interference rights, which is conducive to the idea of limited government. By contrast, 'positive' rights are seen as giving an entitlement to individuals that the State act in a particular way to the benefit of the individual, such as through the provision of education. In this way, duties are imposed on the State to provide the necessary resources to vindicate these positive rights of the citizen.[28]

[1.38] The enforcement of rights against States in international human rights law has often been seen from the perspective of the types of obligations imposed in fulfilment of individual rights.[29] These obligations may be described as an obligation to respect – this means preventing the State from encroaching on recognised rights or freedoms. In the health context this would mean, for example, the State must refrain from denying or limiting access to healthcare services, from marketing unsafe drugs, from imposing discriminatory practices, from limiting access to reproductive health services. The next obligation is to protect – this means obliging the State to take steps to prevent others from violating rights or freedoms. This means that States should adopt measures to ensure, for example, that the private sector must conform to human rights standards in the production of food, medical equipment and medicines. Next is the obligation to fulfil which requires States to actively create, through appropriate legislative, administrative, judicial, promotional and other measures, the conditions within which the realisation of rights can take place.

[1.39] Positive obligations are generally associated with economic, social and cultural rights and commonly entail financial obligations for the State. For example, if an enforceable positive right to health (the obligation to ensure, under the preceding classification) were imposed on a State, the State would be obliged to provide hospitals and medical treatment in realisation of this right. However, it has been argued that these economic, social and cultural rights do not have a binding force in law and are thus legally inferior.[30] This argument is premised on the classification of rights as those that are justiciable, ie enforceable in a court of law or other comparable tribunal, and that social rights are not directed at government action that can be described in legal terms. Therefore, in the absence of an effective enforcement mechanism in international law in respect of economic, social and cultural rights, these are arguably not legal rights at all but rather aspirations.

[1.40] It is argued against this premise that this argument insists on a false comparison between national and international law. The former system encompasses institutional law-making processes, an executive branch of government and a law enforcement

---

28 See further, Steiner and Alston, *International Human Rights in Context* (3rd edn, OUP, 2008).
29 Van Hoof, 'The Legal Nature of Economic, Social and Cultural Rights: A Rebuttal of Some Traditional Views' in Alston and Tomasevski (eds) *The Right to Food*, (Martinus Nijhoff, 1984) 97–119 at 106.
30 Vierdag, 'The Legal Nature of the Rights Granted by the International Covenant on Economic, Social and Cultural Rights' (1978) 9 Netherlands Yearbook of International Law, 69–105.

mechanism. In international law, these functions are generally performed by States themselves in a non-institutionalised way. It is the exception rather than the rule that norms of international law can be enforced through courts of law, but this is an insufficient reason to deny such norms the status of binding rules. The enforcement of such rules through methods that differ from those available at national level does not detract from their efficacy.

[1.41] It is also argued against the legal nature of economic, social and cultural rights that the realisation of these rights entails financial effort on the part of the State that is not required in the realisation of civil and political rights. It is also argued that the latter rights do not require active intervention by the State and are more in the nature of non-interference rights. However, such distinctions are difficult to adhere to in relation to some civil and political rights, such as the right to a fair trial and the right to free elections, both of which involve the State in their active fulfilment and require financial expenditure. In fact, national and international courts are increasingly interpreting civil and political rights in such a way that they not only imply State abstention but also State intervention or action.[31] This is demonstrated by case law under the European Convention on Human Rights, in particular the right to respect for private and family life under art 8.

The right to health in international law

[1.42] The importance of good health is something that is uncontroversial amongst policy-makers; however, the action to be taken in furtherance of good health at the expense of the State is a topic that has exercised many governments, activists, academics and medical practitioners alike. The legal and moral responsibility of the State to prevent disease as well as to promote good health amongst its citizens is the subject of longstanding debate.[32]

[1.43] The concept of a right to health is a relatively fluid or even ambiguous one. What constitutes 'health' may be considered in the light of international statements such as those outlined below but these tend to describe health in terms of well-being, which may be impossible to achieve in a large part of the world where living standards are extremely poor. In legal terms it is difficult to conceptualise the content of the 'right to health' which could in any sense be justiciable if health is defined as broadly as 'a state of complete physical, mental and social well-being'. Therefore there are inherent dangers in a broad definition of a right to health because it is less likely to have clearly defined content than a narrower definition, and this may severely limit its practical impact.[33] It has been suggested that the standard set by some of these documents is not achievable and, even if it were limited to a reasonable rather than an absolute standard, there would be considerable practical difficulties with implementation.

---

[31] Toebes, *The Right to Health as a Human Right in International Law* (Hart/Intersentia, 1999) 232.

[32] Montgomery, 'Recognising a Right to Health' in Beddard and Hill (eds) *Economic, Social and Cultural Rights, Progress and Achievements,* (MacMillan, 1992).

[33] Gostin and Lazzarini, *Human Rights and Public Health in the AIDS Pandemic* (OUP,1997), quoted in Hervey and McHale, *Health Law and the European Union* (Cambridge University Press, 2004) 9.

[1.44] On an international level, the right to health first began to be claimed during the rise of public health programmes, when people began to be aware of the effects of industrialisation on sanitation, pollution and health. Demands began to be placed on governments to guard against the ill-effects of these developments. Similarly, with increased knowledge regarding the spread of disease, demands were placed on governments to instigate programs of vaccination. These rights evolved in the same era that other social rights were being translated into legal rights, such as rights to education and reasonable working conditions.[34] The claim of a right to healthcare was asserted when objections arose to various economic, social or geographic obstacles in the paths of many people who sought adequate healthcare. Underlying the response to these obstacles was the assumption that everyone ought to have equal access to needed healthcare.[35]

[1.45] It is generally acknowledged that the right to health, if it exists, is not a right to be healthy.[36] This is something that would be impossible to guarantee as good health is influenced by several factors that are outside the direct control of States, such as an individual's biological make-up and socio-economic conditions.[37] It is, however, a right to certain health services and a right to be safeguarded from certain threats to health for which the State can be held responsible.[38] Therefore it may be preferable to refer to it as the right to the *highest attainable* standard of health. Gostin and Lazzarini propose that the right to health may be regarded as 'the duty of the state within the limits of its

---

[34] Harron, Burnside and Beauchamp, *Health and Human Values, A Guide to Making your Own Decisions* (Yale University Press, 1983), 116–117.

[35] Harron, Burnside and Beauchamp, *Health and Human Values, A Guide to Making your Own Decisions* (Yale University Press, 1983), at 116.

[36] Disagreement exists as to the correct terminology to use in this context. The term 'right to health' is most commonly used in international treaties and seems to envisage not only a right to healthcare services but also a right to underlying preconditions for health. It is argued that a 'right to health' is awkward, as it suggests that people have an enforceable right to something that is highly subjective and impossible to guarantee:

> Health is a state of being, not something that can be given, and only in indirect ways something that can be taken away or undermined by other human beings. It no more makes sense to claim a right to health than a right to wisdom or courage. These excellences of soul and of body require natural gift, attention, effort, and discipline on the part of each person who desires them. To make my health someone else's duty is not only unfair: it is to impose a duty impossible to fulfil.

Kass, 'Regarding the End of Medicine and the Pursuit of Health' (1975) 40 Public Interest, 11–42 at 40.

[37] Office of the UN High Commissioner for Human Rights, Fact Sheet No 31, The Right to Health, page 5. See also WHO fact sheet on the Right to Health, Fact sheet No 323, November 2013 available at www.who.int.

[38] For example, the Dutch Constitution contains, in art 22(1), the stipulation that 'the authorities shall take steps to promote the health of the population', which is generally referred to as a right to healthcare. Health promotion is interpreted as including protection against threats to health. In cases heard under this section, the Dutch government has been obliged to ensure access to particular necessary treatments and to ensure that patients are not on unacceptably long waiting lists for treatment. See further Toebes, *The Right to Health as a Human Right in International Law* (Hart/Intersentia, 1999) p 203.

available resources to ensure the conditions necessary for the health of individuals and populations.' They agree that many factors which have an impact on an individual's right to health, such as genetics, behaviour and climate, are beyond governmental control. However, the State has the power to ensure conditions under which people are healthy, and therefore it has a responsibility, within the limits of available resources, to intervene to prevent or reduce serious threats to the health of individuals and populations. Thus, the obligations of States to protect human health apply not only to the protection of the health of individuals but also to the health of populations.[39] International human rights law recognises that certain elements of the right to health will take time to realise and therefore the concept of progressive realisation encompasses an obligation to move as expeditiously as possible towards realisation of the right in light of economic conditions in the State.

[1.46] The recognition of economic, social and cultural rights on the international level is often seen as having begun in 1941 with Franklin Roosevelt's Four Freedoms Speech in which he referred, inter alia, to 'freedom from want'.[40] He went on to explain this freedom as 'economic understandings which will secure to every nation a healthy peacetime life for its inhabitants – everywhere in the world.' In 1944 he advocated the adoption in the US of an economic Bill of Rights which would include 'the right to adequate medical care and the opportunity to achieve and enjoy good health.'[41] After the Second World War, these economic, social and cultural rights were included in various international treaties and national constitutions that were drafted around this time.[42]

[1.47] In 1946, representatives of 61 States signed the Constitution of the World Health Organisation (WHO) during the International Health Conference in New York. Its preamble formulates a right to health for the individual as a right to the highest attainable standard of physical, mental and social well-being and not only the absence of infirmity and disease. The WHO Constitution is binding on States that are a party to the WHO, including Ireland.[43] However, the WHO has been criticised for failing to enforce the right to health through the adoption of legislation clarifying the obligations on States in relation to the right to health.[44]

[1.48] A number of other international treaties and declarations also make reference to the right to health.[45] For example, after much discussion, debate and redrafting, the European Social Charter 1961 refers to the right to protection of health whereby the

---

[39] Hervey and McHale, *Health Law and the European Union* (Cambridge University Press, 2004) p 10.

[40] Address to Congress, 6 January 1941.

[41] Address to Congress, 11 January 1944.

[42] Toebes, *The Right to Health as a Human Right in International Law* (Hart/Intersentia, 1999) p 14–15.

[43] For further information on the structure, powers and functions of the WHO, see Toebes, *Right to Health as a Human Right in International Law* (Hart/Intersentia, 1999) p 33.

[44] See generally Taylor, 'Making the World Health Organisation Work: A Legal Framework for Universal Access to the Conditions for Health' (1992) American Journal of Law and Medicine, Vol 18, No 4, 301–346.

[45] Others include The 1965 International Convention on the Elimination of all forms of Racial Discrimination: art 5 (e)(iv); (contd.../)

Contracting Parties undertake to remove, as far as possible, the causes of ill-health, to provide educational and advisory facilities for the promotion of health and the encouragement of individual responsibility in health matters, and to prevent, as far as possible, epidemic, endemic and other diseases.[46] Since revision in 1996 the latter now also includes the prevention of accidents.

[1.49] Article 25.1 of the Universal Declaration of Human Rights states that 'everyone has the right to a standard of living adequate for the health and well-being of himself and his family, including food, clothing, housing and medical care and necessary social services.' Article 12 of the International Covenant on Economic, Social and Cultural Rights 1976 refers to the 'right to the highest attainable standard of physical and mental well-being'. It is recognised that the right to health does not exist in a vacuum but is closely related to and dependent on the realisation of other human rights, such as the right to safe food, adequate nutrition and housing, healthy working conditions, health-related education, human dignity, life, non-discrimination, gender equality and so on. In adopting art 12 of the Covenant, the Third Committee of the UN General Assembly therefore did not confine the right to health to the delivery of healthcare. While recognising that the right to health does not mean a right to be healthy, it does contain both freedoms and entitlements such as the (negative) right to be free from interference in relation to sexual and reproductive choices, and freedom from non-consensual medical treatment. Positive entitlements include the right to a system of health protection that provides equal opportunity to people to attain the highest level of health. Thus the right to health is an inclusive right which contains essential elements of availability, accessibility, acceptability and quality. It must take into account the individual's biological and socio-economic preconditions and the State's available resources.[47]

[1.50] States are obliged by international customary law and international human rights treaties to give effect to the rights contained therein. Article 2(1) of the International Covenant on Economic, Social and Cultural Rights provides that States have the obligation to progressively achieve the full realisation of the rights under the Covenant. 'This is an implicit recognition that States have resource constraints and that it necessarily takes time to implement the treaty provisions.'[48] It means that not all aspects of these rights can be realised immediately but that States must show, at a minimum, that they are making every possible effort within available resources, to better protect and

---

[45] (\...contd) the 1979 Convention on the Elimination of all forms of Discrimination against Women: Arts 11 (1)(f), 12 and 14(2)(b); the 1989 Convention on the Rights of the Child: art 24; The 1990 International Convention on the Protection of the Rights of Migrant Workers and Members of their Families: Arts 28, 43(e) and 45(c); the 2006 Convention on the Rights of Persons with Disabilities: art. 25.

[46] See Roscam Abbing, *International Organisations in Europe and the Right to Health Care* (Deventer, 1979).

[47] For details of the substantive issues arising in the implementation of this covenant, see General Comment No 14 (2000), Committee on Economic, Social and Cultural Rights, available at www.unhchr.ch. See also the Irish national report under the covenant and criticism in the Department of Foreign Affairs human rights unit https://www.dfa.ie/our-role-policies/international-priorities/human-rights/human-rights-in-ireland/.

[48] Fact sheet no 31 at 23.

promote these rights. This requires States to adopt a national strategy to ensure the enjoyment of the right to health based on human rights principles. However, some obligations are regarded as core and must be given priority by States, such as the right to services on a non-discriminatory basis, access to minimum essential food, shelter, sanitation and medicinal drugs.

[1.51] As mentioned earlier, it is sometimes argued that, due to the lack of a clear enforcement mechanism, these international rights are not effective in ensuring the attainment of the right to health. However, monitoring of States' compliance with legal obligations takes place at national, regional and international levels, aiming to ensure accountability and transparency. Implementation of the United Nations human rights treaties is monitored by committees composed of independent experts such as the Committee on the Rights of the Child. This is carried out largely through examination of reports from States on how they are implementing the rights at a national level. The committees discuss these reports with representatives of the States and give observations and recommendations for further implementation. In addition in 2002 the Commission on Human Rights, (replaced in 2006 by the Human Rights Council), established the office of Special Rapporteur on the right to health to gather information, maintain a dialogue with States, UN bodies and others on the right to health, report on the status of the right to health throughout the world, and make recommendations accordingly.[49]

[1.52] Although judicial enforcement mechanisms at a national level depends on the justiciability of these rights in domestic courts, the incorporation into national laws of international instruments recognising the right to health can enable courts to hear cases relating to the right to health. For example, courts in Argentina have ordered the State to ensure the provision of vaccines and other drugs for medical treatment in accordance with the right to health.[50]

Rights to health and the EU

[1.53] Despite the fact that it has little formal competence in this area, the European Union has become increasingly involved in healthcare, an aspect of EU law and policy sometimes referred to as 'creeping competence'. Litigation based on EU law has resulted in a right to receive healthcare services across national boundaries within the EU, which may have financial and other implications for national health systems and the EU has legislated on matters such as clinical trials, marketing of drugs, data protection and product liability. In addition to this example of direct effect, there is also an effect on national health policy through changing international norms and political pressures. Each EU Member State has its own national health policy, which in turn lends itself to differences in approach across the EU in relation to regulatory mechanisms and interpretation of legal measures. However, as Hervey and McHale argue, 'at least at a level of abstraction, 'fundamental values' such as the sanctity of life, dignity, autonomy,

---

[49] www.ohchr.org/EN/Issues/Health/Pages/SRRightHealthIndex.aspx

[50] Supreme Court of Justice, *Campodonico de Beviacqua, Ana Carina v Ministerio de Salud y Accion Social – Secretaria de Programas de Salud y Banco de Drogas Neoplasicas*, 24 Oct 2000, cited in Fact Sheet no 31 at 32.

privacy, justice and solidarity may be said to underpin all health regimes within the EU although the interpretation of those values may differ considerably in practice.'[51]

[1.54] It was originally agreed that national governmental institutions would have primary responsibility for health. As Brooks explains:

> Fiercely defended against interference from 'Brussels', health has traditionally been an area of sole member state competence, with little-to-no basis for EU involvement. Possessing what Steffen et al describes as a 'unique social psychological dimension'[52] it is a central part of government welfare provision and varies dramatically from state to state. These sensitivities, combined with the lack of legal competency granted by the treaties, make a homogenous 'European health policy' almost impossible to achieve.[53]

However a number of influencing factors became prominent within the EU, namely, human rights, and the drive towards the single market with its fundamental freedoms of movement, people and services. In addition, a number of public health policy concerns at a European level led to political agreement on a limited EU competency in that area as discussed below.

[1.55] On the human rights front, statements came from the Council of Europe, in particular the European Convention on Human Rights and Fundamental Freedoms in 1950 (ECHR) rather than the EU itself. This has led to a number of significant challenges to national policy on matters affecting health, in particular mental health. The Convention on Human Rights and Biomedicine was drafted by the Council of Europe in 1996.[54]It contains provisions relating to, inter alia, consent, privacy, genetics, research, organ transplantation and disposal of body parts. The Convention also stipulates that States are obliged to take appropriate measures to provide equitable access to healthcare of appropriate quality, taking health needs and available resources into account. The latter phrase allows States a certain leniency in the provision of healthcare facilities. A number of EU Member States have either not signed or not ratified the Convention, including Ireland.[55] The Charter of Fundamental Rights of the EU, which has the same legal value as the EU treaties since the Treaty of Lisbon in 2009, contains both classic civil and political rights as well as an extensive range of economic, social and cultural rights. Article 35 provides 'Everyone has the right of access to preventive healthcare and the right to benefit from medical treatment under the conditions established by national laws and practices. A high level of human health protection shall be ensured in the definition and implementation of all the Union's policies and activities.' The provisions of the Charter are addressed to EU institutions

---

[51] Hervey and McHale, *Health Law and the European Union* (Cambridge University Press, 2004) p 5.

[52] Steffen et al, 'The Europeanisation of health policies' in Steffen, (ed). *Health governance in Europe: issues, challenges and theories.* (Routledge, 2005.)

[53] Brooks 'Crossing borders: A critical review of the role of the European Court of Justice in EU health policy' (2012) 105 Health Policy 33–37.

[54] Also known as the Oviedo Convention, its full title is the *Convention for the Protection of Human Rights and Dignity of the Human Being with Regard to the Application of Biology and Medicine*, adopted by the Committee of Ministers on 19 November 1996 (DIR/JUR (96) 14). Opened for signature 4 April 1997.

[55] See www.conventions.coe.int/.

and to Member States when they are implementing EU law, but not otherwise. Therefore, 'in the many areas which still fall outside EU law, the Charter is not applicable and forms no part of the constitutional framework. Thus, depending on whether or not a matter falls within the sphere of EU law, different sets of rights and principles may apply as a matter of Irish and EU constitutional law.'[56]

[1.56] In 1994, the WHO (Europe) issued the Amsterdam Declaration on patients' rights in Europe. In some countries, such as the UK, such rights may be seen as encompassed within human rights law through the incorporation into national law of the ECHR. Hervey and McHale argue that while human rights discourse is clearly influential at a rhetorical level and human rights undoubtedly underpin legal engagement with health, there are a number of difficulties with application of a human rights analysis, such as problems of interpretation due to the breadth of human rights provisions, and the problems associated with conflict of rights. Nonetheless, they argue that despite these problems, the application of human rights analysis will continue to play a crucial role in health law in the future.[57] They also refer to art 35 of the Charter of Fundamental Rights of the European Union but they acknowledge that the human rights approach may have both positive and negative effects. In a positive sense, the application of human rights theories and instruments to health law brings with it a 'conceptualisation of health law that includes legal provision for individual patients' entitlements, in the manner of their treatment, for instance, on rights to informed consent and bodily integrity.' However, human rights also have 'limitations as drivers of law and policy. Human rights provisions may be of rhetorical significance, particularly in policy-making debates and, in some circumstances may assist in construction of specific legal instruments, or the determination of their legality. In other cases, however, their practical impacts are likely to be limited …'[58]

[1.57] Despite the reservations expressed above, case law on civil and political rights shows that several health-related issues have been addressed within this framework of human rights. Such cases concerned the obligation to provide access to healthcare facilities, the obligation not to deprive people of medical treatment, and the obligation to offer protection against environmental health threats.[59] In some of these cases, for example, claims were made that expulsion from a Member State would inevitably have a deleterious effect on the claimant's health, bearing in mind the lack of suitable medical facilities in the claimant's own state. It was claimed that the deprivation of medical treatment was inhuman treatment within the meaning of art 3 of the ECHR. For example, in *D v the UK*[60] the European Court held that expulsion from St Kitts of the claimant, who was in the last stage of HIV, would violate art 3. However, the Court pointed out that, in principle, a person subject to expulsion cannot claim any entitlement

---

56 Fennelly, 'Economic, Social and Cultural Rights in Irish Constitutional law' in the *8th Report of the Convention on the Constitution* (March 2014) at 20.

57 Hervey and McHale, *Health Law and the European Union* (Cambridge University Press, 2004) p 25.

58 Hervey and McHale at 27.

59 Toebes, *Right to Health as a Human Right in International Law* (Hart/Intersentia, 1999) p 233.

60 *D v the UK* (2 May 1997), 1997–III, No 37. See also European Commission, No 30240/96, 26 June 1996.

to remain within the territory of a particular state in order to benefit from medical assistance. In a comparable case, *Tanko v Finland*,[61] the expulsion of the applicant from Finland to Ghana was challenged on the basis that it would subject him to the risk of losing his eyesight in view of the lack of suitable medical facilities and treatments for him in Ghana. The Commission held the claim to be inadmissible but said that 'a lack of proper care in a case where someone is suffering from a serious illness could in certain circumstances amount to treatment contrary to art 3.'

[1.58] Other cases have examined the issue of environmental health and the information to be given to residents in a locality in which their health could be affected by pollutants. These cases have decided that the failure to take steps to prevent severe environmental pollution that might affect health and to inform of the risks to health is a violation of the right to respect for private and family life under art 8 of the ECHR.[62] In the context of the discrepancy between public and private healthcare provision by states, the reporting mechanisms imposed by, for example, the European Social Charter[63] and the International Covenant on Economic, Social and Cultural Rights, mean that international expert committees assess the provision by the contracting states of hospital beds, accessible services, highly qualified personnel and so on. States are obliged to reduce infant mortality, to ensure that privatisation does not disadvantage the elderly or other vulnerable groups, provide accessible services in geographically remote areas, ensure that no discrimination exists in the provision of healthcare to socially disadvantaged groups as well as to pursue other important policies in this context. However, whether states organise their healthcare systems publicly or privately is essentially a matter for each state to decide for itself. International treaty provisions do not require states to organise their healthcare system publicly in order to guarantee equality of access and quality of services.[64] In some states there is a strong public national health system, as in the United Kingdom and Canada, whereas in others the healthcare system is privately organised, as in the United States.

[1.59] Although states are not required to provide a free national health service, they cannot abdicate their responsibilities by pointing to the fact that the requisite services are available privately. The international committees, to which states report under international obligations, are concerned about the increasing tendency of states to privatise healthcare. 'They request State representatives to indicate whether disparities exist between the standard of health services offered in the private and public sectors and whether access to healthcare services is the same in both sectors.'[65]

[1.60] In relation to public health, the Treaty of Rome 1958 which established the European Economic Community (EEC) did not contain any formal legal basis for

---

61 *Tanko v Finland*, European Commission, No 23634/94, 19 May 1994.

62 *Lopez Ostra v Spain* 9 December 1994, A 303C (1995); *Anna Guerra v Italy* (App No 14967/89) 19 February 1998. See also *McGinley and Egan v the UK* (9 June 1998) App No 10/1997/794/995–996 and *LCB v the UK* (9 June 1998). App No 14/1997/798/1001.

63 Each state that has ratified the Charter (including Ireland) must submit reports for examination every two years (from June 1997) under the headings of removal of causes of ill-health, advisory and educational facilities and prevention of diseases.

64 Toebes, *Right to Health as a Human Right in International Law* (Hart/Intersentia, 1999) at 248.

65 Toebes, *Right to Health as a Human Right in International Law* (Hart/Intersentia, 1999) at 249.

measures in this area. However, since 1997, a Council of the Ministers of Health began to meet on an occasional basis. These meetings resulted in acts such as 'decisions of the Member States meeting within the Council' or non-binding resolutions. Following the signature of the Single European Act in 1986, instruments of this kind began to proliferate and public health was finally enshrined in the Treaty on European Union (Maastricht Treaty 1992) with the insertion of a 'Public Health' Title, which opened the way to formal cooperation between Member States in this area. It provided for the first time an explicit legal basis for health due to concern that some health policy areas were not capable of resolution within national borders eg HIV/AIDS. art 129 of the EC Treaty states 'the community shall contribute towards a high level of human health protection by encouraging cooperation between Member States, and, if necessary, lending support to their action.' Article 129 was seen as a 'flanking policy', ie the activities of the EU were limited to support and co-ordination of actions directed towards major health problems, eg drug dependence, research into major diseases, and provision of information on health, all of which related to public health issues rather than individual entitlements.

[1.61] In parallel, art 3 raised health protection to the rank of a Community objective. Since then Community measures have focused on horizontal initiatives providing for information, education, surveillance and training in the field of health, the drafting by the European Commission of reports on the state of health in the European Community and the integration of health protection requirements into the Community policies. Moreover, global multiannual programmes have been mounted in priority areas such as cancer, drug addiction, AIDS and transmissible diseases. Community action has also assumed other forms, for example in the fields of transmissible diseases, blood and tobacco and – in the context of completing the Single Market – through the adoption of legislation on veterinary and phytosanitary controls, or again, in the field of biotechnology, through the funding of research work.

[1.62] Article 129 was subsequently revised in the Amsterdam Treaty of 1997 to enable the Community to adopt measures aimed at ensuring (rather than merely contributing to) a high level of human health protection. This provision was inserted in response to the BSE[66] crisis in Europe in the mid-1990's and, in particular, the ineffectiveness of EU institutions to address the crisis in a transparent manner to reassure citizens. The new art 152 of the EC Treaty has a wider scope than before. It provides that 'community action, which shall complement national policies, shall be directed towards improving public health, preventing human illness and diseases, and obviating sources of danger to human health.' Among the areas of cooperation between member states, the article lists not only diseases and major health scourges but also, more generally, all causes of danger to human health, as well as the general objective of improving health. The Council may also adopt measures setting high quality and safety standards for organs and substances of human origin, blood and blood derivatives.

[1.63] The significance of art 152 is that health protection must now be considered in the implementation of all community policies. There is also an increased focus on health

---

[66] Bovine spongiform encephalopathy (BSE), commonly known as mad cow disease, is a fatal neurodegenerative disease (encephalopathy) in cattle that causes a spongy degeneration in the brain and spinal cord.

promotion, for example, the ban on tobacco product advertising. However, the wording of the article which includes provision for 'preventing human illness' may also be seen as a further extension of competence beyond previous public health parameters. Article 152(5) does however maintain national competence over the financing of national health systems by providing that 'community action in the field of public health shall fully respect the responsibilities of the Member States for the organisation and delivery of health services and medical care'.

Single European Market and role of the European Court of Justice

[1.64] The other driver in this extension of competence for health under European law relates to the free movement principles in the single European market. The European Union (EU) created an internal market in Europe based on economic interests. An important part of the EU's policy is the abolition of restrictions on the freedom of movements of persons, services and goods so that healthcare providers are free to offer their services in other member states, and that citizens are free to travel to other member states to receive services. In 2002 Legemaate claimed that the influence of these freedoms on healthcare was already greater than was often assumed at the time.[67] He advised that health policy decision makers should realize that the European Common Market would have a permanent, growing and substantial impact on their healthcare systems. He pointed to an increasing number of cross-border activities of patients, healthcare providers, insurance companies and health hazards. Legemaate predicted that:

> Situations endangering the health of people in one country may easily arise in another, eg through the export of contaminated products or through cross-border pollution. Patients going from one country to another in order to receive healthcare will expect the rights and quality of their country of origin. Health professionals transferring their practices from country A to country B will have to be subjected to professional rules and mechanisms of quality assurance in both countries, preferably in a similar way. These cross-border movements and the expectations of the parties involved will lead to the necessity to lift norms and standards regarding individual rights and the quality of health services from a national to an international level.

[1.65] The European Court of Justice (ECJ) has confirmed on a number of occasions that health, like any other service, is subject to the non-discrimination principles of the internal market, thus creating a basis for EU involvement in health law and policy. The Court's increasing role has given rise to some concern and criticism as it 'means in essence that an unelected and unrepresentative body is in large part constraining the context in which decisions may be taken'.[68] Greer claims that despite constant resistance from member states against formal policy intervention, the environment of health services policy is thus being shaped by EU legislation and jurisprudence.[69] Hervey and

---

[67] Legemaate, 'Integrating health law and health policy: a European perspective' (2002) 60 Health Policy 101–110.

[68] Hancher, 'The EU pharmaceuticals market: parameters and pathways' in Mossialos et al, (eds) *Health systems governance in Europe: the role of European Union Law and policy, European observatory on health systems and policies.* (Cambridge University Press, 2010)

[69] Greer, 'Uninvited Europeanisation: neofunctionalism and the EU in health policy' (2006) 13(1) Journal of European Public Policy.

McHale also describe the legal order of the EU as one with a 'clearly articulated dominant purpose: that of integration of the markets, economies and (ultimately) related policies of the member states.'[70]

[1.66] Perhaps the most significant development by the ECJ in relation to health rights is in the context of cross-border medical treatment and services. Under Regulation (EEC) No 1408/71[71] individuals (and their families) who travelled to other Member States for employment purposes were entitled to the same medical treatment as that which was provided to citizens of the country to which they travelled, at the expense of their home country. This originally only applied to workers and self-employed individuals but was subsequently extended to all citizens who are on a temporary stay in another Member State. Article 22 of the Regulation provides that authorisation [for treatment in the EU]…may not be refused where…the person concerned …cannot be given…treatment within the time normally necessary for obtaining the treatment in question in the Member State of residence, taking account of his current state of health and the probable course of the disease. Under this procedure (known as E112) citizens may make an application to their local Health Authority for authorisation to travel to another Member State of the European Union to receive medical treatment there. For example, it is possible for a citizen resident in Ireland to obtain authorisation to receive medical treatment in Germany or Austria or any other Member State of the European Union. Authorisation is generally required from the Health Authority in the home state where the treatment is not available in the home Member State or where the treatment cannot be provided in the home state without undue delay. If the authorisation to obtain treatment in a hospital or institution in another Member State is granted, the cost of the treatment will be paid for by the Health Authority in the citizen's home state. This means that where a citizen who is resident in Ireland obtains authorisation to receive medical treatment in Germany, the cost of the treatment will be paid by the Irish health service.

[1.67] The criteria for such funding may be summarised as follows: the treatment is not available in the country of origin; there is an *urgent medical necessity* for the treatment; there is a reasonable medical prognosis; the treatment is a proven form of treatment; and the treatment is in a recognised hospital.[72] In *Pierik (No 1)*[73] the European Court of Justice (ECJ) applied these rules in the context of physiotherapy treatment for a rheumatic ailment, where the individual concerned had already received treatment in Germany, and a medical expert in the Netherlands was of the opinion that no treatment

---

[70] Hervey, McHale, *Health Law and the European Union*. (Cambridge University Press, 2004) 31.

[71] Regulation (EEC) No 1408/71 of the Council of 14 June 1971 on the application of social security schemes to employed persons and their families moving within the Community, contained in the Official Journal of the EEC No L230 dated 22 August 1983, and Council Regulation (EEC) No 2001/83, which amends No 574/72 contained in the Official Journal as above.

[72] The EC Regulations in question are Council Regulation (EEC) No 2000/83 which amends No 1408/71 contained in the Official Journal of the EEC No L 230 dated 22 August 1983 and Council Regulation (EEC) No 2001/83 which amends No 574/72 contained in the Official Journal as above.

[73] *Pierik (No1)*, Case 117/77 [1978] ECR 825.

available in the Netherlands would be as effective as the treatment sought. 'This ruling suggests that an individual seeking reproductive treatment according to a procedure which is not available in her own Member State, for instance, an Austrian seeking IVF with gametes donated by someone who is not her husband or cohabitee, could require her Member State's national health insurance to meet the cost.'[74] However, a subsequent ruling on the same issue suggested that the Court would be unlikely to interpret the regulation to this effect.

[1.68] In *Pierik (No 2)*[75] the ECJ was asked to deal with the question of whether the regulation applied where the Member State deliberately excluded a medical treatment from its national health service, inter alia, on ethical grounds. Although the facts of the case did not require the Court to consider this issue, 'the submissions of the Commission suggest that Member States are permitted to refuse authorisation for treatments 'seriously contrary to the ethical rules prevailing' in its jurisdiction, on the grounds that Member States retain competence to regulate public morality'.[76]

[1.69] In 1998, two seminal rulings by the Court dramatically changed the landscape of European healthcare, opening the door to market forces and healthcare provision in other member states.[77] This was also extended to treatments that were available in the patient's home state. As Brooks[78] points out, the *Kohll*[79] and *Decker*[80] cases are widely considered to mark the beginning of the ECJ's role in patient mobility, which saw landmark rulings accumulate to create a substantial body of case-law. In these decisions, both of which involved Luxembourg residents seeking non-hospital care (eyeglasses and orthodontia respectively) in another state, the ECJ found that the refusal of the Luxembourg authorities to reimburse the patients constituted discrimination against the right to use services across borders. In the following decade, the Court extended and refined its judgements, creating a set of de facto guidelines for the provision of cross border healthcare.[81] The Court confirmed that member states are entitled to impose *some* restrictions on the operation of the free movement principles to prevent instability in their national health service,[82] such as through the requirement for prior authorisation from the home state. The court took the view that there is a difference between inpatient

---

74   Hervey, 'Buy Baby: The European Union and Regulation of Human Reproduction' (1998) 18 Oxford Journal of Legal Studies 207–233 at 216.

75   *Pierik (No2)*, Case 182/78 [1979] ECR 1977.

76   Hervey, 'Buy Baby: The European Union and Regulation of Human Reproduction' (1998) 18 Oxford Journal of Legal Studies 207–233 at 216, quoting Watson, *Social Security Law of the European Communities* (Mansell Publishers, 1980), p 258.

77   Wismar, 'ECJ in the driving seat on health policy, but what's the destination?' (2001) 7(4) Euro Health

78   Brooks, 'Crossing borders: A critical review of the role of the European Court of Justice in EU health policy' (2012) 105 Health Policy 33– 37

79   *Kohll v Union des Caisses de Maladie* (Case C-158/96) [1998] ECR I-1931.

80   *Decker v Caisse des Maladie des Employes Prives* (Case C-120/95) [1998] ECR I-1831.

81   *BSM Geraets-Smits v Stichting Ziekenfonds VGZ and HTM Peerbooms v Stichting CZ Groep Zorgverzekeringen* EUR-lex 61999J0157; *Patricia Inizan v Caisse primaire d'assurance maladie des Hauts-de-SeineElchinov* Case C-56/01.

82   *VG Müller-Fauré v Onderlinge Waarborgmaatschappij OZ Zorgverzekeringen UÀ and EEM van Riet v Onderlinge Waarborgmaatschappij ZAO Zorgverzekeringen* Case C-385/99.

and outpatient care in this context, with prior authorisation in the case of inpatient hospital care being justified on the grounds that hospital authorities must be able to properly plan and organise the provision of services in the hospital.

[1.70] Although the Court stated that prior authorisation from the home country is a justifiable restriction on free movement in the case of hospital treatment, it does not give carte blanche to member states to rely on this basis to refuse to fund travel under the Regulations. The Court has firmly advised that all such decisions would be subject to scrutiny. So, for example, although waiting lists in the home country will be justifiable if they are proportionate and necessary, the Court will scrutinise the facts in individual cases to ascertain whether there was 'undue delay' caused to patients by these waiting periods.[83]

[1.71] One of the most important cases in this line of jurisprudence from the ECJ is *R (on the application of Watts) v Bedford Primary Care Trust*.[84] Mrs Watts was a 72 year old woman with osteoarthritis in both hips. In October 2002, her consultant advised that she needed a hip replacement in both hips. There was a standard waiting list in the NHS in England at that time of 12 months. She was not categorised as urgent, and was placed on the waiting list. Due to the pain she was experiencing, her daughter contacted the local primary care trust to authorise treatment abroad for her mother under the E112 procedure described above. The Trust refused on the basis that Mrs Watts' case was not specifically supported by her consultant, the procedure was routine in nature and a 12-month waiting period was not 'undue delay.' Mrs Watts travelled to France in January 2003 where she was seen by a surgeon and anaesthetist who recommended that she should have the procedure by March of that year. Mrs Watts sought judicial review of the Trust's refusal to refer her under the E112 procedure. She was re-examined and re-categorised into the 'soon' category which meant she should be seen within three to four months. Mrs Watts did not want to wait any longer so she proceeded to have the surgery carried out in France and subsequently claimed reimbursement of her costs from the Trust. The Trust refused to pay on the basis that she had not been given prior authorisation. Mrs Watts sought judicial review of their refusal.

[1.72] At first instance Munby J suggested that the original 12-month delay would be an 'undue delay' in Mrs Watts' case but that since her waiting time had decreased to three to four months, she had not in fact suffered undue delay. In the Court of Appeal, the court considered that the waiting time had to be examined in the context of clinical judgment and the impact of the delay for this particular patient but the court sought a preliminary ruling from the ECJ on the question of the inter-applicability of art 49 of the European Treaty, which established the principle of free movement of persons and art 22 of Regulation 1408/71.

[1.73] The ECJ held that citizens had rights under both art 49 of the Treaty and art 22 of Reg 1408/71 to access healthcare in another member state. The criteria under both provisions for measuring whether there was 'undue delay' had to take into account an objective measurement of the impact of the delay on the clinical situation of the

---

[83] *Patricia Inizan v Caisse primaire d'assurance maladie des Hauts-de-Seine* Case C-56/01.

[84] *Watts v Bedford Primary Care Trust and Secretary of State for Health* [2006] ALL ER 220, Case C-372/04. See useful commentary by McHale, 'Rights to medical treatment in EU law' (2007) 15 Medical Law Review 99–108.

particular patient, their illness, prognosis, and the degree of pain and/or disability suffered. Given that there were no set criteria at the time within the NHS setting out how patients could access treatment under these provisions, this was a restriction on patients' rights by making it more difficult for them to gain access to healthcare abroad. The Court found that, where the delay arising from such waiting lists appears to exceed an acceptable period in the individual case concerned having regard to an objective medical assessment of all the circumstances of the situation and the patient's clinical needs, the competent institution may not refuse authorisation on the grounds of the existence of those waiting lists, an alleged distortion of the normal order of priorities linked to the relative urgency of the cases to be treated, the fact that the hospital treatment provided under the national system in question is free of charge, the duty to make available specific funds to reimburse the cost of treatment provided in another Member State and/ or a comparison between the cost of that treatment and that of equivalent treatment in the Member State of residence. It stated that the competent authorities of a national health service, such as the NHS, must provide mechanisms for the reimbursement of the cost of hospital treatment in another Member State to patients to whom that service is not able to provide the treatment required within a medically acceptable period.

[1.74] In addition to the importance of the specific ruling on reimbursement, the significance of the *Watts* case is also that it demonstrates the widening impact of EU law on healthcare law at a domestic level.[85] Patients may now choose to obtain hospital treatment from any foreign healthcare provider (public or private). They must pay the overseas provider for it and then claim reimbursement. This amount may not exceed the cost of treatment, had it been provided within their home country.[86] Veitch suggests that the ruling challenges the political claim of States to legitimately determine the characteristics of their own national health system and provides evidence of the ECJ's desire for individualised clinical judgment and liberalisation of patient mobility. He questions why a state-funded (ie the taxpayer) national health service should be required to fund those who provide medical services privately in other states and why citizens should be entitled to be reimbursed for private medical care received outside their own state when they would not be entitled to receive it for private treatment within the state.[87]

The EU Patients' Rights Directive

[1.75] Directive 2011/24/EC of the European Parliament and of the Council on the application of patients' rights in cross-border healthcare (known as the Patients' Rights Directive) was introduced to improve the functioning of the internal market and the free movement of persons, goods and services and to codify all the ECJ principles in the patient mobility cases discussed above.[88] Thus the principles in the Directive are broadly

---

85 McHale, 'Rights to medical treatment in EU law' (2007) 15 Medical Law Review 99–108, at 108.
86 Veitch, 'Juridification, medicalization, and the impact of EU law: Patient mobility and the allocation of scarce NHS resources' (2012) 20 Medical Law Review 363–398.
87 Veitch, 'Juridification, medicalization, and the impact of EU law: Patient mobility and the allocation of scarce NHS resources' (2012) 20 Medical Law Review 363–398 at 382.
88 See further comprehensive analysis in Quinn and de Hert, 'The European Patients' Rights Directive: A clarification and codification of individual rights relating to cross border healthcare and novel initiatives aimed at improving pan-European healthcare co-operation' (2012) 12 Medical Law International 28–69.

in line with those discussed above. Although the decisions of the ECJ are binding on Member States, placing these principles in a Directive can have important benefits through the transcription of its provisions into national law and thus making them more visible to citizens.

[1.76] The Directive continues the ECJ's justification of restrictions imposed by member states on the basis of the 'planning exception' which ensures states have the ability to plan and deliver a high-quality service even though this might have the effect of restricting a citizen's right to reimbursement of cross-border healthcare. Under the Directive, determinations on prior authorisation must meet the same criteria as in *Watts* case ie objective medical assessment of the particular patient. It provides that prior authorisation may be refused in four circumstances namely: where the requested procedure would, with reasonable certainty, expose the patient to unacceptable risk; where the procedure would expose the public to substantial risk (eg through the transmission of infectious disease); where the standards of the proposed healthcare provider raises serious concerns about compliance with safety and quality standards; or where the healthcare can be provided within the Member State in a timeframe that is medically justifiable taking into account the current state of health and probable course of illness of the individual concerned. Quinn and de Hert suggest that this final ground is extremely broad and weakens the value of the Directive as most EU countries have well developed health systems which means that the majority of healthcare services will likely be available in all member states within a reasonable timeframe. Thus, they argue that unless there are administrative burdens which unjustifiably delay treatment, in most cases the home state will be able to justify refusal of prior authorisation.

[1.77] In addition to clarifying these existing principles from the ECJ case law, the Directive also establishes a requirement for a National Contact Point in each Member State who will disseminate information on healthcare services within their own country. This is again a further effort to ensure that all citizens have access to clear and accurate information which will enable them to travel for healthcare services abroad. It also calls for, inter alia, the electronic transmission of patient records to ensure service providers have access to necessary information regarding the patient, and mutual recognition of prescriptions.

[1.78] The Directive was introduced into Irish law by the European Union (Application of Patients' Rights in Cross-Border Healthcare) Regulations 2014.[89] This means that the Health Service Executive provides for the cost of publicly funded healthcare in Ireland to be availed of and the costs to be reimbursed subject to compliance with the applicable administration processes adopted by the HSE in the administration of the Directive. Therefore patients who are entitled to public health services in Ireland may opt to access those services in another EU member state, the cost of the services will be reimbursed at the cost of the service in the country where you availed of it or the identified cost in Ireland, whichever is the lesser. The HSE advises that the patient must obtain a referral letter from their referring clinician which stipulates the healthcare required, the health professional abroad the patient is being referred to and the clinic/ hospital/location where that health professional operates from. The patient must ensure the service being sought is covered by the provisions of the Directive as the Directive

---

[89] SI 203/2014.

excludes certain health services such as public health services, long term care and organ transplantation. Funding will only be reimbursed for healthcare that is publicly funded and available in Ireland and which is not contrary to Irish legislation and reimbursement will be made in line with published reimbursement rates. If the service being sought involves an overnight or longer stay in hospital then the patient will need prior authorisation.

[1.79] It is important to note that the Directive does not replace the existing schemes by which a citizen can avail of treatment in another state. The Treatment Abroad Scheme remains in operation with different criteria, although the individual may only apply for reimbursement under one of these schemes. Under this scheme the treatment must *not* be available in Ireland, it must be medically necessary and will meet the patient's needs; it must be a proven form of medical treatment and is not experimental or test treatment; and the treatment must be provided in a recognised hospital or other institution under the control of a registered medical practitioner.[90] The European Health Insurance Card scheme applies to citizens who travel to other member states for business or holidays and require emergency healthcare while abroad. Presentation of the EHIC card at the point of care means that the patient will not be charged for services that are available to citizens of that country free of charge.[91]

Right to health in Irish constitutional law

[1.80] Ireland has ratified six of the nine core UN human rights conventions, including the International Covenant on Economic, Social and Cultural Rights and has therefore committed to realise the right to the highest attainable standard of health.[92] Irish national health strategy documents tend to include some provisions and principles that are consistent with human rights law, such as equity, quality and accountability. However, this does not appear to have been done in any systematic way nor is a human rights framework evident from those policy documents. This results in criticism of the health system as failing to integrate adequate monitoring of data to ensure strategic implementation, inequitable and inadequate distribution of resources, barriers to accessibility of services for vulnerable groups, discrepancies between public and private medicine which leads to separate waiting lists for treatment, and insufficient accountability within the Health Service Executive.

[1.81] The Irish Constitution does not make explicit reference to rights relating to individuals' health. Article 40.3.1° of the Irish Constitution 1937 provides that 'the State guarantees in its laws to respect, and, as far as practicable, by its laws to defend and vindicate the personal rights of the citizen.' Subsection 2 of that section provides protection 'in particular' for the 'life, person, good name, and property rights of every citizen'. Other subsections relate to the inviolability of the dwelling, freedom of expression, right to peaceful assembly and the right of association. As the other provisions of art 40 do not specifically protect the citizen's right to life or a good name, the inference has been drawn that those provisions are not an exhaustive enumeration of

---

[90] www.hse.ie/treatmentabroad/.

[91] For useful diagrammatic comparison of the three schemes see www.hse.ie/eng/services/list/1/schemes/cbd/healthcoopeustates/Comparison_TAS_CBD_EHIC.pdf.

[92] See discussion of international right to health in human rights instruments at para 1.42 et seq.

the rights guaranteed.[93] This has led to the development of a category of unenumerated rights by the Irish courts which, although not expressly provided for in the text of the Constitution, are nonetheless constitutionally protected by art 40.3 as coming within the 'personal rights' of the citizen. For example, rights to privacy,[94] to dissociation,[95] to access to the courts[96], to travel,[97] to legal representation[98] and to fair procedures have been recognised within this category. The development of the law in this way has been criticised by some who view the rights thus far granted constitutional protection within this category as coming from a subjective interpretation by judges who have upper-middle-class fundamental values rather than any objective determination of personal rights.[99]

[1.82] The right to protect one's health was the subject of *Ryan v Attorney General*[100] in which the plaintiff claimed that legislation providing for the compulsory fluoridation of public water supplies violated her constitutional rights and those of her family. The main argument in this case was that fluoridation was dangerous to health and therefore compulsory fluoridation violated her constitutional right to bodily integrity. Kenny J in the High Court found that the plaintiff had failed to demonstrate that fluoridation was dangerous to health, and that in fact it was beneficial in the reduction of the incidence of dental disease, a finding upheld by the Supreme Court. In its judgment, the Supreme Court concluded that one of the unenumerated rights protected by art 40.3 of the Constitution was the right to bodily integrity. In the High Court, Kenny J had held that this right meant that:

> [N]o mutilation of the body or any of its members may be carried out on any citizen under the authority of the law except for the good of the whole body and that no process which is or may, as a matter of probability, be dangerous or harmful to the life or health of the citizen or any of them may be imposed (in the sense of being made compulsory) by an Act of the Oireachtas.[101]

However, although the Supreme Court upheld Kenny J's decision, the Court declined to define the right to bodily integrity or comment on Kenny J's definition of it.

[1.83] Ó Dálaigh J observed that the State has an obligation to take the necessary steps to protect persons' health; that the State 'has the duty of protecting the citizens from dangers to health in a manner not incompatible or inconsistent with the rights of these citizens as human persons.'[102] However, 'it was not indicated in what circumstances the

---

[93] Casey, *Constitutional Law in Ireland* (Round Hall, Dublin, 2000) at 394.

[94] For example, *McGee v Attorney General* [1974] IR 284; *Norris v Attorney General* [1984] IR 36; *Kennedy v Ireland* [1987] IR 587; *In Re a Ward of Court (No 2)* [1996] 2 IR 79.

[95] *Educational Co Ltd v Fitzpatrick (No 2)* [1961] IR 345.

[96] *Macauley v Minister for Posts and Telegraphs* [1966] IR 345.

[97] *State(M) v Minister for Foreign Affairs* [1979] IR 73.

[98] *State (Healy) v Donoghue* [1976] IR 325.

[99] See Hogan, 'Unenumerated Personal Rights: *Ryan's* Case Re-evaluated' (1990–92) The Irish Jurist Vols. XXV–XXVII, 95–116. Also Ely, *Democracy and Distrust: A Theory of Judicial Review* (Harvard University Press, 1980).

[100] *Ryan v Attorney General* [1965] IR 294.

[101] *Ryan v Attorney General* [1965] IR 294 at 313–14.

[102] *Ryan v Attorney General* [1965] IR 294 at 348.

Court would order the State to adopt measures necessary to protect health. For instance, if there was no Fluoridation Act on the statute book, in the light of the evidence given in the *Ryan* case, would the Court order that such an Act be introduced?'[103] This case also demonstrates that in some instances public health efforts will conflict with an individual's rights or civil liberties, particularly in the context of compulsory vaccinations and infectious disease control.[104]

[1.84] Perhaps surprisingly, very few cases have mentioned a constitutional right to health. In *Heeney v Dublin Corporation*[105] a group of tenants in social housing high-rise flats in Dublin claimed that the local authority was obliged under their tenancy agreement to provide an efficient lift service. The court accepted that this was the case and said that 'there is a hierarchy of constitutional rights and at the top of the list is the right to life, followed by the right to health.' However in *In the Matter of Art 26 of the Constitution and the Health (Amendment) (No 2) Bill 2004*[106] it was argued that a constitutional right to healthcare could be derived from the right to life, personal dignity and/or the right to bodily integrity. The Court rejected the existence of a right to health where that would create an obligation on the state to provide free healthcare. 'While the right to health in international law similarly does not create a right to free healthcare, this judgment reflects the overall resistance by the Supreme Court to the recognition of economic, social and cultural rights, and their enforcement.'[107]

[1.85] The rights of the citizen in this context are not restricted to the operation of legislation. They also extend to acts or omissions of the executive that could expose the health of the person to risk.[108] However, as with all the unenumerated rights, they are not unqualified. In *State (C) v Frawley*[109] the plaintiff argued that the State was failing to vindicate his constitutional rights by not providing him with a specialised secure unit during which he could serve his prison sentence. He suffered from psychological disturbances, which resulted in the self-infliction of physical harm. The plaintiff argued that, by failing to provide him with a specialised unit, the State was in breach of its duty to vindicate his right to bodily integrity. Also, it was argued that the restrictions placed on him, such as deprivation of items that could be used by him for self-harm, solitary confinement for certain periods, and the use of handcuffs to restrain the plaintiff, were contrary to his personal right to be free from torture and inhuman and degrading

---

[103] Forde, *Constitutional Law of Ireland* (Cork and Dublin: The Mercier Press, 1987) p 541.

[104] Brazier and Harris, 'Public Health and Private Lives' (1996) 4 Medical Law Review 165; Old and Montgomery, 'Law, Coercion and the Public Health' (1992) 304 BMJ 891.

[105] *Heeney v Dublin Corporation* [1998] IESC 26.

[106] *In the Matter of Art 26 of the Constitution and the Health (Amendment) (No 2) Bill 2004* (16 February 2005) SC.

[107] Irish Human Rights Commission (2005) *Making Economic, Social and Cultural Rights Effective*, An IHRC Discussion Document, Dublin IHRC, p 110. See also Amnesty International, *Healthcare Guaranteed? The Right to Health in Ireland*, June 2011.

[108] Where an individual health board or hospital makes a decision that has negative consequences for the individual, it is more likely that such action or omission would be challenged through a negligence action, as in *Healy v North Western Health Board* (31 January 1996) HC, where a health board was found liable in negligence for discharging from a mental institution a man suffering from depression who subsequently committed suicide.

[109] *State (C) v Frawley* [1976] IR 365.

treatment. The Court held that the restrictions imposed on the plaintiff were imposed to prevent self-injury or self-destruction, and were not imposed for any evil purpose. While acknowledging that the right to bodily integrity applied to acts of the executive as much as to the application of legislation and that this right included the right not to have one's health endangered, the Court held that the executive's duty to the plaintiff was not an absolute one, and had not been breached in this case. Finlay J stated, 'I see no reason why the principle [ie the right of bodily integrity as an unspecified constitutional right] should not operate to prevent an act or omission of the Executive which, without justification, would expose the health of a person to risk or danger.'

[1.86] There have been a number of such cases dealing with the lack of provision by the State of secure institutional facilities for young people and prisoners with psychological difficulties where they may be detained and treated. These cases have been brought on the basis of the failure of the State to vindicate the constitutional rights of those in question. While not founded exclusively on the right to protect one's health, these cases may nonetheless be seen as linked to such a right. The courts have taken the view that this right is not exercisable only against the legislature but also extends to acts of the executive which violate the personal rights of citizens. For example, in *DB (A Minor suing by his mother and next friend SB) v Minister for Justice, Minister for Health, Minister for Education, AG and the Eastern Health Board*,[110] Kelly J, in granting an injunction obliging the State to provide suitable places for detention of troubled minors, affirmed that the courts are as entitled to invoke these rights on behalf of a citizen against the executive, as against the legislature, although the courts would not do so lightly. He adopted the position taken by Finlay CJ in *Crotty v An Taoiseach*[111] where he said:

> [W]ith regard to the executive, the position would appear to be as follows:- This Court has on appeal from the High Court a right and duty to interfere with the activities of the executive in order to protect or secure the constitutional rights of individual litigants where such rights have been or are being invaded by those activities or where activities of the executive threaten an invasion of such rights.

[1.87] Other cases relevant in this context have focused on the obligations on the State to provide necessary educational and medical services to those with intellectual disabilities. These cases have not concentrated primarily on the right to protect one's health but have examined the rights of the citizen to education without limitation of age or intellectual ability. Such cases are relevant in the context of the imposition of positive duties on the State within the economic, social and cultural rights categorisation. *O'Donoghue v Minister for Health*[112] involved an application for judicial review to oblige the State to provide for free primary education for the applicant, an eight-year-old boy suffering from severe mental disability. In a lengthy judgment exploring the issue of education for people with disabilities in Ireland, O'Hanlon J concluded that 'there is a

---

[110] *DB (A Minor suing by his mother and next friend SB) v Minister for Justice, Minister for Health, Minister for Education, AG and the Eastern Health Board* [1999] 1 IR 29. Other similar cases include *TD v Minister for Education* [2000] 3 IR 62; *F (N) v Minister for Education* [1995] IR 29.

[111] *Crotty v An Taoiseach* [1987] IR 713 at 773.

[112] *O'Donoghue v Minister for Health* [1996] 2 IR 20.

constitutional obligation imposed on the State by the provisions of art 42.4 of the Constitution to provide for free elementary education of all children.' This was affirmed by the Supreme Court. The Court accepted that the plaintiff's rights had been violated and ordered the State to provide primary education as appropriate. However, this case was firmly grounded on the obligations imposed by art 42 to provide education, and could not be extended to other fundamental rights not specifically imposed on the State.

[1.88] In *Sinnott v Minister for Education*[113] the plaintiff, through his mother, claimed that the State had failed to provide him with free education and had thereby breached its duty to vindicate the plaintiff's constitutional rights in this regard. In the Supreme Court the State conceded the right to free primary education to the age of 18. On the plaintiff's behalf it was argued that the right to primary education endured as long as the student could benefit from it, which in this case would be the remainder of his life. However, it was argued on behalf of the State that although a person such as the plaintiff who suffers from intellectual disability needs education for life, the State is not obliged by the Constitution to provide education after the age of 18. The Supreme Court took the view that the Constitution obliges the State to provide free primary education, the word 'primary' being interpreted as basic or fundamental. This is an absolute duty. However, the plaintiff's right to education did not extend after the age of 18 years, as this would be extending the interpretation of 'primary', which was historically and logically linked with the definition of 'child', such definition applying to persons up to the age of 18 years. Interestingly in the context of healthcare, in his judgment Murphy J also pointed out that the Constitution imposes no obligation on the State to provide healthcare of any description for its citizens.

[1.89] The Irish courts have not yet considered what minimal amount of medical care and hospital services the State is constitutionally obliged to provide to those in need.[114] Based on the foregoing analysis of related case law, it is unlikely that an action taken against the State on constitutional grounds for failing to provide necessary healthcare services would succeed.[115] Despite the lack of jurisprudence on the point, the courts would doubtless be slow to oblige the government to expend huge financial resources on specific healthcare facilities, as this would substantially interfere with the policy-making functions of the executive. The courts have taken the view in other areas of law that it would be a violation of the separation of powers doctrine if the courts were to be concerned with the distribution of national resources.[116] In order for the courts to equip themselves with the ability to make such decisions, it would be necessary to examine the many competing claims on national funds and arguments as to the correct priority to be

---

[113] *Sinnott v Minister for Education* [2001] IESC 39.

[114] Forde and Leonard, *Constitutional Law of Ireland* (Bloomsbury Professional, 3rd edn) para 27.06.

[115] In relation to the non- recognition generally of economic and socio-economic rights under the Constitution, see Murphy, 'Economic Inequality and the Constitution', in Murphy and Twomey (eds), *Ireland's Evolving Constitution 1937–1997* (Hart Publishing, 1998), 163–181. Also Hogan, 'Unenumerated Personal Rights: *Ryan's* Case Re-evaluated' *The Irish Jurist* Vols XXV–XXVII, 95–116, and Humphreys, 'Interpreting Natural Rights' (1993–95) 28–30 *Irish Jurist* 221.

[116] See Morgan, *A Judgment Too Far? Judicial Activism and the Constitution* (Cork University Press, 2001) pp 62–71.

accorded to those claims. Individual judges have expressed the opinion that matters of national policy are outside of the judicial function and it would be wholly inappropriate for the courts to resolve disputes in this context on a case-by-case basis.

[1.90] 'While the 1970s and 1980s saw the Irish courts recognise a wide array of rights not explicitly enshrined in the text of the Constitution, over time the Courts became increasingly reluctant to recognise additional rights as being protected under art 40.3 of the Constitution. Judicial creativity ceded to judicial caution. Thus, when litigants began to invoke further unenumerated economic, social and cultural response, they have met a cooler response.'[117] In *O'Reilly v Limerick Corporation, Minister for the Environment, Minister for Health, Minister for Education, Ireland and the Attorney General*,[118] the plaintiff, who was a member of the travelling community, claimed that the State had violated his constitutional right to be provided with certain resources, specifically a halting site. He claimed that he had a right under the Constitution to basic material conditions to foster his dignity and freedom as a human person, and the authority of the family with which he lived. His argument essentially was that there had been a failure on the part of the State to distribute adequately in the plaintiff's favour a portion of the community's wealth. Costello J reiterated the distinction between negative and positive rights explained above and stated that usually a claim in relation to unspecified rights under the Constitution related to a wrongful interference in some activity which the plaintiff seeks to protect. In this case the claim was entirely different, as the plaintiff was asserting that the State had a duty to provide him with the resources and services he lacked. Although he did not use the floodgates argument as the basis for his decision, he adverted to it in pointing to the homeless and other deprived people in the community to which the State may similarly owe obligations if the plaintiff's case succeeded. He distinguished distributive justice, which is the distribution of common goods and burdens, and commutative justice, which is fixing what is due to one individual from another individual.[119] He classified this claim as involving distributive justice, which does not fall within the administration of justice function given to the courts:

> I am sure that the concept of justice which is to be found in the Constitution embraces the concept that the nation's wealth should be justly distributed (that is the concept of distributive justice), but I am equally sure that a claim that this has not occurred should, to comply with the Constitution, be advanced in Leinster House rather than in the Four Courts.[120]

[1.91] The learned judge felt that if the court adopted the suggested supervisory role, it would have to make an assessment of the validity of the many competing claims on those resources, the correct priority to be given to them and the financial implications of

---

[117] Fennelly, 'Economic, Social and Cultural Rights in Irish Constitutional law' in the *8th Report of the Convention on the Constitution* (March 2014) p 17.

[118] *O'Reilly v Limerick Corporation, Minister for the Environment, Minister for Health, Minister for Education, Ireland and the Attorney General* [1989] ILRM 181.

[119] Morgan, *A Judgment Too Far? Judicial Activism and the Constitution* (Cork University Press, 2001) p 67.

[120] *O'Reilly v Limerick Corporation, Minister for the Environment, Minister for Health, Minister for Education, Ireland and the Attorney General* [1989] ILRM 181 at 195.

the plaintiff's claim. This would involve adjudication on the fairness of the manner in which the State administered public resources. He continued:

> Apart from the fact that members of the judiciary have no special qualification to undertake such a function, the manner in which justice is administered in the courts, that is on a case by case basis, make them a wholly inappropriate institution for the fulfilment of the suggested role. I cannot construe the Constitution as conferring it on them.

[1.92] In *Brady v Cavan County Council*[121] the applicant asked the Court to make an order requiring the local authority for the area in which he lived to keep the roads in the area in good condition. The local authority argued that to do so would leave insufficient funds to discharge some of its other functions such as public housing provision, and water and sewerage facilities. The Supreme Court held, in rejecting the application, that the local authority did not have the means to comply with such an order and it was not known whether central government would assist in this regard. While this case may be confined to the facts which turned on the relative poverty of this particular local authority and the length of time it would have taken to bring the roads into a satisfactory condition, nonetheless the case is also important in that it shows judicial 'sensitivity to the general financial implications of colossal expenditure for public bodies'[122], as it also explored the notion that the Oireachtas was not and could not be a party to these proceedings on the basis of the doctrine of separation of powers.

[1.93] A further case in 2001 demonstrates a similar line of reasoning. In *TD v Minister for Education*[123] the applicants were disadvantaged and vulnerable children who needed accommodation and treatment in high support units. Although there was a policy direction in existence to provide for the care of these applicants, it was argued that the Minister had not taken steps to implement the policy. In relation to the question of whether the applicants had a right to be placed and maintained in a secure residential unit so as to ensure their education, the court expressed 'gravest doubts' as to whether it should at any stage assume the function of declaring socio-economic rights to be unenumerated rights guaranteed by art 40.[124] Hardiman J was of the view that the courts should not assume a policy making role in relation to 'the multitude of social and economic issues which form the staple of public debate.' He said this would involve the transfer of power from the political branches to the courts contrary to the doctrine of the separation of powers; the courts are not democratically accountable to the people as politicians are; the courts do not have any special qualifications or experiences to make such decisions, nor is the adversarial process appropriate for such decision-making.[125]

[1.94] In the context of the imposition of specific obligations on the State regarding the provision of healthcare, it may be argued that the executive should be bound by the Constitution in the same way as any other citizen. If there is a right to health included in the unspecified personal rights protected by art 40.3, the executive as well as the

---

[121] *Brady v Cavan County Council* [2000] 1 ILRM 81.

[122] Morgan, *A Judgment Too Far, Judicial Activism and the Constitution* (Cork University Press, 2001) p 67.

[123] *TD v Minister for Education* [2001] 4 IR 259.

[124] *TD v Minister for Education* [2001] 4 IR 259 at 282.

[125] See counter-arguments from Whyte, in 'The Role of the Supreme Court in our Democracy: A response to Mr Justice Hardiman' (2006) 28 DULJ 1.

legislature should be bound by the terms of the Constitution.[126] However, it has been suggested that a more sophisticated approach to understanding our political system indicates that this was not intended by the drafters of the Constitution. On the contrary, it was feared that putting socio-economic guarantees into the fundamental rights provisions of the Constitution would open the floodgates for the imposition of many difficult and costly obligations on the State. Therefore, these rights were instead inserted into a clause headed Directive Principles of Social Policy, contained in art 45 and devolved exclusively to the Oireachtas by that article. The intention was to ensure that, unlike all the other constitutional rights, they would not be justiciable or cognisable by the courts, a fact that has led to the marginalisation of their impact in constitutional terms. The only exception was the free primary education provisions in art 42.4, the only enforceable socio-economic right in the Constitution.[127]

[1.95] The Report of the Constitution Review Group[128] examined the issue of whether specific socio-economic rights should be included in the Constitution and recommended against such a step. One of the arguments adopted by the Group centred on the fact that the development of fundamental rights is a matter for political decision rather than a judicial function:

> These are essentially political matters which in a democracy it should be the responsibility of the elected representatives of the people to address and determine. It would be a distortion of democracy to transfer decisions on major issues of policy and practicality from the Government and the Oireachtas, elected to represent the people and do their will, to an unelected judiciary.[129]

While favouring the identification of fundamental rights in the Constitution as far as possible, the Group also felt that the concept of unenumerated rights had considerable merit, as it allowed for the evolution of social attitudes and approaches to justice over time. However, the Group was reluctant to entrust the further development of socio-economic rights to 'subjective judicial appraisal' bearing in mind that judges can never be completely independent of the social class, gender, professional background and religion that has shaped their individual attitudes to such issues.

[1.96] The Review Group also stressed the financial cost objection to the inclusion of socio-economic rights in the Constitution. It argued that 'It would not accord with democratic principles to confer absolute personal rights in the Constitution in relation to economic or social objectives, however desirable in themselves, and leave the Oireachtas with no option but to discharge the cost, whatever it might be, as determined by the judiciary.'[130] However, this has been criticised by the Irish Commission for Justice and Peace, which points out that the Group expressly recommends the inclusion of the specific right of access to the courts, acknowledging that such a positive right would

---

[126] As Morgan notes from Kelly J in *DB*, 'the Minister for Health is not immune from a court order vindicating the personal rights of a citizen.' Morgan, *A Judgment Too Far, Judicial Activism and the Constitution* (Cork University Press, 2001) p 69.

[127] Hogan, 'Unelected Judges Cannot Remedy Some Wrongs', (2001) The Irish Times, 14 July.

[128] *The Report of the Constitution Review Group* (Government Stationery Office, 1996).

[129] *The Report of the Constitution Review Group* (Government Stationery Office, 1996) p 235.

[130] *The Report of the Constitution Review Group* (Government Stationery Office, 1996) p 236.

involve financial expenditure and without clarifying exactly how the State is to implement such a right.[131]

[1.97] The Convention on the Constitution also considered the issue of economic, social and cultural rights in 2014. It discussed the complexity of enforceability of such rights generally, the appropriateness or otherwise of effectively placing responsibility for such rights in the hands of the judiciary, the financial implications of explicit constitutional recognition of such rights, the role of the government in determining the allocation of public expenditure, and other options by which such rights might be strengthened. A large majority (85%) of members supported changing the Constitution to strengthen the protection of economic, social and cultural rights. Many supported further consideration of the issue. The Convention recommended progressive realisation of such rights within the State's available resources, and explicitly identified certain rights such as housing and healthcare, which it recommended should be enumerated in the Constitution.[132]

[1.98] In summary, it is unlikely that the Supreme Court would decide that the Constitution gives the judiciary power to investigate and allocate public expenditure in the context of a right to health or any other economic, social and cultural rights.[133] At the present time this would be seen as unjustifiable interference with the power of the executive and a violation of the separation of powers doctrine.[134] Arguably, the cases that have indicated that such a power might be available to the courts have not discussed the

---

[131] Irish Commission for Justice and Peace, *Re-Righting the Constitution, The Case for New Social and Economic Rights: Housing, Health, Nutrition, Adequate Standard of Living.* (Genprint, 1998) at 11–12. This report called for specific inclusion in the Constitution of specific rights such as the right to health in the following terms:

> Each person has the right to health including the right to emergency medical assistance. The enjoyment of this right should in the first place be ensured by the initiative and efforts of each person. Where individual persons or their dependants are unable adequately to exercise or enjoy the right to health, the State shall ensure that this right is respected and protected. As guardian of the common good the State shall take reasonable steps to promote the general and progressive enjoyment of this right, in view of actual conditions, resources and standards, at 27.

[132] *8th Report of the Convention on the Constitution* (March 2014).

[133] Laurie et al take the view that although it may seem surprising that there have not been more actions brought by patients who feel that the State has failed in its duty to provide healthcare services, this is probably due to the 'extreme improbability of a successful outcome.' Laurie, Harmon and Porter, *Law and Medical Ethics* (10th edn, OUP, 2016), para 11.25

[134] The classic case in England is *R v Secretary of State for Social Services, ex parte Hincks* (1979) 123 Sol Jo 436, in which patients in an orthopaedic hospital sought a declaration that the health authorities were in breach of their duty in that the patients had been forced to wait for an unreasonable time for treatment due to a shortage of facilities arising in part from a decision not to add a new block to the hospital on cost grounds. Wien J said it was not the court's function to direct Parliament as to what funds to make available to the health service nor how to allocate such resources as had been made available. The court could only intervene if the Minister acted unreasonably or in frustration of the Act. Similar decisions were made in *R v Central Birmingham Health Authority, ex parte Walker* (1987) 3 BMLR 32, and *R v Central Birmingham Health Authority, ex parte Collier* (6 January 1988). See Newdick, 'Rights to NHS Resources After the 1990 Act' (1993) 1 Med L Rev 53, and Miller, 'Denial of Health Care and Informed Consent in English and American Law' (1992) 18 Am J Law Med 37.

dangers of such an approach as fully as they might have done. 'It seems inappropriate for an unelected body to assert the power... to increase public expenditure.'[135] However, although the separation of powers doctrine has stood the test of time and the public/ private divide may become fragile if too many openings are created for State action and interference, it may in the future be possible to view economic, social and cultural rights in a way that brings them into closer alignment with the separation of powers doctrine.[136]

ALLOCATION OF HEALTHCARE RESOURCES

National policy-making

[1.99] Clearly, good health is vitally important and few would dispute that access to essential healthcare should not hinge on one's ability to pay.[137] However, 'at its most basic level, it is literally impossible for government to guarantee good health to its citizens.'[138] Because of resource scarcity, access to healthcare and related technologies in practice hinges not on legal requirements, but on government budget decisions and, at the private level, on clinical judgements of health professionals and the incomes of individual patients. In keeping with their responsibility to provide for the general welfare, governments have much of the responsibility for defining public health objectives for the whole society and providing the resources to achieve them. Those determinations always involve negotiation, trade-offs, and the balancing of interests.'[139] All are agreed that '[N]o resources are infinite... It is clear that it is impossible to provide every form of therapy for everyone – some sort of selective distribution must be made.'[140] The wide spectrum of decisions that must be made on a national level in the context of resource allocation in healthcare is well described by Kass as follows:

> Personnel and facilities for medical research and treatment are scarce resources. Is the development of a new technology the best use of scarce resources, given current circumstances? How should we balance efforts aimed at prevention against those aimed at cure, or either of these against efforts to redesign the species? How should we balance the delivery of available levels of care against further basic research? More fundamentally, how should we balance efforts in biology and medicine against efforts to eliminate poverty, pollution, urban decay, discrimination, and poor education? This last question about distribution is perhaps the most profound.[141]

[1.100] In relation to the issue of access to or allocation of healthcare services, the principle of justice is one of the most important bioethical principles in this balancing of

---

135 Morgan, *A Judgment Too Far, Judicial Activism and the Constitution* (Cork University Press, 2001) p 70.

136 Quinn, 'Rethinking the Nature of Economic, Social and Cultural Rights', in Costello (ed) *Fundamental Social Rights, Current European Legal Protection and the Challenge of the EU Charter on Fundamental Rights* (Irish Centre for European Law, 2001) No 28 at 35–54.

137 This part is based on the Report of the Expert Panel on Medical Need for Medical Card Eligibility (Sept 2014) Ch 2. See footnote 1 above.

138 Goodman, 'Is there a right to health?' (2005) Journal of Medicine and Philosophy 30:643–662.

139 Goodman, 'Is there a right to health?' (2005) Journal of Medicine and Philosophy 30:643–662 at 655.

140 Laurie, Harmon and Porter, *Law and Medical Ethics*, (10th edn, OUP, 2016), para 11.01.

141 Kass, 'The New Biology: What Price Relieving Man's Estate?' (1971) Science 174; 779.

interests and has been addressed in bioethics literature since the 1980s. If we accept that the health system must be sustainable[142] and that it is impossible for any health system to provide everything for everyone, then setting limits on expenditure of shared societal resources is ethically required and must be done in a just, transparent and compassionate way. Although the word rationing is usually avoided as it raises memories of war-time scarcity and poverty, it is arguably a more honest and accurate description of the reality of healthcare systems worldwide as it refers to the controlled allocation of some scarce resource or goods and it implies that some limits are placed on availability. In healthcare this applies to treatments, services, pharmaceuticals, medical procedures and so on. When healthcare resources are rationed, patients may be restricted to certain treatments or placed on waiting lists for treatments. It means that someone somewhere has made a decision about the limits of what is provided or how it is provided, a priority setting decision.[143] Although rationing of healthcare resources sounds like an unethical proposition as it interferes with individual choices and values, it is inevitable in all healthcare systems around the world. Indeed there are those who argue that healthcare rationing is not only necessary but also desirable. 'The careful rationing of healthcare is one of the factors that make a healthcare system work well. The best healthcare systems in the world do it.'[144]

[1.101] Hard ethical choices are sometimes masked in clinical or technical terms as the idea of rationing is unpalatable and unpopular since it means in reality that some people who may benefit from healthcare may have to do without it. However, it is important to acknowledge that rationing is not limited to state run or sponsored public health systems, it also takes place in private health insurance and in the most affluent of societies. When the government decides which drugs to subsidise, it is engaged in rationing; when it decides where to build a new hospital, it is engaged in rationing; when it introduces a cancer screening programme it is engaged in rationing because as a result of those priority-setting decisions, other drugs, citizens and patients will not be funded. Private insurers carry out the same exercises by loading premiums of new entrants with pre-existing conditions, or by agreeing to only fund certain treatments. It is inevitable that some patients will be disadvantaged by the limits that are set.

[1.102] There are various approaches in moral theory that one might take to this issue: libertarianism, utilitarianism, egalitarianism etc. Nearly all appear to take the view that just societies should provide all their members with guaranteed access to at least a decent minimum of healthcare, although there is little consensus on what the decent minimum entails. The development of any national strategy to deal with these questions must first decide what resources arc available nationally to deal with healthcare. That is essentially a political question. Then it must be determined how the resources are to be divided between all of those who need them. The latter problem is that of distributive justice and involves a determination or prioritisation of needs in the community. The mechanism by which such choices are made is often the subject of intense criticism.

---

[142] Healthy Ireland, a Framework for Improved Health and Wellbeing 2013–2025, Appendix 2 www.hse.ie.

[143] See generally, Bognar and Hirose, *The Ethics of Rationing* (Routledge Press, 2014).

[144] Bognar and Hirose, *The Ethics of Rationing* (Routledge Press, 2014) at 2.

[1.103] There are four main theories of justice that may be useful in this context: utilitarianism, egalitarianism, libertarianism and contractarianism. When applied to healthcare, each of these theories provides guidance on a just system of healthcare distribution. Although this section can only give general indications of how each system might work in practical settings, it is nonetheless useful to examine the different methods briefly to demonstrate the benefits and challenges that each of these theories involves.

[1.104] Firstly, we will look at utilitarianism. The most well-known proponent of this theory of justice, John Stuart Mill, argued that a just allocation provides the greatest good to the greatest number of people.[145] In applying this theory to healthcare allocation, utilitarians would therefore seek to promote the maximum benefit for the greatest number. Thus, they would seek to prevent or cure the most common illnesses, adopt programmes that help many rather than few persons, and generally use funds where they will have the greatest impact for most people. Although this approach certainly has appeal, the consequence of this might be that expensive treatments for few people would not be provided at the expense of programmes to help provide basic care for larger numbers.[146] Although all citizens would potentially benefit from the division of services in this way, utilitarianism would also justify preferential treatment of children on the basis that such treatment will offer the most years of benefit.[147] On this basis, funding of routine care, screening, immunisations, and other prevention programmes would be more beneficial than the development of a few specialised therapies that might save relatively few children. Problems arise in the application of this theory in trying to calculate what is best for the greatest number, and whole groups could be excluded or discriminated against if they have rare or expensive conditions, in the interests of the common good.

[1.105] Secondly, we can look at egalitarianism. This theory attempts to resolve allocation problems by giving similar benefits, goods and services to all on the same basis. It directs us to equalise, as much as possible, in terms of everyone's well-being up to a certain level. Therefore, all similarly situated persons should be able to receive similar goods and services. In relation to expensive treatments or scarce resources, egalitarians might argue that lotteries are the most just way of allocating such finite resources amongst people similarly situated.[148] This would acknowledge the right of each person to gain fair access to the benefits of the treatment in question.[149] However, problems exist in trying to determine what kind of equality is important, ie age, nature of medical condition, life expectancy with/without treatment, family circumstances and so on. Again, here certain groups could be excluded if they fall outside certain parameters.

---

[145] Mill, *Utilitarianism*, (Parker, Son, and Bourn, 1957, edn) (1863). See in particular Chapter 2, 'What Utilitarianism Is'.

[146] Kopelman and Palumbo, 'The US Health Delivery System: Inefficient and Unfair to Children' (1997) 23 Am J L and Med 319.

[147] Callahan, 'Terminating Treatment: Age As a Standard' Hastings Center Report Oct./Nov. 1987, at 21.

[148] Childress, 'Who Shall Live When Not All Can Live?' (1970) 53 Soundings 339, at 347–54.

[149] Kopelman and Palumbo, 'The US Health Delivery System: Inefficient and Unfair to Children' (1997) 23 Am J L and Med 319, at 325.

[1.106] Thirdly, the theory of libertarianism argues that the State should not limit the liberty of competent adults except to prevent harm to third parties.[150] On this basis, market forces and choices about how to use one's own money should shape the kind of healthcare people get. However, concern may be expressed here for the protection of vulnerable groups such as the elderly, the poor, children or incompetent adults, as libertarianism seems to disproportionately favour the wealthy.

[1.107] Finally, we can examine the theory of contractarianism. According to this theory, fair distributions of social goods occur when informed and impartial people agree on the procedures used for distribution. The most well-known proponent of this theory is John Rawls, who contends that people should form a consensus as to allocation of resources within their society.[151] Although he did not specifically address healthcare resources in his writings, his theory has been built on by Daniels, who argues that a just society should provide basic healthcare to all, but redistribute goods and services more favourably to children to provide them with fair equality of opportunity to compete with their peers.[152] Critics argue that it is difficult to apply the equality of opportunity rule fairly and that it seems unsatisfactory to fund expensive treatment of a few disadvantaged people to the detriment of the fulfilment of the needs of many others.

[1.108] It can be seen, therefore, from this very brief sketch of some theories of justice that the application of these theories, while useful in stimulating discussion about priorities and objectives of the healthcare system, are each imperfect. Each theory ranks values differently, from equality to liberty and so on. The difficulty is how to choose between these theories in determining how to prioritise scarce resources, and who is to be the decision-maker in these situations: doctor, patient or politician? Decisions require priority setting between different types of service, which in turn depends on professional medical assessment and advice, public opinion and economic evaluation. Public opinion is a 'fickle measuring instrument' as 'not only can polls be grossly distorted by the way in which questions are put but also opinion is very subject to political and other extraneous influences – particularly that of the media whose circulations depend on maintaining an aggressive and partisan attitude.'[153] However, the importance of transparency in decision-making in rationing resources has become increasingly important in recent years.

Models in other jurisdictions

The Oregon Health Plan

[1.109] An often-quoted process of transparent healthcare allocation decision-making is the Oregon plan which took place in the late 80's following a public outcry after the death of a seven year old boy whose bone marrow transplant, which would have cost

---

[150] The most well-known proponent of this theory was Locke, *Treatise of Civil Government* 18–33 (Blackwell, 1956) (1689). Also see Nozick, *Anarchy, State and Utopia* (Basic Books, 1974) at 120–46.

[151] Rawls, *A Theory of Justice* (1971) (Revised edition, OUP, 1999) and *Political Liberalism* (Columbia University Press, 1996).

[152] Daniels, *Just Health Care* (Cambridge University Press, 1985) at 111–12.

[153] Laurie, Harmon and Porter, *Law and Medical Ethics*, (10th edn, OUP, 2016), para 11.13.

$100,000 was not covered by Medicaid. The State of Oregon realised that it had to balance costs, benefits and access in the face of scarcity of resources. Either it had to limit the Medicaid program to the most cost-effective services or it had to deny healthcare to many people. An open and transparent public consensus model was attempted whereby a policy was devised which tried to compile a list of health services ranked by priority, from the most important to the least important, representing the comparative benefits of each service to the population.[154] This was so as to enable the funding received from central government under the Medicaid scheme (designed to cover those unable to afford health insurance) to be administered according to the net benefit to be obtained and the priorities generally set by the relevant community. A working group was established and agreed on three important principles: access to a basic level of care must be universal; society is responsible for financing care for poor people; a basic level of care must be defined through a public process. A panel of experts known as the Health Services Commission was tasked with formulating a list following extensive public consultation which was declared to be the world's first prioritized list of health services.[155] Services were listed by reference to specific treatments and conditions, distinguishing in seventeen categories as between acute and chronic illness, preventative and curative treatments, illnesses causing death and those causing disability and so on. A separate ranking process took place within each category and only those ranked high on the lists would be funded.

[1.110] The Commission also requested information on public values concerning healthcare. Three methods were used to gather this public input: twelve public hearings in which testimony was taken from Oregonians concerning their healthcare experiences and preferences; approximately fifty focus groups around the state in which facilitators helped citizens to identify health values on which there was some degree of consensus; and finally, a survey of 1001 Oregonians to identify the impact on overall health resulting from a broad range of hundreds of conditions such as shortness of breath, limited range of motion, social dysfunction, and hearing loss. These three methods provided the Commission with a sense of the relative importance of treating a condition as expressed by those who would be covered by the benefit package resulting from the prioritization of services.[156]

[1.111] The first list which was based on a methodology of cost effectiveness analysis yielded some peculiarities, such as possibly covering tooth caps, but not surgery for emergent appendicitis. The results also placed obstetrical care low and infertility treatment high in the priority ranking, causing concern from those administering the scheme. Many conditions were not listed, and problems could arise for patients presenting with more than one condition, some of which were not fundable. The plan was subject to much criticism due to these anomalies and there was also opposition to the plan on grounds that it discriminated against people with disabilities. There was a

---

154 US Congress, Office of Technology Assessment, Evaluation of the Oregon Medicard Proposal, OTA-H-531 (Washington DC: US Government Printing Office, May 1992) available at www.fas.org.ota/reports/9213.pdf; (Honigsbaum, *Who Shall live? Who Shall Die? – Oregon's Health Financing Proposals* (King's Fund, 1993).

155 www.oregon.gov/oha/healthplan/pages/priorlist.aspx.

156 Di Prete and Coffman, 'A Brief History of Health Services Prioritization in Oregon' www.oregon.gov/oha/OHPR/HSC/docs/prioritizationhistory.pdf.

perceived problem that in asking the public for input on social values, the Commission may have come under the influence of biases against people with disabilities. As a result, the Commission was required to remove all public input obtained from the survey. The Commission revised the plan to take these considerations into account with the result that cost-effectiveness was relegated to the back seat.[157] As an example of the commission's work in re-balancing competing claims, the highest-priority categories 1 through 6 subsequently encompassed services such as the 'birth of a child and maternal care' (category 1); 'preventive care;' and 'life-threatening diseases,' each with many line items in the category, whereas lower-ranked categories included nonfatal, self-limiting, elective, or inconsequential conditions and interventions.

[1.112] The Oregon Health Plan was finally accepted in 1993 and the priority list is revised every two years and appears to enjoy significant public support. Although praiseworthy in its attempt to involve the community in the prioritisation of resources, a number of problems became apparent with this methodology as many of those within the population most likely to be affected did not participate in the exercise and the results may indicate that the difficult ethical issues arising in some medical conditions could not be appreciated by those who did not understand the resource implications inherent in their choices. 'As the experiment in Oregon showed, it is difficult to involve a representative cross-section of people in the exercise. Often, particular groups will be involved and some will effectively lobby for funds, but one wonders who will speak up for the less articulate groups such as the mentally handicapped, the elderly, and those with 'unpopular' diseases.'[158] However, although in many ways an imperfect method, many advocates have noted the importance of the list from an ethical point of view in attempting to develop a fair and transparent consultative public process for prioritizing medical services through its laws and regulations.[159]

The National Health Service (UK)

[1.113] Another example of how rationing decisions are made in other jurisdictions can be seen in the model adopted in the UK where healthcare is provided by the publicly funded National Health Service (NHS).[160] In England and Wales, decisions relating to access to healthcare are decentralised and services are organised by regional trusts with the result that there are inequalities between different areas, known as the postcode lottery.[161] Trusts make their own decisions about spending and coverage, so a patient may not be covered for an intervention that another patient living in a different area *would* be covered for. To reduce this inequity, the government asked the National Institute for Clinical Excellence (NICE) to draw up guidelines for coverage and spending decisions. Its guidelines are based on cost-effectiveness analysis, measured by

---

[157] Bognar and Hirose *The Ethics of Rationing* (Routledge Press, 2014) at 61.

[158] Newdick, *Who Should We Treat?* (OUP, 1995) at 36.

[159] See contrasting views of Howard et al 'Oregon's experiment in healthcare delivery and payment reform: co-ordinated care organisations replacing managed care' (2015) 40(1) J Health Polit Policy Law 245, and Chang et al 'Oregon's Medicaid transformation: observations on organisational structure and strategy' (2015) 40(1) J Health Polit Policy Law 257.

[160] See generally Laurie, Harmon and Porter, *Law and Medical Ethics* (10th edn, OUP, 2016) Ch 11.

[161] Bognar and Hirose, *The Ethics of Rationing* (Routledge Press, 2014) at 63–65.

a system known as Quality Adjusted Life Years (QALYs), (discussed below) of new medical technologies and treatments. NICE also instituted Citizen Councils, comprised of representatives of the general population rather than experts in healthcare, to deliberate on the ethical and social issues raised by its guidelines. In common with the Oregon Health Plan, this also demonstrates the importance and value of a fair and transparent consultative public process for prioritizing payment for medical services.

[1.114] A further methodology sometimes used in the context of ensuring cost effectiveness, which is highly relevant to prioritisation decisions, is Health Technology Assessment (HTA). This has been introduced in a number of countries in recent years as a means by which health resources are assessed to ensure that they are being used in a way that maximises the best outcome for patients. For example, in the Member States of the European Union, HTA activities are increasingly visible, and almost all now have a national agency for HTA or its equivalent. HTA involves an assessment of the clinical and cost effectiveness of the medicines, devices, diagnostics, and health promotion used across the health system. It also includes the evaluation of social and ethical issues, quality of life and quality of end of life and cost effectiveness in relation to health technology. The objective of HTAs is to support decision-makers such as the Minister for Health and the HSE to develop policies in relation to health technology which are socially and medically acceptable in the community. The emphasis is on ensuring that the decision-making process itself is fair, open and inclusive of all perspectives.[162] It is important that the decision-maker is as transparent as possible in relation to the ethical stance taken and the values underpinning the decision. Provided the bases for decision-making are flexible in relation to the times, then the underlying system is probably just and likely to produce just results.[163]

[1.115] In Ireland, the Health Information and Quality Authority (HIQA) currently carries out HTAs in order to enable the Minister for Health and Children to make informed decisions on the desirability and effectiveness of investing in new therapies, drugs, equipment or health-promotion activities. For example, some of the HTAs already carried out by HIQA include an assessment of the role of vaccination against human papillomavirus (HPV) in reducing the risk of cervical cancer in Ireland; population-based colorectal cancer screening programme; public access defibrillation; robotic-assisted surgery and many more important technologies and services.[164] HIQA has also developed guidelines which may be used by other organisations involved in such exercises.[165]

Effect of prioritisation on individual patients

[1.116] Although the politician's duty is to make the sort of macro decisions that must be made regarding the provision and funding of expensive treatments generally,[166] at a

---

[162] Drummond et al, 'Key Principles for the Improved Conduct of Health Technology Assessments for Resource Allocation Decisions' (2008) Intl J of Technology Assessment in Health Care 24:3.

[163] Gillon, 'Justice and Allocation of Medical Resources' (1995) 291 BMJ 266.

[164] See www.hiqa.ie/healthcare/health-technology-assessment.

[165] www.hiqa.ie/healthcare/health-technology-assessment/guidelines.

[166] See generally, Hon. Justice Kirby, 'Bioethical Decisions and Opportunity Costs' (1986) Journal of Contemporary Health Law and Policy Vol 2:7–21.

micro level the medical practitioner's ultimate duty is to his patient, and he must also be conscious of the resource implications of his decision-making. How is an individual medical practitioner to decide as between these competing claims? 'Resources have never been infinite and unenviable decisions between patients have always been made, though in a manner less visible in the past. Doctors care for groups of patients and know very well that the use of a bed or operating theatre for one patient may mean that the treatment of another will be delayed or denied altogether.'[167] Those with responsibility for allocation of health resources face difficult dilemmas in deciding whether or not to fund treatments for particular patients.

[1.117] From the perspective of the individual doctor, they are expected not only to treat their patients to the best of their ability, but also to be aware of the economic costs of their treatment decisions. For example, the Medical Council's Guide to Professional Conduct and Ethics[168] advises doctors that, subject to their duty to act in the best interests of patients, they have a responsibility to engage and advocate with the relevant authorities to promote the provision of appropriate healthcare resources and facilities. They also have a duty to assist in the efficient and effective use of healthcare resources and to give advice on their appropriate allocation. Doctors are advised that while balancing a duty of care to the individual patient, they should be aware of the wider need to use limited healthcare resources efficiently and responsibly. For example, they should prescribe bio-equivalent generic medicines where they are safe and effective and only commission investigations if they are clinically indicated.

[1.118] What *are* the criteria that should be used to make decisions of this kind? The first and most obvious one is the probability of successful medical outcome. In itself this appears unproblematic and, indeed, ethically mandatory. However, it is argued that many predictions of successful medical outcome might also be covert value judgments[169] and might in fact be basing decision-making on a second criterion, ie the patient's value or disvalue to society, or where patients have somehow, by their lifestyle or other choices, caused their own illness. This has been debated, for example, in the context of the exclusion of smokers from cardiac surgery,[170] although the potential for such a policy is also evident in relation to persistent drug or alcohol abusers. The question here is whether the patient's own behaviour and quality of life considerations should be relevant in deciding how to allocate scarce resources.[171] While it is generally agreed that individuals have responsibilities as well as rights in relation to their own healthcare, it would be impossible to maintain an exclusionary policy that did not transgress equal status principles of non-discrimination on the basis of disability, age, class or social background.

---

[167] Newdick, *Who Should We Treat?* (OUP, 1995) p 277.

[168] Medical Council, *Guide to Professional Conduct and Ethics* (8th edn, 2016) www.medicalcouncil.ie/.

[169] Stauch, Tingle & Wheat, *Sourcebook on Medical Law* (2nd edn, Cavendish, 1998) p 48.

[170] Underwood and Bailey, 'Coronary Bypass Surgery Should Not Be Offered to Smokers' (1993) 306 BMJ 1047.

[171] For further discussion of this issue see *The Report of the Independent Inquiries into Paediatric Cardiac Services at the Royal Brompton Hospital and Harefield Hospital* (April 2001) available at www.rbh.nthames.nhs.uk.

[1.119] In its report on Social Value Judgements, NICE states that decision-makers should not take into consideration whether or not a particular condition was self-induced. It was often impossible, in an individual, to decide whether the condition was dependent on their own behaviour or not; and receiving NHS care should not depend on whether people 'deserved' it or not. However, if the behaviour is likely to continue and can make a treatment less clinically effective or cost effective, then it may be appropriate to take this into account.[172]

[1.120] Another issue that arises in this context is the relevance of age of the patient. If age is to be considered as a factor in the decision-making process, this might result in older patients being denied access to services on the basis of utility and cost-effectiveness given the comparatively shorter life expectancy of this group. Harris argues that ageism is inherently unethical – it adopts a metric of cost effectiveness that lacks compassion, and discriminates against the old, those with diminished life expectancy, the very ill, or those whose individual circumstances mean they will get less than ideal benefit from treatment and this, he says is 'a perversion of science as well as of morality.' He argues that '[E]ach citizen surely has an equal claim on the protection of the community as expressed by its public healthcare system and this means that each is entitled to an equal chance of having their, necessarily individual and personal and hence different, health needs respected by any publicly funded healthcare system.'[173] Harris argues:

> If you and I are competitors for treatment and I will have a better health outcome from treatment than you, but the treatment offers to each of us the chance of a health gain that is significant and important to us, automatically preferring to satisfy my needs rather than yours, seems unfair. Why should my life or health be judged more worth saving or preserving because I am healthier or younger, or because there are more effective treatments for my condition, (even though the treatments available for your condition—as in the Alzheimer's case, are still valuable, and worth having) rather than because I am more intelligent say, or more useful?

[1.121] Therefore, Harris argues, we each suffer the same injustice if our wish to live the rest of our lives, however long or short a time that might be, is taken from us. Why should something we each value equally be taken from some based on their date of birth? However implausible it might thus seem to distinguish between people on the basis of age, when the boundaries of the argument are pushed to their logical extremes, the ageist argument creeps back in. For example, no one may suggest that a 20-year-old should be treated ahead of a 30-year-old simply on the basis of age, but should a 5-year-old not be treated ahead of an 85-year-old? Harris suggests in reply that one strategy for dealing with this situation would be the 'fair innings' argument, which takes the view that there is some span of years that is considered to be a reasonable life. If a fair share of life is taken at, say, 70 years, then anyone who reaches that age should be relatively satisfied that they have had a fair innings, and that anything beyond that is a bonus rather than an entitlement:

> The attraction of the fair innings argument is that it preserves and incorporates many of the features that made the anti-ageist argument plausible, but allows us to preserve our

---

[172] NICE, *Social Value Judgements* (2nd edn, 2008) https://www.nice.org.uk/.
[173] Harris, 'Its not NICE to discriminate' (2005) 31 J Med Ethics 373–375.

feeling that the old who have had a good run for their money should not be endlessly propped up at the expense of those who have not had the same chance.[174]

[1.122] In the UK, the National Institute for Clinical Excellence (NICE) recommended that age should not be a primary criteria regulating choice. They take the view that health should not be valued more highly in some age groups rather than others (unless age is an indicator of benefit or risk in the particular circumstances) and that individuals' social roles should not influence considerations of cost effectiveness. NICE's general principle is therefore that patients should not be denied, or have restricted access to NHS treatment simply because of their age. However, they may refer to age where there is evidence that age is a good indicator for some aspect of patients' health status and/or the likelihood of adverse effects of the treatment; there is no practical way of identifying patients other than by their age (for example, there is no test available to measure their state of health in another way); or where there is good evidence, or good grounds for believing, that because of their age patients will respond differently to the treatment in question.[175]

Role of the courts

[1.123] While the courts would generally be reluctant to interfere with clinical decisions made by a responsible practitioner, it would not necessarily be sufficient to answer an allegation of negligence against a funding authority that there were not enough resources to provide the requisite care. The courts have jurisdiction through judicial review to inquire into the reasonableness of all such decisions made by funding authorities.[176] However, provided the exercise of such discretionary powers by funding authorities do not exceed 'the loose constraints of 'reasonableness'[177] these decisions are ethically difficult and emotionally agonising but legally undemanding.[178] In England cases have been heard on the basis of the reasonableness or otherwise of the clinical decision not to offer treatment in individual circumstances.

[1.124] In *R v Sheffield Health Authority, ex parte Seale*,[179] the plaintiff was refused in vitro fertilisation treatment because she was deemed to be too old, at 37 years of age. She argued that the setting of a blanket upper age limit failed to take into account her own clinical circumstances and was therefore illegal. The Court of Appeal held that this was not so; the age limit was neither irrational nor absurd for failing to consider individual case merits:

> A clinical decision on a case by case basis is clearly desirable and, in cases of critical illness, a necessary approach. However, it is reasonable, or at least not *Wednesbury*[180]

---

[174] Harris, *The Value of Life* (Routledge, 1985).

[175] NICE, *Social Value Judgements* (2nd edn, 2008) www.nice.org.uk/.

[176] See Newdick, 'Resource Allocation in the National Health Service'. (1997) 23 Am. JL and Med 291.

[177] Wall, '*R v Cambridge Health Authority, ex parte B* (a minor) (1995): A Tale of Two Judgments' in Herring and Wall, *Landmark Cases in Medical Law* (Hart Publishing, 2015) 111–127 at 111.

[178] Foster, 'Simple rationality? The law of healthcare resource allocation in England' (2007) 33 Journal of Medical Ethics 404, 406.

[179] *R v Sheffield Health Authority, ex parte Seale* (1994) 25 BMLR 1.

[180] *Associated Provincial Picture Houses Ltd v Wednesbury Corp* [1947] 2 All ER 680.

unreasonable…of an authority to look at the matter in the context of the financial resources available to it and the many other services for which it is responsible. I cannot say that it is absurd for this authority …to take thirty-five as an appropriate criterion when balancing the need for such provision against its ability to provide it.

[1.125] Such difficult decisions are also made with life or death consequences, as in the case of *R v Cambridge Health Authority, ex parte B*[181] which concerned a 10-year-old child who was suffering from lymphoma had received chemotherapy, radiotherapy and a bone marrow transplant before she relapsed. The medical team were of the view that no other treatment would be beneficial and that her life expectancy was between six and eight weeks. Her father sought a second opinion from doctors in the United States and he received advice which estimated that further chemotherapy treatment and a bone marrow transplant carried a 10–20% chance of success. The cost of the treatment would be £75,000. B's father requested the health authority to fund the treatment but his application was refused. B's father sought judicial review of this decision.

[1.126] In the High Court, Laws J determined that the decision of the health authority conflicted with B's right to life and with her father's right to determine her healthcare. He criticised the health authority for merely tolling 'the bell of tight resources' and he considered that where there was even a slim chance that the child might be saved the authority must do more than consider the financial implications involved. He criticised the authority for failing to provide a substantial justification for its decision and for failing to have regard to the views of B's family. He ordered that the authority's decision be reconsidered. His decision seems to focus on the human rights perspective of the case and the consequences of the decision for B's right to life. It has been argued[182] that viewing the impact on the individual's interests through a human rights framework 'permits the court to shift the terrain on which a resource allocation decision is considered'[183], enables the courts to 'perform their constitutionally-assigned task of protecting human rights'[184], and 'give effect to those clearly defined and enduring values which lie beyond the purviews of statute'.[185] Sheldrick argues that where a statutory decision interferes with a human right, the courts ought to rigorously scrutinise the decision and 'assert their authority and expertise over and above the expertise of policymakers.'[186]

[1.127] On appeal, the Court of Appeal reversed this decision. The court shied away from human rights language emphasising that its role was not to judge the merits of the medical judgment made but to examine the lawfulness of the decision of the authority. It was held that the Authority was not to be criticised for refusing to fund the treatment on grounds that the proposed treatment was experimental as the treatment was not one that

---

[181] *R v Cambridge Health Authority, ex parte B* (1995) 25 BMLR 5; reversed (1995) 23 BMLR 1 CA.

[182] Wall, '*R v Cambridge Health Authority, ex parte B* (a minor) (1995): A Tale of Two Judgments' in Herring and Wall, *Landmark Cases in Medical Law* (Hart Publishing, 2015) 111–127 at 116.

[183] Sheldrick, 'Judicial review and the allocation of health care resources in Canada and the United Kingdom' (2003) 5 Journal of Comparative Policy Analysis: Research and Practice 149,157.

[184] Young, 'In Defence of Due Deference' (2009) 72 Modern Law Review 554, 575.

[185] Palmer, 'Resource allocation, Welfare Rights – Mapping the Boundaries of Judicial Control in Public Administrative Law' (2000) 20 Oxford Journal of Legal Studies 63, 70–71.

[186] Sheldrick, 'Judicial review and the allocation of health care resources in Canada and the United Kingdom' (2003) 5 Journal of Comparative Policy Analysis: Research and Practice 149 at 157.

had a well-tried track record of success. Neither should the Authority be criticised for failing to explain how a limited budget is best allocated to the maximum advantage of the maximum number of patients since the court is not in a position to assess these difficult and agonising judgments. The Court also felt that the authority had adequately considered the parents' wishes, and that it was unrealistic to proceed on the basis that any treatments needed by a patient would be provided, irrespective of the cost. The Court said it could not make a judgment as to how the limited budget of the authority should best be spent, and it was open to the authority to reach the decision it had in fact reached.[187] Sir Thomas Bingham MR said:

> I have no doubt that in a perfect world any treatment which a patient ... sought would be provided if doctors were willing to give it, no matter how much it cost ... It would, however, be shutting one's eyes to the real world if the court were to proceed on the basis that we do live in such a world.[188]

Wall argues that '[M]edical law ultimately defers to the judgment of public healthcare authorities as to how healthcare resources are allocated. As *ex parte B* demonstrates, this deference is despite the life or death consequences of funding decisions.'[189]

Quality adjusted life years

[1.128] An attempt to remove the risks inherent in the exercise of discretion in emotionally charged contexts such as those in *ex parte B,* can be seen in NICE's adoption of the Quality Adjusted Life Years (QALYs) approach.[190] This approach attempts to evaluate healthcare outcomes according to a generic scale, thus removing subjectivity or value judgments being brought into funding allocation decisions. Put simply, it asks for how long a proposed treatment will improve the quality of a patient's life and how much the treatment costs. Each full year of health counts as one, and each year of declining health counts as less than one. Thus, if the patient's improvement is likely to be long-lasting and significant, then the patient accumulates a high score on the quality of life measure. If the cost of the treatment is relatively low, then the cost per unit of quality is also low. 'The theory favours treatments which achieve the greatest increase in the quality of life, over the longest period, for the least cost.'[191]

[1.129] Newdick gives the example of the treatment of premature babies in neonatal intensive care. The number of babies that survive very low birthweight difficulties has grown significantly in the last 20 years but there is still the fact that some will not survive despite best medical efforts, others will survive with varying degrees of

---

[187] As a result of a sympathetic media campaign, B's treatment was funded privately and this extended her life for two further years. See Entwistle, Watt, Bradbury and Pehl, 'Media Coverage of the Child B Case' (1996) 312 BMJ 1587.

[188] *R v Cambridge Health Authority, ex parte B* (1995) 23 MBLR 1 at 8–9.

[189] Wall, '*R v Cambridge Health Authority, ex parte B* (a minor) (1995): A Tale of Two Judgments', in Herring and Wall, *Landmark Cases in Medical Law* (Hart Publishing, 2015) 111–127 at 126–127.

[190] See Williams, 'The Value of QALYs' (1985) Health and Social Services Journal; Harris. 'QALYfying the Value of Life' (1987) 13 Journal of Medical Ethics 117; Newdick, *Who Should We Treat?* (OUP, 1995) p 22.

[191] Newdick, *Who Should We Treat?* (OUP, 1995) p 22.

disability, while others will survive and live a normal, healthy life. It is sometimes difficult to distinguish between these groups at the outset. Economists point to the fact that the cost per QALY for this group of patients is extremely high because of their short life expectancy. Does this mean that we should not treat them if the money can be better expended elsewhere? Although a health economist may argue that strictly speaking this should be the case, and although it may be strictly egalitarian in not favouring one patient over another, it is nonetheless instinctively difficult to accept, as it might result in the withdrawal of pain relief from a cancer patient who is likely to die in any event, non-treatment of a child with cerebral palsy and other decisions that would conflict with the values and objectives in most healthcare systems.

[1.130] Critics of the QALYs system point to the difficulty in scoring the degree of likely improvement of a patient after treatment and point to its subjectivity, something that the system is supposed to avoid. While one patient may be content to live with physical limitations for 10 years after surgery, another patient may prefer to die than be confined to a wheelchair. The system works on the assumption that most rational people would prefer a shorter, healthier life to a longer period of survival in discomfort or disability. However, this would discriminate against disabled and elderly persons from the outset, as they would never be able to achieve the optimum score on an objective assessment of their quality of life. Economists say that such decisions are made every day, they are inevitable and the inherent value of the QALYs system is that it tries to make such decisions on a more rational and transparent basis.

[1.131] It is also argued that rather than treating all needy patients equally, the QALYs system would prefer one person's life over the other's, even if the difference in life expectation was very small, such as two days. Proponents of QALYs rebut this by pointing to the fact that if all needy patients were to be treated equally, then one whose life expectancy was 30 years after treatment would be treated the same as one whose life expectancy was 2 days after treatment.[192]

[1.132] There are conflicting and arguably unrealistic obligations placed on doctors in this context to act as gatekeepers in the management of scarce resources. To what extent can, or should, a doctor serve simultaneously the needs of his patients, his own interests and those of society?[193] As well as having obligations to promote their patients' welfare, doctors are under constraints to restrict the use of expensive medical services, which raises dilemmas in cutting corners and exposing themselves to later allegations of negligence. Harris proposes, as an alternative to QALYs, a random selection of patients or lottery method.[194] Such a method has the advantage of apparent objectivity and could be defended as the morally desirable choice but, as Mason and Laurie point out, it is a bad medical option because it takes no account of the gravity of the patient's condition and no account of medical benefit – it concentrates on justice and ignores welfare. 'Nevertheless it may be the way of allocating scarce resources that the public prefer and it is, in fact, practised in the form of, say, waiting lists for transplantable organs.'[195]

---

[192] See series of articles by Harris and McKie each arguing opposite sides of the QALY debate in (1996) 22 JME 204–21.

[193] Pellegrino, 'Rationing Health Care: The Ethics of Medical Gatekeeping' (1986) Journal of Contemporary Health Law and Policy Vol 2: 23–45.

[194] Harris, *The Value of Life* (Routledge, 1985).

[195] Laurie, Harmon and Porter, *Law and Medical Ethics*, (10th edn, OUP, 2016), para. 11.52.

Chapter 2

Regulation of Medical Practice in Ireland

INTRODUCTION

[2.01] Until the middle of the last century the medical profession was largely, though not always, harmless and essentially ineffective: comfort more than cure.[1] The doctor's primary duty was to diagnose an illness and then track its natural course. Doctors did all they could to help the sick, but they did not have either the tools or the understanding of the body's workings they needed to consistently succeed. It was not until after World War II that biomedical research provided the profession with the tools it needed. 'Doctors were widely hailed as miracle workers, and 'quality' care became synonymous with 'more' care. More doctors. More nurses. More hospitals. More drugs. More diagnostic equipment.'[2] Doctors are now expected to provide safe, high-quality care, participate in research, be effective and compassionate communicators and often to run their own businesses as well.[3] Medicine has become hugely more effective in the last few decades, but this has brought its own challenges, with increasing expectations of the public, use of high-end expensive technology, changes in the dynamic of the doctor-patient relationship, an increased focus on safety and quality improvement alongside pressure on healthcare resources, particularly during recent recessionary times.

[2.02] The tradition in the medical profession was, for much of the last two hundred years, that the patient was the passive recipient of medical care and doctors took it upon themselves to decide what treatment and information should be provided. Doctors were encouraged to protect their patients from information about their own health, in case it made them sicker. This tradition of strong paternalism is particularly evident in the Irish and English legal systems where, in matters of civil liability, the courts allowed doctors to broadly set their own standards.

[2.03] Criticism of medical paternalism is often seen in the context of calls for recognition of patients' rights, whereby the moral agency of the individual and the value of respect for the patient as person is proclaimed. Suppression of the patient's voice is considered incompatible with legitimate expectations about individual choice and freedom to decide what is done to one's body. These expectations argue a right to the

---

[1] Chantler, 'The role and regulation of doctors in the delivery of health care', (1999) Lancet 353:1178.

[2] Millenson, Demanding Medical Excellence, Doctors and Accountability in the Information Age (University of Chicago, 1997) p 4.

[3] For interesting analysis of patients' expectations of doctors, see Madden and O'Donovan, Qualitative Review of Complaints to the Medical Council and doctors' responses (2015) www.medicalcouncil.ie/News-and-Publications/Reports/Listening-to-Complaints-Learning-for-Good-Professional-Practice.html.

kind of disclosure and dialogue that will permit informed decision-making.[4] In recent years there has been a movement in the education and training of doctors, as well as professional guidelines to practitioners, towards encouragement of greater patient participation and a more collaborative approach to medical decision-making. Despite much improvement, however, the traditional approach has not yet completely disappeared, particularly in the hospital environment, where the busy context and hierarchical nature of the organisation can hinder the development of such a partnership model. There are also cultural flaws in the medical profession which Irvine says show up as 'excessive paternalism, lack of respect for patients and their right to make decisions about their care, and secrecy and complacency about poor practice':[5]

> The nature of medical practice may have changed considerably in recent times but the hospital setting still bears the stamp of the Hippocratic tradition. The more impersonal and hierarchical hospital regime still reflects a time-honoured ethos that remains a potent force in medical schools. There are signs that its hold is weakening, in the face of new managerial policies and financial constraints dictated by governmental drive for cost containment and greater accountability. But such developments do not argue a professional conversion to the primacy of patient choice and patient's rights.[6]

[2.04] In the context of general practice, although the traditional paternalistic model was based in part on the belief that keeping negative information from the patient was good for his health, this too has come under attack in recent years. Studies show how failure to involve patients can lead to error in diagnosis and treatment, delay recovery and adversely affect long-term outcomes. To experience a measure of control over one's illness can itself be therapeutic and can reduce levels of anxiety and depression. This has been reflected in more recent literature on medical ethics that stress the doctor-patient relationship as a partnership or a collaborative effort. Patients are unlikely to want to dictate to their doctor or to determine their own treatment. They are more likely to want co-determination and genuine communication.[7]

[2.05] Principles of autonomy and empowerment of the individual have been brought to medical practice with far-reaching consequences for the relationship between medicine and law. Medicine is certainly not alone in feeling the effects of social and cultural changes brought about by increased public education and access to information at the touch of a button. Freedom of information policies and legislation dealing with access to personal records have added to 'the unease of doctors keeping such records and to increased defensiveness in the practice of medicine in Ireland because the documentation of clinical standards and of consent procedures is now readily scrutinised.'[8]

---

4   See generally Teff, Reasonable Care, Legal Perspectives on the Doctor-Patient Relationship (Clarendon Press, 1994).

5   Irvine, 'The changing relationship between the public and the medical profession' (2001) Journal of the Royal Society of Medicine 94: 162–169.

6   Teff, Reasonable Care, Legal Perspectives on the Doctor-Patient Relationship (Clarendon Press, 1994) at xxv.

7   Donnelly, Consent: Bridging the Gap Between Doctor and Patient, (Cork University Press, 2002).

8   Cusack, 'Ireland: Breakdown of Trust Between Doctor and Patient' (2000) The Lancet 356:1431 at 1432.

[2.06] Another issue of importance in the changing medical-legal relationship is the growing recognition and awareness of rights as a precursor to any medical treatment. This has become evident not only in the increase in medical litigation, but also in the ways in which doctors approach the issues of capacity and informed consent. Whereas in the past doctors may have been prepared to treat patients without fully informing them of possible risks and complications where they were of the opinion that the patient did not want the information or would be distressed by it, this approach would generally not be seen as acceptable today. There has also been a move towards patient charters and national guidelines on what patients can expect from their doctor and hospital.[9] While such documents may provide useful benchmarks against which health service providers can measure themselves and be assessed, the language of rights sometimes used in such documents is not necessarily accurate or conducive to a collaborative relationship. The right to healthcare is discussed in more detail in Chapter 1.

[2.07] The common use of the internet has also led to a radical change in the way in which patients come to their doctors for treatment. Whereas the patient traditionally came to the doctor in need of an explanation, a diagnosis and a reassurance that a means could be found to cure the ailment, now patients often search for information on the internet prior to attending the doctor, so they can easily find an explanation for their symptoms and the preferable method of treatment. They may then often present themselves to the doctor already self-diagnosed from a perusal of a vast array of medical information and advice on treatment. While the increase and accessibility of information may be considered a huge advance in educating the public on illness and its management, a note of caution must also be sounded in respect of the accuracy and reliability of some of the websites that may be accessed by the public, which are not based on sound objective facts and may be sponsored by agencies or commercial enterprises with financial interests at stake. Internet advice is often given by people without medical training, is unconventional and may be inappropriate. Therefore, electronic resources should always carry a warning about adherence to their advice.

[2.08] From the perspective of its effect on the doctor-patient relationship, the challenge may be for the doctor to explain and justify any disagreement with this internet diagnosis to which the patient may be wedded, and any deviation from the treatment the patient has come to the doctor expecting to receive. This shift in the balance of information and power has, without doubt, added to the empowerment of the patient, and perhaps the defensiveness of the profession, which feels under more scrutiny than ever before. 'Empowered patients are challenging the professional's medical advice and choices of treatment, sometimes by finding alternative sources or providers of treatment on the Internet.'[10]

[2.09] For doctors, too, the internet has provided a rich source of learning. The technical evolution in the field of therapeutic medicine has been impressive. Although the bases for making a diagnosis today remain the same as 20 years ago, collaboration with

---

9   Health Service Executive, *The HSE and You*, (2010), available at www.hse.ie

10 Cox, *The Impact of the Internet on the Doctor-Patient Relationship*, (Imperial College Management School, 2000). A preliminary study carried out by Cox on the impact of the information revolution reported that 40 per cent of obstetricians interviewed said that use of the internet 'could damage the traditional doctor-patient relationship.'

colleagues nationally and internationally, medical information retrieval and case discussion now takes place faster and with higher degrees of speciality.[11] The expansion of medical knowledge and skill at an unprecedented rate, together with the revolution in information technology has huge implications for the profession.[12] Telemedicine or telehealth[13] is used to more advantage now and, in particular, for remote diagnosis in sparsely populated areas.[14] Robotic surgery may be carried out even where the doctor and patient are not physically present in the same room.[15] However, computer-based technologies could be seen as a double-edged sword, as they also provide the opportunity for the commission of illegal and unprofessional conduct. 'The loss and damage which could result from the improper use of on-line technologies are formidable, both in financial and human terms.'[16] The risks inherent through interception of communications, computer hacking, copyright infringement and breach of confidentiality are just some of the dangers lurking in this form of practice. There are also concerns arising in the area of medical negligence claims that could become even more complicated where medical practice transcends jurisdictional lines, and where the very existence of the doctor-patient relationship may be brought into question.[17]

[2.10] In recent years there has also been an increased focus on health information technology as a means of ensuring patient safety. There have been numerous calls for the introduction of information communication technology in the healthcare system, such as electronic health records, electronic prescribing, disease surveillance databases, electronic adverse-event-reporting systems, digital imaging and transmission of

---

[11] 'Medical Diagnosis in the Internet Age.' (1999) The Lancet Vol 354, supplement 4.

[12] Irvine, 'The performance of doctors: professionalism and self regulation in a changing world', (1997) British Medical Journal 314:1540.

[13] 'Telemedicine' means medicine across distance. X-rays were probably the first documented medical visual communication across distance, being transmitted over telephone lines in 1948. It is now being replaced by 'telehealth', which is the systematic application of telecommunication technology to the field of healthcare.

[14] For an historical overview see Barrett and Brecht, 'Historical Context of Telemedicine' in Viegas and Dunn, *Telemedicine: Practising in the Information Age* (Lippincott Williams & Wilkins, 1998).

[15] The world's first transoceanic operation on humans was recently conducted over high-speed fibreoptic connections. Surgeons in New York successfully used remotely controlled robots to laparoscopically remove a gall bladder from a woman in France. The operation lasted less than an hour, no intraoperative complications occurred and the 68-year-old-patient was discharged within 48 hours after an uneventful hospital stay. BMJ 2001; 323:713 (29 Sept.).

[16] Smith Russell, 'Medicine, Crime and Unprofessional Conduct in the Online World', Medico-Legal Journal 65/3.

[17] It may, for example, be argued that in the absence of any direct contact between the doctor and patient in the practice of telemedicine, that no such relationship is formed, and therefore no duty of care arises. However, if the doctor has participated in the diagnosis of the patient, or prescribed a course of treatment for him, a professional relationship is established. 'All professionals who engage in telemedicine practice should assume that their telemedicine encounters impose on them at least the same obligations arising from a professional relationship as do their non telemedicine encounters.' Blair, Bambas and Stone, 'Legal and Ethical Issues', in Viegas and Dunn, *Telemedicine: Practising in the Information Age* (Lippincott Williams & Wilkins, 1998).

radiological images, GP electronic booking for referrals and hospital appointments, discharge summaries, reporting of laboratory results and so on. National strategy and policy documents all support these measures and the government has accepted the necessity to introduce such technology as part of a patient safety framework proposed by the Commission on Patient Safety and Quality Assurance.[18] The proposed Health Information Bill will put in place the necessary legislative framework to support the introduction of many of these ICT measures. This is discussed further in Chapter 3.

[2.11] Apart from the internet, other new technologies also generate dramatic responses. Medical practice has changed almost beyond recognition in 50 years. Patients with congestive heart failure can now live longer, laparoscopy can be used to perform surgery, anaesthetic techniques enable lengthy and complicated operations to take place and immunisations are available that were not dreamt of then.[19] Technology is expensive but promises more hope than ever before, as does the increasing array of new drugs, devices and procedures launched every year. The increasingly effective use of medical technologies, however, also leads to higher patient expectations and sometimes ethical concerns as to misuse. Difficulties arise regarding the funding of such technology and how scarce resources will be allocated if the technology does become available. Issues arise in relation to reproductive technology, genetic diagnosis and the use of stem cells that were unimaginable 50 years ago and pose huge ethical and legal problems now. The hope held out for the future is set in promising terms – 'Once science enables us to know our own genome, we will be able to anticipate future health problems, change any risk-taking behaviour, and have personalised treatments designed for us.'[20] Yet, this knowledge too may have inherent disadvantages, as it forces individuals to confront their own health and mortality, at perhaps psychological detriment to themselves and their families, and perhaps without holding out any cure for the predicted disease.

MEDICAL ETHICS

[2.12] Medical ethics are vital to the practice of medicine and thus to any understanding of medical law for a number of reasons. Firstly, many practitioners look for guidance in their decision-making to ethics rather than law. Most practitioners will have had the benefit of a module on ethics during their training and may also look to the Medical Council and other sources for guidance on ethics. Secondly some legal principles have been influenced by the evolution of ethical principles – for example, the law of consent to medical treatment is based on respect for autonomy, and attempts to legislate in the area of medical practice are sometimes resisted on grounds of ethical principles such as respect for autonomy and freedom of choice.[21] Thirdly, in Ireland many areas of medical law are as yet undeveloped, with relatively sparse legislation and few judicial precedents. Although the courts are quick to point out that the judicial function is not to be an arbiter of different ethical perspectives, such perspectives nonetheless inform public debate and academic literature on medical law, and undoubtedly influence legal

---

[18] *Building a Culture of Patient Safety.* Section 7.7, available at www.health.gov.ie.

[19] Herman, 'The Good Old Days', (1998) The Lancet, Vol 353 No 9144.

[20] Berger and Smith, 'New Technologies in Medicine and Medical Journals' (1999) BMJ: 319: 7220.

[21] McHale & Fox, *Health Care Law, Text and Materials* (Sweet & Maxwell, 1997) at 71.

thinking. Thus 'it is impossible to study medical law without confronting complex ethical dilemmas.'[22] Jackson gives examples such as when is it acceptable for doctors to withhold treatment from a profoundly disabled baby? Should parents be allowed to choose the sex of their children? Is it wrong to pay someone to donate a kidney? Should voluntary euthanasia be legalised? 'It would be difficult to work out the appropriate *legal* response to such questions without also considering their ethical implications.' For this reason, this section will briefly outline some of the main ethical theories that might be used in discussing and resolving such ethical dilemmas.

[2.13] The word 'ethics' comes from the Greek *ethos*, which means 'custom or practice, a characteristic manner of acting, a more or less constant mode of behaviour in the deliberate actions of men.' Broadly speaking, ethics is the science or study of the morality of human acts through the medium of natural reason.[23] There are a number of approaches to the study of ethics that may be explained briefly. Normative ethics generally tries to evaluate what general norms for the guidance of conduct are morally acceptable and why. It is a 20th century idea that, in theory, satisfies a set of criteria for inquiry into moral concepts and principles. Practical or applied ethics are an attempt to work out the implications of general theories for specific forms of conduct, or for specific professions or public policy. These theories are invoked to help develop guides for action in those contexts. Non-normative ethics are categorised as, firstly, descriptive ethics, which is a factual investigation of how moral attitudes are expressed in practice, codes and policies, and, secondly, metaethics, which involves analysis of the language, concepts and methods of reasoning in ethics. Both of these have as their objective to establish what factually or conceptually is the case, not what ought to be the case.[24]

[2.14] Medical ethics is an application of general ethical principles to the solution of the moral problems of the medical profession and is principally concerned with what it means to be a good doctor. It involves an analysis of the concepts, assumptions, beliefs, attitudes, emotions, reasons and arguments underlying medico-moral decisions.[25] There are many different approaches to medical ethics and the methodologies that may be used when confronted by difficult moral problems. To assist doctors, ethical guidelines are produced by medical professional regulatory bodies to impose rules on doctors to ensure that their conduct towards their patients and colleagues meets certain agreed standards. Some have argued that the focus of medical ethics has been too narrow – in emphasising the duties of doctors, the obligations of patients have been ignored. Draper and Sorrell argue that medical ethics makes very few demands of patients and that 'little is said

---

22 Jackson, *Medical Law, Text, Cases and Materials* (2nd edn, OUP, 2010) p 2.

23 McFadden, *Medical Ethics* (6th edn, FA Davis Co, 1967), p 1.

24 Beauchamp and Childress, *Principles of Biomedical Ethics* (4th edn, New York: OUP, 1994) p 4. Chapter 1, 'Morality and Moral Justification', provides a very useful explanation of the terminology used in the study of ethics and the methodologies that may be employed in problem-solving.

25 Gillon, *Philosophical Medical Ethics* (Wiley, Medical Publications, 1986) p 2. Gillon begins his book with an interesting example of how ethical issues arise in medical situations, and he uses this example as a backdrop for his later discussion of medical ethics. The case is that of Dr Leonard Arthur, who was acquitted of the attempted murder of a newborn infant with Down's syndrome. Dr Arthur had prescribed dihydrocodeine and 'nursing care only' after the baby had been rejected by his mother.

about the kinds of decisions patients *ought* to make. Nor is much said about their responsibilities for making good rather than bad decisions. Indeed... mainstream medical ethics implies that a competent patient's decision is good simply by virtue of having been made by the patient. At times it seems as though patients never make, or cannot make, bad decisions...'[26]

[2.15] Of all the professions, medicine raises the most complex and difficult moral problems, concerned as it is with the intricacies of the beginning and ending of life. Biomedical ethics or bioethics is the application of ethical principles to the biological sciences, medicine and healthcare. It emerged as a discipline in the 1960s in response to technological developments and challenges to medical paternalism, with a corresponding rise in the principle of patient autonomy:[27]

> Traditionally, medical ethics has focussed primarily on the doctor-patient relationship and on the virtues possessed by the good doctor. It has also been very much concerned with relations between colleagues within the profession...Bioethics, on the other hand, is a more overtly critical and reflective enterprise. Not limited to questioning the ethical dimensions of doctor-patient and doctor-doctor relationships, it goes well beyond the scope of traditional medical ethics in several ways. First, its goal is not the development of, or adherence to, a code or set of precepts, but a better understanding of the issues. Second, it is prepared to ask deep philosophical questions about the nature of ethics, the value of life, what it is to be a person, the significance of being human. Third, it embraces issues of public policy and the direction and control of science.[28]

[2.16] There are a number of theories or traditions which inform bioethical debates. Firstly, teleological (derived from the Greek *telos,* meaning consequences) or consequentialist ethics judges the rightness or wrongness of an action based on its consequences. The most well-known theory in this tradition is utilitarianism, which is based on the maximisation of pleasure or happiness for the greatest number of people in society. It emerged as an alternative to Christian ethics in the late 18th and early 19th centuries through the work of Jeremy Bentham and John Stuart Mill. Consequentialists will examine an action not in terms of its intrinsic rightness but rather on the basis of what consequences it may bring for society. For example, in examining arguments for active euthanasia, they may argue that legalising such an activity would have negative consequences for society, as it may damage the doctor-patient relationship. This approach looks at the total welfare of the community rather than that of an individual and may necessitate some ranking or prioritisation of values.

[2.17] Another ethical tradition is deontological ethics (derived from the Greek *deontos* meaning duty), which looks not at the consequences of actions but rather at whether they conform to basic moral principles. For example, in relation to voluntary euthanasia, one might argue that it should be legalised so as to conform to the ethical principle of respecting the autonomous decisions of adults. The best-known example of this ethical tradition is known as Kantianism, named after the famous philosopher Immanuel Kant.

---

[26] Draper and Sorrell, 'Patients' Responsibilities in Medical Ethics' (2002) 16 Bioethics 335–51.

[27] Kuhse and Singer, 'What is Bioethics? A Historical Introduction' in *A Companion to Bioethics* (Blackwell, 1998) 3–11.

[28] Kuhse and Singer, 'What is Bioethics? A Historical Introduction' in *A Companion to Bioethics* (Blackwell, 1998) 3–11.

His writings, and in particular his 'Categorical Imperative' which he described as an unconditional obligation, have been applied in support of autonomy, independence and rationality. Categorical imperatives are principles that are intrinsically valid; they are good in and of themselves; they must be obeyed in all, and by all, situations and circumstances if behaviour is to observe the moral law. It is from the Categorical Imperative that all other moral obligations are generated, and by which all moral obligations can be tested. Kant believed that if an action is not done with the motive of duty, then it is without moral value. He thought that every action should have pure intention behind it; otherwise it was meaningless. He did not necessarily believe that the final result was the most important aspect of an action, but that how the person felt while carrying out the action was the time at which value was set to the result.

[2.18] Kant gave four formulations of the Categorical Imperative, two of which are particularly relevant to bioethics. The First Formulation requires that the maxims be chosen as though they should hold as universal laws of nature, in other words we should act according to consistent and just rules. The Second Formulation requires us to act with reference to every rational being so that it is an end in itself, meaning that the rational being is the basis of all maxims of action and must be treated never as a mere means but as an end at the same time. This means we must not treat other persons (or allow ourselves to be treated) solely to serve another's purpose, or as a means to an end. Kantian ethics place a primacy on rationality and individuality as a basis for qualification as autonomous beings, which may be argued to ask too much of patients. 'This idealistic concept is of little practical relevance in health contexts where patients, on the whole, bear little resemblance to the Kantian free, independent, exclusively rational individual.'[29]

[2.19] A third ethical tradition is virtue ethics, which is derived from Ancient Greek moral philosophy, in particular the work of Aristotle, and which emphasises not only good outcomes but also the character or motivation of the individual carrying out the actions. Virtue ethicists argue that people should always do the right thing for the right reason. For example, they do not hold with the view that patient autonomy trumps all other ethical values. Thus, in relation to euthanasia, the fact that the patient chooses to die does not in itself make euthanasia the right thing to do. Causing a patient to die might only be right if the patient's quality of life lacked basic human goods.

[2.20] While examination of the theories above may help our understanding of ethical dilemmas, it rarely yields a clear solution for doctors faced with the practical difficulty of deciding what to do. The prime question for many doctors is how to make decisions for and with their patients that respects their wishes and at the same time safeguards their well-being. Many different authors who put forward various theories based on moral principles have given answers to this question. For example, Beauchamp and Childress put forward the principle of 'respect for autonomy, beneficence, non-maleficence, and justice'.[30] Downie and Calman indicated the principles of 'utility, justice, non-maleficence, compassion (benevolence) and self-development', governed by the principle of 'respect for the autonomous individual' as the consensus principles.[31]

---

[29] Secker, 'The Appearance of Kant's Deontology in Contemporary Kantianism: Concepts of Patient Autonomy in Bioethics' (1999) 24 Journal of Medicine and Philosophy 43–66.

[30] Beauchamp and Childress, *Principles of Biomedical Ethics* (4th edn, OUP, 1994).

Engelhardt suggested the principles of 'permission' and 'beneficence' as the principles of bioethics.[32] Veatch identified 'utility, veracity, fidelity to promises, avoid killing, justice and autonomy' as principles of right actions.[33] Macer argued that love should be foundation of bioethics in the form of 'self-live (autonomy), love of others (justice), loving life (do no harm), and loving good (beneficence).'[34]

[2.21] The 'four principles' approach put forward by Beauchamp and Childress is generally regarded as the origin of the principles-orientated bioethics method in Western societies. Many professional bodies and associations have thus used these principles as a framework within which to develop their own ethical guidelines and codes of conduct, adding to or elaborating on these principles where appropriate in a given speciality. This approach has also been expanded, particularly in the United States, by a concern for the scope of application of these principles. The 'four principles plus scope' approach claims that the four principles alone do not provide a method for choosing between moral principles in the event that they are in conflict. This may be a source of dissatisfaction for those who want ethics to be a neat set of rules that will provide an exact and complete answer to any ethical problem. However, by looking at the scope of the principles, a common set of moral commitments and a common moral language can be discovered by which to confront moral issues.[35]

[2.22] Each of the four principles will be considered briefly in turn – first, respect for autonomy.[36] Autonomy literally means self-rule, in other words making one's own deliberate decisions. Respect for autonomy therefore is 'the moral obligation to respect the autonomy of others in so far as such respect is compatible with equal respect for the autonomy of all potentially affected.'[37] Respect for autonomy is also sometimes described as treating others as ends in themselves rather than as means to an end. In the medical arena, respect for autonomy is of vital significance in relation to consulting with and informing patients about their healthcare and their choices and respecting the right of competent adults to make decisions about their treatment. It requires doctors to obtain informed consent from patients before any treatment or intervention (except in cases of incapacity or medical emergency). It also requires patient confidentiality to be maintained, appropriate behaviour to be practised and good communication methods to be used.

[2.23] Beneficence and non-maleficence are sometimes considered together as two sides of the same coin, although in some situations one of these duties may exist without the other. The ultimate aim in healthcare is to produce net benefit over harm, while

---

31 Downie and Calman, *Healthy Respect* (2nd edn, OUP, 1994).

32 Engelhardt, *The Foundation of Bioethics* (2nd edn, OUP, 1996).

33 Veatch, 'Theories of Bioethics' in *Global Bioethics: the 4th World Congress of Bioethics Program Book*. Proceedings of a conference presented by the International Association of Bioethics in conjunction with the Asian Bioethics Association, Nov. 1998, Japan.

34 Macer, *Bioethics Is Love of Life: An Alternative Textbook* (Christchurch New Zealand: Eubios Ethics Institute, 1998).

35 Gillon, 'Medical Ethics: Four Principles Plus Attention to Scope' (1994) BMJ 309:184.

36 For a discussion of the history of the concept, see Faden and Beauchamp *A History and Theory of Informed Consent* (OUP, 1986).

37 Gillon, 'Medical Ethics: Four Principles Plus Attention to Scope' (1994) BMJ; 309:184, p185.

recognising that, inevitably, some risk of harm may exist when any medical intervention takes place. Beneficence is the traditional Hippocratic duty to do good, while non-maleficence is the duty not to harm. These duties mean that those who treat patients must be appropriately qualified to do so, otherwise the risk of causing harm becomes disproportionate. The medical profession undertakes to provide extensive training and education to prospective and current practitioners to ensure adequate protection of patients.

[2.24] The duty of justice is generally synonymous with fairness and may thus be described as the moral obligation to act on the basis of fair adjudication between competing claims. This may be subdivided into three categories of obligations: distributive justice, which involves the fair distribution of resources;[38] rights-based justice, which involves respect for people's rights;[39] and legal justice, which involves respect for morally acceptable laws.[40] There are many moral conflicts that can arise in this context, for example how to decide between a number of deserving patients as to provision of a scarce resource.[41] There are also issues in regard to the wider use of resources, conscious that payment must be made for those resources either by the patient, an insurer or the State. For example, one controversial issue here might be whether a doctor may decide to withhold a heart bypass operation from a patient who refuses to give up smoking, or a liver transplant from a patient who refuses to give up alcohol. It may be argued that it is the doctor's responsibility to ensure that scarce resources are allocated not only on the basis of need but also on the basis of maximising the benefit to be obtained from the use of those resources. However, the counter argument is that the doctor's role is not to punish patients for personal habits or lifestyle choices, even though those choices may have contributed to the person's illness and need of those resources.

[2.25] It is important to recognise that these four duties do not and cannot exist separately from each other and, of course, may come into conflict with each other. This requires consideration of the 'scope' of the principles. While ensuring that doctors must do good, it is also necessary to realise that the 'good' may be subjective and may not, in fact, coincide with respect for the choice made by the patient. In such a case, which duty is paramount – beneficence or respect for autonomy? This may arise in relation to treatment which may offer the patient a good chance of survival or recovery from their illness, but may impair their quality of life so much that, in that patient's eyes, life would no longer be worth living. In such a case respect for autonomy must take priority, as

---

[38] See further Rawls, *A Theory of Justice* (Harvard University Press, 1971); Beauchamp and Walters (eds) *Contemporary Issues in Bioethics* (Wadsworth Publishing Co, 1989) at 25–34.

[39] This may be seen, for example, in the context of the abortion debate in Ireland where much debate takes place around the issue of the woman's right to choose an abortion, and the fetus's right to life. For further discussion of the influence of the language of legal rights in the healthcare context, see Montgomery, 'Patients First: The Role of Rights' in Fulford et al (eds) *Essential Practice in Patient-Centred Care,* (Wiley-Blackwell, 1996); Brazier 'Rights and Health Care' in Blackburn (ed) *Rights of Citizenship*, (Mansell Publishing Ltd, 1993); Raz, *The Morality of Freedom* (Clarendon Press, 1986).

[40] Gillon 'Medical Ethics: Four Principles Plus Attention to Scope' (1994) BMJ; 309:184 at 186.

[41] For reflections on this argument in the UK healthcare system, see Newdick, *Who Should We Treat? Law, Patients and Resources in the NHS* (OUP, USA, 1995).

otherwise the patient would be treated without having given a truly voluntary consent, which would be unethical and illegal.[42] This decision becomes more difficult in cases where the choice appears irrational and may cause harm to others, such as in cases of refusal to undergo a caesarean section delivery in order to save the fetus's life.[43] Although the decision to refuse treatment may be unpalatable (which in itself is a subjective judgment on the doctor's part), nonetheless it may be argued that it is the patient's right to make it.

[2.26] Traditional medical paternalism as described by the Hippocratic Oath says only that doctors must work for the benefit of their patients, and says nothing about consulting patients, describing alternatives or even doing what the patient wants. The old (and, in some instances, current) view is that the doctor knows best. Some doctors may argue that, although the explanation of the Oath in such terms seems blatantly outdated, in many cases patients would be best served by not having the information explained to them or choices given to them in circumstances in which they are already terrified by their illness, in severe pain, confused and distressed. Adding to that distress, it is said, would not be in their best interests. Although it is necessary to recognise that some patients do not want to hear bad news, it would, however, be wrong to make such an assumption without clear statements to that effect by the patient. Concealing such information from the patient also sometimes takes place at the request of the patient's family, who would prefer to shelter their parent, sibling or child from such trauma. However, in such a difficult situation, the doctor has to decide whether the subjective decision of a family member on the basis of the patient's welfare takes priority over the individual's right to respect for autonomy. Deceiving the patient in this way breaches the normal rules of medical confidentiality, may cause distress to the family in trying to conceal the truth, engender further alarm and fear in the patient who suspects the truth and cause resentment or anger if the patient later discovers the deceit.[44]

[2.27] An illustration of this difficult balancing act is provided by the controversy that arose as a result of the retention of human organs following post-mortem examination. In the past, in Ireland and elsewhere, organs and tissue were removed and retained from the bodies of persons undergoing post-mortem examination in order to complete a thorough examination and comprehensive diagnosis of the cause of death. Organs were sometimes retained for long periods of time for teaching and research purposes without the knowledge of the deceased's family. It was not hospital or professional policy to inform parents about this practice. The shock, anger and betrayal felt by families at the revelation of these long-standing practices highlighted the existence of a significant communication gap between the medical establishment and the general public. Doctors argued that their reluctance to inform families of the details surrounding the post-mortem examination and retention of organs was to protect rather than insult, that they had a different professional perspective of the body, that the information was likely to

---

[42] This follows John Stuart Mill's argument that restrictions on liberty may only be permissible in the interests of other people, and then only to a strictly limited extent. Restrictions on liberty imposed on a person for his own good may never be justified. JS Mill, *On Liberty,* originally published in 1859, reprinted in 1956.

[43] For example, *Re S (Adult: Refusal of Medical Treatment)* [1992] 4 All ER 671.

[44] See generally Gillon, *Philosophical Medical Ethics* (Wiley Medical Publications, 1986) 60–106.

cause more grief and pain than it alleviated and that therefore they were behaving ethically. In Ireland, the Report on Post Mortem Practice and Procedures (the Madden Report) found that 'this argument has a clear and reasonable humanitarian appeal but rests on a paternalistic basis that patients, parents, and the general public now interpret as unnecessarily secretive and disrespectful. Medical paternalism is unacceptable by modern standards whereby doctor and patient now stand in a different relationship to each other, one that is based on mutual trust and shared understanding.'[45]

THE RELATIONSHIP BETWEEN LAW AND MEDICINE

[2.28] The relationship between law and medicine has not been an easy one. Both have traditionally been regarded as powerful and elite professions and have been at once honoured and attacked on this ground. Both professions have traditionally been self-regulating and have resisted any attempts at State intervention, although this resistance has not proved successful in the face of demands for greater accountability and lay involvement in recent years. The medical profession has tended to resent the interference or encroachment of lawyers into their professional lives and practices, and the interference brought about by spiralling medical litigation. Many blame the legal profession for encouragement of such claims against doctors with little regard for the long-term consequences for medical practice. To doctors, the law constitutes 'a symbolic representation of the limits of medicine's authority' and, commonly armed with only a hazy understanding of medical law, doctors are 'fighting a battle of symbols...to defend their jurisdiction.'[46] The legal profession are perhaps a little sceptical too of the medical profession's ability to find expertise to support wildly differing medical facts and to vouch for medical injuries and ailments that are exaggerated by their clients.

[2.29] The description of law's relationship with medicine has been characterised by the famous quote of Windeyer J in *Mount Isa Mines v Pusey*, where he said that law is seen as 'marching with medicine but in the rear and limping a little'.[47] With the rapid advances witnessed in medicine over the last few decades, the changing structure of the health services and increased medical knowledge in the community, a new conceptualisation of the medical relationship not only between doctor and patient, but also between law and medicine more generally is necessary. Those who criticise the traditional formulation of the medical relationship argue that what is needed is more focus on patients' rights. Others argue that more account needs to be taken of patient welfare. The two approaches are not altogether complementary. 'Should the emphasis be on the accountability of doctors or on their responsiveness, on the legal entitlements of the 'purchaser' of healthcare, or on the therapeutic benefits of being involved in one's treatment?'[48]

---

[45] Report of Dr Deirdre Madden on Post Mortem Practice and Procedures (Government Stationery Office, Dublin, 2005) para 2.4.

[46] Zussman, *Intensive Care* (University of Chicago Press, 1992) 183–185.

[47] *Mount Isa Mines v Pusey* [1970] 125 CLR 383 at 395.

[48] Teff, Reasonable Care, Legal Perspectives on the Doctor-Patient Relationship (Clarendon Press, 1994) at xxvii.

[2.30] Medical litigation is naturally concerned with the resolution of disputes, and therefore the court must make a decision in relation to the rights and duties of the parties involved. Liability for negligence is essentially a form of public ordering, a standardised mechanism for regulating doctors' conduct, because what is in issue is whether the doctor has fallen below the requisite standard of care. Their professional calling is to ensure the well-being of patients, to safeguard their welfare rather than their rights. However, medical litigation should accommodate a medical model of 'therapeutic alliance' which both acknowledges the doctor's responsibility for patient welfare as well as respecting patients' rights. This would have advantageous consequences for both patient and doctor in terms of decision-making and consent to treatment:

> The therapeutic case for a collaborative approach, being medically inspired, rooted in patient welfare, and non-confrontational in nature, is far more likely than an appeal to 'patients' rights' to elicit the sympathy and co-operation of the medical profession, a key practical consideration which is too often neglected. The law obviously cannot determine the nature of medical relationships, but it could have a positive influence on them by proclaiming more responsive standards as norms for medical practice.[49]

[2.31] The attitude of the medical profession to the law is perhaps shaped in part by the traditional lack of education on legal issues in medical training schools. Such education as is given has traditionally focused on forensic medicine, death certification, giving expert evidence and compliance with other relevant statutory provisions. As for the broader legal responsibilities of doctors: 'consent, professional confidence, drug legislation, failure to communicate and the whole expanding field of negligence and malpractice form a minefield into which many new graduates now seem to wander unprotected by little if any knowledge, or even awareness of the problem.'[50] Although the tide is certainly turning in recent years in favour of the teaching of specialised legal subjects dealing with the wider areas of medical jurisprudence, the vast array of medical courses to be digested by medical students tends to swamp any such attempts.

[2.32] The most prominent legal concern of any doctor is inevitably the avoidance of litigation. The natural fear and resentment felt by many doctors towards the prospect of being sued leads to a hostile beginning to the relationship between law and medicine. There are concerns that the law is unduly intrusive and threatening, that it distracts the doctor from his real work of treating patients and that the maze of legal rules and procedures are designed to trip up those who are unfamiliar with the system. Their opinions are often misinterpreted or distorted by opposing legal teams, their answers led by clever advocacy. 'The physician, normally masterful and self-confident in the setting of medicine, becomes infantilised in the setting of adversarial litigation.'[51] The adversarial approach to which our legal system subscribes is not designed to investigate without confrontation. The system tends to encourage hostility and distress and parties are forced into a trial by battle. Doctors are not alone in finding such an approach to the

---

[49] Teff, *Reasonable Care, Legal Perspectives on the Doctor-Patient Relationship* (Clarendon Press, 1994) at xxxi.

[50] Knight and McKim Thompson, 'The Teaching of Legal Medicine in British Medical Schools' (1986) 20 *Medical Education* 246, 247.

[51] Dickens, 'The Effects of Legal Liability on Physicians' Services' (1991) 41 University of Toronto Law Journal 168, 180.

resolution of complicated medical disputes incomprehensible, as patients too are dispirited by the system.

[2.33] In recent years there have been numerous calls for a system of open disclosure which would require patients to be informed promptly and honestly of any adverse event which may have impacted their health.[52] The Commission on Patient Safety and Quality reported in 2008 that a substantial number of patients suffer injuries due to medical interventions while in hospital. When the causes are investigated it is found that most of such injuries are due to errors and are therefore potentially preventable. When an error or adverse event occurs, healthcare professionals may be faced with a difficult dilemma in deciding whether and what to tell the patient. On the one hand disclosure is advocated by patients, safety experts and ethicists; yet on the other hand professionals are conscious and fearful of potential litigation. Although such fears are understandable, studies show that error disclosure reduces patients' inclination to sue and even when they do sue, the financial costs involved to the institution or the insurer are reduced due to the speed of negotiation, the use of alternative methods of dispute resolution, and the consequent decrease in recourse to legal practitioners. Many patients who believe they have been the victim of incompetent care take legal action simply to find out exactly what happened to them and to prevent recurrence. International evidence shows that the vast majority of patients who are injured by medical errors never sue. The Commission concluded that although no approach to disclosure is without risk, there is no evidence to suggest that a policy of open disclosure increases liability.

[2.34] There has been growing support in the international literature for the concept that doctors should make full disclosure of medical errors to their patients. As well as enhancing patient safety by the acknowledgement that an error occurred, it is also in keeping with the ethical commitment of honesty to patients. Failure to communicate effectively with patients following errors therefore damages the integrity of the profession.[53] The Commission on Patient Safety acknowledged that there are significant barriers to communicating with patients and families after an adverse event. These have been identified as including the belief that there was no need to disclose an error if the harm was trivial or if the patient was unaware that the error had taken place; belief that certain patients would not want to know about an error and that informing these patients of an error would diminish patients' trust in their physician. There may be psychological reasons for non-disclosure as acknowledging an error may damage a physician's confidence and self-esteem, and render him/her less effective. Junior and senior physicians may have different reasons for non-disclosure. Junior physicians may be concerned about their professional advancement while senior physicians may have particular concerns about admitting error because they may fear that this will diminish their authority. Fear of litigation has also been identified as an important barrier to disclosure. Such fears may however be allayed by a combination of education and training approaches to support healthcare professionals, and appropriate legislation to protect such disclosures being used in the context of litigation. The overriding principle

---

[52] See discussion and recommendations of the Commission on Patient Safety and Quality (2008) pp 77–82 www.health.gov.ie/wp-content/uploads/2014/03/en_patientsafety.pdf

[53] Report of the Commission on Patient Safety (2008) page 78.

accepted by the Commission is that patients are entitled to expect honest and open communication in relation to adverse events that may have caused them harm.

[2.35] In 2013 the Health Service Executive in Ireland in conjunction with the State Claims Agency, published a new policy on Open Disclosure which will apply throughout the public health and social care service.[54] Open Disclosure is also one of the National Standards of Safer Better Healthcare produced by the Health Information and Quality Authority[55] which will form the basis for licensing of all health establishments in the near future. It is also supported by the Medical Council, professional indemnity bodies and is contained in the National Healthcare Charter in 2012[56] which sets out what patients may expect from the health service, based on principles of access, dignity and respect, safe and effective services, communication and information, participation, privacy, improving health and accountability.

[2.36] In recent years there has been an increased emphasis on consumer awareness and consumer rights in many areas of society, not least in relation to healthcare. Higher public expectations of doctors, greater levels of understanding of illness and medicine and a corresponding ease of access to information and travel has led to a demand for patient charters of rights to which hospitals and doctors may be held to account. However, it has been claimed that a reliance on rights in medical law would lead not only to increased medical litigation but also to an increase in the practice of defensive medicine. Such practices, which encourage doctors to order every possible test or procedure in circumstances in which they may not be clinically justifiable in order to defend themselves against possible future litigation, is seen as potentially damaging to patients, and certainly to the healthcare system in general. If doctors feel that they have to change their medical practices in order to ward off potential claimants, as has been argued in the context of increased rates of caesarean sections and episiotomies, patients, health insurers and the State will ultimately be the losers, as the costs of excessive and unjustifiable tests have to be paid for by someone.

REGULATION OF MEDICAL PRACTICE IN IRELAND

[2.37] What is the role of a profession and why is it considered necessary to regulate those who work within professions? Mills et al describe a profession as 'an occupation in which a trained individual uses an intellectual skill based on an established body of knowledge and practice to provide a specialised service in a defined area, exercising independent judgement in accordance with a code of ethics and in the public interest.'[57] Healthcare is commonly delivered by a range of professionals acting individually or as a team. This can include general practitioners, specialists, nurses, therapists, pharmacists and many health and social care professionals. The common feature shared by these professions is that they are special kinds of knowledge-based occupations. The type of knowledge, the social and cultural value attributed to it and the way in which each

---

[54] The HSE Open Disclosure Policy is available at www.hse.ie/opendisclosure/.

[55] www.hiqa.ie/standards/health/safer-better-healthcare.

[56] www.hse.ie/eng/services/yourhealthservice/hcharter/National_Healthcare_Charter.pdf.

[57] Mills, Ryan, McDowell, Burke, *Disciplinary Procedures in the Statutory Professions* (2011, Bloomsbury Professional) p 6.

occupation handles that knowledge are seen as central to both the process of professionalism and maintaining or extending professional positions. Another factor that commonly distinguishes health professional groups in particular is the requirement to obtain a licence to practise from the State. In this way, health professionals draw a boundary around their knowledge which excludes outsiders. This boundary is usually underpinned by legislation which brings about market control for health professionals in the supply of healthcare.[58]

[2.38] The medical profession in every country in the world has always been held in special esteem. Doctors are respected, trusted and admired as healers, protectors and confidants. Doctors in most communities are regarded as persons with unquestionable authority and with special skills and intellect. Their opinions have therefore traditionally been deemed of the utmost importance, both in terms of clinical advice and psychological support and empathy given to those in distress. Doctors are also scientists who help to develop new technologies and treatments through clinical research and trials, thus improving diagnoses and outcomes for the patients. The medical profession may also be seen as having a political function through involvement in public policy debates about healthcare, lobbying for change on various healthcare provision and patient safety issues and negotiating with the government for better conditions of employment for doctors in the public healthcare system. Similar, though perhaps less publicly visible, roles apply to the other health and social care professions also.

[2.39] In more recent times, the relationship between the doctor and the community has gone through many changes as the layperson has steadily become more informed about healthcare issues and more inquisitive about his choices. This is reflected in the expectations that patients have of their doctors in relation to diagnoses and prescribing practices. The old adage of 'doctor knows best' has almost been consigned to the realms of the history books. These changes have had a huge impact not only on the day-to-day practice of the medical profession, but also on their ethical and legal responsibilities. It has also led to increased public expectation that those who practise any of the health professions will be subject to a system of regulation by which their conduct and competence can be measured. Regulation of the health and social care professions is therefore seen as achieving a number of important objectives in the public interest. Firstly, regulation aims to ensure that those who practise within the relevant profession are bound by appropriate and specific standards of education, training, competence and conduct. Secondly, regulation empowers the regulator to take disciplinary action against those who fall short of those standards.

[2.40] The medical profession in Ireland, as elsewhere, traditionally jealously guarded their professionalism and ability to self-regulate. 'The medical profession of the twentieth century was consistently the master of its own destiny, setting its own conditions of entry to the profession by controlling educational requirements and practice standards.'[59] De Prez argues that such regimes of self-regulation are inevitably controversial as they appear to depart from the rule of law ideal which requires that

---

[58] Report of the Commission on Patient Safety (2008) para 6.3. *Building a Culture of Patient Safety.* Section 7.7.

[59] De Prez, 'Self-regulation and paragons of virtue: the case of Fitness to Practise' *Med Law Review* 10, Spring 2002, pp. 28–56 at 30.

doctors be subject to the law just like anyone else. Proponents of self-regulation argue that it is justified where the practitioners possess an unusual level of skill and knowledge, the trustworthiness of the practitioners means they can work without supervision, and where there are issues of incompetence or unethical conduct, the profession can undertake the necessary disciplinary action itself.[60] Self-regulation also offers the advantages of independence and clinical freedom, bringing insider knowledge to bear on a problem and is more acceptable to those being regulated, thereby encouraging compliance. It is also said to be more responsive, as self-regulating bodies can move faster without the necessity to change legislation, and it is cheaper, as it requires less monitoring.[61] Irvine says that for self-regulation and professional independence to continue 'patients must feel able to trust their doctors and society must feel able to trust the collective medical profession.' However, in recent years public confidence and trust in the profession in Ireland was shaken by a number of medical scandals which led to a perception that the profession was failing to regulate the small number of aberrant doctors who caused harm to patients. It was argued that self-regulating bodies lack legitimacy, are open to accusations of self-protection, fail to provide public accountability and may be dependent on support from members of the profession.

[2.41] Demands for greater openness and accountability was not just a feature of the Irish health system. Internationally, the role of health professions in society and their self-regulatory status has also changed in recent years. This change is driven by a number of trends, such as the decline in public trust in health professions, change in regulatory structures for other professions, challenges to traditional hierarchical structures in the healthcare delivery system through the increase in multi-disciplinary care teams, changes in working arrangements and globalisation of the workforce with increased mobility and diverse expectations. The combination of these factors led to a substantial change in the way in which the medical profession is regulated in Ireland, with the passing of the Medical Practitioners Act in 2007, discussed in more detail below.

[2.42] The main feature of the move away from professional self-regulation has been the establishment of non-professional majorities on regulatory bodies, a significant dilution of the power of the relevant profession which was strongly resisted but ultimately introduced in the Medical Practitioners Act and other statutes regulating the other health and care professions in Ireland.

[2.43] There are a number of professional regulatory bodies in Ireland governing the practice of medicine.

- The Medical Council[62] regulates registered medical practitioners under the Medical Practitioners Act 2007. Its functions include assuring the quality of undergraduate education of doctors; assuring the quality of postgraduate

---

[60] Friedson, *Profession of Medicine* (University of Chicago Press 1988), quoted by de Prez.

[61] See Irvine, 'The performance of doctors: professionalism and self regulation in a changing world' BMJ 1997; 314:1540.

[62] www.medicalcouncil.ie

- training of specialists; registration of doctors; disciplinary functions; and providing guidance on professional standards/ethical conduct.
- The Dental Council[63] regulates dental practitioners under the Dentists Act 1985. Its roles include the maintenance of a register of dentists and dental specialists; assessment of the adequacy and suitability of dental education and training in the dental schools in the State; disciplinary functions; and advising the dental profession and the public on matters relating to dental ethics and professional behaviour.
- The Nursing and Midwifery Board[64] regulates nurses under the Nurses and Midwives Act 2011. The Board's functions include the registration of nurses; provision of education and training; disciplinary functions; giving guidance to the profession; managing a careers centre to provide a centralised system of processing and selection of applicants wishing to enter nursing and provision of careers advice to nurses and midwives.
- The Pharmaceutical Society of Ireland[65] is the regulator of pharmacies under the Pharmacy Act 2007. Its roles include the maintenance of a register of pharmacists and pharmacies; inspection of pharmacy premises; development of codes of conduct for pharmacists; promotion of high standards of education and training; disciplinary functions; and recognition of qualifications of pharmacists from other jurisdictions.
- The Health and Social Care Professionals Council[66] regulates 12 health and social care professions under the Health and Social Care Professionals Act 2005. These cover clinical biochemists, dieticians, medical scientists, occupational therapists, orthoptists, physiotherapists, podiatrists, psychologists, radiographers, social care workers, social workers and speech and language therapists. The functions of the Council include coordination of the activities of the twelve registration boards established for each of the foregoing professions; the enforcement of standards of practice for registrants; disciplinary functions; and promotion of collaboration between the registration boards including in relation to education and training.

This chapter deals primarily with the functions of the Medical Council in relation to education and training, and the maintenance of standards of professional conduct by registered medical practitioners. The other health and social care professionals mentioned above are regulated under a broadly similar legislative framework.[67]

THE MEDICAL COUNCIL

[2.44] The Medical Council of Ireland was established by the Medical Practitioners Act 1978 and commenced operation in April 1979. It has been amended a number of times

---

[63] www.dentalcouncil.ie.

[64] www.nursingboard.ie.

[65] www.thepsi.ie.

[66] www.coru.ie.

[67] For a more comprehensive analysis of the regulation of these professions, see Mills, Burke, McDowell and Ryan, *Disciplinary Procedures in the Statutory Professions,* (2011, Bloomsbury Professional).

since 1978, and was repealed and replaced by the Medical Practitioners Act 2007 (hereafter 'the Act'). It has 25 members, comprised of elected and appointed members. Historically, the Medical Council had a majority of medical members (21 out of a total membership of 25 were doctors) but the 2007 Act substantially changed the composition of the Council by requiring that 10 of the 25 members must be doctors, 11 must not be doctors and the remaining 4 may/may not be doctors, depending on the nominations made by the Health Service Executive (HSE) and approved bodies delivering undergraduate medical education. Therefore the Act facilitates the appointment of a lay majority though it does not guarantee it, as this will depend on the qualifications of those appointed by the latter groups. Members of the Council hold office for five years, renewable up to a maximum of two terms.

[2.45] The Council is a statutory body entrusted with important functions to be performed in the public interest. Section 6 of the Act states that the object of the Council is to 'protect the public by promoting and better ensuring high standards of professional conduct and professional education, training and competence among registered medical practitioners.' Although funded from registration fees paid by medical practitioners, the Council is 'not a body established to manage the affairs of the medical profession or to protect its interests.'[68]

[2.46] The principal functions of the Council are set out by the 1978 Act as amended by the 2007 Act, as: the maintenance of a register of medical practitioners, the supervision of the standards of medical education and training of doctors, the control of postgraduate training of specialists, the imposition of disciplinary procedures and the development of professional standards of ethical conduct. The Council has committees dealing with education and training, registration, health of medical practitioners, maintenance of professional competence, fitness to practise, standards in practice and ethics. The committees generally meet on a monthly to quarterly basis. Under the Act, the Minister for Health has the power to make certain orders relating to the training of doctors or the implementation of European Directives and Regulations and may also give directions to the Council on matters other than professional conduct and ethics or disciplinary matters.

Registration

[2.47] Registration is a key component of professional regulation as it requires the practitioner to comply with minimum educational standards prior to entry into practice, and it enables the regulator to ensure continued compliance with standards of practice throughout the practitioner's career. It therefore provides assurance to the public and employers that only those who have achieved (and maintain) a specified degree of competence in medical practice are on the register. Any member of the public can check the register, using either the name or registration number of the person representing themselves as a doctor, to verify whether in fact this person is legitimately entitled to so represent themselves.[69] Through the registration process, the Medical Council is

---

[68] *Philips v The Medical Council, the Minister for Health, Ireland and the Attorney General* [1991] 2 IR 115, per Costello J.

[69] www.medicalcouncil.ie/Public-Information/Check-the-Register/.

therefore cast in the role of guardian of the public interest.[70] '[T]he existence of a register is both a desirable and an efficient way to offer both protection and information to the general public: protection from those who are not registered and information on those who are.'[71] However it is unlikely that many patients or members of the public use this facility although they probably assume that a doctor is regulated by some authority, even if they do not know the Medical Council by name.

[2.48] A person cannot practise medicine in Ireland unless he or she is registered with the Medical Council.[72] It is an offence to practise medicine within the State while unregistered, with the exception of administering first aid or visiting European Economic Area (EEA) registered doctors attending in an emergency.[73] Section 41 of the Medical Practitioners Act 2007 also provides that certain designated titles may only be used by doctors and that breach of this provision is a criminal offence.

[2.49] Under s 6 of the 2007 Act, the Medical Council is obliged to maintain a Register of Medical Practitioners. This includes establishing procedures and criteria for registration. The register is divided into:

- The General Division – this is open to those who have completed medical training in Ireland, the EU or elsewhere and who have completed required examinations or have satisfactory evidence of experience sufficient to permit registration. Doctors who do not practise in individually numbered, identifiable training posts, who have not been proposed for a post in the Supervised Division, and who have not completed recognised specialist medical training must register under General Registration. This is the only form of registration available to them. Doctors with general registration may practise independently without supervision but may not falsely represent themselves as holding specialist or trainee specialist registration.

- The Specialist Division – this is open to those who have completed specialist medical training in a speciality recognised by the Council and who can provide evidence from an appropriate body that satisfies the Medical Council.

- The Trainee Specialist Division –The Medical Council, in consultation with approved postgraduate training bodies and the HSE, maintains a record of postgraduate training posts within the State. A doctor undertaking postgraduate medical training in a recognised training post must be registered in this division of the register. Medical practitioners can only hold trainee specialist registration while occupying individually numbered, identifiable training posts within the State.

- Internship registration – Internship Registration allows a doctor to carry out internship training in a hospital recognised by the Medical Council. Internship registration is open to both graduates of Irish and EU Member State Medical Schools.

---

[70] De Prez, 'Self-regulation and paragons of virtue: the case of Fitness to Practise' *Med Law Review* 10, Spring 2002, pp. 28–56 at p 34.

[71] Mills, Burke, McDowell and Ryan, *Disciplinary Procedures in the Statutory Professions,* (2011, Bloomsbury Professional) at 21.

[72] Medical Practitioners Act 2007, s 37.

[73] Medical Practitioners Act 2007, s 41.

- Supervised division – Registration in the Supervised Division can only be granted to doctors who are offered a post with the HSE that has been approved as an individually numbered, identifiable post.[74]
- The Visiting EEA Practitioners Division – this is for practitioners who are practising medicine in an EU Member State and who wish to practise in Ireland only on a temporary or occasional basis. The practitioner must be an EU citizen and must be registered with the relevant regulatory body in the other EU Member State. They must notify the Council of intended periods and scope of practice in Ireland and provide certificates of good standing from all regulatory bodies with which they have been registered in the previous five years.

[2.50] It is possible to apply to transfer from one division of the register to another, for example a practitioner on the Trainee Specialist or General division may apply to move onto the Specialist division. Specialist registration is specifically for medical practitioners who have completed specialist training recognised by the Medical Council and can practise independently as a specialist. While external agencies of the Council may advise the Medical Council on individual applications, the final decision on eligibility for entry into the Specialist Division of the Register lies with the Council.

[2.51] The Council is obliged by the Act to publish copies of the Register (and supplements to it) at specified intervals and to keep available for inspection at Council offices the most recently published copy of the Register.[75] The facility for checking the registration status of any medical practitioner is also available online.[76] Only a person registered under the Act may sign a certificate that is required to be signed by a medical practitioner. It is a criminal offence to make any false declaration or misrepresentation to the Council in order to obtain registration. The practitioner must state his registration number on all medical documents, such as prescriptions or other records.

Medical education and training

[2.52] Under s 6(c) of the Medical Practitioners Act 2007, the Medical Council shall 'approve programmes of education and further education necessary for the purposes of registration and continued registration'. This means that the Council is responsible for the accreditation of medical schools in Ireland, for the assessment of the quality of

---

[74] Under the 2007 Act, doctors who entered the General Division of the register could take up any post in Ireland including unsupervised locum general practice positions and could work wholly in private practice. In July 2011, an amendment to the 2007 Act was passed to establish a new Supervised Division of the medical register which ensures that doctors registered in this division will be restricted to working under supervision, only in Council-approved posts, for a period of two years or less. Registration in this division is contingent on doctors satisfying the Council that their education and training in their country of qualification meet required standards and that they have not been subject to disciplinary actions in any country where they previously practised medicine. They will also be required to undertake an examination here related to their chosen specialty which will assess their competence in areas of clinical judgement, communication and data interpretation.

[75] Medical Practitioners Act 2007, s 57.

[76] www.medicalcouncil.ie/Public-Information/Check-the-Register/.

educational programmes and for the registration of graduates as medical practitioners.[77] It must keep these programmes under review and oversee lifelong learning and skills development throughout doctors' professional careers through the establishment of professional competence requirements.

[2.53] Every medical degree programme delivered in Ireland is required to meet the standards set by the Medical Council, which in turn are based upon the World Federation for Medical Education's Global Standards for Quality Improvement in Medical Education.[78] These standards set requirements for programmes, and for the medical schools delivering the programmes. The Medical Council is also obliged to ensure that the minimum standards required by any Directive of the European Community relating to education and training are met by the formal qualifications in the State. The Council must satisfy itself as to the suitability of undergraduate medical education and training provided by recognised medical schools and the standard of theoretical and practical knowledge required at the examinations for primary qualification. It must also satisfy itself as to the clinical training and experience required for the granting of a certificate of experience, and the adequacy and suitability of postgraduate education and training. The Council carries out this function by firstly assessing written submissions from the medical schools, postgraduate training bodies and clinical sites which provide information as to compliance with the required standards. It then forms an accreditation team which visits the medical schools and other sites to discuss the submission and meet staff and students. The Council can then approve, impose conditions, or refuse approval to the medical school or training site depending on the level of compliance.

[2.54] In recent years there has been much discussion in Ireland and elsewhere of the need for continuing education and professional development of healthcare professionals. For example, the Report of the Commission on Patient Safety in 2008 stated:

> It is clear that a health professional can no longer be regarded as trained for life upon qualification. Instead what is required are systems of lifelong learning and professional development, with regular competence assurance to ensure that there is a workforce of skilled professionals who are fit for purpose, competent in managing patients' needs, aware of the limits of their own competency and adaptable and capable of responding to changing needs. Continuing Professional Development (CPD) is a key responsibility of individual practitioners, a core function of training bodies and a crucial component of the professional regulatory reforms eg the Medical Council's Competence Assurance Scheme.[79]

[2.55] The Medical Practitioners Act 2007, s 94 introduced for the first time a legal obligation on registered medical practitioners to maintain their professional competence throughout their working lives. Part 11 of the Medical Practitioners Act provides a statutory basis for the development of Professional Competence Schemes in Ireland. Section 91(1) of the Act provides that 'It shall be the duty of the Council to satisfy itself as to the ongoing maintenance of professional competence of registered medical practitioners.' If a registered medical practitioner refuses or ceases to cooperate with the

---

[77] Review of Medical Schools in Ireland, Medical Council 2007.

[78] Available at www.wfme.org.

[79] *Building a Culture of Patient Safety* (2008), p 99 available at www.health.gov.ie.

Scheme, the Council may make a complaint to the disciplinary or Fitness to Practise section of the Council. Healthcare employers are obliged by s 93 of the Act to facilitate the maintenance by the practitioner of his professional competence. Section 93 provides as follows:

> (1) The Health Service Executive shall facilitate the maintenance of professional competence of registered medical practitioners pursuant to a professional competence scheme applicable to the practitioners concerned.

> (2) An employer of a registered medical practitioner, not being the Health Service Executive, shall facilitate the maintenance of professional competence of registered medical practitioners pursuant to a professional competence scheme applicable to the practitioners concerned.

[2.56] As a result of this provision in the 2007 Act, doctors are now legally obliged to maintain their professional competence by enrolling in professional competence schemes and following requirements set by the Medical Council. Most doctors previously engaged in continuous professional development, however this new system creates a formal process of lifelong learning which highlights doctors' dedication to developing their skills throughout their professional lives. Participation in a Professional Competence Scheme operated by postgraduate training bodies is designed to help registered doctors to demonstrate that they are fulfilling their new statutory duty. Schemes are in place for all registered doctors on the Specialist and General Division of the Medical Register.

[2.57] At a practical level this is a key issue not only for individual practitioners but also for employers, who should have systems in place to ensure that all professional staff participate in Continuing Professional Development (CPD) and are provided with adequate time and resources to do so. CPD involves not only the continuous upgrading of clinical skills but also the development of the necessary skills of accessing and appraising evidence, clinical audit and reflective practice, the application of standards and the monitoring of performance against standards.

Freedom of establishment

[2.58] Under European law, citizens are entitled to freedom of movement, which means that the presence of national borders should not be an impediment to the free market. Therefore, a doctor who is qualified in one EU state should, in principle, be free to travel to and work in another EU Member State. A number of EU Directives were introduced to deal with free movement of persons and freedom of establishment. These were consolidated in 2005 in Directive 2005/36/EC. This was transposed into Irish law in both the Medical Practitioners Act 2007 and the Recognition of Professional Qualifications (Directive 2005/36/EC) Regulations, 2008.[80]

[2.59] Issues that have caused some difficulties in recent years centre on the recognition of qualifications from other countries and language proficiency tests. Under Irish law, the focus is primarily on the qualification held by the applicant, not the applicant's citizenship. EU/EEA and non-EU/EEA citizens are generally treated equally. This means that the Medical Council is not entitled to require evidence of English language

---

[80] SI 139/2008.

proficiency from EU citizens. A person who wishes to carry on a regulated profession in another Member State is obliged to fulfil certain minimum criteria set out in the Directive and provide evidence that he or she has obtained equivalent professional and educational qualifications and training in an EU Member State. If these conditions are met, permission may not be refused to an EU citizen to practise in another Member State. If the training is not deemed equivalent, the host state may offer an aptitude test and period of adaptation in the host country.

Illegal practice of medicine

[2.60] Section 37 of the Medical Practitioners Act 2007 provides that an unregistered medical practitioner shall not practise medicine or advertise his services as a medical practitioner. The expression 'practice medicine' is not clearly defined in the Act; it is simply stated to mean 'to engage in the practice of medicine'. This phrase in turn is defined as including 'the practice of surgery and other disciplines of medicine.' Section 38 of the Act provides that a medical practitioner does not contravene s 37 if:

(a)   the practitioner is a dentist registered under the Dentists Act 1985 who only practices medicine in the course of, and for the purpose of, the lawful practice of dentistry,

(b)   the practitioner is a person registered under the Nurses Act 1985 (as subsequently amended by the Nurses and Midwives Act 2011) who only practices medicine in the course of, and for the purposes of, the lawful practice of nursing or midwifery,

(c)   the practitioner is a registered pharmaceutical chemist or a registered dispensing chemist and druggist, under the Pharmacy Acts 1875 to 1977, who only practices medicine in the course of, and for the purposes of, the lawful practice of pharmacy in accordance with those Acts,

(d)   the practitioner is a person registered under the Health and Social Care Professionals Act 2005 to practice a profession designated under that Act who only practises medicine in the course of, and for the purposes of, the lawful practice of that profession,

(e)   the practitioner only practises medicine in the course of rendering first aid to a person,

(f)   the practitioner only practises medicine in the State pursuant to the provisions of s 50 (this section provides that, subject to the conditions set out in the Act, a medical practitioner who is a national of a Member State and lawfully established in medical practice in a Member State may, on visiting the State, practise medicine on a temporary and occasional basis without first being registered, and advertise the practitioner's services as a medical practitioner for this purpose.)

(g)   the practitioner only practises medicine in any combination of any of the circumstances specified in paragraphs (a) to (f).

[2.61] Section 39 of the Act provides that the Minister for Health may make regulations to designate for the purposes of this Act any title or variants thereof to be used by any registered medical practitioner. This power will only be exercised following consultation with interested parties and organisations, and where the designation of title is deemed to be in the public interest. The Minister will consider the extent to which any class of medical practitioners has a defined scope of practice and applies a distinct and recognised body of knowledge, as well as the degree of risk to the health, safety or welfare of the public from the incompetent, unethical or impaired practice of any class of medical practitioners. If the Minister exercises the power under this Act, s 40 provides that a registered medical practitioner shall not use a designated title other than in accordance with such regulations.

[2.62] Section 41 of the Act provides that a person is guilty of an offence if they practise medicine while unregistered or use a designated title without being so entitled, falsely represent themselves to be a registered medical practitioner, or represent themselves to be registered in a division of the register other than that in which they are so registered. Section 42 provides that an unregistered medical practitioner shall not be entitled to recover fees or expenses incurred in providing services in the course of practising medicine.

DISCIPLINARY FUNCTIONS

Historical background

[2.63] One of the most important ways in which the Medical Council discharges its function of protecting the public is by investigating complaints made against registered medical practitioners and imposing sanctions where the allegations are upheld. The purpose of the imposition of sanctions is not regarded by the Council as a punitive measure but rather as a protective mechanism to safeguard the public from any future aberrations by the practitioner. It is also considered important in the public interest to maintain the reputation and dignity of the profession. 'Preserving the reputation of the profession as ethically superior is of value to the profession in attracting the privileges of social status and respect in society. In this sense the GMC[81] might be regarded as enforcing a mutually beneficial contract with the profession to ensure that such status is maintained by the expulsion of those who attract undesired attention to its members.'[82]This was described by the Privy Council in *Gupta v General Medical Council*[83] as follows: 'where professional discipline is at stake, the relevant Committee is not concerned exclusively, or even primarily, with the punishment of the practitioner concerned.' The Privy Council in that case upheld the approach taken in *Bolton v The Law Society*[84] where Sir Thomas Bingham MR spoke at length about the function of imposing disciplinary sanctions against a professional. He said:

> To maintain this reputation and sustain public confidence in the integrity of the profession it is often necessary that those guilty of serious lapses are not only expelled but denied readmission...A profession's most valuable asset is its collective reputation and the confidence which that inspires...It often happens that a solicitor appearing before the

---

[81] The General Medical Council (GMC) in the United Kingdom with similar functions to the Irish Medical Council.

[82] De Prez 'Self-regulation and Paragons of Virtue: the case of Fitness to Practise' Medical Law Review, 10, Spring 2002, 28–56 at 51.

[83] *Gupta v General Medical Council* [2001] UKPC 61.

[84] *Bolton v The Law Society* [1994] 1 WLR.

tribunal can adduce a wealth of glowing tributes from his professional brethren. He can often show that for him and his family the consequences of striking off or suspension would be little short of tragic. All these matters are relevant and should be considered…[but] the reputation of the profession is more important than the fortunes of any individual member. Membership of the profession brings many benefits, but that is part of the price.[85]

[2.64] The history of investigation into alleged misconduct of medical practitioners dates back to the Medical Act 1858 which established the General Council of Medical Education and Registration in the United Kingdom. This Act provided that if any registered medical practitioner was convicted of any crime or found guilty of 'infamous conduct in any professional respect', the Council could direct the Registrar to erase that practitioner's name from the register. This provision was considered in *Allinson v General Medical Council*[86] following a complaint concerning advertising by Dr Allinson. In the advertisement Dr Allinson had warned the public to avoid other practitioners and recommended them to attend him instead. The Court held that this behaviour amounted to infamous conduct in a professional respect. The Court said 'if it is shown that a medical man, in the pursuit of his profession, has done something with regard to it which would be reasonably regarded as disgraceful and dishonourable by his professional brethren of good repute and competency, it is open to the Council to find that he has been guilty of infamous conduct in a professional respect.' Lord Esher also drew a distinction between the standard of behaviour expected of medical practitioners and that expected of those outside the profession:

> The question is, not merely whether what a medical man has done would be an infamous thing for anyone else to do, but whether it is infamous for a medical man to do it…There may be some acts which, although they would not be infamous in any other person, yet if they are done by a medical man in relation to his profession, that is, with regard either to his patients or to his professional brethren, may be fairly considered 'infamous conduct in a professional respect' and such acts would, I think, come within section 29.

[2.65] The Medical Practitioners Act 1927 established the Medical Registration Council which also had the authority to erase the name of any practitioner who had been found guilty of infamous conduct in a professional respect. In the Medical Practitioners Act 1978 the term 'professional misconduct' was first used in Ireland to describe the conduct for which a practitioner could be sanctioned by the Medical Council. The term 'professional misconduct' is a deliberately broad term designed to cover a range of behaviour. 'Modern definitions of professional misconduct acknowledge the futility of seeking to exhaustively set out its parameters. In particular, they admit that despite the needs of the profession for certainty in this crucial concept, its meaning fluctuates with shifting values in wider society.'[87]

---

85   Although it may be argued that Bingham MR may have gone too far in this passage, 'there is some obvious benefit to both profession and consumer to have elevated personal standards for professional people. The maintenance of high personal moral standards both burnishes the status of the profession and communicates certain assurances to consumers of the profession's services.' Mills et al, *Disciplinary Procedures in the Statutory Professions*, 10.

86   *Allinson v General Medical Council* [1894] 1 QB.

87   Du Prez, 'Self-regulation and Fitness to Practice' Med L Rev (2002) Vol 10(1) 28 at 36.

[2.66] One of the most important decisions in relation to the meaning of professional misconduct under the 1978 Act was *O'Laoire v The Medical Council*.[88] This case involved a breakdown in professional relationships in the neurosurgery department of Beaumont Hospital in Dublin which resulted in consultant neurosurgeon Mr O'Laoire refusing to treat a number of patients on grounds that he did not have the necessary skills, and also Mr O'Laoire making a number of allegations against another neurosurgeon in the department. Mr O'Laoire was the subject of a complaint to the Medical Council and was subsequently found guilty of professional misconduct, suspended for a period of up to eighteen months and censured for his behaviour. The Council's decision was appealed to the High Court, during which Keane J defined professional misconduct as follows:

(1) Conduct which is 'infamous' or 'disgraceful' in a professional respect is 'professional misconduct'...;

(2) Conduct which would not be 'infamous' or 'disgraceful' in any other person, if done by a medical practitioner in relation to his profession, that is, with regard either to his patients or to his colleagues, may be considered as 'infamous' or 'disgraceful' conduct in a professional respect;

(3) 'Infamous' or 'disgraceful' conduct in turn is conduct involving some degree of moral turpitude, fraud or dishonesty;

(4) The fact that a person wrongly but honestly forms a particular opinion cannot of itself amount to infamous or disgraceful conduct in a professional sense;

(5) Conduct which could not properly be characterised as 'infamous' or 'disgraceful' and which does not involve any degree of moral turpitude, fraud or dishonesty may still constitute 'professional misconduct' if it is conduct connected with his profession in which the medical practitioner concerned has seriously fallen short, by omission or commission, of the standards of conduct expected among medical practitioners.

[2.67] Tests (1) to (4) are commonly referred to as the 'infamous or disgraceful conduct test', or the 'moral turpitude test' and test (5) is referred to as 'the expected standards test'. The first limb of Keane J's test was described in *Re Lynch and Daly*[89] as implying 'an element of conscious wrongdoing or the doing of something which a professional person by reason of his training must have realised would cause him to incur shame in the eyes of his professional colleagues.' As shown in *Allison,* considered above,[90] such 'infamous or disgraceful conduct' is considered in the context of the conduct expected of a professional person, thereby holding professionals to a higher standard of conduct than non-professionals. This is also evident from *McCandless v General Medical Council*[91] in which it was argued on behalf of the doctor that his poor treatment of patients was not enough to constitute professional misconduct, as the doctor had been doing his best and may have simply been overworked or just not very good at his job. The Court found that seriously negligent treatment can amount to professional misconduct and upheld the finding against the doctor in question. The Court took the

---

88 *O'Laoire v The Medical Council* (27 January 1995).

89 *Re Lynch and Daly* [1970] IR 1.

90 Para **[2.64]**.

91 *McCandless v GMC* [1995] 1 WLR 169.

view that the public has higher expectations of doctors and that their regulatory bodies are under a duty to protect the public against the genially incompetent as well as the deliberate wrongdoers. It is also important to note that the notion of professional misconduct can change from time to time because of changing circumstances and new eventualities.[92] These tests have been followed in subsequent cases involving both medical and other practitioners including: *An Bord Altranais v O'Ceallaigh*;[93] *Millett-Johnson v Medical Council*;[94] and *Cahill v Dental Council*.[95]

[2.68] Keane J's test of misconduct 'in a professional respect' is relatively straightforward when the allegations relate to conduct in clinical practice. However, it is less so when the alleged conduct falls outside the boundaries of clinical practice. For example, in the English case of *Roylance v General Medical Council*[96] where the Court considered the question of whether a medical practitioner could be found guilty of misconduct in relation to conduct which took place while he was acting in a management position rather than as a clinician. Dr Roylance was the Chief Executive Officer of a hospital in which there had been excessive mortality rates of children who underwent cardiac surgery and it was alleged that he had failed to take steps to deal with the problem. The Court held that a doctor who carried out purely administrative functions within a hospital still had a doctor's duties and was not entitled to disregard his medical responsibility. For a doctor to be found guilty of misconduct, the acts or omissions must be serious and must be linked to the profession of medicine. However, conduct removed from the practice of medicine might also qualify if it was of a sufficiently immoral or outrageous or disgraceful character. This was because the public reputation of and public confidence in the profession could be adversely affected.[97]

[2.69] A further example is *Meadow v General Medical Council*[98] in which a doctor was found guilty of serious professional misconduct arising from evidence he had given in a criminal trial of a mother accused of murdering her children. Although Professor Meadow's appeal to the Court of Appeal was successful, the court was of the view that his conduct in giving evidence was an appropriate matter for the GMC to inquire into. The Court said there was ample authority for the proposition that a professional may face fitness to practise proceedings not just for conduct strictly within his professional capacity, but also for conduct in his private capacity.

---

[92] Per Kelly J in *Prendiville and Murphy v Medical Council* [2007] IEHC 427.
[93] *An Bord Altranais v O'Ceallaigh* [2000] IESC 21, [2000] 4 IR 54 & 102 (17 May 2000).
[94] *Millett-Johnson v Medical Council* (12 January 2001) HC.
[95] *Cahill v Dental Council* [2001] IEHC 97.
[96] *Roylance v General Medical Council* [2000] 1 AC 311.
[97] The Court referred to *A County Council v W (disclosure)* [1997] 1 FLR 574 in which a medical practitioner opposed the General Medical Council's application for disclosure of documents connected with care proceedings in which allegations were made against him of sexual abuse of his daughter. He argued that even if proved, such allegations could not constitute professional misconduct as it was not connected with the carrying out of his profession. The Court disagreed with this contention: 'It seems to me that this doctor can be said, if he has sexually abused his daughter, to have demonstrated conduct disgraceful to him as reflecting on his profession and /or indeed conduct disgraceful to him as a practising doctor.'
[98] *Meadow v General Medical Council* [2007] QB 462.

[2.70] The second limb of Keane J's test is that of 'seriously falling short of standards'. This involves judging the alleged conduct against proper professional standards and therefore will always involve conduct of the practitioner carried out in a professional capacity. However, it is perhaps worth noting the comments of Charleton J in *Barry v Medical Council*[99] in this respect where he said (obiter) that:

> [M]embers of the medical profession are entitled to a degree of latitude with regard to their conduct, engaging as they do in a profession which is both stressful and involves them carrying the physical and psychological burdens of sick people. In that regard the standard to be applied in judging their conduct is that of men and women of professional standards and ethics, and not of angels.

[2.71] In the *O'Laoire* case, Keane J also said that the tests must be read in the context of the definition of professional misconduct set out in the Medical Council's Guide to Ethical Conduct and Behaviour.[100] Although the Guide is intended to be merely a guide, practitioners are entitled to expect that if the definition of misconduct changes or if new categories of conduct are categorised as misconduct, practitioners would be apprised of that fact in the Guide. A significant case in this context is *Prendiville and Murphy v The Medical Council*,[101] in which the applicants sought an order by way of judicial review against the Council to quash a finding of professional misconduct imposed on them following a Fitness to Practise Inquiry. The events arose out of an earlier investigation into the competence and conduct of Dr Michael Neary arising out of a complaint about the number of caesarean or postpartum hysterectomies he had carried out in the previous number of years. Dr Prendiville, Dr Murphy and a third doctor were asked by the Irish Hospital Consultants Association to urgently prepare a report on Dr Neary's practice that could be used to oppose an anticipated application to have him suspended from practice. The doctors were later the subject of a complaint to the Medical Council arising out of the contents of their report, and were found guilty of professional misconduct.

[2.72] Most of the arguments put forward by the applicants in their judicial review application to have the Council's decision quashed related to the process by which the Council reached its decision. It is not necessary to discuss these arguments in detail as most of the points raised, which were upheld by Kelly J, have been addressed in the Medical Practitioners Act 2007 which is discussed below. In the context of the definition of professional misconduct however, the applicants also argued that the Fitness to Practise Committee had applied the wrong test of professional misconduct, in that it had used the 'expected standards' test rather than the 'moral turpitude' test. The former test was first contained in the 2004 edition of the Medical Council's Ethical Guide, although Keane J had adverted to it in *O'Laoire v the Medical Council* in 1998. Kelly J said in the present case that the Committee had applied the expected standards test in circumstances where the alleged misconduct took place in 1998, some years before this test had been included in the Ethical Guide. Therefore the judge said the

---

[99] *Barry v Medical Council* [2007] IEHC 74.
[100] For further discussion of the effect of professional codes of conduct on misconduct, see Mills, Burke, McDowell and Ryan, *Disciplinary Procedures in the Statutory Professions,* (2011, Bloomsbury Professional) at [2.40]–[2.44]
[101] *Prendiville and Murphy v The Medical Council* [2007] IEHC 427.

Committee was not entitled to apply this test, as it was unreasonable and unfair to expect medical practitioners to be subjected to a test of professional misconduct which the Council had not promulgated or notified to the profession until years after the event. As Kelly J stated:

> It would be unreasonable to expect the Council to publish a catalogue of the forms of professional misconduct which may lead to disciplinary action. But if a new test is applied or a new species of conduct is to be regarded as amounting to professional misconduct, then one would expect the Council to notify its members of that.

Fitness to Practise under the Medical Practitioners Act 2007

[2.73] The cases discussed above took place under the statutory framework imposed by the Medical Practitioners Act 1978. This Act was repealed by the Medical Practitioners Act 2007 which, inter alia, made a number of changes to the Fitness to Practise procedure. In addition to complaints of alleged professional misconduct, the Council may now also hear a complaint in relation to an alleged poor professional performance and/or relevant medical disability on the part of a medical practitioner. Poor professional performance is defined in the Act as 'a failure by the practitioner to meet the standards of competence (whether in knowledge and skill or the application of knowledge and skill or both) that can reasonably be expected of medical practitioners practising medicine of the kind practised by the practitioner.' Relevant medical disability is defined as 'a physical or mental disability of the practitioner (including addiction to alcohol or drugs) which may impair the practitioner's ability to practise medicine or a particular aspect thereof.' These are considered further below.

[2.74] Under s 57 of the 2007 Act, an application for an inquiry may be brought on the following grounds:

   (a)   professional misconduct;

   (b)   poor professional performance;

   (c)   a relevant medical disability;

   (d)   a failure to comply with a relevant condition;[102]

   (e)   a failure to comply with an undertaking or to take any action specified in a consent given in response to a request made under s 67(1);[103]

   (f)   a contravention of a provision of the Medical Practitioners Act 2007, and;

   (g)   a conviction in the State for an offence triable on indictment or a conviction outside the State for an offence consisting of acts or omissions that, if done or made in the State, would constitute an offence triable on indictment.

---

[102] This refers to a situation in which a medical practitioner, who has previously been the subject of a Fitness to Practise Inquiry as a result of which conditions were imposed on his registration, fails to comply with any such condition. In such circumstances the doctor may be the subject of a new complaint to the Medical Council.

[103] Medical Practitioners Act 2007, s 67 (1) provides that the Fitness to Practise committee may, at any time after a complaint is referred to it, request the doctor to give an undertaking to not repeat the conduct complained of, or to undertake to be referred to a professional competence scheme and comply with any requirements imposed in that regard, consent to undergo medical treatment, or consent to being censured by the Council.

Section 57(2) provides that a complaint may be made on the grounds of professional misconduct or poor professional performance notwithstanding that the matter to which the complaint relates occurred outside the State.

Meaning of professional misconduct

[2.75] Professional misconduct is not defined in the 2007 Act. However, the meaning of professional misconduct is set out in the Medical Council's Guide to Professional Conduct and Ethics as:

> Conduct which doctors of experience, competence and good repute consider disgraceful or dishonourable; and/or conduct connected with his or her profession in which the doctor concerned has seriously fallen short by omission or commission of the standards of conduct expected among doctors.[104]

The test therefore continues to incorporate both the moral turpitude and the expected standards tests outlined above. It will be a matter for the Fitness to Practise Committee to decide firstly, whether the allegations have been proven against the medical practitioner and secondly, whether the allegations as proven amount to either disgraceful or dishonourable conduct, or whether the facts demonstrate a serious falling short of the standards expected of medical practitioners.

[2.76] Complaints[105] received in relation to professional misconduct are mainly in relation to clinical care such as incompetence, misdiagnosis or lack of diagnosis, poor prescribing practice, adverse outcomes or lack of hygiene. There is also a high rate of complaints in relation to communication such as rudeness, lack of consideration for patients, poor or lack of communication about diagnosis and treatment, and prejudicial remarks. There are also complaints in relation to professional behaviour such as refusal to treat or refer patients, failure to transfer medical records and advertising.[106]

Poor professional performance

[2.77] A new ground of complaint was introduced in the 2007 Act, namely, poor professional performance.[107] Unlike professional misconduct, poor professional performance is defined in s 2 of the Act as follows:

> ...in relation to a medical practitioner, means a failure by the practitioner to meet the standards of competence (whether in knowledge and skill or the application of knowledge and skill or both) that can reasonably be expected of medical practitioners practising medicine of the kind practised by the practitioner.

Although there may be some discussion about the distinction between competence and performance, ie competence may describe knowledge and skill whereas performance

---

[104] Medical Council, *Guide to Ethical Conduct and Behaviour* (8th edn, 2016) para 2.1

[105] Complaints are protected disclosures under the Health Act 2004 as amended by the Health Act 2007.

[106] Details relating to the number and type of complaints made against doctors are available in a report published by the Medical Council in July 2015 called Listening to Complaints - Learning for Good Professional Practice. Available at www.medicalcouncil.ie.

[107] Similar grounds of complaint exist under the Nurses and Midwives Act 2011, the Pharmacy Act 2007 and the Health and Social Care Professionals Act 2005.

may describe what the practitioner does within his/her actual practice,[108] in Ireland the statutory scheme does not distinguish between the two and, as can be seen from the statutory definition above, actually defines performance by reference to competence. It is also clear from the wording above that the conduct in question must relate to the performance of professional duties.[109] The practitioner's conduct must be compared with someone in the same profession and speciality thereof.[110]

[2.78] The distinction between professional misconduct and poor professional performance was discussed in the English case of *R (on the application of Calhaem) v General Medical Council*[111] which concerned a consultant anaesthetist who had been found guilty of misconduct and deficient professional performance arising out of his post-operative management of a patient. In defining deficient professional performance and distinguishing it from professional misconduct, Jackson J set out five principles:

(1)   Mere negligence does not constitute 'misconduct' within the meaning of the Act. Nevertheless, and depending upon the circumstances, negligent acts or omissions which are particularly serious may amount to 'misconduct'.

(2)   A single negligent act or omission is less likely to cross the threshold of 'misconduct' than multiple acts or omissions. Nevertheless, and depending upon the circumstances, a single negligent act or omission, if particularly grave, could be characterised as 'misconduct.'

(3)   'Deficient professional performance' within the meaning of the Act is conceptually separate both from negligence and from misconduct. It connotes a standard of professional performance which is unacceptably low and which (save in exceptional circumstances) has been demonstrated by reference to a fair sample of the doctor's work.

(4)   A single instance of negligent treatment, unless very serious indeed, would be unlikely to constitute 'deficient professional performance.'

(5)   It is neither necessary nor appropriate to extend the interpretation of 'deficient professional performance' in order to encompass matters which constitute misconduct.

---

[108] See further discussion in the 5th Shipman Report, *Safeguarding Patients: Lessons from the Past - Proposals for the Future*, Published 9 December 2004, Cm. 6394 at para 24.10.

[109] In England, the equivalent test is 'deficient professional performance' in respect of which Elias LJ said in *R (on the application of Remedy UK Ltd.) v General Medical Council* [2010] EWHC 1245 at para 37: 'Unlike the concept of misconduct, conduct unrelated to the profession of medicine could not amount to deficient performance putting fitness to practise in question.'

[110] See *Holton v General Medical Council* [2006] EWHC 2960 in which Stanley Burnton J said 'Just as the public is entitled to expect a consultant in any area of medical practice to have a higher standard of work than a practitioner of a lower grade, so the public is entitled to expect that the work of a doctor who occupies a post in any specialty is the standard applicable to that post in that specialty. I add that in my view a practitioner who works outside his specialty is liable to be judged by the standard applicable to the level and the specialty in which he works.' See also *Krippendorf v General Medical Council* [2001] 1 WLR 1054.

[111] *R (on the application of Calhaem) v General Medical Council* [2007] EWHC 2006.

[2.79] In February 2015 the Supreme Court delivered judgment in the case of *Corbally v the Medical Council*[112] in which the Court considered for the first time the meaning of 'poor professional performance'. Given the significance of the case in defining the concept of poor professional performance, the facts of the case are worth outlining in some detail. Professor Corbally had been found guilty of poor professional performance by the Council in respect of a procedure which had been carried out on a young child of two and a half years. The child had presented with a history that the frenulum (fold of tissue) under her top lip was catching, causing an ulcer under that lip and contributing to a gap in her front teeth. Following examination, Professor Corbally recommended division of her upper frenulum, a fairly straightforward and quick surgical procedure. However, in writing up his notes of the consultation, he incorrectly described it as excision of the upper lingual frenulum. The child presented at the hospital some weeks later but on admission, the reference to the upper frenulum was not inputted into the hospital admissions system due to the way in which such procedures were coded in the hospital's computerised system. The theatre list described the required procedure as a 'tongue tie'.

[2.80] Professor Corbally was due to perform the procedure on the child himself but was called urgently to attend another patient in the intensive care unit of the hospital so he delegated the procedure to his specialist registrar. As a result of the way in which the procedure had been inputted into the hospital's computer system, the registrar carried out a different procedure which left the child still requiring the upper frenulum release. Once the error was realised, the child was brought back to theatre a second time and the correct procedure was performed. The child made a full recovery. Professor Corbally acknowledged the inaccuracy in his notes and apologised to the child's parents. However, her parents were upset that the incident had occurred and complained to the Medical Council. A Fitness to Practise inquiry was held into the allegations that Professor Corbally had incorrectly described the required procedure, had delegated the procedure to his registrar without adequately communicating to him the procedure to be performed, and as a result had failed to apply the appropriate standards of clinical judgement that could be expected of a surgeon of his experience and expertise.

[2.81] Professor Corbally was found guilty of poor professional performance and admonished by the Council. He successfully applied to the High Court for judicial review of the Council's decision[113] and the Medical Council subsequently appealed the decision to the Supreme Court. The Council identified the central issue in the case as the extent to which once-off errors such as had occurred in this case, can be the subject of a finding of poor professional performance within the meaning of the Act. It was conceded on behalf of the Council that if a threshold of seriousness was required in order to establish poor professional performance, the Council could not meet the threshold in this particular case.

[2.82] In dismissing the appeal, Mr Justice Hardiman gave the majority decision on behalf of the Court. He stated that before a medical practitioner could be subjected to 'the extremely threatening ordeal of a public hearing before the Medical Council, either

---

[112] *Corbally v the Medical Council* [2015] IESC 9.

[113] Under the 2007 Act there is no appeal in cases where an admonishment is imposed, therefore the only possible option open in this case was to seek judicial review of the decision.

for professional misconduct or for poor professional performance, there must be reason to believe that what can be proved against him is something of a serious nature.'[114] He went on to say that although there may be many matters which may aggrieve patients or their relatives, the Council must be capable of taking the decision that such matters will not proceed to an inquiry unless they are serious in nature. He referred to other non-adversarial strategies that may be utilised in such circumstances.

[2.83] The judgments of the Court demonstrate some dissatisfaction with the wording of the Act and the approach taken by the legislature. Hardiman J pointed out that since there was no distinction in the Act in terms of the sanctions that could be imposed for professional misconduct and poor professional performance, there was 'no sense in which the offence of poor professional performance is intrinsically less serious than professional misconduct.' He said that there may be 'some lacuna in the consideration by the drafters of the measure of what precisely is intended to be the difference between the two delicts and whether it is intended, or not, that one be intrinsically less serious than the other.' He also drew attention to comparable legislation in England where a complaint may be made on grounds of 'deficient professional performance', and which was interpreted by the English courts as requiring a threshold of seriousness to be met.[115] He concluded on this point that if the legislature had intended to make it possible to impose sanctions for non-serious failings by a medical practitioner, 'it would be necessary to use explicit language to bring this about.'[116] Interestingly, although he did not find it necessary to refer to this in his interpretation of the Act, Hardiman J also referred to Parliamentary material in his judgment, specifically an exchange in the Dáil during the passage of the Medical Practitioners Act[117] in which it was suggested that the word 'significant' should be inserted before the words 'failure by the practitioner to meet the standards of competence...' in s 2 of the Act. Assurances appear to have been given that it was not necessary to insert this word because, due to the decision in *O'Laoire*,[118] the wording in the Bill was appropriate and would only deal with a serious falling short of standards.

[2.84] Mr Justice O'Donnell agreed with Hardiman J in holding that only a serious error or a series of errors (which may therefore be serious) could justify a finding of poor professional performance. In common with Hardiman J, he also referred to the 'devastating consequences' a public hearing and finding of guilt can have on the career and livelihood of a medical practitioner and was of the view that such consequences should only be visited upon a practitioner in cases which pass a threshold of seriousness. He stated that:

> It does appear that the 2007 Act was not perhaps fully thought through, and neither adopts the position in the UK (which might have many practical benefits given the professional

---

[114] *Corbally v the Medical Council* [2015] IESC 9 per Hardiman J at paras 50 and 51.

[115] *R (on the application of Calhaem) v General Medical Council* considered above at para **[2.70]**.

[116] *Corbally v the Medical Council* [2015] IESC 9 per Hardiman J at para 19.

[117] Dail Debates 20 March, Vol 634, No 5.

[118] *O'Laoire v the Medical Council* in which Keane J stated that conduct may constitute professional misconduct if 'it is conduct connected with his profession in which the medical practitioner concerned has seriously fallen short, by omission or commission, of the standards of conduct expected amongst medical practitioners.' See para **[2.66]** above.

exchange between the two jurisdictions) nor establishes a fully coherent and independent scheme of professional supervision and discipline.

[2.85] As a result of this case, the test to be applied to all conduct, whether a once-off incident or a series of incidents, is the same test of 'seriousness'. According to the Court, the facts in this case were that Professor Corbally made a slight error or 'a slip of the pen' in circumstances in which he was working under enormous pressure and which did not cause the events complained of. Hardiman J acknowledged that errors are made every day and that it would be 'a very confrontational, legalistic, and defensive world indeed if a person in any occupation could be put on risk of his livelihood and his irreproachable reputation because it could be proved he had made some error even … one which is not serious.'[119]

[2.86] The court also considered but did not deal comprehensively with the question of whether non-causative lapses on the part of the practitioner could give rise to the same findings and sanctions as those which caused a negative outcome or adverse consequence to the patient. The President of the High Court in his judgment said that such non-causative lapses should be seen as less serious in character as those that have caused damage, thereby importing causation as an important element of the test of poor professional performance. However Mr Justice McKechnie in the Supreme Court considered this question differently in stating that 'whilst outcome, adverse consequence or causative effect are not essential, where present, such will be factors for consideration.'[120] Given that any error, whether causative or non-causative of an adverse outcome for a patient, may be a cause for concern in relation to the knowledge and competence of the relevant practitioner, McKechnie J's broad approach of not requiring the presence of adverse consequences but taking them into consideration where such consequences have occurred, would seem to be the preferable approach.

[2.87] Other matters considered by the Supreme Court included the departure by the Fitness to Practise Committee from the advice given to them by the legal assessor in relation to the seriousness threshold. The Court was of the view that, although the Committee was entitled to depart from that advice,[121] the Committee failed to give clear and cogent reasons for not following the advice given, which left Professor Corbally at a disadvantage in not being able to understand the basis on which the Committee approached the issue of poor professional performance.

[2.88] Finally the Court also referred to the fact that under the Act, there is no appeal in circumstances in which the sanction of admonishment is given. This means that the Court has no power to substitute its own view of the merits for those of the primary deciding body. 'Its focus is on how the decision was made, especially in what concerns basic fairness, not the merits of the decision itself.'[122] The lack of appeal has previously been considered in *Akpekpe v Medical Council*[123] in which the High Court upheld this aspect of the statutory scheme as constitutional.

---

[119] *Corbally v the Medical Council* [2015] IESC 9 per Hardiman J at para 49.

[120] *Corbally v the Medical Council* [2015] IESC 9 per McKechnie J at para 93.

[121] See *McManus v Medical Council* (14 August 2013) HC.

[122] *Corbally v the Medical Council* [2015] IESC 9 per Hardiman J at para 10.

[123] *Akpekpe v Medical Council* [2013] IEHC 38, currently under appeal.

[2.89] An outstanding issue arising from this case is the difference in practical terms between professional misconduct and poor professional performance given that both have now been interpreted as requiring the same threshold of seriousness and both expose the practitioner to the same potential sanctions. McKechnie J reflected on this in his judgment and said it was not altogether clear what was intended by the introduction of poor professional performance. He said that if it was intended that the difference between professional misconduct and poor professional performance was a question of degree, with poor professional performance 'being somewhat akin to a summary matter to be dealt with by a summary process', neither the provisions nor the structure of the 2007 Act itself, implemented same.' He said that it might be that the Oireachtas intended to refer to conduct of a different type or quality, something qualitatively different from professional misconduct. 'Again, however, if that was the ambition, the provisions of the Act likewise in my view, failed to reflect it.'

[2.90] The outcome of these comments, and indeed the judgment itself, is that the Supreme Court was unable to ascertain the legislative intent behind the introduction of this new test of poor professional performance and was of the view that the Oireachtas has introduced a confusing regulatory scheme for medical practitioners, which is replicated to some degree in the regulatory schemes for other health professionals also. The consequence of the case is that a threshold of seriousness is applied to all complaints before they proceed to a formal inquiry. In the absence of legislative clarity or further judicial decisions on the distinction between professional misconduct and poor professional performance, it may be that the regulators will proceed by considering conduct issues under the professional misconduct test, and clinical competence issues under the poor professional performance test. It remains to be seen whether this is the correct approach.

Relevant medical disability

[2.91] Under s 45 of the 1978 Act, an inquiry may be held into a medical practitioner's fitness to engage in the practice of medicine by reason of physical or mental disability.[124] The old Act therefore required that the practitioner's disability rendered him unfit to engage in the practise of medicine, which was a high threshold for the Council to establish. In cases where the practitioner was found by the Council to be unfit by reason of a disability, the High Court could subsequently cancel this decision on the ground that by the time the appeal came before the Court, the practitioner had received sufficient medical treatment as to now render him fit to engage in practice again. Issues which have led to findings of unfitness in the past include psychiatric conditions and addiction problems.

[2.92] Under the 2007 Act a complaint may be made to the Medical Council against a registered medical practitioner on grounds of a relevant medical disability.[125] This is now defined by the Act as 'a physical or mental disability of the practitioner (including addiction to alcohol or drugs) which may impair the practitioner's ability to practise medicine or a particular aspect thereof.' This test will require expert evidence to be

---

[124] Considered in *McCarthy v Medical Council* (1984), Costello J and *Victor Moore v Medical Council* (2006), Hanna J.

[125] Medical Practitioners Act 2007, s 57(1)(c).

adduced by the Council to the effect that on the date of the inquiry, the disability is such that the practitioner's ability to practise medicine is impaired. Even if the Council cannot establish this, the Council may attach conditions to his registration which will most likely be monitored by the Health Committee of the Council,[126] for example that the practitioner continue to be treated by a named psychiatrist who will provide regular reports to the Council. The difference between the two tests may be a question of degree but the test of impairment under the new Act would appear to be a broader or perhaps lower test than unfitness.[127] This will undoubtedly be challenged in the future but until then remains a moot point.

INVESTIGATION OF COMPLAINTS

[2.93] A complaint may be made to the Medical Council by patients, family members of patients, employers, other health professionals, another regulatory body or from any other person who has a concern about the conduct or competence of a medical practitioner. 'It is important to observe that there is no requirement for a complainant to have the equivalent of *locus standi*: a complainant need not be a person who has been affected by the conduct of the registrant in question (although it is often the case that the complainant is such a person).'[128] Although in principle it is possible to make an anonymous complaint, this may raise practical challenges for the Council in investigating the complaint and seeking to establish whether the alleged facts took place unless the anonymous complainant is willing to provide evidence of the alleged misconduct. It also raises legal difficulties in terms of holding an inquiry into anonymous allegations as the practitioner would be denied the opportunity to cross-examine his accuser.

[2.94] Once a complaint has been received by the Medical Council, it must be investigated to determine whether there is a prime facie case against the medical practitioner. If the matter is urgent and the Council considers that it is in the public interest that the practitioner be immediately suspended from the register, the Council may apply to the High Court for such an order under s 60 of the 2007 Act. Whether the practitioner is informed of such application depends on the circumstances and urgency of the matter. Section 60(1) allows the Council to make an *ex parte* application in private unless the Court considers it appropriate to hear the application in public. The Court has discretion to make whatever order it sees fit and, mindful of the seriousness of the allegations, the effect of suspension on the practitioner and his/her reputation and right

---

[126] The Health Committee's role is to monitor and support medical practitioners to maintain their registration during illness and/or disability. Such medical practitioners may come to the attention of the Medical Council in a variety of ways, including: self referral; referral by a third party or referral from the Council.

[127] It is consistent with the language used by the General Medical Council which may suspend a doctor's registration where his or her disability 'seriously impairs' their fitness to practise.

[128] Mills, Burke, McDowell and Ryan, *Disciplinary Procedures in the Statutory Professions,* (2011, Bloomsbury Professional) at 3.03.

to earn a livelihood, will usually direct that an inquiry be held into the allegations as expeditiously as possible.[129]

[2.95] Under the Medical Practitioners Act 2007 the Council has two committees dealing with disciplinary matters: the Preliminary Proceedings Committee (PPC), and the Fitness to Practise Committee (FTPC). Under s 20(11) of the Act, all committees of the Council (except the FTPC) must have a medical majority. This means the PPC will have a medical majority and the FTPC will have a non-medical majority. Both of these committees must be chaired by a Council member and both committees may co-opt medical and non-medical members who are not members of the Council. The PPC considers all applications for inquiries. Although the Act does envisage the possibility of oral evidence being heard by the PPC, in practice the PPC makes its decision on the basis of an examination of the written complaint received, any additional material obtained by the Council and the observations and comments submitted by the medical practitioner. By comparison, the FTPC conducts a hearing into the allegations with oral evidence from a number of sources including the complainant and the practitioner, as well as other witnesses and experts.

The Preliminary Proceedings Committee

[2.96] The function of the PPC is to investigate the complaint and determine as expeditiously as possible whether the Council should hold an inquiry into the complaint.[130] On receipt of a complaint, the Council notifies the medical practitioner of the name of the complainant[131] and the nature of the complaint, and seeks observations and comments in response from the practitioner.[132] The Professional Standards department of the Council investigates the complaint and provides a case file for the PPC to consider the complaint. This will include any correspondence received, witnesses interviewed, experts' reports, and any medical records supplied. The PPC may require the complainant to verify the contents of the complaint by affidavit, and may require the complainant to provide more information in relation to the complaint.[133] It will then consider whether the complaint is trivial or vexatious or without substance or made in bad faith and form an opinion as to whether there is sufficient cause to warrant further action being taken in relation to a complaint or the complaint should be referred to another body or authority.[134] If the PPC forms the opinion that there is sufficient cause to warrant an inquiry, it will refer the complaint to the FTPC. If it forms the opinion that there is not sufficient cause to

---

[129] See for example, comments made by Morris J in *Whelan v Medical Council* (20 February 2001) HC relating to the 'very great hardship' on the doctor and his family arising out of the granting of such an order. Also *Medical Council v PC* [2003] IR 600 in which Keane J at p 602 discussed the balancing exercise to be carried out by the Court between the public interest and the constitutional rights of the practitioner.

[130] Medical Practitioners Act 2007, s 57(3).

[131] In the event that the Council receives an anonymous complaint, the Council may itself become the complainant in the matter – Medical Practitioners Act 2007, s 57(1).

[132] Medical Practitioners Act 2007, s 59(5)–(8).

[133] Medical Practitioners Act 2007, s 59(3).

[134] Medical Practitioners Act 2007, s 59(2).

warrant further action being taken, or that the complaint should be referred to another body or to a professional competence scheme or that the complaint is one that could be resolved by mediation or other informal means, it will inform the Council of that opinion.

[2.97] The Council may follow the view of the PPC in this regard and decide not to hold an inquiry or alternatively may direct the PPC to refer the complaint to another body, refer the complaint to a professional competence scheme, or refer it for resolution by mediation. It may also direct that further action be taken, in which case the PPC must refer the matter to the FTPC.[135] It must duly inform the medical practitioner and the complainant of its decision, the nature of the complaint, the evidence supporting the complaint, the right to be legally represented and the right to apply for the inquiry to be held in private.

Interim orders

[2.98] The Council also has an important power under s 60 to make an *ex parte* application (without notice to the doctor) to the Court for an order to suspend a doctor's registration, whether or not the doctor is the subject of a complaint, if the Council considers that the suspension is necessary to protect the public until further steps are taken. Such applications will be heard in private unless the Court considers it appropriate to hear the application in public. The Court may make any order it thinks appropriate on foot of such an application, including suspension of the doctor's registration and may give the Council any further directions it thinks appropriate.

The Fitness to Practise Inquiry

[2.99] In preparation for the Inquiry, the Chief Executive Officer (CEO) (formerly known as the Registrar under the 1978 Act) of the Council collects evidence in the case for presentation to the FTPC.[136] The complainant does not have any formal role in the hearing other than to give evidence if called upon to do so. This may sometimes be the source of some misunderstanding amongst complainants who view the investigation of the complaint and the hearing as a form of private dispute resolution. It is important therefore that it is explained to complainants that once their complaint has been submitted to the Council, their role is limited to providing any further information that may be sought. The complaint is investigated by the Council in furtherance of its statutory duty in regulating the standards of the profession in the public interest.

[2.100] The medical practitioner against whom the complaint has been made is given notice of the evidence in the case and has the opportunity to be present at the hearing of the case, or be legally represented. In practice, both the practitioner and the CEO of the Council are usually legally represented and the procedure is inevitably relatively formal, though perhaps not to the same degree as court proceedings. The Committee has the powers, rights and privileges of the High Court in relation to the calling and examination

---

135 Medical Practitioners Act 2007, s 63.
136 The relationship between the Committee and the Registrar was described by Costello P in *Barry v The Medical Council* [1998] 3 IR 368 as analogous to that between the chairman of a tribunal and solicitor and counsel employed by him to present the evidence, rather than that which exists between prosecutor and the judge in a criminal trial.

of witnesses and the production of documents. Refusal to attend a hearing following a summons by the Committee to do so, or failure to produce documents called for by the Committee, or any other conduct which would constitute a contempt of court, is an offence.[137] Witnesses give their testimony under oath and have the same immunities and privileges as in the High Court. The inquiry team also has the assistance of a legal assessor who is not a member of the Committee but who is present to give legal advice if requested, and to ensure that fair procedures are observed. Any such advice by the legal assessor is given in the presence of all parties to the inquiry and an opportunity is given to the parties or their legal advisors to make representations to the FTPC in respect of any such advice. The FTPC is not obliged to follow the advice of the legal assessor, but in departing from such advice, should give clear reasons for so doing.[138]

[2.101] Given the significant impact that a finding of professional misconduct or poor professional performance may have on a medical practitioner's career and reputation, strict adherence to fair procedures in the conduct of an inquiry is required.[139] These procedural rules are designed to 'provide a just balance between the legitimate expectation of the complainant that a complaint of serious professional misconduct will be investigated and the need for legitimate safeguards for the practitioner, who as a professional person may be considered particularly vulnerable to and damaged by unwarranted charges against him.'[140] Although the balance between these two interests need not be equally weighted given the primacy of public protection, these procedural rules mean, for example, that the medical practitioner must receive a copy of the evidence to be presented at the inquiry.[141] There is no corresponding obligation on the medical practitioner to notify the Council in advance of the evidence he proposes to call in his defence in the inquiry. As Keane CJ said in *Borges v The Fitness to Practice Committee*:[142]

> It is also not in dispute that the practitioner concerned is entitled to have the hearing conducted in accordance with fair procedures and natural justice. That is not to say that a body of this nature may not depart from procedures which would be essential in a court of law, as was made clear by this court in *Kiely v Minister for Social Welfare* [1977] IR 267: in particular, they may act on the basis of unsworn or hearsay evidence. But, as was also made clear in that case, their freedom from the constraints to which courts of law are subject does not permit them to act in a way which is inconsistent with the basic fairness of procedures guaranteed by implication by Article 40.3 of the Constitution.

[2.102] The practitioner must also be given an opportunity to cross examine witnesses and give evidence in rebuttal and in his own defence. This may pose difficulties in circumstances where, for example, the complaint has been submitted to the Council anonymously, or where the alleged incident took place outside the jurisdiction and the

---

[137] Medical Practitioners Act 2007, s 45(7).

[138] *McManus v Medical Council* (14 August 2013) HC; *Corbally v Medical Council* [2015] IESC 9, per Hardiman J at para 54.

[139] In keeping with *In re Haughey* [1971] IR 217.

[140] *R v General Medical Council, ex parte Toth* [2001] 1 WLR 2209.

[141] Section 65 of the Act.

[142] *Borges v The Fitness to Practise Committee* [2004] 1 IR 103.

witnesses are unwilling to travel or appear by video link to give evidence. In *Borges,* the court said:

> It is beyond argument that, where a tribunal such as the Committee is inquiring into an allegation of conduct which reflects on a person's good name or reputation, basic fairness of procedure requires that he or she should be allowed to cross-examine, by counsel, his accuser or accusers. That has been the law since the decision of this court in *In re Haughey* and the importance of observing that requirement is manifestly all the greater where, as here, the consequence of the tribunal's finding may not simply reflect on his reputation but may also prevent him from practising as a doctor, either for a specified period or indefinitely.

[2.103] The facts of the *Borges* case involved an inquiry into the conduct of an obstetrician and gynaecologist who was registered in Ireland and had been erased from the corresponding register in the United Kingdom following allegations of inappropriate and indecent examination of female patients. The witnesses who had given evidence before the inquiry held by the General Medical Council in the UK were not willing to travel to Ireland to give evidence or give evidence by way of video-link. The FTPC therefore sought to rely on the transcripts of evidence given before the GMC as well as the decision of the GMC as ratified by the English court. This was challenged by the medical practitioner as a breach of fair procedures, namely the lack of opportunity to cross-examine witnesses. Keane CJ said:

> [O]ne must bear in mind the reasons which have led courts in this jurisdiction to hold that, in some cases at least, the right of a person to have the evidence against him given orally and tested by cross-examination before the tribunal in question may be of such importance in a particular case that to deprive the person concerned of that right would amount to a breach of the basic fairness of procedure to which he is entitled by virtue of Article 40.1 of the Constitution. It is not simply because the tribunal is in greater danger of arriving at an unfair conclusion, absent the safeguard of material evidence being given orally and tested by cross-examination. Such a departure from the normal rules of evidence might well be justifiable, as I have already noted, in the case of a tribunal of this nature. It is because, depending on the nature of the evidence, its admission in that form may offend against fundamental concepts of fairness, which are not simply rooted in the law of evidence, either in its statutory or common law vesture.

Although the Court was cognisant of the important statutory function to be discharged by the Council in protecting the public, it took the view that such consideration could not relieve the court of the obligation of ensuring that the right of the doctor concerned to a fair hearing is, so far as practicable, upheld.

[2.104] All proceedings of the FTPC must also be cognisant of the provisions of art 6 of the European Convention on Human Rights (ECHR), incorporated into Irish law by the European Convention on Human Rights Act 2003, which requires a 'fair and public hearing within a reasonable time by an independent and impartial tribunal established by law.' This means that the FTPC must be free from both actual and apparent bias as well as any conflict of interest in relation to the allegations or the parties involved. The members of the Committee should not be in a position where there might be a reasonable apprehension that they may have prejudged the issues before the Committee.

[2.105] At the conclusion of the inquiry, the FTPC makes its decision in relation to the allegations of professional misconduct and/or poor professional performance and submits a report to the Council on the inquiry, including recommendations in respect of sanction. Reasons should be given for each finding of misconduct or poor professional performance.[143] Members of the inquiry team are not present for the Council's discussion of the report. Under s 70, if the Committee finds that no allegation against the registered medical practitioner the subject of the complaint is proved, the Council shall dismiss the complaint. If the Committee finds that any allegation against the practitioner is proved, it presents a report on the findings to the Council as well as recommendations for the sanction to be imposed. However, s 71 of the Act stipulates that it is the Council that will decide on the sanction to be imposed on the practitioner. Therefore, the Council is obliged to accept the findings of fact of the FTPC in relation to whether the medical practitioner is guilty of professional misconduct or poor professional performance but has discretion in relation to the sanction to be imposed, if any.

Burden and standard of proof

[2.106] The evidential burden of proof in cases brought before the Committee is on the person making the allegations, in this context, the Chief Executive Officer of the Medical Council.[144] Although FTP inquiries are not criminal prosecutions, the Medical Council and other regulatory bodies generally apply the criminal standard to their disciplinary hearings. Internationally the civil standard of proof is applied by a number of regulatory bodies, including the General Medical Council in the UK since 2008, which takes the view that the disciplinary function is not a criminal court and that the civil standard is consistent with protecting patients and the public interest while at the same time being fair to doctors.[145] The change in the UK followed criticism in the Fifth Report of the Shipman Inquiry,[146] a report from the Chief Medical Officer called *Good Doctors, Safer Patients*,[147] and a Government White Paper called *Trust, Assurance and Safety*,[148] all of which questioned the retention of the civil standard. The Health and Social Care Act 2008 implemented the civil standard for all healthcare regulators in the UK.

[2.107] The law in Ireland on this point was set out in *O'Laoire v Medical Council*,[149] in which the court discussed whether the standard of proof was the civil or criminal standard. The FTPC had decided the case in question on the basis of proof beyond a reasonable doubt. In the High Court Keane J was satisfied that 'the onus lay upon the Council to prove beyond reasonable doubt every relevant averment of fact which was not admitted…and to establish beyond reasonable doubt that such facts, as so proved or admitted, constituted professional misconduct.'[150] This approach was upheld by the Supreme Court with O'Flaherty J taking the view that, although the criminal standard of

---

[143] *Prendiville and Murphy v The Medical Council* [2007] IEHC 427.

[144] *O'Laoire v Medical Council* (27 January 1995) HC per Keane J.

[145] www.gmc-uk.org.

[146] Safeguarding Patients: Lessons from the Past-Proposals for the Future (9 December 2004) Cmnd Paper Cm 6394: www.shipman-inquiry.org.us/reports.asp

[147] Dept of Health (UK) 14 July 2006.

[148] Dept of Health (UK) 21 February 2007.

[149] *O'Laoire v Medical Council* (25 July 1997) SC.

[150] *O'Laoire v Medical Council* (27 January 1995) HC per Keane J at 115.

proof ought best to be confined to criminal trials to which that standard is particularly suited, in civil hearings such as this one the evidential burden must be commensurate with the gravity of the matter at hand. He said:

> The essence of a disciplinary enquiry into alleged professional misconduct, such as concerned the Committee and the trial judge here, is to find out by clear evidence the pith and substance of the misdeed being investigated and decide whether the case has been established against the person, always bearing in mind the grave consequences that such a finding will, in general, have for the person whose conduct is called in question but also remembering that the public has an interest in making sure that proper standards of professional conduct are upheld. The graver the allegation the greater will be the care which the tribunal or court will take to make sure that the case has been brought home against the person whose conduct is impugned.

O'Flaherty J went on to discuss cases from the UK,[151] Canada,[152] Australia[153] and New Zealand[154] with which he was satisfied that the Irish decisions on the point concurred.

[2.108] Since the decision in *O'Laoire*, the application of the criminal standard of proof has been confirmed in a number of other cases including *Millett-Johnson v Medical Council*,[155] *O'Connor v Medical Council*[156] and *Barry v Medical Council*.[157] However, there is no statutory requirement to apply the criminal standard set out in the Act and it may be that the Council may decide to apply the civil standard in an appropriate case in the future. Such a case would undoubtedly result in a legal challenge but may ultimately provide useful clarity for professional regulators.

Private or public hearings

[2.109] An issue which has in the past exercised both the Medical Council and the courts is whether the FTPC should hold its inquiry in public or in private. Traditionally all disciplinary proceedings were held in private. This issue was at the heart of *Barry v The Medical Council*[158] in which the practitioner, who was the subject of an inquiry by the FTPC into allegations that he had secretly recorded consultations with and examinations of some of his patients, wished to have the hearing in public in order to vindicate his character in circumstances in which the allegations against him had received much damaging advance publicity. The Committee refused on the basis that it had discretion under the scheme of the Act in any case and in this case had exercised its discretion in favour of a private hearing. This was grounded on the nature of the allegations against the practitioner, in this case being of an intimate personal nature, a fact that may deter those making the complaints from giving evidence in public.

---

[131] *Reg v Home Secretary, Ex-p Khawaja* [1984] AC 74; *R v Wolverhampton Coroner* [1990] 2 All ER 759.

[152] *Rizzo et al v Hanover Insurance Co* (1990) 68 DLR (4th) 420.

[153] *Neat Holdings PTY Ltd v Karajan Holdings PTY Ltd* 1992 67 ALJR 170.

[154] *Back v National Insurance Company of New Zealand Ltd* [1996] 3 NZLR 363.

[155] *Millett-Johnson v Medical Council* (12 January) HC, Morris J.

[156] *O'Connor v Medical Council* [2007] IEHC 304.

[157] *Barry v Medical Council* [1997] IEHC 204, [1998] 3 IR 368 (11 February 1997).

[158] *Barry v Medical Council* [1998] 3 IR 368.

[2.110] In the High Court the applicant claimed that he had a constitutional right to fair procedures and that this required a public hearing of the allegations made against him. He relied on the provisions of art 6(1) of the European Convention on Human Rights (ECHR), which provides as follows:

> In the determination of his civil rights and obligations or of any criminal charge against him, everyone is entitled to a fair and public hearing within a reasonable time by an independent and impartial tribunal established by law. Judgement shall be pronounced publicly but the press and public may be excluded from all or part of the trial in the interests of morals, public order or national security in a democratic society, where the interests of juveniles or the protection of the private life of the parties so require, or to the extent strictly necessary in the opinion of the court in special circumstances where publicity would prejudice the interests of justice.

[2.111] The applicant accepted that the Convention was not part of Irish law but argued that in giving effect to the notion of fair procedures under art 40.3 of the Constitution, the Court should be guided by internationally accepted norms enshrined in the Convention.[159] He also pointed out that art 34 of the Constitution provides that justice is to be administered in public, save in limited cases prescribed by law. However, the applicant did not argue that the Committee infringed this article, as it was accepted that the Committee does not administer justice as, in order to have any legal effect, the Council must accept the Committee's decision and apply for confirmation to the High Court which, sitting in public, *determines* the dispute. Costello P accepted the Committee's argument that it had a statutory discretion as to whether to hold its hearings in public or in private. In light of the intimate private details of the case and the reluctance of some witnesses to proceed with giving evidence in public, he held that the Committee had correctly applied the principles contained in art 6(1) of the Convention in this case. This was on the basis of the right to privacy of others and the interests of justice.[160]

[2.112] The Supreme Court unanimously agreed that the Committee has discretion under the Act to conduct its proceedings in public. Barrington J said:

> While the Act contemplates that proceedings before the Fitness to Practise Committee shall be in private it does not require it. I can see no reason why the Committee should not hold its proceedings in public if all parties were agreed and if the Committee itself thought it was the proper thing to do.

---

[159] The applicant relied on the decision of the European Court of Human Rights in *Diennet v France* (1995) 21 EHRR 554 where, in similar circumstances, a French doctor successfully argued that art 6(1) of the Convention was breached by the fact that he did not receive a public hearing before the disciplinary section of the National Council of the French Medical Association. However, Barrington J in the Supreme Court pointed out that in this case the applicant had appealed the decision of the Disciplinary Committee to the French *Conseil d'Etat* on a point of law only. There was no rehearing of the case and therefore it was possible for the Court to agree that there had been no public hearing of an issue which touched on the doctor's civil rights, contrary to the Convention. In the instant case the applicant had the right to appeal the decision of the Medical Council to the High Court where he would be entitled to a full rehearing and possibly rehearing in public.

[160] Arguments made on the basis that there was no objective separation of the functions of prosecutor and adjudicating tribunal in this case were also rejected by the Court.

The Supreme Court also agreed that the Committee had properly exercised its discretion on the facts of this case.

[2.113] The *Barry* case has lost its significance somewhat given that s 65 of the Medical Practitioners Act 2007 now provides that a hearing before the FTPC shall be held in public unless the medical practitioner or a witness who will be required to give evidence at the hearing requests that it be held in private and the Committee is satisfied that it would be appropriate in the circumstances to hold the hearing (or part of it) in private. Inquiries are now regularly held in public.[161]

SANCTIONS

[2.114] The purpose of the imposition of sanctions on medical practitioners is not punishment but protection of the public and of the reputation of the profession. In the English case *Meadow v General Medical Council*[162] Sir Anthony Clarke said 'In short, the purpose of [fitness to practise] proceedings is not to punish the practitioner for part misdoings but to protect the public against the acts and omissions of those who are not fit to practise. The [inquiry committee] thus looks forward not back.' Under ss 46–48 of the 1978 Act, the Council was entitled to impose sanctions including erasure or suspension from the medical register, provision of advice, admonishment or censure or the attachment of conditions to the retention of the name of a medical practitioner on the medical register. Section 71 of the Medical Practitioners Act 2007 contains broadly similar provisions and gives power to the Council to impose the following sanctions:

(a)   an advice or admonishment, or a censure, in writing;

(b)   a censure in writing and a fine not exceeding €5,000;

(c)   the attachment of conditions to the practitioner's registration, including restrictions on the practice of medicine that may be engaged in by the practitioner;

(d)   the transfer of the practitioner's registration to another division of the register;

(e)   the suspension of the practitioner's registration for a specified period;

(f)   the cancellation of the practitioner's registration, or;

(g)   a prohibition from applying for a specified period for the restoration of the practitioner's registration.

[2.115] The factors that will be taken into account by the Council in considering which, if any, sanction to impose include deterring the practitioner from carrying out a similar act or omission again, demonstrating the gravity of the offence to other practitioners, and upholding the reputation of the profession and maintaining standards and public confidence in the profession.[163] The Council will also have regard to the principle

---

[161] For further elaboration of the circumstances in which an inquiry might be held in private, see Mills, Burke, McDowell and Ryan, *Disciplinary Procedures in the Statutory Professions,* (2011, Bloomsbury Professional) at 5.43–5.53.

[162] *Meadow v General Medical Council* [2006] EWCA Civ 1390.

[163] See *Ala v General Medical Council* (2000) where the court stated that honesty and trustworthiness were qualities that the public has a right to expect of the profession. See also guidance note on sanctions published by the Medical Council available at www.medicalcouncil.ie/Existing-Registrants-/Complaints/Guidance-on-Sanctions-Imposed-by-the-Medical-Council.pdf.

of proportionality, measuring the nature of the proven allegations against the range of available sanctions. Where a sanction is considered to be excessive or disproportionate by the High Court on appeal, the Court may alter it or set it aside. For example in *Cahill v Dental Council*[164] the Court altered the conditions imposed on the dentist on the basis that they were unnecessarily restrictive. In *Hermann v Medical Council*[165] the Court was of the view that the sanctions of suspension and conditions imposed by the Council were a 'proportionate rehabilitative and punitive response to the findings against the practitioner.'[166]

[2.116] The Council takes the view that the outcome is not necessarily relevant when considering sanction. For example, the fact that a patient ultimately came to no harm may be less relevant than the risk posed by the behaviour of the practitioner. Evidence of the practitioner's understanding of any underlying deficit in his approach to the issue which led to the complaint and his attempts to address it may be considered. This may include an admission of the facts of the case, an admission of professional misconduct and/or poor professional performance and/or relevant medical disability, an apology by the practitioner to the complainant or injured party, efforts made by a practitioner to prevent recurrence and improve deficiencies. Evidence of the practitioner's adherence to important principles of good practice may be taken into account as well as references and/or testimonials presented by the practitioner to demonstrate his good standing.

Cancellation and suspension of registration

[2.117] Removal of the practitioner's name from the Register is the most serious sanction that may be imposed on the practitioner and may result in a life-long bar from practice unless the practitioner subsequently makes a successful application for restoration of his name to the register. The Council may also stipulate a time period within which the medical practitioner is prohibited from applying for restoration to the register. The purpose of cancellation of registration is to protect the public, to deter other practitioners from similar conduct and to protect the reputation and trust-worthiness of the profession. The Medical Council has given indicative guidance on the circumstances in which this sanction may be considered appropriate such as professional misconduct arising from findings of disgraceful or dishonourable behaviour including dishonest/ fraudulent behaviour regarding professional practice ie falsifying records, abuse of patients, inappropriate sexual relations and certain criminal behaviour. Professional misconduct arising from a breach of the 'expected conduct' standard may also result in cancellation of registration in circumstances of reckless and deliberate unskilled practice, breach of confidentiality, inappropriate prescribing and breach of conditions or undertaking to the Medical Council.

[2.118] Suspension from the register for a finite period of time is an alternative option for the Medical Council in cases where it is appropriate to 'send a signal to the doctor, the profession and the public about what is regarded as behaviour unbefitting a registered medical practitioner.'[167] It also has a punitive effect as it prevents the doctor

---

[164] *Cahill v Dental Council* [2001] IEHC 97.

[165] *Hermann v Medical Council* [2010] IEHC 414.

[166] Per Charleton J at para 31.

[167] Indicative Sanctions Guidance for the Fitness to Practise Panel, General Medical Council (UK) (2009) para 69. Available at www.gmc-uk.org.

practising during that period. It may be regarded as appropriate in cases where the misconduct is serious enough that action is required in order to protect the public and maintain confidence in the profession but where the conduct is not regarded as incompatible with continued registration. This may arise in circumstances where the practitioner has displayed good insight into his behaviour and the Council is satisfied that, although serious, the behaviour is unlikely to be repeated. It may also arise where the facts of the case relate to deficiencies in competence or performance which are considered remediable through a period of suspension, rehabilitation and re-training.

Imposition of conditions

[2.119] The Council may consider that a proportionate response to the proven professional misconduct or poor professional performance of the medical practitioner is the imposition of conditions attached to the practitioner's continued registration. These conditions should be relevant to the conduct complained of[168] and will be imposed for a finite period. They may, for example, involve a requirement for re-training to rectify deficiencies in the practitioner's competence, restriction on unsupervised practise in a particular area, or restriction on prescribing certain medications. The conditions are subject to confirmation by the High Court which may vary them as it considers fit. Compliance with the conditions is monitored by the Medical Council and if they are not adhered to, this may be the subject of a further complaint to the Council potentially leading to a more severe sanction.

Other possible sanctions

[2.120] Other sanctions that may be imposed by the Medical Council include the imposition of a fine not exceeding €5,000 and/or advice, admonishment or censure. The Council does not have the power to award compensation to complainants. Advice, admonishment and censure are mechanisms which demonstrate the disapproval of the practitioner's conduct by the Council without affecting his or her registration status. The difference between these reprimands is a question of degree with advice being the least serious and censure being at the higher end of serious reprimand. The important distinction between these sanctions and suspension or cancellation of registration is that they do not restrict the practitioner's ability to practise medicine. Perhaps because they are regarded as therefore less serious and do not affect the practitioner's constitutional right to earn a livelihood, the imposition of these sanctions does not require confirmation from the High Court and cannot be the subject of an appeal. A practitioner who is unhappy with the imposition of such sanctions may therefore only challenge the Council's decision by way of judicial review.

Challenges to power of Council to impose sanctions

[2.121] Given the seriousness of the imposition of any sanctions affecting the practitioner's registration and consequent ability to practise medicine, it is not surprising that such decisions are often appealed or form the basis of applications for judicial review or constitutional challenge. Comparable provisions under ss 45 and 46 of the

---

[168] *Millett-Johnson v Medical Council* (12 January 2001) HC Morris J.

1978 Act were considered in *M v The Medical Council and the Attorney General*[169]in which the plaintiff applied to the High Court under s 46 for an order cancelling the decision of the Council to remove his name from the register. The plaintiff claimed, inter alia, that ss 45 and 46 of the Act were unconstitutional,[170] and that the Council's decision was therefore null and void. He alleged that the powers vested in the FTPC or in the Medical Council by the 1978 Act were powers to administer justice which, due to the fact that their effect would be to deprive him of his livelihood by striking him from the register of medical practitioners, could not be considered to be limited powers under art 37 of the Constitution.[171] He also alleged that the procedures set out by the Act were unfair and inconsistent with art 40 of the Constitution[172] in that his case came before the Court with a predetermination of guilt from the Council. He claimed that there was no prohibition on the Council from publishing its findings that the practitioner was guilty of misconduct, which was a failure to vindicate and defend the practitioner's good name under art 40.

[2.122] The Council argued that its functions did not constitute the administration of justice as it lacked the finality or enforceability necessary to that function by virtue of the fact that the decision of the Council was not effective unless confirmed by the Court. It was also argued that it was in the public interest that publication be made of the fact that his colleagues had found the doctor guilty of misconduct. Finlay P distinguished the facts of *In re the Solicitors Act 1954*,[173] in which the disciplinary committee of the Law Society had the power to determine complaints of professional misconduct against solicitors, strike their names off the register and award restitution and costs. He said that there was 'a very striking difference between the extent and nature of the powers there conferred on the disciplinary committee and the powers conferred by the Act of 1978 on the Committee and the Council.' He went on to explain that the only power the Committee or the Council had was to initiate proceedings in the High Court which may lead to an order suspending the practitioner from his practice, erasing his name from the register or the other sanctions provided by the Act. He adopted the test laid down in the *Solicitors Act* case that the essential question here was whether the tribunal in question had power by its determination to impose liability or affect rights. In this case the only powers of the Council that could be said to be final were the publication of a finding of misconduct or unfitness to practise, and the Council's power to advise, admonish or censure a practitioner. Even if these powers could be said to affect the rights of the

---

[169] *M v The Medical Council and the Attorney General* [1984] IR 485.

[170] Article 34, s 1 of the Constitution provides 'Justice shall be administered in courts established by law by judges appointed in the manner provided by this Constitution, and, save, in such special and limited cases as may be prescribed by law, shall be administered in public.'

[171] Article 37 of the Constitution provides 'Nothing in this Constitution shall operate to invalidate the exercise of limited functions and powers of a judicial nature, in matters other than criminal matters, by any person or body of persons duly authorised by law to exercise such functions and powers, notwithstanding that such person or such body of persons is not a judge or a court appointed or established as such under this Constitution.'

[172] Article 40.3.2° provides 'The State shall, in particular, by its laws protect as best it may from unjust attack and, in the case of injustice done, vindicate the life, person, good name, and property rights of every citizen.'

[173] *In re the Solicitors Act 1954* [1960] IR 239.

practitioner in the present context, these functions would be so clearly limited in their effect and consequence as to come within the exception provided by art 37 of the Constitution.[174]

[2.123] The plaintiff also argued that there was a lack of fair procedure in the manner by which his application came before the High Court, with a badge of guilt arising from a finding of the Committee. In rejecting this contention, Costello P equated any such implication or imputation that might arise from such a finding by a professional body with the implication or imputation which arises from a decision on the part of the Director of Public Prosecutions to prosecute an accused person. Accordingly this ground also failed. However, it may be questioned whether this is in fact a correct interpretation of the position in relation to the Director of Public Prosecutions where it would be inconsistent with the constitutional right to fair procedures to have any implication of guilt arising in a criminal prosecution prior to a court hearing. Despite the seriousness of the decision to strike a practitioner from the Register, it is not a criminal prosecution and the two situations are not directly comparable.

[2.124] The plaintiff also challenged the constitutionality of the Council's power to publish the fact that the Committee had reached a decision as to the practitioner's conduct. Costello P held that art 40.3.2° does not guarantee to protect a person from every statement which may damage his good name. The common good may require, as in these circumstances, that a decision reached as to the conduct of a person carrying out a profession affecting the public be made known to the public:

> In the case of a person practising medicine, the public have a clear and identifiable interest to be informed of a responsible view reached by his colleagues with regard to his standard of conduct or fitness. I cannot see that the absence from the statute of a prohibition on the publication of an adverse finding of the Committee [where they have made a finding of misconduct or of unfitness] can be a failure to protect the good name of the practitioner from an unjust attack.[175]

[2.125] According to the Court, the practitioner's right to have a full public hearing before the High Court during which he may completely vindicate his good name and reputation constituted a sufficient protection of his good name so as to make the scheme of the Act consistent with art 40. This would seem to be a sensible approach bearing in mind the clear necessity of protecting the public from unfit practitioners. Once appropriate safeguards have been observed from a procedural point of view and the Committee has reached a decision on the practitioner's conduct, it would not be inappropriate for the Committee to publish its findings in that regard.

Power to impose sanctions without finding of guilt

[2.126] In *Casey v The Medical Council*,[176] the plaintiff argued that the Council's power to attach conditions to the retention of his name in the register was ultra vires the Council. The plaintiff complained that although the Committee considered that there was insufficient evidence to find him guilty of misconduct, the Council advised him to

---

[174] *M v The Medical Council and the Attorney General* [1984] IR 485 at 497.
[175] *M v The Medical Council and the Attorney General* [1984] IR 485 at 500.
[176] *Casey v The Medical Council* [1999] 2 IR 534.

101

avail of continuing medical education and professional development courses in his field, keep more comprehensive clinical notes, attend a course in communication skills, and, where appropriate, consider the presence of a chaperone when dealing with patients. These conditions were attached to the retention of his name in the register and were to be reviewed after one year. The plaintiff argued that the Council had no power to make such a decision and had therefore acted ultra vires.

[2.127] The plaintiff's argument was grounded on the contention that in the absence of a finding of misconduct by the Committee, the Council had no power under the Act to do any of the things it purported to do. By imposing conditions on the retention of his name on the register the Council was in effect reversing the findings of the Committee, which had heard all the evidence and the witnesses in the case. The plaintiff relied on the judgment of Finlay P in *Re M, a Doctor*,[177] in which the judge was said to have demonstrated the correctness of the plaintiff's case that before a power could be exercised under s 47 of the Act, there must have been a finding of guilt by the Committee. The Council argued that not only was it entitled to invoke the powers in question, but it ought to do so having regard to the public interest and the care of patients. The Council sought to rely on *M v The Medical Council and the Attorney General*[178] in which Finlay P had considered the provisions of s 47. However, in that case he had taken the opposite view, namely that the Council could exercise its powers under the section irrespective of the precise findings of that enquiry by the Committee.

[2.128] Kelly J held that there was nothing in the words of ss 47 or 48 that would require as a condition precedent to their being acted upon by the Council a finding of guilt on the part of the practitioner who has been the subject of an inquiry by the Committee. 'Under the express terms of each section all that is required in order to trigger the entitlement of the Council to utilise them is that there should have been an inquiry held and a report made by the Committee pursuant to s 45 of the Act.' He disagreed with Finlay P in *Re M, a Doctor*, taking the view that the learned judge had not accurately described the statutory provisions in that case. There was, he held, no basis for indicating that the Council's powers could only be exercised where the practitioner had been found guilty of misconduct. Such a view was inconsistent with the express provisions of the Act and also with his own views in the later decision, *M v The Medical Council and the Attorney General*, with which Kelly J agreed.

[2.129] As regards the issue of where the public interest lies in such cases, it had been contended by the plaintiff that s 51 of the Act,[179] which enables the Council to apply to the High Court to suspend a practitioner's registration for a specified period, was sufficient protection for the public. Kelly J took the view that, although it was quite clear from the wording of that section that the Council had a role to play in the protection of the public interest, s 51 was not the only way in which this might be achieved. On the contrary, that section was reserved for exceptional cases in which a doctor ought to be suspended in the public interest:

---

[177] *Re M, a Doctor* [1984] IR 479.

[178] *M v The Medical Council and the Attorney General* [1984] IR 485. Both this and *Re M, a Doctor* [1984] IR 479, discussed above, relate to the same doctor.

[179] Now s 60 of the 2007 Act.

There must be cases where the Council would, from the point of view of protecting the public, wish to bring about an improvement in the standards of an individual practitioner. It would be absurd that in every such case where the Council desired so to do it would have to invoke the provisions of Section 51. To contend that this is the only mechanism that the Council is given by the Legislature in order to address the public interest is, in effect, to advocate the use of the proverbial sledge hammer to crack a nut with consequent hardship being suffered by the unfortunate medical practitioner who would be the recipient of such force.

[2.130] Accordingly, the Medical Council was held not to have acted ultra vires in its decision to attach conditions to the plaintiff's registration. In reaching this decision, the Court recognised the complexity of the medical relationship and the seriousness of any finding of misconduct. On examination of the doctor's conduct in this case the Committee was of the opinion that, although certain aspects of his practice needed improvement, such as communication and note taking, there was not the level of misconduct involved as to justify a recommendation that he be struck off the register. The plaintiff's argument that it was essentially *all or nothing* so far as the imposition of any sanctions was concerned does not take account of the pragmatic approach taken by the Council in fulfilment of its function in protecting the public.

[2.131] This issue has been addressed by s 70 of the Medical Practitioners Act 2007 which provides that if the FTPC finds that no allegation against the practitioner has been proved, the Council shall dismiss the complaint. If the FTPC has found that one or more allegations have been proven, the Council shall decide which sanction to impose under s 71.

[2.132] The power of the Council to 'advise, admonish or censure' a practitioner in relation to his professional conduct was challenged in *Ogochukwu Anachebe v The Medical Council*[180] where it was argued that the sanctions that the Council could impose by way of recommended erasure from the register had such grave consequences for a practitioner that they constituted an administration of justice, a function reserved for the courts by the Constitution. It was for this reason that the confirmation of the High Court was required for such an action and that the practitioner had the right to appeal to the High Court to set such a decision aside. The power of the Council to refuse to renew temporary registration and to censure the practitioner in relation to his conduct were no less serious sanctions for the practitioner, and yet no right of appeal to the High Court was given by the Act to the practitioner in such instances. Morris P held that the power that was exercised in this case was to censure the plaintiff in relation to his professional conduct and that no right is given to the practitioner to apply to the court to set that decision aside. 'This is because the sanction of advice, admonishing and censuring is not of sufficient gravity.' This further recognises the point that a gradation of misconduct exists in relation to medical professionals and that, while serious sanctions may be imposed at one end of the scale, it is also necessary to acknowledge that, in keeping with the Council's role in protection of the public interest, less serious penalties may also be appropriate in certain circumstances. It is seen as being impractical to give a right of appeal in such cases where the livelihood of the practitioner is not threatened.

---

[180] *Ogochukwu Anachebe v The Medical Council* [2000] IEHC 193.

Confirmation of decision and appeals

[2.133] Under s 75(1) of the 2007 Act the practitioner may appeal the Council's decision to impose a sanction (other than one imposed under s 71(1)(a)) within 21 days after receiving notification of the decision from the Council. If the practitioner decides to appeal the decision, the Court will conduct a re-hearing of the case against the practitioner, including the consideration of all evidence adduced against him and the testimony of all witnesses. The Court may either confirm the decision of the Council, cancel the decision, impose a different sanction, or give directions to the Council as appropriate. Where the practitioner does not appeal the decision within the specified time period, the Council must, as soon as practicable after the expiry of the relevant time period, make an application to the Court for confirmation of the decision (other than in the case of sanctions imposed under s 71(1)(a)).

[2.134] Following confirmation of the sanction, the Council is obliged by s 84 to notify the Minister for Health and the Health Services Executive of any sanction imposed on the practitioner other than advice or admonishment. Under s 85 it shall also advise the public of such sanctions if it is satisfied that it is in the public interest to do so. The Council shall also publish the transcript of inquiries after consultation with the FTPC. It is not clear whether the power to publish also applies to cases in which the sanction of advice or admonishment has been imposed. These sanctions are specifically excluded from ss 84 and 85 of the Act and thus it may be argued that the Council does not have the power to publish the details of advice or admonishment of a medical practitioner. However it may be counter argued in an appropriate case that such publicity falls within the Council's general functions to do all things necessary to perform its functions in the public interest under s 7. In this context it is worth mentioning that art 6 of the European Convention on Human Rights specifies that the requirement of fair procedures include the public pronouncement of judgments, and the general framework of the 2007 Act leans in favour of publicity, but ultimately this issue will again fall to be considered by the courts.

Challenges on grounds of delay

[2.135] The investigation and completion of the disciplinary process can sometimes take a substantial amount of time. This may be because the disciplinary inquiry may be adjourned pending a criminal prosecution, or a coroner's inquest, or there may be difficulty in getting patients to provide evidence. There is also the practical complication of recruiting expert witnesses and scheduling an inquiry to be heard by members of the FTPC who also have other professional commitments outside of the Council. The issue of delay may give rise to a challenge on behalf of the doctor in that art 6 of the ECHR provides that persons have a right to be 'tried' within a reasonable time and violation of this right may be an abuse of process. This is an issue that has also arisen not infrequently in the prosecution of criminal offences. If the complaint relates to incidents that are alleged to have occurred years previously, the Committee may have to consider why the complainant did not come forward sooner, is the recollection of events reliable and is the practitioner prejudiced in any way by the passage of time and the inability to provide a substantial defence due to lack of records or recollection. In criminal cases it is not usually sufficient to prevent the hearing of a case to say that the passage of time renders the process contrary to fair procedure unless some specific prejudice can be proven. Similarly, it is unlikely to be successful in relation to disciplinary hearings unless there is a real risk that an inquiry could not be conducted fairly.

PROPOSALS FOR REFORM

[2.136] In recent years there has been discussion about the retention of the disciplinary function by professional regulatory bodies. At the present time, Fitness to Practise inquiries held by the Medical Council are generally heard by a small panel of medical and non-medical members of the regulatory bodies and co-opted members. Such members may sit on inquiries for a number of days per year and each team may be comprised of different members. The Fifth Shipman Inquiry Report in the UK[181] raised a number of concerns in relation to the operation of the Fitness to Practise (FTP) process in the General Medical Council (GMC). One of those concerns was that those adjudicating on FTP panels may each sit for only a few days per year. They will therefore have little opportunity to develop real expertise and there are likely to be problems in ensuring consistency of decision-making. This Report states that since all healthcare regulatory bodies are obliged to appoint and train panellists for the FTP procedures, it would be preferable to appoint a body of full-time or nearly full-time panellists who could sit on panels of all such bodies. This would ensure greater consistency of decision-making as well as clear separation between the power to investigate and the power to adjudicate concerns about health professionals.

[2.137] In Ireland similar recommendations were made in the Report of the Commission on Patient Safety and Quality Assurance in 2008.[182] The Report considered the findings and recommendations of the Shipman Report above and stated that although some changes had been introduced in Ireland in the Medical Practitioners Act 2007, it remained concerned that the members of the Fitness to Practise Committee who will hear the evidence and submissions in the Inquiry and reach conclusions on the allegation of professional misconduct will be members of the same body that will make the final decision as to professional misconduct, although they will not be part of the final decision-making process. The Commission was of the view that 'the appearance of separation of function must be matched by the reality of the processes and procedures.' The Commission was concerned that the current system does not facilitate the development of expertise in relation to the disciplinary process and may result in inconsistencies in the application of standards. In addition, the increase in multi-disciplinary team care and treatment of patients may result in complaints being made against a team rather than an individual practitioner. For example, skills extension for nurses has led to the assumption of specifically defined clinical decision-making, drug-prescribing and the performance of medical procedures such as bronchoscopy and colonoscopy. The Commission was of the view that the current disciplinary structures in the professional regulatory bodies do not facilitate an investigation and hearing of such a complaint, which may therefore fall between the regulatory bodies.

---

[181] Safeguarding Patients: Lessons from the Past – Proposals for the Future (9 December 2004) Cmnd Paper Cm 6394: www.shipman-inquiry.org.us/reports.asp.

[182] *Building a Culture of Patient Safety*, p 13, available at www.health.gov.ie.

[2.138] The Commission therefore recommended that there should be greater separation between the investigation and adjudication functions performed by the professional regulatory bodies so that the public might have greater confidence that the disciplinary functions exercised by those bodies are independent and robust. Although there are arguments for removing the entire disciplinary process from the regulatory bodies, the model preferred by the Commission would maintain the involvement of the regulatory body as arbiter of the first stage of the disciplinary process, ie the regulatory body would make the decision as to whether the professional against whom the allegation was made had a case to answer. The regulatory body would then investigate and prepare a case to be heard by an independent panel of healthcare professionals and lay members. Under the model proposed by the Commission, the regulatory bodies would also have a role in the development of standards, criteria and thresholds for all stages of the process, including the adjudication stage. They would be able to monitor the outcomes of cases and thereby inform themselves of the need for any adjustment in the standards, criteria and thresholds. With this model, a body of full-time or nearly full-time panellists should be appointed who could sit on joint panels of all the healthcare regulatory bodies. This would provide a measure of independence from any one particular regulatory body and would also ensure that panellists developed experience and expertise. A full-time legal assessor would be appointed to sit with all adjudicating panels so as to ensure consistency of standards and to address all legal issues arising. Although these recommendations appear to have support within the majority of the professional healthcare regulatory authorities themselves, it remains to be seen if and how these recommendations might be implemented.[183]

PROFESSIONAL CONDUCT AND ETHICS

[2.139] Section 69(2) of the Medical Practitioners Act 1978 provided that 'it shall be a function of the Council to give guidance to the medical profession generally on all matters relating to ethical conduct and behaviour.' In this context the Medical Council has traditionally published an ethical guide on a five-yearly basis that are designed to be applied by doctors in various situations. This mandate has been reinforced by s 7(i) of the 2007 Act which specifies that the Council shall 'specify standards of practice for registered medical practitioners, including the establishment, publication and maintenance and review of appropriate guidance on all matters related to professional conduct and ethics for registered medical practitioners.'

[2.140] Although the Ethical Guide of the Council does not have any binding force in law, it is important for the internal regulation of the profession and it lays down what is ethical medical practice in Ireland. These guidelines are not rules that will provide the doctor with an answer to every difficult issue. Rather, they are principles that ought to be used by doctors together with their judgment, experience, knowledge and skills in each situation. The Guide therefore does not generally catalogue behaviour which may be deemed to be unprofessional but sets out broad principles against which doctors may judge the situation in which they find themselves.

---

[183] The Report of the Commission was accepted by the Government as providing the framework for patient safety and quality assurance in Ireland and is currently in the process of being implemented. See further www.patientsafetyfirst.ie.

[2.141] It is possible that the Guide may be indirectly incorporated into law through case law in the same way as the guidelines of other professional bodies, such as accountancy bodies in tax and accountancy cases. In the case of the latter, the guidelines are seen as a body of professionally desirable standards for the accountancy profession, departure from which would be strictly scrutinised. Although the Medical Council's current Guide is not as detailed and specific, it could be argued that the principles set out therein should be regarded in a similar fashion. In the absence of legislation, a court may therefore decide that although not of binding legal force, departures from the Guide may constitute a breach of professional duty for the purposes of establishing negligence unless justified by the specific circumstances of the case. A patient may also argue that he had a legitimate expectation that the guide would be adhered to by the doctor and that this formed an implied term of the contract with the doctor.

[2.142] The current Guide (8th edn) published in 2016 covers a broad range of areas of professional conduct under three headings of Partnerships, Practice, and Performance which represent the Council's view of medical professionalism. Under the heading of partnerships, the Council sets out provisions in relation to the relationship between patient and doctor such as guidance on capacity and consent, dignity of the patient, personal relationships with patients, using social media, and treating children and young people. Under the heading of practice, it provides guidance on matters such as confidentiality and disclosure, prescribing, telemedicine, reproduction and end-of-life issues, and employment and indemnity. Finally, under the heading of performance, the Guide sets out provisions on open disclosure, teaching, and raising concerns about colleagues.[184]

---

[184] Guide to Professional Conduct and Ethics (8th edn, 2016). Available at www.medicalcouncil.ie.

Chapter 3

Protection of Personal Health Information

INTRODUCTION

[3.01] Personal health information is information collected from and on behalf of a patient which is retained for the benefit of the patient in his or her current or future treatment. It generally includes clinical information such as blood type, allergies, test results, diagnoses, previous surgeries and medications. Such information is usually entrusted by a patient to a doctor on the strict understanding that it will remain confidential and will not be disclosed to others without the patient's consent. This implicit understanding of confidentiality is central to the trust between patient and doctor.

[3.02] The information which is collected as part of a patient's medical records may later be sought by the patient or by others who may have a financial or social interest in the information. The first part of this chapter will explore the issue of access to personal health information by the patient and by others and, in particular, the framework of access governed by the Freedom of Information Acts. This part will also discuss the broad provisions of the Data Protection Acts, which give very detailed guidance in terms of collection, retention, use and destruction of personal data. This chapter will also examine the duty of confidentiality and the circumstances in which information may be disclosed sometimes even in the absence of the patient's consent. Due to advances in information technology in recent years, some jurisdictions have moved towards the storage of health information on electronic records using unique patient identifiers. E-health, which might be described as the use of information technology in healthcare, will be discussed in the final part of this chapter.

ACCESS TO MEDICAL RECORDS AT COMMON LAW

[3.03] Doctors are ethically obliged to maintain records of their care of patients and many doctors also have a legal obligation to do so under the terms of their General Medical Scheme (GMS) contract[1] with the Health Service Executive (HSE) as well as under the common law duty of care to patients. The length of time for which records should be retained is not set by law and will depend on what kind of record it is and what the nature of the relationship between the doctor and patient is, as well as other issues such as the occurrence of an adverse event or patient dissatisfaction with the outcome of treatment. The HSE has published guidelines setting out a range of retention periods for records which are supported by professional and indemnity bodies.[2] The guidelines

---

[1] The GMS is operated by the HSE, whereby general practitioners provide free primary care to patients with a medical card.

[2] HSE Records Retention Policy 2013 available at www.hse.ie. See also www.medicalprotection.org.

generally advise that records be retained for up to eight years following last treatment or death of an adult patient. In relation to children and young people, records should be kept until the patient's 25th birthday, or 26th if the young person was seventeen at the conclusion of treatment. Records should be kept for longer periods if the contents have relevance to adult conditions or have genetic implications. Maternity records should be kept for 25 years after the birth of the last child.

[3.04] Section 7 of the Civil Liability and Courts Act 2004 provides that in the case of medical negligence causing personal injuries, the patient has either two years from the date of the injury or two years from the date on which the patient discovers that he has suffered an injury through negligence in which to institute legal proceedings. This time period is extended in relation to children as the two-year period does not commence until the child turns 18 years of age. However, even if the action is not statute barred, the defendant may successfully claim that lengthy delay in instituting legal proceedings prejudices his ability to defend the action. For example, in *Toal v Duignan*[3] the plaintiff discovered he was infertile when he was 22 years old and alleged negligence on the part of the doctor in failing to diagnose an undescended testicle after birth. His action was taken within the technical time limit of three years after discovery of the alleged negligence (as noted above, the time limit is now two years). However, his action was unsuccessful due to the time lapse between the alleged negligence and the taking of the action (26 years), despite the fact that the plaintiff could not have reasonably discovered the infertility at any earlier time. Where there is a clear and patent unfairness in asking a defendant to defend a case after a very long lapse of time between the acts complained of and the trial, then if that defendant has not himself contributed to the delay, irrespective of whether the plaintiff has contributed to it or not, the court may as a matter of justice have to dismiss the action. The Court did not specifically address the common law right of access to medical records in this case but indicated that it was unreasonable to expect that medical records would be retained for 26 years.

[3.05] There are a number of ways in which the doctor may store healthcare records. For example, a doctor may keep written manual records locked in a filing cabinet in an office or, more commonly now, the information may be stored on a computer database. In either case, the doctor is in control of the information given to the patient. At common law the legal provisions dealing with access differed depending on the method of storage. This caused difficulties to patients trying to get access to their medical records. At common law the question of control of the record turned on the question of ownership of the record. This, in turn, was dependent on who owned the paper on which the records were written. If the patient was a private patient and he or she had a contract with the doctor, then the contract would determine who owned the records. However, it would not be common practice to include express contractual terms dealing with this issue and courts are generally reluctant to imply terms that are not considered necessary for the efficacy of the contract. If the patient was a public patient, he or she could not claim ownership of the physical records that were provided and paid for by the State.

---

[3]   *Toal v Duignan* [1991] ILRM 135.

[3.06] In theory, the patient could try to assert ownership of the records on the basis that the information contained in records 'belonged' to them.[4] Alternatively, if the patient was a private patient, he or she could claim that the doctor was in a fiduciary relationship with the patient and was obliged by that relationship to hold the information for the benefit of the patient, which included a right of access by that patient. These arguments were considered by Canadian and Australian courts with markedly different judicial views in each. In *McInerney v McDonald*[5] the Canadian Supreme Court considered the question of whether a fiduciary relationship existed between doctor and patient. Mrs McDonald had been treated over a number of years by various physicians before she came to be treated by Dr McInerney. On Dr McInerney's advice she stopped taking medication that had been prescribed to her by a previous physician but became concerned at the care she had received before attending Dr McInerney. She requested Dr McInerney to give her copies of her complete medical file, including reports and correspondence from other doctors that had treated her in the past. Dr McInerney gave her all the notes and reports she had prepared herself but refused to give reports prepared by other doctors as, in Dr McInerney's opinion, these were the property of those doctors and it would be unethical for her to release them.

[3.07] La Forest J identified the central issue in this case as whether, in the absence of legislation, a patient is entitled to inspect and obtain copies of his medical records upon request. He was prepared to accept that the doctor, institution or clinic that compiles the records owns the physical records but the patient has a vital interest in the information contained therein. He said:

> Medical records include information about the patient revealed by the patient, and information that is acquired and recorded on behalf of the patient. Of primary significance is the fact that the records consist of information that is highly private and personal to the individual. It is information that goes to the personal integrity and autonomy of the patient.

[3.08] The judge also examined the nature of the relationship within which such personal information was entrusted to the doctor and found it to be similar in character to that between a priest and confessor, or a lawyer and client. In describing it as a fiduciary relationship, however, La Forest J also made it clear that he did not wish to apply fixed rules and principles to all circumstances of this kind – the rules are shaped by the demands of the situation. Nevertheless some duties do arise from the special relationship of trust and confidence that exists in a fiduciary relationship. 'Among these are the duties of the doctor to act with utmost good faith and loyalty, and to hold information received from or about a patient in confidence.' Information given by a patient in the context of that relationship remains the patient's own and the doctor holds that information in a fashion akin to a trust. While the doctor owns the record, the information contained therein is to be used by the doctor for the benefit of the patient. The beneficial interest of the patient means that, as a general rule, he should have a right

---

[4] For arguments that patients should be allowed to look after their own records, see Gilhooly and McGhee, 'Medical Records: Practicalities and Principles of Patient Possession' (1991) J Med Ethics, 17, 138–143; Gillon, 'Should Patients Be Allowed to Look After Their Own Records?' (1991) J Med Ethics, 17, 115–116; Coleman 'Why Patients Should Keep Their Own Records' (1984) J Med Ethics, 1, 27–28.

[5] *McInerney v McDonald* [1992] 93 DLR (4th) 415.

of access to it and the doctor should be obliged to provide such access. This means that the patient is entitled to examine and copy the records but not to remove them from the doctor's premises, as this would disrupt the doctor's ability to provide future care for the patient.

[3.09] This case is useful because it recognises the fundamental importance of privacy on the one hand, but also stresses that disclosure to the patient reinforces the trust placed in the doctor. The trust given by the patient to the doctor mandates that the flow of information works both ways. It improves patient understanding, cooperation and compliance, which, in turn, promote the well-being of the patient:

> The personal privacy of the patient which he entrusts to a certain extent to the physician must be met with a corresponding openness and full disclosure…Personal privacy and access to medical information are not incompatible partners but interchangeable rights.[6]

The judge rebutted arguments that disclosure may facilitate unfounded litigation by pointing out that in fact denial of access may actually encourage unfounded litigation, as in many cases taking legal action is the only means by which the patient fulfils a strong need to discover information about his medical treatment. Arguments were also put to the Court that the information may be meaningless or may be misinterpreted by the patient but the judge was of the view that this did not justify non-disclosure, as the patient could obtain assistance in understanding the file, and that a more general regime of access might also encourage doctors not to use medical jargon and technical terminology in the patient's file.

[3.10] Another argument frequently used in the debate around access to records is that doctors would be less complete and frank in their note keeping if the patient might get access to them. This was also addressed by La Forest J, who doubted the practical significance of this argument, bearing in mind the ethical and legal obligations on doctors to keep accurate records. Although he recognised that doctors may indeed become more cautious in what they record, this did not necessarily imply that such caution would operate to the detriment of the patient, as any information relevant to the patient's medical care would have to be included on the record in any event.[7]

[3.11] The only argument for non-disclosure in which the judge found merit was if there was a real potential for harm to the patient as a result of the disclosure. However, this should be limited to the most compelling cases, as non-disclosure too can cause harm to the patient, who may speculate as to far worse difficulties than might actually exist. The paternalism evident in such an argument, which relies on the doctor's perception of the patient's best interests, conflicts sharply with the patient's right to self-determination. Both interests are worthy of protection, but as a general rule records should be disclosed to the patient 'unless there is a significant likelihood of a substantial adverse effect on

---

6   Knoppers, 'Confidentiality and Accessibility of Medical Information: A Comparative Analysis' (1982) 12 RDUS 395, at 431, quoted by La Forest J in *McInerney v McDonald* [1992] 93 DLR (4th) 415.

7   In fact, a more open system of access to notes may help to encourage doctors not to use 'offensive surgical witticisms' in medical records such as FLK (funny looking kid) or FTM (first-time mum), or the use of terms such as 'hysterical', 'neurotic', 'senile' or 'geriatric', which have pejorative, even abusive, connotations. See Gillon, 'Should Patients Be Allowed to Look After Their Own Records?' (1991) J Med Ethics, 17 at 116.

the physical, mental or emotional health of the patient or harm to a third party.' This reinforcement of the 'therapeutic privilege' is also significant, as it does allow for exceptional situations in which the doctor's duty to protect the patient outweighs the patient's right to access. However, it is likely that these situations will arise in fewer numbers than before, as patients are now more informed and educated regarding health issues, and also as their contact with any one individual doctor becomes more fragmented in larger clinics and across other health-care environments.

[3.12] In the Australian case of *Breen v Williams*[8] Ms Breen, a former patient of Dr Williams, claimed a legal right of access to records kept by Dr Williams in relation to her treatment. She based her claim on, inter alia, a proprietary right and interest in the actual information in the records, an implied contractual obligation and a fiduciary duty. All of these grounds were rejected by the High Court of Australia.[9] On the first argument based on proprietary interests it was conceded that the doctor owns the paper on which the records are written but it was argued that the records themselves were not owned by anybody, not having been abandoned. The Court held this argument to be ill-founded and contrary to common law. It was held that, in the absence of statutory or contractual provision to the contrary, medical records prepared by a doctor are the property of the doctor and, accordingly, he has the right to refuse access to those records.

[3.13] The Court stated that the doctor-patient relationship was contractual in origin whereby the doctor offers a patient diagnosis, advice and treatment.[10] However, due to the informal nature of the relationship, the terms of this contract are rarely expressly made. Therefore, it was the role of the Court to imply the terms of such a contract according to established legal principles. One of the arguments made by Ms Breen was that it was an implied term of the contract with her doctor that he would act in her best interests, and that this meant that she should be given access to her records should she request it. The Court said that there was an implied obligation on the doctor to exercise reasonable care and skill in the provision of medical care and treatment but that this did not extend to granting the patient access to medical records, unless this would otherwise cause the patient harm. The Court unanimously refused to imply a term that doctors contract to act in the 'best interests' of the patient, noting the general rule that an implied term is based upon the presumed or imputed intention of the parties, meaning that had they put their minds to it they would have expressly agreed to it. The court took the view that it would be a far stretch of this proposition to suggest that a doctor would voluntarily submit himself to a duty to always act in the 'best interests' of the patient given existing tortious duties which obliged the doctor to exercise reasonable care in dealing with patients.

[3.14] As for fiduciary duties, the Court did not recognise the doctor-patient relationship as implying fiduciary obligations as might be found in the relationship between trustee and beneficiary, lawyer and client, agent and principal. Although a patient is dependent on the doctor for advice and treatment, and confides intimate personal details to the

---

8 *Breen v Williams* [1996] 70 ALJR 772, Australian HC.
9 For comment on the case, see Swanton and McDonald 'Patients' Right of Access to Medical Records – a Claim Without a Category' (1997) 71 Aust LJ 413–417.
10 The court cited with approval *Sidaway v Governors of Bethlem Royal Hospital* [1985] AC 871 at 904.

doctor in the course of that treatment, that does not mean that the relationship is a fiduciary one for all purposes, although it may imply fiduciary obligations for some purposes. If Dr Williams owed a fiduciary duty to Ms Breen, the duties and obligations which arose from their fiduciary relationship could only come from those aspects of the relationship which exhibited the characteristics of trust, confidence and vulnerability that typify the fiduciary relationship. They could only attach in respect of matters that relate to diagnosis, advice and treatment.

[3.15] The Court went on to say that a consideration of the fundamental obligations of a fiduciary relationship showed that Dr Williams owed no fiduciary duty to Ms Breen to give her access to the records he had created. The judgment in the Canadian case of *McInerney,* discussed above, was robustly criticised on the basis that the law in Australia does not characterise the doctor-patient relationship as fiduciary and that it is not accurate to describe information in the records as property. The records themselves are the only property in question, and these belong to the doctor. This does not mean that he may misuse the information contained in the records to make a profit for himself at the expense of the patient, but otherwise he may save or destroy them as he wishes. The Court went on to describe the differences between Australia and Canada in the imposition of fiduciary duties and held that in Australia no such fiduciary relationship would be recognised in this case. The High Court was also wary of the floodgate effect the imposition of such positive rights may have on other fiduciary relationships. If positive obligations were to be imposed in a doctor-patient relationship it would follow that in many situations where personal and confidential information is conveyed, such as 'journalists, accountants [and] bank officers', such persons would come under a fiduciary duty to 'give access to their records to the person who gave that information' and such a broad ranging obligation would simply be untenable.[11]

[3.16] The Medical Council's Guide to Professional Conduct and Ethics (8th edn)[12] states in paragraph 33.5 that patients have a right to get copies of their medical records except where this is likely to cause serious harm to their physical or mental health. The Guide also recognises that a patient may also seek access to their medical records in circumstances where they are transferring their care to another medical practitioner or where the patient wishes to seek another opinion. The Guide advises in paragraph 38.4 that doctors should help patients who request another opinion unless this is deemed not to be in the patient's best interests. This includes making copies of all relevant information available to another registered doctor nominated by the patient.

[3.17] The Heads of the proposed Health Information and Patient Safety Bill[13] published in November 2015 further deal with this issue by providing in Head 6 that 'An individual may, by notice in writing, request a health services provider who is providing or has provided health services to the individual to furnish a copy of any health records that the provider holds in relation to the individual to a person who is the provider of a similar health service to the individual specified in the request.' The person to whom the request

---

[11] Brebner, *'Breen v Williams:* A lost opportunity or a welcome conservatism?' Deakin Law Rev 1996; 3:237.

[12] Published in May 2016, available at www.medicalcouncil.ie.

[13] www.health.gov.ie/blog/publications/general-scheme-of-health-information-and-patient-safety-bill/.

is made is entitled to make reasonable inquiries in order to satisfy himself as to the identity of the individual concerned and the identity of the person to whom the records are to be transferred. A health services provider who fails, without reasonable excuse, to forward the relevant health record, as required by this Head, will be guilty of an offence. This Bill has not yet been enacted at the time of writing.

FREEDOM OF INFORMATION ACT 2014

[3.18] The issue of access to records is dealt with in Ireland by the Freedom of Information Act and the Data Protection Acts. The Freedom of Information Act 2014 (the FOI Act), which repealed the earlier 1997 and 2003 Acts, covers official information which an individual may seek to have access to and to have amended if inaccurate. The legislation establishes a presumption in favour of access to information in visual, written or electronic forms. It gives individuals rights to access personal and non-personal information, have personal records amended or deleted where the information is incorrect, incomplete or misleading and to seek reasons for decisions affecting them.

[3.19] Personal information is defined generally in the FOI Act as information about an identifiable individual that (a) would, in the ordinary course of events, be known only to the individual or members of the family, or friends, of the individual, or (b) is held by a public body on the understanding that it would be treated by it as confidential. Such definition is clearly applicable to personal health information and indeed the Act gives illustrative examples of such information as including information relating to the educational, medical, psychiatric or psychological history of the individual.

[3.20] It is important to note that the FOI Act applies only to public bodies.[14] In the health context, this includes government departments, the Health Service Executive and voluntary hospitals. This means that it applies, for example, to records created by a doctor or other health care professional in the carrying out of duties as part of his employment by the State, such as in the treatment of a patient with a medical card, or within a public hospital. It means however that medical records held by private hospitals or clinics, or records created on a private basis between doctor and patient are not accessible under the FOI Act. However, the provisions of the Data Protection Acts, discussed below,[15] apply to all legal entities in this jurisdiction whether Government, private, voluntary or charitable that control personal data. One of the obligations on data controllers under the Data Protection Acts is to give a person a copy of their personal data on request. This obligation is subject to very limited exemptions.

Exemptions

[3.21] Decisions on access to records are made by designated decision-makers or FOI officers within the public body. Although there is a presumption in favour of access by the person whose personal records are held, there are exemptions provided for in Part 4 of the FOI Act which outlines circumstances in which the requested information may not be released. There are two broad categories of exemptions: class exemptions where

---

14 www.foi.gov.ie/faqs/what-bodies-are-covered-by-foi/.
15 Para **[3.42]** et seq.

all records in that class or category are exempt, for example, records to which legal professional privilege attaches and harm-based exemptions where records which might damage a particular public interest are exempt, for example, records which might reveal the negotiating positions of public bodies. Examples of exemptions include circumstances in which disclosure of the record would prejudice the privacy of another person, the request is frivolous, vexatious or voluminous or the record would disclose deliberations of a public body that it would be against the public interest to disclose. Many but not all exemptions may contain what is often referred to as a public interest override, that is, even though a record is exempt under the FOI Act a public body or the Information Commissioner may decide, on balance, that the overall public interest justifies its release. Some exemptions may provide that a public body may refuse to disclose the very existence of a particular record where to do so might disclose exempt information. Some classes of records may also be excluded from the scope of the FOI Act, for example records created by the Attorney General, records relating to the President and the private papers of TDs and Senators. Reasons for refusals of access must be given, and the Office of Information Commissioner has been set up to review decisions by and practices of public bodies as well as the operation of the FOI Act generally.[16]

[3.22] The most relevant exemption in the health care context where access to information may be refused is where it could reasonably be expected to endanger the life or safety of any person[17] or if the information relates to another person who has not given consent to its release.[18] The latter exemption will not apply, inter alia, where the information is available to the general public or where disclosure of the information is necessary in order to avoid a serious and imminent danger to the life or health of an individual.

[3.23] A further exemption is provided where an FOI request relates to (a) a record of a medical or psychiatric nature relating to the requester concerned, or (b) a record kept for the purposes of, or obtained in the course of the carrying out of, social work in relation to the requester, and, in the opinion of the head concerned, disclosure of the information concerned to the requester might be prejudicial to his or her physical or mental health, well-being or emotional condition. In such circumstances s 37(3) provides that access may be denied.[19] Where access is denied, s 37(4) states that the information may be provided through a nominated health professional, such as the patient's general practitioner. This serves to reinforce the position that rights of access to medical records are more restricted than other records, dependent on the decision of either the executive

---

16 For discussion of the operation of these exemptions in practice see report of the OIC at www.oic.gov.ie/en/Publications/Special-Reports/Investigations-Compliance/Compliance-by-Public-Bodies/Chapter-6.html. For comprehensive review of the operation of the Act see generally McDonagh, *Freedom of Information Law in Ireland* (3rd edn, Round Hall, 2015).

17 Section 31(1)(b) of the 2014 Act.

18 Section 37 of the 2014 Act.

19 This is similar to an exemption contained in the Data Protection Act 2003. However refusal of access is discretionary under FOI but mandatory under Data Protection law in such circumstances. There is also a difference in the degree of potential harm to the person seeking access, with FOI law setting a lower threshold where access 'might be prejudicial' than Data Protection.

of the public body in question (who may not have any medical qualifications with which to assess the request for access) or a nominated health professional who will exercise his own medical judgment. Although such refusals are subject to the right of appeal, the individual does not have a broad right to records of his health care, which seems to be in conflict with the overall aim of the FOI Act.[20]

Parental access to records in relation to children

[3.24] An issue which can cause difficulty in practice is in relation to a parent's right of access to the health records of their children. It is worth noting that a child under the FOI Act is defined as a person who has not reached the age of majority, ie eighteen years.[21] Although in principle an FOI request may only be made in relation to one's own personal records and not the records relating to any other person, family relationships require special consideration. The difficulties that may arise in this context are illustrated in *McK v The Information Commissioner*[22] where the issue to be decided by the Court was whether a father, a widower who had been separated from his late wife, and who was joint guardian of his children, was entitled under the Freedom of Information Act 1997 to information, in the form of hospital notes, about an illness of his daughter. The circumstances were that there had been an unproven allegation of sexual abuse by the man of his daughter prior to the couple's separation. As part of the separation agreement, the man had supervised access to his children and the parties were working towards a position of unsupervised access at the time of the wife's death. By agreement, the children went to live with the wife's brother. The father, his brother-in-law and his wife were joint guardians of the children. Following admission of the man's daughter to hospital for an unspecified viral infection, the man sought further information from the hospital, which was not forthcoming. The other joint guardian refused permission for release of the records. On appeal to the Information Commissioner, the Commissioner decided that in any situation in which there is disagreement between parents/guardians regarding the release of records relating to a minor, release will only be directed where there is tangible evidence that such release would actually serve the best interests of the minor.

[3.25] On appeal to the High Court and subsequently to the Supreme Court it was held that the Commissioner had erred in application of the relevant legal test. The Supreme Court held that as a matter of constitutional and family law a parent has rights and duties. In general a parent would expect to be given and would be given medical information about his or her child. It would only be in exceptional circumstances that medical information about a child would not be given to a parent/guardian. This presumption, while not absolute, is fundamental. The 'tangible evidence' test of the

---

[20] The aim of the provision is to give the individual to whom the information relates indirect access to the information and, as it has been expressed in an Australian report, 'to ensure that people receive 'disturbing' information in a supportive environment.' McDonagh, *Freedom of Information Law* (3rd edn, Round Hall, 2015) at 594.

[21] This may cause difficulties in light of the general practice of allowing persons over the age of sixteen years to give their own consent to medical, surgical and dental treatment under s 23(1) of the Non-Fatal Offences Against the Person Act 1997. This is considered in Chapter 11.

[22] *McK v The Information Commissioner* [2006] IESC 2.

Commissioner had reversed the onus of proof by requiring the requester to satisfy the decision-maker that release of the records would be in the best interests of the minor. The Court held that the obverse is the correct approach - the presumption is that the release of such medical information would best serve the interests of the minor. However, evidence may be produced, including reference to the views of the minor herself if appropriate, that it would not serve her interests, and, in considering the circumstances, her welfare is paramount.

[3.26] Regulations were introduced in 2009 to clarify this issue.[23] These provide that where a parent/ guardian requests access to records of their minor child, this request shall be granted where it would, in the opinion of the Head of the FOI body concerned, having regard to all the circumstances and to any guidelines drawn up and published by the Minister, be in the best interests of the minor. Guidance Notes on Access to Records by Parents/Guardians were also issued by the Minister for Finance.[24] The Notes also apply to the records of persons with disabilities. They describe the factors that should be taken into account by a decision-maker in relation to the release of the personal records of the minor to parents or guardians. The first factor is whether the minor would consent to the release of the records. However, the guidance notes point out that consultation with the minor is not compulsory and should be at the discretion of the decision-maker. The fact that a minor might object to release of information to his or her parents/ guardians will not always be enough in itself to justify refusal, but it will be a factor that the decision maker should consider before making a decision. A second factor to consider is whether release of the material would damage the minor in some way. Finally the decision-maker should consider whether the records are held in the minor's own right. If so, the general position is that such records would not be released to a parent or guardian unless such release was in the minor's best interest. Interestingly, the Guidance Notes give an example of a record in this area as certain medical records which may not be appropriate for automatic release to parents/guardians, such as records a GP might have on prescribing contraceptives to a minor.[25] This may be open to challenge by parents who might seek to rely on the constitutional rights of the family, however as the Guidance advises only that such records may not be appropriate for *automatic* release, each case should be decided on its own merits taking into account the best interests of the minor and the other factors considered in the Guidance Notes.

[3.27] The Guidance Notes also provide useful advice regarding consultation with the minor in relation to the release of their records. It advises that the decision-maker should consider the capacity of the person to understand the issues involved. This could depend on the minor's age, intelligence and maturity. The decision to consult with a minor will also depend on factors such as the nature of the record, ie its sensitivity or otherwise. The decision maker should seek to ascertain whether the minor is capable of coming to a mature view as to what is in his or her best interests in the particular circumstances and weigh any opinion that may be got from the child accordingly. In some cases, even young children may be capable of understanding the issues involved and in such event the refusal of the minor to consent to release of a record to a parent or guardian could be

---

[23] SI 387/2009.
[24] www.foi.gov.ie/regulations/regulation-No-387/.
[25] www.health.gov.ie/wp-content/uploads/2014/03/Guidance_Notes-FOI1.pdf.

given a significant weighting. The Notes advise that the decision maker would need to determine the extent to which involvement of a parent or guardian in the consultation process is appropriate. For example, if the record sought contains allegations of abuse or suspected abuse of the child by a parent or guardian, it may not be appropriate for that parent or guardian to be present during consultation with the child. Where records sought are of substantial concern to the minor or incapacitated adult to whom they relate, or they are of an inherently personal and sensitive nature, this will influence the form and extent of consultation undertaken and the weight to be given to the views of the person, eg where records sought relate to personal, including sexual, relationships of the person, it is more likely that the decision-maker would give greater weight to the views of the person in such a case than in others. The decision-maker must also take into account guardianship and custody issues, the preferable format for the consultation, and the best interests of the person to whom the records relate.

Access to records of deceased persons

[3.28] Another issue which can cause difficulties in this context is in relation to access to medical records after death by family members of the deceased, executors of the deceased's estate and others. From an ethical perspective, most professional codes of conduct, including the Medical Council's Guide to Professional Conduct and Ethics for Registered Medical Practitioners,[26] stipulate that the duty to maintain confidentiality extends after death. However, confidentiality is not absolute and is usually qualified by the need to protect third parties or society.[27] The rights of individuals to confidentiality after death can be a difficult and sensitive issue, as views range from those who assert that the deceased have no rights and that therefore information can be disclosed to the deceased's family after death, to those who argue that the principle of confidentiality must be maintained even after death so as not to damage the relationship of trust between doctor and patient.

[3.29] The question arises as to whether disclosure of information after death can cause harm.[28] There are several possible areas of concern that may arise here such as the patient's own expectations, the protection of others and the preservation of societal expectations of confidentiality. For some patients, posthumous disclosure of sensitive information may cause as much fear as contemporaneous disclosure. Such fears affect patient behaviour and candour, which may result in suboptimal care during life. Individuals frequently withhold information from loved ones to protect them, and there is no reason to assume that this should be different after a person's death. An expectation among the living that their private medical information may be released after death may also inhibit the patient-clinician relationship.[29]

[3.30] However, there are circumstances in which it may be in the family's interests to access information relating to the deceased after death, such as where they may be

---

[26] Guide to Professional Conduct and Ethics (8th edn, 2016) para 32.

[27] This is discussed in Part Two of this chapter.

[28] Robinson and O'Neill, 'Access to Health Care Records After Death, Balancing Confidentiality with Appropriate Disclosure' (2007) JAMA Vol 297 No 6, 634–636.

[29] Robinson and O'Neill, 'Access to Health Care Records After Death, Balancing Confidentiality with Appropriate Disclosure' (2007) JAMA Vol 297 No 6, 634–636.

concerned about the care the person received prior to death, or inherited diseases, or their testamentary capacity. In some of these situations, the family may seek a court order for discovery of the medical records such as to confirm the validity of a will. In these circumstances it might be preferable to consider the possibility of controlled release of information in a clinical manner as part of a bereavement care programme involving the patient's doctor. Support could also be given by expert clinicians independent of the particular health-care institution involved in the deceased patient's care. This solution may be considered a balance between the rights of the deceased to privacy (by avoiding indiscriminate release of their healthcare records) and of the living to access information pertinent to their own health and peace of mind (by providing a clinically informed response to their concerns).[30]

[3.31] Section 37(5) of the FOI Act[31] provides that in relation to a request the grant of which would otherwise fall to be refused on the basis that it is personal information (defined as including information relating to a deceased person), the decision-maker may grant the request if, in his or her opinion, the public interest that the request should be granted outweighs the public interest that the right to privacy of the individual to whom the information relates should be upheld, or the grant of the request would benefit the individual. This is referred to as the 'public interest override.' Under the FOI Regulations of 2009,[32] access to health records of a deceased person may be given to three categories of people with specific interests. These are: the deceased person's personal representative acting in the course of the administration of his estate or someone acting with the consent of the personal representative; a person on whom a function is conferred by law in relation to the deceased person or his estate acting in the course of the performance of this function; and, finally, the spouse or a next of kin of the individual where, in the opinion of the head of the public body concerned, the public interest would, on balance, be better served by granting than by refusing to grant the request.[33] Under the Regulations, persons who are neither spouses nor next of kin of the deceased person are ineligible to apply for access to records of deceased persons. This limitation would affect, for example, relatives of the deceased other than next of kin, as well as friends and other interested parties.[34]

[3.32] McDonagh and Donnelly pose the question as to whether the public interest override can be applied in cases where requests for access to records of deceased persons do not meet the conditions for the granting of such access provided for in the Regulations, namely consideration of the public interest and the extent to which release of the records would benefit the individual. In the case of the first condition, it raises issues about the extent to which, if at all, a dead person can be said to enjoy a right to privacy. It also requires an exploration of the public interest factors favouring the granting of requests for access to health information about the dead. The second

---

[30] Robinson and O'Neill, 'Access to Health Care Records After Death, Balancing Confidentiality with Appropriate Disclosure' (2007) JAMA Vol 297 No 6, 634–636 at 635.

[31] Previously s 28(5) of the 2007 Act.

[32] SI 387/2009.

[33] Reg 4(1)(b)(iii).

[34] McDonagh and Donnelly, 'Access to Health Information in respect of deceased persons: The Law in Ireland' (2010) 16(1) MLJI 7–15.

condition raises the question of whether the granting of an FOI request could ever be said to benefit a deceased person. In the same way that the existence of posthumous harm gives rise to significant conceptual challenges,[35] it is difficult to see how recognition could be afforded to the notion of a dead person's enjoyment of a benefit.

[3.33] The introduction of the public interest test by the 2009 Regulations is of central importance to the operation of the access rights of spouses and next of kin.[36] The Minister for Finance published detailed Guidance Notes in relation to the interpretation of 'public interest' in this context. These advise that the following matters should be taken into consideration –

- The confidentiality of personal information as set out in s 28(1) of the Act.
- Whether the deceased would have consented to the release of the records to the requester when living? Has the person outlined arrangements in his will or other instrument in writing consenting to release of personal records?
- Would the release damage the good name and character of the deceased?
- The nature of the relationship of the requester to the deceased and the circumstances of the relationship prior to the death of the deceased.
- The nature of the records to be released.
- Can the requester obtain the information they seek without accessing the records of the deceased, for example from another family source?
- Any other circumstances relevant to the request as set out by the requester.

In relation to medical records, the Guidance Notes also indicate that 'due regard should be had to the confidentiality of medical records in accordance with the Irish Medical Council Guide to Ethical Conduct and Behaviour'.

[3.34] In *Rotunda Hospital v Information Commissioner*[37] the Court had to consider an appeal from the Rotunda Hospital against the decision of the Information Commissioner to grant access to information in a Labour Ward Book and a Porter's Lodge Book in the hospital. This information was sought by Ms Dawn Walsh on behalf of her elderly father Mr Thomas Walsh (who was deceased at the date of the judgment), who had been given up for adoption in 1922. The information related to the age of the woman believed to be registered in the hospital records as Mr Walsh's mother, Bridie Walsh. This was sought by the family in order to assist Mr Walsh in tracing his family roots. The hospital refused access to the information on the grounds that it had a policy of ensuring that women

---

[35] As described by Sperling, *Posthumous Interests: Legal and Ethical Perspectives* (Cambridge University Press, 2008), p15, the difficulty with a concept of posthumous harm is first, how a person can be harmed if they cannot experience the 'evil of harm' and secondly, if a deceased person no longer exists for legal purposes, who is the subject of posthumous harm? Although several commentators have tried to develop theories justifying the conceptual possibility of posthumous harm, (see, for example, Feinberg, *The Moral Limits of the Criminal Law: Harm to Others* (OUP, 1984), pp 89–91; Sperling, *Posthumous Interests*), the issue remains conceptually problematic. For further discussion of the conceptual issues involved, see McDonagh and Donnelly, 'Keeping the Secrets of the Dead: An Evaluation of the Statutory Framework for Access to Information About Deceased Persons' 31(1) *Legal Studies* (2011) 42–70.

[36] Reg 4(1)(b)(iii).

[37] *Rotunda Hospital v Information Commissioner* [2009] IEHC 315.

who came to the hospital have an absolute guarantee of confidentiality, whether it was information required for therapeutic purposes or not. The Information Commissioner overturned the hospital's refusal to grant access to the information sought. The hospital appealed the decision to the High Court. McCarthy J in describing the substance of the appeal said:

> Needless to say there is not now and was never at any time in our law absolute confidentiality in respect of information passed between, say, a patient and doctor or a patient and the servants or agents of a hospital (which amounts to the same thing) so one should proceed, of course, on the basis that what is advanced here is a claim for confidentiality in terms of the Acts, without prejudice to any other circumstance where disclosure could be compelled.

[3.35] One of the issues in contention was whether the age of the woman who had given birth was 'personal information'. Section 28(2)(a) of the 2007 Act removed the ban on access to a record where it would involve disclosure of personal information where the information concerned relates to the requester. However, one may not obtain, as of right, personal information pertaining to oneself if it also relates to another person. It is only if the information is in the public domain or the subject of regulation that disclosure arises as of right. McCarthy J took the view that the mother's age was personal information relating to the requester and therefore subject to the Act.

[3.36] The second issue was whether this information was confidential and therefore subject to a prohibition on disclosure. The Commissioner took the view that since information on age is available through birth, marriage and death certificates, this is information already in the public domain and thus not properly regarded as confidential. The judge considered definitions of confidential information in other jurisdictions as well as Irish authorities, including *House of Spring Gardens Ltd and Others v Point Blank Ltd and Others*[38] in which the Supreme Court said that the issue was to be decided by looking at the relationship between the parties and the nature of the information. McCarthy J also examined case law surrounding the nature of the duty of confidentiality, including *W v Egdell*[39] and *X v Y*.[40] The judge considered whether the mother in this case, presumably now deceased given the passage of time since giving birth in 1922, could enjoy constitutional rights or whether such rights might be exercised on her behalf by her personal representatives.

> She could have no right to life or surely anything of the nature of a right going to the nature of the human personality or freedom of expression or liberty nor a right against self-incrimination or to marry…I find it hard to accept any such right could ever arise. Privacy is a highly personal right and surely it must be the case that such a right could not arise.

The learned judge later went on to say that he was of the opinion that 'no right to privacy exists in deceased persons.' He held that the record did not enjoy the necessary quality of confidentiality for the purpose of prima facie prohibiting disclosure under s 26.

[3.37] On appeal to the Supreme Court,[41] the court, by majority, allowed the appeal and held that the FOI Act *did* apply to the relevant hospital records relating to the age of the

---

[38] *House of Spring Gardens Limited and Others v Point Blank Ltd and Others* [1984] IR 611.

[39] *W v Egdell* [1990] 1 All ER 835.

[40] *X v Y* [1988] 2 All ER 648, discussed below at paras **[3.95]–[3.96]**.

[41] *Rotunda Hospital v Information Commissioner* [2011] IESC 26.

woman who had given birth. The Court held that personal information about Bridie Walsh would have been given to the hospital in confidence and on the understanding that it would be kept confidential, and that the public interest did not justify its release. It is interesting to note Fennelly J's view that this entire case concerned 'an apparently innocuous, and now, after a lapse of many years, even trivial piece of information' about the age of a single woman who gave birth to a child in the hospital in 1922. He said 'It is difficult to avoid the feeling that none of this great litigation would have taken place if it had not been for the Freedom Information Acts and that the information would have been released.'[42] Fennelly J also acknowledged the balancing of two private interests involved here and said that a child seeking information about his or her family may give rise to conflict with a profound wish for privacy on the part of the other party. 'The present case is different but only in degree. Thomas Walsh was seeking information about his mother, who, in all probability, is long since deceased. The Hospital, however, invokes s 26 of the Act to protect from disclosure information communicated to it in circumstances of confidentiality.' The Commissioner had based her decision on the 'public interest in persons generally having the fullest possible information on their origins.' Fennelly J said in response to this point that 'whether people generally should be granted access to information concerning their origins is a matter of policy. It would have been possible to include in the legislation. It has not been included. It is not, in my view, open to the Commissioner to adopt a general policy in the public interest.'[43]

[3.38] Denham J (dissenting) was also of the view that the age of Bridie Walsh at the date of the birth of Thomas Joseph Walsh was prima facie personal information to Bridie Walsh. However, she went on to consider whether this information was also personal information to Thomas Walsh, her son. The learned judge considered that in all probability Bridie Walsh was now deceased and therefore personal information should not be disclosed unless it came within one of the statutory exemptions. Denham J disagreed with the conclusion reached by the Commissioner that the information relating to the age of Bridie Walsh was available to the general public through birth registration records. She said that there are likely to be many people of that name in the Register and therefore further information would be required in order to ascertain which Bridie Walsh was the relevant person sought by the applicant. Denham J said that the Regulations allow records of deceased persons to be made available to next of kin of the deceased, such as Mr Walsh in this instance and that therefore access to the records should have been granted to him.

[3.39] In relation to confidentiality, the hospital argued (and the majority of the Court accepted) that the information had been given by Bridie Walsh to the hospital in the expectation of confidentiality. However, Denham J was of the view that although confidentiality is of considerable importance, a balance must be struck between the confidentiality of the document and the public interest. Each case should be determined on its own facts. Denham J was satisfied that in this case the public interest favoured the requester. She said 'The requester is the son and next of kin of the deceased. This is a factor which carries significant weight. It is an entirely different situation to a request from a person who has not got such kinship connections.'

---

[42] *Rotunda Hospital v Information Commissioner* [2011] IESC 26, Fennelly J at para 28.
[43] *Rotunda Hospital v Information Commissioner* [2011] IESC 26, Fennelly J paras 107–109.

Relationship between FOI and Data Protection

[3.40] As noted above, the Freedom of Information Act grants every person a right, subject to certain restrictions, to access information held by Government Departments, agencies and other designated bodies in receipt of State funding, the essential principle of FOI being that there should be access to records held by or under the control of public bodies 'to the greatest extent possible consistent with the public interest and the right to privacy'.[44] The Act also allows persons to seek access to their own data held by such bodies. Data protection involves 'the protection of individual privacy and the putting in place of safeguards where personal information is collected, used, disclosed or transferred to other persons and/or other countries. It imposes obligations on all individuals, agencies or organisations that keep personal information, and not just public bodies.'[45] Therefore while the FOI Act applies only to public bodies, the requirements of the Data Protection Acts apply to *all* legal entities in this jurisdiction whether Government, private, voluntary or charitable that control personal data. The Data Protection Act places obligations on such entities in terms of how they process personal data. One of these obligations is to give a person a copy of their personal data on request. This right to access personal data is subject to very limited exemptions. When a public body covered by Freedom of Information legislation receives an FOI request from a person for their own information, they are required to also consider the request under data protection requirements and give the person the maximum amount of their information taking account of both sets of legislation.[46] There is a clear overlap between the two frameworks and the protection that they provide. However, there are also differences in terms of the definitions of personal data or information and in relation to the release of information on grounds of public interest.

[3.41] Although the Data Protection Act 1988 applied only to data retained in electronic form, the amending Act of 2003 extended the provisions to personal information in both manual and electronic forms. Not all personal information is covered by data protection law due to the definition used in the Act and, similarly, not all personal information is classed as sensitive information within the Freedom of Information provisions. The Data Protection Act provides in s 1(5)(a) that a right conferred by this Act shall not prejudice the exercise of a right conferred by the Freedom of Information Act. This means that if a request for access to records under the FOI Act is refused, the applicant may nonetheless be able to seek access under Data Protection law. The relevant provisions of the Data Protection Acts are described below.

DATA PROTECTION ACT 2003

[3.42] Patients have an expectation that their privacy will be respected by the professionals and healthcare facilities to which they entrust their personal and often sensitive information. This expectation comes not only from the confidentiality of the doctor-patient relationship but also from the nature of the information that is disclosed.[47]

---

44 Long Title to the FOI Act 1997.

45 Lennon, *Protecting Personal Health Information in Ireland, Law and Practice* (Oak Tree Press, 2005), p 323.

46 www.dataprotection.ie/docs/General/1237.htm#7.

47 *Campbell v Mirror Groups Newspapers* [2004] 2 All ER 995 at para 145.

Principles of confidentiality have consistently been strongly upheld by the courts on the basis that information relating to one's health is central to a sense of personal identity, of fundamental significance to one's private and family life and therefore of the utmost sensitivity.[48] However, it is also important to acknowledge that the use and sharing of health data takes place across the health system for many purposes ranging from clinical, administrative, financial, educational purposes and research. Some of these uses will have a direct impact on the patient through sharing her clinical data with the members of different medical teams providing care to her. Other uses may not have a direct impact on the patient herself but are nonetheless important in ensuring patient safety and quality through analysis of data in education, quality assurance programmes, audit and research. As highlighted in the Department of Health's discussion paper on the proposed Health Information Bill:

> A major debate, internationally, centres on the need to balance potentially competing (individual) rights and (societal) needs. In the health sector, this is about the rights of the patient to determine who has access to his or her medical records and the needs of the health service to use patient information for a range of management and research purposes that stand to benefit both the individual patient directly and society generally, through better service planning and healthcare innovations. The extent to which patient consent should determine the use and disclosure of personal health information is a critical matter.[49]

[3.43] In Ireland the first Data Protection Act was introduced in 1988 to address concerns regarding the protection of data stored on computer.[50] The concerns centred on the ease with which computerised data could be retrieved and transferred without the knowledge of the individuals to whom the data related. This led to fears that the State would have the ability to access sensitive information about every individual and that the information could be stolen or otherwise misused by others who were able to break into the system.[51] This Act was later amended to give effect to the European Data Protection Directive of 1995[52] which was founded on the principle that an individual must give prior consent to the processing of his or her personal data.[53] It also establishes the principle that personal data must be processed fairly and lawfully. The Directive was transposed into Irish law by the Data Protection (Amendment) Act of 2003 (hereafter referred to as 'the Act').

[3.44] The transposition of the Directive in different legal instruments across all the Member States led to a fragmented regulatory system for data controllers operating in the European Union. The Directive has now been replaced by the EU General Data

---

[48] *I v Finland* (Applic No 20511/03; Judgment 17 July 2008, at para 38).

[49] Available at www.hrb.ie/research-strategy-funding/policies-and-guidelines/guidelines/data-protectionhealth-information/.

[50] See Kelleher and Murray, *Information Technology Law in Ireland* (2nd edn, Bloomsbury Professional, 2007).

[51] 375 Dáil Debates, Cols. 2846–7, Mr G Collins TD, then Minister for Justice.

[52] Data Protection Directive 95/46/EC.

[53] Consent is defined in art 2(h) of the Directive as 'any freely given specific and informed indication of his wishes by which the data subject signifies his agreement to personal data in relation to him being processed.'

Protection Regulation (GDPR) 2016.[54] Following a two year implementation period, the GDPR will be applied across the European Union from 25 May 2018. The GDPR is aimed at enhancing data protection rights of individuals and improving business opportunities in the digital single market. As a regulation, the GDPR will be directly applicable in the Member States, without the need for any implementing legislation. This should allow for the application and enforcement of a more standardised data protection law across the EU. The reforms in the Regulation also specifically address technological challenges and opportunities in respect of the processing of personal data in the digital age, including profiling, data portability and the 'right to be forgotten'. However, the core principles around data processing in the Regulation remain largely unchanged from the Directive, but have simply been expanded and clarified to strengthen the rights of data subjects.[55]

[3.45] Personal data is defined in the 2003 Act as 'data relating to a living individual who is or can be identified either from the data or from the data in conjunction with other information that is in, or is likely to come into, the possession of the data controller.' The definition of personal data has been further clarified in the 2016 GDPR to mean 'any information relating to an identified or identifiable natural person ('data subject')'. It goes on to provide that 'an identifiable natural person is one who can be identified, directly or indirectly, in particular by reference to an identifier such as a name, an identification number, location data, an online identifier or to one or more factors specific to the physical, physiological, genetic, mental, economic, cultural or social identity of that natural person.'

[3.46] Sensitive personal data[56] is defined in the 2003 Act as any personal data as to (a) the racial or ethnic origin, the political opinions or the religious or philosophical beliefs of the data subject, (b) whether the data subject is a member of a trade union (c) the physical or mental health or condition or sexual life of the data subject, (d) the commission or alleged commission of any offence by the data subject, or (e) any proceedings for an offence committed or alleged to have been committed by the data subject, the disposal of such proceedings or the sentence of any court in such proceedings. Under art 9 of the GDPR processing of personal data revealing racial or ethnic origin, political opinions, religious or philosophical beliefs, or trade union membership, and the processing of genetic data, biometric data for the purpose of uniquely identifying a natural person, data concerning health or data concerning a natural person's sex life or sexual orientation shall be prohibited, subject to specific exceptions set out in the Regulation. It is also provided that in addition to the these exceptions, Member States may maintain or introduce further conditions, including

---

[54] Regulation (EU) 2016/679.

[55] See generally Hordern, 'The Final GDPR Text and What It Will Mean for Health Data' www.hldataprotection.com/2016/01/articles/health-privacy-hipaa/the-final-gdpr-text-and-what-it-will-mean-for-health-data/.

[56] The Data Protection Acts require additional conditions to be met for the processing of such data to be legitimate. Usually this will be the explicit consent of the person about whom the data relates.

limitations, with regard to the processing of genetic data,[57] biometric data[58] or data concerning health.

[3.47] Where personal data is collected and processed by an individual or organisation, that person/organisation is known as a data controller. The person whose data is collected is referred to as the data subject. In the healthcare context, for patients in public hospitals the Health Service Executive is the data controller and not the treating doctor. However where a doctor has private patients then he/she becomes the controller if he/she is treating them in a private hospital or in his/her private rooms. Under the 2016 GDPR there is now a specific obligation on a controller or a processor to appoint a data protection officer where its core processing activities require regular and systematic monitoring of individuals on a large scale, or where its core activities consist of the processing of sensitive data on a large scale. This obligation could be relevant for a range of participants in healthcare such as healthcare providers and health insurance companies. In any event, the data controller must comply with the Eight Data Protection Principles set out in the Act as follows:

1.   Obtain and process information fairly.
2.   Keep it only for one or more specified, explicit and lawful purposes.
3.   Use and disclose it only in ways compatible with these purposes.
4.   Keep it safe and secure.
5.   Keep it accurate, complete and up to date.
6.   Ensure that it is adequate, relevant and not excessive.
7.   Retain it for no longer than is necessary for the purpose or purposes.
8.   Give a copy of his or her personal data to that individual, on request.

Data collection conditions

[3.48] Section 2 of the Act provides that personal data must be obtained and processed fairly, be accurate and complete and, where necessary, kept up to date. This means the data (i) shall have been obtained only for one or more specified, explicit and legitimate purposes, (ii) shall not be further processed in a manner incompatible with that purpose or those purposes, (iii) shall be adequate, relevant and not excessive in relation to the purpose or purposes for which they were collected or are further processed, and (iv) shall not be kept for longer than is necessary for that purpose or those purposes. The data controller must take appropriate security measures against unauthorised access to, or unauthorised alteration, disclosure or destruction of, the data, in particular where the processing involves the transmission of data over a network, and against all other unlawful forms of processing.

---

[57]   'Genetic data' means personal data relating to the inherited or acquired genetic characteristics of a natural person which give unique information about the physiology or the health of that natural person and which result, in particular, from an analysis of a biological sample from the natural person in question.

[58]   'Biometric data' means personal data resulting from specific technical processing relating to the physical, physiological or behavioural characteristics of a natural person, which allow or confirm the unique identification of that natural person, such as facial images or dactyloscopic data.

Data processing conditions

[3.49] The Act (and GDPR) provides that personal data may only be processed if certain conditions are met. Processing includes almost any use of the data, including collection and storing it, altering, transmitting it to others and deleting it. In relation to the processing of sensitive personal data, such as medical records, the Act sets out detailed conditions, at least one of which must be met before processing such data. These include:

- obtaining the consent of the data subject;
- the processing is necessary for the discharge of a legal obligation;
- the processing is necessary in order to protect the vital interests of the data subject;
- the processing is necessary for the legitimate interests of the data controller or a third party to whom the data is disclosed;
- the processing is necessary in order to obtain legal advice;
- the processing is necessary for medical purposes and is carried out by a health professional or a person who would owe a similar duty of confidentiality.

The term 'health professional' includes a registered medical practitioner, within the meaning of the Medical Practitioners Acts 1978–2007, a registered dentist, within the meaning of the Dentists Act 1985 or a member of any other class of health worker or social worker standing specified by regulations made by the Minister. 'Medical purposes' includes the purposes of preventive medicine, medical diagnosis, medical research, the provision of care and treatment and the management of health-care services.

[3.50] The list above indicates that patient consent is only one of a set of conditions which must be met prior to processing, and is not a necessary pre-condition in itself. In other words it is possible to process personal data without consent if the processing meets any of the other conditions listed above. In addition however s 2D sets out a default position that data is not to be regarded as having been processed fairly unless the data subject has been made aware of the identity of the data processor and the purposes for which the processing is intended. Therefore where data is processed for a purpose other than that which was made known to the data subject or where data is to be shared with a third party, then the data controller is under an obligation to advise the data subject accordingly. There are exceptions to these requirements where the processing is for historical or scientific research or where compliance would be impossible or would involve disproportionate effort.

Consent of the data subject

[3.51] Consent is defined in art 2(h) of the 1995 Directive as 'any freely given specific and informed indication of his wishes by which the data subject signifies his agreement to personal data in relation to him being processed.' The requirement under art 7 of the GDPR for obtaining valid consent is broadly similar to the requirement under the Directive – consent must be a freely given, specific, informed, and unambiguous indication of an individual's wishes. However it is important to note that art 7 provides that if consent is given in a written declaration that also contains other matters, the consent must be clearly distinguishable from those other matters, in an easily accessible form and using clear and plain language, and individuals must be able to withdraw their consent easily. These requirements mean that controllers will need to carefully consider the wording in consent forms and the means by which consent is achieved in the healthcare context.

[3.52] Consent may generally be expressly given in writing by signing a consent form or hospital admission form in which the processing of personal data is indicated, or consent may be implied by the actions of the patient in attending the doctor's clinic or hospital. In such circumstances, however, patients should be made aware by notices or otherwise on display that their personal data will be processed. The Data Protection Commissioner has indicated that the adequacy of such notices will depend on the circumstances and it may not be sufficient to display such a notice in an Accident and Emergency waiting area, as persons attending such areas are likely to be in pain, anxious, and distressed and thus not in a position to properly take note of such notices.[59] Implied consent would generally cover the sharing of information within a clinical team where this is in the interests of providing care to a patient. It would also cover administrative uses of the information, for example sharing certain information with the billing department of a hospital. However, the amount of information and the nature of the data shared should be carefully kept to a minimum and only shared to the extent necessary. It does not cover sharing of information for other purposes such as teaching or research, for which explicit consent is required. Article 7 of the GDPR requires the data controller to be able to demonstrate that the data subject has consented to processing of his or her personal data and therefore the opportunity for implied consent seems to have been significantly restricted by this provision.

[3.53] Another use of patient data may be for clinical audit which is a very important quality improvement process that seeks to improve patient care and outcomes through systematic review of care against explicit criteria and acting to improve care when standards are not met. The process involves the selection of aspects of the structure, processes and outcomes of care which are then systematically evaluated against explicit criteria. If required, improvements are implemented at an individual, team or organisation level and then the care re-evaluated to confirm improvements.[60] Clearly, for some forms of clinical audit, patient data will be used in order to assess, for example, the rate of hospital re-admission within four weeks of discharge, or the length of hospital stays following hip fracture in the elderly etc. The question arises as to whether the use of such data comes within the Data Protection framework and, further, whether consent from patients is required for the use of their data in this context.

[3.54] The Data Protection Commissioner has published guidelines in relation to the operation of the Acts in the context of research in the health sector. In relation to clinical audit, the guidelines state that implied consent is normally all that is required when the audit could be of benefit to the patient or where the audit is being carried out by the health facility itself. Where the audit is being carried out by persons external to the data controller, informed consent from the patient is required. 'In such circumstances,

---

[59] Case study 1/97 of the Data Protection Commissioner, available at www.dataprotection.ie

[60] Commission on Patient Safety and Quality Assurance, *Building a Culture of Patient Safety* (2008) p 152 www.health.gov.ie/wp-content/uploads/2014/03/en_patientsafety.pdf.

informed consent may be captured by the inclusion of the possibility of external clinical audit in the general information material provided to the patient on how their information will be used.'[61] The HSE National Consent Policy[62] similarly states that in general, audit does not require informed consent. If the audit is being conducted by those who are involved in the care of the patient (or support staff) then explicit consent is not required as long as the patient has been informed of the possibility that their data will be used for this purpose and has been given an opportunity to opt out. It goes on to say that where the audit is being conducted by others, then the data must be de-identified. In that way it is no longer personal data within the meaning of the Act, and therefore no consent is required. In cases where the audit can only be carried out using identifiable data, explicit informed consent must be obtained for disclosure to third parties carrying out the audit.

[3.55] In seeking consent, a healthcare data controller also needs to consider the particular data subject, what their understanding is likely to be and therefore what they may reasonably expect. This means having regard to factors such as the individual's age, sex or cultural, linguistic and socio-economic background. If an individual expresses negative views, when made aware of a proposed secondary use or disclosure of their personal information, this would indicate ordinarily that they would not reasonably expect that use.[63]

[3.56] The General Scheme of the proposed Health Information and Patient Safety Bill 2015 contains a number of provisions in relation to clinical audit in this context. It provides in Head 79 that the Minister for Health will issue guidance on carrying out clinical audit in relation to the governance framework and methodology that must be adopted. Head 80 provides that the Minister will decide the format and method of publication of aggregate results of clinical audit but such publication will not contain personal data. Aggregate results are essentially findings from the clinical audit presented in a statistical format. Head 81 provides that the Freedom of Information Act 2014 shall not apply to a record created solely for the purpose of clinical audit where the record is created in compliance with the guidance issued by the Minister and aggregate results are published in accordance with Head 80. Neither will such records be admissible as evidence in civil proceedings (Head 82).[64] It remains to be seen when this Bill will be enacted and commenced and the extent to which, if any, those provisions are altered during the legislative process.

[3.57] The requirement for consent may be waived under s 8 of the 2003 Act where, for example, information is required urgently to prevent injury to an individual. Certain infectious diseases are subject to specific regulations designed to protect public health and which may require disclosure of personal data.[65] Other statutory and legally permitted or required disclosures include disclosure to the National Cancer Registry

---

[61] ww.dataprotection.ie/documents/guidance/Health_research.pdf.

[62] HSE National Consent Policy (2013) p.91.

[63] Available at www.hrb.ie/research-strategy-funding/policies-and-guidelines/guidelines/data-protectionhealth-information/.

[64] These provisions are in keeping with recommendations of the Report of the Commission on Patient Safety and Quality Assurance (2008), available at www.health.gov.ie.

[65] Section 29 of the Health Act 1947.

under the Health (Provision of Information) Act 1997, or disclosures as required by a court of law.

Data protection and newborn screening cards

[3.58] A useful illustration of how data protection can impact on the delivery of health services arises in relation to the controversy that arose in Ireland in 2011–12 in relation to the retention of newborn screening cards.[66] Newborn screening is based on a small sample of blood which is drawn from the heel of an infant a few days after birth, and is commonly known as the heel prick test. The sample of blood taken from the baby is stored on a piece of filter paper often known as a Guthrie card. The card also contains information for identification purposes such as the baby's name, mother's name, date and place of birth. In addition to its primary diagnostic purpose, these cards may be used for a range of secondary purposes such as confirmation of laboratory tests, development of new screening tests, public health research, genetic testing of siblings of a deceased person, and assisting in forensic investigations. Some of these uses require identified samples while others can use anonymised samples. Until 2011 formal consent was not obtained at the time of collection from the parents of the newborn infants for the analysis or storage of these samples. Controversy arose following a complaint to the Office of the Data Protection Commissioner, in relation to whether the samples which had been collected and retained without consent prior to 2011 must be destroyed in order to comply with data protection law.

[3.59] As outlined above, the retention of personal data must satisfy s 2(a) which means establishing that the data was obtained and processed fairly. Fair processing requirements include that the data subject be informed of the identity of the data controller and the purpose or purposes for which the data are intended to be processed. This information was not commonly given to parents of infants undergoing the heel prick test until 2011 and therefore s 2(a) was not satisfied. Although there are exceptions in the Data Protection Acts which allow for the processing of personal data without consent under certain circumstances, these exceptions only apply where the data has been obtained fairly in the first place in compliance with s 2(a).

[3.60] One of the potential uses of the archived screening cards is epidemiological or public health research, for example, to examine the prevalence of particular medical conditions in a cohort of individuals born in a particular time period or location to try to ascertain specific risk factors to which they might have been exposed. Where data is to be used for research purposes the Data Protection Commissioner has advised that although ideally patients should be made aware of these uses, processing of data for such purposes without consent may be permitted as long as no damage or distress is likely to be caused to the individual.[67] The Guidelines issued by the Office of the Data Protection Commissioner further state that anonymised and pseudonymised use of data does not need consent. The application of these guidelines in relation to screening cards would mean that the pre-2011 cards, if anonymised, could be used for research purposes

---

[66] See Madden, 'Retention and use of human biological samples – The Guthrie card problem' in Donnelly and Murray (eds), *Emerging Issues in Medical Law and Ethics* (OUP 2016)

[67] Office of the Data Protection Commissioner, Guidelines on research in the health sector available at www.dataprotection.ie.

without consent. However, some of the potential valuable uses of the cards require the possibility of identifiable data being made available in order, for example, to identify a genetic cause for Sudden Cardiac Death in a family member. It is important to note that in these circumstances, given that the card relates to a deceased individual, the provisions of the Data Protection Acts do not apply in any event.

[3.61] The HSE National Consent Policy[68] states that archived material may be used for research without consent where the material or data is not identifiable and there are no potential harms to the person from whom the material or data was obtained. It also states that where the material is identifiable, a research ethics committee may waive the consent requirement if the use of the material/data without consent is unlikely to adversely affect the welfare of the individual involved, the researchers will take appropriate measures to protect the privacy of individuals and to safeguard the material/data, they will comply with any known preferences of the individuals in relation to their material/data, and it is impossible or impractical to seek consent from individuals to whom the material/data relates.

[3.62] A further important consideration here is that s 8 of the Data Protection Act 2003 provides that any restrictions in the Act on the prohibition on processing do not apply, *inter alia,* if the processing is … (e) required by or under any enactment or by a rule of law or order of a court. Therefore it is possible that the Minister for Health could introduce specific legislation dealing with the retention of screening cards by effectively exempting such collection from the provisions of data protection provisions in the interest of the common good and subject to an appropriate structured governance framework to ensure that individual rights are protected.[69]

CONFIDENTIALITY

[3.63] Confidentiality is one of the most important elements of the relationship between doctors and patients and is a well-accepted principle of medical law. Patients presume when they attend a doctor for diagnosis and treatment that all aspects of their personal information will be kept confidential by the doctor. This aspect of the relationship is fundamental to the trust which patients place in their doctors and has been regarded as a crucial aspect of medical professionalism since the Hippocratic Oath, which stated 'whatsoever I shall see or hear concerning the life of men, in my attendance on the sick, or even apart therefrom, which ought not to be noised abroad, I will keep silence thereon, counting such things to be as sacred secrets'. Although the Hippocratic Oath is no longer commonly sworn by doctors, all professional codes of ethics and international declarations on medical ethics advocate strict adherence to the principle of confidentiality, subject to certain exceptions considered below.[70]

---

[68] Available at www.hse.ie.
[69] It is possible that the collection may come within the definition of 'Health Information Resource' contained in the General Scheme of the proposed Health Information and Patient Safety Bill 2015 but detailed analysis of these provisions is premature at this point.
[70] For example, the Declaration of Geneva and the Irish Medical Council's Guide to Professional Conduct and Ethics for Registered Medical Practitioners (8th edn, 2016)

[3.64] Confidentiality is crucial not only to respect the sense of privacy of a patient but also to preserve his or her confidence in the medical profession. Without such protection, those in need of medical assistance may be deterred from revealing such information of a personal and intimate nature as may be necessary in order to receive appropriate treatment and, even, from seeking such assistance, thereby endangering their own health and, in the case of transmissible diseases, that of the community.[71] In Ireland the duty of medical confidentiality arises from a number of sources, including the constitutional right to privacy, the protection of privacy under art 8 of the European Convention on Human Rights (ECHR), the ethical duties imposed on doctors, possible contractual obligations arising from the doctor-patient relationship and equitable duties imposed by virtue of the relationship and nature of the information disclosed.

[3.65] The right to privacy has been recognised by the Irish courts as an unenumerated constitutional right.[72] In *Kennedy v Ireland*[73] Hamilton P said:

> Though not specifically guaranteed by the Constitution, the right of privacy is one of the fundamental personal rights of the citizen which flow from the Christian and democratic nature of the State…The nature of the right to privacy must be such as to ensure the dignity and freedom of an individual in the type of society envisaged by the Constitution, namely, a sovereign, independent and democratic society.

However, the right to privacy is not absolute. Its exercise may be restricted by the constitutional rights of others or by the requirements of the common good and it is subject to the requirements of public order and morality. The doctor-patient relationship does not come within the relationships typically afforded the right to privacy under the constitution, such as marriage. 'However, in few other relationships is the conflict between the public interest in freedom of information and the need to protect personal privacy more poignantly marked and the boundaries more ambiguous.'[74] It is likely that personal medical information would thus be protected by the right to privacy, although this may be overridden by the public interest in certain circumstances.

[3.66] If an express contract exists between doctor and patient, the obligation of confidentiality may, of course, be specifically included as a term of that contract. The extent of the obligation will depend on the terms used and the interpretation put on the contract. However, it would not be usual for a doctor to have a written contract with his patient and therefore the existence of duty of confidentiality may be implied into the contract. It may be argued by the patient that he had a legitimate expectation that the relationship with the doctor would be governed by the ethical guidelines of the profession and that this encompassed the duty of confidentiality. In this way, the doctor's ethical duties may become part of his legal obligations *vis-á-vis* his patient.

---

[71] *Z v Finland* (1997) BMLR 107.

[72] See *McGee v Attorney General* [1974] IR 284; *Norris v Attorney General* [1984] IR 36; *Madigan v Attorney General* [1986] ILRM 136; *Attorney General (SPUC Ireland Ltd) v Open Door Counselling Ltd* [1987] ILRM 477.

[73] *Kennedy & Arnold v Ireland* [1987] IR 587.

[74] O'Neill, 'Matters of Discretion – The Parameters of Doctor/Patient Confidentiality' (1995) MLJI, 94–104.

[3.67] In the English case *Hunter v Mann*,[75] Boreham J said:

> Medical practitioners and others in a similar position, such as bankers, accountants, priests and journalists are bound by a duty which the law respects and enforces from disclosing without the consent of the patient or client communications or information obtained in a professional capacity, save in exceptional situations in the public interest.

The existence of an equitable remedy for breach of confidence was recognised in the English case of *Attorney General v Guardian Newspapers (No 2)*[76] and in the Irish case of *House of Spring Gardens v Point Blank Ltd*[77] where Costello J said that an action for breach of confidence must consist of the following elements: (i) There must exist from the relationship between the parties an obligation of confidence regarding the information which had been imparted; (ii) the information which had been communicated must properly be regarded as confidential; (iii) The recipient of the information must have breached his duty to act in good faith, ie he must have used the information for a purpose for which it was not imparted to him and to the detriment of the informant.

[3.68] It is also important to recognise the ever-widening circle of health professionals who may legitimately have access to a patient's medical records. This is increased even further in the case of a hospital admission where technical and ancillary staff may also have access.[78] Patient data are generated in many locations in a hospital and handled by a range of different parties. As Jackson says:

> Most obviously, an absolute duty of confidentiality would be incompatible with the reality of medical treatment. For a patient's condition to be diagnosed and treated, it will often be necessary for a number of health care professionals to have access to her records. In hospital, treatment is provided by teams of doctors and nurses. Patients may be referred to specialist consultants, or for diagnostic procedures, such as blood tests, x-rays, and scans. If information about the patient's condition could never be shared with others, the provision of health care would grind to a halt.[79]

---

[75] *Hunter v Mann* [1974] QB 767, [1974] 2 All ER 414.

[76] *Attorney General v Guardian Newspapers (No 2)* [1988] 3 All ER 545, also known as the *Spycatcher* case where Lord Goff accepted 'the broad general principle ...that a duty of confidence arises when confidential information comes to the knowledge of a person in circumstances where he has notice, or is held to have agreed, that the information is confidential, with the effect that it would be just in all the circumstances that he should be precluded from disclosing the information to others.'

[77] *House of Spring Gardens v Point Blank Limited* [1984] IR 611; see also *Cook v Carroll* [1945] IR 515.

[78] See Siegler, 'Confidentiality in Medicine –A Decrepit Concept.' (1982) New Eng J Med, Vol 307 (24) 1518–1521, where it is argued that confidentiality no longer exists, it is old, worn out and useless. Siegler gives one example of a fairly straightforward hospital admission which prompted at least 75 health professionals at the hospital to access the patient's medical records, including doctors, residents, nurses, pharmacists, secretaries, financial officers and medical students, many of whom changed on shift relief. He claims that 'as medicine expands from a narrow, disease-based model to a model that encompasses psychological, social, and economic problems, not only will the size of the health-care team and medical costs increase, but more sensitive information (such as one's personal habits and financial condition) will now be included in the medical records and will no longer be confidential.'

[79] Jackson, *Medical Law: Text, Cases and Materials* (3rd edn, OUP, 2013) p 359.

[3.69] In Ireland the Medical Council, which regulates the medical profession, publishes a Guide to Professional Conduct and Ethics which sets out the standards of behaviour expected of registered medical practitioners. In every edition since its inception, the Guide has contained strong advice to doctors in relation to the maintenance of confidentiality. The Guide provides that confidentiality is central to the trust between doctors and patients and a core element of the doctor/patient relationship.[80] However, it also recognises that confidentiality is not absolute by stating that there may be circumstances in which it is necessary or justifiable to share patient information with others. It advises doctors not to share information with the patient's family members or carers without their consent, or unless disclosure is necessary to protect the patient or others from a risk of serious harm. Doctors may also be obliged by law to disclose patient information such as in the context of court proceedings or by virtue of infectious disease regulations under which notification is mandated in the public interest to prevent the spread of disease.

[3.70] The Guide also states that in exceptional circumstances disclosure of patient information without their consent may be justifiable when it is necessary in the public interest to protect the patient or other identifiable people or the community.[81] Before making such a disclosure the doctor must be satisfied that the possible harm the disclosure may cause the patient is outweighed by the benefits that are likely to arise for the patient or for others. Doctors should only disclose to an appropriate person or authority and include only the information needed to meet the purpose. In all such instances, the patient should be informed about the disclosure unless this would cause them serious harm or undermine the purpose of the disclosure.

[3.71] In relation to the disclosure of patient information to other healthcare professionals, the Guide points out that most patients understand and accept the need for such disclosure, which is done in order to provide the most appropriate care to the patient. Information may also be shared with other staff, particularly in a hospital environment, as part of clinical audit and quality assurance systems, or education and training, which are designed to ensure that patient care is provided in a safe and effective manner now and in the future. Such information should be anonymised where possible and, if this is not possible, the patient should be informed and any objection should be respected.

Consent to disclosure

[3.72] There will be no breach of the duty of confidentiality when a patient expressly consents to disclosure.[82] Consent should be fully informed and freely given, and the subsequent disclosure should not exceed the terms of the consent given. Questions may arise in relation to decision-making capacity of some patients and in such cases care must be taken to ensure that the patient has the capacity to understand the nature and

---

[80] Guide to Professional Conduct and Ethics (8th edn, 2016) para 29.1 available at www.medicalcouncil.ie.

[81] Guide to Professional Conduct and Ethics (8th edn, 2016) para 31.

[82] *C v C* [1946] 1 All ER 562.

implications of the disclosure and is not under undue influence from any third party in giving consent.[83]

[3.73] In the case of minors, the question of legal capacity arises.[84] If the minor is regarded as the patient, does this status of itself infer the obligation of confidence, or does it also depend on the perceived mental capacity or maturity of the minor? The common law does not have a fixed age at which a child is held to have capacity to consent to the disclosure of confidential medical information. In the English case of *Gillick v West Norfolk and Wisbeck Area Health Authority*[85] it was held that a person under the age of 16 years can give consent to medical treatment if she fully comprehends the nature of the treatment and the consequences involved of treatment and non-treatment. By analogy to the question of disclosure it would seem that the young person may consent to disclosure if he understands the nature of secrecy and the consequences of disclosure. However, the *Gillick* case has never been judicially considered in Ireland and may be decided differently in light of the Constitutional provisions in relation to the family.[86]

Court order

[3.74] In the context of personal injury litigation it is usual for the defendant to request disclosure of the medical records pertaining to the plaintiff's case. If the plaintiff refuses to consent to such disclosure, an order for discovery may be sought by the defendant. This will compel production of the relevant documents. Where the patient consents to disclosure of his records, doctors have an ethical responsibility to supply medical reports to solicitors or insurers on behalf of such patients they have seen or treated. These reports must be factual and true and are not to be influenced by the fee involved or by pressure from anyone to omit or embellish details. If the case results in a court appearance by the doctor, all notes, records and conversations with the patient may be disclosed by the doctor without incurring responsibility for breach of duty. He will be entitled to legal professional privilege in relation to the information he discloses in the medical report and in the witness box. The report must have been drawn up for the purpose of litigation in order for the privilege to apply. The doctor may well be uncomfortable when asked questions in the witness box which would involve the disclosure of confidential information about the patient, and a judge may try to clarify whether the disclosure is necessary in the circumstances.[87] However, if pressed to do so,

---

[83] See chapter 9 for discussion of decision-making capacity

[84] See Donnelly, 'Capacity of Minors to Consent to Medical and Contraceptive Treatment' (1995) Medico-Legal J of Ireland 18.

[85] *Gillick v West Norfolk and Wisbeck Area Health Authority* [1985] 3 All ER 402.

[86] This is discussed further in Chapter 11.

[87] In *Hunter v Mann* [1974] QB 767, Lord Widgery stated: 'If a doctor is asked in court a question which he finds embarrassing because it involves him in talking about things which he would normally regard as confidential he can seek protection from the judge and ask if answering is necessary. The judge, by virtue of the overriding discretion to control his court which all ...judges have, could tell the doctor that he does not need to answer the question. Whether or not the judge would take that line depends largely on the importance of the potential answer to the issue being tried.' Such judicial discretion may be exercised following a private examination by the judge of the evidence in question.

the doctor is obliged to answer any question put to him and a refusal may leave the doctor open to a charge of contempt of court.

Disclosure in the patient's best interests

[3.75] Although the patient's consent is always preferable where the doctor wishes to disclose confidential information, it may be possible in certain circumstances for the doctor to justify disclosure on the grounds that it was necessary to protect the interests of the patient. A doctor may believe it is in the best interests of his patient to disclose certain information regarding the patient's health to a relative or carer. The doctor may presume that the patient consents to such disclosure and on the basis that it is in the patient's best interests for close relatives to share this information so as to enable them to provide optimum care and support for the patient. However, unless the patient is not capable of giving consent, the patient's consent should be obtained prior to any disclosure, and if the patient expressly refuses to give consent, the doctor must respect the patient's wishes, even if the doctor is of the opinion that this is contrary to the patient's best interests. In exceptional circumstances where non-disclosure might result in serious harm to the patient or others, the doctor may disclose information but only on a strict need-to-know basis and with minimal sharing of information.

[3.76] In *W v Watters & Mental Health Commission*[88] the Court had to consider whether the release of medical records to a legal representative of a person detained involuntarily under the Mental Health Act 2001 was in that person's best interests. The applicant was a 70-year-old woman suffering from early-onset Alzheimer's disease, who was detained involuntarily in a psychiatric hospital of which the defendant was the clinical director. Under the Mental Health Act 2001 the applicant was entitled to have the admission order reviewed by a mental health tribunal within 21 days of admission. The Mental Health Commission is required to ensure that certain procedures are complied with following the making of an admission order, including the appointment of a legal representative to represent the patient. The Commission appointed a solicitor who sought to interview the applicant and review her medical records. Due to her incapacity, the applicant was unable to give consent to the review of her records or to give instructions to the solicitor. The hospital took the view that it was not authorised to release the medical records in the absence of consent from the patient unless obliged to do so by the Mental Health Tribunal. All parties agreed that it was in the best interests of the patient that her legal representative had access to medical records as early as possible in order to best represent and protect the patient's best interests. The Court heard arguments from counsel in relation to the wording and role of the Medical Council's Guide in relation to confidentiality and the exceptions thereto. Peart J took the view that the disclosure of a patient's medical records to her legal representative, where the patient lacked the capacity to consent to such disclosure, was necessary to protect the interests of the patient and did not contravene the duty of confidentiality.[89]

---

[88] *W v Watters & Mental Health Commission* [2008] IEHC 462.

[89] See further Whelan, *Mental Health Law and Practice* (Round Hall, 2009) at para 7.55.

Protection of another individual

[3.77] The issue has also arisen whether a doctor is justified in disclosing, and indeed has a duty to disclose, confidential information where another individual may be at risk. This has arisen in the context of the treatment of patients diagnosed with HIV infection, and also in psychiatric care where a patient exhibits a threat of violence to an identifiable person.[90] In the context of HIV, infected persons pose a risk to their sexual partners, depending on the nature of the sexual activity and the level of precautions taken. Patients would generally be counselled as to the risks of transmission and would be advised to inform their partners. 'It is unsurprising that there will be some patients who are not prepared to do so nor, indeed, to inform their general practitioners; the doctor is then faced with the problem of whether or not he, himself, should inform those with a need to know'.[91]

[3.78] The Medical Council's Guide provides that in exceptional circumstances disclosure of patient information without their consent may be justifiable when it is necessary to protect the patient or others from serious risk of death or serious harm. Doctors are advised to seek patient consent to such disclosure where possible. Therefore, in the context of HIV transmission, it may be ethically justifiable to disclose to the patient's partner in order to enable that person to seek testing for themselves and so as to ensure that appropriate protection is put in place. Although an action for breach of confidence may be taken by a patient whose spouse or partner was informed in such circumstances, it is possible that the court, in balancing the interests of both parties involved, would take the view that disclosure was justifiable in the interests of protecting others from a possibly fatal risk.[92]

[3.79] In relation to psychiatric care, changes in emphasis in treatment have increased the 'open door' approach, which enables patients to continue to live within the community as much as possible, while being treated as voluntary out-patients with drugs and psychotherapy. In some circumstances it has been argued that it is justifiable, and perhaps even obligatory, for a medical practitioner who is aware of psychiatric difficulties which may give rise to violence, to disclose such a risk to those who may be in direct contact with the patient. The idea that psychiatrists can predict dangerousness in such a person has meant that in some jurisdictions, most notably the United States, a duty has been imposed on doctors to breach the patient's confidentiality in the interests of protecting another person from a predicted violent attack. The psychiatric profession generally objects to the imposition of such a duty on the grounds that (i) not all psychiatric patients are dangerous, (ii) there is no reliable means for predicting danger,

---

[90] For discussion of other issues such as marital violence, contraceptive treatment of minors and sterilisation, see O'Neill, 'Matters of Discretion – The Parameters of Doctor/Patient Confidentiality' (1995) MLJI 94–100 at 99.

[91] Laurie, Harmon and Porter, *Law and Medical Ethics* (10th edn, OUP, 2016) p 195.

[92] For further reading on this point see Neave, 'AIDS: Confidentiality and the Duty to Warn' (1987) 9 Univ. of Tasmania L Rev 1; Gostin and Hodge, 'Piercing the Veil of Secrecy in HIV/ AIDS and Other Sexually Transmitted Diseases: Theories of Privacy and Disclosure in Partner Notification' (1998) 5 Duke J of Gender L & Pol 9; Caswell, 'Disclosure by a Physician of AIDS-Related Patient Information: An Ethical and Legal Dilemma' (1989) 68 Can Bar Rev 225; Patterson, 'AIDS, HIV Testing and Medical Confidentiality' (1991) 7 Otago L Rev 379.

(iii) trust in the relationship is damaged by disclosure, and (iv) disclosure provides a disincentive to discussion of violent fantasies. Some examples from case law are illustrative of this dilemma.

[3.80] The most well-known case in this area is *Tarasoff v Regents of the University of California*.[93] The facts were that a student, Poddar, who was studying at Berkeley, had undergone psychotherapy at the university, during which he had reported to his therapist, Dr Moore, that he intended to kill a girl who was identifiable to Dr Moore as Tatiana Tarasoff, with whom Poddar had a previous short romantic relationship. The doctor concluded that Poddar should be placed under observation in a psychiatric hospital. The doctor notified the campus police and Poddar was taken into custody. However, the police became satisfied that Poddar was rational and released him from custody. Some weeks later Poddar went to Ms Tarasoff's apartment and killed her. Ms Tarasoff's parents sued Dr Moore, the campus police and the university on the basis that they had failed to detain a dangerous patient, and had failed to warn others, and in particular Ms Tarasoff herself, regarding the danger presented.

[3.81] The California Supreme Court upheld the action on the basis that there was a breach of the duty to warn Ms Tarasoff of the danger to herself, despite the fact that she was not a patient of Dr Moore. The Court held that:

> When a therapist determines, or pursuant to the standard of his profession should determine, that his patient presents a serious danger of violence to another, he incurs an obligation to use reasonable care to protect the intended victim against such danger...[This] may call for him to warn the intended victim or others likely to apprise the victim of the danger, to notify the police or to take whatever other steps are reasonably necessary under the circumstances.[94]

Although there was no special relationship in this case between Dr Moore and Ms Tarasoff, the Court imposed liability on the basis that its most important consideration in establishing a duty to warn was forseeability. The Court was of the opinion that a therapist becomes sufficiently involved with his patient that he assumes some responsibility for the safety, not only of the patient, but also of those who are threatened by the patient. It stated that the public policy favouring protection of the confidential nature of patient-psychotherapist communications must yield to the extent to which disclosure is necessary to avoid danger to others. In other words, as the Court put it: 'the protection privilege ends where the public peril begins.'

[3.82] Dissenting judgments in the case were based on the argument that a diagnosis of mental illness is not a prediction of dangerousness and that psychiatrists do not possess a crystal ball with respect to the future actions of their patients. The dissents also concentrated on the relationship between the patient and the therapist, which will only

---

[93] *Tarasoff v Regents of the University of California* 529 P 2d 55 (Cal, 1974); on appeal 551 P 2d 334 (Cal, 1976). For discussion see Kermani and Drob, '*Tarasoff* Decision: A Decade Later Dilemma Still Faces Psychotherapists' (1987) Am J of Psychotherapy, Vol XLI, No 2, 271; Wulsin et al, 'Unexpected Clinical Feature of the *Tarasoff* Decision: The Therapeutic Alliance and the Duty to Warn' (1983) Am J Psychiatry 140:5, 601; deHaan, 'My Patient's Keeper? The Liability of Medical Practitioners for Negligent Injury to Third Parties.' (1986) Professional Negligence, May/June, 86–91.

[94] *Tarasoff v Regents of the University of California* 529 P 2d 55 (Cal, 1974), per Tobriner J.

work successfully if the patient trusts the therapist sufficiently to divulge his fantasies. Critics of the majority decision have argued likewise that 'the imposition of a duty to protect, which may take the form of a duty to warn threatened third parties, will imperil the therapeutic alliance and destroy the patient's expectation of confidentiality, thereby thwarting effective treatment and ultimately reducing public safety'.[95]

[3.83] Following *Tarasoff*, there have been other cases in the US which have further explored this issue. Some cases place a duty to warn of danger in circumstances only where there is a specific threat to a specific individual, as was the case in *Tarasoff*. *Brady v Hopper*[96] provides a celebrated and dramatic illustration. In that case, a psychiatric patient, Hinckley, tried to assassinate President Ronald Reagan in an attempt to impress the actress Jodie Foster. The plaintiff was a presidential aide who was wounded in the attack. He claimed that the psychiatrist treating Hinckley should have known that he had a gun and that he identified with a political assassin in a film in which Ms Foster had appeared. The plaintiff alleged that the doctor was negligent in failing to warn law enforcement officials and Hinckley's parents. The Court rejected the claim on the basis that the plaintiff's injuries were not foreseeable. Hinckley had not made any specific threats against any individual, and had no predisposition to violence. Therefore, the possibility of his injuring someone was 'vague, speculative and a matter of conjecture.'[97] This seems to generally be regarded as a sensible decision not only on the basis of proximity principles in tort law, but also on the basis of medical confidentiality.[98] If the patient's confidences are to be disclosed, then this should only be in clearly exceptional cases. The 'specific threats to specific individuals' test seems a reasonable boundary in this regard.

[3.84] On the other hand, some cases have extended the duty to the prediction of dangerousness generally.[99] In *Lipari v Sears*[100] the patient was under the care of a psychiatrist as an outpatient. He had not displayed any signs of dangerousness and had never threatened anyone. He purchased a shotgun from the defendants and fired it into a crowded nightclub, killing a man and blinding the man's wife. The woman sued Sears for negligence in selling a gun to a mentally ill individual. Sears in turn sued the hospital

---

[95] Stone, 'The *Tarasoff* Decision: Suing Psychotherapists to Safeguard Society' (1976) Harvard Law Review 90: 358–378.

[96] *Brady v Hopper* 570 F Supp 1333 (1983).

[97] See also *Thompson v County of Alameda*, 167 Cal Rep 70 (1980); *People v Murtishaw* 175 Cal Rep 738 (1981); *Mavroudis v Superior Court of County of San Mateo* 161 Cal Rep 724 (1980); *Leedy v Hartnett* 510 F Supp 1125 (MD PA 1981).

[98] See also *Home Office v Dorset Yacht Company Ltd* [1970] AC 1004 where the House of Lords held that although there was no general duty to control the actions of another, the existence in this case of a special relationship between seven Borstal trainees and the three officers supervising their training provided a source for such a duty. As the wrongdoers in this case were under the control of the defendants, and control imports responsibility, the defendants owed a duty to take reasonable care in the exercise of their supervision and control.

[99] See further Mullen, 'Mental Disorder and Dangerousness' (1984) 18 Aust NZ J of Psych. 8; Grisso and Applebaum, 'Is it Unethical to Offer Predictions of Future Violence?' (1992) 16 Law and Hum. Behvr. 621; Rudegeair and Applebaum, 'On the Duty to Protect: An Evolutionary Perspective' (1992) 20 Bull Amer Acad Psych Law 419.

[100] *Lipari v Sears* 497 F Supp 185 (Neb 1980).

at which the patient was being treated for not having recognised the danger. The Court upheld the claim, holding that psychotherapists have a duty to third parties if the patient presents an unreasonable risk of harm. The Court rejected the limitation of this duty to identifiable individuals. In doing so, 'the court essentially imposed a duty on therapists to predict dangerousness in general terms and to protect society at large from all 'dangerous' individuals whom they have occasion to treat.'[101]

[3.85] The extension of the *Tarasoff* case in this way may be argued to be unreasonable, as it obliges doctors to do something which they argue is impossible, that is, to predict dangerousness. It also involves disclosure of confidential information in circumstances which, arguably, falls outside of the ethical principles under which doctors work, as the disclosure is not necessary to protect a particular individual. However, it could conceivably be argued that disclosure to police authorities in circumstances such as occurred in *Lipari* would be in the public interest.[102] It has been claimed, however, that this would turn psychotherapists into law enforcement agents and subject psychiatric patients to indirect police surveillance.[103]

[3.86] In the English case *Palmer v Tees Health Authority*[104] the patient, Mr Armstrong, had been diagnosed as suffering from personality disorder or psychopathic personality. He had been admitted to hospital on a number of occasions. While being treated as an out-patient, he killed a four-year-old child who lived in a neighbouring house. The girl's mother sued the hospital for negligence in discharging Mr Armstrong and for the consequent nervous shock she suffered as a result of her daughter's death. Stuart-Smith J held that there was insufficient proximity between the hospital and the child and that for a duty of care to be established, the victim would have to be identified or identifiable, as in the *Tarasoff* case. He went on to say:

> An additional reason why in my judgement in this case it is at least necessary for the victim to be identifiable…to establish proximity, is that it seems to me that the most effective way of providing protection would be to give warning to the victim, his or her parents or social services so that some protective measure can be made.

The judge also suggested that to impose liability could lead to the practice of defensive medicine. It is argued that this would negatively affect the introduction of new treatments, lead to the confinement of patients exhibiting anti-social behaviour and would generally be a retrograde step for the profession. In the Irish case *C v North Western Health Board*[105] it was held that a health board owed a duty of care to a man who was attacked by a patient who had escaped from a psychiatric hospital, but on the facts it was held that the duty of care had not been breached. White J held that if the

---

[101] Kermani and Drob, '*Tarasoff* Decision: A Decade Later Dilemma Still Faces Psychotherapists' (1987) Am J of Psychotherapy, Vol XLI, No 2, at 278. See also *McIntosh v Milano* 403 A 2d 500 (1979); *Durflinger v Artiles* 673 P 2d 86 (Kan 1983); *Perreira v State* 768 P 2d 1198 (Colo 1989); and *Estates of Morgan v Fairfield Family Counselling Center* 673 NE 2d 1311 (Ohio 1997).

[102] See Jones, *Medical Negligence* (Sweet & Maxwell, 1992) at paras 2.62–2.68.

[103] Kermani and Drob, '*Tarasoff* Decision: A Decade Later Dilemma Still Faces Psychotherapists' (1987) Am J of Psychotherapy, Vol XLI, No 2, 271 at 281.

[104] *Palmer v Tees Health Authority* [1999] EWCA Civ 1533.

[105] *C v North Western Health Board* [1997] Irish Law Log Weekly 133. (Circuit Court).

patient was known to be dangerous, every step possible would have to be taken to prevent him from doing damage.

[3.87] Under the ECHR, breaches of confidentiality may also be justified in certain circumstances. For example in *Andersson v Sweden*[106] where a psychiatrist disclosed concerns regarding the health of a patient's son, the European Commission held there was no case to answer under art 8 of the Convention, as the disclosure of the information pursued the legitimate aims of protecting 'health or morals' and the 'rights and freedoms of others'. A similar finding was made in *TV v Finland*[107] where prison staff were notified of the health status of a prisoner with HIV. These cases are reconcilable with the *Egdell* case discussed below.

Protection of society/public interest

[3.88] This is the most general and controversial exception to the rule of medical confidentiality, due to its possible diversity. On the one hand, situations in which confidentiality may be breached in the public interest are relatively straightforward, such as in relation to statutory obligations imposed on doctors to notify public health authorities of specific conditions they have diagnosed in their patients. This is in order to ensure the health and safety of the community by protective measures, quarantine, monitoring of the spread of disease and so on. The Health Act 1947 entitles the Minister for Health to specify by regulation the diseases that are infectious diseases which require notification to public health authorities. Under the Infectious Diseases Regulations 1981, and subsequent amendments, the Health Protection Surveillance Centre is authorised by law to collect information from doctors and laboratories about diagnoses of certain infectious diseases in Ireland. These diseases are referred to as notifiable diseases. The most recent amendment to the Regulations is the Infectious Diseases (Amendment) Regulations 2011[108] which contains the up to date list of notifiable diseases. When a medical practitioner becomes aware of or suspects that a person on whom he is in professional attendance is suffering from or is the carrier of a notifiable disease, he is required to transmit a written or electronic notification to a Medical Officer of Health. A clinical director of a diagnostic laboratory is subject to the same requirement as soon as an infectious disease is identified in that laboratory and must notify through the Computerised Disease Reporting System (CIDR). Notifications from clinicians are also entered into the CIDR. The notifiable diseases include meningitis, smallpox, measles, tuberculosis, hepatitis and syphilis, some of which are immediately notifiable.[109] Access to the information in CIDR is controlled so that personally identifiable information is visible only to those with a need to manage the individual case. All CIDR information is protected by appropriate security and confidentiality mechanisms and complies with Data Protection legislation.

[3.89] Apart from specific statutory obligations outlined above, a medical practitioner may be justified in disclosing confidential information in order to safeguard the public interest. Some of the issues which have been judicially considered in this context have

---

[106] *Andersson v Sweden* Application No 20022/92, 7 August 1997.
[107] *TV v Finland* [1994] 18 EHRR CD 179.
[108] SI 452/2011.
[109] Available at www.hpsc.ie.

centred on the disclosure of criminal offences committed or likely to be committed by a patient, the disclosure of a patient's HIV status, the patient's capacity to drive and suspected child abuse.

[3.90] In relation to the commission of a criminal offence, it may be justifiable (though not obligatory) for a medical practitioner to provide information to the police if he becomes aware that his patient has committed or is likely to commit a serious criminal offence and if he forms the view that, on balance, to do so is in the public interest.[110] This is a professional judgement to be made in light of the seriousness of the offence and the potential damage to the public arising from non-disclosure.

[3.91] In the case of patients who present a serious risk of violence, is the doctor ethically and legally justified in breaching the patient's confidence in the public interest? In *W v Egdell*[111] a consultant psychiatrist, Dr Egdell, was asked to examine a prisoner, W, in a secure hospital for the purposes of a review of his case with a view to transferring W to another unit. Dr Egdell strongly opposed the transfer and recommended that further tests and treatment were advisable. He drew attention to W's continued interest in firearms and explosives, which was probably of particular relevance in this case as W had been convicted of shooting and killing five people and wounding two others. Dr Egdell subsequently learned that as a consequence of his report W withdrew his application for a transfer and that therefore the medical report had not been seen by anyone other than W's legal team. Dr Egdell decided to disclose his report to the hospital and the Secretary for State.

[3.92] W sought an injunction against the recipients of the report to prevent them from using or disclosing it further and damages for breach of the duty of confidentiality. The Court was of the opinion that the circumstances of the medical examination did import a duty of confidentiality on Dr Egdell so that, for example, he could not have sold the contents of his report to a newspaper. Stephen Brown P referred to Lord Goff's judgment in the *Spycatcher* case[112] where he said that:

> [A]lthough the basis of the law's protection of confidence is that there is a public interest that confidences should be preserved and protected by the law, nevertheless that public interest may be outweighed by some other countervailing public interest which favours disclosure...It is this limiting principle which may require a court to carry out a balancing operation weighing the public interest in maintaining confidence against a countervailing public interest favouring disclosure.

[3.93] He also referred to the General Medical Council's advice on professional conduct and discipline, contained in what is known as the 'Blue Book'. He said that while the rules themselves do not have statutory authority, they were valuable in showing the approach of the General Medical Council to the breadth of the duty of confidence. In the circumstances of the present case Dr Egdell was within the scope of the exception in relation to communicating confidential information to other health professionals

---

[110] See the classic statement by Avory J: 'There are cases where the desire to preserve the confidential relation which exists between the medical man and his patient must be subordinated to the duty which is cast on every good citizen to assist in the investigation of serious crime.' Birmingham Assizes, 1 December 1914. Reported in (1914) 78 JP 604.

[111] *W v Egdell* [1990] 1 All ER 835.

[112] *Attorney General v Guardian Newspapers (No 2)* [1988] 3 All ER 545.

involved in W's treatment. Stephen Brown P held that there were also broader considerations involved. Although the doctor had been engaged on behalf of W his duty was not to W alone. Dr Egdell also owed a duty to the public which 'would require him…to place before the proper authorities the result of his examination if, in his opinion, the public interest so required.' Therefore, Dr Egdell was justified in making the disclosure to those responsible for W's treatment and to the Secretary of State, who was responsible for securing public safety. Bingham J concurred, saying:

> Where a man has committed multiple killings under the disability of serious mental illness, decisions which may lead directly or indirectly to his release from hospital should not be made unless a responsible authority is properly able to make an informed judgement that the risk of repetition is so small as to be acceptable. A consultant psychiatrist who becomes aware, even in the course of a confidential relationship, of information which leads him, in the exercise of what the court considers a sound professional judgement, to fear that such decisions may be made on the basis of inadequate information and with a real risk of consequent danger to the public is entitled to take such steps as are reasonable in all the circumstances to communicate the grounds of his concern to the responsible authorities.

[3.94] This case is relatively straight-forward in demonstrating the balancing act that must be carried out in such circumstances. It would clearly be unrealistic to suggest that confidentiality must be maintained where there is a serious risk of danger to public safety, and the disclosure is measured in terms of those to whom it is made. However, disclosure in such circumstances must be only to those to whom it is necessary to tell and only if the risk is a real rather than fanciful one. In *Stone v South East Strategic Health Authority*[113] it was held that the publication of a report into two homicides carried out by Mr Stone was lawful, even though it included details relating to Mr Stone's medical history. David J held that there was a public interest in knowing the treatment provided, or not, to Mr Stone in order to correctly identify any failures in such treatment and the appropriate steps to be taken to address any deficiencies.

[3.95] Also in the context of the public interest as a justification for disclosure of medical information, the English case *X v Y*[114] provides further authority. In this case some employees of a health authority supplied information to a newspaper which identified two doctors in general practice as having AIDS. The health authority sought an injunction to prevent publication of the names of the doctors. The question arose as to whether the newspaper was justified in publishing this information in the public interest.

[3.96] It was clearly recognised that in the particular case of AIDS it was of vital importance that those affected by the disease would not be inhibited from coming forward for treatment by fears that their confidentiality might be breached. If treatment was not provided to those suffering from the disease not only would the individual patient suffer but also there would be a consequent increase in the spread of the disease. Therefore, the preservation of confidentiality was in the public interest. The newspaper argued strongly in favour of the public interest in freedom of the press and the necessity to foster debate about the issues involved in AIDS, both of which were accepted as valid

---

[113] *Stone v South East Strategic Health Authority* [2006] EWHC 1668. See Munro, 'Privacy v Publication: Homicide Inquiries in the Balance' (2007) 15 Med L Rev 109.

[114] *X v Y* [1988] 2 All ER 648.

by the Court. However, the Court nonetheless held that when balanced against the public interest in confidentiality, the latter was the stronger right generally and particularly in the context of AIDS patients.[115] As for the second point, the Court held that the debate sought by the newspaper in the public interest could take place without identifying the individual doctors involved.

[3.97] In relation to the point made in *Egdell* that disclosure is only justified if made on a need-to-know basis to the appropriate authority, the New Zealand case of *Duncan v Medical Practitioner's Disciplinary Committee*[116] is instructive. In that case a bus driver, Mr Henry, was required under the terms of his licence to furnish a medical certificate on an annual basis for renewal of the licence. Having undergone a triple bypass operation, he later returned to his GP, Dr Duncan, who had referred him for surgery, to request a medical certificate for him to renew his driving licence. The doctor declined to do so on the grounds that Mr Henry was not fit to drive passenger vehicles. Dr Duncan also tried to have the bus driver's licence revoked, told people in the community not to travel in his bus as it was too dangerous, and complained to the police and the media. Mr Henry went to the surgeon who had treated him and the surgeon certified Mr Henry as fit to drive. Mr Henry complained about Dr Duncan to the relevant regulatory authority on grounds of breach of confidentiality. The authority found Dr Duncan to be in breach of professional standards. This was subsequently upheld by the court which held that Dr Duncan was in breach of his duty of confidence to his patient. Jefferies J said that it did not appear to have been a case in which '...a doctor receives information involving a patient that another's life is immediately endangered and urgent action is required.'[117] Jefferies J also said that the doctor should ensure that the '...recipient (of any such information) is a responsible authority.' In this case, for example, if Dr Duncan had made his complaint to an appropriate authority that was responsible for granting bus drivers' licences or controlling standards for bus drivers, it is possible his disclosure may have satisfied the public interest exception.

[3.98] Therefore, if the patient refuses to report a serious disability which may affect his ability to drive safely, and refuses consent for the doctor to do so, it is likely following the *Egdell* line of authority, that protection of the public would justify the doctor in informing the licensing authorities.[118] It has been mooted whether a doctor who knew that an unsafe patient of his (for example, someone suffering from epilepsy) was continuing to drive and who then failed to take any action on the point might be liable in damages for negligence to anyone harmed by his patient on the road.[119] However, in the US case, *Crosby v Sultz*[120] an action against a doctor who allowed a diabetic patient to

---

[115] See also *H (A healthcare worker) v Associated Newspapers Ltd* [2002] EWCA Civ 195.

[116] *Duncan v Medical Practitioner's Disciplinary Committee* [1986] 1 NZLR 513.

[117] 'There may be occasions when a doctor receives information involving a patient that another's life is immediately endangered and urgent action is required. The doctor must then exercise his private judgement based on the circumstances and if he fairly and honestly believes such a danger exists, he must act unhesitatingly to prevent injury or loss of life.' *Duncan v Medical Practitioner's Disciplinary Committee* [1986] 1 NZLR 513.

[118] See O'Neill, 'Matters of Discretion – The Parameters of Doctor/Patient Confidentiality' (1995) MLJI, 94–104, p 98.

[119] See 'Doctors, Drivers and Confidentiality' (1974) 1 BMJ 399.

[120] *Crosby v Sultz* 592 A 2d 1337 (Pa, 1991).

drive was rejected on the grounds that injuries inflicted on a person who could not be notified of the driver's condition were not foreseeable.

[3.99] Although there have not been any cases on breach of confidence in this context in Ireland, it is likely that an interpretation similar to that made in *Egdell* would be made by an Irish court, based on the exception given in favour of the disclosure in the public interest by the Medical Council's Guide, and the recognition that constitutional rights to privacy are limited in favour of the common good.

HEALTH INFORMATION TECHNOLOGY

[3.100] It is vital for any health service to have accurate, meaningful and accessible information to assist patients, the public, healthcare professionals, planners and politicians in improving the safety and quality of the healthcare provided at all levels of the system. Consequently, it is impossible to think about improvements in safety and quality in healthcare, and the development of a high reliability healthcare system, without also considering the health information and health information technology (HIT) developments that are required to enable and sustain these improvements and further the understanding and knowledge of the health system.[121]

[3.101] With increased emphasis in Ireland in recent years on patient safety and the delivery of safe, high-quality care, there has been a recognition that in addition to other quality initiatives, it is necessary to also ensure that high-quality information is at the core of decision-making concerning health at all levels, from individual patient care to the planning and management of services at local and national levels. However, it is also recognised that access to information in healthcare is frequently limited and fragmented, as patient records in many areas of care are paper-based or, if computerised, are in formats that cannot be shared easily between providers.

[3.102] Health information technology (HIT) is commonly regarded as critical to the transformation of healthcare. However, the sector has historically lagged behind other sectors in the adoption of technology, and the underpinning foundations of an effective ICT infrastructure in healthcare were often seen as a low priority, particularly when decisions to invest in ICT to improve patient safety were competing with other service delivery priorities.

[3.103] The *eHealth for Safety: Impact of ICT on Patient Safety and Risk Management Report*,[122] undertaken on behalf of the European Commission, identified that in many European countries, one of the most important developments in eHealth in recent years has been the implementation of electronic health records at national, regional and local levels. This was further acknowledged in the eHealth Task Force 2012 report *Redesigning health in Europe for 2020.*[123] This Report sets out five levers for change to facilitate e-health as follows:

---

[121] *Building a Culture of Patient Safety*, Ch 7, s 7, p 185. Available at www.health.gov.ie.

[122] *eHealth for Safety: Impact of ICT on Patient Safety and Risk Management Report* (European Commission 2007), available at: www.ec.europa.eu/information_society/activities/health/.

[123] www.ec.europa.eu/digital-agenda/en/news/eu-task-force-ehealth-redesigning-health-europe-2020.

- The first lever is referred to as 'my data, my decisions' which is based on the principle that individuals are the owners and controllers of their own health data, with the right to make decisions over access to the data and to be informed about how it will be used.

- The second is 'liberate the data'. This states that large amounts of data currently sit in different silos within health and social care systems. If this data is released in an appropriate manner and used effectively it could transform the way that care is provided. Governments should ensure that health data is robust (accurate and reliable), gathered in a standard way, anonymised and then made freely available to anyone that can add value to it.

- The third lever for change is 'connect up everything'. This acknowledges that the digital environment is growing and evolving rapidly with an increasing trend of interaction and sharing. The popularity of online networking and social spaces has created a parallel digital existence for millions of people. Each person is the publisher of their digital life stream, adding their own content and curating information submitted by other individuals, institutions and applications The plethora of available data can be used by individuals to monitor their physical and emotional wellbeing and share it with others. Much of this data will be geo-tagged, making it extremely valuable for public health surveillance and epidemiology. Public services need to be able to access, and be accessible via, the life-stream.

- The fourth lever calls for full transparency across the health sector so that, armed with data about the performance of health professionals and institutions patients will be able to make more informed choices about where and how they want to be treated. This will have real impact on resource allocation in health, as funding follows the patients.

- The final lever promotes equality and inclusivity by recognising that new ICT tools have the potential to reduce health inequalities but they need to be designed to actively promote and enhance equity. This means ensuring that rural communities have access to services and that products are usable for patients with a diverse range of literacy and technical abilities.

The European Commission subsequently published an eHealth Action Plan 2012–2020[124] to provide a 'roadmap to empower patients and healthcare workers, to link up devices and technologies, and to invest in research towards the personalised medicine of the future.'

[3.104] In the Irish context, the Commission on Patient Safety reported in 2008 that the effective use of quality-based information systems, modern communications technology and the effective use of health information has the potential to make a major contribution to improved patient safety and quality through the following means:

- reducing errors in drug prescribing by flagging allergies and contra-indications and in the dispensing and administration of medications;

---

[124] www.ec.europa.eu/digital-agenda/en/news/ehealth-action-plan-2012–2020-innovative-healthcare-21st-century.

- providing more evidence-based care and seamless integrated care across all healthcare sectors and environments because information will accompany the patient through the system and be available where it is needed and when it is needed;

- empowering patients and other healthcare service-users by opening up health related knowledge bases to assist choice thereby facilitating a new information based relationship between patients and healthcare professionals and health agencies;

- improving planning, management and the delivery of health services and health projects through better information management, enhanced business planning and control and greater risk management;

- better research and disease management outcomes which benefit both individuals and society, due to total population studies rather than limited sample ones;

- establishing new data collections and data sets that will help identify and manage the specific health needs of defined population groups across different care settings;

- mitigating public health and other population threats by improving our ability to detect and respond quickly, for example to disease outbreaks;

- extending the scope of healthcare beyond its current boundaries through, for example, telemedicine and home-based care, especially for patients with chronic conditions, which has particular relevance for rural and island communities;

- more accessible continuing education for healthcare professionals through online training models, and;

- enhancing the privacy, confidentiality, integrity and security of patient information through the computerised tracking and auditing of access to patient records.[125]

[3.105] The importance of health information and HIT to underpin the wider health reform programme, including the safety and quality agenda, has also been set out in a number of other key national strategy documents in Ireland, including *Quality and Fairness – A Health System for You*, the *National Health Information Strategy* and *Primary Care: A New Direction* (2004) and most recently, the important *eHealth Strategy* (2013).[126] This strategy document outlines the important strategic goals to enable Ireland to meet the objectives of successful health reform consistent with the EU eHealth Action Plan 2012–2020. It also established eHealth Ireland[127] to focus on the promotion and implementation of the eHealth agenda. Priority areas for initial development include ePrescribing, online referrals and scheduling, telehealth (particularly relating to the management of chronic disease) and the development of summary patient records. The Office of the Chief Information Officer (OCIO) was also established within the HSE in 2015 with responsibility for the delivery of technology to

---

[125] Report of the Commission on Patient Safety and Quality Assurance 2008, section 7.7. Available at www.health.gov.ie.

[126] www.health.gov.ie/wp-content/uploads/2014/03/Ireland_eHealth_Strategy.pdf.

[127] www.ehealthireland.ie/.

support healthcare across Ireland and 'to turn the eHealth Ireland Strategy into a reality ensuring that technology supports healthcare efficiently and effectively throughout the whole system.'[128]

[3.106] The ability to reliably and rapidly share the right information in the right way and at the right time is regarded as an essential component of ensuring safety in the care of patients. Achieving this requires common standards for information, the ability to correctly match records to the individual patient, appropriate arrangements which govern the handling and use of the information, the necessary legal enablement to share information across institutional boundaries, including the interface between public and private healthcare, and providing healthcare professionals with the business change skills required to adapt to an information-rich environment. The development and implementation of effective health information and HIT solutions are essential in order to address these challenges.

[3.107] Work has been ongoing for a number of years on the proposed Health Information and Patient Safety Bill, published in 2015.[129] In addition to making provision for research ethics approval, reporting of patient safety incidents, clinical audit and other important patient safety matters, the objectives of the Bill in relation to health information are to provide for the setting of standards by the Minister for Health on the efficient electronic exchange (inter-operability) of health information and the setting of voluntary best practice standards by HIQA for health service providers on the processing of health information. It also sets out a regulatory framework for data matching in the health service and a similar framework for health information resources (ie databases, registers) which can have considerable benefits in areas like disease monitoring and health service management. 'While data matching and health information resources can bring undoubted benefits to the health services, they also bring privacy considerations. It is essential therefore that the enabling legislation has the appropriate checks and balances for proper regulation and control and helping to ensure public confidence. In that regard, the Bill sets out a detailed governance framework that will be further underpinned by Regulations and with roles for both HIQA and the Data Protection Commissioner.'[130]

[3.108] An important enabler in promoting eHealth and patient safety is the development of unique health identifiers (a unique, non-transferable number assigned to all individuals using health and social care services in Ireland, which will last for their lifetime) which help to ensure that the right information is associated with the right individual at the right time. They also help to reduce duplication and the risk of mis-identification at the point of care. The Health Identifiers Act 2014 provides the legal basis for individual health identifiers for health service users and health service providers, both public and private. The Act protects the privacy of individuals and complies with data protection legislation by providing that an individual's health identifier is personal data for the purposes of the Data Protection Acts (s 27).

---

[128] www.hse.ie/eng/about/Who/OoCIO/.

[129] www.health.gov.ie/wp-content/uploads/2015/11/Revised-General-Scheme-HIPS-Bill.pdf.

[130] www.health.gov.ie/wp-content/uploads/2015/11/Revised-General-Scheme-of-the-Health-Information-and-Patient-Safety-Bill-RIA.pdf.

[3.109] The Act provides for the establishment of a National Register of Individual Health Identifiers. This will comprise a Register of all recipients of health services. The HSE will be responsible for assigning Individual Health Identifiers to each recipient. This Register will not be publically available and will only be accessible to certain people, including the Minister for Health and other specified persons, which includes the State Claims Agency, Irish Medicines Board and the Chief Inspector of Social Services. The Act also provides for the establishment and maintenance of a National Register of Health Services Provider Identifiers, which will be publicly available. This will comprise a list of all health practitioners and providers, to include employees and agents of health practitioners and providers. The HSE will be responsible for assigning a Health Services Provider Identifier to each practitioner and organisation. Health practitioners will be obliged to place their identifier number on all medical records completed by them, unless they are already required to use a registration number assigned to them by their regulator.

[3.110] Following the commencement of these provisions of the Act in 2015, the Health Information and Quality Authority (HIQA) published Information Governance and Management Standards for the Health Identifiers Operator in Ireland.[131] The Standards consist of basic requirements to support the introduction of individual health identifiers (IHIs) and guidance for the HSE to establish and manage the National Register of Individual Health Identifiers and the National Register of Health Services Provider Identifiers. The HSE commenced a trial of IHIs on a pilot basis in 2015 in certain clinical information systems (the Epilepsy Electronic Patient Record, a multi-GP General Practice and the Electronic Medical Record within a hospice). It is expected that full roll-out of IHIs on a national system wide basis will take a number of years to fully implement.

---

[131] www.hiqa.ie/publications/information-governance-and-management-standards-health-identifiers-operator-ireland.

Chapter 4

Assisted Reproduction

INTRODUCTION

[4.01] The World Health Organisation (WHO) defines infertility as the failure to achieve a clinical pregnancy after at least twelve months of regular unprotected sexual intercourse.[1] It describes infertility as a global public health issue which affects a significant proportion of humanity. The WHO has calculated that over 10% of women are affected – that figure refers to women who have tried unsuccessfully to become pregnant and have remained in a stable relationship for five years or more.[2] The rate of infertility in men is unknown. According to the WHO, the overall burden of subfertility/ infertility is significant, is likely underestimated, and has not displayed any decrease over the last 20 years.[3]

[4.02] Many of the assisted reproduction technologies (ARTs) commonly available today are a phenomenon of relatively recent origin in the context of medical practice, although the first insemination procedures are reported to have been performed in the late 19th century. The Feversham Report in 1960 reported that while there had been isolated cases on insemination in the 19th century, donor insemination was hardly practised at all until the 1920s.[4] Donor insemination appears to have been carried out from the 1930s and 1940s in the United States, the United Kingdom, Australia, Canada, Belgium, Switzerland, Denmark, Italy, Spain and Israel.[5] The second half of the 20th century witnessed stunning changes in the available methods for building families and yet many societies still struggle to find adequate structural mechanisms to deal with the legal, cultural, religious and ethical dimensions of what this progress may mean to individuals, the concept of family and society.[6] Some of the new reproductive technologies that have been developed, and their application in particular circumstances, have caused heated debates around the ethical, philosophical and legal implications of such advances in medical science.

---

[1] International Committee for Monitoring Assisted Reproductive Technology (ICMART) and the World Health Organization (WHO) revised glossary of ART terminology, 2009. Fertility and Sterility, Vol 92, No 5, November 2009.

[2] Estimates in women using a two-year time frame result in prevalence values 2.5 times higher.

[3] www.who.int/reproductivehealth/topics/infertility/perspective/en/.

[4] Earl of Feversham, Report of the Departmental Committee on Human Artificial Insemination (Cmnd 1105) 1960.

[5] Cusine, *New Reproductive Techniques, A Legal Perspective* (Dartmouth Publishing, 1990) Ch 3.

[6] Andrews, 'Regulating Reproductive Technologies' J Legal Med (2000) 21:1 at 1.

[4.03] The 1970s brought a dramatic development in reproductive technologies with the birth in 1978 of the first baby conceived through in vitro fertilisation (IVF). This development was greeted with mixed reactions ranging from delight on the part of infertile couples and many medical practitioners, to horror from those who saw it as a gross interference with nature. Some criticised the development on resource allocation grounds, arguing that medical funds should be spent instead on reducing overpopulation in the world and enhancing the adoption of children with special needs, or on other pressing medical and social problems.[7] Another argument was that since infertility was not a disease in the ordinary sense of the word, treating infertility through IVF was non-therapeutic and artificial since it did not treat the underlying cause of the infertility.[8] Others criticised the technique as unnatural because it separates the physical aspects of conception from the emotional and spiritual aspects, and procreation thereby becomes a mechanical process.[9] Finally, another major concern for many critics was that it represented an unprecedented opportunity for people to apply technology to their own shaping, an inappropriate attempt to 'play God'.

[4.04] It is also important to locate the emergence of reproductive technologies in their modern form at a time when established social boundaries were decomposing. Lee and Morgan point to the waning in the nature and stability of the family and marriage, the increasing acceptability of heterosexual partnerships without marriage and homosexual relationships, and the changing roles and expectations of women in the family and community.[10] The development of reproductive technologies enabled humans 'to access their very genesis and it caused a wave which still impacts on our understanding of ourselves'.[11] Assisted reproduction affects and challenges assumptions about family, kinship, parentage and personal identity with the result that:

> Any change in custom or practice in this emotionally charged area has always elicited a response from established custom and law of horrified negation at first; then negation without horror; then slow and gradual curiosity, study, evaluation, and finally a very slow but steady acceptance.[12]

[4.05] IVF has now gained fairly widespread acceptance, though there remain controversies surrounding the legal repercussions of some associated procedures such as embryo storage, research and destruction, the use of donated gametes and genetic screening of embryos to avoid transmission of disease and for sex and trait selection. The 1980s also brought a further controversial reproductive technology to public attention with the advent of surrogate motherhood in the public domain, which was criticised as facilitating the commodification of children and the exploitation of women. In the 1990s reproductive technologies went one step further and created worldwide

---

[7] See for example, Hellegers and McCormick, 'Unanswered Questions on Test Tube Life' (1978)139 America 74.

[8] See Kass, 'Making Babies' Revisited' (1979) 54 Public Interest 32.

[9] Kerby Anderson, *Genetic Engineering* (Zandervan Publishing House, 1982).

[10] Lee and Morgan, *Human Fertilisation and Embryology, Regulating the Reproductive Revolution* (Blackstone Press Ltd, 2001) at p 2.

[11] Winston, *The IVF Revolution: The Definitive Guide to Assisted Reproductive Techniques* (Vermillion, 1999) at 137.

[12] Kleegman and Kaufman, *Infertility in Women, Diagnosis and Treatment* (FA Davis Co, 1966) at 178.

concern when the first cloned mammal, Dolly the sheep, was created in 1996.[13] Controversy erupted surrounding the possibility that this technology could be used to clone a human. Legislation banning cloning was introduced almost immediately in a number of countries. These techniques are considered in more detail in later chapters.

[4.06] For those who want to have children, infertility can be a devastatingly traumatic experience. They may experience guilt, low self-esteem, depression and isolation, and consequently some couples may suffer marital conflict and sexual dysfunction.[14] Some couples feel that they have nothing to contribute to society and that they do not have a common bond with their friends and the wider community. The treatments may involve physical, emotional and financial hardship, which can continue for several years. Assisted reproduction clinics and practitioners generally offer counselling at all stages of diagnosis and treatment of infertility to help the infertile individual to adjust to and mourn their inability to have a child naturally, and to face the possibility of childlessness if treatments are unsuccessful.

[4.07] Many couples who are infertile desire to have a child with a genetic or biological link to them. Their reasons are no different from those of fertile couples: some believe that having a biological child will give them a sense of immortality while others believe their biological child will be an expression of themselves or their relationship. Other couples stress the significance of child-bearing as an important life experience, with some women expressing the view that they would feel less fulfilled without children. Although adoption may fulfil the desire for parenting for some people, others want to experience pregnancy and see their own features and characteristics expressed in their children.

TREATMENTS FOR INFERTILITY

[4.08] The choice of procedure employed in the treatment of infertility depends on the cause of the failure to achieve or carry a pregnancy to term. If the infertility is caused by female factors such as blocked fallopian tubes, the woman's eggs may be removed from her ovaries and fertilised with the man's sperm in a petri dish in the laboratory (IVF). If fertilisation occurs, the resulting embryo is then transferred to the woman's womb/uterus and it is hoped that a pregnancy will then ensue. This method is not possible where the woman cannot provide the eggs herself, due for example to prior ovarian cancer. Nor will it be possible where the woman has had her womb removed or where her womb is not receptive to the embryo as this would prevent implantation of the embryo in the lining of the womb, thus leading to a miscarriage. In these circumstances, a third party may donate the eggs, embryo or use of her uterus to enable the couple to have a child. Gamete donation could also be sought by couples who, though not necessarily infertile, carry a genetic abnormality that they do not want to risk passing on to their children. If the cause of the infertility is due to male factors such as low sperm count, then the male partner's sperm may still be used to attempt a pregnancy using intra-cytoplasmic sperm injection (ICSI) combined with fertilisation of the egg in vitro

---

[13] www.roslin.ed.ac.uk/public-interest/dolly-the-sheep/a-life-of-dolly/.

[14] Harvard Mental Health letter, Harvard Medical School 'The psychological impact of infertility and its treatment' (2009) www.health.harvard.edu/newsletter_article/The-psychological-impact-of-infertility-and-its-treatment.

and embryo transfer (IVF). If the male partner is unable to provide the sperm, then donor sperm may be used to attempt to achieve a pregnancy (DI).

THE PRINCIPLE OF PROCREATIVE LIBERTY

[4.09] One of the issues which has often caused debate amongst policy makers in the context of assisted reproduction is the extent to which the State should prohibit or regulate the exercise of reproductive choice by those who experience infertility. Western societies generally place a high priority on private choice and decision-making in reproductive matters, for example in relation to the control of fertility and avoidance of pregnancy through the use of contraceptives. However, the right to reproduce – to bear, beget and rear children – has received less explicit recognition. One prominent legal writer, John A Robertson, argues in favour of the presumptive priority of procreative liberty, which he describes as the freedom to decide whether or not to have children and to control the use of one's reproductive capacity.[15] He says that while this value is widely acknowledged when reproduction occurs naturally, 'it should be equally honoured when reproduction requires technological assistance.'[16] His argument is that if there is a moral right to reproduce for those who are fertile then, based on principles of equality and non-discrimination, the same right should apply to those who are infertile. Whether one is born with reproductive potential or not, or whether one loses the potential in the course of one's life, if there is a right to reproduce, the same principles should apply to the fulfilment of that reproductive potential. 'Their infertility should no more disqualify them from reproductive experiences than physical disability should disqualify persons from walking with mechanical assistance.'[17]

[4.10] Robertson argues that procreative liberty should be given presumptive priority in all conflicts due to its central importance to individual meaning, dignity and identity and that there should be a burden on opponents of any particular technique to show that harmful effects from its use justify limiting procreative choice. This means that in cases of conflict involving such a right it should be presumed to take precedence. In his view, procreation is thus regarded as a constitutional right in the same category as liberty and freedom of expression which, though of fundamental importance to each individual in society, similarly do not have a guarantee of absolute protection. This is by virtue of the nature of societies as requiring some safeguarding of the common good, which may require imposition of restrictions on those fundamental rights, such as deprivation of liberty for those who are a danger to society.

[4.11] For those who do not experience infertility, reproduction may not be thought of as being of as vital importance, but to those who suffer the trauma and devastation of infertility, it is the centre of their lives. Robertson's view of the right to reproduce is, however, as a negative one, that is to say, a right 'against the interference of other individuals (or the State) in one's reproductive decisions. However, on this view, the

---

15 Robertson, *Children of Choice, Freedom and the New Reproductive Technologies* (Princeton University Press, 1994) 16.

16 Robertson, *Children of Choice, Freedom and the New Reproductive Technologies* (Princeton University Press, 1994) 16, note 15 at 16.

17 Robertson, *Children of Choice, Freedom and the New Reproductive Technologies* (Princeton University Press, 1994) 16, note 15 at 32.

right to reproduce does not imply a positive right to intervention in order to exercise one's reproductive liberty.'[18] This view of reproduction emphasises genetic reproduction, ie the passing on of one's genes, as a basis for the existence of this right, whether this also includes child rearing or not. It has been argued that this shows a lack of understanding of both 'the nature and value of the right to reproduce' and it is wrong to claim a right in relation to pure genetic reproduction where there is no intent to rear.[19]

[4.12] There are those who argue that such a principle of procreative liberty, if it were to become enshrined as a matter of constitutional law, would be too broad and would not necessarily be in the interests of the child. For example, Bartholet says 'if we really care about children, we should question why there is so much talk of the adult's right to procreate, right to control his or her body, and right to parent, but so little talk of the child's right to anything.'[20] Maclean Massie similarly questions Robertson's assertion that procreative liberty could not be interfered with by claims that the welfare of the child would be in jeopardy.[21] While Robertson acknowledges that the welfare of the child is important, he claims that in all instances existence for the child is better than non-existence. However, Massie cites the example of a HIV-positive applicant for IVF services who, under the presumption of procreative liberty, would be entitled to access to that treatment. The woman's fundamental constitutional right to reproduce would override any interest the State might have in restricting her right (because the resulting child might be HIV-positive and might not have the care of its parent(s) for very long after its birth) on the basis that it would be better for the child to be born than not to be born. Massie says this principle is too broad and that it forecloses important discussions relating to social values and concerns for the future of our society. 'His glib recitation of the rubric that, from the perspective of any individual, it is invariably better to have been born than not to have been born makes too short a shrift of a concern central to the reproductive technologies debate – namely, what we should do to ensure the physical, mental, and psychological well-being of the children whom we are deliberately bringing into existence.'[22]

[4.13] It may be argued that the moral right to reproduce is respected because of the centrality of reproduction to personal identity, meaning and dignity. This importance makes the liberty to procreate an important moral right, both for an ethic of individual autonomy and for ethics of community or family that view the purpose of marriage and sexual union as the reproduction and rearing of offspring. Because of this importance, the right to reproduce is widely recognised as a prima facie moral right that cannot be

---

[18] Quigley, 'A Right to Reproduce?' Bioethics, Volume 24, Issue 8, pages 403–411, October 2010.

[19] Steinbock, 'A Philosopher looks at Assisted Reproduction'. J Assist Reprod Genet 1995; 12: 543–551. Robertson and Steinbock's differing positions are discussed in more detail in Quigley, 'A Right to Reproduce?' Bioethics, Volume 24, Issue 8, pages 403–411.

[20] Bartholet, *Family Bonds: Adoption and the Politics of Parenting* (Houghton Mifflin, 1993), p 229.

[21] MacLean Massie, 'Regulating Choice: A Constitutional Law Response to Professor John A Robertson's Children of Choice' (1995) 52 Wash & Lee L Rev 133.

[22] MacLean Massie, 'Regulating Choice: A Constitutional Law Response to Professor John A Robertson's Children of Choice' (1995) 52 Wash & Lee L Rev 133 at 145.

limited except for very good reason.[23] Sherwin argues that Robertson's claim that reproduction is central to individual meaning and dignity is overstating its importance in the light of practices of sexual promiscuity and some uncaring and irresponsible parental attitudes amongst other interests pursued by many individuals.[24] 'There is simply no argument offered for assuming that genetic connection (or its absence) is so central to the goals of (all) human beings as to merit its being granted pride of place within the generally libertarian schema Robertson supports.' She also criticises the lack of accounting for the effects of such a policy on women in a world in which women are 'systematically oppressed' and 'coercively controlled' in relation to many aspects of reproduction. She claims that although Robertson does deal with the objections of many feminist writers he does not appreciate the gravity of the harm which concerns those writers and is unwilling to consider the impact of his proposed policy on vulnerable groups, such as disadvantaged women, in society.

[4.14] It has also been argued that the principle of procreative liberty espoused by Robertson does not take account of differences in class and wealth which, for some, may make the exercise of procreative choices impossible. The distribution of wealth acts as a prime determinant of who exercises reproductive rights, particularly in access to reproductive technology. However, it is argued by proponents of this principle that questions of social justice are not compelling reasons for limiting the procreative choice of those who can pay for treatment. In other words, 'it does not follow that society's failure to assure access to reproductive technologies for all who would benefit justifies denying access to those who have the means to pay.'[25]

IS THERE A LEGAL RIGHT TO REPRODUCE?

[4.15] If reproduction is to be given the status of a right then this must be because it is an interest worthy of special protection, exceptions to which must require particular justification. The use of the language of rights emanates from the history of the debate on reproductive freedom, which began in the late 19th century. At that time the feminist movement demanded voluntary motherhood and the right to birth control as validating the procreational right of women to choose whether and when to reproduce. This was more of a right *not* to reproduce or control reproduction rather than a right to reproduce in itself but it did prove to be a starting point in the debate on procreational autonomy.

[4.16] In the early years of the 20th century concern began to be expressed in the United States about the ability of another party such as the State to intervene in an individual's right to bodily integrity and right to self-determination. This was evidenced by the condemnation of the eugenics movement, which had been seen in the case of *Buck* v *Bell* in 1927,[26] in which a statute providing for compulsory sterilisation of inmates in a mental hospital was upheld. Eugenics was seen as a means of protecting society from the burden of having to cope with individuals who were considered to be unfit. It was

---

[23] Robertson, *Children of Choice, Freedom and the New Reproductive Technologies* (Princeton University Press, 1994) 16, note 15 at 30.

[24] Sherwin, 'The Ethics of Babymaking' (1995) March-April, Hastings Center Report, 34.

[25] Robertson, *Children of Choice, Freedom and the New Reproductive Technologies* (Princeton University Press, 1994) 16, note 15 at 226.

[26] *Buck v Bell* 274 US 200.

argued that compulsory reproductive control was essential if societies were not to be swamped by the unfit, the disabled, the poor and the shiftless. This argument found favour by drawing on the fears at that time that America would become 'black' and the belief that certain non-white immigrant races were inferior. These theories, which were incorporated into legislation in most American States, were 'surely the clearest example of the non-recognition at that time of a universal right to reproduce.'[27] Reproduction was seen as a duty for those deemed to be biologically superior, and a capacity which could be controlled by State interference for those who did not fall within that elite group. The oft-cited judgment of Holmes J in *Buck* v *Bell* clearly demonstrates the thinking at that time:

> The right to reproduce was not perceived to be a right and it was more as a privilege. We have seen more than once that the public welfare may call upon the best citizens for their lives. It could be strange if it could not call upon those who already sap the strength of the State for these lesser sacrifices, often not felt to be such by those concerned, in order to avoid our being swamped with incompetence. It is better for all the world if instead of waiting to execute degenerated offspring for crime or let them starve for their imbecility, society can prevent those who are manifestly unfit from continuing their kind. The principle that sustains compulsory vaccination is broad enough to cover cutting the Fallopian tubes. Three generations of imbeciles is enough.[28]

[4.17] At the time it was made, this statement reflected the concerns and fears of American society. If nothing else it demonstrates how issues concerning public morality and policy statements are clear indicators of the era in which they are made and should not automatically be presumed to be applicable to every other time and place. However, in *Skinner* v *Oklahoma*[29] the United States Supreme Court moved away from the position discussed above and held unconstitutional a statute which provided for the involuntary sterilisation of certain classes of offenders. The case was decided principally on equal protection grounds but the court also stressed the importance of marriage and procreation as among the basic civil rights of man and noted that marriage and

---

[27] McLean, 'The Right to Reproduce', in Campbell, Goldberg, McLean and Mullen (eds) *Human Rights: From Rhetoric to Reality,* (Blackwell Publishing, 1986) 105. McLean discusses the use of the language of rights in the debate about reproduction and how it has elevated reproduction from a mere capacity that may not be interfered with, to a kind of right which depends on an element of choice. This debate is also linked with the right to self-determination and concern about State intervention in choices made by individuals relating to their reproductive capacities. It is also important to recognise that the use of rights terminology in reproduction does not imply an obligation or duty but rather a choice. McLean examines the social history of the right to reproduce from the right to access to birth-control methods, to compulsory sterilisation cases, to abortion. She also discusses the legal approach to the existence of a right to reproduce, which has been shaped to some extent by the public debates raised by demands for reproductive services. She concludes that although there can be identified the core and scope of a right to reproduce which is deserving of respect, it is unlikely that this guarantees to citizens the ability to insist on provision of services by the State to facilitate the exercise of the right in circumstances such as those relating to the provision in infertility treatments. 'The reality is that the rhetoric of rights has limited practical value in this as in other areas.' p 120.

[28] *Buck v Bell* 274 US 200, 207.

[29] *Skinner v Oklahoma* 316 US 535 (1942).

procreation are fundamental to the very existence and survival of the race.[30] However, this case is not as strong as it may appear at first instance – the right to reproduce was not seen so much as a right deserving of protection but rather a means of resisting unwarranted State interference in decisions involving procreational choices. It is doubtful therefore that this case could be used to found a case against the State to compel the provision of infertility treatments. Although the issue was not specifically addressed by the Court in *Skinner* it is thought that the applicability of the right to reproduce put forward in that case to treatments such as artificial insemination, in vitro fertilisation and surrogacy is open to question. It was concerned with State interference with a civil right to reproduce naturally, not the application by a citizen to enforce his or her procreational choices against the State so as to insist upon the provision of artificial methods of reproduction.

[4.18] On a slightly different point, the substantive content of the right to reproduce was not clarified by the Court in *Skinner v Oklahoma* in terms of eligibility for the right and whether it applied to social as well as biological parenting: that is to say, does the right apply to those who intend to bring up the child after, for example, a surrogate birth? These issues were not directly relevant to the facts of the aforementioned cases, as the concepts of surrogate motherhood and egg donation had not been brought to judicial attention at this stage. The issue turns on whether the right to reproduce is simply a biological right or whether it also encompasses the right to rear a child. In most instances the right to reproduce would include both aspects of parenting but this will not always be the case. It may be, for example, that a woman wishes to conceive and give birth to a child without ever having the intention to raise it, as in surrogacy.

[4.19] *In re Baby M*[31] is an infamous example of a case in which the two aspects – the rights to reproduce and to rear – were seen as separate. The case involved a surrogacy arrangement in which a couple, the Sterns, commissioned a surrogate, Mary Beth Whitehead, to be artificially inseminated with Mr Stern's sperm and carry the child to term, upon which it would be given up to the Sterns. When the child was born, Mrs Whitehead changed her mind and attempted to retain custody of the child. In examining the right to procreation, the New Jersey Supreme Court said:

> The right to procreate very simply is the right to have natural children, whether through sexual intercourse or artificial insemination. It is no more than that ... The custody, care, companionship, and nurturing that follow birth are not parts of the right to procreation.[32]

[4.20] Thus in this case the Court held that the biological and social aspects of parenting are divisible and that the right to procreate necessarily only encompasses the former. Although Mrs Whitehead was given 'parental rights', this did not entitle her to custody of the child, rather she was only given visitation rights. The biological contributors to Baby M's life, Mr Stern and Mrs Whitehead, were both recognised as the child's parents, but due to the circumstances and the conflict involved in the custody dispute, only Mr Stern was given the right to social parenthood, ie the right to rear the child.

---

[30] See further discussion by Dillard, 'Rethinking the Procreative Right' (2014) *Yale Human Rights and Development Journal* Volume 10 Issue 1, Article 1. Available at www.digitalcommons.law.yale.edu/yhrdlj/vol10/iss1/1.

[31] *In re Baby M* 109 NJ 396, 537 A 2d 1227 (1988).

[32] *In re Baby M* 109 NJ at 448, 537 A 2d at 1253 (1988).

[4.21] In the modern era, the classic statement of privacy in the context of reproduction is *Griswold v Connecticut*,[33] which dealt with the constitutionality of statutes prohibiting contraceptive devices. The Court said:

> Would we allow the police to search the sacred precincts of marital bedrooms for tell-tale signs of the use of contraceptives? The very idea is repulsive to the notions of privacy surrounding the marriage relationship. We deal with a right of privacy older than the Bill of Rights. Marriage is a coming together for better or for worse, hopefully enduring, and intimate to the degree of being sacred.

Goldberg J agreed with Marlan J's dissenting judgment in *Poe v Ullman*,[34] in which he said:

> The home derives its pre-eminence as the seat of family life. And the integrity of that life is something so fundamental that it has been found to draw to its protection the principles of more than one explicitly granted constitutional right. Of this whole private realm of family life it is difficult to imagine what is more private or more intimate than a husband and wife's marital relations.

Goldberg J continued: 'The entire fabric of the Constitution and the purposes that clearly underlie its specific guarantees demonstrate that the rights to marital privacy and to marry and raise a family are of similar order and magnitude as the fundamental rights specifically protected'.

[4.22] In the later case of *Eisenstadt v Baird*[35] in which the Court extended the right to obtain contraceptives to unmarried persons, Brennan J said: 'If the right of privacy means anything, it is the right of the individual, married or single, to be free from unwarranted governmental intrusion into matters so fundamentally affecting a person as the decision whether to bear or beget a child'. The importance of these two cases in the context of the recognition of a right to reproduce is that they provide a clear judicial statement that procreational choices made by a husband and wife (or by unmarried individuals) are so personal to them that they must, by necessity, be protected by the constitutional right to privacy. The sacred nature of such private and intimate decisions reached within a relationship must be protected by law.

[4.23] In *Roe v Wade*,[36] which involved a challenge to State criminal abortion legislation, the Court recognised that although not specifically mentioned in the Constitution, a right to privacy does exist and that this extended to activities relating to marriage – procreation, contraception, family relationships and child rearing and education. This case was, and is, of fundamental importance in the context of abortion law, as it sets out the parameters for permissible abortion in the United States, which remain in force today. It recognised that although the right to privacy came under the umbrella of fundamental rights protected by the Constitution and that it included activities relating to procreation and contraception, it was not an absolute right, as some State regulation of these areas must also be acknowledged. The Court was of the opinion

---

[33] *Griswold v Connecticut* 381 US 479, 85 S Ct 1678, 14 L Ed 2d 510 (1965).
[34] *Poe v Ullman* 367 US 497, 551–552 (1952).
[35] *Eisenstadt v Baird* 495 US 438 (1972).
[36] *Roe v Wade* 410 US 113 (1973).

that a State may properly assert important interests in, inter alia, safeguarding health, maintaining medical standards and protecting potential life.

[4.24] These cases and others[37] indicate that there is a constitutional right, in a married couple at least, (and probably unmarried individuals) to resist State interference with the restriction of coital reproduction unless the State can show that great harm would result from the reproduction in question. US courts have not yet directly dealt with the legal claim of a married infertile couple to procreate although, as has been stated earlier in connection with the presumption in favour of procreative liberty, the same underlying principles should apply. If this is so, they would have a constitutional right to access to a wide variety of non-coital technologies to have children. This right, by analogy with the right to procreate given to fertile couples, should only be interfered with if justified by the State on the same standard as applicable to fertile couples. 'Noncoital reproduction should thus be constitutionally protected to the same extent as is coital reproduction, with the state having the burden of showing severe harm if the practice is unrestricted'.[38]

[4.25] The only cases that directly consider the extension of married couples' procreational rights into the realm of non-coital reproduction involve surrogate mother contracts. In *Doe v Kelley*[39] a married couple sought a declaratory judgment establishing their right to contract with a woman who was to be inseminated with the husband's sperm, carry the child and then relinquish it to the couple at birth. The Court of Appeal in Michigan found that the fundamental right to bear or beget a child was not infringed by the State law which prohibited the payment of fees for adoption. The Court noted that the couple was not prevented from having the child, but only from using the State process to effectuate the adoption. It has been suggested by Robertson that the Court should have recognised that by denying the couple access to State adoption procedures, the State was burdening their exercise of the right to bear and beget, and then should have scrutinised the weight of the State interests allegedly served by the prohibition.[40] However, based on the language of rights heretofore used by the courts, this decision is in keeping with the case law in relation to privacy and reproduction. The cases indicate a willingness on the part of the judiciary to resist interference by the State in personal freedoms but a hesitation to enforce positive (perhaps costly) duties against the State. In this case, the State did not choose to interfere directly with the surrogacy arrangement, as this would have been tantamount to an interference with reproductive choices.

---

[37] In another case dealing with abortion, *Casey v Planned Parenthood* 112 S Ct 2791 (1992), the Court stated: 'Our law affords constitutional protection to personal decisions relating to marriage, procreation, contraception, family relationships, childrearing and education. These matters, involving the most intimate and personal choices a person may make in a lifetime, choices central to personal dignity and autonomy, are central to the liberty protected by the Fourteenth Amendment.'

[38] Robertson, *Children of Choice, Freedom and the New Reproductive Technologies* (Princeton University Press, 1994) p 39.

[39] *Doe v Kelley* 106 Mich App 169, 307 NW 2d (1981) The couple had argued that by prohibiting the payment of money in connection with adoption, the legislature was also effectively prohibiting surrogacy, which necessitated recourse to formal adoption procedures. This, the couple argued, denied them their fundamental right to have a child.

[40] Robertson, 'Procreative Liberty and the Control of Conception, Pregnancy, and Childbirth' (1983) 69 Virginia Law Review 428.

However, the State did not consider itself bound to change its laws and policies in relation to adoption in order to effectuate such an arrangement.

[4.26] It may be considered that other cases on surrogacy contracts such as *Syrkowski v Appleyard*[41] and *In re Baby Girl*[42] are also examples of situations in which the courts, by refusing to recognise surrogacy contracts, are unduly restricting the right to reproduce without due regard being had for the need for strict scrutiny of the justification for the infringement of the constitutional rights in question. By contrast, in *Cameron v Board of Education*[43] an Ohio court declared that a woman had a constitutional privacy right to become pregnant by artificial insemination, while in *JR v Utah*[44] the genetic parents of a child born to a surrogate mother successfully argued that the State's mandated determination of parentage in such cases violated their constitutional right to procreative liberty by forcing them to adopt their own genetic child.

[4.27] Even though the US courts have found the right to privacy to exist under the American Constitution, they still reserve for the legislature the power to intervene for the protection of compelling State interests, although this term is neither defined nor explained. Legislative obstacles to the use of assisted reproduction may be seen as excessive even though in some cases, such as prohibition of the use of adoption procedures in surrogate motherhood, they may be indirect. It seems that the broad nature of public morality and the common good is something which the courts will use in order to defend an infringement of the right to privacy, and as these justifications may be of particular relevance to assisted reproduction, it is likely that any supposed interference with the individual's right to have a child through such techniques might be exonerated on these grounds:

> At the very least, state interference which effectively prohibits procreation by the initiating parents must be subject to strict scrutiny. The fundamental interest of begetting a child should not be abrogated without proof that preservation of a compelling state interest justifies the denial of the right and can be achieved by no less restrictive means.[45]

[4.28] The two most likely justifications for denying access to reproductive technology are the State's interest in public morals and its interest in health and safety. In relation to the first, the State might argue that the existence of families created with the aid of reproductive technology would disrupt traditional family values by bringing a third party into the conception of the child and moving away from natural methods of conception. However, the counter argument might be made that most applications of reproductive technology take place within a stable heterosexual relationship, married or unmarried. The family unit thus remains the same irrespective of the method of conception of the child. This can be seen in relation to families with adopted children – the State could not argue that bringing an adopted child into a family would somehow threaten traditional family values.

---

[41] *Syrkowski v Appleyard* 9 Fam L Rep (BNA) 2260 Mich Ct App, 19 January 1983.

[42] *In re Baby Girl* 9 Fam L Rep (BNA) 2348 (Ky Cir Ct 8 March 1983).

[43] *Cameron v Board of Education* 795 F Supp 228, 237.

[44] *JR v Utah* 261 F Supp 2d 1268.

[45] Stumpf, 'Redefining Mother: A Legal Matrix For New Reproductive Technologies' 96 Yale LJ 187 (1986) at 199.

[4.29] The second argument which might be made within the context of the 'common good' justification for State interference concerns the State's interest in health and safety. In other words, 'if a particular reproductive procedure were found to pose a substantial health risk to either children or parents, the State could probably restrict the technique.'[46] However, to date, the technologies do not appear to have raised any such problems, although this argument could, for example, be used as one of a number of reasons to prohibit reproductive cloning which has not been proven to be safe in humans to date.

[4.30] In practice the issue of whether assisted reproduction is a procreative liberty recognisable by law is really a question about who society allows to become a parent. Where a genetic tie exists between the adult and the child, the law generally associates the recognition and promotion of parental rights and responsibilities as a benefit to the child. In this way, the best interests of the child can be promoted through the law's traditional deference to parental rights. However, even where there is a genetic link present, there may sometimes be a different and more complex legal response where third parties such as gestational surrogates become involved. In cases where the genetic relationship is absent such as where sperm or eggs are donated, the best interests of the child also becomes more controversial.[47]

The right to reproduce in Irish constitutional law

[4.31] In Ireland, despite the onus placed on the courts to uphold and vindicate the personal rights of the citizen, the position is not much clearer than the US position outlined above. There are different contexts in which a right to reproduce using ARTs might arise, for example, it might be argued that the State has a positive duty to provide assisted reproduction such as IVF treatments to citizens within the public health system, or to provide pre-implantation genetic diagnosis for families who are carriers of serious genetic diseases. However, the imposition of positive socio-economic duties such as this on the State has not been a strong feature of Irish case law on constitutional rights to date.[48]

[4.32] The right to reproduce has been recognised by the Supreme Court as falling within the ambit of personal rights protected by art 40.3.1° of the Constitution 1937, which provides that 'The State guarantees in its laws to respect, and, as far as practicable, by its laws to defend and vindicate the personal rights of the citizen.' In *Murray v Ireland*[49] the plaintiffs, a married couple, were convicted of the capital murder of a member of the police force. They claimed that their constitutional rights to privacy and procreation were violated by the failure of the State to facilitate conjugal visits. The Court acknowledged the existence of these constitutional rights but held that they were not absolute and must be qualified by the exigencies of the common good, in this case prison security. The significance of the case in the context of assisted reproduction is

---

46   'Reproductive Technology and the Procreation Rights of the Unmarried' (1985) 98 *Harvard Law Review* 669–685 at p 682.

47   Storrow, 'The Bioethics of Prospective Parenthood: In Pursuit of the Proper Standard for Gatekeeping in Infertility Clinics' (2007) Vol 28 (5) Cardozo Law Review 101, at 117.

48   See further discussion of constitutional right to health in Chapter 1 at paras **[1.80]–[1.98]**.

49   *Murray v Ireland* [1991] 1 ILRM 465.

limited as the facts in *Murray* related to natural reproduction and it did not discuss access to ARTs.

[4.33] The only other case to refer to a constitutional right to procreate was *Roche v Roche*[50] which concerned a married couple who underwent successful IVF treatment, following which a number of frozen embryos remained. They subsequently separated and the wife sought to be implanted with the remaining embryos, but her husband refused to consent to this. The case focused on the question of whether the embryos enjoyed a constitutional right to life under art 40.3.3°, and the right to procreate was mentioned only briefly in obiter comments by Denham J as follows: 'The right to procreate was recognised in *Murray v Ireland*. There is an equal and opposite right not to procreate. In the circumstances of this case, while the plaintiff and her husband have family rights, the exercise of a right not to procreate by the husband is a proportionate interference in all the circumstances of the case to the right of the plaintiff to procreate'.[51] It is not clear from this statement whether the right to reproduce referred to exists under the Constitution as a negative or a positive right but it is doubtful whether it could be used to try to establish a right of individuals to access assisted reproduction services.

[4.34] Further scope for recognition of the right to procreative liberty potentially exists within the right to privacy. In this context, the link between privacy and reproduction has been seen in relation to the availability of contraceptives in *McGee v Attorney General*,[52] which considered the constitutionality of a statutory provision which made it a criminal offence to import contraceptives into the State. Mrs McGee was a young married woman who had been prescribed contraceptives by her doctor for medical reasons. At that time contraceptives were not manufactured in Ireland and therefore any contraceptives that were available in Ireland were necessarily imported in breach of the statutory provision. Mrs McGee claimed that this provision was in breach of her personal rights under the Constitution. The Court recognised the necessity of the marital relationship having the protection of a right to privacy.[53] Walsh J said:

---

[50] *Roche v Roche* [2009] IESC 82.

[51] *Roche v Roche* [2009] IESC 82, para 39 per Denham J.

[52] *McGee v Attorney General* [1974] IR 284.

[53] During the 1970s there was an apparent tension between Church leaders and politicians. The Church was anxious that the liberal moral trends they perceived in other jurisdictions would not take hold in Ireland through rights decisions in the courts. Contraception proved to be a contentious issue at this time with bills being raised by backbenchers to relax the prohibition on contraceptives, Church leaders opposed to any such move and party leaders not wanting to hold the 'hot potato'. After *McGee v Attorney General* in 1974, a number of measures were attempted to provide for access to contraceptives, some restrictive and unworkable measures which tried to yield a little to pressure from the Church. Eventually in 1985 the Family Planning (Amendment) Act was passed, which was seen as 'the triumph of pluralist politicians over the Church. Although the hostility of the Church was made very clear, the official stance of the Hierarchy conformed to the 1973 principles: it was for the clergy to give guidance to Catholics and for the politicians to decide. However, some bishops and many other clergy did not adhere to that line, and by adopting a harder and more traditional stance heightened the impression of a confrontation between the Church and the state which the Church lost.' Chubb, *The Politics of the Irish Constitution* (Dublin: Institute of Public Administration, 1991) 53.

The sexual life of a husband and wife is of necessity and by its nature, an area of particular privacy. If the husband and wife decide to limit their family, or to avoid having children, by use of contraceptives, it is a matter peculiarly within the joint decision of the husband and wife and one into which the State cannot intrude unless its intrusion can be justified by the exigencies of the common good.

[4.35] Walsh J went on to explain that public morality does not of itself justify State intervention, as this would be seeking to impose on a married couple a code of private morality which they did not desire. However, unlike the other judges in the Supreme Court, Walsh J did not base the right to marital privacy on art 40.3.1°, but on art 41 of the Constitution, which seeks to protect the family. Since it is 'a matter exclusively for the husband and wife to decide how many children they wish to have' and since the State cannot dictate that they shall have a certain number of children, 'the husband and wife had a correlative right to have no children.'[54] While the Court agreed that, wherever the right was based, the intimacy of married life was possibly the most fundamental situation in which the right to privacy necessarily operated, Budd J took the view that if the State is entitled to prevent people from determining the number of children they shall have, then the constitutional guarantees are virtually meaningless. 'The State guarantees as far as practicable by its laws to vindicate the personal rights of the citizen. What more important personal right could there be in a citizen than the right to determine in marriage his attitude and resolve his mode of life concerning the procreation of children?'[55] Henchy J was of the opinion that the violation by the State of Mrs McGee's right to privacy lay in frustrating and making criminal any efforts by her to effectuate a decision taken, on medical advice, by herself and her husband, to use contraceptives so as to ensure her health and the security of her family.

[4.36] Thus, in this decision, the Supreme Court recognised that a right to privacy was constitutionally guaranteed, whether through art 40.3.1° or art 41. This applied to the broad area of personal marital relations and control of reproduction within the marital relationship. In this sense then it might be used to establish a right of a married couple to make positive decisions regarding the medical treatment of their infertility. That is to say, if a particular infertility treatment were available in Ireland, such as IVF using donated gametes, a married couple would have a constitutional right of access to this treatment, within the limits set by law, without interference from the State. This might be significant in terms of equality and non-discrimination policies if, for example, a couple with prior history of criminal convictions was refused access to treatment. Such an exclusionary rule would have to be justified by reference to the State's imposition of reasonable and proportionate restrictions in the pursuit of legitimate aims such as child protection and welfare. However, the principle itself would not enable a couple to pursue an argument that the State owed them a positive duty to provide such services free of charge within the public health system.

[4.37] The imposition by the State of restrictions on the exercise of the right to privacy was specifically stated in *McGee*. Despite a judgment in favour of the existence of the

---

54 *McGee v Attorney General* [1974] IR 284 at 311.
55 *McGee v Attorney General* [1974] IR 284 at 322.

right to privacy, the court agreed that there remained the possibility of State intervention in the interests of the common good, although no such State interest existed in the circumstances of this particular case. Unfortunately, very little useful definition of the common good may be taken from the judgment, although Walsh J did draw a distinction between public and private morality: 'It is undoubtedly true that among those persons who are subject to a particular moral code no one has a right to be in breach of that moral code. But when this is a code governing private morality and where the breach of it is not one which injures the common good then it is not the State's business to intervene'.[56] Unfortunately he did not clarify how the particular moral code applicable in the public domain was to be ascertained.

[4.38] In *Norris v Attorney General*,[57] which challenged the constitutionality of laws penalising homosexual acts between males, the plaintiff asserted that the State had no business in the area of private morality and for the State to legislate in relation to private sexual conduct between consenting adults was, as O'Higgins CJ put it, 'to shatter that area of privacy which the dignity and liberty of human persons require to be kept apart as the haven for each citizen.' The court accepted, however, that, as a general proposition concerning the purpose of law and with particular reference to the constitutional right to privacy, the State must have an interest in the general moral well-being of society and must be entitled to discourage conduct which is contrary to the values of society. O'Higgins CJ was of the view that there are certain acts which may take place in private which, although they do not harm any other individual, must be condemned by the State on the basis that they are morally wrong such as abortion, incest, suicide attempts, suicide pacts, euthanasia or mercy killing.

[4.39] In keeping with *McGee*, the court further held that a right of privacy can never be absolute. McCarthy J said 'the right to privacy is not in issue – it is the extent of that right – the extent of the right to be let alone.' He referred to the compelling State interest which is necessary in order to justify intrusion into areas within the realm of the right and stated that a 'very great burden lies upon those who would question such personal rights'. The examples of justifiable interference which he gave included the protection of minors or incapacitated persons, and public decency. If none of these obvious justifications exist, then he was of the view that State interference would be of a most grievous kind. Henchy J recognised that there were many aspects to the right to privacy which are as yet judicially undeveloped and that they all seemed to fall 'within a secluded area of activity or non-activity, which may be claimed as necessary for the expression of an individual personality, for purposes not always necessarily moral or commendable, but meriting recognition in circumstances which do not endanger considerations such as State security, public order or morality, or other essential components of the common good'. He therefore recognised that there are activities which may be carried out in private, and which do not contravene policy considerations of the State, which are neither moral nor commendable, but yet should not be condemned by law. The extent of the justification of State policy, particularly in the area of morality, was unfortunately not elaborated on here.

---

[56] *McGee v Attorney General* [1974] IR 284 at 313.

[57] *Norris v Attorney General* [1984] IR 36.

[4.40] On the basis of the consideration of the right to privacy by the Irish Courts[58] it can be said that the development of the right has taken place along similar lines to that taken in the United States.[59] The right is seen as worthy of constitutional protection but not in any absolute form. It is seen as necessarily subject to State interference in the interests of the common good, which is itself a general and undefined term. As Walsh J stated extra-judicially:

> Various justifications are offered for invasions of privacy such as the public interest and these are to some extent recognised by the European Convention of Human Rights in art.8 ... The State's rights as such, can only be upheld if they can be equated with the common good and again a delicate balance has to be preserved between the power of the Oireachtas to decide what is in the common good and the powers of the judge to so decide ... What is, I think, universally acceptable is that the requirements of the public good must depend upon the needs and conditions which exist at any given moment. [60]

[4.41] The case might be made that the right to procreate, which it is thought would come within the realms of the right to privacy, would also be similarly susceptible to State interference along those principles.[61] The phrase 'common good' seems to import notions of public morality, social justice and perhaps good government. It has been said that social justice cannot be considered to be the old standard of 'the greatest good of the greatest number, for, at the present day, it may be considered proper that the claim of a minority be made paramount on some topic.'[62] It is thought that the 'common good' or 'social justice' cannot be regarded as being of a constant quality since considerations in this context will vary with social and economic circumstances which evolve over time:

---

[58] See also *Kennedy & Arnold v Ireland* [1987] IR 587, which involved the interception of telephone conversations of two journalists by order of the Minister for Justice. Hamilton P recognised the general right of privacy and held that the plaintiffs' Constitutional rights had been violated. He also held that the right to privacy was not absolute and was open to exceptions such as the common good, public order and morality, and the Constitutional rights of others. In *Attorney-General (Society for the Protection of the Unborn Child) v Open-Door Counselling Ltd* [1987] ILRM 477, Hamilton P held that the right to privacy could not be invoked to interfere with such a fundamental right as the right to life of the unborn. Although this was because of the express protection of the unborn under art 40.3.3°, the case broadly demonstrates again the limited development and use of the right to privacy in Ireland when faced with competing claims.

[59] Indeed, this similarity has given some commentators cause for concern, as it was thought that the development of individual privacy from the marital privacy protection in *McGee* could provide the opportunity to derive a right to abortion in Ireland, in the same way as in *Roe v Wade*. See Binchy, 'Ethical Issues in Reproductive Medicine: A Legal Perspective' in Reidy (ed), *Ethical Issues in Reproductive Medicine* (Gill & McMillan, 1982) 95–117, at 104.

[60] Walsh, 'The Judicial Power and the Protection of the Right to Privacy' (1977) Dublin University Law Journal 3.

[61] So, in *Murray v Ireland* [1991] 1 ILRM 465, the right to reproduce was seen as necessarily subject to the exigencies of the provision of State security, in the context of a refusal to grant conjugal rights to prisoners in order that they might conceive a child. This was a case in which the Court arguably gave insufficient weight to the couple's reproductive rights and too much weight to the State's claims of administrative inconvenience but, it is submitted that due to the special circumstances of the case, that is to say, the special setting of a prison, it is not a strong precedent for limiting procreative freedom in non-prison settings.

[62] *Pigs Marketing Board v Donnelly (Dublin) Ltd* [1939] IR 413, per Hanna J.

In a court of law it seems to me to be a nebulous phrase, involving no question of law for the courts, but questions of ethics, morals, economics, and sociology, which are, in my opinion, beyond the determination of a court of law, but which may be, in their various aspects, within the consideration of the Oireachtas, as representing the people, when framing the law.[63]

[4.42] The promotion of the common good is also specifically referred to in the Preamble to the Constitution as one of its objectives. The Preamble has been adverted to in a number of cases but no case has been decided solely on the strength of it. For example, it has been said that 'the justice or otherwise of any legislative interference with the right ... [in regard to guarantees for property]... has to be considered in relation, inter alia, to the proclaimed objects with which the Constitution was enacted, including the promotion of the common good.'[64] Although the precise meaning of this phrase has not been elaborated upon, the courts have taken the view that judicial activism may be sanctioned by reference to the changing values to be accorded to the common good. In *McGee*, Walsh J said:

> According to the Preamble, the people gave themselves the Constitution to promote the common good with due observance of prudence, justice and charity so that the dignity and freedom of the individual might be assured. The judges must, therefore, as best they can from their training and their experience interpret these rights in accordance with their ideas of prudence, justice and charity. It is but natural that from time to time the prevailing ideas of these virtues may be conditioned by the passage of time, no interpretation of the Constitution is intended to be final for all time.[65]

[4.43] To return to privacy and procreation rights under the Constitution – these rights, if they exist at all, are not absolute and would seem to be subject to the vagaries of the courts' interpretation of social justice. The courts have not expressed clearly what is intended by the use of the phrase 'the common good' and seem to use it as an all-encompassing formula for principles of public morality and social justice. But, in the particular context of procreational choices, it is difficult to see how the 'common good' could be used in any way other than imposing a set of *moral* principles on a private individual or couple without having to demonstrate harm to any specified person/group of persons. The State would surely have to show a pressing and substantial concern which must be of such sufficient importance to justify overriding a constitutional right, and the infringement on the right ought to be proportionate to the concern to be safeguarded. There are arguably very few circumstances in which such a substantial concern might be demonstrated to be sufficiently weighty so as to justify State intervention in this context. It might occur, for example, in a situation in which it could

---

[63] *Pigs Marketing Board v Donnelly (Dublin) Ltd* [1939] IR 413, per Hanna J.

[64] *Attorney General v Southern Industrial Trust* [1960] 94 ILTR 161 per Davitt P.

[65] *McGee v Attorney General* [1974] IR 284. This approach was endorsed by O'Higgins CJ in *The State (Healy) v Donoghue* [1976] IR 325; and by McWilliam J in the High Court in *Norris v Attorney General* [1984] IR 36. In the latter case McWilliam J considered whether 'the Legislature could now, under current social conditions, having regard to the prevailing ideas and concepts of morality and the current knowledge of matters affecting public health, reasonably come to the conclusion that the homosexual acts declared unlawful by the statutes under challenge were such as ought to be prohibited for the attainment of true social order as mentioned in the Preamble to the Constitution'.

be established with some degree of probability that the conception of the child was sought for some criminal purpose such as child prostitution. These are issues in which the State might be justified in having an interest, for the direct safety and protection of the child to be conceived. Any other vague societal interests claimed by the State under the auspices of the common good would surely require substantial proof of harm directly caused by the exercise of procreative rights by accessing assisted reproduction in the particular circumstances at hand.

Rights to reproduce under international law

[4.44] In international law, the existence of negative and positive rights may also be seen in the language and jurisprudence of human rights conventions. Positive obligations are generally associated with economic, social and cultural rights and commonly have financial obligations. It may be argued, however, that these economic, social and cultural rights do not have a legally binding character and are thus legally inferior.[66] The thrust of this argument is that the term 'right' ought to be reserved for rights which may be enforced in a court of law or in a comparable manner and also that social rights are not directed at government action that can be described in terms of law: 'The creation of social and economic conditions under which social rights can be enjoyed is – as yet – not describable in terms of law. In order to be a legal right, a right must be legally definable; only then can it be legally enforced, only then can it be said to be justiciable'.[67] In the absence of any effective enforcement mechanism in international law in respect of economic, social and cultural rights, these are not legal rights at all. However, it may be argued that the realities of international law are not taken into account in this false comparison between national and international law. There are wide-ranging differences between national communities and the international community based on the vertical structure and central organisation of the one and the horizontal structure and decentralised organisation of the other. National legal systems are usually equipped with an institutionalised law-making process, an executive branch of government and law-enforcement mechanism. In the international context these functions are largely performed in a non-institutionalised way by the states themselves.

[4.45] It is the exception rather than the rule that norms of international law can be enforced through courts of law, or in a comparable manner. However, this is generally considered an insufficient reason to deny to such norms the status of binding rules of international law. Similarly, it does not mean that there is no way to enforce, or rather to implement, such rules of international law. All that it implies is that rules of international law usually have to be enforced or implemented through methods different from those available in municipal legal systems. So even if the availability of enforcement through courts of law constitutes a pre-condition for according a legally binding status to a norm in national legal systems, this does not justify the same conclusion with respect to international law.[68]

---

[66] Vierdag, 'The Legal Nature of the Rights Granted by the International Covenant on Economic, Social and Cultural Rights.' (1978) 9 Netherlands Yearbook of International Law 69–105.

[67] Vierdag, 'The Legal Nature of the Rights Granted by the International Covenant on Economic, Social and Cultural Rights.' (1978) 9 Netherlands Yearbook of International Law 69–105 at 93.

[68] Van Hoof, 'The Legal Nature of Economic, Social and Cultural Rights: A Rebuttal of Some Traditional Views' in Alston and Tomasevski (eds) *The Right to Food*, 97–110, at 101.

[4.46] Article 16(1) of the Universal Declaration of Human Rights 1948 provides that 'Men and women of full age, without any limitation due to race, nationality or religion, have the right to marry and to found a family.' This appears to link marriage and the right to found a family, which perhaps implies that unmarried couples or individuals may not avail of the right. Article 16(3) goes on to provide that the family is 'the natural and fundamental group unit of society' and is therefore entitled to State protection. Article 12 of the European Convention on Human Rights (ECHR) provides that 'men and women of marriageable age have the right to marry and to found a family according to the national laws governing the exercise of this right.' While the values underpinning these provisions are laudable, the scope of the provisions themselves is uncertain. It is thought that the limitations intended by the expression used in the Convention must relate to legitimate purposes such as to prevent incest or bigamy and do not sanction a complete and arbitrary deprivation of rights by national laws. If this were not the case the Convention would be meaningless, as it would entitle national legislatures to ignore its provisions without legitimate justification.[69]

[4.47] In the *Van Oosterwijck* case[70] the complainant argued that the Belgian authorities were violating his right to marry and found a family under art 12 of the ECHR by not permitting him to change his birth certificate to reflect the fact that he had undergone sex reassignment surgery. The Commission upheld his claim under art 8 (right to respect for private and family life) on grounds that the law obliged him to use documents which did not reflect his real identity, and under art 12 (right to marry and found a family). The Commission stated that there was a clear link in art 12 between marriage and procreation but was of the view that a marriage could be valid despite the lack of an intention or capacity to procreate, as the latter is not a prerequisite for marriage: 'Although marriage and the family are in fact associated in the Convention and in domestic legal systems, there is nothing to support the conclusion that the capacity to procreate is an essential condition of marriage or even that procreation is an essential purpose of marriage'.[71] The European Court of Human Rights declined to consider the merits of the case on grounds that there had been a failure to exhaust domestic remedies.

[4.48] As changes continue to take place within society and its perception of the institution of marriage and family, this link between marriage and procreation may be abolished. This may result in demands for reproductive services as rights of the individual rather than the couple. Although the right to reproduce using assisted reproduction has yet to be recognised as a positive right in international law, it is expected that technological developments will increasingly create demands that a right to parenthood be recognised. 'The availability of effective treatments of infertility, embryo transfer, and surrogate motherhood, have created a host of demands for entitlements concerning procreation'.[72]

---

[69] Liu, *Artificial Reproduction and Reproductive Rights* (Dartmouth Publishing Ltd, 1991) at 27–31, and Harris, O'Boyle, Warbrick, *Law of the European Convention on Human Rights* (Butterworths, 1995) 435.

[70] *Van Oosterwijck v Belgium* (ECHR Appl No 7654/76).

[71] Report of 1 March 1979, B 36 (1983) 28–29 at 28.

[72] Tomasevski, 'Women', in Eide, Krause and Rosas (eds) *Economic, Social and Cultural Rights* (Martinus Nijhoff Publishers, Dordrecht, 1995) 273–288, at 281.

[4.49] Even within the marital relationship, there is no right to adopt or found a family by alternative means. The possibility of ARTs being used to create a family was certainly not in the minds of those who drafted the Convention. However, as societal attitudes change and reproductive technologies become more widely available, the substance of an existing relationship should be looked at and its effective enjoyment provided for, rather than confining the protection of 'family life' to formal relationships. This would expand the obligation to protect from discrimination on the basis of marital status or sexual orientation:

> It does not seem likely that the Convention imposes any limits on what choices a state may make and it is probably premature to decide that the Convention imposes a[n]... obligation on a state to legislate to allow any particular technique. However, as the acceptability of those measures which are closest to natural reproduction (eg IVF) increases, states may find themselves having an increasingly heavy burden to explain why married persons may not avail themselves of them. It is much less likely that a positive duty will be placed on the state to provide the appropriate treatment.[73]

[4.50] Even if a positive right to respect for family life (and within this, the right to procreate) were to be established under the Convention, it is likely that individual states would be given a wide 'margin of appreciation' to decide what 'respect' required in the particular circumstances of an individual applicant.[74] What this means in effect is that the State has to have regard 'to the fair balance that has to be struck between the general interest of the community and the interests of the individual, the search for which balance is inherent in the whole Convention.'[75] In balancing the interests of an infertile couple in receiving treatment against the general interest of the community in protecting its traditional respect for the protection of the unborn under the provisions of the Irish Constitution, it may well be that, even if the couple was seen as having a right to assistance from the State in pursuance of trying to have a family, the State may come within this margin of appreciation and avoid obligation. However, it must also be borne in mind that this might be a more difficult argument for the State to make since the Supreme Court decision in *Roche v Roche*[76] which held that the embryo outside the womb does not qualify for constitutional protection.

[4.51] Eijkholt argues that examination of the recent case law of the European Court of Human Rights suggests that art 12 is no longer the vehicle within which to assert the sorts of claims that tend to be made under arguments for a right to procreate. Claims related to assisted reproduction, and access thereto, have been submitted under art 8 which enshrines respect for private and family life. She claims that references to art 12 have been ignored or, possibly, avoided, and art 12 hardly plays any role in cases concerning reproduction. Hence, it seems that art 12 no longer offers the legal basis for

---

[73] Harris, O'Boyle, Warbrick, *Law of the European Convention on Human Rights* (Butterworths, 1995), at 441.

[74] In *Cabales and Balkandali v UK*, A 94 para 67 [1985], the Court said: '...especially as far as those positive obligations are concerned, the notion of 'respect' is not clear-cut: having regard to the diversity of practices followed and the situations obtaining in the Contracting states, the notion's requirements will vary considerably from case to case.'

[75] *Cossey v UK* (1985) 7 EHRR 471.

[76] *Roche v Roche* [2009] IESC 82.

a right to procreate, if it ever did.[77] Eijkholt states that the article's restrictive interpretation is, 'first, a result of its wording':

> Article 12 refers to 'men and women of a marriageable age'. This wording has constrained the Court in its application to, for example, single individuals. Furthermore, the wording obviously refers to heterosexual couples and seems not necessarily to encompass reproductive desires expressed by homosexual couples. Second, Article 12 is limited by a narrow understanding of the notion of 'family'. It extends only fully to cases that concern natural and genetic children, and, by analogy, to 'acts' by which they are reproduced. Where there is no genetic bond, for example, in issues about non-genetically related children or extra-marital children, protection lies in Article 8 instead. Third, the Article seems to have been applied in a conservative way. The Court remains hesitant to go outside the prescribed application.

[4.52] Two cases in particular illustrate the approach taken by the Court in recent years *Sijakova v the Former Yugoslav Republic of Macedonia*[78] and *SH and others v Austria*.[79] In the Sijakova case, a group of parents had applied to the Court on the basis that their right to found a family was violated. Their children had taken holy orders and a vow of celibacy in the Macedonian Orthodox Church, and as a result, the applicants could 'not found a larger family and have grandchildren'. The group of parents argued that the Church's rules were unconstitutional and against their Convention rights. Yet, while declaring the case inadmissible, the Court stated that 'the right to have grandchildren or the right to procreation is not covered by art 12 or any other art of the Convention'.

[4.53] In *SH v Austria,* two couples appealed against the Austrian Artificial Procreation Act. The Act excluded them from fertility treatment, as it did not allow the use of donor gametes. One couple required donor sperm for IVF treatment because the husband was infertile. The other couple required implantation of an embryo created with a donor ovum, since the woman did not produce any ova herself. The Grand Chamber took the view that, within the EU, member states had a very wide margin of appreciation in how to regulate assisted reproduction. 'The use of IVF treatment ... continues to give rise today to sensitive moral and ethical issues against a background of fast-moving medical and scientific developments.' It acknowledged that these are 'areas where there is not yet clear common ground amongst the member states'. The Grand Chamber also made the point that there was no prohibition on Austrian citizens going abroad to seek treatment of infertility that uses artificial procreation techniques not allowed in Austria and that in the event of a successful treatment the Austrian Civil Code contains clear rules on paternity and maternity that respect the wishes of the parents':

> It therefore appeared to be a little easier to justify Austria's wide margin of appreciation because it was also simple for Austrian citizens to avoid its effects by travelling to another country with a more relaxed regulatory regime. In many ways, this is peculiar: it appears to suggest that the harshness of a prohibition can be defended, at least in part, because it is fairly easy to avoid it. If the margin of appreciation is so important to member states, isn't

---

[77] Eijkholt, 'The Right to Found a Family as a Stillborn Right to Procreate?' (2010) Med L Rev 18(2), 127–151.

[78] *Sijakova and Others v The Former Yugoslav Republic* (Application No 67914/01, 6 March 2003).

[79] *SH and others v Austria* (Appl No 57813/00, 15 November 2007).

it a little odd that their citizens are simultaneously given a simple route through which they can access the banned treatment?[80]

[4.54] Hence, despite the fact that procreation was central to both cases, the Court dismissed any claim to a right to procreate under art 12. These judgments reject any argument that the core of art 12, the right to found a family, could be phrased as a right to procreate.[81] By contrast, the right to privacy may provide a more fruitful means to establishing a right to procreate, despite the ambiguous nature of the obligation to 'respect' which is often contained in the wording of relevant articles and constitutional provisions on privacy. Stephens claims that 'the right to privacy is implicated when the State inserts itself into the decision of a person, or a couple to conceive by whatever means they feel are necessary. A limitation on the use of reproductive technologies clearly has the potential to interfere in a person's or a couple's right to found a family, by making it more difficult or impossible to do so.'[82] Of particular interest here is art 8 of the European Convention on Human Rights 1950 which provides:

1. Everyone has the right to respect for his private and family life.

2. There shall be no interference by a public authority with the exercise of this right except as is in accordance with law and is necessary in a democratic society in the interests of national security, public safety or the economic well-being of the country, for the prevention of disorder or crime, for the protection of health or morals, or for the protection of the rights and freedoms of others.'

[4.55] The application of art 8 in the context of assisted reproduction was considered in *Evans v UK* [83] in which a British woman claimed that the UK's Human Fertilisation and Embryology Act of 1990, which required her former partner's consent before the embryos made with their joint genetic material could lawfully be transferred to her uterus, was in violation of her rights under arts 8 and 14[84] of the European Convention on Human Rights, and contrary to the embryo's right to life under art 2.[85] The European Court of Human Rights stated that all parties to the case agreed that the Act did constitute an interference with Ms Evan's rights under art 8(1), however the issue was whether such interference could be justified under art 8(2). The Court was of the view that since there was no clear common ground amongst the Member States on the issues raised by the case, the margin of appreciation to be afforded to the UK must be a wide one which extended both to its decision to regulate the area at all and to the detailed rules it lays down in order to achieve a balance between the competing public and private interests involved. Therefore the Court held that the UK, in adopting the 1990

---

[80] Jackson, 'Commentary on *SH v Austria*' (2012) Reproductive BioMedicine Online, Volume 25 , Issue 7 , 663 – 664.

[81] Eijkholt, 'The Right to Found a Family as a Stillborn Right to Procreate?' (2010) Med L Rev 18(2), p 137.

[82] Stephens, 'The Right To Reproduce And International Law' (2010) Vermont Law School Legal Studies Research Paper Series Research Paper No 10–47.

[83] *Evans v The United Kingdom* [2007] EHRR 728 [71].

[84] The Court found there was no violation of art 14 which prohibits discrimination in the enjoyment of the Convention rights and freedoms.

[85] The Court held that since an embryo does not have any independent rights under English law and therefore cannot claim a right to life, there was no violation of art 2.

Act, did not exceed the margin of appreciation granted to it and therefore there was no violation of art 8.

[4.56] In *Dickson v UK*[86] a prisoner and his wife requested that the Secretary of State provide them with facilities for artificial insemination as the man's wife would be too old to conceive naturally when her husband would be released from detention.[87] The request was refused. The applicants complained that the refusal by the Secretary of State to allow the first applicant access to artificial insemination facilities whilst in prison constituted a breach of the applicants' rights under art 8 (right to private and family life) and art 12 (right to marry and found a family) of the European Convention on Human Rights. The Grand Chamber held that art 8 was engaged, as the complainants' private and family lives incorporated their rights to respect for their decision to become genetic parents. Prisoners retained their Convention rights on imprisonment and any restriction of them must be justified in each case. Whilst the state was entitled to be concerned about the welfare of any child conceived, that obligation could not go so far as to prevent parents from conceiving a child in circumstances such as these, especially as the prisoner's wife was at liberty and could have taken care of any child until the husband's release. It was therefore not necessary to examine the complaint under art 12.

REGULATION OF ASSISTED REPRODUCTION IN IRELAND

[4.57] Although there is no national collation of data on assisted human reproduction (AHR) in Ireland at present, it is estimated that approximately 3,500 IVF/ICSI treatments are performed each year with about 500–800 frozen embryo replacement cycles and 1,000–1,500 intra uterine insemination treatments. The provision of assisted reproduction services is not currently regulated other than by EC Directive 2004/23/EC which lays down standards of quality and safety for the donation, procurement, testing, processing, preservation, storage and distribution of human tissues and cells.[88] The European Communities (Quality and Safety of Human Tissues and Cells) Regulations 2006[89] which transposed the Directive designated the former Irish Medicines Board, now called the Health Products Regulatory Authority (HPRA), as the competent authority for the implementation of this legislation. Any individual or site which carries out any prescribed activity is required to be authorised by the HPRA. In order to obtain a tissue establishment authorisation, an application must be made to the HPRA and compliance with the requirements of relevant Regulations must be demonstrated by applicants. To ensure that compliance with these requirements are maintained, inspectors monitor compliance through regular on-site inspections.

[4.58] For registered medical practitioners working in the area of assisted reproduction, the Medical Council's Guide to Professional Conduct and Ethics is also important. The Medical Council is a statutory body established by the Medical Practitioners Act 1978,

---

[86] *Dickson v The United Kingdom* [2007] 46 EHHR 927 at para 76.

[87] See also *R (Mellor) v Secretary of State for the Home Department* [2001] 3 WLR 533 in which a similar application was refused by the English Court of Appeal on public policy grounds.

[88] An associated Commission Directive 2006/17/EC, sets out technical requirements for the activities of donation, procurement and testing of human tissues and cells and came into force on 1 November 2006.

[89] SI 158/2006.

as amended in 2007, to protect the public by promoting and better ensuring high standards of professional conduct and professional education, training and competence among registered medical practitioners. One of the functions of the Council is to specify standards of practice for registered medical practitioners, including providing guidance on all matters related to professional conduct and ethics. The Council achieves this objective by publishing a Guide to Professional Conduct and Ethics, which doctors are expected to comply with in their professional practice.[90] In relation to assisted reproduction the Guide (8th ed)[91] states:

> 47.1 Assisted human reproduction treatments such as In Vitro Fertilisation (IVF) should only be used after thorough investigation has shown that no other treatment is likely to be effective. You should make sure that patients have been offered appropriate counselling and have had enough time to consider the information before giving informed consent to any treatment.

> 47.2 Assisted human reproduction services should only be provided by suitably qualified professionals, in appropriately accredited facilities, and in line with international best practice. You should do regular clinical audits and follow-up of outcomes.

> 47.3 If you offer donor programmes to patients, you must have strong governance structures and keep accurate records so that the identity of the donor can be traced. Donor programmes should be altruistic and non-commercial. You should also comply with industry accreditation standards for donation programmes.

> 47.4 You must not take part in the creation of new forms of human life solely for experimental purposes. You must not engage in human reproductive cloning.

[4.59] In 2000, the Minister for Health established the Commission on Assisted Human Reproduction (CAHR) to prepare a report on the possible approaches to the regulation of all aspects of assisted human reproduction and the social, ethical and legal factors to be taken into account in determining public policy in this area. The membership of the Commission was comprised of medical, scientific, social and legal expertise. A public consultation exercise was carried out by the Commission as well as a survey of service users, and consultation with medical practitioners working in the area of AHR in Ireland. The Commission also took account of the position in other jurisdictions in its report to the Minister in March 2005.[92] It made 40 recommendations many of which are referred to in subsequent chapters below. As an overarching recommendation the Commission stated that legislation should be enacted to establish a regulatory body which would issue licences to service providers. Despite judicial criticism of the delay in regulating this area and numerous political commitments to do so, the pace of change has been extremely slow. Although some measures have been introduced in the Children and Family Relationships Act 2015 to deal with the parentage issues arising from some assisted reproduction services such as donor insemination and egg donation, the regulation of the facilities which provide these services and other issues such as surrogacy has not yet been dealt with by legislation. The publication of the general

---

[90] The role of the Medical Council is further discussed in Chapter 2.

[91] Medical Council Guide to Professional Conduct and Ethics (8th edn, 2016) www.medicalcouncil.ie.

[92] Report of the Commission on Assisted Human Reproduction (Government Publications Office, 2005), available at www.health.gov.ie.

scheme of a Bill dealing with regulation of assisted reproduction is expected in 2016–17.

REGULATION OF ASSISTED REPRODUCTION IN OTHER JURISDICTIONS

[4.60] Internationally, there is wide divergence in relation to the regulation of AHR. The development of IVF and its subsequent variations and extensions appears to have generated more interest and concern among religious leaders, bioethicists and the general public than any other medical procedure. This widespread interest and concern has consequently attracted the attention of the political process in many countries. As a result of these events, many expert committees have examined the ethical, legal, religious, medical, and public policy aspects of AHR, resulting in the establishment of unofficial guidelines and/or government regulations in many states where AHR is practised. There are several states which have adopted guidelines, described as sets of rules to be followed voluntarily, generally proposed by unofficial organisations such as an infertility society or a society of obstetrics and gynaecology. Other states have passed regulations, that is, sets of rules adopted by legislative action, with assigned penalties for violations. Other states have neither regulations nor guidelines. Due to the pace of change in this area internationally, it is difficult to get a picture of the regulatory landscape other than that which is available as a snapshot in time. An organisation that collates this information on a cyclical basis is the International Federation of Fertility Societies (IFFS) which represents the national fertility societies of approximately 70 states, including Ireland. In its most recent surveillance report in 2013, it stated:

> The practice of ART is extensively influenced by cultural, religious, and political exigencies in each of the locales in which it is practiced. All nations have a legitimate interest in promoting the safety and welfare of its citizens undergoing new medical therapy, and the practice of ART has endured special scrutiny in its regulation. The attention devoted to implementing new ART legislation appears to exceed that given to other medical disciplines. While the plethora of different national laws across the globe may try to ensure safety and implement best practices, they can be influenced by cultural norms, religious ideology, preferences of local officials, ethical opinion, and general public perception.[93]

[4.61] The IFFS Report notes that AHR remains a highly regulated medical discipline. In the 2013 survey of 60 countries, 90% of the respondents surveyed reported some regulation via either legislation or guidelines or a combination of both. Legislation was updated in 43% of the respondent's countries since the previous survey in 2007, demonstrating the continued role of government in regulating the practice of AHR. It concludes that the ultimate benefit and harm of regulation continues to be intensely debated, but the widespread acceptance of the legitimacy of assisted reproduction and society's role in promoting its safe and ethical application are now well established.[94]

[4.62] An example of comprehensive regulation of AHR can be seen in the UK where services are regulated by the Human Fertilisation and Embryology Act 1990, as amended in 2008. Clinics must be licensed by the Human Fertilisation and Embryology

---

[93] IFFS Surveillance 2013 available at www.iffs-reproduction.org/ page 15.
[94] IFFS Surveillance 2013 available at www.iffs-reproduction.org/ page 17.

Authority[95] (HFEA) and must comply with both the Act and the Codes of Practice issued by the HFEA. The HFEA regulates the provision of fertility treatment and the carrying out of embryo research by an inspection and licensing regime. It also maintains a register of information about the provision and outcome of fertility treatments. It publishes a Code of Practice and Directions which gives guidance to clinics about the conduct of activities regulated by the HFEA. This is seen as an advantageous model rather than primary legislation, as it allows flexibility in changing rules to adapt to emerging technologies and clinical practice. Jackson notes that:

> The Code thus has the advantage of being able to respond to a continually shifting evidence base. The legal status of the Code of Practice is, however, a little unclear. A breach of the Code is not a criminal offence, unlike many breaches of the Act itself. Nevertheless, breaches of the Code can be taken into account by a licence committee when deciding whether to vary or revoke a licence.[96]

ACCESS TO AHR AND THE WELFARE OF THE CHILD

[4.63] Access to AHR services in light of considerations of the welfare of the future child is one of the most controversial issues in this area of medical practice. Questions are raised about the suitability of certain family forms in terms of parenting style and lifestyle choices and the right of a child to be raised by its biological parents. The issue confronts societal prejudices about different forms of parenting, discrimination and the legitimacy of interfering with reproductive choice. As discussed above, the Irish courts have recognised a right to privacy and a right to reproduce, both of which are qualified by considerations of the common good, judicial definition of which is unfortunately lacking in this context.

[4.64] In the context of AHR clinics deciding whether or not to provide services for an individual or couple, the welfare of the child is often seen as an important guiding principle. Child welfare is a multi-faceted concept ranging from narrow inquiries about protecting children from physical harm and abusive parents on the one end of the spectrum to expansive questions about what promotes a child's best interests on the other.[97] The concept is described by Lee and Morgan as 'broad and all-embracing', noting that a very wide range of factors must be taken into account when considering the future lives of children who may be born as a result of the treatment.[98] By comparison, parents who can conceive their children naturally generally enjoy a presumption of fitness that frees them to exercise their parental prerogatives without State interference. The courts do not intervene to safeguard the child's welfare other than in exceptional circumstances where this is necessary for the protection of the child.

---

[95] See www.hfea.gov.uk/.

[96] Jackson, *Medical Law: Text, Cases and Materials,* (3rd edn, OUP, 2013), p 775.

[97] Storrow, 'The Bioethics of Prospective Parenthood: In Pursuit of the Proper Standard for Gatekeeping in Infertility Clinics' (2007) Vol 28 (5) Cardozo Law Review 101 at 118 referring to Robertson, 'Procreative Liberty and Harm to Offspring in Assisted Reproduction', (2004) 30 Am J L & Med 7.

[98] Lee and Morgan, *Human Fertilisation and Embryology, Regulating the Reproductive Revolution* (Blackstone Press Ltd, 2001) at p 161.

[4.65] For those who seek to adopt children in Ireland, no parental rights or responsibilities are transferred until the legal eligibility test and suitability to adopt criteria are satisfied. If these requirements are satisfied, the Adoption Authority may make an adoption order in respect of a child under the Adoption Act 2010. Section 19 of the Act states that in any such matter, the welfare of the child shall be the first and paramount consideration. Slightly different wording is sometimes used in relation to medical treatment of children which tends to focus on best interests. The term 'best interests' is also used in the UN Convention on the Rights of the Child 1989 and art 42A of the Irish Constitution, effected by the Thirty-First Amendment of the Constitution (Children) Act 2012. However, any difference between 'welfare' and 'best interests' in this context is unlikely to be significant. The aim is to measure the specific needs of the particular child and how those needs will be met by placement in a particular home.

[4.66] Assisted reproduction legislation in many jurisdictions similarly mandates consideration of child welfare in advance of the child's conception. However, this is more challenging to apply in terms of measuring the specific needs of the particular child as no such child yet exists. The 'welfare' or 'best interests' test is therefore generally couched in very general terms and has consequently often been criticised for its inconsistent and potentially biased application. Some commentators believe that such provisions are inherently speculative given the lack of evidence regarding parenting ability.[99] 'Unless we are concerned to prevent reproduction in anyone who may offer a suboptimal environment for their children's upbringing, then restricting the reproductive options of infertile people on the basis of some vague appeal to child welfare may be both disingenuous and discriminatory.'[100] There are concerns that the welfare test may thus be used in practice as an indirect means of preferring certain kinds of families that fit a particular idealised stereotype.

[4.67] In Ireland, the Equal Status Acts 2000–2004 prohibits direct or indirect discrimination on grounds of, inter alia, disability, sexual orientation, marital status, age, gender, or religion, in relation to the provision of services.[101] 'Service' here includes 'a service or facility of any nature which is available to the public generally or a section of the public'[102] and therefore, in the absence of any future legislative provision to the contrary, would cover clinics providing assisted reproduction treatments. In the context of the provision of AHR services, a refusal by a clinic to treat a person/couple on grounds of marital status or sexual orientation would clearly come within the prohibitions in the Act. However, it is possible that a refusal on grounds of age may be defended by a clinic on clinical grounds in relation to that particular patient,[103] or, where the refusal is on grounds of disability and there is evidence that treatment may result in harm to any child that could be conceived by the treatment.[104]

---

[99] Jackson, *Regulating Reproduction: Law, Technology and Autonomy* 192 (2001).

[100] Jackson, *Regulating Reproduction: Law, Technology and Autonomy* 192 (2001) at 174.

[101] The prohibited grounds or discrimination are set out in the Equal Status Acts 2000–2004, ss 2 and 3.

[102] Defined in the Equal Status Acts 2000–2004, s 2.

[103] Equal Status Acts 2000–2004, s 16(2)(a).

[104] Equal Status Acts 2000–2004, s 4(4).

[4.68] The Commission on Assisted Human Reproduction considered this issue in its Report in 2005.[105] It recommended that services should be available without discrimination on the grounds of gender, marital status or sexual orientation, subject to consideration of the best interests of any children that may be born. It stated that any relevant legislation on the provision of AHR services should reflect the general principles of the Equal Status Acts subject to certain qualifications. These qualifications would support the introduction of an upper age limit on persons seeking treatment in order to confer protection on the future child in respect of its need to have a parent into the child's maturity and also in respect of protection of the health of the person seeking treatment which might be contra-indicated for older persons. The second qualification recommended by the Commission was that legislation may confer on AHR clinics discretion to deny services to a person where there are serious concerns supported by objective evidence that the welfare of any resulting child could otherwise be at risk. The evaluation of such evidence could however be open to challenge by applicants who have been refused access to treatment services.

[4.69] The Commission discussed different ways of evaluating the welfare of the child in this context, such as the maximum and minimum welfare principles.[106] The maximum welfare principle implies that one should not knowingly and intentionally bring a child into the world in less-than-ideal circumstances. Research shows that children need a stable home with mature, caring adults who themselves have a sound relationship. However '[T]he difficulty with the use of this principle is that every characteristic of those who request medical assistance that does not conform to the stereotypical family based on heterosexual married parents and their genetically related children' is assumed to result in negative consequences for the child.[107] The second measure of evaluation of welfare is described as the minimum threshold principle. This principle states that as it may be impossible to reach consensus on what it means to be a good parent, society instead should agree a minimum threshold below which prospective parents must not fall in order to be given access to reproductive technologies. It is likely that a reasonable consensus could be reached on which circumstances would be considered unacceptable, such as previous criminal convictions for child abuse, serious mental illness, history of drug abuse and perhaps severe marital strife. This standard takes the view that a child should not be brought into the world only if it would have been better for that child never to have been born.

[4.70] A middle ground between these two alternatives may be considered the reasonable welfare principle, which does not aim to ensure that the child is perfectly happy, but is reasonably happy. This principle essentially provides that since no parents are perfect and no person is completely happy, parents may make decisions that might potentially negatively impact upon their children, such as moving house or changing schools. If this principle were to be adopted, the State would generally only be able to interfere in very exceptional circumstances when parental decisions have potentially disastrous consequences for their children. So this test would apply to render AHR

---

[105] Available at www.health.gov.ie.

[106] Available at www.health.gov.ie, page 116.

[107] Golombok, 'New Families, Old Values: Considerations Regarding the Welfare of the Child' (1998) Human Reproduction, Vol 13 No 9: 2342–2347.

acceptable when it is expected that the child conceived as a result of treatment will have a reasonably happy life. This would include having a normal range of opportunities, and the abilities to realise goals which in general make human lives happy. True determining factors for a child's well-being (strong desire for parenthood, warm and supportive relationships) do not coincide with and are not (mainly) determined by the sexual orientation, the number of parents or the genetic relatedness.[108] It is therefore argued that if we are seeking to prioritise the welfare of the child, we should focus on characteristics and conditions which have a proven influence on the well-being and happiness of children, and not on ideologically or religiously based features.[109]

[4.71] In the United Kingdom much is left to the discretion of the centres licensed to perform such procedures. Centres are obliged to have an ethics committee to supervise the treatments and research programmes, and they must comply with the Code of Practice of the Human Fertilisation and Embryology Authority (HFEA).[110] Section 13(5) of the 1990 Act provided that one of the conditions of the licences given to centres was that consideration had to be given by the centre to the welfare of the child who may be born as a result of the treatment, including the child's need for a father.[111] Although this condition could be interpreted as including a social as well as biological father, (that is to say someone in the immediate family circle who will take on the role of father to the child), nevertheless this condition may have made some clinics reluctant to give treatment to single persons and gay couples.

[4.72] Section 13(5) was the subject of much debate[112] as to how a clinician could base a decision as to whether to provide AHR services to a particular person in part by a consideration of the future child's welfare. Since the policy of the law generally is to assume a position that existence is better than non-existence, it was difficult to argue that in given circumstances, a child would not be benefited by being brought into existence. Clinicians do not have access to all the relevant information or the specialist training required to make such decisions and it was argued that it would impose an unfair burden on infertile parents to prove their fitness to parent despite the fact that those who are fertile do not have to pass any such test. There are counter arguments to the effect that there is an inherent difference with AHR where medical intervention is necessary to assist in the creation of new life and such intervention brings with it a

---

[108] Golombok, 'New Families, Old Values: Considerations Regarding the Welfare of the Child' (1998) Human Reproduction, Vol 13 No 9: 2342–2347.

[109] Pennings, 'Measuring the Welfare of the Child: In Search of the Appropriate Evaluation Principle' (1999) Human Reproduction, Vol 14, No 5, 1146–1150.

[110] In *R v Ethical Committee of St. Mary's Hospital: ex parte Harriott* (1987) 137 NLJ Reps 1038 a woman was refused IVF treatment because she had a criminal record for prostitution. Her application for judicial review failed on the basis that this was not a decision to which no reasonable consultant could have come. However, the door to judicial review was left slightly ajar in that Schiemann J indicated that a policy by a centre, for example to refuse treatment on the grounds of colour or religion, might be declared illegal.

[111] Human Fertilisation and Embryology Act 1990 (UK), s 13(5).

[112] See for example, Jackson, 'Conception and the Irrelevance of the Welfare Principle' (2002) 65 Mod Law Rev 176–203.

responsibility towards any future children who may be born. In 2005 the House of Commons Science and Technology Committee strongly criticised s 13(5) as follows:

> The welfare of the child provision discriminates against the infertile and some sections of society, is impossible to implement and is of questionable practical value in protecting the interests of children born as a result of assisted reproduction. …The welfare of the child provision has enabled the HFEA and clinics to make judgments that are more properly made by patients in consultation with their doctor. It should be abolished in its current form. The minimum threshold principle should apply but should specify that this threshold should be the risk of unpreventable and significant harm.[113]

[4.73] The amendment of the HFE Act in 2008 resulted in the replacement of the consideration of the child's 'need for a father', with the need for 'supportive parenting'.[114] The HFEA Code of Practice states that the centre should have documented procedures to ensure that proper account is taken of the welfare of any child who may be born as a result of treatment services, and any other child who may be affected by the birth. It also provides that the centre should assess each patient and their partner (if they have one) before providing any treatment, and should use this assessment to decide whether there is a risk of significant harm or neglect to any child who would be born as a result of treatment services or affected by the birth. The centre is expected to consider the wishes of all those involved, and the assessment must be done in a non-discriminatory way. In particular, patients should not be discriminated against on grounds of gender, race, disability, sexual orientation, religious belief or age.

[4.74] Centres are advised that they should consider factors that are likely to cause a risk of significant harm or neglect to any child who may be born or to any existing child of the family. These factors include any aspects of the patient's or (if they have one) their partner's:

(a) past or current circumstances that may lead to any child mentioned above experiencing serious physical or psychological harm or neglect, for example:

    (i) previous convictions relating to harming children

    (ii) child protection measures taken regarding existing children, or

    (iii) violence or serious discord in the family environment

(b) past or current circumstances that are likely to lead to an inability to care throughout childhood for any child who may be born, or that are already seriously impairing the care of any existing child of the family, for example:

    (i) mental or physical conditions

    (ii) drug or alcohol abuse

    (iii) medical history, where the medical history indicates that any child who may be born is likely to suffer from a serious medical condition, or

    (iv) circumstances that the centre considers likely to cause serious harm to any child mentioned above.

[4.75] When considering a child's need for supportive parenting, the HFEA advises centres to consider the following definition: 'Supportive parenting is a commitment to

---

[113] Human Reproductive Technologies and the Law, Fifth Report (2005) para 107.
[114] Human Fertilisation and Embryology Act 2008, s 14(2).

the health, well-being and development of the child. It is presumed that all prospective parents will be supportive parents, in the absence of any reasonable cause for concern that any child who may be born, or any other child, may be at risk of significant harm or neglect. Where centres have concern as to whether this commitment exists, they may wish to take account of wider family and social networks within which the child will be raised.'[115]

ACCESS TO AHR BY SAME SEX COUPLES, COHABITING COUPLES AND SINGLE PERSONS

[4.76] If legislative provisions were introduced in Ireland similar to those in the HFE Act 2008 discussed above, it is possible that a constitutional challenge could be brought in relation to the provision of AHR services to non-marital families under art 41 of the Constitution. It may be argued that, by obliging clinics to provide assisted reproduction treatments without reference to the marital status of the patients, the State would be failing to 'guard with special care the institution of Marriage, on which the family is founded' under art 41.3.1°. In an Appendix to the Report of the Commission on Assisted Human Reproduction, it is noted that this constitutional duty is imposed only on the State and so would not apply in the context of private clinics or hospitals offering services to non-marital families. The success of a constitutional challenge is doubtful as it would require the acceptance of the argument that a legislative requirement obliging clinics to treat non-marital families amounted to an inducement not to marry. 'It remains to be seen whether the courts would agree that a statutory requirement that AHR services be provided to non-marital families satisfied such a test so as to render the requirement unconstitutional.'[116]

[4.77] In 2015 Ireland voted by referendum to amend the Constitution to permit marriage to be contracted by two persons without distinction as to their sex. The amendment was effected by the Thirty-fourth Amendment of the Constitution (Marriage Equality) Act 2015. One of the interesting features of the marriage equality debate in this context was whether such a change in the law would result in a right to reproduce for gay and lesbian couples who, if the referendum was passed, would have the same rights as a married heterosexual couple. There is no positive right to reproduce for heterosexual couples in Ireland and, even when viewed as a negative right, it is seen as subject to proportionate state intervention where this is necessary to safeguard the public interest. The claim to such a right in the context of access to assisted reproduction has not yet been explored in the Irish courts. If legislation were introduced to facilitate access to AHR services for heterosexual couples only and which therefore sought to discriminate against same-sex married couples, such legislation could be challenged on grounds of discrimination. In the absence of compelling evidence to suggest that the welfare of any children born to same sex couples would be negatively impacted as a consequence of their parenting, such a challenge would be likely to succeed as the State would not be justified in discriminating against same sex couples.

---

[115] HFEA Code of Practice (8th edn) para 8.11.
[116] Available at www.health.gov.ie, page 138.

[4.78] The ECHR might be called into service in aid of single persons who seek access to assisted reproductive technologies and the subsequent recognition of their family as deserving respect under the Convention. In *Kerkhoven, Hinke and Hinke v The Netherlands*[117] two women lived together as a family and shared parental authority over a child born to one of them through use of DI. The Commission refused to recognise this as a legal relationship and to grant parental authority to the mother's partner, despite the existence of the factors on which they had denied the right of an unmarried man to seek paternity rights, namely the existence of a stable relationship, the planned birth of the child and the bond between the child and the person seeking to assert parental authority.[118]

[4.79] In *G v The Netherlands*,[119] the Commission noted that cohabitation is only one of the factors to be taken into account in determining the existence of family life under the Convention. In this case, the applicant had donated sperm to a lesbian couple who were known to him. Subsequent to the birth, and having visited the child and the couple on a number of occasions, the applicant wished to establish regular access to the child, whereupon the couple broke off all contact with the applicant. The judge declared that donation of sperm was, in itself, an insufficient basis for the establishment of parental rights and duties, and for the creation of family life under art 8 of the Convention. Before the Commission, the applicant argued that the latter point had not been adequately or properly considered by the judge, as he did have a biological link to the child and had regular contact with her until the couple broke the arrangement. The Commission considered that the situation in which a man donates sperm only to enable DI to take place, does not give the donor a right of respect for family life with the child. The Commission considered that the contacts between the applicant and the child had been limited both in time and intensity. The applicant had also not considered making any contribution to the child's upbringing.

---

[117] *Hinke and Hinke v The Netherlands* 15666/89, (decision of 19 May 1992).

[118] Other cases in point include the English case in *Re W (a minor) (Homosexual adopter)* [1997] 2 FLR 406; the Irish case of *MacD v L* [2009] IESC 81 (discussed in Ch 5); and the judgment of the E Ct HR in *Schalk and Kopf v Austria* (Application No 30141/04) in which the Court noted that 'there is an emerging European consensus towards legal recognition of same-sex couples. Moreover, this tendency has developed rapidly over the past decade. Nevertheless, there is not yet a majority of States providing for legal recognition of same-sex couples. The area in question must therefore still be regarded as one of evolving rights with no established consensus, where States must also enjoy a margin of appreciation in the timing of the introduction of legislative changes.' However, in *obiter* comments, the Court also went on to recognise that stable relationships of cohabiting same-sex couples fall with the notion of family life: 'The Court notes that 'a rapid evolution of social attitudes towards same-sex couples has taken place in many member States. Since then a considerable number of member States have afforded legal recognition to same-sex couples... Certain provisions of EU law also reflect a growing tendency of include same-sex couples in the notion of 'family' ... In view of this evolution the Court considers it artificial to maintain the view that, in contrast to a different-sex couple, a same-sex couple cannot enjoy 'family life' for the purposes of art 8. Consequently the relationship of the applicants, a cohabiting same-sex couple living in a stable de facto partnership, falls with the notion of 'family life', just as the relationship of a different-sex couple in the same situation would.'

[119] *G v The Netherlands* 16 EHRR CD 38, January 1993 (16944/90).

[4.80] In *X, Y and Z v UK*,[120] the Commission dealt with the recognition, for birth certification purposes, of the legal relationship between a child born through DI and its social father, who was in fact a female-to-male transsexual who had been living in a permanent and stable union with the mother of the child. The inability of the partners to marry also led to the inability to adopt the child, and the status of illegitimacy being conferred on the child, which although of little effect in reality, also meant the inability to register the applicant as father. The Commission considered that whether de facto family ties are deemed sufficient to fall within the scope of family life under the Convention will depend on the circumstances of the case, including the existence of blood ties, cohabitation, the nature of the relationships involved and the demonstrable interest, commitment and dependency between them. The Commission recognised that it had yet to find a case for family life that did not involve a blood link or a legal relationship through marriage or adoption. It noted that on the facts of this case, to all appearances, the applicant was the child's father. It distinguished the *Kerkhoven* case on the basis of the medical condition of a transsexual called gender dysphoria by which the person may receive medical treatment to enable the transsexual to become the gender to which he or she has the conviction of belonging.

[4.81] The Commission was of the opinion that the relationships between the applicants had the appearance and substance of family life. The only factor detracting from this was the fact that the first applicant had been registered at birth as a female, with the consequence that he was unable to marry the child's mother or be registered on the birth certificate as the father. Accordingly:

> The Commission is of the opinion that this element, whether seen as biological or historical cannot outweigh the reality of the applicant's situation which is otherwise undistinguished from the traditional notion of family life. It would note that the UK, in the context of children born by artificial insemination by donor has itself for the purposes of the 1990 Human Fertilisation and Embryology Act accepted that there are circumstances where a 'father' need not be linked to a child either by blood or by marriage to its mother and that it was by virtue of UK law in force that the relationships between the three applicants were created.[121]

[4.82] Consequently, the Commission found that the applicants were entitled to enjoy respect for their family life under art 8 of the Convention. The next issue for the Commission to decide was whether respect for family life implies a positive obligation on the State to change its legal system in respect of transsexuals. The Commission noted that, despite the assertion on behalf of the State that the use of a birth certificate is uncommon in the UK, there were circumstances in which it may be required for official or educational purposes. The inability to have the applicant registered as the child's father may cause trauma and upset to the child and to others. Also, due to the inability of the applicant to be regarded as the father of the child, the child had no rights to participate in the distribution of the applicants' estate on intestacy. The Commission regarded the granting of a residence order in favour of the applicant as insufficient recognition of the parental authority of the applicant.

---

[120] Com Rep of 27 June 1995, unreported (21830/93).
[121] Com Rep of 27 June 1995, unreported (21830/93) at para 58.

[4.83] As a consequence of the lack of respect for the family life of the applicants, the Commission was satisfied that the family unit could suffer a lack of security and value and that the child could be affected in her personal development and sense of identity. The Commission found that there had been a violation of art 8 by the UK which had not been sufficiently outweighed by the public interest. Nor was it within the margin of appreciation afforded to States in situations where the issue was controversial, novel and sensitive. 'Having regard therefore in particular to the welfare of the third applicant and her security within the family unit, the Commission finds that the absence of an appropriate legal regime reflecting the applicant's family ties discloses a failure to respect their family life.'[122]

[4.84] The Court disagreed with the Commission, finding that there had been no violation of art 8.[123] The basis for the Court's decision was the lack of consensus in Europe in relation to parental rights to be granted to transsexuals and the legal relationship between a DI child and its 'social' father. This allowed the UK to have a wide margin of appreciation which it had not breached in the circumstances of the case. Although the Court admitted that de facto family ties did exist between the applicants, the community also had an interest in a coherent system of family law which gave priority to the best interests of the child. The Court felt that the disadvantages which might be sustained by the applicant and the child by the failure to recognise the former as the legal father would not cause undue hardship. Further, it was not certain that the registration of the applicant would benefit this child or DI children in general.[124]

---

[122] Com Rep of 27 June 1995 (21830/93) at para 69.

[123] *X, Y and Z v UK*, judgment of 22 April 1997.

[124] Com Rep of 27 June 1992 (21830/93) at para 37. Court decision is reported at (1997) 24 EHRR 143.

Chapter 5

Artificial Insemination and Egg Donation

INTRODUCTION

[5.01] As outlined in Chapter 4, people who seek fertility treatments generally do so with the hope and intention that they will be able to have a genetically related child of their own. Where the couple can provide the sperm and eggs themselves this does not usually cause legal or ethical difficulties as the medical assistance provided does not alter the genetic parentage of the child. However, issues can arise even where the couple are the providers of the genetic material in circumstances where the use of the material is sought by one member of a couple after the death of the other. This chapter will consider the legal difficulties involved in posthumous reproduction such as those that arise in relation to birth registration and succession rights of the child.

[5.02] Depending on the nature and cause of the fertility difficulties experienced, couples may not be able to have a genetic child of their own and it may be necessary to use genetic material donated by another person or couple. This chapter will also outline the legal and ethical difficulties involved in fertility treatments where the sperm or eggs are donated to the person or couple undergoing treatment. These will focus on issues that arise in relation to the separation of genetic and social parenthood which can lead to lack of clarity around the legal status and parentage of children, and the rights of children to access information about their genetic parents. In Ireland there is no sperm donor facility available so individuals or couples who require donor sperm may import it privately themselves or through the services of an Irish clinic. There is currently no regulation in Ireland of the number of children that may be born from a single donor, whether donors may be paid for their donation or other related issues.[1]

[5.03] Artificial insemination may provide assistance to heterosexual couples in circumstances of male infertility as well as to female same sex couples or single women. The technique used is called Intrauterine Insemination (IUI) which firstly involves a man providing a semen sample, which is then filtered using special techniques. The concentrated sperm is then passed directly into the woman's womb through a thin tube called a catheter, usually at a time of ovulation.[2] Generally the procedure is performed by a medical practitioner, although this is not necessary to its success, with some women

---

[1] These matters are expected to be dealt with in the long-awaited Bill on the Regulation of Assisted Reproduction but only limited details of this are available at the time of writing. www.health.gov.ie/blog/press-release/govt-to-legislate-for-assisted-human-reproduction-associated-research/.

[2] The procedure involved in artificial insemination is not a new technological development, the first reported case occurring in 1799 for AIH and 1884 for DI. See Klayman, 'Therapeutic Impregnation: Prognosis of a Lawyer – Diagnosis of a Legislature' (1970) 39 U Cin L Rev 291.

preferring to self-inseminate in the privacy of their own homes. The sperm may be obtained either from the husband or partner of the woman upon whom the procedure is performed or from a third-party donor (Donor Insemination (DI)). Another technique that may be used in the treatment of male sub-fertility is ICSI (intra-cytoplasmic sperm injection), which enables couples in which the man has a very low sperm count to conceive. This procedure takes a single sperm from a semen sample from the male partner and injects it directly into the cytoplasm of the female egg. If this results in fertilisation, the resulting embryo is then transferred to the uterus of the female partner, where it is hoped that a pregnancy will result. The success of this procedure in recent years has led to a decline in the use of sperm donation for couples where male sub-fertility is identified as the cause of the couple's inability to conceive.

[5.04] Egg donation may be used where a woman is unable to produce eggs of sufficiently good quality to enable her to become pregnant. This may be due to ovarian failure, premature menopause, chemotherapy or other medical treatment affecting fertility. In this procedure a woman (the donor) undergoes ovarian stimulation in order to generate eggs for collection, the eggs are fertilised in the laboratory with the recipient partner's (or donor) sperm, and the resulting embryos are transferred to the recipient. The legal issues are broadly the same in relation to both forms of gamete donation in relation to parentage and access to identifying information about the donor.

ARTIFICIAL INSEMINATION BY HUSBAND OR PARTNER

[5.05] The simplest form of artificial insemination is where the sperm used to inseminate the woman is taken from her husband. There are no major legal and ethical issues where the couple are married and using their own sperm and eggs, as the procedure is seen simply as a method of reproduction which bypasses normal intercourse. However, there are objections from some religions which oppose all forms of reproductive technologies on the grounds that such technologies separate the procreative process from the conjugal act within marriage.[3] In a small number of cases an issue may arise where sperm has been stored on behalf of a couple and the man dies before the sperm is used by his partner. This is considered further below.[4]

---

[3] Vatican's Congregation for the Doctrine of the Faith, *Instruction on Respect for Human Life in its Origin and on the Dignity of Procreation,* (1987), published in English by the Catholic Truth Society. The *Instruction* states: 'Homologous artificial fertilisation, in seeking a procreation which is not the fruit of a specific act of conjugal union, objectively effects an analogous separation between the goods and the meanings of marriage.' Ch II, sect 4 at 27. As Coughlan points out '… [H]omologous artificial insemination is accepted as licit only under stringent conditions, viz, only if it serves to facilitate the conjugal act and is not a substitute therefor, or if it does not involve a dissociation of the unitive and procreative meanings of this act. The last point means, for example, that the obtaining of sperm by masturbation, even for the purposes of homologous artificial fertilisation, is not permissible.' Coughlan, *The Vatican, the Law and the Human Embryo* (Iowa City: University of Iowa Press, 1990) at 5.

[4] Posthumous reproduction is discussed at para **[5.26]** et seq.

Parentage

[5.06] The question of parentage in artificial insemination where the recipient woman is married and the sperm used is that of her husband, is straightforward. Under s 46 of the Status of Children Act 1987 if a woman gives birth to a child during a subsisting marriage or within the period of ten months after the termination by death or otherwise of a marriage to which she is a party, then the husband of the marriage shall be presumed to be the father of the child unless the contrary is proved on the balance of probabilities.[5] Therefore if a child is born to a married woman as a result of artificial insemination in which her husband's sperm is used, her husband will be the father in the same way as if the child had been conceived by natural reproduction.

[5.07] Where the father of the child is *not* married to the mother the presumption of paternity does not apply in the same way. The traditional position in relation to children born outside of marriage in Ireland was that the mother was the sole legal guardian and Irish courts were reluctant to accord natural unmarried fathers any rights in respect of their children. This is evident in *State (Nicolaou) v An Bord Uchtála*[6] where the Supreme Court held that there is a significant difference in moral capacity and social function between mothers and fathers of children born outside of marriage. The facts were that the parents of the child were a couple who had lived together for a time and conceived a child together. The mother of the child decided to give the child up for adoption without informing the father. The father subsequently applied to have the adoption declared invalid on the basis that the Adoption Act 1952 was discriminatory in requiring consent to adoption from the child's mother and not the child's father. The Supreme Court felt that such discrimination was justified on the basis that in most cases of this kind where fathers do not have a relationship with the mother, they do not have any interest in the child born out of that relationship.

[5.08] The position therefore was that an unmarried father of the child could be registered as the father only with the consent of the mother or a court order. However, neither birth registration nor a court order of paternity conferred any automatic guardianship rights on the father. Reform of this position was advocated by academics, family law practitioners, advocacy groups and others for many years on grounds that it is in the best interests of the child to know and enjoy a legal relationship with its father, and also to rectify the discrimination against unmarried fathers.

[5.09] In 1986 the European Court of Human Rights held in *Johnston and Others v Ireland*[7] that an illegitimate child 'should be placed, legally and socially, in a position akin to that of a legitimate child'.[8] The Court considered that Ireland's failure to establish an appropriate legal regime reflecting the illegitimate child's natural ties constituted a violation of art 8.1 of the European Convention on Human Rights (ECHR) which provides that 'everyone has the right to respect for his private and family life, his

---

5   This will not apply if the child is born more than ten months after separation of the couple: s 88 of the Children and Family Relationships Act 2015.
6   *State (Nicolaou) v An Bord Uchtála* [1966] IR 1.
7   *Johnston and Others v Ireland* [1986] ECHR 17, 9697/82, [1986] 9 EHRR 203.
8   *Johnston and Others v Ireland* [1986] ECHR 17, 9697/82, [1986] 9 EHRR 203.

home and his correspondence.' Dissenting judge De Meyer J went further in saying that it was not sufficient to state that the illegitimate child's position should be *akin* to a legitimate child. In his view the Court should have been more unequivocal in stating that 'the legal situation of a child born out of wedlock must be identical to that of a child of a married couple'.[9] However, as is pointed out by Meeusen:[10]

> [B]y its refusal to accept the De Meyer rule, the majority made clear that, in spite of its rejection of the restriction of illegitimate's patrimonial rights on the mere basis of their status, States can adopt certain specific regulations concerning children born out of wedlock. The status of illegitimacy as such is not condemned by the Court.

[5.10] In response to this case, the Status of Children Act was introduced in Ireland in 1987 to abolish the presumption of legitimacy[11] and replace it with a presumption of paternity[12]. However, the Act still did not go far enough in recognising the rights of unmarried fathers in respect of their children, and the rights of children to have access to the identity of their genetic fathers. This is illustrated by *Keegan v Ireland*[13] in which the facts were that the applicant had met his girlfriend in May 1986, and they began living together in February 1987. In February 1988, the woman became pregnant and the couple planned to marry. Shortly afterwards, however, the relationship broke down and they ceased to cohabit. After birth the child was placed for adoption by the mother without the applicant's knowledge or consent. The relevant provisions of the Adoption Act 1952 permitted the adoption of a child born outside marriage without the consent of the natural father. The applicant applied to the Circuit Court, under the Guardianship of Infants Act 1964, to be appointed as the child's guardian, which would have enabled him to challenge the proposed adoption. He was appointed guardian and awarded custody of the child. The decision of the Circuit Court was upheld by the High Court, but on appeal the Supreme Court ruled that the wishes of the natural father should not be considered if the prospective adopters could offer a better quality of welfare for the child. The case was remitted to the High Court. At the rehearing, a consultant psychiatrist gave evidence that if placement with prospective adopters was disturbed after a period of over a year, a child would be likely to suffer trauma and to have difficulty in forming relationships of trust. The High Court therefore declined to appoint the applicant as guardian. An adoption order was subsequently made.

---

9   Opinion of Judge De Meyer, III,1, p 39.
10   Meeusen, 'Judicial Disapproval of Discrimination Against Illegitimate Children – A Comparative Study of Developments in Europe and the United States' (1995) 43 The American Journal of Comparative Law 119 at 141. Meeusen discusses US case law concerning the rights of children born outside of marriage. These cases form the basis of the principle that *substantive* discrimination between children born within marriage and those born outside marriage is unconstitutional, but that *procedural* discrimination may be permitted in certain circumstances. He also examines the cases which have come before the European Court of Human Rights and forms the conclusion that the European Court has formulated a similar principle in rejecting discrimination against the illegitimate child but nonetheless falling short of striking down the concept of illegitimacy per se.
11   Status of Children Act 1987, s 44.
12   Status of Children Act 1987, s 46.
13   *Keegan v Ireland* 18 EHRR 342 1994.

[5.11] On appeal to the European Court of Human Rights, the Court held that the notion of the 'family' in art 8 is not confined solely to marriage-based relationships and may encompass other de facto 'family' ties, where the parties are living together outside marriage. 'A child born out of such a relationship is *ipso facto* part of that family unit from the moment of his or her birth, and by the very fact of it. There thus exists between the child and the parents a bond amounting to family life even if at the time of the child's birth the parents are no longer co-habiting or if their relationship has then ended.' The relationship between the applicant and the child's mother lasted more than two years, during one of which they cohabited. The conception was the result of a deliberate decision, and the couple had planned to get married. The Court held that the relationship between the applicant and the child's mother had the hallmark of family life for the purposes of art 8, and accordingly from the moment of the birth a bond amounting to family life existed between the applicant and the child.

[5.12] As regards the alleged violation of art 8, the Court held that the fact that Irish law permitted the secret placement of the child for adoption without the applicant's knowledge or consent, leading to the bonding of the child with the proposed adopters and to the subsequent making of an adoption order, amounted to an interference with the applicant's right to respect for family life. The decision to place the child for adoption without the father's knowledge or consent, and the decisions taken by the courts concerning the child's welfare, were in accordance with Irish law, and pursued the legitimate aim of protecting the rights and freedoms of the child. However, the interference was not necessary in a democratic society as provided for in art 8.2. The placement of the child shortly after birth not only jeopardised the applicant's ties with the child, but also set in motion a process which was likely to prove irreversible, thereby putting the applicant at a significant disadvantage in his contest with the prospective adopters for the custody of the child. The government had advanced no reasons relevant to the welfare of the child to justify this.

[5.13] The Court also held that the adoption process had to be distinguished from guardianship and custody proceedings. The applicant had no rights under Irish law to challenge the decision to place the child for adoption, and indeed had no standing in the adoption procedure generally. His only recourse to impede the adoption was to bring guardianship and custody proceedings. By the time these proceedings were determined, the scales concerning the child's welfare had tilted inevitably in favour of the prospective adopters. His right to a hearing under art 6(1) of the Convention had accordingly been violated.

[5.14] As a result of this case Ireland became obliged to give natural fathers to whom children are born in the context of family life, as interpreted by the European Court of Human Rights, a legal opportunity to establish a relationship with that child. This was interpreted as requiring a legal entitlement to be consulted before the child is placed for adoption, and also possibly rights of access to the child and joint guardianship or joint custody with the natural mother.

[5.15] The Constitution Review Group in its consideration of the constitutional provisions in relation to the family and the unmarried father recognised the difficulties involved in an extension of the definition of 'family' to those not based on marriage.[14] It

---

[14] Available at www.archive.constitution.ie/reports/crg.pdf.

recommended that the Constitution should retain its pledge to safeguard the institution of marriage but that the legislature should not thereby be prohibited from legislating for families not based on marriage. It stated that this might entail a recognition of the de facto family, consistent with the European jurisprudence:

> There has been much criticism of the continued constitutional ostracism of natural fathers. This can be readily understood in relation to those natural fathers who either live in a stable relationship with the natural mother, or have established a relationship with the child. However, there does not appear to be justification for giving constitutional rights to every natural father simply by reason of biological links and thus include fatherhood resulting from rape, incest or sperm donorship.[15]

[5.16] The Review Group considered that the solution lay in following the approach of art 8 of the ECHR in guaranteeing to every person respect for 'family life', which has been interpreted to include non-marital family life but yet requiring the existence of family ties between the mother and the father:

> This may be a way of granting constitutional rights to those fathers who have, or had, a stable relationship with the mother prior to birth, or subsequent to birth with the child, while excluding persons from having such rights who are only biological fathers without any such relationship.[16]

[5.17] In *WO'R v EH & An Bord Uchtála*,[17] the Supreme Court considered the alteration of the relationship between two children and their unmarried father, through the marriage of their mother to another man. The natural father wished to be appointed guardian to the children, with whom he had a relationship through having lived together as a family for a number of years, and thereafter through liberal access arrangements by agreement. The new husband wished to formalise his relationship with his wife's children through adoption, which the natural father would have been opposed to.

[5.18] The Court considered the right of the natural father in this case to be a right to apply for guardianship under the 1987 Act, rather than a right to be appointed guardian. Hamilton CJ accepted a statement made in *JK v VW*, by Finlay CJ in which he stated that 'no constitutional right to guardianship in the father exists.[18] However, he did accept that there may be circumstances in which it may be in the interests of the child's welfare to enjoy the 'society, protection and guardianship of its father'.[19] The Court felt that in circumstances where the child had been born into a stable relationship and had been cared for initially by both parents, the rights of the natural father would be very extensive. However, the Court also had to take into account the interests of the children in this case in the context of the proposed adoption by their mother's husband, particularly when the parties agreed that such an order would not alter the existing arrangements with regard to access to the children.

[5.19] Interestingly, Murphy J, in obiter comments, broached the subject of sperm donors and egg donors in his judgment. He considered that biological fathers, in

---

[15] Available at www.archive.constitution.ie/reports/crg.pdf.
[16] Available at www.archive.constitution.ie/reports/crg.pdf.
[17] *WO'R v EH & An Bord Uchtála* (23 July 1996) SC.
[18] *JK v VW* [1990] 2 IR 437.
[19] *WO'R v EH & An Bord Uchtála* (23 July 1996) SC at 32.

circumstances of sperm donation, would not have any natural or constitutional parental rights, along the same lines as the decision in *Nicolaou*, mentioned above:

> In more recent times one has to recognise a category of biological parenthood within which the male contributes sperm which is provided by means of artificial insemination in a female recipient unknown to the donor. This must be the case by which can be tested the basic proposition whether the mere donation of sperm confers on the donor any natural or constitutional right over the child that may subsequently be identified as having been conceived as a result of such a procedure. In my view that cold and clinical scenario would do much to strengthen the view expressed in the *Nicolaou* case that the mere fact of fatherhood does not give rise to natural; or constitutional rights.[20]

[5.20] Although Murphy J recognised that social and moral attitudes towards children outside marriage had changed significantly in the intervening period since that case, he nevertheless appeared to endorse that decision. Sperm donation was an issue far removed from the facts of the case before the court which involved a relatively long-term relationship with the mother and children, regular access to the children and emotional and financial support being given. It was presumed by Murphy J, without very much analysis, that the fact of mere biological parentage would not entitle the father to any parental rights whatsoever.[21]

[5.21] Barrington J also felt that a blood tie was insufficient to give parental rights to the father. However, he criticised the *Nicolaou* case on the basis that the reasoning in the case was fundamentally flawed and inadequate. He was of the view that in circumstances such as those before the Court, a denial of the relationship between the parent and the child may be a cruel injustice[22] and that a dispute between unmarried parents in such cases should be decided on the same basis as if they were married parents.

[5.22] More recently in *McD v L & Another*,[23] a gay man who had donated sperm to a lesbian couple sought the right to be appointed legal guardian of the child and access to the child. Hedigan J held that the lesbian couple and the child constituted a de facto family and that there was nothing in Irish law to suggest that a family of two women and a child had any lesser right to be recognised than a de facto family comprised of a man and woman unmarried to each other and a child. However, he dismissed the application for guardianship on the basis that it was not in the best interests of the child due in part to the difficult relationship between the man and the couple, particularly the birth mother of the child. The case was appealed to the Supreme Court which held that the man was entitled to access to the child but not guardianship at the present time. The

---

20. *WO'R v EH & An Bord Uchtála* (23 July 1996) SC, per Murphy J.
21. Murphy J also went on to raise the issue of motherhood in the context of gestational surrogacy and asked, 'Who is the mother for the purposes of art 40 of the Constitution? The woman who provided the ovum or the woman who gave birth to the child? These very questions illustrate the fundamental distinction between the line which may have to be drawn between the provision of the genetic material on which life depends and the nurturing of the being not merely from the time of birth but from the moment of conception.' These issues are discussed in Chapter 7 in the context of surrogacy.
22. *WO'R v EH & An Bord Uchtála* (23 July 1996) SC at 37, 38.
23. *McD v L & Another* [2009] IESC 81.

issue of the recognition of the de facto family in the context of art 8 of the ECHR was also discussed. The Supreme Court held that the High Court had no jurisdiction to apply directly the provisions of the Convention to the lesbian couple and the child. Denham J stated that there is no institution in Ireland of a de facto family and that the family in Ireland is defined as that based on marriage. She held that the man had rights as a natural father to apply to be appointed guardian and the Court had to consider such an application using the best interests of the child as its paramount consideration.

[5.23] The case failed to avail of the opportunity to extend the rights of natural fathers in line with even the most conservative decisions of the European Court of Human Rights. The dismissal of the concept of the de facto family as not being within the framework of the Constitution despite the recognition of such families by the European Court, is arguably out of step with societal changes since the days of *Nicolaou,* changes in the legal status of children born outside of marriage, the introduction of divorce to recognise the increase in breakdown of the traditional constitutional family unit and the importance attached by modern commentators to the actuality of family care and support irrespective of legal marital ties. The Law Reform Commission subsequently published a report on Legal Aspects of Family Relationships which recommended that legislation be enacted to provide for automatic joint parental responsibility (guardianship) of both the mother and the father of any child.[24]

[5.24] In 2015 the Children and Family Relationships Act introduced a number of reforms in this context by providing for automatic legal guardianship for unmarried fathers in certain circumstances. A man who is not married to the mother of his child may now acquire guardianship rights in three ways.

i.   The father and mother can complete and sign a statutory declaration for joint guardianship in the presence of a Peace Commissioner or a Commissioner for Oaths.[25] This form declares that the parents have not married each other, they are the parents of the child and they agree to the appointment of the father as a guardian.

ii.   Section 49 of the 2015 Act amends s 6 of the Guardianship of Infants Act 1964 by providing that a father who is living with the mother continuously for 12 months, and at least three of these months are after the birth of the child, will automatically be the guardian of his child.[26]

iii. The father can apply to the local district court to become a joint guardian of his child, whether or not his name is on his child's birth certificate. The court will consider such an application in light of the best interests of the child.

[5.25] Although some welcome progress has therefore been made in relation to the position of fathers of children born outside of marriage, the legal position does not provide automatic guardianship to such fathers in all circumstances. Eligibility for

---

[24] Law Reform Commission, Legal Aspects of Family Relationships, LRC 101–2010 para 2.12.

[25] SI 5/1998.

[26] The cohabitation period can only be calculated going forward from the commencement date of the relevant section of the Children and Family Relationships Act 2015 which was 18 January 2016. This means that guardianship will only be acquired automatically where the parents live together for at least 12 months after 18 January 2016.

guardianship remains contingent on satisfying the statutory conditions outlined above. These provisions would apply whether the child is conceived naturally or using artificial insemination as long as the sperm that is used for the procedure is that of the woman's partner. Separate provisions were introduced in the 2015 Act to deal with donor insemination and these provisions are discussed below.[27]

Posthumous reproduction

[5.26] Although the legal issues involved in artificial insemination of a woman using her husband's sperm are usually straightforward, as outlined above, problems may arise in situations where a widow wishes to use her husband's sperm after his death. The development of cryopreservation (the technology of freezing used to preserve gametes and embryos) has created the potential for posthumous reproduction after death.[28] It has become increasingly common for men to store sperm in advance of chemotherapy treatment,[29] or for soldiers and athletes to store sperm for potential use by their wife or partner in the event of their injury or death. Sperm harvesting, the process by which sperm is extracted following a man's death, has also been the subject of a number of requests from spouses or partners of men who have been hospitalised following road traffic accidents and other catastrophic events.

[5.27] More infrequently, requests have been made by surviving partners or parents for retrieval or use of oocytes or eggs from women who have been hospitalised and later died following accidents or sudden brain injuries and other illnesses.[30] In these cases courts are often asked to determine whether valid consent had been given by the deceased person to the retrieval, storage and use of their gametes after death. A recent

---

[27] Para **[5.58]** et seq.

[28] It is estimated that hundreds of thousands of cryopreserved embryos exist in the United States and the number is climbing as the practice of American soldiers storing their sperm increases, as the practice of harvesting sperm from newly deceased spouses becomes more common and as the technology of cryopreserving ova advances. See The President's Council on Bioethics, *Reproduction and Responsibility: The Regulation of New Biotechnologies* (March 2004), chapter 2, page 17.
www.bioethics.georgetown.edu/pcbe/reports/reproductionandresponsibility/index.html

[29] Deterioration of sperm quality occurs as a result of the damaging effect of chemotherapy. This may be permanent or temporary. Men with cancer diagnoses are now often offered the opportunity to freeze semen samples for possible future use. Knowledge that their fertility potential is secured may also help in the emotional battle against the cancer. See Lass, 'Cancer Patients Should Be Offered Semen Cryopreservation' (1999) 318 British Medical Journal 1556. This facility is available in Ireland, for example see www.rotundaivf.ie/the-journey-through-ivf-treatment/fertility-preservation-for-cancer-patients/.

[30] For example, see case report in the New England Journal of Medicine 15 July 2010. 'Case 21–2010 A request for retrieval of oocytes from a 36-year-old woman with anoxic brain injury' NEJM Vol 363: 276–283 Number 3. The case involved a married woman who had a cardiac arrest after a massive pulmonary embolism resulting from venous thrombosis that occurred while she slept in a sitting position on a long airplane flight. Her husband and parents wished to have her oocytes retrieved (which could then be fertilised with the husband's sperm and carried by a surrogate mother on behalf of the husband) but there was no clear evidence of the patient's own wishes. The request was refused.

example is the English case *R (IM and MM) v HFEA*[31] where the parents of a single 28 year old woman (AM) who had stored her eggs prior to treatment for cancer and later died, sought permission to export her frozen eggs to the United States for fertilisation by donor sperm and embryo transfer to AM's mother. Under the Human Fertilisation and Embryology Act 2008, posthumous reproduction is permitted only if 'effective consent' had been given by the deceased person. The HFEA has discretion to waive the legal requirements that consent must be signed and made in writing when agreeing to the export of gametes for use in treatment abroad, but it can only do so in a way that does not circumvent that legislation. Ouseley J held that the HFEA had correctly refused permission on the basis that AM had not given effective consent. He said:

> There was no evidence that [AM] had ever contemplated or consented to the export of her eggs, or to a sperm donor or overseas sperm donor or one selected by her parents, or had thought through and consented to the implications of foreign law governing the ability of the child to establish the identity of the father and to make contact. There was no evidence that AM had ever discussed the question of donor sperm with anyone. There was no evidence that she understood the implications for her mother's health or the legal implications of her mother acting as surrogate, namely that her mother would be the legal mother of her daughter's child.

[5.28] This case was successfully appealed to the Court of Appeal[32] which held, per Arden J, that the decision of the HFEA (through its Statutory Appeals Committee) was flawed. The court held that although AM had not completed additional written consent forms explaining the terms of her initial consent, all available evidence indicated that she wanted the eggs to be used by her mother after her death, and there was no evidence that she wanted the eggs to be allowed to perish. The Court of Appeal said that it was unreasonable to expect AM to have considered the prospect of export (which she could not have anticipated) or to have set out in detail matters which she had reasonably left to her parents to decide (such as the choice of sperm donor, and the potential risks to her mother in carrying a pregnancy). The court held that the Committee had not properly considered whether AM had given effective consent to the use of her eggs after her death. The Court therefore remitted the decision back to the Committee for further consideration of the appellants' export application.

[5.29] In Ireland there is currently no legislation in relation to posthumous reproduction. Some clinics require couples seeking treatment to sign a consent form which stipulates that if the man dies the sperm will be thawed without transfer. However, in the absence of legislation, it is unclear whether such a provision would be upheld by a court faced with a testamentary provision to the opposite effect and a claim by a widow to have constitutional rights to inherit under her husband's will. As such a case has not yet arisen in Ireland, the legal status of a child born in such circumstances is also uncertain. The court may take the view that the deceased man had ownership rights in relation to his body and its tissue and that therefore he was entitled to bequeath it to his partner. Alternatively, the court could decide that this issue should not be decided on property grounds and should instead be decided on the basis of autonomy and the proven intent of the deceased to become a father after his death. The issue of property rights in the

---

[31]   *R (IM and MM) v HFEA* [2015] EWHC 1706 (Admin).
[32]   *R (IM and MM) v HFEA* [2016] EWCA Civ 611.

human body generally, and specifically in relation to gametes, is considered in detail in Chapter 13.

Parentage issues in posthumous reproduction

[5.30] Under s 46 of the Status of Children Act 1987, where a woman gives birth to a child either during a subsisting marriage or within the period of ten months after the termination by death or otherwise of a marriage to which she is a party, the husband of the marriage shall be presumed to be the father of the child. Therefore if a child is born to a widow within ten months of the death of the child's father, the deceased man will be presumed to be the father of the child. The issue becomes more complicated in cases of assisted reproduction, as children can be born years after the death of the parent and may therefore fall outside of the legislative provisions.

[5.31] Regulation of posthumous reproduction is varied and inconsistent around the world. For example, in the United States, the Uniform Law Commission (ULC)[33] published the Uniform Parentage Act in 2002 which provides that 'if an individual who consented in a record to be a parent by assisted reproduction dies before placement of eggs, sperm, or embryos, the deceased individual is not a parent of the resulting child unless the deceased spouse consented in a record that if assisted reproduction were to occur after death, the deceased individual would be a parent of the child.'[34] This means that, in the absence of a written record to the contrary, the deceased man would not be regarded as the father of a child conceived after his death. This provision is designed primarily to avoid the problems of intestate succession which could arise if the posthumous use of a person's genetic material leads to the deceased being determined to be a parent. An individual who wants to explicitly provide for such children in his or her will may do so by expressly providing for this in a written record to that effect. However, the legislation has thus far been enacted in only a small number of states. Although welcome in providing some clarity in relation to posthumous reproduction, it would preclude a finding of parentage in cases where a man who has never executed such a record dies an untimely death, is relatively young, leaves a spouse, and post-death retrieval of his sperm is possible.[35]

[5.32] Courts in the United States have considered the issue of parental recognition and inheritance in a number of cases dealing with social security and pension entitlements. In 1993, the absence of express statutory provision dealing with the status of a child born to a widow was considered in the context of a social security claim in Louisiana. The circumstances of this case, *Hart v Charter*,[36] were that Mr Hart had deposited sperm in a sperm bank prior to undergoing chemotherapy for a tumour which led to his death a

---

[33] The ULC is also known as the National Conference of Commissioners on Uniform State Laws. It promotes the principle of uniformity by drafting and proposing specific statutes in areas of the law where uniformity between US states is desirable. Although the ULC can only propose new laws and no uniform law is effective until a state legislature adopts it, it is nonetheless influential in raising issues which could benefit from a uniform legal position, researching, drafting and subsequently promoting the enactment of uniform state laws.

[34] Section 707 Uniform Parentage Act 2002 available at www.uniformlaws.org/.

[35] Kindregan, 'Posthumous Reproduction' (2005). *Suffolk University Law School Faculty Publications.* Paper 24 at 10

[36] *Hart v Charter* no 04–3944 (ED La Dismissed 18 March 1996).

short time later. Before undergoing surgery to remove the tumour, Mr Hart told his wife that he wanted her to carry out their plans to have a child even if he should die. Three months after his death, his widow became pregnant using the stored sperm and gave birth to a baby girl in June 1991, 355 days after her husband's death. Mrs Hart applied for social security Survivor's Benefit for her daughter but this was denied on the basis that Mr Hart was not the child's father. Counsel argued that excluding the child from entitlement to obtain benefits was unconstitutional. The Social Security Administration declined to defend against that argument and agreed to pay benefits.

[5.33] A further issue arises in relation to inheritance rights on behalf of the children conceived after the death of their father. 'Given the advances in cryopreservation and the ability to conserve gametes for many years, states must consider enacting legislation in order to safeguard the orderly administration of estates disrupted by claims from posthumously conceived children. A balance must be struck between the child's right to inherit, on the one hand, and the state's interest in the orderly administration of estates on the other, as well as the interests of prior born children.'[37] This is further considered later.

[5.34] In *Estate of Kolacy*,[38] a New Jersey court decided that twins born eighteen months after the death of their father were his legal heirs. The Court took the view that posthumously conceived children should be able to inherit as long as there is evidence of consent from the deceased and unless doing so would unfairly intrude on the rights of other heirs or seriously disrupt the orderly administration of the deceased's estate. Similarly, in *Woodward v Commissioner of Social Security*,[39] a Massachusetts court addressed the question of whether twins conceived from frozen sperm and born two years after the father's death from leukaemia had specific inheritance rights under state law and were consequently eligible for certain federal survivor benefits. After the Social Security Administration (SSA) denied benefits to Mrs Woodward's daughters on the grounds that 'she had not established that the twins were the husband's 'children' within the meaning of the US Social Security Act,' Mrs Woodward brought suit in federal court against the agency. In this case, eligibility for SSA benefits turned on whether the children would be treated as the husband's natural children for the disposition of his personal property under the Massachusetts law of intestate succession. The Supreme Judicial Court ruled that under limited circumstances, posthumously conceived children do have inheritance rights under state intestacy laws if two conditions are met. First, the child's surviving parent or legal representative must establish a genetic relationship between the child and the deceased. Second, the parent or representative must demonstrate that the deceased 'affirmatively consented' to posthumous conception and the support of any resulting child.

[5.35] The *Woodward* Court noted that no American court of last resort had previously considered the question of posthumously conceived genetic children's inheritance rights under other states' intestacy laws. The Court considered three important issues in its decision. First, under the 'best interests of the child' consideration, the Court concluded

---

[37] Kindregan, 'Posthumous Reproduction' (2005). *Suffolk University Law School Faculty Publications*. Paper 24 at 14.

[38] *In re Estate of Kolacy* 753 A 2d 1257 (NJ Super Ct Ch Div 2000).

[39] *Woodward v Commissioner of Social Security*, 435 Mass 536 (2002).

that posthumously conceived children should be, as far as possible, entitled to the same legal rights and protections as children conceived before death. The Court provided a number of factors supporting this conclusion, including the fact that the legislature had expressed its will that all children be entitled to the same legal rights and protections 'regardless of the accidents of their birth' and that intestacy statute provisions had been regularly amended to expand the class of non-marital children eligible to succeed from an intestate estate. It also pointed to the fact that some reproductive technologies, such as sperm preservation, had been performed for a number of years, and in that time the legislature had not acted to preclude posthumously conceived children from inheriting on intestacy.

[5.36] In relation to the need for efficient administration of estates, the Court considered a second important legislative purpose of providing certainty to heirs by effecting the prompt and accurate administration of intestate estates. The Court noted that two issues are critical to these goals, certainty of relationship between the deceased and his 'issue', and limitation periods for the commencement of claims against the estate. The Court addressed the first issue in its requirement of proof of genetic relationship (seen as particularly necessary in light of the possibility of different 'legal' and 'genetic' parentage), and noted that while the second issue of time limitation was highly relevant, it was outside the scope of the facts of this particular case.

[5.37] Finally, the Court considered a third important state interest in honouring the reproductive choices of individuals. The Court found that consent by the deceased to posthumous reproduction as well as to the support of the children was necessary to satisfy the goal of fraud prevention. The Court provided a number of reasons supporting this requirement, including that an individual has a protected right to control the use of his or her gametes, silence should not be construed as consent and that gametes are preserved for a variety of reasons beyond posthumous reproduction. Accordingly, the Court stated, 'where conception results from a third-party medical procedure using a deceased person's gametes, it is entirely consistent with our laws on children, parentage, and reproductive freedom to place the burden on the surviving parent ... to demonstrate the genetic relationship of the child to the decedent and that the decedent consented to reproduce posthumously and to support any resulting child.'

[5.38] In a similar case in Arizona, *Gillett-Netting v Barnhart*,[40] the mother of twins conceived 10 months after their father's death claimed social security survivor benefits. The children had been conceived using sperm their father stored before undergoing chemotherapy treatment for cancer. The Court noted that parentage was not in dispute, as the children were unquestionably the biological children of the deceased and they were therefore deemed dependent under the wording of the Social Security Act.

[5.39] The US case law discussed above thus shows inconsistency on the issue of eligibility for social security benefits in cases of posthumous conception with some courts ruling in favour of granting benefits and others denying benefits. The US Supreme Court has now settled this uncertainty to some extent in *Astrue v Capato*[41] where it was held that a child conceived and born after a parent's death cannot rely

---

[40] *Gillett-Netting v Barnhart* 371 F 3d 593 (9th Cir, Ariz 2004).
[41] *Astrue v Capato* 566 US ___ (2012).

solely on a genetic connection to the deceased parent in order to qualify for Social Security dependent's benefits. The Court held that all children, including those born via assisted reproduction technology, must either demonstrate that they would be eligible to inherit from their late parent under state law or satisfy one of the statutory alternatives to that requirement. The court felt that this interpretation was more consistent with the core purpose of the Act, which is to protect family members who depend on another family member's income from hardship if that family member dies.

[5.40] In the United Kingdom under the Human Fertilisation and Embryology Act 1990, the posthumous use of gametes was not prohibited once effective consent has been provided by the deceased person. However, the child was not recognised as the child of the deceased. Section 28(6)(b) of the 1990 Act provided that where 'the sperm of a man, or any embryo the creation of which was brought about with his sperm, was used after his death, he is not to be treated as the father of the child.' This provision was inserted according to the recommendations of the Warnock report, to ensure that estates could be administered with some degree of finality and to actively discourage such practices in effect. This was apparently due to the feared potential psychological problems which could ensue for a child and its mother as a result of such procedures.

> The instrument which is used is that of punishing the child for what are seen as 'the sins of its mother.' This is an odd, not to say indefensible, way of proceeding ... It seems inconsistent with the general legislative mood of recent years which has sought to minimise or mitigate the differential statuses of children (and the adults they will become) based solely on the conduct of their parents.

[5.41] The 1990 Act was amended in 2008. Section 39(1) of the 2008 Act provides that:

- if a child has been carried by a woman as a result of the placing in her of an embryo or of sperm and eggs or her artificial insemination after the death of the man, and
- the man consented in writing to the use of his sperm after his death, and
- to being treated for the purpose mentioned in subsection (3) as the father of any resulting child, and
- the woman has elected in writing not later than 42 days from the day on which the child was born for the man to be as the father of the child, and
- no-one else is to be treated as the father of the child,
- then the man is to be treated for the purpose mentioned in subsection (3) as the father of the child.

Subsection (3) states that the purpose referred to in subsection (1) is that of enabling the man's particulars to be entered as the particulars of the child's father in a relevant register of births. This means that posthumous conception using the sperm of a deceased man is dependent upon his written consent (as was the case under the 1990 Act). This consent must also confirm the man's intent to be considered as the father of the child for birth registration purposes. These provisions confer parenthood for birth registration purposes only.

Succession rights of posthumously conceived children

[5.42] In relation to succession rights of children conceived after the death of their biological parent, there are two main approaches that may be taken to the resolution of the difficulties posed by inheritance provisions and the administration of estates in the case of posthumously conceived children. Firstly, the law might allow the child to be registered as having a father for administration purposes, for example birth certification, but simply prohibit succession to his estate. Secondly, it might allow the child to inherit only if he or she was born within a stipulated time period after the death of the deceased man. The most commonly suggested time period within which such a child might be eligible is birth within two years of the deceased's death. This time period is taken as reflecting the usual time period within which estates are settled and within which the child might retain a sense of connection to the parent. A longer period might interfere with the administration of the estate while a shorter period might interfere with procreative liberty.[42]

[5.43] This balancing of procreative liberty against an adminstratively workable fixed time period results in an admittedly arbitrary time frame, as it may very easily take longer than two years to conceive and give birth to a child in these circumstances but it seems to offer the best compromise. It offers recognition to procreational autonomy of the individual and legal connection between the child and its father with the attendant financial responsibilities which this entails, while at the same time respecting the right of the State and other interested parties to a relatively normal administration period for the settlement of the estate for the deceased.

[5.44] In the Australian case, *Estate of K*, in 1996[43] the deceased, who died intestate, was survived by a wife, four children and two frozen embryos. His widow wished to have the embryos implanted in her. The question for the administrator of the estate, and ultimately the Court, was whether the frozen embryos were issue of the deceased so as to give them inheritance rights in relation to the estate. Slicer J decided that, once born, the frozen embryo could be regarded as the child of the deceased in the same way as the common law had done for children *en ventre sa mere* born within a defined time of the deceased father's death. He saw no logical distinction between the in vitro child born posthumously who was at birth the biological child of the father and mother, irrespective of the time of implantation, and the child *en ventre sa mere* who had a contingent interest dependent on birth.

[5.45] The conclusion reached in this case has been criticised on the basis that, as a matter of law, the deceased could not be the father of the child, as the legislation in question applies the presumption of paternity to married women only.[44] The death of the child's father terminates the marriage and therefore when the implantation occurs, she is not a married woman and does not come within the terms of the legislation. However, it could be argued that it is the provision of the semen rather than the embryo implantation which is the relevant time to consider the question of paternity. At the time of the

---

[42] Chester, 'Freezing the Heir Apparent: A Dialogue on Postmortem Conception, Parental Responsibility and Inheritance' (1996) 33 HLR 967, 995–996.

[43] *Estate of K* [1996] 5 Tas R 365. For further discussion see Chalmers, 'Frozen Embryos: Rights of Inheritance. *In Re the Estate of the late K*' [1997] Med L Rev 121.

[44] Atherton, 'En Ventre sa Frigidaire: Posthumous Children in the Succession Context' (1999) 19(2) Legal Studies 139–164 at 159.

provision of the semen used to create the embryo, the marriage was still in subsistence and therefore the statutory presumption of paternity should apply.[45]

[5.46] These cases indicate that the issues raised by reproductive technology are 'neither academic nor avoidable'.[46] The social context in which decisions may be made in relation to the child's status must also be considered:

> If a child is born to a man's widow which is genetically his child – and he was a willing participant in the process – then it should be considered his child if indeed the child is born alive. *Not* to reach such a conclusion is historically regressive: placing the children back in the era of bastards, with all their disabilities, if not necessarily the same social stigmas.[47]

[5.47] Consent is not the only consideration to be taken into account here – the best interests of the future child must also be a significant factor in determination of this issue.[48] The European Society of Human Reproduction and Embryology (ESHRE) acknowledges that there is no consensus among the different religions on posthumous conception and that there are different ethical considerations to be taken into account.[49] These include the principle of respect for the autonomy of the individual to decide about reproduction, and the principle of beneficence or concern for the welfare of the future child. No research has been conducted to study the consequences for the child who has been conceived posthumously and it is speculated that a number of factors may be influential here, including being raised in a one-parent family and possible stigmatisation, although there is no empirical evidence about serious harmful effects on the child. On the positive side, the child will have knowledge of its genetic parentage and will see its conception as a story of a much-desired gift from a loving relationship. ESHRE advises an evaluation of the surviving parent's motives and expectations, as there is a danger for the autonomy of the child if the parent sees the child as a commemoration or symbolic replacement of the deceased partner. The society also

---

[45]   See also the recent Australian case of *Ping Yuan v Da Yong Chen* [2015] NSWSC 932 (14 July 2015) in which a woman successfully applied for an order allowing doctors to extract sperm from her husband shortly before his death on the basis that the extraction fell within the meaning of 'treatment' for the purposes of s 40 of the Guardianship Act 1987. This provision enables a person who is responsible for a patient who lacks capacity to give consent for medical treatment of that person. The word 'treatment' is not statutorily defined and the court said it was not always limited to cures for disorders. The court held that it was appropriate to declare that the medical practitioners of the relevant fertility clinic could lawfully act upon the consent of the plaintiff, as the person responsible for the patient, with respect to carrying out the extraction and storage of semen. A declaration was made accordingly and communicated to the medical practitioners concerned. Further use of the semen is dependent upon the clinic being satisfied that the deceased had consented, specifically to the use of the gamete after his death within the terms of s 23(a) of the Assisted Reproduction Technology Act 2007.

[46]   Atherton, 'En Ventre sa Frigidaire: Posthumous Children in the Succession Context' (1999) 19(2) Legal Studies 139–164 p 159.

[47]   Atherton at 159.

[48]   Jones and Gillett, 'Posthumous Reproduction: Consent and Its Limitations' (2008) J Med Law Oct 16(2): 279–87.

[49]   ESHRE Task Force on Ethics and Law 11: Posthumous Assisted Reproduction (2006) Human Reproduction Vol 21, No 12 pp 3050–3053.

recommends written consent from the deceased and a minimum waiting period of one year after death before treatment should be commenced.

Posthumous reproduction in Ireland

[5.48] It remains to be seen what approach the Irish legislature or judiciary will take to this complex area. In the draft Children and Family Relationships Bill it was provided that consent from a deceased person would not be valid for the purposes of assisted reproduction. This would have precluded the use of sperm from a deceased man by his widow. However, this provision was not contained in the final version of the Bill as enacted in 2015, and the Act is now silent on the matter of posthumous reproduction. At the time of writing, the Department of Health has indicated that it plans to introduce legislation to regulate assisted reproduction, and as part of that legislation it will deal with the issue of posthumous reproduction. It is expected that use of stored sperm, eggs or embryos after a person's death by their spouse or civil partner will be permitted if that person gave their consent for such a use prior to their death.[50]

[5.49] In the absence of legislation an Irish court could be asked to decide on the validity of a testamentary disposition of gametes, most usually sperm, to the deceased's partner. Arguments could be made that respect for reproductive autonomy demands that the deceased man's wishes in relation to the posthumous use of his sperm be observed but this may cause problems for the law. The two main difficulties in Ireland, as elsewhere, relate to the status of the child and his/her inheritance rights to the estate of his/her parent. The status of a child born through the posthumous use of sperm is uncertain in Ireland, even where the woman who wishes to use the sperm is the widow of the deceased and his intent to reproduce in this way in clearly evident from a will or other legal document. The marriage of the parties is no longer in existence due to the husband's death and, therefore, in essence the child is born to a single parent and will be a non-marital child. This is curious, as the intent to reproduce is clear and the sperm was donated at a time when the parties were legally married. Perhaps it is due to the focus on the child's right to inherit from its father's estate which at common law was dependent on the child's legitimate status. However, in Ireland, due to the Status of Children Act 1987, distinctions between children on the basis of the marital status of their parents are no longer valid for succession purposes.

[5.50] The difficulty here, however, is that the child would not be recognised as a child of its deceased 'father' at all and would therefore be regarded as legally fatherless rather than simply a non-marital child. This would effectively prohibit the child's inheritance rights and claims to succession. In such circumstances where the child's genetic parentage is clear, it is inconsistent with the best interests of the child. This classification, if used at all, should be reserved for situations in which paternity is unknown or unclear, such as in situations where a single woman gives birth to a child through donor insemination. The problem is a reflection of the common law position under which a child would only be regarded as legitimate if born within the usual period

---

[50] See Department of Health press release (2015) www.health.gov.ie/blog/press-release/govt-to-legislate-for-assisted-human-reproduction-associated-research/.

of gestation (child *en ventre sa mere*) after its married father's death.[51] In this way the court could be satisfied that conception took place within the legitimate bounds of a valid marriage.

[5.51] A further consideration in this context is whether, even if the use of sperm posthumously was considered to be unlawful in Ireland, due, for example, to the absence of written consent, an application to export the sperm to another jurisdiction for lawful use there would be successful. In the English case of *R v Human Fertilisation and Embryology Authority (ex parte Blood)*[52] sperm samples had been extracted from Mr Blood, who was in a coma, at the request of his wife. After his death she applied for permission to use the sperm to become pregnant but permission was refused on the grounds that Mr Blood had not given written consent under the provisions of the then Human Fertilisation and Embryology Act 1990. Mrs Blood sought judicial review of this decision and also of the refusal of a request to allow her to export the sperm to another European country for treatment there.

[5.52] In relation to storage and use in the United Kingdom, the Court held that the Act was clear that no storage of gametes could lawfully take place without written consent. Therefore, the storage of Mr Blood's sperm was prohibited in the absence of written consent and the Authority had no discretion to authorise treatment in the UK. In relation to the issue of export of the sperm, the Court of Appeal held that the decision of the HFEA had been made without due consideration having been taken of the cross-border rights to which Mrs Blood was entitled to under EC law.[53] Although the HFEA was entitled under the EC Treaty to restrict the export of sperm on grounds of public policy, the court was not satisfied that the public interest was served by refusing Mrs Blood's application. The court remitted the decision for re-consideration by the HFEA which subsequently granted Mrs Blood's application.[54]

[5.53] Despite the court in the *Blood* case indicating that this case was a one-off which would not be likely to be repeated, similar facts arose in the later case of *L v Human Fertilisation and Embryology Authority*.[55] In this case H had died suddenly following surgery and an urgent application was made by his widow, L, to authorise the removal of sperm from his body. The application was granted by the court in error on the basis of a misunderstanding that the English Human Tissue Act 2004 allowed posthumous sperm retrieval if the consent of a qualifying relative was obtained. In fact the 2004 Act does not apply to gametes. As H had not given written consent, his sperm could not be used in the UK so L applied for the sperm to be exported. The evidence before the court was that the couple already had a child together and were anxious to have another. Charles J held that although the sperm could not lawfully be used in the UK, the HFEA had a wide discretion to allow export. Taking into account the judgment in the *Blood* case and the

---

51 The Succession Act 1965, s 3(2) provides 'Descendants and relatives of a deceased person begotten before his death but born alive thereafter shall, for the purposes of this Act, be regarded as having been born in the lifetime of the deceased and as having survived him'.

52 *R v Human Fertilisation and Embryology Authority (ex parte Blood)* [1997] 2 WLR 806; [1999] Fam 151 also discussed in chapter 13.

53 EC Treaty, art 59.

54 Mrs Blood exported the sperm to Belgium and subsequently had two children.

55 *L v Human Fertilisation and Embryology Authority* [2008] EWHC 2149 (Fam).

fact that L had rights under both the EC Treaty and arts 8 and 12 of the European Convention on Human Rights, the HFEA subsequently decided to permit export of the sperm to the United States where it could be lawfully used.

[5.54] Other cases also demonstrate the potential complexity of cases where couples are nationals of different European states and reside outside their countries of origin to which they wish to return for fertility treatment. In a recent French case before the Conseil d'Etat,[56] Mrs A (a Spanish woman) and her husband MB (an Italian man) living in France, had taken steps to ensure that they might have a child together despite MB's illness. Given that his treatment carried a risk of infertility, he stored sperm in advance of his treatment intending to benefit later from medical assistance to have a child with his wife when his health improved. However, his health did not improve and he died in 2015. Before his death, MB had explicitly consented that his wife should, after his death, proceed with their plan in Spain, which allows posthumous insemination. After the death of MB, Mrs A, who had by then returned to live in Spain, asked the French administration to allow her to export her husband's sperm to allow the conception of the child in Spain. Her request was rejected, on the ground of the prohibition of posthumous insemination in French legislation.

[5.55] French law allows assisted reproduction only to remedy infertility of a couple or to avoid the transmission of a serious disease. In order for the couple to benefit from such procedure, they have to be alive and of reproductive age. The separation of the couple or the death of either one of them prevents the other from pursuing assisted reproduction. In addition, French law[57] prohibits the export of gametes stored in France for a use that would go against the principles of the French legislation. By comparison, in Spain, posthumous insemination for the benefit of a widow is allowed in the 12 months following the death of her husband, if he gave his consent prior to his death.

[5.56] Mrs A argued that denying the export of the gametes was incompatible with art 8 of the European Convention for the Protection of Human Rights and Fundamental Freedoms (ECHR), which guarantees that 'Everyone has the right to respect for his private and family life'. The Conseil d'État held that the French legislation, taken as a whole, was not incompatible with this article as the margin of appreciation granted by the Convention to States on bioethical matters is wide and both the prohibition to perform a posthumous insemination and the prohibition to export gametes for this purpose falls within the State's margin of appreciation. However, the Conseil d'État noted that Mrs A's situation resulted from the illness and the sudden deterioration of Mr B's health, which prevented the spouses from carrying out their plan to have a child and, in particular, to deposit some gametes in Spain as well, a country which allows posthumous insemination. In those circumstances, Mrs A, who came back to Spain to live there without the intention to bypass the French law, now faced a situation in which the export of the gametes stored in France is the only way for her to exercise her right under Spanish law. The Conseil d'État accordingly concluded in this instance that the denial of Mrs A's application to export her husband's sperm jeopardised her right to respect for private and family life. Therefore, the Conseil d'État ordered that the hospital

---

[56] CE, 31 May 2016, Mme CA, N°396848 http://english.conseil-etat.fr/News/Posthumous-Insemination.

[57] Article L 2141-11-1 of the Code of Public Health.

and relevant authorities take all necessary steps in order to allow the export of the gametes to Spain.

[5.57] These cases demonstrate the relevance and importance of both the cross-border rights of EU citizens under the EC Treaty, and the provisions of the ECHR, in particular arts 8 and 12, in this context. Even if future Irish legislation were to prohibit or restrict the posthumous use of sperm in this jurisdiction, the courts (or any future regulatory authority) here would similarly have to take into account arguments in favour of permitting the export of stored sperm to another jurisdiction where such use is lawful.

DONOR INSEMINATION

[5.58] In this procedure (hereafter referred to as DI) the sperm used to inseminate the woman is that of a donor. There is no donor sperm bank currently in operation in Ireland, although men who are undergoing chemotherapy can store their sperm in advance of treatment. Sperm is imported by some Irish clinics from other jurisdictions on behalf of patients who seek sperm donation in order to conceive. Individuals and couples may also import sperm privately by purchasing it directly through the internet.[58] The legal issues that arise here mainly relate to parentage and the right of the child to information about the donor.

Parentage

[5.59] In Ireland, until recently there were no legislative provisions on the parentage of children born through donor insemination. A child born to a married woman through use of donor sperm was presumed to be that of her husband and he would be registered as the child's father. In the case of an unmarried couple, the man could be registered as the father of the child with the consent of the birth mother but, since he would not be the biological father, he would not be entitled to apply for a court order if she did not consent. In the case of a single woman who had a child through use of donor sperm, no man would be registered as the father.

[5.60] Part 2 of the Children and Family Relationships Act 2015 (which has not yet been commenced at the time of writing) makes provision for parentage of children born following donor-assisted reproduction. Section 5 provides that the parents of a donor-conceived child are the mother and her husband, civil partner or cohabitant as long as that person has given their consent under s 11 of the Act. 'Cohabitant' is defined by s 172(1) of the Civil Partnership and Certain Rights and Obligations of Cohabitants Act 2010 as 'one of two adults (whether of the same or the opposite sex) who live together as a couple in an intimate and committed relationship and who are not related to each other within the prohibited degrees of relationship or married to each other or civil partners of each other.' Therefore, the parentage provisions will apply only where the mother is married (same sex or opposite sex marriage), in a civil partnership (entered into prior to the Marriage Act 2015) or cohabiting (same sex or opposite sex) within the terms of the 2010 Act. Couples who do not live together would not appear to comply with the provisions of the Act and therefore the parentage provision would not apply.

---

[58] This option is regarded by clinicians as raising potential safety issues in relation to the health screening of donors in an unregulated internet environment.

[5.61] These provisions apply only where the procedure has been performed in a DAHR (Donor-Assisted Human Reproduction) facility. This is to ensure that there is clear evidence of the parents' intentions about fatherhood and perhaps also to ensure that appropriate screening of donors has taken place in a clinical environment. The Act requires relevant information on parenthood to be given by the operator of such a facility to the donor, the intending mother and the husband, civil partner or cohabitant prior to the giving of consent.

Rights and responsibilities of sperm donors

[5.62] Section 5 of the Children and Family Relationships Act 2015 makes it clear that a donor of a gamete that is used in a DAHR procedure is not the parent of a child born as a result of that procedure and has no parental rights or duties in respect of that child. However, as mentioned above, these provisions apply only where the procedure has been performed in a DAHR facility.

[5.63] In some circumstances children may be conceived using donor sperm where the identity of the donor is known. This sometimes occurs in situations where the mother is a single woman or in a same sex relationship and although not necessarily infertile, the intending mother seeks the assistance of a male friend in order to have a child.[59] Although the 2015 Act does allow donors to make 'directed donations' to a particular woman or couple under s 6(4), the parties may choose not to avail of the service of a DAHR facility and carry out the insemination themselves in private. In these circumstances the provisions of the Act will not apply. In many cases of this kind, it is agreed between the parties that the man will not have any financial responsibilities to the child but will play a role in the child's life such as that of an uncle or godfather. However, if this arrangement breaks down, the man may seek to formalise his access to the child by applying for recognition as the biological father.

[5.64] In one of the first reported cases on this issue, the American case *CM v CC*, in 1977[60] a sperm donor sought parental rights to the child conceived as a result of donor insemination using his sperm. The donor was known to the mother at all times and claimed that he believed that he would be treated as, and wished to be treated as, the child's father. The question for the Court was whether a sperm donor should be treated as the natural father of the child, thereby entitling him to visitation rights. Based on family law principles in relation to parentage, the New Jersey Appeal Court found the case to be analogous to Artificial Insemination by Husband in that the donor was known to the mother and intended to have a parental role in relation to the child. The Court held that 'if an unmarried woman conceives a child through artificial insemination from a known man, that man cannot be considered to be less a father because he is not married to the woman.' The Court also relied on policy considerations in deciding that it was in a

---

[59] The woman may choose instead to import sperm from abroad which will be delivered to her home for self-insemination. It is important that any woman considering this option would choose from a reputable organisation that carefully selects and screens donors. It is also preferable that the woman would be treated by a doctor or clinic who can carry out a comprehensive medical examination, diagnosis, scanning, timing, and hormonal stimulation if required.

[60] *CM v CC* 152 NJ Super 160, 377 A 2d 821.

child's interests to have two parents wherever possible. This case is important because it refused to distinguish, for the purposes of visitation and custody rights, between a child conceived by natural means and a child conceived by artificial insemination.

[5.65] In an Irish case involving a known sperm donor, *McD v L & Another*,[61] a man donated sperm to a same sex couple on the understanding that he would have a role in the child's life such as that of a godfather or favourite uncle. The relationship between the man and the couple, particularly the birth mother, deteriorated after the child's birth due to disagreements regarding the extent of the relationship between the man and the child. The man sought the right to be appointed legal guardian of the child and access. The High Court dismissed the action on the basis that it was not in the best interests of the child. Hedigan J held that the couple and the child constituted a de facto family and that there was nothing in Irish law to suggest that a family of two women and a child had any lesser right to be recognised than a de facto family comprised of a man and woman unmarried to each other and a child.

[5.66] The case was appealed to the Supreme Court which held that the man was entitled to access to the child but not guardianship at the present time. The Court unanimously held that the agreement between the parties prior to the conception of the child was unenforceable but nonetheless relevant as a factual background and context to the case. All judges were also unanimous in stating that the welfare of the child, as the first and paramount consideration, was central to the determination of the issues in this case as provided by s 3 of the Guardianship of Infants Act 1964.

[5.67] The issue of the recognition of the de facto family in the context of the application of art 8 of the ECHR was also discussed by the Court. The Court held that the High Court had no jurisdiction to apply directly the provisions of the Convention to the same sex couple and the child. Denham J stated that there is no institution in Ireland of a de facto family and that the family in Ireland is defined as that based on marriage.[62] She held that the man had rights as a natural father to apply to be appointed guardian and the Court had to consider such an application using the best interests of the child as its paramount consideration. She also held that there is benefit to a child in having the society of its father and that it was unfortunate that the parties had not been able to agree between them on what form of contact the child should have with his father. Geoghegan J held that:

> Even within the narrow confines of a sperm donor situation, as in this particular case, there may be wholly different sets of circumstances. There may be the anonymous donor who afterwards purports to claim such rights. There may be the known donor, as in this case, but with quite different types of side agreements (whether binding or not). In either of those situations, the donee may be married or unmarried and may be living in a heterosexual or homosexual relationship or none. In all these cases, the judge dealing with the application, must stand back and consider what is the just and common sense solution, always bearing in mind that the child's welfare is the first and paramount consideration.

[5.68] He also recognised that it was well-known from adoption situations that a child not brought up by and out of contact with his or her natural parents will frequently have

---

[61] *McD v L & Another* [2009] IESC 81.

[62] See also the decision of the European Court of Human Rights in *Schalk and Kopf v Austria* (Application No 30141/04).

a real interest at some stage in making such contact. Therefore, the blood link is always a factor to be taken into account in considering the child's best interests but any conclusions will vary enormously depending on the circumstances of the particular case. He was of the view that if there was to be any contact between a sperm donor father and the child, the only viable role was that originally agreed by the parties, that is of a 'favourite uncle'. The learned judge felt that 'any connection closer than that, at least in the absence of complete agreement, would be bound to be wholly disruptive and against the child's interests'.

[5.69] The Court allowed the appeal on the issue of access and remitted the matter to the High Court for determination. Despite the decision not to grant guardianship in this case based on the application of the best interests of the child test in light of the poor relationship between the mother and father of the child, the decision is positive in its recognition that it is generally in the best interests of children to know who their fathers are and to have a relationship with them where possible. However, although the man was described by the court as a sperm donor, these circumstances were unusual in that he was a known donor who from the outset wanted some form of relationship with the child. These factors are not usually present in sperm donation and therefore the case is distinguishable on its facts from more usual sperm donation scenarios where the donor is not known to the recipient and does not intend to play a role in the child's life.

[5.70] There have also been cases brought under the ECHR in an attempt to establish a legal relationship between the father/donor and the child. For example, in *M v the Netherlands,* an application was brought under art 8 of the ECHR (though held to be inadmissible) by a man who had agreed to be a sperm donor for a lesbian couple.[63] The man had kept in regular contact with the couple during the pregnancy and with the resulting child. He did not make any financial contribution to the child's upbringing. Disagreements arose as to his visitation rights to the child and he instituted court proceedings in the Netherlands claiming an entitlement to contact with the child. The Dutch Supreme Court denied his application on the basis that biological fatherhood alone was not sufficient to establish 'family life' within the meaning of art 8. The applicant complained to the Commission, which also required close personal ties such as cohabitation to establish a relationship within art 8. It found that donation of sperm by itself could not found a claim to family life. Although he had some limited contact with the child, this was held to be insufficient to form the close personal ties required.

[5.71] The position under Irish law therefore is that under s 5 of the 2015 Act, a man who has donated sperm for a procedure to be carried out in a DAHR facility will not be regarded as the father of any resulting child. A man who has provided sperm to a woman other than in a DAHR facility may not however be exempted from parentage under the 2015 Act. If both parties intend that he would have a relationship with the child, he may be registered on the birth certificate and acquire guardianship with the consent of the mother or by order of the court.[64] If he sought to be registered as the father and to

---

[63] *M v Netherlands* (1993) 74 DR 120.

[64] The automatic guardianship provision for unmarried fathers introduced in the Children and Family Relationships Act 2015 would not usually apply in this situation as it requires the man to have cohabited with the child's mother for 12 consecutive months, including 3 months following the child's birth.

acquire guardianship rights in respect of the child without the consent of the mother, this would be decided on the best interests of the child test as illustrated by *McD v L*. The court would examine the circumstances within which the child was conceived, the relationship between the parties, and the best interests of the child in having a relationship with its father where possible. This will be based on considerations of the child's welfare. If he did not seek to be registered as the father nor to have any parental rights or responsibilities, the mother could nonetheless seek child support from him in the same way as from any other man who is the genetic father of a child.

Disclosure to the child about their donor conception

[5.72] Traditionally couples undergoing DI treatment were advised and often chose to keep this fact a secret as they believed this was the best way to protect their family's privacy as well as possible social disapproval and stigmatisation. Due to matching of physical characteristics such as hair and eye colour of the donor with those of the male partner, and the confidentiality of relationship between the couple and the medical practitioner, it was easy for couples to believe that no-one need ever know about the procedure. In recent years there has been increasing recognition of the negative effects of secrecy within families and the child's right to know the circumstances of its conception and the identity of its genetic parents.[65] However, despite strong arguments in favour of disclosure, studies show that many couples do not tell their children that they were donor-conceived.[66] It is argued that the maintenance of secrecy demonstrates that the paramount concern here is for the parents and not the child.[67] The debate surrounding disclosure of donor identity is typically framed as a tension between the rights of donors and parents on one hand, and those of donor-conceived children on the

---

[65] 'The young child's partial overhearing of mysterious allusions, and his sense of parental lies, half-truths and evasions may incur confusion, suspicion and anxiety for which he needs his parents' help – instead he feels cut off from them by a conspiracy of silence.' Holland, 'Adoption and Artificial Insemination: Some Social Implications.' (1971) 50(4) Soundings: An Interdisciplinary Journal 302 at 305. Similarly, Triseliotis argues: 'It can now be claimed with some confidence from the available evidence that there is a psychological need in all people, manifest principally among those who grow up away from their original families, to know about their background, their genealogy, and their personal history if they are to grow up feeling complete and whole'. Triseliotis, 'Obtaining Birth Certificates' in Bean, (ed) *Adoption* (Tavistock Publication, 1984) at 38. Also see Macklin, who remarks that: 'Donor offspring ... rarely find out the truth of their origins. But, some of them do, and we must listen to them when they speak of their anguish, of not knowing who fathered them; we must listen when they tell us how destructive it is to their self-esteem to find out their father sold the essence of his lineage for $40 or so, without ever intending to love or take responsibility for them.' Macklin, 'Artificial Means of Reproduction and Our Understanding of the Family' (1991) 21 Hastings Center Report 5, 11.

[66] The rates vary with different studies, for example: Brewaeys et al 'Anonymous or Identity-Registered Sperm Donors? A Study of Dutch Recipients' Choices' (2004) 20 Human Reproduction 820, finding that only 17% of parents intended to disclose; Klock et al 'A Prospective Study of Donor Insemination Recipients: Secrecy, Privacy and Disclosure' (1994) 62 *Fertility and Sterility* 477 finding that 27% of couples planned to disclose. See further discussion at para **[5.77]**.

[67] Snowden and Mitchell, *The Artificial Family* (Allen & Unwin, 1981) 79.

other. It is argued that donors have a right to maintain anonymity in order to avoid potential future liabilities and interference with their lives, and parents have a right to keep the circumstances of conception private as this is something intensely personal to their family. On the other hand, it is argued that donor-conceived children and adults have a right to know who their genetic parents are.

[5.73] It has long been argued that with the development of a sense of personal identity usually during adolescence comes an identification with one's family and past. This necessitates a connection with those to whom the person is genetically related. If the child or young adult is separated from genetic relatives this can disrupt the development of the individual leading to identity confusion. Much of the evidence used in the debate about disclosure is drawn from research and literature on adoption. 'It is now accepted that open communication between adoptive parents and their children, such that children are given developmentally appropriate information about their adoption and feel free to discuss adoption-related issues as they arise, is important for positive adult-child relationships and the psychological well-being of adopted children.'[68] Golombok explains that there are potentially negative psychological consequences of keeping children's origins secret because secrets create boundaries between those who know the secret and those who do not and can create anxiety when topics related to the secret are discussed. Children can often sense when they are not being told something and may become confused, anxious, and can even develop symptoms of psychological disorder as a result.[69] In relation to donor conception, similar arguments may be made as it is thought that children can pick up signals from their parents that they are in some way different, such as if the parents become uncomfortable in talking about family resemblances or similar topics. Family therapy practitioners claim that openness and honesty are preferable and that basing family life on deception and secrecy can cause stress and anxiety within the family.[70]

[5.74] A further issue that may arise here is whether the absence of a genetic relationship between the child and one of its parents is detrimental to family functioning. Studies on adopted children indicate, on average, higher rates of emotional and behavioural problems than non-adopted children.[71] However, these problems tend to be related to factors associated with the adoption such as children's experiences of abusive or neglectful parenting before the adoption takes place rather than the absence of a genetic link with the adoptive parents. The situation of donor conceived children is different from adoptees as they have not been relinquished by or removed from their genetic parents, they are not exposed to the adverse experiences of prior abusive parenting and they are usually raised by one genetic parent. They would not therefore be

---

[68] Golombok, *Modern Families, Parents and Children in New Family Forms* (Cambridge University Press 2015) at 94.

[69] Golombok, *Modern Families, Parents and Children in New Family Forms* (Cambridge University Press 2015) at 95.

[70] Frith, 'Gamete donation, identity, and the offspring's right to know.' Virtual Mentor, Sept 2007, Vol 9, No 9:644–648.

[71] Palacios and Brodzinsky, 'Adoption research. Trends, topics, outcomes.' (2010) International Journal of Behavioural Development, 34(3), 270–284.

expected to show increased rates of psychological problems resulting from these factors.[72]

[5.75] Although there are differences between adopted and donor-conceived children, they may share an interest in knowing about their origins and the absence of such information can represent a missing part of their lives. 'While the analogy between donor offspring and adoptees is not a perfect fit, it appears that these two groups often have similar concerns about their genetic identity.'[73] This has also been referred to in the context of gamete donation as 'genealogical bewilderment' meaning that the donor child can be curious about the physical characteristic, family aptitudes, and medical history of the donor:[74]

> The first generation of donor-conceived offspring is now becoming young adults who are beginning to share their unique perspectives. Many are telling a story of psychological distress. They describe a strong need to know 'where they came from;' to know their genetic origins as an essential part of constructing their identities.[75]

[5.76] Donor-conceived adults advocate openness from an early age so that there is never a time in the child's life when disclosure comes as a shock to them. Donor conceived children who find out later in life about their conception report numerous negative consequences, including mistrust within the family, lack of genetic continuity, poor self-perception, feeling that they did not fit in with their families because of physical differences, being aware from a relatively early age that something was not said within the family, learning about their conception in shocking and unexpected circumstances, or finding out later in life which provoked anger, resentment or upset.[76] By comparison, children who are told early about their donor conception tend to respond in a factual non-emotional way.[77] Children who are told about their donor conception in their preschool years respond neutrally, or with curiosity, rather than distress.[78] However, they have little understanding of gamete donation until about age 10. In a study of the thoughts and feelings of adolescents who had grown up with the knowledge that they were donor conceived, the majority reported feeling comfortable

---

[72] Golombok, *Modern Families, Parents and Children in New Family Forms* (Cambridge University Press 2015) at 97

[73] Frith, 'Gamete donation, identity, and the offspring's right to know.' Virtual Mentor Sept 2007, Vol 9, No 9:644–648.

[74] McWhinnie, 'Gamete donation and anonymity.' Hum Reprod 2001; 16(5): 807–817.

[75] Ravitsky, 'Knowing Where You Come From': The Rights of Donor-Conceived Individuals and the Meaning of Genetic Relatedness' (2010) Minnesota Journal of Law, Science & Technology; 11(2):655–84.

[76] Van den Akker, 'A review of family donor constructs: Current research and future directions.' Hum Reprod Update (March/April 2006) 12(2) 91–101.

[77] Blake et al 'Daddy ran out of tadpoles: how parents tell their children that they are donor-conceived and what their 7 year olds understand' (2010) 25(10) Human Reproduction 2527–2534.

[78] Golombok, *Modern Families, Parents and Children in New Family Forms* (Cambridge University Press 2015) at 105.

about their donor conception and felt that learning about their donor conception had not had a negative impact on their relationships with their parents.[79]

[5.77] The child's parents are often reluctant to tell the child about their donor conception as they may want to keep the matter private and protect the child against possible negative reactions.[80] They may worry that the child will be upset, shocked and confused by the knowledge that they are not genetically related to one of their parents.[81] They may fear the disruption of their family life if the donor's identity were made known, as the child may attempt to establish a relationship with the donor, which might result in a sense of loss to the parents.[82] They may have unresolved feelings about not being the child's genetic parent[83] and they may also fear interference from the law in granting the donor parental rights in respect of the child at some point in the future.[84] As a result the rates of disclosure by parents has traditionally been very low with only around 10 per cent of parents in European countries telling their children by early adolescence.[85] In recent years there has been a rise in the number of parents who intend to tell their children, for example in a longitudinal study of children born through assisted reproduction in the UK, 46 percent of parents of children born through donor insemination and 56 percent of parents of children born through egg donation stated that they planned to tell their children. However despite these intentions, many parents do not actually disclose the information with only 28 percent of donor insemination parents and 41 percent of egg donation parents doing so by the time the child was 7 years old.[86]

[5.78] Clinicians working in this area have also traditionally been reluctant to advocate disclosure as they fear that disclosure leads to many donor-conceived children and adults seeking to know the identity of their sperm donor. There is a fear that this in turn may lead to a decrease in the number of men willing to act as donors with the result that

---

[79] Golombok, *Modern Families, Parents and Children in New Family Forms* (Cambridge University Press 2015) at 105.

[80] Lalos et al 'Legislated right for donor-insemination children to know their genetic origin: a study of parental thinking.' Human Reproduction Vol 22, No 6: 1759–1768 (2007).

[81] Golombok, *Modern Families, Parents and Children in New Family Forms* (Cambridge University Press 2015) at 99.

[82] They may also fear that the child will suffer negative reactions in society and they may wish to hide their infertility. See Kirkman, 'Parents' Contributions to the Narrative Identity of Offspring of Donor-Assisted Conception' 57 Social Science and Medicine 2229 (2003); Nachtigall et al 'The Disclosure Decision: Concerns and Issues of Parents of Children Conceived Through Donor Insemination' (1998) 178 American Journal of Obstetrics and Gynaecology 1165.

[83] Crammond, (1998) 'Counselling needs of patients receiving treatment with gamete donation.' J Commun Appl Soc Psychol 1, 313–321.

[84] For example, *Jhordan C v Mary K,* 179 Cal App 3d 586 (1986) in which the donor was granted legal rights to visitation, as well as a legal responsibility to support the child.

[85] Golombok, *Modern Families, Parents and Children in New Family Forms* (Cambridge University Press 2015) at 98–99. The rates rise slightly in some countries by the time the child turns 18, and the rates sometimes vary when the child was born as a result of embryo rather than egg or sperm donation.

[86] This is the age by which most adopted children have been told about their adoption. Golombok, *Modern Families, Parents and Children in New Family Forms* (Cambridge University Press 2015) at 101.

clinics will no longer be able to offer this service. It is believed that the sperm donor may have a strong interest in remaining anonymous and may not welcome a potentially traumatic disruption of his family life by the appearance of a child of whose existence he was not aware. He may not have a developed perception of the needs of the child and may simply see it as an unwanted intrusion.[87] He may fear the imposition of legal responsibility on him for the child and maintenance obligations. However, this may also depend on social or cultural factors. Surveys suggest that most donors have serious misgivings about their legal responsibility for offspring that might cause them to stop donating if their identities were revealed without legal protection. Even in the absence of such legal risks where legislation exempts donors from legal responsibility, anonymity remains important to some donors due to the risk that a donor offspring would appear in their later lives.

[5.79] In the United States, disclosure is not regulated and donor anonymity is still the norm. However, practice varies between states and between various clinics. Some clinics offer a double-track policy, which offers recipients of DI treatment the option of choosing a traditional anonymous treatment or an open donation/identity release treatment in which they agree that identifying information will be shared with offspring years later. In other jurisdictions the practice also varies with a number of European countries introducing legislation in recent years prohibiting anonymity, for example Norway, Sweden, Austria, Switzerland, the Netherlands, the UK and Finland. New Zealand and three Australian states similarly prohibit anonymity.[88] There is anecdotal evidence that the removal of donor anonymity in some of these countries has resulted in an increase in the proportion of parents who tell their children about their donor conception but there is little systematic data yet on the impact of the removal of donor anonymity on disclosure rates.[89]

[5.80] Donor-conceived persons claim that the right to know one's genetic parentage is a basic human right and that knowledge of one's origins is essential for psychological well-being and the establishment of healthy family relationships. They argue that there

---

[87] Some studies, however, show the contrary, that is, that the donor *does* have an interest in his potential children. In a study in New Zealand, 80 per cent of donors wanted to know if children were conceived. See Purdie, Peek, Irwin, Ellis, Graham & Fisher, 'Identifiable Semen Donors – Attitudes of Donors and Recipient Couples' (1992) New Zealand Med J 27–28. This is similar to previous studies in Australia, New Zealand and USA. See Kovacs, Clayton & McGowan, 'The Attitudes of Semen Donors' (1983) 2 Clin Reprod Fertil 73–5; Rowland, 'Attitudes and Opinions of Donors on an Artificial Insemination by Donor (AID) Programme' (1983) 2 Clin Reprod Fertil 249–59; Daniels, 'Semen Donors in New Zealand: Their Characteristics and Attitudes' (1987) 5 Clin Reprod Fertil 177–90; Daniels, 'Semen Donors: Their Motivations and Attitudes to Their Offspring' (1989) 7 J Reprod Infant Psychology 121–7; Handelsman, Dunn, Conway, Boyland & Jansen, 'Psychological and Attitudinal Profiles in Donors for Artificial Insemination' (1985) 43 Fertil Steril 95–101; Sauer, Gorrill, Zeffer & Bustillo, 'Attitudinal Survey of Sperm Donors to an Artificial Insemination Clinic' (1989) 34 J Reprod Med 362–4. Some of these studies show that many donors often think about their DI children.

[88] New South Wales, South Australia and Western Australia.

[89] Golombok, *Modern Families, Parents and Children in New Family Forms* (Cambridge University Press 2015) at 101.

are four important aspects to the right to know one's origins. The *medical* aspect points towards the right to know one's full medical history and to know medically relevant genetic information about the donor.[90] 'Not only is it helpful in diagnosing medical problems to know of family history, but certain hereditary diseases such as haemophilia or Huntington's Chorea, must be of concern to persons planning to have children of their own.'[91] The *identity* aspect points towards the right to personal information about the donor as a person (narrative information) that would assist offspring in overcoming identity issues. The *relational* aspect points towards the right to know the full identity of the donor (and perhaps other siblings) in order to contact him or her and attempt to establish a relationship.[92] Finally, the *parental disclosure* aspect relates to the right to know the truth about the circumstances of one's conception as trumping parents' right to privacy.

[5.81] Some of these arguments were put to the Supreme Court of British Columbia in *Prattan v British Columbia (Attorney General)*.[93] In this case the Court found that donor offspring justifiably fear that their health may be seriously compromised by the lack of information about their donor. Even with the availability of genetic testing, family history is more predictive, and genetic testing is best interpreted in the context of a

---

[90] There are many reasons why a person might need to know his/her genetic background, such as the ability to preserve one's health by altering behaviour to prevent problems; cautioning proper diet if there is a history of heart disease in the family; avoiding alcohol if there may be a predisposition to alcoholism; advising regular mammograms if there is a history of breast cancer; or by enabling kidney or bone marrow transplants to be made between compatible relatives if necessary. It also helps parents to avoid passing on certain genetic defects to their children. Obviously, this does not necessitate the identity, as opposed to genetic health, of the donor being made available. Swanson, 'Donor Anonymity in Artificial Insemination: Is It Still Necessary?' (1993) 27 Columbia J of Law and Social Problems, 151 at 174.

[91] O'Donovan, 'A Right to Know One's Parentage' (1988) 2 I J of Law and the Family 27–45 at 30. O'Donovan questions the existence of a general right to access information regarding one's parentage and claims that there are three interests which may be benefited by such information – medical, legal and psychological. She argues that if access to genetic and identifying information is regarded as an important interest in the case of those who have been adopted, then there is no legitimate distinction which may be drawn between those children and children born as a result of reproductive technology. She also points to the inconsistency in the position of the medical profession who, on the one hand encourage a person to be aware of his/her medical history but, on the other hand, make no attempt to record it in the case of adopted children or those born through donor insemination. The arguments for and against openness in this context are examined by O'Donovan, who concludes that there is a strong and powerful case to be made out in favour of telling a child of its genetic origins, but that there are wider issues which should be confronted in society such as why we put such an emphasis on genes at all when we allow children to be brought up on a separate, social basis.

[92] Research shows that sometimes donor conceived people are more interested in forming relationships with donor siblings than with the donor. They may want to know information about the donor and even to meet him, but often they want to stay in touch with siblings. Golombok, *Modern Families, Parents and Children in New Family Forms* (Cambridge University Press 2015) at 113–114. 'It seems that a new phenomenon is taking place – family relationships based on genetic connections between children who were not previously aware of each other's existence are being created across multiple family units.' Golombok at 116.

[93] *Prattan v British Columbia (Attorney General)* [2011] BCSC 656.

family history. Because of a lack of information, donor offspring can face delayed medical treatment, and an inability to have conditions that are inherited or genetic diagnosed and treated. Adair J held that it is therefore important, psychologically and medically, for donor offspring to have the ability to know identifying and non-identifying information about their donor. The learned judge held that their psychological and medical needs in that respect are substantially the same as adoptees. Donor offspring also commonly, and legitimately, fear inadvertent consanguinity. Without further biological testing, many do not have the information required to determine if another individual is a biological half-sibling. Judge Adair found that the secrecy that often surrounds the process of conception, even when done with the best of intentions, can have devastating effects on donor offspring when the truth is revealed. 'Knowing the truth (that the other biological parent was a donor), but having no means to discover what the truth means for one's life, can be a significant source of anxiety, depression and frustration for donor offspring.'

[5.82] Adair J found that the legislature's failure to address the needs of donor offspring to obtain information about their biological fathers discriminated against them on the basis of the manner of their conception. Unlike adoptees who, once they reach the age of majority have qualified access to their adoption order and registration of birth, donor-conceived people have no right to know their origins or prevent the destruction of records that would help identify their biological parents.

[5.83] However the Court of Appeal later reversed Adair J's decision.[94] The Court held that it is open to the legislature to provide adoptees with the means of accessing information about their biological origins without being obligated to provide comparable benefits to other persons seeking such information. The Court held that Ms Pratten's argument that s 7 of the Canadian Charter of Rights and Freedoms[95] guarantees the right 'to know one's past' also failed. Frankel J said 'However desirable it may be that persons have access to information about their biological origins, Ms Pratten has not established that such access has been recognized as so 'fundamental' that it is entitled to independent constitutionally protected status under the Charter.'[96] He was of the view that 'what Ms Pratten seeks is far more extensive than what is enjoyed by most people in Canada and would result in state intrusion into the lives of many.' Ms Pratten's attempt to appeal to the Supreme Court of Canada was unsuccessful.

[5.84] Other than Victoria, Australia discussed below, none of the countries which have prohibited anonymity (Sweden, Norway, the Netherlands, Switzerland, New Zealand and the UK) have introduced a system for ensuring that the child is informed; that decision is left to the parents.[97] Although there are strong arguments in favour of the creation of a legal mechanism which would ensure that the child is told of its origins such as through the issuing of a donor conception certificate which would be attached to

---

[94] *Prattan v British Columbia (Attorney General)* 2012 BCCA 480.

[95] Section 7 provides that 'Everyone has the right to life, liberty and security of the person and the right not to be deprived thereof except in accordance with the principles of fundamental justice.'

[96] *Prattan v British Columbia (Attorney General)* 2012 BCCA 480 at para 50.

[97] Frith, 'Beneath the Rhetoric: The Role of Rights in the Practice of Non-Anonymous Gamete Donation', (2001) 15 Bioethics 473 at 477.

a child's birth certificate, or the insertion of the words 'by donation' on the birth certificate, this remains a highly controversial proposition.[98] On the one hand a policy which forces parents to disclose is in keeping with a true understanding of genetic relatedness and also obliges the State not to collude in the deception of the child. It may be argued that genetic relatedness is of such importance to the child as to warrant such intrusion into the family.

[5.85] On the other hand, such a policy would infringe upon the parents' right to privacy as well as their fundamental Constitutional right to make decisions regarding their children's welfare. The Ethics Committee of the American Society for Reproductive Medicine takes the view that although disclosure is in the best interests of the child, the decision is a highly personal one about which parents may differ. Ultimately it must be the choice of the recipient parents as to whether to disclose the fact of donor conception to their offspring.[99] This is also the approach recommended by the Nuffield Council on Bioethics which concluded that:

> It is not the role of state authorities, whether through direct contact with donor conceived people as they reach adulthood, or through the use of official documentation such as birth certificates, to intervene to ensure that all donor-conceived people know of the circumstances of their conception.[100]

The middle ground currently adopted in most jurisdictions in which anonymity is prohibited is through education and public awareness campaigns aimed at social change, and access to information for the donor-conceived person who has been told of the circumstances of their conception. Thus, encouraging telling rather than forcing telling through legal means, appears to be the most common approach.

[5.86] In Victoria, Australia, a different approach has been taken.[101] Victoria was the first Australian state and the first jurisdiction in the world to enact legislation regulating assisted reproductive treatment. The Infertility (Medical Procedures) Act 1984 came into effect in 1988 and was later amended by the Infertility Treatment Act 1995 (effective from 1 January 1998), and the Assisted Reproductive Treatment Act 2008 (effective from 1 January 2010). These Acts incrementally introduced provisions allowing donor-conceived people to access information about their donors, with the Infertility (Medical Procedures) Act 1984 allowing post-1988 donor-conceived people to obtain identifying information with the donor's consent, and the Infertility Treatment Act 1995 introducing the right for all post-1998 donor-conceived people to obtain identifying information about their donor in all cases. This meant that rights of access to information by donor-conceived people were essentially determined by the date at which the gametes used in their conception were donated. People conceived from gametes donated before 1 July 1988 had no rights to access information about their donors under

---

[98] Blyth, 'The Role of Birth Certificates in Relation to Access to Biographical and Genetic History in Donor Conception' (2009) 17 International Journal of Child Rights 207.

[99] ASRM 'Informing offspring of their conception by gamete or embryo donation: a committee opinion.' Fertility and Sterility Vol 100 No 1 July 2013 45–9.

[100] Nuffield Council on Bioethics: Donor conception: ethical aspects of information sharing (2013) para 6.8. Available at www.nuffieldbioethics.org.

[101] See Johnson et al 'Donor conception legislation in Victoria, Australia: The 'Time to Tell' campaign, donor-linking and implications for clinical practice.' (2012) 19 JLM 803.

legislation, although they could obtain information through a voluntary register. People conceived from gametes donated between 1 July 1988 and 1 January 1998 were entitled to receive non-identifying information about their donors, and identifying information with their donors' consent. People conceived from gametes donated after 1 January 1998 were entitled to obtain non-identifying and identifying information about their donors.

[5.87] A further important feature of the 2008 Act is that it provided that when a donor-conceived person born after 1 January 2010 reaches adulthood and applies for a birth certificate, an addendum stating that further information is available will be provided by the Victorian Registry of Births, Deaths and Marriages. Those who contact the Registry will be informed that their details appear on the Donor Central Register, ie that they were donor-conceived.[102] They can then apply to the Register to obtain details about their donor if they wish. 'Unless they have already been informed about being donor-conceived, young adults born under the current legislation may find out about their donor origins in this manner. This legislation provides a strong incentive for parents of donor-conceived children to inform them of their donor origins.'[103] The Victorian Assisted Reproductive Treatment Authority (VARTA) runs 'Time to Tell' education seminars and provides other supports for parents to assist them in telling their children. Although it was feared that the introduction of this legislation would dissuade men from donating, the number of donors has thus far remained steady, thus confirming that identity release may not in fact deter donors.[104]

[5.88] The perceived inequality of the position under the 2008 Act by which rights for access to information by donor-conceived people was determined by the date at which the gametes used in their conception were donated, was examined by the Law Reform Committee in Victoria in 2012.[105] The Committee acknowledged that donors were promised anonymity when making donations prior to 1 January 1998, and providing donor-conceived people with access to identifying information may constitute an unreasonable breach of donors' privacy. However, the Committee determined that the right of a donor-conceived person to have access to identifying information about his or her donor is paramount. The Committee therefore recommended that the Victorian Government introduce legislation to allow all donor-conceived people to obtain identifying information about their donors. However, in order to provide some assurance to donors and donor-conceived people that they will not consequently experience unreasonable interference in their lives, the Committee also recommended that both parties be able to lodge a contact veto to prohibit contact with each other.

[5.89] These recommendations were accepted and amendments to the Assisted Reproductive Treatment Act 2008 were subsequently passed in February 2016 by the Victorian Parliament. The key elements of this legislation included provisions to the

---

[102] Assisted Reproductive Treatment Act 2008 (Vic) ss 153, 17B(2).

[103] Johnson et al 'Donor conception legislation in Victoria, Australia: The 'Time to Tell' campaign, donor-linking and implications for clinical practice.' (2012) 19 JLM 803 at 806.

[104] Johnson et al 'Donor conception legislation in Victoria, Australia: The 'Time to Tell' campaign, donor-linking and implications for clinical practice.' (2012) 19 JLM 803 at 806 at 808.

[105] Available at www.parliament.vic.gov.au.

effect that all Victorian donor-conceived people, regardless of when they were born, will have a right to identifying information about their donor, without having to receive consent from their donor. This will mean that donor-conceived people born before 1998 will have the same rights as those born after 1998. Contact preferences will be made available to donors and donor-conceived people, allowing them to determine the way in which contact with those with whom they are linked will occur. People will also have the option to choose a 'no contact' preference. If a contact preference is breached, a significant penalty may apply. Contact preferences will also be extended to those legal children of donors or donor-conceived people who are under the age of 18 years. The legislation will be implemented from 1 March 2017.

[5.90] In the United Kingdom, the Human Fertilisation and Embryology Act 1990 provided that children conceived using donated gametes could apply to the Human Fertilisation and Embryology Authority for certain information when they reached the age of 18 years, or 16 years if they were getting married and wanted to find out if their spouse could be related to them. The information that could be disclosed under the Act was restricted to non-identifying information such as physical description (height, weight, eye and hair colour), year and country of birth, ethnicity, whether the donor had any children at the time of donation and any additional information the donor chose to supply such as occupation, religion, interests and a brief self-description. This principle of donor anonymity was challenged in *Rose and anor v Secretary of State for Health and Human Fertilisation and Embryology Authority*[106] in which two donor-conceived adults sought access to information about their donors. They argued that donor anonymity breached their right to private life under art 8 of the European Convention on Human Rights. Scott Baker J agreed that art 8 was engaged but postponed his decision to enable the Government to review arrangements and hold a public consultation on the information to be provided to donor-conceived people.

[5.91] Regulations were subsequently introduced in 2004 which allowed details about egg donors and sperm donors registered after 1 April 2005 to be passed on to the offspring, including the name and last address of the donor.[107] In 2007 the Joint Committee of the House of Lords and House of Commons which was established to undertake pre-legislative scrutiny of the draft Bill which was to become the Human Fertilisation and Embryology Act of 2008, recommended that the fact of donor conception should be registered on a person's birth certificate.[108] 'This proposal was founded on the Joint Committee's concerns that the intention of the legislature removing donor anonymity could be thwarted because too few donor-conceived people were aware of the nature of their conception in the first place.'[109]

[5.92] This recommendation was not implemented in the 2008 Act. Section 31ZA of the Human Fertilisation and Embryology Act 2008 provides that a person over 18 may

---

[106] *Rose and anor v Secretary of State for Health and Human Fertilisation and Embryology Authority* [2002] EWHC 1593.

[107] Human Fertilisation and Embryology Authority (Disclosure of Donor Information) Regulations 2004 (SI 1511/2004).

[108] House of Lords and House of Commons, 2007 a: Recommendation 28, para 276).

[109] Blyth et al, 'The role of birth certificates in relation to access to biographical and genetic history in donor conception.' Intl J of Children's Rights 17 (2009) 207–233.

request the Authority to give notice as to whether or not the person was conceived using donated gametes, and if so, must give the person information relating to the donor (including identifying information such as name, date of birth and last known address) and any half-siblings (non-identifying information only unless the half-siblings consent otherwise). The applicant must be given a suitable opportunity to receive proper counselling about the implications of compliance with the request. If the applicant is under the age of 18 years, the Authority cannot be required to release identifying information. Donors can be told the number, age, sex of any children born from their donation but not the children's identity.

[5.93] The applicant may apply under s 31ZB for information as to an intended spouse. This information may show whether the applicant might be related to a specified person whom they propose to marry, enter into a civil partnership with or with whom they are in an intimate physical relationship. The applicant must be over the age of 16 years to avail of this provision. Donors can be informed that a person conceived using their gametes has made a request for identifying information, though the identity of the applicant for information will not be disclosed to the donor.

The right to know one's identity under the European Convention on Human Rights

[5.94] In the international arena, the law of human rights may be considered as providing a means through which a child could claim a right to information as to its parentage. Indeed the child's right to know his or her origins is now broadly recognised and respected.[110] It has also been guaranteed by international human rights law and in particular the case law of the European Court of Human Rights since 1989 based on the ECHR (1950), the Convention on the Rights of the Child (1989) and the Hague Convention on the Protection of Children and Co-operation in Respect of Intercountry Adoption (1993).

[5.95] Article 8 of the ECHR provides that:

(1) Everyone has the right to respect for his private and family life, his home and his correspondence.

(2) There shall be no interference by a public authority with the exercise of this right except such as is in accordance with the law and is necessary in a democratic society in the interests of national security, public safety or the economic well-being of the country,

---

[110] Beeson, 'Enforcing the Child's Right to Know Her Origins: Contrasting Approaches Under the Convention on the Rights of the Child and the European Convention on Human Rights' (2007) International Journal of Law, Policy and the Family, 21, 137–15. See also Triselotis, *In Search of Origins: The Experiences of Adopted People* (Routledge, 1973); O'Donovan, 'A Right to Know One's Genetic Parentage?' (1988) International Journal of Law Policy and the Family, 2, 27 – 45; Stewart, 'Interpreting the Child's Right to Identity in the UN Convention on the Rights of the Child' (1992) Family Law Quarterly, 26, 221 – 33; Hodgson, 'The International Legal Protection of the Child's Right to a Legal Identity and the Problem of Statelessness' (1993) International Journal of Law, Policy and the Family 7, 255–270; Freeman, 'The New Birth Right?: Identity and the Child of the Reproductive Revolution' (1996) 4 International Journal of Children's Rights, 3, 273–97; Frith, 'Gamete Donation and Anonymity: The Ethical and Legal Debate' (2001) 16 Human Reproduction, 5, 818–824.

for the prevention of disorder or crime, for the protection of health or morals, or for the protection of the rights and freedoms of others.

[5.96] Although it does not contain any express reference to any aspects of the child's identity, art 8(1) has been interpreted by the European Court of Human Rights in *Gaskin v UK*[111] as requiring that everyone should be able to establish details of their identity as individual human beings. However, this right has not been very clearly defined by the European Court of Human Rights. It is said to cover the right of an adult placed in care as a child to consult his personal file (*Gaskin v UK*[112]), the right of a child to identify her father through DNA testing (*Mikulic v Croatia*[113] and *Ebrü v Turkey*[114]), and the right of an adult to obtain a post-mortem DNA sample of his presumed father (*Jäggi v Switzerland*[115]). However, the Court in *Odièvre v France* rejected the claim that the absolute birth secrecy granted in France violates art 8.[116]

[5.97] Article 7 of the Convention on the Rights of the Child (CRC) provides that 'The child shall be registered immediately after birth and shall have the right from birth to a name, the right to acquire a nationality and, as far as possible, the right to know and be cared for by his or her parents.' The term 'parents' has been argued to include not only social or legal parents, but also biological or genetic parents.[117] Article 8 provides:

(1) States Parties undertake to respect the right of the child to preserve his or her identity, including nationality, name and family relations as recognized by law without unlawful interference.

(2) Where a child is illegally deprived of some or all of the elements of his or her identity, States Parties shall provide appropriate assistance and protection, with a view to re-establishing speedily his or her identity.

[5.98] The right is both a negative and a positive right, meaning that it protects a person from active violations by State authorities but also protects against a passive omission by the State. This is important in the imposition of obligations on states to establish and maintain registers of birth data to which the child can have later access in fulfilment of the right to know his or her origins. Beeson claims that this is a 'truly innovative provision. It is the first time an international instrument guarantees identity rights, and to children.'[118] However, despite its apparently innovative nature, she points out that it does not define the concept of identity. She also argues that although States are the main

---

[111] *Gaskin v UK* [1990] 1 FLR 167, 10454/83 [1989] ECHR 13 (7 July 1989).

[112] *Gaskin v UK* [1990] 1 FLR 167, 10454/83 [1989] ECHR 13 (7 July 1989).

[113] *Mikulic v Croatia* 53176/99 [2002] ECHR 27 (7 February 2002).

[114] *Ebrü v Turkey* 60176/00 [2006] ECHR (30 May 2006)

[115] *Jäggi v Switzerland* 58757/00 [2006] ECHR (13 July 2006).

[116] *Odièvre v France* 42326/98 [2003] ECHR 86 (13 February 2003).

[117] Freeman, 'The New Birth Right?: Identity and the Child of the Reproductive Revolution' (1996) 4 International Journal of Children's Rights, 3, 273–97.

[118] Beeson, 'Enforcing the Child's Right to Know Her Origins: Contrasting Approaches Under the Convention on the Rights of the Child and the European Convention on Human Rights' (2007) International Journal of Law, Policy and the Family, 21, at 143. She notes that it was introduced following an Argentinean proposal due to the disappearance of many children in Argentina during the 1970s and 1980s.

duty-bearers in respect of this right, perhaps individuals, for example mothers, should also be imposed with direct duties pertaining to the right.

[5.99] Difficulties may arise in this context where the fundamental rights and values of various parties involved are in conflict. As described above, the rights and interests of the genetic parents and the legal parents may often be very different. The genetic parent(s) may wish to keep their identity secret and the legal parents may not wish to have their social ties to the child affected by revelations regarding the circumstances of the child's conception. Balancing of rights is therefore necessary at a policy level. Articles 7 and 8 of the CRC do not adjudicate on the issue of how this balance should be struck. It may be argued that since art 7 grants the child the right to know 'as far as possible' this may be interpreted as conditional on granting respect for other legal rights and duties. Beeson argues that this interpretation is too limited, however. 'A more complete interpretation is that the right to know is granted only as far as this is possible within the limits of the legal order and that illegal restrictions to the right to know are prohibited.'[119] There is no mechanism for individual petition under the CRC, and therefore it is difficult to draw from the CRC any criteria by which such conflicts might be resolved. As a result, states are given a wide margin of appreciation in relation to their compliance with arts 7 and 8.

[5.100] In relation to the ECHR, art 8 (2) acknowledges the possible restriction of the right to know in circumstances when it conflicts with the rights of others. The case law of the Commission and the European Court of Human Rights also confirms its interpretation of art 8 as not intending to grant an absolute right to know one's origins. In balancing this right with the rights of others, the Court also grants states a wide margin of appreciation. For example, in *MB v UK*,[120] the Commission decided that the national authorities' refusal to order blood tests to enable an unmarried man to discover whether he was the father of a child born to a married woman was reasonable in the circumstances. The Commission was influenced by the fact that the alleged father had never lived with the mother, had not planned for the child and did not see the child or form any bond with her. The authorities had defended their refusal to order blood tests on the basis of the best interests of the child being the maintenance of a stable private life in the family unit within which she was being brought up. The Commission found that this approach was justifiable in giving greater weight to the child's interests than to the ascertainment of a biological fact which may be to the detriment of the child and the family.

[5.101] In *Odièvre v France*[121] the applicant argued that the French practice of anonymous birth ('under X') by which her mother was allowed to retain her anonymity

---

[119] Beeson, 'Enforcing the Child's Right to Know Her Origins: Contrasting Approaches Under the Convention on the Rights of the Child and the European Convention on Human Rights' (2007) International Journal of Law, Policy and the Family, 21, at 150.

[120] *MB v UK*, dec of 6 April 1994, DR 77A, p 108 (22920/93). Although the applicant attempted to bring an action also in the child's name, this was refused, as he did not have any responsibility for the child under national law.

[121] *Odièvre v France* 42326/98 [2003] ECHR 86 (13 February 2003).

from the applicant, who was her daughter, infringed art 8. The French authorities were prepared to give the applicant non-identifying information, and legislation in 2002 would enable an independent council to waive anonymity, but only with the mother's consent. The Court said:

> Article 8 protects a right to identity and personal development and the right to establish and develop relationships with other human beings and the outside world...The preservation of mental stability is in that context indispensable precondition to effective enjoyment of the right to respect for private life. Matters of relevance to personal development include details of that person's identity as a human being and the vital interest protected by the Convention in obtaining information necessary to discover the truth concerning important aspects of one's personal identity, such as the identity of one's parents. Birth, and in particular the circumstances in which a child is born, forms part of a child's, and subsequently the adult's private life guaranteed by Article 8 of the Convention. That provision is therefore applicable in the instant case.

[5.102] The Court went on to say that the child's vital interest in its personal development is also widely recognised in the general scheme of the Convention. On the other hand, a woman's interest in remaining anonymous in order to protect her health by giving birth in appropriate medical conditions cannot be denied. The two private interests with which the Court was confronted in the present case are not easily reconciled. The Court took the view that the State had provided evidence that it had made an effort to balance competing interests and that its decision came within the margin of appreciation given to individual states. The case has been criticised, however, as according too much weight to the margin of appreciation and for effectively giving the birth mother an absolute veto in respect of the release of information, thereby negating any real balancing of rights.[122]

[5.103] The two later cases of *Ebrü v Turkey*,[123] and *Jäggi v Switzerland*[124] may demonstrate a different approach by the Court. In *Ebrü*, the applicant brought a paternity suit in Istanbul against a well-known Turkish folk-singer, Emrah Ipek, claiming that he was her child's biological father. The Court attributed paternity to Ipek, on the basis of the blood and genetic test results, and all the other evidence before it. It ordered the registrar-general to amend the child's birth certificate accordingly. The Appeal Court later quashed this judgment and remitted the case for further consideration on the basis of additional forensic tests. Ipek did not attend any of the appointments made for forensic testing and the Court decided to lodge a complaint for abuse of authority with the public prosecutor against the police officers responsible for executing an arrest warrant. It also decided to notify Ipek that failure on his part to submit to DNA tests would be construed as an admission of paternity. On the basis of further tests the court later ruled that Ipek was the father. The various stages of the

---

[122] Beeson, 'Enforcing the Child's Right to Know Her Origins: Contrasting Approaches Under the Convention on the Rights of the Child and the European Convention on Human Rights' (2007) International Journal of Law, Policy and the Family, 21 at 151.

[123] *Ebrü v Turkey* 60176/00 [2006] ECHR (30 May 2006).

[124] *Jäggi v Switzerland* 58757/00 [2006] ECHR (13 July 2006).

proceedings, which lasted over eight years, received wide media coverage because of Ipek's national celebrity status.[125]

[5.104] The Court found that the civil proceedings had failed to strike a fair balance between the applicants' right to establish the truth as to the boy's paternity without undue delay, and the right of the alleged father not to have to undergo DNA tests. In conclusion, the inability of the domestic courts to settle the paternity issue in a timely manner had left the applicants in a prolonged state of uncertainty as to the child's individual identity.[126] The applicants' right to respect for their private life had thus been breached and the Court held that there had been a violation of art 8.[127]

[5.105] In *Jäggi*, the Swiss authorities refused an adult man the right to obtain a post-mortem DNA sample from his dead father. Shortly before the applicant's birth in 1939, his mother brought an action against AH, his putative father, seeking a declaration of paternity and the payment of a contribution towards his maintenance. The action was dismissed by the Geneva Court of First Instance in 1948. On registering the applicant's birth, his mother declared that his father was AH. The applicant was placed with a foster family. He was informed by his mother in 1958 that AH was his father.

[5.106] The applicant asserted that he had had regular contacts with AH and had received presents from him and money every month until he came of age. AH's family rejected those allegations, and AH always refused to submit to tests to establish his paternity. In 1999 the applicant applied for revision of the judgment of 1948, requesting a DNA test on the remains of AH. His application was refused by the trial courts. The Federal Court dismissed an appeal by the applicant on the ground that at the age of 60 he had been able to develop his personality even in the absence of certainty as to the identity of his biological father. The applicant brought an action to the European Court of Human Rights alleging violation of art 8.[128]

[5.107] The Court considered that persons trying to establish their ancestry had a vital interest, protected by the Convention, in obtaining the information they needed in order to discover the truth about an important aspect of their personal identity. However, the need to protect third parties might exclude the possibility of compelling them to submit

---

[125] The applicants complained of the excessive length of the proceedings and of the lack of a judicial forum to which a complaint might be submitted. They argued that, throughout that period, they had been in the media spotlight because Ipek was a celebrity, and that if they had received maintenance, the child would have had a better life and education. They relied on art 6(1) (right to a fair hearing within a reasonable time), art 13 (right to an effective remedy) and art 8 (right to respect for private and family life).

[126] The Court noted that a period of over eight years and nine months was excessive, particularly in view of the applicants' interest in the dispute, and did not meet the reasonable-time requirement. Accordingly, the Court held unanimously that there had been a violation of art 6(1).

[127] The Government had failed to indicate the existence of any specific remedy by which the applicants might have complained about the length of the proceedings. Accordingly, the Court held unanimously that there had been a violation of art 13 because of the lack in domestic law of a remedy allowing the applicants to assert their right to a ruling on their case within a reasonable time.

[128] He also alleged violation of art 14 (prohibition of discrimination).

to any kind of medical analysis, particularly DNA tests. The Court would therefore weigh against each other the conflicting interests, namely the applicant's right to discover his parentage against the right of third parties to the inviolability of the deceased's body, the right to respect for the dead and the public interest in the protection of legal certainty.

[5.108] The Court considered that an individual's interest in discovering his parentage did not disappear with age and that the applicant had always shown a real interest in discovering his father's identity, since he had tried throughout his life to obtain reliable information on the point. Such conduct implied moral and mental suffering, even though this had not been medically attested. The Court noted that in opposing the DNA test, which was a relatively unintrusive measure, AH's family had not cited any religious or philosophical reasons. The Court observed that the private life of the deceased person from whom it was proposed to take a DNA sample could not be impaired by such a request since it was made after his death. The Court considered that Switzerland had not secured to Jäggi the right to respect for his private life and held that there had been a violation of art 8.

[5.109] These cases illustrate a different approach being taken in recent years to the interpretation of art 8 and in particular the balancing of conflicting rights at national level. The Court seeks to ensure that States do not grant absolute protection to either the child's right to know or the parents' right to privacy but rather examines the specific context in which the conflict has arisen and the interests to be protected. Beeson argues that the Court considers some interests to be more fundamental than others and that those interests, such as the right to know one's origins, form part of the inner core of the right to respect for private life and must be respected as such.[129]

The right to know one's identity under Irish law

[5.110] Until 2015 the only analogous situation in Ireland pertaining to the right to know one's origins was in relation to adoption. Historically most adoptions were arranged through adoption agencies which sought to preserve the anonymity of the parties involved. In recognition of the desire that many adoptees and their birth parents have for contact, the Adoption Authority of Ireland now maintains a National Adoption Contact Preference Register. This enables adopted people, natural parents and any natural relative of an adopted person to sign up to facilitate contact and meetings. Participation is voluntary and contact through the register will only be initiated where both parties register. It also includes an option to have no contact with the other party to the adoption although the Adoption Authority recommends that even if this option is chosen, information on medical background would be made available to the adopted person.

[5.111] Section 84 of the Adoption Act 2010 requires the Registrar General of Births, Deaths and Marriages to maintain an Adopted Children's Register. Section 86 of this Act further provides that the Registrar General 'shall keep an index to make traceable the connection between each entry [in the Adopted Children's Register] and the

---

[129] Beeson, 'Enforcing the Child's Right to Know Her Origins: Contrasting Approaches Under the Convention on the Rights of the Child and the European Convention on Human Rights' (2007) International Journal of Law, Policy and the Family, 21 at 152.

corresponding entry in the register of births.' It further states that 'that index shall not be open to public inspection and no information from it shall be given to any person except by order of a Court or the [Adoption] Authority'. Section 86 of the Adoption Act 2010 therefore enables the Adoption Authority or a Court to direct that the adopted person be given access to the original entry of his or her birth in the records maintained by the Registrar General of Births, Deaths and Marriages.

[5.112] In *IO'T v B and the Rotunda Girls' Aid Society*[130] it was held that the right to be told the identity of a natural mother is not absolute, and must be balanced against the natural mother's right to privacy. This was a case stated from the Circuit Court pursuant to the provisions of s 16 of the Courts of Justice Act 1947, and the plaintiffs were children born before the enactment of the Adoption Act 1952 (and were 'informally adopted' in 1941 and 1951 respectively). It is clear from the report that they were born out of wedlock. By a majority (Keane J dissenting), and as appears from the judgment of Hamilton CJ, it was held that the right to know the identity of one's natural mother is a basic right flowing from the natural and special relationship which exists between a mother and her child, which relationship is clearly acknowledged in passages quoted from the judgments of the Supreme Court in *The State (Nicolaou) v An Bord Uchtála*[131] and *G v An Bord Uchtála*.[132] He further said that:

> The existence of such right is not dependent on the obligation to protect the child's right to bodily integrity or such rights as the child might enjoy in relation to the property of his or her natural mother but stems directly from the aforesaid relationship. It is not, however, an absolute or qualified right: its exercise may be restricted by the constitutional rights of others, and by the requirement of the common good. Its exercise is restricted in the case of children who have been lawfully adopted in accordance with the provisions of the Adoption Act 1952 as the effect of an adoption order is that all parental rights and duties of the natural parents are ended, while the child becomes a member of the family of the adoptive parents as if he or she had been their natural child.

[5.113] As to the rights of the natural mother (giving rise to a restriction on such right of the child), Hamilton CJ said:

> While they enjoy the constitutional right to know the identity of their respective natural mothers, the exercise of such right may be restricted by the constitutional right to privacy and confidentiality of the natural mothers in respect of their dealings with … [a society which had provided for an 'informal' adoption] … whether they are so restricted depends on the circumstances of the case and whether they, or either of them, wish to exercise this right to privacy.

And further:

> [Where] there is a conflict of constitutional rights, the obligation on the courts is to attempt to harmonise such rights having regard to the provisions of the Constitution and in the event of a failure to so harmonise, to determine which right is the superior having regard to all the circumstances of the case. So far as the applicant and the plaintiff are

---

[130] *IO'T v B and the Rotunda Girls' Aid Society* [1998] 2 IR 321.
[131] *The State (Nicolaou) v An Bord Uchtála* [1966] IR 567.
[132] *G v An Bord Uchtála* [1980] IR 32.

concerned, the court must decide whether their constitutional rights outweigh the constitutional and legal status of their natural mothers.

[5.114] The Adoption Authority will release birth certificates where the natural mother has been consulted about the application and is agreeable to the birth certificate being released or where the natural mother is deceased. The Authority may refuse to release a birth certificate in cases where the natural mother has been consulted and is opposed to its release, or where it considers the natural mother's privacy or safety might be put at risk by the release of the document.[133]

[5.115] At present, sperm donation is facilitated by the importation of sperm into Ireland from other jurisdictions, usually Denmark and the UK. Centres in the UK are permitted to export sperm under certain conditions. If the importing country is within the EEA (European Economic Area) the person responsible must obtain and retain (for three years) written evidence that the receiving or sending centre is accredited, designated, authorised or licensed in accordance with the requirements of the 2004 European Tissues and Cells Directive.[134] In all cases, all the requirements in the relevant HFEA Directions on import and export of gametes and embryos relating to identification, consent, parenthood, payment of the donor, use of the gametes and embryos and screening must be met.[135] So, if a child is born in Ireland using sperm that was imported from the UK, the question arises as to whether the child would be entitled to seek information from the HFEA on reaching the relevant age.

[5.116] Section 31 of The Human Fertilisation and Embryology Act 1990 (as amended in 2008), requires the Human Fertilisation and Embryology Authority (HFEA) to maintain a Register of licensed fertility treatment carried out in the UK, and to respond to requests for information from persons entitled to information held on the Register, such as persons who are donor-conceived. The Act requires HFEA-licensed centres to supply the HFEA with the necessary information which then enables the HFEA to respond to individual requests from the register. The HFEA, however, is not permitted to hold data about treatment cycles held outside of a UK licensed centre. As a result, it would not be able to provide register information to persons who were conceived following treatment outside of a UK licensed centre, such as in Ireland.

[5.117] In 2005, the Commission on Assisted Human Reproduction recommended that gamete and embryo donation should be permitted in Ireland, subject to regulation by a licensing body. It considered at length the issues relating to donor anonymity and concluded that the best interests of children born through AHR required that they be facilitated in accessing information relating to their genetic parentage. The Commission therefore recommended that 'any child born through the use of donated gametes or embryos should, on maturity, be able to identify the donor(s) involved in his/her conception.'[136]

[5.118] The Children and Family Relationships Act 2015 fundamentally changed the legal landscape for donor-conceived adults. Although not yet commenced, Part 3 of the

---

[133] http://www.aai.gov.ie/index.php/tracing/release-of-original-birth-certificate.html.

[134] Directive 2004/23/EC of the European Parliament and of the Council of 31 March 2004.

[135] For further details see www.hfea.gov.uk/.

[136] Available at www.health.gov.ie.

Act provides for the establishment of a national donor-conceived person register which will record information on donor-conceived children, donors and parents for the purpose of enabling a donor-conceived child to trace his or her identity. Section 24 prohibits a Donor Assisted Human Reproduction (DAHR) facility from acquiring anonymous gametes or embryos. This would also apply to importation of gametes with the result that those who seek to use anonymous sperm imported from countries such as Denmark will be unable to do so with the assistance of a clinic and will only be able to do so in a private capacity. However s 26 provides that the facility may use anonymous gametes for up to three years from commencement of the Act where an intending parent wishes to use the gametes in order to have a genetically related sibling for an existing child. This means where a child has already been born using anonymous sperm before the commencement of the Act, the parents may seek to use sperm from the same anonymous donor to conceive a second child who will be a genetic sibling of the first child. The facility may also continue indefinitely to use embryos created before the Act even if created using donor gametes.

[5.119] Section 28 provides that the DAHR facility must retain and provide information to the Minister for Health on the donor and intending parent(s) as well as the name, date of birth, sex and address of the resulting child. Section 33 provides for the establishment of a national donor-conceived person register which will record information on the child, the donor, the parents, and the facility at which the procedure took place. Section 34 sets out the information that each category of person will be entitled to receive from this register. A donor-conceived child who has reached the age of 18 or the parent of a donor-conceived child will be able to access non-identifying information on the donor and whether any related siblings exist, their sex and year of birth. The donor will also be able to get information as to whether children have been born from their donation, and the sex and year of birth of each of them.

[5.120] Section 35 provides that a donor-conceived child over 18 can apply to the Minister for Health for all information in relation to the donor maintained on the register. The Minister must inform the donor that this request has been made and the donor then has 12 weeks within which to object to the release of such information on the grounds that the safety or well-being of the donor or child would be affected by the release of the information. The Minister will decide if there are sufficient reasons to withhold or release the information. If the donor does not respond within 12 weeks, the information will be released. A similar procedure exists for donors to access identifying information in respect of any child born as a result of their donation. The child will be notified that the donor has sought the information only if that child has previously given their consent to contact from the donor.[137] Section 37 sets out a similar procedure to be followed in relation to donor-conceived siblings.

[5.121] Section 39 sets out how the donor register described above will interact with the birth register. When an entry is made on the donor-conceived person register, the Minister for Health must notify the General Register that a record on the child is held on the donor-conceived person register. The General Register must note this fact on the Register of Births. If a person over 18 applies for a copy of his or her birth certificate, he/she will be informed that further information relating to the person is available from

---

[137] Section 35 of the 2015 Act.

the donor-conceived person register. This means that the first time that a person discovers that they were donor-conceived may be when this information is provided to them by the Registrar of Births. The Act does not stipulate the mechanism by which the person is given this information but since this procedure will not become available until the first child born after commencement of this Part of the Act reaches 18, it is expected that the details of how this information will be disclosed, whether counselling will be offered and so on, will be worked out in the intervening years.[138]

EGG DONATION

[5.122] In the past, oocyte (egg) storage raised difficult clinical challenges and it was therefore a procedure that was relatively uncommon and regarded as experimental. However, the use of the procedure has grown recently, with the advent of vitrification, a technique that is gradually replacing slow freezing. The technique is currently being used not only for egg donation, but also for women undergoing oncological treatment or other therapies which could damage their fertility. It is also available in some countries for women electing to postpone childbearing for personal or professional reasons.[139]

[5.123] Egg donation may be sought if, for example, the woman's ovaries were damaged during treatment for cancer[140] or if she suffered from Turner's syndrome in which she was born without ovaries, or she had non-functioning ovaries due to premature ovarian failure or premature menopause. The procedure itself is time-consuming and invasive, as the donor must undergo medical and genetic screening, blood tests, the administration of fertility drugs and hormone injections, and ultrasound-guided retrieval of the eggs. Risks to the donor include ovarian cysts, caused by stimulation of the ovaries, and possible bleeding, injury, or infection of internal organs during the process of egg retrieval.[141] For the recipient, too, the procedure involves physical risk and intrusion. Synchronisation of the recipient's ovulatory cycle with the donor's ovulatory cycle

---

[138] Translating the *idea* of openness into *practice* is not as straightforward as one might think. Openness can lead to a series of dilemmas in personal life such as in the context of decisions about disclosure and the issue of family boundaries; when to share information with the child; sharing information with the wider family; and moral dimensions embedded in the idea of disclosure and so how to share information in the 'right way'. Nordqvist, 'The Drive for Openness in Donor Conception: Disclosure and the Trouble with Real Life.' Int J Law Policy Family (2014) 28 (3): 321–338.

[139] International Federation of Fertility Societies, Surveillance 2013, p 58 available at www.iffs-reproduction.org.

[140] Some of these difficulties might be avoided in future years due to recent reported successes in freezing ovarian tissue. The ovarian transplant technique has been pioneered primarily to help women facing early menopause or sterility caused by chemotherapy treatment. In such cases the ovaries would be removed before treatment, frozen and later re-implanted to give the woman back the ability to produce eggs.

[141] However, thus far no major long-term harmful effects have been demonstrated. Most studies have reported a high level of donor satisfaction, with almost all donors (99%) in a recent study reported to be either satisfied or very satisfied with their decision to donate and 95% would warmly recommend it to other women. Viveca Söderström-Anttila et al 'Short- and long-term health consequences and current satisfaction levels for altruistic anonymous, identity-release and known oocyte donors.' Hum Reprod (2016) 31 (3): 597–606.

requires close monitoring and, in the case of recipients with ovarian failure, estrogen and progesterone replacement to achieve endometrial maturation. The donation may be followed by fertilisation of the egg in vitro with the recipient's husband's sperm, (or donor sperm), and then transferred to the uterus of the recipient. Alternatively it may be transferred together with the sperm to the fallopian tube where it is hoped that fertilisation will occur (Gamete Intra Fallopian Transfer).

[5.124] Most European countries allow egg donation, with the exceptions of Austria, Italy, Norway, and Switzerland. Egg donors generally tend to be women who are undergoing surgical procedures which would allow access to the eggs, women who specifically want to become egg donors, such as sisters or friends of an infertile woman, or women who are undergoing IVF and who produce more eggs than they require for their own treatment, although this 'egg sharing' facility is not widely available. In the UK and most European countries, egg donors must be under the age of 35. Egg donation programmes are available in Ireland with the donors commonly being friends or relatives of the couple undergoing treatment or the donors being recruited in other countries through partner clinics. In some countries some of these women may be compensated or paid expenses,[142] while others may be offered their own medical procedure (such as sterilisation) free in return for the eggs.

[5.125] The question arises whether payment of money or provision of discounted medical treatment should be regarded as ethically acceptable. The issue here is largely one of public policy rather than law. Most societies regard some values as impossible to put a price on, such as personal relationships, justice, health and children. The challenge here, however, is to decide where to draw the line between what is necessary in the public good and therefore ought to be encouraged at whatever price, and that which is considered to be too valuable to be priced, despite the cost to those who need it. It may be argued that a regime whereby gametes could be bought and sold encourages the correlation of procreation and commerce that undermines the dignity of the child and the parents. 'Certain things should be above the hustle and bustle of the market-place so as to preserve their dignity.'[143]

[5.126] Another much-voiced concern here is the possibility for exploitation of impoverished women by offering them financial inducements to enter into a procedure which is invasive and risky. The prospect of payment may therefore have a coercive effect for some of these women, thereby negativing their free consent to the procedure. The counter-argument to this is that by prohibiting payment, society is being unduly

---

[142] In the United States, in the absence of regulation, eggs may be bought and sold for profit. Ikemoto gives an example of an advertisement for 'High IQ eggs' for $10,000 which appeared on a student's Facebook news feed. Clinics and agencies look for evidence of test scores, IQ, and college ranking. High scores and enrolment at prestigious universities are central to the egg market as well as other traits such as youth, good health, race, ethnicity, religion, good looks, height, and athleticism among the characteristics used to solicit, profile, and select women. Demand for eggs from Asian women exceeds supply so the prices offered to Asian women for their eggs sometimes exceed the prices offered to women of other races. However, it is the elitist criteria – near-perfect SAT scores and a place at a top-ten university – that consistently command the higher prices. "High IQ Eggs Wanted" – ads appeal to ego and altruism, offer $10,000 (Mar 19 2015). Available at www.biopoliticaltimes.org.

[143] Prichard, 'A Market for Babies?' (1984) 34 U Toronto LJ 341, 352.

paternalistic as regards women who may exercise their autonomy to utilise their bodies in any way they so wish.

[5.127] The predominant negative effect of the prohibition of payment for eggs is that the supply of an already scarce commodity will diminish even more, thereby perhaps reducing even further the opportunity for infertile couples to conceive. Although the evidence suggests many women donate for altruistic reasons, most would not donate without financial compensation. The compromise position that has been adopted in many countries is to allow for the payment of expenses to the donor to compensate her for the risk, discomfort and inconvenience involved in the procedure. It is unclear what position will be adopted in relation to payment to gamete donors in the promised Bill to regulate assisted reproduction. There are however indications that reasonable expenses may be permitted for surrogate mothers and therefore it is likely that a similar position will be adopted for gamete donors.[144]

Legal maternity

[5.128] One of the most interesting legal questions to arise from egg donation is well expressed by an English judge, Scott Baker J who noted that:

> Until recently, when the advance of medical science created the possibility of *In Vitro* Fertilisation, it was not envisaged that the genetic mother and the carrying mother could be other than one and the same person. The advent of *In Vitro* Fertilisation presented the law with a dilemma: who should the law regard as the mother?[145]

To ask the question another way: is the legal mother to be the genetic mother who donated her eggs or the gestational mother who carried the child to term and gave birth to it?[146] Many definitions of motherhood have been put forward, some of which emphasise the importance of the nine-month gestation period during which the mother's body supplies physical and emotional protection to the developing child. Others argue that gestation is 'an experience of identity or, more precisely, of undifferentiation' and that pregnancy is experienced 'not so much as presence of a separate entity in the womb, but as an alteration of the entire body.'[147]

[5.129] The Warnock Report in the UK in 1984 concluded 'where a woman donates an egg for transfer to another the donation should be treated as absolute and that, like a male donor, she should have no rights or duties with regard to any resulting child.'[148] Section 33 of the Human Fertilisation and Embryology Act 2008, (as also provided by the preceding 1990 Act s 27(1)) provides that a woman who carries a child as a result of the placing in her of an embryo or of sperm and eggs, and no other woman, is to be

---

[144] http://health.gov.ie/blog/press-release/govt-to-legislate-for-assisted-human-reproduction-associated-research/.

[145] *Re W (Minors)(Surrogacy)* [1991] 1 FLR 385.

[146] This same question was posed in Ireland, obiter, by Murphy J in *WO'R v EH & An Bord Uchtála* [1996] 2 IR 248.

[147] Ashe, 'Law-Language of Maternity: Discourse Holding Nature in Contempt' (1988) 22 New Eng L Rev 521–549.

[148] *Report of the Committee of Inquiry into Human Fertilisation and Embryology* (1984) Cmnd. 9314, HMSO, London.

treated as the mother of the child. This seeks to emphasise the social, psychological and nurturing aspect of motherhood and gives these elements priority over the genetic link.

[5.130] In Ireland s 4 of the Children and Family Relationships Act 2015 (which has not yet been commenced) defines the child's 'mother' as the woman who gives birth to the child.[149] Section 5 provides that the parents of a donor-conceived child are the mother and her husband, civil partner or cohabitant. It is specifically provided that the donor of a gamete is not the parent of any resulting child and has no parental rights or duties. The provisions in Part 3 of the Act in relation to access by donor-conceived children to information relating to sperm donors also apply to children conceived using donated eggs.[150]

---

[149] This is consistent with the judgment of the Supreme Court in *MR and DR (suing by their father and next friend OR) and CR and An t-Ard -Chlaratheoir, Ireland and the Attorney General & another* [2014] IESC 60, where the court interpreted the meaning of 'mother' for birth registration purposes as the birth mother. This is discussed further in relation to surrogacy in Ch 7.

[150] Para **[5.118]** et seq.

Chapter 6

In Vitro Fertilisation

INTRODUCTION

[6.01] One of the main treatments for female infertility is IVF (in vitro fertilisation). This treatment may help women who have been diagnosed with conditions such as blockage of the fallopian tubes or endometriosis. The procedure usually requires the woman to take ovarian stimulation drugs for a period of time to stimulate the ovaries to produce a number of eggs (optimally six to eight) which are retrieved vaginally or by laparoscopy. The eggs are then incubated with sperm in a petri dish in a laboratory so that fertilisation can take place. If fertilisation occurs, approximately 18 hours after insemination visible changes can be seen under microscopic examination with pronuclear development of the embryo. Depending on the practice of the clinic, within a few days after fertilisation, the embryos will be transferred to the woman's uterus, or may be stored for future use. Since the first IVF baby, Louise Brown, was born in 1978 6.5 million children have been born worldwide through this technique.[1] However, although IVF has largely become more acceptable in most societies, there are still controversies surrounding its use in certain circumstances.

[6.02] Female fertility decreases with age so a woman may have difficulty conceiving after her mid-thirties. For a woman who may wish to postpone having a family until this age or later, she could consider storing her eggs for her own future use. Eggs used to be scarcer and more difficult to handle than sperm, but with advances in technology in recent years,[2] this form of 'social egg freezing' has now become a more feasible option.[3] Eggs may also be frozen in advance by a woman undergoing medical treatments such as chemotherapy or radiotherapy which could damage her fertility. If on the other hand, the woman does not have eggs, for example due to ovarian failure or premature menopause, or where the eggs cannot be used due to poor quality, she may become pregnant using egg donation. This is where a woman (the donor) provides several eggs in order to help another woman (the recipient) become pregnant. The procedure involves both donor and recipient going through IVF treatment at the same time. The donor's ovaries are

---

[1] https://focusonreproduction.eu/2016/07/05/6-5-million-ivf-babies-since-louise-brown/ (July 2016).

[2] Eggs have a high water content, so the slow-freezing techniques used for freezing sperm and embryos were not as successful. With slow freezing, ice crystals can form, and when the eggs are thawed, those ice crystals can fracture and damage the egg. In recent years, a new freezing process called vitrification has grown in popularity. Vitrification is an ultra-rapid process that prohibits the formation of ice crystals. It also involves the use of new cryoprotectants, which are substances that protect tissue from freezing damage.

[3] Cobo et al 'Use of cryo-banked oocytes in an ovum donation programme: a prospective, randomised, controlled, clinical trial' (2010) 25 Human Reproduction 2239–46.

stimulated in order to generate eggs for collection, the eggs are fertilised in the laboratory with the recipient partner's sperm and at the same time the recipient's body is prepared for embryo transfer. In some cases, a couple will seek embryo donation if they are unable to provide the eggs or sperm themselves but the woman can still carry the pregnancy. In this situation a couple who have already been through IVF may have more embryos than they intend to use for their own reproductive purposes so they may decide to donate them to another couple. The legal and ethical issues associated with gamete donation are discussed in Chapter 5.

[6.03] If a couple has more than one fertilised egg or embryo available for transfer, the question arises as to how many embryos should be transferred to the woman's uterus. Multi-fetal pregnancies are recognised as a major problem associated with assisted reproduction. The incidence of twin and high-order multiple births has quadrupled since 1980. This very significant increase has been attributed to three major factors: 'the delay of first childbirth with a corresponding higher incidence of multiple pregnancy in women of advanced maternal age, the increased use of ovulation induction and insemination procedures for infertile patients, and the more prevalent use of IVF'.[4] This is a matter of considerable concern for obstetricians and paediatricians as these pregnancies can lead to 'an increase in perinatal mortality primarily due to premature delivery, but also to utero-placental compromise and an increased rate of congenital anomalies among these infants. Maternal complications of triplet and high-order multiple births include pregnancy-induced hypertension, antepartum and postpartum haemorrhage, and severe anaemia.'[5]

[6.04] During the past 10 years, these risks have become more widely acknowledged and many countries have established either legislation or guidelines with the intent of limiting the number of embryos for transfer. Studies from Australia, Sweden, Denmark, the Netherlands, and Belgium have shown that single embryo transfer achieves pregnancy and live birth rates equivalent to the transfer of two and even three embryos, without the complications of twin and higher order pregnancies and births.[6] Several countries now have firm guidelines or regulations permitting only single embryo transfers for certain categories of patients.[7] Despite the fact that in Ireland it is estimated that at least 1 percent of all births result from assisted reproduction,[8] there are no regulations in place dealing with embryo transfer.[9] As a result of the lack of regulation, and also due to the fact that there is no public funding of IVF in Ireland, there are

---

[4] International Federation of Fertility Societies, Surveillance 2013 available at www.iffs-reproduction.org.

[5] International Federation of Fertility Societies, Surveillance 2013 available at www.iffs-reproduction.org.

[6] Chambers et al, 'Assisted reproductive technology: public funding and the voluntary shift to single embryo transfer in Australia' Med J Aust 2011; 195 (10): 594–598.

[7] International Federation of Fertility Societies, Surveillance 2013 available at www.iffs-reproduction.org.

[8] ESHRE. 'Assisted reproductive technology in Europe 2009. Results generated from European registers by ESHRE' (2013) Human Reproduction 2318–31

[9] There are limited guidelines in the Medical Council's Guide to Professional Conduct and Ethics (8th edn, 2016) available at www.medicalcouncil.ie, discussed further at **[6.10]**.

concerns that 'in many cases the market incentive to attract patients may override more conservative embryo transfer practices.'[10]

Development of the early embryo

[6.05] The process of formation of an embryo begins with the production of gametes, that is, the eggs and sperm, within the bodies of the woman and the man. The eggs are collected following ovarian stimulation and the man produces a semen sample. In IVF, the sperm and egg are placed together in a petri dish in the laboratory and the fertilisation process begins with the sperm making its way through the cells surrounding the egg. The sperm then reaches the zona or shell of the egg, with which it binds. It passes through the zona into the space between the zona and the egg by releasing special enzymes, which help dissolve the area of the zona immediately in front of the sperm head. The sperm is then drawn into the egg cytoplasm and the chromosome sets of the egg and sperm forming the female and male pro-nucleus join in a process called syngamy about 28–30 hours after the beginning of the process. The fertilisation process is only completed by formation of the single celled zygote 26–32 hours after the first contact between egg and sperm. In some cases a variant of IVF called Intra Cytoplasmic Sperm Injection (ICSI) is used when semen quality is poor.[11] This involves directly injecting a single moving sperm into the egg. Very few sperm are required for this technique and the ability of the sperm to penetrate the egg is not important as this has been assisted by the injection of the sperm directly into the egg. The success rates for IVF and ICSI are considered to be the same[12] and there are no distinct legal or ethical issues involved in ICSI.

[6.06] After the formation of the zygote, which is a single pluri-potent and toti-potent cell[13] with its complement of 46 chromosomes, the process of cell division continues. In IVF, the embryo is usually transferred to the uterus 3-5 days after fertilisation. After 5 days, when there are between 64 and 128 cells present, the blastocyst begins to form in which cells begin to differentiate into the future embryo, the placenta and other membranes. In sexual reproduction up to 80 per cent of blastocysts may be lost spontaneously and unnoticed around this stage. This may be due to abnormalities in these blastocysts or other factors such as the uterus not being fully receptive, which

---

[10] Submission by the Institute of Obstetricians and Gynaecologists to the Department of Health http://health.gov.ie/wp-content/uploads/2015/02/Institute-of-Obstetricians-and-Gynaecologists.pdf.

[11] Further techniques, Percutaneous Epididymal Sperm Aspiration (PESA) and Testicular Sperm Extraction (TESE) have been developed to recover sperm from from men who have no sperm in the ejaculate, either due to congenital reasons or acquired as a result of vasectomy.

[12] Success rates are not collated nationally in Ireland but the Human Fertilisation and Embryology Authority in the UK which collates data from all licensed fertility centres in the UK states that the success rate is 32.2% for women aged under 35 and it declines thereafter for women over 35. http://www.hfea.gov.uk/ivf-success-rate.html

[13] Totipotency means the cell can develop into any other cell or even into an entire new embryo; pluripotency means the cell may develop into many different cell types, but not all. The cells of the early embryos are totipotent, in that they have the ability to form all the different cell types of the body, including the stem cell of the next stage, the blastocyst. Stem cells are said to be pluripotent in that they have the ability to form multiple cell types.

would actively inhibit implantation. At about the fifth or sixth day after fertilisation the blastocyst begins to attach to the lining of the uterus. This process of implantation is a crucial point in the development of the embryo because, without implantation, the embryo will not survive as it requires oxygen and nutrients from the mother to be able to grow.

[6.07] At around the 14th day after fertilisation, a line known as the primitive streak is identifiable on the surface of the embryonic disc. This is the precursor of the development of a nervous system and is another important stage in the development of the embryo. It is at this point that twinning will become evident, as the number of embryos will be determined by the number of primitive streaks that develop. Some commentators and scientists argue that this is the most important stage in the development of the new human being:

> To me the point at which I began as a total whole individual human being was at the primitive streak stage ... If one tries to trace back further than that there is no longer a coherent entity. Instead there is a larger collection of cells, some of which are going to take part in the subsequent development of the embryo and some of which aren't.[14]

The significance of this stage is that under the terms of the Human Fertilisation and Embryology Act, clinics in the UK may not be licensed to keep or use a human embryo after the appearance of the primitive streak.[15] After the development of the primitive streak, the pre-embryonic phase is over and the embryonic phase begins.[16] Thus, fertilisation should be understood not as a moment in time but rather as a process which takes place over many hours and has two important consequences, namely that the egg is activated to continue development and that a single set of chromosomes from each parent combines to produce a new unique double set in the zygote.

[6.08] In so-called 'simple' IVF, where a married couples' own gametes are used, the process presents no major legal problems. 'The genetic and natural parentage of the resulting infant are not disputed. All that has occurred is that a technique has been substituted for a natural process; if any would protest that this is in some way immoral, they would, at the same time, have to contend that the surgical treatment of any disease is similarly immoral'.[17] The main ethical and legal issues that arise in the context of IVF occur due to the cryopreservation or storage of embryos. In the absence of legislation, this practice can sometimes lead to disputes in relation to the status of the embryo and the locus of decision-making authority in respect of the embryos.

---

[14] McLaren, 'Prelude to Embryogenesis' in Bock and O'Connor (eds), *Human Embryo Research* (Tavistock Publications, 1986) 22.

[15] Section 3 Human Fertilisation and Embryology Act 1990 (UK) as amended in 2008.

[16] In coming to an understanding of the status of the early embryo, it is important to recognise that conception is a process or series of phases of development rather than one single moment. 'The idea of a moment of conception when a new human being is miraculously created is over-dramatised, and results from ignorance of modern biology. The 'moment' when two gametes (the sperm and the ovum) fuse resolves itself under the microscope into a succession of clearly discernible stages, which may take 24 hours or more to complete. No one of these stages identifies itself as obviously the 'moment of conception'. However you date man's beginning, it is, like his ending, a process.' Williams, 'The Fetus and the 'Right to Life'' (1994) Cambridge Law Journal, 71–80 at 76.

[17] Laurie, Harmon and Porter, *Law and Medical Ethics* (10th edn, OUP, 2016) para 8.51.

[6.09] Due to the stimulation of the ovaries for the purposes of IVF, a number of eggs may be retrieved from the woman. This averages about six but may be as high as ten or more. Although egg freezing has become more technically successful, it is common practice to fertilise the eggs with sperm in order to create embryos which can be stored more successfully. As mentioned above, in order to avoid multiple pregnancies, best medical practice indicates that no more than two or, at a maximum three, embryos should be transferred and several countries now have firm guidelines or regulations permitting only single embryo transfers for certain categories of patients. This means that a decision must be made as to what will happen to embryos that are not used for transfer. In most countries in which IVF is practised, the remaining embryos may be cryopreserved or frozen for future use. The first successful birth from a frozen and thawed embryo was in 1983:

> It would now be considered dangerous for an IVF clinic not to have an embryo freezing programme available to cope with instances where a 'freeze-all' is indicated on safety grounds, such as where ovarian hyperstimulation syndrome (OHSS) is very likely. If there are additional embryos available surplus to requirement for immediate transfer, these can be stored for future cycle usage, sparing the couple the full procedure should the present one not succeed or they wish to try to procreate again if it does. Importantly, freezing allows the number of embryos transferred in one cycle to be reduced and with that, the chances of multiple pregnancy.[18]

[6.10] In the absence of legislation dealing with these issues, medical practitioners in Ireland observe international best practice guidelines, guidelines of the Irish Fertility Society[19] and the provisions of the Medical Council's Guide to Professional Conduct and Ethics. The Medical Council's Guide (8th edn) does not specifically mention embryo transfer or storage and therefore it might be argued that doctors are not obliged to limit the number of embryos for transfer. However, the Guide does state that 'assisted reproduction services should only be provided by suitably qualified professionals, in appropriately accredited facilities and in line with international best practice'.[20] It is therefore possible that clinicians who do not follow international best practice in relation to embryo transfer in order to reduce the risk of multi-fetal pregnancies could be the subject of a complaint to the Medical Council which could result in a Fitness to Practise Inquiry and sanctions being imposed where appropriate.[21]

ETHICAL ISSUES IN IVF

[6.11] Before discussing the legal issues arising in relation to the status of the embryo, this section will briefly examine some of the ethical issues in IVF. Any public debate about the regulation of assisted reproduction in Ireland will inevitably involve

---

[18] Harrison, *The Smart Guide to Infertility* (Hammersmith Press, 2009) at p 230.
[19] Para 3.3 of the Irish Fertility Society's Consensus document states 'Freezing of embryos is a requirement in the development of effective single embryo transfer policies and the reduction in multiple pregnancy rates.' It further advises that 'Appropriate protocols should be in place in each unit to govern the transfer (to the uterus), freezing, storage and disposal of frozen embryos.'
[20] Guide to Professional Conduct and Ethics (8th edn, 2016). Para 47.2 www.medicalcouncil.ie
[21] See Chapter 2 for discussion of the role of the Medical Council and Fitness to Practise inquiries.

arguments relating to the moral status of the embryo as well as other ethical objections. The moral issue that has perplexed many philosophers in relation to IVF revolves around the question of 'when does life begin?' It has been argued, however, that this question is unanswerable and indeterminate from a scientific point of view and that therefore the question should be 'when does life begin to matter morally?' or 'when does life begin to have that special value we believe attaches to human life?'[22] 'The question is not whether the conceptus is human but whether it should be given the same legal protection as you and me.'[23] By defining what significance the embryo has, society can lay down the parameters within which the embryo may be accorded rights and privileges in the legal context. However, in an attempt to clarify the issue, perhaps this argument ought to be reversed. It might well be that it is by discovering what we are prepared to do with the embryo that we can determine what its status is, as opposed to the other way around.[24]

[6.12] For those who take the position that human life begins at the point at which the sperm penetrates the egg, then experimentation or destruction of the fertilised egg is immoral. However, if human life is not perceived to begin until some later point, such as: syngamy (when the chromosomes from the male and female fuse); or implantation (when the embryo implants in the lining of the uterus); or at the emergence of the primitive streak, then before these various stages the embryo egg could be stored for future use or used for research purposes without transgressing the principle of dignity and respect for human life. After human life has been established the application of this principle of respect and dignity would ensure that no intervention could be made which would harm the developing embryo.[25]

[6.13] There are many different approaches to the question of when life begins to matter.[26] Some of these arguments look at whether one can describe the embryo as 'a life', while still recognising that it is human and living tissue. Thus the issue for consideration is whether the cell mass that is the embryo constitutes a human life in its own right, thereby according to it moral and legal rights and placing corresponding duties on others. This is not to say that if it does not constitute a human life that it is

---

22   Harris, *The Value of Life* (1985) p 8.
23   Williams, 'The fetus and the 'right to life'' (1994) Cambridge Law Journal p 78.
24   Evans, 'Pro-Attitudes to Pre-Embryos', in Evans (ed) *Conceiving the Embryo* (Martinus Nijhoff Publishers, 1996) 27. Evans considers the character of, what he terms, 'pro-attitudes to pre-embryos', in attempting to come to a conclusion on the status of the embryo. He argues that science alone cannot determine the issue, as scientists too are divided on when life begins. He asks whether philosophical reflection can assist in the discussion and demonstrates that here too the debates are split. In the face of such division and disagreement he queries whether regulation would be proper and concludes that a minimalist programme of regulation which would broadly give respect for human life would be the most we could hope for in this debate.
25   Madden, '*In Vitro* Fertilisation: the Moral and Legal Status of the Human Pre-Embryo' (1997) 3(1) Medico-Legal Journal of Ireland, 12–20 at 13.
26   Harris argues that there are only two types of answer which might be given to when does the embryo begin to matter morally. One is in terms of what the embryo *is*, the other is in terms of what it will *become*, that is to say, its *potential*. See Dyson and Harris, *Experiments on Embryos* (Routledge, 1990) p 67.

worthy of *no* protection or *no* respect, but rather that it is deserving of less respect and protection than a human life.

Personhood

[6.14] The definition of person is usually derived from Boethius, a philosopher and theologian from the 5th century, who defined 'person' as 'an individual substance of a rational nature'.[27] Aquinas later indicated that this definition applies to human beings because they are separate from each other, thus they are individuals, and because they are rational, that is 'they have control over their own actions and are not only acted upon as are all other beings, but act of their own initiative'.[28] He considered the term *person* to be a special name differentiating substances of a rational nature from other substances based on their intrinsic nature, not decisions based on social acceptance or law. As Aquinas uses the term, 'the mere presence of the intellective soul is sufficient for personhood.'[29] In more modern times, Locke further defined a person as:

> [A] conscious thinking thing (whatever substance made up of, whether spiritual or material, simple or compounded, it matters not) which is sensible, or conscious of pleasure and pain, capable of happiness or misery, and so is concerned for itself, as far as that consciousness extends.[30]

[6.15] Many modern bioethicists have focused on the issue of consciousness as the necessary component of personhood although this is controversial as it excludes those without capacity. According to this definition, it is possible to be a human being in the sense of being a member of the *homo sapiens* species, but yet not be a person. Engelhardt claims:

> Not all humans are persons…Fetuses, infants, the profoundly mentally retarded, and the hopelessly comatose provide examples of human nonpersons. Such entities are members of the human species but they do not in and of themselves have standing in the moral community. They cannot blame or praise or be worthy of blame or praise…For this reason, it is nonsensical to speak of respecting the autonomy of fetuses, infants, or profoundly retarded adults, who have never been rational.[31]

[6.16] On the other hand, many bioethicists do not exclude from personhood human beings who have lost or never attained consciousness. The Roman Catholic Church's position was espoused by Pope John Paul II: 'A man, even if seriously ill or disabled in the exercise of his highest functions, is and always will be a man, and he will never become a vegetable or an animal.'[32] O'Rourke and other Catholic theologians claim

---

27 Boethius, 'De Duabis Naturis' 3 in Migne, *Patrologia Latina*, vol 64, 1343. Quoted in O'Rourke, 'The Embryo as Person' (2006) Essays, National Catholic Bioethics Center, 241–251 at 243.

28 St Thomas Aquinas, *Summa Theologiae*, I, Q 29.1.

29 O'Rourke, 'The Embryo as Person' (2006) Essays, National Catholic Bioethics Center, 241–251 at 243.

30 Locke, *An Essay Concerning Human Understanding* (OUP, 1975) 62, quoted in O'Rourke.

31 Engelhardt Jr, *The Foundations of Bioethics*, (OUP, 1986) 107; Also Lizza 'Persons and Death' (1993) Journal of Medicine and Philosophy 18.4: 351–374.

32 John Paul II, 'On Life-Sustaining Treatments and the Vegetative State' (March 20, 2004) National Catholic Bioethics Quarterly 4.3.

unequivocally that the embryo is a person from fertilisation and that therefore society has a responsibility to protect them from that point. This approach, that what matters morally is being a member of the human species and that membership begins at fertilisation, has been described by Harris as 'the hedgehog's approach to the moral status of the embryo.'[33] Harris claims that this approach does not deal with the fact that fertilisation is a continuous process which would not be possible without a process of development and maturation of the egg that begins at a much earlier stage.[34] So, too, the sperm is alive before it penetrates the egg.[35] So if the egg and sperm are alive before conception, it is difficult to state that life begins at that moment when the sperm successfully penetrates the egg.[36]

[6.17] Another argument sometimes used in favour of conferring personhood on the embryo from fertilisation stems from the conviction that there is no stage of early embryonic development which is as significant as this point in time. In other words, everything that occurs after fertilisation is simply a development of the potential attributes with which the embryo was bestowed at that time:

> The embryo or foetus possesses its fundamental right to life from the moment of conception. From that moment the foetus is already provided with all the genetic elements that will shape its future development as an adult human person. To use the language of genetics, the embryo, from the instant of the meeting of the mother and father cells, is already equipped with the entire 'programme' of its future physical characteristics, right down to the minutest detail...as well as of its basic mental capacity and personality traits.

---

[33] Harris takes this description from a famous essay on Leo Tolstoy, called *The Hedgehog and the Fox*, by Isaiah Berlin. 'Berlin takes a fragment of Greek poetry and uses it to create a celebrated typology of human thought. 'The fox knows many things, but the hedgehog knows one big thing.' There are those, according to Berlin, who pursue many ideas and those who like to bring everything under one central vision or organising principle. The latter are hedgehogs, the former are foxes.' Harris describes the fox's approach to this problem as being more sophisticated. The fox will attempt to identify morally relevant features of the embryo or foetus (such as its form, development of functioning organs, sentience and so on), and argue that in virtue of its possession of these characteristics, it is worthy of protection. Harris, *Experiments on Embryos* (Routledge, 1990) pp 67–68.

[34] Harris, *The Value of Life* (Routledge, 1985) p 10.

[35] The argument, between the spermatozoists and the ovists, as to the relative significance of the sperm and the ovum in reproduction was seen in the 17th Century, with each group of the opinion that preformed human life was in the preferred gamete and the corresponding dormant partner gamete either sparked off the growth of the preformed embryo (the role of the sperm according to the ovists), or provided the necessary context for the growth of the preformed embryo (the role of the ovum according to the spermatozoists). See Evans, 'Pro-Attitudes to Pre-Embryos', in Evans (ed) *Conceiving the Embryo* (Martinus Nijhoff Publishers, 1996) 27, p 32.

[36] It has been known for some time that sperm entry is not the only stimulus for cleavage to begin. Parthogenic activation of early development can be achieved in some mammalian species including humans. Braude and Johnson ask 'how should we regard, in philosophical terms, these unfertilised but cleaving "pre-embryos"?' 'The Embryo in Contemporary Medical Science' in Dunstan, *The Human Embryo: Aristotle and the Arabic and European Traditions* (University of Exeter Press, 1990) 208–221, p 218.

> Everything that education and environment will later have to work on is already present in the embryo.[37]

[6.18] Other philosophers argue that certain criteria must be satisfied before personhood is possible. In other words, there should be at least a biological stability or organisation in the embryo before it will be granted the privilege of personhood. Some call it a 'spatially-defined entity', while others refer to the fact that preliminary developments in the fertilised egg are not the development of the embryo proper but rather the establishment of the trophoblast, or feeding layer, that is crucial to any future development. The Catholic Church's teaching has been criticised for not distinguishing between genetic individuation and developmental individuation in this regard:

> There is no awareness that in the embryo's early stages neighbouring cells are loosely associated, that the cells of the inner cell mass of the early blastocyst are... 'little different in developmental capability from the zygote. Each can contribute to any part of the embryo, and separation of the mass into two parts can still yield two or more embryos.'[38] It shows no awareness that only with the process of implantation do we eventually attain primary embryonic organisation.[39]

The position of the Roman Catholic Church

[6.19] Although Ireland has in recent years become a more multi-cultural and multi-denominational country, in the population census carried out in 2011, 84.2 per cent of the Republic's population described themselves as Roman Catholic, with other religious communities such as Protestant, Muslim, Jewish, Jehovah's Witnesses, and Orthodox faiths increasing steadily.[40] Although art 44 of the Irish Constitution guarantees freedom of conscience and the free profession and practice of religion to all citizens, the Roman Catholic tradition has had a significant influence on the development of health policy in Ireland. Indeed, McDonnell and Allison claim that in relation to bioethical issues, the Catholic Church 'is not simply asserting its voice of dissent in the context of public debate as one voice amongst a plurality of other voices, but to shape the emerging debate as a powerful, institutional actor.'[41] They state that Ireland has been slow to debate or regulate bioethical issues, including assisted reproduction:

> The apparent reticence of policy makers to engage in the emerging international bioethical discourse on advances in biomedical science and biotechnology reflects, in large part, the legacy of...the 'moral monopoly' of the Catholic Church over questions of identity, ethics and public morality in Ireland.[42]

---

[37] Bishops of Ireland, 'Yes to Life', Extract From the Pastoral Letter 'Human Life is Sacred', in 'Abortion, Law and Conscience' (May/June 1992) 42(5) Doctrine and Life 326–335 at 328.

[38] Quoting Grobstein, *Science and the Unborn* (Basic Books, 1988).

[39] McCormick 'Who or What is the Preembryo?' (1991) 1 Kennedy Institute of Ethics Journal 1 p 8.

[40] http://www.cso.ie.

[41] McDonnell and Allison, 'From Biopolitics to Bioethics: Church, State, Medicine and Assisted Reproductive Technology in Ireland' (2006) Sociology of Health and Illness Vol 28 No 6 p 817–837.

[42] McDonnell and Allison, 'From Biopolitics to Bioethics: Church, State, Medicine and Assisted Reproductive Technology in Ireland' (2006) Sociology of Health and Illness Vol 28 No 6 p 818.

[6.20] The Catholic Church is opposed to IVF and other forms of assisted reproduction on the grounds that it is contrary to the teachings of the Church and the dignity of the human being. '[A]ll the teaching of the Church in regard to medical ethics results from the Christian understanding of the worth and activity of the human person.'[43] This understanding may be paraphrased as being based on the view that God creates the human person in his own image and likeness and possessing a spiritual intelligence and free will. According to traditional Catholic views, beginning at conception the embryo has moral status as a human being, and this means that most assisted reproductive technologies are forbidden. 'Although the human body is brought into being through the cooperation of human parents, the creation of the human soul is a direct act of God'.[44] The Catholic Church states that procreation must conform to the dignity of the person. The only possible way in which to procreate in such conformity is to respect the link between the meanings of the conjugal act and respect for the unity of human beings:

> In his unique and irrepeatable origin, the child must be respected and recognised as equal in personal dignity to those who give him life. The human person must be accepted in his parents' act of union and love; the generation of a child must therefore be the fruit of that mutual giving which is realised in the conjugal act ...He cannot be desired or conceived as the product of an intervention of medical or biological techniques; that would be equivalent to reducing him to an object of scientific technology. No one may subject the coming of a child into the world to conditions of technical efficiency which are to be evaluated according to standards of control and dominion.[45]

[6.21] Another objection taken to IVF by the Catholic Church is based on the sanctity of human life from its beginning. Pope Paul VI in 1973 said the State's protection of human life should begin at conception, 'this being the beginning of a new human being.'[46] The Congregation for the Doctrine of the Faith issued a Statement on Procured Abortion in 1974, which also dealt with the status of the embryo. It states that '[F]rom the time that the ovum is fertilised, a life is begun which is neither that of the father nor the mother, it is rather the life of a new human being with his own growth. He will never become human if he were not human already.'[47] The Catholic Church asserts that modern genetic science confirms this position because it shows that from the very beginning, the

---

[43] Ashley and O'Rourke, *Health Care Ethics* (2nd edn, Catholic Health Association of the United States, 1982) p 162.

[44] O'Rourke and Boyle, *Medical Ethics: Sources of Catholic Teachings* (2nd edn, Georgetown University Press, 1993) p 4.

[45] Congregation for the Doctrine of the Faith, 'Instruction on Respect for Human Life in its Origin and on the Dignity of Procreation' (1987) 16 Origins at 706.

[46] *Pourquois l'Eglise Ne Peut Accepter l'Avortement'* (1973) 70 Documentation Catholique, 4–5. English translation: (1973) 17 The Pope Speaks, 333–335.

[47] Congregation for the Doctrine of the Faith (1974) p 9. The final sentence of this statement has been troublesome for many theologians in terms of Christian teaching. This is due, in part, to its contradiction of the principle developed by St. Thomas Aquinas known as hylomorphism, which became the dominant theory in the theology of the Middle Ages from 600–1500 AD. The concept defines the human being as a unity of two elements: primary matter, which represents the potentiality of the body; and substantial form, which represents the actualising principle of the soul. 'It implies that hominisation is delayed to some point after the embryo has become a fully human body. Despite the body's potential as primary matter, there is no human person without the actualising principle of the substantial form, the soul. (contd.../)

complete genetic package is in place. However, this refers only to genetic individuality and not developmental individuality.[48] The Declaration of the Congregation of the Faith also states that it is leaving aside the thorny question of when the moment of animation occurs. It expressly refrains from stating that the soul is present from the beginning but yet human life must be protected from the time of fertilisation. It states: '[F]rom a moral point of view this is certain: even if a doubt existed concerning whether the fruit of conception is already a human person, it is objectively a grave sin to dare to risk murder.'[49] The Declaration therefore admits to the presence of a doubt about personhood but claims that it is immoral to act when such a doubt is present: 'It calls to mind the age-old chestnut: when the hunter is uncertain whether it is an animal or human moving in the underbush there is a certain obligation not to shoot.'[50]

Human dignity

[6.22] Objection is sometimes taken to IVF and associated practices on the basis that it is contrary to human dignity. The classical definition of human dignity comes from Greek and Roman antiquity, with the expressions *dignus* and *dignitas* expressing the notions of 'worthiness for honour and esteem'. This notion of dignity as something rare and exceptional retains some power in modern times in relation to our respect for those who are somehow distinctive and admirable due to their courage, heroism, athleticism, or selflessness in the service of others. But Schulman says if we are to speak about 'human dignity' there must be something in the nature of human beings per se that makes them worthy of respect.[51] He argues that the classical notion of dignity lends

---

[47] (\...contd) This substantial form, or soul, can only be present in a body capable of receiving it, one that has developed beyond the earliest stages of pregnancy.' Hurst, *The History of Abortion in the Catholic Church – The Untold Story,* (Washington DC Catholics for a Free Choice, 1989) p 13. This doctrine thus defines human beings as a unity of body and soul, not as a potential inherent in a developing body, which will eventually gain a human soul. In claiming that the fertilised egg 'would never be made human if it were not human already', the Church has changed the terms of arguments without confronting hylomorphism and the delayed hominisation principle. Hurst p 21.

[48] McCormick, 'Who or What is the Preembryo?' (1991) 1 Kennedy Institute of Ethics Journal 1, p 6. McCormick sees this as a fatal flaw in the reasoning behind the document, as it misunderstands the meaning of individuality and does not cater for the scientific knowledge, which clearly points to the conclusion that the embryo is not developmentally individual at this stage.

[49] McCormick, 'Who or What is the Preembryo?' (1991) 1 Kennedy Institute of Ethics Journal 1, at p 10.

[50] McCormick, 'Who or What is the Preembryo?' (1991) 1 Kennedy Institute of Ethics Journal 1, at p 7. However, as mentioned earlier, this tutiorist argument is only relevant in circumstances in which the doubt is a reasonable one. It has no place in modern discussions relating to the embryo due to the knowledge now available in relation to the development of the early embryo. Any doubt in respect of whether the embryo is a human individual at this stage in its development is, it may be argued, an unreasonable one and therefore should not be used in a tutiorist argument in favour of a prohibition on any action in relation to the embryo other than transfer to the uterus.

[51] Schulman, *Bioethics and Human Dignity*, The President's Council on Bioethics, Working Paper 2003.

itself to invidious distinctions between human beings, and is not fully at home with democratic ideals of equality, freedom and tolerance. He says that 'to make the case for human dignity as a robust bioethical concept for our age, one would have to show that dignity can be something universal and accessible to all human beings as such.'

[6.23] Kantian philosophy states that dignity is the intrinsic worth that belongs to all human beings and to no other beings in the natural world. All men possess dignity because of their rational autonomy, ie their capacity for free obedience to the moral law of which they themselves are the authors. Kant's doctrine of human dignity demands equal respect for all persons and forbids the use of another person merely as a means to one's own ends. Yet there are problems with this theory, too. If dignity depends on rational will and the capacity to act autonomously, does this imply that those who do not have such capacity, for example, intellectually disabled persons, infants or persons in a comatose state, are not worthy of human dignity?[52]

[6.24] Some commentators take the view that the vague and illusory nature of the concept of human dignity begs the question as to whether it has any place in bioethical discourse at all.[53] Examples of the use of the concept of human dignity in bioethics show how it can be manipulated to serve opposing sides of the same issue, such as end-of-life decision-making where both proponents and opponents of voluntary euthanasia appeal to human dignity in their arguments. This is perhaps due to the fact that the idea of human dignity emanates from a number of different sources, each of which brings with it its own difficulties.

[6.25] Many international declarations, such as the Universal Declaration of Human Rights (1948), the Universal Declaration on Bioethics and Human Rights (2005), and various national constitutions refer to human dignity, yet its meaning and content is never expressly defined. This reflects a political consensus among groups that may well have different beliefs about what human dignity means and what it entails. In effect, it serves as a placeholder for whatever it is about human beings that entitles them to basic human rights and freedoms.[54] This made a lot of practical sense after World War II when the most important issue was to ensure that agreement was reached that the atrocities inflicted at concentration and death camps would never be repeated. The 'inviolability of human dignity' was thus enshrined in some of these international documents to prevent a second Holocaust. However, although a baseline of inviolable rights is undoubtedly welcome, some argue that the same objective could be achieved by invoking the concept of 'respect for persons' instead.[55]

---

[52] Schulman, *Bioethics and Human Dignity*, The President's Council on Bioethics, Working Paper 2003.

[53] Macklin, 'Dignity is a Useless Concept' (2003) BMJ 327:1419–1420.

[54] Shultziner 'Human Dignity – Functions and Meanings' (2003) Global Jurist Topics 3:3.

[55] For example, Macklin argues that this ensures voluntary informed consent, the protection of confidentiality, and the need to prevent discrimination and abusive practices. Macklin, 'Dignity is a Useless Concept' (2003) BMJ 327:1419–1420.

Individuality

[6.26] An argument commonly raised to oppose the proposition that personhood begins at fertilisation is that multiple births such as twinning can occur after formation of the embryo. In the case of identical or monozygotic twins, each of these twins, when born, will be accorded the status of individuals.[56] Thus, the question arises whether there was one person present or two people present at the formation of the embryo. If there was only one person, what happened to this person when the second person appeared, and if there were two people to begin with, did they inhabit the same body? One response to this argument is what may be called the 'I'm in there somewhere' approach, which takes the view that because the embryo contains some cells which will later become the foetus, the entirety should be treated as if it had the potential to be human.[57] However, this approach may be criticised on the basis that it does not advert to the lack of the 'spatially-defined entity'. Also the fact that some cells may form the later foetus does not mean that they are singled out at this early stage as having that destiny. This is a gradual process that takes place over time, each cell having the potential to develop into many different parts of the body as well as the potential to develop into extra-corporeal matter. So it becomes very difficult to identify the person who is said to be 'in there somewhere'. The taking of the time of fertilisation as the starting point for the granting of protection is not necessarily logical. 'The pro-lifers think they solve the problem by admitting that the development of the foetus is continuous; they say that because no line can be drawn, the law must protect the human organism from the time of fertilisation. But what is the logic (never mind the practicality) of beginning with fertilisation? It is an essential stage in our development but so are all the others':[58]

> Life is a continuum which semantics, ethics and the law force us to divide at arbitrary points ... To pursue a less emotive parallel from postnatal life, we would not in a democracy give the vote to a child of 6 months or withhold it until an individual is 60, but whether the franchise is given at 18, 20 or 30 is an arbitrary decision.[59]

[6.27] Since twinning can occur prior to the emergence of the primitive streak, it is argued that individuality is not yet certain. 'Developmental individualisation is completed only when implantation has been completed, a period of time whose outside time-limits are around fourteen days'.[60] A human individual is not divisible, therefore an entity that *is* divisible and therefore lacks continuity of existence cannot be individual. Therefore, the answer to the question – how could a human individual not be a human

---

[56] Dunstan states: 'It is axiomatic in Western philosophy that there can be no personality without discrete individuality'. Dunstan and Seller (eds) *The Status of the Human Embryo. Perspectives From Moral Tradition* (King Edwards Hospital Fund, 1988) p14.

[57] See Holland, 'A Fortnight of My Life Is Missing: A Discussion of the Status of the Human Pre-Embryo' (1990) 7(1) Journal of Applied Philosophy 25.

[58] Williams, 'The Fetus and the 'Right to Life'' (1994) Cambridge Law Journal p 77.

[59] Potts, 'Postcoital contraception or abortion?' The Lancet Vol 322, Issue 8343, p 223, 23 July 1983.

[60] McCormick, 'Therapy or Tampering: the Ethics of Reproductive Technology and the Development of Doctrine' in *The Critical Calling, Reflections on Moral Dilemmas since Vatican II* (Georgetown University Press, 1989) Ch 19, 329–352 at 346.

person? – is, 'by not being, yet, a human individual.'[61] It may be counter argued however that developmental individualisation, or the phenomenon of twinning, is a special case and should be treated as the exception which proves the rule. In other words, personhood should be conferred on the embryo at the time of conception but, for twins, their personhood only begins at the 14-day stage when individuality becomes evident.[62] It is argued in relation to the problem of twinning that a living being as a whole does not turn into two or more living beings. But *parts* (such as cells or tissues) of the living being can be detached and added to other beings. This is not a division of the whole.[63] The biological picture which is given in relation to twinning has been criticised as being constructed out of what is seen through mechanistic or dualistic 'mental spectacles' – the early embryo, which is a conglomerate of undifferentiated cells, may enter or be brought into subsequent cellular divisions and aggregations of various kinds. It is only when such divisions and combinations can no longer be brought about, that there exists a stable individual that is not capable of becoming two or more by twinning.

The potentiality argument

[6.28] Many commentators argue that although life itself may not begin at conception, nevertheless at least the potential for human life begins there. Since the fertilised egg is a *potential* human being it must be accorded the same rights and privileges as an *actual* human being. However, there are a number of difficulties with this argument. The first is the logical premise that even if something will become X, this does not mean that it has the right now to be treated as if it were X.[64] There is no certainty that the fertilised egg will ever become an embryo, or that the embryo will become a foetus, but even if this were an accepted scientific fact it would not of itself give the fertilised egg the rights and privileges accorded to human beings.[65] In other words 'the fact that an entity can

---

61 McCormick, 'Therapy or Tampering: the Ethics of Reproductive Technology and the Development of Doctrine' in *The Critical Calling, Reflections on Moral Dilemmas since Vatican II* (Georgetown University Press, 1989) Ch 19, 329–352, p 345.

62 Gardner, an ordained Protestant minister and consultant gynaecologist, in his justification of abortion, considers that the soul does not enter the body until the child takes its first breath. Three scientific points are made to support this argument: First, the question of monozygotic twins, where the embryo splits in two. Gardner says '[U]nless we are to agree with the suggestion that the soul splits likewise we are driven to conclude that in some cases at least its infusion is not before the fourth week of intrauterine life.' Secondly, drawing attention to the high rates of fetal wastage, or spontaneous miscarriage, he considers it inconceivable that God should fill his heaven with these young lives, and concludes that it is evidence of the absence of 'spiritual status' on the part of the fetus. Thirdly, to suggest that embryos created in vitro, experimented on, and disposed of possess a soul, would be to trivialise the 'meaning of the soul'. Gardner, *Abortion: The Personal Dilemma* (Exeter: The Paternoster Press, 1972) pp 123–131.

63 Iglesias, *IVF and Justice* (Linacre Centre for Health Care Ethics in London, 1990) p 11.

64 Dyson and Harris, *Experiments on Embryos* (Routledge, 1990) p 70.

65 Dunstan says that it is insufficient to rest a claim to the status and rights of a person on the 'potential' for personality in the embryo. 'Roger Bacon, among the Scholastic philosophers of his day, disposed of that argument seven centuries ago. The argument will not bear the weight put upon it.' Dunstan and Seller (eds) *The Status of the Human Embryo. Perspectives from Moral Tradition* (King Edwards Hospital Fund, 1988) 14.

undergo changes that will make it significantly different does not constitute a reason for treating it as if it had already undergone those changes. We are all potentially dead, but no-one supposes that this fact constitutes a reason for treating us as if we were already dead.'[66] It is argued that we must take into account the probabilities of whether a potentiality may be realised, as otherwise our notion of potentiality would be 'too promiscuous' to be of any use in our ethical deliberations.[67] An embryo requires many external factors, such as implantation in a hospitable womb and nutrition, in order for it to develop intellect, will and other characteristics of personhood.

[6.29] Another difficulty relates to the chronology of human development in that while the fertilised egg may have the potential to become a human being, it is also true to say that the unfertilised egg and sperm are equally potential human beings. A fertilised egg will only have the potential to become human if certain stages in its development are passed, such as cleavage, implantation, emergence of the primitive streak and other developmental milestones, and if some things do not happen to it, such as a miscarriage. The same can be said of the egg and sperm: 'if certain things happen to the egg (like meeting a sperm) and certain things happen to the sperm (like meeting an egg) and thereafter certain other things do not (like meeting a contraceptive), then they will eventually become a new human being':[68]

> Given the appropriate conditions, these entities have the potential to develop into persons and so we would have to accord them the same moral status as the embryo. Moreover, if every cell in our body could be used for reproductive cloning, every cell would then have the potential for personhood. If we wish to deny the potential for personhood to gametes and these other cells, we must deny it to the embryo. In all these cases, external factors must be added or assumed in order to attribute the potential for personhood to the entity.[69]

[6.30] So, the argument logically concludes with an assertion that the sperm and egg also have a right to life and therefore any form of contraception is murder. As Lizza points out, this argument is a *reduction ad absurdum* criticism of the claim that the human embryo has the potential for personhood in a morally relevant sense. Evans illustrates the point thus:

> For example was the sperm which played a part in my generation potentially me? Was it also potentially a multiplicity of other people who never materialised (because my father happened to have had relations with different women from my mother)? Do all sperm have the potential to become people (given that they outnumber the oocytes in the world by a factor of millions in any given week)?[70]

---

[66] Dunstan and Seller (eds) *The Status of the Human Embryo. Perspectives from Moral Tradition* (King Edwards Hospital Fund, 1988) 14.

[67] Lizza, 'Potentiality and Human Embryos' (2007) Bioethics Vol 21 No 7 379–385 at 380.

[68] Harris, *The Value of Life* (Routledge, 1985) p 12.

[69] Lizza, 'Potentiality and Human Embryos' (2007) Bioethics Vol 21 No 7 379–385 at 381.

[70] Evans (ed), *Conceiving the Embryo, Ethics, Law and Practice in Human Embryology* (Martinus Nijhoff, 1996) 3 at 6. Although Evans recognises that for some people this sort of argument is absurd and illogical and therefore the whole principle should be discarded. However, he counters that such a discard would be mistaken without at least careful deliberation on this important question. Although absolute certainty is impossible and unrealisable here, it does not mean that it is not safe to act. (contd.../)

[6.31] Most of those who argue for potentiality distinguish between the fertilised egg and the sperm so as to accord the former the status of a full human being, but not the latter. One way in which this argument is made is to point out that fertilisation is the beginning of a process, which, if left alone, will result in a baby. On the other hand, the sperm and egg unjoined, if left alone, will not develop into anything. However, even leaving apart the very poor rates accorded to natural reproduction,[71] this argument is difficult to apply to embryos conceived in vitro. A fertilised egg in vitro has no chance of becoming anything unless someone intervenes to transfer it to a receptive uterus.[72] In this sense it is the same as the unfertilised egg and sperm, in that something has to be done in order for it to achieve a pregnancy:

> If it is claimed that gametes are not potential people, because they will not, on their own, develop into human beings, then it must be acknowledged that precisely the same is true of extra corporeal embryos. At least in the context of IVF, there does not seem to be an enormous moral difference between the zygote in the petri dish just after fertilisation has occurred and the sperm and the ovum in the petri dish just prior to fertilisation.[73]

Scientifically, the embryo has a dynamic structure of human cells with a wide range of potentialities. 'For example, it could develop into one or more human beings, or it could just form a troublesome mole or cyst in the womb. At its earliest stages, the embryo is no more the individual human being into which it may come to grow, than the clay on the potter's wheel is already a particular pot.'[74]

---

[70] (\...contd) We rarely in life enjoy absolute certainty in respect to the consequences of our actions, and our actions should be judged in light of this fact. Evans discusses the principle of moral theology called tutiorism, which bases itself on the understanding that we should be judged on the basis of what it is reasonable to believe in any given situation rather than on what is demonstrably certain. However, he says that this does not require us to err on the side of caution in relation to embryos, as the doubt in question in relation to whether they are persons is not a reasonable one. This does not mean they may be destroyed at will, as we may still have certain moral responsibilities to the embryos.

[71] See para **[6.06]**.

[72] Laurie, Harmon and Porter also take the view that 'no moral value can be attributed to the embryo by virtue of its potential for personhood – for no such potential exists in the medium of the petri dish.' *Law and Medical Ethics* (10th edn, 2016) at 8.77

[73] Steinbock, 'The Moral Status of Extra-Corporeal Embryos: Pre-Born Children, Property or Something Else?' in Dyson and Harris (eds) *Ethics and Biotechnology* (Routledge, 1994) at 85. Steinbock cites an example from George Annas in 'A French Homunculus in a Tennessee Court' (Nov/Dec 1989) 19:6 Hastings Center Report 22, where he poses the question of who would be saved if a fire broke out in a laboratory in which seven embryos were stored and there also happened to be a two-month-old child. If only the embryos or the child could be saved, he argues, no one would hesitate before saving the child. This shows that no one really equates embryos and children and the 'absurdity of a best-interests analysis applied to blastocysts.'

[74] Coughlan, 'From the Moment of Conception ... The Vatican Instruction on Artificial Procreation Techniques' (1988) 2 Bioethics No 4, 194 at 213. Coughlan wonders why the Vatican's Instruction does not injunct civil authorities to act on the basis of the moral weight of the principles outlined in the document. A clear demand for action from civil authorities is only made in relation to the prohibition of experimentation, mutilation or destruction of human beings, even at the embryonic stage. He claims that if civil authorities are to be expected to act in relation to this principle there should be a convincing exposition by the Vatican, which could stand independently of religious persuasion, as to the justification of this view. (contd.../)

Independent moral status

[6.32] Even if one were to take the view that the embryo outside of the body does not have any moral value, this does not necessarily mean that it is not due the same respect as would be shown to any other living human tissue. There is public concern and disagreement about any perceived interference in the reproductive process and some controls are therefore required in order to allay fears that the human embryo would be treated as any other product in a laboratory. An intermediate or compromise position which might be adopted here is to recognise that the embryo is a living entity deserving some respect, though not the same protection as human persons:

> The embryo is at least potential humanity, and as such it elicits, or ought to elicit, our feelings of awe and respect. In the embryo ... we face a mysterious and awesome power, a power governed by an imminent plan that may produce an indisputably and fully human being. It deserves our respect not because it has rights or claims or sentience (which it does not have at this stage), but because of what it is, now and prospectively.[75]

[6.33] For those for whom the embryo 'is not nothing', this argument has some merit. The collection of cells that make up the embryo is living and may have the potential for human life in the future. This does not mean that it is a new human life or that consequently it is deserving of the same rights as the foetus in vivo. For the embryo in vitro there is no potential to become a human life unless and until it is transferred to the uterus and implants in the uterine wall. Nevertheless the fertilised egg is alive, it is human in origin and it therefore is deserving of some protection. This argument is not based on the grounds of its potential to become a person, for this is not sufficient to distinguish it from the unfertilised egg, which also has the potential to become a person, but is perhaps based on its symbolic status.

[6.34] This intermediate approach has been adopted in many official and professional reports, such as the Ethics Advisory Board in the United States, which found that 'the human embryo is entitled to profound respect; but this respect does not necessarily encompass the full legal and moral rights attributed to persons.'[76] This position was also adopted by the Warnock Committee in the United Kingdom: 'The human pre-embryo[77] ... is not under the present law of the United Kingdom accorded the same status as a living child or adult, nor do we necessarily wish it to be accorded the same status. Nevertheless, we were agreed that the pre-embryo of the human species ought to have a

---

[74] (\...contd) His article is an examination of the defence offered in the Instruction for this principle. He concludes that the lack of persuasive revelation-independent justification given by the Instruction forfeits the authority to press the case on legislators for the inclusion of the moral principles espoused by the document.

[75] Kass, 'Ethical Issues in Human In Vitro Fertilisation, Embryo Culture and Research, and Embryo Transfer.' This was a submission to the Ethics Advisory Board, US Dept of Health, Educ. & Welfare, in Appendix (No 2) (May 4, 1979): *HEW Support of Research Involving Human In Vitro Fertilisation and Embryo Transfer.*

[76] Department of Health and Human Services, the Ethics Advisory Board in the United States, US Department of Health, Education and Welfare, Ethics Advisory Board, *HEW Support of Research Involving Human In Vitro Fertilisation and Embryo Transfer*, 44 Fed Reg 35,033 (1979).

[77] The term 'pre-embryo' or 'conceptus' was commonly used to designate the fertilised egg up to the end of the implantation stage.

special status.'[78] The logic of this argument is that the biology of the early embryo supports the view that it is not a person or a rights-bearing entity but, despite this, it may yet be the subject of duties created to demonstrate a commitment to human life and persons generally. Once this basis for valuation is clear then it may be acceptable to accord the embryo a higher value than accorded to other human tissue in order to symbolise respect for human life. However, such symbolic valuation must be balanced against the procreative liberty of the couple involved and the restriction of activities with the embryos that could be of benefit to society through the advancement of medical knowledge in the treatment of disease and disabilities.[79]

Welfare of children

[6.35] Apart from those objections to IVF considered above, which are based on theological or philosophical grounds, there are also a number of fundamental objections to IVF based on the claim that the procedure commodifies children and treats them as a means to an end rather than an end in themselves. This view is based on the belief that by translating the wish to have children into a moral or legal right to reproduce, the child's human dignity is instrumentalised from the start – the child is conceived to satisfy the couple's ego. Practices which presently allow couples to select the sex of their child (primarily for medical reasons) may in the future enable couples to 'design' traits (such as intelligence, personality, appearance) in the children they conceive through IVF. This contradicts the principle of unconditional acceptance by which parents should love their children as equals, and instead treats them as objects to be designed according to specifications and susceptible to rejection if they fall short of expectations.[80]

---

[78] *Report of the Committee of Inquiry into Human Fertilisation and Embryology* (1984) United Kingdom, Department of Health and Social Security.

[79] See also Robertson, 'In the Beginning: the Legal Status of Early Embryos' (1990) 76 Virginia Law Review 437 at 444–450. Robertson expounds his theory in relation to the principle of according respect to the embryo as a matter of choice. However, he goes on to say that the notion of respect here must mean something – that it is not just empty rhetoric. It must at some point confront the situations in which the content of respect must be constituted. There must be some limits on the actions which may be taken in relation to embryos if respect for them is to mean anything. Such conflicts involve a trade-off between the differing interests at stake and the competing values which they encompass rather than a consideration of whether the embryo is a prenatal subject of rights.

[80] O'Donovan, *Begotten or Made?* (OUP, 1984). O'Donovan distinguishes the child-as-object from the child-as-equal as follows: 'That which we beget is like ourselves. Our offspring are human beings, who share with us one common nature, one common human experience and one common human destiny...But that which we make is unlike ourselves...it is the produce of our own free determination. We have stamped the decisions of our will upon the material, which the world has offered us, to form it in this way and not in that. What we 'make', then, is alien from our humanity. In that it has a human maker, it has come into existence as a human project, its being at the disposal of mankind...That which we beget can be, and should be, our companion; but the product of our art...can never have the independence to be that 'other I', equal to us and differentiated from us which we acknowledge in those who are begotten...A being who is the maker of any other being is alienated from that which he has made, transcending it by his will and acting as the law of its being. To speak of 'begetting' is to speak of quite another possibility than this: the possibility that one may form another human being who will share one's own nature, and with whom one will enjoy a fellowship based on radical equality.'

[6.36] It is argued that a basic demand of all human beings is to be loved and respected for our own sakes and not for any instrumental gains that others may seek from us. The concern expressed by those who oppose IVF is that 'a child tends to be thought of merely as an object that satisfies a need. If desired, anything will be done to have it; if not desired it will be rejected, even to the point of being destroyed. This attitude of regarding children as commodities will be fostered by IVF programmes.'[81]

> Owing to the stressful nature of infertility and its treatment, which often lasts for many years, it was thought that parenting difficulties might arise following the eventual birth of a long-awaited baby. Specifically, it was argued that parents who had had difficulty in conceiving might become emotionally over-invested in their much wanted children, and that those who had become parents after a period of infertility may be over-protective of their children or have unrealistic expectations of them or of themselves as parents.[82]

However, children born through IVF are not and should not be regarded as any different from children conceived naturally. The motivation and desire for parenting of would-be parents for whom IVF is a last resort, is the same as that of parents who can conceive without assistance. Mary Warnock, Chairman of the Committee of Inquiry into Human Fertilisation and Embryology in the UK, stated that with improvements in the success rates for IVF, she believed that it would come to be regarded as a more or less routine procedure. She went on: '[C]hildren born by IVF will, I believe, be no more remarkable than children born by caesarean section. It is impossible to see that they could suffer in any way from the technical method of their birth.'[83] Many years after the Warnock Report it now appears that her prediction about the normalisation of IVF has been realised with over 6.5 million children having been born worldwide by 2016.

[6.37] Welfare of the child issues have been considered in many official reports around the world, such as that published by the Victorian Law Reform Commission in Australia in 2004.[84] This report concludes that the concerns that Assisted Reproductive Technology (ART) parents may have dysfunctional parenting styles due to the intensive and interventionist nature of conception are not borne out in research. 'ART parents are found not to be over-protective, not to have unrealistic expectations of the child, nor to have increased marital problems following fertility treatment. The non-biological parent of a donor-conceived child is found to accept the child as his or her own, and to be just as effective as the biological parent.' In common with studies in the UK,[85] the report also found that a number of positive differences have been found in the quality of parenting

---

[81] Iglesias, *IVF and Justice: Moral, Social and Legal Issues Related to Human In Vitro Fertilisation* (Linacre Centre for Health Care Ethics in London, 1990) p 53.

[82] Golombok, *Modern Families, Parents and children in new family forms* (2015 Cambridge University Press) at 73–74.

[83] Warnock, 'The Good of the Child' (1987) 1 (2) Bioethics 141–155 at 147.

[84] Victorian Law Reform Commission (2004) Outcomes for Children Born of ART in a Diverse Range of Families.

[85] MacCallum, 'Embryo Donation Parents' Attitudes Towards Donors: Comparison With Adoption' (2009) Human Reproduction, 25, 517–523; MacCallum & Keeley, 'Embryo Donation Families: A Follow-Up in Middle Childhood' (2008) Journal of Family Psychology, 22, 799–808; MacCallum, Golombok & Brinsden, 'Parenting and Child Development in Families With a Child Conceived Through Embryo Donation' (2007) Journal of Family Psychology, 21 (2), 278–287; (contd.../)

within ART families when compared with natural conception families – mothers express more warmth toward their child; mothers and fathers are more emotionally involved and interact more with their child; mothers and fathers are less stressed by parenting; fathers who have children through ART are less authoritarian than fathers of naturally conceived children, regardless of whether they are biologically related to them or not; and children report less parental criticism than natural or adoptive children. In addition it found that the psychological development of children in ART families is no different to that of children in naturally conceived families. Similarly, Golombok states that 'in general, mothers and fathers whose children have been conceived through IVF appear to be highly committed and involved parents – a finding that is perhaps not surprising given the obstacles they faced in their quest for a child.'[86]

[6.38] Another factor thought to influence parent–child relationships in the case of assisted reproduction is the experience of infertility. Since the advent of IVF, it has been speculated that parents who have used assisted reproduction may be overprotective of their children because of the emotional, financial and psychical obstacles they had to overcome in order to conceive. However, 'contrary to the fears voiced in the early days of IVF, children conceived in this way appear to show low levels of emotional and behavioural problems and no evidence of cognitive impairment. Although there is some evidence of temperamental problems in infancy, this may reflect the perceptions of anxious mothers, rather than the difficulties of their infants. IVF children are just as likely as their naturally conceived counterparts to be securely attached to their mothers.'[87] When it comes to older children and adolescents, does fertility treatment lead to overprotective parents who hinder the emotional development of their children at adolescence? 'Or will the overcoming of infertility produce parents who are more resilient and who pass this along to their children at a time when they are becoming

---

[85] (\...contd) Golombok, 'Parenting and the Psychological Development of the Child in ART Families' in Vayena, Rowe & Griffin, (eds) *Current Practice and Controversies in Assisted Reproduction: Report of a Meeting on Medical, Ethical and Social Aspects of Assisted Reproduction* (Report of a Meeting on 'Medical, Ethical and Social Aspects of Assisted Reproduction', 2002) World Health Organization, Geneva; Golombok, 'Preface' in Singer & Hunter (eds) *Assisted Human Reproduction: Psychological and Ethical Dilemmas.* (Wiley, 2003); Golombok, 'The Potential Impact of Removing Donor Anonymity on Donors, Parents, Offspring and Service Provision' (2003) Report commissioned by the Department of Health UK; Golombok, 'Reproductive Technology and its Impact on Child Psychosocial and Emotional Development' (2003) in Tremblay, Barr & Peters (eds) *Encyclopedia on Early Childhood Development,* 1–7 [online]. Centre of Excellence for Early Childhood Development. Canadian Institute of Child Health, Montreal; Golombok, 'Assisted Reproduction Families: Key Policy Issues. Report to House of Commons Science and Technology Committee Review of Human Reproductive Technologies and the Law' (2004); Golombok, 'Unusual Families' in Edwards (ed) 'Ethics, Science and Moral Philosophy of Assisted Human Reproduction' (2005) Vol 10, Supplement 1; Middelburg et al, 'Neuromotor, Cognitive, Language and Behavioural Outcome in Children Born Following IVF or ICSI – A Systematic Review' (2008) Hum. Reprod. Update 14 (3): 219–231.

[86] Golombok, *Modern Families, Parents and children in new family forms* (2015 Cambridge University Press) at 81.

[87] Golombok, *Modern Families, Parents and children in new family forms* (2015 Cambridge University Press) at 84.

more autonomous?'[88] Research shows that parent–adolescent relationships in IVF families did not differ from naturally conceived families in terms of parental control, warmth and conflict, or parental dependability and sensitivity towards the child. More specifically, IVF adolescents reported high levels of warmth and low levels of conflict in their relationships with their parents, and this level was no different from adolescents in naturally conceived families. Additionally, no differences were found in parental self-reports, or adolescent reports of parenting style or stress between IVF and natural conception parents. These findings suggest that the 'positive relationships between parents who used IVF and their children persist into adolescence.'[89]

[6.39] As IVF and other assisted reproductive technologies have become more commonplace, it has been possible to carry out important research in relation to the outcomes for children born through these techniques and the experiences of their parents. The general conclusion thus far is that 'It seems that families created with these technologies function well, and the fears expressed about the potentially negative impact these technologies may have on parenting and child development are unfounded.'[90]

LEGAL ISSUES IN IVF

Embryo custody disputes

[6.40] Of all the controversies surrounding the creation and use of IVF embryos, disputes over the fate of the embryos which sometimes arise between the parties concerned are particularly difficult.[91] Such disputes raise issues around ownership of embryos and decision-making control in circumstances which are often characterised by disagreement between the gamete-providers, the end of a family relationship between them through death or separation, the symbolic representation of the embryo as an unborn child, and the finality of the last opportunity for some parties to become a genetic parent. Yet the law must intervene to find a solution in these difficult embryo-custody disputes.

[6.41] In law it is usual to categorise things into property, which can be owned and controlled, and persons who cannot. It is difficult to decide which of these categories is most appropriate for the embryo. On the one hand, if the embryo were property then this would signify that the providers of the genetic material from which it is conceived could be said to own it. This, in the absence of regulation, would enable the couple to determine the disposition of the embryo in any way they wished, subject to legislative policy. On the other hand, it is difficult to apply the notion of personhood to the early

---

[88] Ilioi and. Golombok, 'Psychological adjustment in adolescents conceived by assisted reproduction techniques: a systematic review' Hum. Reprod. Update (January/February 2015) 21 (1): 84–96.

[89] Ilioi and Golombok, 'Psychological adjustment in adolescents conceived by assisted reproduction techniques: a systematic review' Hum. Reprod. Update (January/February 2015) 21 (1): 84–96.

[90] Golombok, *Modern Families, Parents and children in new family forms* (2015 Cambridge University Press) at 90.

[91] Chan and Quigley, 'Frozen Embryos, Genetic Information and Reproductive Rights' (2007) Bioethics Vol 21(8) p 439.

embryo for both biological and moral reasons as outlined earlier. To say that the embryo outside the womb is a person is to accord it the full rights and protections accorded to a living human person. This position might therefore require it to be given an opportunity for implantation so that its right to life may be upheld, and to prohibit any action that might harm the embryo, such as freezing. The context in which these difficult questions have come before the courts has often been where couples have stored embryos during fertility treatment and subsequently separate without reaching agreement about the fate or disposition of those stored embryos.

US case law

[6.42] The first case to come before the courts in this context was the US case of *Davis v Davis*,[92] in which a dispute arose during a divorce settlement in relation to who should have custody of seven frozen embryos stored in a fertility clinic at the couple's request. At first instance the wife wished to use the embryos herself in an attempt to become pregnant after the divorce, a plan to which the ex-husband was opposed. By the time the case was finally decided by the Tennessee Supreme Court she had remarried and no longer wished to use the embryos herself but to donate them to an infertile couple. The ex-husband maintained throughout the case that he did not want the embryos to be used at all, as it would be an interference with his procreational autonomy in forcing him to become a parent against his wishes. He argued that whether his ex-wife used them or an anonymous couple were given them as a donation, he would consider himself to have fathered a child somewhere in the world. His position was that he would feel a responsibility to seek the child out and maintain it even if it was born to someone else. Therefore, he preferred to see the embryos kept in storage until he decided whether or not he wanted to become a parent outside of marriage.

[6.43] At first instance the trial court decided that the embryos were human beings from the moment of fertilisation and awarded custody to the wife on the basis that she should be given the opportunity to bring them to term through implantation. The Court of Appeals reversed this decision, holding that the husband had a constitutionally protected right *not* to beget a child where no pregnancy had taken place. The Court gave joint control to the couple. This was, in effect, giving a veto to each party in respect of decisions the other might make in relation to the embryos.

[6.44] Before the Supreme Court, the parties' positions had altered in that the ex-wife no longer wished to use the embryos herself, and the ex-husband preferred to have them discarded rather than donated to another couple. This change in positions meant that the Court, in weighing each party's procreational rights against the other's, was able to conclude that the ex-husband's rights in seeking to avoid the burden of parenthood were greater than the ex-wife's right to know that her genetic material contributed to the bringing into existence of children somewhere by another couple. The Court admitted that the case would have been more difficult to decide if the wife wanted to use the embryos herself in circumstances in which she was unable to achieve a pregnancy by attempting IVF again. On the question of ownership of genetic material, the Court held that the embryos occupied an interim category between persons and property, which entitled them to special respect because of their potential for human life. The Court said:

---

[92] *Davis v Davis* 842 SW 2d 588 (Tenn 1992).

Pre-embryos are not, strictly speaking, either 'persons' or 'property', but occupy an interim category that entitles them to special request because of their potential for human life. It follows that any interest that …[the couple] have in the pre-embryos in this case is not a true property interest. However, they do have an interest in the nature of ownership, to the extent that they have decision-making authority concerning disposition of the pre-embryos, with the scope of policy set by law.

[6.45] Even though the bundle of rights over the embryo has been judicially described as 'dispositional control' rather than as ownership, it may be argued that the rights given are, in effect, a property right akin to ownership. It gives the individuals who provided that genetic material the right to decide which of several options may be legally taken in respect to the embryo. A small number of cases in the US seem to support the right of ownership of embryos albeit perhaps indirectly. In *Del Zio v Columbia Presbyterian Hospital*[93] a jury awarded \$50,000 to a couple whose embryos had been destroyed by a doctor who objected to their attempts to have IVF done without obtaining review board approval. This decision recognises that negligent or intentional destruction of embryos would be actionable due to the significant financial, emotional and physical loss involved for the couple. 'Only difficulties in calculating damages, and not doubts about the ownership rights of the couple, would stand in the way of tort remedies for negligent destruction of pre-embryos.'[94]

[6.46] In *York v Jones*[95] a couple who moved from Virginia to California wished to have 'their' embryos, which were stored at a clinic in Virginia, released and transported to California to be transferred to the wife's uterus by a doctor there. The clinic refused to release the embryos for transportation on various grounds, including the demeaning effect of shipping human embryos by air in the same way as cattle. The Court found that the Virginia clinic was merely a temporary custodian of the embryos and had no right to keep them against the couple's wishes. This case is significant because the court 'assumes without question that embryos are the property of the gamete providers, and finds that any transfer of their dispositional authority must be explicitly stated in the documents of participation provided by the program.'[96]

[6.47] In other embryo custody cases in the United States, the issue has not been centred on ownership per se, but rather on the interpretation of contractual provisions between the couples and the clinics involved, and the question of whether one party should be facilitated in a change of mind subsequent to marital separation or divorce. In *Kass v Kass*,[97] Mrs Kass had undergone 10 unsuccessful IVF attempts over a 3-year period prior to the final attempt which, for the first time, included cryopreservation or freezing of the surplus embryos. The couple signed four consent forms drafted by the hospital, one of which stated that in the event of divorce all surplus embryos would be used for scientific research and destroyed. A number of embryos were transferred to Mrs Kass' sister, who had volunteered to be a surrogate mother, but this was unsuccessful. The remaining embryos were frozen. The couple applied for a divorce shortly after the last

---

[93] *Del Zio v Columbia Presbyterian Hospital* No 71–3588 (SDNY 1978).
[94] Robertson, *Children of Choice* (Princeton University Press, 1994) p 105.
[95] *York v Jones* 717 F Supp 421 (ED Va 1989).
[96] Robertson, *Children of Choice* (Princeton University Press, 1994) p 106.
[97] *Kass v Kass* 663 NYS 2d 581 (1997).

unsuccessful attempt. Mrs Kass applied for sole custody of the embryos, an application which was opposed by Mr Kass. The Court decided that the parties' prior statement of intent with regard to the embryos, as demonstrated by the signed consent forms, should be given a clear and unambiguous reading. The Court therefore granted Mr Kass's application for specific performance of the consent form. It stated as follows:

> We find that the decision to attempt to have children through IVF procedures and the determination of the fate of cryopreserved pre-zygotes resulting therefrom are intensely personal and essentially private matters which are appropriately resolved by the prospective parents rather than the courts. Accordingly, where the parties have indicated their mutual intent regarding the disposition of the pre-zygotes in the event of the occurrence of a contingency, that position must be scrupulously honoured and the courts must refrain from any interference with the parties' expressed wishes. The documentary evidence overwhelmingly demonstrates that the parties in this case made such a clear and unequivocal choice, and the plaintiff's subsequent change of heart cannot be permitted to unilaterally alter their mutual decision.[98]

[6.48] In *AZ v BZ*[99] a couple underwent IVF treatment for a number of years and had twins following IVF in 1991. During that attempt surplus embryos were formed and two vials containing embryos were stored on behalf of the couple for possible future transfer. In 1995, the wife had one of these embryos transferred without her husband's knowledge. Her husband received a letter from his health insurance company informing him of the treatment. Relations between the couple subsequently deteriorated and the husband sought a divorce. At the time of the divorce there was one vial containing four embryos in storage at the clinic. At each stage during the couple's treatment by the clinic, the couple had signed a consent form. The consent forms contained a blank line to permit couples to insert their preferred option in the event of separation, divorce or death. The first form was filled out by the wife to the effect that in the event of separation, they agreed that their embryos would be returned to the wife for implantation. The husband signed this first form after it was completed. Six further consent forms were signed over the years of treatment but these were all signed in blank by the husband for convenience, and later filled in by the wife to the same effect as the first form. When the couple divorced, the husband sought to avoid enforcement of the consent form.

[6.49] This was the first reported case in the US concerning the disposition of frozen embryos in which a consent form signed between the couple and the clinic provided that, on the couple's separation, the embryos were to be given to one of the parties for implantation. The Court took the view that given the purpose of the form (which was drafted by and to give assistance to the clinic) and the circumstances of its execution, it could not be said with certainty to represent the intent of the husband and wife as to the

---

98   Although sympathetic to the physical and emotional strain endured, particularly by Mrs Kass, the Court dismissed the notion that the disposition of the embryos involved reproductive liberty or privacy concerns. The court reasoned that because the embryos were not yet implanted, the fundamental rights that arise with a traditional pregnancy were not implicated. For criticism of this approach see Daar, 'Assisted Reproductive Technologies and the Pregnancy Process: Developing an Equality Model to Protect Reproductive Liberties' (1999) 25 Am JL and Med 455.

99   *AZ v BZ* 725 NE 2d 1051 (2000).

disposition of the embryos. Therefore, the Court concluded that it should not be enforced in the circumstances of this case.

[6.50] The basis for the Court's decision rested on a number of grounds. Firstly, the Court held that the consent form's primary purpose was to explain to the couple the benefits and risks of freezing, and to record their desire for disposition of the frozen embryos at the time the form was executed in order to provide the clinic with guidance if the couple later decided they did not wish to use the embryos. The form did not indicate that the couple intended the consent form to act as a binding agreement between them in the event of a later dispute. Secondly, the form did not contain a duration provision and the Court was of the opinion that there was no evidence from which it could be assumed that the parties intended it to govern the disposition of the embryos four years after it was signed, especially in light of the fundamental change in their relationship.

[6.51] Thirdly, the form used the term 'should we become separated' in reference to the disposition of the embryos but because this dispute arose in the context of a divorce, the Court said it could not conclude that the consent form was intended to govern in these circumstances as separation and divorce have different meanings in law. Fourthly, the Court took into account the circumstances in which the husband had signed the consent forms in blank before the wife had filled in the form, indicating that the embryos would be returned to her following separation. The Court said it was unable to conclude that the consent form represented the true intention of the husband. The Court also said that the consent form was not a separation agreement and was legally insufficient in a number of respects to be considered as an enforceable contract.

[6.52] The Court also stated that even if the husband and wife *had* signed an unambiguous agreement, it would not be enforceable in the circumstances where this would force one person to become a parent against their will. It stated that:

> As a matter of public policy, we conclude that forced procreation is not an area amenable to judicial enforcement. It is well-established that courts will not enforce contracts that violate public policy. While courts are hesitant to invalidate contracts on these public policy grounds, the public interest in freedom of contract is sometimes outweighed by other public policy considerations; in those cases the contract will not be enforced.

[6.53] In *JB v MB*[100] the couple had signed a consent form provided by the clinic prior to undergoing IVF. The form described the IVF procedure and contained provisions discussing the control and disposition of the embryos, which indicated that the embryos 'belonged' to the patient and her partner. JB gave birth to a daughter but the couple divorced a short time later. She sought an order for destruction of the embryos on the ground that she had intended only to use the embryos during her marriage to MB and that they had never discussed the disposition of the embryos in the event that the marriage were to end. MB disputed this on the basis that, after having long discussions with JB about his Catholic beliefs, they had agreed to donate any surplus embryos to other infertile couples. The Supreme Court of New Jersey held that the consent form did not manifest a clear intent regarding disposition of the embryos in the event of divorce. It also accepted that where the procreational interests of both parties are in conflict, the right not to procreate outweighs the right to procreate. Therefore, the Court suggested

---

[100] *JB v MB* WL 909294 (NJ 2001).

that since JB did not oppose continued storage, MB could continue storage if he paid the storage fees, but that otherwise the embryos would be destroyed.[101] Thus the position in the US seems to favour upholding the terms of the written agreement between the couple and the clinic, but nonetheless facilitating a change of mind by one of the parties in circumstances where upholding the contract would impose unwanted parenthood.

English case law

[6.54] In the UK, the Human Fertilisation and Embryology Act 1990, as amended in 2008, does not refer to ownership of embryos but recognises that the gamete providers have decision-making authority in relation to what may be done with the embryos created from their eggs and sperm. At the start of treatment, the couple must sign a consent form indicating to what use the embryos may be put and what is to happen to the embryos in the event of the death or separation of the couple. However, despite the apparent clarity of the position taken by the Act, it has not provided a permanent resolution for custody disputes as evidenced by *Evans v Amicus Healthcare Ltd, Hadley v Midland Fertility Services Ltd.* [102]

[6.55] In the *Evans* case, the Court was asked to consider whether consent to storage and use of the embryos given at the time of their creation was capable of being withdrawn following a change of mind by the male partners in each case. The two women, Ms Evans and Mrs Hadley, each sought injunctions to restore their former partner's consent, declarations that they could be treated lawfully under the terms of the 1990 Act, and a declaration that the restrictions imposed by the 1990 Act were incompatible with the Human Rights Act 1998, which gave effect to the European Convention on Human Rights (ECHR).

[6.56] Under the 1990 Act, clinics which provide IVF treatment services must do so pursuant to the terms of a licence provided by the Human Fertilisation and Embryology Authority established under the Act. One of the conditions imposed on every licence is that the provisions of Schedule 3 of the Act must be complied with. Schedule 3 sets out provisions in relation to necessary consents to be obtained prior to the storage or use of gametes or embryos. Paragraph 2 provides that effective consent must specify the purposes for which the embryo may be put, the maximum storage period agreed and what is to be done with the gametes or embryos in the event of death or incapacity of the person giving consent. Paragraph 4 provides that the consent may be varied or withdrawn by the person who gave the consent by giving notice at any time to the clinic,

---

[101] 'Although the court suggested it was willing to enforce embryo disposition contracts, its rule ultimately renders all such contracts unenforceable. Because mere disagreement by either party vitiates the contract in favour of balancing the procreative rights of the parties, there is really no contract.' Glenn Cohen, *Case Comment on JB v MB* [2001] Harvard L Rev Vol 115 p 701. See also *Litowitz v Litowitz* 146 Wash 2d 514 (2002) and *Roman v Roman* 193 SW 3d 40 (Tex App-Hous (1 Dist) 2006).

[102] *Evans v Amicus Healthcare Ltd, Hadley v Midland Fertility Services Ltd* [2003] 4 All ER 903. See Mason, 'Discord and Disposal of Embryos' (2004) 8 Edin L Rev 84; Alghrani, 'Deciding the Fate of Human Embryos' (2005) 13 Med L Rev 244; Annett, 'Balancing Competing Interests Over Frozen Embryos: The Judgment of Solomon' (2006) 14 Med L Rev 425; Enright, 'Justice, Convention and Anecdote: *Evans* and the Right to Become a Mother' [2006] 4 Irish Journal of Family Law 11.

unless the embryo has already been used in the provision of treatment services or for research purposes. Paragraph 5 provides that a person's gametes must not be used for the purposes of treatment other than in accordance with an effective consent given by that person. Paragraph 6 provides that an embryo must not be used for any purpose unless there is an effective consent by each person whose gametes were used to bring about the creation of the embryo.

[6.57] Since the male partners in each of these cases had withdrawn their consent to the use of the embryos by their former partners, the Court refused to grant the injunctions and declarations sought on the grounds that there was no 'effective consent' as required by the provisions of the Act. In the absence of consent, the clinics were not authorised to store or use the embryos. The Court recognised that the two pillars of the statutory scheme embodied in the Act were consent and the welfare of the child. The clear policy of the Act is to ensure continuing consent from the commencement of treatment to the point of implantation. The Court said it would be 'extremely slow to recognise or to create a principle of waiver that would conflict with the Parliamentary scheme.'

[6.58] In relation to the application for a direction that the restrictions imposed by the Act were incompatible with human rights, the Court principally addressed arts 8 and 14 in respect of the women's rights, and arts 2 and 8 in relation to the embryos. Article 8(1) of the ECHR provides that 'everyone has the right to respect for his private and family life, his home and his correspondence.' Article 8(2) provides that there shall be no interference with the exercise of this right except such as is in accordance with the law and is necessary in a democratic society in the interests of national security, public safety or the economic well-being of the country, the prevention of disorder or crime, the protection of health or morals, or for the protection of the rights and freedoms of others.

[6.59] It was accepted that the refusal of treatment to the women at the centre of these cases was an interference with, and therefore a failure to respect, their private life. The question for the Court was therefore whether such interference was prescribed by law and necessary for the protection of the rights and freedoms of others, namely the male gamete providers. The Court of Appeal said that 'while legislation modifying private law liabilities can be expected not to infringe their Convention rights without clear justification, legislation directed to the implementation and management of social policy may well have to infringe some individuals' Convention rights in the interests of consistency.' The Court stressed that the question was whether a less drastic means could be used to achieve the same end without infringing the rights of the claimant. The less drastic means argued for in this case would be a rule that would make the withdrawal of consent by her former partner, Mr Johnston, non-conclusive. This would enable Ms Evans to continue treatment due to her inability to conceive by any other means. However, the Court said that unless it gave weight to Mr Johnston's firm wish not to be a father to a child born to Ms Evans, such a rule would diminish his right to respect for private life in direct proportion as it enhanced the respect accorded to hers. Arden LJ said that if Ms Evans' argument succeeded, 'it would amount to an interference with the genetic father's right to decide not to become a parent. Motherhood could surely not be forced on Ms Evans and likewise fatherhood cannot be forced on Mr Johnston.' The Court therefore concluded that 'the sympathy and concern which anyone must feel for Ms Evans is not enough to render the legislative scheme of Schedule 3 disproportionate.'

[6.60] Another ground for Ms Evans' appeal was based on unlawful discrimination contrary to art 14 of the Convention. Article 14 provides that the enjoyment of the rights and freedoms set out in the Convention shall be secured without discrimination on any ground such as sex, race, colour, language, religion, political opinion, origin and so on. Ms Evans claimed that she was being discriminated against in that she was treated differently to fertile women in that the consent of a male partner could not be withdrawn in natural reproduction at any time following the fertilisation of the egg. Under the scheme of the Act, in the case of IVF the male partner was permitted to withdraw his consent subsequent to fertilisation at any time prior to implantation. Therefore, Ms Evans argued that this differential treatment of infertile women was unjustifiably discriminatory. Although Arden LJ agreed that, seen from this perspective, there was discrimination in that the genetic father was allowed to withdraw his consent in IVF later than he could so in normal sexual intercourse, she was of the view that the conditions imposed by the Act were objectively justified for the reasons given above in relation to art 8.

[6.61] An argument was also made under art 2 of the Convention, which provides that 'everyone's right to life shall be protected by law'. Ms Evans argued that although the embryo has no right to life in the sense that a human being has such a right, an embryo does have a qualified right to life which is consistent with its mother's wishes. Arden LJ acknowledged that neither the Convention nor English law provided a clear-cut answer to the question as to what point human life attained the right to legal protection. She took the view that while an embryo has the potential to become a person, it is not itself a person since further changes must take place. She was of the view that an embryo does not have a qualified right to life given that the Act provided that embryos must be destroyed after the expiration of the maximum statutory storage period or if either party withdrew consent to storage. She therefore concluded that 'the embryo has no right to life which trumps the right to choose of a person whose ongoing consent to its use or storage is required under the 1990 Act.'

[6.62] Ms Evans' appeal was declined on all grounds by the Court of Appeal and she subsequently challenged the legislation at the European Court of Human Rights.[103] The Court, like the national courts, had great sympathy for the plight of the applicant who, if implantation did not take place, would be deprived of the ability to give birth to her own child. However, the panel majority found that, even in such exceptional circumstances as Ms Evans', the right to a family life enshrined in art 8 could not override Mr Johnston's withdrawal of consent. The court also held that the UK's policy lay within a national jurisdiction's margin of appreciation when determining the balance to be struck between the rights of both parties. Ms Evans' appeal to the Grand Chamber was similarly unsuccessful.[104]

---

[103] Application 6339/05, Fourth Section Judgment of 7 March 2006: *Evans v United Kingdom* (2006) 43 EHRR 21.

[104] *Evans v United Kingdom* App No 6339/05 (2007) 10 March 2007 (2008) 46 EHRR 34.

[6.63] In both the Chamber and Grand Chamber, the European Court of Human Rights accepted that the 'bright-line' approach taken by the UK legislation, which was to require continuing consent from both parties to the use and storage of embryos, was consistent with promoting certainty and consistency in the law. Dissenting judges and commentators argue however that this approach has a disproportionate effect on the rights of the woman. Enright suggests that the 'conflict of rights' model, where the right to avoid parenthood (usually on the part of the male partner) is set against the right to become a parent, is the basic foundation for decided embryo custody cases.[105] She argues that the *Evans* decision suggests an equality theory, namely that male and female rights are absolutely equivalent and therefore decisions regarding the embryo must be made on an equal basis – a mutual consent requirement must be adhered to. In the US and Israel, the courts have adopted a clear hierarchy of rights - 'in the American courts the 'right not to procreate' has become the default rule; it trumps the 'right to parenthood' even in the most difficult circumstances and no matter whether the court decides on the basis of contractual or constitutional principle.' In Israel, it appears that the female right takes precedence over the male.[106] Thornton also criticises the equality approach on the basis that it operates inconsistently and arbitrarily in terms of its real, differential impact on the female and male gamete providers. She suggests that:

> if a bright-line approach is desirable at all, then why should it be fixed…at the time of implantation rather than allowing male consent to be withdrawn only up to the point of fertilisation (as, for instance in Austria and Estonia). The latter threshold would both recognise the greater impact of the decision on the female partner and mirror more closely the situation of natural conception.[107]

[6.64] Enright suggests that these cases 'push men's procreative rights far beyond their expected boundaries.'[108] Where the man's refusal to consent will result in the destruction of the embryo, it is argued that the right claimed is not the right 'not to procreate' but the right to stop the procreative process once it has begun. Traditionally, that it is a right available to women in countries where abortion is permitted, but which is not afforded to men. Enright argues that in circumstances where the use of the embryos represent the woman's last chance to have a genetic child (as in *Evans*), the man's refusal is not merely a cancelling out, or a restoration of the position that existed prior to the IVF attempt. In such cases the woman is not restored to her previous position, as the man, in many ways, is:

> Her important expectation interests in becoming a mother are irretrievably breached. She is further harmed because she cannot recoup her emotional and material investments in

---

[105] Enright, 'Justice, Convention and Anecdote: *Evans* and the Right to Become a Mother' [2006] 4 Ir J Fam Law 11.

[106] *Nachmani v Nachmani* AH 2401/95, 50(4) PD 661. The Israeli Supreme Court decided by a seven-to-four majority that the ex-wife's right to have a child trumped her ex-husband's right not to have one, in particular since she had no more eggs and therefore had no other means of having a genetic child of her own. See Chen, 'The Right to Her Embryos: An Analysis of *Nachmani v Nachmani* and its Impact on Israeli In Vitro Fertilisation Law' (1999) 7 Cardozo J I & Comp L 325.

[107] Thornton, 'European Court of Human Rights: Consent to IVF treatment' (2008) 6 Intl J Const Law 317–330.

[108] Enright, 'Justice, Convention and Anecdote: *Evans* and the Right to Become a Mother' [2006] 4 Ir J Fam Law 11, p 13.

the reproductive process. He, on the other hand, gains or is healed by his refusal; he obviates a future harm and relieves himself of present stress and worry.[109]

This is echoed by Lind who says that if Mr Johnston had fathered a child accidentally during sexual intercourse, he would have been denied the level of control over his procreation that the statute gives him.[110]

[6.65] Enright concludes that the Court in *Evans* used the principle of equality in order to put distance between the law and the emotive facts of the case. However, in doing so it 'eschewed individualised decision-making in favour of essentialist dogmatic presumption'. She argues that a case-by-case analysis is preferable, which reflects the differences between men and women, but also the argument between the individual man and woman in dispute.[111] This would enable the court to consider the effect of the decision on the individuals concerned; for example, the burden that unwanted paternity would impose on the man, and the deprivation of the last opportunity for genetic maternity for the woman. 'Such an approach accords meaningfully and readily with the law's stated concern for reproductive autonomy and the interests of the warring couple.'

[6.66] Chan and Quigley are of the view that the *Evans* case demonstrates the tremendous importance that is placed on genetic relationship by many people in modern society, particularly when it comes to reproduction:[112] 'The extensive use of artificial reproductive technologies and the attention devoted to extending the limits of these methods in order to allow more people to reproduce genetically illustrate the value that is placed on genetic relatedness as a part of parenthood, in addition to birth parentage and upbringing.' They advocate a different approach to embryo disputes based on a property framework in respect of genetic information. They acknowledge that the law governing genetics is confusing in that it is drawn from a multitude of sources, both common law and statutory, some of which contain conflicting ideals. However, they say that nonetheless the law does recognise some rights of confidentiality, privacy and control in both our genetic material and genetic information. Property rights might be accorded to genetic information in the context of, for example, locating a previously unknown gene, determining its function and making it accessible for further exploitation.[113] Such rights can be transferred or ceded, for example when sperm is donated to a sperm bank for the purpose of transfer to another person for reproductive purposes:

---

[109] Enright, 'Justice, Convention and Anecdote: *Evans* and the Right to Become a Mother' [2006] 4 Ir J Fam Law 11, p 16.

[110] Lind, 'Evans v UK – judgments of Solomon: Power, Gender and Procreation' (2006) 18 Child and Fam Law Quarterly 576.

[111] Sheldon says that the robustness of the consent process should be investigated to ensure that the couple had privacy, space and time to discuss the ramifications of their decision. Sheldon, 'Case commentary: revealing cracks in the 'twin pillars'?' (2004) 16 Child and Fam Law Quarterly 437.

[112] Chan and Quigley, 'Frozen Embryos, Genetic Information and Reproductive Rights' (2007) Bioethics Vol 21(8) p 439–448.

[113] Laurie, 'Patenting and the Human Body', in *Principles of Medical Law*, Grubb (ed) (2nd edn, OUP, 2004) 1079–1102 at 1085.

When gametes fuse to form an embryo in the process of in vitro fertilisation, the individual rights which the gametic progenitors have over the separate gametes are altered. There can be no property or rights claims over those gametes because the two separate gametes no longer exist. In their place there is an embryo. Embryos can also be viewed as a type of genetic material containing physical and informational property, but both the physical and informational components are contributed to by both parents.[114]

[6.67] Chan and Quigley argue that when the partners agree to attempt IVF in order to have a child, they cede any rights they might have had not to become a parent as soon as the egg is fertilised with the sperm. Therefore, once the embryo is created, the male partner no longer has the right to prevent its birth on the grounds of not wanting a genetically related child:

> The implication of this is plain and simple: once you have given up your genetic informational rights in this manner you cannot take them back. The creation of IVF embryos involves both parents giving up some rights over their genetic information in pursuit of the creation of the embryos. Once this has occurred, any right of the parents not to have those embryos created (as new genetic entities from their genetic information) is lost, and only the physical rights to the embryos persist.

[6.68] They do not claim that there are no circumstances under which embryo transfer can be stopped once the embryo has been created, as they do acknowledge that, for example, there may be some exceptional child-welfare issues which might be of such significance as to alter the situation. However, this does not detract from their central argument that there can be no right not to have a child once the embryos have been created. As seen above, however, the English and American courts do not appear to have accepted this argument, and have generally given priority to the party who does not want to have a genetically related child.

'Reproductive blunders'

[6.69] In recent years there have also been a small number of embryo custody cases in which mistakes have been made in the course of egg fertilisation or embryo transfer which have resulted in women giving birth to children who are genetically related to another couple being treated at the same clinic at the same time. These cases give rise to 'very interesting and complex questions about genetic origins, genetic identity and the desirability or undesirability of full knowledge disclosure and access to all the types of relatedness that can exist between human beings.'[115]

[6.70] Prior to the advent of IVF and associated technologies, laws determining parentage and parental rights flowed directly from the laws of nature. Under common law, maternity was easily established by the biological fact that pregnancy occurred as a result of natural sexual intercourse, a foetus was carried to term by the woman and maternity was thus established from the moment of birth.[116] Paternity was less easily

---

[114] Chan and Quigley, 'Frozen Embryos, Genetic Information and Reproductive Rights' (2007) Bioethics Vol 21(8) p 445.

[115] Harris, 'Assisted Reproductive Technological Blunders (ARTBs) (2003) J Med Ethics; 29:205–206.

[116] This is recognized by the ancient maxim *mater est quam gestation demonstrat* (by gestation the mother is demonstrated).

established and courts relied on certain presumptions or social policy to assign paternity on the basis of the man's relationship with the birth mother. Thus the presumption of paternity applies to a married man to ensure that he is recognised as the legal father of a child born to his wife. Establishing paternity for men outside marriage was more problematic at common law and relied on the testimony of the woman. Advances in medical technology, blood and DNA tests have now made it easier to establish a biological link between father and child.

[6.71] In assisted reproduction disputes, the courts in other jurisdictions have taken diverse approaches based on property law, contract law, causation, public policy, constitutional rights, intent, and the best interests of the child. Some commentators argue that a 'bright-line test' ought to be agreed in order to establish certainty and avoid disputes. This could be, for example, a presumption that placement with the gestational mother is always in the child's best interests, or conversely, that the child's interests are best served by being with its genetic mother. Others argue for a multi-factorial best interests analysis, such as that used in custody disputes in a divorce setting.[117] The former has appeal, as it allows parentage to be established with certainty from the moment of birth whereas the latter would hold parental status in limbo pending a judicial determination.

[6.72] There is considerable disagreement between those who favour the genetic mother and those who favour the gestational mother in such disputes. Those who favour the genetic mother focus on the bonds of nature, ie the concept of genetic identity. Those who favour the gestational mother prioritise the social bonding that occurs between the mother and child during the pre-natal and post-natal nurturing. This is resonant of the well-rehearsed nature versus nurture debates in human psychology, to which there is no clear answer.

[6.73] A best interests approach combined with an analysis of the intent of the parties has been suggested as the most appropriate solution in cases where genetic material has been mistakenly switched. The first step of such a test would be to establish who had the intent to parent the child, starting from the presumption that the birth mother is the legal mother. Her intent to procreate and raise the child may be implied from her participation in the IVF process. On this basis she has an exclusive claim to parental rights in the absence of a claim from the genetic mother, who may establish her genetic link to the child, that her genetic material was used without her consent and that she has not abandoned her parental rights to her child. Thus, both women have sufficient *locus standi* to claim parental rights to the child and the outcome should be determined by application of the best-interests-of-the-child test.[118]

[6.74] In *Perry-Rogers v Fasano*,[119] two couples, the Fasanos and the Perry-Rogers, went for treatment to an IVF clinic in New York on the same day. Due to a clinical error that

---

[117] Noble-Allgire, 'Switched at the Fertility Clinic: Determining Maternal Rights When a Child is Born From Stolen or Misdelivered Genetic Material' (1999) Vol 64(3) Missouri Law Review 517 at 577.

[118] Noble-Allgire, 'Switched at the Fertility Clinic: Determining Maternal Rights When a Child is Born From Stolen or Misdelivered Genetic Material' (1999) Vol 64(3) Missouri Law Review 517 at 589.

[119] *Perry-Rogers v Fasono* 715 NYS 2d 19 (App Div 2000).

caused an embryo mix-up that day, six of the Perry-Rogers' embryos were transferred to Mrs Fasano along with at least one of the Fasano's embryos. She became pregnant and gave birth to twin boys, one of whom was Caucasian like the Fasanos and the other of whom was African-American like the Perry-Rogers couple. The Fasanos were happy to raise both boys but once the Perry-Rogers couple discovered the mistake and the birth of the twins, they insisted on genetic tests being undertaken, which revealed that one of the twins was their genetic child. They applied for a declaration of parentage and custody. The case was settled on the basis that the Fasanos agreed to relinquish custody to the Perry-Rogers couple on the understanding that they would have visitation rights. The baby was handed over when he was almost five months old. However, two weeks later the Perry-Rogers couple sued for exclusive custody in contravention of their written agreement. The Court initially granted the Fasanos extensive visitation but on appeal by the Perry-Rogers couple, the Appeal Court held that the Fasanos had no standing to claim visitation rights to the child and had no parental rights to ask the Court to enforce the visitation agreement. They did not have the opportunity to petition the Court in relation to the child's best interest, nor was the other twin granted any visitation rights as a sibling. The decision was based on the wording of the New York statute, which provided that only parents could be accorded visitation and in the circumstances of this case the Fasanos did not qualify under the statutory provisions. The Court held that where a child is properly in the custody of its parents, those parents are accorded extremely broad rights to exclude any visitation, even by a person who has raised and nurtured the child as his or her own.

[6.75] The Court stressed that it was not making its decision based solely on a prioritisation of genetics over other biological or social factors. However, its decision in favour of the genetic parents without providing the gestational mother an opportunity to make a contrary argument seems to suggest otherwise. The Court also said that once the Fasanos became aware of the mistake during pregnancy it was incumbent on them to have the mistake rectified as soon as possible after birth rather than allow a bond to develop with the child and subsequently use this bond as a basis upon which to deny custody to the genetic parents. It has been argued that the application of this equitable 'dirty hands' argument is deeply flawed both in principle and in fact, as denial of the right to visitation seems a disproportionately harsh punishment for forming a bond with the child, and also the Perry-Rogers couple could be said to have acted badly in agreeing to visitation in order to regain custody of the child and then immediately violating the terms of the agreement.[120]

[6.76] Bender states that mistakes such as that which occurred in this case force us to confront the underlying assumptions in our legal notions of kinship and the values we want to reflect in our applications of law. She says that society cannot expect to use technologies without mistakes, whether negligent, reckless or intentional. Although tort actions may serve important social justice goals in these cases, they do not resolve who will be the parents of the child. All too often, courts are expected to resolve these cases without legislative guidance and are bound to get it wrong in some cases.[121]

---

[120] Bender, 'Genes, Parents and Assisted Reproductive Technologies: ARTs, Mistakes, Sex, Race and Law' (2003) 12 Columbia Journal of Gender and Law 1.

[121] Bender, 'Genes, Parents and Assisted Reproductive Technologies: ARTs, Mistakes, Sex, Race and Law' (2003) 12 Columbia Journal of Gender and Law 1 at 26.

[6.77] In a comparable English case, *Leeds Teaching Hospital NHS Trust v Mr & Mrs A & Others*[122] two couples, the A's and the B's, were attending the same hospital for infertility treatment. Mr and Mrs A, a white couple, consented to Mrs A's eggs being fertilised with Mr A's sperm and any resulting embryos to be transferred to Mrs A Mr and Mrs B, a black couple, gave consent to similar IVF procedures for themselves but Mr B also expressly refused to allow his sperm to be used for research purposes. Following a mix-up at the clinic, Mr B's sperm was used to fertilise Mrs A's eggs. She became pregnant and later gave birth to twins. The mistake only became apparent when the twins were delivered, as they were of mixed race. It was confirmed that Mr B was the father of the twins but they continued to live with the A's and he had no contact with them. All of the parties agreed that it was best for the children to reside with the A's but the High Court was asked to resolve the issue of paternity of the children.

[6.78] The Human Fertilisation and Embryology Act 1990 (subsequently amended in 2008) provides in s 28 that where a woman is married, her husband is the father of any child born to her unless he did not consent to the treatment she received. Although Mr A gave his consent to the IVF procedure, his consent was limited to the creation of an embryo using his sperm, not that of Mr B. Therefore the Court said 'Mr A did not consent to the placing in his wife of the embryo which was actually placed. Accordingly, s 28(2) does not apply.' The only possible outcome was to revert to the common law assumption that Mr B, who had been shown to be the genetic father, was also the legal father. Butler-Sloss J held that he had the same legal status as an unmarried father, ie he had no automatic rights to the children.[123]

[6.79] Ford and Morgan take the view that rather than prioritising a social view of parenthood, the case favours a biological accident by declaring the gamete provider rather than the man with whom the children have a familial bond to be their legal father. Butler-Sloss J considered the impact of art 8 of the Human Rights Act 1998 in connection with the right of the children to know the identity of their biological father. She said:

> To refuse to recognise Mr B as their biological father is to distort the truth about which some day the twins will have to learn through knowledge of their paternal identity. The requirement to preserve the truth will not adversely affect their immediate welfare nor their welfare throughout their childhood. It does not impede the cementing of the permanent relationship of each with Mr A who will act as their father throughout their childhood.

The court therefore concluded that the children would remain within a loving and stable home and their rights would be safeguarded by appropriate family or adoption orders.

[6.80] Another error came to light in the Northern Irish case of *A and B (by C, their mother and next friend) v A (Health and Social Services Trust)*[124] where donor sperm from a South African donor was used in the treatment of a white couple resulting in dark coloured twins. The children later alleged that they had suffered racial harassment at

---

[122] *Leeds Teaching Hospital NHS Trust v Mr & Mrs A & Others* [2003] EWHC 259.

[123] All parties were agreed that the children should remain in the A's custody and that Mr A should be able to acquire fatherhood by adoption.

[124] *A and B (by C, their mother and next friend) v A (Health and Social Services Trust)* [2011] NICA 28.

school and sued the Trust for harm sustained as a result of the error. The case, which was essentially based on a wrongful conception argument, failed on the grounds that they had not sustained a recognisable injury.[125]

[6.81] Although not an error per se, a further case also demonstrates the complexity of some arrangements which the courts are asked to untangle and the dangers of an unregulated environment despite the existence of comprehensive legislation. In the English case of *M v F (Legal Paternity)*[126] M, the mother, and H, her husband, were unable to conceive. Following communication between M and F though an internet website on which F advertised as an unpaid sperm donor, they met over a period of time and a child was conceived. M and F disputed how the child was conceived. M claimed it was as a result of sexual intercourse, which would mean that F was the legal parent. F claimed it was as a result of artificial insemination, in which case parentage would depend on the application of the provisions of the Human Fertilisation and Embryology Act 2008. The mother applied for a declaration that F was the legal parent and for financial provision under the Children Act 1989. The judge considered both M and F to have been deceitful but ultimately M was believed in relation to how the child was conceived, namely by sexual intercourse. Accordingly, F was the legal parent.

Embryo disputes in Ireland

[6.82] The only Irish case to date to deal with a dispute in relation to the disposition of stored embryos arose in 2006 in *MR v TR & Ors*[127] (also known as *Roche v Roche*). The facts of this case were that MR and TR were married in 1992 and sought fertility advice from their general practitioner in 1994. They were referred to the National Maternity Hospital for specialist treatment and subsequently had a son in 1997. Shortly after the birth of the child, MR underwent ovarian surgery as a result of which she sought fertility treatment at an IVF clinic in 2001. In January 2002, the couple attended the clinic and signed a number of documents covering consent to treatment and the cryopreservation of the embryos.

[6.83] TR signed a form in which he acknowledged that he was MR's husband and consented to the fertilisation of her eggs and the transfer of three embryos to her uterus. He also acknowledged that he would become the legal father of any resulting child. As a result of the treatment, six viable embryos were created. Three were transferred to MR's uterus and the remaining three were frozen. MR became pregnant and gave birth to a daughter in October 2002. Marital difficulties arose between the couple and they subsequently separated. The case arose as a result of the fact that MR wished to have the three frozen embryos transferred to her uterus whereas TR did not wish this to happen nor to become the father of any child that might be born as a result of such a treatment.

[6.84] There were a number of issues before McGovern J in the High Court. The first related to the extent to which TR could be held to have agreed to the transfer of the embryos to MR and whether such an agreement was binding on the parties in the circumstances of their marital separation. The second issue in relation to the

---

[125] See Sheldon, 'Only skin deep? The harm of being born a different colour to one's parents.' (2011) 19 Med L Rev 657

[126] *M v F (Legal Paternity)* [2013] EWHC 1901.

[127] *MR v TR & Ors* [2006] IEHC 359.

constitutional protection of the unborn is considered later.[128] In relation to the question of consent, McGovern J held that there was no agreement between the parties as to what would happen to the frozen embryos if the first embryo transfer was successful and resulted in pregnancy. The Court held that TR did not give his consent, either express or implied, to the transfer of the frozen embryos and acknowledged that the clinic was unwilling to release the embryos into the custody of MR in the absence of such consent. On appeal to the Supreme Court, the Court unanimously upheld the decision of the High Court that the husband had not given consent, either expressly or impliedly to the transfer of embryos to his wife.[129] The Court held that the forms signed by the husband were not contractually binding and were simply medical consent forms. There was no question of an offer or acceptance or consideration, or an intention to create a legal contract, nor was the man bound by the application of equitable principles to permit the frozen embryos to be implanted.

[6.85] Consent is a crucial aspect of all medical treatment and, in the case of IVF, would appear to be required from both partners at all stages of the process from fertilisation until embryo transfer. There is an argument to the effect that an implied consent arises by virtue of the couple presenting for IVF treatment together and that any subsequent dispute should be resolved in favour of the party seeking to procreate, as that was the original intention of the treatment.[130] On this basis 'voluntary participation in the IVF process could be regarded as conduct reasonably leading to the assumption that both parties have committed to reproduction. In the event of changed circumstances, the doctrine of promissory estoppel becomes essential, as the party who subsequently seeks to use any non-transferred embryos relies, to his or her detriment, on the other party's commitment to reproduce jointly.'[131] Therefore, the partner who opposes implantation of the embryos should be estopped from asserting his or her right not to reproduce. This argument was put to the Court in the present case, to the effect that the husband was estopped from withholding consent to embryo transfer after the creation of the embryos and the use of some of them in an earlier, successful IVF cycle, was not upheld by the Court. Denham J stated that even if the husband had entered an agreement on this issue, it would not necessarily be irrevocable and that the Court would have to take all the circumstances into account, including whether the use of the embryos at issue represented the last opportunity for either party to have a biological child of their own.[132] In acknowledging the existence of a right to procreate, which was recognised in *Murray v Ireland*,[133] she said that:

> There is an equal and opposite right not to procreate. In the circumstances of this case, while the plaintiff and her husband have family rights, the exercise of a right not to

---

[128] Para **[6.92]**.

[129] *Roche v Roche* [2009] IESC 82.

[130] Waldman, 'The Parent Trap: Uncovering the Myth of Coerced Parenthood in Frozen Embryo Dispute' (2004) Am Univ Law Rev 53:1021; Apel, 'Cryopreserved Embryos: A Response to 'Forced Parenthood' and the Role of Intent' (2005) Fam Law Q 39: 663.

[131] Sills and Murphy, 'Determining the Status of Non-Transferred Embryos in Ireland: A Conspectus of Case Law and Implications for Clinical IVF Practice' (2009) Philosophy, Ethics and Humanities in Medicine 4:8.

[132] *Roche v Roche* [2009] IESC 82 at para 38.

[133] *Murray v Ireland* [1991] 1 ILRM 465.

procreate by the husband is a proportionate interference in all the circumstances of the case to the right of the plaintiff to procreate.

[6.86] The forms used by the clinic in this case did not deal with the position of the parties in respect of any frozen embryos. It did not stipulate, therefore, what the parties intended should happen to such embryos in the event that a pregnancy was achieved on the first attempt, or that the couple separated, divorced or died. The legal insufficiencies of the forms used in this case provide a clear illustration of the need for clarification and guidance in Ireland on legal issues relating to IVF. The Commission on Assisted Human Reproduction recommended in 2005 that appropriate guidelines should be put in place by the regulatory body proposed by the Commission, to govern the options available for excess frozen embryos. These would include voluntary donation to other recipients, donation to research or allowing the embryos to perish. It also recommended that 'the regulatory body should, in accordance with statutory guidelines, have power to address cases where embryos are abandoned, where the commissioning couple cannot agree on a course of action, where the couple separates or where one or both partners dies or becomes incapacitated.'[134] There has been no legislative action taken to date to implement these recommendations.

Constitutional protection of the unborn

[6.87] Article 40.3.3° of the Irish Constitution 1937 states:

> The State acknowledges the right to life of the unborn and, with due regard to the equal right of life of the mother, guarantees in its laws to respect, and, as far as practicable, by its laws to defend and vindicate that right.[135]

The most important word, from the perspective of IVF, is the word 'unborn'. For the purposes of IVF if the 'unborn' includes the pre-implantation embryo, then the application of the constitutional protection in art 40.3.3° would have implications for IVF practices insofar as embryo freezing may not be permissible, at least unless there was a guarantee that the embryo would subsequently be transferred to a receptive uterus. This would be necessary due to the interpretation of the 'right to life' as meaning the right to have the opportunity to grow and develop in the uterus and be born. This is evident from *G v An Bord Uchtála*[136] in which Walsh J stated:

> [A child] has the right to life itself and the right to be guarded against all threats directed to its existence whether before or after birth ... The right to life necessarily implies the right to be born, the right to preserve and defend, and to have preserved and defended, that life ....

[6.88] The use of the word 'unborn' in the Constitution is unfortunate because it introduces uncertainty into the law regarding the presumed intention of the People that is reflected in that document. If the 'unborn' means 'not yet born' or 'with the potential to be born' then, in the light of the biological development of the early embryo and the

---

[134] Report of the Commission on Assisted Human Reproduction (Government Publications Office, 2005) p 17 available at www.health.gov.ie.
[135] Inserted by the Eighth Amendment of the Constitution in 1983.
[136] *G v An Bord Uchtála* [1980] IR 32.

absence of potential in the pre-implantation embryo, it is likely that the embryo in the laboratory does not qualify for this Constitutional protection. In its report the Constitutional Review Committee said in relation to art 40.3.3°:

> There is no definition of 'unborn' which, used as a noun, is at least odd. One would expect 'unborn human' or 'unborn human being'. Presumably the term 'unborn child' was not chosen because of uncertainty as to when a fetus might properly be so described. Definition is needed as to when the 'unborn' acquires the protection of the law. Philosophers and scientists may continue to debate when human life begins but the law must define what it intends to protect. 'Unborn' seems to imply 'on the way to being born' or 'capable of being born'. Whether this condition obtains from fertilisation of the ovum, implantation of the fertilised ovum in the womb, or some other point, has not been defined.[137]

[6.89] This expression 'on the way to being born' reinforces the view that the pre-implantation embryo is not covered by the Constitutional provision as it stands. The embryo at this stage, without implantation, is neither on the way to being born nor capable of being born. It may not even be human nor individual unless it is transferred to the uterus, implants in the uterine wall and develops a primitive streak. Whereas arguments may continue in relation to the embryo in the womb and whether and at what stage it is 'on the way to being born' so as to prohibit abortion, these arguments do not apply to the embryo outside the body, which will only qualify for the same protection if it is transferred to the uterus. Williams dismisses claims that the embryo is an 'unborn child' as follows:

> In the early stages of fetal development some people, not only lawyers, would incline to think the phrase 'unborn child' out of place. It would certainly be odd to refer thus to a microscopic fertilised ovum, or to the mass of cells into which it shortly develops – cells nearly all of which will be shed as part of the afterbirth. To call this an 'unborn child' would be a flight of fancy.[138]

[6.90] In the case of *Attorney General v X* in 1992,[139] the Supreme Court considered art 40.3.3° in the context of whether a young girl who was at risk of suicide could travel abroad to obtain an abortion. The Court held that the interpretation of the provision required that the termination of pregnancy was permissible only when it was established as a matter of probability that there was a real and substantial risk to the life of the mother if such termination were not provided. For the purposes of a consideration of the meaning of the provision in relation to the pre-implantation embryo, the judgment of the Court is not of great assistance. It must be borne in mind that the Court, in referring to

---

[137] Report of the Constitution Review Group (1996) at 275.

[138] Williams, "The Fetus and the 'Right to Life'" (1994) Cambridge Law Journal at 73.

[139] *Attorney General v X* [1992] 1 IR 1. This case appears to have been followed by the Court in a case in which a pregnant 13-year-old girl, who had allegedly been raped, was allowed to travel to the UK for an abortion on the grounds that she would commit suicide if she had to continue with the pregnancy. The facts were seen as coming within the precedent set by the *X* case and therefore it was unnecessary to go into the meaning of 'unborn' or the protection given by the Constitution. An unusual aspect of this case was the fact that this girl was in the care of the health board at the time of the application and subsequent journey to the UK and therefore the abortion was carried out at the expense of the State. See *A and B v Eastern Health Board* [1998]1 IR 464.

the 'unborn' in the course of the judgment were doing so in light of the facts of the case, which involved a pregnancy already begun, an embryo 'on the way to being born'. For this reason, much of the judgment of the Court is not applicable to the embryo outside the body, which is not 'on the way to being born' unless implantation takes place. In instances where the meaning of 'unborn' is indirectly adverted to, it is spoken of in relation to 'the life of the infant in the womb'. This has no application to the embryo *outside* the womb.

[6.91] According to Hederman J (dissenting), the objective of the constitutional provision is the protection of human life. He states:

> The Eighth Amendment establishes beyond any dispute that the constitutional guarantee of the vindication and protection of life is not qualified by the condition that the life must be one which has achieved an independent existence after birth. The right of life is guaranteed to every life born or unborn. One cannot make distinctions between individual phases of the unborn life before birth, or between unborn and born life.[140]

This extract from the judgment of Hederman J is the closest the Court gets to discussing what is meant by the expression 'unborn' used in the Constitution, yet it does not go far enough. Even if it is accepted that distinctions cannot be made as between the foetus at 6 weeks (or earlier) and the foetus at 36 weeks for the purposes of the Constitutional protection they both may enjoy, it may be argued that this does not apply to the embryo outside the body. In this instance the embryo is not 'an autonomous human being'[141] (another phrase used by Hederman J) because it can never become human unless it is transferred to the uterus, (which depends on the actions of someone else), nor does it establish a pregnancy (in which the right to life of the mother may be given priority over the right to life of the embryo). It does not share any of the characteristics possessed by the foetus in the womb except that it is human in origin. It is not sentient, it has no 'potential' to become anything while it remains in the petri dish in the laboratory. Therefore, it may be argued that the Constitutional provision has no application to the pre-implantation embryo.

[6.92] The first judicial consideration of the application of art 40.3.3° to embryos took place in *MR v TR & Ors*[142] (also known as *Roche v Roche)*, the facts of which are outlined above.[143] On the constitutional issue, the Court was asked to consider whether art 40.3.3° applied to the frozen embryos which were the subject of the dispute between the estranged couple in this case. The High Court heard from a number of witnesses who gave their view as to when life begins. Some argued that 'from the moment of fertilisation of the ovum by the sperm a new human life begins.' Others argued that 'it was only when the embryo became implanted in the uterus that the potential to be born existed and that human life began at that point'. Yet other witnesses stated that 'human life began at the formation of the primitive streak' and others took the view that it was impossible to say when human life begins. In this regard, McGovern J stated that:

> It is possible for scientists and embryologists to describe in detail the process of development from the ovum to the embryo and on to the stage when it becomes a foetus

---

[140] Williams, 'The Fetus and the 'Right to Life'' (1994) Cambridge Law Journal, p 72.

[141] *Attorney General v X* [1992] 1 IR 1.

[142] *MR v TR & Ors* [2006] IEHC 359.

[143] Para **[6.84]**.

after implantation of the embryo in the wall of the uterus, but in my opinion, it is not possible for this Court to state when human life begins.

[6.93] The judge went on to acknowledge that the point at which people ascribe human characteristics to genetic material depends on other issues besides science and medicine, and is dependent upon one's own moral or religious beliefs. He stressed that it was not the function of the Court to choose between competing moral beliefs and that the only issue that he had to decide was whether the three frozen embryos in this case were 'unborn' within the meaning of art 40.3.3° of the Constitution. In deciding upon this important point, McGovern J first stated that in considering the words in art 40.3.3° the Court could have regard to the legislative history of the Constitutional amendment but not to debates in the Oireachtas in order to clarify what was in the contemplation of the People in passing the amendment. He also referred to the Medical Council's Guide to Ethical Conduct and Behaviour (in its previous edition dated 2004), the Report of the Constitution Review Group and the Report of the Commission on Assisted Human Reproduction, also mentioned above. McGovern J concluded that there had been:

> [N]o evidence adduced that it was ever in the mind of the people voting on the Eighth Amendment to the Constitution that 'unborn' meant anything other than a foetus or child within the womb. To infer that it was in the mind of the people that 'unborn' included embryos outside the womb or embryos in vitro would be to completely ignore the circumstances in which the amendment giving rise to Article 40.3.3 arose. While I accept that Article 40.3.3 is not to be taken in isolation from its historical background and should be considered as but one provision of the whole Constitution, this does not mean that the word 'unborn' can be given a meaning which was not contemplated by the people at the time of the passing of the Eighth Amendment and which takes it outside the scope and purpose of the amendment.

[6.94] Consequently, the Court held that the word 'unborn' within art 40.3.3° does not include embryos in vitro and therefore did not include the three frozen embryos in this case. McGovern J stated that in the absence of any regulation in this country 'embryos outside the womb have a very precarious existence' and that 'until the law or the Constitution is changed this issue remains within the sphere of ethics and morality.' On appeal to the Supreme Court,[144] the judges all took the view that decisions in relation to the definition of life or adjudications on matters of science, theology or ethics were not appropriately made by a court of law. The court's function was to make a legal decision on the interpretation of an article of the Constitution, and it was a matter for the legislature to make policy choices in relation to the regulation of assisted human reproduction and the protection of the embryo. The Court said that the provision had been inserted into the Constitution to deal with termination of pregnancy and the balancing of rights between the foetus and the mother. The language and intent of the article envisages a specific constitutional and legal relationship between the unborn and the mother which only exists by virtue of a physical connection between them. This only happens after implantation and therefore an 'unborn' under art 40.3.3° is established when an embryo implants in the womb.[145]

---

[144] *Roche v Roche* [2009] IESC 82.
[145] [2009] IESC 82, per Denham J para 60.

[6.95] Denham J also said that the concept of 'unborn' envisages a state of being born, the potential to be born or the capacity to be born, which occurs only after implantation.[146] She said that if embryos were considered to be 'unborn' within the Constitution, the State would have an obligation to protect all embryos in the State in every clinic and hospital and would have to intervene to facilitate their implantation irrespective of the parents' wishes, and this would be inconsistent with the rights of the family.[147]A similar point was made by Hardiman J who expressed concern that if respect for the embryo were carried to the point of equating it to a life in being, that view would lead to the outlawing of one of the most widely used methods of contraception, the morning-after pill, which operates by prevention of implantation.

[6.96] All five judges of the Supreme Court said that legislation should be introduced to deal with the legal issues arising in assisted human reproduction. In February 2015 the Cabinet authorised the Department of Health to prepare legislation on Assisted Human Reproduction and associated research but the Heads of Bill have not yet been published.[148]

---

[146] Denham J para 61.

[147] Denham J para 67.

[148] health.gov.ie/blog/press-release/govt-to-legislate-for-assisted-human-reproduction-associated-research/.

Chapter 7

Surrogacy

INTRODUCTION

[7.01] Surrogacy is not a modern development; indeed, in a simpler form, it has been in existence for centuries.[1] In modern practice, surrogacy is an arrangement whereby a woman agrees to be artificially inseminated (known as traditional or partial surrogacy), or have an embryo transferred to her uterus (known as gestational or full surrogacy) in order to become pregnant and carry a child to term, with the intention of relinquishing custody of that child upon birth to the couple with whom she has made the agreement. The couple is usually referred to either as 'the intended parents' or 'the commissioning couple'.[2] In commercial surrogacy, the surrogate mother is paid a fee, which can range from €10,000 to €50,000 or more depending on the jurisdiction in which it takes place. In addition, medical and other expenses as well as a fee to the clinic which facilitates the arrangement may be payable. Altruistic surrogacy arrangements may be made between family members or friends in which no money is paid other than reimbursement of medical and out-of-pocket expenses.

[7.02] Surrogacy might be an option where, for example, a woman has severe pelvic disease which cannot be remedied surgically, or where she has no uterus following a hysterectomy. It might also be used in situations where a woman has uterine insufficiency as a result of which she has suffered repeated miscarriages and, although she can produce eggs, she is unable to carry a pregnancy to term. Traditional surrogacy, in which the surrogate mother's egg is fertilised by the intended father's sperm, can be performed without the assistance of a doctor or any modern technology as impregnation can occur by intercourse or through self-insemination methods. Due to the fact that no medical assistance is required, regulation of this form of surrogacy is very difficult as it may occur without formal oversight. Gestational surrogacy, on the other hand, does require medical assistance as the surrogate is the carrier of an embryo which has been created by the intended parents using their own sperm and eggs or gamete donors where

---

[1] Biblical examples of surrogacy are often cited as an example, eg Genesis, Chapter 16: 4–7, where Abraham's wife Sarah could not bear a child so Abraham lay with a slave-girl, Hagar, in order to found a family through her. Hagar duly bore Abraham a son, Ishmahel. Unfortunately, there was not a happy ending to this tale, as Sarah became bitter and jealous and cast out Hagar and Ishmahel, who later returned only to be again rejected by Abraham and Sarah. Ishmahel grew into a 'wild ass of a man, his hand against every man and every man's hand against him.' 16:12. See also *Briody v St. Helen's Knowsley Health Authority* [2000] EWHC QB 178, per Ebsworth J at 19; and Eriksson, *Reproductive Freedom in the Context of International Human Rights and Humanitarian Law* (Martinus Nijhoff Publishers, 2000) at 207.

[2] A surrogacy arrangement could also be made by a single person using donated gametes to create an embryo which is then transferred to the surrogate mother.

necessary. In this case the embryo transfer would be carried out by an embryologist in an IVF clinic and therefore this form of surrogacy is more readily amenable to regulation.

[7.03] In the 1980s, surrogacy sparked off controversies unheard of before.[3] Issues such as the meaning of motherhood, the role of gestating a baby, the consequences for women, the importance of the mother-child bond, payment for gestational services and the valuation of parenthood were debated as the result of a small number of high-profile cases which caught the public's attention. Surrogacy became 'the whipping post for the moral backlash against the brave new world of technological rationality and scientific finality.'[4] The tug-of-love scenario usually conjured up when surrogacy was discussed also demonstrated the role of the media in focusing on the sensationalist angle of surrogacy, drawing attention to the very few cases in which the surrogate changes her mind and decides to keep the child.[5]

[7.04] In the cases in which surrogacy has come to judicial and public attention, much energy and public debate is expended on the ethical issues involved in this practice, some of which are discussed below. However, from a legal perspective when surrogacy cases have come before the courts, judges have tended to take a pragmatic view of surrogacy determining that the morality of the practice is irrelevant to the legal determination of parentage which must be decided on the basis of the best interests of the child.

ETHICAL ISSUES IN SURROGACY

[7.05] A range of ethical issues arise in relation to surrogacy from concerns about the splitting of motherhood between a number of different women, the commodification of

---

3   Perhaps the reason for the discomfort which usually characterises public reaction to surrogacy is the change which technology brings to familiar traditions and structures. 'We need not look too deeply into history to understand that technology consistently places old questions in new contexts. Technology usually unsettles settled expectations; it often jars and frightens; it has a way of disorienting us by wresting away our confident assumptions from a simpler past. Occasionally, it forces us to rethink our very moral fabric, or at least to explore our values anew to determine how they apply in wholly unprecedented contexts. So it is, in my judgement, with surrogacy.' Bezanson, 'Solomon Would Weep: A Comment on *In the Matter of Baby M* and the Limits of Judicial Authority' (1988) 16:1–2 Law, Medicine and Health Care 126–130 at 126.

4   Morgan and Lee, *Human Fertilisation and Embryology, Regulating the Reproductive Revolution* (Blackstone Press, 2001) at 191.

5   It is difficult to assess with accuracy the number of cases in which breaches of the arrangement take place, as it is impossible to know how many surrogacy cases occur at all. However, those involved in arranging surrogacy believe that the incidence is very low. See Schuck, 'Some Reflections on the *Baby M* Case' (1988) 76 Geo LJ 1793 at 1801 fn.30, recording an interview with a lawyer dealing in surrogacy transactions. It was claimed that there were 9 problem cases out of about 600, and 4 (including the infamous *Baby M* case, which is discussed later) that ended up in court. A report in the UK estimates that it is only in 4–5 per cent of cases that the surrogate refuses to hand over the child. Surrogacy: Review for Health Ministers of Current Arrangements for Payments and Regulation (Cm.4068) (Department of Health, 1998) at para 3.38. In the Republic of Ireland, no cases of this nature have been brought to judicial attention, although there have been children born to Irish couples through surrogacy arrangements made in the US, Ukraine, India, Romania and other jurisdictions.

children, the potential for exploitation of women and concern for the welfare of children.[6] Although courts generally do not engage in making judgments on ethical issues as this is not a judicial function, they are of course obliged to consider the issues relating to child welfare, validity of consent and the public policy considerations which may arise in relation to enforceability of the contract and conflict with adoption laws. Many of these cases that have arisen are in the context of commercial surrogacy rather than altruistic surrogacy due to the issue of payment involved.

Baby selling

[7.06] One of the most widely used moral arguments for the prohibition of commercial surrogacy has been to consider it an example of baby selling.[7] It is argued that surrogacy is unethical because the payment of money commodifies the child and treats it as a product rather than a person. For example, Anderson claims that commercial surrogacy substitutes market norms for some of the norms of parental love.[8] She states that the surrogate mother renounces her parental responsibilities not for the sake of the child but for her own sake and that therefore both she and the commissioning couple treat her rights as a kind of property right. 'They thereby treat the child itself as a kind of commodity, which may be properly bought and sold.'

[7.07] This view of surrogacy is echoed in one of the first reported cases, *In Re Baby M*,[9] in which the New Jersey Supreme Court stated: 'This is the sale of a child, or, at the very least, the sale of a mother's right to her child, the only mitigating factor being that one of the purchasers is the father. Almost every evil that prompted the prohibition of money in connection with adoptions exists here.' However, others dispute the use of the term 'baby selling' as the baby itself is not being sold as an object; rather, parental rights are being exchanged for a fee.[10] It is therefore argued that it is possible to maintain that a baby is 'sold' only if persons with no genetic association purchase an infant that is

---

[6] See useful discussion by the Danish Council of Ethics, *International Trade in Human Eggs, surrogacy and organs* (2013) 53 – 63.

[7] The offensive notion of paying a price for a human being was the driving force behind the Surrogacy Arrangements Act 1985 in the UK. However, the Act merely prohibits payments to third parties or brokers in relation to surrogacy. It does not ban payments to the surrogate herself due to concerns about the effect on the child born to a woman who is subject to the taint of criminality.

[8] Anderson, 'Is women's labour a commodity?' (1990) 19 Philosophy and Public Affairs 71–92.

[9] *In re Baby M*, 525 A, 2d 1128, 217 NJ Super 313 (Superior Ct Chancery Div 1987), reversed on appeal, 1988 West Law 6251 (NJ Supreme Ct, 3 February 1988).

[10] Shapiro argues that the child is not 'conceived in order to be given away', as this would imply that the child would be handed over to the first person who came along. He argues that: '[T]he child is not being conceived because the transfer of the child is itself the intrinsically valuable goal of the arrangement. The child is conceived as part of the formation of a nuclear family – with all the bonds, relationships and duties for which one hopes. That is the purpose of the overall transaction. The new family is, of course, not that of the birth mother, so transfer is a necessary mechanism. The transfer is not the purpose or goal, but the means.' Shapiro, 'How (Not) to Think About Surrogacy and Other Reproductive Innovations' (1994) 28 University of San Francisco Law Review 647 at 657.

already in being.[11] It is thus more logical to regard the transaction as payment for gestational expertise or 'services rendered', with a crucial distinction being drawn between reasonable recompense and inducement to gestate.[12] By comparison, Brazier argues that such a distinction is specious unless the usual consequences of paid employment ensue and the contract is regarded as enforceable in the same way as other contracts for services.[13] The reproductive labour which commissioning couples are prepared to pay for is inevitably 'the labour of having a child *for them* – they are paying for their child.'[14] The only difference from a baby market is that the child is genetically related to one or both of the commissioning parents. Brazier questions whether this is sufficient to distinguish surrogacy from adoption, where payments are explicitly prohibited.

[7.08] The connotations of buying and selling infants are instinctively unpleasant to most people. This is especially true when economic or market language enters familial relationships. In 1979, Posner and Landes controversially explained how a market in babies should be regarded and regulated.[15] They began by pointing out the shortage of babies for adoption in the United States. This was due, largely, not to the increased availability of contraception and abortion, as might have been thought, but to the fact that a larger proportion of parents of illegitimate children were keeping them instead of giving them up for adoption:

> This trend may be due to inexplicable (on economic grounds) changes in moral standards; or it may be due to the fact that the increased opportunities for women in the job market have made them less dependent on the presence of a male in raising a child. An additional feature is that, given the increased availability of contraception and abortion, an illegitimate baby is more likely than formerly to be a desired baby.[16]

[7.09] The effect of the shortage is obvious – some couples have to wait for years to get a baby, others never get one and others are put off by the size of the queue from even applying. Where demand outstrips supply, and where there are restrictions on payment, as there are in connection with adoption, it is understandable that surrogacy, with clandestine payments or payments of only medical expenses, could be seen as providing a solution. This may lead to a black market situation in which surrogates use their genetic backgrounds to make the sale to prospective commissioning couples. The legal sanctions that may apply to such an arrangement may lead to the risks being overcome by an increase in the financial incentives involved. It may also be the case that these

---

[11] Laurie, Harmon and Porter *Law and Medical Ethics* (10th edn, OUP, 2016) para 8.116

[12] Laurie, Harmon and Porter *Law and Medical Ethics* (10th edn, OUP, 2016) para 8.116. See also Freeman 'Does Surrogacy Have a Future After Brazier?' (1999) 7 Med L Rev 1 at 9; Dickenson, *Property, Women and Politics* (Rutgers University Press, 1997) at 160–165; Purdy *Reproducing Persons*, (Cornell University Press, 1996) at 47.

[13] Brazier 'Can You Buy Children?' (1999) Child and Fam Law Quarterly Vol 11 No 4, 345–354.

[14] Brazier 'Can You Buy Children?' (1999) Child and Fam Law Quarterly Vol 11 No 4, 345–354 at 351.

[15] Landes and Posner, 'The Economics of the Baby Shortage' (1979) 7 Journal of Legal Studies 323.

[16] Landes and Posner, 'The Economics of the Baby Shortage' (1979) 7 Journal of Legal Studies 323 at 325.

sanctions may lead to fraud, dishonesty, misrepresentation and blackmail on the part of the surrogate who is selling her services.

[7.10] It may be argued that all of the potential ill effects in relation to the market in babies are as a result of the fact that the market is an illegal one. Although these arguments are directed towards a legal market in adoptions, an analogy may be drawn with surrogacy. Landes and Posner argue that a legal market would allow: enforceability of contracts (which would decrease the risks involved for both parties); increase in consumer satisfaction (due to the higher-quality package of rights thereby obtained); decrease in the price to be paid (the net medical costs would be cancelled out by the fact that paying the surrogate's medical bills are comparable to the hypothetical costs of the commissioning couple's medical bills had they been able to conceive themselves); and allow more lower-income families to obtain a child (as the cost of acquiring a baby would often be small).

[7.11] Although there may be some attraction in the economic analysis, there are many obvious criticisms of a legal market in babies, most importantly the issue of protection of the child. A free market in adoptions does not necessarily coincide with the objective of the adoption process, which is to ensure that the child's best interests are safeguarded.[17] Usually a free market increases the satisfaction of those trading in it, but this does not take account of the fact that the product being sold in this instance is a child whose individual welfare and interests society is committed to protect. 'The question is whether the price system would do as good a job as, or a better job than, adoption agencies in finding homes for children that would maximise their satisfactions in life.'[18]

[7.12] In looking at the practice of adoption, one can see that the screening process is an obvious attempt to safeguard the welfare of the child by eliminating any unfit parents from consideration as adopters. However, once the couple makes it onto the waiting list, the allocation of children then usually works on a 'first-come, first-serve' basis, so that those who are best suited as parents do not necessarily get priority on the list. Also important is that the adoption agency does not know what the individual needs of the particular child will be in the future, apart from necessities such as love, warmth, food and shelter:

> One cannot read from the face of a new born whether he or she will be of above or below normal intelligence, or be naturally athletic, musical, or artistic. Hence agencies cannot be presumed to match these very real, if inaccessible, qualities of infants with the qualities of the adoptive parents any more effectively than a market would.[19]

Thus, it is argued that if the commissioning couple is screened for suitability in the same way as prospective adopters, the newborn child's best interests may be as well served by placement with that couple as they would with an adoptive couple.

---

[17] Landes and Posner, 'The Economics of the Baby Shortage' (1979) 7 Journal of Legal Studies 323 at 342.

[18] Landes and Posner, 'The Economics of the Baby Shortage' (1979) 7 Journal of Legal Studies 323 at 342.

[19] Landes and Posner, 'The Economics of the Baby Shortage' (1979) 7 Journal of Legal Studies 323 at 343.

[7.13] Another concern in relation to the market in babies is the equation of property rights with human beings, with its resonances of slavery. The idea that one is purchasing a baby gives the impression that one is thereby free to do with one's property whatever one likes. However, it may be counter argued that this is untrue in relation to adoption and surrogacy because, *even* if one is said to buy a baby, this does not mean that the baby can be abused or neglected or mistreated,[20] as the laws forbidding such activities still apply to adoptive or commissioning parents. 'The laws against child abuse have never distinguished among different methods of acquiring custody of the child. Natural parents are not permitted to abuse a child because they are natural rather than adoptive parents.'[21]

[7.14] A problem that may arise in this context if one were to accept the market principle is to determine the outcome when the child is born disabled.[22] If this were treated as the purchase of a product, the buyer could reject the child as 'defective goods', but parents (whether they are natural or adoptive parents) are not permitted to reject their baby because it does not conform with their expectations, although of course parents (natural or adoptive) may abandon the child into the care of the State. In any such case the welfare of the child must be considered along with that of the contracting parties, as 'the child is an interested third party whose welfare would be disserved by a mechanical application of the remedies available to buyers in the market for inanimate goods.'[23]

[7.15] Posner deals specifically with the market engendered by surrogacy by claiming that the case for making surrogacy contracts legally enforceable from an economic perspective is straightforward. Such contracts are made by the parties in the belief that they will be mutually beneficial:

> The father and wife must believe that they will derive a benefit from having the baby that is greater than $10,000, or else they would not sign the contract. The surrogate must believe that she will derive a benefit from the $10,000 (more precisely, from what she will use the money for) that is greater than the cost to her of being pregnant and giving birth and then surrendering the baby. So *ex ante*, as an economist would say (ie before the fact), all the parties to the contract are made better off.[24]

---

[20] There is no evidence to establish that children born of surrogacy arrangements are faced with any different problems than other children. Gostin states that there is 'no data to demonstrate that children born as the result of surrogacy contracts are worse off by any measure – that they suffer more neglect, abandonment, and physical abuse, or that they receive less nurturing and love.' Gostin, 'A Civil Liberties Analysis of Surrogacy Arrangements', in Gostin, (ed) *Surrogate Motherhood* (Indiana University Press, 1990) 3.

[21] Posner, 'The Regulation of the Market in Adoptions' (1987) 67 Boston University Law Review 59 at 66.

[22] This issue was raised in the case of Baby Gammy in 2013 where an Australian couple engaged the services of a Thai woman to act as surrogate. She conceived twins, one of whom (Gammy) was born with Downs' Syndrome. The couple returned to Australia without Gammy, which sparked an international outcry that the child had been rejected as a result of his intellectual disability.

[23] Posner, 'The Regulation of the Market in Adoptions' (1987) 67 Boston University Law Review 59 at 67.

[24] Posner, 'The Ethics and Economics of Enforcing Contracts of Surrogate Motherhood' (1989) 5 Journal of Contemporary Health Law and Policy 21 at 23.

[7.16] However straightforward such an approach might appear, this analysis fails to consider the effects of the contract on the non-party most closely affected by the contract, the child. However, Posner claims that it is more likely that the child is made better off by surrogacy than worse off. This is on the basis that without the contract the child would not be born at all, whereas with the contract the child becomes part of a family with at least one if not both genetic parents involved in its upbringing. Although studies on surrogate children are still at their early stages, there is no evidence thus far that such children grow up to regret that they were ever born or that they are any less stable or happy than natural children. The possibility that knowledge of the circumstances of his birth and the payment involved will have detrimental effects on the child is no less than the possible effect on a child born through IVF or artificial insemination who will also at some point understand that his parents spent large sums of money to bring about his conception. Any such detriment remains unproven at present.[25]

Protection of the surrogate mother

[7.17] Another common objection to commercial surrogacy is the potential for the economic exploitation of women. It is argued that 'the application of commercial norms to women's labour reduces the surrogate mothers from persons worthy of respect and consideration to objects of mere use.'[26] In addition to the principled objection to the use of women in this way, concern has also been voiced in relation to offering women money to bear a child particularly where the surrogate mothers live in poor socio-economic climates as these women may be financially impoverished and have few employment prospects. Thus, it is said they are women whose financial circumstances therefore may make them more likely to be influenced by the prospect of the monetary compensation offered by surrogacy and may be tempted to participate against their better judgment.

[7.18] It has been argued that a typical payment of $10,000 for nine months work is equivalent to a wage of $1.54 per hour, and that this is similar to 'sweat-shop' wages which are clearly exploitative.[27] This issue was explored in *Johnson v Calvert*[28] in which

---

25 Golombok, Blake, Casey, Roman & Jadva, (2013) 'Children born through reproductive donation: A longitudinal study of child adjustment.' *Journal of Child Psychology and Psychiatry, 54,* 653–660; Ilioi & Golombok (2015). 'Psychological adjustment in adolescents conceived by assisted reproductive techniques: A systematic review'. *Human Reproduction Update, 21(1),* 84–96.

26 Anderson, 'Is women's labour a commodity?' (1990) 19 Philosophy and Public Affairs 71–92

27 Hessenthaler, 'Gestational Surrogacy: Legal Implications of Reproductive Technology' (1995) 21 North Carolina Central Law Journal 169 at 176. This article gives a detailed description of the facts of the *Calvert* case, the trial proceedings, and the concurring and dissenting judgments. The author disputes the Supreme Court's assertion that Constitutional rights were not implicated in the case because the surrogate was free to terminate the pregnancy at will. She says that the decision is lacking in substance and is patronising to women by paying mere lip-service to the importance of the gestator's role in bringing the child into existence. She takes the view that although surrogacy has enabled women to fulfil their maternal instincts in circumstances where the infertility would otherwise have prevented this, the masses of women who are physically and psychologically harmed by surrogacy far outweigh those who gain by it. The unanswered question resulting from the *Calvert case* is whether satisfaction of the strong desire to have one's own child is worth the social price of surrogacy.

28 *Johnson v Calvert* (1993) 851 P 2d 776 (Cal Sup Ct).

the Court acknowledged that women of lower means typically served as surrogates but the Court said that there was no proof that surrogate contracts exploited these women to any greater degree than the general exploits of poorly paying and undesirable employment.[29] The Court pointed out that the wages being paid to surrogates are on a par with the wages being paid to the same category of women hired as childcarers and housekeepers, work which also takes them away from their own homes and families:

> Why is it 'exploitation' to give these women the free choice of opting to earn money while remaining at home, or perhaps earning more money while performing their previous jobs and, at the same time, also serving as a gestator? Rather than exploiting women, commercial surrogacy will liberate many women by allowing them to engage in employment that is less distasteful and more remunerative than their present choices.[30]

It may be argued that opposition to surrogacy on this basis is paternalistic and elitist.[31] Although the women who choose to act as commercial surrogates tend to be poor and to have few attractive work options, this may not be a reason to ban surrogacy as this would only serve to further restrict their options. 'The thought that commercial surrogacy should be banned because the poor working women who mostly choose it are too incompetent to be entrusted to make their own decisions in this sphere has an ugly, elitist sound.'[32]

[7.19] Although a practice that exploits people or violates human dignity may be universally agreed to be immoral, surrogacy is not necessarily guilty on either of these counts.[33] The mere fact that pregnancy is risky does not make surrogate agreements exploitative or morally wrong, as people often do risky things for money. In relation to

---

[29] *Johnson v Calvert* (1993) 851 P 2d 776 (Cal Sup Ct) at 785.

[30] Ingram, 'Surrogate Gestator: A New and Honorable Profession' (1993) 76 Marquette Law Review 675 at 684. Ingram criticises the application of old legal codes and principles to new disputes as looking backward when science is looking forward. He examines the participants in gestational surrogacy arrangements, the reasons for their choices and the objections that have been taken thereto. He takes perhaps a rather simplistic view that because society generally does not consider it exploitative to expect people to perform difficult and dangerous tasks that they have freely undertaken, society should view gestational surrogacy in the same light. It must, however, be recognised that such an approach is naïve in its assumption that all dangerous tasks are equivalent in moral terms, as the potential for loss of life and limb which may be inherent in, say military combat, are very different considerations from the bringing into existence of a new life with all its inherent demands and possibilities, which occurs in surrogacy. In the former, one may make such a choice concerning one's own life but, in the latter, choices are being made about another person's life and very existence and therefore demand greater attention and consideration. He suggests that all couples should be obliged to adopt, as their third child, a hard-to-place child before being allowed to conceive again naturally, in order to draw attention to, what he considers, to be the unfairness of limiting potential opportunities available to infertile couples who have not chosen to be in the situation in which they find themselves.

[31] Arneson, 'Commodification and commercial surrogacy' (1992) 21 Philosophy and Public Affairs 132–64.

[32] Arneson, 'Commodification and commercial surrogacy' (1992) 21 Philosophy and Public Affairs 132–64.

[33] Steinbock, 'Surrogate Motherhood as Prenatal Adoption' (Law, Medicine and Ethics, 1988) 16: 1–2, p 47.

the motivation of surrogate mothers and the extent to which it might be argued that financial reward might influence their decision-making such as to negate their appreciation of the risks and consequences of their participation, research shows that the typical surrogate mother, at least in the Western World, does not appear to be so economically desperate that the promise of financial reward would coerce her into doing something she does not want to do. There may however be other considerations at play in jurisdictions which are characterised by economic deprivation. This is discussed further in the context of surrogacy tourism later.

[7.20] One of the first studies done in the 1980s in the United States indicated that surrogate mothers are largely drawn from the middle-class and have sufficient experience and education to understand the physical and emotional risks involved.[34] Parker found that there were several factors involved in the women's agreement to become a surrogate mother – the financial advantages, enjoyment of pregnancy and the perception that the advantages of relinquishment outweighed the disadvantages. This was based on two components – firstly, the wish to give the gift of a child to a couple who could not have one, and, secondly, for some of the women it enabled them to master unresolved feelings they had in relation to a previous voluntary loss of a child. A further English study in 2003 showed similar results with some women giving multiple reasons for their decision to become a surrogate mother. The most common motivation reported by 91% of the women interviewed was 'wanting to help a childless couple', 15% gave 'enjoyment of pregnancy' as a reason for opting for surrogacy, and 6% gave 'self-fulfilment' as the reason. Only one surrogate mother said that payment was a motivating factor.[35]

[7.21] Many surrogates report having chosen the surrogate role primarily because the fee provides a better economic opportunity than alternative occupations, but also because they enjoy being pregnant. Some derive a feeling of self-worth from an act they regard as highly altruistic: providing a couple with a child they could not otherwise have. 'If these motives are present, it is far from clear that the surrogate is being exploited. Indeed, it seems objectionably paternalistic to insist that she is.'[36] Similarly many surrogates report 'the tremendous psychic benefits they received from the feeling that they were helping someone meet a joyous life goal.'[37]

> Many viewed themselves as feminists who were exercising reproductive choice and demonstrating an ethic of care. It seems crass not to try to understand the arrangement from the surrogate's vantage point, in which this type of employment is viewed as a higher calling, like being a healthcare professional or educator, and may consequently be preferable to working as a check-out clerk in a grocery store or at some other minimum wage job.[38]

---

[34] Parker, 'Motivation of Surrogate Mothers: Initial Findings' (1983) 140 Am J Psychiatry 117.

[35] Jadva et al, 'Surrogacy: The Experiences of Surrogate Mothers' (2003) Human Reproduction Vol 18, No 10 pp 2196–2204.

[36] Steinbock, 'Surrogate Motherhood as Prenatal Adoption' (Law, Medicine and Ethics, 1988) 16: 1–2, p 48.

[37] Andrews, 'Beyond doctrinal boundaries: a legal framework for surrogate motherhood.' (1995) 81 Virginia Law Review 2343–75

[38] Andrews, 'Beyond doctrinal boundaries: a legal framework for surrogate motherhood.' (1995) 81 Virginia Law Review 2343–75.

[7.22] These studies show that many women, at least in developed countries, volunteer to become surrogates for reasons other than financial ones. Some women choose surrogacy not only for the fee involved but also because they enjoy being pregnant and the respect and attention that it draws.[39] Generally, the concept of remuneration is de-emphasised by both the surrogate mothers and the intended parents, which fosters the sense of the pregnancy being a 'gift' from the surrogate to the couple, and also conforms to the culturally held belief that children are priceless. However, most surrogates feel that it would be unreasonable to expect them to give birth and relinquish the child with no compensation, even if this only covers reimbursement of expenses. In a study of women taking part in surrogacy in the US, it was noted that the women rarely spent the money on themselves, but used it to buy things for their families, perhaps as a reward for the disruption to their home and family life during the pregnancy.[40] Altruism, as a motivation for surrogates, can be seen from the applications of some surrogates as including enjoyment of pregnancy, a protest against abortion, having a perfect birth and a wish to give a baby to a couple who could not have one.[41] Some women applied who had previously had an abortion or given a baby up for adoption, surrogacy allowing them to assuage the guilt they may have felt. While this may seem strange to many, for behavioural scientists it is a well-known aspect of some gift relationships. It provides a means of redressing balances that have been upset.[42]

[7.23] Surrogacy has also been a divisive issue in the feminist community, as the issues involved focus on the potential exploitation of women, the paternalism of men, the stereotypical image of women as nurturers and the capability of women to enter into contracts involving their reproductive capacity for profit.[43] On one hand, concerns have been raised about exploitation, with images depicted of poor, uneducated women enlisted to produce babies for wealthy men and their wives, either because of fertility problems or because pregnancy is simply too inconvenient for those women who can afford to hire someone to do it for them. On the other hand, it is argued that the State

---

[39] Robertson, 'Surrogate Mothers: Not So Novel After All' (1983) 13 Hastings Center Report, No 5.

[40] Ragone, *Surrogate Motherhood: Conception in the Heart* (Westview Press, 1994).

[41] In her study, Ragone noted that the majority of surrogates were either housewives and mothers or were in occupations with limited prospects. She hypothesised that a highly attractive aspect of surrogacy was the opportunity it gave them to transcend their everyday roles, and to participate in something where everybody treated them as special. This was also touched on by four of Blyth's subjects, who perceived surrogacy as doing something valuable and unusual. One woman said, 'I wanted to do something that was out of the ordinary and that made me a little bit special'. While there is no intrinsic harm in this motivation, problems may arise when the pregnancy is over, the child is relinquished and the surrogate mother is no longer receiving this special attention.

[42] For example, see Schwartz, 'The Social Psychology of the Gift' (1967) Am J Soc 1.

[43] Seven different feminist positions on surrogacy may be detected, ranging from liberalist; through acceptance with strict regulation; acceptance of traditional though not gestational surrogacy; acceptance of familial surrogacy only; acceptance of same-race surrogacy only; acceptance of contract surrogacy on certain conditions; and acceptance on the fulfilment of certain medical prerequisites by the commissioning parents. Van Dyck, *Manufacturing Babies and Public Consent* (New York University Press, 1995) at 172–3. See also Mahoney, 'An Essay on Surrogacy and Feminist Thought' (1988) 16 Law, Medicine and Health Care 81.

should not pass laws that tell women what they can and cannot do with their bodies. The traditional patriarchal allegations that 'biology is destiny' have always infuriated feminists, who claim rather that it is male domination and oppression that have cast women into the role of homemaker and mother. Some feminists argue that if surrogacy is prohibited by legislation, this will be unduly restrictive of women's reproductive choices. After all, men are free to donate or, in some countries, sell their sperm so women should also be able to donate or sell their reproductive potential. Any difference in treatment between the male and female roles might thus be argued to be discriminatory against women. However, if anti-surrogacy legislation was framed as prohibiting baby selling rather than as protecting women, and if it applied to prevent both men and women from entering into surrogacy contracts, it would be less likely to be viewed as discriminatory.[44]

[7.24] A further argument is that surrogacy contracts should not be enforced on the grounds that women who enter into these arrangements are not giving a fully informed consent. It is claimed that the surrogate does not know when she enters into the contract how she will be affected by the hormonal changes brought about by pregnancy and the bonding process which may take place with the growing foetus.[45] There is a concern that either the surrogate mother would find it very difficult to hand over the child to the commissioning couple, or that she may distance herself from the pregnancy by reinforcing the belief that the child is not hers, thus making her more likely to put her health and that of the child at risk. The risk of post-natal depression and feelings of anger or guilt may all put a further strain on her psychological health. There may also be a negative impact on her partner and children, with the potential for ostracisation in the community. However, it is argued that these are matters which may form part of the detailed prior discussions and counselling that should take place with the surrogate to ensure she is fully informed and prepared for such possibilities and do not provide sufficient justification for banning or even condemning surrogacy.[46]

[7.25] As some of the most contested ethical issues in surrogacy relate to the welfare and motivation of surrogate mothers, it is important to look at the research that has been carried out in this regard. A study of surrogate mothers in the UK in 2003 found that surrogate mothers do not generally experience major problems in their relationship with the commissioning couple, in handing over the baby or from the reactions of those around them. The emotional problems experienced by some surrogate mothers in the weeks following the birth appeared to lessen over time. The study also showed that surrogate mothers were generally open with family and friends about the arrangement and while some received initial negative reactions, these people later accepted the idea and the majority of surrogate mothers reported that their partners and children were positive and supportive:

---

[44] Mahoney, 'An Essay on Surrogacy and Feminist Thought' (1988) 16 Law, Medicine and Health Care at 82.

[45] Hassenthaler, 'Gestational Surrogacy: Legal Implications of Reproductive Technology' (1995) 21 North Carolina Central Law Journal 169 at 177.

[46] Wilkinson, *Bodies for Sale: Ethics and Exploitation in the Human Body* (Routledge: London, 2003) 171–173.

Overall, surrogacy appears to be a positive experience for surrogate mothers. Women who decide to embark upon surrogacy often have completed a family of their own and feel they wish to help a couple who would not otherwise be able to become parents. The present study lends little support to the commonly held expectation that surrogate mothers will experience psychological problems following the birth of the child.[47]

[7.26] More recent studies also show that the psychological well-being of surrogate mothers did not change ten years following the birth with all remaining positive about the surrogacy arrangement and the majority continuing to report good mental health.[48] None expressed regret about being a surrogate. In three-quarters of surrogacy arrangements the surrogate mothers had stayed in touch with the children they had carried, and almost half of the surrogate's own children were in contact with the surrogacy child. The findings from the few studies of surrogacy that currently exist indicate that families formed in this way are generally functioning well with harmonious relationships between the surrogate mothers' families and the families these surrogates have helped to create.[49] The issues arising in the context of foreign surrogacy arrangements are considered later.

Welfare of the child

[7.27] Irrespective of whether the surrogacy arrangement is altruistic or commercial, it is often argued that surrogacy is potentially harmful to the child due to the psychological problems it may suffer as a result of the method of its conception. Particularly in cases of commercial surrogacy, concern is expressed that the child may feel like a commodity, may struggle not to disappoint its parents who went to great lengths to have a child, and may be emotionally challenged by the fact of being given up by its birth mother. Radin claims that if a baby industry were to come into being we could not avoid measuring, even subconsciously, the monetary value of children. She asks 'how could our children avoid being preoccupied with measuring their own dollar value? This makes our discourse about ourselves (when we are children) and about our children (when we are parents) like our discourse about cars.'[50]

[7.28] However, others dispute this point on grounds that it is fallacious to suggest that surrogacy is degrading to the child because the child will have been bought for money. For example Freeman characterises the payment of money in surrogacy as payment for services and as compensation for the burden of pregnancy. He says 'the child may have a right not to be sold, but that is a distortion of what is happening, even in cases of commercial surrogacy.'[51] In addition, it is argued that although feelings of worthlessness

---

[47] Jadva et al, 'Surrogacy: The Experiences of Surrogate Mothers' (2003) Human Reproduction Vol 18, No 10 pp 2196–2204.

[48] Jadva, Imrie, Golombok, (2014) Surrogate mothers 10 years on: a longitudinal study of psychological well-being and relationships with the parents and child Hum. Reprod. 30 (2): 373–379.

[49] Golombok, *Modern Families, Parents and Children in new family forms* (Cambridge University Press, 2015) at 136–137.

[50] Radin, 'Market Inalienability' (1987) 100 Harvard Law Review 1849–1937.

[51] Freeman, 'Is surrogacy exploitative? in McLean (ed) *Legal Issues in Human Reproduction* (Gower: London, 1989) 164–184.

are harmful and can prevent people from living happy, fulfilling lives, a surrogate child, even one whose life is miserable because of those feelings, cannot claim to have been harmed by the surrogate agreement:

> Without the agreement, the child would not have existed. Unless she is willing to say that her life is not worth living because of these feelings, that she would be better off never having been born, she cannot claim to have been harmed by being born of a surrogate mother.[52]

[7.29] Although there have been only a small number of reliable studies carried out in relation to the impact of surrogacy on children, the evidence thus far suggests that any fears are unfounded. The only longitudinal study on surrogacy in the world has shown that surrogacy does not appear to impact negatively on parenting or child development.[53] This is consistent with previous studies of assisted reproduction families that showed greater warmth and emotional involvement between parents and children than in natural conception families. The authors say this may be explained by the view that these couples who have gone to great lengths to have a child are thus more likely to be highly motivated and committed parents. The children themselves did not differ from naturally conceived children with respect to socio-emotional or cognitive development. The study also examined the issue of whether it makes a difference if the surrogate mother is also the genetic mother of the child. 'It appears not, as no differences were found in the quality of the surrogacy parents' parenting according to whether or not the surrogate was the genetic mother of the child.'[54] It appears therefore from this research that a gestational or genetic bond with the child is of less importance for the child than a strong desire for parenthood by the child's parents.

[7.30] In recent follow-up studies when the children in this study were older, researchers found that most children who are aware of their surrogacy conception are able to show some understanding of surrogacy by age 7 years and most children were positive about their surrogacy birth at age 10 years.[55] During early adolescence around age 14, the research shows positive mother-child relationships and high levels of psychological adjustment by children. The findings from these studies also show that the majority of families kept in contact with their surrogate mother and maintained a good relationship with her over the course of the first ten years of the child's life, thus allaying commonly voiced concerns that this relationship would present difficulties as the child grows up. It is important to note however that the children in the study were all born using non-commercial surrogacy as commercial surrogacy is prohibited in the UK, and the study did not involve international surrogacy arrangements. Further research is required in

---

[52] Steinbock, 'Surrogate Motherhood as Prenatal Adoption' (Law, Medicine and Ethics, 1988) 16: 1–2, p 49.

[53] Golombok et al, 'Surrogacy Families: Parental Functioning, Parent-Child Relationships and Children's Psychological Development at Age 2' (2006) Journal of Child Psychology and Psychiatry 47:2 pp 213–222 at 213.

[54] Golombok, *Modern Families, parents and children in new family forms* (Cambridge University Press 2015) at 126

[55] Jadva et al, 'Surrogacy families 10 years on: relationship with the surrogate, decisions over disclosure and children's understanding of their surrogacy origins' Hum Reprod (2012) 27 (10): 3008–3014.

relation to these types of surrogacy, as well as further follow-up studies on children during older adolescence when identity issues become of prime concern.

[7.31] Concerns have also been raised about the effect of surrogacy on the surrogate mother's own children if she has any. Those children will of course be aware of the pregnancy and the relinquishment of the child and therefore may potentially be emotionally affected by the situation. However, in the first study to investigate the experiences of surrogacy and the psychological well-being of surrogates' children from the perspective of the children themselves, Jadva and Imrie show that overall the children of surrogate mothers do not experience negative psychological health or family functioning, irrespective of whether or not the surrogate uses her own egg. Most (86%) children of surrogates held a positive view of their mother's involvement in surrogacy with many expressing pride in what their mother had done for another family, and the remaining 14% reporting a neutral/ambivalent view.[56]

LEGAL ISSUES IN SURROGACY

[7.32] Surrogacy has received a mixed response around the world, with some states refusing to enforce it on grounds of public policy, others dealing with it solely as a custody dispute between the birth mother and biological father, and others enforcing it on contractual grounds. Where surrogacy has been the subject of legislation setting out rules for determining parentage, it is common to require a court declaration of parentage either before, during or after the birth of the child rather than simply assign parentage by way of an administrative procedure. These court proceedings are usually uncontested applications which confirm compliance with statutory provisions and conditions. Contested cases that have come to judicial attention have largely been in the context of custody disputes between the intended parents and the surrogate mother, although these are few in number.

The surrogacy contract

[7.33] One of the central issues in dealing with surrogacy from a policy perspective is whether it should be regarded and treated simply as a contractual agreement, or a family law issue. 'The central policy issue is settling on the paradigm that should govern surrogate motherhood, a model of family relations (adoption) or of contractual relations (sale of a product or service). And the central legal issue is whether any restrictions on personal choice that follow from the policy selected – and especially from a rejection of the contractual model with its implication of free choice – are constitutionally permissible.'[57] Although surrogacy may be largely considered as a family law matter, it has its legal roots in the bargain made between the surrogate and the commissioning couple. 'A surrogate mother provides a strange blend of intimate services and products. She permits a doctor to artificially inseminate her, carries a child to term, and in nine months delivers a new born child to whoever hired her. She sells her ovum, her ability to

---

[56] Jadva and Imrie, 'Children of surrogate mothers: psychological well-being, family relationships and experiences of surrogacy', Hum Reprod (2014) 29 (1): 90–96.

[57] Capron and Radin, 'Choosing Family Law Over Contract Law as a Paradigm for Surrogate Motherhood' (1988) Law Medicine & Health Care Vol 16:1–2 at 37.

nurture a single cell into an infant and all her future claims to rear the child she bears.'[58] In the small number of cases where the surrogate mother changes her mind and refuses to relinquish the baby, a number of legal issues arise for determination such as whether the contract between the parties is enforceable, whether the contract is void on public policy grounds, whether the surrogate mother has a stronger claim to custody of the child even if she is not the genetic mother, and where the best interests of the child are best protected.

[7.34] One of the first cases to come to judicial attention in the United States was the *Baby M* case.[59] In this well-known case, Mary Beth Whitehead, a married mother of two children, agreed to be inseminated with the sperm of William Stern and to carry a child for Mr and Mrs Stern for a fee of $10,000. Mr Stern was a biochemist and his wife, Elizabeth, was a paediatrician who had multiple sclerosis which, although it did not render her infertile, would have been exacerbated by pregnancy. When the baby was born, Mrs Whitehead handed her over to the Sterns as promised but, a few days later, changed her mind and asked the Sterns to let her have custody of the child for a short while. The Sterns reluctantly agreed to this course of action. Mrs Whitehead, however, subsequently refused to give the child back to the Sterns and fled the jurisdiction. After a period of some months the police seized the child and returned her to the Sterns, whereupon a lengthy custody battle ensued.

[7.35] At the initial hearing, Sorkow J held that the surrogacy contract was valid and that specific performance of it was in the best interests of the child. He said the contract was not baby selling: 'The money to be paid to the surrogate is not being paid for the surrender of the child to the father ... he cannot purchase what is already his.' He felt the contract was merely a contract for services. Immediately following his decision he also enabled Mrs Stern to legally adopt the baby. The decision was appealed to the New Jersey Supreme Court, which reversed Sorkow J's decision in relation to the validity of the contract. The Court held that a surrogacy contract, which provides for payment to the surrogate and for her irrevocable consent to the surrender of her child at birth, is invalid and unenforceable.[60] As a result, the adoption order granted by Judge Sorkow was

---

58 'Rumpeltstiltskin Revisited: The Inalienable Rights of Surrogate Mothers' 99 Harvard Law Review 1936.

59 *In re Baby M*, 525 A, 2d 1128, 217 NJ Super 313 (Superior Ct Chancery Div 1987), reversed on appeal, 1988 West Law 6251 (NJ Supreme Ct, 3 February 1988).

60 It has been argued that the application of existing legal precepts to this novel situation was misguided, as the courts are not equipped to deal with matters of social policy. Bezanson argues thus: 'The surrogacy dispute in *Baby M* provided the court with an issue as to which there is no law. Existing statutory provisions and common law doctrines are relevant to the surrogacy question only as they are grounded on assumptions about parentage, family, and the reproductive process. But these assumptions are simply irrelevant to the dilemmas posed by surrogacy arrangements, and by many other reproductive technology issues as well. There was no right or wrong answer in the *Baby M* case, but there is a lesson to be learned. Courts are not equipped to create fundamental social policy. Our society's basic moral and ethical values must be shaped and expressed through the pluralistic legislative process, not in court. The *Baby M* court should have decided only the question of *Baby M*'s custody, based on its determination of the child's best interests.' Bezanson, 'Solomon Would Weep: A Comment on *In the Matter of Baby M* and the Limits of Judicial Authority' (1988)16:1–2 Law, Medicine and Health Care 126–130, at 126.

improperly granted and Mrs Whitehead was the child's legal mother.[61] However, it was further decided that the sole determining factor in a custody dispute was the child's best interests, and in the instant case this meant that the child should remain in the custody of the Sterns. It was also provided that the surrogate mother should have visitation rights in respect of the child. The result reached in this case – that Mr Stern was the child's legal father and Mrs Whitehead was her legal mother, was described by some as 'the worst result possible'.[62]

[7.36] The sensationalist facts of this case led to the kind of media attention and public outrage that one has come to expect from a custody battle of this nature.[63] The public were caught up in the intricacies of Mrs Whitehead's relationship with her husband and children, the financial details of both couples, the suitability of both women as mothers, and the psychological well-being of all of the parties. The case also raised comments about the needs of children, such as whether the courts should focus on financial and educational benefits or emotional bonds. It conjured up fears that surrogacy would be used for the convenience of wealthy professional couples who could exploit an impoverished woman in order to avoid the inconvenience of being pregnant. Many commentators criticised the assessment made of Mrs Whitehead's ability to be a good mother as being based on middle-class prejudices and the evidence of mental health officials who testified at the hearing. The Court did not find her to be an unfit mother to her other children as 'she was portrayed as immature, untruthful, hysterical, overly identified with her children, and prone to smothering their independence.'[64] As the New

---

61 When Baby M (Melissa Stern) turned 18 years of age she initiated the process of allowing Elizabeth Stern to adopt her, terminating Whitehead's parental rights.

62 Bezanson, 'Solomon Would Weep: A Comment on *In the Matter of Baby M* and the Limits of Judicial Authority' (1988)16:1–2 Law, Medicine and Health Care 126–130, at 126.

63 There was a flood of academic writing on the case at the time. See, for example: Brandel, 'Legislating Surrogacy: A Partial Answer to Feminist Criticism' (1995) 54 Maryland Law Review 488; Steinbock, 'Surrogate Motherhood as Prenatal Adoption' in Gostin (ed) *Surrogate Motherhood: Politics and Privacy* (Indiana University Press, 1990) 123–28. Carney, 'Where Do the Children Go? – Surrogate Mother Contracts and the Best Interests of the Child' (1988) XXII Suffolk Univ Law Review 1187; Dolgin, 'Status and Contract in Surrogate Motherhood: An Illumination of the Surrogacy Debate' (1990) 90 Daily Journal Report 2; Hey, 'Assisted Conception and Surrogacy – Unfinished Business' (1993) 26 The John Marshall Law Review 775; Klinke, 'The *Baby M* Controversy: A Class Distinction' (1993) 18 Oklahoma City Univ. Law Review 113; Johnson, 'The *Baby M* Decision: Specific Performance of a Contract for Specially Manufactured Goods' (1987) 11 Southern Illinois Univ LJ 1339; Recht, "M' is for Money: *Baby M* and the surrogate motherhood controversy'(1988) 37 The American Univ. Law Review 1013.

64 Steinbock, 'Surrogate Motherhood as Prenatal Adoption' (Law, Medicine and Ethics, 1988) 16: 44 at 46. Steinbock says that it is clear that Mrs Whitehead should not have been accepted as a suitable surrogate mother in the first place and that her uncertainty about giving up the child during the pregnancy should have alerted others to the potential problems which lay ahead. Also, it is unusual for the surrogate to be given the baby; rather, the adoptive parents are involved in the birthing process and are handed the child at birth, which serves to promote their bonding and lessen the surrogate mother's pain at the separation.

Jersey Supreme Court concluded, the application of the best-interests test boils down to a judgment call regarding the "likely future happiness of a human being."[65]

[7.37] There have been many criticisms of this case such as the belief that if Mrs Whitehead had not fled the jurisdiction, which led Sorkow J to order the return of the baby to the Sterns, and which also influenced the subsequent decision that the child had been so long in the custody of the Sterns that it would be detrimental to the child to reverse that order, the decision may have been different. Nevertheless on the actual facts of the case, there is general consensus that the issue of custody appears to have been correctly decided. The instability of the Whitehead's marriage, concerns for the child and the period of time spent in the care of the Sterns, all combine to suggest that the child's best interests were correctly served by granting custody to the only parents she had known in her life at that stage. Commentators also criticised the granting of visitation rights to Mrs Whitehead on the grounds that this was not likely to be in Baby M's best interests and would serve to undermine the Stern's parental authority.

[7.38] On what grounds could a court decline to enforce a surrogacy contract? Contracts may generally be invalidated through the operation of the doctrines of mistake, misrepresentation, duress and undue influence, incapacity and illegality. In surrogacy the terms of the contract are not generally unduly complex or difficult to understand. The parties agree that the surrogate mother would be inseminated or have an embryo transferred to her uterus, would carry the child to term, and upon its birth would relinquish custody to the commissioning couple (usually) in exchange for a sum of money agreed between them. This does not leave very much scope for mistake or misrepresentation between the parties, unless on some minor matter. More important in this context then are arguments that, due to an inequality of bargaining power between the surrogate mother and the commissioning couple, the validity of the contract must be in doubt.

[7.39] In the debate over surrogate motherhood, different perspectives about the nature of human choice tend to become entangled with moral judgments about the mother's decision to surrender custody of her child. Those who view the mother's decision to surrender custody as unnatural or reprehensible explain her decision in terms of financial pressures 'overcoming' her free will. Those who emphasise the benefit to infertile couples from surrogacy arrangements are more likely to view the mother's choice as a rational decision in which the financial payment makes more attractive an option which could be justified on non-monetary grounds.[66] Whether contract principles

---

[65] *In re Baby M* 217 NJ Super, 313, 525 A 2d 1128 (NJ Super Ct Ch Div 1987) at 2024. See also Goldstein, Freud and Solnit, *Beyond the Best Interests of the Child* (New York, Free Press, 1973).

[66] Carbone, 'The Role of Contract Principles in Determining the Validity of Surrogacy Contracts' (1988) 28 Santa Clara Law Review 581 at 600. Carbone examines the validity of using contract principles in domestic arrangements and why they have not been so used traditionally. She analyses the different characteristics present in commercial and domestic arrangements, such as the difference in equality between the parties, the implications for those outside the contract and the willingness of the judiciary to interfere in any dispute which may arise. She finds that contract has not been seen as the governing principle in family relationships due to these differences where status is seen as more important in determining rights and obligations. (contd.../)

can offer any solutions to reconcile these opposite viewpoints is very much open to question.[67]

[7.40] Although there is a traditional reluctance to involve the law in domestic matters, the role of contract in governing family relationships is growing. 'Family matters, and, indeed, intimate relationships generally, are no longer a separate world into which contract and the courts dare not tread.'[68] In relation to solving custody disputes in surrogacy, apart from a symbolic affront to traditional values in ensuring mothers' commitment to their children, it is difficult to identify a societal interest that is in fact injured by surrogacy arrangements.[69] The pregnancy is not accidental, indeed the parents conceive the child with far more advance thought, care and commitment than attends the conception of most children. The mother is not abandoning the child, she is simply agreeing that the child's father, who can be screened for fitness, will have custody.[70]

[7.41] It is often argued that a woman ought to be able to change her mind about relinquishment of the baby as she is not capable of knowing in advance whether she will be able to relinquish custody of the child she has carried and therefore her consent was not truly informed. In an ordinary pregnancy many factors, biological, emotional and social, may combine to reinforce a woman's bond with the unborn child. Do these factors suggest that no woman can give a truly informed consent to an agreement to surrender custody of a child until after she has experienced the birth of that child? Or does it mean that a decision made at a time prior to conception would be more likely to be more dispassionate and more presumptively valid?[71] Conclusions about the utility

---

[66] (\...contd) However, she also examines the increasing willingness to incorporate contract principles into family law on a case-by-case basis to overcome specific problems. Public policy is also of relevance here in the reinforcement of traditional morality and societal norms and presumptions. In *Re Baby M*, the Court phrased much of its discussion, according to Carbone, on contract principles but interprets and applies those principles using a moral bias derived from normative standards. In the absence of legislative intervention, she concludes that the uncertainty inherent in such compromises is more dangerous to the children, the couples and society than the agreements themselves could ever be.

[67] Freeman says that the law of contract is 'a blunt instrument which cannot adequately tackle the problems spawned by the issue of surrogacy.' He demonstrates this by examining the question of remedies. The enforcement of a surrogacy arrangement by specific performance of the contract, he says, would 'smack of a form of slavery' and would not be contemplated by any court. Freeman, 'Children's Rights in Surrogacy' 16 Childright 8. Similarly, Singer and Wells, 'The Reproduction Revolution: New Ways of Making Babies' (OUP, 1984) at 122 say: '[t]he compulsion involved would be of a uniquely odious form. The contract is not like an ordinary contract for services, since its fulfilment involves a physical invasion of the contractor's body. The surrogate could not, like any other contractor, walk out of the work-place. She is the work-place.'

[68] Carbone, 'The Role of Contract Principles in Determining the Validity of Surrogacy Contracts' (1988) Vol 28 Santa Clara Law Rev 581 at 589.

[69] Carbone, 'The Role of Contract Principles in Determining the Validity of Surrogacy Contracts' (1988) Vol 28 Santa Clara Law Rev 581 at 594.

[70] Carbone, 'The Role of Contract Principles in Determining the Validity of Surrogacy Contracts' (1988) Vol 28 Santa Clara Law Rev 581 at 594.

[71] Carbone, 'The Role of Contract Principles in Determining the Validity of Surrogacy Contracts' (1988) Vol 28 Santa Clara Law Rev 581 at 597.

and morality of surrogacy will colour discussion of these questions, as those who object to surrogacy are more likely to argue that women who enter into such contracts underestimate the bonding process, and thus any subsequent change of mind on the surrogate mother's part is both valid and correct. Proponents of surrogacy will argue that changes of mind are precisely the type of changes the contract is designed to guard against and that the appropriate response is counselling, independent legal advice and emotional support for the surrogate mother prior to making the commitment, and at the time of relinquishment of the child.

[7.42] Some commentators argue that there should be a change of heart period in order to challenge the notion that contracts are more important than people and must be honoured no matter what.[72] 'A deal is not always a deal – at least not when one is trading in some of the deepest emotions human beings can ever feel. Any approach that *binds* women to reproductive decisions – as does the contract approach – must be regarded with deep suspicion.' On this basis it is argued that it would be unwise to allow specific enforcement of surrogacy contracts as 'wanting to keep one's children, even where one has previously agreed otherwise is not pathological or wrong, but rather understandable and defensible.'[73]

[7.43] It is counter-argued however that if the surrogate mother changes her mind, the loss to the intending parents should not be ignored. 'A reproductive agreement creates expectations regarding the opportunity to parent a child; those expectations have vital importance to those who hold them.'[74] It is argued that it would be unfair to disregard these expectations which are 'intense and significant'. If surrogates but not others are entitled to change their minds, this reinforces the stereotype of women as unstable, unable to make decisions and stick to them, and as vulnerable because of hormonal and emotional influences. 'In particular, it exalts a woman's experience of pregnancy and childbirth over her formation of emotional, intellectual and interpersonal decisions and expectations, as well as over others' reliance on the commitments she has earlier made.'[75]

[7.44] It has also been suggested that the failure to enforce surrogacy contracts may persuade women to become surrogates even if they are not completely sure that they will be able to give up the baby, as they know the law will not force them to do so.[76] Allowing the surrogate to keep the child and the payment under the agreement might thus provide an opportunity for extortion as the intending parents might be open to threats from the surrogate mother that she will keep the baby or abort unless they pay her more money.[77]

---

[72] Tong, 'Feminist perspectives and gestational motherhood: the search for a unified legal focus', in Callahan (ed) *Reproduction, Ethics and the Law: Feminist Responses* (Indiana University Press: Bloomington) 1995, 55–79.

[73] Bartlett, 'Re-expressing parenthood.' (1998) 98 Yale Law Journal 293, 333.

[74] Shultz, 'Reproductive technology and Intention-based parenthood: an opportunity for gender neutrality' (1990) Wisconsin Law Review 297–398.

[75] Shultz, 'Reproductive technology and Intention-based parenthood: an opportunity for gender neutrality' (1990) Wisconsin Law Review 297–398.

[76] Jackson, *Medical Law, Text, Cases and Materials,* (3rd edn, 2013 OUP) 868.

[77] In Greece, a surrogate mother who refuses to relinquish the child under a court-approved surrogacy arrangement, may be forced to do so as the intending mother is presumed to be the legal mother of the child (art 946 Code of Criminal Procedure). (contd.../)

By comparison, in Israel a rigorous approval process precedes any surrogacy arrangement lessens the chance that there will be a change of mind.[78] The physician involved must declare that he has explained to the surrogate the consequences of her agreement. An approvals Committee must then be satisfied that the surrogate mother has received independent legal advice from a suitably qualified lawyer and the Committee will interview the surrogate mother to ascertain whether her consent is voluntary and informed. Although the law does allow for a change of mind by the surrogate mother, this is very limited in that she would have to convince the court of a change in circumstances that justifies her change of mind, and a welfare officer would have to agree that this is in the child's best interests.[79] There does not appear to have been any cases where the surrogate mother has changed her mind. Schulz suggests that:

> One reason for this may be the screening by the Approvals Committee. While, of course, we cannot be sure that there would have been problems if arrangements had gone ahead which the birth mother rejected as unsuitable, it seems likely that the Approvals Committee is in a better position than the intended parents to judge the suitability of the birth mother both because of the professional skills and experience of the Approvals Committee members and because they are more likely to be objective. Childless couples, with limited options open to them, perhaps need protecting against possible rashness and lack of judgement in choosing a birth mother.[80]

Adoption

[7.45] Rather than use a contract law model it has been suggested that surrogacy should be dealt with by way of adoption since existing law is inadequate to deal with surrogacy and the emergence of surrogacy as a social practice does not require major law reform. Families in modern society have many different forms and, although certain core values are recognised by states as matters of legitimate concern for the state, nonetheless there is increasing latitude given to private ordering of families without State interference. The core values that are of relevance to surrogacy would include the protection of children's welfare and interests and the prevention of human exploitation. In light of concern for those values, states have introduced laws about parentage and adoption which aim to provide certainty and protection for children:

> These legal rules serve children's interest in having clearly identified people recognised from the moment of birth as their legal parents, with all the obligations and expectations consequent to this role. If the status of adult parties in relation to a newborn child is dependent on any contracts or other agreements they may have reached, then this status – and the rights and responsibilities that flow from it – may be thrown into doubt when

---

[77] (\...contd) The surrogacy contract is deemed to be valid and enforceable so if the surrogate absconds with the child, she may be criminally prosecuted for child abduction (art 324 Greek Criminal Code).

[78] Schulz, 'Surrogacy in Israel: an analysis of the law in practice' in Cook, Sclater and Kaganas (eds) *Surrogate Motherhood: International Perspectives* (Hart, 2003) 35–53

[79] Horsey and Neofytou, 'The fertility treatment time forgot: what should be done about surrogacy in the UK?' in Horsey, *Revisiting the Regulation of Human Fertilisation and Embryology* (Routledge) 2015, 130.

[80] Schulz, 'Surrogacy in Israel: An analysis of the law in practice' in Cook, Sclater, Kaganas (eds) *Surrogate Motherhood: International Perspectives* (Hart, Oxford 2003) 35–53.

contractual terms are unclear or when the contract is disavowed due to alleged breaches or other disagreements.[81]

[7.46] In many jurisdictions, agreements to relinquish parental rights are not permitted prior to the child's birth. Adoption statutes typically provide for a period of time after relinquishment of the baby during which the birth mother may change her mind. Such provisions aim to balance several interests. On the one hand, the child needs unqualified acceptance and stability in its surroundings. This need is fostered by ensuring the people who are serving as caregivers are appropriate for that role and are confident that they will be able to keep the child. On the other hand, permitting the birth mother to change her mind reinforces a societal respect for biological ties and recognises that circumstances might force a woman to make a decision immediately after birth of a child that does not reflect her true wishes.[82]

[7.47] It may be argued that the law should not differentiate between women who become pregnant pursuant to surrogacy contracts from those who become pregnant by other means. Thus, the normal rules of adoption would apply to the transfer of parental status to the intended who will raise the child as their own. Any element of uncertainty created by restricting specific performance and allowing the surrogate to change her mind would simply serve to underline the need for caution by all parties involved. A key advantage of bringing surrogacy within the ambit of existing adoption law is that it would involve the State in the process through assessment of the prospective parents by social workers as well as oversight by the court procedure which is necessary to approve the adoption. This would mean that the child's best interests were protected by the rigorous screening procedures that exist prior to a couple being deemed suitable adopters. However, this may prove to be contentious in a case where the prospective adopters were deemed unsuitable, for example on age grounds or other criteria. In a case of gestational surrogacy where the prospective adopters are the genetic parents of the child, would commitment to the principle that the child's best interests are paramount result in a refusal to allow the child to be adopted by its genetic parents? This would mean that the care of the child would remain with the surrogate mother if she was willing to take on that responsibility, or the child being adopted by an unrelated couple if she was not willing to do so.

Custody disputes

[7.48] Although very rare, an obvious conflict that could potentially arise in a surrogate agreement involves both the surrogate and the couple seeking custody of the child.[83] In most jurisdictions the paramount consideration in such instances is that of the best

---

[81] Capron and Radin, 'Choosing Family Law Over Contract Law as a Paradigm for Surrogate Motherhood' (1988) Law Medicine & Health Care Vol 16:1–2 at 35.

[82] Capron and Radin, 'Choosing Family Law Over Contract Law as a Paradigm for Surrogate Motherhood' (1988) Law Medicine & Health Care Vol 16:1–2

[83] The numbers of cases in which this occurs is actually very small. In the US it is estimated at about 1 per cent – See Schuck, 'Some Reflections on the *Baby M* Case' (1988) 76 Geo LJ 1793 at 1801 fn 30, and in the UK about 4–5 per cent – see Surrogacy: Review for Health Ministers of Current Arrangements for Payments and Regulation (Cm 4068) (Department of Health, 1998) at para 3.38.

interests of the child. The requirement that the child's best interests should inform decisions made about the child is a well-established legal principle. The principle has been used to guide decision-making in family law for decades and it is contained in family law statutes in many jurisdictions around the world. Best interests are determined on a case-by-case basis with an examination of the needs of the child and the ability of the parties to provide for those needs from a financial, psychological and emotional perspective. As a result the best interests test has been criticised as vague and subjective.[84] In his seminal work on best interests in 1975, Mnookin says:

> Deciding what is best for a child poses a question no less ultimate than the purposes and values of life itself. Should the judge be primarily concerned with the child's happiness? Or with the child's spiritual and religious training? Should the judge be concerned with the economic 'productivity' of the child when he grows up? Are the primary values of life in warm, interpersonal relationships, or in discipline and self-sacrifice? Is stability and security for a child more desirable than intellectual stimulation? Those questions could be elaborated endlessly. And yet, where is the judge to look for the set of values that should inform the choice of what is best for the child?[85]

[7.49] Best-interest determinations may thus remain dependent on the values and choices of particular judges, thereby ensuring wide differences in the character of decisions made in custody cases. A well-intentioned judge, anxious to discern a child's best interests in a custody case must consider 'the lives and personal characteristics of potential custodians. That task encourages courts to compare these adults. In making such a comparison, it is easy to weight the balance in favour of one potential custodian by focusing on negative behaviours associated with another.'[86]

[7.50] In surrogacy cases, unless a different approach is mandated by legislation, the judiciary has tended to adopt the same approach to the determination of custody disputes as in other cases. This can be seen in the classic US case *In Re Baby M* in which the New Jersey Supreme Court held that the sole determining factor in a custody dispute was the child's best interests. Reliance on the best interests of the child standard in these cases may yield the result that the child is adopted by the commissioning couple, who perhaps can afford to care for and educate the child to a higher standard than the surrogate mother. However, the welfare of the child depends not only on financial well-being but also, more importantly, on psychological security. In this sense, each party may be equally well placed to provide the care and nurturing necessary to rear a child. The court would no doubt be influenced by whether the surrogate mother had 'bonded' with the child or had relinquished custody at birth, although courts have in recent years accepted that ties of attachment have less to do with biological links and more to do with the psychological attachment that takes place after the child has reached the age of six months.

---

[84] For discussion of best interests see Goldstein, Freud & Solnit, *Beyond the Best Interests of the Child* (1973), *Before the Best Interests of the Child* (1979), and *In the Best Interests of the Child* (with Goldstein, 1986); See critique by Mnookin, 'Child-Custody Adjudication: Judicial Functions in the Face of Indeterminacy' (1975) 39 *Law & Contemporary Problems* 226.

[85] Mnookin, 'Child-Custody Adjudication: Judicial Functions in the Face of Indeterminacy' (1975) 39 *Law & Contemporary Problems* 226.

[86] Dolgin, *Why Has the Best Interest Standard Survived?: The Historic and Social Context*, 16 Child Legal Rts J 2 (1996).

[7.51] A different approach, which has been taken in some jurisdictions, focuses on the intention of the parties when they deliberately chose to bring the child into existence. Thus, the contractual intent is enforced through recognition of legal parentage in the commissioning couple.[87] This can be seen in *Johnson v Calvert*,[88] in which the Supreme Court of California ruled that in a case of gestational surrogacy, the legal mother of the child is the genetic mother. The facts of this case involved a couple who agreed with a surrogate mother to pay her $10,000 in return for the surrogate bringing to term a child created from the gametes of the couple. During the course of the pregnancy the relationship between the couple and the surrogate mother deteriorated, and each party applied to court for a declaration of parentage. In relation to the contractual issue, the Court held there was no question of coercion or duress involved and it was unconvinced that such contracts generally would exploit or dehumanise women of lower economic status.[89] It also dismissed any claim that by enforcing surrogacy contracts, the Court was recognising that children could be treated as mere commodities.[90]

[7.52] The Court held that in theory each woman had a claim to be declared the legal mother of the child under existing Californian law: the surrogate by reason of having given birth to the child, and the commissioning mother on the basis of blood tests which showed her to be the genetic mother. An argument was put to the court by *amicus curiae* that in this situation the child should be recognised as having two legal mothers, but the Court rejected this approach.[91] The Court preferred the claim of the genetic mother to be regarded as the legal mother, not, however, simply on the basis of the genetic link, but

---

[87] This effectively allows the birth certificate of the child to record the commissioning couple as the legal parents. This may raise conflict of laws issues if the arrangement is entered into by non-US nationals who subsequently bring the child back to their own jurisdiction.

[88] *Johnson v Calvert* 851 P 2d 776 (Cal 1993).

[89] The Court said that 'there has been no proof that surrogacy contracts exploit poor women to any greater degree than economic necessity in general exploits them by inducing them to accept lower-paid or otherwise undesirable employment'. *Johnson v Calvert* 851 P 2d 776 (Cal 1993) at 785.

[90] The case has been criticised on many fronts. It has been argued that the facts of this case show how exploitative surrogacy can be in relation particularly to class and race distinctions, as the surrogate in this case was black, of African-American ancestry, had one child of her own and was on welfare. It may be argued that African-American and Hispanic women, who have fewer economic choices than Caucasian women, will be hired as gestators because they will accept lesser fees than Caucasian women. Russell-Brown describes the decision as 'a modern version of reproductive slavery.' Russell-Brown, 'Parental Rights and Gestational Surrogacy: An Argument Against the Genetic Standard' (1992) 23 Colum Hum Rts L Rev 525.

[91] For further discussion of the possibility of 'child sharing' between two mothers in surrogacy, see Wallbank, 'Too many mothers? Surrogacy, kinship and the welfare of the child.' Med L Rev 10 (2002) 271–294. Wallbank suggests that perhaps the law should adopt a model that recognises that all the parties involved have an interest in the child's welfare and cases should not be decided on an either/or basis. Rather than preferring one mother over the other, she suggests that child sharing should become the norm. See also judgment of Clarke J in *MR and DR (suing by their father and next friend OR) and CR and An t-Ard -Chlaratheoir, Ireland and the Attorney General & another* [2014] IESC 60 discussed at para **[7.114]** below.

rather on the basis of the parties' intention when the surrogacy arrangement began. Panelli J, giving the majority judgment, said:

> The parties' aim was to bring Mark's and Crispina's [the commissioning couple] child into the world, not for them to donate a zygote to Anna [the surrogate]...Although the gestative function Anna performed was necessary to bring about the child's birth, it is safe to say that Anna would not have been given the opportunity to gestate or deliver the child had she, prior to implantation of the zygote, manifested her own intent to be the child's mother... she who intended to procreate the child – that is, she who intended to bring about the birth of a child that she intended to raise as her own – is the natural mother under California law.[92]

[7.53] The Court in this case concentrated on what has been described as the intent or 'intellectual conception' of the child, and the 'but for' test in deciding the issue of parentage.[93] In other words, without the intention of the commissioning couple, this child would never have come into existence. The reliance on intention in family law matters is a relatively new trend, although it does have a weak precedent in relation to adoption and guardianship applications whereby an adult forms the intention to become a social parent and acts on that intention in order to legalise his/her relationship with the child. The law is perhaps becoming more cognisant of the idea of social or psychological parenting, which de-emphasises genetic or gestational parenting and concentrates on the rearing of the child. Such a position would appear consistent with the research findings discussed earlier in relation to the psychological outcome for children born as a result of surrogacy arrangements.[94]

[7.54] Reliance on intent may also be seen in a case which came before the California Supreme Court in 1998, *In Re Marriage of Buzzanca*.[95] The convoluted circumstances of this case are interesting, as they show just how complicated assisted reproduction may become. A married woman (Mrs X, who remained anonymous) decided to become an egg donor, on condition that she and her husband would have the opportunity to approve who was to get her eggs. One particular couple (Mr and Mrs Davidson) were approved for the donation. Seventeen eggs were harvested from Mrs X and fertilised with Mr

---

[92] Russell-Brown, 'Parental Rights and Gestational Surrogacy: An Argument Against the Genetic Standard' (1992) 23 Colum Hum Rts L Rev 525.

[93] Douglas, 'The Intention to Be a Parent and the Making of Mothers' (1994) 57 Modern Law Review 636. Douglas examines the focus in the *Johnson* case on intention and the consequences this may have for our attitudes to parenthood and family life generally. Due to men's physical incapacity to produce a child, is the reliance on intention to reproduce a convenient way to reinforce the male experience of reproduction and a concentration on the assertion of their parentage? If intention is to be the determining factor, how does this fit in with traditional norms of a two-parent heterosexual family? There would also be the difficulty of accommodating the welfare and interests of the child within this model, which itself is unpredictable and subjective. Proof of intention may not always be easy to find unless written evidence were forthcoming and it implies a willingness to consider children as forms of property that are freely alienable. Underlying this article is the presumption that society retains its abhorrence of surrogacy and is still clinging on to traditional models of family life from which surrogacy radically departs. Douglas concludes that the *Johnson* case is a step closer to recognition of social as opposed to biological parenthood.

[94] See discussion at paras **7.29–7.30**.

[95] *In Re Marriage of Buzzanca* 61 Cal App 4th 1410, 72 Cal Reptr 2d 280 (1998).

Davidson's sperm. Four were implanted in Mrs Davidson, who gave birth to twins. The others were then available for further donation according to the consent form signed by Mr and Mrs Davidson (seemingly without the knowledge of the initial egg donor Mrs X or her husband). One of the embryos was implanted in the uterus of a surrogate, Mrs Snell, on behalf of another couple Mr and Mrs Buzzanca. A few weeks before the birth of the child, Mr and Mrs Buzzanca separated and divorce proceedings were instituted.

[7.55] In the divorce Mrs Buzzanca tried to get maintenance for the child but the Court ruled that Mr Buzzanca was not the child's legal father, as he had not contributed the sperm. Further, Mrs Buzzanca was held not to be the legal mother because she was neither the genetic nor the gestational mother. The surrogate was not the legal mother due to a contractual provision between the parties to that effect. The gamete donors and their spouses were unknown to the Court and not parties to the case. So the child, theoretically, had eight parents, but legally had none. The California Supreme Court eventually overturned this decision by relying on a principle that people should be held responsible for the reproductive outcomes of their actions. Therefore, Mr Buzzanca, who had consented to the surrogacy arrangement and intended to raise the resulting child, was imposed with legal fatherhood. Similarly, although Mrs Buzzanca was neither the genetic nor the gestational mother, she intended the child to be born, and she was held to be the legal mother. The case was simplified somewhat by the fact that the surrogate withdrew her claim for custody and the gamete providers were not involved.[96]

[7.56] Other states in the US also hold that intent manifested in a surrogacy agreement offers another way, besides procreation and adoption, by which parentage can be established.[97] Thus courts have upheld surrogacy arrangements on contract principles,[98] or on the basis of the commissioning couple's genetic tie to the child.[99] For example, Nevada law provides that a person identified as an intended parent in a surrogacy contract must be treated in law as a natural parent under all circumstances.[100] Similarly, Arkansas law provides that a child born to a surrogate mother is presumed to be the child of the biological father and the intended mother as long as the father is married.[101]

---

[96] For further discussion see generally Pitt, 'Fragmenting Procreation: In re Marriage of Buzzanca,' Yale Law Journal Vol 108, No 7 (May, 1999), pp. 1893–1900; O'Hara and Vorzimer, 'In re Marriage of Buzzanca: Charting a New Destiny', 26 W St U L Rev 25 (1999).

[97] Spivack, 'The Law of Surrogate Motherhood in the United States' [2010] Am J of Comp Law Vol 58, 97–114.

[98] *PGM v JMA*, 2997 WL 4304448 (Minnesota Court of Appeals) – the Court held that the parties had entered into a valid agreement that reflected their joint intention, were not coerced and did not contravene state policy.

[99] *Clark v Belsito* 644 N E 2d 760 (Ohio 1994) where the Court ruled that 'the law requires that those who provided the child with its genetics…must be designated as the legal and natural parents'. See also *Perry-Rogers v Fasano* 715 NYS 2d 19 (NY App Div 2000), in which two embryos were transferred to Ms Fasano, one of which was genetically related to Ms Fasano and her husband, but the other of which was unrelated and transferred to her by mistake. Ms Fasano gave birth to two children of different races. The Court appears to have relied in part on genetics in ruling that Ms Fasano was a mere gestational carrier for the child to whom she was not related.

[100] Nev Rev Stat 126.045 (2001).

[101] Ark Code Ann §9–10–201.

[7.57] A common criticism of the approach taken in these cases is that by concentrating on intent, the court is implicitly refusing to give the surrogate parental rights over the child she carried. This amounts to a denial of the fundamental importance of her role in nurturing the child for nine months in her womb. Essentially, the surrogate has complete control over the health and safety of the foetus, as it will be affected by her lifestyle, habits, diet and arguably her psychological and emotional health. Her choices as to consumption of alcohol, drugs, cigarettes, nutritional food, vitamin supplements and so on may, to a larger or lesser degree, have permanent effects on the developing child. The argument, therefore, is that if effects on the child are seen as sufficient to recognise the importance of the genetic input of the commissioning parents, then the surrogate should also be regarded as having made a vital contribution to the developing child. This argument does not, however, advance the question of who should have custody of the child in the event of a dispute as between the genetic and gestational mother.

[7.58] The use of intent in the determination of parenthood is significant, as it respects the understanding upon which the parties have relied in their arrangement. The parties rely on this understanding of their roles in their appreciation of the financial and emotional costs of becoming involved in surrogacy. Any rules which negative these commitments or create ambiguities where there were none in the minds of those who participated in the programme are, arguably, destructive of the autonomy of the individuals in shaping their reproductive futures. Since both the gestational and genetic mother play an essential role in the creation of the child, a legal determination of which of the two roles is more important is arbitrary.[102]

[7.59] There are however objections to contract law principles being used in relation to parental status, such as in the inappropriateness of using commercial law doctrines in familial disputes, the failure of contract law to safeguard the best interests of the child, and the lack of appreciation of the emotional involvement of the parties. However, these objections may be countered by recognition that, while in sexual reproduction the intentions of the partners as to parenthood may be blurred, in cases of surrogacy the demarcation lines are firmly drawn in advance of the process taking place. It may thus be argued that the law should recognise the importance for the parties involved of being able to deliberately plan and negotiate their roles unhindered by traditional notions of parenthood that are inapplicable to their relationship.

[7.60] In reconciling the intent-based determination of parenthood with the need to secure the best interests of the child, it may be argued that adhering to the pre-conception agreement as articulated by the parties will generally coincide with the most positive outcome for the child. Those who are strongly motivated and act upon their intentions regarding parenthood are most likely to be motivated and fill those intentions consistently and well.[103] It also reduces the necessity of litigation, as the predictability of the outcome will deter frivolous applications to court that would ultimately only serve to destabilise the child and its relations with others. There may well be situations in which the upholding of the parties' intentions may conflict with the child's best interest and in such circumstances the court must decide which interest is more important. There

---

[102] Reichman Schiff, 'Solomonic decisions in Egg Donation: Unscrambling the Conundrum of Legal Maternity', 80 Iowa L Rev (1995) 265 at 277.

[103] Para **[7.29]**.

should, in such cases, be a presumption in favour of upholding the agreement made but this should not be conclusive in cases where it would be detrimental to the child.

[7.61] A different approach is evident in the first litigated surrogacy case in Australia, *Re Evelyn*.[104] The facts here were that two couples were friends for a number of years. Mr and Mrs Q were unable to conceive, Mrs Q having had a total hysterectomy arising from ovarian cancer. They had an adopted son who was aged three at the time of the trial. Dr and Mrs S had three children of their own aged between three and seven years. Mrs S offered to be inseminated with Mr Q's sperm and then to carry the child with a view to handing it over to the Q's after birth. The arrangement was entirely altruistically motivated. Baby Evelyn was born in December 1996 and was taken by the Q's to their home a week later. Mr Q was registered as the father on the birth certificate. It had been intended that the couples would remain in close contact, particularly between Mrs S and the baby. Mrs S became frustrated at the level of communication which she perceived as inadequate and she also began to attend grief counselling and a relinquishing mothers' support group. She decided that she could no longer abide by her decision to relinquish the baby and in July 1997 she travelled to the Q's home and took the baby from them. An initial hearing returned the baby to the Q's with a contact order in favour of the S's. By the time the trial came to full hearing, the baby was one year old and had been living with the Q's for most of her young life. The judge refused to criticise the couples for having become involved in this arrangement and concentrated instead on the paramount importance of the child's welfare. He took the view that the arrangement had been entered into with the noblest of motives and that all the adults involved were genuine and well intentioned.

[7.62] The trial judge stated that the agreement between the parties was void and unenforceable but nonetheless he said that 'whilst, of course, such considerations are secondary to an independent determination of what is in Evelyn's best interests, the circumstances surrounding her creation are pertinent to such an assessment.'[105] However, he held that public policy considerations prevailed over the expressed intention of the parties, and that Evelyn's best interests were the paramount consideration. He took the view that Evelyn should reside with the S's (the surrogate mother and her husband) although contact was arranged with the Q's and they were to have shared long-term responsibility for her care, welfare and development. Although the judge said that he was satisfied that both couples would be capable of providing Evelyn with the highest standard of care, he focused on the long-term implications for Evelyn, having regard to the special circumstances of her conception. He found that Evelyn would be likely to suffer identity problems during her adolescence and that her biological mother, Mrs S, was better equipped to deal with those problems. Mrs S also had a more flexible attitude to future contact in the event her application was successful than did the Q's. Jordan J also found that the loss to Evelyn of not growing up with her half-siblings outweighed the loss to her of her relationship with her adopted brother.

[7.63] An appeal to the Full Court of the Family Court and ultimately to the High Court by the Q's was unsuccessful. The Full Court of the Family Court held that as a matter of principle, there was no presumption in favour of a biological parent and that although

---

[104] *Re Evelyn* [1998] Fam CA 103.
[105] *Re Evelyn* No BR 7321 of 1997 at 29.

Jordan J had given a preferential position to the biological mother in this case, this was done on the basis of his evaluation of the personal qualities of the parties, their parenting capacities and the expert evidence before him. The Court concluded that the judge was entitled to place greater emphasis on the long-term rather than short-term issues for the child. Evelyn was ultimately handed over to the S's in September 1998, when she was almost two years old.

[7.64] Legal provisions in force in Australia at the time of this case meant that Mrs S, as the birth mother, was deemed to be the legal mother and her husband was the legal father. The biological father, Mr Q, was characterised almost in the same way as a sperm donor and was presumed not to be the father as Mr S was married to the legal mother and enjoyed a presumption of paternity. Thus, the legal provisions of parentage operated to deny the commissioning parents the possibility of establishing legal parentage through the use of their genetic material. This does not make any allowance for the existence of agreements between the parties and their joint intention that Mr Q would be the legal father, as evidenced by his registration on the birth certificate as such. Despite the conclusion reached in this case, it would be a mistake to overstate the significance of legal parentage rules, as Jordan J clearly stated that the parentage rules must be read as subject to the paramountcy principle. He said he would 'consider the case on its merits without being unduly fettered by legal fictions based on broad considerations of public policy'. The Full Court did not consider this issue further.[106]

SURROGACY IN THE UK

Background

[7.65] The Warnock Report on Human Fertilisation and Embryology, which was published in 1984 in Britain, was one of the first reports worldwide to consider the implications of biotechnology for human reproduction. The committee gave its blessing to IVF, artificial insemination, egg donation and, to a more limited extent, embryo donation. It recommended that each of these practices be regulated by a new statutory licensing authority which would gather empirical data, issue guidelines and guard against potential abuses. Surrogacy is the only reproductive alternative to receive outright condemnation. The Committee said, 'It is inconsistent with human dignity that a woman should use her uterus for financial profit and treat it as an incubator for someone else's child.'[107] The Committee recommended that the commercialisation of surrogacy arrangements by an agency should be a criminal offence. This recommendation was enacted in the Surrogacy Arrangements Act 1985,[108] following the

---

[106] See further discussion of this case in Otlowski, '*Re Evelyn* – Reflections on Australia's First Litigated Surrogacy Case' Med Law Review (Spring 1999) 7, p 38–57.

[107] Report of the Committee of Inquiry into Human Fertilisation and Embryology (1984) Cmnd. 9314, para. 8.10. Mary Warnock subsequently stated that the committee had been influenced in its views by public concerns about the operation of unscrupulous US agencies coming to the UK and that she had changed her mind about surrogacy in the intervening years since the Warnock Report was published. http://www.bionews.org.uk/page_611935.asp

[108] The Parliamentary debates at the time the Bill was being passed are instructive. Surrogacy was condemned as: 'sick' (Peter Bruinvels HL Vol 77 Col.42); 'totally immoral' (Ian Paisley, Vol 68 Col 555); (contd.../)

public debates brought about by the *Baby Cotton* case.[109] The Act was designed to prohibit any arrangement that held the possibility of payment, but it did not deal with altruistic or family arrangements or those that had been assisted by a charitable organisation. The Act was criticised by many as a stop-gap measure which would have the undesirable effect of driving some aspects of surrogacy underground rather than having them dealt with by professionally qualified advisors.[110] It is not an offence under the Act to enter into a surrogacy arrangement but the agreement itself is unenforceable, meaning that the commissioning couple has no legal redress if the surrogate mother decides to keep the baby, nor may the surrogate mother sue the couple for payment or force them to take the child. There is a criminal sanction for commercial agencies negotiating or making surrogacy arrangements.[111] This Act remains in force at the present time although non-profit making agencies may now charge a reasonable fee in order to recoup their costs and parentage provisions have been introduced in the Human

---

[108] (\...contd) 'repugnant' (W Benyon, Vol 68 Col 582); 'the sale of children' (Jill Knight, Vol 68 Col 565); 'trafficking in human beings' (Patrick Cormack, Vol 74, Col 1193); an 'extremely distasteful matter' (Roger Sims, Vol 74 Col 1189); a 'well defined evil' (Norman Fowler, Vol 74 Col 1193); and 'sheer effrontery' (AJ Beith, Vol 77 Col 33).

[109] *Re C (a minor)* [1985] FLR 846. The consequence of this first commercial surrogacy case, which occurred in January 1985, has been described as a 'moral panic', defined by Cohen as 'a condition, episode, person or group of persons which emerge to become identified as a threat to societal values or interests'. Cohen, *Folk Devils and Moral Panics* (MacGibbon and Kee Ltd, 1972) at 9. Kim Cotton, the surrogate mother involved, overnight became a 'folk devil', a 'visible reminder of what we should not be.' Dyer, 'Baby Cotton and the Birth of Moral Panic', *The Guardian*, 15 January 1985. 'The intermingling of commerce and the family, the public realm and the private sphere, prompted a government, committed to free enterprise on the one hand and valorisation of the family on the other, to take swift action.'

[110] Eaton criticises the Act on the basis of a logical inconsistency between its objectives and methods. The Act clearly purports to combat the perceived evils of commercialism, but there is no prohibition against the couple paying a surrogate a substantial fee for her services. 'It is difficult to see how a fee is any less commercial, coercive or exploitative if offered by the couple rather than through their commercial agent'. The most serious danger posed by this 'piecemeal legislation' is its encouragement of amateurish agreements. The definition of the offence is broad enough to include legal, medical and psychological counsellors who, for a fee, might otherwise assist the parties. 'They are left to stumble through the process without advice. It is most unfortunate that a law that does not condemn the agreement itself does not permit the parties to pursue it in a professional manner.' Eaton, 'The British Response to Surrogate Motherhood: An American Critique' 19 The Law Teacher 163. See also Freeman, 'After Warnock: Whither the Law?' (1986) 39 Current Legal Problems 33. Freeman says the Act is 'short-sighted and ultimately self-defeating'. He believes that criminalisation of surrogacy will not prevent its occurrence and that regulation is the best solution. 'It is inevitable that we will have to recognise that surrogacy is a legitimate response to a felt need and that it requires regulation to ensure it is practised so as to promote the best interests of all involved.'

[111] Section 2 of the 1985 Act. See comments of Ebsworth J in *Briody v St Helen's and Knowsley Health Authority* [2000] 2 FCR 13. This was quite an unusual case in that it involved a claim for damages for medical negligence that had allegedly resulted in the plaintiff being unable to bear children. The plaintiff claimed for the cost of commercial surrogacy entered into in California. This was dismissed by the Court, as such an award would enable an unenforceable and unlawful contract to be entered into, which was contrary to public policy and would not be allowed.

Fertilisation and Embryology Act discussed later. In reality, surrogacy arrangements are made not only on an altruistic basis between family members and friends but also for payment of between £10,000 and £15,000.

[7.66] The Human Fertilisation and Embryology Act 1990 ('the HFE Act') which was introduced to regulate clinics providing assisted reproduction services did not expressly deal with surrogacy but provided that any medical treatment used as part of a surrogacy arrangement, such as the donation of eggs or sperm, or embryo transfer, must take place in a licensed treatment centre. Therefore, 'although the Authority [Human Fertilisation and Embryology Authority (HFEA)] does not directly regulate surrogacy, licensed treatment services provided to establish a surrogate pregnancy will be carried out under its auspices.'[112] In circumstances where the creation and transfer of embryos is involved, as in gestational surrogacy, this can only be done in centres licensed by the HFEA. This means that clinical, scientific, counselling and legal services should be available to commissioning couples and surrogate mothers under the Code of Practice issued by the HFEA.[113] The Act also provided for the making of parental orders in favour of commissioning couples if certain conditions were met.[114]

[7.67] The Brazier Committee[115] was established to examine surrogacy arrangements from the perspective of public policy, the designation of parenthood and the meaning of 'reasonable expenses' which may be paid to the surrogate mothers. The Report of the Committee acknowledged that there was a policy vacuum and an absence of a coherent policy in relation to surrogacy. The Committee believed that it was anticipated that the Surrogacy Arrangements Act 1985 would be effective in deterring commercial surrogacy, which would then 'largely disappear'[116] or 'wither on the vine'.[117] This has not occurred, and in fact the number of surrogacy arrangements is on the increase.[118] The Report also estimated that, contrary to early fears, it is only in a handful of cases (4–

---

[112] Morgan and Lee, *Human Fertilisation and Embryology, Regulating the Reproductive Revolution* (Blackstone Press, 2001) at 199.

[113] See http://www.hfea.gov.uk.

[114] Section 30 of the 1990 Act. These provisions were largely replicated in the 2008 Act discussed below.

[115] *Surrogacy: Review for Health Ministers of Current Arrangements for Payments and Regulation* (Cm. 4068) (Department of Health, 1998). The review was prompted in part by a highly publicised dispute between a married surrogate, Karen Roche, and a Dutch couple who paid her £12,000, three days after she became pregnant with the man's sperm. The relationship deteriorated and the surrogate told the couple, falsely, that she had terminated the pregnancy. She had also contracted with another couple to give them custody of the child. She subsequently decided to keep the baby, who then became the subject of a custody battle. 'The Baby Market' (1997) The Lancet; 349:1487; The Independent, 20 January 1997. Freeman claims that the review was also sparked off by the arrival in the UK of an American, Bill Handel, 'who 'advertised' his presence in the UK [without breaching the 1985 Act] and let it be known that payments of between £30,000 and £45,000 were available for willing surrogates.' Freeman, 'Does Surrogacy Have a Future After Brazier?' (1999) 7 Medical Law Review, 1–20 at 2, n.14.

[116] Brazier Report at para 3.5.

[117] Brazier Report at para 3.44.

[118] Freeman 'Does Surrogacy Have a Future After Brazier?' (1999) 7 Medical Law Review, 1–20 at 3.

5 per cent) that 'the nightmare scenario occurs and a surrogate refuses to hand over the child.'[119]

[7.68] The concerns in relation to surrogacy, as seen by the Committee are: '…whether the law and practice adequately safeguard the welfare of the child; whether it protects the interests of the surrogate, her family and the commissioning couple…and whether it should do so; and whether payment of the surrogate is acceptable.'[120] The ethical issues in surrogacy, therefore, remain largely the same as they were when considered by the Warnock Committee in 1984. The danger of exploitation of women, and the subjection of others as a means to an end, is always open to objection. The Committee takes the view that payment increases the risks of exploitation if it is an inducement to participate in an activity whose risks the surrogate cannot predict.[121] Although the Committee's remit did not include a consideration of whether to outlaw surrogacy, the Report takes the view that surrogacy should not become an acceptable occupation, and that there is sufficient cause for concern to make regulation of the practice essential.

[7.69] The Report made recommendations in relation to payments to surrogates, the regulation of surrogacy and new legislation. It also proposed a new code of practice for dealing with surrogacy arrangements. In relation to the question of payments, the evidence before the Committee was that in only three per cent of cases was payment more than £10,000. The Committee recommended that payments should cover only genuine expenses associated with the pregnancy (a list is provided), and actual loss of earnings (the difference between the surrogate's usual earnings and State benefits). The reasons for this are as follows: firstly, children are not commodities to be bought and sold; secondly, it is in line with emerging policy in relation to gamete donors; thirdly, women should not be attracted to surrogacy by the lure of financial reward; and fourthly, it is not in the child's best interests to learn that their surrogate mother benefited financially from giving them up.[122]

[7.70] In relation to the regulation of surrogacy, the Committee was of the view that regulation might reduce the hazards to the child and the others involved. It rejects the idea of giving regulatory powers to infertility clinics,[123] preferring the option of having surrogacy agencies registered with the Department of Health, who would impose a statutory Code of Practice. It recommended a new Surrogacy Act to deal with the main legal principles governing surrogacy arrangements and to offer a Code of Practice. This Act would continue existing prohibitions in relation to commercial activity in surrogacy

---

[119] Freeman 'Does Surrogacy Have a Future After Brazier?' (1999) 7 Medical Law Review, 1–20 at 3.

[120] Freeman 'Does Surrogacy Have a Future After Brazier?' (1999) 7 Medical Law Review, 1–20 at 4, quoting from the Brazier Report at para 4.6.

[121] Freeman says of this point: '[t]he prospective surrogate's autonomy must, it seems, be protected by a healthy injection of paternalism.' 'Does Surrogacy Have a Future After Brazier?' (1999) 7 Medical Law Review, 1–20 at 5.

[122] For a criticism of these reasons, see Freeman, 'Does Surrogacy Have a Future After Brazier?' (1999) 7 Medical Law Review, 1–20 at 9–10.

[123] Staff at infertility clinics have expertise in medical and scientific matters but such skills are not usually required in surrogacy. The skills required in surrogacy are more likely to be found in adoption-like agencies.

arrangements; define and limit lawful payments to surrogates; and set out a Code of Practice for agencies with the child's interests of paramount concern. In terms of eligibility, the Committee believed that there should be a minimum and maximum age for commissioning parents, and for the surrogate mother. The surrogate should have had a child and have one still living with her; a period of two years between pregnancies; a maximum number of surrogate births (usually one); independent counselling; comprehensive information regarding risks; legal advice; and a period of reflection before conception is attempted. The relationship between the surrogate and the commissioning couple should be based on a memorandum of understanding which, though not legally binding, would clarify the expectations of the parties from the outset regarding contact, the welfare of the child and information to be given to the child regarding his/her origins. The Committee's recommendations were not implemented in the 2008 Act discussed below.

Legal parentage

[7.71] The HFE Act was amended in 2008 but the provisions in relation to surrogacy remained substantially unchanged and the prohibition on commercial involvement in surrogacy is still in place thereby preventing professional advice being given to couples and potential surrogates. In relation to legal parentage, s 33 of the 2008 Act provides that 'the woman who is carrying or has carried a child as a result of the placing in her of an embryo and of sperm and eggs, and no other woman, is to be treated as the mother of the child.' The Act does not differentiate between genetic and gestational surrogacy so the surrogate will always be the legal mother irrespective of whether she is genetically related to the baby. Jackson believes that the principal merit of this approach is that 'it unambiguously identifies the child's legal mother.'[124] She says although it might be possible to use a genetic test as an alternative mechanism, this would produce different results depending on the type of arrangement. Although a test based on intention may be open to dispute, it would have certain advantages if, for example, a couple refused to accept a child born with disabilities, they would be held to their agreement based on their pre-conception intention to be parents of this child. 'The UK's approach instead puts the surrogate mother in the difficult position of having prima facie responsibility for a child that she never wanted, and leaves the commissioning couple with no legal responsibility for a child whose creation they brought about.'[125]

[7.72] Paternity is dealt with by s 38 of the 2008 Act. It provides that the surrogate mother's husband (if she has one) is treated as the father of the child unless it can be shown that he did not consent to her treatment.[126] If the surrogate is unmarried but has a partner, he may be treated as the father if he satisfies the 'agreed parenthood' conditions[127] in the Act but this is unlikely unless he and the surrogate decide to keep the baby. The intended father would not usually avail of the 'agreed fatherhood' provisions

---

[124] Jackson, *Medical Law: Text, Cases and Materials* (3rd edn, OUP, 2013) at 843.

[125] Jackson, *Medical Law: Text, Cases and Materials* (3rd edn, OUP, 2013) at 843.

[126] See *Re G (Surrogacy: Foreign Domicile)* [2007] EWHC 2814 (Fam).

[127] These conditions in s 37 of the Act essentially require a written notice from the man and the woman involved that they consent to the man being treated in law as the father of any resulting child.

as these apply to men whose sperm was not used in the procedure. In surrogacy, it is usual for the intended father's sperm to be used unless a donor is required.

Parental orders

[7.73] Since the surrogate mother is regarded as the legal mother under the Act, the intended parents will require a transfer of parental rights and responsibilities for the child either through adoption or a parental order which essentially enables the parties to avoid the cumbersome aspects of the adoption procedure if certain conditions are met. Section 54 of the Act provides that on an application made by two people (the applicants) the court may make an order providing for a child to be treated in law as the child of the applicants if, inter alia, (a) the child has been carried by a woman who is not one of the applicants, as a result of the placing in her of an embryo or sperm and eggs or her artificial insemination, (b) the gametes of at least one of the applicants were used to bring about the creation of the embryo. When such an order is made, the child's birth is re-registered and, as with adoption, it will not be possible for the public to make a link between entries in the register of birth and the parental order register. However, the child will have access to its original birth certificate on reaching 18 years of age and having been offered appropriate counselling.

[7.74] The parental order provisions are aimed at a situation where, for example, a woman can donate eggs but cannot carry a child to term. She and her partner or husband may agree with a surrogate mother that the surrogate will carry to term an embryo created by the fertilisation of the wife's eggs and the husband's sperm. The Act thus allows the court to make an order providing for the child carried by the surrogate to be treated in law as the child of the intended parents, provided that the gametes of one or both have been used and they are adult and married, in a civil partnership or living as partners in an enduring family relationship.[128]

[7.75] This provision in s 54 in relation to the status of the applicants was recently successfully challenged in *In the matter of Z (A Child) (No 2)*[129] in which Z, who is the biological son of the applicant father, was carried to birth by a surrogate mother. The father argued that the provisions of s 54, which provides that an application for a parental order can be made only by *two* people, were a discriminatory interference with a *single* person's rights to private and family life, and therefore inconsistent with articles 8 (right to respect for private and family life) and 14 (prohibition of discrimination based on sex, race, colour, language, religion, political or other opinion, national or social origin, association with a national minority, property, birth or other status) of the European Convention on Human Rights. The Secretary of State conceded that the facts fell within the ambit of art 8 and that art 14 was also engaged. It was accepted that there is a difference in treatment between a single person entering into a lawful surrogacy arrangement and a couple entering the same arrangement. This difference in treatment, namely the inability to obtain a parental order, is on the sole ground of the status of the commissioning parent as a single person versus the same person were he part of a couple. The Secretary of State accepted that, in light of the evidence and the

---

[128] For useful synopsis of legal provisions in the UK and relevant case law see http://www.nataliegambleassociates.co.uk/.

[129] *In the matter of Z (A Child) (No 2)* [2016] EWHC 1191 (Fam).

jurisprudential developments both domestic and in Strasbourg, including for example *Mennesson v France*[130] and *Wagner v Luxembourg*,[131] this difference in treatment on the sole ground of the status of the commissioning parent as a single person versus being part of a couple, could not be justified within the meaning of art 14. The court accordingly made a declaration of incompatibility with the ECHR and the Secretary of State has indicated that the government in the UK is considering how to amend the law to remedy the breach.

[7.76] Section 54 of the 2008 Act also provides that a parental order is also subject to other conditions, including the consent of the surrogate, her husband and the genetic father where applicable and where they can be found. The application must be made within six months of the child's birth and no money or payment other than reasonable expenses must be involved in the agreement unless authorised by the court. The child must be living with the intended parents both at the time of the application and at the time of the making of the order. Either or both of the intended parents must be domiciled in the UK, the Channel Islands or the Isle of Man.[132]

Payment to surrogate mothers

[7.77] The issue of authorisation of payments to surrogate mothers has arisen in a number of cases as, although the Act prohibits payment of anything other than reasonable expenses, the courts may under s 54(8) exercise discretion to authorise payments in excess of reasonable expenses if this is in the best interests of the child. For example in *Re C (Application by Mr and Mrs X under section 30 of the Human Fertilisation and Embryology Act 1990)*[133] the couple had paid the surrogate £12,000, a sum which Wall LJ stated was clearly not 'expenses reasonably incurred'. However, the judge went on to say that the couple had entered into the arrangement in good faith. 'They were not buying a baby. They were paying a figure for expenses which they had been advised was on the high side, but which was not disproportionate.' The couple was unaware that the surrogate mother was also claiming social welfare benefits until after they found out she was pregnant, at which time it was too late for them to withdraw from the arrangement. The judge said that they were a genuine couple who had spent many years attempting to have a child, the child was much loved and cherished by them and therefore it was 'manifestly in her interests that she should be treated in law as the child of Mr and Mrs X, and that both should have parental responsibility for her.' Therefore the judge exercised his discretion to authorise the payment.

[7.78] This issue also arose in *Re X and Y (Foreign Surrogacy)*.[134] In this case, a British couple went to the Ukraine to avail of a surrogacy programme there. They conceived twins through use of an anonymous egg donor's eggs, which were fertilised by the commissioning father's sperm, and carried by a Ukrainian surrogate mother. The

---

[130] *Mennesson v France* Appl No 65192/11.

[131] *Wagner v Luxembourg* Appl No 76240/01.

[132] For case law in relation to domicile for the purposes of parental orders see *AB v SA* [2013] EWHC 426 (Fam); *CC v DD* [2014] EWHC 1307 (Fam).

[133] *Mr and Mrs X under section 30 of the Human Fertilisation and Embryology Act 1990)* [2002] EWHC 157 (Fam).

[134] *Re X and Y (Foreign Surrogacy)* [2009] 1 FLR 733.

commissioning couple agreed to pay the surrogate mother €235 per month plus a lump sum of €25,000, which she intended to use to help her to buy a flat for her family. They were assured that the legalities were straightforward but this turned out not to be the case, despite the fact that Ukrainian law regarded the commissioning couple as parents of the twins and absolved the Ukrainian surrogate mother and her husband of any legal responsibility for them. However, this was directly contrary to the position under English law by virtue of which the legal parents of the twins were the surrogate mother and her husband, and the commissioning parents had no responsibility for them:

> The practical effect of this conflict over legal parenthood was that each system of law abdicated parental responsibility for each set of parents. The children were, therefore, born parentless, and, by extension, stateless (entitled to neither British nor Ukrainian citizenship).[135]

[7.79] The twins were thus stuck in a legal vacuum without parents and with no right to either enter the UK or remain in the Ukraine. The British parents took responsibility for them from birth but they had only a limited visa and would be forced to leave the children in a Ukrainian orphanage if the legal difficulties were not resolved. DNA tests were undertaken to establish that the commissioning man was the biological father of the twins and the children were given discretionary leave to enter the UK 'outside the rules' for 12 months to enable the couple to apply for a parental order. The main difficulty was that the surrogate mother had received payment which was in excess of reasonable expenses and therefore the Court had to consider whether to authorise the commercial payment so that a parental order could be made.

[7.80] Hedley J considered that there were three issues involved in deciding whether or not to approve the payment. The first was whether the sum paid was disproportionate to reasonable expenses. He noted that reasonable expenses will vary from country to country and heard evidence about the cost of living in the Ukraine. He concluded that the sum was not so disproportionate that the granting of the order would be an 'unacceptable affront to public policy'. The second issue was whether the applicants were acting in good faith and without 'moral taint' in their dealings with the surrogate mother. On this point Hedley J held that there was no doubt that this was so, and was satisfied that no advantage was taken of the surrogate mother who was herself 'a woman of mature discretion'. The third issue was whether there had been any attempt to defraud the authorities and on this point Hedley J held that in fact the opposite was true in that the applicants had sought at all times to comply with the requirements of English and Ukrainian law.

[7.81] The Court also had, of course, to consider the welfare of the children in this case. Conscious of the fact that the children were stateless and parentless unless the order was granted, Hedley J said that this made the granting of the order 'most uncomfortable'. He recognised that what he was being asked to do was to balance two potentially irreconcilably conflicting principles in that Parliament expected the courts to implement its policy decision in relation to commercial surrogacy, but at the same time the rigour of such implementation must be mitigated by considerations of the welfare of the child. He added: 'The difficulty is that it is almost impossible to imagine a set of circumstances in

---

[135] Gamble and Ghevaert, *'Re X and Y (Foreign Surrogacy)*: A Trek Through a Thorn Forest' (2009) Fam Law 239.

which by the time the case comes to court the welfare of any child (particularly a foreign child) would not be gravely compromised (at the very least) by a refusal to make an order.' The effect of this judgment is, as Gamble and Ghevaert, point out that:

> [T]he only sanction the court holds against commercial surrogacy (ie to refuse a parental order) has the effect of punishing an innocent child, and it would be difficult – even impossible – for an English family court to do this, no matter how badly the parents had infringed public policy. The case therefore goes a significant way to allowing fully commercial surrogacy in the UK, particularly where the court is in practice presented with a *fait accompli*.[136]

[7.82] Other cases have made similar orders in prioritising the best interests of the child. In *Re S*,[137] a case which involved a Californian surrogacy arrangement in which $23,000 was paid, Hedley J again considered the issue of authorisation in respect of a payment for a commercial surrogacy arrangement and set out further the approach the court should take. He noted that it was unclear what the proper approach should be where those who cannot do something lawfully in the UK, go overseas to do it perfectly lawfully according to the country in which the surrogacy is carried into effect and then seek retrospective approval in the UK. He said that this clearly raised matters of public policy to ensure that commercial surrogacy agreements are not used to circumvent childcare laws, to ensure that the courts were not involved in anything that looks like the simple payment for effectively buying children overseas, and also to ensure that sums of money which might look modest in themselves are not in fact of such a substance that they overbear the will of a surrogate. Hedley J decided that the parental order would be made in this case as the applicants would not have been prevented from parenting children in the UK, and the sums involved were not greatly disproportionate to expenses reasonably incurred.

[7.83] Following these decisions Parental Order Regulations[138] were introduced in the UK in 2010 to provide that the child's welfare must now be the court's paramount consideration throughout the child's lifetime. The impact of these changes can be seen in *Re L (Commercial Surrogacy)*[139] in which a child had been born in Illinois in the USA as a result of a commercial surrogacy arrangement which would have been unlawful in the UK due to the level of payment made to the surrogate mother. The parents applied for a parental order under the 2008 Act. The order was made, but in doing so the court had to give retrospective approval to the payments. Hedley J emphasised that the consequence of statutory developments is that 'welfare is no longer merely the Court's first consideration but becomes its paramount consideration.' He said 'it will only be in the clearest case of the abuse of public policy that the court will be able to withhold an order if otherwise welfare considerations support its making.' It is of course open to speculation as to what the learned judge meant by 'clearest case of abuse' and what the outcome of such a finding might mean for the child in circumstances where the surrogate mother does not want custody of the child. The obvious concern is that the

---

[136] Gamble and Ghevaert, '*Re X and Y (Foreign Surrogacy)*: A Trek Through a Thorn Forest' (2009) Fam Law 239.

[137] *Re S* [2009] EWHC 2977 (Fam).

[138] SI 2010/986.

[139] *Re L (Commercial Surrogacy)* [2010] EWHC 3146 (Fam).

court might refuse to make a declaration of parentage with the result that the child would end up in state care, an option that would clearly not be in the child's best interests.

[7.84] This approach was also followed in *J v G*[140] where the payment to the surrogate mother was the highest to come before an English court to date. The applicants were civil partners in the UK who entered into a surrogacy arrangement through a surrogacy agency in California as a result of which twins were born. The twins were genetically the children of one of the applicants. Since their birth the children were in the full time care of the applicants who obtained US passports for the children and returned to the UK with them. They subsequently applied for a parental order in respect of the children. One of the issues for the court was whether to authorise the payment of $56,750 as reasonable expenses under the provisions of s 54. Theis J held that the payments in this case were not so disproportionate to expenses reasonably incurred that the granting of an order would be an affront to public policy. 'There is no evidence to suggest that they were of such a level to overbear the will of the surrogate. The surrogate was an experienced surrogate; she had been one twice before. She is a mature woman with financial means. She had legal advice before entering into the agreement and was able to command a higher compensation fee because of her proven track record.' Theis J was satisfied that the applicants had acted in good faith at all stages. The judge said 'Their journey to have a family has clearly been a long and arduous one, both emotionally and financially. There is no suggestion they have used surrogacy as a means of circumventing child protection laws. They are a loving and committed same sex couple with a stable home environment.' They had taken all proper steps to comply with the legal parentage requirements in both the US and in the UK. The court therefore exercised its discretion pursuant to s 54(8) and authorised the payments made other than for expenses reasonably incurred.

[7.85] The result of these cases is that the provisions in relation to payment to surrogates are completely ineffective. 'If the people applying for a parental order are decent or even adequate parents, it is almost impossible to imagine the circumstances where the fact that they engaged in commercial surrogacy, in which the surrogate was paid, would prevent them from being granted a parental order.'[141] A Report from the Surrogacy UK Reform Group in 2015 also states:

> It appears that what might be considered payments beyond 'reasonable expenses' or compensation (as certainly happens in some overseas surrogacy arrangements) will generally always be authorised by a court unless there is *another* reason for the court to consider that the granting of a parental order to the intended parents would not be in the best interests of the child.[142]

---

[140] *J v G* [2013] EWHC 1432. See also similar approach in *Re X (Children) (Parental Order: Retrospective authorisation of payments)* [2011] EWHC 3147 where the court authorised the payment of over £27,000.

[141] Jackson, *Medical Law, Text, Cases and Materials* (3rd edn, OUP, 2013) at 851.

[142] Surrogacy in the UK, Myth busting and reform available at www.kent.ac.uk/law/research/projects/current/surrogacy/.

Time limits

[7.86] This approach of prioritising the best interests of the child in circumstances where the provisions of the Act have not been complied with can also be seen in cases involving non-adherence to time limits set out in the Act. Section 54 of the 2008 Act specifies that the applicants for a parental order must apply during the period of six months beginning with the day on which the child is born. In *Re X (A Child) (Surrogacy: Time limit)*[143] the intended parents had married in 1998 and in 2011 they made a surrogacy agreement in India with the surrogate mother which was accepted by all parties to be valid under Indian law. The surrogate mother conceived using eggs donated by a third party and the intended father's sperm. The child, X, was born in India on 15 December 2011. X entered the UK on a British passport on 6 July 2013. On 4 August 2013 the surrogate mother and her husband confirmed, in separate written documents, that they wished to relinquish all their parental rights and responsibilities in respect of X, which they confirmed on 1 December 2013. In June 2013 the intended parents separated but did not divorce. In July 2013 the intended father applied in the Birmingham County Court for a residence order in respect of X but the six month requirement in s 54 had not been complied with in this case as the intended parents were unaware of the need to apply for a parental order. In the absence of a parental order being made, they did not have parental responsibility for X and the surrogate parents remained X's legal parents.

[7.87] Munby P held that contrary to previously decided cases,[144] he did have power to make an order notwithstanding the expiry of the six-month time limit. He took the view that parental orders went to the most fundamental aspects of status and to the very identity of the child and have a transformative effect on the child's legal relationships with the surrogate and commissioning parents and the practical and psychological realities of the child's identity, thus having an effect extending far beyond the merely legal, which is, for all practical purposes, irreversible. He said he could not think that Parliament had intended that the gate to the making of an order should be barred even if the application was one day late. Such a result would be 'almost nonsensical' given the myriad potentially innocent reasons there might be for non-compliance with the time limit. He held that the commissioning parents should be allowed to pursue an application notwithstanding that it was made two years and two months after X's birth. Although the delay was a long time, given that a parental order went to both status and identity as a human being and the court was looking to a future stretching many decades, the court was entitled, in consideration of the welfare of the child to take a more liberal and relaxed approach to time limits in this case.[145]

[7.88] Munby P also had to consider other conditions set out in s 54, namely whether a parental order could be made in favour of applicants who were no longer living together.

---

[143] *Re X (A Child) (Surrogacy: Time limit)* [2014] EWHC 3135 (Fam).

[144] *In re X (Children) (Parental Order: Foreign Surrogacy)* [2008] EWHC 3030 (Fam), [2009] Fam 71, [2009] 1 FLR 733, *Re S (Parental Order)* [2009] EWHC 3146 (Fam), [2010] 1 FLR 1156, *JP v LP and others* [2014] EWHC 595 (Fam) and *Re WT (A Child)* [2014] EWHC 1303 (Fam).

[145] A similar decision was reached in *Re A and B (Children) (Surrogacy: Parental Orders: Time Limits)* [2015] EWHC 911 (Fam).

The Act specifies that 'the child's home must be with the applicants at the time of the application for the parental order'. In this case the parents were separated and not living together at the time of the application. However, Munby P held that the couple remained husband and wife for the purposes of the application and that X's 'home' was with 'them' at the time of the application notwithstanding that he was splitting his time between their separate homes. He also considered that he should exercise his discretion to authorise payments made to a mediator and the surrogate mother under s 54(8) which he held had been made in good faith and without moral taint. He therefore made the parental order sought on the basis of X's best interests.

Proposals for reform

[7.89] Similarly in *Re A and B (Children) (Surrogacy: Parental Orders: Time Limits)*[146] an application for parental orders was made in respect of two children who were born as a result of gestational surrogacy agreements entered into in the USA in 2006 and 2009. At the time of the application A was 8 years old, and B was 5 years old. The applicants, had complied with all requirements in the USA and orders were made confirming that they were the legal parents of both children. British passports were obtained for the children and the applicants travelled to the UK with the children. The applicants stated that they were not aware of the need to apply for orders in the UK to ensure they had the same legal parental status as they had obtained in the USA. Russell J considered s 54(3) which imposes the six-month time limit. She considered whether it was right in this case that the principle in *Re X* should be followed. She also considered that she must weigh public policy concerns against the welfare of the subject children. In light of case law in relation to s 54(8) the judge considered that the paramountcy principle of the children's welfare must be applied unless the case was one of a clear abuse of public policy. It was accepted that the sole reason the applicants did not apply within the six-month time limit was because they did not realise that the legal parental status obtained in the USA was not recognised in the UK. Russell J concluded that although the time that had elapsed far exceeded the six-month time limit provided for in s 54(3), parental orders best fitted the children's needs and welfare throughout their lives, both retrospectively as well as for the future. Accordingly, parental orders were made.

[7.90] In addition to the problems identified in the cases discussed above, cross-national surrogacy arrangements are also on the increase with couples from the UK travelling to India, Thailand, Ukraine, United States and elsewhere for commercial surrogacy.[147] This can result in complicated jurisdictional and conflict of laws problems to determine the parentage of the child. There is no straightforward way to bring a child born abroad through surrogacy into the UK, with the result that sometimes the child will be 'stateless' pending a decision to grant a passport. It has been claimed that 'UK law makes it deliberately hard for parents to find a surrogate in the UK, and creates a regulatory vacuum in which intended parents have to fend for themselves with no guidance on which surrogacy services being offered in the UK and abroad are safe and reputable.' When these laws were initially introduced in the 1980s it was hoped that

---

[146] *Re A and B (Children) (Surrogacy: Parental Orders: Time Limits)* [2015] EWHC 911 (Fam).
[147] Discussed further below at paras **7.117–7.131**.

these restrictive surrogacy laws would make surrogacy go away, but given today's global surrogacy market that no longer seems a realistic objective.[148]

[7.91] The issues discussed above demonstrate the challenge of legislating in this area as legislative policies in relation to expenses and time limits have consistently been overridden in the best interests of the child. This has led to calls for reform of surrogacy law in the UK over recent years on the grounds that firstly, prohibition of commercialisation has failed to prevent the routine payment of sums of £10,000 to £15,000 to surrogate mothers in the UK, and considerably more in some overseas arrangements. Secondly, the Human Fertilisation and Embryology Act's fatherhood provisions are intended to cover cases in which donated sperm is used, and they apply awkwardly and inappropriately to surrogacy arrangements. Thirdly, the complexity of the rules governing the transfer of legal parenthood undoubtedly deters some commissioning parents from acquiring a formal relationship with 'their' child, and this is clearly not in the child's best interests. Fourthly surrogacy arrangements are not properly regulated, and agreements are often made without legal advice, with potentially disastrous consequences for all concerned.[149]

[7.92] A Surrogacy Law Reform project which was published in 2015 in the UK states that the 30-year old law regulating surrogacy in the UK is out of date and in dire need of reform. The authors are of the view that the law must recognise the correct people as parents of children born through surrogacy and it recommends that parental orders should be pre-authorised so that legal parenthood is conferred on intended parents at birth. Parental orders should also be available to intended parents where neither partner has used their own gametes ('double donation'). The Report recommends that the time limit for applying for a parental order should be removed and that the rules on surrogacy-related advertising and the criminalisation of this should be reviewed in the context of non-profit organisations.[150]

SURROGACY IN THE UNITED STATES

[7.93] In the United States, there are few ground rules for surrogacy. There are no national laws or regulations related to surrogacy and each of the fifty states has its own approach with some states embracing commercial surrogacy, others allowing only

---

[148] Gamble, 'The Indian surrogacy industry – and why we need to reform UK surrogacy law,' BioNews 2 June 2012 http://www.bionews.org.uk.

[149] Jackson, *Medical law: Cases, Text and Materials* (3rd ed.2013 OUP) 861. For example of the negative consequences that can flow from private surrogacy arrangements see *Re T (a child) (surrogacy: residence order)* [2011] EWCH 33 (Fam) in which a surrogacy arrangement was made over the internet without the benefit of advice or counselling from any of the UK's not-for-profit surrogacy agencies. The relationship between the parties subsequently broke down, the surrogate mother decided to keep the baby and the court awarded custody to the surrogate mother. For commentary see Alghrani, 'Surrogacy: A Cautionary Tale' *Med L Rev* 20, Autumn 2012 pp 631–641. See also similar private arrangements made through Facebook in *Re Z (surrogacy agreements) (Child arrangement orders)* [2016] EWFC 34, and *Re A, B and C (UK surrogacy expenses)* [2016] EWFC 33.

[150] Surrogacy in the UK: Myth-busting and Reform, Report of the Surrogacy UK Working Group on Surrogacy Law Reform www.kent.ac.uk/law/research/projects/current/surrogacy/.

altruistic arrangements, and others banning all types of surrogacy. There is no authority deciding on the fitness of the commissioning couple to become parents, or no independent screening process to decide if the woman is suitable to act as surrogate. Surrogacy appears to be controlled mainly by doctors and private agencies, some of which adhere strictly to voluntary guidelines, and some of which do not. The US has become a hub of surrogacy tourism, especially surrogacy friendly states such as California. No regulatory body tracks exactly how many international parents commission surrogate babies in the US. Recent accounts suggest that this practice represents a growing portion of the surrogacy market in the US.[151]

[7.94] Mohapatra says there are many reasons why this surrogacy tourism trend has emerged in the US. First, the US allows for birth citizenship for a baby born in the US regardless of the baby's parents' country of origin. Therefore, unlike in some countries, such as India where surrogacy arrangements have created stateless babies,[152] babies born in America are citizens of the US. Also, many states allow for commercial surrogacy, and some states allow unmarried or lesbian, gay, bisexual, or transgender individuals to be an intended parent.[153] Many individuals seek out surrogacy arrangements in the US because such arrangements are illegal in their home countries or they (particularly LGBT individuals) are banned from participating in such surrogacy agreements in their home countries.[154]

[7.95] The disadvantages of the US system are firstly that it is the most expensive in the world with typical prices of between $75,000 and $120,000.[155] Secondly the inconsistency of the laws that exist with regard to surrogacy even between states just a few miles from one another can result in confusion and conflict of laws problems. It may also result in surrogacy agreements providing that the surrogate cannot travel during her pregnancy to deliver in order to make sure the child is not born in a State with an unfavourable surrogacy law.[156]

---

[151] Mohapatra, 'States of Confusion: Regulation of Surrogacy in the United States' in Rainhorn & Boudamoussi (eds) *Commodification of the Human Body: A Cannibal Market* Editions de la Fondation Maison des Sciences de l'Homme, Paris, 2015.

[152] Smerdon, 'Crossing Bodies, Crossing Borders: International Surrogacy Between the US and India', 39 Cumb. L Rev 15, 24 (2008–2009).

[153] For example in California an 'Intended Parent' is 'an individual, married or unmarried, who manifests the intent to be legally bound as the parent of a child resulting from assisted reproduction.' California Family Code, s 7690(c). Defining 'Intended Parent' as an 'individual' whether 'married or unmarried,' alters the traditional conceptions of who is a parent, minimizing the potential for discrimination against single or unmarried intended parents and same sex domestic partners according to Vorzimer and Randall (2013) 'California passes the most progressive Surrogacy Bill in the world.' http://www.path2parenthood.org/blog/california-passes-the-most-progressive-surrogacy-bill-in-the-world/.

[154] Mohapatra, 'States of Confusion: Regulation of Surrogacy in the United States' in Rainhorn & Boudamoussi (eds) *Commodification of the Human Body: A Cannibal Market* Editions de la Fondation Maison des Sciences de l'Homme, Paris, 2015.

[155] Hartocollis, 'And Surrogacy Makes 3', *New York Times.* (February 19, 2014). www.nytimes.com.

[156] Mohapatra, 'States of Confusion: Regulation of Surrogacy in the United States' in Rainhorn & Boudamoussi (eds) *Commodification of the Human Body: A Cannibal Market* Editions de la Fondation Maison des Sciences de l'Homme, Paris, 2015.

[7.96] Legal limitations on traditional surrogacy are common in the United States.[157] In a number of states, paid traditional surrogacy is prohibited, sometimes with penalties for participation.[158] In other states, traditional surrogacy contracts are not prohibited, but they also are not enforceable. If the surrogate wants to claim her parental status, she may do so.[159] In contrast, a number of states permit and enforce contracts for gestational surrogacy, in which the surrogate carries the pregnancy but does not have a genetic relationship with the child.[160] Even though gestational surrogacy is permitted in many states, it is prohibited in other states.[161] In some states parents must go through a formal adoption process to gain legal custody but often this is done after the child has been born and is in the care of the commissioning couple, in effect leaving the courts with little option but to approve the adoption.

[7.97] In some states, judicial pre-authorisation of the surrogacy arrangement is required by law in order to validate the arrangement.[162] For example, New Hampshire in the United States has a very extensive statutory scheme to regulate surrogacy arrangements.[163] Under that scheme, the intended parents must be married to each other and one of them must be genetically related to the child. The surrogacy arrangement must be judicially preauthorised. Evaluations and counselling of the parties must be conducted prior to impregnation of the surrogate. Such evaluations include home studies of all parties; the surrogate, the intended mother and the intended father. The agreement must be submitted in the form of a petition to Probate Court. At the hearing, the probate judge validates the surrogacy agreement after meeting with the parties, reviewing the agreement's terms and conditions, verifying that all the required counselling and appropriate evaluations have occurred and, finally, determines whether everything will be ultimately in the best interest of the resulting child. The birth mother has the right to take all health-care decisions concerning the foetus, including any decision to abort. After the birth, the surrogate has 72 hours in which to decide whether to keep the child. Once parental rights are transferred to the intended parents, they have a duty to support the child. The child born under surrogacy is considered to be the legitimate child of the intended parent. Fees for surrogacy as negotiated between the parties are limited to medical expenses, lost wages, insurance, legal costs and home studies. New Hampshire

---

[157] See further Orentlicher, 'Societal Disregard for the Needs of the Infertile' Oxford Handbook of Reproductive Ethics (2016).

[158] See, eg, Ky Rev Stat § 199.590(4); NY Dom Rel Laws §§ 122 (with civil and criminal sanctions in § 123); Mich Comp Laws § 722.855 (with criminal sanctions in § 722.859).

[159] See, eg, Fla Stat § 63.213 (giving the surrogate up to 48 hours after birth to rescind her agreement); *RR v MH* 689 NE 2d 790 (Mass 1998) (also rejecting compensation beyond pregnancy-related expenses).

[160] See, eg, 750 Ill Comp. Stat § 47/15; *Culliton v Beth Israel Deaconess Medical Center* 756 NE 2d 1133 (Mass. 2001); *JF v DB* 879 N Ed 2d 740 (Ohio 2007). For a helpful discussion of the societal trend in support of gestational surrogacy and the important factors that have influenced the debates over traditional and gestational surrogacy, see Scott, 'Surrogacy and the Politics of Commodification,' Law & Contemporary Problems 72 (2009): 109–146.

[161] See, eg, Ariz Rev Stat § 25–218 (also prohibiting traditional surrogacy); DC Stat § 16–401–402 (also prohibiting traditional surrogacy).

[162] For useful source of information on legal provisions in all US states, see http://adoption.uslegal.com/surrogacy/.

[163] New Hampshire statute RSA §§ 168–B:1–B:32.

laws prohibit fees for arranging a surrogacy contract. There are also provisions addressing issues of the contract being breached or terminated, termination and transfer of parental rights to intended parents, and intestate and testate succession in the context of children born in surrogacy.

[7.98] California has the richest case law and history with surrogacy in the US, and is often thought of as the 'surrogacy capital' of the US with one of the most legally permissive approaches to surrogacy when compared to other states. Californian courts have upheld the validity of surrogacy contracts with the result that the commissioning couple is likely to get custody of the child in the event of a dispute other than in exceptional circumstances such as where this is not in the best interests of the child. Legislation was introduced in 2012[164] to codify existing California law that already recognised the validity of gestational surrogacy arrangements and the parental relationships that flow from these agreements.[165] The law requires a surrogate mother and the intended parent or parents to be represented by separate independent counsel prior to executing an assisted reproduction agreement for a gestational carrier. The law prohibits any administration of medicines or embryo transfer procedures until full execution and notarization of the agreement. The parent-child relationship can be established in the agreement before the child's birth under the statute. A copy of the agreement must be filed with the court, and the records are sealed to all but the intended parents, surrogate, attorneys, and the state Department of Social Services.

SURROGACY IN IRELAND

[7.99] There is no mention of surrogacy anywhere in enacted legislation in Ireland at present.[166] However, Irish couples are known to travel to other jurisdictions to avail of surrogacy arrangements,[167] and there have been a small number of familial surrogacy cases reported in medical journals.[168] The legal issues that arise here stem from the potential application of the adoption legislation, conflict of laws difficulties for couples who travel abroad for surrogacy and constitutional issues in the event of a custody dispute between the commissioning couple and a surrogate mother who changes her mind.

---

[164] AB 1217.

[165] Mohapatra, 'States of Confusion: Regulation of Surrogacy in the United States' in Rainhorn & Boudamoussi (eds) *Commodification of the Human Body: A Cannibal Market* Editions de la Fondation Maison des Sciences de l'Homme, Paris, 2015.

[166] A framework for surrogacy was comprehensively provided for in the original published draft of the General Scheme of the Children and Family Relationships Bill which, although imperfect, represented the first legislative attempt in Ireland to grapple with the difficult legal issues involved. However, this part of the Bill was deleted from the final version as enacted in 2015. The Department of Health is expected to publish the heads of a bill dealing with the regulation of assisted reproduction, including surrogacy, in 2016–17 http://health.gov.ie/blog/press-release/govt-to-legislate-for-assisted-human-reproduction-associated-research/.

[167] 'Surrogacy: the babies born into legal limbo'. Irish Times Nov.22, 2011.

[168] Sills et al, 'First Irish Pregnancies after IVF with Gestational Carrier' (2009) Irish Medical Journal Vol 102 (2).

[7.100] In order for an intending parent of a child born through surrogacy to gain legal recognition, there must be a parental link between the person and the child which fits into the legal definition of 'father' or 'mother' under Irish law.[169] The position for the male partner is more straightforward than for the female because the intending father often provides the genetic material used in the surrogacy arrangement and therefore he more easily fits the definition of legal father. As a result he can, amongst other things, seek and obtain a declaration of parentage under the Status of Children Act 1987, seek to be appointed guardian of the child under the Guardianship of Infants Act 1964, seek custody of the child under the Guardianship of Infants Act 1964, and obtain Irish citizenship for his child.

[7.101] Even where he is the biological father, it is important to note that, until recently, a man who was not married to the mother of the child did not have any automatic right to guardianship of his child. He could obtain guardianship either through agreement with the mother and a statutory declaration filed to that effect, or a court application establishing biological parentage. The court has discretion in this regard and will only make a guardianship order where this is regarded as being in the best interests of the child. This position has recently been changed by the Children and Family Relationships Act 2015 by virtue of which an unmarried biological father may obtain automatic guardianship in circumstances where he has lived with the child's mother for 12 consecutive months, including at least three months with the mother and the child following the child's birth. However this is unlikely to apply in a surrogacy arrangement and therefore the biological father's guardianship of the child will depend on either the surrogate mother's consent or a court order appointing him as guardian if this is consistent with the best interests of the child. If the sperm used in the arrangement is that of a donor, no legal paternity arises for the intending father and he cannot avail of any of the above provisions.

[7.102] In the case of the intending mother in gestational surrogacy, she may or may not be the provider of the genetic material. To a large extent this is, however, irrelevant as the legal definition of mother in Irish law is the woman who gives birth to the child, ie the surrogate.[170] This means that the intending mother cannot be regarded as the legal mother and cannot seek any legal remedies despite the fact that she will be a joint carer of the child in circumstances where her husband has been granted guardianship of the child as biological father. This could cause serious difficulties in the event of death of the father or if the couple were to divorce, as the intending mother would have no legal relationship with the child she is raising. This is an issue which is of serious concern to couples who seek gestational surrogacy and also has repercussions in other areas such as birth certification, passport applications, medical decision-making, and inheritance rights.

[7.103] One potential mechanism by which the mother could seek legal recognition of her relationship with the child is through adoption. The Adoption Authority was

---

[169] The material in this section has been adapted from Madden, 'Gestational surrogacy in the Republic of Ireland' in Sills (ed) *Handbook of Gestational Surrogacy: International Clinical Practice & Policy Issues* (Cambridge University Press, 2016).

[170] *MR and DR (suing by their father and next friend OR) and CR and An t-Ard -Chlaratheoir, Ireland and the Attorney General & another* [2014] IESC 60 (2014).

established under the Adoption Act 2010 to improve standards in both domestic and Inter-country adoption and does not purport to deal directly with surrogacy. However, some of the legislative provisions pertaining to adoption may impact upon surrogacy in situations where the commissioning couple choose to adopt the child born through a surrogacy arrangement in order to establish a legal relationship with it. These provisions relate primarily to the issue of payment and private placement of a child, both of which are prohibited or restricted by the legislation. Section 125 of the 2010 Act states that a child may not be given to a person for adoption unless the adoptive parent is a parent, relative or spouse of a parent of the child. All other adoptions must go through an accredited adoption society or the Health Service Executive and be approved by the Adoption Authority. Therefore if the commissioning father is biologically related to the child and can establish parental rights through guardianship, then it is possible that he and his wife may apply for an adoption. However, if the genetic link with the child is through the intending mother, this does not appear possible as she will not be regarded as the legal parent.

[7.104] Section 145 of the 2010 Act provides that it is a criminal offence to give or receive any payment or other reward in consideration of the adoption of a child. This does not apply to accredited bodies' reasonable costs and expenses related to their functions, including reasonable fees paid as remuneration for professional services. This means that a commissioning couple cannot agree to give, and a surrogate mother cannot receive, any payment in consideration of the making of arrangements to have the child adopted by the couple, such as the surrogate mother signing the necessary consents for the adoption. Whether the Adoption Authority would consider medical expenses and reimbursement of other costs to the surrogate mother as a prohibited 'payment or other reward' is not clear as it is not defined in the Act and has not been the subject of any reported judicial interpretation to date.

[7.105] In the event that the surrogate mother changes her mind about relinquishment of the child and refuses to sign the necessary consents for adoption, an adoption application would not be likely to succeed, even where the intending parents are the full genetic parents of the child. The rights of an unmarried mother in relation to her child, including the right to custody of the child, have been held to be personal rights protected by art 40.3 of the Irish Constitution 1937. These rights can be transferred (by adoption), or lost if she abdicates her rights and duties, but otherwise the mother would have very strong constitutional rights to retain custody of the child as against the commissioning couple. This is a considerable source of worry to couples who seek gestational surrogacy arrangements in Ireland as the surrogate mother would be regarded as the legal mother, and in the event of a dispute, would therefore be likely to retain custody of the child.

[7.106] The only surrogacy case to come before the Irish courts to date is *MR and DR (suing by their father and next friend OR) and CR and An t-Ard -Chlaratheoir, Ireland and the Attorney General & another*.[171] In this case a married woman and her husband entered into an altruistic surrogacy arrangement with the woman's sister who agreed to act as the gestational surrogate. The genetic material was provided by the couple. Twins

---

[171] *MR and DR (suing by their father and next friend OR) and CR and An t-Ard -Chlaratheoir, Ireland and the Attorney General & another.* [2014] IESC 60.

were born and there was no dispute between any of the parties involved that the twins would be raised by the genetic parents. The legal issues which arose in this case involved the registration of the birth of the children as the children of the surrogate mother rather than the genetic mother. The court had to consider for the first time the question of who is the legal mother in Irish law in circumstances of surrogacy.

[7.107] The State argued that the gestational mother must be regarded as the legal mother on the basis of the Latin maxim '*mater simper certa est*' (motherhood is always certain). It was argued that this maxim expressed an irrebuttable presumption as to who the mother of a child must be, based on gestation and birth. On the other hand the applicants argued that this maxim and maternal certainty was no longer clearly applicable in the post-IVF era and that the law must take account of developments in reproductive medicine. It was argued that the birth certification process should recognise that the child was genetically that of the commissioning couple, who remained the intended parents, and that the mother-to-child blood-link was a sacred 'primordial constitutional principle'. In the High Court Abbott J found in favour of the applicants and declared the genetic, intended mother to be the legal mother on the basis that the old maxim no longer applied.[172] Abbott J also drew a comparison between the basis upon which legal paternity was recognised ie the genetic link, and stated that:

> While the input of the gestational mother is to be respected, the predominant determinism of the genetic material in the cells of the foetus permits a fair comparison with the law and standards for the determination of paternity. It would be invidious, irrational and unfair to do otherwise...To achieve fairness and constitutional and natural justice for both the paternal and maternal genetic parents, the feasible inquiry in relation to maternity ought to be made on a genetic basis and, on being proven, the genetic mother should be registered as the mother.

[7.108] Although courts must always prioritise the best interests of the child affected by any dispute, the learned judge stated that in most cases, if not all, the interests of the child 'would be best served by an inquiry of the genetic interest.' The case raised very interesting questions about the role of genetics in situations where the eggs and/or sperm were donated by anonymous donors, but neither this issue nor the distinction between altruistic and commercial surrogacy were discussed in the judgment.

[7.109] The decision was appealed by the State to the Supreme Court which, by majority, overturned the findings of the High Court and held that the gestational mother should be regarded as the legal mother unless and until the legislature provided otherwise. The court interpreted the meaning of 'mother' for birth registration purposes as the birth mother and any change in this position was a matter for the legislature not the courts. Denham CJ acknowledged that the Constitution does not define the word 'mother' and held that 'there does not appear to be any authority to suggest that it [the principle of *mater simper certa est*] is either an irrebuttable presumption or that it is enshrined as a maxim of 'Irish public law'.' However, that did not necessarily determine the issue. Denham J went on to recognise that any law on surrogacy 'affects the status and rights of persons, especially those of the children; it creates complex relationships,

---

[172] *MR and DR (suing by their father and next friend OR) and CR and An t-Ard -Chlaratheoir, Ireland and the Attorney General & another* [2013] IEHC 91.

and has a deep social content. It is, thus, quintessentially a matter for the Oireachtas.'[173] Under the current legislative framework she concluded that it is not possible to address issues arising on surrogacy, including the issue of who is the mother for the purpose of the registration of the birth. She upheld the appeal and quashed the order of the High Court.

[7.110] Hardiman J said the question of what is motherhood 'cannot be answered by any technical legal exegesis or even by any purely logical process. This is because, at bottom, the question raised is not a legal question or a purely logical question. It is a question of values and attitudes so deep that it is an understatement to call it a matter of policy.' The learned judge expressed concern that if the High Court judgment in favour of the genetic mother were to stand, the legislature's hands might be tied in respect of any attempts to legislate in relation to the position of a woman who gave birth to a child using donated eggs, as it would be the donor and not the birth mother who would be determined to be the legal mother.[174]

[7.111] O'Donnell J said this was not an issue of validity or enforceability of surrogacy contracts. 'Nor does it involve any dispute between a commissioning parent and a surrogate mother and equally clearly it does not involve the question of the constitutional validity of any legislation regulating or even prohibiting surrogacy agreements.'[175] The learned judge outlined in some detail the range of difficult questions that arise in relation to surrogacy and strongly lamented the lack of legislation in the area. He said this case was a simple question of statutory interpretation: what does the 2004 Act mean when it refers to 'mother'? In particular, does it mean in this case the woman whose egg is fertilised and which develops through pregnancy into the baby who is born, or does it mean the woman who gives birth to the baby, or perhaps to both?

> This is not an easy question but it is useful to identify just what is not involved. This is not a question of whether a genetic or a gestational mother provides more genetic material to a child. Nor does it involve a question of policy as to who *should* be registered as a mother where the gestational and genetic mothers are not the same person, now that we know for the first time in human history that it is possible to separate the functions of reproduction and birth into at least two if not more parts which can be carried out by at least two, if not more, people.[176]

[7.112] O'Donnell J concluded that the purpose of the Civil Registration Act 2004 (and the Births and Deaths Registration Act (Ireland) 1880) is plain. 'It is to establish and maintain a system of registration. That registration in this case is of the fact of birth. The Act operates by reference to the date of birth and requires compliance within a fixed period thereafter. While a birth certificate has subsequent importance as evidence, its original and basic function is demographic.

> From the function it was intended to fulfil and the circumstances in which it operated, it seems clear that under the Act, the person to be registered on the birth certificate as mother under both the 1880 Act and the 2004 Act is unsurprisingly, the person giving

---

[173] Denham CJ, para 113.
[174] Hardiman J, para 18–19.
[175] O'Donnell J, para 3.
[176] O'Donnell J, para 27–28.

birth. Science may have undermined or at least qualified the assumptions upon which the Act was based, but that does not alter the interpretation of the Act.[177]

[7.113] In conclusion O'Donnell J also recognised the human cost of entering into surrogacy arrangements in the absence of clear legislative guidance. He held that the registration system, in recording the fact of birth, was permissible but that there were serious constitutional issues arising if this position were maintained as an absolute principle for all purposes.

> From a human point of view it is completely wrong that a system, having failed to regulate in any way the process of assisted reproduction, and which accordingly permits children to be born, nevertheless fails to provide any system which acknowledges the existence of a genetic mother not merely for the purpose of registration, but also in the realities of life including not just important financial issues such as inheritance and taxation, but also the many important details of family and personal life which the Constitution recognises as vital to the human person.

[7.114] An interesting dissenting judgment was written by Clarke J who was not satisfied that the common law in Ireland defined mother in a way which confined that term to birth mother to the exclusion of genetic mother.[178] He said the common law regarded both the genetic mother and the birth mother as being the mother of a child for the simple reason that there was, in practical reality, no distinction between them. He was not satisfied that the language of either the Status of Children Act 1987 or the 2004 Civil Registration Act was sufficiently clear to alter that pre-existing position.[179] He stated that both the genetic and gestational mothers had characteristics of mothers as that term is currently used. He said that 'there may well be cases where the merits would overwhelmingly favour declaring either a birth mother or a genetic mother as being properly regarded as the mother to the exclusion of the other. But there is just no legal framework in which such a decision can properly be taken which differentiates between one case and another. In the absence of legislation the law must be the same in all cases.' He concluded:

> There is no doubt that the idea that two persons may, in different ways, be regarded as the mother of a child is counter-intuitive. But so also is not regarding the person who gives birth to a child as being its mother, and, equally in not so regarding the person who has given the female half of the genetic material which underlies such a child's makeup. Advances in reproductive science have led to a situation where, in the absence of legislation, whatever the law determines as the meaning of mother will, to an extent, be counter-intuitive in some cases. It may well be that the proper answer to the question as to who should be recognised as a mother in the often complex situations which can arise in this field is 'it depends'.[180]

Therefore he concluded that his preference would have been for the Court to make a declaration to the effect that the genetic mother is the mother of the twins without prejudice to the status of the birth mother and that the Registrar should be ordered to

---

[177] O'Donnell J, para 32.
[178] Clarke J, para 5.13.
[179] Clarke J, para 7.3.
[180] Clarke J, para 8.8.

take whatever steps might be necessary to ensure that the registration of the birth of the twins reflects the status of the genetic mother thus declared.

[7.115] All of the Supreme Court judges made strong statements in this case regarding the obligation on the legislature to urgently deal with the issues raised by this case and assisted reproduction generally and some referred to the fact that it was disturbing that many years after the report of the Commission on Assisted Human Reproduction, the government still had not enacted legislation in this area. Murray J said 'How these complex issues concerning such rights, status and welfare can be addressed, taking account of competing, or even conflicting, values, is quintessentially a matter for the legislature. The courts do not, in my view, have at their disposal objective criteria to lay down some golden rule or series of principles which would govern such matters.' Hardiman J stated 'I wish to join with my colleagues in pointing out the urgency of the need for legislation on this topic. There is at present a serious disconnect between what developments in science and medicine have rendered possible on the one hand, and the state of the law on the other. It is as if Road Traffic law had failed to reflect the advent of the motor car.'

[7.116] The Report of the Commission on Assisted Reproduction which was published in 2005 on possible approaches to the regulation of all aspects of assisted human reproduction and the social, ethical and legal factors to be taken into account in determining public policy in this area recommended that a new Act should be passed to establish a regulatory body to regulate AHR services in Ireland.[181] The majority of the Commission concluded that surrogacy should be permitted subject to regulation.[182] It also recommended that the proposed regulatory body could ensure that appropriate screening procedures should be employed to ensure the suitability of surrogate mothers and commissioning parents. Counselling as well as medical, legal and psychological supports could be provided prior to conception of the child in order to ensure voluntary and informed consent from all parties and to guard against any exploitation. Reviews of procedures and fees could be conducted periodically by professionals and the optimum conditions for a safe and successful outcome ensured as far as possible. The Commission also recommended that surrogate mothers should be entitled to receive reimbursement of pregnancy-related expenses, and that surrogacy-born children should be able to access the identity of the surrogate mother. In relation to parentage the Commission recommended that the child born through surrogacy should be presumed to be the child of the commissioning couple. The Commission came to this conclusion because the word 'presumed' allows some flexibility in relation to the legal parentage of the child in the case of some fundamental change in the circumstances under which the surrogate mother consented to the arrangement. [183]

---

[181] Report of the Commission on Assisted Human Reproduction (2005) available at www.health.gov.ie.

[182] Report of the Commission on Assisted Human Reproduction (2005) available at www.health.gov.ie, chapter 7.

[183] Report of the Commission on Assisted Human Reproduction (2005) page 53. The Commission acknowledged that implementation of some of these recommendations may require amendment of the Constitution. See also dissent to these recommendations by O'Rourke at pages 76–77 of the Report.

INTERNATIONAL SURROGACY ARRANGEMENTS

[7.117] The global industry of commercial surrogacy has now overtaken inter-country adoption and is estimated to be worth approximately $6 billion annually.[184] The phenomenon of couples or individuals travelling to other jurisdictions to avail of reproductive services is often known as fertility tourism or even circumvention tourism as it is designed to avoid restrictive laws in the country of residence of potential parents.[185] Commercial surrogacy arrangements have been entered into in other jurisdictions such as India,[186] Thailand, Ukraine, Russia, Mexico, Nepal, Poland, Georgia and the United States, by couples who wish to be parents and for whom other options are not available. In general, couples go to these specific countries in order to avail of birth certification processes in those countries which state that the intended parents are the legal parents of the child, thus making them very attractive destinations for potential parents. However, the difficulty is that such birth certificates do not necessarily determine parentage under the law of the country of residence of the intending parents and consequent conflict of laws difficulties may arise in trying to bring the child into the country and establish legal parentage.

[7.118] This is illustrated by cases before the European Court of Human Rights in *Mennesson v France*[187] and *Labassee v France*[188] which concerned the French refusal to grant legal recognition in France to parent-child relationships that had been legally established in the United States between children born as a result of surrogacy treatment and the couples on whose request the treatment was performed. The European Court of Human Rights held that there had been a violation of the European Convention on Human Rights, in particular the children's right to respect to private life, but no violation of the right of the children or intended parents to respect of family life. The Court stressed that there was a wide margin of appreciation for States in making decisions in relation to surrogacy in view of the difficult ethical issues involved and the lack of consensus on these matters in Europe. Nevertheless, that margin of appreciation was narrow when it came to parentage, which involved a key aspect of individuals' identity. The Court also had to ascertain whether a fair balance had been struck between the interests of the State and those of the individuals involved, bearing in mind the fundamental principle that the best interest of the child must prevail.

[7.119] The Court said that the parents' family life had been affected by the French legal position on surrogacy but the obstacles they had faced had not been insurmountable. However, with regard to the children's right to respect for their private life, the Court noted that they were in a state of legal uncertainty as French authorities had denied them

---

[184] Deonandan, 'Recent trends in reproductive tourism and international surrogacy: ethical considerations and challenges for policy'. Risk Management and Healthcare Policy 2015:8 111–119.

[185] For interesting analysis of interviews with couples who chose to undertake international surrogacy, see Riggs, Narratives of Choice amongst white Australians who undertake Surrogacy Arrangements in India J Med Humanit DOI 10.1007/s10912-015-9330-z.

[186] In India surrogacy is estimated to be worth approximately $400 million annually, generated from the country's approximately 3,000 specialty clinics.

[187] *Mennesson v France* E Ct HR Appl No 65192/11.

[188] *Labassee v France* E Ct HR Appl No 65941/11.

the status of the legal children of their parents. This undermined the children's identity within French society as well as causing worrying uncertainty regarding their nationality. Further, their inheritance rights were less favourable than legally recognised children. This was particularly relevant because the children were biologically related to the male applicant in each case. The Court held:

> Given the importance of biological parentage as a component of each individual's identity, it could not be said to be in the best interests of the child to deprive him or her of a legal tie of this nature when the biological reality of that tie was established and the child and the parent concerned sought its full recognition.

Consequently, in preventing the recognition of the children's legal relationship with their biological father, the French State had overstepped the permissible margin of appreciation. The Court held that the children's right to respect for their private life had been infringed, in breach of art 8.

[7.120] The European Court of Human Rights again considered the issue of international surrogacy arrangements in *D and Others v Belgium*[189] in which a married couple, Mr D and Ms R, were Belgian nationals who travelled to Ukraine for a surrogacy arrangement. After the child was born they obtained a Ukrainian birth certificate for the child which recorded Mr D as the father and Ms R as the child's mother. They applied to the Belgian embassy for a passport for the child but this was refused on the basis that they were unable to produce certain documents proving the existence of their family relationship with the child. They were forced to return to Belgium without the child as their residence permit in Ukraine expired. A nanny looked after the child in their absence and they returned to Ukraine as frequently as possible. They subsequently produced additional documentation and obtained travel documentation for the child who was then able to return with them to Belgium.

[7.121] The Court held that the separation of the child from its parents for four and a half months was an interference in the applicants' right to respect for their family life, however this was not an unreasonably long period and the couple ought reasonably to have foreseen this problem as they had been advised by both a Belgian and Ukrainian lawyer. The Court again stressed that States have a relatively wide margin of appreciation in this area and held that in this case the Belgian State had acted within the limits of that by following a procedure, known to the applicants, to ensure that certain legal checks would be carried out to establish the existence of a legal relationship with the child.

[7.122] In a further surrogacy case heard by the European Court of Human Rights, *Paradiso and Campanelli v Italy*,[190] the Court held that public policy considerations could not take precedence over the best interests of the child. This case was unusual in that there was no biological link between the child and the intended parents. The child had been removed from their custody on grounds that the birth certificate obtained in Russia, where the child was born through surrogacy, had misrepresented the child's parentage by referring to the applicants as the child's parents. The Court held that the removal of the child was a justified interference with the applicants' private life in

---

[189] *D and Others v Belgium* E Ct HR Appl No 29176/13.
[190] *Paradiso and Campanelli v Italy* E Ct HR Appl No 25358/12.

accordance with law as the child had been removed to put an end to an unlawful situation. However, the State should also have taken into consideration the best interests of the child, irrespective of the parental relationship, genetic or otherwise. The threshold for removal of a child from a family setting was a very high one which, the Court found, had not been met in this case. Thus, the authorities had failed to strike a fair balance between the interests at stake in this case, in violation of art 8. However, although there had been a violation, the Court did not order the return of the child who had by that time developed emotional ties with the foster family with which he had been living since his removal from the applicants.

[7.123] These cases clearly illustrate some of the risks undertaken by couples seeking surrogacy arrangements in countries which appear to be surrogacy-friendly in circumstances where their own country of residence does not facilitate or recognise such arrangements. Indeed fertility, or more specifically surrogacy, tourism poses risks to all parties involved as well as the states in which the services are provided and the country of residence of the parties themselves. The risks experienced by the country of origin of the fertility tourist are mainly of a legal or economic nature. In addition, to the extent that regulatory issues reflect societal values, elements of the source country's values system may also be affected.

> Economically, one of the common arguments against any kind of medical tourism is that the traveller is spending his or her money in a foreign country rather than in their home jurisdiction. Their expenditure includes both payment for medical treatments and payment for services associated with travel. This is not an inconsequential amount, given the size and value of the industry, representing a loss of income opportunity for the source country. Legally, if travellers are crossing borders to avoid restrictions in the source country, then that country's ability and willingness to enforce its restrictions comes into question.[191]

[7.124] The risks to the country where the service is provided are also legal, financial and values-based. For countries such as India,[192] the financial benefits are substantial but although the medical education, expertise and resources have been paid for by Indian taxpayers, it is the surrogacy tourists who derive most benefit. As a result of the financial incentives involved, it is possible that a sufficiently powerful industry may influence national laws to reflect its needs instead of the values of the citizens. From a cultural perspective the rapid growth of the industry and its globalized nature necessarily introduce practices and values from different countries into a milieu that may be culturally unprepared for such rapid change.[193]

---

[191] Deonandan, 'Recent trends in reproductive tourism and international surrogacy: ethical considerations and challenges for policy'. Risk Management and Healthcare Policy 2015:8 111–119 at 113.

[192] In 2015 the Indian government published a draft Assisted Reproductive Technology (Regulation) Bill designed to curb surrogacy tourism by restricting surrogacy to individuals with a link to India (ie overseas citizens of India, people of Indian origin, non-resident Indians and foreigners married to an Indian citizen). The Bill has not been enacted at the time of writing.

[193] Deonandan, 'Recent trends in reproductive tourism and international surrogacy: ethical considerations and challenges for policy'. Risk Management and Healthcare Policy 2015:8 111–119 at 113–114.

[7.125] Those who travel to other countries to avail of surrogacy and the surrogate mothers are also at risk, as demonstrated by the European Court of Human Rights cases discussed above.

> People traveling internationally and spending large amounts of money to create their families are by their very nature vulnerable. They have typically struggled with biological infertility (or in the case of same-sex couples, social infertility) for many years, and have chosen the international surrogacy route after much travail. The threat is high for unsupported promises, by disreputable clinics and brokers, of high success rates, seamless legal procedures, uncomplicated surrogacy negotiations, and comfortable travel experiences.[194]

Risks to the surrogates can be of a social, legal, physical, or emotional type, and all can be placed somewhere on the continuum between respect for autonomy and exploitation of that autonomy. While the biological risks to surrogates are those shared by all pregnant women, in the case of assisted reproduction procedures, there are heightened risks for multiple pregnancies, which are problematic for both the surrogate and foetuses. The emotional risk faced by all surrogates is the potential emotional attachment to a child that she must give away immediately after delivery. Additionally, economically poor surrogates in countries like India face particular social risks, including potential disapproval from their communities and rejection by their husbands.[195]

[7.126] Studies in India show that the typical surrogate is poor, lives in a rural area, is undereducated, married young, and lives in an extended family that includes her in-laws.[196] The language and ideals of autonomy may not be as relevant to such a woman as it may be for a white, middle class woman that liberal feminism often speaks for.[197] Such a woman may think of herself as part of a larger family rather than an individual. It is argued that being a surrogate in India or similarly situated countries should be considered a form of labour or work, rather than an autonomous choice. Such work should therefore be compared to the other job prospects women who become surrogates actually have.[198]

[7.127] For those who travel to other countries to avail of surrogacy, conflict of laws problems may ensue when they try to bring the child back into their country of residence as demonstrated by the *Mennesson* and *Labassee* cases above.[199] Although the legal position in the country where the child was born may recognise the commissioning

---

[194] Deonandan, 'Recent trends in reproductive tourism and international surrogacy: ethical considerations and challenges for policy'. Risk Management and Healthcare Policy 2015:8 111–119.

[195] For discussion of the extent to which surrogacy in India is exploitative see Kirby, 'Transnational Gestational Surrogacy: Does It Have to Be Exploitative?' Am. J of Bioethics 14(5) 24–32 (2014).

[196] Amrita Pande, 'Commercial Surrogacy in India: Manufacturing a Perfect Mother-Worker', 35 J of Women in Culture and Society 969, 974 (2010).

[197] Cyra Akila Choudhury, Exporting Subjects: Globalizing Family Law Progress Through International Human Rights, 32 Mich J Int'l L 259 (2011).

[198] Quoted by Mohapatra, 'Achieving Reproductive Justice In The International Surrogacy Market' (2012) 21 Annals Health L 191.

[199] Para **[7.118]**.

couple as the legal parents, when registering a child's birth the country of residence usually applies its own internal law in relation to who the legal parents are and may therefore take the opposite view and regard the surrogate mother (and her husband if she is married) as the legal parents. Authenticity of foreign birth certificates and proof of family relationships are also very important for birth registration, as demonstrated by *D v Belgium*,[200] and sometimes a further legal procedure is required to legally recognise documents from other states. However, despite these difficulties, national reports on surrogacy show that couples (and individuals) are willing to go to great lengths to circumvent the law and find alternative ways to bring about their intended parenthood.[201] 'Resort to these various, and imperfect, mechanisms is particularly problematic when the child has subsequently to cross national borders.'[202]

[7.128] In recent years there have been numerous calls for an international effort to reach consensus on a convention on surrogacy to deal with these difficult jurisdictional differences and problems.[203] This includes not only academic commentators but also judges who have been called upon to adjudicate in such cases. 'There is, in my view, a compelling need for a uniform system of regulation to be created by an international instrument in order to make available an appropriate structure in respect of what can only be described as the surrogacy market.'[204] The Report from the Hague Conference on Private International Law (2014)[205] which has focused on surrogacy in recent years, demonstrates huge diversity of regulatory approaches in this area and issues relating to international surrogacy were discussed at the UN Committee on the Rights of the Child in two different State reporting procedures in 2014, demonstrating the significant concern in relation to the issue worldwide.[206]

[7.129] In 2015, the Council on General Affairs and Policy of the Hague Conference decided that an Experts' Group should be convened to explore the feasibility of advancing work in this area. In 2016 this Group recognised that the absence of uniform private international law rules or approaches with respect to the establishment and

---

[200] Para **[7.120]**.

[201] For comprehensive description of the conflict of laws problem, see Trimmings and Beaumont (eds), *International Surrogacy Arrangements: Legal Regulation at the International Level* (Hart Publishing, 2013). See also Brunet *et al*, *A Comparative Study on the Regime of Surrogacy in EU Member States* (European Union, 2013), www.europarl.europa.eu/studies.

[202] Fenton-Glynn, 'Human Rights And Private International Law: Regulating International Surrogacy' Vol 10 No 1 Journal of Private International Law 157.

[203] Evidenced by *Re X and Y (Foreign Surrogacy)* [2009] 1 FLR 733, discussed at para **[7.78]**.

[204] Per Moylan J in *Re D (A Child)* [2014] EWHC 2121.

[205] https://www.hcch.net/en/projects/legislative-projects/parentage-surrogacy.

[206] See also House of Representatives Standing Committee on Social Policy and Legal Affairs, Parliament of the Commonwealth of Australia, *Inquiry into the regulatory and legislative aspects of international and domestic surrogacy arrangements* (April 2016) para 1.69 where the Committee noted that 'a large proportion of the Australians who have a child through surrogacy do so by entering into offshore commercial surrogacy arrangements.' The Committee found that extra-territorial offences in these States have not deterred intended parents from accessing commercial surrogacy services, and no one has ever been prosecuted under those laws.

contestation of parentage can lead to conflicting legal statuses across borders and can create significant problems for children and families, eg, uncertain paternity or maternity, limping parental statuses, uncertain identity of the child, immigration problems, uncertain nationality or statelessness of the child, abandonment including the lack of maintenance. The Group recognised that common solutions are needed to address these problems[207] but determined that, owing to the complexity of the subject and the diversity of approaches by States to these matters, definitive conclusions could not be reached at this time as to the feasibility of a possible work product in this area and its type or scope. Work will continue in this area to try to find an international solution.

[7.130] Trimmings and Beaumont also carried out a comprehensive analysis of the legal provisions in relation to surrogacy in 24 countries. They concluded that traditional rules on jurisdiction and applicable law are inefficient when responding to the reality of international surrogacy arrangements, leading to 'considerable legal uncertainty for intended parents, and to some children falling through the gaps between incompatible regimes'.[208] They are of the view that attempts to impose a complete prohibition on cross-border surrogacy arrangements are doomed to failure,[209] and, as a result, see international regulation as the lesser of two evils to avoid black market practices and exploitation. They suggest a convention that would 'harmonise private international law in this area to ensure the allocation of responsibility regarding various components concerning the surrogacy, and the mutual recognition of arrangements made under this instrument.'[210]

[7.131] Pending the introduction of legislation in Ireland to deal with domestic and international surrogacy, guidelines from the Department of Justice[211] provide that an Irish passport may be obtained if a child is born abroad to an Irish parent. They also state that the woman who gives birth is the legal mother even if she does not have a genetic link to the child. Therefore either the genetic father or the surrogate mother must be Irish in order to apply for a passport, most usually this will be the commissioning father. All guardians of the child must give their consent to the issuing of the passport, or have their consent dispensed with by an Irish court. The authorities in Ireland may grant Emergency Travel Certificates (ETC) where the child is an Irish citizen, the application is made by a parent or guardian of the child, consent has been given by all

---

[207] Report of the February 2016 Meeting of the Experts' Group on Parentage/Surrogacy www.hcch.net/en/projects/legislative-projects/parentage-surrogacy.

[208] Fenton-Glynn, 'Human Rights And Private International Law: Regulating International Surrogacy' Vol 10 No 1 Journal of Private International Law 157 at 160.

[209] It may be argued that the pragmatic approach which would see prohibition as futile in the face of global demand and ease of travel, fails to acknowledge the important communicative, expressive and anthropological meaning and function of national laws. See Van Beers, 'Is Europe 'giving in to baby markets?' Reproductive tourism in Europe and the gradual erosion of existing legal limits to reproductive markets.' Med L Rev Vol 23, No 1 pp 103–134.

[210] Fenton-Glynn 'Human Rights And Private International Law: Regulating International Surrogacy' Vol 10 No 1 Journal of Private International Law 157 at 160–161.

[211] Citizenship, Parentage, Guardianship And Travel Document Issues In Relation To Children Born As A Result Of Surrogacy Arrangements Entered Into Outside The State available at www.justice.ie.

guardians of the child, and the issuing of an ETC is in the best interests of the child. The adults caring for the child will have to undertake to notify local health officials of the child's presence within two days of their arrival in the State and the genetic father will have to undertake that he will apply to the Court for a declaration of parentage and guardianship in relation to the child within ten working days.

Chapter 8

Genetics

INTRODUCTION

[8.01] The last 60 years have seen unprecedented breakthroughs in the biological sciences with the development of the so-called 'new genetics' which has increased capacity to test for genetic diseases and to develop cures as well as advancing knowledge about the workings of the human body. However, although there is much anticipation and optimism for the future potential application of this knowledge, there is also concurrent unease and fear about the dangers of unregulated developments leading to eugenic tendencies slipping into policy-making, and the manipulation of human genes for commercial purposes. Genetics is 'a science that elicits vastly different reactions: at one pole we find celebration and boundless optimism; at the other, we have profound suspicion and dire prediction; and, between these extremes, there is a broad spectrum of opinion in which a positive view of genetics is qualified by expressions of caution and concern.'[1]

[8.02] In 1953 Crick and Watson published an explanation of the spiral structure of DNA and the way in which the genes operated through coded messages and sequences of letters.[2] A gene may be defined as the fundamental physical and functional unit of heredity. It is an ordered sequence of nucleotides located in a particular position on a particular chromosome that encodes a specific functional product, a protein.[3] Proteins are therefore made according to a specific 'recipe' set out in that coded message. Gene expression is the process by which the gene's coded information is converted into the structures present and operating in the cell. The structure of DNA (deoxyribonucleic acid) consists of an estimated three billion pairs of nucleotides, called base pairs, fitted together like steps of a twisting ladder at regular intervals, held together by sugar molecules and phosphates. DNA has been described as 'the true chemical of life ... the essential component from which our genes are made. In it is encoded the genetic language that controls our destinies.'[4] Numerous breakthroughs in biological techniques followed Crick and Watson's elucidation of DNA, and this explanation now forms the

---

1   Brownsword, Cornish and Llewelyn, 'Human Genetics and the Law: Regulating a Revolution' (1998) 61(5) Mod. L Rev 593.

2   The story of the discovery of DNA is told in the autobiography of James D Watson, *The Double Helix* (New York: Atheneum, 1968). See also Judson, *The Eighth Day of Creation* (Simon & Schuster, 1979).

3   *A Primer on Molecular Genetics* (1992) US Dept of Energy, Office of Energy Research, Office of Health and Environmental Research, Washington, 36.

4   Bodmer and McKie, *The Book of Man: The Quest to Discover Our Genetic Heritage* (Little Brown and Company, 1994) p 10.

central thesis of molecular biology. In the 1970s, the genetic basis of some genetic conditions was acknowledged and the revolution began:

> We are witnessing a revolution brought about by scientific and technological advances, one in which change occurs at an accelerated pace. By 1945 we had the ability to destroy life on a large scale. By 2045, only a hundred years later, we ought to be able to create life from scratch, both in real space and in cyberspace.[5]

[8.03] In 1990 it was decided to sequence the entire human genome, which is the complete set of genes and chromosomes of the human organism. The intention was to construct a high-resolution genetic, physical and transcript map of the human, with ultimately, a complete sequence. The Human Genome Project, which was completed in 2003, was the largest research project ever undertaken with the intention of analysing the structure of human DNA and determining the location of the estimated 25,000 human genes.[6] It was heralded as having three main advantages, namely improved diagnostics, new approaches to the prevention of disease and gene replacement therapy. As the President's Council on Bioethics in the United States put it at that time:

> By all accounts we have entered upon a golden age for biology, medicine and biotechnology. With the completion of [the DNA sequencing phase of] the Human Genome Project and the emergence of stem cell research, we can look forward to major insights into human development, normal and abnormal, as well as novel and more precisely selected treatments for human disease...In myriad ways, the discoveries of biologists and the inventions of biotechnologists are steadily increasing our power ever more precisely to intervene into the workings of our bodies and minds and to alter them by rational design.[7]

[8.04] Gene defects are estimated to underlie approximately 4,000 different diseases, and this estimation does not include polygenic diseases where there is interaction between certain genes and the environment.[8] In reality very few diseases are unifactorial and 'the great majority of genetic disorders result from multifactorial traits which are believed to be the result not only of the effects of one or several genes but also of a combination of genetic and environmental factors.[9] Tests are already available for many genetic diseases, such as cystic fibrosis, which enables carriers to be identified and more accurate genetic counselling to be offered. Individuals who may be susceptible to diseases such as schizophrenia, where many genes interact with environmental factors, may be targeted with preventative regimes. Personalised medication may in the future be developed according to the specific genetic profiles of individual patients. This is the objective of pharmacogenetics which aims at understanding how genetic variation contributes to variations in response to medicines. The variation that exists in all genes

---

[5]   Baldi, *The Shattered Self: The End of Natural Evolution* (MIT Press, 2002) at 163.

[6]   The new genetics has led to a 1,000-fold increase in capacity to read a DNA sequence and a 10,000-fold reduction in the cost of DNA sequencing. House of Lords Science and Technology Committee, *Human Genetics: The Science and its Consequences* (July 1995) para 71.

[7]   President's Council on Bioethics, *Beyond Therapy*, (2003) at 5–6, quoted by Brownsword in 'Human Dignity, Ethical Pluralism, and the Regulation of Modern Biotechnologies', Murphy (ed) *New Technologies and Human Rights* (OUP, 2009) 19–85 at 19.

[8]   Wexler, 'Disease Gene Identification: Ethical Considerations' (October 15 1991) Hospital Practice 145.

[9]   Laurie, Harmon and Porter, *Law and Medical Ethics,* (10th edn, OUP, 2016) para 7.07.

causes different people to express different forms of proteins, including those that metabolise drugs. This can lead to different responses to those drugs. Genetic databases which bring together several streams of data about individuals – molecular genetic data, standardised clinical data, data on health, lifestyle and environment and so on – will enable correlations to be made which will guide mechanistic, pharmaceutical and other investigations. Measuring the genetic differences in this way will help predict the variation in response to the medicine and enable doctors to identify patients with a greater chance of effective response and reduced risk of adverse reactions.[10] It is anticipated that drug development will also become faster and more efficient.

[8.05] If the predictions prove to be correct, the new genetics could represent a major advance in general health.[11] Thus, embracing genomic medicine could be legitimately seen as an economic necessity in order to fast-track new forms of preventative medicine for both poor and rich countries. The development of effective vaccines at low cost, based on DNA or related genomic research, could offer assistance to poor countries which carry huge burdens of infectious disease.[12] However, some geneticists advise against being seduced by 'genohype' and are concerned that the clinical benefits that will accrue from the application of genetics for therapeutic purposes have been exaggerated. For example, they argue that it will be almost impossible to find the genes involved in polygenic forms of common diseases where the clinical outcome is determined by complex gene, environmental and behavioural interaction, and similarly it will be difficult to develop useful and reliable predictive tests for them.[13]

[8.06] The medical, as opposed to the scientific, view of the value of the new genetics is also noteworthy. Many medical practitioners feel that their knowledge of genetics is lacking and that genetic advances will have little effect on the management of common diseases. However, the likely increases in availability of DNA-based tests and demand by patients for genetic information and advice mean that general practitioners will need to become genetically literate[14] as they have an important role in recognising the features of common genetic conditions, providing basic genetic information to patients, recognising the psychosocial issues for a family affected by a genetic condition and other vitally important services. Issues in genetic medicine that may be relevant in primary care would include reproductive risk, adult-onset genetic disorders, genetic variations in immune response and drug metabolism. Family history is currently used in determining risk of some specific cancers and informing decisions about early screening or genetic testing.[15] However, for other genetic conditions some practitioners may feel

---

10   Roses, 'Pharmacogenetics and the Practice of Medicine' (2000) Nature; 405: 857–865.

11   McLean, 'Interventions in the Human Genome' (1998) 61(5) Mod L Rev 681 at 682.

12   Richards, 'Three Views of Geneticists: The Enthusiast, the Visionary, and the Sceptic' (2001) 322 BMJ 1016. See also 'Genetics and Developing Countries' (2001) 322 BMJ 1006.

13   Richards, 'Three Views of Geneticists: The Enthusiast, the Visionary, and the Sceptic' (2001) 322 BMJ 1016.

14   Emery and Hayflick, 'The Challenge of Integrating Genetics Medicine into Primary Care' (2001) 322 BMJ 1027.

15   For discussion of how giving patients information about their genetic risk of developing common diseases will be helpful if they can be persuaded to adopt healthy lifestyles that reduce risk, see Marteau and Lerman, 'Genetic Risk and Behavioural Change' (2001) 322 BMJ 1056.

that it is unethical to inform patients that there may be a genetic risk in their family in the absence of effective screening technologies and therapies to reduce that risk.

[8.07] In addition to the potential benefits of genetic testing, new treatments may also be developed to counteract diseases caused by a specific gene defect such as Severe Combined Immune Deficiency in which patients cannot deal with infection and have to live in sterile environments. It is possible to treat these patients by way of gene therapy, whereby normal genes are inserted into their blood cells which, along with other treatment, would enable these patients to live a normal life.[16]

[8.08] There are many issues raised by genetics, in particular how to assimilate the mass of new information and translate it into clinical practice which both fulfils scientific criteria and respects ethical and social concerns.[17] The importance of evaluating public attitudes toward genetic testing is critical in appreciating patient response to future screening and in developing public policy. The need for greater general public understanding of genetics is evident in reports from bodies such as the Nuffield Council on Bioethics, the British Medical Association, the European Commission, the World Health Organisation and the National Institute of Health in the United States.

[8.09] From a legal perspective, the picture is not particularly clear or satisfactory. Tension exists between those who promote principles of scientific freedom and those who fear social engineering, invasions of privacy and a loss of control over the uses to which increased knowledge will be put.[18] As a result, there is a 'paucity of legal protection or acknowledgement of the commercial implications of scientific research. Legislators in many countries, including Ireland, seem reluctant to involve themselves in these issues and it may be argued that rapid developments in biotechnology appear to render it unsuitable to cumbersome legal machinery. Moreover, a legal response has the potential to frustrate and hinder scientific progress.'[19] It is argued that the legal community is not well equipped to deal with the revolution in biotechnology, particularly one of the proportions indicated by modern genetics. Law has traditionally been reactive rather than proactive, responding to specific developments rather than establishing structures within which flexibility is possible by monitoring advances on the one hand while accommodating changing knowledge and capacity on the other.[20] The pace of change in this area, the need for flexibility, and the importance of developing public understanding through education and debate, means that any legislative intervention should be passed with as full as possible an appreciation of the consequences, and kept under periodic review.[21]

---

[16] See Nevin, 'Advances in Genetics: Spiralling into Trouble?' (2001) 68(4) Medico-legal Journal 4–12.

[17] Duboule, 'The Evolution of Genomics' (1998) 278 Science 555.

[18] See Smith, 'Genetic Enhancement Technologies and the New Society' (2000) 4 Med Law I 85–95.

[19] Gannon, 'The Science of Biotechnology: Present, Past and Future Quagmires' in Petersen, *Intersections: Women on Law, Medicine and Technology* (Dartmouth Publishing, 1997) p 216.

[20] McLean, 'Interventions in the Human Genome' (1998) 61(5) Mod L Rev 681 at 695.

[21] See recommendations of the UK Select Committee on Science and Technology, Third Report, *Human Genetics: The Science and its Consequences*, HC 1994–95, HC Paper 41, paras 2 and 3.

[8.10] At a European level, there have been attempts to harmonise the response to developments in genetics through the Council of Europe Convention on Bioethics and Biomedicine (also known as the Oviedo Convention) in 1997.[22] However, the Convention has not received widespread acceptance with a number of European countries such as Ireland and the UK declining to sign it. The Convention acknowledges that progress in genetics will enable advances to take place in disease prevention, diagnosis and treatment but also warns that the risks should not be ignored, as it is no longer the individual or society that may be at risk but the human species itself. The Convention marks a significant attempt to address the diverse dilemmas of bioethics through the use of a human rights framework. It was drafted in an attempt to keep pace with biomedical developments and to close legal loop-holes that might exist within Europe where scientists could exploit lack of regulation in order to evade the legal restrictions in force in their own countries. The underlying principles contained in the Convention are autonomy and informed consent, although it is open to question whether such a model would provide effective protection against powerful bodies such as employers and insurers.[23] Cloning is specifically prohibited in a Protocol to the Convention[24] and the granting of patents for cloning processes has been prohibited by the Directive on the Legal Protection of Biotechnological Inventions.[25]

[8.11] UNESCO has also played an important role in setting ethical standards internationally in the area of genetics. It stated that:

> Genetic data can be used for medical diagnosis, disease prevention and population genetics studies. As each person's genetic heritage is unique, forensic science and the judicial system also use them for identification purposes. The number of genetic databanks is rising, with some containing more than a million records. Some are maintained at a national level and contain samples from virtually entire national populations. In this rapidly developing field, many people fear that human genetic data will be used for purposes contrary to human rights and freedom. Governments, non-governmental organizations, the intellectual community and society in general are calling for guidelines at the international level.[26]

As a result, it published the International Declaration on Genetic Data in 2003[27] which lays down the ethical principles that should govern the collection, processing, storage and use of human genetic data. The Declaration's stated aim is to ensure the respect of human dignity and the protection of human rights. It states that the collection of human genetic material should be based on 'prior, free, informed and express consent, without

---

[22] Convention for the Protection of Human Rights and Dignity of the Human Being with regard to the Application of Biology and Medicine: Convention on Human Rights and Biomedicine (1997).

[23] McGleenan, 'Legal Regulation of Genetic Technology' in *The Concise Encyclopaedia of the Ethics of New Technologies,* Chadwick (ed) (Academic Press, 2001) 199.

[24] Additional Protocol to the Convention for the Protection of Human Rights and Dignity of the Human Being with regard to the Application of Biology and Medicine, on the Prohibition of Cloning Human Beings (Paris, January 1998).

[25] Directive of the European Parliament and of the Council on the Legal Protection of Biotechnological Inventions, No 98/44/EC of 6 July 1998, OJ L213, 30/7/98, p 13.

[26] www.unesco.org/new/en/social-and-human-sciences/themes/bioethics/human-genetic-data/.

[27] www.unesco.org/new/en/social-and-human-sciences/themes/bioethics/human-genetic-data/.

inducement by financial or other personal gain', and states that data collected for one purpose should not be used for a different purpose that is incompatible with the original consent. More generally, the Declaration also calls for the promotion and establishment of independent multidisciplinary ethics committees at national, regional, local or institutional levels, and for the conclusion of bilateral and multilateral agreements that will enable developing countries to participate in generating and sharing the scientific knowledge resulting from the investigation of human genetic data.

[8.12] UNESCO also decided that it was opportune and desirable to set universal standards in the field of bioethics with due regard for human dignity and human rights and freedoms, while respecting the spirit of cultural pluralism inherent in bioethics. It stated:

> A growing number of scientific practices have extended beyond national borders and the necessity of setting universal ethical guidelines covering all issues raised in the field of bioethics and the need to promote the emergence of shared values have increasingly been a feature of the international debate. The need for standard-setting action in the field of bioethics is felt throughout the world, often expressed by scientists and practitioners themselves and by lawmakers and citizens. States have a special responsibility not only with respect to bioethical reflection but also in the drafting of any legislation that may follow.[28]

[8.13] UNESCO subsequently published the Universal Declaration on Bioethics and Human Rights in 2005, which attempts 'to balance the somewhat divergent claims of social solidarity with the protection of individual human rights'.[29] 'It protects the rights and liberties of individuals and also enshrines the role of science and knowledge in helping civilisation to progress. The Declaration is also designed to remind the international community of its duty of solidarity towards poorer countries from the benefits of biomedical progress.'[30] It has been suggested that the key feature of the Declaration is 'the continuing commitment to ethically clean science coupled with a willingness to engage with cultural diversity.'[31] The UNESCO Declarations promote the idea that while science and technology have the capacity to function as a positive force, they must be compatible with respect for human rights and human dignity.

[8.14] As well as concerns arising about the need for regulation, there are also many social concerns arising from the availability and use of genetic information.[32] These involve issues of fairness in the use of genetic information; ownership, privacy and

---

[28] www.unesco.org/new/en/social-and-human-sciences/themes/bioethics/bioethics-and-human-rights/.

[29] McGleenan, 'Legal Regulation of Genetic Technology' in *The Concise Encyclopaedia of the Ethics of New Technologies,* Chadwick (ed) (Academic Press, 2001), at 201.

[30] Lenoir, 'UNESCO, Genetics and Human Rights' (1997) 7 Kennedy Inst. of Ethics Journal 31.

[31] President's Council on Bioethics, *Beyond Therapy,* (2003) at 5–6, quoted by Brownsword in 'Human Dignity, Ethical Pluralism, and the Regulation of Modern Biotechnologies', Murphy (ed) *New Technologies and Human Rights* (OUP, 2009) 19–85 at 19.

[32] It is important to avoid an approach labelled as 'geneticisation' whereby human beings are regarded essentially as gene carriers, and issues of nature, functioning, health and disease are all characterised in the language of genetics. This tendency would distract from explanations based on social, environmental or economic conditions and result in less resource allocation for social research and policy. (contd.../)

confidentiality; psychological impact and possible stigmatisation; use of genetic information in reproductive decision-making; the ethics of testing for late-onset diseases or those for which no treatment is available; environmental issues; patenting of DNA sequences; and issues around the lines to be drawn between treatment and enhancement, acceptable diversity, freewill and genetic determinism.

ETHICS AND GENETICS

[8.15] It has been argued that the development of the Human Genome Project raises no new ethical problems and few legal ones.[33] Such problems as there are come from the development of new therapeutic opportunities rather than the acquisition of the new knowledge itself.[34] On the other hand, what *is* arguably unique about genetics is the advance realisation that serious ethical and policy issues are raised by the research and that pre-emptive steps must be taken to assure the maximisation of the benefits of the knowledge and the minimisation of the 'potential dark-side'.[35] No branch of science has created more acute or more subtle and interesting ethical dilemmas than genetics. Although other areas of science, such as nuclear physics, may create problems of greater moral importance, 'it is genetics that makes us recall, not simply our responsibilities to the world and to one another, but our responsibilities for how people will be in the future. For the first time we can begin to determine not simply who will live and who will die, but what all those who live in the future will be like.'[36]

[8.16] One of the features of the 'dark-side' is the fear of eugenics which has been defined as the 'conscious selection of humans by encouraging the production of those with desired inherited characteristics and for restricting those with undesirable inherited characteristics.'[37] The notion that humanity can and should be bettered by such conscious selection, and that science can be trusted with this task, forms the roots of eugenic policies. There are both negative and positive aspects to such policies on the wider population or societal level. On the one hand, negative eugenics policies would involve the imposition of restrictions on sexual freedom on those deemed 'unfit' to reproduce, whereas positive eugenics might, theoretically, promote the representation of certain genes in the gene pool of future generations.[38]

---

[32] (\...contd) It may also result in changes in reproductive decision-making as the traditional emphasis on parenting is replaced by the genetic quality in reproduction. Fatalistic attitudes may develop which avoid social and moral responsibility by referring to one's inability to avoid one's genetic heritage. See Nuffield Council on Bioethics, *Mental Disorders and Genetics: The Ethical Context*, (1998) at para 1.5–1.7, and Lippman, 'Led (Astray) by Genetic Maps: the Cartography of the Human Genome and Healthcare' (1992) 35 Social Science and Medicine 1469–76.

[33] Report of the Clothier Committee on the Ethics of Gene Therapy (1992) Cm 1788.

[34] Maddox, 'New Genetics Means No New Ethics' (1993) 364 Nature 97.

[35] Annas, *Standard of Care* (OUP, 1993) 149–50. See also Morgan, *Issues in Medical Law and Ethics* (2001) Ch 9.

[36] Burley and Harris (eds) 'Introduction' in *A Companion to Genethics* (Blackwell Publishing, 2002) at 1.

[37] Rothley and Casini, 'Ethical and Legal Problems of Genetic Engineering and Human Artificial Insemination' (1990) EU Committee on Legal Affairs and Citizen's Rights.

[38] Kelves, *In the Name of Eugenics: Genetics and the Uses of Human Heredity* (Knopf, 1985).

[8.17] The historical connotations associated with eugenic policies and programmes present obvious reminders of the dangers of abuse in the concept that humankind should be bettered.[39] In the United States in the 1920s it was thought that genetics provided evidence of the inferiority of certain minorities.[40] This was clearly the motivation behind the judgment of the Supreme Court in *Buck v Bell*[41] in 1927 where a law requiring the sterilisation of hospital inmates was upheld on the basis that 'three generations of imbeciles is enough.'[42] In European history, the horrors of the Nazi era provide the clearest context for discussion of the dangers of eugenics.[43] In the mid to late 1930s the idea of racial purity and a healthy population led to the policy that has subsequently been identified as the 'ultimate eugenic nightmare'.[44] The identification and elimination of those deemed responsible for the degeneration of human kind, such as those suffering from blindness and epilepsy[45] as well as those from 'inferior' races such as the Jews, was based on genetics. This also led to human experimentation carried out in order to attain the utopian dream of the perfect society.

[8.18] Germany's involvement in eugenic policies and negative population genetics, racist discrimination in the United States and sex selection in India and China has shaped international reaction to developments in genetics. While on the one hand science marches on regardless of moral values and concerns, on the other hand, calls for legal regulation of scientific developments continue to be made. The possibility for prospective parents to avoid passing on inherited diseases to their future children is extremely tempting, and some might say, coercive. There is a corresponding anxiety, however, that this will in time lead to the spectre of 'designer babies' and the search for the perfect child.[46] The elitism inherent in such a pursuit may seem to be dangerously close to the notion of the master race that successfully persuaded many followers of Hitler to the eugenic creed. The arguments used here are emotive and perhaps

---

[39] See Haker's discussion of the history of eugenic thought in the 20th century in 'Human Genome Analysis and Eugenics', Haker, Hearn and Steigler (eds) *Ethics of Human Genome Analysis, European Perspectives* (1993, Attempto Verlag Tubingen) p 293.

[40] Norton, 'Unnatural Selection: Non Therapeutic Pre-Implantation Genetic Screening and Proposed Regulation' (1994) 41 ICLA Law Rev 1586.

[41] *Buck v Bell* (1927) 274 US 200.

[42] *Buck v Bell* (1927) 274 US 200 at 207.

[43] See 'Eugenic Origins of Medical Genetics' in Paul, *The Politics of Heredity* (State University of New York Press, 1998) Ch 8.

[44] 'Justice and Eugenics' in Vollrath, *Science and Moral Values* (1990) at 107.

[45] Huntington's disease was listed as one of the disorders suitable for compulsory sterilisation in German law in 1933. It is thought that there were up to 5,000 sterilisations of those from families with the disease. See Muller-Hill, *Murderous Science* (Cold Spring Harbor Laboratory Press, 1998); Burleig, *Death and Deliverance, Euthanasia in Germany 1900–1945* (New York: Cambridge University Press, 1991); Harper, 'Huntington's Disease and the Abuse of Genetics' in Harper and Clarke, *Genetics, Society and Clinical Practice* (Garland Science, 1997) Ch 17.

[46] Negative interventions designed to avoid suffering seem to be less threatening and more acceptable than positive interventions designed to promote desirable characteristics. Harris argues that this is not necessarily plausible. He gives the example of an intervention designed to promote intelligence in children and says that to prohibit such an intervention is akin to 'inventing antibiotics but declining to put them into production'. See Harris, *The Value of Life* (Routledge, 1985) 150.

sensationalist as each side tries to capture the moral 'right'. The value of promoting 'genetic responsibility' or 'responsible parenting' so as to avoid increasing the transmission of deleterious genes in society, as opposed to the recognition of the intrinsic worth of every individual irrespective of their genes, raises an argument which it seems impossible to resolve. An example of the ethical issues that may arise in this context is given by the suggestion that there is a genetic basis to certain forms of criminal behaviour and that a predisposition to violence, or sexual deviance, could in some way excuse such behaviour on the grounds that the individual was compelled by his genetic make-up and thus had no free will. The likelihood of such an argument being successfully used in the criminal justice system is doubtful but whether it would reinforce the tendency to 'control, categorise and label people' is open to broader debate.[47]

[8.19] The concept of human dignity has been prioritised in all of the many international documents that have emerged since the recognition of the importance of the explosion of new information available. For example, the Preamble to the Council of Europe's Convention on Human Rights and Biomedicine states that States must take necessary measures 'to safeguard human dignity and the fundamental rights and freedoms of the individual with regard to the application of biology and medicine.'[48] Similarly, in the Preamble to UNESCO's Universal Declaration on the Human Genome and Human Rights[49] it is stated that research on the human genome 'should fully respect human dignity, freedom and human rights.' Some commentators argue that appeals to the concept of human dignity are 'comprehensively vague'[50] or that, though seemingly simple, it is an expression 'full of fragility'.[51]

[8.20] Dignity may be interpreted in two senses - the first, which is common in debates around instrumentalisation, is that dignity relates to the intrinsic value of persons and that therefore it is wrong to treat persons as mere things, or as means to an end. This is classically expressed by Kant's formulation of the Categorical Imperative: 'Act in such a way that you always treat humanity, whether in your own person or in the person of any other, never simply as a means, but always at the same time as an end.'[52] For Kant, every human being has a legitimate claim to respect from other human beings and, in turn, is bound to respect every other. Secondly, and less importantly in the context of human genetics, there is the idea that dignified conduct is a kind of virtue. In other words, the

---

[47] See further Wells, "'I Blame the Parents': Fitting New Genes in Old Criminal Laws" (1998) 61(5) Mod L Rev 724–739.

[48] Council of Europe, Convention for the Protection of Human Rights and Dignity of the Human Being with regard to the application of Biology and Medicine: Convention on Human Rights and Biomedicine (DIR/JUR (96) 14) Strasbourg: Directorate of Legal Affairs, November 1996.

[49] Adopted by the General Conference on 11 November 1997.

[50] Harris, *Clones, Genes and Immortality* (OUP, 1998) 31.

[51] Bedjaoui, *Proceedings of the Third Session of the International Bioethics Committee of UNESCO*, Sept. 1995: Vol 1 at 144, quoted in Beyleveld and Brownsword, 'Human Dignity, Human Rights, and Human Genetics' (1998) 61(5) Mod L Rev 661.

[52] See Paton, *The Moral Law* (Kant's groundwork of the metaphysic of morals: first published 1785) (1948) at 91, quoted by Beyleveld and Brownsword, 'Human Dignity, Human Rights, and Human Genetics' (1998) 61(5) Mod L Rev 661 at 666.

way in which a person presents himself socially, and the manner in which he handles adversity, is understood as a sign of a person's dignity.[53]

[8.21] It is argued that it is an abuse of the concept of human dignity to operate it as a veto on any practice that is intuitively disliked. It may rightly be used to require that agents, that is, those who have the capacity freely to select and act for purposes, should be treated as ends and not mere things. Complementary to that is the principle that the freedom and well-being of agents should not be interfered with against their own will, so that if they choose to participate in genetic research or to sell their genes, it is argued that any interference with such actions on the grounds of human dignity would be misguided paternalism.[54] Therefore:

> [T]he concept of human dignity has a legitimate place in debates about human genetics. However, it is something of a loose cannon, open to abuse and misinterpretation; it can oversimplify complex questions; and it can encourage a paternalism that is incompatible with the spirit of self-determination that informs the mainstream of human rights thinking.[55]

GENETIC TESTING AND SCREENING

[8.22] Genetic disorders are diseases and malformations caused entirely, or to a substantial extent, by a series of alterations in the genome. They are traditionally divided into three categories. First, there are unifactorial disorders caused by changes in single genes. These disorders may be classified into dominant, recessive and x-linked inheritance patterns which reflect the probability of inheriting a genetic defect. If the gene in question is dominant, a single gene inherited from one parent will cause the disease. An example is Huntington's disease which is a fatal neurological degenerative disease which affects people usually between the ages of 30 and 50 and causes progressive deterioration of bodily functions and cognitive ability, and death within 15–20 years. If the gene is recessive, a person will only develop the disease if they inherit the gene from both parents. An example of a recessive genetic condition is cystic fibrosis, a lung condition with a reduced life expectancy. People who only have one copy of this gene are carriers and they will not develop the disease themselves but if they have a child with another carrier, there is a one-in-four chance that the child may have a double dose of the gene and will therefore have the disease. X-linked disorders are triggered by a mutation on the X chromosome. Women have two X chromosomes so they will usually have a second normal X chromosome to compensate for the defective

---

[53] Beyleveld and Brownsword, 'Human Dignity, Human Rights, and Human Genetics' (1998) 61(5) Mod L Rev at 667, see also President's Council on Bioethics, *Beyond Therapy*, (2003) at 5–6, quoted by Brownsword in 'Human Dignity, Ethical Pluralism, and the Regulation of Modern Biotechnologies', Murphy (ed) *New Technologies and Human Rights* (OUP, 2009) 19–85 at 19.

[54] Beyleveld and Brownsword, 'Human Dignity, Human Rights, and Human Genetics' (1998) 61(5) Mod L Rev at 680, referring to the central contention in Gewirthian moral theory that agents are bound by the Principle of Generic Consistency under which agents have reciprocal rights and duties to respect one another's freedom and well-being. Gewirth, *Reason and Morality* (University of Chicago Press, 1978).

[55] Beyleveld and Brownsword, 'Human Dignity, Human Rights, and Human Genetics' (1998) 61(5) Mod L Rev 661 at 662.

one and therefore they will usually only be carriers of these diseases themselves, but risk passing on the disease to any male children. An example is Duchenne Muscular Dystrophy. Secondly, there are polygenic disorders which occur as a result of the absence or interaction of more than one gene. Information may be limited on these disorders due to a multiplicity of gene combinations and environmental factors. Many forms of cancer have an inherited genetic basis which may be triggered by environmental factors. Thirdly, there are chromosomal disorders caused by a rearrangement of chromosomes, such as Down Syndrome.[56] In recent years there has been further research done in the area of susceptibility genes, which are genes that increase a person's risks of developing a condition but do not mean that the condition is inevitable, for example certain types of cancer.

[8.23] Genetic testing is not a single technology. It refers to a broad range of methods for gauging the presence, or absence of activity, of genes in cells. There are different types of genetic testing, ranging from requests from relatives of patients with a late-onset genetic disorder, to population screening, testing of symptomatic individuals, and susceptibility testing for common disorders.[57] It is not currently possible to test for all genetic disorders as the responsible gene(s) may not yet have been identified. In practice, individuals and families affected by or at risk of a genetic disorder may attend a geneticist for diagnosis. Once a diagnosis has been made, families are then advised on the interpretation of the test results and given non-directive counselling about related risks. Families may then seek further clinical care from their general practitioner or appropriate consultants.

[8.24] Perhaps the most straightforward form of testing is diagnostic testing as the test seeks to identify the cause of the existing symptoms in the individual. However, individuals with a mutation or aberration affecting chromosomes or genes that cause disease later in life may not have any symptoms until early adulthood or later. In some cases the underlying mutation may be diagnosed by predictive genetic testing by way of chromosome and DNA analysis. This will provide information about the likelihood of the disorder appearing in the individual at some future time. Predictive genetic testing can be performed on individuals, members of a family at risk, specific sections of the population, or the general population as a whole. By contrast with a conventional medical diagnostic test which provides information as to the patient's current state of health, a predictive genetic test provides information about a future medical condition that may or may not develop. Although the identified risk might sometimes be high (as in Huntington's disease), there will always be an element of uncertainty about whether the condition will develop, when it will appear, and how severe the symptoms will be in this particular patient. The possible interventions for the condition may also be untested and recommendations may be based on presumed benefit rather than on observations of outcomes.[58] The notion of genetic 'report cards' that would successfully predict at birth

---

[56] Brown and Gannon, 'Confidentiality and the Human Genome Project: A Prophecy for Conflict?' in McLean (ed) *Contemporary Issues in Law, Medicine and Ethics* (Dartmouth, 1996) Ch 11.

[57] For discussion, see Schwartz Cowan's *Heredity and Hope, The Case for Genetic Screening* (Harvard University Press, 2008) Ch 1.

[58] Evans et al, 'The Complexities of Predictive Genetic Testing' (2001) 322 BMJ 1052–1056; Burke W et al, 'Recommendations for Follow-Up Care of Individuals with an Inherited Predisposition to Cancer' (1997) 277 JAMA 997–1003 and 915–919.

the future health of the individual are, as yet, illusory and misrepresentative of the possibilities offered by predictive testing.[59] However, some argue that:

> It is not at all fanciful to foresee a day in which a single drop of blood from a newborn child provides the template upon which a completely automated system checks for the presence of a hundred different genetic conditions. A similar level of scrutiny will be available for the fetus, and, in time, premarital screening will routinely apprise couples of how they might fare in the genetic lottery occurring with each conception.[60]

[8.25] The availability of genetic tests has sometimes been accompanied by confusion in people's minds about what exactly will be achieved by the test. Genetic tests do not provide a cure for genetic disease, in fact in many cases in which genetic disease is indicated by the test result, no cure is possible. In relation to late-onset disorders, those who seek predictive testing usually perceive themselves to be at risk due to relevant family history. These kinds of tests are generally regarded as more problematic for ethical reasons. The benefits of testing in those cases would be the possibility of preventative measures or early treatment; the ability to plan major life events and make decisions; and the awareness of passing on the risk to future family members.[61] However, the result of such a test rarely gives information on when the symptoms of the disorder will appear or how severe they may be, and a positive test result may lead to severe psychological problems.

[8.26] Although the futility of discovering that one is going to become ill with an incurable disease may mean that some people would rather not have that information, the reason that many do wish to have the test done is to prepare themselves for their future ill-health, both emotionally and financially. Those who may have intended to start a family may make a more informed decision about whether to take the risk of passing on the genetic disorder to future children. It has been argued, however, that this advance knowledge may not always be advantageous to the individual. There is evidence, for example, that the suicide rate among young Caucasians who know that they carry the gene for Huntington's disease (a late-onset neurological disease for which there is no cure) is at least four times higher than that of the national average for a comparable group of their peers.[62] Knowledge that one's health is going to deteriorate can cause psychological distress for many people, who then become self-obsessed and subject to feelings of victimisation. They may sometimes behave as though they already have the

---

[59] See Khoury et al, 'Challenges in Communicating Genetics: A Public Health Approach' (2000) 2 Genetics in Medicine 198–202.

[60] Reilly, 'Public Policy and Legal Issues Raised by Advances in Genetic Screening and Testing' (1993) XXVII Suffolk University Law Review 1327 at 1329.

[61] See detailed discussion in the former UK Advisory Committee on Genetic Testing, *Report on Genetic Testing for Late Onset Disorders* (1998).

[62] See Andrews, 'Legal Aspects of Genetic Information' (1990) 64 Yale J Biol Med 29. A more recent study states that the rate is up to 10 times higher: Almqvist et al, 'A Worldwide Assessment of the Frequency of Suicide, Suicide Attempts, or Psychiatric Hospitalisation After Predictive Testing for Huntington's Disease' (1999) 64 Amer J of Human Genetics 1293. See further Hayden, 'Predictive Testing for Huntington's Disease: Are We Ready for Widespread Community Implementation?' 40 Am J Med Gen 515; Brandt et al, 'Presymptomatic Diagnosis of Delayed-Onset with Linked DNA Markers: The Experience with Huntington's Disease' (1989) 216 JAMA 3108.

disease. The necessity of having counselling both prior to and after receiving genetic testing is self-evident so that individuals are given the necessary information upon which to base an informed choice and also the time for reflection before making that choice, as well as before receiving the results of the test.

[8.27] As mentioned above, predictive testing may be able to offer significant benefits to individuals carrying a particular genetic trait, in terms of improved duration and quality of life by early warning, and, in some cases, avoidance of exacerbating factors. However, the dangers of misuse are also clear, whether it be by virtue of inadequate methodology,[63] lack of adequately trained test providers or lack of understanding of genetics by health care professionals and the public at large.[64] The psychological burden to the patient in knowing that he carries a predisposition to a specific disorder, the social pressures to act on that knowledge, the reduction in tolerance and discrimination in cases of genetic dysfunction,[65] as well as the possibility of misuse by third parties such as employers, insurers and the State,[66] all lead to the conclusion that a policy of caution is advisable in this context.

[8.28] A significant distinction between predictive testing and other diagnostic tests is that the latter do not usually have significance for other family members, except where the condition is communicable, such as an infectious disease. With predictive testing there may be direct implications for family members who share the same gene pool. The impact on individual autonomy, the possibility of making informed choices and the nature of the relationship between individuals and society are issues to be examined not only by the clinicians considering what tests to carry out, but also by those who choose to present for testing.[67]

[8.29] The systematic search for persons having particular genetic characteristics is called 'genetic screening'. In contrast to diagnostic genetic testing described above, screening is not usually sought by the person tested, but rather it is initiated by the provider of the test, such as public health authorities who may want to screen the general population for a particular genetic disease.[68] Governments have great expectations of[68]

---

[63] The NIH Task Force on Genetic Testing recommends that 'the genotypes to be detected by a genetic test must be shown by scientifically valid methods to be associated with the occurrence of a disease. The observations must be independently replicated and subject to peer review.'

[64] Holtzman, Proceed with Caution. Predicting Genetic Risks in the Recombinant DNA Era (John Hopkins University Press, 1989).

[65] See Markel in Holtzman and Watson (eds) *Promoting Safe and Effective Genetic Testing in the United* States (1997) Task Force of the National Institutes of Health on Genetic Testing, Appendix 6.

[66] For consideration of whether pre-symptomatic individuals who have tested positive for a specific genetic disease, such as Huntington's, should come within the meaning of 'persons with disabilities' so as to prevent unlawful discrimination in employment opportunities, see Gin, 'Genetic Discrimination: Huntington's Disease and the Americans with Disabilities Act' (1997) 97 Columbia Law Review 1406–1434.

[67] For a discussion on the relationship between genetics and behaviour, see Nuffield Council on Bioethics, *Genetics and Human Behaviour: The Ethical Context* (2002).

[68] In the US in the 1960s and early 1970s, when the biochemical basis of Tay–Sachs disease (an autosomal recessive genetic disorder which causes deterioration of physical and mental capacity and commonly results in childhood death) was first becoming known, no mutations had been sequenced directly for any genetic diseases. (contd.../)

screening, as do caregivers, private individuals and other groups within the healthcare sector.[69] It is thought that new forms of screening will help people to live longer, healthier lives and avoid symptoms of disease. However, screening almost always has some drawbacks.

> It is not merely that false-positive test results ('false alarms') and over-diagnosis (an anomaly is identified but it is not one that without screening would have led to symptoms of disease) are associated with unnecessary feelings of fear and uncertainty, they can also result in damage to health from high-risk follow-up tests or therapeutic interventions. False-negative results may lead to unfounded reassurance.[70]

[8.30] Screening can take the form of large-scale programmes, such as the national newborn screening programme for PKU, or all men or women of a certain age, such as the national breast[71] and cervical screening[72] programmes. It could also entail a group of patients being invited to a preventative blood pressure screening by their GP, employees being offered tests by their employers, or people responding to advertisements in the media for a health check examination with a particular clinic. The acceptability of genetic screening is likely to be very diverse, reflecting 'the variety of social and medical impact genetic information can have, and the varying degrees to which various populations have access to those benefits and confidence in legal protection of social status.'[73] 'The use of genetic screening for public health purposes will tend to be most effective when it serves a clear population goal, has a healthy ratio of overall economic and social benefits to costs, entails a just use of resources, and is acceptable to the populations it targets.'[74]

[8.31] There are ethical concerns that not only might genetic screening lead to stigmatisation, particularly since certain genetic defects are more prevalent in particular ethnic groups, but that the concept itself 'smacks of the turn-of-the-century eugenics movement in the United States when laws were passed to sterilise people who were thought to have the genes for feeblemindedness, epilepsy, prostitution, and pauperism.'[75] In the early days of large-scale genetic screening programmes, a lack of understanding of the complexities involved resulted in organizing efforts that were premature, poorly designed and had inadequate safeguards. Health officials, understandably wanting to bring the benefits of promising new technology to the public as rapidly as possible, frequently did not give adequate consideration to possible negative psychosocial and

---

[68] (\...contd) Researchers of that era did not yet know how common polymorphism would prove to be and it was thought that a single mutation must have spread from one population into another. Subsequent research has proven that a large number of HEXA mutations can cause some form of the disease. Tay–Sachs disease was one of the first genetic disorders for which widespread genetic screening was possible.

[69] Health Council of the Netherlands (2008) *Screening: Between Hope and Hype* at 13.

[70] Health Council of the Netherlands (2008) *Screening: Between Hope and Hype* at 16.

[71] www.breastcheck.ie.

[72] www.cervicalcheck.ie.

[73] Burris and Gostin, 'Genetic screening and public health' in Burley and Harris (eds) *A Companion to Bioethics* (Blackwell 2004) 455–463 at 462.

[74] Burris and Gostin at 462.

[75] Andrews, 'Genetic Fallout: New Technologies Are Changing the Legal Landscape' (1995) Trial 20 at 23.

economic consequences. Thus carriers were sometimes denied employment and life insurance because genetic traits and genetic diseases were confused.[76]

[8.32] Genetic screening may also generate anxieties and concerns in people who are identified as carriers. They will never benefit from being identified as such because their partners are not carriers or they are not planning to have children or are not inclined to alter their life or reproductive plans as a result of their carrier status. Although carriers of genetic disease will not be affected themselves, studies have shown that many carriers suffer anxiety about their health, lower self-esteem and feelings of shame.[77] Such screening could therefore be seen as unduly burdensome to them, and the impact on their well-being must be considered in deciding whether to proceed with such screening. The Nuffield Council on Bioethics recommends that the factors to be taken into account in relation to any proposed screening programme should include: the predictive power and accuracy of the test; the benefits of informed personal choice; the psychological impact of the outcome for the individuals and families; therapeutic possibilities; possible social and economic disadvantage; and the resource implications of the programme.[78]

[8.33] It is likely that requests for genetic information will become more commonplace as genetic research expands and as more patients become informed about genetics and seek testing for predisposition to chronic illnesses. The importance of providing accurate information and counselling is crucial to ensure that people understand the meaning and implications of the information they are given.[79] Recent advances in direct-to-consumer (DTC) testing[80] or self-testing kits which allow individuals to order in-home saliva-based kits which will be used to provide reports on over 100 health conditions and traits, have led to concern in relation to their scientific validity, consumer protection, assignment of legal responsibility, efficacy of national regulation in the face of worldwide internet access and so on.[81] According to the European Society of Human Genetics, experience in relation to DTC advertising of prescription medicine has shown that this has created an inappropriate demand for medications. Moreover, it has shown that various advertisements for drugs have been misleading. 'Overstatement of effectiveness or minimization of risk has led to inadequate or inappropriate changes in medication, diet or lifestyle by consumers. DTC advertising of genetic tests for health related purposes runs the same risks as DTC advertising of prescription medicine in this regard. Aggressive marketing strategies and slogans for DTC genetic testing might

---

[76] Kenen and Schmidt, 'Stigmatization of Carrier Status: Social Implications of Heterozygote Genetic Screening Programs' (1978) American Journal of Public Health, Vol 68, No 11.

[77] Clarke, 'Genetic Screening and Counselling' in Kuhse and Singer, *A Companion to Bioethics,* (Blackwell, 1998) at 221.

[78] Nuffield Council on Bioethics, *Genetic Screening: Ethics Issues* (1993). www.nuffieldbioethics.org.

[79] See discussion in Jordan and Fu Chang Tsai 'Whole-genome association studies for multigenic diseases: ethical dilemmas arising from commercialisation – the case of genetic testing for autism' (2010) 36 J of Med Ethics 440–444.

[80] See for example www.23andme.com/en-eu/.

[81] See Berg and Fryer Edwards 'The ethical challenges of Direct-to Consumer genetic testing' (2007) 77 Journal of Business Ethics 17. See also Bortolotti and Widdows 'The right not to know: the case of psychiatric disorder' (2011) 37 J of Med Ethics 673–676.

overstate the potential for predictive information of such tests and overrate its future health implications:[82]

> It is important that the technology is regulated to ensure that: information is accurate; individuals are provided with information about the identified problem in order to make informed choices; the implications for relatives of those tested are clearly understood by the individual undergoing the test; testing does not result in unfair discrimination at work or for life and health insurance; and priorities and resource allocation decisions are based on as sound evidence as possible taking account of the state of the art.[83]

Privacy and the interests of family members

[8.34] The current revolution in genetic science has enabled us to examine our own genetic make-up for the first time. This has led to a greater understanding of known diseases, an improved ability to predict future health, an increased understanding of behaviour traits and a wider range of reproductive options. However, a genetic test result may have implications not only for the person tested, but also for blood relatives who share a common gene pool. With this genetic revolution, and in particular the predictive power of genetic tests, have come ethical and legal problems, including the issues of privacy and confidentiality. The crucial issues here in relation to access to genetic information are: what are the rights of the individual, and what are the rights of third parties with a legitimate interest in the information?

[8.35] The presence of a genetic mutation within a family is significant for a number of reasons. Any genetic information about a person may indicate that blood relatives should also be tested, particularly where there are interventions available to alleviate the condition. Even if there is no treatment or cure for the condition, information can give a level of preparedness to individuals so that they can make life-choices and reproductive decisions in light of the available facts.[84] However, 'those individuals who are directly affected may suffer anxiety, fear, depression, guilt and the stress of being the bearer of bad news to the family.'[85] In relation to some genetic conditions it may also be necessary to test family members in order to refine the risk to one member. It is not difficult to imagine situations in which families may be split over the question of genetic testing. These might include situations where one family member will not provide a tissue sample necessary for a complete diagnosis within the family, or the person tested refuses to inform relatives that they may be affected by a positive test result, or there are debates within the family over whether to have a child tested for a late-onset disorder for which

---

[82] European Society of Human Genetics: 'Statement of the ESHG on Direct-to-Consumer Genetic Testing for Health-Related Purposes' (2010) European Journal of Human Genetics, 1– 3. See also concerns expressed in February 2011 by the American Medical Association regarding the importance of medical supervision of genetic testing: www.ama-assn.org/ resources/doc/washington/consumer-genetic-testing-letter.pdf.

[83] Kinderlerer and Longley, 'Human Genetics: the New Panacea?' (1998) 61(5) Mod L Rev 603 at 613.

[84] Laurie, Harmon and Porter, *Law and Medical Ethics* (10th edn, OUP 2016) at 7.31

[85] Skene, 'Legal Regulation of Genetic Testing, Balancing Privacy and Family Interests' in Iltis, Johnson and Hinze (eds) *Legal Perspectives in Bioethics* (Routledge, 2008) at 208. See also O'Donovan K and Gilbar R 'Consent and confidentiality in genetics: whose information is it anyway?' (2003) 29 Journal of Medical Ethics 16–18.

there is no effective intervention.[86] Where one family member refuses to undergo testing, this may effectively block other members' ability to discover their risk factor.

[8.36] The ethical and legal difficulties that may arise here centre on the value of the right to know one's genetic make-up and the right to refuse to be tested for genetic disorder. If the relative refuses to be tested due to a wish not to be informed of their own genetic risk, it may be possible to inform other relatives without informing the donor of the tissue, but this may not always be appropriate.[87] 'There is then an inevitable tension between an individualistic model of confidentiality, in which a person's health information is regarded as paradigmatically private, and the inherently shared nature of genetic information.'[88]

[8.37] An important aspect of the dilemma posed by the existence of the competing interests here is: who is the patient, is it the individual or is it the family?[89] The importance of genetic testing for the person tested is that it gives him or her information about future health, some of which information may be utilised in behavioural change so as to delay the ill-health. It is argued that the same reasons point to disclosure to the relatives so that they can prepare themselves for what lies ahead. Genetic information may also be important for those who are planning to have children so that they can have pre-implantation genetic testing carried out in order to ensure that their children do not have the particular disease. 'In many ways, therefore, the information is also theirs. The family has a claim as a collective, as does each of the individuals who make up that collective.'[90] 'Hereditary information is a family possession rather than simply a personal one.'[91] This reinforces the view often expressed by clinicians who work in the area of genetics, that is, that the family is the patient. If that is the case, then the duty of confidentiality owed by the doctor is owed, not to the individual tested, but to each member of the family.[92] In that way, the doctor is justified, and indeed in some jurisdictions may be obliged, to inform affected relatives. This is often referred to as a 'communitarian' or 'family' approach.[93]

---

[86] Reilly, 'Public Policy and Legal Issues Raised by Advances in Genetic Screening and Testing' (1993) XXVII Suffolk University Law Review 1327 at 1335.

[87] Obviously in a case of identical twins, any genetic diagnosis will affect both individuals.

[88] Jackson, *Medical Law: Text, Cases and Materials* (3rd edn, 2013) 413.

[89] Laurie, 'Genetics and Patient's Rights: Where Are the Limits?' (2000) Med L I Vol 5, 255–44. See also Bell and Bennett, 'Genetic Secrets and the Family' Med L Rev (2001) Vol 9:130–161; Skene, 'Genetic Secrets and the Family: A Response to Bell and Bennett' Med L Rev (2001) Vol 9: 162–169; Skene, 'Patient's Rights or Family Responsibilities? Two Approaches to Genetic Testing' (1998) 6 Med L Rev 1.

[90] Laurie, 'Genetics and Patient's Rights: Where are the Limits?' (2000) Med L I Vol 5, 25–44, p 29.

[91] Wertz and Fletcher, (1991) 'Privacy and disclosure in medical genetics examined in an ethics of care' *Bioethics* 5, 212–232.

[92] There may be difficulties in determining where the duty on the doctor ends in this context in terms of contacting relatives. Questions arise as to how this communication is to take place, whether counselling is to be offered to each relative, at what level of dilution of the risk does the duty end, and so on.

[93] See also Kent, 'Consent and confidentiality in genetics: whose information is it anyway?' (2003) 29 Journal of Medical Ethics 16–18.

[8.38] There have been calls for a familial approach to genetics which would stress the need for a shift in focus away from the idea that the individual 'owns' his genetic material, towards the idea that patients should consider more than what will affect their own health.[94] Generally patients seek genetic tests as a member of a family, because of a shared family history. This context adds to the responsibility to be placed on patients and doctors to inform other members of the family thus affected.[95] It has therefore been suggested that in instances where the propensity to the disease is high and the symptoms serious, the doctor may be justified in informing other relatives, despite objections from the person tested. Disclosure may take place, if practicable, without identifying the particular person tested. Even if disclosure of the person's identity is inevitable, their genetic status need not and should not be revealed without specific consent. This would be in line with general principles regarding confidentiality in other clinical contexts where exceptions to strict confidentiality may be justified where necessary to protect others from serious harm.[96]

[8.39] Despite the strong appeal of the notion of the family as patient in the context of genetics, others argue that genetic filiation is not enough in itself to warrant setting aside important legal and ethical protections.[97] There are also concerns about putting the doctor or genetic counsellor in the role of enforcing commendable social goals and of assuming a position of knowing what is best for the family.

> Family dynamics, as well as the understanding of what a family is, are not uniform or determined solely by biological connection. While medical professionals may have superior insight into the strictly medical aspects of the dilemma, even there we do not ordinarily presume that superior medical insight entitles them to override the purely medical aspects of their patients' decisions...Healthcare professionals do not train to be clairvoyants or family values police; nor should we want them to.[98]

[8.40] If the person tested refuses to inform relatives who may also be affected, the doctor may have to consider whether to disclose relevant information without the person's consent. Trust is a crucial element of the relationship between doctor and patient – the doctor trusts that the patient is disclosing all the facts relevant to his condition and the patient trusts that the doctor will respect his privacy and will not disclose confidential information about him to others. Doctors thus have legal, ethical and professional obligations to respect patient confidentiality. Genetics has a significant

---

[94] Anti-Cancer Council of Victoria, Cancer Genetics Ethics Committee, *Ethics and Familial Cancers: Including Guidelines on Ethical Aspects of Risk Assessment, Genetic Testing and Genetic Registers* (March 1997), discussed by Bell and Bennett, 'Genetic Secrets and the Family' Med L Rev (2001) Vol 9:130–161, p 133.

[95] For consideration of the issues in the US, see Parker, 'Camping Trips and Family Trees: Must Tennessee Physicians Warn Their Patients' Relatives of Genetic Risks?' (1998) 65 Tennessee Law Review 585; Deftos, 'Genomic Torts: The Law of the Future: The Duty of Physicians to Disclose the Presence of a Genetic Disease to the Relatives of Their Patients with the Disease' (1997) 32 Univ of San Fran L Rev 105.

[96] See discussion in Chapter 3 para [3.77] et seq.

[97] See Suter, 'Whose Genes Are These Anyway? Familial Conflicts Over Access to Genetic Information' (1993) 91 Mich L Rev 1854.

[98] Powers, 'Privacy and genetics' in Burley and Harris (eds) *A Companion to Genethics* (Blackwell, 2004) 364–378 at 375.

bearing on confidentiality as information concerning others may become apparent due to the fact that genes run in families. Therefore 'when genetic testing of one person can benefit another family member, privacy and autonomy interests of the former may collide with the relative's interests in protecting her health or planning her future.'[99] Thus the doctor has to reconcile his duty of confidentiality to his patient with a duty to safeguard the welfare of others:

> On the one hand, it is necessary to recognise individuals as autonomous moral agents, who should be free to make decisions regarding their own health care. However, when these autonomous agents make decisions that may prove detrimental to the health of others, problems arise. This is especially so when omitting to provide relatives with information interferes with their autonomy by restricting their present and future life choices and decisions.[100]

[8.41] There has been debate in recent years about the extent to which genetic information is unique and requires a legal framework different from that which is applicable to other forms of medical information. 'Many privacy advocates favour stronger privacy protections for genetic information than for other types of medical information based on the premise that genetic information and its unwanted dissemination have potentially greater adverse consequences than the loss of privacy with regard to other types of medical information.'[101] This is referred to as 'genetic exceptionalism'.[102] Skene thus argues that genetic information is different and that disclosure may be justified even in circumstances which would not ordinarily come within the confidentiality exceptions. However, she is of the view that for the confidentiality exception to be applicable the threat of harm to the other person must be serious and imminent. A genetic risk, though serious, is unlikely to be regarded as 'imminent' and therefore the common law justification of disclosure is not sufficient in these circumstances.[103] Jackson also points out that our current capacity to treat genetic disease is limited so disclosing genetic information to relatives would not necessarily prevent serious harm but 'in the future, however, as it becomes possible to successfully treat more genetic diseases, there will be increasing pressure on the principle of confidentiality in the context of genetic disease, and the balancing exercise between the public interest in disclosure and the public interest in confidentiality will become even more finely balanced and complicated.'[104]

[8.42] It is also important to note that genetic information covers 'a broad spectrum from highly monogenic disorders through susceptibility genes and on to a simple family history...Not every class of this information is predictive of future ill health – indeed,

---

[99] Suter, 'Whose Genes Are These Anyway? Familial Conflicts Over Access to Genetic Information' Mich Law Rev 9, June 1993 at 1855.

[100] Clarke, 'Genetic Screening and Counselling' in Kuhse and Singer, *A Companion to Bioethics,* (Blackwell Publishing, 1998) at 222.

[101] Powers, 'Privacy and genetics' in Burley and Harris (eds) *A Companion to Genethics* (Blackwell, 2004) 364–378 at 368.

[102] See Gostin and Hodge, 'Genetic Privacy and the Law: An End to Genetic Exceptionalism' (1999) 40 Jurimetrics 21.

[103] Skene, 'Genetic secrets and the family: a response to Bell and Bennett' (2001) 9 Med Law Rev 162–169.

[104] Jackson, *Medical Law, Text, Cases and Materials* (3rd edn, 2013) at 416.

many examples of genetic information are no more predictive than is general health information.'[105] On this basis the uniqueness of genetic information may be disputed and genetic information may not be deemed sufficiently different from other medical information to justify a deviation from ordinary principles of confidentiality. Using these principles, existing exceptions to confidentiality would be applicable in circumstances where there is a serious risk of harm to another such as where a relative refuses to inform other family members who may be at risk.[106]

[8.43] In Ireland the Medical Council's Guide to Professional Conduct and Ethics states that there are some circumstances in which a doctor may justify a breach of confidentiality. Paragraph 31.3 of the Guide states that disclosure in the public interest may be made to protect the patient, other identifiable people, or the community more widely. Before making a disclosure, the doctor must satisfy himself that the possible harm the disclosure may cause the patient is outweighed by the benefits that are likely to arise for the patient or for others. The information should be disclosed to an appropriate person or authority and include only the information needed to meet the purpose.[107] Whenever a doctor exercises this discretion in this context, he must be prepared to justify his decision and if he has exercised it incorrectly, he may be liable to sanction. The question is whether the court would accept that the public interest in warning an individual at risk of genetic disease outweighed the public interest in maintaining the confidentiality of his patient.

[8.44] In considering whether to disclose information and breach confidentiality, the doctor should therefore firstly consider the severity of the disease in question as any potential breach of confidentiality is justifiable only if the harm sought to be avoided by the disclosure is serious. Secondly, the doctor should assess the availability of treatment for the disease as it may cause significant distress to know that the disease is untreatable but it may also offer opportunities for family members to make reproductive choices to ensure that they do not pass on the gene to their children. The accuracy and reliability of the test must also be considered as well as the availability of expertise to interpret the information for the family appropriately.[108] Evidence that these considerations were taken into account may provide a defence for a clinician who decides to divulge genetic information to a family member to enable that person to seek medical attention. A doctor might for example be less inclined to disclose information about a condition for which nothing can be done and which has relatively mild symptoms.[109]

---

[105] Laurie, Harmon and Porter, *Law and Medical Ethics,* (10th edn, OUP, 2016) at para 7.28.

[106] Bell and Bennet, 'Genetic secrets and the family' (2001) 9 Med Law Review 130–61.

[107] Guide to Professional Conduct and Ethics (8th edn, 2016) www.medicalcouncil.ie.

[108] Laurie, 'The Most Personal Information of All: An Appraisal of Genetic Privacy in the Shadow of the Human Genome Project' (1996) 10 I J of Law, Pol & the Family 74 at 85. See also Brownrigg, 'Mother still knows best: Cancer-related gene mutations, familial privacy and a physician's duty to warn.' (1999) 26 Fordham Urban Law Review 247, 273. See discussion in Jackson *Medical Law: Text, Cases and Materials* (3rd edn, 2013) 414–415.

[109] The President's Commission on Bioethical Issues in the US favours a legal duty to disclose medical information, including genetic tests, when it might prevent harm to third parties. (contd.../)

[8.45] There have been no reported cases in Ireland to date on the issue of whether doctors are under a duty to warn a patient's relatives that they are at risk of genetic disease. Two cases in the US illustrate how this action might arise. In *Pate v Threlkel*,[110] Dr Threlkel had operated on Marianne New, the mother of Heidi Pate, for thyroid cancer three years before Pate's own thyroid cancer was diagnosed and treated, but had not warned Pate of the hereditary nature of her mother's condition. Pate and her husband alleged that the physicians knew or should have known of the likelihood that New's children would have inherited the condition genetically; that the physicians were under a duty to warn New that her children should be tested for the disease; that had New been warned in 1987, she would have had her children tested at that time; and if Pate had been tested in 1987, she would have taken preventative action, and her condition, more likely than not, would have been curable. Pate claimed that as a direct and proximate cause of the physicians' negligence, she suffered from advanced medullary thyroid carcinoma and its various damaging effects.

[8.46] The Court took the view that the duty to warn of the genetic nature of the disease was satisfied by informing the patient herself; there was no duty to inform the patient's children:

> If there is a duty to warn, to whom must the physician convey the warning? Our holding should not be read to require the physician to warn the patient's children of the disease. In most instances the physician is prohibited from disclosing the patient's medical condition to others except with the patient's permission ... Moreover, the patient ordinarily can be expected to pass on the warning. To require the physician to seek out and warn various members of the patient's family would often be difficult or impractical and would place too heavy a burden upon the physician. Thus, we emphasize that in any circumstances in which the physician has a duty to warn of a genetically transferable disease, that duty will be satisfied by warning the patient.

[8.47] However, in *Safer v the Estate of Pack*[111] this narrow approach was not followed. During the 1950s, Dr George Pack had treated Donna Safer's father for a cancerous blockage of the colon and multiple polyposis. In 1990, Safer was diagnosed with the same condition, which she claimed was inherited, and, if not diagnosed and treated, invariably would lead to metastatic colorectal cancer. Safer alleged that Dr Pack knew the hereditary nature of the disease, yet failed to warn the immediate family, thus breaching his professional duty to warn. The Court said that although an overly broad and general application of the physician's duty to warn might lead to confusion, conflict or unfairness in many types of circumstances, the duty to warn of avertible risk from genetic causes, by definition a matter of familial concern, is sufficiently narrow to serve the interests of justice. This duty was owed not only to the patient himself but also 'extends beyond the interests of a patient to members of the immediate family of the

---

[109] (\...contd) They recommend that an attempt ought first to be made to persuade the patient to disclose, there must be a high probability of harm without disclosure and a high probability that the disclosure will avert the anticipated harm, the potential harm must be serious, and only the least amount of detail necessary to avert the harm should be disclosed. *President's Commission for the study of ethical problems in medicine and biomedical and behavioural research: Screening and Counselling for genetic conditions* (Washington DC 1992).

[110] *Pate v Threlkel* 661 So. 2d 278 (Fla 1995).

[111] *Safer v Estate of Pack* 677 A 2d 1188 (NJ 1996).

patient who may be adversely affected by a breach of that duty.' The Court did not decide how precisely that duty is to be discharged, especially with respect to young children who may be at risk, except to require that reasonable steps be taken to assure that the information reaches those likely to be affected or is made available for their benefit. The Court further acknowledged the potential conflict between the physician's broader duty to warn and his fidelity to an expressed preference of the patient that nothing be said to family members about the details of the disease. Unfortunately the Court did not advise on how such a conflict could be resolved.

[8.48] A separate but related issue in relation to duties to disclose test results that may arise in practice is where test results indicate misattributed paternity. This may occur when a woman gives birth to a child with an autosomal recessive disorder (meaning that the disorder is inherited from both parents, who are usually themselves unaffected) and the husband is found not to be a carrier, or when linkage studies with other family members show that the child's genetic markers are incompatible with being the child of the presumed father.[112] This is certainly not a novel problem but the question arises as to whether the doctor or geneticist is under a duty to disclose the facts to the family. The practice in many laboratories appears to be simply to answer the clinical question asked and avoid reporting information that is not medically relevant. Alternatively, the geneticist may meet the woman alone to report the finding, the husband is not directly informed and the biological facts are avoided. 'In such situations, the justification is that the geneticist owes a higher allegiance to the integrity of the family than to any one member. Disclosing the full truth to the husband might do more harm than good. Although it may be defensible ethically, the practice of deceiving the husband has shaky legal foundations.'[113] An alternative approach would be to ensure both parties know in advance of the test about the risk of discovering a false paternity, thus giving them the possibility to choose whether they will be informed in cases of such a result, and only if they have so chosen does the geneticist or counsellor have the duty to disclose the incidental finding.[114]

The right not to know

[8.49] In relation to the information to be provided to other family members who may be affected,[115] there is also the issue that some people may prefer not to have advance knowledge of future ill-health.[116] 'Knowledge of one's own genetic constitution and of possible future ill health can have profound effects on one's sense of 'self'. And, while

---

[112] Reilly, 'Public Policy and Legal Issues Raised by Advances in Genetic Screening and Testing' (1993) XXVII Suffolk University Law Review 1327 at 1335.

[113] Reilly at 1338.

[114] Tozzo, Caenazzo, Parker 'Discovering misattributed paternity in genetic counselling: different ethical perspectives in two countries' J Med Ethics 2014;40:177–181.

[115] Andrews, 'Gen-Etiquette: Genetic Information, Family Relationships and Adoption' in Rothstein, *Genetic Secrets: Protecting Privacy and Confidentiality in the Genetic Era* (Yale University Press, 1997) Ch. 14; Deech, 'Family Law and Genetics' (1998) 61 MLR 697.

[116] Ngwena and Chadwick, 'Genetic Diagnostic Information and the Duty of Confidentiality: Ethics and Law' (1993) 1 Med Law International 73. Craufurd et al also report that fewer than 15 per cent of at-risk individuals opt to be tested for Huntington's disease. 'Uptake of Presymptomatic predictive testing for Huntington's Disease.' (1989) 334 Lancet 603.

an individual who seeks out genetic testing might have prepared himself for possible bad news, can the same be said of that person's relative who might suspect nothing as to the presence of genetic disease in their family?'[117] Knowledge can be useful and important where there is something that can be done with the knowledge in order to avoid future ill-health. However, in circumstances where individuals do not currently display symptoms of disease, have no knowledge that they might be affected by disease, and where there is no effective intervention available, the benefit of knowledge is less obvious. Laurie says that:

> To argue that this promotes preparedness for the onset of disease presupposes that people are able to prepare adequately for the harm to come. Moreover, it ignores the possibility of causing psychological harm by burdening people with information which forces them into a period of self-reflection and self-reassessment which they would not otherwise have experienced.[118]

[8.50] Studies show that, contrary to what might be expected, both positive and negative results can have psychological effects on those tested. For example, one study found that 58 per cent of asymptomatic carriers and 24 per cent of non-carriers were depressed in the months after being tested.[119] Other studies have found that some of those who tested negative for the gene reported being rejected by their families once it became apparent that they no longer shared a bond which had previously brought the family closer.[120]

[8.51] Knowledge of genetic disease can also lead to what the Danish Council of Ethics called 'morbidification' which it says is the notion of falling victim to some inescapable fate through knowledge about risk of disease.[121] This can affect the way people feel about themselves as well as how they treat their children, whether or not they are affected by the disease.[122] Thus, giving a person information that they have expressly refused, is disrespectful of autonomy as 'control of information about ourselves must be an essential part of any concept of ourselves as autonomous persons,' and this control does not simply refer to controlling who has access to that information but also should include the facility not to accept the information.[123]

[8.52] The right not to know has been recognised in the Council of Europe Convention for the Protection of Human Rights and Dignity of the Human Being with regard to the

---

[117] Mason and Laurie, *Law and Medical Ethics* (8th edn, OUP, 2010) para 7.31 (now in its 10th edn, 2016)

[118] Laurie, 'Genetics and Patient's Rights: Where Are the Limits?'(2000) Med Law International Vol 5 pp 25–44 at 34.

[119] Gargiulo, 'Long-term outcome of presymptomatic testing in Huntington's disease' (2009) 17 *European Journal of Human Genetics* 165–71, cited by Jackson at 404–5.

[120] Tibben, et al, 'Testing for Huntington's disease with support for all parties' (1990) 335 Lancet 553. Cited by Jackson, *Medical Law, Text, cases and materials* (2nd edn) 404–5.

[121] Danish Council of Ethics, *Ethics and Mapping of the Human Genome*, (1993 Copenhagen) page 60.

[122] Laurie, 'Genetics and Patient's Rights: Where Are the Limits?'(2000) Med Law International Vol 5 pp 25–44 at 34.

[123] Laurie, 'In defence of ignorance: genetic information and the right not to know' (1999) 6 Eur J of Health Law 119–32.

Application of Biology and Medicine (Oviedo Convention 1997)[124] and the UNESCO Universal Declaration on the Human Genome and Human Rights.[125] It is questionable, however, whether the grounding of a right not to know solely in terms of choice is effective:

> The principle of respect for autonomy requires that we see the individual as a 'moral chooser'. In order to choose meaningfully we require full information about the range of options available and the consequences of any particular choice. Unfortunately, this paradigm breaks down in the context of an interest in not knowing genetic information. Here, the choice is about knowledge itself.[126]

In other words, there is no way to exercise the choice of not knowing because by the doctor or geneticist asking if the person wants to know whether they are at risk the essence of the information has already been made known.[127] Thus it is not only direct disclosure that threatens respect for the right not to know as just telling relatives that information exists and asking them if they wish to receive it, lets them know that there may be something they need to know.[128]

Interests of insurance companies and employers

[8.53] Other parties may also claim an interest in the information revealed by genetic tests. Much controversy has arisen in relation to the interest of insurance companies and employers, both of whom have financial interests in the information, as well as the State, which has an interest in the protection of public health and the reduction of financial expenditure in this regard.[129]

---

[124] Council of Europe, Convention for the Protection of Human Rights and Dignity of the Human Being with regard to the Application of Biology and Medicine, Oviedo 1997, art 10 (2): 'Everyone is entitled to know any information collected about his or her health. However, the wishes of individuals not to be so informed shall be observed.'

[125] Adopted in Paris in 1997. Article 5c provides 'The right of every individual to decide whether or not to be informed of the results of genetic examination and the resulting consequences should be respected.'

[126] Laurie, Harmon and Porter, *Law and Medical Ethics* (10th edn, OUP, 2016) para 7.39.

[127] Wertz and Fletcher 'Privacy and disclosure in medical genetics examined in an ethic of care' (1991) 5 Bioethics 212.

[128] Jackson, *Medical Law, Text, Cases and Materials* (3rd edn, 2013) at 417.

[129] It is not proposed to deal with the mandatory screening of infants here. However, it is important to note the Supreme Court case of *North Western Health Board v HW and CW* [2001] 3 IR 622, [2001] 3 IR 635, [2001] IESC 90, where the issue of testing for phenylketonuria (PKU) was at issue. The parents of a young child refused permission for the test to be carried out by the 'heel test' method as, for them, this was the infliction of pain on their child. The Health Board stressed the importance for the child of this screening programme in order to make any necessary diagnosis early enough to be able to treat the serious disease that may result. The Supreme Court focused on the rights of the family under the Constitution to make such decisions in relation to the children of the family. It held that 'While there may inevitably be tensions between laws enacted by the State for the common good of society as a whole and the unique status of the family within that society, the Constitution firmly outlaws any attempt by the State in its laws or its executive actions to usurp the exclusive and privileged role of the family in the social order.' (contd.../)

The overriding fear is that the information will be used in a way which will discriminate against those who may have inherited a genetic disease.[130]

[8.54] Insurance is a way of mitigating the effects of harmful events of uncertain incidence by pooling modest premiums which provide the resources to make large payments selectively to those who suffer such events.[131] The types of policy for which it is argued that genetic information may have relevance, are health and life insurance. Private health insurance is an important feature of the healthcare landscape in Ireland as the purchase of such policies can enable the insured person to get faster access to tests and treatments. Life insurance policies are of huge significance in relation to a person's ability to purchase a house and apply for a mortgage, as a policy of life insurance is generally a requirement of any financial institution before any loan is given. Insurance contracts are contracts *uberrima fides*, ie of the utmost good faith, which means that full disclosure must be made by the applicant of all material facts relevant to the risk to be undertaken by the insurer. In life insurance, it is argued that the insured person is at an advantage in having all the information pertaining to his health and family background, information which would obviously be highly relevant to the insurer in deciding whether to insure and what premium to charge in recognition of the risk presented. To redress this 'imbalance', insurance contracts place a legal obligation on persons applying for insurance to disclose all material facts. This will include all relevant medical history and family background. If such information is not disclosed, the insurance contract could later be avoided by the insurers.

[8.55] In the context of genetic information there is a fear that if insurers were to be entitled to gain access to the results of genetic tests, this information would be used to discriminate against the insured by either refusing to provide cover, or by charging excessive premiums. Studies in the US have shown, for example, that 85 per cent of the population are concerned about access to genetic test results by insurers and employers and would not take genetic tests if such access were permitted.[132] There are two different ways in which the insurer could seek such information. It could be made a term of the contract that the insured disclose the results of any genetic tests undertaken, or the insurer could oblige the insured to undertake certain genetic tests and disclose the results.

[8.56] In many instances, insurers argue that genetic information is no different from other medical information about which the insured has no difficulty in disclosing. If the insured is prepared to disclose a family history of heart disease or cancer, the disclosure

---

[129] (\...contd) There is no mandatory obligation on parents to submit their child to this test, and if such was to be enforced by legislation, it would be open to review on grounds of interference with the jurisdiction of the family. Therefore, unless the State could clearly justify, in the interests of the common good, population screening for genetic diseases, it is likely that the privacy and authority of the family would usurp any such attempt to gain access to genetic information. Medical treatment decisions on behalf of children are dealt with in Chapter 11.

[130] See generally Sorrell, 'The Insurance market and discriminatory practices' in Burley and Harris (eds) A Companion to Bioethics (Blackwell 2004) 398–407.

[131] O'Neill, 'Insurance and Genetics: the Current State of Play' (1998) 61:5 Modern Law Review at 716.

[132] Dept of Labour, Dept of Health and Human Services, Equal Employment Opportunity Commission, Dept of Justice *Genetic Information and the Workplace*, Washington DC 1998.

of a genetic test result indicating the same information should not be treated any differently. It has been argued that individuals should pay a premium for life assurance that is commensurate with the risks they bring to the insurance pool.

> If a genetic test with demonstrable predictive efficiency predisposes an individual to a particular disease that is actuarially relevant, fairness demands that they are charged a higher premium for commercial insurance or are denied coverage. Those who argue that we should privilege such individuals, and bestow on them a specific right of non-disclosure, appear to permit inequity in the market.[133]

[8.57] One of the concerns here is that compulsory disclosure of test results would deter individuals being tested in the first place, which would have deleterious effects on health.[134] As regards insurers obliging individuals to be tested, there is concern that this would lead to the development and proliferation of predictive genetic testing,[135] (which may not be accompanied by necessary counselling) and that there would be a danger that the individual would not validly consent to such tests, due to the pressure of needing to get life assurance. The Council of Europe Recommendation on the protection of medical data states that medical data (including genetic information) should only be processed for preventative treatment, diagnosis or treatment of the data subject, scientific research, judicial procedure or criminal investigation.[136] The Explanatory Memorandum states that 'a candidate for employment, an insurance contract or other services or activities should not be forced to undergo a genetic analysis, by making employment or the insurance dependent on such an analysis, unless such dependence is explicitly provided for by the law and the analysis is necessary for the protection of the data subject or a third party.'[137]

[8.58] In Ireland, s 42 of the Disability Act 2005 provides that genetic testing shall not be carried out on a person unless (a) the testing is not prohibited by law, and (b) the consent of the person to the processing of any genetic data to be derived from the testing has been obtained in accordance with the Act. This prohibition applies to employment, health insurance, life assurance, occupational pensions and mortgages. Therefore, insurers are not permitted to use genetic tests in relation to health or life assurance policies. However, it is important to note that insurers still require patients to declare family history so if, for example, a woman's mother had young-onset breast cancer, that woman could still have her insurance premium increased or loaded. Even if the woman's mother were found to have a BRCA mutation (a genetic mutation linked to an increased risk of breast and other cancers), and the woman herself did not have her mother's BRCA mutation, the woman could still be loaded by the insurer by virtue of family history alone. Therefore there is a gap in protection regarding family medical history in

---

[133] Mittra, 'Predictive genetic information and access to life assurance: the poverty of genetic exceptionalism' (2007) 2 BioSocieties 349–73. See also Hoyweghen et al, 'Genetic 'risk carriers' and lifestyle 'risk takers'. Which risks deserve our legal protection in Insurance?' (2007) 15 Health Care Analysis 179.

[134] UK House of Commons Science and Technology Committee *Human Genetics: The Science and its Consequences*, Third Report, 6 July 1995.

[135] Chadwick and Ngwena, 'The Human Genome Project, Predictive Testing and Insurance Contracts: Ethical and Legal Responses' (1995) 1 Res Publica 115.

[136] Council of Europe, *The Protection of Medical Data* Rec. No (97) 5.

[137] Explanatory Memorandum para 103.

Irish law. This means that there is protection accorded to the individual and family for the results of genetic tests that is not accorded currently to the gathering and use of family history information.[138]

[8.59] Insurers also now commonly ask if a person is having regular screening for a condition (without mentioning genetics), and if they are, their insurance premiums may be loaded. Insurance companies argue that in the absence of such information, there is an imbalance in the insurance application process because an applicant for insurance may be aware of the results of a genetic test but the insurer will not be privy to such information. This is referred to as adverse selection. When this situation arises, it can be expected that high-risk people will purchase a disproportionate amount of insurance. The problem this creates is not simply a threat to insurers' profits. When insurers expect or experience adverse selection, they are forced to raise their rates across the board to anticipate it, because they are not able to identify those at higher risk whose rates they should selectively increase.[139] The Disability Act also allows the Minister for Justice to regulate the use of family history in assessment of insurance and/or employment, but no such regulations have yet been introduced.

[8.60] In 2013 the Irish Data Protection Commissioner approved a Code of Practice for Insurance which provides that an Insurer will not request an applicant to have a genetic test.[140] Application forms which ask health questions of an individual or their doctor must not include any question about genetic tests. Forms which ask health questions directly of the individual, or their GP, must include a form of words bringing to their attention the fact that they should not disclose a genetic test result. In the event of a genetic test result coming into the possession of an insurer, the genetic test result must be ignored and not taken account of by the insurer in any way whatsoever. This applies both to positive and negative test results.

[8.61] In relation to employment, the issues and concerns are similar in the sense that the employer has a financial interest in the health of the person he chooses to employ. If the employee is likely to become seriously ill, then his productivity will decrease, thus affecting the employer's profits. He may also fear that the work environment may exacerbate the symptoms of the employee's disease, thus causing ill-health earlier than perhaps might be expected.[141] As well as the human concern that might be behind such fears, there is perhaps also the concern that the employer might be sued for compensation in such cases for failing to provide a safe workplace for the employee. Therefore, as with the insurer, the employer may argue that he is entitled to ask, before hiring, for results of any genetic tests undertaken, or perhaps to ask for those tests to be undertaken. Epstein argues that people ought to be obliged to inform their employers if they know they are at risk of a serious inherited disease.

---

[138] Consultation on Part 4 of the Disability Act (Genetic Testing) Submission by the Neurological Alliance of Ireland available at www.nsai.ie.

[139] Hall and Rich, 'Laws Restricting Health Insurers' Use of Genetic Information: Impact on Genetic Discrimination' (2000) Am J Hum Genet; 66(1): 293–307.

[140] Available at www.insuranceireland.eu.

[141] Capron, 'Which ills to bear? Re-evaluating the 'threat' of modern genetics' (1990) 39 Emory Law Journal 665, 692.

It is critical to note that the plea for privacy is often a plea for the right to misrepresent one's self to the rest of the world...No doubt the individual who engages in this type of deception has much to gain. But equally there can be no doubt that this gain exists in all garden variety of fraud as well. To show the advantage of the fraud to the party who commits it is hardly to excuse or to justify it, for the same can be said of all cases of successful wrongs. On the other side of the transaction, there is a pronounced loss from not knowing the information when key decisions are made.[142]

[8.62] The same concerns pertain here relating to the discriminatory effects of disclosure of genetic test results in the employment context. In a report by a number of government departments in the US in 1998, it was stated that genetic information could be used to unfairly discriminate against individuals in the workplace, for example by denying them jobs on the basis that they might be more likely to take sick leave, resign or retire early for health reasons, creating extra costs in recruiting and training new staff.[143] The Nuffield Council on Bioethics in the UK recommended that legislation should be introduced to protect the privacy of genetic information and that employers should not be entitled to access the results of genetic tests, except where specifically relevant to the work environment within which the individual works.[144] The former UK Human Genetics Commission also recommended specific legislation prohibiting genetic discrimination but the House of Lords Science and Technology Committee decided that there was no evidence that genetic discrimination was occurring at present and would keep the matter under review.[145]

[8.63] In the United States, the Genetic Information Non-Discrimination Act 2008 (GINA) was introduced to provide federal protection from genetic discrimination in health insurance and employment. The Act makes it illegal for health insurance providers to use or require genetic information to make decisions about a person's insurance eligibility or coverage. It also makes it illegal for employers to use a person's genetic information when making decisions about hiring, promotion and several other terms of employment. However, the Act does not apply to life assurance, disability insurance and long-term care insurance. 'This means that, despite the existence of

---

[142] Epstein, 'The legal regulation of genetic discrimination: old responses to new technology' (1994) 74 Boston Univ Law Review. Epstein also argues that, for example in the case of Huntington's disease, this duty of disclosure should extend to potential spouses who should have a right to know that the person they are marrying will develop a terminal degenerative disease in middle age.

[143] Dept of Labour, Dept of Health and Human Services, Equal Employment Opportunity Commission, Dept of Justice *Genetic Information and the Workplace*, Washington DC 1998.

[144] Nuffield Council on Bioethics *Genetic Screening: Ethical Issues* (1993), and House of Commons Science and Technology Committee, *Human Genetics: The Science and its Consequences*, Third Report, 6 July 1995 at 231–233. For a criticism of these recommendations see Rothstein, 'Genetic Discrimination in Employment: Ethics, Policy and Comparative Law' in Guillod and Widmer (eds) *Human Genetics Analysis and the Protection of Personality and Privacy* (Zurich: Schulthess Poylygraphischer Verlag, 1994). See also Olick, 'Genes in the Workplace, New Frontiers for ADA Law, Policy and Research' in Blanck (ed) *Employment, Disability and the Americans with Disabilities Act: Issues in Law, Public Policy and Research* (Northwestern University Press, 2000) 285.

[145] Science and Technology Committee, 2nd Report of Session 2008–09, Genomic Medicine, HL Paper 107–I available at www.publications.parliament.uk.

GINA, people may continue to be deterred from undergoing genetic testing in case it increases their insurance premiums for these excluded types of insurance.'[146] A further issue is that GINA does not protect people who are already symptomatic with the disease. This means that even though disability discrimination is prohibited in the US people might find themselves in a legal limbo when they first become symptomatic as GINA will not provide them with protection, but neither are they covered by anti-discrimination legislation until they become disabled within the meaning of such legislation.[147]

[8.64] It has been suggested that GINA is flawed in promoting genetic exceptionalism, that is, the idea that genetic information is different and needs special treatment. The question is if a number of individuals can each suffer from the same disease but the cause of the disease may be different for each of them, (genetic, environmental, behavioural, life-style choices) why should employers be prohibited from discriminating only against those for whom the disease was caused by genetic factors. Passing antidiscrimination legislation for genes, but not for other factors, 'seems at best an unfinished job.'[148]

[8.65] In the Irish context s 6(1) of the Employment Equality Act 1998 provides that discrimination shall be taken to occur where a person is treated less favourably than another person is, has been or would be treated in a comparable situation on any of the grounds specified in subs (2). One of the 'discriminatory grounds' listed is that of disability. Disability is defined in the Act as the absence of bodily or mental functions, the presence in the body of organisms likely to cause illness or disease, the malfunction or disfigurement of part of a person's body, a condition which results in a person learning differently, or a condition, illness or disease which affects a person's thought processes, perceptions of reality, emotions or judgment. The definition includes a disability which exists at present or which previously existed or may exist in the future. These provisions mean that an employer may not discriminate between individuals on the basis that one person has a genetic predisposition to disease which might come within the definition of a disability that may exist in the future.

Genetic testing of children

[8.66] Genetic testing of children raises particular difficulties as young children cannot make decisions for themselves and symptoms of the diseases for which they are being tested may not present until later in life. The American Society of Human Genetics considers that genetic testing of children requires special consideration for a number of reasons:

> Informed consent to genetic and genomic testing is a core principle for which there are few exceptions. Young children lack decision-making capacity, so decisions about testing must be conducted through surrogates, usually the parents, and must be done with the child's best interest at heart. The notion of 'best interest' is intended to place the child's welfare foremost in medical decision making. However, given the subjective nature of the interests of those who cannot speak for themselves, defining an individual child's 'best

---

[146] Jackson, *Medical Law, Text, Cases and Materials* (3rd edn, 2013) at 429.
[147] Jackson, *Medical Law, Text, Cases and Materials* (3rd edn, 2013) at 429.
[148] (2009) 122 Harvard Law Review 1038.

interest' is often complex and controversial, particularly in medical circumstances involving burdensome treatments and profound disabilities. Surrogate decision making is also an ethically freighted concept, because although parents are the appropriate surrogates for their children in almost all cases, controversies arise when parents make decisions that seem contrary to the best interest of their child. As children age, they gain decision-making capacity and experience with health conditions. Therefore, including children to various degrees as they age in genetic- and genomic-testing decisions and responses is important but challenging. Finally, because children are young, decisions for them, and by them, might have implications for the course of their lives.[149]

Controversies have arisen both in the context of screening newborns as well as infants and older children. Newborn screening is generally recommended only when there is a clear indication of benefit to the newborn, where there is a system in place to confirm the diagnosis and where treatment is available for those affected.[150]

[8.67] The most common type of newborn screening is for phenylketonuria (PKU) which was introduced in Massachusetts in the United States in 1962 and in Ireland in 1966.[151] The screening is based on a small sample of blood which is drawn from the heel of the infant a few days after birth, known as the heel prick test. If a baby has PKU the long-term benefit of early treatment is much greater than the small discomfort they may feel when the blood sample is taken. Parents are now also offered newborn screening for other conditions such as homocystinuria, maple syrup urine disease, clinical galactosaemia, cystic fibrosis and congenital hypothyroidism. The National Newborn Bloodspot Screening Programme in Ireland currently stores screening cards from heel prick tests carried out since 1984.[152]

[8.68] Traditionally the benefits of such screening were generally considered so great as to obviate any need for detailed explanation or information for parents and it was not until 2011 in Ireland that formal consent was not obtained at the time of collection from the parents of the newborn infants for the analysis or storage of these samples.[153] 'Studies of parental knowledge of newborn screening have shown that few parents even

---

[149] Botkin et al, 'Points to Consider: Ethical, Legal, and Psychosocial Implications of Genetic Testing in Children and Adolescents' (2015) The American Journal of Human Genetics , Volume 97, Issue 1, 6 – 21.

[150] Institute of Medicine, Andrews et al (eds) Assessing Genetic Risks: Implications for Health and Social Policy (1994) at 10.

[151] Ireland has a high rate of PKU, around 1 in 4,500. This is much greater than in the US, where the incidence is about 1 in 12,000. http://www.pkunews.org/research/yap.htm.

[152] Older cards were also stored from 1966 but in 1984, due to flooding in the storage facility, archived screening cards were destroyed. The current archive contains newborn screening cards from all babies tested from around 1984 to the current time – about 1.5 million cards. www.hse.ie/eng/health/child/newbornscreening/newbornbloodspotscreening/disposal/disposalqa.html.

[153] 'Obtaining truly informed permission for NBS during the postnatal period is challenging because of the hectic environment, the short hospitalization for many newborns, and the many competing priorities for parents and newborn-care providers. Further, signatures to document permission can be obtained in a perfunctory fashion, so requiring signatures per se does not assure a meaningful informed-permission process.' Botkin et al 'Points to Consider: Ethical, Legal, and Psychosocial Implications of Genetic Testing in Children and Adolescents' (2015) The American Journal of Human Genetics, Volume 97, Issue 1, 6 – 21. (contd.../)

know for what conditions their infants are screened.'[154] Screening for other conditions, such as muscular dystrophy[155] or chronic lung disease, has been seen as more questionable based on studies that have shown adverse impact on families and the emotional trauma of early diagnosis in some cases.[156] However, more recent studies have shown that there is medium- or long-term benefit to the child as a result of newborn screening for cystic fibrosis,[157] and many centres world-wide are introducing this as a practice. On the other hand, the avoidance of prolonged uncertainty during lengthy diagnostic processes, and the ability to plan for the future, may tip the balance in favour of screening in some situations.[158] It has been argued, however, that in requesting testing, parents typically think only of the benefits of a negative test result and not of the potentially damaging effects of a positive one.[159] Some studies have also shown evidence

---

[153] (\...contd) For discussion of challenges involved in the retention of newborn screening cards see Madden, 'Retention and use of human biological samples – The Guthrie card problem' in Donnelly and Murray (eds) *Ethical And Legal Debates In Irish Healthcare, Confronting complexities* (2016) Manchester Univ Press.

[154] Clarke 'Genetic Screening and Counselling' in Kuhse and Singer, *A Companion to Bioethics* (Blackwell Publishing, 1998) at 220.

[155] Duchenne muscular dystrophy is a genetic disease which, in two out of three cases, is transmitted on the X chromosome to male offspring of female carriers; in the other cases the gene mutation happens as a sporadic event. Muscle wasting is one of the devastating symptoms of this disease, which usually manifests itself at around two years of age. It begins with developmental and motor delay, clumsiness and falling over. By the age of 11, 90 per cent of those suffering from the disease are wheelchair bound. Some live until their 20s, but the average age is about 17, with death resulting from respiratory infection or heart failure. Parsons and Bradley, 'Ethical Issues in Newborn Screening for Duchenne Muscular Dystrophy: the Question of Informed Consent' in Clarke (ed) *Genetic Counselling* (Taylor & Franus, 1994) at 99. This essay discusses the introduction of testing for DMD in Wales, which according to the authors, is a good example of the tension between the power of the technological imperative and the protection of the individual.

[156] In 1972 the Swedish government initiated national newborn screening for a condition known as alpha –1 antitrypsin deficiency, which is common in those with Scandinavian ancestry. For those infants who tested positive for the predisposition, preventative measures were recommended to avoid exposure to environmental antagonists. Follow-up studies demonstrated that more than half of the families suffered severe psychological consequences, some of which were still present five to seven years after testing. As a consequence of early feedback on these negative effects, the government discontinued the programme after just two years. See McNeil et al, 'Psychosocial Effects of Screening for Somatic Risk: The Swedish Alpha-1 Antitrypsin Experience' (1988) 43 Thorax 505–7; Clarke, 'Genetic Screening and Counselling' in Kuhse and Singer, *A Companion to Bioethics* (Blackwell Publishing, 1998) at 220.

[157] See Farrell et al, 'Nutritional Benefits of Neonatal Screening for Cystic Fibrosis' (1997) 337 (14) NEJM 963–967.

[158] See Holtzman, 'What Drives Neonatal Screening Programs?' (1991) 325 NEJM 802–4; Farrell and Mischler, 'Newborn Screening for Cystic Fibrosis' (1992) 39 Advances in Pediatrics 66. For similar studies in the area of muscular dystrophy see Bradley et al, 'Experience with Screening Newborns for Duchenne Muscular Dystrophy in Wales' (1993) 306 BMJ 357–61.

[159] Hoffman and Wulfsberg, 'Testing Children for Genetic Predispositions: Is It in Their Best Interest?' (1995) 23 Journal of Law, Medicine and Ethics 331–44 at 333. (contd.../)

of a 'vulnerable child syndrome', where parents of a child with a genetic predisposition become over-protective, restricting the child's activities unnecessarily.[160]

[8.69] If a young child has a health problem where management would be aided by accurate genetic diagnosis, it would seem to be in the best interests of the child to carry out genetic tests. A similar situation would apply if a healthy child is being tested for a late-onset disorder of which there is family history, and for which early intervention or treatment might be of benefit. However, the situation becomes more problematic where the test is for a late-onset disorder for which there is no medical benefit in early detection.[161] There has been much debate about whether such testing should be performed at the request of parents on the basis that the information may be beneficial to the family, even though there may be little benefit to the child itself.[162]

[8.70] The ethical difficulties in predictive or pre-symptomatic testing are that firstly, it removes the right of the child to make an autonomous decision on reaching maturity whether to have the test or not; secondly, the confidentiality that would be accorded to an adult patient in such circumstances is not applicable to a young child; and thirdly, a positive test result may lead to deleterious social consequences, as the parents may relate to the child differently and may have different expectations of the child.[163] Sometimes parents may request testing for their child for the parents' benefit rather than the child's, as the parents may want to reassure themselves that their 'genetic curse' was not passed on to their children or may want to prepare themselves emotionally or organise their home environment to cater for the future illness of their child. It may be argued that such a decision should focus exclusively on the child's best interests but it may also be suggested that parental well-being also has a significant impact on children regardless of whether the child's well-being or best interest is at the core of the parent's desire to know. Therefore, perhaps an exclusive focus on the child's interest is too narrow, and

---

[159] (\...contd) See also Wertz et al, 'Genetic Testing for Children and Adolescents: Who Decides?' (1994) 272 JAMA 875 at 878 and Fanos, *Developmental Consequences for Adulthood of Early Sibling Loss* (University of Michigan Microfilms, 1987).

[160] Tluczek et al, 'Parents' Knowledge of Neonatal Screening and Response to False-Positive Cystic Fibrosis Screening' (1992) 13 Journal of Developmental and Behavioural Pediatrics 181–86.

[161] The Working Party of the Clinical Genetics Society in the UK recommended that predictive testing not be carried out on children if the child is healthy and there are no effective medical interventions in the event of a positive test result. See 'The Genetic Testing of Children' (1994) 31 J of Med Genetics 785.

[162] See further Fost, 'Genetic Diagnosis and Treatment: Ethical Considerations' (1993) 147 Am J of Diseases of Children 1190–95; Wertz et al, 'Genetic Testing for Children and Adolescents: Who Decides?' (1994) 272 JAMA 875–82; Harper and Clarke, 'Viewpoint: Should We Test Children for 'Adult' Genetic Disease?' (1990) 335 Lancet 1205–06.

[163] 'Testing a child carries no medical advantage but puts the child at risk of harm, as a high-risk result may prejudice upbringing by either natural or adoptive parents, and may even result in stigmatisation. It also removes the child's future autonomy regarding the decision to be tested.' Ball, Tyler and Harper, 'Predictive Testing of Adults and Children: Lessons from Huntington's Disease' in Clarke (ed) *Genetic Counselling, Practice and Principles* (Routledge, 1994) at 74. See also Robertson and Savulescu, 'Is There a Case in Favour of Predictive Genetic Testing in Young Children?' (2001) Bioethics Vol 15(1) 26; Otlowski, 'An Exploration of the Legal and Socio-Ethical Implications of Predictive Genetic Testing of Children' (2004) Aus J Fam Law Vol 18.

clinicians should respect parental decisions that take into account familiar psychosocial factors, at least in relation to conditions that present in childhood.[164]

[8.71] It is clear that in deciding whether to test for late-onset disorders, the geneticist should prioritise the best interests of the child, bearing in mind that 'best interests' are not limited to medical factors, but also include psychological health and relationships with other family members. If the symptoms of the disease running in the family are likely to manifest themselves in adolescence, it may be appropriate to prepare the child in advance. It has also been argued that children ought to be told about genetic conditions that are known to exist in the family on the basis that keeping secrets may result in more harm than good and that keeping information from children is an affront to their identity.[165] Such at-risk children should also be tested for their genetic status, as knowing their genetic make-up may benefit them by offering them important choices that they would otherwise not have, and by allowing them to assimilate such knowledge into their identity so that the knowledge simply becomes a part of who they are. The former UK Advisory Committee on Genetic Testing (later the Human Genetics Commission) recommends that careful consideration be given to the separate and potentially conflicting interests of children, parents and other family members in assessing the best interests of the child in this context. 'Where there is a particular concern over what is in the best interests of a child in certain circumstances, including where there is any dispute between those with parental responsibility for the child, it may first be necessary to seek an order from the court that the child be tested.'[166]

[8.72] Given the traditional deference shown by the courts to parental authority, it may be argued that the courts would permit the parents to make a decision in favour of testing the child, as long as the child's life would not be endangered by the test itself. However, depending on the likely onset of symptoms and any clinical benefit for the child arising from the test, genetic testing is not necessarily analogous to situations in which medical treatment or surgery is recommended for a child, and refused by a parent. If the geneticist is reluctant to perform the test where no clinical benefit to the child would be obtained, and the parents insist upon it in order 'to satisfy their own curiosity', in light of the fact that the courts have traditionally taken the view that parents may not demand treatment for their children, particularly where this contravenes medical opinion, it is likely that a court would decide to refuse testing until the child is mature enough to make his own decision.[167]

---

[164] Friedman Ross, 'Predictive Genetic Testing for Conditions That Present in Childhood' (2002) Kennedy Inst of Ethics J 12.3: 225 244.

[165] Malpas, 'Why Tell Asymptomatic Children of the Risk of an Adult-Onset Disease in the Family But Not Test Them For It?' (2006) JME 32:639–642.

[166] UK Advisory Committee on Genetic Testing, at 27. In the UK, the Children Act 1989, s 8 enables the court to make a 'specific issue order' for the purpose of resolving a specific question in connection with any aspect of parental responsibility for a child, such as consent for a genetic test.

[167] See discussion in Hoffman and Wulfsberg, 'Testing Children For Genetic Predispositions: Is It in Their Best Interest?' (1995) 23 Journal of Law, Medicine and Ethics 331 at 335–336. See also Clayton, 'Removing the Shadow of the Law From the Debate About Genetic Testing of Children' (1995) 57 Am J of Med Genetics at 630.

[8.73] Various professional bodies and health organisations have developed guidelines in relation to predictive genetic testing of children, including the World Health Organisation (WHO),[168] the American Society of Human Genetics,[169] the Nuffield Council on Bioethics,[170] and the Human Genetics Society of Australasia.[171] These expert groups have generally concluded that predictive testing for adult-onset disease for which there is no known treatment or preventive strategy has no immediate benefits and should be deferred until adulthood, or at least until the person is able to appreciate the relevant genetic facts, as well as the emotional and social consequences of what predictive genetic testing entails. The American Society of Human Genetics stated in its 2015 guidance that facilitating predictive or pre-dispositional testing of children for adult-onset conditions can be justified in certain circumstances. 'For example, after careful deliberations with the family and older child, testing can be justified to alleviate substantial psychosocial distress or to facilitate specific life-planning decisions. The impact of predictive testing on children and families remains uncertain and therefore can be justified in specific cases when it is requested by families after informed deliberations and when the testing is not clearly inconsistent with the welfare of the child.'[172]

[8.74] The availability of medical benefit is regarded as the most important justification for performing predictive testing in minors, regardless of the onset of the disease. Therefore the absence of medical benefit is the most important reason to delay testing until the adolescent or adult is able to make a personal decision following full exploration of the issues.[173] If a mature minor requests genetic tests, the geneticist should take into account the competence of the minor to understand the complex issues involved and, having explored them fully, may carry out the testing on the basis that it confers medical, psychological or emotional benefits on him.[174] If the request is made by a parent or other family member, the views of the minor should be obtained and consent given if he is competent. If there is disagreement between the minor and his parents as to whether testing should be carried out, although the geneticist should perhaps recommend delaying the tests until the age of majority is reached, the competent minor should be entitled to make a decision on this matter after full exploration of the issues

---

[168] WHO, *Proposed International Guidelines on Ethical Issues in Medical Genetics and Genetics Services,* 1997.

[169] ASHG/ACMG Report 'Points to Consider: Ethical, Legal and Psychological Implications of Genetic Testing in Children and Adolescents' (1995) 57 Am J Hum Gen 1233.

[170] Nuffield Council on *Bioethics, Mental Disorders and Genetics* 1998.

[171] Human Genetics Society of Australasia, *Predictive Testing in Children and Adolescents* (1999).

[172] Botkin et al, 'Points to Consider: Ethical, Legal, and Psychosocial Implications of Genetic Testing in Children and Adolescents' (2015) The American Journal of Human Genetics, Volume 97, Issue 1, 6 – 21.

[173] See further Borry et al, 'Presymptomatic and Predictive Genetic Testing in Minors: A Systematic Review of Guidelines and Position Papers' (2006) Clin Genet 70:374–381.

[174] The Nuffield Council recommends that caution be exercised before a child under the age of 16 be allowed to make a decision of this nature, as genetic testing may be seen to be in a novel category raising complex issues of benefit and possible harm, particularly if the testing is of no therapeutic benefit and cannot be categorised as treatment. Nuffield Council on Bioethics, Genetic Screening: Ethics Issues (1993) para 5.29.

and appropriate counselling.[175] Disclosure of the test results will also necessitate a finding as to the minor's competence to understand and willingness to know the implications of the results. Whether the results of the test should remain confidential to the minor, unless he consents to disclosure to parents or other family members and the information is relevant to the current care of the minor, is also currently open to question. Under freedom of information legislation in Ireland, the parents of the child would have a presumptive entitlement to access the child's medical records.[176]

[8.75] In relation to diseases for which there is no treatment such as Huntington's disease, many centres have refused to test children under the age of 18 for the gene, as it is perceived that the potential harms of testing in that age group are greater than the benefits. The reasons for such refusals are that:

> Children clearly cannot make an informed decision about whether to participate in predictive testing. The request is made by a third party, in this instance a parent. The only justification for doing predictive testing in childhood is if an advantage can clearly be demonstrated for the child. There is currently no known treatment which might prevent or delay the age of onset for HD. Such testing may be disadvantageous for the child, either because of possible distortion of parent/child or sib/sib relationships or because of limitation of resources for the child shown to be at increased risk. The self-esteem and sense of worth of a developing child may be profoundly and negatively affected. The attitude of society and its agencies toward high-risk individuals has not yet been clarified. Since no treatment is available and there is the possibility of harm, we oppose the testing of children.[177]

[8.76] The International Huntington's Disease Association has also recommended that minors should not be tested for Huntington's disease until they turn 18:[178]

> Persons who learn that they are carriers are at risk for severe reactive depression, and it is known that among carriers the suicide rate is four-fold, higher than in the general population. In families with several children, survival guilt may be a serious problem as the child who learns that he or she does not have the gene, but that a sibling does, may have great difficulty resolving the issue of 'why him and not me?' While learning early that one has *not* inherited the gene eliminates years of anxiety for the adolescent, it should be noted that half the time the hopes of both parent and child are dashed by a positive diagnosis.[179]

Genetic testing and mental disorders

[8.77] The range of ethical issues raised by genetic information expands when the information concerns mental disorders. Some of these additional issues cluster around the notion of personal well-being, of how one views oneself and is viewed by others;

---

[175] Former UK Advisory Committee on Genetic Testing, *Genetic testing for late-onset disorders* (1998) at 28.

[176] See further discussion in Ch 3 at para **[3.24]** et seq.

[177] Bloch and Hayden, 'Opinion: Predictive Testing for Huntington Disease in Childhood: Challenges and Implications' Am J Hum Genet 46:1–4, 1990.

[178] MacLeod et al, 'Recommendations for the predictive genetic test in Huntington's disease', Clinical Genetics Volume 83, Issue 3, 221–231, March 2013.

[179] Reilly, 'Public Policy and Legal Issues Raised by Advances in Genetic Screening and Testing' (1993) XXVII Suffolk University Law Review 1327 at 1340–41.

others concern reproductive decisions and some arise from the fact that mental disorders are often stigmatised.'[180] The term 'mental disorder' is described by the WHO as implying 'the existence of a clinically recognisable set of symptoms or behaviour associated in most cases with distress and with interference with personal functions.'[181]

[8.78] In relation to single-gene disorders a genetic test may yield a high degree of certainty as to whether the individual will or will not develop a particular disorder. If the disorder has already been seen in the family, the individual member of the family already has information upon which to base a decision about whether to request testing or not. However, where the test is for a gene variant associated with relatively slight predispositions to a disorder, the issues are more difficult, as susceptibility is markedly different from certainty, although susceptibility may be relevant in making certain life-style choices. Most common disorders, both physical and mental, are influenced by variants in several or many genes, with each one having a relatively small effect. In addition, susceptibility may be affected by environmental factors. This means that differences in individuals' genetic make-up may lead them to experience the same environment, such as traumatic life events, differently.[182]

[8.79] In relation to mental disorders, the genetic information obtained by way of testing might raise serious questions about the person's functional abilities and reproductive choices. In some cases, the acquisition of such knowledge might lead to extreme distress and anxiety, which might even precipitate the onset of the condition. The potential stigmatisation of mental disorder for both the patient and family members must also be taken into account here, as the availability of genetic tests for such disorders may not necessarily serve to lessen this problem.[183] Although it has been claimed that gene identification will be very valuable in personalising risks of mental disorder and that the increase in precision provided by the ability to calculate risks on an individual basis will be of enormous clinical benefit, this has been doubted by the Nuffield Council on Bioethics, which states that the evidence to support such claims is currently lacking.[184] As with all genetic tests, specialist counselling should be provided before such tests are undertaken, particularly as people with psychiatric problems have low self-esteem, and

---

[180] Nuffield Council on Bioethics, *Genetic Screening: Ethics Issues* (1993) at 1.19.

[181] WHO, *The Classification of Mental and Behavioural Disorders: Clinical Descriptions and Diagnostic Guidelines* (1992) at 5. Most psychiatrists diagnose mental disorders only when an individual is unable to achieve realistic personal goals due to psychiatric symptoms. See Nuffield at para 2.1. For discussion about the difficulties of defining mental illness, and the distinction between illness and social deviance, see Nuffield Council on Bioethics, *Genetic Screening: Ethics Issues* (1993) at 2.1 – 2.11.

[182] See further Rutherford et al, 'Genetic Influences on Eating Attitudes in a Normal Female Twin Population' (1993) 23(2) Psychological Medicine 425–36; Rutter and Plomin, 'Opportunities for Psychiatry from Genetic Findings' (1997) 171 British J of Psychiatry 209–19; Nuffield at 3.16–3.20.

[183] Stigmatisation results from ignorance and misconceptions about mental disorders. While less than 3% of mentally ill patients could be categorised as dangerous, 77% of mentally ill people depicted on prime-time television are presented as dangerous. See Dubin and Fink, 'Effects of Stigma on Psychiatric Treatment' in Fink and Tasman (eds) *Stigma and Mental Illness* (American Psychiatric Press Inc, 1992) at 3.

[184] Nuffield Council on Bioethics *Genetic Screening: Ethics Issues* (1993) at 4.16.

they may believe that positive test results confirm this opinion. This may cause fatalistic attitudes to develop towards their problem, and decrease their motivation to resolve it.[185]

[8.80] In order to give informed consent to be tested, the law presumes that the person has capacity to understand the information they are given about the nature of the test and its benefits and risks. Understanding the complexities of genetics is not easy, particularly given the variety of scientific, psychological, familial and social issues involved. Information should always be given in a clear and balanced way, using non-technical language as far as possible, so as to facilitate the necessary level of understanding to be reached in order that the person has an informed choice as to whether to be tested.

PRENATAL DIAGNOSIS

[8.81] Approximately 8 million children are born worldwide with serious illnesses with a genetic cause every year. At least 3.3 million children less than 5 years of age die annually because of serious birth defects, defined as any serious abnormality of structure or function. An estimated 3.2 million of those who survive may be mentally and physically disabled for life.[186] For some couples, the birth of a child with a serious medical condition is the first indication that one or both of the parents carries a genetic mutation. Others may be aware of a family history of genetic disorder and may therefore know that they are at risk of conceiving a child with the particular disorder. Prenatal tests have been available for many decades which make it possible for parents to assess the severity of the risk that a child will be born with a genetic defect. If a genetic defect is identified in the foetus, the parents may nonetheless make a decision to continue with the pregnancy but there is psychological and practical value in being aware of the condition of the foetus at an early stage.

[8.82] There are a number of different techniques that can be used at the pre-natal stage. Non-invasive screening tests, such as nuchal thickness screening, serum screening or cell-free DNA screening which screens non-fetal DNA in the maternal bloodstream, can estimate the risks of a pregnancy giving rise to a baby with specific chromosome abnormalities such as Down's syndrome, but these are only risk-based tests and not absolute diagnostic tests. Prenatal diagnosis (PND) in the form of amniocentesis was first reported in 1930 and is relatively simple to perform. A small amount of amniotic fluid is removed from the pregnant woman at 16 weeks of pregnancy in order to identify specific genetic disorders. Chorionic villus sampling removes placental tissue at 11 weeks to detect foetal abnormalities. Both of these diagnostic tests are invasive and carry some risks for the pregnancy and would usually be used if a screening test or prenatal cell-free DNA screening indicates a possible problem, or the woman's age, family history or medical history puts her at increased risk of having a baby with a

---

[185] Nuffield Council on Bioethics *Genetic Screening: Ethics Issues* (1993) at 5.5.
[186] Christianson, Howson and Modell, *The March of Dimes Global Report on Birth Defects: The Hidden Toll of Dying and Disabled Children* (2006).

genetic problem. Screening for neural tube defects is almost always done by way of antenatal ultrasound.

[8.83] In jurisdictions where abortion is permissible, couples face the dilemma of having to decide after diagnosis of a serious abnormality whether or not to terminate the pregnancy. In Ireland the dilemma effectively begins at an earlier stage as the couple has to decide whether or not to have the test done bearing in mind that a termination of the pregnancy will not be possible in this jurisdiction unless the woman's life is endangered by the pregnancy.[187] In circumstances where a diagnosis of serious abnormality is made, where the medical condition suffered by the foetus is such that it is believed to be incompatible with life outside the womb, the couple will have to choose whether to continue with the pregnancy until natural delivery, knowing that the baby will not survive, or to travel to another jurisdiction (usually the UK) for a termination of the pregnancy there.[188]

Ethical issues

[8.84] Any discussion of the ethical issues of genetic counselling and prenatal diagnosis is unavoidably haunted by a ghost called the morality of abortion. This section will not discuss the issues involved in abortion generally, but will look at ethical issues that arise in the case of prenatal diagnosis leading to abortion for foetal indications, sometimes referred to as genetic abortion.

[8.85] Arguments in favour of genetic abortion rest on a few principles, firstly that it is a private matter for the couple to decide, based upon their own values and determination of what is in the best interests of their family, the number and health of their children if this is scientifically possible. If they believe that the birth of a child with a serious disease or disability would be psychologically, emotionally and financially harmful for themselves or their other children, they should therefore be permitted to reach the decision to abort such a foetus. Secondly it may be said that society has a legitimate interest in the pursuit of genetic fitness of its members. It is thus argued that the financial implications of caring for people with disabilities could be more productively spent on caring for those who are likely to give something back to society.[189] This does not however take account of the financial resources expended on public health and education of healthy citizens, nor does it take into account the immeasurable contributions that people with disabilities can make in society, such as the provision of comfort and practical help to others living with disabilities, as well as teaching the value of patience, kindness and understanding to those with whom they come into contact.[190]

[8.86] The third justification could be described as 'the natural standard'. It is argued here that, due to our increasing knowledge of genetic diseases, it is known that those

---

[187] Protection of Life during Pregnancy Act 2013.

[188] This issue is currently a matter of considerable political and public debate in Ireland with many calls being made for the repeal of the 8th Amendment to the Constitution to enable the 2013 Act to be amended to allow termination of pregnancy in cases of fatal fetal abnormality.

[189] See generally Kaplan, 'Prenatal Screening and its Impact on Persons with Disabilities' in Kuhse and Singer, *A Companion to Bioethics* (Blackwell Publishing, 1998) at 130–136.

[190] Buck, Foreword to *The Terrible Choice: The Abortion Dilemma* (Bantam Books, 1968).

who suffer from certain diseases will never live the full life of a human being.[191] They will not be able to live independent lives, care for themselves, nor, in some cases, develop the distinctively human capacities for thought or self-consciousness. Nature has caused miscarriage to occur in many of these cases, or early death in others. Therefore, the altruistic argument is that we should not strive to keep alive people born with such conditions, and we should try to avoid their conception or birth if possible. By permitting prenatal screening or genetic abortions, we are thus 'saving potential future children from pain and harm.'[192] The logic of this argument is that standards in these cases are objective and of general application, thus avoiding the relativity and subjectivity of societal and parental interests.[193] However, the counter argument is that the boundaries between potentially human and potentially not human are ambiguous and can lead to value judgments on the meaning of 'severe' and 'disability'. Even the notion that there is a norm of perfection to which nature strives is difficult to accept given that many of us would fall short of such a norm.

[8.87] There is also the argument that we should try to provide every child with a normal opportunity for health, even if this duty requires us to refrain from reproduction. Although this may again seem to incorporate unsatisfactory appeals to what may be considered 'normal', bearing in mind the worldwide differences in such measurements, another way of looking at it would be to say that parents ought to try to provide for their children health normal for that culture, although it may be inadequate if measured by other standards.[194] The argument is based on prospective views rather than retrospective ones, and therefore does not impinge on the value of those people already living with genetic disorders. It is based on the opinion that, for example, a world where nobody is at risk for Huntington's disease, must be preferable to the current situation where children are born with a 50 percent chance of suffering from this serious disease. It is thus regarded as defensible to prevent the birth of possible persons, who are not thereby deprived or injured if they do not exist. This is premised on the argument that possible persons do not exist, nor do they have any right to exist, and therefore they do not have any experiences or interests that might suffer if they are not brought into existence.[195]

---

[191] There is an assumption that there is a relationship between genetic conditions and a negative life experience. For less severe genetic conditions, this may not be a correct assumption. 'The disability rights movement certainly agrees that there are economic and social disadvantages that are associated with disability. However, the fact that so many persons with disabilities are engaging in ordinary lives with satisfying jobs, happy family situations, and a variety of community roles suggests that these disadvantages can be eliminated without eliminating persons with disabilities.' Kaplan, 'Prenatal Screening and its Impact on Persons with Disabilities' in Kuhse and Singer, *Bioethics* (Blackwell Publishing,1998) at 135.

[192] Kaplan, 'Prenatal Screening and its Impact on Persons with Disabilities' in Kuhse and Singer, *Bioethics* (Blackwell Publishing,1998) at 133.

[193] Kass, 'Implications of Prenatal Diagnosis for the Human Right to Life' in Hilton et al (eds) *Ethical Issues in Human Genetics: Genetic Counselling and the Use of Genetic Knowledge* (New York: Plenum Press, 1973) 185–199.

[194] Purdy, 'Genetic Diseases: Can Having Children Be Immoral?' in Kuhse and Singer (eds) *Bioethics, An Anthology* (Blackwell Publishing, 1999) 123–129 at 126.

[195] Purdy, 'Genetic Diseases: Can Having Children Be Immoral?' in Kuhse and Singer (eds) *Bioethics, An Anthology* (Blackwell Publishing, 1999) 123–129 at 126.

[8.88] The slippery slope argument arises here too, in that if pre-natal diagnosis and abortion are permitted for what might be accepted as a serious condition, it is argued that a further extension of pre-natal diagnosis for 'minor' genetic abnormalities may become commonplace in the future. The ethical objections to such an extension rest on grounds of irrationality, discrimination, rationing of resources, reduced genetic diversity, harm to the foetus, distinction between social terminations and terminations following pre-natal diagnosis, and harm to society.[196]

PRE-IMPLANTATION GENETIC DIAGNOSIS

[8.89] Developments in in vitro fertilisation (IVF)[197] and embryo micromanipulation techniques led in 1989[198] to the ability to determine genetic diagnoses in early embryos prior to implantation of the embryo in the uterus.[199] Since then there has been in excess of 10,000 births worldwide from IVF-PGD cycles.[200] Pre-implantation genetic diagnosis (known as PGD or PID) most commonly involves the removal of a single cell from an embryo created through IVF[201] which has been cultured in carefully controlled conditions until 6 to 12 discreet cells are present. This usually occurs about three days following fertilisation. Each of these cells contains the full genetic material of the baby that would develop if the embryo were to implant in the womb. The DNA contained in the cell is amplified and tested to determine whether or not the embryo from which the DNA was extracted carries a genetic mutation known to be carried by one or both parents. In this way, only unaffected embryos will be selected for transfer to the uterus.[202] The most common uses of PGD are for cystic fibrosis, sickle-cell disease, thalassaemia, Tay-Sachs mutations, X-linked diseases, Duchenne's muscular dystrophy and some chromosomal abnormalities. Tests for other genetic mutations may be possible depending on current knowledge of the genetic code underlying the disease.[203] PGD may

---

[196] Boyle and Savulescu, 'Prenatal Diagnosis for Minor Genetic Abnormalities is *Ethical*' (2003) Am J of Bioethics Vol 3 No 1.

[197] See Ch. 6 for further discussion of IVF.

[198] The first successful PGD was reported in 1990 when two sets of twin girls were produced where families were at high risk of passing on a serious X-linked disorder. See Handyside et al, 'Pregnancies From Biopsied Human Preimplantation Embryos Sexed by Y Specific DNA Amplification' (1990) 344 Nature 768–770. The first autosomal recessive disorder where PGD resulted in the birth of an unaffected child was cystic fibrosis. See Handyside et al, 'Birth of a Normal Girl After IVF and Preimplantation Diagnostic Testing for Cystic Fibrosis' (1992) 327 NEJM 905–909.

[199] See generally Hildt and Graumann, *Genetics in Human Reproduction* (Ashgate Publishing, 1999).

[200] Simpson, Rechitsky, Kuliev, 'Next generation sequencing for preimplantation genetic diagnosis'. Fertil Steril. 2013 Feb 13.

[201] The removal of one cell from an embryo does not seem to impair the viability of that embryo.

[202] For detailed discussion of the development of the technique, see Edwards and Schulman, 'History of and Opportunities for Preimplantation Diagnosis' in Edwards (ed) *Preconception and Preimplantation Diagnosis of Human Genetic Disease* (New York: Cambridge University Press, 1993) 3–40.

[203] For comment on the issues affecting couples who choose PGD, see Botkin, 'Ethical Issues and Practical Problems in Preimplantation Genetic Diagnosis' (1998) 26 JME 17.

also be used for sex selection and for HLA tissue typing but these uses are more controversial and will be discussed further later.

[8.90] The significance of PGD is that it offers high-risk couples the chance to have a child free from specific disorders without having to undergo invasive prenatal diagnostic procedures or terminations. Both PGD and PND (pre-natal diagnosis during pregnancy) can be used in an attempt to avoid the birth of a child with a genetically inherited condition or defect, although the use of genetic tests will never achieve 'perfection' due to the fact that most people carry at least four or five recessive genes. When used for such a purpose, the chief moral advantage generally claimed for PGD over PND is that PGD does not involve terminating a pregnancy. 'This will not impress those who believe that a biologically human being has an inviolable 'right' to life from conception, but it does recommend PGD to those who believe that the embryo achieves this status only at the moment of implantation.'[204] 'Since embryos with genetic abnormalities are discarded, PGD requires couples to make a moral distinction between termination of an implanted pregnancy and the discarding of affected, non-transferred embryos.'[205]

[8.91] Considerable differences in regulatory oversight of PGD exist among countries, ranging from total bans on any embryo manipulation to the almost complete absence of any regulations or authority. For example in the UK, an embryo may be tested to establish whether it has a particular chromosomal abnormality only if a) that abnormality may affect its capacity to result in a live birth, or b) there is a particular risk that it has that abnormality, and where the Human Fertilisation and Embryology Authority (HFEA), which licenses centres to provide this service, is satisfied that there is a significant risk that a person with that abnormality will have or develop a serious medical condition.[206]

[8.92] Recommendations and regulations governing its use often draft the criteria for PGD broadly in line with the criteria for selective abortion, where such is permitted by law. PGD is becoming increasingly available throughout the world, although often in only limited circumstances. The International Federation of Fertility Societies Surveillance in 2013 reports that PGD is increasingly available worldwide. 'It provides easily proven benefits, is generally considered safe, and has a low frequency of errors...PGD clearly prevents women from delivering offspring with serious genetic disorders, avoids terminations, and brings peace of mind to many couples that otherwise are fearful or simply would not have children.[207]

[8.93] Those most likely to benefit from the technique include couples known to carry a genetic mutation who have a moral objection to termination of pregnancy following prenatal testing, women who are infertile and at risk of carrying a particular genetic disease and so-called 'genetic disaster' families who have already conceived children

---

[204] Beyleveld, 'Does PID Solve the Moral Problems of Prenatal Diagnosis? A Rights Analysis'. Beyleveld uses the acronym PID for preimplantation genetic diagnosis and PD for prenatal diagnosis.

[205] Simpson, 'Preimplantation genetic diagnosis at 20 years.' Prenat Diagn. 2010 Jul;30(7):682–95.

[206] See list of conditions for which licences may currently be given by the HFEA at www.hfea.gov.uk/cps/hfea/gen/pgd-screening.htm.

[207] www.iffs-reproduction.org at 105.

with the disease.[208] Almost all genetically inherited conditions that are diagnosed in the prenatal period can also be diagnosed in the pre-implantation period. As technology continues to develop it is argued that the temptation to subject embryos to a 'genetic check-up' prior to implantation will increase, although it will never ensure the birth of a completely 'normal' baby,[209] as it will be impossible to check for polygenic or multifactorial disorders or to rule out the possibility of the child being affected with diseases other than those already present in the family. It is also unlikely that PGD will ever be employed on as broad a basis as prenatal testing as it is only available in conjunction with IVF, which is a complex and costly procedure,[210] and also because of the very small number of viable offspring that result from its use.[211]

[8.94] In relation to the importance of genetic counselling[212] of couples seeking PGD it has been argued that, although the standard view is that non-directive counselling should be given, it is not possible, and may not be desirable, to do so in relation to PGD. This is due to the vulnerability of the couple, the social context and attitudes to disability and the structure of the genetic services offered.[213] Chadwick explains this firstly by the fact that in professional-client relations, there is typically an imbalance of power due to the difference in knowledge and, often, social status, between the parties. In reproductive counselling this is exacerbated by the extra vulnerability of pregnancy and in PGD, by the strains of the IVF process. Secondly, the significance of negative social attitudes towards disability will inevitably play a role in advancing the perception that PGD is preferable to prenatal diagnosis and that this will also affect the practice of genetic counselling. Thirdly, the fact that genetic counselling is available for certain conditions would seem to indicate that these conditions are more undesirable than others. So 'although there is explicit adherence to the ideal of choice, implicitly certain decisions are expected.'[214] Non-directive counselling may not be desirable in this context, as it may not be what couples want, being perceived as cold and unhelpful. Also it is argued

---

[208] Penketh, 'The Scope of Preimplantation Diagnosis' in Edwards (ed) *Preconception and Preimplantation Diagnosis of Human Genetic Disease* (New York: Cambridge University Press, 1993) at 82–84.

[209] The definition of 'normal' is obviously a matter of crucial debate in this context, as is any attempted definition of 'severe' or 'serious' disorder. Values differ amongst families, societies and ethnic groups and may change over time. It is difficult, therefore, to compile any list of disorders for which it would be ethical to test. The standard used in the context of PND in the UK is where there is a precise diagnosis and a 'substantial risk' of 'serious handicap.'

[210] PGD is not commonly carried out in Ireland so couples may travel to the UK, where a small number of clinics are licensed by the Human Fertilisation and Embryology Authority to carry out such testing. Alternatively, cells removed from embryos in Irish clinics may be sent to licensed clinics in other countries for diagnostic testing.

[211] Human Genetics Commission, Response to the HFEA on the Consultation on PGD (2001) para 4.

[212] For further explanation of the issues involved in genetic counselling, see Clarke 'Genetic Counselling' in Chadwick, *The Concise Encyclopedia of the Ethics of New Technologies* (Academic Press, 2001) at 131–146.

[213] Chadwick, 'Preimplantation Diagnosis – Implications for Genetic Counselling' in Hildt and Graumann, *Genetics in Human Reproduction* (Ashgate Publishing, 1999) at 253.

[214] Chadwick, 'Preimplantation Diagnosis – Implications for Genetic Counselling' in Hildt and Graumann, *Genetics in Human Reproduction* (Ashgate Publishing, 1999) at 254.

that the principle of autonomy as the underpinning of such counselling may not be appropriate here as reproductive decisions should be made in the light of as much information as possible.[215] The suggestion of such a duty 'marks a move away from autonomous decision-making about reproduction to the suggestion that there are certain constraints on what decisions we ought to make.'[216]

[8.95] One of the issues that arises here is the extent to which the prospective parents' views about foetal disability should be taken into account. It has been argued that '[t]he vast majority of people hope that their children will be healthy and free from disability. This does not mean that they will not love and care for a child born with a disability. However, the impact on the quality of life of a child born with a disability, as well as their families will depend on a number of factors. These will include the seriousness of the disability, the circumstances of the family, as well as the emotional and material support available. Each family should be free to make their own choices in this respect and their view will be one of the most important determining factors in assessing the justification for PGD.'[217]

[8.96] People vary in their reaction to the possibility of foetal abnormality: 'there are reasons to want to prevent the birth of a child affected by impairment which do not reflect discrimination against disabled people: for example, the desire to avoid the early death or suffering of a loved child, or a feeling that a family will be unable to cope with the strain of looking after a very impaired member.'[218] The difficulty is that moving to a rights-based system which accords full decision-making authority to the prospective parents, whether it be in relation to genetic abortion, PND or PGD, could lead to abortion on demand, whereas putting limits on decision-making authority interferes with reproductive autonomy.[219] While selection of an embryo to avoid serious impairment may be morally justifiable, the definition of 'serious' is problematic when we move beyond extreme conditions such as Tay-Sachs disease, which can include symptoms such as blindness, deafness, loss of intellectual and motor skills, feeding difficulties and seizures. Many reports and commentaries on this issue state that the task of defining 'serious' in this context is impossible. In cases where there is a reasonable disagreement between the prospective parents and the health professionals on whether a condition is 'serious', it may be argued that the parents' views should carry the most weight since they will have the responsibility of caring for and raising the child.

---

[215] Botkin suggests that 'it would make little sense to go through IVF procedures and genetic analyses only to be nondirective about which embryos to place in the uterus. The purpose of PGD is not simply to inform a couple about the genetic nature of their embryos. The explicit purpose is also to transfer healthy embryos and to discard those destined to be affected. Once a couple has chosen PGD, nondirectiveness is no longer relevant.' Botkin, 'Ethical Issues and Practical Problems in Preimplantation Genetic Diagnosis' (1998) 26 JME 17.

[216] Chadwick, 'Preimplantation Diagnosis – Implications for Genetic Counselling' in Hildt and Graumann, *Genetics in Human Reproduction* (Ashgate Publishing, 1999) at 254.

[217] Human Fertilisation and Embryology Authority and Advisory Commission on Genetic Testing, *Consultation Document on PGD* (1999).

[218] Shakespeare, 'Choices and Rights: Eugenics, Genetics and Disability Equality' (1998) 13(5) Disability and Society 665, 672.

[219] See further discussion by Scott, 'The Uncertain Scope of Reproductive Autonomy in Preimplantation Genetic Diagnosis and Selective Abortion' (2005) Med Law Rev Vol 13: 291–327.

[8.97] There are many ethical issues associated with PGD, including whether moral status is accorded to the embryo from conception,[220] and the inherent 'selection' that PGD seems to offer.[221] PGD has sometimes been represented as the technique enabling parents to create 'designer babies' by selecting embryos with desired genes for intelligence, sporting ability, musical talent and so on.[222] Thus, it may be argued that 'once we decide to begin the process of human genetic engineering, there is really no logical place to stop. If diabetes, sickle cell anaemia, and cancer are cured by altering the genetic makeup of an individual, why not proceed to other 'disorders': myopia, colour-blindness, left-handedness?'[223] Even if it is accepted that PGD should be available for serious or severe conditions, how may lines be drawn between severe conditions and non-severe conditions? 'Severity varies not only historically but according to the precise social context of each affected person.'[224] However, even if it were technically possible to select embryos on the basis of desired genes, the ethical implications of using the procedure for non-disease genes or for social characteristics would be hard to overcome.[225]

[8.98] It may be argued that PGD, as a negative selection tool, meets the definition of eugenics, as it excludes the implantation of certain embryos after genetic defects are discovered, or prefers certain embryos on the basis of desired characteristics.[226] Article 3.2 of the EU Charter of Fundamental Rights 2000 proclaims the right to the integrity of the person and states that 'the prohibition of eugenic practices, in particular those

---

[220] See Chapter 6 for detailed discussion of this issue.

[221] As Glover asks, 'how far should we go in choosing what kinds of people should be born?' Glover, 'Eugenics: Some Lessons from the Nazi Experience' in Harris and Holm (eds) *The Future of Human Reproduction* (Clarendon Press, 1998) 55 at 57. See also Krahn, 'Regulating Preimplantation Genetic Diagnosis: The Case of Down's Syndrome' (Spring 2011) 19, Medical Law Review, pp 157–191.

[222] For arguments that couples should be allowed to select embryos which are most likely to have the best life, based on available genetic information, including information about non-disease genes, see Savulescu, 'Procreative Beneficence: Why We Should Select the Best Children' (2001) 15 (5/6) Bioethics 413–426.

[223] This statement was made in the context of gene therapy but the sentiment applies equally here. Rifkin, cited in Holtug, 'Human Gene Therapy: Down the Slippery Slope?' (1993) 7(5) Bioethics 402–419.

[224] Holm, 'Ethical Issues in Pre-Implantation Genetic Diagnosis' in Harris and Holm (eds) *The Future of Human Reproduction* (Clarendon Press, 1998) at 184.

[225] PGD 'could signify the reduction of human life to the sum of its genes'. Decisions based on quality of life criteria should be scrutinised on the basis of the distinction between illness and enhancement. See Mieth, 'In Vitro Fertilisation: From Medical Reproduction to Genetic Diagnosis' (1996) 1 (1) Biomedical Ethics 6–8.

[226] Advances in non-invasive prenatal testing may yield similar outcomes through testing of maternal plasma. Recent research shows that among high-risk pregnancies clinically indicated for invasive prenatal diagnosis, non-invasive detection of foetal trisomy 21 (Down's syndrome) can be achieved with the use of sequencing of maternal plasma DNA. It is thought that the sequencing test could be used to rule out trisomy 21 among high-risk pregnancies before proceeding to invasive diagnostic testing to reduce the number of cases requiring amniocentesis or chorionic villus sampling. Chiu et al, 'Non-Invasive Prenatal Assessment of Trisomy 21 by Multiplexed Maternal Plasma DNA Sequencing: Large Scale Validity Study' BMJ 2011; 342: c7401.

aiming at the selection of persons' must be respected.[227] This provision may be interpreted as precluding PGD.[228] In addition to arguments that this comes close to eugenics, it may also be claimed that testing the embryo for specific genes interferes with the child's right to an open future.[229] Davis explains that 'good parenting requires a balance between having a child for our own sakes and being open to the moral reality that the child will exist for her own sake'.[230] For example, an embryo might be selected for its perfect musical pitch[231] yet the child has an interest in not having the way she is raised unduly affected by her parents' expectations consequent on their PGD decisions – she needs to be able to reject music if she wishes.[232]

[8.99] It is also argued that the use of PGD devalues people with disabilities, as it is akin to stating that they should not have been born. The purpose of PGD is not just to inform couples about the genetic conditions of their embryos but to enable them to avoid having a child with a disability. Perfection will thus become the norm in society, which will increase the stigmatisation of those who choose not to undergo such testing. The counter argument is that it is ethically acceptable to choose not to have a child with a particular disorder, while at the same time agreeing that any affected person would have the same rights and worth as any other member of society. Asch acknowledges that although society can do a great deal to offer opportunities to people with disabilities, not all disabilities can be overcome – this is not a matter of social prejudice but of reality. She says:

> Not all problems of disability are socially created and, thus, theoretically remediable…The inability to move without mechanical aid, to see, to hear, or to learn is not inherently neutral. Disability itself limits some options. Listening to the radio for someone who is deaf, looking at paintings for someone who is blind, walking upstairs for someone who is quadriplegic, or reading abstract articles for someone who is intellectually disabled are precluded by impairment alone…It is not irrational to hope that children and adults will live as long as possible without health problems or diminished human capacities.[233]

[8.100] Is it possible to view PGD as a form of disease prevention, comparable to recommending folic acid supplements to pregnant women to prevent the births of

---

[227] See http://www.europarl.europa.eu/charter/pdf/text_en.pdf.

[228] Somsen, 'Regulating Human Genetics in a Non-Eugenic Era' in Murphy (ed) *New Technologies and Human Rights* (OUP, 2009) 85–127.

[229] Feinburg, 'The Child's Right to an Open Future' in Aiken and LaFollette (eds) *Whose Child? Children's Rights, Parental Authority and State Power* (Rowman and Littlefield, 1980).

[230] Davis, 'Genetic Dilemmas and the Child's Right to an Open Future' (1997) Hastings Centre Report 27(2) 7 at 12.

[231] Robertson argues that selecting embryos for perfect pitch or other non-medical reasons may be justifiable, depending on the importance of the reproductive choice being asserted, the burdens of the selection procedure, its impact on offspring and its implications for deselected groups and society generally. Robertson, 'Extending Preimplantation Genetic Diagnosis: Medical and Non-Medical Uses' J Med Ethics (2003) 29: 213–216.

[232] Scott, 'Choosing Between Possible Lives: Legal and Ethical Issues in Preimplantation Genetic Diagnosis' (2006) 26(1) Ox J Leg Studies 153–178 at 170.

[233] Asch, 'Reproductive Technology and Disability' in Cohen and Taub (eds) *Reproductive Laws for the 1990s* (Humana Press, 1988) p 69–124. Quoted by Steinbock, 'Preimplantation Genetic Diagnosis and Embryo Selection' in Burley and Harris (eds) *A Companion to Genethics* (Blackwell Publishing, 2002) 175 at 180.

children with neural tube defects? Both measures are designed to reduce the number of individuals born with disabilities but no one claims that recommending folic acid constitutes discrimination against people with spina bifida. Steinbock thus argues that 'there is no inconsistency in thinking, 'if I have a child who has a disability or becomes ill, or has special needs, I will love and care for that child; but this is an outcome I would much prefer to avoid.'[234] Savulescu goes further in advocating a principle of procreative beneficence which states that couples should select the child, of the possible children they could have, who is expected to have the best life, or at least as good a life as the others, based on the relevant available information.[235]

[8.101] Another issue is whether carrier or affected embryos should be transferred to the uterus in any circumstances. In some cases PGD will identify not only embryos directly affected by the genetic disorder but also those who may be carriers of recessive disorders. If there are not many embryos available for transfer the couple may choose to transfer a carrier embryo even though the child will face difficult reproductive decisions of its own at some future time. The former Human Genetics Commission in the UK was of the view that if it is possible to exclude affected embryos without discovering the carrier status of others, and without compromising the accuracy of the test, then this is to be preferred. 'This will result in an increased chance of the couple achieving an unaffected pregnancy. It will also protect the unborn child's subsequent right to decide for themselves whether or not to be tested for their carrier status.'[236]

[8.102] It is also possible that a couple may specifically wish to transfer an affected embryo, although this would be regarded as highly unusual and ethically problematic. An example of this occurred in 2002 when a deaf couple in the United States chose to transfer an embryo carrying the gene for deafness because they were of the opinion that a hearing child born into their environment would be alienated and disadvantaged in the deaf community. They did not see deafness as a disability and saw it rather as defining their cultural identity. They regarded sign language as a sophisticated, unique form of communication.[237] Whether it is ethically acceptable to deliberately cause a child to be born with, what may be perceived as, a disability is open to question, given that the welfare of any resulting child should be considered before embarking on any IVF programme. However, it is also important to note the danger here of slipping down a slippery slope[238] where screening then becomes an obligation or inherent in responsible procreation.[239]

---

[234] Steinbock, 'Preimplantation Genetic Diagnosis and Embryo Selection' in Burley and Harris (eds) *A Companion to Genethics* (Blackwell Publishing, 2002) 175 at 182.

[235] Savulescu, 'Procreative Beneficence: Why We Should Select the Best Children' (2001) Bioethics 15(5/6) 414–425.

[236] Former Human Genetics Commission, Response to the HFEA on the Consultation on PGD (2001) p 4.

[237] See discussion in Savulescu, 'Deaf lesbians, 'designer disability,' and the future of medicine.' British Medical Journal. 2002;325(7367):771–773.

[238] See further McGleenan, 'Reproductive Technology and the Slippery Slope Argument: A Message in Blood' in Hildt and Graumann (eds) *Genetics in Human Reproduction* (Ashgate Publishing, 1999) 273–283; and McGleenan, 'Human Gene Therapy and Slippery Slope Arguments' (1995) 21 JME 350–355.

[239] 'With the availability of genetic tests, bringing an affected child into the world could be construed by some as reproductive irresponsibility. (contd.../)

PGD for sex selection

[8.103] PGD allows for the chromosomal evaluation of embryos and therefore for the selection of embryos by sex prior to transfer to the uterus. Although sperm-sorting techniques had been available for this purpose for many years, PGD is a more effective and accurate method of selection. Many international bodies such as the United Nations,[240] the International Federation of Gynaecology and Obstetrics[241] and the American College of Obstetricians and Gynaecologists[242] oppose sex selection for non-medical reasons on the basis that it is sexist and therefore discriminatory against women, and that it might lead to gender imbalances in the general population, as reported in India and China, where societies clearly favour male over female children. There is also a suggestion that evidence from evolutionary psychology and biology suggests that the sex of the offspring in mammals may not be a matter of chance. Instead, sex allocation may be the result of a finely tuned adaptive process involving the suitability of the mother to conceive a child of a particular sex. Therefore, more information needs to be obtained before a social policy is determined which could have disadvantageous consequences for children, their parents and society.[243]

[8.104] Although pre-conceptive sex and race selection enhance procreative liberty, the procedures are regarded by some as disturbing because they potentially reflect parental expectations of gender-appropriate stereotypical behaviour.[244] However, it may also be said that these arguments allow political correctness to abridge individual reproductive choice.[245] It is a presumption of liberal democracies that the freedom of citizens should not be interfered with unless good and sufficient justifications can be produced for so doing. As Dworkin puts it:

> The right of procreative autonomy has an important place...in Western political culture more generally. The most important feature of that culture is a belief in individual human dignity: that people have the moral right – and the moral responsibility – to confront the most fundamental questions about the meaning and value of their own lives for themselves, answering to their own consciences and convictions...The principle of

---

[239] (\...contd) This irresponsibility may be in respect of the child if born, or in respect of the community whose scarce resources will be used to support that child through its disability.' Whittaker, 'The Implications of the Human Genome Project for Family Practice' 35(3) J of Fam Practice 294 at 296.

[240] United Nations, 'Gender Equality, Equity and Empowerment of Women' in Population and Development: Programme of Action Adopted at the International Conference on Population and Development, Sept 1994, Cairo: New York UN 1995, 17–21.

[241] FIGO, Committee for the Ethical Aspects of Human Reproduction and Women's Health, 'Ethical Guidelines on Sex Selection for Non-Medical Purposes' I J Gyn Obst 2006; 92:329–330.

[242] ACOG, Committee on Ethics. Sex Selection, Committee Opinion Number 360; Feb 2007; Obstet Gynecol 2007; 109:475–478.

[243] Grant, 'Sex Predetermination and the Ethics of Sex Selection' Hum Reprod Vol 21 No 7 pp 1659–1661, 2006.

[244] Berkowitz, 'Sexism and Racism in Preconceptive Trait Selection' (1999) 71(3) Fertility and Sterility 415–417.

[245] Paulson, 'Political Correctness and the Abridgement of Reproductive Choice' (1999) 71(3) Fertility and Sterility 418–419.

procreative autonomy, in a broad sense, is embedded in any genuinely democratic culture.[246]

[8.105] However, others argue that although personal freedom is important, 'it is an inadequate ethic if it effectively forecloses moral evaluation of any activity where harms have not yet been empirically demonstrated – especially where the nature of those possible harms makes them difficult to demonstrate'.[247] Williamson claims that advocates of an expansive concept of personal freedom have not shown that restricting some choices, such as selecting the traits of children, will have an adverse effect on the exercise of personal freedom in areas in which they are most significant or result in a slippery slope of ethical micro-management by an interfering State.

[8.106] It may also be argued that 'sex selection is intrinsically sexist in that it is based on assumptions about future individuals from differences that are socially constructed or at least mediated, rather than on experience of individual identity.'[248] This may cause harm to the child that is selected because the parents may, consciously or unconsciously, express their expectations to the child. Failure to fulfil those expectations might result in parental disappointment, and discovery of the selection decision might result in a child perceiving parental love as conditional.

[8.107] Any social changes brought about by technologies such as PGD are likely to reflect the existing imbalance of power between males and females.[249] Thus, it has been asserted that the widespread commercial availability of this technique would reduce the size of the female population – 'Given the well-documented societal preference for male children – and the fact that millions of women, as well as men, in the western world, not just third world countries, still react to the births of daughters with disappointment, sorrow, and even economic and social penalties – the potential widespread commercial availability of sex pre-selection techniques opens up ominous possibilities'.[250] Although it might be thought that a smaller female population might prove advantageous to women, studies of populations with sex-ratio imbalances have shown that such societies are characterised by 'bride-price and bride-service, great importance attached to virginity, emphasis on the sanctity of the family ... proscriptions against adultery ... marriage at an early age, and [prejudice against] women ... regarded as inferior to men ... [in] reasoned judgement, scholarship and political affairs.'[251] Thus, it is argued,

---

[246] Dworkin, *Life's Dominion* (Harper Collins, 1993). See also Harris, 'Sex Selection and Regulated Hatred' J Med Ethics 2005;31: 291–294 and Baldwin 'Reproductive Liberty and Elitist Contempt: Reply to John Harris' J Med Ethics 2005; 31:288–290.

[247] Williamson, 'Sex(ist) Selection?' Med Law I 2004, Vol 6 pp 185–206 at 194.

[248] Williamson, 'Sex(ist) Selection?' Med Law I 2004, Vol 6 pp 185–206 at 193.

[249] See Bubeck, 'Sex selection: The Feminist Response', in Burley and Harris (eds) *A Companion to Genethics* (Blackwell Publishing, 2002) 216–228.

[250] Steinbacher, 'Sex Choice: Survival and Sisterhood' 5–6 (April 1984) (Paper presented at the Second International Interdisciplinary Congress on Women, Women's Worlds: Strategies for Empowerment, in Gronigen, Netherlands).

[251] Holmes and Hoskins, 'Prenatal and Preconception Sex Choice Technologies: A Path to Femicide?' April 1984 (paper presented at the Second International Interdisciplinary Congress on Women, Women's Worlds: Strategies for Empowerment, in Gronigen, Netherlands, quoting Guttentag and Secord, *Too Many Women? The Sex Ratio Question* (Sage Publications, 1983) p 79.

technologies such as this would have the effect of furthering the imbalance of power and ultimately benefiting men to the cost of women.

[8.108] The importance of sex predetermination may be seen in the context of three population variables: first-child patterns, family size and the sex ratio.[252] In many countries, studies reflect a preference among both men and women for a boy for the first child and a consequent inclination to reduce family size if the desire for a particular sex is met with the first child or first two children. Possible reasons for the preference for a son are given as the tradition of carrying on the family name, the value they may have as adults in their chosen profession and a traditional wish among women to please their husbands. Girls would seem to be less valued, as their futures as wives and mothers may be less surprising and perhaps less financially valuable. Their birth is seen as less likely to please their fathers, as they are thought to be harder and more costly to raise. What is interesting about these studies is the fact of the societal preference itself, suggesting that if sex pre-determination were to become widely available, it would be taken advantage of by a large percentage of the population:

> Sex predetermination is unlikely to change the patriarchal emphasis of our society but, adopted on a wide-scale, and this depends on the technique developed, it offers the possibility of strengthening son preference and daughter non-preference, of reinforcing sex roles by under-writing the conflation of sex and gender, of altering the sex ratio further in favour of males, of placing greater restriction on women's limited control over their reproductive capacities.[253]

[8.109] Although behaviour patterns in some countries suggest a societal preference for male offspring, this would not necessarily be the case in other countries such as the US, Australia and most European states, where in fact a preference for female children may be evident.[254] Thus, it may be argued that the technique is not inherently discriminatory towards women. Although sex determination contributes to the devaluation of the female sex, this may be a good reason for considering it to be undesirable but not a sufficient reason for legal prohibition. Women and girl children may in fact be worse off in other ways as a result of prohibiting sex determination than they would be if the practice were to be legally tolerated, such as that they are obliged to have more children than they want or than is healthy for them until they have the required number of sons; some go to private doctors for sex determination, which may be more costly and less safe than it would be in public hospitals; and those who do not bear sons are at risk of desertion by their husbands, leaving them with no financial means.[255] In countries such as India and China, it is thus argued that social reforms rather than prohibition of sex determination are more likely to achieve the desirable effects of increasing respect for women and enhancing their status. Given the expense and inaccessibility of the technique for the vast majority of the population, it is also unlikely to be used so

---

[252] Hanmer, 'Sex Predetermination and Male Dominance' in Roberts (ed) *Women, Health and Reproduction* (Routledge, Kegan & Paul, 1981) 163–190 at 166.

[253] Hanmer agrees with other authors who see women's reproductive role in society as becoming more important as their proportionate numbers decrease, almost like the queen bees to be given as rewards to outstanding males. At 185

[254] Gleicher and Barad, 'The Choice Of Gender: Is Elective Gender Selection Indeed Sexist?' Hum Reprod 2007; 22: 3038–3041.

[255] Macklin, 'The Ethics of Sex Selection' (1995) Indian J of Med Ethics 3: 61–64.

extensively as to contribute to societal sex-ratio imbalances.[256] However, it is important to note the increased availability of non-invasive prenatal diagnosis through genetic testing of maternal blood for free foetal DNA containing a Y chromosome at seven weeks of pregnancy.[257] This can be used for women who carry X-linked conditions, but is also now available worldwide via finger prick testing direct to the consumer at relatively inexpensive prices. These may replace poor-quality ultrasound in India and China for social sex selection.

[8.110] Another use of PGD for sex selection is where family balancing is sought by the couple. This may occur where a couple seeks variety or balance in the gender of offspring because of the different rearing experiences that come with rearing children of different genders.[258] Although there is not yet strong evidence of a substantial need or desire for gender variety in children, it may be that if such evidence were presented, the use of PGD to choose a gender opposite to that of an existing child or children may be much less susceptible to a charge of sexism. In other words, the case for allowing PGD for the first child may be weak as this carries a risk of promoting sexist social mores, but it may be acceptable for gender variety in a family as the risk of sexism is lessened.[259] However, it may be counter-argued that *any* attention to the gender of offspring is inherently sexist.

[8.111] Sex selection techniques may also be very important in the detection of serious heritable sex-linked diseases. The use of such techniques in these instances would mean predetermining the sex of the child but the selection itself is not a sexist act, as no gender-based stereotypical assumptions are made by the prospective parents who seek to avoid the genetic illness in their child. This was approved in Ireland by the recommendations of the Commission on Assisted Human Reproduction but has not yet been enacted in legislation.[260]

Pre-implantation tissue typing

[8.112] Pre-implantation tissue typing is a technique which allows the selection of embryos in order to bring about the birth of a child who can provide a matched tissue donation to an existing sibling, either as the sole clinical objective or in combination

[256] Robertson, 'Extending Preimplantation Genetic Diagnosis: Medical and Non-Medical Uses' J Med Ethics 2003; 29: 213–216. See also Ashcroft, 'Back to the Future: Response to Extending Preimplantation Genetic Diagnosis: Medical and Non-Medical Uses' (2003) J Med Ethics; 29:217–219.

[257] Wright and Chitty, 'Cell-Free Fetal DNA and RNA in Maternal Blood: Implications for Safer Antenatal Testing' BMJ 2009; 339: b2451.

[258] Robertson, 'Extending Preimplantation Genetic Diagnosis: Medical and Non-Medical Uses' J Med Ethics 2003; 29: 213–216.

[259] See also Savulescu and Dahl, 'Sex Selection and Preimplantation Diagnosis, A Response to the Ethics Committee of the American Society of Reproductive Medicine' Hum Reprod Vol 15 No 9, 1879–1880 (2000); and Pennings, 'Ethics of Sex Selection for Family Balancing' Hum Reprod Vol 11 No 11 pp 2339–2345 (1996).

[260] The Commission recommended that 'Preconception sex selection should be permitted only for the reliable prevention of serious sex linked genetic disorders but not for social reasons' available at www.health.gov.ie.

with PGD to avoid a serious genetic disorder in the resulting child.[261] The test involves taking a cell sample from the embryo at the eight-cell stage and testing it for the same genetic disorder as an existing child. In addition to enabling the parents to avoid having another child with the same genetic disorder, it also enables the clinician to establish whether the embryo would be a tissue match for the existing child. The first baby, or 'saviour sibling', born following application of this technique was in the United States in 2001.

[8.113] The ethical issues raised by this procedure centre on the instrumentalisation of children, in other words the child who is conceived in this way becomes an instrument to cure another child. It is argued that this is contrary to the Kantian imperative which is one of the fundamental rules underlying Western moral thinking: 'Act in such a way that you always treat humanity, whether in your own person or the person of any other, never simply as a means, but always at the same time as an end.'[262] However, there are a number of difficulties with the application of this principle in this context. Firstly, Kant defines personhood with reference to rationality, which is a characteristic that embryos do not exhibit. Secondly, it is not always clear how it should be decided when someone is treated as a mere means and no longer as an end in himself. Furthermore, Kant's dictum says that an action should only be condemned when it treats a person *solely* as a means. Children are often conceived for a purpose or unconditional ends, such as to care for parents, to be a companion for a sibling or to run the family business. This is not to say that such children are not also valued for themselves.[263] It may thus be asked, 'Who is harmed by allowing PGD to be performed solely for the benefit of a relative? Not the couple who wish to produce an embryo. Nor the child who would not otherwise have existed. Nor the person who receives the stem cell transplant that might save his or her life.'[264]

[8.114] What is the legal and ethical basis for the decision to carry out the stem cell transplant? The usual approach to the question of whether a medical intervention is acceptable is to seek the informed consent of the patient. This will not be possible in the case of infants or very young children. In such circumstances the decision is generally made following consideration of the best interests of the child. In the context of tissue typing, it may be argued that the child has an interest in growing up in an intact family and that the child will benefit if the older sibling survives. 'However vague, the underlying idea is that the social, emotional and psychological interests of a person depend on the happiness in the family in which he grows up'.[265] It may be argued that the child will feel diminished when informed about the reason for his existence or that it will give the child a sense of unworthiness or deficiency if the transplant fails, though the latter is unlikely given the age of the donor child. But it could be countered that being told that one was conceived to help a sibling may give the child a greater sense of

---

[261] HFEA Report, Preimplantation Tissue Typing (2004).

[262] Kant, *Groundwork of the Metaphysics of Morals*, (Harper and Row, 1964).

[263] Pennings, Schots and Liebaers, 'Ethical Considerations on Preimplantation Genetic Diagnosis for HLA Tissue Typing to Match a Future Child as a Donor Of Haematopoietic Stem Cells to a Sibling' (2002) Hum Reprod Vol 17 (3) 534–538.

[264] Boyle and Savulescu, 'Ethics of Using Preimplantation Genetic Diagnosis to Select a Stem Cell Donor for an Existing Person' (2001) 323 BMJ 1240–1243.

[265] Savulescu, 'Substantial Harm but Substantial Benefit' (1996) BMJ 312, 241–242.

self-esteem and self-worth, as there are few things that are as valuable as saving the life of another person.[266]

[8.115] It may also be claimed that the donor child will be at life-long risk of exploitation, of being a tissue source for the sibling, of being repeatedly subjected to testing and harvesting procedures, and of being pressurised despite protestations.[267] However, this ignores the purpose of tissue typing, which seeks only to use the stem cells available in the umbilical cord of the newly born child, a procedure which is not harmful to the child or its mother. Although it is true that the child might later in life become a candidate for bone marrow donation for its sibling, a child born in this way is no different from a naturally conceived child who is protected by law. 'Thus, just as no naturally conceived tissue matched child could legally function as a source of spare parts for its sibling, no child intentionally conceived as a tissue match could legally fill such a role.'[268]

[8.116] The question arises in this context, as in many others in the area of reproduction, whether the State is justified in interfering with a couple's decision to avail of such a procedure. In modern societies which are more pluralistic than in the past, the prospect of regulation that is both effective and judged to be legitimate seems like an increasingly elusive concept.[269] Thus, in a community of rights, even allowing for a precautionary threshold for legitimate state intervention, the arguments for prohibiting a consenting couple's access to reliable reproductive technologies are weak.

[8.117] In 2001 the Human Fertilisation and Embryology Authority in the UK adopted a precautionary approach when first considering this procedure and decided that it should only be permitted when it was combined with tests to enable parents to select embryos which are free from a serious genetic disorder. This was due to the invasive nature of the technique and the concern about a potential risk of damaging the embryo, so tissue typing was only allowed on cells which had already been taken from the embryo for genetic diagnosis. This policy was challenged by an interest group called CORE (Comment on Reproductive Ethics) which brought an application for judicial review on the grounds that the policy was ultra vires.

[8.118] In *Quintavalle (on behalf of Comment on Reproductive Ethics) v HFEA*[270] the facts involved a child called Zain Hashmi, who was six years of age and suffering from a serious genetic disorder called beta thalassaemia major. His bone marrow did not produce enough red blood cells and he needed daily drugs and regular blood

---

[266] Thomasna, 'Ethical Issues and Transplantation Technology' (1991) Cambr Quart Healthcare Ethics 4, 333–343. See also discussion of possible tort actions in circumstances where the treatment is unsuccessful by Chico, 'Saviour Siblings: Trauma and Tort Law' (2006) Med Law Rev 14: 180–218.

[267] Wolf et al, 'Using Preimplantation Genetic Diagnosis to Create a Stem Cell Donor: Issues, Guidelines and Limits' J Law Med Ethics 2003; 31: 327–39. See also a fictional depiction of such a scenario in Picoult, *My Sister's Keeper* (Atria Books, 2004).

[268] Ram, 'Britain's New Preimplantation Tissue Typing Policy: An Ethical Defence' (2006) J Med Ethics 32: 278–282.

[269] Brownsword, 'Happy Families, Consenting Couples and Children with Dignity: Sex Selection and Saviour Siblings' (2005) Child and Fam Law Quarterly Vol 17 No 4 pp 435–473.

[270] *Quintavalle (on behalf of Comment on Reproductive Ethics) v HFEA* [2005] UKHL 28.

transfusions to keep him alive but he could be restored to normal life by a transplant of stem cells from a tissue-compatible donor. His parents wanted to use PGD to select a suitable embryo which would be free of the disease and a compatible donor for their son. The Court had to consider whether tissue typing fell within the list of approved purposes for which the HFEA was empowered to grant a licence. The 1990 Act provided that the Authority may license treatment services, including those designed to secure that embryos are in a suitable condition to be placed in a woman or to determine whether embryos are suitable for that purpose. The HFEA argued that tissue typing fell within that definition, as a woman would be entitled to regard an embryo as unsuitable unless it was free of abnormality and also a perfect tissue match for an existing child.[271] CORE argued for a narrower construction to the effect that 'suitable' must mean capable of becoming a healthy child free of abnormalities, not ensuring that the child would be a compatible donor. The House of Lords found that the HFEA was acting within its powers in providing a licence for tissue typing to enable the Hashmis to select an embryo which would be a good match for their son. Lord Hoffman stated that allowing the Hashmis greater control in their reproductive decision-making saved them from 'having to play dice with conception'.

[8.119] In 2004, the HFEA revised its view on this matter on the basis that the risk to the resulting child associated with embryo biopsy is not enough to warrant a policy which distinguishes between cases in which preimplantation tissue typing is used in combination with PGD for serious disease and where discovering tissue type is the sole treatment objective. The Authority found no evidence that adverse psychological effects would result from the procedure but recommended that further follow-up studies of these children and their families should be conducted. It concluded that the technique should be available subject to appropriate safeguards, in cases where there is a genuine need for potentially life-saving tissue and a likelihood of therapeutic benefit for an affected child. The new guidance differed from the policy position established in November 2001 in that it recognised that pre-implantation tissue typing may be acceptable in cases in which the embryo to be tested was not itself at risk from the condition affecting the existing child, and depending on the indications for the existing child, it may be acceptable to use pre-implantation tissue typing with a view to using bone marrow from the resulting child.[272]

[8.120] PGD was not available in Ireland for many years due to concerns that the destruction of embryos with genetic abnormalities might be contrary to the provisions of art. 40.3.3 of the Constitution by which 'the State acknowledges the right to life of the unborn and, with due regard to the equal right to life of the mother, guarantees in its laws to respect, and, as far as practicable, by its laws to defend and vindicate that right.' These fears have been allayed by the Supreme Court in *MR v TR*[273] in 2009, which held that the embryo outside the body is not within the definition of 'unborn' in art 40.3.3°. The

---

[271] Sheldon states that this is consistent with a healthy respect for women's or couple's autonomy in reproductive decision-making, as the embryo must not only be suitable in medical terms but also taking account of the wishes of Mrs Hashmi. See Sheldon. 'Saviour Siblings and the Discretionary Power of the HFEA' (2005) Med Law Rev 13: 403–411.

[272] http://www.hfea.gov.uk/515.html.

[273] *Roche v Roche* [2009] IESC 82 discussed in Chapter 6 at para **[6.92]** et seq.

Commission on Assisted Human Reproduction recommended in its Report in 2005 that PGD should be allowed for tissue typing but only for serious diseases that cannot otherwise be treated.[274] A small number of clinics in Ireland now provide this service in collaboration with partner testing laboratories abroad. No legislation has yet been introduced to provide a legal framework within which such services should be provided.

GENE THERAPY

[8.121] As well as the advances in genetic testing and diagnosis brought about by increased knowledge of genetic disorders, it has become possible in recent years to manipulate the genes of existing and, possibly, future individuals by way of gene therapy.[275] 'Like most new developments in medicine and biotechnology, human gene therapy holds out the promise of substantial benefits to humanity while threatening both specific health hazards and fundamental damage to human dignity, and challenging us to consider the very limits of humanness.'[276] The main purpose behind gene therapy is to provide a patient with healthy copies of missing or flawed genes.[277] There are two types – somatic or germ-line gene therapy.[278] Somatic gene therapy attempts to remedy defects within the patient by inserting genetic material to perform a function which the patient's own genetic material is not achieving.[279] Germ-line gene therapy involves either the insertion of genes into the germ cells of the patient, which will have no direct consequences for him but will have results in his children; or by insertion of genes into the early embryo. Both types of germ-line therapy are intended to cause children to be born with or without certain characteristics, and both are highly controversial.

[8.122] Somatic gene therapy is regarded as the simplest and least controversial form of gene therapy[280] as in many ways it is similar to other forms of medical treatment such as organ or tissue transplantation, drug therapy or surgical intervention. As somatic gene

---

[274] Available at www.health.gov.ie.

[275] See generally Walters and Palmer, *The Ethics of Human Gene Therapy* (OUP, 1997).

[276] Dworkin, 'Law and Ignorance: Genetic Therapy and the Legal Process' (1996) Jahrbuch für Recht und Ethik, Annual Review of Law and Ethics, Volume 4.

[277] 'Gene therapy is the use of genetic information to intervene in the DNA of a human cell to relieve the symptoms and prevent the causes of diseases with a genetic component.' Hedgecoe, 'Gene Therapy' in Chadwick, (ed) *The Concise Encyclopedia of the Ethics of New Technologies* (Academic Press, 2001) 123.

[278] Other potential types of therapy could be described as enhancement genetic engineering, which would involve the insertion of a gene to enhance a known characteristic such as a growth hormone, and eugenic genetic engineering, which would be an attempt to alter or improve complex human traits coded by a large number of genes, such as intelligence, personality and character. See generally French Anderson, 'Human Gene Therapy: Scientific and Ethical Considerations' in Chadwick, (ed) *Ethics, Reproduction and Genetic Control* (Croom Helm Ltd, 1987) at 147; Torres, 'On the Limits of Enhancement in Human Gene Transfer: Drawing the Line' (1997) J Med & Phil Vol 22 No 1: 43–53.

[279] See further Walters and Palmer, *The Ethics of Human Gene Therapy* (OUP, 1997) Ch 2.

[280] This form of therapy is not scientifically unproblematic. For an overview of some of these difficulties, see Kinderlerer and Longley, 'Human Genetics: the New Panacea?' (1998) 61(5) Mod L Rev 603 at 615–618.

therapy generally affects only non-reproductive cells,[281] none of the genetic changes produced by this form of therapy will be passed on to the patient's children.[282] Also, the products of the modified cells are, in some cases such as enzyme therapies, similar to medications that the patient can take as an alternative.[283] The Clothier Committee in the UK in 1992 viewed the therapy as uncontroversial, though novel, and felt that it gave rise to no new ethical issues.[284] This view is shared by advisory bodies to the European Commission,[285] although it was advised that research be restricted to serious diseases at present,[286] and also by similar bodies in the US.[287]

[8.123] Germ-line gene therapy on the other hand has raised a number of ethical issues due to its capacity to change future individuals.[288] 'The theory is that at a very early stage of an individual's development, perhaps even before conception, changes could be made to a person's genome that would have an effect on every single cell of their body (since all other cells would develop from those early ones) and upon children that they have (and upon all subsequent generations).'[289] The ethical issues here focus on human dignity, enhancement and eugenics,[290] similar to those arguments outlined above in relation to PGD.[291] In germ-line gene therapy, however, some of the changes that may

---

[281] Although it is possible that a gene delivered to one tissue may pass into the gonads, ie ovary or testis, and carry consequences for that person's offspring. All participants in gene therapy trials are advised to avoid pregnancy.

[282] For further information, see Friedmann, 'The Origins, Evolution, and Directions of Human Gene Therapy' in Friedmann (ed) *The Development of Human Gene Therapy* (CSHL, 1999).

[283] Walters and Palmer, *The Ethics of Human Gene Therapy* (OUP, 1997) at 36.

[284] Report of the Committee on the Ethics of Gene Therapy (1992).

[285] Opinion of the Group of Advisors on Ethical Implications of Biotechnology of the European Commission, *The Ethical Implications of Gene Therapy* (1994).

[286] In 1999 a young man, Jesse Gelsinger, died in the US during the course of a clinical trial on gene therapy run by the University of Pennsylvania. An investigation into his death carried out by the Food and Drug Administration found a number of breaches of rules such as the inclusion of Gelsinger as a substitute for another volunteer who dropped out, despite Gelsinger having high ammonia levels that should have led to his exclusion from the trial; failure by the university to report that two patients had experienced serious side effects from the gene therapy; and failure to mention the deaths of monkeys given a similar treatment in the informed consent documentation. See the useful discussion by Berry, 'Health Care and the Human Genome' in Iltis, Johnson and Hinze (eds) *Legal Perspectives in Bioethics* (Routledge, 2008) 95–125. For issues relating to how ethics committees should evaluate research protocols in this area, see Dettweiler and Simon, 'Points to Consider for Ethics Committees in Human Gene Therapy Trials' (2001) 15 (5/6) Bioethics 491–500.

[287] Report and Recommendations of the Panel to Assess the National Institutes of Health Investment in Research on Gene Therapy (1995).

[288] For an interesting view on legal remedies that might be called into action in cases where gene therapy is unsuccessful for a particular patient, see Marshall, 'Medical Malpractice in the New Eugenics: Relying on Innovative Tort Doctrine to Provide Relief When Gene Therapy Fails' (2001) 35(4) Georgia L Rev 1277–1327.

[289] Hedgecoe, 'Gene Therapy' in Chadwick (ed) *The Concise Encyclopedia of the Ethics of New Technologies* (Academic Press, 2001) p124.

[290] For a summary of the issues, see Graumann, 'The Debate About the Moral Evaluation of Germ Line Therapy – A Critical Overview' (1997) 1 (2) Biomedical Ethics 12–16.

[291] See discussion of the arguments for and against germ-line gene therapy in Walters and Palmer, *The Ethics of Human Gene Therapy* (OUP, 1997) at 80–92.

theoretically be possible may turn out to be universally acceptable, such as the ability to ensure that carriers of serious genetic disorders will not pass on the disorder to their children.[292]

[8.124] An interesting concept raised in recent debates in this area is that of intergenerational justice,[293] which suggests that current genetic knowledge *should* be used in ways which enhance the health and well-being of children yet to be born. It is thus argued that in considering the issues raised by the new genetics, there is a responsibility to take into account the implications for future generations, as it is their genome project also.[294] If research into germ-line gene therapy is prohibited, it may be that the obligation to protect future children from genetic compromise will not be fulfilled:

> The completion of the human genome project will provide a basis for acting on a moral obligation for *future* generations, a claim that has appeared weak in the past. A generation *with* such knowledge who neglected to use it to minimise the risks in reproduction could hardly be said to respect the requirements of intergenerational justice.[295]

[8.125] The concerns about risks and benefits to future children focus on the social and psychological consequences to engineered children arising out of the cure of a disease or the enhancement of a feature. However, advocates argue that such concerns are overblown and that we should embrace the possibility of future generations who might be disease-free, long-lived, intelligent, strong, agile and free of hyper-aggressiveness. While genetic engineering might be a novel technique, they argue that it is no different from parents vaccinating their children against disease, or undertaking other healthcare or educational initiatives to increase their children's longevity, enrich their intellect, build their fitness and so on.[296]

[8.126] However, as is the case in much of the debates involving genetics, the danger of the slippery slope into eugenics[297] causes concern about this form of genetic engineering.[298] 'Once we decide to begin the process of human genetic engineering, there is really no logical place to stop. If diabetes, sickle cell anaemia, and cancer are to be cured by altering the genetic make-up of an individual, why not proceed to other 'disorders': myopia, colour-blindness, left-handedness? Indeed, what is to preclude a

---

[292] It may be asked why germ-line therapy should be condemned since it would spare future children the requirement of therapy for a gene defect, which perhaps could have been removed before birth.

[293] See further Lappe, 'Ethical Issues in Manipulating the Human Germ Line' in Kuhse and Singer (eds) *Bioethics, An Anthology* (2nd edn, Blackwell, 2006), pp 198–208 at 155–164.

[294] Macer, 'Whose Genome Project?' (1991) 5 Bioethics 183 at 209.

[295] Fletcher and Wertz, 'An International Code of Ethics in Medical Genetics Before the Human Genome is Mapped' in Bankowski and Capron (eds) *Genetics, Ethics and Human Values: Human Genome Mapping, Genetic Screening and Therapy* (World Health Organisation, 1991) 97 at 103.

[296] Berry, 'Health Care and the Human Genome' in Iltis, Johnson and Hinze (eds) *Legal Perspectives in Bioethics* (Routledge, 2008) 95–125.

[297] See Harris, 'Is Gene Therapy a Form of Eugenics?' in Kuhse and Singer (eds), *A Companion to Bioethics* (Blackwell Publishing, 1998) 165–170.

[298] For discussion of 'slippery slope' arguments in this context, see Pattinson, 'Regulating Germ-Line Gene Therapy to Avoid Sliding Down the Slippery Slope' (2000) 4 Med Law I 213–222.

society from deciding that a certain skin colour is a disorder?[299] Such slippery slope arguments have led a number of advisory and governmental bodies to ban the practice.[300] Legislation in Austria, Denmark, France, Germany and Sweden all prohibit the practice. The Council of Europe initially recommended a complete ban on this form of therapy on the grounds of human dignity, but later allowed germ cell manipulation for therapeutic purposes.[301] While many would support such a position, it remains difficult to draw fine lines between therapeutic purposes and enhancement objectives in some situations.[302] If it does become possible to draw such lines 'it should be necessary to forbid *all* work in this area only if it is felt that the demarcation line can never be held.'[303]

[8.127] It has been speculated that any pressure to introduce germline gene therapy will be most likely to come from parents who want to improve the chances for their children to function more effectively.[304] Once the new technologies are proven to be safe and effective, choice may thereby become the prime policy driver.[305] Laurie, Harmon and Porter say the irony of this position is that the development of human rights discourse and the commitment to individualism was driven in response to eugenic practices, albeit at the hands of states.[306] They query whether eugenic practices, such as those represented by the application of some of these new technologies, are any less offensive if they are dressed up in the guise of autonomous choices?[307] The Nuffield Council on Bioethics believes that if these new techniques are proven to be safe and effective, 'it would be ethical for families to use them if they wish to do so and have been offered an appropriate level of information and support.'[308]

---

[299] Rifkin, *Algeny: A New Word – A New World*, in collaboration with Perlas, (Viking Press, 1983) p 232.

[300] For a critique of such arguments, see Pattinson, 'Regulating Germ-Line Gene Therapy to Avoid Sliding Down the Slippery Slope' (2000) 4 Med Law I 213–222.

[301] The Oviedo Convention provides in art 13 that 'an intervention seeking to modify the human genome may only be undertaken for preventative, diagnostic or therapeutic purposes and only if its aim is not to introduce any modification in the genome of any descendants.'

[302] 'For example, gene therapy might be used to increase the height of children with growth hormone deficiency to that of the norm in the population. This would count as therapy. But the same (or similar) techniques could be used to increase the height of a normal child so that they were of above average height. This would be enhancement of characteristics.' Hedgecoe, 'Gene Therapy' in Chadwick (ed) *The Concise Encyclopedia of the Ethics of New Technologies* (Academic Press, 2001) at 125. See also Smith, 'Genetic Enhancement Technologies and the New Society' (2000) Med Law I Vol 4 pp 85–95.

[303] Laurie, Harmon, Porter *Law and Medical Ethics* (10th edn, OUP, 2016) at 7.98.

[304] Capecchi 'Human germline gene therapy' in Stock and Campbell (eds) *Engineering the Human Germline: An Exploration of the Science and Ethics of Altering the Genes that we pass to our children* (2000) at 31.

[305] Laurie, Harmon, Porter, *Law and Medical Ethics* (10th edn, OUP, 2016) at 7.99.

[306] Laurie, Harmon, Porter, *Law and Medical Ethics* (10th edn, OUP, 2016) at 7.99.

[307] Referring to Coutelle and Ashcroft 'Risks, benefits and ethical, legal, and societal considerations for translation of prenatal gene therapy to human application.' (2012) 891 Methods Mol Biol 371.

CLONING

[8.128] In July 1996 in Scotland, a famous sheep called Dolly was born following the application of cloning techniques.[309] This involved taking a normal diploid[310] adult cell from the udder of a sheep, removing the genetic material from it and implanting that material within the membrane of an egg cell, which had already had its own genetic material removed. The resulting cell, which consisted of adult genetic material and the egg cell membrane, was transferred to the uterus of another sheep. The Dolly technique was regarded as an enormous development because her birth resulted from the transfer of the nucleus of a somatic (non-reproductive) cell into an enucleated egg cell. This showed that genetic material could be reprogrammed or reactivated well into the chronological life of the cell.[311] After Dolly's birth, concern began to be expressed as to whether this might be replicated in humans.

[8.129] Human cloning might be suggested for a variety of reasons: as a means for an infertile couple to have a child, to bring back a lost relative, to have a child as a copy of a person held in high esteem, or fourthly as a source of tissue for a sick person.[312] Therefore if cloning was safe, it would add to the reproductive options already available and enhance procreative choice for the infertile.[313] For couples unable to take advantage of conventional fertility treatments, cloning one of the partners may be the only way of having a genetically related child.[314] It may also be a means of ensuring that a hereditary genetic disease is not transmitted from an adult to a future child, to produce a replica of a dying child, to produce a genetically identical child for tissue transplantation or to engineer a child with particular desirable characteristics. Attempts to produce a person with particular characteristics would therefore be to 'attempt to prescribe a theme to the nascent life.' The parents would therefore have a standard to which the child was supposed to conform, perhaps considering children who did not measure up to be failures, or the children themselves might consider themselves defective if they did not measure up.[315]

[8.130] Those wishing to use cloning technology for any of the reasons mentioned above may assert a fundamental right to reproductive autonomy, including the right to produce a cloned child.[316] The importance of the right to procreative autonomy has been

---

[308] Nuffield Council on Bioethics, *Novel Techniques for the prevention of mitochondrial DNA disorders: an ethical review* (2012).

[309] The team involved in Dolly's birth claim to have been motivated by the desire to produce transgenically modified animals which would contain valuable substances in their milk.

[310] Diploid means having two homologous sets of chromosomes, such as is found in adult cells.

[311] National Bioethics Advisory Commission, *Cloning Human Beings* (1997).

[312] Ian Wilmut, 'Cloning in Biology and Medicine: Clinical Opportunities and Ethical Concerns' in Burley and Harris (eds), *A Companion to Genethics* (Blackwell Publishing, 2002) 33 at 36.

[313] Robertson, 'Liberty, Identity and Human Cloning' (1998) 76 Texas Law Review 1371 at 1372. See also Bell, 'Human Cloning and International Human Rights Law' (1999) 21 Sydney Law Review 202, and Beyleveld and Brownsword, 'Human Dignity, Human Rights and Human Genetics' (1998) 61(5) MLR 661.

[314] Robertson, 'Two Models of Human Cloning' (1999) 27 Hofstra Law Review 609, 618–627.

[315] Kitcher, 'Creating perfect people' in Burley and Harris (eds), *A Companion to Genethics* (Blackwell Publishing, 2002) at 239.

considered in detail in Chapter 4.[317] This right has generally been seen as a negative right and one that is restricted to issues such as sterilisation, contraception and abortion, although it may be that future policies and judicial decisions will see an extension of the right to cover assisted reproduction.[318] It has been argued further that the principles of self-determination, autonomy and privacy would encompass the right to engage in reproductive cloning:[319]

> We have the right to make decisions on issues important to us – and have those decisions respected by the state and other persons (the right to moral integrity). The right to moral integrity, and to a lesser degree the right to physical integrity, affords us the opportunity to function freely, and the possibility of self-definition and 'self-creation'...A human rights regime which recognised the value of individual self-determination would not interfere in the right of persons to...clone themselves – unless there could be shown a good argument to the contrary.[320]

[8.131] Similarly, the right to procreative liberty might logically entail the right to choose which gametes and embryos to use.[321] This choice then extends naturally to negative selection of the embryos on the basis of genetic characteristics. The next important step in extending the right to cloning seems, to some, to be perfectly natural, quite insignificant and thus convincing.[322] When one looks at the most likely application of cloning techniques, to enable infertile couples to procreate genetically related children, it might be argued that cloning shares many features with assisted reproduction and genetic selection. The motive behind the cloning should be considered as irrelevant, in the same way as motive is not considered when fertile couples reproduce. However, the argument in favour of reproductive cloning is much weaker where a fertile couple seeks, for narcissistic or eugenic reasons, to use the technique in order to have a child with a particular genome or relationship to the couple. In such cases, cloning in lieu of sexual reproduction would not seem to come within the meaning of procreative liberty as it is currently understood.[323]

[8.132] In relation to the question of whether a right to engage in human reproductive cloning might be protected by international human rights law, the basis upon which such

---

[316] For detailed consideration, see Harris-Short, 'An Identity Crisis in the International Law of Human Rights? The Challenge of Reproductive Cloning', Conference paper given August 2002 at the 11th World Conference of the I Soc of Fam. Law: *Family Life and Human Rights*.

[317] At para **[4.09]** et seq.

[318] See Jackson, 'Conception and the Irrelevance of the Welfare Principle' (2002) 65(2) MLR 176; Harris, 'The Right to Found a Family' in Ladd (ed) *Children's Rights Re-visioned – Philosophical Readings* (Belmont: Wordsworth Knopf, 1996) 66; Liu, *Artificial Reproduction and Reproductive Rights* (Dartmouth, 1991).

[319] See Harris 'Goodbye Dolly? The Ethics of Human Cloning' in Kuhse and Singer, *A Companion to Bioethics* (Blackwell Publishing, 1998) at 149–50; Dworkin, *Life's Dominion* (Vintage Books, 1993) at 148 and *Freedom's Law* (OUP, 1996) at 237–8.

[320] Wheatley, 'Human Rights and Human Dignity in the Resolution of Certain Ethical Questions in Biomedicine' (2001) 3 EHRLR 312 at 313–4.

[321] See also Feuerberg Duffy, 'To Be or Not to Be: The Legal Ramifications of the Cloning of Human Embryos' (1995) 21 Rutgers Computer And Technology Law Journal 189–223.

[322] Robertson, 'Two Models of Human Cloning' (1999) 27 Hofstra Law Review 609.

[323] Robertson, 'Two Models of Human Cloning' (1999) 27 Hofstra Law Review 609 at 627–633.

a claim could be currently grounded is weak.[324] However, it might be argued that 'given the relatively recent interest in reproductive rights, there is a strong possibility of future significant expansion in this field. Any future developments are likely to move towards providing greater support for recognition of a right to access to artificial reproductive techniques, which will, in turn, open up the possibility of more far-reaching claims to engage in genetic manipulation and cloning.'[325] Another, perhaps remote, possibility would be to claim that a total prohibition on cloning violates the right to respect for private and family life under art 8 of the European Convention on Human Rights (ECHR). However, it is likely any attempt to challenge a legislative prohibition on cloning on such grounds would be easily met by art 8(2) which justifies interference with this right where it is in accordance with law and necessary in a democratic society in the interests of, inter alia, the protection of health or morals.

[8.133] Cloning may also be of benefit in other ways. Although human cloning is ethically unacceptable, research stimulated by the birth of Dolly will lead to many new therapies in human medicine:

> It is a superficial paradox that the technique that could be used to make identical copies could, in principle, provide a means of introducing precise genetic change. This ability will generate the means to provide organs, such as kidneys or hearts, from animals for transplantation to human patients. In addition, cell therapy will provide more effective treatment of diseases associated with damage to cells that are not repaired or replaced: diseases such as Parkinson's disease, heart attack, blindness caused by macular degeneration or diabetes Type 1. This could be achieved with cells from animals, or by taking cells from the patient, growing them in the laboratory, treating them so as to obtain cells of the damages type, and returning these to the patient.[326]

[8.134] It is necessary in any discussion about cloning to distinguish between the different types of cloning that are at least theoretically possible. On the one hand there is reproductive cloning where a cell containing the donor's DNA is transferred to the enucleated egg. It is activated to begin cleavage and transferred to the uterus to grow into a foetus. The child would therefore be born with the same DNA as the DNA donor alone. Therefore, the clone is not the genetic *child* of the DNA donor but rather his/her 'identical' twin sister or brother, and the genetic child of the DNA donor's own genetic parents.[327] However, it is important to recognise that the child would not truly be identical due to differences in uterine environment, social environment and other factors. Clones would be less alike than genetically identical twins, because in most cases they would be derived from a different recipient egg, develop in a different womb, be fed by a different mother, brought up in a different era and subject to a different chapter of accidents and illnesses.[328]

---

[324] See Chapter 4 at para **[4.44]** et seq

[325] Harris-Short, 'An Identity Crisis in the International Law of Human Rights? The Challenge of Reproductive Cloning', Conference paper given August 2002 at the 11th World Conference of the I Soc of Fam Law.

[326] Wilmut, 'Cloning in Biology and Medicine: Clinical Opportunities and Ethical Concerns' in Burley and Harris (eds) *A Companion to Genethics* (Blackwell Publishing, 2002) 33.

[327] Harris, 'Goodbye Dolly? The Ethics of Human Cloning' in Kuhse and Singer, *A Companion to Bioethics* (Blackwell Publishing, 1998) at 148.

[8.135] Alternatively, reproductive cloning could be achieved by cell mass division or embryo splitting, where the early embryo is divided or split into two or more parts, each of which will continue to cleave and develop into a child. This is similar to the process by which monozygotic or identical twins occur in natural reproduction.[329] Legal and ethical issues in reproductive cloning include considerations of the scientific difficulties, such as the very high rates of miscarriage,[330] early postnatal death in animal cloning and the ethics of incurring those difficulties in humans. Other issues address the dignity of the human person, such as the argument that cloning instrumentalises the person by treating it solely as a means to an end, that it would be open to exploitation by the production of clones to be used as sources of spare parts and that it would severely disrupt family relationships. These issues are considered further below.

[8.136] Another use of the technique is in therapeutic cloning, referred to variously as somatic cell nuclear transfer (SCNT), or nuclear transplantation. As with reproductive cloning, a patient's DNA is transferred to an enucleated egg and activated. It behaves as an embryo and starts to split into cells which may be a source of stem cells for treatment of the patient. These cells are totipotent,[331] which means they may have huge potential for medical treatment in the future. The theory is that once the activated egg has subdivided sufficiently to yield over a hundred cells, it is broken open, the inner cells removed and the stem cells harvested. It is hoped that these stem cells may then be grown into a variety of cells for transplantation in human patients. The advantages of this procedure would be that, if used for transplantation in the person from whom the DNA was derived, the cell line would be free of contamination, would not be rejected by the patient's immune system, and would be capable of multiplying indefinitely in the laboratory, thus providing a wealth of transplant material.

[8.137] Whether it is possible to allow therapeutic cloning and prohibit reproductive cloning, is a matter of debate, given that the techniques involved are the same in both cases. The fear is that once cloned embryos are created in the laboratory for any purpose, there will be no way of policing the use of that embryo to ensure that it is not transferred to a woman's uterus to produce a cloned child. On the one hand, it is argued that it is possible and important to avoid this particular slippery slope by criminalizing reproductive cloning while recognising the significant potential offered by continuing efforts in therapeutic cloning.[332] However, it must also be recognised that once the scientific feasibility of reproductive cloning exists, although reputable scientists will observe legal prohibitions, a small number of persons might be prepared to violate such a law.[333]

---

[328] Wilmut, 'Cloning in Biology and Medicine: Clinical Opportunities and Ethical Concerns' in Burley and Harris (eds) *A Companion to Genetics* (Blackwell Publishing, 2002) at 36.

[329] Harris argues that, as there are no ethical issues raised by the natural phenomenon of identical twins, why should there be apprehension when such twins are deliberately created? Harris, Goodbye Dolly? The Ethics of Human Cloning' in Kuhse and Singer, *A Companion to Bioethics* (Blackwell Publishing, 1998) at 144.

[330] Dolly was born after 277 attempts.

[331] 'Totipotent' means that its potential is total, in the sense that it may develop into an embryo, or into other tissue or organs.

[332] Report of the Commission on Assisted Human Reproduction (Dublin, 2005) at 61.

Ethical issues

[8.138] For many, Dolly was a shocking symbol of biotechnology raging out of control, warranting a swift and decisive halting of any further experimentation in the cloning arena before its inevitable spillover to the human race. For a smaller group, Dolly was a marvellous and long-awaited sign that a century-old inquiry into the possibility of asexual reproduction had yielded a tentative answer.[334] Those who advocate cloning argue that there are people for whom cloning might offer the only plausible reproductive option if they wish to avoid the use of donated gametes or for those who wish to avoid the transmission of deleterious genes. A further benefit might be to assist single individuals and same-sex couples to reproduce or to aid parents who have suffered the loss of a child. There are also those for whom the duplication of their own genetic material holds a special appeal, usually for various dubious and narcissistic reasons.

[8.139] The ethical issues here revolve around the status of the human embryo, how it should be respected, and whether there is a difference between embryos that remain unused after IVF attempts, and embryos deliberately created for research purposes.[335] SCNT involves the deliberate creation and destruction of an embryo, which many people fear will lead to the instrumentalisation of human life and the erosion of other protections for participants in research. The validity of some of these objections presupposes that the embryo has the status of a human being so as to warrant prohibiting its use as a source of cells or tissues. Such an approach would be rejected by those who take a developmental approach, which accords lesser weight to the embryo in its earliest stages when there has been no differentiation yet between different tissues and organs. On this view, research on such embryos that could provide significant therapeutic benefit may be ethically justified.

[8.140] The first argument most commonly raised against reproductive cloning is that it is not safe for use in humans. Animal cloning has not yet reached the minimum level of safety and efficacy that is needed before research on human cloning could even begin. In the research leading to the birth of Dolly the sheep, 62 per cent of foetuses were lost, many were born with serious abnormalities and many died soon after birth. It also appears that there may be other long-term deleterious effects in animals. It is unclear the extent to which the advanced age of the cloned adult cell affects the ageing process in the cloned animal. Given these concerns, it would not be considered ethical to consider applying these techniques in humans. In addition it is argued that reproductive cloning is contrary to human dignity, would lead to identity confusion and consequent disruption of family relationships and that it would lead to a decrease in genetic diversity.

[8.141] A further argument against cloning is based on respect for the moral status of the human embryo. In international literature three views are generally put forward of

---

[333] Robertson, 'Two Models of Human Cloning' in (1999) 27 Hofstra Law Review 609 at 614; also in Steinbock (ed) *Legal and Ethical Issues in Human Reproduction* (Ashgate Publishing, 2002) Ch. 11 at 352. Harris, 'Goodbye Dolly? The Ethics of Human Cloning' (1997) 23 Journal of Medical Ethics, pp 353–360.

[334] Daar, 'The Prospect Of Human Cloning: Improving Nature or Dooming The Species?' (2003) 33 Seton Hall L Rev 511.

[335] See Lanza et al, 'The Ethical Validity of Using Nuclear Transfer in Human Transplantation' (2000) 284 (24) JAMA.

the moral status of the embryo. The first is the right-to-life position, which maintains that embryos have the same moral status as human persons, irrespective of their stage of development. On this view, therapeutic cloning would be similar to creating a baby to harvest its organs, which would be clearly abhorrent. The second view is the person view, which maintains that moral status is not a matter of species membership but rather of psychological features, such as the ability to think and feel and experience. On this view, human embryos are not persons nor are they deserving of the same status as that conferred on human persons.[336] In between these two views is the position that even though embryos do not have moral status, they are a form of human life and, as such, deserving of respect.[337] Those who adopt this view may view therapeutic cloning as acceptable in exceptional and well-defined circumstances.

[8.142] It is sometimes said that cloning, if permitted, would change our perception of personhood. While cloned human beings would be recognised as fully human and entitled to the same respect as any other, 'permitting and engaging in human cloning would intrinsically violate our conception of human dignity.'[338] Cloning would oblige us to regard people as repeatable, which would diminish the value of personhood:

> Deliberately cloning human beings is a threat to human identity, as it would give up the indispensable protection against the predetermination of the human genetic constitution by a third party. Further ethical reasoning for a prohibition to clone human beings is based first and foremost on human dignity which is endangered by instrumentalisation through artificial human cloning.[339]

[8.143] Human dignity is a 'very broad and fiercely contested concept. At its core, however, is the idea that every human being has an intrinsic value: that human life is beyond price.'[340] In its deliberations on stem cell research, the UK House of Lords Select Committee found the concept of human dignity to be ill-defined,[341] but expressed concern that 'the range of ambiguities introduced into family relationship by cloning

---

[336] Steinbock, *Life Before Birth: the Moral and Legal Status of Embryos and Fetuses* (1992) 51–58.

[337] The meaning of 'respect' is not clear and has been criticised as an empty phrase designed to make us feel better about killing embryos. Callahan, 'The Puzzle of Profound Respect' (1995) 25(1) Hastings Center Rep. 39–40. Callahan takes the view that it is not that we should not use embryos for research, but rather that the interests to be served by the research should be shown to be compelling and unreachable by other means.

[338] Kaebnick and Murray, 'Cloning' in Chadwick (ed) *The Concise Encyclopedia of the Ethics of New Technologies* (Academic Press, 2001) 51 at 60.

[339] Council of Europe, Additional Protocol to the Convention on Human Rights and Biomedicine on the Prohibition of Cloning Human Beings, Explanatory Report (ETS No 168) Para 3.

[340] Harris-Short, 'An Identity Crisis in the International Law of Human Rights? The Challenge of Reproductive Cloning', Conference paper given August 2002 at the 11th World Conference of the I Soc of Fam Law: *Family Life and Human Rights*, quoting Beyleveld and Brownsword D and Brownsword R, 'Human Dignity, Human Rights and Human Genetics' (1998) 61(5) MLR 661 at 666.

[341] Harris also claims that appeals to the concept of human dignity are universally attractive, but comprehensively vague. Harris, 'Goodbye Dolly? The Ethics of Human Cloning' in Kuhse and Singer, *A Companion to Bioethics* (Blackwell Publishing, 1998) at 145.

from a close relative would be large and the possibility for emotional confusion and uncertainty – not only on the part of the cloned child – considerable.'[342]

[8.144] The idea that cloning would involve a process similar to 'photocopying' an individual on an automated production line[343] seems to violate an inherent respect for human dignity. It is assumed that each one of us has a right to our own genetic uniqueness, which would somehow be denigrated by such a technique. However, geneticists have claimed that this is in fact an inaccurate representation of genetics.[344] The most usual way of demonstrating this is by use of the example of monozygotic or identical twins.[345] As the name suggests, the twins share the same DNA, but would clearly be regarded as separate individuals. As each twin grows and develops, its experiences and environment will shape its unique identity. In the case of a clone and its DNA source, the two will not share the same uterus, or mitochondrial DNA, and each will have a different childhood and environment.[346] Therefore, it is claimed that they will be less alike than identical twins in both character and appearance.[347] Thus, it is argued that:

> [T]o produce another Mozart, we would need not only Wolfgang's genome but mother Mozart's uterus, father Mozart's music lessons, their friends and his, the state of music in eighteenth century Austria, Haydn's patronage, and on and on, in ever-widening circles...we have no right to the...assumption that his genome, cultivated in another world at another time, would result in an equally creative musical genius.[348]

[8.145] Despite the refutation of this claim that the clone will be a replica of the DNA donor, nevertheless there is a planned similarity that cannot easily be achieved through current reproductive technology. As with germ-line gene therapy, this element of control is perhaps the most unsettling aspect of cloning as we speculate the future of the human gene pool. It is argued that the expectations placed on the cloned human to be similar to its twin, impairs that person's right to an individual identity and an open future.[349] If the child grows up in the shadow of such assumptions of its ability and has its future pre-

---

[342] Report from the Select Committee: Stem Cell Research, HL 83(i), HMSO, 2002.App. 6, para 6.

[343] Wellcome Trust, Report on Public Attitudes to Human Cloning (1998) at 13.

[344] The US National Bioethics Advisory Commission points out that the belief that a person's genes bear a simple relationship to the physical and psychological traits that compose that individual is based on misunderstanding. Such a belief is referred to as 'genetic determinism'. The Commission is of the view that the great lesson of modern molecular genetics is the profound complexity of both gene-gene interactions and gene-environment interactions in the determination of whether a specific trait or characteristic is expressed. 'In other words, there will never be another you'.

[345] The natural occurrence of monozygotic or identical twins is one in 270 pregnancies.

[346] Kaebnick and Murray, 'Cloning', in Chadwick (ed) *The Concise Encyclopedia of the Ethics of New Technologies* (Ashgate Publishing, 2001) 51 at 60.

[347] Cloned individuals will never be identical in the sense of looking identical at the same moment in time. The further separated in time the DNA source and clone are, the less likely they are to have similarities in character. Harris, 'Goodbye Dolly? The Ethics of Human Cloning' in Kuhse and Singer, *A Companion to Bioethics* (Blackwell Publishing, 1998) at 144.

[348] Eisenberg, 'Are Cloned Sheep Really Like Humans' (1999) 340 NEJM 471.

[349] Putnam, 'Cloning People' in Burley (ed) *The Genetic Revolution and Human Rights* (1999) at 11 suggests that cloning might give rise to a new human right – the right to be a complete surprise to one's parents.

determined, this will impair its own development and be contrary to its best interests. However, this does not take into account the expectations that most parents have of their children, for example, to follow their parents' or older siblings' footsteps in relation to career paths. The clone would not be identical to its twin; its health, appearance and personality would all be different, so in this sense it is difficult to accept this argument as a sound basis for rejection of cloning.

[8.146] The concept of identity is one that has become the focus of much debate in recent years, particularly in relation to adoption and assisted reproduction. In relation to cloning the issue is not only whether the child should be told the truth about its parentage but also whether cloning itself violates the child's right to his/her own identity. Freeman describes the concept in the following way: 'Identity is what we know and what we feel is an organising framework for holding together our past and our present and it provides some anticipated shape to future life. It is an inner personal landscape, a 'feeling of being at home in one's own body'.'[350] Whereas in adoption and gamete donation the concern is that there will be gaps in the child's genetic story, in reproductive cloning the argument is that the story itself will be harmful to the child.[351] The knowledge of being profoundly different from other normal families as well as the huge problems of establishing parentage[352] may also increase the danger of identity confusion for the child. In conclusion on this point it would seem that 'given the strengths of the concerns raised about the effect of reproductive cloning on the fundamental rights and interests of the resulting child, there is a growing consensus among the international community that the risks posed to the child currently outweigh any competing rights and interests of the procreating adult (assuming they can be successfully established) and a total ban on reproductive cloning is thus fully justified.'[353]

[8.147] The slippery slope argument is also used here to suggest that even if permitted in exceptional and tightly regulated circumstances, there will always be the potential that these exceptions could be widened over time and that cloning could be put to abusive uses. The fictional notion that uncontrolled scientists could clone replicas of dictators caught the public imagination: 'scenarios of armies of Hitlers, clones used as organ farms for already existing individuals, and the imaginative portrayal in a Woody Allen

---

[350] Freeman, 'The New Birth Right? Identity and the Child of the Reproductive Revolution' (1996) 4 I J of Children's Rights 273 at 283.

[351] For critical comment on the possible 'right to have two parents' or the 'right to be the product of the mixture of the genes of two individuals' see Harris, 'Goodbye Dolly? The Ethics of Human Cloning' in Kuhse and Singer, *A Companion to Bioethics* (Blackwell Publishing, 1998) at 147–8.

[352] Harris-Short gives the example of 'the creation of a clone using the DNA of the intended child's social father: the social father would be the child's trans-generational identical twin sibling, the child's social grandparents would be the child's genetic parents and the child's social siblings would be in some sense his/her niece or nephew.' Harris-Short, 'An Identity Crisis in the International Law of Human Rights? The Challenge of Reproductive Cloning' Conference paper given August 2002 at the 11th World Conference of the I Soc of Fam Law.

[353] Harris-Short, 'An Identity Crisis in the International Law of Human Rights? The Challenge of Reproductive Cloning' Conference paper given August 2002 at the 11th World Conference of the I Soc of Fam Law.

movie of cloning the nose of a dictator, are only some of the images television news broadcasts presented to viewers…Science fiction stories that involve cloning have not portrayed the evils of producing human beings by this method but rather, the abuses of one application in the production of multiple clones of consummately evil people.'[354] Trust in the medical and scientific professions has decreased over the last few decades, and many people fear that it would be inevitable that illegal research would be impossible to patrol and prevent.[355]

International regulation

[8.148] After the birth of Dolly was announced in late February 1997, there was a worldwide rush to legislate for a ban on human cloning. In early March 1997, US President Clinton issued an immediate moratorium on the use of federal funds for human cloning and requested scientists in the private sector to voluntarily comply with the ban. In the UK, the House of Commons Select Committee on Science and Technology issued a report urging the Government to tighten existing law to ensure that human cloning did not take place in the UK. France, Italy, Norway and Germany all took similar steps. The European Parliament issued a resolution opposing human cloning, the Group of Advisors on the Ethical Implications of Biotechnology to the European Commission issued an opinion that cloning was unacceptable and the Council of Europe drafted an additional Protocol to the existing Convention for the Protection of Human Rights and Dignity with Regards to the Application of Biology and Medicine which stated that any intervention seeking to create a human being identical to another human being is unacceptable, although it left to domestic law the precise definition of 'human being'. UNESCO declared that cloning was unacceptable because it undermines genetic indeterminability, it overrates the biological link and it is contrary to human dignity. The World Health Assembly issued a statement in May 1997 which stated that cloning was contrary to human integrity and morality and requested the WHO to consult with other international organisations and governmental agencies on the matter.

[8.149] Why did the prospect of cloning provoke such swift and strong reactions? It is open to question whether widespread revulsion, if it exists, provides good grounds for instituting legal prohibitions. Although revulsion is not an argument, it is 'the emotional expression of deep wisdom, beyond reason's power fully to articulate it'.[356] However, it might be argued that to base public policy on 'what we intuit and feel' is questionable at best, and irrational at worst.[357] Macklin claims there is no evidence that human dignity, whatever it means, has been compromised by assisted reproduction, nor is it threatened by cloning:

---

[354] Macklin, 'Cloning and Public Policy' in Burley and Harris (eds), *A Companion to Genethics* (Blackwell Publishing, 2002) 206 at 209.

[355] Wellcome Trust, *Report on Public Attitudes to Human Cloning* (1998).

[356] Kass 'The Wisdom of Repugnance' The New Republic, June 2 1997, p 20.

[357] Macklin, 'Cloning and Public Policy' in Burley and Harris (eds) *A Companion to Genethics* (Blackwell Publishing, 2002), at 212.

Rhetorical flourishes, even eloquent appeals, and vague references to human dignity are no substitute for reason and argument...Dignity is a fuzzy concept, and appeals to dignity are often used to substitute for empirical evidence that is lacking or sound arguments that cannot be mustered. If objectors to human cloning can identify no greater harm than a supposed affront to the dignity of the human species, that is a flimsy basis on which to erect barriers to scientific research and its applications, and to enact prohibitionist legislation.[358]

[8.150] The regulatory approaches taken in the EU, in particular the UK, as well as Canada and the US are divergent but generally prohibitive.[359] However, much of this legislation was drafted prior to the creation of Dolly the sheep, and needs to be interpreted very broadly in order to encompass the technique by which she was created. One might also question whether cloning can harm the resulting clone, thus perhaps rendering the technique immoral. 'The issue is whether merely allowing or causing the conception or birth of a child can ever constitute a wrong to that child.'[360] Many philosophers argue that a child cannot be harmed by conduct causing it to be conceived, where the only alternative is not to have been conceived at all. In other words, existence must be better than non-existence. Others agree in principle subject to the proviso that the child's condition must not be so severe as to render his life not worth living. Thus, unless the cloning technique itself causes the cloned embryo to be worse off relative to its alternatives, a cloned individual's rights cannot have been violated merely by its cloning.

Ireland

[8.151] In its Report to the Irish Government in 2005, the Commission on Assisted Human Reproduction discussed the scientific background to cloning as well as the arguments in favour and against the application of this technique to humans. It recommended that human reproductive cloning should be prohibited. In relation to therapeutic cloning, although the Commission recommended that the generation of embryos through IVF specifically for research purposes should be prohibited, it felt that an exception should be made for regenerative medicine. 'This exception is made on the basis that regenerative medicine is not actually IVF. The objective is to generate a stem cell line that in turn can be used to generate a particular tissue for treatment of a specific disease and one of the main potential advantages of this procedure is that the cloned embryonic stem cells are genetically identical to the host and will not generate an immune response following transplantation.' The majority of the Commission recommended that regenerative medicine (or therapeutic cloning) should be allowed under regulation.[361]

---

[358] Macklin, 'Cloning and Public Policy' in Burley and Harris (eds) *A Companion to Genethics* (Blackwell Publishing, 2002), at 212.

[359] Pattinson, 'Reproductive Cloning: Can Cloning Harm the Clone?' (2002) 10 Med Law Rev, 295–307.

[360] Pattinson, 'Reproductive Cloning: Can Cloning Harm the Clone?' (2002) 10 Med Law Rev, 295–307 at 303.

[361] Available at www.health.gov.ie.

[8.152] The legal position in relation to cloning in Ireland in the current absence of legislation is the same as for embryos created through in vitro fertilisation. Irrespective of the method of its creation, it follows from the Supreme Court decision in *MR v TR* in 2009 that the embryo outside the womb does not qualify for the protection of art 40.3.3°.[362] Thus, there is no current constitutional or legislative impediment to therapeutic or reproductive human cloning in Ireland.

[8.153] For medical practitioners in Ireland, the Guide to Professional Conduct and Ethics published by the Medical Council is of significance, as it provides in para 47.4 that doctors must not engage in reproductive cloning.[363] It is important to note, however, that the Guide is applicable to registered medical practitioners only and has no relevance to other health professionals or scientists working in the fields of embryology or research.

EMBRYONIC STEM CELL RESEARCH

[8.154] In human reproduction, the fertilised egg develops from a single cell into a small, hollow ball of cells termed a blastocyst. The blastocyst has an outer layer of cells which will go on to form the placenta and other supporting tissues needed for foetal development, and an inner cell mass which will go on to form virtually all of the tissues of the human body. These inner cells are pluripotent, which means they can give rise to many types of cells and will undergo further specialisation into stem cells that perform a particular function such as blood stem cells which form blood cells and platelets, or skin stem cells which give rise to skin cells.

[8.155] The potential applications of pluripotent stem cells in research include developing a better knowledge of cell specialisation, which could help understanding of diseases such as cancer and birth defects. It could also change the way drugs are developed and tested for safety by using cell lines to analyse the safety and efficacy of medication prior to animal and human testing. According to the National Institute of Health in the US, the most far-reaching potential application of human pluripotent stem cells is the generation of cells and tissue that could be used for cell therapies.[364] Many diseases and disorders result from disruption of cellular function or destruction of tissue in the body. Pluripotent stem cells, stimulated to develop into specialised cells, offer the possibility of a renewable source of replacement cells and tissue to treat a myriad of diseases, conditions and disabilities including Parkinson's and Alzheimer's disease, spinal cord injury, burns, stroke, diabetes, arthritis and epilepsy, as well as provide heart muscle cells for congestive heart failure, arrhythmias and cardiac tissue scarred by heart attacks. Another important potential development would be to trigger stem cells to differentiate into cells of the blood and bone marrow in order to treat disorders such as multiple sclerosis, rheumatoid arthritis and other autoimmune diseases.[365]

---

[362] *MR v TR* [2009] IESC 82, discussed in Chapter 6 at para **[6.92]**.
[363] The Medical Council, Guide to Professional Conduct and Ethics (8th edn, 2016) available at www.medicalcouncil.ie.
[364] See stemcells.nih.gov/info/basics/basics6.asp.
[365] The embryonic stem cell has been referred to as a 'factory-in-a-dish' by Regalado, 'The Troubled Hunt for the Ultimate Cell' (1998) Technology Review 35.

[8.156] Pluripotent stem cells may be derived from the inner cell mass of embryos at the blastocyst stage. This requires that the blastocyst is disaggregated or broken up into single cells which are then no longer able to make a whole organism. ES cells are capable of extensive self-renewal (where a cell makes an identical copy of itself) in the culture dish.[366] The first hESC line was derived in 1998, ushering in 'one of the most public, spirited, and intractable debates in research ethics: the moral status of the embryo from which hESCs are derived.'[367] These debates arose because, as King and Perrin explain, to harvest hESCs, it is first necessary to destroy the 5-day-old preimplantation embryo. Opponents of hESC research argue that because the embryo is capable of developing into a human being, it has significant moral standing; therefore, its destruction is unethical. Some proponents of hESC research deny that the embryo has any moral status; others grant it limited moral status but argue that the value of this limited status is far outweighed by the potential benefits that can result from hESC research.[368]

[8.157] While ES cell research shows much promise, much work still remains to be done before this potential might be realised, and the technologies incorporated into clinical practice. Basic research must be carried out to understand the cellular events leading to cell specialisation in the human so as to be able to direct the stem cells to become the type of tissue needed. Also the problem of immune rejection must be overcome. If the stem cells are taken from unrelated embryos or foetuses, their DNA would be different from that of the recipient. However, if the stem cells are derived by virtue of cell nuclear transfer (or therapeutic cloning) they would be genetically identical to the patient, there would be no rejection and no need for immuno-suppressants.

[8.158] Controversy about the derivation and use of hESCs led investigators to seek less ethically fraught but maximally useful types of stem cells. However, the discovery of other highly multipotent stem cell types (such as induced pluripotent stem cells or iPS cells) and alternative methods of isolating and creating highly multipotent stem cells has raised further questions and concerns.[369] Issues that may arise in this area of research include 'the minimization of risks of harm; the importance of information disclosure and informed consent; the potential for overpromising, over-expectations, and the therapeutic misconception; and the pressure from disease constituencies and commercial entities to move quickly into the clinic, too often at the expense of understanding basic mechanisms.' [370]

---

[366] Svendsen, 'Stem Cells' in Burley and Harris (eds) *A Companion to Genethics* (Blackwell Publishing 2002) at 8.

[367] King and Perrin, 'Ethical issues in stem cell research and therapy' Stem Cell Research & Therapy 2014, 5:85.

[368] King and Perrin, 'Ethical issues in stem cell research and therapy' Stem Cell Research & Therapy 2014, 5:85.

[369] King and Perrin, 'Ethical issues in stem cell research and therapy' Stem Cell Research & Therapy 2014, 5:85.

[370] King and Perrin, 'Ethical issues in stem cell research and therapy' Stem Cell Research & Therapy 2014, 5:85.

[8.159] A further possible way to avoid some of the ethical issues associated with hESC research is to use stem cells from some types of adult tissue. Some scientists are of the view that adult stem cells, already committed to the development of one line of specialised cells, would not have the capacity to be reprogrammed into other types of specialised cells and therefore provide less therapeutic potential. However, research is continuing into ways in which the adult cells might be redirected. If successful, the adult stem cells could be taken from a patient, coaxed to divide and directed to specialisation. They could then be transplanted back to the same adult. The use of adult stem cells in this way would have medical advantages in not being rejected by the recipient, and would have ethical advantages in avoiding the use of cells from human embryos or foetal tissue. However, even if successful, there are limitations in that stem cells have not yet been isolated for all tissues of the body, such as cardiac or pancreatic stem cells. Also adult stem cells are often present in tiny quantities, are difficult to isolate and their numbers may decrease with age. If the patient has a genetic disorder, the genetic error may also be present in the patient's stem cells, and therefore would not be appropriate for transplantation. They may also contain more abnormalities caused by exposure to environmental factors such as toxins or sunlight. Adult stem cells are difficult to grow in a laboratory and their potential to reproduce diminishes with age so obtaining significant amounts of adult stem cells may prove difficult. There are no perceived ethical or legal difficulties associated with adult stem cells research, which should be governed by normal research criteria.

Ethical issues

[8.160] The main arguments in relation to human embryology stem cell (hESC) research are in relation to the scientific evidence supporting claims made by both advocates and opponents, and ethical disagreement about the status of embryos and the cells derived from them. These disagreements are unlikely to be resolved by philosophical argument.[371] 'While everyone has views about the moral status of the embryo and some of those who have views even have arguments to support their views, attempts to solve problems about issues which depend on the use of embryonic or foetal material by recourse to establishing the moral status of the embryo have proved intractable.'[372]

[8.161] Many of those who oppose hESC research do so on the basis that the embryo is a human person deserving respect and protection. The moral status of the embryo is not just a philosophical question and will also have important practical implications.

> Each definition has a practical intent. Once we ascribe human life and personhood to an entity we want to protect it. If one wants to give maximum protection, one has to use a

---

[371] Solbakk and Holm, 'The Ethics of Stem Cell Research: Can the Disagreements Be Resolved?' (2008) Vol 34 J Med Ethics 831. See also Holm, 'Going to the Roots of the Stem Cell Controversy' (2002) Vol 16 (6) Bioethics 493; Savulescu, 'The Embryonic Stem Cell Lottery and the Cannibalization of Human Beings' (2002) Vol 16 (6) Bioethics 508; Green, 'Benefiting From 'Evil': An Incipient Moral Problem in Human Stem Cell Research (2002) Vol 16 (6) Bioethics 544; and Agar ,'Embryonic Potential and Stem Cells' (2007) Vol 21 (4) Bioethics 198.

[372] Harris, 'The Ethical Use of Human Embryonic Stem Cells in Research and Therapy' in Burley and Harris (eds), *A Companion to Genethics* (Blackwell Publishing) at 163.

minimal definition, such as the new genetic unity created by egg and sperm. A maximal definition of human life, such as the ability to communicate, or to act independently, offers minimal protection to the stages prior to these competencies and after they have been lost.[373]

This view is shared by the Catholic Church which states that fertilisation is critical in terms of acquisition of personhood, and opposes all forms of research on embryos.[374] There are also those who accept that the embryo is not yet a person but that it has moral status due to its potential to become a person. For example, Marshall regards the potential to become a human person as of tremendous importance and even though by opposing experimentation on embryos he recognises that some scientific advances may be lost, he does not believe the loss will be as great as scientists would have us believe. 'On this argument, because the entity has the potential to become a person, one affirms that it should *not* be interfered with, that *nothing* should be done that prevents it realising its potential, and that things *can* be done which will help it to attain that potential.'[375]

[8.162] Advocates for hESC research dispute the claim for personhood based on potential on the basis that moral rights are based on actuality not potential. 'The embryo's potential to become a person is relevant to the moral status it will have if and when it does become a person, but it does not confer the moral status on it when still an embryo that it will have later when it has become a person.' [376] Brock argues that since there are numerous excess embryos stored in IVF clinics on behalf of couples who will never use them, nothing is lost by allowing couples to choose to donate these embryos for research purposes rather than have them destroyed or stored indefinitely. 'If one believes that human embryos are neither human persons nor beings deserving of respect that is incompatible with their destruction, then this reasoning provides strong support for use of surplus embryos for hESC research.'[377] The 'nothing is lost' principle will not justify such research for those who believe that embryos are human persons or beings deserving of respect that is incompatible with their destruction. However, Brock argues that few who hold this view accept its full implications. He says that embryos lost in natural reproduction are not grieved over in the same way as the death of a foetus or child.[378] He also quotes from Sandel's hypothetical example of a fire in a fertility laboratory where one could save a tray of ten surplus embryos or one eight-year-old

---

[373] Junker-Kenny, 'The moral status of the embryo' in Messer (ed) *Theological issues in bioethics: an introduction with readings* (Darton, Longman and Todd: London 2002) 8–75.

[374] Congregation for the Doctrine of the Faith *Instruction Dignitas Personae* on certain bioethical questions (Vatican 2008). See further discussion in Ch 6 at para **[6.19]** et seq.

[375] Marshall J, 'The case against experimentation' in Dyson and Harris (eds), *Experimentation on Embryos* (Routledge, London 1990) 55–64.

[376] Brock, 'Is a Consensus Possible on Stem Cell Research? Moral and Legal Obstacles' (2006) J Med Ethics 32: 36–42.

[377] Brock, 'Is a Consensus Possible on Stem Cell Research? Moral and Legal Obstacles' (2006) J Med Ethics 32: 36–42.

[378] Brock says that it is well known that for each embryo born alive from sexual reproduction at least three are created who will die before birth.

child, but not both, virtually everyone would save the child.[379] This suggests that people do not view embryos as morally comparable to born human beings or persons.

[8.163] Those who do not believe that a human embryo is a full human person nevertheless believe it is not mere human tissue to be discarded at will. Instead it is a morally significant entity deserving of serious moral respect. There is concern that as a society we do not want to see embryos treated as products,[380] as this would cheapen reproduction and the value of parenting. As Robertson puts it:

> Although embryos do not themselves have rights, they are an occasion for expressing or symbolising one's views about the importance or value of human life, thereby constituting one's moral or national character in the process. People differ, however, over the degree and intensity of the symbolic associations that attach to non-rights-bearing entities such as embryos. The importance of signifying or constituting a highly protective attitude towards human life by objecting to certain kinds of embryo research is thus more determined by personal or public preferences than it is by the obligations of moral duty.[381]

This compromise position therefore treats the embryo as 'special' because it is a member of the human species, but this does not require us to treat the four-cell embryo the same status as a human person. This position was adopted by the Warnock Committee in the UK which recommended that embryo research should be permitted in certain circumstances.[382] This was subsequently embodied in the Human Fertilisation and Embryology Act in the UK (1990 and 2008) which permits embryo research up to 14 days after fertilisation subject to licence from the Human Fertilisation and Embryology Authority.

[8.164] The President's Council on Bioethics in the US took the view that human embryos have some form of intermediate moral status between full human persons and morally insignificant things and said that it was incoherent and self contradictory to claim that embryos deserve special respect and yet to endorse research that requires the creation, use and destruction of those organisms.[383] However, Brock argues with this conclusion by drawing an analogy with the respect commonly shown to domestic pets or

---

[379] Brock, 'Is a Consensus Possible on Stem Cell Research? Moral and Legal Obstacles' (2006) J Med Ethics 32: 36–42. See also Harris, 'On the moral status of the embryo' in Dyson and Harris (eds) Dyson and Harris (eds), *Experimentation on Embryos* (Routledge, London 1990) 65–81; Singer and Dawson 'IVF Technology and the argument from potential' in Singer et al (eds) *Embryo experimentation* (CUP: Cambridge 1990) 76–89.

[380] The use of embryos for commercial purposes is very controversial. The legal issues involved in patenting discoveries derived from stem cell research are not discussed in this book. However, readers may wish to note the EU Directive 98/44/EC on legal protection of biotechnological invention and the case of *Brüstle v Greenpeace eV* (Case C–34/10).

[381] Robertson: Presentation to Smithkline Beecham Ethics and Public Policy Board, Chewton Glen, July 11 1999; quoted by Harris, 'The Ethical Use of Human Embryonic Stem Cells in Research and Therapy' in Burley and Harris (eds), *A Companion to Genethics* (Blackwell Publishing) at 163.

[382] Report of the Committee of Inquiry into Human Fertilisation and Embryology (1984).

[383] The President's Council on Bioethics, *Human Cloning and Human Dignity: An Ethical Inquiry* (US Government Printing Office, 2002) at 154.

primates such as monkeys. He says that these animals are not mere things to be used for human purposes in any way we wish, as their capacity to suffer underpins their intermediate moral status. Yet these animals are bred and sometimes killed in the course of biomedical research aimed at treating serious human disease. Many people accept such a practice as morally permissible yet oppose the use of animals for other less significant purposes such as cosmetic research. The difference between these purposes lies clearly in the seriousness and importance of the two activities. Brock says it is incompatible with the intermediate moral status of the animals to destroy them for a trivial purpose and that by limiting their use to important valuable research aimed at treating serious illness, this shows them special respect. Likewise, human embryos could be shown the special respect that intermediate moral status requires by limiting their use to equally important human purposes that have reasonable promise of alleviating serious human disease.[384]

[8.165] In 2007 researchers announced that they had produced induced pluripotent cells (IP cells) from human adult somatic cells.[385] These cells are very similar to hES cells in that they are pluripotent and therefore have the capacity to differentiate into specific cell types. These findings have significant implications for stem cell ethics, as the production of these cells do not involve the contentious issue of embryo destruction as they are derived from skin cells not embryos. The ongoing research in relation to IP cells aims to produce the same ends as therapeutic cloning without destroying any embryos and therefore has attracted much attention as an ethical breakthrough. However, the matter is not so straightforward:

> It has sometimes been argued that an embryo has the right to life by virtue of its interest in experiencing what has sometimes been called a 'future of value', because of its potential to be a person. Yet if skin cells and possibly other cells can be reprogrammed to embryonic status, are all of these now embryos *in potentio* in the same way as in some sense, an embryo is a person *in potentio*? Those who value the embryo for its potentiality might well feel obliged to value all cells that might be reprogrammable for the same reason.[386]

[8.166] It is also argued that the social acceptability of scientific progress should not be determinative of whether IP cells should be preferred to hES cells. 'It would be a bad day for scientific progress and for human welfare if priority-setting in science were dictated by the degree of opposition to a particular practice.' This does not mean that scientists should not be accountable by having to justify their research and obtain ethics committee approval but rather that they should not have to prioritise their research in terms of public approval ratings.

[8.167] Although the development of IP cells may be seen as a major breakthrough in stem cell research, it is also important to note that many scientists caution against

---

[384] Brock, 'Is a Consensus Possible on Stem Cell Research? Moral and Legal Obstacles' (2006) J Med Ethics 32: 36–42.

[385] Takahashe et al, 'Induction of Pluripotent Stem Cells From Adult Human Fibroblasts by Defined Factors' (2007) Cell; Vogel and Holden 'Developmental Biology. Field Leaps Forward With New Stem Cell Advances' Science 2007; 318:1224.

[386] Chan and Harris. 'Adam's Fibroblast? The (Pluri) Potential of iPCs' (2008) J Med Ethics 34:64–66.

abandoning hESC research at this stage for a number of reasons. Firstly, it is too early to know whether stem cells produced in this way will prove as effective as hES cells. Both IP cells and hESC research are directed towards similar goals and until there is evidence that one approach rather than the other is more effective in achieving those goals, many would argue that both should be pursued in tandem. Secondly, the use of hES cells is also essential in increasing scientists' understanding of IP cells; if an alternative to ES cells is to be produced, it is necessary to know everything about ES cells first. Thirdly, there is also concern that because IP cells are heavily manipulated to drive somatic cells back in developmental time and then to drive them down a specialised pathway, they may end up losing their immune compatibility along the way, making them less beneficial for the patient from whom the skin cells have been derived.[387]

[8.168] The use of stem cells in medical treatment has also been controversial with reported success in China, India and elsewhere on spinal injuries and other disabilities. However, these treatments have not been validated in clinical trials and the International Society for Stem Cell Research is concerned about the safety of these procedures, which are offered without proper scientific validation to vulnerable patients, and the risk of maverick practitioners in an area of rapidly evolving technology. It has published guidelines for the clinical translation of stem cell research to ensure rigorous standards in the development of stem cell therapies, including stringent evaluation and oversight, a thorough informed consent process and transparency in operations and reporting.[388]

International regulation

[8.169] By comparison to the almost universal opposition to reproductive cloning, there is less consensus in relation to embryonic stem cell research. In Europe four different approaches might be described amongst those countries that have legislated on this issue.[389] Those with permissive legislation include Belgium, Sweden, Finland, Spain and the UK. These countries allow SCNT and stem cell research under certain conditions. A large group of countries pursue a compromise position which allows hESC research only on surplus IVF embryos and prohibits the use of SCNT or therapeutic cloning for this purpose. This group includes France, Denmark, the Netherlands, Norway, Portugal and Switzerland. Germany and Italy have a more restrictive compromise which allows hESC research only on cell lines created before a certain date. Countries with a prohibitive position include Poland, Austria and Slovakia. Similar groupings are evident in the United States, Asia and Oceania.

[8.170] In the United States, in addition to discussions about the ethics of stem cell research, there has also been much debate about the funding of hESC research since its inception. In 2001 President Bush decided that federal funding of research would be allowed only using existing stem cell lines of which he understood there were about 60.

---

[387] In 2008 Doug Melton from Harvard University reported that he had been able to short-circuit the process of reprogramming an adult cell into a differentiated cell of another kind in mice through a process called 'lineage reprogramming.' However, it is unclear whether cells can be fully converted in this way. Zhou and Melton, 'Extreme Makeover: Converting One Cell Into Another' (2008) Cell Stem Cell 3(4): 382–388.

[388] See www.isscr.org/About_Stem_Cell_Treatment.htm.

[389] For up-to-date information on legislation and policy, see www.hinxtongroup.org.

He banned federal funding for research using stem cells derived from frozen embryos, about 100,000 of which existed at fertility labs across the country. In 2005, the Stem Cell Research Enhancement Act of 2005 was passed by the House of Representatives and in 2006 it was passed by the Senate. However, President Bush opposed embryonic stem cell research on ideological grounds and he exercised his first presidential veto when he refused to allow the Act to become law. On March 9, 2009, President Obama, by Executive Order, lifted the Bush administration's eight-year ban on federal funding of embryonic stem research.[390]

[8.171] Funding for research from commercial sources is often predicated on the potential to derive intellectual property rights from the work and therefore the issue of patenting the findings of any such research is of huge practical significance. In *Brüstle v Greenpeace*[391] the German Federal Court of Justice asked the Court of the European Union (CJEU) to define what is meant by the term 'human embryos' in art 6(2)(c) of the European Parliament and Council Directive on the legal protection of biotechnological inventions.[392] The Directive considers unpatentable uses of human embryos for industrial or commercial purposes. The Directive did not mention human embryonic stem cells, as the technology had not been developed at that stage. But in 2005, a resolution of the European Parliament declared that 'the creation of human embryonic stem cells implies the destruction of human embryos and... therefore the patenting of procedures involving human embryonic stem cells or cells that are grown from human embryonic stem cells is a violation'.

[8.172] The Court defined the concept of human embryos broadly, since it was of the view that the European Union legislature intended to exclude any possibility of patentability in situations that could potentially affect the respect for human dignity. The Court took the view that although the Directive seeks to promote investment in the field of biotechnology, use of biological material originating from humans must be consistent with regard for fundamental rights and, in particular, the dignity of the person. Accordingly, the Grand Chamber of the Court ruled 'any human ovum after fertilization, any non-fertilised human ovum into which the cell nucleus from a mature human cell

---

[390] In lifting the ban President Obama said, 'In recent years, when it comes to stem cell research, rather than furthering discovery, our government has forced what I believe is a false choice between sound science and moral values. In this case, I believe the two are not inconsistent. As a person of faith, I believe we are called to care for each other and work to ease human suffering. I believe we have been given the capacity and will to pursue this research – and the humanity and conscience to do so responsibly.... I can also promise that we will never undertake this research lightly. We will support it only when it is both scientifically worthy and responsibly conducted. We will develop strict guidelines, which we will rigorously enforce, because we cannot ever tolerate misuse or abuse. And we will ensure that our government never opens the door to the use of cloning for human reproduction. It is dangerous, profoundly wrong, and has no place in our society, or any society.' For more information see, http://stemcells.nih.gov/policy/defaultpage.asp.

[391] Court of Justice of the European Union (2011). *Oliver Brüstle v Greenpeace* Judgment of the Court (Grand Chamber) of 18 October 2011. Case C-34/10.

[392] European Union (1998). Directive 98/44/EC of the European Parliament and of the Council of 6 July 1998 on the legal protection of biotechnological inventions, Official Journal of the European Communities, L 213/13.

has been transplanted, and any non-fertilised human ovum whose division and further development have been stimulated by parthenogenesis constitute a 'human embryo', and may not be the subject of a patent. The result of this case is that hESC research is not prohibited but scientists will not be able to patent their work in the European Union, therefore making it difficult to commercialise or get funding for their research.

[8.173] Problems were identified with the Court of Justice's ruling on this issue on the basis that its definition of human embryos failed to examine the differences between hESC and iPS cells. Indeed, it was argued that the Court seemed to equate cells with human embryos, which has been described as 'a definitional misstep that contorts our common understanding of developmental biology.'[393] European authorities and patent offices had up to that point continuously denied patents on human totipotent cells, which are those cells that have the ability to make the embryo proper as well as the extra-embryonic tissues necessary to support its development, such as the placenta. By comparison, pluripotent cells make the many different types of cells, tissues, and organs of the embryo. It is therefore important to ask whether a cell can contribute whole or in part to a fully developed organism.

> To bypass its troubles with biological terminology, the CJEU seemingly refrained from using the term totipotent and instead used the descriptive criterion of a cell's 'capability of commencing the process of development of a human being.' Broadening the criterion ignores the scientific subtleties of human development and ignores the actions taken in order to prove a cell can commence the process of human development.[394]

[8.174] Scientists involved in this area of research argued that the Court had, by an overbroad and ill-conceived ruling, thus extended the definition of human dignity to 'entities that in no way resemble fertilized human embryos awaiting potential implantation into a female uterus via in vitro fertilization.'[395] Thus, it was argued that:

> Human dignity is a noble concept, but it is useful insofar as it is concerned with the well-being of actual human beings. Europe should focus more on protecting the human dignity of terminally ill patients eagerly awaiting novel stem cell treatments than on safeguarding the human dignity of each and every somatic cell in our body.

[8.175] Clarification was received on some of these issues in the later case of *International Stem Cell Corporation v Comptroller General of Patents, Designs and Trade Marks*,[396] in which the Court of Justice ruled that egg cells incapable of developing into humans cannot be considered human embryos under the Directive. The

---

[393] Triller Vrtovec and Scott, 'The European Court of Justice Ruling in Brüstle v. Greenpeace: The Impacts on Patenting of Human Induced Pluripotent Stem Cells in Europe' Cell Stem Cell 9, December 2, 2011, 502.

[394] Triller Vrtovec and Scott, 'The European Court of Justice Ruling in Brüstle v. Greenpeace: The Impacts on Patenting of Human Induced Pluripotent Stem Cells in Europe' Cell Stem Cell 9, December 2, 2011, 502.

[395] Triller Vrtovec and Scott, 'The European Court of Justice Ruling in Brüstle v. Greenpeace: The Impacts on Patenting of Human Induced Pluripotent Stem Cells in Europe' Cell Stem Cell 9, December 2, 2011, 502.

[396] *International Stem Cell Corporation v Comptroller General of Patents, Designs and Trade Marks* Case C364/13, 18 Dec 2014.

case was brought in Britain by a US company, International Stem Cell Corporation, against the UK Intellectual Property Office for refusing to grant it two patents covering the use of human egg cells. The British authorities had argued that since the eggs involved were active and developing organisms, even though they were not fertilised by male sperm, the *Brüstle* case prevented the company from securing a patent on them. The company argued that the eggs, activated by a chemical process known as parthenogenesis, could not develop into human beings as they lacked the full parental DNA required and therefore did not come within the definition of human embryo of the Court in *Brüstle.*

[8.176] The Court held that it had been previously decided in *Brüstle* that any human ovum must, as soon as it is fertilised, be regarded as a 'human embryo' within the meaning and for the purposes of the application of art 6(2)(c) of the Directive, since fertilisation commences the process of development of a human being. The Court said that it had specified in that judgment, that that classification must also apply to a non-fertilised human ovum into which the cell nucleus from a mature human cell has been transplanted and a non-fertilised human ovum whose division and further development have been stimulated by parthenogenesis. Although those organisms have not, strictly speaking, been the object of fertilisation, due to the effect of the technique used to obtain them, they are capable of commencing the process of development of a human being just as an embryo created by fertilisation of an ovum can do so. The Court held that, following the judgment in *Brüstle,* a non-fertilised human ovum must be classified as a 'human embryo', within the meaning of art 6(2)(c) of Directive 98/44, in so far as that organism is 'capable of commencing the process of development of a human being'.

[8.177] Consequently where a non-fertilised human ovum does not fulfil that condition, the mere fact that that organism commences a process of development is not sufficient for it to be regarded as a 'human embryo', within the meaning and for the purposes of the application of Directive 98/44. In the current case the Court was satisfied that, according to current scientific knowledge, a human parthenote, due to the effect of the technique used to obtain it, is not as such capable of commencing the process of development which leads to a human being. Accordingly the Court held that art 6(2)(c) of Directive 98/44/EC of the European Parliament and of the Council of 6 July 1998 on the legal protection of biotechnological inventions must be interpreted as meaning that an unfertilised human ovum whose division and further development have been stimulated by parthenogenesis does not constitute a 'human embryo', within the meaning of that provision, if, in the light of current scientific knowledge, it does not, in itself, have the inherent capacity of developing into a human being, this being a matter for the national court to determine.

[8.178] In this case the Court also held that the term 'human embryo', within the meaning of art 6(2)(c) of the Directive, must be regarded as designating an autonomous concept of EU law which must be interpreted in a uniform manner throughout the territory of the Union thereby obliging harmonisation of the definition of this term at least for the purposes of patentability. However, on the broader question of regulatory harmonisation of hESC research, it has been debated whether this is possible or even desirable. In principle, harmonisation is seen as having a number of important benefits by facilitating international trade, the avoidance of uncertainty about national regulation, and the elimination of expense and effort involved in monitoring compliance with the regulatory requirements of different countries.[397] In the context of stem cell research, harmonisation may be desirable also for ethical reasons so that researchers worldwide would be required to conform to the same ethical standards. It would also help increase public confidence in this area of science by highlighting the need to ensure that it is carefully monitored and regulated. Many countries have no legislation or policy in this area so 'the creation of international standards could fill this gap where it exists, and it might also prompt jurisdictions without any regulatory scheme to either directly adopt the standards or craft their own laws and policies in a manner consistent with the harmonised guidelines.'[398]

[8.179] One of the difficulties inherent in the harmonisation process where so many diverse views are present is the risk of reducing harmonised principles to 'the lowest common denominator'. For countries with rigorous regulations already in place, this could result in significant downgrading of domestic legal norms. Another difficulty exists in relation to cultural diversity, as the way in which countries respond to issues such as stem cell research is related to their cultural perceptions and values:

> A country's historical experiences, religious values and its social and legal understandings of the human embryo all play a critical role in shaping its regulatory approach to stem cell research and cloning technology. Because these factors are so varied from one jurisdiction to the next, devising a single set of regulatory guidelines to which the entire international community must adhere would be a formidable task.[399]

[8.180] Campbell and Nycum advocate a harmonisation process developed by an independent non-political international agency marked by diversity in terms of culture and disciplinary expertise. The entity would strive for the creation of harmonised legal norms governing stem cell science which are clear enough to be implemented in all countries and could be revised as appropriate to consider new emerging knowledge and challenges. Although the enforceability of such norms would pose significant problems, they argue that by inclusion in the drafting of such norms, the scientific community would be persuaded to abide by the norms in their research. 'This model thus aims to reconcile the ongoing tension between the desire to create harmonised standards that are internationally perceived as desirable, legitimate and as having normative force, while at the same time ensuring that the harmonisation process does not negate local cultural values, norms and approaches to the governance of science.'

Ireland

[8.181] In Ireland there is no specific legislation governing the use of human embryos or stem cell research. The Commission on Assisted Human Reproduction recommended in

---

[397] Campbell and Nycum, 'Harmonising the International Regulation of Embryonic Stem Cell Research: Possibilities, Promises and Potential Pitfalls' (2005) Med Law International Vol 7, pp 113–148.

[398] Campbell and Nycum, 'Harmonising the International Regulation of Embryonic Stem Cell Research: Possibilities, Promises and Potential Pitfalls' (2005) Med Law International Vol 7, pp 113–148, at 126.

[399] Campbell and Nycum, 'Harmonising the International Regulation of Embryonic Stem Cell Research: Possibilities, Promises and Potential Pitfalls' (2005) Med Law International Vol 7, pp 113–148, at 130.

2005[400] that the embryo formed by IVF should not attract legal protection until placed in the human body and that embryonic stem cell research should be permitted on surplus embryos for specific purposes and under stringently controlled conditions. The Irish Council for Bioethics published a report on stem cell research in 2008 in which it also advocated in favour of permitting embryonic stem cell research within certain limits.[401] The Medical Council in its Guide to Professional Conduct and Ethics in 2009 stated in para 47.4 that doctors must not participate in creating new forms of life solely for experimental purposes. It also states that doctors must not engage in human reproductive cloning but there is no reference to embryonic stem cell research or regenerative medicine.[402]

[8.182] It had been speculated for some time that the destruction of embryos might be unconstitutional in Ireland in light of the provisions of art 40.3.3°. However, in 2009 the Supreme Court delivered its long-awaited judgment in the case of *MR v TR*, also known as *Roche v Roche*.[403] The facts of this case involved a dispute between a separated couple in relation to the disposition of frozen embryos which they had stored during a previous IVF attempt.[404] One of the issues arising before the Court was whether these frozen embryos qualified for constitutional protection under the provisions of art 40.3.3°, which acknowledges the right to life of the unborn. In a unanimous judgment of the Court, it was held that the word 'unborn' did not extend to pre-implantation embryos and therefore the frozen embryos in this case did not qualify for constitutional protection. As a result of this case, there is no constitutional or legislative prohibition in Ireland at present on the use or destruction of human embryos for research purposes. This case is discussed in more detail in Ch 6.

---

[400] Report available at www.health.gov.ie.

[401] The Irish Council for Bioethics was disbanded in 2008 but its report on stem cell research is available at http://www.bioethics.ie/index.php/reports-and-opinions.

[402] Medical Council, *The Guide to Professional Conduct and Ethics* (7th edn, 2009), available at http://www.medicalcouncil.ie/.

[403] *Roche v Roche* [2009] IESC 82.

[404] For further discussion, see Ch 6 at para **[6.92]**.

Chapter 9

Capacity and Assisted Decision-Making

INTRODUCTION

[9.01] It has been said that non-disclosure and deference have been the hallmarks of the paternalistic tradition that has dominated orthodox medical practice over a period of some 2,500 years.[1] Traditional medical ethics were based on the Hippocratic Oath, which obliged the doctor to use his skill to the best of his ability and to abstain from harming the patient. These obligations did not require the doctor to consult with or seek permission from the patient for any medical intervention. The common understanding of the relationship between them was that since the doctor had more knowledge about the patient's condition, he would do what was best for the patient and the patient did not need to be informed. This form of decision-making is now referred to as paternalism, defined by Dworkin as 'interference with a person's liberty of action justified by reasons referring exclusively to the welfare, good, happiness, needs, interests, or values of the person being coerced.'[2]

[9.02] It was only in the 1960s that attitudes began to change, particularly in the United States, and questions began to be raised about whether in fact the doctor was in a better position to make healthcare decisions for the patient than the patient himself. Donnelly says that the shift in emphasis occurred for a number of reasons. Firstly, challenges to medical authority were part of a broader picture of challenges to traditional authority, campaigns for civil rights and the rise of feminism which were prevalent at this time. Secondly, there were specific concerns about certain medical practices, in particular in relation to persons with a mental disorder, and abuses in medical research such as the infamous Tuskegee Syphilis Trial.[3] These factors led to a mistrust of the profession and reluctance to accept medical views unquestioningly.[4]

[9.03] Mounting criticism of the paternalistic approach has taken a variety of forms but a central theme is concern that the patient's voice is insufficiently heard.[5] 'The assertion of patients' rights is presented as a natural antithesis to medical paternalism, proclaiming the moral agency of the individual and the intrinsic value of respect for the patient as person.' The influential Belmont Report, which was published in the US in

---

[1]   Pellegrino and Thomasma, *A Philosophical Basis of Medical Practice* (OUP, 1981).

[2]   Dworkin, 'Paternalism' (1972) *The Monist* 56, p 65.

[3]   For further information, see Final Report of the Tuskegee Syphilis Study Legacy Committee May 20, 1996; and Jones, *Bad Blood: The Tuskegee Syphilis Experiment* (Free Press, 1993).

[4]   Donnelly, *Healthcare Decision-making and the Law, Autonomy, Capacity and the Limits of Liberalism* (Cambridge University Press, 2010) 14.

[5]   Teff, *Reasonable Care, Legal Perspectives on the Doctor-Patient Relationship* (Oxford, Clarendon Press 1994) at xxiv.

1978, advocated a principles-based approach to medical research involving human participants.[6] Around the same time Beauchamp and Childress wrote one of most widely read and influential texts on medical ethics in which they proposed four governing principles for bioethics: autonomy, beneficence, non-maleficence and justice.[7] Although they did not prioritise amongst these four principles, autonomy quickly became regarded as the most important. Some ethicists, such as Gillon,[8] are of the view that this is the correct approach whereas others, such as Callahan,[9] feel that the failure to engage with the other principles results in an impoverished ethical framework.

[9.04] Despite the societal changes which led to the dominance of autonomy in healthcare ethics, paternalism has been remarkably resilient.[10] The medical profession has undoubtedly increased its emphasis on communication skills and ethics in medical education and training in recent years but some resistance remains. Rights-based criticisms have originated mainly from outside the world of medicine but within it patient welfare as traditionally conceived still takes pride of place, particularly in hospital settings where hierarchical and more impersonal regimes still often reflect a time-honoured ethos which has not converted to the primacy of patient choice and patients' rights.[11] On a practical level, some doctors claim that pressures of work and scarcity of time often constrain their ability to make a more conscious effort to involve the patient in his illness and treatment. Patients may also be reluctant to know the precise details of their condition and may prefer to leave the treatment in the doctor's expert hands. While this may also be seen as an exercise of autonomy in that the patient is making a choice not to know, there is a danger that the habit of decision-making on the patient's behalf may become a routine part of the doctor's management of all of his patients.[12] 'Practitioners are trained to make decisions for patients, and to put those decisions in the form of advice…The emphasis on giving advice rather than explanation has led practitioners (doctors, nurses and paramedics) to be more skilled at persuasion than at discussion, more dependent on authority than on rationale. And it has sometimes tempted them to take short cuts in gaining or assuming consent.'[13]

---

[6] National Commission for the Protection of Human Subjects of Biomedical and Behavioural Research, *Ethical Principles and Guidelines for the Protection of Human Subjects of Research* (Dept of Health, Education and Welfare, 1979).

[7] Beauchamp and Childress, *Principles of Biomedical Ethics* (1st edn, OUP, 1979).

[8] Gillon, 'Ethics Needs Principles – Four Can Encompass the Rest – And Respect for Autonomy Should Be First Among Equals' (2003) 29 Journal of Med Ethics 307.

[9] Callahan, 'Autonomy: A Moral Good, Not a Moral Obsession' (1984) 14 Hastings Center Report 40, quoted by Donnelly, *Healthcare Decision-making and the Law, Autonomy, Capacity and the Limits of Liberalism,* (Cambridge University Press, 2010) 15.

[10] Teff, *Reasonable Care, Legal Perspectives on the Doctor-Patient Relationship* (Oxford, Clarendon Press 1994) at 69.

[11] Teff, *Reasonable Care, Legal Perspectives on the Doctor-Patient Relationship* (Oxford, Clarendon Press 1994) at xxv.

[12] See discussion by Brazier, 'Patient Autonomy and Consent to Treatment: The Role of the Law?' (1987) 7 Legal Studies at 169–193 at 174.

[13] Williamson, *Whose standards? Consumer and professional standards in health care* (Open University Press, 1992) p 110–111.

Respect for autonomy

[9.05] Respect for the principle of individual autonomy is now regarded as central to healthcare decision-making.[14] This ethical principle has been reiterated by the law, as seen in the classic statement by Justice Cordozo: 'Every human being of adult years and sound mind has a right to determine what shall be done with his own body and a surgeon who performs an operation without his patient's consent commits an assault, for which he is liable in damages'.[15] Yet it is not entirely clear what autonomy means in some contexts, what respect for it entails, and whether there are circumstances in which other ethical principles or values should take precedence over autonomy. 'The status of autonomy within ethical discourse has been challenged for almost as long as the principle has been revered, while in a legal context the degree of respect accorded to the principle of autonomy has varied depending on the circumstances in which the principle is called into action.'[16]

[9.06] The central idea of autonomy is that one's actions and decisions are one's own.[17] Some people regard it as a distinctively human ability to be able to reflect on and adopt attitudes towards one's desires, intentions and plans. For example, Dworkin describes autonomy as 'a second-order capacity to reflect critically upon one's first-order preferences and desires, and the ability either to identify with these or to change them in light of higher-order preferences and values. By exercising such a capacity we define our nature, give meaning and coherence to our lives, and take responsibility for the kind of person we are.'[18] One gives meaning to one's life in any number of ways, and the equality that is accorded to every human person demands that recognition is given to the way that each person has chosen to value and define his or her life. There is something special about the role of autonomy in healthcare when the doctor's functions are examined in that context. A doctor cares for the health of the body, but the care of the body is intrinsically linked with our identity as persons. A doctor is not so much the preventer of death but rather the preserver of life capacities for the realisation of a reasonable, realistic life plan of the patient.[19] Beauchamp says that autonomy is associated with several ideas such as privacy, voluntariness, self-mastery, the freedom to choose and accepting responsibility for one's choices. 'To respect an autonomous agent is to recognise with due appreciation the person's capacities and perspective, including his or her right to hold certain views and to take certain actions based on personal values and beliefs.'[20]

---

[14] McCall Smith criticises the prioritisation of autonomy as the 'passive acceptance of a one-dimensional perspective' and questions the 'liberal individualist consensus' which dominates the debate. He says that 'the assertion that patient autonomy is a firm rule restricts discretion and places physicians in a straitjacket.' See McCall Smith, 'Beyond Autonomy' [1997] J of Contemp Health L & Policy Vol 14:23–39.

[15] *Schloendoff v Society of New York Hospital* 211 NY 125 (1914).

[16] Donnelly, *Healthcare Decision-making and the Law, Autonomy, Capacity and the Limits of Liberalism,* (Cambridge University Press, 2010) at 1.

[17] Dworkin, *The Theory and Practice of Autonomy* (Cambridge University Press, 1998) at 108.

[18] Dworkin at 108.

[19] Fried, *Medical Experimentation: Personal Integrity and Social Policy* (American Elsevier, 1974) 98.

[20] Beauchamp 'Informed Consent' in Veatch (ed) *Medical Ethics* (2nd edn, Jones and Bartlett Publishers, 1997) 185 at 195.

[9.07] Respect for autonomy means that decisions about what form of treatment to undergo, the probabilities of cure and of side effects, whether to spend one's last days at home or in hospital and so on, are not to be regarded as solely clinical judgments to be made by medical professionals alone. 'To suppose that these are matters of expertise, decisions to be taken by experts, represents a denial of autonomy'.[21] Such a denial of autonomy is particularly damaging because one's body is irreplaceable and inescapable. As it is impossible for the patient to escape his body, and because he *is* his body, it is a particularly insulting denial of autonomy to fail to respect the patient's wishes in respect of his body. For others, autonomy is predicated on independence, individualism, and freedom from external influences. This view is well described by Berlin:

> I wish to be an instrument of my own, not of other men's, acts of will. I wish to be a subject, not an object; to be moved by reasons, by conscious purposes, which are my own, not by causes which affect me, as it were, from outside. I wish to be somebody, not nobody, a doer – deciding, not being decided for, self-directed and not acted upon by external nature or by other men as if I were a thing, or an animal, or a slave incapable of playing a human role, that is, of conceiving goals and policies of my own and realising them.[22]

[9.08] This definition of autonomy excludes the patient who lets the doctor make decisions for him, as he would then not be making an independent or self-sufficient judgment. This approach has been criticised as not reflecting the reality of medical practice in which patients may want to have the necessary information about their medical problem but may not want to be the one to make the important decisions about what treatment to take.[23] In the context of informed consent, there is also evidence that patients who are given comprehensive information about their treatment fail to understand or even remember the information given to them[24] yet perhaps this is based in part on the adequacy and comprehensibility of the explanation given or due to lack of effective communication skills on the doctor's part. Low socioeconomic status, poor education, old age, lengthy hospital stay, stress, language barriers, and misinterpretation of probabilistic data, as well as poor disclosure practices contribute to poor outcomes in terms of reflecting genuinely autonomous choices.[25] As a result of some of these difficulties, some bioethicists argue that the legal doctrine of informed consent is a 'cruel hoax'[26] or a myth, as it is unachievable and perhaps even undesirable.[27] However, although the ideal of informed consent may be aspirational rather than attainable, it

---

[21] Dworkin, *The Theory and Practice of Autonomy* (Cambridge University Press, 1998) at 113.

[22] Berlin, *Four Essays on Liberty* (OUP, 1969) 131.

[23] Donnelly, *Consent: Bridging the Gap between Doctor and Patient* (Cork University Press, 2002) p 12. See also Jenkins, 'Consent: A Matter of Trust Not Tort' (1996) MLJI 83.

[24] President's Commission for the Study of Ethical Problems in Medicine, *Making Health Care Decisions* (US Government Printing Office, 1982).

[25] Epstein, 'Why Effective Consent Presupposes Autonomous Authorization: A Counterorthodox Argument' (2006) J Med Ethics 32:342–345.

[26] Katz, 'Disclosure and Consent' in Milunsky and Annas (eds) *Genetics and the Law, Vol II* (Plenum Press, 1980) 122, 128.

[27] Freedman, 'A Moral Theory of Informed Consent', Hastings Center Report (1975) 5:32–39.

nonetheless serves as an ideal benchmark against which the moral adequacy of legal and institutional practices should be evaluated.[28]

[9.09] Respect for autonomy not only encompasses the right to consent to treatment, but also crucially, the right to refuse medical treatment. This aspect of autonomy has sometimes caused difficulty for healthcare professionals and courts as they struggle to respect the rights of the individual without allowing harm to be caused to that person or another person as a consequence. It is also important to note that there are circumstances in which it is justifiable for the doctor to proceed to provide emergency treatment to a patient in the absence of consent, such as where the patient is unconscious. Decision-making for persons whose mental capacity is in question is considered further later.

[9.10] In recent years there has been an increased emphasis on a model of collaborative autonomy or a patient-doctor partnership which balances the doctor's responsibility for the patient's welfare with due respect for patients' rights and choices. It is thought that such an approach, which is premised on genuine patient involvement and mutual trust, will also lead to therapeutic benefits for the patient.[29] This approach can be seen in the adoption of a patient-centred test of information disclosure in the context of informed consent which is discussed in more detail in Chapter 10.

DECISION-MAKING CAPACITY

[9.11] Respect for autonomy entails enabling people to make decisions for themselves. This provides the ethical underpinning for the law relating to informed consent which is discussed in detail in Chapter 10. One of the constituent elements of a valid consent to treatment is that the decision-maker has the ability to understand the information relevant to the choice he is making and has the capacity to make decisions for himself. The law has used this requirement for capacity as a means by which to determine difficult cases, enabling a (sometimes problematic) distinction to be drawn between those whose decisions will be respected and those whose decisions will be set aside. In adopting any principles in respect of capacity, the law makes normative choices.[30] As the President's Commission in the US said: '[A] conclusion about a patient's decision-making capacity necessarily reflects a balancing of two important, sometimes competing objectives: to enhance the patient's well-being and to respect the person as a self-determining individual.'[31]

---

[28] Faden and Beauchamp, *A History and Theory of Informed Consent*, (OUP, 1986): 274–297.

[29] Failure to involve patients can lead to error in diagnosis and treatment, delay recovery and adversely affect long-term outcomes. Patients who experience a measure of control over their illness may have reduced levels of anxiety and depression as a result. See Teff, *Reasonable Care, Legal Perspectives on the Doctor-Patient Relationship* (Oxford, Clarendon Press 1994) at xxvi.

[30] Donnelly, *Healthcare Decision-making and the Law, Autonomy, Capacity and the Limits of Liberalism*, (Cambridge University Press, 2010) at 90, referring to Buchanan and Brock, *Deciding For Others: The Ethics of Surrogate Decision-Making* (Cambridge University Press, 1989) p 47.

[31] President's Commission for the Study of Ethical Problems in Medicine and Biomedical and Behavioural Research, *Making Health Care Decisions: A Report on the Ethical and Legal Implications of Informed Consent in the Patient-Practitioner Relationship* (US Superintendent of Documents, 1982) p 57.

[9.12] A decision in relation to a person's capacity is of huge significance from a legal and practical perspective in terms of making their own decisions, and a psychological perspective in relation to that person's autonomy, dignity and privacy. The consequences of a person being found to lack capacity are as follows:

> A designation of incapacity has enormous practical, legal and psychological significance for the individual involved. Following the designation, she loses the freedom to make decisions for herself, at least in relation to the matter(s) to which the incapacity relates. Instead, others will decide for her on the basis of what they believe to be in her best interests. Depending on the circumstances, she may be told where to live, what medical treatment to have, what contracts she may enter, whether she may bequeath her property and whether or not she may marry or have a sexual relationship. Thus, her fundamental rights to liberty, to autonomy and to privacy will be significantly undermined by the designation of incapacity. Psychologically, too, a designation of incapacity may have an adverse impact on the individual who has to contend with both the practical limitations on her freedom and the stigmatising effect of being labelled 'incapable'. For these reasons, the way in which capacity is assessed must be monitored carefully in order to ensure that a designation of incapacity is made only where it is necessary and appropriate. [32]

Presumption of capacity

[9.13] Cognisant of the consequences outlined above and in keeping with its respect for autonomy, the law presumes that all adults have decision-making capacity. This was affirmed in England in *Re C (Adult: refusal of treatment)*,[33] in which a man suffering from paranoid schizophrenia objected to amputation of his foot as a result of gangrene. The consultant was of the view that he had only a 15 per cent chance of survival if the foot was not amputated below the knee. C refused the operation, saying that he would rather die with two feet than live with one. The hospital questioned C's capacity to make this decision and an application was lodged on C's behalf seeking an injunction against the hospital proceeding with the operation without C's consent. Thorpe J held that there is a rebuttable presumption in favour of capacity which had not been displaced by the evidence in this case.[34] The judge was satisfied that although C's general capacity was impaired by schizophrenia, he nonetheless understood the nature, purpose and effects of the proposed treatment in coming to his decision. Thorpe J said:

> I am completely satisfied that the presumption that C has the right to self-determination has not been displaced. Although his general capacity is impaired by schizophrenia, it has not been established that he does not sufficiently understand the nature, purpose and effects of the treatment he refuses. Indeed, I am satisfied that he has understood and

---

[32] For a comprehensive discussion of the issues involved in assessing legal capacity, see Donnelly, 'Assessing Legal Capacity: Process and the Operation of the Functional Test' (2007) 2 Judicial Studies Institute Journal 141.

[33] *Re C (Adult: refusal of treatment)* [1994] 1 All ER 819.

[34] This presumption of capacity has now been enshrined in legislation in England by virtue of s 1(2) of the English Mental Capacity Act 2005 and discussed in *PH v A Local Authority and others* [2011] EWHC 1704; *CC v KK* [2012] EWHC 2136 (COP); *Re TZ No 2* [2014] EWCOP 973; *PC and NC v City of York Council* [2013] EWCA Civ 478; *King's College Hospital NHS Foundation Trust v C and V* [2015] EWCOP 80 (MacDonald J); *Re Z and others* [2016] EWCOP 4 (Cobb J).

retained the relevant treatment information, that in his own way he believes it, and that in the same fashion he has arrived at a clear choice.

This meant that C was entitled to refuse the treatment even if the consequences of this would be that C would die. The case reaffirmed the principle of respect for patient autonomy and also demonstrated that incapacity in one area does not lead to a finding of incapacity in other areas, nor does it mean that one cannot refuse treatment. This principle was also confirmed in *Re B (adult: refusal of medical treatment)*[35] in which a 43 year old patient who was paralysed and wanted her ventilator to be removed was found to be competent to make this decision and those treating her against her wishes were found to be guilty of a technical assault.[36]

[9.14] The presumption of capacity was also affirmed in Ireland in *Fitzpatrick and Another v K and Another*[37] in which Laffoy J held that 'there is a presumption that an adult patient has the capacity, that is to say, the cognitive ability, to make a decision to refuse medical treatment, but that presumption can be rebutted.' The presumption of capacity has now been enshrined in s 8(2) of the Assisted Decision-Making (Capacity) Act 2015 which is discussed in detail later. This statutory presumption is important in affirming that in keeping with respect for autonomy, the patient is not required to 'prove' her capacity and the presumption may only be rebutted if certain conditions are met.

[9.15] There is no statutory guidance on when an assessment of capacity is appropriate. However the HSE National Consent Policy[38] advises that 'an important implication of the presumption of capacity is that this presumption should not be challenged unless an adequate 'trigger' exists. All service users may experience temporary lack of capacity due to severe illness, loss of consciousness or other similar circumstances.' The Policy advises that the possibility of incapacity and the need to assess capacity formally should only be considered, if, having been given all appropriate help and support, a service user is unable to communicate a clear and consistent choice or is obviously unable to understand and use the information and choices provided. Significantly this duty to communicate in a manner appropriate to the person concerned and provide support to enable the person to make a decision is also included in the guiding principles set out in s 8 of the Assisted Decision-Making (Capacity) Act 2015 which provides that a person 'shall not be considered as unable to make a decision in respect of the matter concerned unless all practicable steps have been taken, without success, to help him or her to do so.'

[9.16] In circumstances where such a 'trigger' exists for a capacity assessment, the individual's capacity must be assessed bearing in mind the gravity of the treatment or procedure proposed, in other words, 'the more serious the decision, the greater the capacity required'.[39] General capacity implies that most of the time the person can

---

[35] Also known as *B v NHS Hospital Trust* [2002] 2 All ER 449.

[36] See Commentary 'The case of Ms B' (2002) 28 J Med Ethics 232

[37] *Fitzpatrick and Another v K and Another* [2008] IEHC 104 discussed further below at para **[9.30]**.

[38] Available at www.hse.ie, para 5.4.

[39] *Re T (an adult: refusal of treatment)* [1993] Fam 95; *Re MB (An adult: medical treatment)* [1997] 2 FCR 541; *Fitzpatrick and Another v K and Another* [2008] IEHC 104.

adequately do the things he needs to do in everyday life.[40] Specific capacity means that the person has capacity to do one specific thing, and perhaps may not have the capacity to do other things. In other words, a person may have capacity to make a healthcare decision but may be assessed as not generally having the capacity to manage other areas of his life, such as making important financial decisions.[41]

Assessment of capacity

[9.17] In recent years there has been much discussion in relation to what test should be adopted in relation to the assessment of capacity. Three methods will be mentioned here – the status approach, the outcome approach and the functional approach. A status approach makes a decision on the individual's capacity on the basis of membership of a particular diagnostic category or legally defined group. In other words this approach looks at the patient's status or medical condition in determining, by virtue of that fact alone, whether the person is capable of making the decision.[42] For example, such an approach might take the view that a person over the age of 80 or a person with a diagnosis of dementia, by virtue of their age or diagnosis alone, lacks capacity to make their own decisions. This clearly violates the principle of respect for autonomy and undermines the rights of the individual.

> The fundamental flaw in the status approach is that it takes no account of the individuality of each person. Respect for autonomy, however, involves respect for each person's individuality. It demands, therefore, that any criterion intended to determine when someone is incapable of being autonomous should, equally, be respectful of that person's individuality. Merely placing him in a class is far too gross a test of incapacity. It denies respect to the individual as an individual, and must therefore be rejected.[43]

[9.18] Another approach sometimes taken is referred to as the outcome approach which assesses the decision made by the person and determines whether it was a 'good' decision. In other words, a decision is made on the individual's capacity based on an assessment of the consequences of their decision making choices so that a decision that appears unwise or foolish to others will be taken as evidence of lack of capacity. This is again a clear interference with respect for autonomy which must, if it is to mean anything, include respect for decisions with which others do not agree.

[9.19] A third form of assessment is a 'functional' or decision-specific approach to defining decision-making capacity in keeping with respect for the autonomy of the individual, so that the individual's capacity is assessed in relation to a particular decision to be made, at the time it is to be made, rather than being a more general judgement about their cognitive ability. In other words the assessment should be issue specific and time specific and dependent upon the ability of an individual to comprehend, reason with and express a choice with regard to information about the specific decision. A

---

40 Abernethy describes it as appropriate functioning in 'an array of cognitive and interpersonal domains'. Abernethy, 'Compassion, Control, and Decisions about Competency' (1984) American Journal of Psychiatry 141:53–60 at 57.

41 See discussion in Cox White, *Competence to Consent* (Georgetown University Press, 1994) 59 *et seq.*

42 Law Reform Commission, *Vulnerable Adults and the Law* (LRC 83–2006).

43 Kennedy, *Treat Me Right* (OUP, 1988) 57.

person might thus have capacity to make some decisions and not others. This approach recognises that there is a hierarchy of complexity in decisions and also that cognitive deficits are only relevant if they actually impact on decision making.[44] Although this is 'undoubtedly autonomy-enhancing'[45] it has been argued that it also means that in theory a person's capacity must be assessed afresh in relation to each decision that arises about their treatment. 'Not only might this be rather time-consuming, but it also inevitably means that the Act places considerable reliance on the judgement of the person charged with assessing capacity.'[46] However, while there may be a tendency to assume that there will thus be an increased emphasis on capacity assessments for each and every decision that a person is asked to make, it is important to remember that one of the guiding principles of the law is that every adult is presumed to have capacity to make those decisions unless an adequate trigger exists to challenge that presumption. If one starts from this presumption then it will mitigate against the increased burden of carrying out capacity assessments with the frequency alluded to above.

English Mental Capacity Act 2005 and relevant case law

[9.20] The functional test was adopted in the Mental Capacity Act 2005 in England and Wales, which defines a person as being without capacity if at the relevant time, he is unable, by reason of mental disability, to make a decision for himself on the matter in question, or is unable to communicate that decision.[47] A person is unable to make a decision if he is unable to understand or retain the information relevant to the decision or is unable to make a decision based on that information. Mental disability is defined as a disability or disorder of the mind or brain, permanent or temporary, which results in an impairment or disturbance of mental functioning.[48] Section 2(1) of the Act is the 'core determinative provision,'[49] which together with the other provisions of ss 2 and 3 flesh out what are traditionally called the two limbs of the capacity test, by asking whether the individual is unable to make a decision for himself (the functional test), and whether that inability is because of 'an impairment of, or a disturbance of the functioning of, the mind or the brain' (the diagnostic test).

[9.21] The English two part test therefore requires firstly that clinicians provide a diagnosis in keeping with the statutory definition and advise whether any such impairment or disturbance in the functioning of the mind or brain is temporary (due to acute illness, medication, shock etc.) or permanent. The Mental Capacity Act Code of Practice[50] provides some examples of such an impairment or disturbance in the functioning of the mind – dementia, significant learning disabilities, delirium,

---

[44] HSE National Consent Policy para 5.1.

[45] Jackson, *Medical Law, Text, Cases and Materials* (3rd edn, 2013) 225.

[46] Jackson, *Medical Law, Text, Cases and Materials* (3rd edn, 2013) 225.

[47] See Donnelly, 'Capacity assessment under the Mental Capacity Act 2005: delivering on the functional approach?' (2009) 29 LS 464.

[48] Examples are provided in the Mental Capacity Act Code of Practice para. 4.12: dementia, significant learning disabilities, long term brain damage, concussion, delirium (not an exhaustive list).

[49] *PC and NC v City of York Council* [2013] EWCA Civ 478 at paragraph 56.

[50] Available at www.gov.uk, para 4.12.

concussion following a head injury, long-term effects of brain damage. Once this diagnostic requirement has been satisfied, it is then necessary to assess whether the person is able to make a decision for himself. The elements of this second part of the test, ie the functional test, are found in s 3(1) of the Act which essentially re-states the common law position set out in *Re C*[51] that the person is regarded as unable to make a decision for himself if he is unable:

- to understand the information relevant to the decision; or
- to retain that information; or
- to use or weigh that information as part of the process of making the decision; or
- to communicate his decision (whether by talking, using sign language or any other means).

[9.22] The key test for capacity is therefore whether the person can understand and use the information relevant to the decision and make a choice. The courts have had to examine whether 'information relevant to the decision' should be interpreted broadly or narrowly. In *A Local Authority v A*,[52] A was a woman with severe learning disabilities who met the first limb of the two part test in the Act and the court then had to decide if she had the capacity under the second part set out above to make a decision about receiving contraceptive treatment. Brody J held that it was not necessary for her to be able to foresee all the possible consequences of having a baby in order for her to have capacity to make this decision. She needed to be able to understand the reason for contraception, the types available and the advantages and disadvantages of each, possible side effects, the effectiveness of the different options and so on. Although A was able to understand these issues, Brody J found she was unable to weigh the information due to the overpowering control exerted over her by her husband. Therefore she was held to lack capacity to make the decision. This interpretation has been criticised on the basis that 'someone who might otherwise be judged competent could be found to lack capacity on the grounds that someone else has put them under pressure in relation to that decision'.[53]

[9.23] The English Mental Capacity Act 2005 also provides in s 1(4) that a person is not to be treated as unable to make a decision merely because he makes an unwise decision. This is consistent with the common law approach illustrated by Lord Donaldson in *Re T*[54] where he said 'the patient's right of choice exists whether the reasons for making that choice are rational, irrational, unknown or even non-existent.' However, while laudable in respecting the person's right to make a decision contrary to medical or other advice, Jackson claims it is sometimes difficult to distinguish between a person's bizarre and irrational wishes, which must nevertheless be respected, and a person's inability to use

---

[51] *Re C (Adult: Refusal of medical treatment)* [1994] 1 All ER 819. See also *Re MB (An adult: medical treatment)* [1997] 2 FLR 426.

[52] *A Local Authority v A* [2010] EWHC 1549 (Fam).

[53] The person would also of course have to have met the diagnostic test of having an impairment or disturbance of the brain. Jackson, *Medical Law: Text, cases and materials* (3rd edn, 2013) at 226.

[54] *Re T (an adult: refusal of treatment)* [1992] 4 All ER 649, [1993] Fam 95.

and weigh information, which may mean that they fail the test for capacity.[55] Butler-Sloss LJ said in *Re MB* 'panic, indecisiveness and irrationality in themselves do not as such amount to incompetence, but they may be symptoms or evidence of incompetence.'[56] However it may be the case that there may be assumptions made about different people's capacity according to whether they suffer from a mental health problem. So, a middle-class professional who refuses conventional cancer treatment might be viewed as making an irrational decision yet this decision would likely be respected whereas a person who has a borderline personality disorder and seeks to make a similar decision might have her capacity called into question.[57]

[9.24] A case which illustrates some of the difficulties in this area is *CC v KK & STCC*[58] decided by Baker J in the Court of Protection. KK was an 82-year old woman with Parkinson's disease, vascular dementia, and paralysis down her left side. Following the death of her husband, she moved and settled in a rented bungalow. However, incapacity and best interests' determinations had resulted in her being placed in a nursing home. Mr Justice Baker was called upon to determine whether she had capacity to make decisions about her residence and care.[59] It was the unanimous view of all the health professionals and the independent expert psychiatrist that KK lacked capacity. Baker J heard evidence from KK in both written and oral form in court.

[9.25] One of the interesting aspects of Baker J's judgment was his discussion of the 'protection imperative', that is, the perceived need to protect the vulnerable adult.[60] He said there was a risk that all professionals involved with treating and helping that person may feel drawn towards an outcome that is more protective of the adult and thus, in certain circumstances, fail to carry out an assessment of capacity that is detached and objective. On the other hand, the court must be equally careful not to be influenced by sympathy for a person's wholly understandable wish to return home.

> In this case, I perceive a real danger that in assessing KK's capacity professionals and the court may consciously or subconsciously attach excessive weight to their own views of how her physical safety may be best protected and insufficient weight to her own views of how her emotional needs may best be met.[61]

[9.26] He found that this was linked to the problem that the local authority had not put in place a care and support plan that could be available to KK in her own home. Therefore she had not been given 'relevant information' including 'what the likely consequences of a decision would be (the possible effects of deciding one way or another)'. In order to understand the likely consequences of deciding to return home, KK would have to be given full details of the care package that would or might be available. The choice which KK should be asked to weigh up is not between the nursing home and a return to the

---

[55] Jackson, *Medical Law: Text, cases and materials* (3rd edn, 2013) at 227.
[56] *Re MB (An adult: medical treatment)* [1997] 2 FCR 541.
[57] Jackson, *Medical Law: Text, cases and materials* (3rd edn, 2013) at 228.
[58] *CC v KK & STCC* (2012) EWHC 2136 (COP).
[59] There were also other issues involved in this case relating to deprivation of liberty which will not be discussed here.
[60] Also referred to in *Oldham MBC v GW and PW* [2007] EWHC 136 (Fam); *PH v A Local Authority, Z Ltd and R* [2011] EWHC 1704 (Fam).
[61] *CC v KK & STCC* (2012) EWHC 2136 (COP) at para 67.

bungalow with no or limited support, but rather between staying in the nursing home and a return home with all practicable support. KK was found to be clear, articulate, and betrayed relatively few signs of the dementia which afflicted her. She understood that she needed total support and carers visiting four times a day. Whilst she may have underestimated or minimised some of her needs, she did not do so to an extent that suggests that she lacked capacity to weigh up information:

> In weighing up the options, she is taking account of her needs and her vulnerabilities. On the other side of the scales, however, there is the immeasurable benefit of being in her own home. There is, truly, no place like home, and the emotional strength and succour which an elderly person derives from being at home, surrounded by familiar reminders of past life, must not be underestimated. When KK speaks disparagingly of the food in the nursing home, she is expressing a reasonable preference for the personalised care that she receives at home. When she talks of being disturbed by the noise from a distressed resident in an adjoining room, she is reasonably contrasting it with the peace and quiet of her own home.

[9.27] The judge indicated that her testimony demonstrated that she had weighed up the risks involved in going home. In an observation which has come to identify this case, he said that KK's statement that 'if I fall over and die on the floor, then I die on the floor' demonstrated to him that she was aware of, and has weighed up, the greater risk of physical harm if she went home. The judge said that this was not an unreasonable view to hold:

> It does not show that a lack of capacity to weigh up information. Rather it is an example of how different individuals may give different weight to different factors. This case illustrates the importance of the fundamental principle enshrined in s 1(2) of the 2005 Act – that a person must be assumed to have capacity unless it is demonstrated that she lacks it. The burden lies on the local authority to prove that KK lacks capacity to make decisions as to where she lives. A disabled person, and a person with a degenerative condition, is as entitled as anyone else to the protection of this presumption of capacity. The assessment is issue-specific and time specific. In due course, her capacity may deteriorate. Indeed that is likely to happen given her diagnosis. At this hearing, however, the local authority has failed to prove that KK lacks capacity to make decisions as to where she should live.

[9.28] This case provides an important and useful analysis of the application of the functional test under the English Mental Capacity Act 2005.[62] The judge identified the difficulties involved in identifying the decision the person is being asked to make and the information that the person must be given in order to equip them to make that decision. The details of the home care package that ought to be in place before KK went home was an important aspect of this information so as to enable KK to correctly weigh the risks of going home (with adequate support) with the disadvantages of staying in the nursing home. Baker J's insightful comments about the protection imperative also serve to emphasise the balance that must be struck between protection against risk and the person's own wishes. This has been echoed by other judges also such as Munby J in *Re MM (An Adult)*:[63]

---

[62] The MCA Code of Practice is also very useful in setting out the crucial elements in the English legislative scheme, available at www.gov.uk.

[63] *Re MM (An Adult)* [2007] EWHC 2003 (Fam).

The emphasis must be on sensible risk appraisal, not striving to avoid all risk, whatever the price, but instead seeking a proper balance and being willing to tolerate manageable or acceptable risks as the price appropriately to be paid in order to achieve some other good – in particular to achieve the vital good of the elderly or vulnerable person's *happiness*. What good is it making someone safer if it merely makes them miserable?'

Capacity assessment in Ireland prior to 2015 Act

[9.29] In Ireland, until recently there were no legislative provisions in place to guide medical and social care practice in relation to capacity. However that is not to say that health and social care practitioners were unaware of the movement towards the functional test of capacity and assisted or supported decision-making. Since 2009 the Medical Council, which is the regulatory body for registered medical practitioners, has advised doctors to use the functional test of capacity[64] and the National Consent Policy in 2013[65] has advised all health and social care professionals to adopt the same broad principles which are now contained in the Assisted Decision-Making (Capacity) Act 2015.

[9.30] There have not been many reported cases in Ireland exploring the test of capacity and those that have arisen have generally been in the context of an adult refusing treatment with potentially serious consequences. The most important case is *Fitzpatrick and Another v K and Another*[66] in which K, a 23-year-old African woman from the Congo, had given birth to a baby in an Irish hospital. Shortly thereafter she suffered a massive post-partum haemorrhage resulting in cardiovascular collapse. As blood was being prepared for transfusion, K said that she would not accept blood for religious reasons. The medical team was concerned that K would die without a blood transfusion and called the Master of the hospital.[67] Following discussions with K, during which she repeated her refusal of blood, the Master had doubts regarding her capacity to make such a decision and decided to apply to the High Court for an emergency order giving the hospital authority to transfuse K.

[9.31] Although the judge was of the view that K's capacity was not impaired, he considered that the rights of her newborn child must be taken into consideration in his decision. He made the order authorising the hospital to administer blood to K, including all appropriate steps by way of restraint as necessary. The Master informed K of the court order and she was transfused following the administration of a sedative. She subsequently made a full recovery. She later claimed that the court order should not have been given, that the transfusion was unlawful and therefore constituted an assault and trespass to her person, and that she was entitled to refuse all or any medical treatment by virtue of her constitutional rights and under arts 8 and 9 of the European Convention on Human Rights (ECHR).

---

[64] Medical Council, The Guide to Professional Conduct and Ethics (7th edn, 2009). The Guide is now in its 8th edition, published in May 2016 www.medicalcouncil.ie.

[65] HSE National Consent Policy (2013) available at www.hse.ie.

[66] *Fitzpatrick and Another v K and Another* [2008] IEHC 104.

[67] The Master is the most senior obstetrician in the maternity hospital with responsibility for clinical governance.

[9.32] In the High Court, Judge Laffoy was of the view that it could not be argued that a competent adult is not free to decline medical treatment. Thus, the question that arose on the facts of this case was whether K had capacity to refuse the blood transfusion. This question had not been determined by an Irish court up to this point and therefore Laffoy J examined relevant case law from other jurisdictions in her judgment. She also referred to the Law Reform Commission's Report on *Vulnerable Adults and the Law*[68] in which the Commission recommends that 'capacity will be understood in terms of an adult's cognitive ability to understand the nature and consequences of a decision in the context of available choices at the time the decision is made'.

[9.33] Laffoy J held that the principles applicable to the determination of capacity are as follows:

- There is a presumption that an adult patient has the capacity, that is to say, the cognitive ability, to make a decision to refuse medical treatment, but that presumption can be rebutted.

- In determining whether a patient is deprived of capacity to make a decision to refuse medical treatment whether (a) by reason of permanent cognitive impairment, or (b) temporary factors..., the test is whether the patient's cognitive ability has been impaired to the extent that he or she does not sufficiently understand the nature, purpose and effect of the proffered treatment and the consequences of accepting or rejecting it in the context of the choices available (including any alternative treatment) at the time the decision is made.

- The patient's cognitive ability will have been impaired to the extent that he or she is incapable of making the decision to refuse the proffered treatment if the patient –

    (a) has not comprehended and retained the treatment information and, in particular, has not assimilated the information as to the consequences likely to ensue from not accepting the treatment,

    (b) has not believed the treatment information and, in particular, if it is the case that not accepting the treatment is likely to result in the patient's death, has not believed that outcome is likely, and

    (c) has not weighed the treatment information, in particular, the alternative choices and the likely outcomes, in the balance in arriving at the decision.

- The treatment information by reference to which the patient's capacity is to be assessed is the information which the clinician is under a duty to impart – information as to what is the appropriate treatment, that is to say, what treatment is medically indicated, at the time of the decision and the risks and consequences likely to flow from the choices available to the patient in making the decision.

- In assessing capacity it is necessary to distinguish between misunderstanding or misperception of the treatment information in the decision-making

---

[68] (LRC 83–2006).

process....on the one hand, and an irrational decision or a decision made for irrational reasons, on the other hand. The former may be evidence of lack of capacity. The latter is irrelevant to the assessment.

- In assessing capacity, whether at the bedside in a high dependency unit or in court, the assessment must have regard to the gravity of the decision, in terms of the consequences which are likely to ensue from the acceptance or rejection of the proffered treatment.

[9.34] Having regard to the nature of the evidence presented in relation to K's capacity, the Court was satisfied that K had been given the information necessary, in layman's terms, to enable her to make an informed decision in relation to the blood transfusion. The relevant factors to be taken into account in this case were that K's medical status was seriously compromised following a long labour, a difficult delivery and a massive haemorrhage. There were communication difficulties due to the fact the K's first language was not English, and the hospital believed that K had no family members in the country to support her at that time. Laffoy J concluded that K's capacity at the relevant time was impaired to the extent that she did not have the ability to make a valid refusal to accept the appropriate medical treatment which was proffered to her, a blood transfusion. Therefore, the administration of the transfusion was not unlawful or in breach of her constitutional rights.

[9.35] This decision was highly significant and welcome in setting out clearly the test for the assessment of capacity in the healthcare context in Ireland. It closely followed the approach set out in the English case of *Re C*, described above,[69] in relation to the three issues that must be considered, ie whether the patient has understood the information provided, has weighed it in the balance and applied it to his or her own situation in reaching a decision. As this was the first case on this issue in Ireland, its value in emphasizing the presumption of capacity and the right of a competent adult to refuse medical treatment cannot be understated. On the particular facts of this case the judge took the view that K lacked capacity to make her own decision, although at the interlocutory stage this had not been the view of the Master of the High Court on the evidence before him at that point in time. Although the factors taken into account by Laffoy J in assessing capacity were significant, it may be tempting to deduce that other women might similarly be assessed as lacking capacity during or following delivery, with the consequent overriding of their decisions made in those circumstances. Due to the finding of incapacity, Laffoy J did not consider the issue of whether the rights and interests of K's newborn child ought properly to have been taken into account in reaching the decision to override K's wishes. Thus, any consideration of a hierarchy of constitutional rights in such contexts will have to await further judicial consideration.[70]

---

[69] Para **[9.21]**.

[70] Further consideration of the right of a competent adult to refuse treatment is considered in Ch 10 at para **[10.80]** et seq.

Assisted Decision-Making (Capacity) Act 2015

[9.36] The common law principles outlined earlier have now been underpinned by statute in the form of the Assisted Decision-Making (Capacity) Act 2015.[71] The genesis of this Act begins in part with the Report of the Law Reform Commission (LRC) in 2006 on 'Vulnerable Adults and the Law' after which the Government undertook to introduce legislation to incorporate many of the recommendations in that report to protect adults who, due to illness, accident or intellectual disability, are unable to make decisions for themselves or exercise their legal capacity. In advocating for the introduction of a new system of protection for vulnerable adults, it was often argued that current laws in this area may be in violation of Constitutional and human rights law. For example, the Irish Constitution 1937 and the European Convention on Human Rights provide for the protection of property rights, and any restriction of a property right must be subject to rigorous procedural safeguards. Given that wardship proceedings tended to be instigated in relation to the property of persons considered to be lacking decision-making capacity, the LRC suggested that some elements of the wardship procedures may conflict with the guarantee of a fair hearing required under art 6 of the ECHR.[72]

[9.37] A further influencing factor in the drafting of the 2015 Act was that Ireland was one of the first signatories to the UN Convention on the Rights of Persons with Disabilities[73] (albeit the last to proceed to ratification) which was drafted to ensure recognition for 'the inherent dignity and worth and the equal and inalienable rights of all members of the human family.' The Act was deemed necessary in order to ensure that Ireland complies with obligations under the Convention, in particular art 12 which provides for equal recognition before the law. Article 12(2) provides that States Parties shall recognise that persons with disabilities enjoy legal capacity on an equal basis with others in all aspects of life and art 12(3) provides that States Parties shall take appropriate measures to provide access by persons with disabilities to the support they may require in exercising their legal capacity. Article 12(4) obliges States Parties to ensure that all measures that relate to the exercise of legal capacity provide for appropriate and effective safeguards to prevent abuse in accordance with international human rights law. 'Such safeguards shall ensure that measures relating to the exercise of legal capacity respect the rights, will and preferences of the person, are free of conflict of interest and undue influence, are proportional and tailored to the person's circumstances, apply for the shortest time possible and are subject to regular review by a competent, independent and impartial authority or judicial body. The safeguards shall be proportional to the degree to which such measures affect the person's rights and interests.' Article 12(5) obliges States Parties to take all appropriate and effective

---

[71] The Act has not yet been commenced at the time of writing but is expected to commence before the end of 2016 in order to enable the government to proceed with ratification of the Convention on the Rights of Persons with Disabilities.

[72] LRC Consultation Paper on Capacity, para 4.12 on notice requirements and para 4.15 concerning the inquiry process, see also para 2.07 of the LRC Report on Vulnerable Adults and the Law (LRC 83–2006), on the ECHR.

[73] Convention on the Rights of Persons with Disabilities (adopted 13 December 2006, entered into force 3 May 2008) 2515 UNTS 3 (CRPD). http://www.un.org/disabilities/convention/conventionfull.shtml.

measures to ensure the equal right of persons with disabilities to own or inherit property, to control their own financial affairs and to have equal access to bank loans, mortgages and other forms of financial credit, and shall ensure that persons with disabilities are not arbitrarily deprived of their property.

[9.38] There is a body of academic opinion which takes the view that art 12 does not permit perceived or actual deficits in mental capacity to be used as justification for denying legal capacity, even in respect of a single decision.[74] As a result it is argued that functional tests of mental capacity that lead to denials of legal capacity violate art 12 if they are either discriminatory or they disproportionately affect the right of persons with disabilities to equality before the law. Flynn and Arstein-Kerslake argue that the text of art 12 doesn't explicitly require the abolition of substituted decision making but it switches the focus from deficits to supports that all people use in exercising legal capacity.[75] It is also argued that functional tests of capacity are applied in a discriminatory way to persons with disabilities and the test itself presumes to be able to assess the inner-workings of the human mind. There thus remains some opposition to attempts to legislate for the functional approach and for any provisions which introduce substitute decision-making. These provisions are discussed in detail later.

[9.39] Notwithstanding these concerns, the Government enacted the Assisted Decision-Making (Capacity) Act in 2015 and stated its intention to proceed to ratify the Convention accordingly. The Act has received broad welcome from advocacy groups and human rights organisations for its movement away from a 'paternalistic stance of looking after what we decide are people's 'best interests', and move towards recognising a person's right to make decisions about their own lives, and to enable them to be supported to make decisions.'[76] Indeed this aspect is a notable distinction between the Irish and English Acts as the Irish Act does not refer to best interests whereas the English Mental Capacity Act requires decisions to be made on the basis of the person's best interests.[77] In this respect the Irish Act is perhaps closer to the Scottish provision in s 1(2) of the Adults with Incapacity (Scotland) Act 2000, which provides 'there shall be no intervention in the affairs of an adult unless the person responsible for authorising or effecting the intervention is satisfied that the intervention will benefit the adult and that such benefit cannot reasonably be achieved without the intervention'. The question of what is meant by benefit is considered later.

---

[74] See for example Flynn and Arstein-Kerslake, 'Legislating personhood: realising the right to support in exercising legal capacity' [2014] 10 International Journal of Law in Context 81; Flynn and Arstein-Kerslake, 'The Support Model of Legal Capacity: Fact, Fiction, or Fantasy?' [2014] Berkeley Journal of International Law 124; Doyle and Flynn, 'Ireland's ratification of the UN convention on the rights of persons with disabilities: challenges and opportunities' (2013) 41 British Journal of Learning Disabilities 171.

[75] Flynn and Arstein-Kerslake 'Legislating personhood: realising the right to support in exercising legal capacity' [2014] 10 International Journal of Law in Context 81at 89.

[76] Inclusion Ireland 'Persons with disabilities waiting eight years for Irish Government to ratify the CRPD' 30 March 2015.

[77] Section 4 of the Mental Capacity Act 2005.

Functional test of capacity

[9.40] One of the most important aspects of the Act is contained in s 3 which stipulates that the functional approach to capacity assessment must be adopted: 'A person's capacity shall be assessed on the basis of his or her ability to understand, at the time that a decision is to be made, the nature and consequences of the decision to be made by him or her in the context of the available choices at that time.' This firmly establishes that the assessment is issue and time-specific and is complemented by the guiding principle in s 8(2) which provides that a person is presumed to have capacity unless the contrary is shown. Section 3 further provides that 'a person lacks capacity to make a decision if he or she is unable –

- to understand the information relevant to the decision,
- to retain that information long enough to make a voluntary choice,
- to use or weigh that information as part of the process of making the decision, or
- to communicate his or her decision (whether by talking, writing, using sign language, assistive technology, or any other means) or, if the implementation of the decision requires the act of a third party, to communicate by any means with that third party.'

This is in keeping with the common law tests outlined in the English *Re C*[78] case and Laffoy J's decision in *Fitzpatrick v K*[79] outlined above.

[9.41] Other significant features of s 3 of the Act are that it provides that a person is not to be regarded as unable to understand information if he or she is able to understand an explanation given in a way that is appropriate to that person's circumstances. This is complemented by s 8(3) which provides that a person shall not be considered as unable to make a decision unless all practicable steps have been taken, without success, to help him or her to do so. These provisions are important in setting out the requirement to provide assistance and information to the person in a manner that is tailor-made to that person's needs, thus recognising that a repertoire of diverse communication styles may be required in order to enable people with differing abilities to make their own decisions. The provisions here are similar to the wording used in the English Mental Capacity Act (MCA) and there is useful guidance in the MCA Code of Practice on the kinds of support people might need to enable them to make a decision such as using non-verbal communication, providing information in a more accessible form, helping the person to learn new skills or treating a medical condition which might be affecting the person's capacity.[80]

[9.42] Sometimes a question arises in practice in relation to retention of information as some of those who may require assistance with decision-making may have short-term memory deficits which makes retention of information difficult. The question is whether a person can be said to have made a decision on the basis of information which they understood at the time it was given but of which they have no recollection a short

---

[78] Para **[9.13]**.
[79] Para **[9.30]**.
[80] MCA Code of Practice para 2.7.

time later. Section 3(4) clarifies this by providing that the fact that a person is able to retain information for a short period only does not prevent him or her from being regarded as having the capacity to make the decision.

[9.43] Other important provisions include s 3(5) which provides that the fact that a person lacks capacity in respect of a decision on a particular matter at a particular time does not mean that the person will not have capacity to make decisions on the same matter at another time, thus underlining the principle that capacity is time specific. Thus, a person may be unable to decide a particular matter today due to, for example, illness, stress, grief but this does not mean that the person is to be regarded as incapable of making such a decision at a future time. This is also complemented by s 8(9) which provides that in the case of an intervention in respect of a person who lacks capacity, regard must be had to the likelihood of the person recovering capacity to make the decision themselves, and the urgency of making the intervention prior to such recovery. For example if a person has a serious infection and is assessed as unable to make a decision in respect of a medical procedure, the doctor must consider whether the medical procedure is urgent or whether it can be postponed until the person has sufficiently recovered from the infection to be able to decide for themselves whether to go ahead with the medical procedure.

[9.44] Section 3(6) underscores the principle that capacity is issue specific by providing that the fact that a person lacks capacity in respect of a decision on one particular matter does not prevent him or her from having capacity in relation to other matters. Thus, for example, a person might be regarded as having capacity to make a decision about where they want to live or about financial matters, but not be regarded as having capacity to make a decision in relation to a complex medical intervention despite efforts to communicate the necessary information in an appropriate manner and to support and assist the person in making their own decision. The person must also be given information about other available choices and the reasonably foreseeable consequences of not making the decision.[81]

[9.45] Section 8 subs (4) precludes use of the outcome test outlined earlier[82] in that it states that a person 'shall not be considered as unable to make a decision in respect of the matter concerned merely by reason of making, having made, or being likely to make, an unwise decision.' This is consistent with Laffoy J's judgment in *Fitzpatrick v K*[83] where she said that in assessing capacity it is necessary to distinguish between misunderstanding or misperception of the treatment information in the decision-making process on the one hand, and an irrational decision or a decision made for irrational reasons, on the other hand. 'The former may be evidence of lack of capacity. The latter is irrelevant to the assessment.' Therefore, a person who makes an unwise or seemingly irrational decision, is nonetheless entitled to the presumption of capacity (unless there is sufficient reason to carry out an assessment of capacity) and entitled to have their decision respected.

---

[81] Section 3(7).

[82] Para **[9.18]**.

[83] Para **[9.30]**.

GUIDING PRINCIPLES FOR INTERVENTIONS

[9.46] Section 8 sets out Guiding Principles that apply for the purposes of an intervention[84] in respect of a relevant person (defined in s 2(1) as a person whose capacity is in question or may shortly be in question, or a person who lacks capacity). Section 8(5) provides that 'there shall be no intervention in respect of a relevant person unless it is necessary to do so having regard to the individual circumstances of the relevant person'. Subs (6) provides that an intervention must be made in a manner that minimises the restriction of the person's rights and freedom of action, have due regard to the need to respect the person's right to dignity, bodily integrity, privacy, autonomy and control over his or her financial affairs and property, be proportionate to the significance and urgency of the matter the subject of the intervention, and be as limited in duration as practicable. These provisions mean that when deciding on how to proceed in the case of a relevant person, the option chosen (if action is deemed necessary at all) should be the least restrictive one. This might, for example, result in alternative medical management of a person's condition rather than proceeding with a surgical procedure.[85] These principles are likely to be significant in cases where, for example, medical treatment is considered urgently necessary and the relevant person is unconscious and has no decision-making support structure in place.

[9.47] Section 8(7) of the Act provides that an intervener (a person who makes an intervention) shall: permit, encourage and facilitate as far as practicable the person to participate as fully as possible in the intervention; give effect as far as practicable to the past and present will and preferences of the person in so far as they are reasonably ascertainable; take into account the beliefs and values of the person in so far as they are reasonably ascertainable and any other factors the person would be likely to consider if he or she were able to do so in so far as these factors are reasonably ascertainable; unless it would be inappropriate or impracticable to do so, consider the views of any person named as a person to be consulted and any decision-making assistant, co-decisionmaker, decision-making representative or attorney for the relevant person; act at all times in good faith and for the benefit of the relevant person; and consider all other circumstances which it would be reasonable to regard as relevant. The intervener may also consider the views of any carer of the relevant person, anyone who has a bona fide interest in the welfare of the relevant person, or healthcare professionals.[86]

[9.48] This provision therefore refers to the need to 'give effect to' the relevant person's will and preferences, to 'take into account' the relevant person's beliefs and values, and to 'consider' the views of those who have been appointed to act as decision-making

---

[84] Defined in s 2 as 'an action taken under this Act, orders made under this Act or directions given under this Act in respect of the relevant person by – (a) the court or High Court, (b) a decision-making assistant, co-decisionmaker, decision-making representative, attorney or designated healthcare representative, (c) the Director, (d) a special visitor or general visitor, or (e) a healthcare professional.'

[85] See for example the English case of *A Local Authority v K* [2013] EWHC 242 (COP) where the court refused to order the sterilisation of a 21 year old woman with Down's syndrome on the basis that sterilisation would be a disproportionate step to achieve contraception for K and there were less restrictive options available.

[86] Subs (8).

supports for the relevant person. This emphasis on the relevant person's own will and preference is important in emphasising the need to respect the autonomy of the person and their right to be treated equally. However, in some circumstances it may not be possible to ascertain their views if the relevant person has never been competent or expressed an opinion which might enable the intervener to assess the person's will and preference, beliefs and values. Having ascertained the will and preference, beliefs and values of the relevant person if possible, and considered the views of the decision-making supporters, the intervener will make a decision in good faith which gives effect to the wishes of the relevant person while at the same time acting for the benefit of the relevant person.

[9.49] It will be interesting to see how the courts in Ireland interpret this provision – clearly the expression 'best interests' which appears in the English Act was avoided in order to move away from the paternalistic approach to persons who lack capacity which has been heavily criticised as not being compliant with the rights of persons with disabilities. In practice there will undoubtedly be circumstances in which the objective view of what would be of benefit to the relevant person will be in conflict with the relevant person's will and preference, beliefs and values. For example, an intervener may consider that it would be more beneficial for the relevant person to be cared for in a nursing home where their medical, nutritional and hygiene needs could be more easily taken care of. However, the relevant person's preference might be to live at home even where the environment is less than ideal. It is noteworthy that the Act states that the person's will and preference must be given effect as far as practicable. This differs from the English Act which requires that the person's wishes must be *considered* by the intervener.[87] The weight given to the person's own wishes is therefore of a much higher order under the Irish Act and the courts may be asked to interpret 'as far as practicable' in resolving conflicts in this regard.

[9.50] It is also worth looking at how the views of family members or others are regarded under the Act. Section 8(7)(d) states that the intervener shall, unless the intervener reasonably considers that it is not appropriate or practicable to do so, consider the views of (i) any person named by the relevant person as a person to be consulted on the matter concerned or any similar matter, and (ii) any decision-making assistant, co-decisionmaker, decision-making representative or attorney for the relevant person. This deals with situations where the relevant person has nominated someone to assist them in making decisions or a decision-making representative has been appointed to make decisions for the relevant person. It is consistent with respect for the person's autonomy to require the intervener to consult with those who have been selected by the relevant person to assist or act in these circumstances, as that person will presumably act in accordance with the relevant person's wishes. The same rationale does not necessarily apply to decision-making representatives who have been appointed by the court rather than by the relevant persons themselves.

[9.51] Section 8(8) goes on to provide that the intervener may consider the views of (a) any person engaged in caring for the relevant person, (b) any person who has a *bona fide* interest in the welfare of the relevant person or (c) healthcare professionals. In this

---

[87] See discussion by Donnelly, 'Best interests, patient participation and the Mental Capacity Act 2005' (2009) 17 Med Law Rev 1–29.

instance where the relevant person has not nominated a carer to be consulted in this context, and there is no decision-making support structure in place, the intervener is not obliged to consult carers but may do so at his or her discretion. The discretionary approach is useful here as the intervener may be aware that family members and carers are in disagreement about what the relevant person would have wanted, or be concerned that family members and carers may exert influence over the relevant person's own views.[88] Donnelly says that care must always be taken in considering representations made by family members about the views of the relevant person.[89]

> While the consultative model is a good one, it is important to remember that even close friends or family members cannot always know the past preferences or the relevant beliefs and values of the person lacking capacity. Statements such as 'I would rather die than be dependent' may reflect a desire for reassurance, or may be a result of temporary depression or fear, and may not represent the person's considered views on future care should they lose capacity.[90]

ASSISTED DECISION-MAKING

[9.52] An important aspect of the Assisted Decision-Making (Capacity) Act is that it provides for a range of decision-making support options designed to enable and support the relevant person to make their own decisions in keeping with obligations under the Convention. (The provisions of the Act in relation to assessment of capacity have been outlined earlier.[91]) These options support the shift away from the idea of capacity as an 'all or nothing' status and put in place a flexible functional approach which supports people at all stages and of all abilities to make their own decisions. The options include a decision-making assistant or a co-decisionmaker either of which may be appointed by the relevant person. If the relevant person cannot make decisions without the assistance of either a decision-making assistant or a co-decisionmaker but there is no suitable person to act in either role, or the court makes a declaration that the relevant person lacks capacity even with the assistance of a decision-making assistant or a co-decisionmaker, the court may appoint a decision-making representative. Other options include creating an Enduring Power of Attorney and/or making an advance healthcare directive. Each of these options will be considered in turn.

Decision-making assistant

[9.53] Part 3 of the Act provides for the making of a decision-making assistance agreement whereby a person (over 18) (hereinafter called the appointer) who considers

---

[88] See for example the English case of *A Primary Care Trust v P* [2008] EWHC 1403.

[89] See English case of *Re M* [2011] EWHC 2443 (COP) where M's family were of the view that M, who was in a minimally conscious state, would not have wanted to be kept alive on artificial nutrition and hydration as she had made general comments to them about not wanting to be dependent. By contrast, M's professional carers expressed a different view about M's best interests which ultimately carried more weight with the judge.

[90] Donnelly, 'Best interests, patient participation and the Mental Capacity Act 2005' (2009) 17 Med Law Rev 1–29.

[91] Para **[9.40]**.

that his or her capacity is in question or may shortly be in question[92] may appoint another person (over 18) (hereinafter called the assistant) to assist them in making one or more decision in relation to personal welfare and/or property and affairs.[93] The appointment is to be made in compliance with regulations to be made by the Minister in respect of the form, procedures and requirements of such an agreement. Such regulations will also prescribe the information that must be included in such an agreement, a statement of understanding by both the appointer and the assistant, the specification of the personal welfare or property and affairs of the appointer, and other matters. More than one assistant may be appointed but the Act precludes certain persons from acting as assistants such as any person who has been convicted of an offence in relation to the person or property of the appointer, a person who has been the subject of a barring order in relation to the appointer, an undischarged bankrupt or someone who has been convicted of offences involving fraud or dishonesty, a person who is the owner or provider of a designated centre or mental health facility in which the appointer resides.[94] The Act contains further provisions in relation to disqualification in s 13.

[9.54] The functions of the assistant are set out in s 14 of the Act and include –

- assisting the appointer to obtain relevant information,
- advising the appointer by explaining relevant information and considerations relating to a decision,
- ascertaining the will and preferences of the appointer on a relevant matter and assisting the appointer to communicate them,
- assisting the appointer to make and express a decision, and
- endeavouring to ensure that the appointer's decisions are respected.

The assistant is not entitled to make a decision either jointly with or on behalf of the appointer. Thus it is clear that the assistant is not in the role of substitute decision-maker for the appointer; the assistant's role is to assist, advise and support the appointer to make his/her own decision.

[9.55] There is no registration procedure for decision-making assistance agreements provided for in the Act. Section 15 provides that a complaint may be made to the Director of the Decision Support Service that the assistant has acted outside the scope of the agreement, is unable to perform the functions, or that fraud, coercion or undue pressure was used to induce the appointer to make the agreement. The Director may investigate the matter and make an application to the court for a determination that the assistant shall no longer act in that role in relation to the appointer. The functions and powers of the Director of the Decision Support Service are considered later.[95]

Co-decisionmaker

[9.56] Part 4 of the Act provides that a person (over 18) (hereinafter called the appointer) who considers that his or her capacity is in question or may shortly be in

---

[92] This definition suggests that this is a subjective determination by the appointer him or herself as to their capacity.

[93] Section 10.

[94] See s 11 for a complete list of persons who are ineligible to be assistants.

[95] Para **[9.69]**.

question may appoint another person (over 18) (hereinafter called the co-decisionmaker) to jointly make with the appointer one or more decision in relation to the appointer's personal welfare and/or property and affairs. A person is suitable for appointment as a co-decisionmaker if he or she is a relative or friend of the appointer who has had such personal contact with the appointer over a period of time that a relationship of trust exists between them, and is able to perform such functions. The appointment must be in writing and in compliance with regulations to be made by the Minister. Section 18 sets out a list of persons who are not eligible to be co-decisionmakers which is similar to the list of ineligible persons set out for decision-making assistants described above. [96]

[9.57] The functions of the co-decisionmaker are listed in s 19 of the Act:

- advise the appointer by explaining relevant information and considerations relating to a relevant decision,
- ascertain the will and preferences of the appointer and assist the appointer with communicating them,
- assist the appointer to obtain relevant information,
- discuss with the appointer the known alternatives and likely outcomes of a relevant decision,
- make a relevant decision jointly with the appointer,
- make reasonable efforts to ensure that a relevant decision is implemented as far as practicable.

Thus, a person who understands that he or she is unable, or will shortly become unable, even with access to information and options, to properly use that information and consider the options on their own without the input/advice of someone else can appoint another person to help them make that decision by working through information and options with them and then making it along with them. One of the main points of distinction between a decision-making assistant and a co-decisionmaker is that the former does not have any role in decision-making whereas the latter makes the decision jointly with the appointer. It is important to understand that co-decision-making is not a form of substitute decision-making on behalf of the appointer as s 19(5) provides that the co-decisionmaker shall acquiesce with the wishes of the appointer unless it is reasonably foreseeable that such acquiescence will result in serious harm to the appointer or another person.

[9.58] A co-decisionmaker is entitled to reimbursement of reasonable expenses out of the appointer's assets but is not entitled to remuneration for the performance of his or her functions. A further point of distinction between a decision-making assistance agreement and a co-decision-making agreement is that the latter must be registered before it can take effect. Registration must take place within five weeks of signature of the agreement and must be in the form set by regulations to be made by the Minister. The appointer and co-decisionmaker must give notice and a copy of the agreement to the spouse, civil partner, cohabitant, adult children of the appointer as well as any decision-making assistant, decision-making representative, attorney, designated healthcare representative or other co-decisionmaker of the appointer. Any of these persons may, within five weeks of notification, notify the Director of the Decision Support Service

---

[96]   Para **[9.53]**.

that he or she objects to the registration on any of the grounds listed in s 24.[97] The Director must consider such objection and decide whether it is well founded before proceeding with registration. Section 21 sets out further provisions in relation to statements that must accompany an application for registration of the agreement. Registration is contingent on the completion of enquiries by the Director to ensure that the agreement meets the criteria set out in s 22 of the Act.

[9.59] The co-decisionmaker must, within 12 months of appointment, and within every 12 months thereafter submit a report to the Director of the Decision Support Service as to the performance of his or her functions during the relevant period. This report must be approved by the appointer and be in such form as prescribed by regulations to be made by the Minister. The report must contain details of all transactions relating to the appointer's finances which are within the scope of the agreement, all costs and expenses reimbursed to the co-decisionmaker and any other prescribed matters.[98] Sections 28 and 29 make provision for variation and revocation of agreements and s 30 provides for complaints to be made to the Director of the Decision Support Service in relation to co-decisionmakers. It is also worth noting that under s 34 it is an offence to use fraud, coercion or undue influence to force another person to make, vary or revoke a co-decision-making agreement.

Court applications

[9.60] Both the decision-making assistant and the co-decisionmaker are persons appointed by the relevant person to assist in decision-making. There may however be circumstances in which the relevant person does not have the capacity to make a decision to appoint someone under these provisions. Under Part 5 of the Act applications may be made to court by any person (over 18) who has a bona fide interest in the welfare of a relevant person.[99] The application, which must be on notice to the relevant person, must state the applicant's connection to the relevant person, the benefit to the relevant person sought by the application and the reasons for the application, in particular why the benefit cannot be achieved by less intrusive means. The applicant must inform the court if he or she is aware of any decision-making assistance agreement, co-decision-making agreement, enduring power of attorney or advance healthcare directive created by the relevant person or any decision-making representation order made in respect of the person. The relevant person may be represented in court by a legal representative or assisted by a court friend[100] unless there is a decision-making assistant, co-decisionmaker, attorney or designated healthcare representative in place for the relevant person. If no person is available, suitable or

---

[97] These include that the agreement was not signed or witnessed in accordance with the Act, that the appointer lacks capacity to make the agreement or has capacity to make decisions without assistance, that the agreement is not in keeping with the will and preferences of the appointer, that the co-decisionmaker is not a suitable person to be appointed, that the application for registration includes a false statement, or that fraud, coercion or undue influence was employed to induce the making of the agreement.

[98] Section 27.

[99] Section 36.

[100] See para **[9.73]**.

willing to act in any of these capacities, the court may direct the Director to appoint a court friend for the relevant person. Court hearings are to be conducted as informally as possible and heard in private. An interesting and welcome provision in s 36(11) provides that judges and legal practitioners involved in such hearings shall not wear wigs and gowns. This is intended to help the relevant person to feel at ease with the proceedings and not to be intimidated or frightened by the court environment.

[9.61] At such a hearing the court may make a declaration that the relevant person lacks capacity to make decisions in relation to his or her personal welfare, property or affairs, without the assistance of a suitable person as a co-decisionmaker, or a declaration that the relevant person lacks capacity even with such assistance. The court may allow the relevant person time to register a co-decision-making agreement if appropriate or may make a declaration as to the lawfulness of a proposed intervention in respect of the relevant person. Rules of court will provide further guidance on the form and manner of such proceedings and the presentation of evidence. The Circuit Court will have jurisdiction on most issues arising under this legislation and it is envisaged that specialist judges will undertake this work. The Act provides that the High Court will have jurisdiction in relation to matters relating to withdrawal of life-sustaining treatment and donation of an organ from a living donor.

Decision-making representatives

[9.62] Where the court has made a declaration that a relevant person lacks capacity to make decisions without the assistance of a co-decisionmaker but there is no suitable person to act in that role, or that a co-decision-making agreement has not been properly registered, or that the relevant person lacks capacity even with the assistance of a co-decisionmaker, s 38 provides for the appointment by the court of a decision-making representative who will act as the agent of the relevant person for the purposes of making one or more specified decisions in relation to a person's personal welfare (including healthcare) or his/her property and affairs, or appointed generally to make all decisions on behalf of a person. The court may alternatively order the making of the decision concerned if the matter is urgent or it is otherwise expedient to do so. In either case the court must consider the terms of any advance healthcare directive made by the relevant person and ensure that the order of the court or the functions of the decision-making representative are not inconsistent with such directive. Similar considerations apply to the terms of any enduring power of attorney made by the relevant person.[101]

[9.63] In considering the appointment of a decision-making representative the court must consider the known will and preferences of the relevant person, the desirability of preserving existing relationships between the family of the relevant person, the relationship between the relevant person and the proposed representative, the compatibility of the proposed representative and the relevant person, whether the proposed representative will be able to perform the relevant functions, and whether there is any conflict of interest. Subs (6) sets out the matters which the court must consider in appointing a decision-making representative such as the complexity of the affairs to be managed and the expertise of the proposed representative. If no suitable person is

---

[101] Para **[9.66]**.

available, the court shall request the Director to nominate two or more persons from a panel established for such purposes. Certain persons are ineligible or otherwise disqualified from acting as representatives.[102] The decision-making representative is entitled to reimbursement of reasonable expenses out of the assets of the relevant person and, where the court so directs, shall also be entitled to remuneration. The Director must maintain a register of decision-making representation orders in such form as is considered appropriate.

[9.64] Section 43 sets out the scope of a decision-making order or decision-making representation order relating to property and affairs, such as for example as to whether the representative can make disposals of property by way of gift. The representative may not prohibit contact between the relevant person and any other person, may not refuse consent to the carrying out or continuation of life-sustaining treatment or consent to its withdrawal. The representative cannot restrain either physically or by chemical means the relevant person unless there are exceptional emergency circumstances which justify such restraint to prevent an imminent risk of serious harm to either the relevant person or any other person and the restraint is a proportionate response to the likelihood and seriousness of such harm. As with co-decisionmakers, the decision-making representative must, within 12 months of appointment, and within every 12 months thereafter submit a report to the Director of the Decision Support Service as to the performance of his or her functions during the relevant period. This report must be approved by the appointer and be in such form as prescribed by regulations to be made by the Minister. The report must contain details of all transactions relating to the appointer's finances which are within the scope of the agreement, all expenses reimbursed and remuneration paid to the decision-making representative and other matters set out in s 46. Complaints in relation to the decision-making representative may be made to the Director.[103]

REFORM OF LAW ON WARDSHIP

[9.65] Another significant aspect of the 2015 Act is its reform of the archaic wardship regime in place in Ireland since the Lunacy Regulations of 1871 and which have been repealed by s 7 of the 2015 Act. Part 6 of the Act commits that within three years from commencement the capacity of all existing Wards of Court to make various decisions on various matters concerning his/her personal welfare and property and affairs will be reviewed in accordance with the functional test for capacity. Section 55 provides that the court will either declare that:

- the ward does not lack capacity (in which case the person is discharged from wardship and has his or her property returned to him or her) or
- the ward lacks capacity unless the assistance of a co-decisionmaker is available, (in which case the ward shall be discharged as soon as a co-decision-making agreement is registered) or
- the ward lacks capacity even with the assistance of a co-decisionmaker.

---

[102] Sections 39 and 40.
[103] Section 47.

If the court makes a declaration that the ward lacks capacity unless the assistance of a co-decisionmaker is available and no suitable person is available or an agreement is not registered, the court shall make such orders it thinks fit under Part 5 (considered above) and order the property of the former ward to be returned to him or her upon the appointment of a decision-making representative by the court. Similar provisions apply where the court makes a declaration that the ward lacks capacity even with the assistance of a co-decisionmaker.

ENDURING POWERS OF ATTORNEY

[9.66] The Powers of Attorney Act 1996 provides that a person may appoint another as decision-maker in case of the donor's subsequent mental incapacity. The Act makes provision in relation to the form and registration of an enduring power of attorney and the protection of those relying on it. The attorney is empowered to make personal care decisions on behalf of the donor, including decisions on (a) where the donor should live, (b) with whom the donor should live, (c) whom the donor should see and not see, (d) what training or rehabilitation the donor should get, (e) the donor's diet and dress, (f) inspection of the donor's personal papers, (g) housing, social welfare and other benefits for the donor. There is no provision empowering the attorney to make healthcare decisions for the donor.

[9.67] Part 7 of the Assisted Decision-Making (Capacity) Act 2015 rectifies this lacuna in the 1996 Act by making provision for an Enduring Power of Attorney ('EPA') which is a document in a prescribed form made by a person called 'the donor' appointing one or more persons as attorneys to manage the donor's personal welfare and/or property and affairs at any subsequent time when the donor lacks capacity to do so. The attorney must do so in accordance with the donor's will and preferences, beliefs and values as expressed in advance to the attorney. The EPA instrument must comply with the conditions set out in s 60, such as including a statement from a legal practitioner that the donor understands the implications of creating the power and is not being coerced to do so, and a statement by a medical practitioner that the donor had capacity at the time of creating the power. The donor must give notice to certain persons prescribed by the Act that he or she has executed an EPA and the document must also be registered in accordance with s 69 of the Act.

[9.68] Where an attorney is given authority by the donor under an EPA to act on the donor's behalf in relation to personal welfare and/or property and affairs, this includes matters such as accommodation for the donor (for example whether the donor should reside at home or in a nursing home), social activities, legal and financial matters, or providing for the needs of dependants. However, s 62(5) provides that healthcare decisions made by an attorney cannot include power to refuse life-sustaining treatment or authorise the attorney to make a decision which is the subject of an Advanced Healthcare Directive made by the donor. Other provisions in this Part relate to eligibility and disqualification of attorneys, registration of EPAs, reports by attorneys, complaints against attorneys, and offences.

DIRECTOR OF THE DECISION SUPPORT SERVICE

[9.69] Part 9 of the 2015 Act also establishes a new office called the Director of the Decision Support Service, to be appointed by the Mental Health Commission. Section 95 sets out the functions of the Director as follows:

(a) to raise public awareness of the Act;

(b) to promote public confidence in the process of dealing with matters which affect persons who require or may shortly require assistance in exercising their capacity;

(c) to provide information to relevant persons in relation to their options under this Act for exercising their capacity;

(d) to provide information to decision-making assistants, co-decisionmakers, decision-making representatives, designated healthcare representatives and attorneys in relation to the performance of their functions under this Act;

(e) to supervise, in accordance with the provisions of this Act, compliance by decision-making assistants, co-decisionmakers, decision-making representatives and attorneys in the performance of their functions under this Act;

(f) to provide information in relation to the management of property and financial affairs to relevant persons and to decision-making assistants, co-decisionmakers, decision-making representatives and attorneys;

(g) to provide information and guidance to organisations and bodies in the State in relation to their interaction with relevant persons;

(h) to provide information and guidance to organisations and bodies in the State in relation to their interaction with decision-making assistants, co-decisionmakers, decision-making representatives, attorneys and designated healthcare representatives;

(i) to identify and make recommendations for change of practices in organisations and bodies in which the practices may prevent a relevant person from exercising his or her capacity under this Act;

(j) to establish a website on the internet or provide, or arrange for the provision of, other electronic means by which to disseminate information to members of the public relevant to the performance of the Director's functions and which will, in the opinion of the Director, assist members of the public to understand the operation of this Act and the Director's role in relation thereto;

(k) to make recommendations to the Minister on any matter relating to the operation of this Act.

[9.70] Since the supports established by the 2015 Act are new to the Irish system and there may be a period of time during which persons and organisations are unsure about the application of the Act and their legal powers and functions under its provisions, it will be important and useful for the Director of the DSS to provide information and guidance as set out in s 95 above. Section 103 of the Act states that the Director may publish Codes of Practice to provide guidance (i) for persons, including healthcare professionals, assessing whether a person lacks capacity in relation to any matter; (ii) the guidance of decision-making assistants; (iii) the guidance of co-decisionmakers; (iv) the guidance of decision-making representatives; (v) the guidance of attorneys; (vi) the guidance of special visitors; (vii) the guidance of general visitors; (viii) the guidance of court friends; (ix) the guidance of healthcare professionals as respects the circumstances in which urgent treatment may be carried out without the consent of a relevant person and what type of treatment may be provided; (x) the guidance of persons acting as advocates on behalf of relevant persons; and (xi) the guidance of other persons (including healthcare, social care, legal and financial professionals) acting on behalf of relevant persons.[104]

[9.71] Another important function of the Director is to investigate, either on his or her own initiative or in response to a complaint made to him or her by any person, complaints in relation to any action of a decision-making assistant, co-decisionmaker, decision-making representative, designated healthcare representative or attorney for a relevant person which may involve a breach of his or her functions as decision-making assistant, co-decisionmaker, decision-making representative, designated healthcare representative or attorney, as the case may be, or a breach of a provision of this Act. This investigation will take place in private and the Director has been given the power to summon witnesses, hear evidence on oath, and require the production of documents.

[9.72] The Act also provides for the appointment of persons to visit the relevant person and their assisted decision supporter to carry out an assessment of the arrangement and presumably to ensure that the relevant person's rights and interests are being protected. Section 99 provides that the Director may appoint a person to be a special visitor or general visitor to visit a person for whom there is a decision-making assistant, co-decisionmaker, decision-making representative, designated healthcare representative or attorney and to make a report to the Director on such matters as the Director specifies. A special visitor is a registered medical practitioner who has particular knowledge, expertise and experience as respects the capacity of persons, or is a person who, although not a registered medical practitioner, is, in the opinion of the Director, a person who has particular knowledge, expertise and experience as respects the capacity of persons. A general visitor is a person who, in the opinion of the Director, is a person who possesses relevant qualifications, or has other relevant expertise or experience, to assist the Director in performing his or her supervisory function.

[9.73] A further important provision is the appointment by the Director under s 100 of a person called a court friend to attend with the relevant person during court applications or other meetings and consultations. This is designed to provide support for those who, for example, may not have family members or friends to provide emotional assistance during such formal processes which can otherwise prove distressing and intimidating to some people. A court friend for a relevant person will assist and attend with the relevant person in court or, if the relevant person is not attending the hearing concerned, promote the interests and the will and preferences of the relevant person in court. A court friend for a relevant person may also attend and represent the relevant person at any meeting, consultation or discussion. The Director will establish a panel of suitable persons willing and able to act as (a) decision-making representatives, (b) special visitors, (c) general visitors, and (d) court friends.

[9.74] When all Parts of the Act have been commenced this legislation will provide much-needed reform of the law in relation to persons who may lack capacity to make their own decisions. The long-awaited repeal of the legal provisions in relation to

---

[104] The Director of the Decision Support Service has not yet been appointed at the time of writing.

wardship, the clear guiding principles on capacity, the statutory reinforcement of the functional test, and the structured decision-making supports that have been put in place by the Act will both require and bring about a culture shift in health and social care practice which will ensure that the person whose capacity may be in question is given all necessary help and support to make their own decision wherever possible.

Chapter 10

Consent and Refusal of Treatment

INTRODUCTION

[10.01] The principle of self-determination requires that every person has the right to have his or her bodily integrity protected against unlawful invasion.[1] Touching the body of another person by way of medical treatment even where designed to help that person is potentially a battery unless the person has given their consent. Therefore it is a fundamental legal and ethical requirement that consent must be obtained from a patient before treatment or care is given.

[10.02] Consent must usually be given expressly, either orally or in writing, but there are some limited situations in which implied consent may be acceptable such as where the patient is informed about the necessity for a blood test and raises her arm to facilitate the blood being extracted. In this case consent may be implied by the patient's actions. In exceptional circumstances treatment may be given without consent under the doctrine of necessity where, for example, the patient is admitted to hospital unconscious following a road traffic accident. The application of the doctrine of necessity legitimises what would otherwise be an unlawful act of interfering with the person's body without their consent, as long as the treatment is confined to only what is necessary to preserve the life and health of the patient. For example, in a Canadian case *Murray v McMurchy*,[2] the plaintiff succeeded in an action for battery against a doctor who performed a sterilisation operation by tying the plaintiff's fallopian tubes without her consent during a caesarean section. He defended the allegations on the basis that the condition of her uterus was such that further pregnancies would be dangerous to her health. However, the court held that this procedure did not need to be done at that particular time even though it may have been more convenient to do so. The surgeon should have postponed the sterilisation until the plaintiff had had the opportunity to give her consent.

[10.03] Similarly in *Williamson v East London and City Health Authority*[3] damages were awarded to a plaintiff for a mastectomy carried out by a surgeon without consent. The plaintiff had agreed to undergo a procedure to remove and replace a leaking breast implant but during the surgery the surgeon found her condition to be more serious than anticipated and performed a mastectomy. Although the procedure would have been necessary at some time in the future, the court held that it did not have to be performed at this particular time and the surgeon should therefore have waited until the plaintiff had the opportunity to give her consent.

---

[1] This is also protected by art 8 of the ECHR as recognised in *YF v Turkey* (2004) 39 EHRR 34.

[2] *Murray v McMurchy* [1949] 2 DLR 442.

[3] *Williamson v East London and City Health Authority* (1998) 41 BMLR 85.

[10.04] In practice much confusion has been caused by a tendency to defer to family members of a patient for consent in circumstances when the patient is too unwell to give their own consent. Family members often assume that they have such a role and this may cause difficulties when doctors decide to proceed with treatment in the absence of consent. The legal position is that relatives or next-of-kin do not have legal authority to give consent for treatment unless they have been given such authority by the patient or the court under the provisions of the Assisted Decision-Making (Capacity) Act 2015 discussed in Chapter 9. Parents who are legal guardians may give consent for children.[4]

[10.05] The term 'consent' in medical practice is usually conflated with 'informed consent' even though the former also includes issues around voluntariness. This feature of consent is aimed at ensuring that the patient's decision is a voluntary one so it looks at the existence of control or manipulative influence by others in the patient's decision. That is not to say that others, such as family members or friends, should not be involved in the decision-making process if this is what the patient wants, but their role must be limited to supporting the patient to make his or her own decision. The law has long recognised that a consent coerced by threats or manipulated by misrepresentation is invalid.

[10.06] In the context of vulnerable patients, such as those in residential care, choices are often made for those patients on a daily basis in order to promote the efficient running of the facility. These may be in relation to the timing and content of meals, the taking of baths, and administration of medicine and so on. The liberty of competent residents to live their lives in accord with their preferences and life plans must often be balanced against protecting their health, protecting the interests of others, promoting safety and efficiency in the facility, and allocating limited financial and other resources. Although respect for autonomy suggests individualized care in the nursing home setting, such care can rarely be individualized in the ways we expect outside such institutions.[5] To say that decision-making in an institutional setting is coercive is probably an exaggeration, indeed it could be said that by entering the institution the person consented to its rules and regulations. Whether the person entered the facility voluntarily or under some persuasion from family is another matter.

[10.07] The term coercion is best used to describe a situation where a person intentionally uses a threat of harm to control another. It is not immediately relevant to the healthcare context, although it could be used in a prison or psychiatric hospital where patients are involuntarily detained. Persuasion is where a person is convinced by another's reasoning to adopt a certain course of action. Manipulation might take place in healthcare decision-making when a person makes a decision on the basis of information given to him in such a way as to alter the person's understanding of the decision to be made and its consequences. This may be in relation to the use of 'routine' tests, or the alternatives to a procedure deemed to be medically desirable. It has been suggested that:

> [C]lients are more often bullied than informed into consent, their resistance weakened in part by their desire for the general service if not the specific procedure, in part by the oppressive setting they find themselves in, and in part by the calculated intimidation, restriction of information, and covert threats of rejection by the professional staff itself.'[6]

---

4   This is discussed in detail in chapter 11.
5   Beauchamp and Childress, *Principles of Biomedical Ethics* (4th edn, OUP, 1994).
6   Freidson, *The Profession of Medicine* (Harper and Row, 1970) p 376.

[10.08] The most important question in this context is whether the person is sufficiently free to perform his or her own actions. In cases of deception, exaggeration, misleading management and withholding of information, the patient's autonomy is overridden and any consent given does not qualify as an informed choice. The same is true of the more subtle form of manipulation where offers and rewards are used to influence a decision. The example commonly given of this kind of scenario is the Tuskegee syphilis experiments, where various methods were used to sustain the interest of participants in a study.[7] The subjects, who were socio-economically deprived, were offered free burial assistance and insurance, free transportation, free medicines and a hot meal on the day of the examination, offers which were not easily refused by those particular individuals.[8]

[10.09] While doctors may, of course, recommend certain courses of action to their patients, it may be questioned how far the doctor may go in persuading the patient to choose a certain option without transgressing the necessary voluntariness of informed consent. The doctor must be able to accept the patient's choice even if he or she does not agree with it, otherwise the whole rationale for informed consent is lost. There are no neat answers to the dilemma of how to persuade without taking control. 'Each situation needs a judgment which can only be made if the professional has experience, knowledge of the situation and of the patient and, most crucially, an inherent respect for the patient's right to make his own decision.'[9]

Lack of consent – battery or negligence?

[10.10] The tort of battery involves touching another person without consent or other lawful reason. It might therefore be thought that this might provide a potential breeding ground for cases involving medical procedures where valid consent had not been given. However, the tort of battery has not generally been employed in such circumstances by the courts, and it is thought that it would only be of use where there was a fundamental mistake on the patient's part in giving consent, such as where the patient consented to touching on the basis that it was therapeutic, when in fact it was for a research paper, financial gain or sexual gratification of the doctor.[10] Another possibility would be if the patient claimed to have consented to a specific surgeon carrying out the procedure, and a different surgeon performs the operation instead.[11] However, it would be difficult for the patient to make such a case if all that he could show was that he consented to the

---

[7] This case is discussed in more detail in chapter 14 at para [14.22].

[8] Veatch, *Medical Ethics* (2nd edn, Jones and Bartlett, 1997) p 201.

[9] Donnelly, *Consent: Bridging the Gap Between Doctor and Patient* (Cork University Press, 2002) p 21.

[10] Skegg, 'English Medical Law and 'Informed Consent': An Antipodean Assessment and Alternative' (1999) Med L Rev at 142.

[11] In *Walsh v Family Planning Services* [1992] 1 IR 496, a vasectomy operation was extensively assisted by a third party under the close supervision of the performing surgeon. The patient was operated on under local anaesthetic and was therefore aware of this, although he had not given his prior consent. McKenzie J in the High Court held that a 'technical assault' had been committed. However, the majority of the Supreme Court disagreed on the basis that the patient had given his consent to the procedure on the basis that it would be carried out by a person with the requisite skill and competence, and that this in fact had been done. He had not specifically consented on the basis that only a particular surgeon would carry out the procedure.

procedure being performed by a person with the requisite skill and experience, as opposed to an identifiable person.[12] If the patient consented to the medical procedure, and later complained that he would not have consented had the true facts been disclosed, this is unlikely to be treated as a battery, given that the treatment was provided in good faith believing the patient to have consented. Allegations of failure to obtain informed consent are more usually dealt with by the tort of negligence.

[10.11] An important aspect of the tort of negligence relates to causation.[13] The court must be satisfied that the patient's injury was caused by the doctor's failure to obtain informed consent. The traditional approach has therefore been to assess whether the patient would have undergone the relevant procedure anyway even if the risks had been disclosed to her. If the court is satisfied that the patient would have proceeded in any event, then the failure to disclose risks to the patient has not caused the injury complained of by the patient. As Lord Bingham put it in *Chester v Afshar*:

> [A] claimant is not entitled to be compensated, and a defendant is not bound to compensate the claimant for damage not caused by the negligence complained of. The patient's right to be appropriately warned is an important right, which few doctors in the current legal and social climate would consciously or deliberately violate. I do not for my part think that the law should seek to reinforce that right by providing for the payment of potentially large damages by a defendant whose violation of that right is not shown to have worsened the physical condition of the claimant.[14]

[10.12] However, the majority of the House of Lords in *Chester* held that although the patient in that case could not say that she would not have had the surgery had she been warned of the risks involved, she should nonetheless be awarded compensation for the injuries sustained. This decision represents a departure from the principles of causation which had previously been employed by the courts. The House of Lords was prepared to depart from these principles in the interests of justice, as otherwise the patient would have been left without a remedy. The Court held, in facts similar to those in *Sidaway*, that if she had been warned, the plaintiff would not have gone ahead when she did, that she would have discussed the matter with others and explored other options. Although the inherent risk would have been precisely the same if she had had the surgery at another time or with another surgeon, and therefore the doctor's breach of duty did not cause or increase the risk of injury to the plaintiff, the issue of causation could not be separated from the issue of policy. Lord Hope started with the proposition that the law which imposed the duty to warn on the doctor has at its heart the right of the patient to make an informed choice as to whether, and if so when and by whom, to be operated on. Some patients will find such a choice difficult and will require time to think, take advice and weigh up the alternatives, whereas others will find the decision easy. The same duty to warn is owed to both, so to leave the patient who would find the decision difficult without a remedy would render the duty useless and would discriminate against those

---

[12] Donnelly, 'Confusion and Uncertainty: The Irish Approach to the Duty to Disclose Risks in Medical Treatment' (1996) MLJI 3.

[13] For detailed analysis of the tort of medical negligence see Healy, *Medical Malpractice Law* (Round Hall, 2009).

[14] *Chester v Afshar* [2004] UKHL 41 para 9.

who cannot honestly say they would have declined the operation had they been warned. He went on to say:

> The function of the law is to enable rights to be vindicated and to provide remedies when duties have been breached. Unless this is done the duty is a hollow one, stripped of all practical force and devoid of all content. It will have lost its ability to protect the patient and thus to fulfil the only purpose which brought it into existence.

[10.13] The Court referred to the Australian High Court decision in *Chappel v Hart*,[15] in which a patient complained that she had not been warned of the risk that an operation on her oesophagus might result in perforation of the oesophagus which could damage her vocal chords. The plaintiff claimed that if she had been informed, she would have deferred the operation and had it performed instead by the most experienced surgeon in the field then available. The majority of the Court held in favour of the plaintiff, with Kirby J stating that:

> The 'commonsense' which guides courts in this area of disclosure supports Mrs Hart's recovery. So does the setting of standards which uphold the importance of the legal duty that was breached here. This is the duty which all healthcare professionals in the position of Dr Chappel must observe: the duty of informing patients about risks, answering their questions candidly and respecting their rights, including (where they so choose) to postpone medical procedures and to go elsewhere for treatment.

Irish case law on informed consent and causation is discussed later.

Evolution of 'informed' consent

[10.14] The Hippocratic tradition in medicine did not discuss any obligations of disclosure on the physician, nor did any of the ancient or even early modern medical ethics literature, although concern did exist about how to make disclosures to the patient without harming him. Benevolent deception was the main practice in the 19th century, with the patient's right to be informed being overruled by the duty to benefit the patient in cases where the information may harm the patient. Up to the 1950s, permission for surgery was sought from patients in a fairly rudimentary way that absolved the physician of responsibility in cases of malpractice. The concept of 'informed consent' to medical treatment only emerged around the 1960s although perhaps one of the most influential cases, *Schloendorff v Society of New York Hospitals*,[16] had come in the United States in 1914. This case was important because it developed the use of rights language in relation to the obligation to obtain the consent of the patient. Self-determination began to be recognised as the primary justification for legal requirements of consent. As Cardozo J famously said:

> Every human being of adult years and sound mind has a right to determine what shall be done with his own body; and a surgeon who performs an operation without his patient's consent commits an assault for which he is liable in damages.[17]

[10.15] In the middle of the 20th century other societal changes began also to impact upon the culture of consent such as a growing concern for issues of equality and civil

---

[15] *Chappel v Hart* [1998] 195 CLR 232.
[16] *Schloendorff v Society of New York Hospitals* (1914) 211 NY at 125.
[17] *Schloendorff v Society of New York Hospitals* (1914) 211 NY at 128.

rights, consumerism and an increasingly technologically driven healthcare system. Knowledge became the fundamental constituent of self-determination. However, although the courts were clear on the link between respect for autonomy and the requirement for consent, in fact many of the cases which came to judicial attention related to the right to refuse treatment rather than give consent to it.

[10.16] The term 'informed consent' is often used to describe the process whereby a healthcare professional discloses all necessary information to a patient prior to obtaining consent to go ahead with a procedure. It is an expression which has been imported into England and Ireland from the United States in a manner often criticised as a lazy, undiscriminating repetition of an easy formula.[18] In many of the English cases in which it has been used, it has invited judicial disapproval of the term, and Kennedy and Grubb refer to it as an 'unfortunate phrase and one prone to mislead.'[19] This has also been seen in Canadian[20] and Australian[21] decisions. It is a useful term, however, to remind those involved in healthcare decision making that an *uninformed* consent may not be valid in law. Despite its wide usage in practice to cover all aspects of consent, in practice it has limited application to aspects of a valid consent such as competence or voluntariness, as its sole purpose is to ensure that sufficient information has been provided to the patient prior to giving consent to medical treatment. The Australian judge Kirby J, writing extra-judicially, defined informed consent as 'that consent which is obtained after the patient has been adequately instructed about the ratio of risk and benefit involved in the procedure as compared to alternative procedures or no treatment at all.'[22] Although useful, the definition should perhaps also have included the necessity of giving basic information about the procedure itself and who will perform it.[23]

Difference between ideal and reality of informed consent

[10.17] One of the difficulties in the area of consent is that there may be a substantial difference between the ethical ideal of informed consent and the reality of what happens in daily medical practice. From a moral perspective, consent is the means by which respect for patient autonomy is ensured through respecting the choices that patients make and in turn fostering trust in the doctor-patient relationship. However, from a legal perspective, informed consent is unfortunately sometimes reduced to patients being asked to sign a lengthy form written in medical terminology that is incomprehensible to the average person but which is seen by the service provider as a defence to potential medical litigation claims in the future. Seeking informed consent then loses all significance, as it becomes an undemanding formality that must be complied with for

---

[18] Skegg, 'English Medical Law and 'Informed Consent': An Antipodean Assessment and Alternative' (1999) Med L Rev at 142.

[19] Kennedy and Grubb, (eds) *Principles of Medical Law* (OUP, 1998) at para 3.86.

[20] The Canadian Supreme Court said that it would be better to abandon the term, in *Reibl v Hughes* [1980] 2 SCR 880,889.

[21] The High Court of Australia said that the phrase is apt to mislead, as it suggests a test of the validity of a patient's consent, in *Rogers v Whitaker* (1992) 175 CLR 479,490.

[22] Kirby, 'Informed Consent: What Does It Mean?' (1983) 9 Journal of Medical Ethics 69.

[23] Skegg, 'English Medical Law and 'Informed Consent': An Antipodean Assessment and Alternative' (1999) Med L Rev at 142.

legal purposes.[24] 'It may be relatively straightforward for a medical practitioner to escape liability if all that is required is a regimented disclosure of all risks, followed by a subsequent signature on a form. This may be a legally valid consent; it is not informed consent, and for all intents and purposes it never will be.'[25] It is argued, however, that if the process of seeking informed consent becomes too demanding in terms of what is to be disclosed to and understood by the patient, then it will never be achievable.

[10.18] Many doctors misinterpret the obligation to obtain informed consent as a simple requirement to disclose facts and receive a signature rather than a process of discussion of facts and getting permission.[26] In that context then perhaps there are two ways of defining 'informed consent'. In one sense, an informed consent is an autonomous authorisation by individual patients or subjects. In the second sense, informed consent is analysable in terms of institutional and policy rules of consent that collectively form the social practice of informed consent in institutional contexts.'[27] In the first meaning a person gives an informed consent only if they voluntarily give permission having had disclosure of the medical facts and options, and having understood that information. In the second meaning a person gives consent if they sign an approval that complies with the institution's rules, policies and guidelines. The difference between these two meanings of consent may be described as the difference between the ideal and the reality.[28]

[10.19] As leading ethicists Faden and Beauchamp point out, the fundamental characteristics of the ideal of informed consent are that the patient substantially understands both the nature of the procedure he is authorising and the fact that he is authorising it, in other words, that he has a choice in the matter. Many patients feel that they are simply being informed as to what is about to happen to them and that their

---

24 'For those who consider that informed consent is merely a medico-legal requirement which must be endured in order to protect the doctor, there is a danger that they will engage in a formulaic process which does little to inform the patient, and, ironically, just as little to protect the doctor.' Jones, 'Informed Consent and Other Fairy Stories' (1999) 7 Med L Rev 103–134 at 126.

25 Heywood, 'Excessive Risk Disclosure: The Effect of the Law on Medical Practice' (2005) *Med Law I* 93–112 at 105.

26 In many instances, the most inexperienced member of the surgical team is sent 'to consent' the patient, a term which itself suggests that something is done to the patient, usually for the purposes of avoiding legal liability, not a process that the patient participates in, or indeed controls. Junior medical staff may not be able to answer reasonable questions from patients, and may have an understandable difficulty in explaining operative procedures to patients that they have never even witnessed, let alone performed. This is discouraged by the HSE National Consent Policy (2013) para 7.2, and the Medical Council's Guide to Professional Conduct and Ethics (8th edn, 2016) para 13.2. See Jones, 'Informed Consent and Other Fairy Stories' (1999) 7 Med L Rev 103–134 at 125. See also *Learning from Bristol: the Report of the Public Inquiry into Children's Heart Surgery at the Bristol Royal Infirmary 1984–1995* (2001, Cm 5297(1)), available at www.bristol-inquiryorg.uk/final_report/.

27 Faden and Beauchamp, *A History and Theory of Informed Consent* (OUP, 1986).

28 Donnelly, *Consent: Bridging the Gap Between Doctor and Patient* (Cork University Press, 2002) p 15.

signature is an acknowledgement of their having been informed.[29] It is important that those who criticise the ideal of informed consent on the basis of its impossibility or at least impracticability, realise that the ideal situation is not necessarily that the patient have *full* understanding of the medical facts, but rather a *substantial* understanding. Complicated medical information that may be difficult to comprehend may be explained in lay language, using common everyday analogies and numerical explanations of risk factors. The core information relevant to the medical procedure to be carried out would be that which patients usually regard as relevant, such as the success rates, risks, alternatives, costs, experience of the doctor and the doctor's recommendation. Additional information may also be required depending upon the patient's own concerns and wishes. How are doctors to know what information that patient deems worthy of consideration?

> The deceptively simple answer is that a doctor will only find out what is relevant to the patient by listening to the patient. This focus on the individual patient regards communication of information as a two-way process. Achieving the ethical ideal of informed consent is therefore not just about imparting information but also about listening to the patient.[30]

[10.20] In fact, the legal action for failing to obtain informed consent is designed to encourage doctors to enquire more of a patient before the patient commits to a choice. In this way it benefits doctors, as it absolves them of the legal complications that may ensue when a patient submits to a particular treatment which ultimately proves unsuccessful.[31] By ensuring that the patient was sufficiently informed before giving consent, the patient thereby shares responsibility for the decision.[32] Communication is therefore regarded as crucial to the informed consent process, as it enables the context, background knowledge and commitments and competences of patient and doctor to be discussed.[33] Unfortunately good communication appears to be lacking to a significant degree in healthcare decision-making. 'In study after study, patients have indicated that they do not understand the consent form they are signing and that they quickly forget

---

[29] See Cassileth et al, 'Informed Consent – Why Are Its Goals Imperfectly Realized?' (1980) NEJM 896; Boisaubin and Dresser, 'Informed Consent in Emergency Care: Illusion and Reform' (1987) 16 Annals of Emergency Medicine 62, quoted in Donnelly, *Consent: Bridging the Gap Between Doctor and Patient* (Cork University Press, 2002) p 16.

[30] Donnelly, *Consent: Bridging the Gap Between Doctor and Patient* (Cork University Press, 2002).

[31] When a medical accident occurs, patients generally seek answers and information regarding what went wrong and why. The failure to provide such information is perhaps an understandable reaction on the part of the doctor, due to the fear of litigation that may ensue. However, ironically, the failure to provide information itself is a factor leading to a complaint or claim for negligence. See Vincent, Young and Phillips, 'Why Do People Sue Doctors?' (1994) 343 Lancet 1609; also the Wilson Report in the UK – *Being Heard – Report of the Review Committee on NHS Complaints Procedures* NHSE, 1994.

[32] Healy, 'Duties of Disclosure and the Elective Patient: A Case for Informed Consent' (1998) MLJI 25–29 at 26.

[33] Manson and O'Neill, *Rethinking Informed Consent In Bioethics* (Cambridge University Press, 2007) p 56.

even the most basic information relating to the procedures consented to.'[34] It is crucial that consent must be regarded as a process of communication and not a once-off event. The doctor must be conscious that a highly technical explanation with very detailed information will not help the patient to understand the proposed treatment and even if the patient signs the consent form, this will not necessarily provide an adequate defence where the patient subsequently alleges that she did not understand what she was signing.

INFORMED CONSENT AND STANDARD OF CARE

[10.21] The tort of negligence is generally concerned with breaches of doctors' duties which caused harm rather than vindication of patients' rights to respect for autonomy.[35] Therefore, it might be difficult to see why and how this form of action is employed in cases where it is alleged that there was a failure to obtain consent from the patient prior to treatment. Jones suggests that there is an inherent imbalance of power in the relationship between doctor and patient, which is remedied by the legal requirement to provide the patient with adequate information.[36] However, since litigation for medical negligence is founded upon the establishment that harm was caused to the patient, doctors are primarily concerned with the disclosure to the patient of information relating to the risk of harm. This reinforces the view that although the ethical concept of consent is concerned with respect for the autonomous choice of patients, in legal terms 'informed consent' has more to do with the liability of professionals as agents of disclosure.

[10.22] Failure to provide certain information in advance of obtaining consent to medical treatment may lead to the imposition of liability in the law of tort. In relation to what information must be disclosed, however, there has historically been a divergence of opinion. The test which had traditionally been adopted until recently in England is that of the 'reasonable doctor' or the professional standard which enables doctors to decide what is appropriate to disclose to patients by reference to what other doctors would have disclosed in similar circumstances. By comparison, the test which has been adopted in Ireland and elsewhere is that of the 'reasonable patient', or the patient standard which is seen as more consistent with respect for patient autonomy. These tests and the relevant case law are discussed below.

[10.23] One of the landmark cases in the development of the doctrine of informed consent is the American case of *Canterbury v Spence*[37] where a 19-year-old plaintiff had been suffering shoulder pains, the cause of which the doctor suspected was a ruptured disc. He recommended surgical removal of the bony arches of the patient's vertebrae to expose his spinal cord. The patient was told that the procedure was not any more serious

---

[34] Donnelly, *Healthcare Decision-making and the Law*, at 85, referring to Bergler et al, 'Informed Consent: How Much Does the Patient Understand?' (1980) 27 Clinical Pharmacology and Therapeutics 435; Cassileth et al, 'Informed Consent – Why Are Its Goals Imperfectly Realised?' (1980) 302 New Eng J Med 896; Jones, 'Informed Consent and Other Fairy Stories' (1999) 7 Medical Law Review 103.

[35] Maclean, 'The Doctrine of Informed Consent: Does It Exist and Has It Crossed the Atlantic?' (2004) 24 Legal Studies 386, 404–6.

[36] Jones, 'Informed Consent and Other Fairy Stories' (1999) 7 Med L Rev 103–134 at 129.

[37] *Canterbury v Spence* (1972) 464 F 2d 772.

than any other operation and consent was given to proceed with the surgery. Shortly after the surgery, the patient fell from his bed and experienced paralysis from the waist down. The surgeon performed another surgery and the patient's condition improved. However, despite extensive medical care, the court found that he never got back to where he was before the surgery. 'Instead of the back pain, even years later, he hobbled about on crutches, a victim of paralysis of the bowels and urinary incontinence.' The patient sued on the grounds that the doctor did not inform him of the potential risks of the surgery. He also sued the hospital for not equipping his bed with a bed rail and for not having a nurse present to assist him at the time of his fall.

[10.24] At the trial the doctor argued that disclosure of minute risks of complication (in this case, a 1 per cent risk of paralysis) was not sound medical practice, as it could deter patients from undergoing necessary surgery. In essence, he was arguing that the doctor himself should decide how much to tell his patient. The judge rejected the argument that the standard of disclosure should be assessed in the light of professional custom and instead proposed that the court should assess whether the patient had been given enough information to enable him to make an intelligent choice between alternative courses of treatment. To this end, a doctor must disclose all risks that might materially affect the patient's decision. The court should assess materiality by how a reasonable person, in what the physician knows or should know to be the patient's position, would be likely to attach significance to the risk or cluster of risks in deciding whether or not to forego the proposed therapy.[38]

[10.25] In this case, the patient's right to self-determination was affirmed as the primary motivation behind the Court's decision.

> The patient's right of self-decision shapes the boundaries of the duty to reveal. That right can be effectively exercised only if the patient possesses enough information to enable an intelligent choice. The scope of the physician's communications to the patient, then, must be measured by the patient's need, and that need is the information material to the decision. Thus the test for determining whether a particular peril must be divulged is its materiality to the patient's decision: all risks potentially affecting the decision must be unmasked. And to safeguard the patient's interest in achieving his own determination on treatment, the law must itself set the standard for adequate disclosure.[39]

[10.26] However, there were also other factors that led to the Court's rejection of the professional standard of disclosure, such as the difficulty in achieving a meaningful consensus within the medical community as to communication of risk information and the inevitable conclusion that a professional standard would leave the decision to the individual physician. In replacing the professional standard of disclosure, the Court opted for an objective reasonable patient standard. In terms of the scope of the disclosure the doctor is legally obliged to make, the court said 'It seems obviously prohibitive and unrealistic to expect physicians to discuss with their patients every risk of proposed treatment – no matter how small or remote - and generally unnecessary from the patient's viewpoint as well.' It was therefore a matter for the doctor, on the basis of his medical training and expertise, to assess the severity of the risk by reference

---

[38] See generally Healy, *Medical Negligence: Common Law Perspectives* (Sweet and Maxwell, 1999) 91 *et seq*.

[39] *Canterbury v Spence* (1972) 464 F 2d 772.

to the patient's own circumstances. The court held that 'risk is thus material when a reasonable person, in what the physician knows or should know to be the patient's position, would be likely to attach significance to the risk or cluster of risks in deciding whether or not to forego the proposed therapy.'

[10.27] Later decisions have further elucidated this important theory by shifting the focus away from disclosure as an isolated right, to a duty which is rooted in the doctor's own vocation.[40] As a general rule, the courts began to find that the greater the risks to the patient which the doctor knows or should know, but which the patient cannot be expected to know, the greater is the duty on the doctor to give the necessary information. In the Australian decision, *Chappel v Hart*,[41] a patient who was suffering with a persistent sore throat and difficulties in swallowing, attended an ear, nose and throat specialist. He recommended surgery but failed to advise the patient that there was a small but known risk that her vocal cords could be damaged as a result of the surgery. The operation was performed with due care but the risk materialised nonetheless and the patient suffered serious voice loss. It was accepted by the Court that the patient had expressed concern to the doctor regarding the possibility of voice loss. Gummow J held that a doctor has a duty to warn a patient of a 'material risk' inherent in a proposed treatment and that a 'risk is material if, in the circumstances of the particular case, a reasonable person in the patient's position, if warned of the risk, would be likely to attach significance to it or if the medical practitioner is or should be reasonably aware that the particular patient, if warned of the risk, would be likely to attach significance to it.'

[10.28] The *Chappel* case also adopted a subjective approach in considering what the particular patient's response would have been if the proper information had been given. This approach 'accords maximum weight to the patient's interest in making their own decision about whether or not to have a given treatment.'[42] Kirby J noted that a more objective approach had been adopted in Canada and the US where the courts looked at what the response of a reasonable person in the patient's position would have been, rather than at the particular patient. He acknowledged the possibility that patients may use the subjective approach to bring claims with the benefit of hindsight, but felt that these dangers should not be overstated: 'Tribunals of fact can be trusted to reject absurd, self-interested assertions.'[43]

[10.29] One of the important features of this case is that, although the patient would probably have consented to the operation even if the risk had been disclosed to her, she would have taken more time over her decision, would have sought a second opinion, would have sought the most experienced surgeon and would have chosen the time of the operation. Thus, the High Court held that 'in all likelihood she would not have suffered the random chance of injury to her vocal cord.' This represented 'nothing more than an acceptance that such injury was an extremely rare occurrence.'[44] The principal reason

---

[40] Healy, *Medical Negligence: Common Law Perspectives* (Sweet and Maxwell, 1999) p 108.

[41] *Chappel v Hart* (1998) 72 ALJR 1344.

[42] Stauch, 'Taking the Consequences for Failure to Warn of Medical Risks' (2000) 63 MLR 261 at 262.

[43] *Rogers v Whitaker* (1992) 175 CLR 479 at para 93.7.

[44] *Rogers v Whitaker* (1992) 175 CLR 479 per Kirby J at para 91.

for the development of the imposition of a duty to warn of risks therefore was not to reduce the likelihood of the risks materialising, as that is, to some extent, unavoidable in the medical context. Rather, it was to promote the patient's decision-making autonomy: the latter's right 'to decide for himself whether or not to submit to the treatment in question'.

> Making one's own choice in this context necessarily includes assessing the various risks and benefits presented by the available treatment options (including non-treatment) and deciding, in the light of one's general goals and values, which of those risks one is prepared to run. The doctor, who, even with the best of intentions, offers an incomplete picture of the therapy he proposes by withholding information as to risks, usurps this right of choice.[45]

[10.30] In Australia, the case of *Rogers v Whitaker*[46] also raised the issue of the information to be given to the inquiring patient. In this case the patient became almost totally blind after surgery conducted by an ophthalmic surgeon. The surgery was performed with the required skill and care but the patient complained that the surgeon had failed to warn her that, as a result of surgery on her right eye, she might develop a condition known as sympathetic ophthalmia in her left eye. The development of this condition and the consequent loss of sight in her left eye were particularly devastating for the patient, who had lost sight in her right eye as a child due to an injury. When she went for an eye examination in relation to getting reading glasses she was referred to a consultant surgeon for possible surgery on her right eye. She was advised that surgery would improve the appearance of her eye and would probably restore significant sight to it. Not only did the surgery not improve the sight in her right eye, but it also led to loss of sight in her left eye (a 1 in 14,000 chance). As a result, the patient was left almost totally blind. Except for death under anaesthetic, it was the worst possible outcome for the patient.

[10.31] This patient had incessantly questioned the doctor as to possible complications and was keenly interested in the outcome of the proposed surgery, including the danger of accidental interference with her good left eye. On the day before the surgery she asked whether something could be put over her good eye to ensure that nothing happened to it and an entry was made in the hospital notes to the effect that she was very worried that the wrong eye would be operated upon. She did not ask the specific question as to whether an operation on her right eye could affect her left eye. There was a body of medical opinion to the effect that only if she had asked that specific question should she have been told about the danger of sympathetic ophthalmia. However, the judge was satisfied that although she may not have asked the right question, she made it clear that her great concern was that no injury would befall her good eye. This was reasonable in the circumstances of an elective procedure.[47]

---

[45] Stauch, 'Taking the Consequences for Failure to Warn of Medical Risks' (2000) 63 MLR 261 at 267.

[46] *Rogers v Whitaker* [1992] 67 ALJR 47 (Australian High Court).

[47] Skegg argues that in cases such as this it might be possible to bring an action for deceit as well as negligence on the basis that the doctor has made a false representation of fact, by omitting a vital piece of information, with the intention that the patient should rely on it. (contd.../)

[10.32] In the context of disclosure a distinction is sometimes drawn between elective and non-elective procedures. Where a treatment is immediately therapeutic, there may be little choice for the patient but to give consent to the treatment, particularly in an emergency and therefore the amount of information given may necessarily be abbreviated in light of the urgent circumstances. However, where the procedure is elective, the patient has more time to consider the information, weigh the risks and benefits, examine the alternatives and reflect on the decision. Therefore, in these circumstances the decision is much more of a choice to be made on the basis of substantial understanding of the procedure and its consequences, rather than a medical necessity which the patient cannot afford to refuse in any event.[48]

[10.33] In this context it may also be useful to remember that illness and admission to hospital affects people in different ways and that a person who is usually confident and articulate may find themselves feeling alienated and infantilised by the hospital environment even where the procedure is an elective one.

> Illness disrupts one's natural equilibrium, one's perspective on life, and one's customary ability to translate will to action. It renders the person vulnerable; the temptation to exalt the one who potentially can help grows accordingly. In a hospital ward, the patient is sartorially and behaviorally exposed. Bed-bound and bed-clothes, encompassed by sickness, the distinct scents of the hospital, and the dominant colour of white, the patient is very much a person in alien surroundings, 'a 'captive' who cannot leave the hospital without serious consequences to himself'.[49]

English case law on risk disclosure

[10.34] Although Dunn LJ once said 'The concept of informed consent forms no part of English law'[50] it is thought that he was referring to the concept of the reasonable patient test expounded in the US case of *Canterbury v Spence* discussed above[51] as informed consent is most certainly a strong component of the English case law discussed below

---

[47]   (\...contd) Although the patient may experience difficulty in establishing that the doctor knew that the representation was false, the patient could also claim that the doctor was negligent in not knowing. If the doctor claimed that he did know, then his only defence would be to claim that non-disclosure was in the interests of the patient, which would be extremely difficult in the case of a patient who makes specific enquiries and has shown herself to be extremely worried about the risk which subsequently transpires, as in the *Rogers* case. See Skegg, 'Informed Consent to Medical Procedures' (1974) 15 Medical Science Law 124 at 131. Healy admits that such an action would not be likely to float in the Irish or English jurisdiction, as the tort of deceit has not been seen to arise in the medical context where half-truths and therapeutic lies have been implicitly accepted by the courts. See Healy, 'Duties of Disclosure and the Inquisitive Patient: A Case for Informed Consent' (1998) MLJI 69–73 at 71.

[48]   Healy, *Medical Negligence: Common Law Perspectives* (Sweet and Maxwell, 1999) p 149–150.

[49]   Healy, 'Duties of Disclosure and the Inquisitive Patient: A Case for Informed Consent' (1998) MLJI 69–73 at 71, quoting from Tagliacozzo and Mauksch, 'The Patient's View of the Patient's Role' in *Patients, Physicians, and Illness: A Sourcebook In Behavioral Science* (3rd edn, New York: Free Press, 1979) p 196.

[50]   *Sidaway v Board of Governors of Bethlem Royal Hospital* [1984] QB 493 at 517.

[51]   *Canterbury v Spence* (1972) 464 F 2d 772. See para **[10.23]** above.

although the courts there were, at least until recently, more traditionally deferential to the medical profession and less inclined towards the reasonable patient test.[52] A landmark English case in the area of medical negligence was *Bolam v Friern Hospital Management Committee*[53] where it was alleged that the plaintiff, who was a voluntary patient at a psychiatric hospital being treated for depression, was offered electroconvulsive therapy and consented to this. Unfortunately he suffered serious fractures as a result of the procedure and took action on the basis that he had not been warned of the risks involved in electroconvulsive therapy, thereby negating the possibility that he might have the opportunity to decide whether he wanted to take those risks. He also argued that he should have been given relaxant drugs and that there should have been more effective manual restraints which might have lessened the risk of fracture. McNair J noted that the doctor had followed the practices he had been taught and that were in operation at the hospital at that time. The question was whether this was a practice that a reasonable doctor would adopt.

[10.35] McNair J directed the jury that they had to consider whether the doctor had fallen 'below a proper standard of competent professional opinion'. This instruction has come to be known as the '*Bolam* test' and has been applied in many cases in the UK since the 1980s although some would argue that the expansion of *Bolam's* remit went way beyond what was intended by McNair J[54] 'According to this test, practitioners are not negligent if they act in accordance with a practice accepted at the time as proper by a responsible body of medical practitioners.'[55] This test restricts the ability of patients to sue for negligence as the doctor merely has to provide evidence from other doctors that they might have done the same thing in the circumstances. Although the test in the case was originally designed to deal with matters of technical competence, it was subsequently expanded to cover other areas such as informed consent, contraception and sterilisation of persons with learning difficulties.[56]

[10.36] The expansion of *Bolam* into the area of informed consent can be seen in case of *Sidaway v Board of Governors of Bethlem Royal Hospital*[57] which provided a good opportunity for the House of Lords to consider the application of the *Bolam* test to the duty to disclose. In this case, the plaintiff, who had suffered recurrent pain in her neck,

---

[52] Laurie, Harmon and Porter, *Law and Medical Ethics* (10th edn, 2016) 113–4.

[53] *Bolam v Friern Hospital Management Committee* [1957] 1 WLR 582.

[54] The House of Lords affirmed the *Bolam* test in the context of treatment in *Whitehouse v Jordan* [1981] 1 WLR 246, and in relation to diagnosis in *Maynard v West Midlands Regional Health Authority* [1984] 1 WLR 634. Miola argues that the decision in Bolam was 'interpreted in such a way that made the chances of plaintiffs winning cases in negligence close to non-existent and denied the courts the power of oversight over medical conduct, but it also expanded a long way beyond its intended boundaries to the point where it became virtually ubiquitous within medical law.' Miola, '*Bolam v Friern Hospital Management Committee* [1957]: Medical Law's Accordion' in Herring and Wall, *Landmark Cases in Medical Law* (Hart Publishing, 2015) 21–37.

[55] Skegg, 'English Medical Law and 'Informed Consent': An Antipodean Assessment and Alternative'(1999) Med L Rev 142.

[56] Miola refers to this as '*Bolam*-isation' in Brazier and Miola 'Bye-bye *Bolam*: a medical litigation revolution?' (2000) 8 Med Law Rev 85.

[57] *Sidaway v Board of Governors of Bethlem Royal Hospital* [1985] AC 871.

shoulder and arms underwent an operation performed by a senior neurosurgeon at the defendant's hospital. The operation carried an inherent risk (1–2 per cent) of damage to the spinal column and nerve roots. As a consequence of the operation the plaintiff was severely disabled. The judge found that the surgeon did not tell the plaintiff that this was an operation of choice rather than necessity and did not tell her of the risk of damage to the spinal cord. This appeared to be consistent with medical practice in that speciality at the time. The House of Lords agreed that doctors must disclose to patients all material risks inherent in a procedure but they disagreed about how materiality should be determined.

[10.37] In the judgments of the House of Lords two opposite positions were adopted in relation to the disclosure of information to patients. Firstly, Lord Scarman took the view that autonomy was a fundamental human right and full disclosure should be made of all material risks inherent in the proposed treatment so that the patient, not the doctor, could make the decision whether to undergo treatment or not. He said:

> It would be a strange conclusion if the courts should be led to conclude that our law, which undoubtedly recognises a right in the patient to decide whether he will accept or reject the treatment proposed, should permit the doctors to determine whether and in what circumstances a duty arises requiring the doctor to warn his patient of the risks inherent in the treatment which he proposes.

The opposite position adopted by Lord Diplock, who was the only judge to wholeheartedly take on the *Bolam* test, is that once the doctor has decided what treatment is in the patient's best interests, he should not alarm the patient by volunteering a warning of any risk involved, however grave and substantial, unless asked by the patient. He was satisfied that the decision as to what information to disclose was that of the doctor in the exercise of his professional skill and judgment in the same way as any other aspect of the doctor's duty of care towards his patient.

[10.38] Lord Bridge agreed that the issue of disclosure was to be decided on the basis of expert medical evidence but that there were some risks that were so obviously necessary to disclose that no reasonable doctor would fail to disclose them. He gave an example of a 10 per cent risk of a stroke, as being a substantial risk of grave adverse consequences.[58] Lord Templeman did not believe that the patient was entitled to know everything, nor that the doctor was entitled to decide everything. He said, 'the duty of the doctor in these circumstances, subject to his overriding duty to have regard to the best interests of the patient, is to provide the patient with information which will enable the patient to make a balanced judgment if the patient chooses to make a balanced judgment.'

[10.39] The test of the reasonable patient put forward in the US case of *Canterbury v Spence*,[59] was regarded by the majority of the Court as impractical in application for a number of reasons. First, it was thought unrealistic to expect the doctor to seek to educate the patient to his own standard of medical knowledge of all the relevant factors

---

[58] The formulation of risks as a percentage has the drawback that it may reduce the law's approach to an arithmetical one, which is concerned with experts' views of percentages. It also presumes that there is a level of harmonisation of views within the profession in relation to the level of risk that ought to be disclosed, whereas in reality experts will inevitably disagree as to what is the precise level of risk in any given case.

[59] *Canterbury v Spence* (1972) 464 F 2d 772. See para **[10.23]** above.

that may be involved in the decision to be made by the patient. Secondly, the test was so imprecise as to be meaningless in the sense that if it were to be left to individual judges to decide for themselves what a reasonable patient in this particular person's position would want to know, the outcome of litigation in this area would be unpredictable. The Court also noted that there seemed to have been a move away from this concept in the United States with many states enacting legislation curtailing the operation of the doctrine. The Court therefore rejected this approach as a solution to the problem of safeguarding the patient's right to decide whether to undergo a treatment proposed by their doctor. It was held that sufficient information had been given to the patient in this case for her to make an informed decision as to the operation and therefore the doctor had not breached his duty to her.

[10.40] Despite the fact that Lord Diplock was in a minority of one in relation to the applicability of the '*Bolam* test' to disclosure, his view was the one accepted in the first Court of Appeal decision to consider the applicability of *Sidaway*.[60] In *Gold v Haringey Health Authority*[61] the Court of Appeal adopted the *Bolam* test as set out by Lord Diplock in *Sidaway* in holding that although all the expert witnesses (including those called on behalf of the defendant) stated that they would have disclosed the risk of a sterilisation operation failing to achieve complete sterility, there was nonetheless a responsible body of opinion within the profession at the time the procedure was carried out who would not have disclosed the risk. This position was also adopted in *Blyth v Bloomsbury Health Authority*[62] in which Neill LJ said that even where questions were asked by the patient or doubts were expressed, the doctor was not under an obligation to put the patient in possession of all the information. He said 'the amount of information to be given must depend on the circumstances, and as a general proposition it is governed by what is called the *Bolam* test.'

[10.41] There was a movement away from *Bolam* in subsequent years as seen for example in *Bolitho v City and Hackney Health Authority*[63] where the House of Lords modified the test by stating that the court *could* reject medical evidence adduced by the defendant and that the doctor's actions had to be able to withstand logical analysis as well as being in accordance with responsible medical opinion. Although it is a departure from *Bolam*, the bar was set very high in that the court could only reject the medical evidence if it lacked logic.[64] Although the court did not go as far as many might have liked in its movement away from *Bolam*, 'what the case does do is demonstrate that at the very least a blind adherence to medical practice would no longer be the approach of the courts'.[65]

---

[60] Donnelly, 'Confusion and Uncertainty: The Irish Approach to the Duty to Disclose Risks in Medical Treatment' (1996) MLJI 3–8 at 4.

[61] *Gold v Haringey Health Authority* [1988] QB 481.

[62] *Blyth v Bloomsbury Health Authority* [1993] 4 Med LR 151.

[63] *Bolitho v City and Hackney Health Authority* [1998] AC 232.

[64] Miola, '*Bolam v Friern Hospital Management Committee* [1957]: Medical Law's Accordion' in Herring and Wall, *Landmark cases in medical law* (Hart Publishing, 2015) 21–37 at 30.

[65] Miola, '*Bolam v Friern Hospital Management Committee* [1957]: Medical Law's Accordion' in Herring and Wall, *Landmark cases in medical law* (Hart Publishing, 2015) 21–37 at 30.

[10.42] This shift in judicial approach is also seen in *Pearce v United Bristol Healthcare NHS Trust*[66] in which a couple whose child had died in utero almost three weeks overdue, sued their doctor for failing to disclose the risks of foetal death in the womb as a result of a delay in delivery. Although the Court endorsed *Sidaway* and accepted *Bolam* as the relevant test, it also held that 'significant risks' must be disclosed to enable the patient to make a balanced decision. Lord Woolf said:

> In a case where it is being alleged that a plaintiff has been deprived of the opportunity to make a proper decision as to what course of action he or she should take in relation to treatment, it seems to me to be the law…that if there is a significant risk which would affect the judgment of a reasonable patient, then in the normal course it is the responsibility of the doctor to inform the patient of that risk, if the information is needed so that the patient can determine for him or herself as to what course he or she would adopt.

The Court did not clarify what it meant by 'significant' risks, although Lord Bridge's example of a 10 per cent risk in *Sidaway* was cited with approval by Lord Woolfe.

[10.43] Further examples of this movement away from the *Bolam* standard in relation to information disclosure include *Smith v Tunbridge Wells Health Authority*[67] in which a surgeon failed to inform a 28 year old man undergoing treatment for rectal prolapse, of the risk of impotence and bladder dysfunction. This failure to inform was held to be negligent despite medical support for the decision not to inform the patient. Also *Birch v University College London Hospital NHS Foundation Trust*[68] where the plaintiff suffered a stroke as a result of a cerebral catheter angiogram, liability was imposed for failure to discuss with the patient the different imaging methods of an MRI scan and an angiogram and the comparative risks and benefits associated with each. Lord Cranston said that a patient should be informed not only of the objectively significant risks of the proposed procedure but also how this risk compared to the risks associated with other procedures which might be relevant to the patient. He said:

> [T]he duty to inform a patient of the significant risks will not be discharged unless she is made aware that fewer, or no risks, are associated with another procedure. In other words, unless the patient is informed of the comparative risks of different procedures, she will not be in a position to give her fully informed consent to one procedure rather than another.[69]

[10.44] In *Chester v Afshar*[70] a surgeon treating a patient for back pain did not disclose a low risk (1–2%) of nerve damage and paralysis which unfortunately later manifested in this particular patient. It was accepted that the risk was an integral aspect of this surgery and while the patient did not argue that she would not have undergone the surgery even if she had been warned, she did claim that if she had been warned she would not have proceeded with it so quickly and would have first sought further advice on alternatives. While there was some discussion in the case regarding whether or not the plaintiff must prove causation in order to succeed in claiming damages on ordinary principles of tort law, three of the judges argued that there ought to be a departure from these principles

---

[66] *Pearce v United Bristol Healthcare NHS Trust* (1999) 48 BMLR 118.
[67] *Smith v Tunbridge Wells Health Authority* [1994] 5 Med LR 334.
[68] *Birch v University College London Hospital NHS Foundation Trust* [2008] EWHC 2237.
[69] See Heywood, 'Medical Disclosure of Alternative Treatments' (2009) 68 CLJ 30.
[70] *Chester v Afshar* [2004] UKHL 41.

on the basis that negligence actions in these circumstances are essentially concerned with protecting autonomy and therefore a special rule was needed. Lord Walker said a claimant such as this one 'ought not to be without a remedy, even if it involves some extension of existing principle.' Lord Hope further elaborated on the justice of the position in saying:

> To leave the patient who would find the decision difficult without a remedy, as the normal approach to causation would indicate, would render the duty useless in the cases where it may be needed most. This would discriminate against those who cannot honestly say that they would have declined the operation once and for all if they had been warned. I would find that result unacceptable. The function of the law is to enable rights to be vindicated and to provide remedies when duties have been breached. Unless this is done the duty is a hollow one, stripped of all practical force and devoid of all content. It will have lost its ability to protect the patient and thus to fulfil the only purpose which brought it into existence. On policy grounds therefore I would hold that the test of causation is satisfied in this case. The injury was intimately involved with the duty to warn. The duty was owed by the doctor who performed the surgery that Miss Chester consented to. It was the product of the very risk that she should have been warned about when she gave her consent. So I would hold that it can be regarded as having been caused, in the legal sense, by the breach of that duty.[71]

[10.45] A more recent Supreme Court ruling in the Scottish case, *Montgomery v Lanarkshire Health Board*,[72] has further clarified the duty of disclosure in the context of antenatal risk. In this case the plaintiff, who was a diabetic and of short stature, brought an action against a consultant obstetrician who had delivered her son. It was accepted that the risk of shoulder dystocia[73] in diabetics whose babies weigh over 4 kg was about 9–10 per cent but in the majority of cases this could be dealt with by a simple procedure. The obstetrician did not inform the plaintiff of the risk or advise her to have a caesarean section as she felt it was unnecessary to provide this information and she also took the view that it was not generally in the maternal interest for women to have caesarean sections.[74] During the labour the baby's head was delivered and he showed signs of shoulder dystocia. The rest of his body was delivered approximately 12 minutes later, during which time he sustained acute hypoxia resulting in renal damage, epileptic seizures and cerebral palsy, as well as other injuries. In addition to a claim for negligence in the management of her labour, the plaintiff also alleged that no ordinary competent obstetrician acting with reasonable skill and care would have failed to advise

---

[71] Green argues that 'in order to serve preconceived notions of justice, the House of Lords sacrificed the coherence of the causal inquiry in negligence…It stands out as a case which is neither consonant with orthodox causal principles, nor justified by reference to any established exception to those principles.' Green, 'Chester v Ashfar [2004]' in Herring and Wall, *Landmark Cases in Medical Law* (Hart Publishing, 2015) 239–253.

[72] *Montgomery v Lanarkshire Health Board* [2015] UKSC 11.

[73] This can occur after the delivery of the head when the baby's shoulder cannot pass below the pubic bone, or requires significant manipulation to do so. Shoulder dystocia is an obstetrical emergency, and foetal disability or death can occur if the infant is not delivered quickly due to compression of the umbilical cord within the birth canal.

[74] This aspect of the case was noted in Lady Hale's judgment where she observed that this seemed like a moral rather than a medical opinion which might deny a pregnant woman the opportunity to obtain important information about her medical care and treatment options.

her of the risks of shoulder dystocia during vaginal delivery and failed to offer her the option of a caesarean delivery.

[10.46] The Supreme Court held that Mrs Montgomery's obstetrician should have disclosed the risk of shoulder dystocia associated with a vaginal delivery, which was substantial, as well as the alternative option of a caesarean section, which was low risk for the mother and virtually no risk for the baby.[75] The Court formally overruled the position of the majority in *Sidaway* on the basis that it was unsatisfactory in applying the *Bolam* text to risk disclosure. This failed to take into account the social changes that had taken place in the intervening years with increased emphasis now being placed on patient autonomy and patients' rights. The court described the modern position in relation to risk disclosure as follows:

> An adult person of sound mind is entitled to decide which, if any, of the available forms of treatment to undergo, and her consent must be obtained before treatment interfering with her bodily integrity is undertaken. The doctor is therefore under a duty to take reasonable care to ensure that the patient is aware of any material risks involved in any recommended treatment, and of any reasonable alternative or variant treatments. The test of materiality is whether, in the circumstances of the particular case, a reasonable person in the patient's position would be likely to attach significance to the risk, or the doctor is or should reasonably be aware that the particular patient would be likely to attach significance to it.

[10.47] The Court clarified that the issue of materiality is not a matter of percentages as the nature of risk, its likely effect on the patient, the importance of the intervention for the patient, and any alternative treatments must also be considered. Furthermore, the information must be communicated to the patient in a way that she can understand. It has been argued that by refraining to identify a specific percentage threshold above which risks must be disclosed, the meaning of materiality remains ambiguous with the result that this could prompt doctors to disclose even low inherent risks associated with treatments so as to avoid negligence claims.[76]

[10.48] Although heralded as a significant advance in the evolution of patient-centeredness in relation to disclosure, the significance of *Montgomery* is arguably open to question given that the reality is that healthcare practice and consent in the UK has for the last ten years focused principally on a reasonable patient test anyway according to Farrell and Brazier.[77] They argue that the Supreme Court endorsed a view of consent that most lawyers and doctors thought already prevailed and largely reflects professional guidance on the issue. Other commentators are troubled by the decision on grounds that the Supreme Court reinforced a stereotypical interpretation of the relationship between the patient and her doctor which assumes that the patient is infantalised and intimidated by the doctor rather than a woman who, as found by the lower court, was intelligent, articulate, independent and well-supported.[78] 'In order to justify a finding of liability, she is, thus, reduced by the Supreme Court from the 'highly intelligent person' who gave

---

[75] The court awarded £5.25 million in compensation.

[76] Laurie, Harmon and Porter, *Law and Medical Ethics* (10th edn) at 4.140.

[77] Farrell and Brazier, 'Not so new directions in the law of consent? Examining *Montgomery v Lanarkshire Health Board*' J Med Ethics 2016; 42: 85–88.

[78] Montgomery and Montgomery, 'Montgomery on informed consent: an inexpert decision?' J Med Ethics 2016; 42:89–94.

evidence to the trial judge into an anxious patient, unable to ask about what she really wants to know.'[79]

[10.49] Questions have also been raised about the Supreme Court's handling of the evidence in relation to clinical guidelines for management of such pregnancies. The obstetrician in this case had followed professional guidelines which indicated that it was not appropriate to offer a caesarean section unless it was clinically indicated. The clinical indication for such a procedure was when the baby's weight was estimated to be over 4.5kg. In this case, the weight of the baby was estimated at 3.9kg and therefore the obstetrician decided that a caesarean section was not clinically appropriate, and this decision was supported by clinical guidelines and experts on both sides of the case. Yet the Court decided that it should have been offered to the plaintiff. It has thus been argued that the decision is difficult to reconcile with the long accepted legal principle that decisions as to the appropriateness or otherwise of treatment are a matter for clinical rather than judicial assessment.[80] The result is that 'a clinician seeking to avoid legal liability can therefore no longer regard compliance with professional guidelines as a protection but must consider which aspects will be accepted by the judiciary and which not.'[81]

[10.50] The issue of materiality was subsequently taken up by the court in *Spencer v Hillingdon Hospital NHS Trust*[82] in which the plaintiff had received a warning of some risks associated with a hernia operation but was not informed about the risks of deep vein thrombosis (0.7 per cent) or pulmonary embolism (0.9 per cent). The judge held in favour of the plaintiff on the basis that the doctor had a legal duty to inform the patient of any material risks involved. He was of the view that the ordinary sensible patient would feel aggrieved not to have been informed about such risks and that even where the risk was small, alerting patients to the symptoms would enable them to seek post-operative care if needed.

[10.51] The guidelines of the medical profession itself might also be read as an indication of the level of risk to be disclosed to patients, although as noted above the Supreme Court in *Montgomery* did not appear to accept clinical guidelines as a justification for non-disclosure of risk in that case. The General Medical Council (GMC) states that the information that patients want or ought to know before treatment may include details of the diagnosis and prognosis, uncertainties about the diagnosis, options for alternative treatment or non-treatment, the purpose of the proposed intervention, explanations as to the likely benefits and any serious or frequently occurring risks, and details of the experience of the doctor responsible for the treatment.[83] It goes on to advise doctors on the best time to discuss treatment with patients, to be part of a continuing dialogue with patients regarding changes in their

---

[79] Montgomery and Montgomery, 'Montgomery on informed consent: an inexpert decision?' J Med Ethics 2016; 42:89–94 at 90.

[80] Montgomery and Montgomery, 'Montgomery on informed consent: an inexpert decision?' J Med Ethics 2016; 42:89–94 at 91.

[81] Montgomery and Montgomery, 'Montgomery on informed consent: an inexpert decision?' J Med Ethics 2016; 42:89–94 at 89.

[82] *Spencer v Hillingdon Hospital NHS Trust* [2015] EWHC 1058.

[83] General Medical Council (UK) Guidance on Consent. Available at www.gmc-uk.org.

condition, to provide clear explanations and answers to questions, to provide information in a considerate way, to allow time for reflection, and to involve other members of the team in discussions.

[10.52] The question of whether a doctor must disclose information which he believes to be potentially harmful to the patient or of which the patient has declined to know, remains controversial. Traditionally if the doctor could explain his failure to warn of risks on the basis that such a warning would cause undue distress and anxiety that would somehow harm the patient, then he could bring himself within a responsible body of medical opinion that would not make such disclosure, and escape liability under the *Bolam* test. In *Sidaway*, Lord Scarman said that even if the risk was material, the doctor would not be liable for non-disclosure if, having made a reasonable assessment of the patient's condition, he took the view that a warning would be detrimental to the patient's health. The defence of 'therapeutic privilege' thus allowed doctors to withhold information from patients on the basis that it might cause them harm.

[10.53] In *Montgomery*[84] the Supreme Court confirmed the traditional position that there may be exceptions to the doctor's duty to disclose material risks if such disclosure is considered to be seriously detrimental to the patient's health. The Court considered these exceptional circumstances to be very limited and that this should not be used to prevent the patient making an informed decision which the doctor considers not to be in her best interests. This appears to be consistent with professional guidelines from the General Medical Council which state that doctors should not withhold information from patients unless giving it would cause the patient serious harm. In this context 'serious harm' means more than that the patient might become upset or decide to refuse treatment. The doctor must record the reason for withholding information in the patient's medical records, and be prepared to explain and justify that decision. The decision should be regularly reviewed in order to consider whether the information could be given to the patient later without causing them serious harm.[85]

[10.54] A further issue arises in the suggestion that patients might be allowed to waive their right to make an informed decision. In this way the patient's autonomy remains intact in that the patient, as ultimate decision-maker, decides that she does not want any or detailed information about the treatment. However, there are no legal precedents in England or Ireland to suggest that such a waiver would excuse a doctor for treating patients who suffer a risk inherent in the procedure which they chose not to receive information about. Heywood argues that the courts would be likely to recognise the waiver in terms of information about risks and alternatives, providing there was strong evidence that the original intention of the doctor was one of disclosure. He argues that doctors ought to recognise waivers as an exercise of autonomy, as forcing information on patients who have made it clear that they do not wish to know certain things may be said to represent bad medical practice.[86]

---

[84] *Montgomery v Lanarkshire Health Board* [2015] UKSC 11. Para **[10.49]** above.

[85] General Medical Council, Guidance on Consent available at http://www.gmc-uk.org/guidance/

[86] Heywood, 'Excessive Risk Disclosure: The Effect of the Law on Medical Practice' (2005) Medical Law International Vol 7, at 101. See also Kihlbom, 'Autonomy and Negatively Informed Consent' (2008) J Med Ethics 34: 146–149.

Irish case law on risk disclosure

[10.55] The law relating to medical negligence in Ireland emanates from a test put forward by the Supreme Court in the seminal case of *Dunne v National Maternity Hospital*[87] in which an infant plaintiff who had sustained irreversible brain damage at birth and his mother (on his behalf) took a negligence action for damages. The Court held that to establish negligence the plaintiff would have to prove that the defendant doctor had been 'guilty of such failure as no medical practitioner of equal specialist or general status and skill would be guilty of if acting with ordinary care.'[88] The fact that the negligence allegation is based on the fact that the medical practitioner deviated from a general and approved practice will not establish negligence unless it is also proved that the course he took was one which no medical practitioner of like specialisation and skill would have followed had he been taking the ordinary care required of a person with his qualifications. This is clearly an endorsement of the professional standard, or 'reasonable doctor' test of negligence. The Court, however, did not adopt the *Bolam* test completely, as the Court also held that the doctor would not be protected by general and approved practice if this practice has inherent defects that would be obvious to anyone giving it due consideration. 'General and approved practice' need not be universal but must be approved of and adhered to by a substantial number of reputable practitioners holding the relevant specialist or general qualifications.

[10.56] Two other principles established by the court in this case are also important to note. Firstly Finlay CJ stated that an honest difference of opinion between doctors as to which are the better of two ways of treating a patient does not provide grounds for a judge to make a finding on negligence and secondly, it is not for a judge to decide which of two alternative courses of treatment is preferable, his function is to decide whether the course of treatment followed by the defendant practitioner, on the evidence, complied with the careful conduct of a medical practitioner of like specialisation and skill. Although treatment is referred to in some of the statements of principle mentioned above, these principles apply in identical fashion to questions of diagnosis. The *Dunne* principles have been applied in many medical negligence cases since 1989, some of which are set out below.

[10.57] In terms of disclosure of information to patients, the courts have not always been inclined to oblige doctors to be forthcoming. For example, in *Daniels v Heskin*[89] the Supreme Court considered the duty of a doctor to tell his patient that a broken part of a needle had been left in her body during stitching after childbirth. The doctor had left instructions that the patient should be x-rayed within six weeks if the needle had not been found. When this was done and an examination was carried out by a different doctor, an operation was performed to remove the needle. The majority of the Supreme Court held that there was no obligation on the doctor to inform the plaintiff or her husband of the presence of the needle at the time of giving birth. Lavery J, with whom Murnaghan and O'Byrne JJ agreed, was of the view that if a dangerous operation was planned, then the doctor must disclose the risks involved. However, in other situations,

---

[87] *Dunne v National Maternity Hospital* [1989] IR 91.
[88] *Dunne v National Maternity Hospital* [1989] IR 91 at 109.
[89] *Daniels v Heskin* [1954] IR 73.

the doctor could decide for himself whether or not to make disclosure. Kingsmill-Moore J said 'I cannot admit any abstract duty to tell patients what is the matter with them... All depends on the circumstances – the character of the patient, her health, her social position, her intelligence, the nature of the tissue in which the needle is embedded...' The court accepted that the doctor could therefore decide not to tell the woman until she had recovered from childbirth. The decision is regarded as being of limited value in the sense that it is unclear to what Lavery J was referring as a 'dangerous' operation, and it has not been referred to by many later judgments on the issue.

[10.58] A more important case in the development of the doctrine of informed consent in Ireland is *Walsh v Family Planning Services*[90] where the plaintiff had had a vasectomy operation for contraceptive purposes. Prior to the operation he had been told that there might be some discomfort and swelling after the operation and that, very rarely, some patients experience pain for some years later. The patient suffered a variety of problems after the operation which included severe groin pain, impotence and eventual removal of his left testicle. Expert evidence showed that he suffered from a rare, but known, possible consequence of vasectomy, called orchialgia. At the time of the operation there was no known practice regarding disclosure of the risk of this possible condition.

[10.59] Finlay CJ was the only judge to adopt the reasonable doctor test put forward in *Dunne,* with the caveat that if the nature of the warning given was inherently defective, the court might be more prepared to judge that the doctor had not fulfilled the duty of disclosure prior to obtaining consent. He also accepted that when the procedure was elective, the courts might more readily decide that there were inherent defects in a standard medical procedure, such that the patient should have been warned about them. The Chief Justice said that he was satisfied that:

> [T]here is, of course, where it is possible to do so, a clear obligation on a medical practitioner carrying out or arranging for the carrying out of an operation, to inform the patient of any possible harmful consequence arising from the operation, so as to permit the patient to give an informed consent to subjecting himself to the operation concerned. I am also satisfied that the extent of this obligation must, as a matter of common sense, vary with what might be described as the elective nature of the surgery concerned. The obligation to give a warning of the possible harmful consequences of a surgical procedure which could be said to be elective may be more stringent and onerous.

[10.60] In fact, for all the judges, the fact that this was an elective procedure (described by O'Flaherty J as one that was 'not essential to health or bodily well-being') was of importance in deciding the extent of disclosure required. The element of choice involved meant that the doctor did not have to weigh up on the risks of not performing the surgery against the risks involved in the procedure.[91] O'Flaherty J took a clear approach to the issue in determining that it should be a matter for the trial judge to decide on general negligence principles. He said: '... [in the case of elective surgery] if there is a risk – however exceptional or remote – of grave consequences involving severe pain stretching for an appreciable time into the future and involving the possibility of further operative

---

[90] *Walsh v Family Planning Services* [1992] IR 496.
[91] Donnelly, 'Confusion and Uncertainty: The Irish Approach to the Duty to Disclose Risks in Medical Treatment' (1996) MLJI 3 at 6.

procedures, the exercise of the duty of care owed by the defendants requires that such possible consequences should be explained in the clearest language to the plaintiff.'

[10.61] In *Farrell v Varian*[92] O'Hanlon J was concerned with whether the plaintiff should have been warned that an operation aimed at curing a particular hand condition, could actually make the condition worse. The judge did not refer to *Walsh* but rather to the *Sidaway* case and in particular where Lord Bridge referred to the issue of disclosure as coming within the realms of clinical judgment unless the matter was so obviously necessary to disclose, that no medical professional would fail to disclose it. On that basis the warning given in this case was sufficient, as the risk was a slight one.

[10.62] A further case in the evolution of the test for disclosure of risk is *Bolton v the Blackrock Clinic, Wood and Cumiskey*[93] where the plaintiff sought treatment for a pulmonary condition and surgery was recommended. She later complained that she had not been given sufficient information regarding the risks involved in this surgery, in particular the risk of narrowing of the bronchus which might require removal of the lung. This is fact occurred in the case and the plaintiff underwent a second operation in which her laryngeal nerve was damaged. Geoghegan J in the High Court found that the defendants had not been negligent in their diagnosis and treatment of the plaintiff, which finding was later affirmed by the Supreme Court. In relation to the question of disclosure, Geoghegan J was of the view that this was to be determined on ordinary principles of negligence and that in this case the risks had been properly disclosed. The Supreme Court upheld this finding of fact and held that the matter should be determined on the basis of the principles in *Dunne*.

[10.63] The case of *Geoghegan v Harris*[94] is of considerable importance in setting out clearly that the standard of risk disclosure is that of the 'reasonable patient'. In this case the plaintiff alleged negligence in the carrying out of a dental implant by the defendant dentist, during the course of which a bone graft was taken from the plaintiff's chin. This was alleged to have damaged a nerve in the front of the chin and left the patient with chronic neuropathic pain. It was alleged that the dentist failed to disclose in advance of the operation the risk that such pain might be a consequence of the procedure and the plaintiff said that he would not have undergone the procedure if he had been warned of the risk. The defendant argued that he had warned of the risk but that even if he had not, he was not under an obligation to warn as the risk was too remote. He was of the view that he had a duty to give information about rare complications only where the risk exceeded 1%.

[10.64] The court held, applying the principles in the *Walsh* case outlined above, that the defendant was obliged to warn of the risk of pain. However, Kearns J departed from the reasonable doctor test in stating that the reason for warning the patient was that it was a 'material risk' that a reasonable patient would want and expect to be told. He said 'Each case it seems to me should be considered in the light of its own particular facts, evidence and circumstances to see if the reasonable patient in the plaintiff's position would have

---

[92] *Farrell v Varian* (1995) MLJI 29.

[93] *Bolton v the Blackrock Clinic, Wood and Cumiskey* (20 December 1994) HC.

[94] *Geoghegan v Harris* [2000] 3 IR 536 (Kearns J).

required a warning of the particular risk.' He went on to say that the court must ultimately decide what is material and that the concept of materiality includes considerations of both the severity of the consequences and the statistical frequency of the risk. 'That both are critical is obvious because a risk may have serious consequences and yet historically or predictably be so rare as not to be regarded as significant by many people.'[95] He also said:

> The reasonable man, entitled as he must be to full information of material risks, does not have impossible expectations nor does he seek to impose impossible standards. He does not invoke only the wisdom of hindsight if things go wrong. He must be taken as needing medical practitioners to deliver on their medical expertise without excessive restraint or gross limitation on their ability to do so.

[10.65] The judge also adopted the reasonable patient standard in relation to causation, in other words, the patient had to convince the court that a reasonable patient would not have proceeded with the procedure had the information been disclosed. 'The problem for claimants is that, because in the vast majority of cases the risks in a procedure are quite small and the potential benefits are quite large, most claimants cannot convincingly argue that they would have acted any differently even if they had been provided with a full picture.'[96] In this case, Kearns J considered whether a reasonable person in the plaintiff's position would have consented to the operation even if informed of the remote risk. The judge noted that the patient had been very keen to proceed with the surgery and thus held that a reasonable person in his position would have consented. The patient therefore failed to show that his injury was caused by the failure to disclose the risks and was unsuccessful in his claim.

[10.66] The importance of this case arises principally from the requirement that the doctor must give a warning of material risk which, in elective treatment, is any risk of grave consequences no matter how remote the doctor deems the possibility of the risk materialising. This clearly and definitively upholds the right of the patient to choose her treatment with full knowledge of all material facts. Although the case involved elective treatment, it nevertheless represented an important indication of judicial willingness to move in the direction of greater recognition of patient autonomy generally.

[10.67] The *Geogeghan* case was not appealed to the Supreme Court so it remained for some time unclear whether the High Court judgment in favour of the 'reasonable patient' test would be approved by the Supreme Court. The matter was settled by *Fitzpatrick v White*[97] in which there was an alleged failure to give a warning to a patient prior to eye surgery. Kearns J reaffirmed the position adopted in *Walsh* that a warning must in every case be given of a risk, however remote, of grave consequences involving severe pain continuing into the future and involving further operative intervention. He went on to say:

---

[95] He also quoted from Healy, *Medical Negligence Common Law Perspectives,* (Round Hall, 1999) p 99: 'Materiality is not a static concept. If the assessment of materiality is to 'abide by a rule of reason' any absolute requirement which ignores frequency seems at variance with any such rule.'

[96] Donnelly, *Consent: Bridging the Gap Between Doctor and Patient,* (Cork University Press, 2002) p 31.

[97] *Fitzpatrick v White* [2007] IESC 51.

[T]he argument that the giving of an adequate warning, far from being a source of nuisance for doctors, should be seen as an opportunity to ensure they are protected from subsequent litigation at the suit of disappointed patients. I am thus fortified to express in rather more vigorous terms than I did in *Geoghegan v Harris* my view that the patient centred test is preferable, and ultimately more satisfactory from the point of view of both doctor and patient alike, than any 'doctor centred' approach favoured by part of this Court in *Walsh v Family Planning Services.*

[10.68] Kearns J held that a risk may be seen as material if, in the circumstances of the particular case, a reasonable person in the patient's position, if warned of the risk, would be likely to attach significance to it. Although the plaintiff's case failed on the basis that the warning given to him was in fact adequate, another noteworthy point from the judgment is in relation to the timing of seeking informed consent. In this case the plaintiff accepted that a warning had in fact been given but alleged that a warning which was given only shortly before the procedure was carried out was insufficient to discharge the duty of care on the doctor. In this case, the plaintiff had his eyesight fully tested and evaluated four months before his operation and the options for surgical intervention were plain from the orthoptist's report from that time. The plaintiff was seen on three occasions prior to his operation. The judge took the view that the risks associated with squint surgery could have easily been explained to the plaintiff at any of these meetings, or certainly well in advance of the time when they were explained – a mere 30 minutes before his operation. The judge said:

There are obvious reasons why, in the context of elective surgery, a warning given only shortly before an operation is undesirable. A patient may be stressed, medicated or in pain in this period and may be less likely for one or more of these reasons to make a calm and reasoned decision in such circumstances.

[10.69] In this case, the plaintiff gave no evidence of being unduly stressed or anxious on the day of his operation, he was not in pain and had not been sedated prior to his operation. He was facing into what could fairly be described as a minor operation only. His evidence suggested he was in a clear and lucid mental state on the day of the operation and well capable of making a decision. He described how his conversation with the doctor was both cordial and relaxed. While the plaintiff said he would have 'walked straight out of the hospital' had he been warned on the day, he did not say he could not deal with a warning given at that point in time. In fact he said the opposite. In the absence of clear evidence that the plaintiff was actually disadvantaged in some material way by the lateness of the warning, the judge held that he would not declare or find the warning given to be invalid because it was given at a late stage. He went on to say that there was nothing in the evidence to suggest the plaintiff could not assimilate or properly understand what he was being told. He said, 'I would make the point strongly however that in other cases where a warning is given late in the day, particularly where the surgery is elective surgery, the outcome might well be different.'

[10.70] Other Irish cases have considered the issue of the validity of consent forms as a representation that the plaintiff accepted the risks of treatment. The patient's signature on a consent form does not always necessarily relieve the doctor from liability in the event of negligence on the doctor's part. In *Byrne v Ryan*,[98] the High Court was asked to

---

[98] *Byrne v Ryan* [2007] IEHC 207.

award damages to a woman whose tubal ligation procedure had failed, with the result that she bore two subsequent children. Although Kelly J denied the plaintiff's claim for the costs of rearing the two children in question on policy grounds,[99] he did award damages for personal injury in relation to the necessity for the plaintiff to undergo a second sterilisation procedure some years later. In relation to the issue of consent, the plaintiff had signed a consent form which acknowledged the possibility that it might not render her sterile. The defendant argued that by signing this document the plaintiff consented to that risk of failure, thus relieving the doctor of any liability. Kelly J did not accept this proposition. He said that the document in its terms was a consent to the operation being carried out and the administration of an anaesthetic. 'It is not a consent to the carrying out of a failure; still less is it a consent to the carrying out of the operation in a negligent fashion. It merely records the plaintiff's understanding that there is a possibility of failure. It might be possible to draft a form of consent which would exclude liability on the part of a doctor for negligent treatment but there is no attempt to do so here.'

[10.71] Although the law in relation to disclosure of risk remains as described by the Supreme Court in *Fitzpatrick*, two other recent cases are also worthy of note in the context of informed consent. The first is *Healy v Buckley*[100] in which the plaintiff had been diagnosed with a pituitary tumour in 1982. She underwent surgery at which a small sample of the tumour was removed for biopsy but the large growth was left in situ and she was put on medication which improved her condition. The plaintiff was under the mistaken impression that the surgeon had removed almost all of the tumour, leaving only a tiny amount behind. From 1994 to 2000, she was under the care of a different medical team, including the defendant Dr Buckley who was a consultant endocrinologist, during which time she had further tests and treatments. In 2000 she underwent an MRI scan which showed a large pituitary mass and she also had another test which indicated excess secretion of growth hormone. In discussions with Dr Buckley about plans for her treatment, the plaintiff misunderstood that the tumour had begun to grow again very rapidly and that her condition had significantly deteriorated. In fact the MRI scan did not show any significant change in relation to the tumour compared with the scan done in 1982. Dr Buckley did not tell the plaintiff that the tumour was growing but he did tell her that it was very unsatisfactory, as a result of which the plaintiff was very alarmed at what she thought was a significant deterioration in her health.

[10.72] Dr Buckley recommended a new drug which he believed to be effective in reducing excess growth hormone levels and which he hoped would also reduce the size of her tumour. The plaintiff agreed to take the drug but experienced gastrointestinal problems for which she had to be admitted to hospital. She was diagnosed with hypothyroidism, which is a side-effect of this particular drug. She later sued Dr Buckley for negligence in prescribing this drug and also claimed that her consent to this treatment was vitiated by lack of sufficient information or misrepresentation concerning her condition and the appropriateness of the drug as a treatment for it.

---

[99] 'The value which the Constitution places upon the family, the dignity and protection which it affords to human life are matters which are, in my view, better served by a decision to deny rather than allow damages of the type claimed.' Per Kelly J.

[100] *Healy v Buckley* [2015] IECA 251.

[10.73] The High Court applied the *Dunne* principles and found that Dr Buckley was not negligent in prescribing the drug as it was a therapeutic option which was appropriate to her condition and it had been prescribed in a manner that was compliant with the manufacturer's indications. The trial judge found that it was not simply that there was a body of opinion that supported the course of action taken by Dr Buckley, but rather that the expert evidence showed that this practice was entirely appropriate in the circumstances. In relation to consent, the High Court held that Dr Buckley had not breached his duty of care to the plaintiff in the information and advice given to her and there was no failure to give warnings concerning the harmful risks or potential side effects from her treatment such as to vitiate her consent.

[10.74] On appeal, the Court of Appeal upheld the High Court's decision on both issues. The court referred to the leading cases of *Geoghegan*[101] and *Fitzpatrick*[102] cases discussed earlier, in accepting the reasonable patient test of disclosure. The court also noted the English case of *Montgomery v Lanarkshire Health Board* discussed earlier[103] which it described as reflecting 'the enhanced status of the patient as the chooser of treatment'. The court said that it would be unjust to apply any new standard to Dr Buckley's treatment fifteen years ago but commented that 'the law on consent in this jurisdiction may require to be re-considered in light of developments, especially in regard to the patient's capacity to choose between treatment and no treatment. However, any expansion of patient power will require careful delineation.'[104] The court did not accept the plaintiff's argument that Dr Buckley should have discussed with the plaintiff the option of doing nothing:

> When the plaintiff has a serious medical condition and has presented herself to the doctor through the agency of her general practitioner in quest of treatment to alleviate her condition, it is difficult to see how he ought to be considered negligent for not debating the merits of doing nothing as compared with treatment that is effective, minimally invasive and safe ie not known to pose a grave danger to her life or health.

[10.75] The court accepted that in other circumstances where the choice was to perform a difficult and dangerous operation, the doctor would and should discuss in detail the various options, including doing nothing. But in this case the doctor recommended what he believed to be good effective drug treatment which had a risk of unpleasant side effects but potentially substantial benefit for the patient. The fact that she had gone to him in the first place was in some sense an implicit rejection of the 'do nothing' option. The court also held that Dr Buckley was not at fault for not being aware of the mistaken impression the plaintiff was under in relation to the earlier removal of the tumour. As a result, the doctor was not negligent in relation to consent and the appeal was dismissed.

[10.76] In *O'Leary v the Health Service Executive and others*[105] an action was taken on behalf of a young man against the HSE in relation to consequences allegedly suffered by the plaintiff following the measles vaccination he received as a baby. It was alleged that the doctor who had carried out the vaccination had failed to obtain the consent of the

---

[101] *Geoghegan v Harris* [2000] 3 IR 536 (Kearns J). See para **[10.63]**.
[102] *Fitzpatrick v White* [2007] IESC 51. See para **[10.67]**.
[103] *Montgomery v Lanarkshire Health Board* [2015] UKSC 11. See para **[10.45]**.
[104] *Healy v Buckley & Ors* [2015] IECA 251 at para 59.
[105] *O'Leary v the Health Service Executive and others* [2016] IECA 25.

plaintiff's mother (who was now deceased) and that therefore the vaccination constituted a battery by the doctor. The medical notes of the visit at which the vaccination had been given did not record any warnings or advices given by the doctor to the plaintiff's mother about the risks of the vaccine and the doctor. There was no evidence as to what the plaintiff's mother would have done if a warning had been given.

[10.77] The Court of Appeal upheld the High Court's dismissal of the action. In relation to the absence of a note recording that the plaintiff's mother had given consent, the court held that 'as a matter of logic and evidence, failure to record can only be considered relevant if there was an obligation to make a note or if it was an accepted practice to do so.' The High Court had not made any finding on this point but said that since there was no evidence that the mother would not have consented even if a warning had been given, the case could not succeed in any event due to failure of causation. The Court of Appeal took the view that it was difficult to see how the trial judge could have come to any other conclusion and dismissed the appeal.

[10.78] In addition to ensuring that they are compliant with legal standards in relation to consent, doctors will also be mindful of professional and organisational guidelines and policies on this issue. The Medical Council, which is the regulatory body for the medical profession in Ireland,[106] publishes guidance for the profession in relation to professional conduct and ethics. The 8th edition of the Guide published in 2016[107] provides that when patients give consent, they are making a voluntary choice. Doctors should help patients to make decisions that are informed and right for them and should not give patients the impression that their consent is simply a formality or a signature on a page. It advises that patients must be given enough information, in a way that they can understand, to enable them to exercise their right to make informed decisions about their care. It also sets out the information that patients generally want and should know before making a treatment decision.

[10.79] The Health Service Executive (HSE) also published a National Consent Policy in 2013 which applies to all health and social care interventions.[108] This Policy is in four parts detailing guidance on general principles of consent, giving consent for children and minors, consent in research contexts, and Do Not Attempt Resuscitation Orders. The principles set out in the Policy are consistent with the legal principles developed in the case law set out above and aim at providing information in relation to these principles in an accessible and user-friendly format for health and social care professionals as well as service-users. The Health Information and Quality Authority also published guidance in 2016 on Supporting People's Autonomy which is aimed at helping services to demonstrate how they show respect for human dignity, how they provide person-centred care, and how they ensure an informed consent process that values personal choice and decision-making.[109] Further guidance is also available from other regulatory bodies and professional indemnity organisations.

---

[106] See further Chapter 2 for discussion of the role of the Medical Council.

[107] Medical Council, *The Guide to Professional Conduct and Ethics* (8th edn, 2016), available at www.medicalcouncil.ie para. 9.

[108] National Consent Advisory Group. National Consent Policy. Dublin: Health Service Executive (HSE); 2013. Available at www.hse.ie.

[109] Available at www.hiqa.ie.

REFUSAL OF TREATMENT BY AN ADULT

[10.80] The right of a patient to refuse medical treatment brings into conflict two ethical principles: respect for autonomy and beneficence. Apart from cases involving terminally ill patients or patients in a persistent vegetative state, there have also been a number of difficult cases before the courts in relation to refusal of blood transfusions by Jehovah's Witnesses, amputation of limbs, feeding of an adult anorexic patient, refusal by parents of treatment for their children for religious and non-religious reasons[110] and refusal of caesarean sections by pregnant women. In some of these cases, the doctors and the courts took the view that no reasonable person in the patient's position would refuse the proposed medical treatment, and that therefore the patient must be regarded as temporarily lacking capacity. Refusal of consent is seen 'not as an assertion of will, but rather as a symptom of unsoundness of mind.'[111] A decision could then be made to proceed with treatment in the 'best interests' of the patient. The difficulty for the courts in cases of refusal of treatment is that there is a stark decision to be made between the fundamental values of choice and health, or in some instances, life itself. Courts have commonly in such situations acknowledged the right of autonomy, but have expressly provided that such rights are not and cannot be absolute in any society. The preservation of life then comes within one of the exceptional situations in which societal interests override the value of self-determination. As will be seen in the discussion of the case law below, this attitude has changed in recent years with an increasing recognition that refusal of treatment is within the decision-making authority of the individual patient, even where the consequences of the refusal may be death or serious harm.

[10.81] The right to refuse treatment is contained within the respect for autonomy enshrined in art 40.3.1° of the Irish Constitution 1937. This has been recognised in a number of cases before the Supreme Court including *Re a Ward of Court*,[112] *JM v Board of Management of St Vincent's Hospital*[113] and *Fitzpatrick v K*[114] where Laffoy J said that it 'could not be argued that a competent adult is not free to decline medical treatment. Section 83(2) of the Assisted Decision-Making (Capacity) Act 2015 also now states that an adult with capacity is entitled to refuse treatment for any reason (including a reason based on his or her religious beliefs) notwithstanding that the refusal appears to be unwise, not based on sound medical principles, or may result in his or her death. This provision explicitly therefore puts on a statutory footing the principles arising from existing case law in relation to contemporaneous refusals of treatment.

[10.82] Before considering the case law on refusal of treatment in Ireland and the UK, it is also important to note the relevance of arts 2, 3, 8, 9, and 12 of the European Convention on Human Rights in relation to the right to refuse treatment.[115] Under art 2 'everyone's right to life shall be protected by law...'. This has relevance for the area of

---

[110] See Chapter 11 for further discussion of parental authority in the treatment of sick children.

[111] Kennedy, *Treat Me Right: Essays in Medical Law and Ethics* (Clarendon Press, 1991) at 337.

[112] *Re a Ward of Court* [1996] 2 IR 79.

[113] *JM v Board of Management of St Vincent's Hospital* [2003] 1 IR 321.

[114] *Fitzpatrick v K* [2008] IEHC 104.

[115] See detailed discussion by Wicks, 'The right to refuse medical treatment under the European Convention on Human Rights' (2001) 9 Med L Rev 17–40.

euthanasia and refusal of life-sustaining treatment. Article 3 prohibits inhuman or degrading treatment, which may encompass non-consensual medical treatment. Degrading treatment has been defined as treatment or punishment of an individual which 'grossly humiliates him before others or drives him to act against his will or conscience.'[116] Although in one case an intention to humiliate was held to be necessary under art 3, the court has generally not imposed such a requirement.[117] Such a requirement would certainly make it almost impossible to succeed in relation to the imposition of medical treatment, as the doctor's intentions would be unlikely to include humiliation of the patient.[118] The emphasis on humiliation, however, seems to indicate a leaning towards the protection of human dignity as opposed to the concept of autonomy and therefore it may be argued that it excludes non-consensual medical treatment from its ambit. However, it is also clear that non-consensual medical treatment deprives a person of the freedom of choice over his own body, which is a fundamental part of individual dignity.[119]

[10.83] In *X v Denmark*[120] the Commission held that 'medical treatment of an experimental character and without the consent of the person involved may under certain circumstances be regarded as prohibited by art 3.' The issue of experimentation is, of course, a particularly sensitive one, given the context within which the Convention was drafted and the response to the atrocities that took place in Germany and elsewhere during and after the Second World War. However, it is unlikely that medical treatment designed and intended to benefit the patient, albeit without the patient's consent, could be held to come within the term 'experimentation.' In the *Herczegfalvy* case,[121] the Court held that 'a measure which is a therapeutic necessity cannot be regarded as inhuman or degrading.' The Court must be satisfied of the medical necessity of the treatment, but once this is established, the imposition of the treatment without consent will not violate art 3.[122]

[10.84] Article 8 provides that 'everyone has the right to respect for his private life.' This has been interpreted as including the 'physical integrity' of the person.[123] Although limitations to this right are possible on the basis of societal interests, such as the protection of health through compulsory vaccination against disease, such limitations are not likely to apply to an individual case of non-consensual medical treatment. In *X v Austria*[124] the Commission specifically stated that a 'compulsory medical intervention,

---

[116] *Denmark, Norway, Sweden and the Netherlands v Greece* [1969] 12 YB 1 at 186.

[117] *Abdulaziz, Cabales and Balkandali v UK* [1985] Series A No 94, para 91.

[118] Wicks, 'The right to refuse medical treatment under the European Convention on Human Rights' (2001) 9 Med L Rev 17–40 at 21, fn 16.

[119] Wicks, 'The right to refuse medical treatment under the European Convention on Human Rights' (2001) 9 Med L Rev 17–40 at 22.

[120] *X v Denmark* [1983] 32 DR 282.

[121] *Herczegfalvy* [1992] Series A, No 244, para 82.

[122] See Wicks, 'The right to refuse medical treatment under the European Convention on Human Rights' (2001) 9 Med L Rev 17–40 at 24 for further discussion of the meaning of 'medical necessity' in light of the possibility of differing bodies of profession opinion on a particular treatment.

[123] *X and Y v Netherlands* [1986] 8 EHRR 235 at para 22.

[124] *X v Austria* [1980] 18 DR 154.

even if it is of minor importance, must be considered as an interference with this right.' However, the protection of the right probably only applies where the adult is competent to make decisions and has been informed of the consequences of the decision. 'Where consent is normally required, as in the case of medical treatment, action without consent will not be an interference if the state can show that the individual was not in a position to give informed consent.'[125] The European Court of Human Rights stated in *Pretty v the UK*[126] that the right of autonomy comes within the protection of art 8 and that this permitted the refusal of medical treatment, even if this would lead to the patient's death. The Court said that the imposition of treatment on a capable adult patient without consent 'would clearly interfere with a person's physical integrity in a manner capable of engaging the rights protected under art 8(1) of the Convention.'[127] This was also affirmed in *Tysiac v Poland*.[128]

[10.85] Article 9 provides protection of freedom of thought, conscience and religion. In many cases, discussed below, medical treatment may be refused on religious grounds. The most striking example of this occurs in the Jehovah's Witness faith, which is opposed to blood transfusions. In *Hoffmann v Austria*[129] the Austrian courts had refused to award custody of children to a woman, in part because she was a Jehovah's Witness and would have refused blood transfusions for her children. Although the European Court concentrated on violations of arts 8 (interference with private life) and 14 (prevention of discrimination) in the circumstances of this case, it also accepted that her opposition to transfusions was a manifestation of her religious beliefs. 'In doing so, the Court seems to have accepted that art 9(1) may prima facie protect a refusal by Jehovah's Witnesses to consent to blood transfusions.'[130]

[10.86] Article 12 provides the 'right to found a family' subject to 'national laws governing the exercise of this right'. This may be of relevance in the non-consensual sterilisation cases where patients incapable of giving consent are sterilised in their best interests. These cases are considered below. In relation to Convention rights, the right to found a family is not an absolute one, as is clear from the express limitation in favour of national laws. However, it has been held that such restrictions as may be imposed by national authorities must not be such as to restrict the right in such a way or to such an extent 'that the very essence of the right is impaired.'[131] In most non-consensual sterilisation situations where the patient is incompetent to give or refuse consent, it would be incumbent on the hospital, in the UK at least, to seek court approval of the procedure. This may be perceived by the European Court as sufficient to provide protection of the rights of the individual patient, given the limitations on the right as previously noted.

---

[125] Harris, O'Boyle and Warbrick, *Law of the European Convention on Human Rights* (1995) at 337–8.

[126] *Pretty v the UK* [2002] 35 EHRR 1.

[127] *Pretty v the UK* [2002] 35 EHRR 1, para 63.

[128] *Tysiac v Poland* [2007] 45 EHRR 42, para 107.

[129] *Hoffmann v Austria* [1993] Series A, No 255.

[130] Wicks, 'The Right to Refuse Medical Treatment Under the European Convention on Human Rights' (2001) 9 Med L Rev 17–40 at 31.

[131] *Rees v UK* [1986] Series A, No 106, para 50.

[10.87] The ECHR may therefore be seen as protecting the ability to choose or refuse medical treatment in a number of ways discussed above. 'The key arts are 3 and 8 which, taken together, will ensure that treatment is consensual or, if the patient is genuinely incapable of consent, therapeutically necessary.' The test of capacity is crucial to any protection provided. Thus, there is a danger that decisions which are deemed unreasonable, irrational, or unorthodox, may be overridden on the basis of incapacity, and will not be protected by the Convention. However, as society becomes more rights-conscious and more concerned about individual autonomy, the courts may find more incompatibility between such interests and the traditional perception of the duties of the medical profession.

English case law on refusal of treatment

[10.88] The classic statement on the right to refuse treatment is found in the judgment of Lord Donaldson MR in *Re T (Adult: Refusal of Medical Treatment)*:

> An adult patient who, like Ms T suffers from no mental incapacity has an absolute right to choose whether to consent to medical treatment, to refuse it or to choose one rather than another of the treatments being offered. This right exists notwithstanding that the reasons for making the choice are rational, irrational, unknown or even non-existent.[132]

Butler-Sloss LJ agreed, stating that 'a man or woman of full age and sound understanding may choose to reject medical advice and medical or surgical treatment either partially or in its entirety. A decision to refuse medical treatment by a patient capable of making the decision does not have to be sensible, rational or well-considered.' Lord Goff further strengthened this in *Airedale NHS Trust v Bland*:

> It is established that the principle of self-determination requires that respect must be given to the wishes of the patient, so that if an adult patient of sound mind refuses, however unreasonably, to consent to treatment or care by which his life would or might be prolonged, the doctors responsible for his care must give effect to his wishes, even though they do not consider it to be in his best interests to do so.[133]

[10.89] These statements provide very powerful affirmation of the right to self-determination even where the exercise of such right is contrary to medical and non-medical recommendations. In practice there may well be circumstances where patients are very stressed and frightened at the prospect of medical intervention and they may make decisions which they subsequently regret. It has been argued that in such cases the patient's refusal should be assigned less weight even if the person has full capacity. 'By permitting a patient to die avoidably, when it is virtually certain that were he saved against his present protest he would be grateful, one is granting that person his short-term 'autonomous' wish while depriving him of his long-term autonomy.'[134] Nonetheless the courts have clearly stated that an adult patient may decide for himself whether to accept or refuse medical advice.

[10.90] However, although the courts have given strong statements in relation to the respect to be afforded to an autonomous refusal, when it comes to applying this principle

---

[132] *Re T (an adult: refusal of treatment)* [1992] 4 All ER 649, [1993] Fam 95 at 102.
[133] *Airedale NHS Trust v Bland* [1993] 1 All ER 821 at 864.
[134] Glick, 'The morality of coercion' (2000) 26 Journal of Medical Ethics 393–5.

in hard cases, the courts have sometimes used the determination of capacity as a way of avoiding the implementation of this principle.

> While recognising a right to refuse treatment, courts have been careful as regards how this right has been applied in practice...[T]he most common reasons that the right has been held not to apply is because of the patient's lack of capacity. This capacity has acted as a safety-valve, allowing courts to endorse the right to refuse treatment while, at the same time, avoid applying it in practice.[135]

Refusals during pregnancy

[10.91] A particularly difficult set of issues arises in cases involving refusals of treatment by pregnant women as these oblige the courts to balance the right to autonomy of the woman with the right to life of the foetus. Where the courts have ordered women to undergo caesarean sections, it is suggested that this is not only a violation of their right to autonomy but also might result in a negative clinical outcome:

> In addition to being an unlawful infringement of the competent adult patient's right to refuse unwanted medical treatment, forcing women to have caesarean sections against their will is ultimately likely to result in poorer outcomes for foetuses in general, since women who object to surgical delivery might be deterred from seeking any medical attention during pregnancy and labour.[136]

[10.92] In some of the earlier cases on this point the courts took the view that the woman lacked capacity and therefore treatment was authorised in her best interests. In *Re T (an adult: refusal of treatment)*[137] T was a 34-week pregnant woman who was involved in a car accident and subsequently refused blood transfusions after speaking with her mother. Although she had been brought up by her mother who was a Jehovah's Witness, she was not practising this religion at the time of her hospitalisation and had a partner who was not of the same faith. Her condition worsened and a caesarean section was recommended to deliver the baby. While she was in intensive care following the section, it was considered medically advisable to administer a blood transfusion, but the hospital felt constrained by T's prior refusal. T's father and her partner sought a declaration that the transfusion would be lawful despite T's refusal of consent.

[10.93] The order authorising transfusion was granted and upheld by the Court of Appeal which was of the opinion that T's own adherence to the Jehovah's Witness faith was no longer as strong as when she had resided with her mother. In addition, she had not been fully informed by the medical team regarding the consequences of her refusal. Given her pregnancy, medication, after-effects of the accident, and severe pneumonia, the Court was prepared to hold that she lacked capacity at the time of her refusal. The Court was of the view that T had also been unduly influenced by her mother, as her refusals had come after time spent alone with her mother on each occasion and her mother declined to give evidence of the content of the conversations. As the critical

---

[135] Donnelly, *Healthcare Decision-making and the Law, Autonomy, Capacity and the Limits of Liberalism,* (Cambridge University Press, 2010) at 57.

[136] Jackson, *Medical Law: Text, cases and materials* (2nd edn) p 222.

[137] *Re T (an adult: refusal of treatment)* [1992] 4 All ER 649, [1993] Fam 95.

medical situation in which she later found herself constituted an emergency, treatment could take place without her consent in her best interests. The significance of the case is in the unanimous recognition by the Court of Appeal of the right to refuse treatment, which was described by Lord Donaldson MR as 'absolute'. However, he also said that the only possible qualification was where the refusal might lead to the death of a viable foetus, which was not at issue in this case, and which would involve the court in a 'novel problem of considerable legal and ethical complexity.'

[10.94] In the same year as *Re T,* another case arose in which the difficulties mentioned by Lord Donaldson had to be decided by the court. In *Re S (Adult: refusal of medical treatment)*[138] a 30-year-old woman was admitted to hospital in spontaneous labour. The woman and her husband refused to consent to a caesarean section on religious grounds. The hospital applied to court for an order compelling the patient to undergo the procedure against her wishes. Sir Stephen Brown did not discuss the issue of the woman's competency, and dealt with the matter on the basis that the life of the foetus took precedence to the right to self-determination of the mother.[139]

[10.95] Despite heavy criticism,[140] this case seems to have been followed in *Rochdale Healthcare (NHS) Trust v C*[141] where a pregnant woman refused a caesarean section because of back pain and pain around the scar she experienced following a previous caesarean section. The patient was deemed incompetent to make a treatment decision, due in part to the fact that 'she was in the throes of labour with all that is involved in terms of pain and emotional stress.' The Court ordered the procedure 'in the best interests of the patient'. The foetus seems to have been regarded by the judge as the 'patient' in this case, not the pregnant woman.[142] The difficulty with this approach is that since almost any labour involves stress and pain, this could mean that every woman in labour can be found incompetent.[143] 'Rather than subscribing to the established law on this issue, the courts have interpreted the law in such a way as to create an imbalance between the interests of the foetus and the woman. In doing so, pregnant women have become a new category of incompetent adults.'[144]

---

[138] *Re S (Adult: refusal of medical treatment)* [1992] 4 All ER 671.

[139] See Thomson, 'After *Re S*' (1994) 2 Med L Rev 127–148; Stern, 'Court-Ordered Caesarean Sections: In Whose Interests?' (1993) 56 Med L Rev 238–243.

[140] Harrington argues that Stephen Brown favoured the medically and socially orthodox way of proceeding to the point where he was prepared to allow the forced subjection of the patient to invasive treatment. 'The repugnance of *Re S* to many commentators is perhaps due to the fact that it represents an open endorsement of medically sanctioned standards of behaviour which also occurs in other, less controversial cases, though behind a veil of incompetence.' Harrington, 'Privileging the Medical Norm: Liberalism, Self-Determination and Refusal of Treatment.' (1996) Legal Studies, Vol 16 No 3 348–367 at 360.

[141] *Rochdale Healthcare (NHS) Trust v C* [1997] 1 FCR 274.

[142] Fovargue and Miola, 'Policing Pregnancy: Implications of the *Attorney General's Reference (No 3 of 1994)*' (1998) 6 Med L Rev 265–296 at 282.

[143] Herring, *Medical Law and* Ethics (4th edn, Oxford University Press, Oxford 2012) 345.

[144] Fovargue and Miola, 'Policing Pregnancy: Implications of the *Attorney General's Reference (No 3 of 1994)*' (1998) 6 Med L Rev 265–296 at 281.

[10.96] The opportunity arose for the Court to again consider the balance struck in this 'maternal-foetal conflict' in the landmark case of *Re MB (adult: medical treatment).*[145] In this case a 23 year old pregnant woman, MB, was admitted to hospital at 40 weeks pregnant and found to be in immediate need of a caesarean section, to which she consented. However, when she became aware of the necessity of the administration of an anaesthetic, she refused consent for the procedure to be performed. A consultant psychiatrist met MB and formed the view that she was suffering from an 'abnormal mental condition' of needle phobia which meant that 'at the actual point she was not capable of making a decision at all, in the sense of being able to hold information in the balance and make a choice.'[146] Anaesthesia by mask was suggested, to which MB initially agreed but subsequently withdrew her consent. The hospital applied for a declaration that it would be lawful to perform the procedure in the absence of consent. The High Court granted the declaration on grounds that MB was overcome by her needle phobia and was incapable of considering the matter lucidly.

[10.97] On appeal, Butler-Sloss LJ for the Court, held that a competent adult may 'for religious reasons, other reasons, for rational or irrational reasons, or for no reason at all, choose not to have medical intervention even though the consequence may be the death or serious handicap of the child she bears, or her own death.' However, there was a distinction between fear of an operation that may be a rational reason for refusing medical treatment, and therefore not impugning the person's competence, and fear that paralyses the will and therefore voids the patient's competence.[147] The Court held that MB was suffering from an 'impairment of her mental functioning which disabled her' rendering her 'temporarily incompetent' due to panic caused by her phobia of needles. It held that the anaesthetic could be administered if this was in the patient's best interests, which included but was not limited to her medical interests, but also took into account relevant information about her circumstances and background.

[10.98] This position might be taken to imply that 'a competent adult may refuse to consent to a caesarean section *provided* that she does not do so because of any form of phobia, rather it is better for her to refuse to give a reason for her lack of consent, and

---

[145] *Re MB (adult: medical treatment)* [1997] 2 FLR 426, [1997] 8 Med L Rev 217. See discussion by Fox and Moreton '*Re MB (adult: medical treatment)* [1997] and *St George's Healthcare NHS Trust v S* [1998]: The dilemma of the 'court-ordered' caesarean' in Herring and Wall, *Landmark cases in medical law* (Hart Publishing, 2015) 145–174.

[146] *Re MB (adult: medical treatment)* [1997] 2 FLR 426, [1997] 8 Med L Rev 217 at 221.

[147] Michalowski argues that the rationality of the patient's fear should be of no more significance than the rationality of other reasons of the patient to refuse treatment. 'While it is perfectly true that fear can exclude capacity if it overrides the patient's ability to understand and weigh treatment information, the Court should not betray its own principles, as irrational fear does not necessarily negate the patient's ability to consent to medical treatment. The only criterion should therefore be whether or not the patient's fear resulted in an inability to understand, retain, believe and weigh the treatment information presented, and not whether or not the patient's fear was rational or irrational.' Michalowski, 'Court-Order Caesarean Sections – The End of a Trend?' (1999) 62 *Modern Lr* 115 at 118. See also Morris, 'Once Upon a Time in a Hospital...The Cautionary Tale of *St. George's Health Care NHS Trust v S*' (1999) 7 Feminist Legal Studies 75–84.

then there will be no attempt to deem her incapable to provide such consent.'[148] The case is important because it gives strong statements regarding the protection of the right of self-determination, but when it comes to applying those principles, the Court appears to have spent little time on the application of those principles to the case in hand.

[10.99] A further case one year later seems to have put an end to the practice of using temporary incapacity in relation to pregnant women. *St George's Healthcare NHS Trust, R v Collins and others, ex parte S*[149] concerned S, a 28-year-old woman with a long-standing aversion to medical intervention. She consulted a doctor when she was 36-weeks pregnant and was diagnosed as having severe pre-eclampsia. She was told that this condition posed a serious risk to her life and the life of the foetus. S declined the recommended treatment, which included an early induced delivery, believing that nature should take its course. She was interviewed by a social worker and two doctors but continued to refuse treatment. S was then admitted against her will to hospital under the Mental Health Act 1983, and subsequently transferred to another. Despite consulting solicitors and repeating her refusal orally and in writing, the hospital applied *ex parte* for a declaration that treatment, including caesarean section, was lawful. The judge was under the mistaken impression that S had been in labour already for some time, and authorised the procedure. S was delivered of a daughter and two days later her detention was terminated and she discharged herself. She later sought to challenge her admission, detention and treatment, as well as appealing the granting of the declaration authorising the operation.

[10.100] The Court of Appeal held that the caesarean section and accompanying medical procedures performed on S amounted to a trespass, and that in the extraordinary circumstances of the case the court declaration provided no defence to a claim for damages against the hospital. The Court held that the detention of the patient under the Mental Health Act was unlawful, as the mental disorder must be such as to warrant detention for assessment, and treatment must be integral to the mental disorder. S had only been detained in order to treat her pregnancy, (had she not been pregnant, her mental condition would not have warranted any medical interest) and was discharged shortly after the baby had been delivered.

[10.101] The Court went to great lengths to affirm the right of autonomy, even where the patient's own life is at stake. It resolved the conflict as between the exercise of individual autonomy and the paternalism of the medical profession very firmly in favour of the individual. In relation to the conflict between the right of the competent patient to refuse medical treatment and the right to life of the unborn child, the Court upheld previous decisions[150] in stating that the unborn child only acquires legal personality at birth, although at 36 weeks it is certainly 'not nothing'. The Court refrained from commenting further on the status of the foetus at this stage, as the conflict, as the Court saw it, was not between the mother and child, but between the woman and the paternalism of the

---

[148] Fovargue and Miola, 'Policing Pregnancy: Implications of the *Attorney General's Reference (No 3 of 1994)*' (1998) 6 Med L Rev 265–296 at 283, emphasis in original.

[149] *St George's Healthcare NHS Trust, R v Collins and others, ex parte S* [1998] 2 FLR 728.

[150] *Paton v British Pregnancy Advisory Service Trustees* [1979] QB 276; *Re F (in utero)* [1988] Fam. 122; *Attorney-General's reference (No 3 of 1994)* [1997] 3 WLR 421; *Re MB (medical treatment)* [1997] 2 FLR 426.

medical profession. While the unborn child was recognised as having interests, as opposed to rights, these must necessarily be subordinated to the woman's absolute right to self-determination.

> In our judgment while pregnancy increases the personal responsibilities of a woman it does not diminish her entitlement to decide whether or not to undergo medical treatment. Although human, and protected by the law in a number of ways...an unborn child is not a separate person from its mother. Its need for medical assistance does not prevail over her rights. She is entitled not to be forced to submit to an invasion of her body against her will, whether her own life or that of her unborn child depends on it. Her right is not reduced or diminished merely because her decision to exercise it may appear morally repugnant.[151]

[10.102] This case is important as it clearly states the law to be firmly opposed to non-consensual medical interventions in pregnancy, irrespective of the rationale for the woman's decision and irrespective of the consequences for the foetus.[152] It is also significant in its condemnation of the use of mental health legislation in circumstances where a woman is exhibiting a thinking process that is unusual or even bizarre and irrational. In doing so it also 'put paid to any notion that women's mental condition in advanced pregnancy is synonymous with incapacity'.[153] The court stressed that a person detained under mental health legislation could only be compulsorily treated for conditions connected with mental disorder and pregnancy was not such a condition.

[10.103] It is worth noting that despite the avowed promotion in this case of the right to autonomy of pregnant women who refuse treatment, the judgment was made in circumstances where the baby had already been delivered and was therefore not in jeopardy. Judges to whom emergency applications are made are faced with the enormity of making a decision within a very short time frame which could result in the death of the foetus. 'Clearly then it would be a brave first instance judge who, confronted with an emergency situation, would choose to uphold the woman's right to refuse treatment in the face of medical evidence that a possible outcome was death.'[154]

Refusals in other circumstances

[10.104] Where there is doubt about the capacity of the patient to understand the consequences of their refusal, or where a change in circumstances challenges the continued validity of an advance refusal, the courts will generally resolve the doubt in favour of the preservation of life. In *HE v A Hospital NHS Trust*[155] the father of AE, a 24-year-old woman who was a Jehovah's Witness, applied for a declaration that a blood

---

[151] *St George's Healthcare NHS Trust, R v Collins and others, ex parte S* [1998] 2 FLR 728 at 746 per Judge LJ.

[152] For further discussion of the woman's moral duty to the foetus, see Scott, 'The Pregnant Woman and the Good Samaritan: Can a Woman Have a Duty to Undergo a Caesarean Section?' (2000) Oxford J of Legal Studies Vol 20, No 3, 407–436.

[153] Bailey-Harris, 'Patient autonomy: a turn in the tide?' in Freeman and Lewis (eds) *Law and Medicine: Current Legal Issues* Vol 3 (2000) 127.

[154] Fox and Moreton '*Re MB (adult: medical treatment)* [1997] and *St George's Healthcare NHS Trust v S* [1998]: The dilemma of the 'court-ordered' caesarean' in Herring and Wall, *Landmark Cases in Medical Law* (Hart Publishing, 2015) 145–174 at 157.

[155] *HE v A Hospital NHS Trust* [2003] EWHC 1017 (Fam.).

transfusion should be administered to her despite her prior refusal. AE had recently become engaged to a Turkish man and it had been a condition of her marriage that she would reject her Jehovah's Witness faith and become a Muslim. She had not attended any religious services in the two months prior to her illness. Munby J said that in cases of doubt, there must be clear and convincing evidence of the continued validity of the advance refusal. He also said that such a refusal would not be valid in the event of a material change in circumstances, as had occurred here. This case leaves genuine doubts about what AE would have wished to happen due to the social context in which AE lived, her desire to please her fiancé and the fact that she had not destroyed the treatment refusal form.[156]

[10.105] A case in which it might have appeared at first glance that the Court might have decided that the patient lacked capacity due to his psychiatric condition and which demonstrates the dangers of a status approach to capacity is *Re C (adult: refusal of medical treatment)*[157] in which a 68-year-old man suffering from paranoid schizophrenia developed gangrene in his foot. He was told that there was a significant chance that he would die unless the leg was amputated. C refused to consent to the operation, stating that he would prefer to die with two feet than live with one. He sought an injunction preventing the hospital from carrying out such a procedure without his consent in the future. The medical evidence was, perhaps unusually, divided on the question of C's capacity. It was held that the test of capacity is that the patient understands or at least is capable of understanding the nature and effects of the proposed treatment in broad terms, to believe the information concerning this, and to weigh the information so as to make a choice. Thorpe J held:

> Applying that test to my findings on the evidence, I am completely satisfied that the presumption that C has the right to self-determination has not been displaced. Although his general capacity is impaired by schizophrenia, it has not been established that he does not sufficiently understand the nature, purpose and effects of the treatment he refuses. Indeed, I am satisfied that he has understood and retained the relevant treatment information, that in his own way he believes it, and that in the same fashion he has arrived at a clear choice.[158]

[10.106] This case is important in confirming the courts' commitment to patient autonomy through the adherence to the presumption of capacity and the requirement of evidence of its displacement where appropriate. In *Re C*, Thorpe J was also clear in his judgment that C was not to be regarded as lacking capacity on the basis of his diagnosis of schizophrenia or by virtue of the fact that he lacked capacity in other areas of his life. In granting the injunction against the hospital in relation to any future attempts to carry out this procedure without his consent, the court was also giving recognition to advance refusals of treatment which are now enshrined in the English Mental Capacity Act 2005. However, the lack of clarity in the judgment has also been questioned as it does not set out what the patient must understand in order to make a decision. 'The decision talks of the 'nature, purpose and effects' of the treatment. This is potentially very broad and can

---

[156] Donnelly, *Healthcare Decision-making and the Law, Autonomy, Capacity and the Limits of Liberalism,* (Cambridge University Press, 2010) at 65.

[157] *Re C (adult: refusal of medical treatment)* [1994] 1 All ER 819.

[158] It is worth noting that, despite his refusal of the amputation, C survived without any deterioration in his health as a less invasive procedure was carried out successfully.

encompass elements ranging from the general aim of the procedure to the risks and the consequences of refusal and beyond.' [159]

[10.107] In cases where it is clear from the evidence before the court that the patient has full capacity to make the decision in question, the English courts have upheld the importance of respect for the autonomy of the patient and stated that the right to refuse treatment is absolute. For example, in *Re AK*[160] a 19 year-old with motor neurone disease, which is a progressive, incurable and fatal condition, had lost all limb movements, speech and the ability to swallow. He was unable to initiate communication or show any emotion and his only means of communication was a tiny movement of one eye which was soon to be lost. When this happened he would be 'locked-in' in the sense that he would hear, see and feel but have no means of communication whatsoever. Motor neurone disease does not affect intellectual capacity and therefore AK had full decision-making capacity as a competent adult. He informed his medical team that he wished his ventilator to be switched off in the event that he lost the ability to communicate.

[10.108] The health authority applied for a declaration that it would be lawful to act on AK's wishes to discontinue treatment two weeks after he lost all ability to communicate. The Court held in granting the declaration that doctors are not entitled to treat a person who, being of sound mind and full capacity, has let it be known that such treatment is against his wishes. The case thus reinforces the principle that a competent adult has an unassailable right to refuse all treatment at common law, even if it will lead to death. Hughes J said that in situations such as this, where communication is very difficult, doctors must exercise great caution, as there is a danger that the patient's wishes might not be properly understood and that external factors such as pain, stress or medication may affect his ability to exercise rational judgment. He said, however, that in this case AK was not influenced by external factors, was fully aware of his situation and demonstrated immense courage and maturity in reaching his decision.

[10.109] A similarly strong example of judicial support for the right to refuse treatment where there was no evidence of incapacity on the part of the patient is *Re B (Adult: Refusal of medical treatment).*[161] In this case a 43-year-old paralysed woman was held entitled to have artificial ventilation removed notwithstanding that this would result in her death. She was found to be a well-informed woman with a high degree of mental competence. Dame Butler-Sloss P held that the physically disabled patient enjoys the same right to personal autonomy as the able-bodied patient and that where capacity is not an issue, the wishes of the patient have to be respected by doctors irrespective of outcome; clinical views as to the patient's best interests are therefore irrelevant. She was also entitled to damages for the prior interference with her right to refuse the treatment.[162]

---

[159] Laurie, Harmon and Porter, *Law and Medical Ethics* (10th edn, 2016) at 4.40
[160] *Re AK* [2001] 1 FLR 129.
[161] *Re B (Adult: Refusal of medical treatment)* [2002] 2 All ER 449.
[162] She sought and was awarded nominal damages only.

The right to refuse treatment in Ireland

[10.110] Even prior to the recent enactment of the Assisted Decision-Making (Capacity) Act 2015 it was beyond doubt that an adult with capacity has the right to refuse medical treatment in Ireland. The Irish courts have expressly stated this principle in a number of cases such as *In Re a Ward of Court*,[163] which dealt with the cessation of artificial nutrition and hydration of a woman in a near persistent vegetative state. In this case the Supreme Court recognised that competent adults had the right to refuse medical treatment, even though such refusal may lead to death. Loss of capacity does not result in the loss of the personal rights protected by the Constitution, including 'the right to life, the right to bodily integrity, the right to privacy, including self-determination, and the right to refuse medical care or treatment.' O'Flaherty J agreed that 'there is an absolute right in a competent person to refuse medical treatment even if it leads to death.'

[10.111] Denham J pointed out that medical treatment may be refused for a variety of reasons, some of which may not be regarded as 'good' or rational decisions, but they must be respected nonetheless. She also said that there were a few rare exceptions to the principle that treatment may not be given to a competent adult without his consent, such as in relation to contagious disease control. In relation to the right to life, Denham J stated that while respect for the right to life is absolute, the right to life itself is not absolute, as the State is required to defend and vindicate life 'as far as practicable'. She said that the State's respect for the life of the individual encompasses the right of the individual to refuse a blood transfusion for religious reasons. In relation to the right to privacy under art 40.3.1°, the Supreme Court held that this right includes a right to refuse medical treatment even where this would lead to death. The case is crucially important due to the court's focus on the right to self-determination despite the consequences of the exercise of that right.

[10.112] The cases on refusal of treatment in Ireland to date have largely focused on the right of Jehovah's Witnesses to refuse blood transfusions. While it is generally accepted that an adult with capacity has the right to refuse treatment, difficulties have arisen in practice where such refusals are made for religious reasons or where the patient is a pregnant woman. In *JM v The Board of Management of St Vincent's Hospital*[164] an application was made by the husband of an African woman who was unconscious, that she should be given a blood transfusion despite the fact that she had refused this treatment while conscious. The woman had become a Jehovah's Witness on marriage and according to Finnegan P had refused treatment 'because of her cultural background and her desire to please her husband and not offend his sensibilities.' The judge felt therefore, in granting the application, that the woman was 'preoccupied with her husband and his religion as Jehovah's Witness rather than with whether to have the treatment and her own welfare.'[165] This is despite the fact that her husband told her that she should not feel obliged to refuse to consent to the transfusion.

---

[163] *In Re a Ward of Court* [1996] 2 IR 79.

[164] *JM v The Board of Management of St Vincent's Hospital* [2003] 1 IR 321.

[165] *JM v The Board of Management of St Vincent's Hospital* [2003] 1 IR 321 at 325.

[10.113] This case is not easy to reconcile with legal principle. The decision shows both the dangers of taking a social or relational approach to agency and the dangers of not doing so.[166] The woman had indicated her refusal of treatment in advance of loss of capacity and there was no suggestion that her husband had pressurised her into doing so. Therefore, it might be questioned as to what basis existed to subject her autonomous decision to the wishes of her husband. On the other hand, there was also clearly a cultural element to this case in which the woman's primary motivation appeared to be to please her husband and therefore she would have agreed with his wish for her to have the transfusion.

[10.114] In a more considered judgment in *Fitzpatrick and Another v K and Another*[167] the High Court was again asked to consider the right of an adult to refuse a blood transfusion. The facts of this case were that K, a 23-year-old African woman from the Congo, gave birth to a baby in an Irish hospital in 2006. Shortly thereafter she suffered a massive post-partum haemorrhage resulting in cardiovascular collapse. As blood was being prepared for immediate transfusion, the medical team was informed that K would not accept blood for religious reasons. The medical team was concerned that K would die without a blood transfusion and called the Master of the hospital (the most senior obstetrician in the maternity hospital with responsibility for clinical governance). Following discussions with K, during which she repeated her refusal of blood, the Master had doubts regarding her capacity to make such a decision and decided to apply to the High Court for an emergency order giving the hospital authority to transfuse K.

[10.115] The judge made the order authorising the hospital to administer blood to K, including all appropriate steps by way of restraint. The Master informed K of the court order and she was transfused following the administration of a sedative. She subsequently made a full recovery. She later claimed that the court order should not have been given, that the transfusion was unlawful and therefore constituted an assault and trespass to her person, and that she was entitled to refuse all or any medical treatment by virtue of her Constitutional rights and under arts 8 and 9 of the ECHR. In the High Court, Laffoy J was of the view that it could not be argued that a competent adult is not free to decline medical treatment and referred to the *Ward of Court* case cited above in support of this conclusion. Thus the question that arose on the facts of this case was whether K had capacity to refuse the blood transfusion. She decided that on the facts of this case K did not have such capacity and therefore the hospital had lawfully administered the transfusion.

[10.116] Although the judgment is strongly supportive of the right to refuse treatment in principle, the issue was ultimately decided on capacity grounds. It is open to speculation what the court's decision might have been if K had not been determined to lack capacity at the relevant time. The circumstances in which an emergency application might be made in such a situation are 'replete with a sense of emergency and panic'[168] with judges

---

[166] Donnelly, *Healthcare Decision-making and the Law, Autonomy, Capacity and the Limits of Liberalism,* (Cambridge University Press, 2010) at 62.

[167] *Fitzpatrick and Another v K and Another* [2008] IEHC 104. See also Chapter 9 para [9.30] et seq.

[168] Gies, 'Contesting the rule of emotions? The press and enforced caesareans' (2000) 9 Social and Legal Studies 515 at 523

undoubtedly also cognisant of negative public reactions if the patient were allowed to die. It has been argued that these pressures facilitate judicial manipulation of the concept of capacity to enable the courts to conclude that the patient lacks the capacity to refuse medically sanctioned intervention.[169]

Refusal of caesarean sections in Ireland

[10.117] In cases where woman refuse medical intervention during pregnancy, it has been suggested that 'cultural and medical norms combine to cast the actions of the pregnant woman who refuses recommended medical treatment as aberrational and beyond comprehension, leaving it open to judges to find her incompetent to decide, thereby legitimising violation of her bodily integrity.'[170] In the Irish context the position is complicated further by the provisions of the Constitution which oblige the State to protect the right to life of the unborn, as well as granting rights to privacy and bodily integrity. There have not been any reported Irish cases in relation to the refusal of caesarean sections to date.[171]

[10.118] The right to bodily integrity under the unenumerated rights in art 40.3.1° might appear to be the most obvious place within which to locate a right of a pregnant woman to refuse to submit to a caesarean section. Article 40.3.1° provides that 'the State guarantees in its laws to respect, and, as far as practicable, by its laws to defend and vindicate the personal rights of the citizen.' In *Ryan v Attorney General*[172] Kenny J in the High Court said that this right means that 'no mutilation of the body or any of its members may be carried out on any citizen under the authority of the law except for the good of the whole body...' The Supreme Court agreed that a right to bodily integrity existed, but did not comment further on the definition given by Kenny J.

[10.119] In relation to the maternal-foetal conflict inherent in the refusal of a caesarean section, the right to life of the unborn is of crucial importance. Article 40.3.3° of the Constitution states: 'The State acknowledges the right to life of the unborn and, with due regard for the equal right to life of the mother, guarantees in its laws to respect, and as far as practicable, by its laws to defend and vindicate that right.' This 'very unique private right' is also 'a human right which there is a public interest in preserving.'[173] However:

> In examining the manner in which Article 40.3.3° might apply in a case of caesarean
> section refusal, the lack of clarity around Article 40.3.3° makes it difficult to assess its

---

[169] Fox and Moreton '*Re MB (adult: medical treatment)* [1997] and *St George's Healthcare NHS Trust v S* [1998]: The dilemma of the 'court-ordered' caesarean' in Herring and Wall, *Landmark Cases in Medical Law* (Hart Publishing, 2015) 145–174 at 158.

[170] Fox and Moreton '*Re MB (adult: medical treatment)* [1997] and *St George's Healthcare NHS Trust v S* [1998]: The dilemma of the 'court-ordered' caesarean' in Herring and Wall, *Landmark Cases in Medical Law* (Hart Publishing, 2015) 145–174 at 159.

[171] See useful discussion by Wade, 'Refusal of Emergency Caesarean Section in Ireland: A Relational Approach' Med Law Rev (Winter 2014) 22 (1): 1–25. Wade refers to media reports of two unreported cases involving refusals of treatment by pregnant women but in neither case was a judgment necessary as the women acceded to the hospitals' application.

[172] *Ryan v Attorney General* [1965] IR 294.

[173] *Society for the Protection of Unborn Children v Coogan* (1989) IR 734 per Walsh J.

potential effect. While it was held in *X* that an abortion is permissible in Ireland, if there is a substantial risk to a woman's life, there is no guidance regarding the distinction between life and health in this context. It is clear that there must be a risk to a woman's life, in order to justify the subordination of the right to life of the unborn. However, it is unknown what level of risk to a woman's life is required. The uncertainty around the meaning of the right to life of the woman also makes it difficult to ascertain what the outcome might be in a case where a woman's quality or longevity of life might be affected as a result of a caesarean section.[174]

[10.120] In *Attorney General v X*[175] the Court considered for the first time a conflict between the rights of the mother and the foetus and certainly seems to indicate 'a less absolutist approach to art 40.3.3°'s guarantee of unborn life than the prior Supreme Court decisions.'[176] The Court held that a termination of pregnancy was permissible under the Constitution if it is established as a matter of probability that there is a real and substantial risk to the life, as distinct from the health, of the mother and that that risk can only be avoided by the termination of her pregnancy. However, Wade is of the view that the meaning and scope of the right to life of the unborn in this case is uncertain and the guidance in *X* is difficult to apply to a caesarean section refusal which is distinct from an abortion, the result of which is the death of a foetus. 'A caesarean section refusal, on the other hand, may carry a *risk* of death to the foetus. In this regard, it is unclear what level of risk to the life of the foetus must be reached in order for the State to intervene to protect its life.'[177] Another issue here is whether the right to life means a right to be born alive or whether it entails a right to be born in the healthiest state possible. This would be relevant if a refusal to consent to caesarean section were to lead to severe disability of the foetus, which could have been averted by the intervention.

[10.121] The importance of the decision here is in relation to the question of whether or not all Constitutional rights are equal, or whether there is a hierarchy of rights in cases where it is impossible to harmonise interacting rights. Finlay CJ was of the view that although the Court's first objective should always be to interpret the Constitution harmoniously, where this is not possible there may be 'a necessity to apply a priority of rights.' He said that where there was a stark conflict between the right to travel and the right to life, 'the right to life would necessarily have to take precedence over the right to travel.' Egan J agreed on this point referring to *People v Shaw*[178] where Kenny J stated that there was a hierarchy of Constitutional rights and, when a conflict arises between them, that which ranks higher must prevail:

> This cannot be taken to mean that an immutable list of precedence of rights can be formulated. The right to life of one person (as in Shaw's case) was held to be superior to the right to liberty of another but, quite clearly, the right to life might not be the paramount right in every circumstance. If, for instance, it were necessary for a father to kill a man engaged in the rape of his daughter in order to prevent its continuance, I have no doubt but

---

[174] Wade, 'Refusal of Emergency Caesarean Section in Ireland: A Relational Approach' Med Law Rev (Winter 2014) 22 (1): 1–25.

[175] *Attorney General v X* [1992] 1 IR 1.

[176] Casey, *Constitutional Law in Ireland*, (3rd edn, Round Hall, 2000) at 400.

[177] Wade, 'Refusal of Emergency Caesarean Section in Ireland: A Relational Approach' Med Law Rev (Winter 2014) 22 (1): 1–25.

[178] *People v Shaw* [1982] IR 1.

that the right of the girl to bodily integrity would rank higher than the right to life of the rapist.

[10.122] Egan J went on to say that in cases where the right to travel was explicitly stated to be with the intent to have a termination of pregnancy, the right to life of the unborn must take precedence: 'In the face of a positive obligation to defend and vindicate such a right (the right to life of the unborn) it cannot reasonably be argued that a right to travel *simpliciter* can take precedence over such a right.' Given that Egan J considered that the termination of pregnancy in the circumstances of this case would not be unlawful, the young girl could not be prevented from exercising her right to travel. McCarthy J sought to find a harmonious interpretation of the various Constitutional rights, stating that 'the guarantee to the unborn was qualified by the requirement of due regard to the right to life of the mother and made less than absolute by recognising that the right could only be vindicated as far as practicable.' He went on to extract Walsh J's judgment in *SPUC v Grogan*,[179] where he asked whether the right to bodily integrity involves the right to control one's own body:

> When a woman becomes pregnant she acquires rights which cannot be taken from her, namely, the right to protect the life of her unborn child and the right to protect her own bodily integrity against any effort to compel her by law or by persuasion to submit herself to an abortion. Such rights also carry obligations the foremost of which is not to endanger or to submit to or bring about the destruction of that unborn life.

[10.123] However, McCarthy J (with whom O'Flaherty J agreed on this point) disagreed with the Chief Justice in relation to the curtailment of the right to travel, stating that as between the right to life of the unborn and the woman's right to travel, 'if it were a matter of a balancing exercise, the scales could only tilt in one direction, the right to life of the unborn, assuming no threat to the life of the mother. In my view, it is not a question of balancing the right to travel against the right to life; it is a question as to whether or not an individual has a right to travel – which she has. It cannot, in my view, be curtailed because of a particular intent.' In discussing the relationship between the rights of the mother and the unborn, Hederman J, who was the only dissenting judge, said:

> The State's duty to protect life also extends to the mother. The natural connection between the unborn child and the mother's life constitutes a special relationship. But one cannot consider the unborn life only as part of the maternal organism. The extinction of unborn life is not confined to the sphere of private life of the mother or family because the unborn life is an autonomous human being protected by the Constitution. Therefore the termination of pregnancy other than a natural one has a legal and social dimension and requires a special responsibility on the part of the State. There cannot be a freedom to extinguish life side by side with a guarantee of protection of that life because the termination of pregnancy always means the destruction of an unborn life. Therefore no recognition of a mother's right of self-determination can be given priority over the protection of the unborn life. The creation of a new life, involving as it does pregnancy, birth and raising the child, necessarily involves some restriction of a mother's freedom but the alternative is the destruction of the unborn life.

[10.124] The final two sentences of this extract from Hederman J's dissenting judgment, although made in the context of a termination of pregnancy as opposed to a refusal of a

---

[179] *SPUC v Grogan* [1989] IR 753 at p 767.

caesarean section with the death of the foetus as a probable consequence, are very firm in their refutation of the possibility that a woman's right to self-determination could outweigh the right to life of the unborn.[180] The case 'graphically illustrates one potential shortcoming of the hierarchy of rights approach, since such *a priori* ranking of such rights (eg life over liberty, liberty over free speech etc) focuses on philosophical abstractions which, if inflexibly employed, would tend to lead to the pre-determination of the outcome of particular litigation, at the expense of the flexibility which is desirable in any judicial appraisal of the relevant facts of each case and the competing merits of particular arguments.'[181] Thus, although the case law around art 40.3.3° has been concerned with the direct termination of the unborn life, as opposed to the death of the foetus as an indirect consequence of the woman's decision to refuse medical treatment, there are indications in some of the majority judgments in the Supreme Court that may be useful here. When read in conjunction with the robust statements in *Re a Ward of Court*[182] as to the importance of the right to self-determination, it is not clear whether the right to refuse treatment (in this case a caesarean section) would take precedence over the right to life of the unborn.

[10.125] In *South Western Area Health Board v K and Anor*[183] the court seemed to indicate that a woman's autonomy could be subordinated to the interests of her foetus. In this case, a woman refused to undergo treatment which would reduce the risk of transmitting HIV to her foetus. Finnegan P advised the woman that if she refused to give birth in a hospital, he would have to make 'much more serious orders affecting her bodily integrity'. It is not known whether such orders could mean forced confinement, twenty-four hour supervision, or the forced administration of medicine, as further details were not given.[184] However, whether a caesarean section, as opposed to forced supervision or administration of medicine, could be imposed to safeguard the right to life of the unborn is open to question.[185]

[10.126] In *HSE v F*[186] a pregnant woman refused to consent to the administration of drugs to her baby on birth, which was medically advised in order to reduce the risk of transmission of HIV. She also refused a caesarean section on the day that it was medically advised, but agreed to have it four days later. In the interim, she wanted the Court to determine whether it was in the child's best interests to be treated with the drugs. The HSE secured a High Court order allowing a doctor to administer the drugs to the baby. It was reported that 'Justice George Birmingham had earlier stated that she could not be forced to have a caesarean section and said no order could be made requiring her to undergo such a procedure'. However, as Wade notes, 'since no further

---

[180] This view has also been expressed in Sheikh and Cusack, 'Maternal Brain Death, Pregnancy and the Foetus: The Medico-Legal Implications' (2001) 7(2) MLJI 75 at 78.

[181] Kelly, *The Irish Constitution* (3rd edn, Butterworths, 1994) at cvii.

[182] *Re a Ward of Court* [1996] 2 IR 79.

[183] *South Western Health Board v K and Anor* (19 July 2002) HC, *ex tempore,* P Finnegan.

[184] Casey, 'Pregnant Woman and Unborn Child: Legal Adversaries' (2002) 8(2) MLJI 75, 75.

[185] Wade, 'Refusal of Emergency Caesarean Section in Ireland: A Relational Approach' Med Law Rev (Winter 2014) 22 (1): 1–25.

[186] *Health Service Executive v F* (20 November 2010) HC, *ex tempore,* Birmingham J, discussed in Wade, 'Refusal of Emergency Caesarean Section in Ireland: A Relational Approach' Med Law Rev (Winter 2014) 22 (1): 1–25.

details on the case are available, it is unknown how such a conclusion was reached and how the constitutional rights of the woman and the unborn are to be balanced in a case of caesarean section refusal.'[187]

[10.127] In 2013 media reports indicate that a hospital made an emergency application to carry out a caesarean section on a woman who refused the intervention, as she wanted the baby to be born naturally.[188] The Court was told that the baby could die or have severe brain damage and the mother would be at serious risk of haemorrhage if the procedure were not carried out. However, when the case was called, the woman reconsidered and consented to the procedure. It was reported that 'Judge Hedigan said that if it is not necessary, then it is appropriate that no court order is made'. Thus, the matter of caesarean section refusal was not addressed. Thus, 'in the two Irish cases involving caesarean section refusal, the women eventually agreed to the procedure.'[189]

[10.128] Although not related to the issue of refusal of caesarean sections, it is of interest to note the decision of the Supreme Court in *North Western Health Board v HW and CW*[190] dealing with parental authority to refuse consent for a test (known as 'the PKU test') to be carried out on their child in order to detect certain biochemical or metabolic disorders. The facts of the case are discussed in more detail in Chapter 11.[191] In holding that the Court should not intervene to order the screening test on the child, some of the judgments demonstrate again a firm commitment to the values of autonomy and privacy. Denham J repeated her position in *Re a Ward of Court*[192] where she stated that 'medical treatment may not be given to an adult person of full capacity without his or her consent.' Although there are some exceptions, these are rare and only applicable in the interests of public health, such as control of contagious disease. In any other case where medical treatment is given without consent, 'it may be trespass against the person in civil law, a battery in criminal law, and a breach of the individual's constitutional rights.' A refusal of consent by a competent adult may be made for various reasons, including non-medical reasons or reasons that others may not regard as rational, but the choice is theirs.

[10.129] Denham J saw it as important to consider the effect that the granting of an order obliging the parents to allow this test to be carried out on their child would have on other medical tests and vaccinations. 'If the responsibility for making this decision is transferred from the parents to the State then it would herald in a new era where there would be considerably more State intervention and decision making for children than has occurred to date.' She also said that in exceptional circumstances, such as where an emergency order was sought to treat a child in a way that had been refused by its parents, it may be 'within the range of responsible decisions' that may be taken by the parents.

---

[187] Wade, 'Refusal of Emergency Caesarean Section in Ireland: A Relational Approach' Med Law Rev (Winter 2014) 22 (1): 1–25.

[188] Reilly, 'Hospital Sought Court Order to Force Mother to have C-Section', *Irish Independent* (10 March 2013).

[189] Wade, 'Refusal of Emergency Caesarean Section in Ireland: A Relational Approach' Med Law Rev (Winter 2014) 22 (1): 1–25.

[190] *North Western Health Board v HW and CW* [2001] IESC 90.

[191] At para **[11.18]** et seq.

[192] *Re a Ward of Court* [1996] 2 IR 79.

'This may occur where a child is suffering a terminal illness and parents decide responsibly that he or she has suffered enough medical intervention and should receive only palliative care.' Denham J was concerned that by making the order sought by the Health Board in this case, the Court would effectively be making the test compulsory for children, without the analysis and policy framework that usually precedes legislation. 'Such an outcome would be at odds with the approach previously taken in Ireland that medical tests or procedures not be compulsory.' It would mean that parents have no right to refuse, which would have a far-reaching effect.

[10.130] Hardiman J examined the few statutory provisions in Ireland dealing with consent, such as the Health Act 1953, which states in s 4 that nothing in the Act imposes an obligation on any person 'to avail himself of any service provided under this Act or to submit himself or any person for whom he is responsible to health examination or treatment.' The history of this and other pieces of legislation demonstrate the legislature's commitment to the principle of voluntarism.[193] 'It appears to me that the principle of voluntarism in respect of medical treatment is plainly established in so far as public medical services are concerned. This extends to a patient himself or to a person making decisions as to medical treatment for another person for whom he is responsible.'

[10.131] Hardiman J also referred to exceptions relating to infectious or communicable disease. He, too, went on to consider medical treatment at common law where consent is the basis of any lawful medical treatment, and he endorsed the statement of Denham J referred to above regarding consent. He said that the order sought by the Health Board was to deny the child's parents their right not to consent to the test being carried out on their child, to compel them to consent to it and to compel them to present their child for a test which was contrary to their religious beliefs. If the Court compelled the parents to present their child for a public health service against their will, this would be contrary to, at the least, the spirit of s 4 of the 1953 Act. Such an order would have a 'chilling effect' on other persons sharing the views of these parents. However, he also said that this did not preclude the courts from acting to enforce the rights of a plaintiff, or infant, in a situation of emergency. He agreed with the trial judge when he said:

> If the State were entitled to intervene in every case where professional opinion differed from that of the parents, or where the State considered that the parents were wrong in their decision, we would be stepping rapidly towards the Brave New World in which the State always knows best. In my view that situation would be totally at variance with both the spirit and the word of the Constitution.

[10.132] Hardiman J took the view that if it were thought necessary to compel parents to submit their children for screening, this would be something for the legislature to consider, bearing in mind whether such compulsion was proportionate or desirable in the circumstances. 'Compulsory medical diagnosis or treatment in any form is…a topic regarded with some unease throughout the civilized world.' Whether such unease should be recognised and legitimate fears allayed, and whether the benefits of the medical test were sufficient to justify coercion, were matters to be addressed legislatively. It would

---

[193] He later said that a salient feature of this claim was that there was no legislation on this topic, other than that mentioned in his judgment, whose effect is to enshrine voluntarism and parental responsibility.

then be for the court to decide whether such legislation was consistent with the provisions of the Constitution.

[10.133] This case reinforces the strongly held views previously expressed in *Re a Ward of Court* in relation to self-determination and consent to treatment. It also clearly resists State interest or intervention in what the Court regarded as parental decision-making. Concerns were expressed regarding the nature of any state in which medical choices could be overridden by a paternalistic interpretation of 'best interests'. In that sense, it could be argued that the case provides further indications that if a competent adult woman were to refuse to submit herself to a caesarean section, particularly if such could be shown to present a serious risk to the woman's own life,[194] the court would not compel her to do so, notwithstanding the rights of the foetus. However, in the absence of clear authority to that effect, it is impossible to predict the outcome of such a case with any real degree of certainty.

Refusals of treatment under the Assisted Decision-Making (Capacity) Act 2015

[10.134] Section 83(2) of the Assisted Decision-Making (Capacity) Act 2015[195] states that an adult with capacity is entitled to refuse treatment for any reason (including a reason based on his or her religious beliefs) notwithstanding that the refusal appears to be unwise, not based on sound medical principles, or may result in his or her death. This provision explicitly therefore puts on a statutory footing the principles arising from existing case law in relation to contemporaneous refusals of treatment. It does not specify what the position should be if the person refusing treatment is a pregnant woman.

[10.135] The provision on refusals of treatment is contained in Part 8 of the Act which also deals with advance healthcare directives, considered in more detail later. It is noteworthy that this Part does deal with advance directives during pregnancy in s 85(6)(a) which provides that where a person making an advance directive is pregnant and her directive does not specifically state whether or not she intended her refusal of treatment to apply if she were pregnant, and the healthcare professionals involved in her treatment consider that her refusal would have a deleterious effect on the unborn, there is a presumption in favour of providing or continuing the relevant treatment. Section 85(6)(b) provides that where the woman has specified that her refusal should apply even if she were pregnant and the healthcare professionals involved in her treatment consider that her refusal would have a deleterious effect on the unborn, an application should be made to the High Court to determine whether or not the treatment should be provided.

---

[194] A caesarean section is major surgery, and, as with other surgical procedures, there are risks involved. The estimated risk of a woman dying after a caesarean birth is less than one in 2,500 (the risk of death after a vaginal birth is less than one in 10,000). Other risks for the mother include the following: infection, increased blood loss, decreased bowel function, respiratory complications, longer hospital stay and recovery time, reactions to anaesthesia and risk of additional surgeries.

[195] The Act has not been commenced at the time of writing.

[10.136] The Act provides that the High Court must consider the potential impact of the refusal on the unborn, the invasiveness and duration of the treatment and the risk of harm to the woman if the treatment were to be provided. Therefore it might be the case that if the refusal by a pregnant woman is contemporaneous rather than contained in an advance directive, the spirit of s 85(6)(b) would be considered to be an appropriate mechanism by which to deal with the maternal-foetal conflict issue discussed above. This would mean that a High Court order should be sought in relation to whether the treatment should be provided and the considerations listed above would be taken into account by the court.

ADVANCE DIRECTIVES

[10.137] In some circumstances people may wish to make a refusal of treatment in advance of losing capacity.[196] These statements of wishes are referred to as 'advance directives', which may be oral or written statements. The word 'directive' is often criticised by medical practitioners and others as it implies that the patient is requiring the doctor to treat the patient in a particular way, whereas the ideal situation is that patients and doctors are regarded as partners in discussing the patient's situation and values with a view to coming to an agreement on end-of-life care that both patient and doctor are comfortable with. For those who hold that view, the use of terms such as 'anticipatory decisions' or 'advance healthcare plans' is preferable. However, the traditional terminology in legal and ethical discourse still refers to advance healthcare directives and, as will be discussed later, this is the term used in the Assisted Decision-Making (Capacity) Act 2015 which gives legislative validity to such statements for the first time in Ireland.

[10.138] As discussed above, the courts in Ireland and elsewhere have clearly stated that an adult patient with capacity is entitled to refuse medical treatment irrespective of the fact that the refusal may cause serious consequences or even death.[197] However, the facts of such cases have often involved contemporaneous as opposed to anticipatory decisions. By comparison with a contemporaneous refusal of treatment, an advance directive is a statement made in advance of an illness about the type and extent of treatment one does not want to receive, on the assumption that one may be incapable of participating in decision-making about treatment when the need arises.[198] Advance directives are regarded as a means of limiting life-prolonging treatment, rather than as a means by which to request the provision of all possible treatments, as it is generally acknowledged that it would not be ethically defensible to require a doctor to provide

---

[196] See Gillon, 'Why I wrote my advance decision to refuse life-prolonging treatment: and why the law on sanctity of life remains problematic' (2016) Journal of Med Ethics 42: 376–382.

[197] See Canadian decisions *Malette v Shulman* [1990] 72 OR (2d) 417 (CA) in which the Court said that a doctor is obliged to observe the previously stated wishes of a Jehovah's Witness patient to refuse a blood transfusion; and *Nancy B v Hotel Dieu de Quebec* [1992] 86 DLR (4th) 385 where a young woman on a ventilator, suffering from Guillan Barre syndrome, succeeded in her wish to have the machine switched off in order to end her life. The Court in the latter case emphasised that no criminal liability would attach to the doctor who acceded to her request, as death would occur as a result of nature taking its course.

[198] Capron, 'Advance Directives' in Kuhse and Singer, *A Companion to Bioethics*, (Blackwell, 1998) 261–271.

treatment which may not be beneficial to the patient. For this reason, although an advance request may be made by a patient, it is not regarded as legally binding[199] but should be taken into account by the healthcare provider.[200]

[10.139] Advance directives were first introduced as a means of addressing the difficult impasse that may occur when a decision has to be made as to whether to continue with treatment of someone who is unable to communicate his own views. Family members, doctors and nurses often find it extremely difficult to make such decisions where the consequence will be the patient's death. Luis Kutner, a US lawyer involved in a right-to-die organisation, drafted what he termed a 'living will' in 1967 to allow a person to give instructions for medical care at the end of life.[201] It was viewed as having three purposes: first, it relieved the patient's family of the burden of decision-making; second, it enabled the incompetent patient to participate in decision-making despite loss of communicative capacity; and third, it helped to raise public and professional awareness that life-prolonging treatment isn't necessarily always a good thing.

[10.140] There are concerns that in giving effect to advance directives, the person may unwittingly be depriving himself of beneficial advances in medical science that take place after the living will was drafted, and that he may not fully understand the nature of the intervention in question. Others argue from a more philosophical perspective that the person in persistent vegetative state (PVS) is not the same person that made the advance directive and, therefore, that treatment decisions should be made in the best interests of the present patient.[202] Maclean uses Parfit's view of personal identity to explain this as follows:

> If advance directives are predicated on the basis of personal autonomy then…their authority only applies to an individual if he or she is the same moral entity that created the directive. This means that for an advance directive to have the necessary moral force there must be a sufficiently close relationship of psychological connectedness and continuity between the past and present selves…Because the necessary relationships are a matter of degree, it requires a normative judgment to determine whether the past and present selves are identical persons.[203]

[10.141] He goes on to use Parfit's theory to argue that when a person undergoes a catastrophic change that severs the necessary psychological continuity which would otherwise have existed, such as occurs with dementia, head injuries and strokes for example, this might mean that there are some human beings who lack a sufficient connection to their previous self for an advance directive to be morally or legally binding. He acknowledges the problems that the application of such a theory would encounter and suggests that 'although the backward-looking psychological connections

---

[199] *R (Burke) v GMC* [2005] EWCA Civ 1003 at [31–32].

[200] See discussion of the relevant provisions of the Assisted Decision-Making (Capacity) Act 2015 at para **10.153**.

[201] Capron, 'Advance Directives' in Kuhse and Singer, *A Companion to Bioethics*, (Blackwell, 1998) p 262.

[202] See, for example, Bernat, 'The Living Will: Does an Advance Refusal of Treatment Made with Capacity Always Survive Any Supervening Incapacity?' (1999) Med Law I Vol 4 1–21.

[203] Maclean, 'Advance Directives, Future Selves and Decision-Making' (Autumn 2006) Medical Law Review 14, pp 291–320 at 298, quoting Parfit, 'Personal Identity' (1971) 80 The Philosophical Review 3.

may be severed, the asymmetrical prospective relationship, along with the connections maintained by the relationships that the human being exists within, justify the former competent self having decisional authority.' This authority should not be absolute but should be subject to the limitation that other interested parties may challenge the former self's advance decision.[204]

[10.142] In the context of psychiatric care, the advance directive also poses particular problems. Mental disorder covers many conditions which challenge paternalistic assumptions. The question that arises in this context is whether a competently executed advance directive by a person with a fluctuating mental disorder, made at a time of full competence, can be binding on a health professional. The example of anorexia nervosa is illustrative, where the patient is usually competent but refuses food to the point of death. What is the situation if such a person makes an advance refusal of food and subsequently becomes unconscious due to very low body weight? The strong autonomy argument states that if the patient is competent at any time and states that in the event of future lack of competence, certain treatments are not to be given, then the professional must observe such refusal. The strong paternalism argument takes the view that the advance refusal should be respected until such point as the patient's life is in danger as a result of mental disorder, and it then becomes acceptable to treat the patient in his best interests. The rights-based argument provides that an advance refusal of treatment made by a competent person should be respected except where the person has a mental disorder that requires that they be compulsorily detained for treatment under statutory authority.

[10.143] The English case of *Re C (Refusal of Medical treatment)*[205] is instructive here. In this case a 68-year-old man suffering from paranoid schizophrenia, who had been a long-term patient at a mental institution, developed gangrene in his right foot. Doctors recommended amputation of the leg below the knee in order to save his life. C refused to consent to amputation under any circumstances, now or at any future time. Alternative treatment was provided and the immediate threat to his life receded but there was a chance that it might recur in the future. C was concerned that this might happen at a time when his capacity to refuse consent might be diminished and that the hospital would perform the operation in his 'best interests'. Therefore, he applied to the Court for an injunction restraining the hospital from amputating his foot in the future without his express consent. The High Court granted the injunction. Thorpe J held that despite the patient's chronic mental illness, there was a rebuttable presumption that an adult has the capacity to decide whether to consent to medical treatment. This presumption had not been displaced in this case. As well as laying down helpful guidelines for the determination of patient competence, the decision clarified that advance refusals were not only directory in nature but were binding as well.

[10.144] This was fleetingly referred to in the recent English case of *Re QQ*,[206] where an application was made to court in March 2016 in respect of a patient who was 26 years of

---

[204] Maclean, 'Advance Directives, Future Selves and Decision-Making' (Autumn 2006) Medical Law Review 14, pp 291–320 at 320.

[205] *Re C (Refusal of Medical treatment)* [1994] 1 FLR 31. See commentary by Grubb, 'Treatment Without Consent: Adult: *Re C (Refusal of Medical Treatment)*' [1994] 2 Med L Rev 92.

[206] *Re QQ* [2016] EWCOP 22.

age and had a diagnosis of an emotionally unstable personality disorder and schizophrenia. QQ's treating clinician who had been treating her for 12 months prior to this application was of the view that she lacked capacity to make decisions on the issue of her treatment in relation to receiving anticoagulation medication. QQ had made an advance directive refusing this medication in August 2015. The court held that at the time of making this directive she lacked capacity and therefore it was not a valid directive. However interestingly, Keehan J also said that even if he was wrong on that issue (in other words QQ *did* have capacity at the relevant time), the contrary views that QQ had recently and fleetingly expressed from time to time, namely that she *would* accept treatment, would not of themselves invalidate what would otherwise have been a valid advance decision.

[10.145] Strict application of agency law, under which one person (the principal) appoints another (the agent) to carry out instructions on his behalf, would generally negate the operation of the living will, as the agency is deemed to be terminated when the principal becomes incompetent. This would mean that 'applied to the medical context, traditional agency law renders instructions in a living will non-binding at the very moment when they are intended to go into effect.'[207] Doctors seeking to justify overriding such instructions frequently used the non-binding nature of advance directives in their reasoning. Legislation began to be introduced following the decision of the New Jersey Supreme Court in *Re Quinlan*,[208] although there was no advance directive in that case. The plight of Karen Quinlan and her family reinforced in the public perception the horrific scenario of being maintained by machines indefinitely in a hospital room with doctors controlling the time and means of death. Advance directives are embodied in federal policy by the Patient Self-Determination Act 1990 (PSDA) which requires medical institutions to give patients information about their rights, which include being given written notice upon admission to the healthcare facility of their decision-making rights, and policies regarding advance healthcare directives in their state and in the institution to which they have been admitted. It also includes the right to have their healthcare decisions facilitated, the right to accept or refuse medical treatment and the right to make an advance healthcare directive. Facilities must inquire as to the whether the patient already has an advance healthcare directive, and make note of this in their medical records.

[10.146] As a result of the PSDA, almost all states in the US provide for living wills, and most states have two statutes, one establishing a living will and the other establishing a proxy or durable power of attorney for healthcare. Issues have arisen in relation to the precision with which the wording of the directive must be drawn so as to specifically deal with the situation that later arises, and the definition of terms often used such as 'terminal illness' or 'heroic measures'. It has been suggested that a checklist approach would be preferable, which would indicate in much more detail exactly what the patient would or would not want to be done to him. Despite the legislative provisions, in practice it appears that in the United States less than one third of the population have advance directives, many of them do not give them to their doctors and studies indicate

---

[207] Capron, 'Advance Directives' in Kuhse and Singer, *A Companion to Bioethics*, (Blackwell, 1998) p 263.

[208] *Re Quinlan* 355 A 2d 647, 97 ALR 3d 205 (S Ct of New Jersey).

that surrogate decision-makers often find it difficult to interpret the wishes of the patient. 25 per cent of patients receive care inconsistent with their living wills, 29 per cent of patients change their minds about life-sustaining treatment over time and 64 per cent of dying patients' living wills do not cover the clinical realities they face.[209] Rich says that one of the reasons why so few people execute advance directives is due to reluctance to contemplate the prospect of life-threatening illness:

> In addition, people often make two false assumptions. First, they assume that advance directives are unnecessary because those closest to them will know intuitively what should be done in the unlikely event that life-threatening illness should strike. Second, they assume that those persons will be empowered to act as surrogates. Regrettably, nothing could be further from the truth, at least when the action is withdrawing life support and there is a lack of consensus among family members.[210]

[10.147] Outside of the US, legislation on advance directives has been enacted in a number of European jurisdictions, including the UK, Austria, the Netherlands, Finland, Denmark and Germany. The Council of Europe Convention for the Protection of Human Rights and Dignity of the Human Being with regard to the Application of Biology and Medicine: Convention on Human Rights and Biomedicine (Oviedo 1997) also makes reference to advance directives under art 9, which states that 'the previously expressed wishes relating to a medical intervention by a patient who is not, at the time of the intervention, in a state to express his or her wishes shall be taken into account'. Ireland has not signed this Convention.

[10.148] The legislation in most jurisdictions that provide for advance directives usually require them to be in written form and to either set out specific treatments that are refused in advance, and/or nominate a person to make decisions on behalf of the author of the directive. The latter allows more flexibility, as the specific circumstances and treatments are not restricted to what has been written in the directive. However, it is also important to recognise that the emotional burden on surrogate decision-makers related to their role in determining a loved one's care can last for months and even years after the treatment choice. It has been noted that the circumstances of decision-making have an impact on how deeply surrogates are affected by stress and guilt in relation to their decision-making, with a substantial reduction in situations where the patient has an advance directive that specifies the patient's wishes.[211]

[10.149] The English Mental Capacity Act 2005 requires that although advance directives generally do not need to be in writing, where an advance directive encompasses a refusal of life-sustaining treatment, it requires a level of formality in order to be considered valid. Such a directive must explicitly state that it applies where life is at risk, it must be in writing and executed in the presence of an independent witness.[212] These procedural formalities provide an opportunity to check the patient's capacity and voluntariness and although some argue that such formalities are unduly

---

[209] Fagerlin and Shneider, 'Enough: The Failure of the Living Will' (2004) 34(2) Hastings Center Report, 30–42.

[210] Rich, 'The Ethics of Surrogate Decision Making' (2002) West J Med 176:127–129.

[211] Wendler and Rid, 'Systematic Review: The Effect on Surrogates of Making Treatment Decisions for Others' (2011) Annals of Internal Medicine, Vol 154, no 5, pp 336–346.

[212] Mental Capacity Act 2005, s 25 (5), (6).

onerous, they may be seen as a 'reasonable compromise between facilitating the uptake of advance directives and protecting vulnerable patients'.[213]

[10.150] Although there is some evidence from the United States that those making advance directives are poorly informed,[214] the English legislation only *recommends* that advance directives are made with medical advice, it does not require it. Maclean explains that this was because the English government took the view that to make this a requirement would be inappropriate and unduly intrusive. However, 'while this approach impacts less on the present person's current autonomy, it makes that person's autonomous choice far more vulnerable at a point when he or she will be incompetent and unable to do anything about it.'[215] Thus, if an individual has not received good medical advice prior to drafting their directive, they may not be able to predict their future medical state and the possible options open to them. This makes their choice inherently vulnerable to being overridden by the court on the grounds that their ignorance meant the person did not fully appreciate the precise circumstances that have now arisen and therefore the directive is not applicable.

[10.151] One of the main practical difficulties with advance directives is ensuring that they anticipate the circumstances that may arise in the future. A directive that is drafted in very general terms is unlikely to be upheld if it is considered to lack the degree of specificity deemed necessary by the courts. Section 24 of the English Mental Capacity Act 2005 provides that an advance decision must relate to a 'specified treatment' although this may be phrased in lay language rather than medical terminology. It is unclear how this term will be interpreted, so for example, would it be sufficiently clear for a patient to refuse 'any life-saving treatment'? 'Although the restriction will provide a safeguard against the inadvertent exclusion of treatments not anticipated by the decision-maker, it also provides the courts with another means to invalidate decisions with which they are uncomfortable.'[216]

[10.152] In relation to the length of time which may have elapsed between the making of the directive and the circumstances which have now arisen, there is nothing in the case law which indicates that the expiry of a particular length of time should affect its validity. However, in general, the older the directive, the closer the scrutiny it will receive by a court which is trying to ascertain whether it continues to reflect the current wishes of the patient. The Code of Practice for the English Mental Capacity Act suggests that anyone who has made an advance directive is advised to regularly review and update it as necessary.[217] Although the setting of a time limit for the validity of an

---

[213] Maclean, 'Advance Directives and the Rocky Waters of Anticipatory Decision-Making' (Spring 2008) Med Law Review 16, pp 1–22 at 11.

[214] Dresser, 'Precommitment: A Misguided Strategy for Securing Death with Dignity' (2003) 81 Texas Law Review 1823, quoted by Maclean, 'Advance Directives and the Rocky Waters of Anticipatory Decision-Making' (Spring 2008) Med Law Review 16, pp 1–22 at 15.

[215] Maclean, 'Advance Directives and the Rocky Waters of Anticipatory Decision-Making' (Spring 2008) Med Law Review 16, pp 1–22 at 15.

[216] Maclean, 'Advance Directives and the Rocky Waters of Anticipatory Decision-Making' (Spring 2008) Med Law Review 16, pp 1–22 at 17.

[217] Code of Practice for the Mental Capacity Act 2005, para 9.29.

advance directive has sometimes been recommended,[218] it has been seen as preferable to leave the question of applicability of the directive to the relevant healthcare professional rather than to set an arbitrary time limit.[219] The professional is protected from liability by s 26 of the Act if he treats a patient in circumstances when he is not satisfied that a valid and applicable advance directive exists. The Act thus gives considerable discretion to the doctor in charge of the patient's care, as his satisfaction as to the validity of the directive is not required to be reasonable. Maclean concludes that the Act provides symbolic support for individual autonomy while providing sufficient scope for interpretation to allow many advance directives to be judged invalid or inapplicable when the likely consequences are contrary to the healthcare professional's or judge's view of an appropriate outcome.

Advance Healthcare Directives under the Assisted Decision-Making (Capacity) Act 2015

[10.153] Until 2015 it was unclear whether advance directives would be upheld by Irish courts as there had been no case directly in point.[220] It was surmised from judicial statements that such a decision by a patient would be recognised as legally valid if the patient was competent and informed when the directive was made, and that it was clear and specific to the patient's current situation. It was generally thought that as long as the directive was lawful, the courts would uphold its validity. This is consistent with the clear statements of the courts which point to a right to refuse contemporaneous medical treatment. Although in the case of advance directives the choice or refusal of medical treatment is made in anticipation of incapacitating illness rather than contemporaneously, it was felt that the court would be likely to hold that the same principle applies if the patient's decision was clearly established and applicable in the circumstances in which the patient now presents.[221]

[10.154] In 2007 the Irish Council for Bioethics published its opinion that 'competent adults should have the right to prepare an advance directive, stemming from their right

---

[218] UK Joint Committee on Human Rights. *Fourth Report of 2004* (2005), para 4.22.

[219] Maclean, 'Advance Directives and the Rocky Waters of Anticipatory Decision-Making' (Spring 2008) Med Law Review 16, pp 1–22 at 19.

[220] It is not known how many people in Ireland have made advance directives, as no case has yet come before the court dealing with them. The Law Reform Commission stated in its Report in 2009 that many people have prepared written advance care directives, sometimes with the benefit of medical and legal advice, and general hospitals deal on a regular basis with patients who verbally express treatment preferences, including refusals of treatment and 'do not resuscitate' requests. The Commission quotes from a study conducted in 2003 in which 27 per cent of physicians had experience of advance care directives made by Irish patients. (Fennell, Butler, Saaidin and Sheikh, 'Dissatisfaction with Do Not Attempt Resuscitation Orders: A Nationwide Study of Irish Consultant Physician Practices' (2006) 99(7) Irish Medical Journal 208). The Commission also received information during its consultation process that a number of hospitals in Ireland have developed guidelines and protocols to deal with advance care directives, based on best practice models from other states, notably the UK. See also Campbell, 'The Case for Living Wills in Ireland' (2006) *Medico-Legal Journal of Ireland*, 12 (1): 2–18.

[221] Affirmed in the UK by *Re T (Adult: refusal of treatment)* [1992] 4 All ER 649, [1993] Fam 95; *Airedale NHS Trust v Bland* [1993] AC 789.

to self-determination and their related rights to bodily integrity, privacy and dignity.' It took the view that the instrument of the advance directive allows individuals to govern their future medical treatment and care, should they become incapacitated, in a way that reflects their personal values and beliefs.[222] In 2009 the Law Reform Commission published its Report on Advance Directives in which it recognised a growing momentum in Ireland favouring the introduction of a legislative framework for advance care directives.[223] It concluded that 'to the extent that case law in Ireland, notably *In re a Ward of Court (No 2)* and *Fitzpatrick v FK*, has addressed this matter, it is clear that an advance care directive made by a person with full capacity would be upheld.' It recommended that an appropriate legislative framework should be enacted for advance care directives as part of the reform of the law on mental capacity.

[10.155] Part 8 of the Assisted Decision-Making (Capacity) Act 2015[224] now provides for advance healthcare directives which are defined in s 82 as 'an advance expression made by the person, in accordance with section 84, of his or her will and preferences concerning treatment decisions that may arise in respect of him or her if he or she subsequently lacks capacity.' Section 83(1) provides that the purpose of this Part is to enable people to be treated according to their will and preference and to provide healthcare professionals with information about people's treatment choices. Subs (2) goes on to explicitly state that an adult with capacity is entitled to refuse treatment for any reason (including a reason based on his or her religious beliefs) notwithstanding that the refusal appears to be unwise, not based on sound medical principles, or may result in his or her death.

[10.156] These provisions clearly put on a statutory footing the principles adopted by the Irish courts in relation to contemporaneous refusals of treatment which have been outlined earlier in this chapter. It is interesting that the drafters felt it necessary to explicitly make reference to religious beliefs as a valid basis for decision-making since, as we have seen above, most of the cases before the courts to date have related to refusals based on religious grounds. This legislation puts the matter beyond doubt that a person with capacity can refuse treatment irrespective of the reason for, wisdom of or consequence of their decision. A person may also choose to appoint a named individual as his or her 'designated healthcare representative' to ensure that the terms of the advance healthcare directive are complied with. The designated healthcare representative may be given the power to advise and interpret the directive-maker's will and preferences regarding treatment, and the power to consent to or refuse treatment, including life-sustaining treatment, based on the directive-maker's will and preferences.[225]

[10.157] Section 84 of the Act sets out the requirements for the making of a valid advance healthcare directive and provides that a refusal of treatment in such a directive 'shall be complied with' if three conditions are met:

---

[222] The Irish Council on Bioethics is no longer in existence but its publications are available at www.health.gov.ie

[223] Report on Bioethics: Advance Care Directives (LRC 94–2009) available at www.lawreform.ie

[224] This Act has not been commenced at the time of writing.

[225] Section 88 of the 2015 Act.

- At the time in question the directive-maker lacks capacity to give consent to the treatment;
- The treatment to be refused is clearly identified in the directive;
- The circumstances in which the refusal of treatment is intended to apply are clearly identified in the directive.

Section 86 of the Act provides that if the conditions set out in Part 8 are complied with, a refusal of treatment in an advance healthcare directive 'is as effective as if made contemporaneously by the directive-maker when he or she had capacity to make that decision.'

[10.158] Section 84 further provides that the directive must be in writing, contain the details set out in subs (5), and be signed and witnessed. A request for a specific treatment is not legally binding but must be taken into consideration where relevant. If such a request is not complied with, the healthcare professional must record in the person's healthcare record the reasons for not complying and give a copy of those reasons to the person's designated healthcare representative (if any) within seven days. Advance directives may be altered or revoked in accordance with s 84(7). A directive made outside the State will have the same effect as if it were made in the State as long as it substantially complies with the requirements of Part 8. The Minister for Health is given the power to make regulations specifying the form of advance directives and setting out notice requirements. The Minister may also require the Director of the Decision Support Service to establish and maintain a register of advance healthcare directives.

[10.159] Section 85 sets out a number of provisions in relation to the validity and applicability of advance healthcare directives. It provides that advance healthcare directives are not valid if the person did not make the directive voluntarily, or if while he or she had capacity, had done anything clearly inconsistent with the relevant decisions in the directive. The directive is only applicable in circumstances where the person lacks capacity to make a contemporaneous decision and will not apply if the treatment in question is not materially the same as the treatment refused by the terms of the directive. Similarly it will not apply if the circumstances set out in the directive as to when the treatment is to be refused are absent or not materially the same. A directive made by a person whose treatment is regulated by Part 4 of the Mental Health Act 2001 or who is the subject of a conditional discharge order under s 13A of the Criminal Law (Insanity) Act 2006 is not legally binding unless the directive relates to an unrelated physical illness rather than a mental disorder.

[10.160] Further significant provisions in s 85 are that an advance healthcare directive will not apply to life-sustaining treatment 'unless this is substantiated by a statement in the directive by the directive-maker to the effect that the directive is to apply to that treatment even if his or her life is at risk.'[226] An advance healthcare directive does not apply to the administration of basic care which includes warmth, shelter, oral nutrition, oral hydration and hygiene measures but does not include artificial nutrition or artificial hydration. This means that a person may refuse medical treatment, including for example artificial nutrition or artificial hydration, but may not refuse basic care such as

---

[226] Section 85(3).

those items listed above (not an exhaustive list). Basic care such as the offer of food and water, or hygiene measures such as washing, do not come within the definition of medical treatment and are generally felt to be consistent with maintaining the dignity and comfort of the person even where medical treatment is to be withdrawn.

[10.161] If there is any ambiguity in the wording or applicability of the directive, s 85(5) provides that the healthcare professional must consult with the person's designated healthcare representative (if any), or the person's family and friends, and seek the opinion of a second healthcare professional in order to try to resolve the ambiguity. If resolution is not possible and the ambiguity remains, it should be resolved in favour of the preservation of the life of the directive-maker.

[10.162] Section 85(6)(a) provides that where a person making an advance directive is pregnant and her directive does not specifically state whether or not she intended her refusal of treatment to apply if she were pregnant, and the healthcare professionals involved in her treatment consider that her refusal would have a deleterious effect on the unborn, there is a presumption in favour of providing or continuing the relevant treatment. Section 85(6)(b) provides that where the woman has specified that her refusal should apply even if she were pregnant and the healthcare professionals involved in her treatment consider that her refusal would have a deleterious effect on the unborn, an application should be made to the High Court to determine whether or not the treatment should be provided. The Court must consider the potential impact of the refusal on the unborn, the invasiveness and duration of the treatment and the risk of harm to the woman if the treatment were to be provided.

[10.163] One of the issues that has been the subject of discussion in other jurisdictions is what the consequences of disregarding an advance directive should be. For example, Michalowski argues that no compelling reasons justify departure from the normal principles of tort law where a patient claims compensation for having had a refusal of life-saving treatment disregarded, and that damages should be available where the cause of action is established and it can be shown that the patient suffered harm as a result.[227] The compensable harm should therefore include all physical and mental pain and suffering caused by the unwanted treatment. 'Where a patient wants to live by his/her religious beliefs or wishes to preserve personal dignity, the harm will be mental distress; where the patient wants to prevent life in a painful condition, or medical problems potentially following the administration of life-saving treatment, such as a stroke or the loss of bodily functions, the harm is physical suffering, probably often accompanied by mental suffering.' The compensable harm is not the patient's existence as such, but the suffering caused by the unwanted treatment. She also states that in addition to liability under tort law, there is also the possibility of disciplinary sanctions in case of a violation of the patient's declared wishes. Indeed the Guide to Professional Conduct and Ethics of the Medical Council provides that 'an advance treatment plan has the same ethical status as a decision by a patient at the actual time of an illness and should be respected' if certain requirements are met.[228]

---

[227] Michalowski, 'Trial and Error at the End of Life – No Harm Done?' (2007) Oxford Journal of Legal Studies Vol 27, No 2:257–280 at 270.

[228] These requirements are set out in para. 16.2 of the Guide to Professional Conduct and Ethics of the Medical Council (8th edn, 2016).

[10.164] Section 86 of the 2015 Act provides that nothing in the Act imposes any civil or criminal liability on a healthcare professional who complies with an advance healthcare directive believing on reasonable grounds that the advance healthcare directive was valid and applicable. Therefore the family of a deceased person could not take legal action against a doctor who acceded to the wishes of the deceased in withdrawing life-sustaining treatment in circumstances where the doctor believed the advance healthcare directive to be valid and applicable. The Act also provides that nothing in the Act imposes any civil or criminal liability on a healthcare professional who has not complied with an advance healthcare directive believing on reasonable grounds that the advance healthcare directive was invalid and/or inapplicable. This might occur for example if the healthcare professional was unaware of the existence of the directive, or knew it existed but did not have access to it and the urgency of the situation was such that he or she could not delay taking appropriate action. It also specifically states that the provisions of this Act do not affect the law relating to murder or manslaughter, or the operation of the provisions of s 2 of the Criminal Law (Suicide) Act 1993 dealing with assisted suicide.

Chapter 11

Medical Treatment of Children and Minors

INTRODUCTION

[11.01] The medical treatment of children and minors raises unique issues in law and ethics. The interaction of rights and interests between the child, its parents or guardians and the medical profession, often poses difficult questions for the courts. As discussed in Chapter 10, in general the law accords central importance to the individual's right of autonomy, and consent is required for any form of medical treatment other than in limited emergency circumstances. However many of the legal authorities in this area have been decided in the context of adult patients who have full capacity to give consent. When the patient is a child who does not have legal capacity to make such decisions, someone else, usually a parent or legal guardian, must give consent on her behalf. This does not detract from the ethical value of respecting the autonomy of the child and ensuring that she participates as much as possible in decision-making about her own health. Communication to and with children in a way they can understand, as well as to parents or guardians is vital if meaningful collaboration with relevant medical professionals is to take place in making such decisions.

[11.02] The treatment of very young children or infants who have been born with life-limiting conditions further demonstrates the importance of collaboration between medical and parental interests, both of whom are presumed to act in the child's best interests. Non-treatment of severely compromised infants raises difficult ethical and legal issues as to the subjectivity of determinations as to the value of life, and how best to safeguard the best interests of such a child. The difference in perception between parents and doctors as to where those best interests lie have posed problems in a number of difficult cases discussed later. The limits of parental decision-making is an issue not yet definitively decided in Ireland, although it is expected that the constitutional rights of the family would play a vital role in setting any limit in this regard. This chapter also examines case law from other jurisdictions in assessing to what extent parental consent to, or refusal of consent for, treatment of children has influenced judicial decisions here, or may in the future.

[11.03] As the child develops towards maturity, its understanding and independence from its parents grows. Adolescents often seek to exert their own independence in all forms of decision-making as they mature and this may be relatively unproblematic unless a decision is made that does not coincide with parental views or professional advice, for example when an adolescent refuses medical treatment. The law in Ireland in relation to the capacity of minors to refuse treatment is unclear and will be discussed later in this chapter.

CONSENTING TO TREATMENT OF YOUNG CHILDREN

[11.04] In the ordinary course of events infants and young children are brought by their parents to healthcare service providers for routine medical treatment without any serious legal or ethical issues arising. The same general principles in relation to capacity and consent set out in Chapters 9 and 10 apply in relation to the adults who have legal authority to give such consent on behalf of the child. However, an issue that may sometimes uniquely arise in this context is who has such legal authority to give consent on behalf of the young child. While parents usually assume that they have automatic legal authority to give consent, the legal position differentiates between parents and legal guardians as not all parents are legal guardians under Irish law. Where a child accesses a health or social care service in the company of an adult, the adult should therefore be asked to confirm that they are the child's legal guardian and this should be documented in the child's healthcare record. In the event that they indicate that they are not the child's legal guardian, contact should be made with the child's legal guardian in order to seek appropriate consent.

[11.05] The term 'legal guardianship' refers to the right of a parent to be involved in all major decisions affecting the welfare and upbringing of a child including decisions relating to education, health, religious, monetary and moral concerns. Under the Children and Family Relationships Act 2015, the following guardianship rules apply:

- Where parents are married, the child's mother and father are the legal guardians.
- Where a child has been jointly adopted, the adoptive parents are the child's legal guardians.
- Following a separation or divorce, both parents remain the child's legal guardian even if the child is not living with them and they have not been awarded custody of the child.

[11.06] Where the child's parents are not married:

- The child's mother is an automatic legal guardian.
- The child's father is an automatic legal guardian if he has lived with the child's mother for 12 consecutive months (after commencement of the Act[1]) including at least 3 months with the mother and child following the child's birth.
- The mother and father of the child may make a statutory declaration to the effect that they agree to the appointment of the father as legal guardian.
- The father may apply to court to be appointed legal guardian.

[11.07] Any adult may apply to court for legal guardianship:

- If he or she is married to or in a civil partnership with, or has been cohabiting for at least 3 years, with the child's parent and has shared parental responsibility for the child's day-to-day care for at least 2 years.
- If he or she has provided for the child's day-to-day care for a continuous period of more than 12 months and the child has no parent or guardian who is able or willing to act as guardian.

---

[1] The relevant Part of the Act commenced on 18 January 2016.

A guardian may nominate another person to act as temporary guardian in the event of the guardian's incapacity. This is subject to court approval. A guardian may also appoint a person to act as the child's guardian in the event of the guardian's death.

[11.08] Where both parents are legal guardians a further issue that may arise in practice is whether both must give joint consent to medical treatment on behalf of the child, or whether the consent of one is sufficient. There is no legislation on this point in Ireland so in the absence of legislative clarity on this issue the HSE National Consent Policy (2013)[2] discusses the matter in some detail. The Policy states that on the one hand, it may be argued that the consent of both parents/legal guardians is required prior to treatment of the child on the basis of the rights of the parents/legal guardians in keeping with art 41 of the Constitution which recognises the family as the natural primary and fundamental unit group of society and the Guardianship of Infants Act 1964. However, seeking joint parental consent may cause delays in children receiving services and potential logistical difficulties in ensuring that all forms are co-signed, eg parents/legal guardians working abroad. In addition the requirement for joint consent may be perceived by those parents/legal guardians not in dispute to be bureaucratic.

[11.09] Conversely, it may be argued that seeking the consent of only one parent/legal guardian is widely recognised in health and social care practice and is considered to be more practical for safe, timely and effective service provision. It is generally accepted in other jurisdictions from a legal perspective that, in protecting health professionals from an action in battery,[3] the consent of one parent or legal guardian (or in their absence, that of the court) is sufficient. The National Consent Policy policy continues that 'the acceptance of consent of one parent/legal guardian assumes that the child's welfare is paramount, which is in line with the Child Care Acts 1991 and 2001, and that the health and social care professional is proposing a treatment or intervention in the child's best interests. It also assumes that both of the parents/legal guardians are concerned with the child's welfare.'

[11.10] The provisions of the Irish Constitution 1937 acknowledge the important role and responsibility that all parents and legal guardians have to safeguard the welfare of their children in relation to decisions in many different contexts, including health, social development, education and so on. As a corollary to the rights given to parents as legal guardians of their children, there are also duties imposed on them to act in the best interests of their children. In the health and social care context this requires parents and legal guardians to engage with health and social care service providers to ensure that the child receives the best possible care and services. The National Consent Policy recommends that such involvement by parents and legal guardians should be encouraged and facilitated by service providers as much as possible.

[11.11] The National Consent Policy policy advises that where both parents/legal guardians have indicated a wish and willingness to participate fully in decision making for their child, this must be accommodated as far as possible by the service provider. This also imposes a responsibility on the parents/legal guardians to be contactable and

---

[2] HSE National Consent Policy 2013 available at www.hse.ie.
[3] Battery is a form of trespass to the person resulting from proof of contact with the body without consent.

available at relevant times when decisions may have to be made for the child. Even where both parents/legal guardians have not clearly indicated their wish to be involved in decision making, if the decision will have profound and irreversible consequences for the child, both parents/legal guardians should be consulted if possible. However if urgent care is required and the second parent/legal guardian cannot be contacted despite reasonable efforts to do so, the service provider has a paramount duty to act in the best interests of the child.

[11.12] The National Consent Policy advises that apart from the circumstances outlined above and in keeping with the prioritisation of the best interests of the child, 'the consent of one parent/legal guardian will provide sufficient authority in respect of any health or social care intervention in relation to a child.' In emergency circumstances where neither parent/legal guardian is contactable, the general doctrine of necessity applies and the service provider is obliged to act in the best interests of the child. It is of course possible that the position adopted by this policy might be challenged in the future on grounds that it potentially excludes one of the child's legal guardians from decision-making. However, until the courts have adjudicated on the matter to the contrary, the principle set out in the policy is justified on the basis of prioritisation of the welfare of the child requiring treatment.

[11.13] It is possible that disagreements may arise between legal guardians as to the appropriateness of treatment of a young child. Where attempts at mediation of the dispute fail, this is a matter that may require court application. The courts have held that there is no hierarchy of rights or 'pre-determined constitutionally protected veto' as between two legal guardians and that the decision will be made by the court in the child's best interests.[4]

Constitutional position of the family

[11.14] There have been very few reported cases in Ireland dealing with parental authority in the treatment of children. The provisions of the Irish Constitution 1937 are considered to be very important here. Article 41.1.1° provides that 'the State recognises the Family as the natural primary and fundamental unit group of Society, and as a moral institution possessing inalienable and imprescriptible rights, antecedent and superior to all positive law.' Article 41.1.2° provides that the State guarantees 'to protect the Family in its constitution and authority, as the necessary basis of social order'. Article 42.1 provides that the State acknowledges that 'the primary and natural educator of the child is the Family' and goes on to guarantee to respect the right and duty of parents to provide for the education of their children. These principles place the family in a predominant position in terms of its place in society and as regards State intervention.[5]

---

[4] See example of media reports of a High Court application in a case in which separated parents were in disagreement regarding the vaccination of their child. 'Mother loses court bid to prevent son's MMR vaccination' *Irish Independent* 19 December 2013.

[5] In *In Re Tilson* [1951] IR 1 Gavan Duffy J said that the articles dealing with the family 'exalt the family by proclaiming and adopting in …the Constitution…the Christian conception of the place of the family in society and in the State.' p 14.

[11.15] These articles were used as a basis for argument in *Ryan v Attorney General*[6] in which the plaintiff claimed that the fluoridation of water violated her rights and those of her children under art 40.3 of the Constitution, that they were a violation of the authority of the family under art 41, and a violation of the family's right to physical education of the children under art 42 of the Constitution. In rejecting the plaintiff's case, the Supreme Court held that there was nothing in the Health (Fluoridation of Water Supplies) Act 1960 which could be said to be a violation of the guarantee on the part of the State to protect the family in its constitution and authority, neither did the allegations come within the meaning of education under the Constitution. The Court held that '[E]ducation essentially is the teaching and training of a child to make the best possible use of his inherent and potential capacities, physical, mental and moral…To give [a child] water of a nature calculated to minimise the danger of dental caries is in no way to educate him, physically or otherwise, for it does not develop his resources.'[7] However, the Court also stated that one of the duties of parents was to avoid dangers to the health of a child. 'There is nothing in the Constitution which recognises the right of a parent to refuse to allow the provision of measures designed to secure the health of his child when the method of avoiding injury is one which is not fraught with danger to the child.'[8]

[11.16] The Irish courts have, where necessary, applied the provisions of the Child Care Act 1991 to protect vulnerable children from neglect and to vindicate the child's best interests. This interference with parental authority was regarded by the courts as consistent with art 42.5. This provision was repealed by the Thirty-First Amendment of the Constitution (Children) Act 2012, and replaced by art 42A.2.1°. The new article makes broadly the same provision as before in envisaging exceptional circumstances in which the State may intervene to protect children where the parents have failed in their duty:

> In exceptional cases, where the parents, regardless of their marital status, fail in their duty towards their children to such extent that the safety or welfare of any of their children is likely to be prejudicially affected, the State as guardian of the common good shall, by proportionate means as provided by law, endeavour to supply the place of the parents, but always with due regard for the natural and imprescriptible rights of the child.

[11.17] The ability and duty of the State to intervene in family life was considered in *Re Article 26 of the Constitution and the Adoption (No 2) Bill 1987*[9] where Finlay CJ said: 'In the exceptional circumstances envisaged by [art 42] where a failure in duty has occurred, the State by appropriate means shall endeavour to supply the place of the parents, This must necessarily involve … the parental duty to cater for the personal rights of the child.' Failure by the parents in this context has been held to include not only physical but also psychological damage sustained by a child.[10]

[11.18] In *North Western Health Board v HW and CW*[11] the Supreme Court was asked to decide whether the parents of a 14-month-old child could be required to permit the

---

[6] *Ryan v Attorney General* [1965] IR 294.
[7] *Ryan v Attorney General* [1965] IR 294 at 350.
[8] *Ryan v Attorney General* [1965] IR 294 at 350.
[9] *Re Article 26 of the Constitution and the Adoption (No 2) Bill 1987* [1989] IR 656.
[10] *Southern Health Board v Bord Uchtála* [2000] 1 IR 165.
[11] *North Western Health Board v HW and CW* [2001] IESC 90.

Health Board to conduct a medical test on the child to ascertain whether the child was suffering from certain biochemical or metabolic disorders. The test, known as the PKU or heel test, is carried out by way of a pinprick to the baby's heel within a few days of birth, extracting a small sample of blood which is then tested for these disorders. The risk to the child involved in taking the blood sample is regarded as minimal and there is no indication of adverse consequences ever having occurred in Ireland as a result of the test since it was introduced in 1966. The relevant disorders are treatable if diagnosed at an early stage, but if untreated could have extremely serious consequences for the child, such as severe mental handicap.

[11.19] In this case the parents of the child had no objection in principle to the test being carried out by non-invasive measures, such as through hair or urine samples, but they refused to allow blood samples to be taken, as samples could only be obtained by invasive measures such as puncturing a blood vessel, to which they were opposed. The couple had previous children who had been tested and none of whom had the genetic condition, therefore lowering the familial risk to this particular child. The Health Board claimed that it was in the child's best interests to have the test carried out and that the refusal of his parents to consent to the test was a failure on their part to vindicate his personal rights. They also claimed that using alternative methods of testing would not be reliable or feasible.

[11.20] In the High Court, McCracken J said that while the State had a duty to vindicate the personal rights of citizens, this was not an unlimited or universal obligation. The Court only had a jurisdiction to interfere or provide for children by virtue of the Child Care Act 1991 in exceptional cases where the parents for physical or moral reasons had failed in their duty towards their children. In this case the objective medical evidence clearly indicated that it was in the child's best interests to undergo the test, but the judge also looked at the policy of the State in relation to other facilities such as vaccination against infectious disease, where the decision is left to the parents. McCracken J took the view that the parents in this case, who were regarded as caring and conscientious parents, had made a decision that was contrary to medical opinion but that such a decision could not be said to constitute an exceptional case such that the State could interfere in it. It was not sufficient for the Health Board to claim that the child's welfare was the only factor to be considered, as the 1991 Act also obliges the Health Board to fulfil its statutory functions subject to the Constitutional rights of the parents and the family as a unit. If the State considered that an injustice was being done to the child, then it could provide for compulsory testing by legislation, which would then be tested for its constitutionality. He said:

> If the State were entitled to intervene in every case where professional opinion differed
> from that of parents, or where the State considered the parents were wrong in a decision,
> we would be rapidly stepping towards the Brave New World in which the State always
> knows best. In my view that situation would be totally at variance with both the spirit and
> the word of the Constitution.

[11.21] McCracken J said that the rights of the family are in a very special position under the Constitution. When seeking to balance parental rights as against a child's rights, where medical opinion was to the effect that it was in the child's best interests to undergo the test, the latter might override parental rights. However, the parents' refusal to consent did not come within the realms of 'exceptional cases' envisaged by the

Constitution, as it was within the permissible range of risk that did not affect the very life of the child.[12] It has been argued that McCracken J's approach to the balancing of rights was flawed in not taking account of the child's rights in the case. 'Unfortunately there are no procedures in such cases as this for the appointment of a guardian *ad litem* to represent the views of the child particularly where medical consent is the salient issue and where the application/non-application of the test could have a profound effect on the short or long-term quality of life of the child.'[13] The inclusion in the Constitution of a provision that, in the event of conflict between child rights and parental rights, all decisions should be made taking the child's best interests as the paramount consideration, would resolve any conflict in favour of the child.[14]

[11.22] On appeal to the Supreme Court, it was submitted that the Court had jurisdiction to intervene to protect the interests of a minor where his personal rights were under threat. It was submitted that the welfare of the child must always be the guiding principle for the court in any proceedings concerning the upbringing of a child and that the power of the court to intervene was not limited to 'exceptional cases.' It was argued on behalf of the parents that a vast range of decisions are made by parents on a daily basis for their children and that few of those decisions had been overridden by the courts, even where they appeared to be wrong or reckless. It was submitted that there were some decisions that could be overridden, such as refusal of blood transfusions in a life-threatening situation, but that this particular refusal did not come into that category. The Supreme Court upheld the High Court decision by majority of four to one with Keane CJ dissenting.

[11.23] Denham J said that art 42.5 envisages State intervention in exceptional cases where the parents failed to protect the child's interests. She said that it was clear from that provision that 'the State is the default parent and not the super parent'. Essentially, the issue before the Court was the balance of responsibility between parental rights, the Health Board and the child's rights as a member of a family and as a person. In trying to find the balance in any case, the threshold would depend on the circumstances, so that if the child's life were in immediate danger, there would be a heavy weight to be put on the child's personal rights as opposed to parental wishes. However, in exceptional cases, such as where the child needed acute medical care, if parents decided that the responsible decision was to refuse such care, that may well come within the range of responsible decisions to be taken by parents. Denham J was concerned that an order in this case in favour of the test would effectively make the test compulsory for all children in the State and that this would turn departmental policy into law, which is a matter more appropriately decided at an executive or legislative level. She said that in the circumstances, she would not interfere with the decision of the parents, as this was not an exceptional case justifying the intervention of the State into the Constitutional rights

---

12 See discussion by Martin, 'Parental Rights to Withhold Consent to Medical Treatment for Their Child: A Conflict of Rights?' (2001) 7 Irish Law Times 114; and Arthur, '*North Western Health Board v HW and CW* – Reformulating Irish Family Law' (2002) 3 Irish Law Times 39.

13 Martin, 'Parental Rights to Withhold Consent to Medical Treatment for Their Child: A Conflict of Rights?' (2001) 7 Irish Law Times 114 at 117.

14 This was suggested by the Whitaker Report on the Constitution in 1996, which recommended amending the Constitution to include explicit rights for children. *Report of the Constitution Review Group* (Government Publications, 1996) p 330.

of the parents. Murphy and Murray JJ took a similar view, although both admitted to being concerned by the possibility that the child would be affected by any of the disorders in question, and to finding the parents' decision unwise and disturbing.

[11.24] Hardiman J regarded this case as seeking to establish a position in which a public authority could compel parents to subject a child to an invasive medical test, which was 'an entirely novel proposition.' He said that lessons to be learned from the compulsory sterilisation cases in the US were that it was 'better to hesitate at the threshold of compulsion, even in its most benevolent form, than to adopt an easy but reductionist utilitarianism whose consequences may be unpredictable.' The principle of voluntarism in respect of medical treatment was plainly established and extended to a person making decisions for himself or for another person for whom he is responsible. The orders sought by the Health Board were directed at denying the right of the parents not to consent to the test, to compel them to consent and to compel them to present their child for the test. Hardiman J concluded that there was a presumption that 'where the constitutional family exists and is discharging its functions as such, and the parents have not for physical or moral reasons failed in their duty towards their children, their decisions should not be overridden by the State and in particular by the Courts in the absence of a jurisdiction conferred by statute...The presumption is not of course conclusive and might be open to displacement by countervailing constitutional considerations as perhaps in the case of an immediate threat to life.' In this case the State could only intervene where the parents failed in their duty towards their child. A conscientious disagreement with the Health Board did not constitute a failure of their duty such as to justify State intervention.

[11.25] Keane CJ (dissenting) traced the origins of our democratic system of government back to Locke and Rousseau, who believed that civil government is the result of a contract between the people and their rulers and 'the family existed before that unit and enjoys rights which, in the hierarchy of rights posited by the Constitution, are superior to those which are the result of the positive laws created by the State itself.' Although tensions between the State and the family may exist from time to time, the Constitution 'firmly outlaws any attempt by the State in its laws or its executive actions to usurp the exclusive and privileged role of the family in the social order.' The learned judge then examined case law from the UK, Canada and Australia in which courts had been asked to override parental decisions in relation to the medical treatment of children.

[11.26] Keane CJ referred to the English case of *Re C (HIV test)*,[15] where the Court had taken the view that a baby born to a HIV positive woman should be tested for HIV despite the parents' refusal of consent, on the basis that the medical case for testing the baby was overwhelming. He also considered *Re T (a minor) (wardship: medical treatment)*,[16] where a mother's refusal of a liver transplant for her young son was upheld by the Court of Appeal on the basis that the trial judge had failed to take into account the weight of the mother's concerns regarding the proposed treatment, as well as the reservations expressed by consultants about coercing the mother into playing a crucial

---

[15] *Re C (HIV test)* [1999] 2 FLR 1004 considered further at para **[11.83]**.

[16] *Re T (a minor) (wardship: medical treatment)* [1997] 1 All ER 906, considered in detail later at para **[11.73]** et seq.

part in the child's care after a treatment to which she was opposed. Keane CJ said he had no doubt that Waite LJ in *Re T* accurately described the position that would apply in Ireland when he said:

> All these cases depend on their own facts and render generalisations – tempting though they may be to the legal or social analyst – wholly out of place. It can only be said safely that there is a scale, at one end of which lies the clear case where parental opposition to medical intervention is prompted by scruple or dogma of a kind which is patently irreconcilable with principles of child health and welfare widely accepted by the generality of mankind; and that at the other end lie highly problematic cases where there is genuine scope for difference of view between parent and judge. In both situations it is the duty of the judge to allow the court's own opinion to prevail in the perceived paramount interest of the child concerned, but in cases at the latter end of the scale, there must be a likelihood (though never of course a certainty) that the greater the scope for genuine debate between one view and another the stronger will be the inclination of the court to be influenced by a reflection that in the last analysis the best interests of every child include an expectation that difficult situations affecting the length and quality of its life will be taken for it by the parent to whom its care has been entrusted by nature.

[11.27] Keane CJ adopted this principle while saying that the Constitution does not oblige the State to allow the wishes of parents, no matter how irrational they appear to be, to prevail over the child's best interests. Such an approach would gravely endanger the child's right to a happy and healthy life and his rights as a member of the family. Keane CJ took the view that in this case the parents had refused to protect the child's Constitutional right to be guarded against unnecessary and avoidable dangers to his health, and that the Court should intervene in the child's best interests.

[11.28] It has been argued that this case errs too far in the direction of protection of parental rights and is, on the whole, unreceptive to the claims of children. It would also 'almost certainly make it impossible to introduce a compulsory vaccination programme for some childhood illnesses.'[17] The case may be seen as pushing the right of parents too far in the direction of absolute decision-making power in relation to their children, and identifying child rights only in the context of parental rights.[18] However, it should also be said that the Supreme Court acknowledged that each case of this kind requires a balancing of parental autonomy against the rights and interests of the child. Thus 'as the consequences of parental refusal become more serious or the grounds for the parents' objections become less serious, the justification for interference with parental autonomy grows. When the threat to the child's welfare becomes too great, it is both ethically desirable and legally justifiable to interfere.'[19] It is thought that disputes in relation to consent to medical treatment of children are likely to continue to grow in Ireland 'particularly as Irish society becomes more culturally diverse...There may be an

---

[17] Donnelly, *Consent: Bridging the Gap between Doctor and Patient* (Cork University Press, 2002) at 40.

[18] Arthur, '*North Western Health Board v HW and CW* – Reformulating Irish Family Law' (2002) 3 Irish Law Times 39.

[19] Donnelly, *Consent: Bridging the Gap between Doctor and Patient* (Cork University Press, 2002) at 41.

increase in the circumstances where medical norms may be challenged by parents from diverse backgrounds concerning their children's health and well-being.'[20]

[11.29] Exceptional circumstances have arisen where Irish courts have granted orders in favour of treatment of children against the wishes of their parents, for example, where a pregnant HIV positive woman refused to give birth in hospital, (although she subsequently agreed) Finnegan J directed that the child's welfare demanded that it be made a ward of court on birth, enabling the child to be tested and treated appropriately. The judge also reportedly said that he would have been prepared to consider making more intrusive orders had the woman not agreed to give birth in hospital, and had she intended to breast feed the baby.[21] This could be criticised on the basis that it does not enable the mother to prove her capacity for motherhood before making the child a ward of court. It appears that the judge presumed that by virtue of her decisions in relation to her pregnancy to date, she was to be considered an unfit mother. This appears to follow the line that the reasonableness or otherwise of parental decision-making is not at issue, rather the court must consider as paramount the welfare of the child, which in this instance mandated the testing and treatment if appropriate.

[11.30] In cases involving the refusal of treatment by Jehovah's Witness parents on behalf of their child, the court may make a temporary care order to facilitate the giving of a blood transfusion in accordance with the child's best medical interests.[22] In *Temple Street v D and another*,[23] an order allowing for the transfusion of a seriously ill three-month-old baby was made against the wishes of his parents. The baby's haemoglobin was at a level where transfusion was absolutely necessary but the parents, who were Jehovah's Witnesses, were opposed to the treatment. The hospital applied to the High Court for an emergency hearing at which the consultant treating the child gave evidence that the child's life was in immediate danger and that there were no alternatives to a transfusion. The parents refused to grant consent for the procedure but appeared resigned to having their wishes overruled, as this had occurred previously with another of their children.

[11.31] Hogan J granted the emergency order and in his judgment, delivered at a later date, he said that there was no doubting the sincerity of the parents' beliefs and their anxiety for the welfare of their child. He took as his starting point the protection of the

---

[20] Martin, 'Parental Rights to Withhold Consent to Medical Treatment for Their Child: A Conflict of Rights?' (2001) 7 Irish Law Times 114 at 119.

[21] See reports in The Irish Times, 20 July 2002.

[22] For example, a newspaper report in 2000 discusses the case of a young boy who was injured in an accident near his home, and required blood transfusions to save his life. His parents were Jehovah's Witnesses and refused consent for the transfusions. The South Eastern Health Board applied for an order taking the child into temporary care under the Child Care Act, s 12. This enabled the hospital to act in accordance with the child's best medical interests and carry out the transfusion. The child was returned to the custody of his parents within 72 hours. See report in The Irish Times, 3 March 2000. See discussion generally by Bridge, 'Religion, Culture and Conviction – The Medical Treatment of Young Children' (1999) Child and Fam L Q Vol 11 No 1, 1–15, in which she argues that the physical integrity of a young child who is too young to make decisions for himself must be accorded total respect and that parents cannot determine life and death matters, irrespective of their religious convictions.

[23] *Temple Street v D and another* [2011] IEHC 1.

free profession and practice of religion under art 44.2.1° of the Constitution, which provides a vital safeguard for minority religions whose tenets are regarded by some as unconventional. The judge said that most Irish people would express unease about a religious belief that required abstaining from an essential medical treatment, but those who held that faith regard the prohibition of blood as scripturally ordained and as a test of their faith. He also said that the right of a properly informed adult with full capacity to refuse medical treatment, whether for religious or other reasons, is constitutionally protected.[24] Of course, this case involved not an adult but a very young baby so different considerations arose.

[11.32] Hogan J said that while parents have the right to raise their children in accordance with their own religious views, this is not an absolute right and different considerations have to be taken into account to ensure that children are protected. The State has a vital interest in intervening in exceptional circumstances where there has been a failure on the part of the parents to protect the child's life or welfare. The test of whether the parents had failed in their duty under the Constitution is an objective one, judged by the secular standards of society in general and of the Constitution in particular, irrespective of the subjective and religious views of the parents. He said that the High Court has a jurisdiction and a duty to override the religious objections of parents where those beliefs threaten the life and welfare of their child and it was for this reason that he granted the declaration. Importantly, Hogan J also said that the declaration was limited to the particular clinical events and was not to be construed as giving clinicians an open-ended entitlement into the future to administer such treatment to the child.

[11.33] This case is important in recognising the constitutional right to free practice of religion but it also recognises that this, like other constitutional rights, is not absolute. The Court clearly stated the right of a competent adult to refuse medical treatment for any reason but noted that in circumstances where the patient is a child and therefore not capable of making such a decision, the State must step in where the parents fail in their duty to protect the life and welfare of their child. This is consistent with previous decisions in this context, but the case is significant as the first written High Court judgment on the matter. The restriction of the declaration to the immediate clinical circumstances also ensures that the infringement of parental authority is limited to the extent necessary to safeguard the child's welfare and is not to be taken as providing a *carte blanche* to clinicians in the future care of the child.

[11.34] As mentioned above, the Thirty-First Amendment of the Constitution (Children) Act 2012[25] removed art 42.5 of the Constitution and inserted art 42A. This provides that 'the state recognises and affirms the natural and imprescriptible rights of all children and shall, as far as practicable, by its laws protect and vindicate those rights.' Article 42A.2.1° provides that 'in exceptional cases, where the parents, regardless of their marital status, fail in their duty towards their children to such extent that the safety or welfare of any of their children is likely to be prejudicially affected, the state as guardian of the common good shall, by proportionate means as provided by law, endeavour to supply the place of the parents, but always with due regard for the natural and

---

[24] *Fitzpatrick v FK (No 2)* [2008] IEHC 104, [2009] 2 IR 7.
[25] This was signed into law in April 2015 following unsuccessful court challenge.

imprescriptible rights of the child.' The article also provides that in any proceedings concerning adoption, guardianship or custody of, or access to, any child, the best interests of the child shall be the paramount consideration. It further provides that in any such proceedings in respect of any child who is capable of forming his or her own views, the views of the child shall be ascertained and given due weight having regard to the age and maturity of the child.

[11.35] Article 42A.2.1° is important in shifting the trigger of intervention from focusing solely on the parents' failure to the impact of that failure on the child.[26] It also provides the State with the power to act when the safety or welfare of a child is likely to be prejudicially affected. It is thought that this new wording 'should encourage the State to intervene earlier in families that are struggling to offer them support and better protect the child.' But importantly, it also contains safeguards to protect against over-intervention by the State, by retaining the phrase 'exceptional cases' and introducing the term 'proportionate' in relation to the proposed intervention. It also provides for the first time the same threshold of protection to all children regardless of whether their parents are married or unmarried. O'Mahony argues that 'art 42A.1 is intended to signal a clear intention to protect the individual rights of all children, regardless of marital status. Its symbolic value is clear, but one cannot help wondering what its practical impact will be. It must be viewed as a relatively minor part of a very complex bigger picture.'[27]

Making decisions for infants with life-limiting conditions

[11.36] The treatment of critically ill newborns with life-limiting conditions is a matter of extreme concern for doctors and parents. While on the one hand decisions in relation to treatment of such a child are profoundly personal and private, there are also questions about law and public policy that need to be addressed. The overriding concern of the medical team caring for and treating the infant is the best interests of the child. This is true whether or not they are born with serious disabilities or are likely to develop such disabilities as they grow. However, as medicine becomes more advanced and more technologically capable of keeping such infants alive, the issue arises as to whether prolongation of life in such situations is always in the best interests of the child.[28]

[11.37] There may be situations where an exception exists to the general presumption in favour of providing life-sustaining treatment, for example where there is an irreversible progression to imminent death, where treatment would clearly be ineffective or harmful, where life would be severely shortened regardless of treatment, where non-treatment would allow a greater degree of caring and comfort than treatment, or where the child's life would be one of intolerable pain and suffering.[29] In many of these situations, the best interests of the child are uncertain because medicine is not an exact science and it may

---

[26] See www.childrensrights.ie for further discussion and submissions in relation to the referendum.

[27] http://humanrights.ie/constitution-of-ireland/legal-analysis-of-the-childrens-referendum-article-42a-1/.

[28] Bioethics Committee, Canadian Paediatric Society 'Treatment Decisions for Infants and Children' (2000).

[29] Bioethics Committee, Canadian Paediatric Society 'Treatment Decisions for Infants and Children' (2000).

not be possible to predict whether a particular treatment will work or, if it does work, what the outcome for the child will be in the long term. As a result, questions arise in relation to the wisdom or utility of trying to save all babies in this situation, particularly when they are born extremely prematurely. It is in these situations that the law has sometimes been asked to intervene to provide an objective determination of where the balance lies in protecting the child's best interests.

[11.38] This issue raises discussion of medical futility or the likelihood of benefit to the child from the proposed treatment. Although perhaps more commonly arising in the context of end-of-life care, 'futility is hardly a novel idea in medicine. Its roots in ancient medicine go back at least to the fifth-century BC physician Hippocrates. Yet debates over its meaning and ethical implications are surfacing with growing frequency. Increasingly, physicians seek to limit the lengths to which they must go to sustain the lives of patients who have lost the ability for conscious, interactive, and meaningful functioning.'[30] It is important that this discussion is not linked or confused with the question of rationing of healthcare resources, as these are entirely separate issues.[31] Respect for the dignity of all patients demands that consideration be taken only of their medical and emotional needs and interests, and that decisions be taken on that basis.

[11.39] The concept of futility should therefore be regarded within the medical rather than the economic sphere and may be described as a treatment 'which cannot give a minimum likelihood or quality of benefit'.[32] It may be argued that the term 'futility' is not always useful in the context of severely disabled infants for whom the question may not be one of life or death, but rather the possibility of sustaining an unacceptable quality of life. Pelligrino says that the term 'futility' suffers from 'vagueness in definition, clinically unpleasant connotations, and intense criticisms by credible bioethicists' but that there is nevertheless a role for the idea of futility where treatment cannot achieve anything and therefore 'futility is the inevitable corollary of the fact of human mortality.'[33] However, there are 'positive dangers of abuse if the term 'futile treatment' is adopted uncritically within the medical vocabulary. These include the resurgence of inappropriate paternalism, the erosion of patient autonomy, the unjustified avoidance of the duty to treat – or the creation of an ephemeral duty not to treat – and the introduction of disguised and arbitrary rationing of resources.'[34] It may be that the term 'non-productive treatment' better serves to place the problem firmly in the medical field and also clarifies the intention of the decision-makers.[35] As can be seen from the case law below, the courts have tended not to use the language of 'futility' or 'non-productive

---

[30] Jecker and Pearlman, 'Medical Futility: Who Decides?' (1992) 152(6) Arch Intern Med 1140.

[31] See *R v Cambridge Health Authority, ex parte B* (1995) 25 BMLR 5, rev'd [1995] 2 All ER 129 and discussion by Wall, in '*R v Cambridge Health Authority, ex parte B* (1995): A Tale of Two Judgments' in Herring and Wall, *Landmark Cases in Medical Law* (Hart Publishing, 2015) 111– 127. See also Koch, 'Care, compassion or cost? Redefining the basis of treatment in ethics and law' (2011) 39(2) J Law, Med and Ethics 130.

[32] Schneiderman and Jecker, 'Futility in Practice' (1993) 153 Arch Intern Med 437.

[33] Pelligrino, 'Futility in Medical Decisions: The Word and the Concept' (2005) 17 HEC Forum 308 at 309.

[34] Wreen, 'Medical Futility and Physician Discretion' (2004) 30 J Med Ethics 275.

[35] Laurie, Harmon and Porter, *Law and Medical Ethics* (10th edn, OUP, 2016) para 15.06.

treatment' but have focused on 'intolerability' in an adjudication of the best interests of the child.

[11.40] The issue of selective non-treatment of neonates or young babies is obviously one that is fraught with difficulty. While deliberate non-treatment at any age is problematic, the newborn baby born with seemingly insurmountable difficulties raises emotive ethical and legal issues around disability and the protection of the dignity of all human life. Parents who are faced with this dilemma are shocked, vulnerable, and probably inexperienced in medical language and decision-making of this kind. Therefore, in the majority of situations, the parents of the child will agree with the medical advice regarding their child and it is only in the rare instances where the family and the medical team have disagreed regarding treatment that the question has reached the courts. Doctors who work in the neonatal intensive care unit are highly qualified, technically skilful and motivated by the desire to do good.[36] Although the traditional model of deference to the profession has been challenged in recent years by a decline in trust, a focus on autonomy and patient-centred care and a rise in consumerism, nonetheless it appears that conflicts between doctors and parents in the neonatal care unit are rare and most parents are content to comply with medical advice.[37]

[11.41] Some disagreements, however, can arise from parental adherence to a particular religious belief or from an inability to comprehend the severity of the problems or an unwillingness to accept the prognosis despite unanimous medical evidence. Where this occurs, the relationship between the parents and clinicians can deteriorate and the hospital may seek judicial sanction for the proposed treatment decisions, as seen in the cases discussed below:

> Treatment decisions taken immediately after birth concern human beings who are at the most vulnerable period of their lives – human beings, moreover, who cannot express their feelings for the present or the future and who clearly cannot have indicated their references to their surrogates. Parents faced with decision making at this point may agree with their medical advisors simply because they have no evidence on which to *disagree*.[38]

[11.42] Another facet of the dilemma facing doctors in this area is the risk of contravening the criminal law by facilitating the death of the severely disabled infant. Killing a child or any other person is murder and even where the actions of the doctor were those of omission rather than commission, he might still be charged with manslaughter.[39] This risk is illustrated by *R v Arthur*[40] in which a doctor was prosecuted for the attempted murder of a newborn child. The facts of this case involved a baby born with Down's syndrome who was otherwise believed to be healthy but whose parents did

---

[36] Morris, 'Selective Treatment of Irreversibly Impaired Infants: Decision-Making at the Threshold' (2009) 17 Med Law Review pp 347–376, at 363.

[37] McHaffie et al, 'Deciding for Imperilled Newborns: Medical Authority or Parental Autonomy?' (2001) 27 JME 104.

[38] Laurie, Harmon and Porter, *Law and Medical Ethics* (10th edn, OUP, 2016) at para 15.09.

[39] See Cuttini, 'End of Life Decisions in Neonatal Intensive Care: Physicians' Self-Reported Practices in Seven European Countries' (2000) 355 Lancet 2112; Barton and Hodgman, 'The Contribution of Withholding or Withdrawing Care to Newborn Mortality' (2005) 116 Pediatrics 1487.

[40] *R v Arthur* [1981] 12 BMLR 1.

not want him to survive. Dr Arthur noted the parents' wishes on the baby's chart and prescribed 'nursing care only' in addition to prescribing medication to be administered at regular intervals to keep the baby sedated. The baby did not receive nourishment or sustenance and died within a few days of birth. It was alleged against the doctor that by prescribing nursing care only, he took steps to bring about the baby's death and intended that the baby should die. In his defence, Dr Arthur argued that his actions constituted acceptable medical practice and not murder. The doctor was initially charged with murder, but it transpired through the forensic evidence that the baby was not physically healthy in any event so the charge was reduced to attempted murder, and Dr Arthur was acquitted.

[11.43] In Farquharson J's summing up to the jury he discussed the careful and agonising consideration that had to be given in relation to the best interests of a child born with Down's syndrome, bearing in mind the 'most appalling' handicap facing the child, and in this case the rejection of the child by the parents. At the centre of the case was the fact that although doctors do not have the right to kill children who are handicapped or seriously disadvantaged, it is sometimes difficult to decide whether a doctor is carrying out a positive act or allowing a course of events to ensue, ie the difference between commission and omission. Evidence was given to the effect that allowing a newborn baby with serious handicap to die was not rare and that Dr Arthur's treatment of the baby was within responsible medical practice. One expert called to give evidence said 'There is an important difference between allowing a child to die and taking action to kill it. Withholding food is, I think, a negative, not a positive act. It is not a positive step to cause the child's death. The doctor indeed has a duty to order feeding, but if he orders food to be withheld, and he does it with the knowledge and wish of the parents, then that is permissible.' The President of the Royal College of Physicians at the time said:

> Where there is an uncomplicated Down's case and the parents do not want the child to live...I think there are circumstances where it would be ethical to put it upon a course of management that would end in its death ...I say that with a child suffering from Down's and with a parental wish that it should not survive, it is ethical to terminate life.[41]

It has been argued that this is a 'remarkable interpretation of both medical and parental responsibilities and powers' and that 'the acquittal of Dr Arthur should be seen as an anachronism' which would not be acceptable today.[42]

[11.44] The prosecution of Dr Arthur for his management of this baby led to a storm of protest from the medical profession, largely on the basis of the passive-active distinction.[43] It was argued that Dr Arthur should not have been prosecuted at all for treating a patient in a manner that most paediatricians would have seen as acceptable medical practice at that time. However, it appears that the reason the doctor was prosecuted may have been because the baby was 'treatable', in that he was in no physical pain and required no intervention as far as the doctors knew at the time. Death therefore

---

[41] *R v Arthur* [1981] 12 BMLR 1 at 21–2.

[42] Laurie, Harmon and Porter, *Law and Medical Ethics* (10th edn) at para 15.19.

[43] Laurie, Harmon and Porter, *Law and Medical Ethics* (10th edn) at para 15.18. See also 'Paediatricians and the Law' (1981) 283 BMJ 1280; 'After the Trial at Leicester' (1981) 2 Lancet 1085.

depended on someone deciding to withhold nourishment from this baby in circumstances which appear to have been based on social rather than medical grounds.

[11.45] Interestingly, another case decided in the same year in the UK also dealt with the question of treatment or non-treatment of a baby with Down's syndrome and is in direct conflict with the *Arthur* case. In *Re B (a minor)*[44] B was an infant whose Down's syndrome condition was complicated by intestinal obstruction, which would be fatal in the absence of surgical intervention. The parents took the decision that the kindest thing for B would be not to have her go through the surgery and for her to die, a decision described by the Court as 'entirely responsible'. The baby was made a ward of court and the question thus came before the Court as to whether she should be treated. In granting the application to authorise the surgery, Dunn LJ said that B 'should be put in the position of any other mongol[45] child and given the opportunity to live an existence.' Templeman LJ was concerned that the judge at first instance in refusing the operation had placed too much emphasis on the wishes of the parents and not enough on the interests of the child. The issue was simply whether to allow an operation to take place which may result in the child living for 20 or 30 years as a mongoloid or whether to terminate the life of a mongoloid child because she also happened to have an intestinal complaint:

> It devolves on this court…to decide whether the life of this child is demonstrably going to be so awful that in effect the child must be condemned to die or whether the life of this child is still so imponderable that it would be wrong for her to be condemned to die….Faced with the choice, I have no doubt that it is the duty of this court to decide that the child must live.[46]

[11.46] Templeman LJ did, however, concede that there may be situations in which the damage to the child is so severe and the child's future so certain to be full of pain and suffering, that the court may come to a different conclusion. In this case the Court of Appeal found no evidence that B's life would be 'intolerable' and held therefore that it was in her interests to have the operation. The case is important as it was the first time that the courts made it clear that in cases involving disputes about medical treatment of children, it is for the courts, not the parents, to decide. It also put it beyond doubt that the practice of allowing children to die simply on the basis that they were disabled was not lawful.[47] The case lays the foundation for 'a quality of life therapeutic standard rather than one based on a rigid adherence to the principle of the sanctity of human life.'[48]

[11.47] There were a series of English cases from the late 1980s and 1990s decided by Donaldson MR relating to the treatment of infants which 'can be viewed as establishing

---

[44] *Re B (a minor) (Wardship: medical treatment)* [1990] 3 All ER 927, [1981] 1 WLR 1421, CA. See discussion by Herring '*Re B (a minor) (Wardship: medical treatment)*: 'The child must live': disability, parents and the law' in Herring and Wall, *Landmark Cases in Medical Law* (Hart Publishing, 2015) 63–82.

[45] Mongol was a term used until the late 1970s as a synonym for persons with Down's syndrome but is no longer considered acceptable.

[46] *Re B (a minor)* [1990] 3 All ER 927 at 929, [1981] 1 WLR 1421 at 1424. See Raphael, 'Handicapped Infants: Medical Ethics and the Law' (1988) 14 J Med Ethics 5.

[47] Kennedy, 'Reflections on the Arthur trial', New Society, 7 Jan 1982, 13

[48] Laurie, Harmon and Porter, *Law and Medical Ethics* (10th edn, OUP, 2016) para 15.23.

the framework for tackling a spectrum of cases that explores the gamut of variables, from the (non)-relevance of distinguishing between withholding and withdrawing treatment to the difference between letting nature take its course and intervening to cause death.'[49] In the first of these cases, *Re C (A minor) (wardship: medical treatment)*,[50] C was a newborn baby suffering from congenital hydrocephalus. She was also a ward of court for other reasons. The local authority sought the determination of the Court as to how she should be treated in the event of a serious infection or in the event of her feeding regimes becoming unviable. C's prognosis was very poor, she was severely brain-damaged, blind, probably deaf, had spastic cerebral palsy of all four limbs and was not absorbing food. By contrast with *Re B*, the evidence here was that C was dying and there was nothing that the medical team could do to alter that fact. The Court held that C should be treated in a manner appropriate to her condition and that measures should be taken to ease her suffering rather than prolong her life. *Re B* was distinguished on the basis that in this case there was no option for the child to have a normal life span and that the child's life would be demonstrably awful and intolerable with no capacity to interact on any level, seemingly coming within the kind of exceptional situation envisaged by Templeman LJ in *Re B*.

[11.48] *Re J (a minor) (wardship: medical treatment)*[51] also concerned the question of whether treatment should be withheld from a baby with severe disabilities. J was a ward of court who had been born prematurely, had suffered very severe and permanent brain damage, was epileptic, and would be quadriplegic, blind and deaf. By contrast with *Re C*, J's life expectancy was uncertain but he was expected to die before late adolescence. He had been ventilated twice for long periods but it was the opinion of the medical team treating J that any further collapse requiring ventilation would be fatal. The question for the Court was whether the medical staff should re-ventilate him in the event of a further collapse. The Court held that even though J was not dying, life-sustaining treatment need not be given where the physical disabilities were so grave that the infant's life would be intolerable. However, the Court could never sanction positive steps to terminate the life of a person. The Court had to perform a balancing exercise between J's right to survive and the pain and suffering he would continue to experience for as long as he did survive. It was held that having regard to the invasive and hazardous nature of re-ventilation, the risk of further deterioration, and the extremely unfavourable prognosis, it would be in J's best interests that he not be re-ventilated. The court was keen to emphasise that the issue here was not about terminating life but about whether to withhold treatment which was designed to prevent death from natural causes.

[11.49] Lord Donaldson MR stated that no one could dictate the treatment to be given to a child, neither court, parents nor doctors. There must be checks and balances in the system such that doctors may recommend one treatment or refuse to adopt another treatment on medical grounds. The court or parents can refuse to consent to treatment but cannot insist on any particular treatment in its place. 'The inevitable and desirable result in that choice of treatment is in some measure a joint decision of the doctors and the court or parents.' The Court rejected submissions that respect for the sanctity of life

---

[49] Laurie, Harmon and Porter, *Law and Medical Ethics* (10th edn, OUP, 2016) para 15.24

[50] *Re C (A minor) (wardship: medical treatment)* [1990] Fam 26.

[51] *Re J (a minor) (wardship: medical treatment)* [1990] 3 All ER 930.

means that there should be no instance in which life-saving treatment should be withheld, irrespective of the side effects of treatment and the quality of life of the child thereafter. It held that there was no authority on principle or precedent for such an absolute position and that there was only one test, namely, the paramount nature of the child's best interests. Consideration of those interests might involve the court determining that deliberate steps should not be taken to artificially prolong the miserable life of a child doomed to incurable pain and suffering.

[11.50] These cases show a firm commitment to the welfare of the child as the paramount concern for the court, as well as strong opposition to any notion that the court could sanction any measures designed to end life. The court will therefore be most concerned with consideration of the pain, distress and suffering likely to be suffered by continuation of the child's life. In another case, also called *Re J (a minor) (medical treatment)*[52] a mother attempted to insist on treatment for her son, who was profoundly mentally and physically handicapped as a result of a fall when he was one month old. He suffered from microcephaly, cerebral palsy, blindness, and severe epilepsy. He was fed by nasogastric tube and was unlikely to progress beyond his present state. His life expectancy was uncertain but likely to be shortened. His convulsions required him to be resuscitated in hospital. The paediatrician considered that it would be medically inappropriate to use mechanical ventilation in any future resuscitation. The health authority, which shared parental responsibility for J, sought the Court's direction as to whether life-saving measures should be administered to J in the future if he suffered a life-threatening event.

[11.51] The Court held that the Court could not order a medical practitioner to treat a patient contrary to his clinical judgment and professional duty. The proper approach was for the Court to consider the options available to it in light of the paramountcy of the child's best interests and to authorise or refuse to authorise a proposed treatment in light of that consideration. The Court was of the view that this was largely a matter of clinical judgment and was not prepared to direct that any particular treatment should be given that might conflict with such judgment.

[11.52] These cases taken together demonstrate the reluctance of the courts to stray into the area of clinical autonomy or judgment. The courts have stated on many occasions that a doctor could not be forced to provide a treatment to which he was professionally and ethically opposed on the grounds that it was not in his patient's best interests. Therefore, parents can never have a right to treatment for their child where this is considered medically inappropriate. The courts seem to support a wide-ranging clinical discretion whereby the *clinical* judgment of the doctor is applied to the 'best interests' of the patient, even though those interests involve issues beyond diagnosis and prognosis.[53] It is not clear what the courts would decide in less clear-cut cases than those discussed above where the medical evidence is less than unanimously in favour of non-treatment of the child, although the general tenor of the judgments of the courts suggests that it would be more likely to opt for the salvaging of life.

---

[52] *Re J (a minor) (child in care: medical treatment)* [1993] Fam 15. [1992] 4 All ER 614.
[53] Morris, 'Selective Treatment of Irreversibly Impaired Infants: Decision-Making at the Threshold' (2009) 17 Med Law Review, 347–376 at 354.

[11.53] In *Re C (a minor) (medical treatment)*[54] the Court again had to consider whether to authorise non-treatment of a young child. In this case C was 16 months old and suffered from spinal muscular atrophy, as a result of which she suffered occasional respiratory arrest for which she had to be ventilated. At the date of the hearing she was on ventilation in hospital, which delayed her death but did not alleviate her suffering. The doctors were of the opinion that ventilation should not be continued indefinitely and that it should not be reintroduced in the event of further respiratory arrests. The parents felt unable to consent to this course of action on the basis of firmly held religious views. The Court reiterated the statement expressed in previous cases that a doctor should not be required to treat a child contrary to his clinical judgment and that, if upheld, the parents' insistence on ventilation in the event of further respiratory arrests would oblige the doctors to undertake a course of treatment that they were unwilling to do on clinical grounds.

[11.54] The Court held therefore that on the evidence, it was in C's best interests to be taken off ventilation and that she should not be re-ventilated in the event of further respiratory failures. This case demonstrates again how parent and child interests might come into conflict. C's parents were unable to face losing their daughter yet the Court determined that their assessment of her best interests should be overruled. Although they wanted her to live as long as possible, the Court held that it was not in her interests to continue to suffer. It is interesting to note that the parents' opposition in this case stemmed from the fact that they were Orthodox Jews who believed in the sanctity of life at all costs. This is however a principle to which the courts have not ascribed, holding that it may not always be in a child's best interests to be kept alive, especially where the child will have a life full of suffering and distress.

[11.55] In *An NHS Trust v D*,[55] the Court was asked to consider the treatment of a 19-month-old child who had been born prematurely with serious disabilities, in particular a severe, chronic, irreversible and worsening lung disease, giving him a very short life expectancy. He also had heart failure, hepatic and renal dysfunction and severe developmental delay. The NHS Trust involved in his care applied for a declaration that in the event of any future respiratory or cardiac failure, it was in his best interests not to resuscitate him but to apply palliative measures to permit him to die peacefully. The medical evidence was that the child's condition could not improve and that invasive treatment would cause distress, discomfort and pain. His parents strongly opposed the application on the grounds that it was premature.

[11.56] Cazelet J outlined four legal principles applicable to this case as follows: firstly, the Court's paramount consideration must be the best interests of the child. This involves consideration of the parent's views, but such views cannot override the Court's views of the child's best interests. Secondly, the Court must respect the sanctity of human life and is obliged to take all steps to preserve life, save in exceptional circumstances. Thirdly, the Court could never approve a course designed to terminate life or accelerate death. It should only be concerned with whether to prolong life. Fourthly, the Court should not direct a doctor to provide treatment that he is unwilling to give according to that doctor's clinical judgment. Having regard to these principles and the minimal quality of life that

---

[54] *Re C (a minor) (medical treatment)* [1998] 1 FLR 384.
[55] *A NHS Trust v D* [2000] Fam Law 803; [2000] 2 FLR 677.

the child had in the short life span left to him in any event, the judge weighed any possible short-term extension to his life against the increasing pain and suffering caused by further ventilation.

[11.57] A declaration was granted to the effect that withholding ventilation would be lawful but, in essence, the decision would be that of the paediatrician in charge of the child's care. This re-affirms previous decisions on the principle that the best interests of the child do not demand heroic measures to be performed in order to prolong life where the child's life expectancy is short and the quality of life is poor. The Court appears to have preferred the opinion of the consultant in charge of the baby's care, who said he had 'minimal awareness' despite the views of his parents and community health workers who had noted improvements in his condition in preceding months. Parental wishes are taken into consideration but are not determinative of the issue, which must be decided on clinical grounds.[56]

[11.58] In *Re Wyatt (A child) (Medical Treatment: parent's consent)*,[57] a baby girl had been born prematurely at 26 weeks gestation, and suffered from severe and repeated respiratory failure with associated heart and renal failure. She was blind, deaf and could make no voluntary movements. Medical evidence was unanimously of the view that she would have minimal cognitive function but would be able to experience the pain of any future medical treatment. Her treating doctors were of the view that further ventilation was not in her best interests, as it would require a tracheotomy and this would subject her to pain and distress without any chance of restoring her to health or prolonging her life significantly. Her parents, who were devout Christians, disagreed. Hedley J held that artificial ventilation, which was not recommended by the medical team, would not be in the child's best interests. Applying the 'intolerability' test of previous cases, the judge was influenced by the medical views that even if she were to survive re-ventilation, her condition was likely to deteriorate and the experience of intensive care treatment would imperil a peaceful death.

[11.59] On appeal, an argument was put to the Court that indeed the proper test to apply was whether the child's life was 'intolerable' but her parents were of the view that her condition had improved to the extent that it could not be described as intolerable. However, the Court said that 'intolerability' was only a potentially valuable guide towards the determination of best interests and that any improvement in her condition was minimal. In refusing the appeal, the Court of Appeal held that:

> The intellectual milestones for the judge in a case such as the present are, therefore, simple, although the ultimate decision will frequently be extremely difficult. The judge must decide what is in the child's best interests. In making that decision, the welfare of the child is paramount, and the judge must look at the question from the assumed point of view of the patient. There is a strong presumption in favour of a course of action which will prolong life, but that presumption is not irrebuttable. The term 'best interests' encompasses medical, emotional, and all other welfare issues. The court must conduct a

---

[56] For analysis of the position in the Netherlands, see Brownstein, 'Neonatal Euthanasia Case Law in the Netherlands' (1997) 71 Aus LJ 54. See also Moor, 'Euthanasia in Relation to Newborn Babies – A Comparative Study of the Legal and Ethical Issues' (1996) 15 Med Law 295.

[57] *Re Wyatt (A child) (Medical Treatment: parent's consent)* [2004] EWHC 2247.

balancing exercise in which all the relevant factors are weighed and a helpful way of undertaking this exercise is to draw up a balance sheet.

[11.60] This case was different from some of the others discussed above in that the question here was not about whether the baby should live or die but *how* and *when* she should die. The media and public attention surrounding this case led to it becoming something of a 'battleground in the defence of the sanctity of life', with Brazier referring to the transformation of private tragedy to public spectacle as disturbing.[58] 'There is no right answer to the dilemma in *Re Wyatt*. Resolution in the courts may indeed exacerbate a tragedy nature created. But is there any alternative?'[59] Hedley J stated that any civilised society must have the means by which intractable disputes are to be resolved and that although a judge will be aware of his own limitations in deciding cases such as these, he or she must nonetheless reach a decision. 'It may well be that an external decision is in the end a better solution than the stark alternatives of medical or parental veto.'[60]

[11.61] Brazier also questions how the initial decision to treat Charlotte was taken, given that the longer the child lives, the more the child appears to have a will to live, and the more agonising the decision of the parents becomes. Although the principles applied in this case were by and large those used previously, nevertheless 'the furore surrounding the case indicates a deep-seated unease about any decision that suggests a life is not worth living.'[61] It may also be questioned why only relatively few cases of conflict arise between doctors and parents, how they arise and whether the courts are the best place to resolve them:

> There are, also, wider considerations of the role of the medical profession, the 'rights' of parents and – underlying it all – the ultimate question of the value of life, including lives affected by physical or mental impairments. Changing attitudes to disability have been due in part to an increasing determination by those with impairments to have their voices heard, and some vociferously oppose the notion that anyone should, as they see it, decide that another person's impaired life is not worth living. Others, who accept that sometimes difficult decisions have to be made, are concerned to establish a transparent ethical and legal framework. The dilemmas raised by these babies encompass the limits of medical technology, professional ethics, parental responsibility, and the role of law in setting standards for society.[62]

[11.62] The balance sheet approach referred to above is illustrated by *An NHS Trust v MB*,[63] where MB had a severe form of spinal muscular atrophy which is fatal without artificial ventilation but MB also had the normal cognition of an 18 month old child. The unanimous medical opinion was that M's quality of life was so low and the burden of living was so great that it was unethical to continue treatment. However, Holman J

---

58 Brazier, 'An Intractable Dispute: When Parents and Professionals Disagree' 13 Med L Rev (2005) 412–418 at 413–414.

59 Brazier, 'An Intractable Dispute: When Parents and Professionals Disagree' 13 Med L Rev (2005) 412–418 at 418.

60 *Re Wyatt (A child) (Medical Treatment: parent's consent)* [2004] EWHC 2247 at para 4.

61 Morris, 'Selective Treatment of Irreversibly Impaired Infants: Decision-Making at the Threshold' (2009) 17 Med Law Review, pp 347–376 at 347.

62 Morris, 'Selective Treatment of Irreversibly Impaired Infants: Decision-Making at the Threshold' (2009) 17 Med Law Review, pp 347–376 at 347–348.

63 *An NHS Trust v M* [2006] EWHC 507.

said that he was being asked to approve, against parental wishes, the removal of life support from a conscious child with sensory awareness and assumed normal cognition. Taking the balance sheet approach, he noted M's inability to move or communicate as well as his pleasure in his family and his soft toys. He said M's life was helpless and sad but he had a relationship of value with his family as well as other pleasures from sight, touch and sound. He held that the burdens of treatment did not outweigh the benefits and he refused to grant the declaration sought by the hospital to discontinue ventilation and provide palliative care only. Holman J set out ten propositions which summarised the jurisprudence in this area, which included the principles that 'considerable weight must be attached to the prolongation of life but the principle is not absolute and may be outweighed if the pleasures and the quality of life are sufficiently small and the pain and suffering or other burdens of living are sufficiently great.' He also said that the wishes of the parents are irrelevant to the objective best interests of the child save to the extent that they may illuminate the quality and value to the child of the parent-child relationship. The case is significant in that it shows that courts *can* sometimes direct doctors to treat even where doctors are of the view that it would be unethical, and this can itself create practical dilemmas for the daily care and treatment of the patient.[64]

[11.63] Other cases include *Re K (a minor)*[65] where the court issued a declaration to enable the medical staff of the Trust to remove from K's abdomen a tube necessary to maintain her nutrition, and to move to a regime of palliative care in order to allow her to die peacefully over a short period of time as there was no realistic sense in which she could have the simple pleasure of being alive. Also relevant is *Re OT*[66] in which a nine-month-old baby required continuous ventilation to live, and sometimes required further intensive medical treatment. The trust wanted to discontinue ventilation and treatment on the basis of the distressing and futile nature of the treatment but the parents wanted all steps to be taken to sustain life. The court held that although the application itself was made in an emergency as a result of a sudden deterioration in the child's condition, the parents had a fair opportunity to prepare their case both before and during the hearing and therefore there was no flaw in the process breaching ECHR rights. Declarations were made permitting the clinicians to treat OT according to their clinical discretion (including not escalating treatment) and to cease ventilation immediately.

[11.64] These cases, and others,[67] show the tragic and difficult circumstances that courts sometimes have to deal with by balancing considerations of best interests, clinical opinion and parental wishes. The is again illustrated by the recent case of *Central Manchester University Hospitals NHS Foundation Trust v A and others*[68] where the

---

[64] Morris, 'Selective Treatment of Irreversibly Impaired Infants: Decision-Making at the Threshold' (2009) 17 Med Law Review, at 369.

[65] *Re K (a minor)* [2006] 2 FLR 883.

[66] *Re OT* [2009] EWHC 633.

[67] See also *NHS Trust v Baby X* [2012] EWHC 2188 (Fam); *An NHS Foundation Trust v AB* [2014] EWHC 1031; *King's College Hospital NHS Foundation Trust v T* [2014] EWHC 3315 (Fam); *King's College Hospital NHS Foundation Trust v Y (By Her Children's Guardian) MH* [2015] EWHC 1966 (Fam); *An NHS Trust v Child B and others* [2014] EWHC 3486 (Fam); *Re A (a child)* [2015] EWHC 443 (Fam).

[68] *Central Manchester University Hospitals NHS Foundation Trust v A and others* [2015] EWHC 2828 (FAM) 12 October.

court was asked to make a declaration authorising the withdrawal of life support from identical twin boys aged 14 months both of whom were suffering from a progressive neuro-degenerative disorder. The boys were non-responsive to stimuli, had increased muscular spasms, increased dystonia and recent onset of seizure activity. The disorder had no known diagnosis and was considered untreatable and completely incurable. Without artificial ventilation they would die but the medical team considered that it was unethical to maintain the ventilation and that they were needlessly prolonging pain and suffering for each boy. The parents did not consent to the ventilation being withdrawn.

[11.65] The court once again held that the test is the best interests of the patient. 'Best interests are used in the widest sense and include every kind of consideration capable of impacting on the decision. These include, non-exhaustively, medical, emotional, sensory (pleasure, pain and suffering) and instinctive (the human instinct to survive) considerations. The court said that although considerable weight must be attached to the prolongation of life because the individual human instinct and desire to survive is strong and must be presumed to be strong in the patient, this is not absolute, nor necessarily decisive; and may be outweighed if the pleasures and the quality of life are sufficiently small and the pain and suffering or other burdens of living are sufficiently great.'

[11.66] The court held that the views and opinions of both the doctors and the parents must be carefully considered. Where, as in this case, the parents spend a great deal of time with their child, the court held that their views may have particular value because they know the patient and how he reacts so well; although the court needs to be mindful that the views of any parents may, very understandably, be coloured by their own emotion or sentiment. The court went on to say that the parents' wishes, 'however understandable in human terms, are wholly irrelevant to consideration of the objective best interests of the child save to the extent in any given case that they may illuminate the quality and value to the child of the child/parent relationship.' The court held that, in the circumstances, 'to artificially prolong their lives... lacks any purpose, confers no benefit at all apart from the fact of physical survival, and involves perpetuating the infliction of pain and discomfort for no gain or purpose. It is not in the best interests of either boy that the process be artificially prolonged, and it is in their best interests that nature should now be permitted to take its inevitable course. That is the tragic genetic destiny of each of these boys.' Ventilation was withdrawn a few days later and the boys died.

[11.67] The Royal College of Paediatrics and Child Health in England has issued useful guidance in this area for many years.[69] In its most recent guidance in 2015 it reiterates the importance of ongoing discussion between clinicians and parents to try to resolve conflicts, using second opinions and mediators if necessary. The College states that there are five situations in which it is ethical and legal to consider withholding or withdrawing treatment from a child. These range from children with advanced progressive incurable disease, children whose death is expected in the near future, children in whom there is a risk of death from a sudden acute crisis in the condition,

---

[69] *Making decisions to limit treatment in life-limiting and life-threatening conditions in children: a Framework for Practice*, (RCPCH, 2015). See also BMA guidelines, *Withholding and Withdrawing Life-Prolonging Medical Treatment: Guidelines for Decision-Making* (3rd edn, BMJ Books, 2007).

children in whom sudden catastrophic events have produced a life-threatening situation, and children in whom the prospect of survival is small, for example some extremely premature infants. Where the child's condition does not fit any of these categories, the child's life should be safeguarded as much as possible.

[11.68] The question of whether to treat extremely premature infants is also a difficult one as although medical advances in recent years mean that it may be technically possible to do so, there is evidence that at least some of these children will suffer ongoing consequences and disadvantages. In 2006 the Nuffield Council on Bioethics published its Report on *Critical Care Decisions in Fetal and Neonatal Medicine*,[70] which proposed guidelines based on gestational age for deciding on the initiation and continuation of intensive care. At 25 weeks gestation and above, it recommended that intensive care should be initiated unless the baby is affected by some severe abnormality incompatible with any significant period of survival. Between 24 and 25 weeks it recommended that a baby should normally be offered intensive care unless parents and clinicians are agreed that in light of the baby's condition, or likely condition, it is not in his best interests to start intensive care. Between 23 and 24 weeks, it is recommended that precedence should be given to the wishes of the parents regarding resuscitation and intensive care but that 'when the condition of the baby indicates that he or she will not survive for long, clinicians are not legally obliged to proceed with treatment wholly contrary to their clinical judgment, if they judge that treatment would be futile.' Parents may decline intensive care because, the Report recognises, 'it will be the parents who will live with the consequences.'[71] Between 22 and 23 weeks, standard practice should be not to resuscitate unless parents request it and the clinicians agree that it is an exceptional case and the resuscitation is in the baby's best interests. Below 22 weeks it is recommended that resuscitation should not be attempted unless it is within an approved research study.

[11.69] The Report received a mixed response, with some commenting that the guidelines were to be 'commended for striving for transparency' and for taking account of factors other than purely medical considerations such as the child's capacity to experience pleasure and form relationships.[72] Others such as the British Medical Association called them 'blanket rules' smothering clinical discretion. On charges that the report treated newborn life as of lesser value than the lives of older children by pointing to the fact that few people insist that when life can be prolonged for however short a time, it must be, the Chairperson Margaret Brazier responded 'What the baby, older child or adult is entitled to, morally and legally, is appropriate care. Neonatal intensive care is invasive and burdensome. A baby may be subjected to 200 or so intrusive and painful procedures in one fortnight. He or she is isolated from the love and warmth of their family, and deprived of the care that should be the birthright of any

---

[70] Nuffield Council on Bioethics, Report on *Critical Care Decisions in Fetal and Neonatal Medicine*. Available at www.nuffieldbioethics.org

[71] Nuffield Council on Bioethics, Report on *Critical Care Decisions in Fetal and Neonatal Medicine,* para 9.17.

[72] Morris, 'Selective Treatment of Irreversibly Impaired Infants: Decision-Making at the Threshold' (2009) 17 Med Law Review, at 350–351.

newborn. When insisting on treatment imposes an intolerable burden on the baby, such treatment becomes inhumane.'[73]

[11.70] One of the important features of the Report is the emphasis on listening to parents' views, and, similar to the Royal College of Paediatrics and Child Health, it recommends a partnership model between clinicians and parents. The question arises, however, to what extent parents' views will be considered in reality, as there is a vast difference between parents being informed as to what will happen and, on the other hand, parents being asked to make the final choice. McHaffie wonders whether parents are really sharing decision-making or 'are neonatologists practising a form of benevolent paternalism?'[74] Although parents may perceive that they have been involved in decision-making, in many instances they will simply have been agreeing with the clinical recommendation. McHaffie believes that parents have 'an impressive ability to understand the issues and weigh up the consequences for their own child' and where the child spends a lengthy period of time in intensive care, the parents will become very familiar with procedures and medical terminology and can participate effectively in decision-making. The Nuffield Report also recognises that in some cases consensus between clinicians and parents will not be achieved, and in most of these situations the parents' views should take priority. It recommended that every effort should be made to resolve disputes without judicial intervention, such as mediation and the use of clinical ethics committees, which are more prevalent in the United States, to assist in providing advice in individual cases.

[11.71] It is interesting to note the different legislative approach taken in the Netherlands where the Coroners Act was amended in 1993 to provide that doctors who carried out euthanasia upon request, or actively terminated a patient's life without request, should report the case to the coroner who would inform the District Attorney. No judicial inquiry would be started if the circumstances indicated that the doctors acted with due conscientious care.[75] The requirements of good medical practice were not explicitly mentioned in the Act. During 1995 two test cases concerning neonatal euthanasia came before the Dutch courts. In the first case, Dr Kadijk administered a combination of lethal drugs to a 25-day-old neonatal girl at the request of the parents.[76] He was charged with murder under the Penal Code. The baby had been born with Patau Syndrome, or Trisomy 13, which caused her to have a cleft lip and palate, skull defects, overlapping fingers and microphthalmia. Ninety per cent of children born with this condition died within the first year of life with serious mental retardation, multiple neurological defects, convulsions and motor retardation. She had a cardio-respiratory arrest shortly after birth and was resuscitated, subsequently evidence of renal failure was also noted. It was decided that should another arrest occur, no further resuscitation would be attempted and she was discharged home. One of her scalp defects became

---

[73] Brazier and Archard, 'Letting Babies Die' (2007) JME 33:125–126; See also April and Parker, 'End of Life Decision-Making in Neonatal Care' (2007) JME 33:126–127.

[74] McHaffie et al, 'Deciding for Imperilled Newborns: Medical Authority or Parental Autonomy?' (2001) 27 JME 104.

[75] Fenigsen, 'The Netherlands: New Regulations Concerning Euthanasia Issues' (1993) 9 (2) Law Med 167.

[76] Judgment of the Groningen District Court in the *Kadijk* case, Parket Nummer: 070093–95, Public Prosecutor's Office, the Hague, Netherlands, 7 November 1995.

infected and she experienced convulsions, spinal fluid leakage and other difficulties. Analgesics and sedatives were considered unsuitable, as they would have caused her death due to her other medical problems. The doctors and parents took the view that no other option was available than ending of her life. The doctor complied with the necessary regulations and notified the coroner before the death of the child. Dr Kadijk was acquitted, with the Court noting that he had acted with scientific responsible medical insight and in accordance with accepted norms of medical ethics.

[11.72] The second case heard on the same day in 1995 involved Dr Prins, who was charged with murder for administering lethal medication to a three-day-old neonate suffering from hydrocephalus and spina bifida.[77] The baby was in severe pain with grossly deformed and paralysed limbs and a poorly developed brain. The medical prognosis was that she faced a short life of pain from several weeks to six months. Following detailed discussion, the parents requested termination of her life with lethal injection. Legal regulations were complied with and the doctor was again acquitted. In both cases the courts acquitted on grounds of *force majeure* in an emergency situation.[78]

The 'difficult' case of *Re T*

[11.73] One particular English case stands out from the rest in relation to the weight to be given to parental authority.[79] In *Re T (a minor) (wardship: medical treatment)*[80] the child in question had been born with a life-threatening liver defect for which he underwent an operation at almost one month old. The operation was unsuccessful and caused the child pain and distress. The prognosis was that he would not live beyond two-and-a-half years without a liver transplant. The evidence before the Court was to the effect that, although liver transplantation was complicated surgery, the operation had a good chance of success for the child, and if successful, the child would go on to have many years of normal life. The mother refused to give her consent for the surgery on the basis that she did not wish the child to undergo the pain and distress of further surgery.[81]

[11.74] On an application by the local authority at the instigation of the consultants dealing with the care of this child, the trial judge held that the mother's decision was not that of a reasonable parent and directed that the child should have the surgery. On appeal, the Court of Appeal recognised the importance of the mother's support for the surgery especially in terms of the necessary aftercare of the child. The mother's concerns as to the benefits of the surgery, the dangers of failure and the possibility of the need for future transplants, and the effect on the child of these concerns were all factors

---

[77] Verdict of the Amsterdam Court of Appeal in the *Prins* case, Arrest Number 23:002076–95. Public Prosecutor's Office, The Hague, Netherlands, 7 November 1995.

[78] See Brownstein, 'Neonatal Euthanasia Case Law in the Netherlands' (1997) 71 Aust LJ 54–58.

[79] Freeman refers to this case as 'the nadir of judicial thinking in this area.' See Freeman, 'Whose Life is it Anyway?' (2001) 9 Med L Rev 259 at 273.

[80] *Re T (a minor) (wardship: medical treatment)* [1997] 1 All ER 906. This case has generated much academic comment. For example, Fox and McHale, 'In Whose Best Interests?' (1997) 60 MLR 700; Freeman, 'Whose Life is it Anyway?' (2001) 9 Med L Rev 259; Loughrey, 'Medical Treatment – The Status of Parental Opinion' [1998] Fam Law 146.

[81] The parents were not married, so only the mother had parental responsibility. Both parents were healthcare professionals.

to be taken into account by the Court. The fact that the mother would be in a position whereby she had to care for the child without the support of the child's father, who lived outside the jurisdiction, and that she would be forced to provide a commitment to the care of her child after surgery which she did not support, all combined to persuade the Court that it would not be in the child's best interests to require him to undergo the surgery.

[11.75] There are a number of aspects of this decision which merit discussion. Until *Re T* all the cases decided by the English courts had shown deference to medical opinion where there was disagreement with parents in relation to the treatment to be provided to their child. The question was always whether the proposed treatment was in the best interests of the child, rather than whether parental wishes should be respected. The other cases involved severely disabled infants who had little or no prospect of improvement and had little or no interaction with their environment. The child in *Re T* did not fall into that category. The Court in *Re T* held that it had to take into account a range of factors in reaching its decision as to the welfare of the child. These factors included the wishes of the parents, who in this case happened to be healthcare professionals themselves, the child's life expectancy, the circumstances of the mother in having to return to the jurisdiction without her partner, and the reluctance of the doctors to perform the surgery in the face of parental opposition. Therefore, the Court took into account other factors apart from the clinical factors. This was unusual in that the medical evidence was unanimously in favour of the surgery on the basis that the prognosis was good.

[11.76] Waite LJ was of the view that one of the distinguishing factors in *Re T* was that the opposition of the parents was not due to dogma or strict principle that may be considered contrary to the principle that the child's best interests should always be paramount, but rather their opposition was due to concerns based on their professional healthcare experience and their child's previous surgical experiences. This would seem to be directed at cases involving Jehovah's Witnesses where parents have been opposed, as a matter of religious principle, to the transfusion of blood to their children.[82] In such cases the courts have generally refused to allow religious beliefs to take precedence over the child's best medical interests.[83] However, in *Re T* the Court took a very different view of the rationale behind the parent's opposition, despite stating that the reasonableness of their refusal was not an issue for the Court to decide.

[11.77] It may be questioned why parental refusal should be accorded more respect in one case rather than the other. 'One distinction may be that the court is prepared to give weight to non-metaphysical factors such as concerns about treatment, but will not consider an assessment of metaphysical factors to be within its competence.'[84] In this case the treatment proposed was unanimously recommended on clinical grounds, it had a relatively minor risk factor that was regarded as well worth taking in light of the fact that it may extend the child's life expectancy considerably. This was not a case where the parents objected to an unusual or experimental treatment that had a poor success rate. It may be argued that parental opposition to treatment should only be relevant where such opposition would jeopardise the chances of success of the treatment, or alternatively

---

[82] For example *An NHS Trust v Child B and others* [2014] EWHC 3486 (Fam).
[83] See *Re S (a minor) (medical treatment)* [1993] 1 FLR 376.
[84] Loughrey, 'Medical Treatment – The Status of Parental Opinion' [1998] Fam Law 146 at 147.

where the relationship between the child and its parents would be so adversely affected that it would not be in the child's best interests to proceed with the treatment in question.

[11.78] Butler-Sloss LJ based her decision on the basis that the mother's total commitment to the surgery was essential to its success, and that forcing the mother to take on this commitment where she did not believe that it was the right thing for her son, would not be in the best interests of the child. While the first of these grounds comes within a traditional interpretation of clinical factors to be taken into consideration, the second arguably goes more towards parental interests. This is seen also in the statement of Butler-Sloss LJ where she describes the mother and child as one – 'the welfare of the child depends upon its mother.' In fact, the converse could be said to be true in this particular case, where the interests of the mother and child were in direct conflict. 'The impact of the situation upon the mother may have been severe, but how conscious would the child have been of the difficulties? It may have been preferable from the child's point of view to be in care with a good chance of survival if the mother could not cope.'[85]

[11.79] Another interesting point of distinction here is the aftercare element that played an important role in shaping the attitude of the Court to the mother's refusal. The Court was of the view that this child's problems required major and complicated surgery and many years of aftercare and administration of medication by the mother. However, when one examines the previous cases, such as *Re C* where the parents of a child with Down's syndrome had refused consent to surgery for an intestinal complaint, it is apparent that in some of these other cases the aftercare involved was as onerous if not more so than in *Re T*. Indeed, if anything, when one compares the case of *Re B*, the child in that case was likely to entail an even greater commitment to caring than the child in the present case, given that after the operation the parents in *Re B* were faced with caring for their disabled child for her remaining lifespan, which was estimated to be 20–30 years.[86]

[11.80] On the question of the rights of the child, the Court did not seem to accept any arguments on this basis, saying that this was not an occasion to talk of the rights of the child. Waite LJ said that in cases such as this, the best interests of the child include an expectation that difficult decisions affecting the length and quality of its life will be taken for it by the parent to whom its care has been entrusted. This may seem to be a throwback to common law notions of the natural rights of parents over their children.[87] Freeman criticises the case on the basis that the Court, while stating that the paramountcy principle must be applied, did not do so wisely. Waite LJ's 'unfortunate dismissal' of rights language is not 'calculated to respect the integrity, individuality, or the citizenship of children.'[88] Freeman claims that the Court was:

> [O]ver-influenced by parental wishes, taken in by their professional knowledge, over-emphasised the logistic problem of returning the child to the jurisdiction…and too little concerned with the interests of a very sick child…Its decision is a hangover from an era in which the unimpeachable parent held sway, when courts were convinced by the validity of

---

[85] Bainham, 'Do Babies Have Rights?' (1997) 56(1) CLJ 48.

[86] Fox and McHale, *Health Care Law, Text and Materials* (Sweet & Maxwell, 1997) pp 703–704.

[87] Bainham, 'Do Babies Have Rights?' (1997) 56(1) CLJ 48.

[88] Freeman, 'Whose Life is it Anyway?' (2001) 9 Med L Rev 259 at 263.

such pseudo-scientific notions as the blood tie and judges could refer to parents' rights (more commonly fathers' rights) as sacrosanct.[89]

[11.81] There has been much criticism of the Court's emphasis on the parents' status as healthcare professionals with experience of paediatric care. 'The Court of Appeal was clearly impressed by their understanding of the situation – so much so that, at times, the mother's views appear to take on the significance of another expert medical opinion.'[90] It is generally considered advisable that medical professionals do not treat members of their own family. The distinction drawn in this case was between 'treatment' and 'caring', which is a distinction fraught with difficulties even apart from the fact that the carers here were health professionals.[91] It is not clear from the judgments why more emphasis was put on the implications for the carers if a decision was made with which they did not agree, than the medical evidence in favour of performing the surgery.

[11.82] *Re T* is probably best regarded as a problematic case in the line of precedents in the UK on medical treatment of young children. The application of the best interests test here appears to have conflated the interests of the child with those of the parents without recognising the danger of according too much weight to parental views. 'Despite the protestations of all three judges, and despite the court's repeated assurance as to the responsibility and devotion of the parents, an unavoidable impression remains that their interests weighed heavily in the balance at the expense of the paramountcy of those of the child.'[92] The case 'highlights the need for a more sophisticated method of adjudicating in cases where such multi-factored decision-making is at issue.'[93] It has been argued that an alternative would be to adopt the practice of using *amicus curiae* briefs where interested parties can assist in providing expert advice, and help to assess alternative legal arguments and judicial conclusions.[94]

---

[89] Freeman, 'Whose Life is it Anyway?' (2001) 9 Med L Rev 259 at 258–259.

[90] Laurie, Harmon and Porter, *Law and Medical Ethics* (10th edn, OUP, 2016) para 15.63.

[91] Fox and McHale, *Health Care Law, Text and Materials* (Sweet & Maxwell, 1997) p 704.

[92] Laurie, Harmon and Porter, *Law and Medical Ethics* (10th edn, OUP, 2016) para 15.64.

[93] Fox and McHale, *Health Care Law, Text and Materials* (Sweet & Maxwell, 1997) p 709.

[94] Fox and McHale, *Health Care Law, Text and Materials* (Sweet & Maxwell, 1997) p 709. For comparative case law see *In the Matter of Baby K* 832 F Supp 1022 (ED Va 1993), affd 16 F 3d 590 (4th Cir, 1994); Flannery, 'One Advocate's Viewpoint: Conflicts and Tensions in the *Baby K* Case' (1995) 23 Law Med & Ethics 7; Clayton, 'Commentary: What is Really at Stake in *Baby K?*' (1995) 23 Law Med & Ethics 13. In this case an anencephalic baby was placed on a ventilator but was expected to die within days. Treatment was considered medically and ethically inappropriate. However, the mother insisted on ventilation of the baby despite medical advice to the contrary. The Court decided on the basis of its interpretation of the relevant statute that stabilising measures had to be given for the infant's respiratory distress, rather than on any application of a best interests test. The Court also held that the parents of a child have the Constitutional right to make decisions on behalf of their children, unless the result will be to cause harm to the child. In the Canadian case *Re Superintendent of Family and Child Service and Dawson* [1983] 145 DLR (3d) 610, the Court held that parental refusal to allow replacement of a shunt for the alleviation of hydrocephalus might result in more pain and disability for the child, and therefore the procedure was authorised. See Dickens, 'Withholding Paediatric Medical Care' (1984) Can BR 196.

Relevance of parents' wishes

[11.83] Conflict between parents and healthcare professionals is not an infrequent occurrence[95] and this has sometimes led to courts having to make difficult decisions, often contrary to the parents' wishes. 'In a medical context, the potential for dispute between clinicians and parents over treatment for children is both apparent and real, arising whenever questions are raised about the welfare of a child and what may or may not be in that child's best interests.'[96] For example, in *Re C (HIV Test)*[97] a local authority applied for an order that a baby born to an HIV positive mother be tested for HIV. The mother had refused medication during the pregnancy and intended to continue to breast feed the child until the child was two years old. The judge found that there was a 20–25 per cent risk that the baby was infected with HIV and that this risk was increased by breast feeding. Both parents were strongly opposed to the HIV test and to any form of medical intervention.

[11.84] The Court of Appeal concluded that although parental views were an important consideration, the arguments for overriding their wishes in this case were overwhelming. The child had rights in national and international law, such that her interests and welfare must be paramount. The test provided a relatively unintrusive way of determining the child's medical status, enabling those concerned with her future welfare to be better informed as to appropriate avenues of treatment. The Court did not deal with the question of how to treat the child and how to deal with the risks associated with breast feeding at this stage.[98] Whether a court would in fact make an order compelling a woman to refrain from breast feeding her baby is open to question, as it would be highly intrusive of the family's rights and would be impossible to police. An alternative would, of course, be to take the child into care, if the child's welfare was deemed to be sufficiently at risk.[99]

[11.85] The European Convention on Human Rights Act 2003 is also likely to become of increasing relevance in such disputes. Article 8 of the Convention protects the right to private and family life and thus may protect a parent's right to make decisions for their child. In *Glass v the UK*[100] the European Court of Human Rights held that the United Kingdom was in breach of art 8 in circumstances where the hospital treating Mrs Glass's 14-year-old son, who had physical and intellectual disabilities, placed a Do Not

---

95 Moore and Kordick, 'Sources of conflict between families and healthcare professionals' (2006) 23 Journal of Paediatric Oncology Nursing 82.

96 *Re B (a minor)* [1981] 1 WLR 1421 quoted by Heywood, 'Parents and medical professionals: conflict, cooperation and best interests.' (2012) *Med Law Review* 20, pp 29–44.

97 *Re C (HIV Test)* [1999] 2 FLR 1004.

98 At the date of the appeal, the Court learned that the couple had disappeared from their home with the baby, and they did not appear at Court for the appeal.

99 At the trial of this action, Wilson J made no order forbidding the breast-feeding, stating that 'the law could not come between the baby and the breast'. Downie suggests that since there was evidence that breast feeding doubled the risk of the HIV virus being passed from mother to child, it might seem that the threshold criteria for the making of a care order could be established in such circumstances. See Downie, 'Consent to Medical Treatment – Whose View of Welfare?' [1999] Fam Law 818 at 819.

100 *Glass v the UK* [2004] ECHR 102.

Resuscitate (DNR) order on him without her knowledge or consent. They also administered a pain-relieving drug to him contrary to his mother's wishes, as she believed this would accelerate his death. The Court found this action to be in breach of the boy's right to private life and physical integrity and his mother's right to respect for her family life. The Court said that before a decision was taken to impose a treatment on a child contrary to the wishes of the parents, the matter should be referred to a court for decision. This provides guidance to healthcare professionals faced with circumstances in which there is an intractable dispute with parents in relation to treatment of their children, as it appears that under human rights law, all such cases should be referred to a court as final arbiter.

[11.86] An unusual set of circumstances arose in 2014 in the case of *Ashya King* who was a young child with a brain tumour whose parents sought permission to take him to Prague for a form of treatment which was not available in the UK. This treatment, in the parents' opinion, would be better for their son as it would cause less radiation and tissue damage than the conventional radiotherapy he was offered in the hospital where he was receiving treatment. The NHS was not prepared to fund the therapy and the parents decided to remove the child from hospital without permission and travel to Spain. The local authorities raised an alarm with the result that arrest warrants were issued in respect of the parents and the child was made a ward of court. There was intense media interest in the story and agreement was finally reached by which the proton therapy sought by the parents would be provided on the basis that this was a reasonably course of treatment which was consistent with the child's best interests.[101]

[11.87] Baker J said that this was not a case where the parents were withholding consent to an essential therapy for the child or insisting on a wholly unreasonable course of treatment. He said any parents in their position would do whatever they could to explore all the options. Some parents might choose to follow the conventional route of radiotherapy recommended by the doctors, others would prefer a relatively untested route in the hope that the toxic effects of radiation would be reduced.[102] He concluded: 'Both courses are reasonable and it is the parents who bear the heavy responsibility of making the decision. It is no business of this court, or any other public authority, to interfere with their decision.'

[11.88] In the King case the parents views were seen as reasonable even though the therapy they wanted for their son was relatively untested. By comparison in *Re JM (a child)*[103] the court had to decide in the case of a ten year old boy with an aggressive form of cancer, whether he should undergo surgery that was refused by both him and his

---

[101] *Re Ashya King* [2014] EWHC 2964. See discussion by Bridgeman, 'Misunderstanding, threats, and fear of the law in conflicts over children's healthcare: In the matter of Ashya King' (2015) 23 Med Law Review 23(3) 477–489.

[102] Bridgeman questions the basis on which Baker J came to the conclusion that it was in the child's best interests to receive this therapy and asks 'What would the court require before it could conclude that treatment, of uncertain benefit, not yet approved in clinical trials, is in a child's best interests?' Bridgeman, 'Misunderstanding, threats, and fear of the law in conflicts over children's healthcare: In the matter of Ashya King' (2015) 23 Med Law Review 23(3) 477–489 at 487–488.

[103] *Re JM (a child)* [2015] EWHC 2832 (Fam).

parents who wanted him to be treated with Chinese medicine instead. The parents were very frightened that their son would blame them for the disfigurement he was likely to sustain as a result of the surgery but it was put to the court that, even though it had been explained to them, the parents did not fully understand that if he did not have the surgery, the prospect of his survival was completely impossible. The court had no difficulty reaching the conclusion that the surgery was in J's best interests and while being conscious that it was a 'strong thing' for a judge who is a stranger to override the wishes of J and his parents, the judge had 'no doubt that J must be given the chance, a very good chance, of a long and fulfilling life rather than suffering, quite soon, a ghastly, agonising, death.' Therefore the parents' views in this case were seen as unreasonable and capable of being overridden on the basis of J's best interests.

[11.89] How are these cases to be distinguished? Parents are under a legal duty to provide adequate medical care for their children and have the right to consent to treatment accordingly. However their power to give consent is limited to treatment that is deemed in the best interests of their child and they may not refuse treatment if that might jeopardise their child's health. In the *King* case the parents were not refusing treatment for their son, rather they were proposing an alternative that the judge found to be a reasonable option, whereas in *Re JM* the court demonstrated the traditional interventionist approach usually favoured by courts in England where parents refuse treatment that is deemed necessary to save the life of a child. These cases also show the enormous challenges facing not only parents and clinicians but also the courts in trying to find the best solution, sometimes in the full glare of the media and consequent public attention which usually supports the parents in such conflicts.[104] Heywood comments that the facts of these cases are seldom reported in their entirety and 'very little consideration is given to the difficult position that healthcare professionals find themselves in and also the problems faced by the courts.'[105]

Conjoined twins

[11.90] The limits of parental authority has also been sharply tested in relation to a particular human tragedy involving the separation of conjoined or Siamese twins. While the birth of such babies is still, fortunately, a rare event, it has provoked legal and ethical debate as to whether and how to separate the twins where it is likely to cause the death of one twin. The very nature of conjoined twins has always proved to be a source of fascination for doctors and society in general. The most famous conjoined twins were born in Siam in 1811, thus the description 'Siamese twins' thereafter for such a phenomenon. The twins lived for over 60 years and were exhibited around the world as part of a circus act. Siamese twins continued to be referred to as 'freakish' 'double-

---

[104] See for example media description of recent English case by Sims, 'Parents anguish as High Court says doctors should not artificially prolong boys life' in The Independent 18 May 2016

[105] Heywood, 'Parents and medical professionals: conflict, cooperation and best interests.' (2012) Med Law Review 20, pp 29–44 at 31.

headed monsters', well into the 20th century, denying them the routine respect and care given to other infants.[106]

[11.91] Conjoined twins are the result of a single ovum or egg which is fertilised by a single sperm and then attempts to split into two identical twins. For some reason not yet fully understood, whether genetic or environmental or otherwise, the egg fails to split completely, leaving the twins joined, most commonly at the chest and sharing a single heart. In this category it is thought extremely difficult to successfully separate such twins, and even if possible by sacrificing one twin, historically the surviving twin has generally not lived for more than a few months after separation.[107] It is also difficult to keep such twins alive without separation for longer than nine months or so, as the strength of the single heart is generally insufficient to maintain both bodies.[108] Where the twins are joined at another part of the body and do not share vital organs, separation is difficult but sometimes possible.[109]

[11.92] In the United States in 1977 conjoined twins were born in circumstances where survival of both twins after separation was impossible, and the survival of one unlikely. The parents were deeply religious Jews and refused to consent to sacrificing one twin so that the other might have a chance to live. Their religious advisors informed them that if one of the twins was 'designated for death' it was acceptable to sacrifice that twin so that the other might live. A family court heard an application by the surgeon to perform the separation and seemed to accept this line of thinking. The procedure was authorised and the separation was successful. However, the surviving twin died a few months later. Similar cases occurred the same year in another part of the US and again 10 years later. In each case it is interesting that the surgeons first sought and received assurances that no criminal prosecution would be brought against them if the procedure were performed.

[11.93] Annas argues that the closest legal precedents deal with the doctrine of necessity, actions taken in response to natural disasters and acts of God. He cites the example of the sinking lifeboat where lots are cast to determine who is thrown overboard in order to save the others from certain death. In these examples, 'having the stronger throw the weaker overboard is not justified by the circumstances.' In the case of conjoined twins if the separation is medically reasonable and the choice of which twin to let die is made fairly, Annas claims that society would probably regard it as justifiable to kill one twin to save the other, although flipping coins would probably be fairer. On this basis it is relevant to examine medical criteria to decide which twin is most likely to survive the separation. This maintains the 'fiction that the decision was an act of God.'

---

[106] Annas, 'Siamese Twins: Killing One to Save the Other' in *Standard of Care, The Law of American Bioethics* (OUP, 1993) 234.

[107] Marin-Padilla et al, 'Cardiovascular Abnormalities in Thoracopagus Twins' (1981) 23 Teratology 101–113.

[108] Annas, 'Siamese Twins: Killing One to Save the Other' in *Standard of Care, The Law of American Bioethics* (OUP, 1993), 234.

[109] In April 2010 conjoined twins from Cork, Ireland, Hassan and Hussein Benhaffaf, successfully underwent separation surgery in London.

[11.94] The use of a best interests test in this context is arguably straining its logic as the best interests of both cannot be simultaneously protected. Although separation is in the best interests of the twin chosen to survive, it cannot be in the best interests of the twin 'designated for death' since that twin is alive, is not suffering, and is now about to have its life cut short by deliberate decision. Annas concludes that both law and ethics support reasonable medical attempts to separate conjoined twins on the basis that it is better to intervene to try and save one life rather than to passively watch two lives end.[110] However, it remains an unmet challenge to develop a fair and useful procedure to apply rationale to the decision to be made.

[11.95] The most widely reported and debated case on conjoined twins to date is the English case of *Re A (Conjoined twins: medical treatment)*.[111] The case of the 'Manchester conjoined twins' captured the public imagination worldwide, as the Court was asked to adjudicate on the legitimacy of killing one of the twins in order to save the life of the other. The facts of the case were that the parents of the twins came to Manchester from the Maltese island of Gozo in order to get the best possible medical care for their children.[112] The twins were born in August 2000, their bodies fused from the umbilicus to the sacrum, and the lower ends of their spines and spinal cords were also fused. They shared a common bladder. The smaller and weaker twin, known as Mary, had a non-functional heart and lungs and her supply of blood came from her twin, known as Jodie. Mary had severe brain malformations and abnormal neurological responses although she was not vegetative or in a coma, whereas Jodie appeared neurologically normal. The medical evidence was that without separation, Jodie's heart and lungs would slowly become affected by the strain of providing blood for both bodies and both twins would die, or that Mary would die from thrombosis of major vessels, and it would be necessary to perform an emergency separation to save Jodie. It was agreed that any separation would lead to Mary's death and that, although Jodie would have to undergo a series of operations throughout her childhood, she would be able to lead a substantially normal life if separated from Mary.

[11.96] The parents of the twins consistently opposed the separation on religious grounds, preferring that nature take its course.[113] They were of the view that one of their daughters should not be killed in order that the other should live. The hospital sought a declaration from the Court that it would be lawful to perform the separation, thus overriding the parents' wishes. This declaration was granted, and an appeal dismissed.

---

[110] Sheldon and Wilkinson predicted that in order to avoid the obvious conclusion that separation in these circumstances would be murder, the court would try to find a solution whereby all concerned could feel a comfortable sense of having saved a life. See Sheldon and Wilkinson, 'Conjoined Twins: the Legality and Ethics of Sacrifice' (1997) 5 Med L Rev 149.

[111] *Re A (Conjoined twins: medical treatment)* [2000] 4 All ER 961; [2001] 1 FLR 1.

[112] See discussion by Harris, 'Human Beings, Persons and Conjoined Twins: An Ethical Analysis of the Judgment in *Re A*' (2001) 9 Med L Rev, 221–236.

[113] Harris points out that although the parents were devout Catholics, it is not clear that Catholicism would demand that the separation not take place. It might in fact be justifiable on the basis of the doctrine of double effect, whereby the act of separation is not intended to cause the death of one, but rather to save the life of the other. Harris, 'Human Beings, Persons and Conjoined Twins: An Ethical Analysis of the Judgment in *Re A*' (2001) 9 Med L Rev, 221–236.

The separation was performed in November 2000, with the result that Mary died. Jodie is expected to enjoy a reasonable quality of life.[114]

[11.97] All of the judges involved in the case, both in the High Court and the Court of Appeal, found in favour of the separation, although for different reasons. The Court of Appeal held that separation was in Jodie's best interests but contrary to Mary's. The difficulty for the Court, then, was in balancing those competing interests. It decided that the balance lay in giving Jodie the chance of life and that such an operation would not violate the criminal law. The complex questions raised by this case include - When does a human being become a person? What role can the characteristic of physical separation play in establishing this status? When should considerations of quality of life outweigh the sanctity of life? What is the significance of the distinction between acts and omissions? Who should decide what is in the best interests of a child? What factors should be taken into account in that decision?[115] It is not proposed to address all of these questions here but in summarising the various points made by the judges, it is interesting to note that what is abundantly clear from the array of issues dealt with by the judgments is the impossibility of separating the legal issues from the ethical ones, both in use of concepts and language. [116]

[11.98] The academic commentary on this case has been predictably extensive, with the case drawing sharp criticism for its reasoning, language and failure to justify the overriding of the parents wishes.[117] The Court of Appeal's decision has been 'both attacked as a dangerous breach of the sanctity of life and an unjustifiable erosion of parental authority, and heralded as a triumph of common sense over religious fundamentalism and a creditable act of judicial support for the well intentioned acts of doctors trying to salvage a life from a no-win situation.'[118] One of the criticisms of the Court of Appeal's ruling in *Re A* centres on the implication of the judgments that Mary's

---

[114] See comments of one of the consultant surgeons in The Times, 18 June 2001, where he said in relation to Jodie that 'she has come on really well, better than expected. Everything works and everything is where it should be, as it is in a normal baby. There are no plans for further surgery and we are confident she will have an excellent quality of life.'

[115] Sheldon and Wilkinson, 'On the Sharpest Horns of a Dilemma: *Re A (Conjoined Twins)*' (2001) 9 Med L Rev 201 at 204.

[116] For arguments as to whether the courts and/or the legislature should have a role in deciding whether to separate conjoined twins, see Excitable, 'Separation of Conjoined Twins: Where Next for English Law?' [2002] Crim L Rev 459–470.

[117] See (2001) 9 Med L Rev, which is entirely devoted to various articles on this case, some of which are mentioned below. Also Bainham, 'Resolving the Unresolvable: The Case of Conjoined Twins' (2001) 60 CLJ 49; Gillon, 'Imposed Separation of Conjoined Twins: Moral Hubris by the English Courts?' (2001) 27 JME 3; McCall Smith, 'The Separating of Conjoined Twins' (2000) 321 BMJ 782; Ratiu and Singer, 'The Ethics and Economics of Heroic Surgery' (March–April 2001) 31 Hastings Center Report 47; Huxtable, 'The Court of Appeal and Conjoined Twins: Condemning the Unworthy Life?' (2000) 162 Bulletin of Medical Ethics 13; Huxtable, 'Logical Separation? Conjoined Twins, Slippery Slopes and Resource Allocation' (2001) 23(4) *J of Social Welfare and Fam Law* 459–471; and Munro, 'Square Pegs and Round Holes: The Dilemma of Conjoined Twins and Individual Rights' (2001) 10 Social and Legal Studies 4.

[118] Sheldon and Wilkinson, 'On the Sharpest Horns of a Dilemma: *Re A (Conjoined Twins)*' (2001) 9 Med L Rev 201 at 207.

death was not murder, even though it was a foreseen, and some would say, intended, consequence of the separation of the twins. Uniacke argues that the Court was confused on some important conceptual matters due, in part, to the legacy of cases dealing with the withdrawal of treatment, which considered these to be omissions as opposed to positive acts.[119] While the judges all agreed that the separation was lawful homicide of Mary, they based their judgments on different reasons.[120]

[11.99] Ward LJ was of the view that the killing was justified on the basis of self-defence or defence of another person, as he perceived that Mary was harming Jodie's chances of life. He said that there was no difference between 'legitimate self-defence and the doctors coming to Jodie's defence and removing the threat of fatal harm to her presented by Mary's draining her life blood.' He argued that as Mary was killing Jodie, to kill Mary in defence of Jodie's life would not violate Mary's right to life. The right to life, for Ward LJ, was not an absolute right not to be killed, but a right not to be killed unjustly. Killing Mary would be legitimate defence of Jodie and therefore would not be murder. However, it has been counter-argued that Mary's relationship with Jodie cannot be characterised in terms of her killing Jodie, although her existence certainly constituted a threat to Jodie's life. Mary was an 'entirely passive recipient of oxygenated blood' from Jodie.[121]

[11.100] Brooke LJ argued that the killing was justified on the basis of the defence of necessity or duress of circumstances. Up to *Re A* it was considered that the defence of necessity was not available on a criminal charge and a jury would not have been allowed to consider it. It has been argued that the judges in *Re A*, by allowing necessity as a defence to the killing of Mary, may have made a fundamental change to criminal law doctrine, the effects of which would be profound. For example, a parent could claim that she killed her severely disabled child out of necessity to spare her any further suffering. 'The Court of Appeal has opened the door to lawful acquittal where euthanasia is the reason for a killing, and it can only be a matter of time before such cases are before the courts.'[122] McEwan argues that the means chosen by the Court of Appeal in order to achieve a utilitarian goal of saving at least one life where two are at stake, places the law at risk of having to condone euthanasia by private citizens who raise the defence of necessity.

[11.101] Walker LJ distinguished Mary's death as a foreseen, though not intended, killing. The latter argument is based on the doctrine of double effect, whereby the clamping of the shared artery between Mary and Jodie was intended as a means of saving Jodie's life, and Mary's death was an incidental consequence of that act. However, as Uniacke argues, 'the legal specification of an action's intended effects includes effects that, while incidental to the actor's aim or purpose, are foreseen as virtually certain. This would include Mary's death as the inevitable consequence of the

---

[119] Uniacke refers in particular to *Airedale NHS Trust v Bland* [1993] AC 789. See Uniacke, 'Was Mary's Death Murder?' (2001) 9 Med L Rev 208 at 209.

[120] See also similar Australian case of *Queensland v Nolan* [2001] QSC 174, and commentary in [2002] Med L Rev 100–102.

[121] Uniacke, 'Was Mary's Death Murder?' (2001) 9 Med L Rev 208 at 212.

[122] See discussion by McEwan, 'Murder by Design: The 'Feel-Good Factor' and the Criminal Law' (2001) 9 Med L Rev 246–258 at 248.

separation surgery.'[123] Similarly, Harris argues that 'the denial that the operation involves the deliberate or intentional killing of Mary is unsustainable.'[124]

[11.102] Another argument that features in this case is the belief that Mary was somehow 'designated for death' and that this justified the deliberate choice to kill her. This is sharply criticised by Harris on the basis that the method by which one would be so designated is unclear and leaves no room for misdiagnosis.[125] To say that someone is 'designated for death', who is going to 'die anyway' is to correlate the value of life with life expectancy, which Harris argues, is profoundly unjust and unethical.[126] Where a person with a short life expectancy has a life to lead and wants to lead it for as much time as is left, 'it would seem inconceivable that they would be killed against their will by a decision of the courts.'[127] However, where the quality, as opposed to the duration, of the life available is such that the person could not benefit from its continuation, it may be relevant to take this into account.

[11.103] The nature of personhood is a notoriously difficult concept to define, and different ethicists define it in different ways. Thus, Harris argues that Mary was not a person at the time of the operation, in the sense that he defines persons as individuals with a biographical life and full moral status. He believes that persons are characterised by having the capacity to value existence and that non-persons lack such capacity. Therefore, persons can be harmed by being killed, as they lose something they value, whereas non-persons cannot, by definition, lose something they could be said to value. On this basis non-persons would include embryos, anencephalic infants and individuals in persistent vegetative state. Therefore, at the time of the operation neither Jodie nor Mary were persons on this understanding of personhood. This, for Harris, is the only ethical basis upon which it can be said that the Court's decision was justified. However, he also feels that the Court should have declared the operation lawful but not mandatory, and in that way left the decision to the parents of the twins. He describes the Court's ruling as so confused and inconsistent that it fails to justify the overruling of the parent's wishes. Gillon also argues that the parents' wishes should not have been overruled as they were 'neither incompetent nor negligent – the standard justifications for depriving parents of such authority – and their reasoning was not eccentric or *merely* religious, but was widely acceptable moral reasoning – as was the contrary moral reasoning justifying an operation.'[128]

---

[123] Uniacke, 'Was Mary's Death Murder?' (2001) 9 Med L Rev 208 at 220.

[124] Harris, 'Human Beings, Persons and Conjoined Twins: An Ethical Analysis of the Judgment in *Re A*' (2001) 9 Med L Rev, 221 at 229.

[125] See discussion in Harris, 'Human Beings, Persons and Conjoined Twins: An Ethical Analysis of the Judgment in *Re A*' (2001) 9 Med L Rev, at 230–232.

[126] See Harris, 'The Concept of the Person and the Value of Life' (1999) 9 (4) Kennedy Inst of Ethics J, 293–308.

[127] Harris, 'Human Beings, Persons and Conjoined Twins: An Ethical Analysis of the Judgment in *Re A*' (2001) 9 Med L Rev, at 232.

[128] Gillon, 'Imposed separation of conjoined twins – moral hubris by the English courts?' (2001) 27 Journal of medical ethics 3–8; See also Hewson, '*A (Children)* – Cruel and Unnatural' (2000) 150 New LJ 1562; and Knowles, 'Hubris in the Court' (2001) 31(1) Hastings Center Report 50.

[11.104] By contrast, Freeman argues that parental autonomy should not be prioritised and that, at least on this ground, the Court of Appeal came to the right decision.[129] He discusses the limits placed on parental authority such that parents cannot, for example, consent to a procedure to be carried out on their child for the benefit of themselves or the child's sibling. Similarly, parents cannot consent to certain procedures, such as the non-therapeutic sterilisation of a disabled child, and previous judgments have shown that parental decision can be overridden in the best interests of the child.[130] In *Re A* the Court of Appeal specifically recognised the importance of the parents' wishes, especially insofar as they were based on religious convictions,[131] but said that the Court could override them, as 'it is the child's best interest that are paramount, not the parents'.

[11.105] Freeman analyses why parents have rights at all, and finds that they are traditionally based on the fundamental importance of family integrity.[132] He is of the view that those who seek to protect the family from interference derive this argument from a mistaken reliance on classic liberalism, the most obvious source being John Stuart Mill's *On Liberty*, which makes the case that the State should stay out of its citizens' lives out of respect for their moral autonomy and human dignity. But, according to Freeman, 'the paradigmatic family conflict is not between the citizen and the state: it is between two persons. If the state removes itself from concern with this type of conflict…the weak can easily be sacrificed to the strong. There is no moral autonomy or human dignity then for those whose interests can so routinely be trampled upon.'[133]

[11.106] The granting of parental rights has often been seen as based on biology, in the sense that individuals are given rights to their genetic offspring. However, this is not universally true, as is evident both from considerations of the law relating to children born through donation of eggs or sperm, and from the fact that unmarried men have always had a struggle to establish a legal relationship with their biological children. Although the law has, at least in modern times, tended to avoid the ascription of rights on the basis of property interests, towards a more child-centred approach, there is still 'a tendency for the child's best interests to be over-identified with the parents' interests.' Freeman argues that the presumptions that children are best placed with their parents, and that parents know what is in their child's best interests, may not provide empirically sound bases upon which to base legal principle.[134] Other bases for granting rights to

---

[129] Freeman, 'Whose Life is it Anyway?' (2001) 9 Med L Rev 259–280.

[130] Freeman cites *Re D* [1976] Fam. 185; *Re B* [1981] 1 WLR 1421; *Re B* [1991] 2 FLR 426; and *Re C* [1998] 1 FLR 384.

[131] *per* Walker LJ at 118.

[132] Freeman quotes from Goldstein, Freud, Goldstein and Solnit, *The Best Interests of the Child* (Free Press, 1996): 'The child's need for security within the confines of the family must be met by law through its recognition of family privacy as the barrier to state intrusion upon parental autonomy. These rights – parental autonomy, a child's entitlement to autonomous parents, and privacy – are essential ingredients of family integrity.' This is reminiscent of the Supreme Court's interpretation of the Constitutional protection of the family in *North Western Health Board v HW and CW*, considered above at para **[11.18]**.

[133] Freeman, 'Whose Life is it Anyway?' (2001) 9 Med L Rev 259 at 270.

[134] Freeman refers to Bartholet, *Family Bonds: Adoption and the Politics of Parenting* (Houghton Mifflin, 1993) at 174–81.

parents, such as intention (which may be relevant in relation to assisted reproduction) and marriage, are unpersuasive in relation to parental authority generally. He concludes that the foundations upon which parents are granted rights are shaky and limited, a factor that must be taken into account in deciding whether those rights should be prioritised in the event of conflict.

[11.107] In trying to accommodate the judgments in *Re T*,[135] where the wishes of the mother of a child in need of a liver transplant were prioritised over the unanimous medical evidence in favour of the surgery, with *Re A* where the wishes of the parents were overruled, Freeman says that 'it would be easy to conclude that the judges speak in the rhetoric of children's rights only when they believe the parents' decision is manifestly wrong.' He questions whether the religious and cultural background of the parents influenced the Court's decision and whether, if their objections had been on grounds other than religion, the Court would have been less inclined to overrule them.[136] However, he believes that the Court's decision to separate the twins was ultimately the right decision, albeit for the wrong reasons. The Court was wrong to prioritise Jodie's interests – both were persons with equal rights – but it was in the best interests of both that they should be separated. He argues that Mary's life was not worthwhile – if she had been born a single baby, she would have been considered non-viable and would not have been resuscitated. She had a right to life but inherent in the right to life is the right to die with dignity. As treatment would have achieved nothing for Mary on the basis that her body could not sustain life, 'the decision is one which upholds dignity: the right of Jodie to live with dignity, the right of Mary to die with dignity.'

[11.108] In conclusion, although compromise and a partnership approach between parents and healthcare professionals is the best solution in all of these difficult cases involving infants and young children, there will inevitably be occasions when this is not possible and a decision of the courts will be required. 'When this happens, perhaps one should not be too critical of any decision taken by the courts and recognise that they are faced with a thankless task of having to adjudicate in a forum that requires a more pragmatic than academic perspective. They can weigh up the advantages and disadvantages of each possible course of action, but in the end they have to make a decision.'[137] Heywood concludes that in the end medical factors are most persuasive in relation to the evaluation of best interests and that although this is the most pragmatic approach, it does not necessarily follow that it is always correct.

Irish case law on treatment of critically ill children

[11.109] There have not been many Irish cases dealing with such difficult and emotive issues so it is difficult to anticipate the outcome were such circumstances to arise as in some of the cases discussed above. The guidance obtained in relation to parental authority from the Supreme Court in *North Western Health Board v HW and CW*[138] is not directly analogous as the court in that case was not dealing with the parents refusing

---

135 *Re T (a minor) (wardship: medical treatment)* [1997] 1 All ER 906 discussed earlier at **[11.73]**.
136 Freeman, 'Whose Life is it Anyway?' (2001) 9 Med L Rev 259 at 275.
137 Heywood, 'Parents and medical professionals: conflict, cooperation and best interests.' (2012) *Med Law Review* 20, pp 29–44 at 44.
138 *North Western Health Board v HW and CW* [2001] IESC 90.

treatment in the immediacy of a life-limiting or life-threatening disorder which could prove fatal to the child. Nor was this a case where the court was faced with a child whose clinical prognosis was 'demonstrably awful' and where the choice was whether to continue to provide medical treatment judged by clinicians to be simply prolonging the suffering of the child, or to withhold treatment in the event of an acute deterioration of the child's condition in order that he or she might die peacefully.

[11.110] The court's respect for parental authority here might indicate that in cases of parental and professional conflict, priority would similarly be given to parental opinion. However, context is very important here and the child in this case was not in imminent danger by virtue of any medical condition, rather the parents chose to refuse to have their healthy child screened for a medical condition that could be serious if found to exist. Hardiman J outlined the position as follows:

> Where the constitutional family exists and is discharging its functions as such, and the parents have not for physical or moral reasons failed in their duty towards their children, their decisions should not be overridden by the State and in particular by the Courts in the absence of a jurisdiction conferred by statute...The presumption is not of course conclusive and might be open to displacement by countervailing constitutional considerations as perhaps in the case of an immediate threat to life.

The final sentence in this extract indicates the balancing of considerations that must inevitably take place in these cases and that where there is a serious risk to the life of the child, parental authority may have to yield to the child's constitutional right to life.

[11.111] In a small number of court applications in recent years the High Court appears to have adopted the 'best interests of the child' approach in relation to cases involving resuscitation or other life-prolonging treatments for young children. In 2012 the High Court granted a declaration permitting the non-resuscitation of a six year old boy who had serious debilitating conditions but was not terminally ill or reported to be in pain.[139] The child had suffered a near-drowning accident shortly before his second birthday which resulted in prolonged cardiac arrest which left him with extensive brain damage, severe spastic quadriplegic cerebral palsy and he was also blind and incontinent. Kearns P adopted the best interests of the child test but tempered it by referring to what the child would choose if he was in a position to make a sound judgment. He went on to say that the court should not impose its own view on whether the quality of life the child would enjoy would be intolerable but should determine the best interests of the child subjectively.[140]

[11.112] A further High Court application was made in 2015 in the case of a 10 year old acutely ill and profoundly disabled girl in State care that she should not be resuscitated or receive emergency life-saving intervention. Media reports record O'Malley J as stating that the Court was obliged to act in the child's best interests and that the child should receive all palliative care but doctors could lawfully follow their clinical judgment not to provide resuscitation, surgery, artificial ventilation or general anaesthesia. The judge took account of her illness, quality and length of life, the

---

[139] *SR (a ward of Court)* [2012] 1 IR 305.

[140] See discussion of the 'legal fiction' inherent in the substituted judgment approach to decision-making by Somers, 'Deciding Obliquely and by a Side-Wind: Substituted judgment and end-of-life decisions for minors' (2013) 19 1 MLJI 11–27.

suffering inherent in aggressive treatment, the views of her parents and doctors. The judge also said, as did Kearns P in the previous case, that it was not for her to impose her own views as to whether the child's potential quality of life would be tolerable but to ask what would the child do if she were in a position to make a sound judgment.[141]

[11.113] In cases involving refusal of treatment by Jehovah's Witness parents on behalf of their children where the risk of harm to the child is high, the courts do not have any difficulty in overriding the wishes of the parents in order to safeguard the life of the child.[142] This can be seen in *Temple Street v D and another*,[143] where Hogan J held that the State has a vital interest in intervening in exceptional circumstances where there has been a failure on the part of the parents to protect the child's life or welfare. He said that the High Court has a jurisdiction and a duty to override the religious objections of parents where those beliefs threaten the life and welfare of their child and he therefore granted the declaration allowing a transfusion to be given to the child despite parental objections. In cases where the child has a serious progressive incurable disease or where the child's death is considered inevitable in the near future but the parents do not agree with the withholding or withdrawing of treatment, the authority of the parents must similarly give way to the best interests of the child. The court must carefully consider the benefits and burdens of treatment for the child and unfortunately in cases where the child's quality of life is small and the pain and suffering of the child is great, this may mean that the child may die earlier than he or she might otherwise have done.

OLDER CHILDREN'S PARTICIPATION IN DECISION-MAKING

[11.114] In the context of the treatment of children it is equally important that respect for the voice and autonomy of the child is integrated into any medical decision-making. This does not mean that the interests and views of parents will be displaced, as in most instances the child's interests will be best represented by its parents, though their interests are not the same. Although as we have seen in the case law discussed above in relation to very young children, parents are generally given authority to make decisions on behalf of their children, legal provisions also exist to deal with situations in which parents breach their obligations towards their children. The courts may also intervene to make decisions for children in circumstances where parents refuse treatment deemed to be in the child's best interests. Those who provide medical treatment for children must be careful not to infringe the autonomy and privacy of the family while at the same time acting as an advocate for the child's interests. The case law shows that walking this tightrope is not an easy task.

[11.115] Whenever a child contracts a chronic or potentially fatal disease, questions arise as to whether to tell the child, how much information to tell them, to what extent

---

[141] See case report by Carolan, 'Court rules girl (10) should not be resuscitated.' The Irish Times July 10, 2015.

[142] See English case of *NHS Trust v Child B* [2014] EWHC 3486 where the parents of a young child refused to consent to treatment for severe burns including skin grafts and blood transfusions on the basis that they were devout Jehovah's Witnesses. The court was satisfied that it was in the child's best interests to receive the transfusions and made the order sought by the Trust.

[143] *Temple Street v D and another* [2011] IEHC 1.

should they be told about the risks and benefits of treatment and whether or not they can refuse treatment. If the child, parents and healthcare team are all in agreement as to the care plan for the child, the situation is unlikely to cause conflict but sometimes the three interests – that of the child to bodily self-determination, of parents to make decisions for their children and the State to impose decisions in the best interests of the child – do not always coincide.[144]

[11.116] Respect for the autonomy of the child entails the facilitation, wherever possible, of the child's right to make his own decisions. Guidelines on treatment of children generally provide that the child's wishes should be taken into account and, as the child grows towards maturity, given more weight accordingly. Children may have strong views about their own healthcare and their responses may range from enthusiastic agreement to absolute rejection without clear or consistent reasons for those views.[145] Medical decisions are rarely clear-cut choices between life and death, as statistical chances of success vary between treatments and between particular patients. Decision-making, therefore, involves a balancing of risks and possible benefits, weighing up potential quality of life with dignity and a pain-free existence. In order to participate in decision-making, children should be given the necessary information in a way that they can understand so that they can adequately comprehend the consequences of the medical decision, and, as far as possible, be given the ability to make such decisions without the influence of parents or doctors.

[11.117] Many professional organisations have recommended that decision-making involving the healthcare of older children and adolescents should include, to the greatest possible degree, the assent of the child, as well as the participation of the parents and doctors. For example, the Committee on Bioethics of the American Academy of Paediatrics states that while paediatricians need not necessarily treat children as rational, autonomous decision-makers, they should give serious consideration to each patient's developing capacities for participating in decision-making, including rationality and autonomy. This would involve helping the patient to achieve an appropriate awareness of the nature of his condition, telling him what he can expect with tests and treatment, making a clinical assessment of his understanding of the situation and how he is responding and soliciting an expression of his willingness to accept the proposed care. Where the patient will have to receive medical care despite his objection, he should not be deceived regarding that fact.[146] 'As children develop, they should gradually become the primary guardians of personal health and the primary partners in medical decision-making, assuming responsibility from their parents.'[147]

---

[144] Walker, 'Meaningful Participation of Minors with HIV/AIDS in Decisions Regarding Medical Treatment – Balancing the Rights of Children, Parents, and State' (2002) I J of Law and Psych 25, 271–297.

[145] See Donnelly and Kilkelly 'Child-Friendly Healthcare: Delivering on the Right to Be Heard' (2011) Med Law Review Vol 19, pp 27–54.

[146] American Academy of Paediatrics, Committee on Bioethics, 'Informed Consent, Parental Permission, and Assent in Paediatric Practice' (1995) Paediatrics Vol 95(2) 314–317.

[147] American Academy of Paediatrics, Committee on Bioethics, 'Informed Consent, Parental Permission, and Assent in Paediatric Practice' (1995) Paediatrics Vol 95(2) 314–317.

[11.118] The HSE National Consent Policy published in 2013 also supports the importance of children's participation in healthcare decision making.[148] It states:

> Involving children in decision-making may be different from obtaining consent in the adult context due to the age or capacity of the child to understand and participate in the decision and the role of the parents and/or legal guardians in decision-making. However, even where children are unable to give a valid consent for themselves, they should nonetheless be as involved as possible in decision-making as even young children may have opinions about their healthcare and have the right to have their views taken into consideration by giving their assent to the proposed treatment or service. This principle is in keeping with legal and international human rights standards and ethical guidance which provide that the child's wishes should be taken into account and, as the child grows towards maturity, given more weight accordingly.

[11.119] Friedman Ross counter argues that children under the age of majority should *not* be empowered to make medical decisions for three reasons.[149] Firstly she says that allowing children to make their own decisions fails to recognise the child's need to gain the skills and virtues necessary to make decisions that promote the child's lifetime well-being. She says 'children need a protected period in which to develop 'enabling virtues' – habits, including the habit of self-control, which advance their life-time autonomy and opportunities.' Secondly allowing children to make their own decisions fails to recognise the parents' role in helping to define the child's well-being and conception of the good. 'By protecting the child from his own impetuosity, his parents help him to obtain the background knowledge of the world and the capacities that will allow him to make decisions that better promote his life plans'. Thirdly allowing children to make their own decisions fails to respect the parents' interest in child-rearing.

> In general, parental autonomy promotes the interests and goals of both children and parents. It serves the needs and interests of the child to have autonomous parents who will help him become an autonomous individual capable of devising and implementing his own life plan. It serves the adults' interest in having and raising a family according to their own vision of the good life. These interests do not abruptly cease when the child becomes competent. If anything, now parents have the opportunity to inculcate their beliefs through rational discourse, instead of through example, bribery, or force.

[11.120] Friedman Ross also argues that those who advocate in favour of respect for autonomy of the child in healthcare do so because they see healthcare as an exception and they do not advocate for child autonomy in other spheres and contexts. She argues that this is inconsistent and asks why should a child who is considered competent to make life or death healthcare choices not be considered competent to make other decisions such as to marry, have sexual relations, buy alcohol or drop out of school.

[11.121] Article 12 of the United Nations Convention of the Rights of the Child[150] requires that 'State Parties shall assure to the child who is capable of forming his or her own views the right to express those views freely in all matters affecting the child, the views of the child being given due weight in accordance with the age and maturity of the

---

[148] HSE National Consent Policy (2013) Available at www.hse.ie.
[149] Lainie Friedman Ross, 'Health care decision-making by children: is it in their best interest?' Hastings Center Report, November/December 1997, Vol 27, p 41–45.
[150] General Assembly Resolution 44/25, November 1989, art 12. The Convention has been ratified by 194 members of the United Nations, with the United States as a notable exception.

child.' Ireland signed up to this Convention in 1992. However, participation in decision-making is different from autonomous decision-making.[151] In the latter situation, responsibility for the decision lies wholly with the decision-maker whereas in the former situation, the participator is listened to, their views are taken into account, they are involved in the decision-making process and share in the responsibility for the decision. In the context of healthcare decisions involving children under the legal age for consent, power is shared between children and adults but if the child's participation is to be meaningful, their views and preferences as to their best interests should be sought and listened to in making this assessment. If the child's preference is overridden, this should be explained to them in language that they can understand.

[11.122] The Committee on the Rights of the Child monitors states' reporting obligations under the Convention, including how art 12 is enshrined in legislation. In its Report in 2009, the Committee recommended that in addition to the introduction into law of an age at which children can consent to medical treatment, states should ensure that where a younger child can demonstrate capacity to express an informed view on his or her treatment, this view is given due weight.[152]

[11.123] Arguments in favour of children's participation are based on both ethical and pragmatic principles. It has been argued that children, as much as adults, must be treated with dignity, and have their personal decision-making respected.[153] 'Nothing is more fundamental to the experience of being taken seriously than simply having a say and having one's perspective considered – in effect, being part of a conversation about matters of personal significance.'[154] On a practical level, ensuring patient choice enhances compliance and facilitates goal achievement, two elements associated with treatment success.[155] Studies have shown that, as compared to those who have not been involved, minors who have been involved in treatment decisions have had improved and more rapid psychological and physical recovery from surgery, increased compliance with recommendations and improved perceptions of the efficacy of treatments.[156]

[11.124] There are also arguments against children's art 12 participation rights, similar to those put forward by Friedman Ross above, based on the child's immaturity, the increase of conflict, and the removal of protection from the child.[157] Firstly, in relation to

---

[151] Donnelly and Kilkelly, 'Child-Friendly Healthcare: Delivering on the Right to Be Heard' (2011) Med Law Review Vol 19, pp 27–54 at 29.

[152] Committee on the Rights of the Child, General Comment No 12 (2009) *The Right of the Child to Be Heard,* UN Doc CRC/C/GC/12, para 102.

[153] Walker and Melton, 'The Smallest Democracy' (1998) 2(4) Family Futures 4; Weithorn, 'Youth Participation in Family and Community Decision-Making' (1998) 2 (4) Family Futures 7.

[154] Melton, 'Parents *and* Children' (1998) 2(4) Family Futures 10 at 12.

[155] See Winick, 'Competency to Consent to Treatment: The Distinction Between Assent and Objection' (1991) 28 Houston Law Review 15; Tremper and Kelly, 'The Mental Health Rationale for Policies Fostering Minors' Autonomy' (1987) 10 I J of Law and Psychiatry 111.

[156] Carter and St Lawrence, 'Adolescents' Competency to Make Informed Consent Birth Control and Pregnancy Decisions: An Interface for Psychology and the Law' (1985) 3 Behavioral Sciences and the Law 309.

[157] See Hafen and Hafen, 'Abandoning Children to Their Autonomy: The UN Convention on the Rights of the Child' (1996) 37 Harvard I LJ 449.

immaturity, it has been argued that the peculiar vulnerability of children and their inability to make critical decisions in an informed manner leads to the conclusion that their Constitutional rights cannot be equated with those of adults.[158] As children are thought to have an incomplete understanding of the finality of death, they should not be considered competent to refuse treatment.[159] Secondly, it has been suggested that giving a child autonomy leads to inevitable and unnecessary conflict.[160] By permitting children to exercise rights of self-determination, parental authority and protection of the child will be seriously damaged. Thirdly, it is argued that where children participate in their own treatment decisions they are conferred with a range of adult burdens and responsibilities, which removes them from 'the protection rights of childhood.'[161]

MATURE MINORS AND CONSENT TO TREATMENT

[11.125] It is a fundamental principle of medical ethics and medical law that where a patient is a competent adult, the patient's autonomy must be respected by seeking consent from the patient prior to providing medical treatment. There are different concepts of what autonomy means but they generally refer to the ability to think for oneself, to make decisions about what one wants in life taking account of one's own values, and then to act on those decisions. As Dworkin puts it, being able to make decisions about my life not only promotes well-being but it is also valuable because 'it makes my life mine'.[162] 'Given the value that we place on being treated as if we have the capacity for autonomy, to fail to treat someone as having that capacity would constitute a failure to respect them as a person, and doing so can be very hurtful for the person concerned.'[163] Walker argues that 16 and 17 year olds similarly have an interest in being recognised as being able to make decisions for themselves and that 'the importance of shaping our own lives and making our own decisions, and of being treated as an equal in this respect, is not something that comes on overnight. It develops over time and as it does so our interest in being treated like an adult develops with it.'[164] The cases discussed below demonstrate the challenging issues raised where young people try to make decisions for themselves which are either in conflict with their parents or healthcare professionals or both.

[11.126] Before examining the legal position in Ireland, it is worthwhile to examine the case law in England which is based on similar legislation. In England s 8(1) of the

---

[158] Per Justice Lewis Powell in the American case *Bellotti v Baird* [1979] 443 US 622 at 634.

[159] See Walker et al, *Children's Rights in the United States: In Search of a National Policy* (Sage Publications Inc, 1998) Ch 7.

[160] Hafen and Hafen, 'Abandoning Children to Their Autonomy: The UN Convention on the Rights of the Child' (1996) 37 Harvard I L J, at 484.

[161] Hafen and Hafen, at 461.

[162] Dworkin, *The Theory and Practice of Autonomy* (Cambridge Univ Press 1988) at 111

[163] Walker, 'If they can consent, why can't they refuse?' in Donnelly and Murray (eds) *Ethical and Legal debates in Irish Healthcare, Confronting Complexities* (Manchester Univ Press 2015) 71 – 83 at 77.

[164] Walker, 'If they can consent, why can't they refuse?' in Donnelly and Murray (eds) *Ethical and Legal debates in Irish Healthcare, Confronting Complexities* (Manchester Univ Press 2015) 71 – 83 at 78.

Family Law Reform Act 1969 gives a minor aged over 16 years powers to consent to medical and surgical treatment equivalent to those of an adult. It is silent in respect of minors under the age of 16. This provision was considered in the leading English case of *Gillick v West Norfolk and Wisbech AHA*.[165] In this case a circular had been issued by the Department of Health and Social Security to the effect that if a young girl, under 16, requested contraceptives, a doctor would not be acting unlawfully in providing them in order to protect the girl from the harmful consequences of sexual intercourse. It was also stated that although the doctor should seek to involve the girl's parents, in exceptional circumstances contraceptives could be provided without parental consent. The plaintiff in this case had five daughters under 16 years of age. She sought an assurance from her local Health Authority that her daughters would not be given contraceptives without her prior consent. The Health Authority refused to give such an assurance and the plaintiff sought a declaration from the Court that the advice contained in the circular was unlawful and in breach of her parental rights.

[11.127] By 3:2 majority decision, the House of Lords found in favour of the Health Authority on the basis that parental rights were limited and that the imposition of a strict age rule failed to take into account the growing understanding of the child. Lord Scarman said that 'the parental right to determine whether or not their minor child below the age of 16 will have medical treatment terminates if and when the child achieves reaches a sufficient understanding and intelligence to enable him or her to understand fully what is proposed.'[166] He went on to explain that the assessment of the competence of the individual to consent must involve not only an evaluation of whether the patient understands the nature of the advice being given, but also whether the patient has sufficient maturity to understand what is involved.[167] In the specific context of contraceptive advice for young girls he was of the view that 'there are moral and family questions, especially her relationship with her parents; long-term problems associated with the emotional impact of pregnancy and its termination; and there are the risks to health of sexual intercourse at her age, risks which contraception may diminish but cannot eliminate.' This has been interpreted as imposing such a high standard of understanding that many adults would fail to pass this threshold.[168]

[11.128] Lord Fraser took the view that there was no distinction to be drawn between consent to medical treatment generally and consent to contraceptive treatment. Therefore, if the argument put forward by the plaintiff were accepted, it would mean that

---

[165] *Gillick v West Norfolk and Wisbech AHA* [1986] AC 112.

[166] *Gillick v West Norfolk and Wisbech AHA* [1986] AC 112.

[167] This approach was also taken in Canada in *Johnston v Wellesley Hospital* [1970] 17 DLR 3d 139, and in Australia in *The Secretary, Dept. of Health and Community Services v JWB and another* [1992] 106 ALR 385 (known as Marion's case). For analysis of the Australian position see Lennings N 'Forward, Gillick: Are competent children autonomous medical decision makers? New developments in Australia.' (2015) Journal of Law and the Biosciences (July 2015) 2 (2): 459–468.

[168] 'The concept of competence, arguably a more rigorous test of understanding and intelligence than is applicable to adults, was intended to be a major hurdle on the way to autonomous decisions-making.' Bridge, 'Adolescents and Mental Disorder: Who Consents to Treatment?' (1997) 3 Med Law I 51 at 54. Also see Montgomery, 'Children as Property?' (1988) 51 MLR 323.

a minor under 16 years of age could not consent to any kind of medical advice, treatment or examination of his or her own body. That proposition was 'so surprising' and 'absurd' that the Court could not accept it. He went on to say that:

> [P]rovided the patient, whether a boy or girl, is capable of understanding what is proposed, and of expressing his or her own wishes, I see no good reason for holding that he or she lacks the capacity to express them validly and effectively and to authorise the medical man to make the examination or give the treatment which he advises.

[11.129] Lord Fraser went on to set out several conditions that should be satisfied before a doctor should offer contraceptive advice to a minor without her parents' knowledge. These have become known as the Fraser Guidelines and provide that the doctor should be satisfied

   i.   that the girl (although under the age of 16) will understand his advice;

   ii.   that he cannot persuade her to inform her parents or to allow him to inform the parents that she is seeking contraceptive advice;

   iii.   that she is very likely to continue having sexual intercourse with or without contraceptive treatment;

   iv.   that unless she receives contraceptive advice or treatment her physical or mental health or both are likely to suffer;

   v.   that her best interests require him to give her contraceptive advice, treatment or both without the parental consent.

[11.130] Lord Bridge expressly agreed with Lord Fraser and Lord Scarman. Both Lord Brandon and Lord Templeman dissented on the issue of whether a doctor could give contraceptive advice or treatment to a girl under 16 without parental knowledge or consent. Lord Templeman said that 'an unmarried girl under the age of sixteen does not, in my opinion, possess the power in law to decide for herself to practise contraception.' He was of the view, therefore, that the parent had the right to decide on behalf of the minor all matters which the minor was not competent to decide. A doctor should not prescribe contraceptives to such a person on clinical grounds, or on the best interests of the minor because his clinical judgment will be based only on the information provided to him by the minor without a full picture of her family circumstances, the parents will find out the truth at some future time which will rupture good relations in the family and with the doctor and the provision of contraception could encourage participation in sexual activities which may cause her harm.[169] If discretion were given to doctors to provide contraception without parental knowledge simply on the basis that the young person was at risk of becoming pregnant, this 'would enable any girl to obtain contraception on request by threatening to sleep with a man.'

[11.131] Although much public attention was focused on the issue of the provision of contraception to minors as a result of this case, over subsequent years the decision also had implications beyond that specific matter. In 2006 it was established in *R (on the application of Axon) v Secretary of State for Health*[170] that the *Gillick* principle also applied to abortion. On facts that were broadly similar to those in *Gillick*, a mother

---

[169] For discussion of the doctor's position in relation to *Gillick*, see Williams, 'The *Gillick* Saga' (1985) 135 NLJ 1156.

[170] *R (on the application of Axon) v Secretary of State for Health* [2006] EWHC 37 (Admin).

claimed that guidance from the Department of Health on sexual and reproductive matters was unlawful in suggesting that people under the age of 16 years could expect confidentiality in relation to advice on contraception and abortion. She said that this interfered with her rights under art 8 of the European Convention on Human Rights which gives a right to respect for private and family life. Silber J dismissed her complaint on the grounds that *Gillick* was not confined to contraception only but extended to other sexual matters and he stated that he was fortified in coming to this conclusion by the fact that young women would be deterred from seeking advice without the assurance of confidentiality. This, he said, would have 'very undesirable and far-reaching consequences.' In relation to the claim that art 8 had been breached, Silber J said the autonomy of the mature young person undermines any art 8 rights of a parent to family life. [171]

[11.132] It was anticipated that the case would spark new developments in the area of children's rights that would change the way in which disputes involving children had traditionally been decided, on a consideration of children's welfare rather than rights.[172] However, as can be seen from many of the subsequent cases dealing with the refusal of treatment by a minor, the courts seem to have retreated somewhat from such a development. In the *Gillick* case, neither Lord Fraser nor Lord Scarman specifically dealt with the competence of the minor to refuse consent to treatment, although both judgments refute the suggestion that parents have absolute control over children until the age of majority. Both judges pointed out that the rights accorded to parents only existed for the benefit of the child, and to permit parents to discharge their duties towards their children. While Lord Scarman suggests, obiter, that the minor assumes power both to consent to and refuse treatment once she has reached capacity, Lord Fraser does not go beyond the provision of consent *to* treatment.[173] Thus, the difficult issue of whether a competent minor can refuse medical treatment remained open after *Gillick*. The contexts in which this issue has commonly arisen are considered below.

---

[171] This approach has been questioned on the basis that family life does not necessarily or even usually cease to exist when the child reaches maturity. Family life depends on close personal ties and parents usually share these ties with their dependent minor children. Taylor suggests that an alternative approach could have recognised that Ms Axon did enjoy family life with her children but that interference with those rights was justified under art 8(2) by the child's art 8 right to have her autonomy respected. See Taylor, 'Reversing the Retreat from Gillick? *R (Axon) v Secretary of State for Health*' (2007) 19 Child and Family Law Quarterly 81.

[172] At common law a father's authority over his children was regarded as absolute, in the absence of gross misconduct on his part. 'Since Victorian times this has been gradually whittled away, first by conferring equality on the father and mother in relation to custody proceedings, secondly by the recognition of the equally parental authority of the father and mother, and thirdly by the emergence of the child's welfare as the paramount consideration overriding the claims of parents where the child's custody or upbringing is brought before the courts.' Bainham, 'The Balance of Power in Family Decisions' (1986) Camb LJ 262 at 268.

[173] For discussion, see Eekelaar, 'The Emergence of Children's Rights' (1986) 6 Ox J of Legal Studies 161.

Minors under psychiatric care

[11.133] A number of cases have considered the application of *Gillick* in the context of minors with psychiatric difficulties, often in circumstances where the minor is refusing treatment recommended by treating clinicians. For example in *Re R (a minor) (wardship: consent to medical treatment)*[174] a 15-year-old girl, R, who was on the local authority's at-risk register, was received into voluntary care and placed in a children's home after a fight with her father. She began to suffer hallucinations and her mental health deteriorated. Her behaviour also became more disturbed and she threatened suicide and attacked her father on one occasion when she had absconded from the home. The local authority obtained place of safety and care orders, and placed her in an adolescent psychiatric unit. Her behaviour remained very disturbed and the unit sought permission to administer anti-psychotic drugs to her. During lucid periods when R was capable of understanding the nature and effect of the medication, she objected to taking the drugs. The unit was unprepared to continue caring for her without permission to administer the medication,[175] and therefore the Local Authority began wardship proceedings seeking permission from the Court to give R the drugs with or without her consent. The Court had to consider whether R was *Gillick* competent and, if so, whether her refusal of the drug treatment could be overridden.

[11.134] Lord Donaldson MR was of the view that *Gillick* did not determine that parental rights to consent terminate with the achievement by the child of competence. Capacity to consent will vary from child to child, and according to the treatment under consideration. If it were the position that when the child was regarded as competent a transfer of rights between parents and child took place, doctors would be faced with 'an intolerable dilemma', particularly when the child was close to 16 years of age and refusing consent. He was of the opinion that a *Gillick* competent child can consent to treatment but if he refuses or declines treatment, consent may be given by someone with parental rights. If all those with power to consent decline or refuse to do so, that creates a veto on treatment. Farquharson LJ said that it was difficult to apply *Gillick* to the facts of this particular case, as R's understanding and capacity was fluctuating from day to day according to the effect of her illness.[176] He said he would 'reject the application of the *Gillick* test to an on/off situation of that kind.' Whether the Court in this instance approached the question from the point of view of competence, or from the perspective of R's welfare as the paramount consideration, the result would have been the same.

[11.135] The Court held that the *Gillick* test had no application in wardship cases, which had to be determined in accordance with the best interests of the ward. Thus, even if the ward was considered to be *Gillick* competent, her refusal to consent to medical treatment

---

[174] *Re R (a minor) (wardship: consent to medical treatment)* [1991] 4 All ER 177.

[175] It may be argued that this is indicative of the manipulation by adults of the acquisition of capacity by children. Bainham, 'The Judge and the Competent Minor' (1992) 108 LQR 194 at 200.

[176] The Court held that R was not competent even in her lucid intervals. 'This is a curious conclusion to reach, since it allows competence to be judged not on the present but on the past or the predicted mental condition of the person.' Elliston, 'If You Know What's Good For You: Refusal of Consent to Medical Treatment by Children' in McLean (ed) *Contemporary Issues in Law, Medicine and Ethics* (Dartmouth Publishing, 1996) 29 at 32.

could be overridden by a court in her best interests.[177] 'Hers is a limited autonomy. If she is sixteen her statutory right to authorise treatment cannot be overruled by parents even though their rights co-exist with her own until she is of full age, but if she objects to treatment, the power of parents or the court, can provide the necessary 'flak jacket' and enable lawful treatment.'[178] Lord Donaldson MR introduced the concept of consent providing the key to the therapeutic door and, in the case of the mature minor, there are two keyholders – the minor and the parents. Either keyholder may *enable* treatment to be lawfully given, but this did not *determine* that treatment should be given. This analogy was heavily criticised and appears to have been later regretted by Lord Donaldson as discussed below.

[11.136] In *South Glamorgan County Council v W and B,*[179] A was a 15-year-old girl who had suffered psychiatric disturbance following her parents' divorce when she was aged 7. She lived with her father and an older brother in the family home and rarely saw her mother. She had received virtually no schooling for a number of years, and lived as a recluse in a room in her home. She was abusive to her family and threatened harm to herself or others if they did not comply with her wishes as to domestic tasks and privacy. Following the recommendation of a number of child psychiatrists, the local authority began care proceedings and sought Court permission for A to be removed from her home for assessment and treatment. A's father opposed the application.

[11.137] The Court considered the provisions of the Children Act 1989, which provides, inter alia, that local authorities can invoke the inherent jurisdiction of the court where the child could probably suffer significant harm.[180] The Act obliges the court 'to have regard to the ascertainable wishes and feelings of the child concerned (considered in the light of his age and understanding)'[181] and also appears to grant a minor a statutory right to refuse to submit to medical or psychiatric examination or treatment where he has 'sufficient understanding to make an informed decision.'[182] It was argued that where a child exercises this statutory right to refuse, the court has no power to override such refusal. The Court did not accept this argument, saying that the Act had specifically preserved the inherent jurisdiction of the High Court with respect to children. In considering whether the Court should exercise that power the child's welfare had to be the paramount consideration, taking into account also the child's wishes in the matter. Balancing these considerations, the Court gave the Local Authority leave to remove A

---

[177] For discussion of parental rights in the context of refusal of consent by a minor, see Thornton, 'Multiple Keyholders – Wardship and Consent to Medical Treatment' [1992] CLJ 34; Bainham, 'The Judge and the Competent Minor' (1992) 108 LQR 194; Grubb, 'Treatment Decisions: Keeping it in the Family' in Grubb (ed) *Choices and Decisions in Health Care* (Wiley, 1993) 60–65.

[178] Bridge, 'Adolescents and Mental Disorder: Who Consents to Treatment?' (1997) 3 Med Law I 51 at 55.

[179] *South Glamorgan County Council v W and B* [1993] 1 FLR 574.

[180] The Children Act 1989 'severely prunes the local authority's access to the wardship jurisdiction. Wardship cannot be used to place a child in care or under supervision, nor to confer parental responsibility on the local authority.' Brazier and Bridge, 'Coercion or Caring: Analysing Adolescent Autonomy' (1996) Legal Studies 84.

[181] The Children Act 1989, s 1(3)(a).

[182] The Children Act 1989, ss 38(6), 43(8), and 44(7).

from her home and take her to a unit for assessment and treatment. In this case the Court was in the difficult position of deciding to override the wishes of a competent minor.[183] Although she did have a statutory right to refuse treatment, the Court chose to adopt an unsatisfactory route of using its inherent jurisdiction to achieve its intended result.[184] It has been suggested that the judgment 'conveys to children the message that they cannot trust that the clearly expressed 'rights' given by Parliament will be safe in the hands of the judges.'[185]

[11.138] While this case deals with conflict between the minor and the medical profession or local authority regarding her care, it does not deal with the situation that may arise where parents and older children or adolescents disagree, particularly where the adolescent refuses treatment. It is sometimes argued that consent is different to refusal, as the reasons for the refusal may be more 'teenage angst'[186] than principled objection, and the consequences of refusal are usually more serious and potentially dangerous and imply a conflict with profession decision-making.[187] However, if the *Gillick* test is to determine whether a minor has sufficient intelligence and understanding to seek and consent to her own treatment, it may be questioned whether non-application of this principle to refusals of treatment is overly paternalistic.[188] The interpretation of the law as retaining parental power to give consent despite the refusal of a competent minor has been described as 'driving a coach and horses through

---

[183] Brazier and Bridge suggest that criticism of the case is misplaced and that the Court could not simply wash their hands of A 'The unfortunate feature of the judgment was to suggest A was capable of autonomous choice, to find her 'not' *Gillick* incompetent.' 'Coercion or Caring: Analysing Adolescent Autonomy' (1996) Legal Studies 84 at 101.

[184] An alternative approach would have been seen if a family member of A's had intervened and made an application for a 'specific issue order' under the Children Act 1989, s 8. This is an order 'giving directions for the purpose of determining a specific question which has arisen, or which may arise, in connection with any aspect of parental responsibility for a child.' In such a case the child is not granted a right of veto over action considered necessary by the courts. The Court does not assume parental responsibility as it does in wardship but, more simply, exercises control over a single issue affecting a child. It is thought to be particularly useful to deal with disputes involving medical treatment, for example where parents themselves are in conflict regarding appropriate treatment, or where both parents refuse consent. However, a Local Authority cannot apply for such an order. See Brazier and Bridge, 'Coercion or Caring: Analysing Adolescent Autonomy' (1996) Legal Studies 84 at 100–101.

[185] Lyon, 'What's Happened to the Child's Right to Refuse?' (1994) 6 Journal of Child Law 84 at 87.

[186] A minor may refuse treatment for a variety of reasons such as rebellion, resentment of adult control, miscommunication, misunderstanding or fear. Bridge, 'Adolescents and Mental Disorder: Who Consents to Treatment?' (1997) 3 Med Law I 51 at 61.

[187] Pearce, 'Consent to Treatment During Childhood: The Assessment of Competence and Avoidance of Conflict' (1994) 165 British Journal of Psychiatry 713.

[188] Elliston argues that it is illogical to distinguish between the ability to consent and the ability to refuse, as 'the right to say yes must carry with it the right to say no. If one is able to weigh up the considerations in order to agree to treatment, surely one is equally capable of weighing up the same considerations even though arriving at a different conclusion?' Elliston, 'If You Know What's Good for You: Refusal of Consent to Medical Treatment by Children' in McLean (ed) *Contemporary Issues in Law, Medicine and Ethics* (Dartmouth, 1996) 29 at 34.

Gillick.'[189] However, the alternative would be to accede to the minor's wishes when competent and to treat her when incompetent under the mantle of necessity. This issue is considered further below.

[11.139] In *Re K, W and H (Minors) (Medical Treatment)*[190] three young people, two aged 15 and one nearly 15 years old, were receiving specialist psychiatric treatment in a secure unit at a hospital. Following a number of complaints from children being treated at the unit, the hospital sought court permission to administer emergency medication. The Court held that none of the three patients were *Gillick* competent[191] and, even if they were, their refusal could be overridden on the basis that the patients' parents had all consented in writing to the administration of emergency medication. Thorpe J was of the view if a *Gillick* competent minor refused treatment, consent could be given by someone else with parental rights. Where more than one person has power to consent, only a refusal of all having that power will create a veto. He held that the application in this case was 'misconceived and unnecessary' on the basis that parental consent was in existence and, whether the minor patients were competent or not, their refusal could be overridden. This case 'denies the young person any forum in which to object to medical treatment'[192] and permits compulsory psychiatric treatment based upon parental consent. 'The doctor has his flak jacket. Any ethical concern he may have about whether to proceed against the child's will he must resolve alone.'[193]

[11.140] In the 1990s a number of cases came before the English courts in relation to the forcible feeding of patients suffering from anorexia, bulimia or abstention from eating due to a personality disorder. Despite the refusal of consent to feeding by these patients the courts invariably found ways to allow their detention and feeding under the umbrella of 'best interests.' The first of these cases was *Re W (a minor) (medical treatment: court's jurisdiction)*[194] which provided the Court with the opportunity to consider whether it had the power to sanction medical treatment of a 16-year-old girl against her wishes. The facts of *Re W* concerned a 16-year-old girl suffering from anorexia. She was admitted to a specialist residential unit and fed by nasogastric tube. Due to continued deterioration in her condition the Local Authority became concerned that she may begin to reject all treatment. The authority applied for permission to move her to a new unit and to treat her without consent under the inherent jurisdiction of the Court under the Children Act 1989. The Court of Appeal granted the application. It held that competent children do not have an absolute power of veto in relation to their medical treatment – the Court could overrule their views in an appropriate case. The Court confirmed the view taken in *Re R* that all that *Gillick* had decided was that a competent child under 16 could give a valid consent to medical treatment. 'It was *not* to be taken as establishing

---

[189] Kennedy, 'Consent to Treatment: The Capable Person' in Dyer (ed) *Doctors, Patients and the Law* (Scientific Publications, 1992) Ch 3.

[190] *Re K, W and H (Minors) (Medical Treatment)* [1993] 1 FLR 854.

[191] It is unclear where this finding came from since there was no evidence given on this issue. See Bates, 'Children on Secure Psychiatric Units – *Re K, W and H* – Out of Sight, Out of Mind?' (1994) 6 Journal of Child Law 131 at 135.

[192] Fox and McHale, *Health Care Law, Text and Materials* (Sweet & Maxwell, 1997).

[193] Brazier and Bridge, 'Coercion or Caring: Analysing Adolescent Autonomy' (1996) Legal Studies 84 at 102.

[194] *Re W (a minor) (medical treatment: court's jurisdiction)* [1992] 4 All ER 627, [1993] 1 FLR 1.

that such children have a power of veto over treatment, nor was it to be regarded as determining the court's power to sanction or prohibit medical treatment whatever the child's (or parents') views.'[195]

[11.141] Lord Donaldson MR was of the view that 'good parenting involves giving minors as much rope as they can handle without an unacceptable risk that they will hang themselves.' The point at which the court must intervene occurred when the child, refusing treatment, would be facing death or severe permanent injury. He said that anorexia was a condition that could destroy a person's ability to make an informed choice. On the facts of this case the application should be granted to save W from martyring herself. Some commentators regard *Re W* as a pragmatic remedies approach well-suited to the common law tradition:

> It takes a case-by-case approach to individual problems without showing an excessive desire to formulate legal principles. *Gillick*, however, was a rights-based approach where the court advocated a view of rights that was broad and general in terms. That approach has now had its wings clipped. Whether one uses Lord Donaldson MR's 'keyholder analogy' or his 'flak jacket' approach, the effect is the same. It enables the court to prevent... 'permanent disability' or 'unnecessary pain and suffering'.[196]

[11.142] On the other hand the judgment has also been criticised, as it runs directly counter to the *Gillick* principle that was interpreted as meaning that a child who has reached a certain level of intelligence and understanding should be given the right to decide whether to have any proposed medical treatment.[197] Lord Donaldson's view, albeit obiter, that no minor, whatever her age, could, by refusing treatment, override a consent to treatment given by someone with parental authority has been seen as 'a fundamental incursion into the adolescent's right to self-determination.'[198] The case poses difficulties by virtue of the nature of the illness itself, which is characterised by a desire not to be treated. Therefore, if a wish not to be treated is part of the illness, it is difficult to conclude that the refusal is a voluntary exercise of the patient's autonomy, since this has been shaped by the illness. 'However, such a finding should be made only with a great deal of care, since it may be all too easy to subvert the concept of

---

[195] Lowe and Juss, 'Medical Treatment – Pragmatism and the Search for Principle' (1993) 56 Modern L Rev 865 at 867.

[196] Lowe and Juss, 'Medical Treatment – Pragmatism and the Search for Principle' (1993) 56 Modern L Rev 865 at 871.

[197] Freeman argues that Lord Donaldson may have displayed some understanding of adolescence but little of anorexia, and in *Re W* because W's ability to make her own choices was removed in order to save her life, this was at the price of undermining her identity and integrity. He argues that decisions like *Re W* would create more anorexics and more disturbed adolescents. Freeman, 'Removing Rights from Adolescents' (1993) 17 Adoption & Fostering 14. This is criticised in turn by de Cruz, who says that this argument 'overstates the case for adolescent autonomy and overlooks the life-saving motives for acting in the child's best interests'. De Cruz, 'Adolescent Autonomy, Detention for Medical Treatment and *Re C*' (1999) 62 Mod L Rev 595 at 603. See also Dickenson, 'Children's Informed Consent to Treatment: Is the Law an Ass?' (1994) 20 JME 205; Masson, '*Re W*: Appealing from the Golden Cage' (1993) J Child Law 37.

[198] Bridgeman, 'Old Enough to Know Best?' (1993) 13 Legal Studies 69; Lewis, 'Feeding Anorexic Patients Who Refuse Food' (Spring 1999) Med Law Rev 7, 21–37.

---

competence in order to hold that a patient's desire not to be treated is a symptom of mental disorder, rather than an expression of their autonomy.'[199]

[11.143] Lord Donaldson regretted his earlier keyholder analogy 'because keys can lock as well as unlock'. In this case he used a new analogy - the legal 'flak jacket' which he said:

> [P]rotects the doctor from claims by the litigious whether he acquires it from his patient who may be a minor over the age of sixteen, or a *'Gillick'* competent child under that age or from another person having parental responsibilities which include a right to consent to the treatment of the minor. Anyone who gives him a flak jacket (ie consent) may take it back, but the doctor only needs one and as long as he continues to have one he has the legal right to proceed.[200]

Again Lord Donaldson has been subjected to criticism for this analogy, which seems to place more emphasis on protecting doctors from litigation than on patient autonomy. 'Flak jackets conjure up a scenario where health professionals quite sensibly become concerned to grab a jacket, get a signature on the consent form, and then proceed to do what they think best.'[201] Although the courts seem concerned with the ethical principle of autonomy and the respect to be accorded to the wishes of the minor, it may be argued that they are reluctant to import it into legal principle.

[11.144] In *Re C (Detention: medical treatment)*,[202] the Court again dealt with a 16-year-old girl suffering from anorexia nervosa. C's family was described as 'highly dysfunctional' and C had a history of being sexually abused by her brother over a substantial period of time. She suffered from the illness for two years and was on a re-feeding programme, funded by the Local Authority, at a private clinic specialising in the treatment of eating disorders. After her discharge from the clinic, C's health deteriorated rapidly and she was re-admitted. Her behaviour was disturbed, aggressive and sometimes suicidal. She absconded regularly from the clinic and her weight fell to a dangerously low level. The clinic sought an order for her detention on the basis that it believed the treatment would only be successful if she could be forced to stay at the clinic. The Court granted the application on the basis that detention was in C's best interests at this time whether or not she consented to the treatment, and held that she should be detained with reasonable force if necessary, albeit with the least distress and greatest dignity possible.

[11.145] In this case it was held that C was not *Gillick* competent, as she was not capable of evaluating the relevant information concerning her treatment in order to make a balanced choice. Therefore, she could not give a valid consent or refusal of treatment. As in *Re W,* her purported refusal could be overridden in her best interests under the inherent jurisdiction of the Court. Her detention was not solely to deprive her of her liberty but was also justified on the basis that her history demonstrated that she was

---

[199] Elliston, 'If You Know What's Good for You: Refusal of Consent to Medical Treatment by Children' in McLean (ed) *Contemporary Issues in Law, Medicine and Ethics* (Dartmouth, 1996) 29 at 34.

[200] *Re W (a minor) (medical treatment: court's jurisdiction)* [1992] 4 All ER 627 at 635.

[201] Brazier and Bridge, (1996) 'Coercion or Caring: Analysing Adolescent Autonomy' Legal Studies 84 at 87.

[202] *Re C (Detention: medical treatment)* [1997] 2 FLR 180.

unable to follow a re-feeding regime outside of the clinic, and since this treatment was in her best interests, detention was also regarded as an essential part of that treatment. Reasonable force was permitted in her detention but not in the feeding since this would be contrary to the ethos of the clinic.

[11.146] *Re C* continues 'the paternalistic line of authority of cases such as *Re W* and negates adolescent autonomy in anorexia cases, but it also enunciates safeguards to protect the child's interests.'[203] It reinforces the message that 'an anorexic adolescent's autonomy ends where her refusal of medical treatment begins to endanger her life – that, in some cases, respecting adolescent autonomy may be simply too high a price to pay.'[204] Although the courts have suggested that the wishes of a child should carry more weight as the child grows more mature, this would appear to be simply paying lip-service to autonomy, since there have been no English cases in which a refusal of medical treatment by a minor has been respected.[205] In all of these cases the courts have relied heavily on the evidence of medical professionals in reaching their decisions. This is probably due to a number of factors, including the traditional deference shown to the profession in medical litigation, the fact that most of these cases are life-threatening and do not allow for lengthy legal research and argument and that the applications are generally brought by institutions with recourse to lawyers and expert witnesses familiar with the issues involved.[206] The result of these cases is that mature and competent minors in the UK can have their decisions respected if, but only if, they know what is good for them and accept the treatment that is offered:[207]

> If society is not prepared to allow adolescents to court unfavourable outcomes in judgments relating to medical treatment, we should say so openly. The law should not pretend to apply a 'functional' test of autonomy to every patient when younger patients are in fact subjected to an 'outcome' test.[208]

Refusal of treatment by minors on religious and other grounds

[11.147] Apart from cases where a young person's refusal of medical treatment is due to mental disturbance or illness, there is also a category of cases where such a refusal is prompted by adherence to strong religious beliefs opposing the medical intervention in question. The problem generated by these 'children of conscience' is how a court should

---

[203] De Cruz, 'Adolescent Autonomy, Detention for Medical Treatment and *Re C*' (1999) 62 Mod L Rev 595 at 603.

[204] De Cruz, at 603. See also Lewis, 'Feeding Anorexic Patients Who Refuse Food' (1999) 7 Med L Rev 21–37.

[205] Elliston, 'If You Know What's Good for You: Refusal of Consent to Medical Treatment by Children' in McLean (ed) *Contemporary Issues in Law, Medicine and Ethics* (Dartmouth, 1996) 29 at 39.

[206] Elliston, 'If You Know What's Good for You: Refusal of Consent to Medical Treatment by Children' in McLean (ed) *Contemporary Issues in Law, Medicine and Ethics* (Dartmouth, 1996) 29 at 48.

[207] Elliston, 'If You Know What's Good for You: Refusal of Consent to Medical Treatment by Children' in McLean (ed) *Contemporary Issues in Law, Medicine and Ethics* (Dartmouth, 1996) 29 at 52.

[208] Brazier and Bridge, 'Coercion or Caring: Analysing Adolescent Autonomy' (1996) Legal Studies 84 at 109.

deal with a decision made by a mature, intelligent minor to refuse medical treatment on the basis of religious conviction. Respect for freedom of religion and the right of self-determination would seem to demand that the choice made by a competent minor should be upheld in the same way as if that minor were an adult person making the same choice for the same reasons.

[11.148] In *Re E (A minor) (Wardship: medical treatment)*[209] E, a young man of fifteen and three quarters, was suffering from leukaemia. He and his parents were Jehovah's Witnesses and all three refused consent to the administration of blood and some particular drugs. They gave consent to a different form of drug therapy that had a much lower chance of success. The hospital began wardship proceedings and sought the Court's permission to treat E conventionally if and when his condition became so bad that he would be at risk of death from heart attack or stroke. E's parents were of the view that his decision should be respected, particularly as he was so close to the age of 16, when his consent would be required by statute. However, the judge instead considered whether E was *Gillick* competent, in order for him to be able to refuse treatment.

[11.149] Ward J found that E was a person of sufficient intelligence to be able to take decisions about his own well-being, but that there was a range of decisions that were outside of his ability to fully comprehend. He found that, although E spoke intelligently, calmly and confidently about the consequences of his refusal of treatment, he did not really appreciate the pain, distress and fear that he would face, as well as the implications for his family. Ward J was therefore of the view that E was not *Gillick* competent, but even if he had been, his veto would not have been binding on the basis that the Court would decide the issue on welfare grounds. He was not satisfied that E's decision was truly free of the influence of his religious beliefs and those of his parents. He accepted that forced transfusion would be traumatic for E but found that E would accept the Court's decision. He said that it was 'essential for his well-being to protect him from himself and his parents' and so overrode E's decision.[210]

[11.150] This case raises questions about the level of understanding required of minors and whether a higher standard is expected of them than could be attained even by adult patients. It is not clear from this case why age alone should be a sufficient determinant of competence, as E was evidently intelligent, mature and content in his understanding of the consequences of his decision. The Court seems to have been influenced by the strength of religious belief with which E grew up, E having had these convictions instilled in him throughout his life by his parents. This led to the Court probing whether E's choice was really a free one. E's death two years after the judgment could be regarded as the Court's decision either having prolonged the waiting period in a distressing manner with unwanted treatment being forced on him, or as having given E the opportunity to mature and become even more convinced of the correctness of his decision.

[11.151] Similar issues arose in *Re S (A minor) (medical treatment)*[211] where a young girl aged 15 and a half had suffered from a life-threatening illness since birth. She had

---

[209] *Re E (A minor) (Wardship: medical treatment)* [1993] 1 FLR 386.

[210] On reaching maturity, E exercised his right to refuse further blood transfusions and subsequently died.

[211] *Re S (A minor) (medical treatment)* [1994] 2 FLR 1065.

endured blood transfusions on a monthly basis and daily injections throughout her life. As a result of irregularity in iron ingestion she did not grow normally and suffered much abuse from her peers in this regard. When S was 10, S's mother converted to the Jehovah's Witness faith and began taking S to meetings with her. S's mother influenced her to stop the treatments and S failed to turn up for transfusions. The Local Authority requested the High Court to exercise its inherent jurisdiction and override S's refusal to have further treatment. Johnson J found that S had only come to this decision recently, was disillusioned with treatment, was influenced by her mother's religious convictions and did not understand the full implications of what would happen to her if she did not receive the transfusions. Her capacity was deemed not to be commensurate with the gravity of the decision to be made. He said that it was not enough that S knew that she would die, although she clearly hoped for a miracle cure. 'For her decision to carry weight she should have a greater understanding of the manner of the death and pain and the distress.' Therefore, Johnson J held that S was not *Gillick* competent and that her decision should be overridden.

[11.152] There are distinctions to be drawn between the facts of *Re E* and *Re S* on grounds of understanding, commitment to religious conviction and influence of others. S was fed up with her debilitating illness and, although she hoped that God might spare her, she felt that she 'might as well die'. She did not display full understanding of why God might want her to refuse transfusions and considered it a possibility that the doctors were wrong in their diagnosis of her illness. E, on the other hand, was committed to his religion from childhood, understood why his religion opposed transfusions and appreciated the fact of his own death, if not the distressing manner of it. Despite the differences between these two young people, both were treated the same by the court and both had their competence questioned and their decisions overruled. This seems to be based, then, not on assessments of competence but on age alone. This ignores the development of the individual and 'flies in the face of evolving autonomy … Rationality appears to be acquired on a person's eighteenth birthday.'[212]

[11.153] In *Re L (Medical treatment: Gillick competency)*[213] again the Court was faced with the question of whether to override the wishes of L, a Jehovah's Witness girl aged 14, in relation to refusal of blood transfusions. L was a firm believer in her faith and had signed a directive that, in the event of an accident, she should not be given blood. She had renewed this directive a short time before an accident in which she sustained very severe burns. Her medical condition demanded at least three operations in order to ensure survival. The anaesthetist was not prepared to proceed with the operation without the availability of blood for the necessary transfusions. The Court was presented with a 'very stark dilemma'. If L received the treatment, her prognosis was very optimistic. If she did not, gangrene was expected to develop and she would, according to the burns consultant, inevitably die a 'horrible death'. The harrowing manner of her death had not been disclosed to L. She was described as 'very religious', 'mature', 'a model of a

---

[212] Brazier and Bridge, 'Coercion or Caring: Analysing Adolescent Autonomy' (1996) Legal Studies 84 at 107. See also Dickenson and Jones, 'True Wishes: Philosophical and Clinical Approaches to the Developing Case-Law on Consent in Children' (1995) Philosophy, Psychiatry and Psychology 4.

[213] *Re L (Medical treatment: Gillick competency)* [1998] 2 FLR 810.

young person…not attracted by some of the more undisciplined pursuits of youth.' She was clearly a serious, intelligent girl from a sheltered family, immersed in church activities.

[11.154] The hospital authority sought and received permission from the Court, exercising its inherent jurisdiction, to administer blood as necessary during L's treatment. This was on the basis that L's welfare demanded that she be protected against a distressing death, even though this overrode her autonomy. There was no hint of any coercion or that L's community would reject her if she received the transfusions. Her family were supportive of her, irrespective of the Court's decision. However, L's religious convictions, though seriously held, were seen as rigid and inflexible, lacking the constructive formulation that an adult might have. Ultimately, her religious beliefs, understanding and maturity 'were weighed alongside the prospect of an outcome which the majority of the community would deplore.'[214]

[11.155] In this case the Court was influenced by a number of factors, including L's firmly held religious views. The Court seemed to take the view that because L was unquestioning of her religion, this demonstrated an immaturity on her part. However, it has been argued that 'absolute faith or the espousal of views in a very black and white manner is itself a feature of any fundamentalist religious belief. Does this mean therefore that a choice of faith over treatment is the preserve of the adult and that the beliefs of the fourteen or fifteen year old lack the validity of adult faith?'[215] Religious belief itself could be said to defy rationality, as it cannot be based on evidence or established truths. Therefore, if the mature, competent minor is under no coercion, misunderstanding or deception, it may be questioned why her belief should not be respected in the same way as an adult's. The Court also relied on her upbringing within a close family circle founded on religious beliefs, as having sheltered her from external experiences that might have contributed to her understanding of her situation. The fact that she had deliberately not been told, at her family's request, of the nature of her death, meant that the Court was able to find that she could not properly understand her situation and could not make a valid refusal of treatment. Rather than order that L be given the requisite information in order to establish whether her understanding increased, and her decision held steadfast, the Court was content with holding that she was not *Gillick* competent.

[11.156] Other jurisdictions also find the issue of respecting adolescent autonomy in cases of religious refusals challenging. In the Canadian case of *AC v Manitoba*[216] C was admitted to hospital when she was 14 years, 10 months old, suffering from lower gastrointestinal bleeding caused by Crohn's disease. She was a devout Jehovah's Witness and, some months before, had signed an advance medical directive containing her written instructions not to be given blood under any circumstances. Her doctor believed that internal bleeding created an imminent, serious risk to her health and perhaps her life. She refused to consent to the receipt of blood. Under s 25(9) of the Manitoba Child

---

214 Bridge, 'Religious Beliefs and Teenage Refusal of Medical Treatment' (1999) 62 Mod L Rev 585 at 587.

215 Bridge, 'Religious Beliefs and Teenage Refusal of Medical Treatment' (1999) 62 Mod L Rev 585 at 588.

216 *AC v Manitoba* [2009] 2 SCR 181.

and Family Services Act it is presumed that the best interests of a child 16 or over will be most effectively promoted by allowing the child's views to be determinative, unless it can be shown that the child does not understand the decision or appreciate its consequences. Where the child is under 16, however, no such presumption exists. The judge ordered that C receive blood transfusions, concluding that when a child is under 16, there are no legislated restrictions of authority on the court's ability to order medical treatment in the child's 'best interests'. C and her parents appealed the order arguing that the legislative scheme was unconstitutional because it unjustifiably infringed C's rights under the Canadian Charter of Rights and Freedoms.

[11.157] The majority of the Supreme Court of Canada held, in dismissing arguments that the Act was unconstitutional, that when the young person's best interests are interpreted in a way that sufficiently respects his or her capacity for mature, independent judgment in a particular medical decisionmaking context, the constitutionality of the legislation is preserved. The Court held that the statutory scheme 'strikes a constitutional balance between what the law has consistently seen as an individual's fundamental right to autonomous decision making in connection with his or her body, and the law's equally persistent attempts to protect vulnerable children from harm.' The 'best interests' standard in the Act operates as 'a sliding scale of scrutiny, with the child's views becoming increasingly determinative depending on his or her maturity.' The more serious the nature of the decision and the more severe its potential impact on life or health, the greater the degree of scrutiny required. The result of this interpretation is that young people under 16 will have the right to demonstrate mature medical decisional capacity. The Court was satisfied that this protects both the integrity of the statute and of the adolescent.

[11.158] In assessing an adolescent's maturity in a best interests analysis, the court held that a judge should take into account the following factors:

- the nature, purpose and utility of the recommended medical treatment and its risks and benefits;
- the adolescent's intellectual capacity and the degree of sophistication to under-stand the information relevant to making the decision and to appreciate the potential consequences;
- the stability of the adolescent's views and whether they are a true reflection of his or her core values and beliefs;
- the potential impact of the adolescent's lifestyle, family relationships and broader social affiliations on his or her ability to exercise independent judg-ment;
- the existence of any emotional or psychiatric vulnerabilities and the impact of the adolescent's illness on his or her decisionmaking ability.

Any relevant information from adults who know the adolescent may also factor into the assessment.

[11.159] Justice Binnie (dissenting) described forced medical treatment as one of the most egregious violations of a person's integrity, and stated that every competent individual is entitled to autonomy to choose or not to choose medical treatment except where that autonomy may be limited or prescribed within the framework of the Constitution. 'The rights under s 2(a) of the Charter (religious freedom) and s 7 (liberty and security of the person) are given to everyone, including individuals under 16 years old.' He went on to hold that the state's interest in controlling the medical treatment of minors ceases where a minor, though under the age of sixteen, demonstrates maturity and thus has no need for any overriding state control; the legitimate basis of state intervention has, by reason of the finding of maturity, disappeared, and the minor is entitled to live or die by her decision.[217]

[11.160] Although this case is important in clarifying the common law of consent to medical treatment for adults and mature minors and in reasonably and clearly outlining the proper process under this particular statutory scheme for assessing maturity and approaching decisions with respect to minors of different ages, it has been argued that the case is ambivalent when it comes to the value of autonomy.[218] Harmon argues that 'the case explicitly recognizes the tensions between our demands for autonomy, on the one hand, and our lingering (if often un-vindicated) sense of responsibility toward others, including minors, on the other hand.'

[11.161] Refusals may of course be made on grounds other than religion, as demonstrated for example in *Re M (child: refusal of medical treatment)*[219] where M, a girl aged 15 and a half, suffered heart failure. Despite medical treatment, her condition deteriorated and it was concluded that the only course of action to save her life would be a heart transplant. M refused to give her consent for the operation as she did not want to have someone else's heart, and did not want to take medication for the rest of her life. Equally, however, she did not want to die. An emergency application was made to the Court to override M's wishes. The Court held that although M's wishes were important, they were not conclusive. There were risks attached to the surgery, to rejection of both the transplanted heart and continued treatment, and there was also a danger that M might always resent what had been done to her. However, when those risks were matched against the certainty of death, the Court was of the opinion that what was best for M was to give authority for the operation.

[11.162] Johnson J said that in the circumstances of this case, consent could have been given by M herself, by her mother who had parental responsibility for her, or by the Court. Although M's wishes were important, they were not decisive. He felt that M had been overwhelmed by her circumstances and the decision she was being asked to make. 'Events have overtaken her so swiftly that she has not been able to come to terms with her situation.' As a result, M was deemed to be incompetent to decide.

[11.163] This case does not provide any new insights into assessment of the competence of adolescents, nor does it deal with the difficulties of balancing the autonomy of minors with judicial and medical perceptions of their welfare.[220] It again displays the apparent

---

[217] *AC v Manitoba* [2009] 2 SCR 181 at paras 221–224.

[218] Harmon, 'Body Blow: Mature Minors and the Supreme Court of Canada's Decision in *AC V Manitoba*' (2010) *McGill Journal Of Law And Health* Vol 4 No 1 84–96 at 92.

[219] *Re M (child: refusal of medical treatment)* [1999] 2 FCR 577 [1999] Fam Law 753.

[220] In a study of children undergoing paediatric orthopaedic surgery, patients, parents and health professionals were asked for their views on when children could decide for themselves whether they wanted surgery or not. Interestingly, the children themselves set the highest threshold age for self-determination at 14 years; the parents put it slightly lower at 13.9 years and the health professionals chose the lowest figure, 10.3 years. See Alderson, *Children's Consent to Surgery* (Open University Press, 1993) at 9. Also Shield, 'Children's Consent to Treatment' (1994) 308 BMJ 1182–1183.

inconsistency between the courts' avowed adherence to principles of self-determination for adult patients, irrespective of the consequences, and their unanimous unwillingness to apply those principles to competent minors. It may be distasteful for judges to contemplate any alternative solution than that displayed in the long line of cases discussed above, particularly where life and death issues are at stake. However, there does not seem to be any attempt on the part of the judiciary to admit this inconsistency for what it is, and stand behind their decisions to overrule minors' autonomy on the basis of age, status and outcome.

[11.164] Common sense might seem to suggest that where the life of the minor is at stake, a higher degree of competence should be required, however it should not be set so high that even competent adults would have difficulty attaining that standard.[221] This is an artificial and disingenuous means of avoiding having to justify distinctions between individual patients on the basis of their age alone. In the same way that it would be considered wrong to give an adult treatment that she has refused because this would be a violation of her autonomy, it would also be wrong to do this to a young person as it would similarly fail to respect their interests in making, and being regarded as competent to make, decisions about what is to happen to them:[222]

> To believe in autonomy is to believe that anyone's autonomy is as morally significant as anyone else's. Nor does autonomy depend on the stage of life that a person has reached …To respect a child's autonomy is to treat that child as a person and as a rights-holder.[223]

[11.165] These decisions demonstrate that the court's powers can always be exercised to protect minors' welfare. It seems disingenuous, then, to go through the motions of assessing the competence of a minor when the court's decision will clearly be based on the outcome of the minor's refusal. If mature minors can never refuse treatment, can it be said that their consent is entirely voluntary?

> A patient's voluntary agreement to have a certain treatment indicates that they have decided of their own free will to have that treatment rather than some other treatment or no treatment at all. In contrast, their saying they agree to the treatment in a situation where they believe it will be given to them even if they refuse indicates no such thing. In this case the choice they face is not between having this treatment and not having it (or having

---

[221] 'It is arguable that a right to consent is meaningless without a corresponding right to refuse and that the Courts have adopted a strict test in determining necessary competence which even those patients for whom competence is assumed (those over 16) are unlikely to satisfy. The British Medical Association (BMA) believes that 'minors who are clearly competent to agree to treatment must be acknowledged as also having an option to refuse treatment if they understand the implications of so doing.' It is accepted that the level of competence necessary to validly refuse life-prolonging treatment is very high but the BMA hopes that the exploration of treatment options and young people's wishes and values will allow agreement to be reached.' BMA, *Withholding and Withdrawing Life-Prolonging Medical Treatment: Guidance for Decision-Making* (2nd edn, 2001) para 16.2. See also BMA *Medical Ethics Today: Its Practice and Philosophy* (1993).

[222] Walker, 'If they can consent, why can't they refuse?' in Donnelly and Murray (eds) *Ethical and Legal debates in Irish Healthcare, Confronting Complexities* (Manchester Univ Press 2015) 71–83 at 78.

[223] Freeman, 'Taking Children's Rights More Seriously' in Alston, Parker and Seymour (eds) *Children, Rights and the Law* (OUP, 1992) 52 at 64–65.

some other treatment), it is between going along with something that is going to happen anyway or resisting it. Their saying they agree to have the treatment in this case does not mean they have voluntarily agreed to have the treatment but rather that they have acquiesced to being given it. And acquiescing to something we take to be inevitable does not constitute giving permission (and hence does not constitute giving consent) for it to be done.[224]

[11.166] If the consequences of refusal by a minor are too serious for the court to sanction, it would be more acceptable to enshrine this in the law, rather than have the court go through a pretence of assessing competence, as if an evaluation in the minor's favour would somehow result in the court upholding the right to refuse treatment. Whether the final decision in *Re L* or any of the other cases on adolescent autonomy was correct or not, the judgments demonstrate a pragmatism and determination to reach a desired result rather than a reasoned analysis of the legal issues. It may thus be argued that:

> Judges should not go through the pretence of applying a functional test of capacity when the outcome of the young persons' decision is not one that they, or probably society, would countenance. The law should openly declare that welfare reigns when grave decisions with momentous outcomes are considered and recognise that adolescent autonomy is, inevitably, circumscribed.[225]

[11.167] Walker also argues that it is not always wrong to give a competent young person medical treatment they refuse because doctors are not only obliged to respect autonomy – they also have other obligations to act on the duties of beneficence, non-maleficence and justice as discussed in Chapter 2.[226] These duties come into conflict with each other, such as where respect for autonomy would result in acceptance of a patient's refusal of treatment, but the doctor's duty to act for the benefit of the patient would require the treatment to be given. In these situations the conflicting obligations must be weighed against each other to see which is the most important. 'What this means is that something could be *prima facie* wrong on the grounds that it fails to respect a person's autonomy, but not wrong all things considered. This would be the case where some other obligation, such as the obligation to do what is best for the patient, outweighs the obligation to respect their autonomy.'[227] Therefore Walker argues that where treatment is required to provide significant benefit to the young person who is refusing it, the doctor's obligation to do what is best for the patient can override his obligation to respect the patient's autonomy.

Irish law on mature minors

[11.168] As discussed above, the law across many jurisdictions does not consistently recognise adolescent autonomy. Similarly in Ireland, there is no single age at which a

---

[224] Walker, 'If they can consent, why can't they refuse?' in Donnelly and Murray (eds) *Ethical and legal debates in Irish healthcare, Confronting Complexities* (Manchester Univ Press 2016) 71–83 at 73–4.

[225] Bridge, 'Religious Beliefs and Teenage Refusal of Medical Treatment' (1999) 62 Mod L Rev 585 at 594.

[226] Para **[2.20]** et seq.

[227] Walker, 'If they can consent, why can't they refuse?' in Donnelly and Murray (eds) Ethical and legal debates in Irish healthcare, Confronting Complexities (Manchester Univ Press 2016) 71–83 at 79.

person is entitled to all the rights and responsibilities of adulthood. The law instead sets various thresholds such as 16, 18 and 21 years at which the young person gradually moves from childhood to adulthood. For example, at 16 some restrictions on employment are lifted and young people may choose to leave school whereas the Age of Majority Act 1985 provides that a person becomes an adult for the purposes of civil law at 18 years. In terms of health care, 16 is largely accepted in practice as the age of consent to medical treatment in a number of countries, including Ireland. A person aged 16 years can choose their own doctor, obtain a medical card and give consent to an operation. In general, young people are not treated in paediatric hospitals once they reach 16.

[11.169] In relation to giving consent to medical treatment, the Non-Fatal Offences Against the Person Act 1997 provides in s 23(1):

> The consent of a minor who has attained the age of 16 years to any surgical, medical or dental treatment which, in the absence of consent, would constitute a trespass to his or her person, shall be as effective as it would be if he or she were of full age; and where a minor has by virtue of this section given an effective consent to any treatment it shall not be necessary to obtain any consent for it from his or her parent or guardian.

This Act implemented the recommendations of the Law Reform Commission (LRC) in its 1994 Report on Non-Fatal Offences against the Person.[228] The LRC emphasised in this report the distinction between criminal and civil liability and limited its recommendations to the criminal law context. In a later Consultation Paper in 2009, the LRC took the view that since the Act originated from recommendations of the Commission in 1994, 'it is unlikely that s 23 could be interpreted as applying in the civil law context.' The LRC stated 'there is a fundamental difference between, on the one hand, the limited nature of a defence to the criminal offence of assault provided for in s 23 of the 1997 Act and, on the other, the wider acknowledgement of a minor's entitlement to exercise a right concerning their autonomy in terms of healthcare.'[229]

[11.170] However, it might be counter-argued that there is no reference to criminal proceedings in s 23. One would expect that if the provision were intended to relate solely to criminal prosecutions, the terms assault and battery would have been used rather than the term 'trespass to the person' which, as noted above, is a civil as well as a criminal wrong. The wording in s 23 is precisely the same as the wording in s 8 of the English Family Law Reform Act 1969 which is clearly not a criminal law statute. There has been no Irish court judgment to date that has held that this provision applies only to criminal proceedings. It has largely been accepted in practice that persons over 16 years can give valid consent to healthcare interventions. This position has been accepted by the HSE in its National Consent Policy,[230] the Medical Council,[231] the Office of the Data Protection Commissioner[232] and others.[233]

---

[228] LRC Report 45 – 1994 available at www.lawreform.ie.
[229] LRC Consultation paper 59–2009 at 4.03.
[230] HSE National Consent Policy (2013) Part Two Children and Minors www.hse.ie.
[231] Guide to Professional Conduct and Ethics (8th edn, 2016) para 18 available at www.medicalcouncil.ie
[232] http://www.dataprotection.ie/docs/Age-of-Consent/212.htm.
[233] The Medical Protection Society www.medicalprotection.org; Medisec Ireland www.medisec.ie; Irish College of General Practitioners www.icgp.ie.

[11.171] Section 23 does not make any reference to those under the age of 16. There are various possible interpretations of this. One interpretation is that the Act provides for consent by a person over 16 without necessarily preventing those under 16 from giving consent. Another interpretation is that the Act prevents those under 16 giving consent. The issues of adolescent autonomy and the 'mature minor' have not yet been judicially considered in Ireland[234] and therefore it is unclear whether the Irish courts would adopt a principle of individualised assessment of competence similar to *Gillick*.[235] Whether the courts would distinguish between contraceptive treatment/advice and other medical treatment is also open to question given the moral and social connotations involved in this issue in the Irish context. It has been consistently recommended by legal commentators as well as the Law Reform Commission and the Office of the Ombudsman for Children[236] that the law should be clarified on this matter.

[11.172] It is also unclear whether the ability to give consent also implies the ability to refuse treatment, or whether the Irish courts would follow their English counterparts in rejecting the ability of minors to refuse medical treatment. 'On the one hand, it might be argued that the right to refuse must complement the right to consent, otherwise this becomes the rather thin 'right' to agree with the doctor's recommendation. A right to agree, unless accompanied by the parallel right to disagree, could hardly be said to protect patient autonomy.'[237] Similarly Harris argues:

> The idea that a child (or anyone) might competently consent to a treatment but not be competent to refuse it is a palpable nonsense, the reasons for which are revealed by a moment's reflection on what a competent consent involves. To give an informed consent you need to understand the nature of the course of action to which you are consenting, which, in medical contexts, will include its probable and possible consequences and side effects and the nature of any alternative measures which might be taken and the consequences of doing nothing. So, to understand a proposed treatment well enough to consent to it is to understand the consequences of a refusal. And if the consequences of a refusal are understood well enough to consent to the alternative then the refusal must also be competent.[238]

[11.173] The impact of the Irish Constitution in this context is also a matter for consideration. The personal rights recognised by the Constitution clearly apply equally to children as to adults. As Walsh J said in *G v An Bord Uchtála* [239] 'The child's natural

---

[234] For discussion, see Donnelly, 'Capacity of Minors to Consent to Medical and Contraceptive Treatment' (1995) MLJI 18–21; Donnelly, *Consent: Bridging the Gap Between Doctor and Patient* (Cork University Press, 2002) at 35–36. See also Rooney, 'The Medico-Legal Impact of Consent to Treatment of Under-Aged Drug Users' (1998) MLJI 74–75.

[235] *Gillick v West Norfolk and Wisbech AHA* [1986] AC 112.

[236] The OCO recommends that the State should enact legislation that provides comprehensively for children and young people's consent to and refusal of medical treatment. This legislation must be rooted in the Convention and underpinned by a clear recognition of children's evolving capacities. Report to the UN Committee on the Rights of the Child on the occasion of the examination of Ireland's consolidated Third and Fourth Report to the Committee (April 2015) available at www.oco.ie April 2015.

[237] Jackson, *Medical Law, Text, Cases and Materials* (OUP, 3rd edn) at 273.

[238] Harris, 'Consent and end of life decisions' (2003) 29 Journal of Medical Ethics 10–15, 12.

[239] *G v An Bord Uchtála* [1980] IR 32.

rights spring primarily from the natural right of every individual to life, to be reared and educated, to liberty, to work, to rest and recreation, to the practice of religion, and to follow his or her conscience.'[240] Therefore a child has a right to privacy and to bodily integrity, which might enable an argument to be made that the child has the right to consent to or refuse medical treatment. Whether this would extend to the provision of contraception would have to be viewed in the light of interpretations of the common good and the rights of the parents or family under arts 41 and 42 of the Constitution.

[11.174] The question of whether respect for the autonomy of the mature minor would interfere with the rights of the family under the Constitution has not been considered in the medical context in any judgment of the Supreme Court to date. In *Attorney General v Edge*[241] the Court appeared to envisage some constitutional difficulty with a rule of law that permitted a boy of 14 to exercise an absolute discretion over where he lived, although Gavan Duffy J was of the view that if the legislature were to pass a statute recognising the common law age of discretion of 14 and its legal consequences, this would not be ultra vires.[242] In *Ryan v the Attorney General*,[243] the Supreme Court rejected the plaintiff's claim that the State policy of water fluoridation constituted an unjustifiable attack on the authority of the family and her right to educate her child. The Court was of the view that there was 'nothing in the Constitution which recognises the right of a parent to refuse to allow the provision of measures designed to secure the health of his child.'[244]

[11.175] Other relevant cases in the context of parental authority include *North Western Health Board v HW and CW*,[245] where the Supreme Court upheld the High Court decision in favour of allowing the parents of a young child to refuse a screening test designed to discover whether the child could have a number of serious metabolic disorders. There is also some limited guidance to be obtained from the Supreme Court's decision in *McK v the Information Commissioner*[246] in which Denham J stated that the views of the minor who was then almost 18 in relation to whether her father should have access to her medical records under the Freedom of Information Acts were 'very relevant'. This was in the context of the legislative provisions in the Freedom of Information Act that provide that a parent or guardian may access personal information of their child who has not yet reached the age of majority (18 years). Although Denham J indicates that the views of the almost 18 year old were 'very relevant' this does not however definitively state that the minor's opposition to the release of the records would be determinative and therefore it does not provide strong support for the principle of adolescent autonomy in that context. The case also demonstrates the strong presumption accorded to parental rights under the Constitution which would undoubtedly prove

---

[240] *G v An Bord Uchtála* [1980] IR 32 at 69.

[241] *Attorney General v Edge* [1943] IR 115.

[242] Donnelly, 'Capacity of Minors to Consent to Medical and Contraceptive Treatment' (1995) MLJI 18 at 20.

[243] *Ryan v the Attorney General* [1965] IR 294.

[244] *Ryan v the Attorney General* [1965] IR 294 at 350.

[245] *North Western Health Board v HW and CW* (November 8 2001) SC discussed above at para **[11.18]**.

[246] *McK v The Information Commissioner* [2006] IESC 2 considered in Chapter 3 at para **[3.24]**.

challenging to a young person's attempt to refuse medical treatment against parental wishes.

[11.176] In *HSE v JM and RP* in 2013,[247] a 15 year old girl with bipolar disorder refused to comply with her treatment regime or to allow a blood sample to be taken from her to monitor her condition. She was assessed by a consultant adolescent psychiatrist as mature enough to understand the necessary information regarding her diagnosis and treatment, and as being at significant risk of suicide to the extent that her judgement was impaired and she was unable to make clear decisions about her future. The Mental Health Act 2001 defines a child as a person under the age of 18 years. The judge took the view that she lacked the capacity to refuse consent to the taking of blood samples.

[11.177] In discussing s 23 of the 1997 Act Birmingham J stated that although the consent of a minor aged 15 years and 11 months would not provide a statutory defence to what would otherwise be a trespass, this is 'not at all to suggest that the views of a minor of that age ought not to be treated with respect, they most certainly should be.' He went on to say:

> I am not to be taken as being of the view that there are no decisions of a medical nature which XY would not have the capacity to take. Neither am I laying down any general principle that young people aged 15 going on 16 should always be regarded as lacking capacity.

[11.178] In relation to the question of whether *Gillick* competence forms part of Irish law, the court noted that this approach had found favour in a number of common law jurisdictions but did not comment on whether it formed part of Irish law, the judge stated only that, even assuming for the purpose of this case only that the concept forms part of Irish law, XY was not in fact *Gillick* competent. Birmingham J also said 'there is a distinction to be drawn between capacity to consent to medical treatment that is proposed and capacity to refuse medical treatment. This is a theme that was addressed in the case of in *Re. R (a minor) (Wardship; consent to treatment)*.' He commented that the court in that case had held that a court in the exercise of its wardship or statutory jurisdiction had power to override the decision of a '*Gillick* competent' child as much as those of parents or guardians.

[11.179] In a later hearing of the same case, subsequently referred to as *XY, a minor suing by her Guardian ad Litem Raymond McEvoy v HSE*,[248] Birmingham J stated that the arguments on behalf of the plaintiff did not take into account 'the central role of parents when it comes to the taking of decisions in relation to their child and their central role in determining if it is in the best interests of a child'. He said 'it will ordinarily be the case that decisions in relation to a child's medical treatment will be taken on behalf of a child by his or her parents. That is so whether the child has or has not mental health issues.' In again referring to *Gillick*, he stressed the significance of the context in which the court had to examine the issue of the mature minor:

> It seems to me that the considerations that apply in deciding whether a sexually active teenager should be permitted to access contraception are of an altogether different order to those that apply in deciding whether a troubled teenager should be permitted to refuse

---

[247] *HSE v JM and RP* [2013] IEHC 12.

[248] *XY, a minor suing by her Guardian ad Litem Raymond McEvoy v HSE* [2013] IEHC 490.

medical treatment so as to advance a determination to commit suicide. A capacity or entitlement to refuse is not necessarily to be equated with a capacity or entitlement to consent to treatment.

[11.180] Unfortunately this case does not provide a comprehensive analysis of the possible application of the *Gillick* test in Ireland. Although Birmingham J does touch on the issue of context by referring to the fact that *Gillick* was a case that involved the sensitive issue of sexual health and reproduction, the case at hand did not require thorough consideration of whether the principles in that case, even if applicable in Ireland at all, might be broadened to apply to other healthcare contexts. In relation to refusals of treatment Birmingham J appears to agree with the decisions of the English courts which differentiate between consent to and refusal of treatment but a more expansive judicial consideration of the issues is required before a definitive interpretation of the law will become clear.

[11.181] In 2011 the Law Reform Commission (LRC) published its Report on *Children and the Law: Medical Treatment*[249] in which it stated that issues of consent and refusal should not be treated differently, as the literature, clinical practice and case law in this area generally treats refusal as the corollary of consent. '…[t]o treat them differently would create an unworkable distinction because the standard needed to satisfy the capacity test would rise, or fall, in accordance with whether a person was consenting to or refusing treatment.'[250] The Commission therefore concluded that the general recommendation concerning 16 and 17 year olds should apply to consent to, and refusal of, treatment.

[11.182] The Commission recommended that legislation should clearly provide that, in general, a person who is 16 or 17 years of age is presumed to have capacity to consent to, and refuse, healthcare treatment. The Commission states that the effect of this would be to clarify that, for the purposes of civil liability a 16 and 17 year old is presumed to have the same capacity, as far as healthcare is concerned, as an 18 year old has under the current law. The Commission considers that the current wording of s 23 of the Non-Fatal Offences against the Person Act 1997 provides a useful statutory precedent in this respect, subject to the need to provide that the proposed statutory framework would apply to the civil liability setting and that it would, in general, deal with refusal of treatment and not merely consent to treatment. A 16 and 17 year old would therefore not be subject to any countervailing test, such as whether the specific treatment is in their 'best interests.'

[11.183] The Commission did however state that while, in general, consent and refusal should be treated similarly, additional considerations need to be taken into account where life-sustaining treatment is refused. This is in keeping with the Commission's general approach that the law in this area should operate on the basis of a presumption in favour of life, which in turn is derived from the important and high status given to the right to life in the Constitution of Ireland and, in international human rights documents such as art 2 of the Council of Europe's 1950 Convention on Human Rights and Fundamental Freedoms. Accordingly, the Commission recommends that in cases where an individual under the age of 18 refuses life sustaining treatment, an application should

---

[249] (LRC 103–2011).
[250] Para **[2.149]**.

be made to the High Court to adjudicate on the refusal. In such a case, the High Court could intervene to order treatment that is necessary to save life and where this is in the best interests of the young person. In the event of such an application, the Commission also recommends that the person under 18 shall be separately represented.

[11.184] In relation to young persons under the age of 16 years the Commission takes the view that a prescriptive approach, in which age rather than maturity is the determining factor, does not reflect the literature on child development and the reality of gradual maturing and understanding during adolescence. It recommends that, for those under 16, a non-prescriptive approach should be taken in which the proposed legislative framework should not include a presumption of capacity for those under 16, but should provide that he or she may consent to, and refuse, healthcare treatment where it is established that the person under 16 has the maturity and understanding to appreciate the nature and consequences of the specific healthcare treatment decision. The Commission also recommends that, in the case of healthcare treatment involving those under 16, the usual situation should be that parents or guardians, who have the primary responsibility for the upbringing and development of children are involved in the decision-making process. The Commission also recommends that the person under 16 should be encouraged and advised to communicate with and involve his or her parents or guardians. The Commission therefore also recommends that it is only in 'exceptional' circumstances, and having regard to the need to take account of an objective assessment of both the rights and the best interests of the person under 16, that healthcare treatment would be provided for those under 16 without the knowledge or consent of parents or guardians.

[11.185] In keeping with the House of Lords decision in *Gillick* and in reference to the sliding scale approach adopted by the Supreme Court of Canada in 2009 in *AC v Manitoba (Director of Child and Family Services),*[251] the Commission further recommended that the proposed legislative framework should provide that, in determining whether a minor under 16 has the maturity and capacity to consent to, and to refuse, healthcare treatment, the following factors should be taken into account:

(a) whether he or she has sufficient maturity to understand the information relevant to making the decision and to appreciate its potential consequences;

(b) whether his or her views are stable and a true reflection of his or her core values and beliefs, taking into account his or her physical and mental health and any other factors that affect his or her ability to exercise independent judgement;

(c) the nature, purpose and utility of the treatment;

(d) the risks and benefits involved in the treatment, and

(e) any other specific welfare, protection or public health considerations, in respect of which relevant guidance and protocols such as the *2011 Children First: National Guidelines for the Protection and Welfare of Children* (or any equivalent replacement document) must be applied.

---

[251] *AC v Manitoba (Director of Child and Family Services)* [2009] 2 SCR 181 discussed above at para **[11.156]**.

[11.186] At the time of writing there is no published plan to introduce legislation to implement these LRC recommendations. The HSE National Consent Policy[252] acknowledges that in health and social care practice it is usual to involve parent(s)/legal guardian(s) and seek their consent when providing a service or treatment to a minor under 16. However, the minor may seek to make a decision on their own without parental involvement or consent. 'In such circumstances it is best practice to encourage and advise the minor to communicate with and involve their parents or legal guardians. It is only in exceptional circumstances that, having regard to the need to take account of an objective assessment of both the rights and the best interests of the person under 16, health and social care interventions would be provided for those under 16 without the knowledge or consent of parent(s) or legal guardian(s).' The Policy advises that in assessing the maturity of the minor, the considerations set out by the LRC above should be taken into account.

---

[252] HSE National Consent Policy (2013) available at www.hse.ie.

Chapter 12

Medical Treatment at the End of Life

INTRODUCTION

[12.01] 'Life and death are one. Though life comes before death, and though death is the threshold of a new life for some, the progression from life to death is unique to each of us; it can happen at any age, at any time, in any place. It is not as amenable to control as we might wish.'[1] All of us hope for a peaceful, pain-free death and most of us would prefer our death to take place in the comfort of our own homes surrounded by family and friends.[2] However, in Ireland, as in many other countries, the reality is all too often very different with only one in four people dying at home and 48% dying in acute hospitals.[3] It has been argued that 'modern scientific capability has profoundly altered the course of human life. People live longer and better than at any other time in history. But scientific advances have turned the processes of aging and dying into medical experiences, matters to be managed by healthcare professionals.'[4] The success of medical technology has thus led to the increasing medicalisation of the dying process,[5] the inexorable rush to hospitalisation of the dying person, the anonymisation of the environment in which the person spends their last days, and the invasiveness of machines, tubing, noise and indignity.[6] This raises concerns about 'the social isolation of dying patients in hospital, of dehumanised dying, and of the failure of medical technology to co-exist appropriately with dignified dying.'[7]

---

[1] Report of the Forum on End-of-Life (2009) page 14 available at www.hospicefoundation.ie.

[2] See Irish Hospice Foundation, *National Audit of End-of-Life Care in Hospitals*, available at www.hospicefoundation.ie.

[3] www.hospicefoundation.ie.

[4] Gawande, *Being Mortal. Illness, Medicine, and What Matters in the End* (Profile Books 2014) at 6.

[5] Ivan Illich was a powerful critic of the technological management of death which he referred to as 'the medicalisation of death'. This is characterised by a failure to accept death and suffering as meaningful aspects of life, being at 'total war' against death at all stages of the life cycle, a crippling of personal and family care, a devaluing of traditional rituals surrounding dying and death, and a form of social control in which a rejection of 'patienthood' by dying or bereaved people is labelled as a form of social deviance. Illich, *Limits to Medicine: Medical Nemesis – the expropriation of health* (London, Marion Boyars, 1975); see also Illich, 'Death undefeated: from medicine to medicalisation to systematisation' (1995) 311 BMJ 1652. See also Tercier, *The Contemporary Deathbed* (Basingstoke, New York: Palgrave Macmillan 2005).

[6] Madden, 'Is there a right to a good death?' (2013) Medico-Legal Journal of Ireland 19(2) 60–68.

[7] Seymour, *Critical moments – death and dying in intensive care* (Buckingham: Open University Press, 2001).

[12.02] The medical treatment of very sick and elderly patients at the end of life brings with it in addition to concerns about relief of pain and other distressing symptoms, consideration of issues of dignity and self-determination. As life begins to draw to a close, decisions may have to be made in relation to the continuance or discontinuance of life-prolonging treatment, or whether medical intervention is beneficial in the particular patient's circumstances.[8] Some people unfortunately suffer from conditions of increasing debilitation accompanied by periods of excruciating pain which is difficult to manage by way of medication. Their deaths may thus come 'not as the peaceful conclusion to a life, but as a violent and cruel destroyer. What it destroys, along with the life in question, is the possibility for release among those left behind. People say that for a long time afterwards, the memory of a painful death-struggle obliterates the much more precious images that they want to preserve.'[9] In order to avoid such circumstances, some people may seek to have control over their deaths and may seek assistance from family, friends or doctors in doing so. The question of whether and how far society should go in allowing people to have this control is discussed in more detail later. Indeed Gawande disputes whether people can ever have control as physics, biology and accident may intervene. He says that 'our most cruel failure in how we treat the sick and aged is the failure to recognise that they have priorities beyond merely being safe and living longer.'[10].

[12.03] The arguments that arise for discussion in the context of end-of-life decision-making focus on the sanctity of life, autonomy, compassion, the slippery slope, fear of being a burden, the impact on the doctor-patient relationship, devaluing disability, respect for human dignity and recognition that assistance with dying is happening anyway.[11] A further underlying issue is the extent to which patients are actually informed about their diagnosis, their fears and anxieties are listened to and their choices about the end of their lives are respected. In some ways this is about communication skills and training, and in other ways it is reflective of the value placed on respect for autonomy.

[12.04] Patient surveys consistently demonstrate dissatisfaction with the amount of information provided to patients by their doctors. In circumstances where communication is poor or even absent,[12] as is unfortunately too often the case where the

---

[8]   Doctors sometimes continue treating patients for too long due to pressure from relatives according to a 2016 report from the British Medical Association. The Report advises that medics should be encouraged to view death differently and to identify and accept when patients are coming to the end of their lives without viewing this as failure. It says doctors and the public should be reminded that all treatment should be appropriate and proportionate, with the aim of providing a net benefit to the patient rather than pursuing aggressive but non-beneficial attempts to prolong life. Available at www.bma.org.uk

[9]   Woodman, *Last Rights: The Struggle over the Right to Die* (Plenum Trade, 1998) at 25.

[10] Gawande, *Being Mortal. Illness, Medicine, and What Matters in the End* (Profile Books 2014) at 243.

[11] McLean, *Assisted Dying: Reflections on the Need for Law Reform* (Routledge-Cavendish, 2007) Ch 2.

[12] See Simpson et al, 'Doctor-Patient Communication: The Toronto Consensus Statement' BMJ 303 (1991) 1385. Also Vincent, 'Information in the ICU: Are We Being Honest with Our Patients?' (1998) 24 Intensive Care Medicine 1251, which reports on a survey of doctors from 16 Western European countries in which only 25% responded that they would give complete information to patients, and (contd.../)

patient is elderly or very ill,[13] the scope for misunderstanding may be exacerbated if care and time is not taken to talk and listen to the patient. Such patients may not have a clear picture of their illness, and may not have worked out for themselves what they want to ask or what way they wish to be treated.[14] If elderly, they may be imbued with the notion that the doctor knows best, having grown up with this tradition of not asking questions.[15] However, such an assumption should not be made for any patient irrespective of age in the absence of personal knowledge of the patient, their values, beliefs and cultural and religious backgrounds, which may be of huge importance in this context. It should be presumed that all patients are entitled to be told the truth about their medical condition and treated with respect for their dignity:

> In medical decisions near the end of life, and in particular in decisions about life-sustaining treatment, these values if anything strengthen the general case for patients' rights to make treatment decisions. In the debilitated and severely compromised condition of many patients near the end of life, patients often become more concerned with maintaining their comfort, quality of life and dignity than with extending their lives. Patients sometimes reach a point at which they decide that the best life possible for them with life-sustaining treatment is sufficiently poor that it is worse than no further life at all, and so decide to forgo any further life-sustaining treatment. But there is no objectively correct point for all persons at which further treatment and the life it sustains are no longer a benefit, but are instead a burden and without value of meaning. There are only the decisions of different competent patients about that point.[16]

[12.05] An argument has also been made that in some circumstances we may have a duty to die. Although we like to think of modern medicine as 'all triumph with no dark side', Hardwig argues that medicine also delivers many of us over to chronic illnesses and 'enables us to survive longer than we can take care of ourselves, longer than we know what to do with ourselves, longer than we even are ourselves.'[17] This argument in favour of a duty to die is based on what Hardwig calls the 'individualistic fantasy', which is the idea that we may like to think that our lives are separate and unconnected and that the way each of us chooses to live is nobody else's business. However, this is 'morally obtuse', as 'we are not a race of hermits'. Most of us are part of a circle of family and friends bound together by legal relationships, obligations, shared living and working spaces, intertwined finances, common projects and shared histories. The fact of

---

[12] (\...contd) 75% accepted the right of patients to refuse treatment. For statistics in the Irish context, see *National Patients Perception of the Quality of Healthcare Survey 2002,* available at www.isqh.ie and discussed by Donnelly, *Consent: Bridging the Gap between Doctor and Patient* (Cork University Press, 2002).

[13] See Ajaj, Singh and Abdullah, 'Should Elderly Patients Be Told They Have Cancer?' (2001) 323 BMJ 1160.

[14] See generally Wilkes, 'Ethics in Terminal Care' in Dunstan and Shinebourne (eds) *Doctors' Decisions, Ethical Conflicts in Medical Practice* (OUP, 1989) p 197–204.

[15] However, a survey carried out by Ajaj, Singh and Abdullah shows that 88% of elderly patients living in the community would wish to know the nature of their illness, even if it was cancer. Ajaj, Singh and Abdullah, 'Should Elderly Patients Be Told They Have Cancer?' (2001) 323 BMJ 1160.

[16] Brock, 'Medical Decisions at the End of Life' in Kuhse and Singer *A Companion to Bioethics,* (Blackwell Publishing, 1998) 231, p 232–233.

[17] Hardwig, 'Is There a Duty to Die?' (1997) The Hastings Center Report, Vol 27 pp 34–42 at 35.

deeply interwoven lives 'debars us from making exclusively self-regarding decisions, as the decisions of one member of a family may dramatically affect the lives of all the rest.'

[12.06] Hardwig argues that the lives of our loved ones can be seriously compromised by caring for us, with the burden of providing care 24 hours a day, 7 days a week, sometimes becoming overwhelming. The health, finances, social life and friendships of our loved ones can be destroyed in the process. Hardwig thus maintains that a duty to die may develop in such circumstances in order to protect our loved ones from such harm. He does acknowledge that caring for a sick and dying relative may also bring rewards in bringing a family closer, but says that we should not assume that this will be the case. He argues 'if I love my family, I will want to protect them and their lives. I will want not to make choices that compromise their futures…' He also argues that we are so busy trying to postpone death that we do not seek to find meaning in it, with the result that:

> We fear death too much. Our fear of death has led to a massive assault on it. We still crave after virtually any life-prolonging technology that we might conceivably be able to produce. We still too often feel morally impelled to prolong life – virtually any form of life – as long as possible. As if the best death is the one that can be put off longest.[18]

[12.07] Discussions about end of life care generally arise in the context of incurable disease or terminal illness. However, it is also important to note that 30 million people per year die of age-related causes such as heart disease, cancer, stroke, respiratory disease, Alzheimer's disease, diabetes, influenza, kidney disease, accidents or infection. Nuland argues that clinicians should not be obliged to name a disease as the cause of death as this distorts what is really happening and puts a biomedical world view on the 'sluggish circulation and an antique heart'. When a person dies, calling the cause heart disease or pneumonia or osteoporosis or vascular dementia is both arbitrary and beside the point. In fact, everything stops working because the person's time is up. 'The thing that peters out is nothing other than the life force.'[19] Why then do death certificates not describe the cause of death as old age, something that is inevitable and universally shared? If the leading cause of death among the very old was simply 'old age' then public policy might take more seriously the issues around long-term care, its costs and indignities.[20]

[12.08] By comparison with old age, terminal illness may be defined as any chronic illness associated with a high chance of dying, and may be seen as beginning when three conditions are satisfied, namely, that diagnosis of the illness has been made and other remedial conditions eliminated; that the advent of death is certain and not too far off; and that medical care has turned from the curative to the palliative.[21] Therefore, in relation to the terminally ill patient, death is often not an idea that is unknown to them. If their illness has been protracted, death may have been expected for a period of time. The various component processes involved in dying must be understood as a whole so as to give effect to all the aspects of the patient's quality of life. People often speak this in the

---

[18]   Hardwig, 'Is There a Duty to Die?' (1997) The Hastings Center Report, Vol 27 pp 34–42 at 40.

[19]   Nuland, *How we die: Reflections of life's final chapter'* (Chatto & Windus 1994).

[20]   Gross, 'The immediate cause of death' *New York Times,* Oct 23 2008.

[21]   Calman, 'Ethical Implications of Terminal Care' in Freeman (ed) *Medicine, Ethics and Law* (Stevens and Sons, 1988) 103–119, p 104.

sense of hoping for a 'good death'.[22] By this they usually mean that they will not be in physical pain, that their emotional reaction and psychological coping mechanisms will enable them to let go of the world in peace, that the social impact of the patient's death on their family will be eased by the gentle manner of their passing, and their spiritual and intellectual strength will enable the patient to work through their anxieties and die on their own terms.

[12.09] One of the primary difficulties in treating terminal illness is the level of uncertainty involved. The doctor may not know whether a particular treatment is going to be effective or whether the patient will respond, when exactly death will occur or whether the patient would like to talk about it. Patients and their families may have misconceptions about the facts underlying the illness and may have false expectations of recovery. Communication and truth-telling are very important but also very difficult aspects of the relationship between patient and doctor in this regard. A fundamental question that patients will often ask is what length of time they have left, a question that is not always possible to answer with any degree of certainty. The doctor may be reluctant to give bad news if it is felt that this will cause a further setback to the patient, and may in fact have been asked by the relatives not to inform the patient of the bleak prognosis. In such cases, the challenge for the doctor is how to balance the patient's autonomy with beneficence.[23]

[12.10] Several recent Irish studies indicate that most patients (over 80%) who are terminally ill want to be told the truth about their diagnosis and prognosis.[24] However, even though patients may want to be informed, Irish research suggests that, in general, relatives are more likely to be informed about patients' illnesses than patients themselves.[25] The research also suggests that there is a gap between what relatives think patients want to know and what patients actually want to know: patients want to be informed even though their relatives believe that they do not.[26] One approach to this would view compassion and beneficence as taking priority over autonomy in these

---

[22] See *Report on End of life Care* from the British Medical Association in 2016 which consulted with the medical profession and the public in to what was considered a 'good death'. Available at www.bma.org.uk

[23] See generally McCarthy et al, *Ethical Framework for End-of-Life Care* (2013) Module 2: The Ethics of Breaking Bad News, available at www.hospicefoundation.ie.

[24] Keating, Nayeem, Gilmartin, & O'Keeffe, 'Advance directives for truth disclosure.' (2005) Chest, 128(2), 1037–1039; O'Keeffe, Noone, & Pillay, 'Telling the truth about cancer: views of elderly patients and their relatives.' (2000) Irish Medical Journal, 93(4), 104–105; Weafer, *A qualitative study of public perceptions of end of life issues.* (2009) Dublin: Irish Hospice Foundation; Weafer, *The views of political representatives.* (2009) Dublin: Irish Hospice Foundation; Weafer, McCarthy, & Loughrey, *Exploring death and dying: the views of the Irish general public.* (2009) Dublin: Irish Hospice Foundation. Quoted by McCarthy et al, *Ethical Framework for End-of-Life Care* (2013) Module 2: The Ethics of Breaking Bad News, available at www.hospicefoundation.ie.

[25] Keegan, McGee, Hogan, Kunin, O'Brien, & O'Siorain, 'Relatives' views of health care in the last year of life.' (2001) International Journal of Palliative Nursing, 7(9), 449–456; O'Keeffe, Noone, & Pillay, 'Telling the truth about cancer: views of elderly patients and their relatives.' (2000) Irish Medical Journal, 93(4), 104–105.

[26] O'Keeffe, Noone, & Pillay, 'Telling the truth about cancer: views of elderly patients and their relatives.' (2000) Irish Medical Journal, 93(4), 104–105.

circumstances and would withhold the information from the patient unless directly asked. However, this may also put other medical professionals, such as the nursing team, in a compromising position where they are complicit in the non-disclosure and are expected to keep up pretences with the patient.[27] A position which prioritises respect for the patient's right to make his own decisions would view truth-telling as more in keeping with the patient's dignity and integrity.[28] This dilemma is something that ought to be addressed if possible at an earlier stage of treatment between the patient and those involved in the patient's care, and an agreement reached as to how to deal with problems that might be expected to arise in this regard.

FUTILE OR NON-BENEFICIAL MEDICAL TREATMENT

[12.11] Demographic changes will occur in Ireland in coming decades as people are living longer, fertility is decreasing and the gap between active life expectancy and death is widening. Although people are living longer, they may often be increasingly dependent on others and may use more healthcare resources in the last year or months of life. This has led to the challenging question of whether scarce resources are being 'wasted' on the dying, resources that could be spent more productively on other patients.[29] It is generally agreed that medical futility should not be used as a method of resource allocation, which would be both ageist and discriminatory. However, it must also be acknowledged that in reality a decision not to treat one patient frees up resources to treat another. Although decisions on resource allocation may be most appropriately decided on the basis of therapeutic benefit, the danger of arbitrary decision-making is high. 'In view of the practical limitations on the availability of medical resources, some consideration of the appropriate allocation of scarce resources and of cost-effectiveness inevitably must come into the decision-making'.[30]

[12.12] In some situations the question may arise as to whether it is right to prolong life in circumstances where treatment may simply delay death for a period of time with no appreciable benefit to the patient. This raises issues of futility or non-beneficial treatment which either has no medical effect or benefit for the patient. In the last few decades the role of the doctor has evolved in many respects from being a life saver to being a quality of life provider – the goal is no longer solely the prolongation of life but also the achievement of a particular standard or quality of life. With this change in emphasis comes the question of futility. 'Whilst there is widespread agreement that there are limits on the duty of doctors to treat terminally ill patients, the difficulty lies in determining the precise *scope* of that duty and at what point the doctor's duty ceases.'[31]

---

[27] Calman, 'Ethical Implications of Terminal Care' in Freeman (ed) *Medicine, Ethics and Law* (Stevens and Sons, 1988) 103–119, p 110.

[28] See also useful discussion of the value of hope as a factor in decision-making in Berlinger, Jennings, Wolf, *The Hastings Center Guidelines for decision on life-sustaining treatment and care near the end of life* (Oxford University Press 2013).

[29] Scitovsky and Capron, 'Medical Care at the End of Life: The Interaction of Economics and Ethics' (1986) Ann. Rev Public Health 7:59–75.

[30] Otlowski, *Voluntary Euthanasia and the Common Law* (OUP, 1997) at 34.

[31] Otlowski, *Voluntary Euthanasia and the Common Law* (OUP, 1997) at 34.

It is no longer a question of whether the patient's life can be saved. It is also now a question of what kind of life the patient will have if it is possible to save him.

[12.13] The notion of 'medical futility' first appeared in the 1980s and its function was to put a limit to the increasing requests for treatment that patients felt entitled to make to doctors. 'After the 1960s and the 1970s, the principle of patient autonomy was interpreted in a more and more radical way. Besides feeling that they had the right to *refuse* an unwanted medical intervention, with increasing frequency patients (or their family or representatives) were *demanding* specific treatments that doctors had not offered.'[32] There are many definitions of medical futility,[33] some of which focus on whether the treatment accomplishes its objectives, some of which examine survival rates and others that look at the quality of benefit to be achieved by the treatment.[34] Some argue that the absence of any universally agreed definition is unexceptional and necessary.[35] If one judges the technique or treatment in terms of its success, this too will be subjective. For some doctors a 10 per cent success rate means the treatment is not futile, while for others it is. Success is not something that can be measured accurately, reliably or consistently and does not have the 'ring of clarity' often associated with decisions in this context.[36] If, on the other hand, one judges futility in terms of quality rather than quantity of life to be obtained as a result of the treatment, this incorporates the patient's own wishes and ambitions in an assessment of whether the treatment would be worthwhile in accomplishing those goals.

[12.14] The use of the term 'futility' may itself be criticised as an emotive term depicting hopelessness, when judgments on such issues ought to be made on clearly rational grounds.[37] The term 'non-productive treatment' or 'non-beneficial treatment' is sometimes used as an alternative.[38] In Irish hospitals 'withdrawal of invasive interventions in hopeless cases is not uncommon in intensive care.'[39] A study in 2006

---

[32] Moratti, 'The Development of 'Medical Futility': Towards a Procedural Approach Based on the Role of the Medical Profession' (2009) J Med Ethics 35: 369–372 at 369.

[33] See Lamb, *Therapy Abatement, Autonomy and Futility: Ethical Decisions at the Edge of Life* (Ashgate Publishing, 1995), Chapter 5.

[34] Jecker and Pearlman, 'Medical Futility: Who Decides?' (1992) 152 Arch Intern Med 1140; Schneiderman and Jecker, 'Futility in Practice' (1993) 153 Arch Intern Med 437; Cranford and Gostin, 'Futility: A Concept in Search of a Definition' (1992) 20 Law, Med, & Health Care 307.

[35] Tomlinson and Czlonka, 'Futility and Hospital Care' (1995) Hastings Center Report 31.

[36] Saunders, 'Medical Futility: CPR' in Morgan and Lee (eds) *Death Rites: Law and Ethics at the End of Life* (Routledge, 1994) p 85.

[37] Gillon, 'Futility – Too Ambiguous and Pejorative a Term?' (1997) 23 J Med Ethics 339.

[38] See analysis of terminology and prevalence of non-beneficial treatments (NBTs) in Cardona-Morrell et al, 'Non-beneficial treatments in hospital at the end of life: a systematic review on extent of the problem' Int J Qual Health Care (2016).The authors conclude that 'given the uncertainty of prognosis on time to death, the social and ethical pressures, and the compassionate recommendation for trial ICU admissions while families come to terms with the inevitable, it appears that a certain level of NBT must always be present, but this does not mean that its prevalence should not be reduced.'

[39] Phelan and Kinirons, 'Withdrawal of Futile Interventions in Intensive Care – An Everyday Ethical/Critical Care Issue' (1996) MLJI 49.

indicates that 69 per cent of deaths in ICU in Ireland occur in association with the limitation of futile life-sustaining treatments.[40] This usually involves withholding CPR (cardio pulmonary resuscitation) and stopping inotropic and dialysis treatment. Extubation or stopping ventilation is less common and usually occurs after other life-sustaining treatments have already been limited.[41]

[12.15] The notion of medical futility has been the object of strong criticism since its first appearance and it has been argued that the topic is fraught with difficulties and contradictions.[42] Some saw it as an attempt to reintroduce medical paternalism by allowing doctors to justify a unilateral decision to withhold or withdraw treatment. Thus, it was argued that doctors should not be given the power to impose on their patients their own personal values under the guise of medical expertise. In the 1990s the debate shifted to the issue of whether futility could be measured according to a quantitative and qualitative parameter. Schneiderman and others argued that an intervention could be defined as quantitatively futile if doctors concluded through personal experience, experiences shared with colleagues or consideration of reported empiric data that in the last 100 cases a certain intervention was 'useless',[43] meaning it failed to benefit the person, even if it contributed to the functioning of the organism. A 'qualitatively futile' intervention was described as 'any treatment that merely preserves permanent unconsciousness or that fails to end total dependence on intensive medical care.' Both definitions were criticised on the grounds that the notion of quantitative futility involves value judgment, as it presupposes a certain definition of what a 'person' is. Also the notion of 'qualitative futility' refers only to conditions associated with overwhelming suffering for a predictably short time and excludes patients whose conditions require frequent hospitalisation, or patients who have severe disabilities.[44]

[12.16] Since the mid-1990s, it seems to be accepted that no consensus may be reached on a definition of futile treatment and that a better approach would be to seek to reach consensus about the way in which the decision should be made by those most closely involved. The American Medical Association takes the view that such a consensus-driven process should aim to promote communication, minimise conflicts between the various actors (potentially) involved and avoid (where possible) polarisation of conflict and mobilisation of formal legal institutions.[45]

[12.17] A distinction is sometimes made in discussions about life-prolonging treatment between ordinary and extraordinary treatment, the former being treatment that the

---

40 Collins, Phelan and Carton, 'End of Life in ICU – Care of the Dying or 'Pulling the Plug'?' (2006) Irish Medical Journal Vol 99 No 4, p 112.

41 See generally Lyons, 'Improving end-of-life care in intensive care units' in Donnelly and Murray (eds) *Ethical and Legal Debates in Irish Healthcare, Confronting Complexities* (Manchester University Press 2015) 236–250.

42 Laurie, Harmon and Porter, *Law and Medical Ethics* (10th edn 2016) at 15.06

43 Schneiderman et al, 'Medical Futility: Its Meaning and Ethical Implications' (1990) Ann Intern Med 112: 949.

44 See response to criticisms by Schneiderman et al, 'Medical Futility: Response to Critiques' (1996) Ann Intern Med 125: 669.

45 Report of the Council on Ethical and Judicial Affairs of the American Medical Association, *Medical Futility in End-of-Life Care* (1999) JAMA 281:937–41.

patient is obliged or assumed to accept, the latter being a matter of choice for the patient. There are many different ways in which the distinction can be drawn. For example, one could distinguish on grounds of the level of invasiveness involved, the degree to which the treatment is considered common practice, the extent to which the treatment is technology-based, the costs of the treatment and so on. However, these various methods of distinction are not helpful in explaining why some treatments are obligatory and others optional. 'What seems morally important and determines whether any treatment should be employed in particular circumstances with a particular patient is not whether the treatment employs high technology or is simple, but whether the patient judges it to be on balance beneficial.'[46]

[12.18] The distinction between ordinary and extraordinary or heroic measures in Ireland and elsewhere was probably influenced by the theology of the Roman Catholic Church where extraordinary treatment is regarded as treatment which is excessively burdensome or without benefit for the patient.[47] It is possible to classify different treatments, such as nutrition and hydration, as always either ordinary or extraordinary, and so as always obligatory or optional. However, this does not take into account the particular patient's condition and wishes and has been increasingly regarded as causing confusion in the debate on end-of-life treatment decisions.[48] It has therefore been argued that '[t]he language of ordinary and extraordinary means of treatment should be discarded because of its imprecision and its tendency to support strong paternalism.'[49]

[12.19] There have been a number of judicial decisions dealing with futile treatment, some of which will be explored in more detail in other contexts later in this chapter. The first cases dealt with the right of patients to refuse treatment being offered by a physician on grounds that it was futile. For example, in *In re Quinlan*[50] the New Jersey Supreme Court stated in relation to Karen Ann Quinlan's wishes concerning life-sustaining treatment: 'She was said to have firmly evinced her wish, in like circumstances, not to have her life prolonged by the otherwise futile use of extraordinary means.' Other cases have followed suit in emphasising the futility of the life-sustaining treatment as one of the reasons for ordering the withholding or withdrawal of treatment.[51] The decisions of the courts were principally based on the right to self-

---

46 Brock, 'Medical Decisions at the End of Life' in Kuhse and Singer *A Companion to Bioethics*, (Blackwell Publishing, 1998) 231 at 235.

47 Kelly, 'The Duty to Preserve Life' (1951) Theological Studies 12 550. See Moratti, 'Italy: The Position of the Roman Catholic Church' in Griffiths J et al (eds) *Euthanasia and Law in Europe* (Hart Publishing 2008) 397.

48 Kearon argues that whether a medical treatment is ordinary or extraordinary is a judgment that can only be made by the patient or from his perspective. '*Re a Ward of Court:* Ethical Comment' (1995) MLJI 58.

49 Childress, *Who Should Decide? Paternalism in Healthcare* (OUP, 1982) at p 166.

50 *In re Quinlan* 70 NJ 10, 355 A 2d 647 (1976) 21.

51 *In re Dinnerstein* 6 Mass App 466, 380 NE 2d 134 (Ct App 1978); *Barber v Superior Court* 147 Cal App 3d 1006, 195 Cal Rptr 484 (Ct App 1983); *Bartling v Glendale Adventist Medical Center* 184 Cal App 3d 961, 229 Cal Rptr 360 (Ct App 1986); *In re Westchester County Medical Center* 72 NY 2d 517, 531 NE 2d 607 (1988); *Westhart v Mule* 213 Ca App 3d 542, 261 Cal Rptr 640 (Ct App 1989); *In re Greenspan* 137 Ill 2d 1, 558 NE 2d 1194 (1989); *In re Lawrence* 579 NE 2d 32 (Ind. 1991).

determination, but the fact that the treatments in question were considered futile made such decisions easier to make.

[12.20] In the Irish context, there have not been many opportunities for the courts to consider the issue of medical futility.[52] However, in *In Re a Ward of Court*[53] the Supreme Court had to consider the question of whether life support, in the form of nutrition and medical treatment, could be withdrawn from a woman in a near persistent vegetative state, at the request of her family. The hospital where the woman was being cared for was opposed to the withdrawal of treatment and nutrition on ethical grounds. The majority of the judges held that the right to life under the Constitution necessarily implies the right to let nature take its course and to die a natural and dignified death and, unless the individual chooses otherwise, not to have life artificially maintained by the provision of nourishment which has no curative effect and merely prolongs life. The principle on which this was based is that the Constitution provides a right to self-determination in the rights to privacy and bodily integrity, and as part of that right a competent adult has the right to forego or discontinue life-saving medical treatment.

[12.21] Hamilton CJ said: 'There is no doubt but that the ward, if she were mentally competent, had the right, if she so wished, to forego such treatment or at any time, to direct that it be withdrawn, even though such withdrawal would result in her death.' He regarded the provision of nutrition in this case, by way of a surgical tube implanted in the woman's stomach, as an abnormal means of nourishment which constituted an interference with the integrity of her body. He agreed with an opinion expressed by Costello P, writing extra-judicially, in which he said that there were powerful arguments to support the view that the dignity and autonomy of the human person oblige the State to recognise that decisions relating to life and death are ones which competent adults should be free to make without undue interference or restraint by the State.[54] Although there might be circumstances in which the State might have a valid interest in restricting such decisions, such as in the case of contagious diseases, 'in the case of the terminally ill, it is very difficult to see what circumstances would justify the interference with a decision by a competent adult of the right to forego or discontinue life saving treatment'.

[12.22] Although the patient in this case did not have decision-making capacity herself, O'Flaherty J also clearly took the view that a person with decision-making capacity had the right to refuse medical treatment even if it leads to death, calling it 'an absolute right' and one which he said was not in dispute in this case. He grounded the right in common law as well as the constitutional rights of bodily integrity and privacy. Blayney J said 'where a person who is *compos mentis* has a condition which, in the absence of medical intervention, will lead to death, such a person has a right in law to refuse such intervention.' Denham J took the same view, saying that medical treatment given without consent may be a trespass, a battery and a breach of Constitutional rights. She continued:

---

[52] See discussion in Charleton and Bolger, 'The Law at Life's End' (1995) Gazette 29. For discussion of the practical points and medical specialist's perspective, see Phelan and Kinirons, 'Withdrawal of Futile Interventions in Intensive Care – An Everyday Ethical/Critical Care Issue' (1996) MLJI 49–51.

[53] *Re a Ward of Court* [1996] 2 IR 79.

[54] Costello, 'The Terminally Ill – The Law's Concerns' (1986) 21 Ir Jurist 35.

The consent which is given by an adult of full capacity is a matter of choice. It is not necessarily a decision based on medical considerations. Thus, medical treatment may be refused for other than medical reasons. Such reasons may not be viewed as good medical reasons, or reasons most citizens would regard as rational, but the person of full age and capacity may make the decision for their own reasons.

This principle has been further affirmed in *Fitzpatrick and Another v K and Another*[55] discussed in Chapter 9.[56]

DO NOT ATTEMPT RESUSCITATION ORDERS (DNARS)

[12.23] There has been a growing trend in some countries towards laws dealing with Do Not Attempt Resuscitation orders (DNARs) (also referred to as DNRs). A DNAR is a doctor's written order not to attempt cardiopulmonary resuscitation (CPR) on a particular patient on the basis that CPR would be futile or not in the best interests of the patient. It has been described as 'a crucial decision point in the limiting of treatment…a point at which doctors and nurses clarify their therapeutic goals and reconsider the appropriateness of further life-sustaining treatment.'[57] CPR was originally designed to treat unexpected cardiac and respiratory arrests after surgery or accidents,[58] but is now commonly used to treat any patient who arrests, on the assumption that all patients would want to receive CPR.[59] It has been argued that in the large majority of cases the procedure is not employed to long-term effect and that, if the patient is expected to die, 'a procedure less dignified and peaceful could hardly be devised'.[60] Routine use of CPR will not always be in the patient's best interests and therefore the practice has developed of making a DNAR order to indicate that CPR is inappropriate. This does not mean that other medical treatment, such as antibiotics, will not be given where appropriate.

[12.24] The futility of attempting CPR in circumstances where it would be unlikely to be successful was considered by the court in *Re R (adult: medical treatment).*[61] R was a 23-year-old man who was born with a serious malfunction of the brain and cerebral palsy. He was not in a permanent vegetative state but had minimal awareness, severe epilepsy, was believed to be deaf and blind, and had to be fed through a syringe. In the year leading to the making of the DNAR decision, R was hospitalised five times due to recurrent infections, constipation, ulceration, fits, dehydration and under-nutrition. The treating doctor and R's parents agreed that if, in future, R suffered a life-threatening condition, CPR should not be given. Some members of the residential home objected to the DNAR decision and an application was brought by way of judicial review to quash it. The judge heard evidence that if CPR was attempted it would be a dangerous

---

[55] *Fitzpatrick and Another v K and Another* [2008] IEHC 104.
[56] See para **[9.30]**.
[57] Smidira et al, 'Withholding and Withdrawal of Life Support from the Critically Ill' (1990) 322 New England J of Med 309.
[58] Kùowenhoven, Jude and Knickerbocker, 'Closed Chest Cardiac Massage' (1960) 173 JAMA 94.
[59] Florin, 'Do Not Resuscitate Orders: The Need for a Policy' (1993) 27 J of the Royal College of Physicians 135.
[60] Saunders, 'Who's for CPR?' (1992) 26 Journal of the Royal College of Physicians 254.
[61] *Re R (adult: medical treatment)* [1996] 2 FLR 99.

operation having regard to R's frailty and might even cause further brain damage. The chances of a successful CPR being performed on someone like R by the staff of a residential care facility were almost nil. The judge was persuaded by the evidence that CPR in this case would be unlikely to be effective or successful and held that it would be lawful for the doctor to withhold such treatment.

[12.25] The decision to record a DNAR is influenced by a combination of medical and non-medical factors. If it is possible to consult with the patient, then a refusal of CPR by the patient must be adhered to in this respect. As a general principle, if the patient is not competent to make such a decision then the doctor, following consultation with the medical and nursing team as well as the patient's family, will make the decision in the patient's best interests. If the patient wishes to have CPR performed no matter what the medical likelihood of success, the doctor is not obliged to comply with such wishes in the event that CPR would be futile.[62]

[12.26] In the United States, hospitals began developing policies on DNARs in the 1970s, most of which stipulate that the consent of either the patient or the surrogate decision-maker must be obtained before the order can be issued.[63] However, a few statutes dealing with medical futility in the context of advance directives provide that consent need not be obtained where, in the opinion of the doctor, the procedure cannot benefit the patient. The healthcare provider would thus be entitled to decline a particular advance instruction or directive from a patient where it would involve medically ineffective healthcare or care contrary to generally accepted healthcare standards.[64]

[12.27] In New York in 1988 legislation was passed decreeing that consent for CPR was to be presumed (and that it was to be employed, unless medically futile) unless there was a formally obtained and recorded DNR order for a patient.[65] Article 29–B of the Consolidated Laws of the State of New York provides that before giving consent to a DNR, the patient must be given information about his diagnosis and prognosis, the reasonably foreseeable risks and benefits of CPR for him, and the consequences of the DNR order. The patient must consent either in writing or orally, in each case before two witnesses, one of whom must be a hospital doctor. Once consent has been given, the DNR order is recorded in the patient's medical record. Where the patient's doctor is of the opinion that the patient would suffer immediate and severe injury from a discussion of CPR, the doctor may make a DNR without the patient's consent. This must be recorded and seconded by another doctor, and the consent of the patient's surrogate decision-maker must be obtained. The DNR order must be reviewed every week for a

---

[62] See detailed discussion in Boozang, 'Death Wish: Resuscitating Self-Determination for the Critically Ill' (1993) 35(1) Arizona Law Review 24.

[63] See discussion in Finucane, 'Thinking About Life-Sustaining Treatment Late in the Life of a Demented Person' (2001) Georgia Law Review Vol 35: 691; Pickering, 'Decisionmaking at the End of Life: Patients with Alzheimer's or other Dementias' (2001) Georgia Law Review Vol 35:539.

[64] The Uniform Health Care Decisions Act, enacted in Maine: Me Rev Stat Tit 18–A, 5–807[f].

[65] Hendrick and Brennan, 'Do Not Resuscitate Orders: Guidelines in Practice' (1997) 6(1) Nottingham Law Journal, 25–45 at 26. See also McGinn, 'New York May Point the Way for Irish Law' (2001) St Paul Ireland Newsletter; Sheikh, 'The Status of the 'Do Not Resuscitate' Order (DNR) in Irish Law and Medicine' (2001) St Paul Ireland Newsletter.

hospital patient, and every two months for a nursing home resident. Provision is made in the statute for mediation in instances where the patient and doctor do not agree in relation to the making of a DNR order. It also provides for immunity from prosecution or civil liability for any health professional who complies with a DNR or initiates CPR when unaware of a DNR order in respect of that patient.

[12.28] The futility of treatment in circumstances where the patient or her family wish treatment to be continued was considered in *Gilgunn v Massachusetts General Hospital*.[66] In this case a jury decided that doctors were not negligent in withdrawing mechanical ventilation and issuing a DNR order despite the objections of the patient's daughter and their apparent belief that the patient herself would have wished to continue treatment. The decision was made on the basis that the treatment was futile. The case was taken after the death of the patient and may well have been decided differently if it had been heard during the patient's lifetime in an application to have treatment withdrawn. This case is seen as problematic because it enables unilateral decision-making to be made by the doctors without taking into account either the patient's own wishes or the wishes of the patient's family[67] and therefore it appears to be inconsistent with increased recognition of patient autonomy.

[12.29] In the UK, guidelines have been published by the British Medical Association (BMA), the Resuscitation Council and the Royal College of Nursing to deal with DNAR decisions.[68] These advise doctors and nurses[69] to consider the appropriateness of such a decision where the patient's condition is such that CPR is unlikely to be successful, where CPR is not in accord with the recorded wishes of the patient, and where, if successful, CPR would be likely to be followed by a length and quality of life which would not be acceptable to the patient. The guidelines advise that individual decisions must be taken in the care of each patient, and that a hospital policy of DNR would be unacceptable. The consultant in charge of the patient's care should discuss the circumstances with the others in the medical and nursing team, and, if possible, with the patient and the patient's close family.[70] The guidelines have been described as 'well-meaning' but 'it is clear that they conceal a hornet's nest of moral dilemmas.'[71]

---

[66] *Gilgunn v Massachusetts General Hospital* No 922–4820 (Mass. Super Ct Civ Action Suffolk Co April 22 1995).

[67] Capron, 'Abandoning a Waning Life' (1995) Hastings Center Report 24 (July-Aug): 24–6.

[68] British Medical Association, Resuscitation Council & Royal College of Nursing *Decisions Relating to Cardiopulmonary Resuscitation*.(3rd edn, 2014) www.resus.org.uk/dnacpr/ decisions-relating-to-cpr/. Further changes to this guidance in light of recent English case law are anticipated.

[69] The involvement of nurses in decision-making on DNAR orders is particularly important, as they may often have a greater insight into the patient's beliefs and wishes, as well as extensive contact with the patient's family. It is also important to note that if the patient goes into cardiac arrest, it is often the nursing staff who have to implement the DNAR order by not calling for a crash team to resuscitate the patient. See further, Marchett et al, 'Nurses' Perceptions of the Support of Patient Autonomy in DNR Decisions' (1993) 30 I J of Nursing Studies 37.

[70] See discussion of an inherent ageism in the making of DNARs by Ebrahim, 'Do Not Resuscitate Decisions: Flogging Dead Horses or a Dignified Death?' (2000) BMJ 320: 1155–1156, and various letters in reply (2001) BMJ: 322:7278.

[71] Laurie, Harmon and Porter, *Law and Medical Ethics* (10th edn, 2016) para 18.30.

Questions arise as to when and at what stages of disease a person should be denied resuscitation, how a patient's quality of life is to be measured, and who should make the decision.

[12.30] The English Court of Appeal recently considered DNARs in *R (on the application of Tracey) v Cambridge University Hospitals NHS Foundation Trust*[72] in which a husband objected to the policy of placing of a DNAR order on his wife by the hospital. On 5 February 2011, Mrs Tracey had been diagnosed with lung cancer with an estimated life expectancy of 9 months. On 19 February, she sustained a serious cervical fracture after a major road accident and was admitted to hospital. She was placed on a ventilator but did not respond well to treatment and subsequent attempts to wean her off the ventilator were unsuccessful. Her treating doctors decided that Mrs Tracey should be taken off the ventilator. The question arose as to what would happen if she suffered a cardio-respiratory arrest. A DNAR notice was placed on her chart which was seen by one of her daughters who strongly objected to it, with the result that the notice was removed. A few days later Mrs Tracey's health deteriorated further and she declined discussion of resuscitation. A second DNAR notice was later put on her chart with the family's agreement and Mrs Tracey subsequently died.

[12.31] The deceased's husband argued that this policy was in breach of her rights under art 8 of the ECHR as it did not involve consultation with the patient and her family, did not require notification or a second opinion, and was not clear or unambiguous. An action was also brought against the Secretary of State for failing to produce national guidelines on this matter. The Court of Appeal granted a declaration against the Trust that it violated Mrs Tracey's article 8 right to respect for private life in failing to involve her in the process which led to the first notice. Lord Dyson MR said 'A decision as to how to pass the closing days and moments of one's life and how one manages one's death touches in the most immediate and obvious way a patient's personal autonomy, integrity, dignity and quality of life.'[73] The court was of the view that there was a breach of the art 8 procedural obligation to involve Mrs Tracey before the first notice was completed and placed in her notes. Ryder LJ said:

> The duty to consult is integral to the procedural obligation to ensure effective respect for the article 8 right, without which the safeguard may become illusory and the interest may not be reflected in the clinical judgment being exercised. That interest is the autonomy, integrity, dignity and quality of life of the patient. It is accordingly critical to good patient care. The duty to consult is of course part of a clinical process. That process is individual to each patient albeit that it is informed by good clinical practice.

[12.32] In relation to the argument that Mrs Tracey and her family should have been offered a second opinion, the court held that there was no obligation to offer to arrange a second opinion in a case such as that of Mrs Tracey where the patient is being advised

---

[72] *R (on the application of Tracey) v Cambridge University Hospitals NHS Foundation Trust* [2015] 1 All ER 450; [2014] EWCA Civ 822. See commentary by Samanta, 'Tracey and respect for autonomy: Will the promise be delivered?' (2015) Med Law Review, Vol 23 No 3 pp 467–476; See also *County Durham & Darlington NHS Foundation Trust v PP* [2014] EWCOP 9.

[73] *R (on the application of Tracey) v Cambridge University Hospitals NHS Foundation Trust* [2015] 1 All ER 450; [2014] EWCA Civ 822, para 32.

and treated by a multi-disciplinary team all of whom take the view that a DNAR notice is appropriate. The case is important in establishing a legal presumption that patients should be involved in making DNAR decisions unless clinical staff can clearly show that such participation would cause the patient harm. The clinician is not entitled to decline to discuss it with the patient simply on the basis that the clinician is of the view that CPR would be futile.[74] Although the courts will not compel a doctor to provide CPR in circumstances where the doctor believes it would be futile, nonetheless 'the patient is entitled to know that such an assessment has been made.'[75]

[12.33] In the later case of *Winspear v City Hospitals Sunderland NHS Foundation Trust*[76] the question arose as to whether and how the principles in *Tracey* should apply in circumstances where the patient lacked capacity under the English Mental Capacity Act 2005. In this case the patient was a 28 year old man with cerebral palsy, epilepsy, spinal deformities and other associated health conditions. He was admitted to hospital with a chest infection and during the night a DNAR order was placed on his medical notes without discussion with his mother with whom he lived. Although the notice was later removed following objection from the patient's mother, the patient was subsequently transferred to the Intensive Care Unit and died. The patient's mother claimed that the placing of the notice on her son's notes without any consultation with a person who had been caring for or representing his interests was a procedural failure and resulted in her son's right to respect for private life under art 8 of the European Convention on Human Rights (ECHR) being interfered with without justification.

[12.34] The Court in the *Tracey* decision had made it clear that an adult patient must be consulted about decisions to withhold CPR. The issue in *Winspear* was the extent to which the principles in *Tracey* could apply to an adult patient without capacity. Blake J held there was nothing in the case of *Tracey* to suggest that the concept of human dignity applies any less in the case of a patient without capacity. He therefore accepted the claimant's case that the core principle of prior consultation before a DNAR decision is put into place applies in cases both of capacity and absence of capacity. Although there are different communication challenges in relation to a patient who lacks capacity, the Mental Capacity Act spells out when and with whom a decision taker must consult. The hospital had argued that it was not practicable to contact the patient's mother in the middle of the night when the DNAR notice had been put on the patient's notes but Blake J did not accept that argument and upheld the claim that there had been a breach of the procedural requirement under art 8(2) of the ECHR.

[12.35] Health professionals tend to find discussions about resuscitation difficult and sensitive. Whether those conversations are appropriate will depend ultimately on a difficult clinical judgement. It has been suggested that such discussions should take place in the context of treatment plans rather than as separate resuscitation consultations.[77] These treatment plans should be discussed at a stage in the patient's care

---

[74] Samanta, 'Tracey and respect for autonomy: Will the promise be delivered?' (2015) Med Law Review, Vol 23 No 3 pp 467–476 at 471.

[75] Laurie, Harmon and Porter, *Law and Medical Ethics* (10th edn, 2016) para 18.31.

[76] *Winspear v City Hospitals Sunderland NHS Foundation Trust* [2015] EWHC 3250 (QB).

[77] Samanta, 'Tracey and respect for autonomy: Will the promise be delivered?' (2015) Med Law Review, Vol 23 No 3 pp 467–476 at 475.

at which the patient can participate as fully as possible in deciding on resuscitation for him or herself.

[12.36] In England the development of 'care pathways' has also been the subject of some controversy in recent years. These pathways or plans for patient care are based on a multidisciplinary assessment of the needs of a patient who is estimated to be very close to death, in order that the patient might achieve as dignified a death as possible.[78] Consultation with the patient and the patient's family was considered an important part of such plans. The most well-known model in this context was referred to as the Liverpool Care Pathway which became the subject of significant criticism as a 'tick box exercise' with patients inadequately assessed as being terminally ill, heavily sedated and denied water. Hospitals were also given financial incentives to meet targets according to the number of patients dying on the pathway. It was subsequently discredited and abandoned following an independent review.[79]

[12.37] In Ireland, DNAR orders are made in hospitals although there is no legislative authority or judicial precedent upholding their legality. The practice appears to be for the medical team to consult with the patient's family and with nursing staff to ensure that such a decision is unanimous and to avoid any possibility that the decision would later be challenged. A study in a large Irish hospital in 2004 found that the majority of DNAR orders were clearly documented by senior doctors and had been discussed with the patient or with the relatives.[80] However, it is not clear to what extent the practice in this hospital is reflective of national practice. The Association of Anaesthetists of Great Britain and Ireland published guidelines on DNAR orders in 2009,[81] which state that the management of patients with DNAR decisions in the perioperative period should focus on what resuscitative measures *will* be embarked on rather than on what *will not* be done. It advises that a review of the DNAR decision by the anaesthetist and surgeon with the patient, proxy decision-maker, other doctor in charge of the patient's care, and relatives or carers, if indicated, is essential before proceeding with surgery and anaesthesia. In an emergency, the doctor must make decisions in the best interests of the patient using whatever information is available.

[12.38] The HSE National Consent Policy[82] deals with the consent issues in DNAR orders in detail in Part Four of the document. It states that DNAR orders must be made separately for each individual based on an assessment of his/her case, and not on the basis of age or disability.[83] Decisions should be made in the context of the likelihood of success and the potential risks as well as the individual's overall goals and preferences

---

[78] Marie Curie Palliative Care Institute, *What is the Liverpool Care Pathway for the Dying Patient?* (April 2010).

[79] Independent Review of the Liverpool Care Pathway, *More Care, Less Pathway* (2013) available at www.gov.uk

[80] McNamee and O'Keeffe, 'Documentation of Do-Not-Resuscitate Orders in an Irish Hospital' (2004) Ir J Med Sci.;173(2): 99–101.

[81] Association of Anaesthetists of Great Britain and Ireland 'Do Not Attempt Resuscitation Decisions in the Perioperative Period', (May 2009). Available at www.aagbi.org

[82] HSE National Consent Policy (2013) available at www.hse.ie

[83] The Policy states 'An individual should not be obliged to put a DNAR order in place to gain admission to a long-stay facility such as a nursing home', p 98.

for his/her treatment and care. This requires discussion with the individual him/herself. The individual may also choose to have family or friends involved in the discussion.

[12.39] The National Consent Policy distinguishes between situations in which cardiorespiratory arrest is unlikely, inevitable, or possible. The first of these situations applies to the general population who are healthy individuals for whom a cardiorespiratory arrest would be an unanticipated emergency. In such cases it is unlikely that the person would have considered or discussed their wishes and therefore there is a general presumption in favour of CPR in such cases. The second situation is where cardiorespiratory arrest is considered inevitable as a terminal event. This applies to individuals who are so unwell that death is considered to be imminent. In such cases CPR would not be clinically indicated and attempting CPR may cause harm to the individual and result in a traumatic and undignified death. Communication with the individual in relation to the severity of their condition should be undertaken, where possible, as part of a sensitive discussion of end-of-life care. This does not mean that the clinician should 'offer' CPR where this would be futile. The third situation arises where individuals have an acute severe illness or multiple medical conditions and there is an identifiable risk of cardiorespiratory arrest. For these individuals advance care planning, including the issue of CPR, should occur in the context of a general discussion about the individual's prognosis, their values, concerns and expectations of care.

[12.40] DNAR orders should be clearly and accurately documented in the individual's medical record along with how the decision was made, the rationale for it, and who was involved in making the decision. The order should be reviewed if the individual's clinical condition changes, their preferences regarding CPR change, an individual who previously lacked decision-making capacity regains capacity, or clinical responsibility for the individual changes such as when they are transferred or discharged.

WITHDRAWAL OF TREATMENT FROM PATIENTS IN PERSISTENT VEGETATIVE STATE

[12.41] Deprivation of oxygen from the brain through hypoxia can result in varying degrees of intellectual disability, depending on how quickly the brain is oxygenated. The extent of cognitive ability retained depends on the degree of damage to the cortex. The brain stem can continue to function even if the cortex is destroyed, leading to what is known as persistent vegetative state (PVS). The condition is characterised by an irregular but cyclic state of circadian sleeping and waking unaccompanied by any behaviourally detectable expression of self-awareness, specific recognition of external stimuli, or consistent evidence of attention or inattention or learned responses.[84] Such patients are not immobile and do retain certain reflexes, including those related to auditory and visual stimuli, depending on the degree of damage to the brain. Thus, the patient in PVS is alive, may have periods of wakefulness but is nonetheless unconscious,

---

[84] Multi Society Task Force on PVS, 'Medical Aspects of the Persistent Vegetative State' (1994) 330 NEJM 1499 (Pt 1), 1572 (pt 2).

has a beating heart and can breathe but cannot have any contact with the outside world.[85] If well managed, a patient in PVS can live for many years.[86]

[12.42] 'Having reached a diagnosis, however, we are left with what may well be regarded as the ultimate tragedy in human life – a human being who is alive in the cardiovascular sense in that he or she can breathe and maintain a heart beat, and who, at the same time, has no contact with the outside world and will never have such contact again.'[87] Ethical and legal difficulties arise in relation to patients in PVS where it may be suggested that treatment should be withdrawn. This raises discussion about medical futility and euthanasia, with the lines between them often indistinct. Decision-making in this context has been based on a number of standards: the subjective, the substituted judgment, and the best-interests test. The subjective test is only applicable in circumstances where the patient has at some time expressed his wishes as to treatment. The substituted judgment test is based on what it is believed the patient would have decided had he been competent to do so, according to his character and stated opinions. The best-interests test is based on the court's interpretation of what is preferable to be done for the patient, in line with good medical practice. Of these tests, the one that most closely adheres to principles of autonomy and self-determination is the subjective, or at the very least, the substituted judgment test which endeavours to treat the patient as he would have wished, rather than according to what others might presume for him.

US case law

[12.43] The volume of cases in the US and the decisions of more than 50 jurisdictions make it unrealistic to expect any uniform or even consistent approach to such a difficult issue. However, it is instructive to examine some of the most important cases, beginning with the classic PVS cases *Re Quinlan*[88] and *Cruzan v Director, Missouri Department of Health.*[89] In *Quinlan* a 22-year-old woman, Karen Ann Quinlan, was in a persistent vegetative state as a result of hypoxia from unknown causes. Her parents sought to remove her from intensive care and sought a declaration that they could give consent on her behalf to the switching off of the life support machine. It was believed that Karen could not survive for very long without the assistance of the respirator, although the exact period of survival could not be estimated. The doctors treating Karen testified that removal of the respirator would be contrary to medical practices, standards and traditions.

[12.44] The Court considered in depth the constitutional right of privacy. It said that if Karen were herself miraculously lucid for a brief interval, she could decide for herself upon discontinuance of the life-support machine, even if the consequences would be death. There was no compelling external interest of the state to force Karen to endure

---

[85] See further useful discussion in Laurie, Harmon and Porter, *Law and Medical Ethics* (10th edn, 2016) paras 15.82–15.90.

[86] For further discussion, see McMahan, 'Brain Death, Cortical Death and Persistent Vegetative State', in Kuhse and Singer, *Companion to Bioethics* (Blackwell, 1998) at 250–260.

[87] Laurie, Harmon and Porter, *Law and Medical Ethics* (10th edn, 2016) at para 15.90.

[88] *Re Quinlan* 355 A 2d 647, 97 ALR 3d 205 (S Ct of New Jersey).

[89] *Cruzan v Director, Missouri Department of Health* 110 S Ct 2841 (1990).

the unendurable where there was no possibility of returning to any semblance of cognitive life:

> We think that the State's interest ... weakens and the individual's right to privacy grows as the degree of bodily invasion increases and the prognosis dims. Ultimately there comes a point at which the individual's rights overcome the state interest. It is for that reason that we believe Karen's choice, if she were competent to make it, would be vindicated by the law.

In view of Karen's incompetence to make such a decision herself, the Court held that her right to privacy could be asserted on her behalf by her guardian in consultation with an ethics committee constituted to consider whether any change in Karen's circumstances was possible.[90] The court reasoned that to refuse Karen's father the authority to exercise Karen's right of privacy would effectively nullify the right altogether.[91] The court stated:

> If a putative decision by Karen to permit this noncognitive, vegetative existence to terminate by natural forces is regarded as a valuable incident of her right of privacy…then it should not be discarded solely on the basis that her condition prevents her conscious exercise of the choice. The only practical way to prevent destruction of the right is to permit the guardian and family of Karen to render their best judgment…as to whether she would exercise it in these circumstances.

[12.45] In some cases patients in PVS do not require ventilator support but do require to be maintained on artificial nutrition and hydration (ANH). The termination of ANH can be a source of distress and disagreement within families, between families and doctors, or between doctors and other healthcare staff.[92] In *Cruzan v Director, Missouri Department of Health*[93] the patient was in a similar situation to that of Karen Quinlan, except that she did not require a ventilator. After three years in PVS, her parents requested that feeding and hydration be discontinued, on the basis of their interpretation of her wishes when she was competent. The Missouri court refused permission and the case went to the US Supreme Court on the question of whether states could, under the Constitution, require clear and convincing evidence of a person's expressed wishes while competent, before hydration and nutrition could be withdrawn. The Court agreed with this requirement but also stated that:

> No right is held more sacred, or is more carefully guarded…than the right of every individual to the possession and control of his own person, free from all restraint or interference of other, unless by clear and unquestionable authority of law.

[12.46] Other cases are perhaps not as straightforward as *Quinlan* and *Cruzan*. For example, in *In the matter of Claire Conroy*[94] the Court had to consider the circumstances in which life-sustaining treatments may be withheld or withdrawn from incompetent, institutionalised elderly patients with severe and permanent mental and physical

---

[90] Karen lived for nine years after the machine was switched off.

[91] See discussion of this case by Falck, '*In Re Quinlan:* One Court's Answer to the Problem of Death With Dignity' (1977) 34 Wash & Lee L Rev 285.

[92] Halliday, Formby and Cookson, 'An assessment of the court's role in the withdrawal of clinically assisted nutrition and hydration from patients in the persistent vegetative state' (2015) 23(4) Medical Law Review 556–587 at 558.

[93] *Cruzan v Director, Missouri Department of Health* 110 S Ct 2841 (1990).

[94] *In the matter of Claire Conroy* (1985) 486 A 2d 1209 (NJ S Ct).

disability, and a limited life expectancy. In this case Ms Conroy was not in a persistent vegetative state but her intellectual capacity was very limited and was unlikely to improve. She suffered from heart disease, hypertension and diabetes. Her leg was gangrenous, she could not control her bowels nor speak nor swallow. On the other hand she did have some limited interaction with her immediate environment in that she had some changes in facial movements in response to various things, her eyes followed individuals in the room, and she sometimes moaned when being fed or having bandages changed.

[12.47] The Court recognised the right of a terminally ill patient to reject medical treatment as that person's right to choose a preferred manner of ending life. The Court also looked at the situation where the person is unable to speak for him or herself, but nonetheless has a right to self-determination. 'The right of an adult who, like Claire Conroy, was once competent, to determine the course of her medical treatment remains intact even when she is no longer able to assert that right or to appreciate its effectuation.' The Court took that view that decision-making for incompetent patients should try to effectuate as far as possible the decision that the patient would have made if competent (the substituted judgment test). In this important sense then the decision is a subjective one, based on the particular patient's character and wishes as expressed by family members and friends, rather than an examination of what a reasonable person would decide in the circumstances. In the present case, there was insufficient evidence of Ms Conroy's wishes on the matter for the Court to use this test to decide whether she would have wanted the life-sustaining treatment to cease.

[12.48] In *Conroy* and an earlier case, *Superintendent of Belchertown v Saikewicz*,[95] the Court considered the balancing of interests as between the incompetent patient and the state. While the patient had a constitutional right to privacy which clearly encompassed the right to refuse medical treatment, the state also had interests in maintaining life and protecting innocent third parties or dependants. The state was entitled to maintain policies discouraging suicide and also had to consider the preservation of the integrity of the medical profession. In each of these cases the patient's right outweighed those of the state.

[12.49] More difficult cases have arisen where the patient is not in PVS but is minimally conscious and unlikely to ever improve beyond his current capacity. The courts have been asked to give decisions in relation to whether artificial feeding and hydration should be continued indefinitely in such cases. An illustrative case is *Conservatorship of Wendland*[96] in which a 48-year-old man, Robert Wendland, was left profoundly brain damaged from injuries sustained in a car accident. He emerged from a coma after 16 months, with severe cognitive impairment and paralysis on his right side. He could not swallow, control his bowel or bladder, communicate or act volitionally. He was, however, able to perform simple tasks with repeated prompting, such as catching a ball, or placing a coloured peg in a hole or moving his wheelchair. His family believed that he did not recognise them. The doctors treating him concluded that he had no reasonable chance of further improvement. Wendland's wife and children sought to have the artificial feeding discontinued on the basis that he would not have wanted to exist in this way. Wendland's

---

[95] *Superintendent of Belchertown v Saikewicz* (1977) 370 NE 2d 417 (Mass Sup Jud Ct).
[96] *Conservatorship of Wendland* 26 Cal 4th 519 (2001).

mother and sister strongly opposed such a move.[97] By the time that the case got to the Supreme Court of California, Wendland had already died of pneumonia, but the ruling of the Court is instructive nonetheless. Case law up to that point had established a right for a competent patient or a surrogate decision-maker to request the withdrawal of artificial feeding. However, the Court recognised that the situation of Wendland fell between PVS and competency, and was therefore unprecedented in California.[98]

[12.50] The important issue for the Court was the standard of proof required to establish a patient's wishes in relation to life-prolonging treatment. It was held that the law requires 'clear and convincing evidence' of the patient's wishes where the patient is incompetent but conscious. There was a distinction, according to the court, between a decision-maker appointed by the patient himself, such as by advance directive, and a conservator appointed by the court. While the former might be expected to have some special knowledge of the patient's wishes, the latter may not necessarily have the same degree of intimate knowledge. In light of the fact that Wendland had not made an advance directive, the Court had appointed his widow as conservator. The Court held that the law requires clear and convincing evidence of the patient's wishes when a conservator seeks to withdraw life-sustaining treatment from a conscious, incompetent patient who has not left legally cognisable instructions for healthcare or appointed a surrogate to make healthcare decisions. It was not satisfied in this case by statements made by Wendland that he would not want to be kept alive artificially. The case provides a strong incentive for those who want to be able to have their wishes in end-of-life situations followed, to execute an advance directive to that effect.[99]

[12.51] The much publicised case involving Terry Schiavo[100] also demonstrates the public and media attention surrounding these tragic cases. Ms Schiavo had been in PVS since an accident in 1990 and ten years later her husband, who was also her guardian, sought to discontinue her feeding and hydration on the basis of the statutory test that this is what she would have chosen. Ms Schiavo's parents objected on religious grounds and

---

97 A similar case decided by the Michigan Supreme Court ruled that life support could not be discontinued on the basis that general statements made by the patient before his injuries did not apply, as they did not provide clear and convincing evidence that the patient would have wanted life support to be withdrawn. *In re Martin* 538 NW 2d 399 (Mich, 1995).

98 *Barber v Superior Court* 147 Cal App 3d 1006 (1983) allowed discontinuance of artificial feeding where the patient was in a coma; *Bartling v Superior Court* 163 Cal App 3d 186 (1984) where a competent patient suffering from an aneurysm and cancer was entitled to request that his ventilator be removed; *Bouvia v Superior Court* 179 Cal App 3d 1127 (1984) where a quadriplegic woman with cerebral palsy was enabled to request doctors to withdraw artificial feeding; *Conservatorship of Drabick* 200 Cal App 3d 185 (1988) where the Court said that a court-appointed conservator could require doctors to withdraw artificial feeding from a patient who had been in PVS for five years following an accident; and *Conservatorship of Morrison* 206 Cal App 3d 304 (1988) where doctors who refused to comply with the request of the conservator of an elderly woman in PVS to withdraw artificial feeding were obliged to transfer the patient to another facility where other doctors would do so.

99 Eisenberg and Kelso, 'Legal Implications of the Wendland Case for End-Of-Life Decisionmaking' (2002) West J Med 176:124–127; Rich, 'The Ethics of Surrogate Decision Making' 2002 West J Med 176:127–129.

100 *Schindler v Schiavo* 851 So 2d 182 (Fla 2d DCA, 2003); *Bush v Schiavo* 23 Sept 2004, No SC04–925.

also because they disputed that this was what she would have wanted, but their objection was overruled by the Florida Circuit Court. The Governor subsequently became involved in the dispute and ordered that the feeding tube should be reinstated but this was deemed unconstitutional by the Florida Supreme Court. The case ultimately, and unusually, came before the US Senate which passed legislation directly applying to Ms Schiavo.[101] The authority to remove her nutrition and hydration was ultimately upheld[102] on grounds that she would not have wished to continue life-prolonging measures and Ms Schiavo died.

[12.52] The US cases indicate a judicial unwillingness to decide 'quality of life' issues where these may be avoided by choosing the 'substituted judgment' test. This enables the court to avoid making a decision that it is in the individual's best interests not to be alive and leaves the decision to surrogate decision-makers appointed either by the person themselves through an advance healthcare directive, or empowered according to a designated statutory hierarchy beginning with the person's spouse and followed by an adult child, parent, brother or sister. Donnelly says that the issue here is not whether in the *Schiavo* case the husband was right and the parents were wrong or vice versa but that 'any system whereby decisions about life or death (and the manner of these) are made on the basis of who happens to be at the top of a list of surrogates fails to accord sufficient respect to the individual, treating her ultimately as a means towards an end rather than as an end in herself.'[103]

English case law

[12.53] The starting point for discussion of the English cases is the important case of *Airedale NHS Trust v Bland*.[104] This case arose out of the tragic incident which took place at the Hillsborough football stadium in 1989 when many fans were crushed during a soccer match. Tony Bland was a 17 year old fan who sustained severe anoxic brain damage, as a result of which he was in PVS. While he had a heartbeat and could breathe unaided, he had to receive nutrition and hydration through a naso-gastric tube. There was no chance of his regaining any cognitive function or sensory capacity. Butler Sloss LJ said that he existed in a 'twilight world'[105] and Lord Goff described his state as a

---

[101] The Schiavo case involved 14 appeals and numerous motions, petitions, and hearings in the Florida courts; five suits in federal district court; extensive political intervention at the levels of the Florida state legislature, then-governor Jeb Bush, the US Congress, and President George W Bush; and four denials of certiorari from the Supreme Court of the United States. The case also spurred highly visible activism from the pro-life movement, the right-to-die movement, and disability rights groups.

[102] *Schindler v Schiavo* 404 F 3d 1282 and 403 F 3d 1289 (2005).

[103] Donnelly, 'Patient-centred dying: the role of law' in Donnelly and Murray (eds) *Ethical and Legal Debates in Irish Healthcare, Confronting Complexities* (Manchester University Press 2015) 222–235 at 230.

[104] *Airedale NHS Trust v Bland* [1993] AC 789 [1993] 1 All ER 821.

[105] *Airedale NHS Trust v Bland* [1993] AC 789 at 816. For discussion of how these descriptions accord with the views of the patients' family see Halliday, Formby and Cookson, 'An assessment of the court's role in the withdrawal of clinically assisted nutrition and hydration from patients in the persistent vegetative state' (2015) 23(4) Medical Law Review 556–587 at 567.

'living death.'[106]After three years without improvement the hospital sought a declaration that it would be lawful to discontinue all life support, and that any further treatment should be given only to enable him to die in dignity.[107]

[12.54] The case eventually came before the House of Lords, which decided that the question should be decided on the best-interests test. As an adult, treatment of Tony Bland in the absence of his consent was only lawful under the doctrine of necessity. Treatment could only be said to be necessary if it could be shown to be in his best interests. As it was immaterial to the unconscious Tony Bland whether he lived or died, it could not be shown that life-prolonging treatment was in his continued best interests. Essentially, he had no interests at all. Therefore, the House of Lords held that it would be lawful to cease treatment, even though the consequence would be that Tony Bland would die. All of the opinions stressed that it was not a matter of it being in the best interests of Tony Bland to die, but rather that it was not in his best interests to keep him alive in circumstances where such medical treatment was futile. In making its decision, the Court had to consider whether such conduct would be in conflict with the criminal law, bringing about, as it did, the death of another human being. The Court also had to consider how its judgment fitted in with the duty of the medical profession to care for patients' best interests.

[12.55] The Court recognised that the doctor has a duty to treat his patient in a patient's best interests. However, if it is accepted, as in the present case, that further treatment is futile, then it cannot be in the patient's best interests to receive that treatment. Although the principle of sanctity of life was important, Lord Keith said 'it does no violence to the principle to hold that it is lawful to cease to give medical treatment and care to a PVS patient who has been in that state for over three years, considering that to do so involves invasive manipulation of the patient's body to which he has not consented and which confers no benefit upon him.'

[12.56] As the proposal in this case was a failure to continue to feed and hydrate rather than an act to cause death, the Court was comfortable in describing this as an omission and not an act. Criminal liability may only be imposed on foot of an omission where there is a duty to act. In this case, as there was an assessment that further treatment would be futile, there was no duty to act imposed on the doctors. This was not, according to the Court, a case of euthanasia, which is a positive act carried out to bring about the death of another, but rather a case of futile treatment. The focus on futility is demonstrated in this extract from the judgment of Lord Goff:

> I cannot see that medical treatment is appropriate or requisite simply to prolong a patient's life, when such treatment has no therapeutic purpose of any kind, as where it is futile because the patient is unconscious and there is no prospect of any improvement in his condition. It is reasonable also that account should be taken of the invasiveness of the treatment and of the indignity to which, as the present case shows, a person has to be subjected if his life is prolonged by artificial means, which must cause considerable distress to his family – a distress which reflects not only their own feelings but their

---

[106] *Airedale NHS Trust v Bland* [1993] AC 789 at 863.

[107] See analysis of the five judgments in the House of Lords by Foster, '*Airedale NHS Trust v Bland* [1993]' in Herring and Wall, *Landmark Cases in Medical Law* (Hart Publishing, 2015) 83–110.

perception of the situation of their relative who is being kept alive. But in the end, in a case such as the present, it is the futility of the treatment which justifies its termination. I do not consider that, in circumstances such as these, a doctor is required to initiate or to continue life-prolonging treatment or care in the best interests of his patient.

[12.57] The court in *Bland*, as in many of the other cases on this point, have chosen to classify feeding and hydration as medical treatment, such that it can be withdrawn on medical criteria. Others argue that food and water is not in any way 'medical', that it does not take medical expertise to administer either of these things, and that both are better classified as a basic need of any human being which it would be unethical to deny.[108] Also the distinction drawn in this case between an act and an omission, while necessary in the Court's view to avoid the label of euthanasia, is open to criticism on the grounds of verbal gymnastics. 'Is the physical withdrawal of the feeding tube an 'act' or merely a failure to continue to feed? Even if we leave the feeding tube in place until the patient is dead, is the writing-up of the decision in the patient's notes not an 'act' from which the negative treatment flows? Which is the morally or legally significant event?'[109] It is said that these cases are not examples of *active* euthanasia but they come within the description of *passive* euthanasia: allowing another to die when a decision is taken that that life should be ended by inaction and when action could sustain the life in question.[110]

[12.58] A number of judges also made comments relating to the role of parliament in matters such as this. Lord Browne-Wilkinson said it was imperative that the moral, social and legal issues raised by the case of Tony Bland should be considered by Parliament. The judicial function is to apply the principles which society adopts through the democratic process, not to impose the judge's own standards on society. He went on to remark that although criminal law draws distinctions between commission of a positive act and the omission to do an act, this could be said to introduce 'intolerably fine distinctions' in cases such as this. He said that it might seem irrational to allow a patient to die over a period of weeks from lack of food but unlawful to produce his immediate death by a lethal injection which might save his family further ordeal. The learned judge admitted to finding it difficult to come to a moral justification of the distinction albeit that it did represent the legal position on the matter. Lord Mustill also said that 'the whole matter cries out for exploration in depth by Parliament and then for the establishment by legislation not only of a new set of ethically and intellectually consistent rules, distinct from the criminal law, but also of a sound procedural framework within which the rules can be applied to individual cases.'

[12.59] The House of Lords' reliance on best interests has been the subject of some commentary given that in the particular case of a patient who is in PVS, the court accepted that such a person has ceased to have any interests at all. Treatment is therefore

---

[108] Keown, 'Restoring Moral and Intellectual Shape to the Law After Bland' (1997) 113 LQR 481. See also McLean, 'From Bland to Burke: the law and politics of assisted nutrition and hydration' in McLean (ed) *First Do No Harm* (Ashgate 2006) 431–46.

[109] Mason and Laurie, 'Negative Treatment of Vulnerable Patients: Euthanasia by Any Other Name?' (2000) Jur Rev Vol 3, 159–178 at 165.

[110] Mason and Laurie, 'Negative Treatment of Vulnerable Patients: Euthanasia by Any Other Name?' (2000) Jur Rev Vol 3, 159–178 at 165.

neither a benefit nor a burden to a person who is insentient. However, it could be argued that this is demeaning and that the manner of one's death is of interest to an individual and their family, for example Lord Hoffman said Tony Bland had an interest in putting to an end 'the humiliation of his being and the distress of his family.'[111] That being said, it is hard not to agree with Lord Browne-Wilkinson's comments about finding it difficult to see why it is lawful to allow a patient to starve to death rather than administering a lethal injection.

[12.60] A year after *Bland* another case came before the English courts dealing with the same issues yet seemed to be decided on less clear and unanimous evidence, thus adding to fears of a slippery slope having been created by the House of Lords. *Frenchay Healthcare NHS Trust v S*[112] concerned an application for a declaration that a feeding tube which had become detached from the patient, a 21-year-old man who had been in apparent PVS for two and a half years following a drug overdose, need not be replaced. Due to the short period of time within which this application was made and disposed of by the Court, there was not a great deal of time spent on obtaining independent medical opinion of S's capacity. In granting the application, Bingham MR accepted that the medical evidence was not as emphatic as that in *Bland* but said that he was satisfied that the diagnosis of PVS was correct, that there was no prospect of recovery and that S had no real cognitive function. This was a case that deserved more judicial attention rather than less due to the very fact pointed out by the judge that the medical evidence was less emphatic than in *Bland*. The case is perceived by some as a rubber-stamping exercise whereby the courts agree with the medical evidence provided by the treating doctors, without hearing independent evidence and a properly prepared defence to the application.[113]

[12.61] In the Scottish case of *Law Hospital NHS Trust v Lord Advocate*,[114] a ruling was sought from the Court of Session that it was lawful to remove artificial feeding and hydration from a woman in PVS. Medical experts agreed that her case was hopeless and that there were no further avenues to explore. Her family agreed with the doctors that feeding and hydration should be discontinued, thus allowing her to die. The Court held that where capacity to consent was lacking, the question as to whether it would be lawful to discontinue treatment was a matter not for doctors, but for the courts in the absence of legislation to the contrary. The test to be applied was whether the proposed course of action was in the patient's best interests, and if the treatment could not be of any benefit to her, there were no longer any best interests to be served by continuing it.[115]

[12.62] A more unusual case arose on the facts of *R (Burke) v The General Medical Council*.[116] The patient, Mr Burke, suffered from a degenerative brain condition which

---

[111] See further discussion in Dresser, 'Missing persons: Legal perceptions of incompetent patients' (1994) 46 Rutgers Law Review 609; Glover, *Causing death and saving lives* (Penguin 1977).

[112] *Healthcare NHS Trust v S* [1994] 2 All ER 403.

[113] Unger, 'In Whose Interests?' (1994) Gazette 91/ 29, 18–19.

[114] *Law Hospital NHS Trust v Lord Advocate* 1996 SC 301, 1996 SLT 848.

[115] Other relevant cases include *Re G* [1995] 3 Med L Rev 80; *Swindon and Marlborough NHS Trust v S* [1995] 3 Med LR 84; *Re D* (1997) 38 BMLR 1; *Re H* (1997) 38 BMLR 11.

[116] *R (Burke) v The General Medical Council* [2004] EWHC 1879; [2005] EWCA Civ 1003; *Burke v United Kingdom* (Appl No 19807/06) 11 July 2006.

would inevitably lead to the need for artificial nutrition and hydration at some point in the future. He argued that the guidelines of the General Medical Council (GMC) on the withdrawal of treatment were inconsistent with his right to medical treatment and respect for his wishes. The guidelines at the time stated that the doctor must make the decision about whether to withhold or withdraw life-prolonging treatment taking into account the views of the patient or those close to the patient. It also stated that 'where death is not imminent, it usually will be appropriate to provide artificial nutrition or hydration. However, circumstances may arise where you judge that a patient's condition is so severe, the prognosis so poor, and that providing artificial nutrition or hydration may cause suffering or to be too burdensome in relation to the possible benefits.' Burke was concerned that doctors may deny him treatment and artificial nutrition and hydration irrespective of his own views.[117] He emphatically did not 'want to die of thirst.' He therefore brought judicial review proceedings against the GMC claiming that the guidelines were incompatible with his rights under the European Convention on Human Rights, namely art 2 (right to life), art 3 (prohibition of inhuman and degrading treatment), and art 8 (right to respect for private and family life).

[12.63] In the High Court, Munby J declared that the guidance was unlawful for a number of reasons, including that it did not recognise the patient's right to require treatment and it did not acknowledge the doctor's duty to go on providing treatment even where he was unwilling to do so, until he could find another doctor to continue treatment. However, the Court of Appeal (and subsequently the European Court of Human Rights) allowed the appeal by the GMC, stating that the guidelines did not contradict the legal requirement that a doctor must take reasonable steps to keep a competent patient alive if that was his expressed wish, nor the obligation to treat an incompetent patient in his best interests. The Court rejected Munby J's rights-based approach and said that a patient cannot insist on treatment above and beyond the doctor's general duty to care for the patient.[118] The Court said that if a doctor deliberately allows a patient to die contrary to his wishes, there would be a violation of art 2 of the European Convention on Human Rights (ECHR) (right to life) and possibly a charge of murder. Therefore, the law protects the patient to the extent that his wish to remain alive is respected as far as possible.[119] On the subject of withdrawing treatment from incompetent patients (which was not an issue in the present case), the Court of Appeal emphasised that whether or not treatment should be withdrawn is based on a test of 'best interests' only and that intolerability was not the test of best interests, which was to be

---

[117] See discussion by Pattinson, '*R (Burke) v The General Medical Council* [2004]; *Burke v United Kingdom* [2006]. Contemporaneous and Advance Requests: The Fight for Rights at the End of Life' in Herring and Wall (eds) *Landmark Cases in Medical Law* (Hart Publishing, 2015) 255–269.

[118] Pattinson says that this case is thus an exception to the general direction of medical law over the last few decades away from medical paternalism towards patient autonomy. Pattinson, '*R (Burke) v The General Medical Council* [2004]; *Burke v United Kingdom* [2006]. Contemporaneous and Advance Requests: The Fight for Rights at the End of Life' in Herring and Wall (eds) *Landmark Cases in Medical Law* (Hart Publishing, 2015) 255–269, at 269.

[119] Gurnham, 'Losing the Wood for the Trees: Burke and the Court of Appeal' (2006) Med Law Review 14(2) 253–263.

determined based on the circumstances of each case.[120] The European Court of Human Rights said the claim was 'manifestly unfounded' and that English law adequately protected the applicant's rights under the relevant articles of the ECHR. The Court was satisfied that 'the presumption of domestic law is strongly in favour of prolonging life where possible, which accords with the spirit of the Convention.'

[**12.64**] As seen in the cases discussed above, the best-interests test is therefore the one that has traditionally found most favour with the English courts rather than the substituted judgment approach. This is also evident in *W Healthcare NHS Trust v H and another*[121] where KH, who had lived with multiple sclerosis for 30 years, required 24-hour nursing care and artificial feeding, but was nonetheless conscious albeit she could not speak or recognise anybody. Her carers wanted to replace her feeding tube that had fallen out but her family was opposed to this as they said KH would not have wanted to live in this undignified state. The court held in favour of continuing the feeding on the basis of her best interests since the alternative would mean KH would starve to death. KH was not in PVS and would have some minimal awareness of the process. Brooke LJ said 'the Court cannot in effect sanction the death by starvation of a patient who is not in a PVS state other than with their clear and informed consent or where their condition is so intolerable as to be beyond doubt.'

[**12.65**] Some patients may not be in PVS but rather are in 'minimally conscious' states. The English courts have used the balance sheet approach of pros and cons in this context, similar to cases involving newborns with critical life-limiting conditions discussed in chapter 11. For example in the first English case on patients in this condition, *W v M*,[122] M was a 43 year old woman who was in a minimally conscious state having suffered from viral encephalitis which left her with extensive and irreparable brain damage. Her parents wanted to remove her nutrition and hydration, but the healthcare team was opposed to this. The court said that using the balance sheet approach resulted in withdrawal of treatment decisions being made in PVS cases for whom treatment was inevitably futile, but for patients who were in minimally conscious states, each case would be decided on its own merits, depending on the facts and evidence before the court. The court was aware of changing technology which meant that over the patient's lifetime, a patient who was minimally conscious could become aware of pain and of the withdrawal of nutrition and hydration, which was not the case with patients in PVS. Despite evidence from her family that M would definitely not have wanted to be kept alive in such circumstances, it was held to be in her best interests that treatment would be continued as she did have some positive experiences. The court also confirmed sanctity of life as its fundamental starting point, an issue that has been criticised as not respecting a person's previously expressed wishes.[123]

---

[120] See discussion by Coggon, 'Could the Right to Die with Dignity Represent a New Right to Die in English Law?' (2006) Med Law Review 14(2) 219–237.

[121] *W Healthcare NHS Trust v H and another* [2004] EWCA Civ 1324.

[122] *W v M* [2011] EWHC 2443 (COP).

[123] Donnelly says 'the dismissal of the patient's views, as communicated through her partner and family, reflects an underlying difficulty which the law encounters in responding to conditions of uncertainty.' (contd.../)

[12.66] Jackson says there is a sharp distinction drawn between patients in PVS and those with limited or minimal consciousness (Minimally Conscious State or MCS).[124] For PVS patients a diagnosis of PVS is sufficient to justify the conclusion that life-prolonging treatment is futile. However, for non-PVS patients, the presumption seems to be reversed and it is much harder to justify treatment withdrawal.

> The concern of courts…is that the minimally conscious patient might want to live, but is unable to express that desire. The epistemic uncertainty about the mental lives of MCS (minimally conscious state) patients warrants due consideration, but it cuts both ways. If we do not know if an individual desires to continue living, we also do not know if they wish their lives to end. The irony is that the MCS patient might actually have preferences – although it is by no means settled that they do – whereas the vegetative state patient certainly does not. Yet, we are more likely to honour the self-determination by proxy of the vegetative state patient, someone who is beyond suffering, than we are to honour it in a person who is minimally conscious.

[12.67] Other recent English cases include *An NHS Trust v L*[125] in which the court said that family and patient views were just one part of the equation to be taken into account by the court in relation to the question of whether to intervene in the event of further deterioration of the patient's condition. The court also said it could not require healthcare professionals to treat against their clinical judgement. In this case the only treatment that could have been of benefit to L, who had an extremely rare form of anorexia and was close to death, was force feeding. The judge held that it would not be in her best interests to provide the treatment as it was unlikely to save her life and would certainly cause her distress as 'every calorie that enters her body is an enemy to Ms L.' In *United Lincolnshire Hospitals NHS Trust v N*[126] the court held that in determining the patient's best interests it was necessary to consider whether it would be futile to continue to treat or whether the treatment was likely to be ineffective or of no benefit to the patient. The court said this did not mean that the treatment would have to be able to cure the patient or return him to reasonable health, but it should be capable of allowing the recovery of a quality of life which the patient would regard as worthwhile. In *St George's Healthcare NHS Trust v P*[127] the court found in favour of the continuation of renal replacement therapy for a patient in minimally conscious state on the basis that it could extend P's life for another four years, that P benefitted from his family's love and affection, that the treatment was not unduly burdensome, and had a prospect of success.

[12.68] Finally the case of *Aintree University Hospitals NHS Foundation Trust v James and others*[128] is instructive in relation to the meaning of best interests. The patient was described as having limited rather than minimal awareness and the question was whether

---

[123] (\…contd) She says the courts in such circumstances will ultimately be drawn to concepts they can work with such as the preservation of life or the right of autonomy. Donnelly, 'Patient-centred dying: the role of law' in Donnelly and Murray (eds) *Ethical and Legal Debates in Irish Healthcare, Confronting Complexities* (Manchester University Press 2015) 222–235 at 231. See also critique by Gillon, 'Sanctity of life has gone too far' BMJ 2012: 345:e4637.

[124] Jackson, *Medical Law: Text, cases and material* (3rd edn, 2013) at 966.

[125] *An NHS Trust v L* [2013] EWHC 4313.

[126] *United Lincolnshire Hospitals NHS Trust v N* [2014] EWCOP 16.

[127] *St George's Healthcare NHS Trust v P* [2015] EWCOP 42.

[128] *Aintree University Hospitals NHS Foundation Trust v James and others* [2013] UKSC 67.

treatment should be withheld even though this might lead to the patient's death. The patient's family took the view that he gained benefit from seeing his family and had overcome all infections and was determined to beat his condition. The Supreme Court said the question was not whether it is lawful to withhold treatment but rather whether it is lawful to *give* the treatment in the patient's best interests. Lady Hale said the court must look at the patient's welfare in the widest sense, not just medical but also social and psychological. The court must consider the nature of the medical treatment in question, what it involves, its prospects of success, and the likely outcome for the patient. The court must also consult others who are interested in the patient's welfare and try to ascertain what the patient's own wishes would be.[129] The latter introduces an element of substituted judgement into the judicial approach although it is but one of a range of considerations for the court and is not determinative of the court's decision.[130] These principles also appear to have been followed in *M and Mrs N and a care provider.*[131]

Irish case law

[12.69] There have not been many cases in Ireland on the issue of withdrawal of treatment. However, the Supreme Court did have the opportunity to examine issues of futility and best interests in *In re a Ward of Court*[132] where the ward was a 45-year-old woman who had suffered irreversible brain damage as a result of cardiac arrest during a minor gynaecological operation in 1972. Since then she had been in an almost persistent vegetative state.[133] The trial judge described her condition as follows: 'She is spastic as a result of brain damage. Both arms and hands are contracted. Both legs and feet are extended. Her jaws are clenched and because she had a tendency to bite the insides of her cheeks and her tongue, her back teeth have been capped to prevent the front teeth from fully closing. She cannot swallow. She cannot speak. She is incontinent.'[134]

---

[129] See commentary by Wise, 'Withdrawal and withholding of medical treatment for patients lacking capacity who are in critical condition – reflections on the judgment of the Supreme Court in *Aintree University Hospitals NHS Trust v James*' (2014) 82(4) Med Leg J 144.

[130] This approach is described by Donnelly as 'messy' as it 'lacks the kind of precision with which lawyers and legal decision-makers are most comfortable'. However, if we accept what Donnelly describes as 'patient-centred dying', it may offer an ethically more defensible position because 'it affords a space for patients' voices to be heard.' Donnelly, 'Patient-centred dying: the role of law' in Donnelly and Murray (eds) *Ethical and Legal Debates in Irish Healthcare, Confronting Complexities* (Manchester University Press 2015) 222–235 at 232.

[131] *M and Mrs N and a care provider* [2015] EWCOP 76. For further discussion see Gillon, 'Why I wrote my advance decision to refuse life-prolonging treatment: and why the law on sanctity of life remains problematic' J Med Ethics (2016) 42:376–382.

[132] *In re a Ward of Court* [1996] 2 IR 79.

[133] Lynch J in the High Court held that the ward was not terminally ill, in the sense that she would not, in her present condition, die within a few months. As long as her condition was stabilised, she could live for many more years. In the Supreme Court, Hamilton CJ disagreed, stating that the ward was terminally ill since she was kept alive by artificial means which, if withdrawn, would result in her death. Denham J said the classification was irrelevant since the decision to withhold treatment or not would have to be made irrespective of the classification of the illness. Tomkin and McAuley argue that what is important is whether the patient may or may not recover cognition, in '*Re a Ward of Court*: Legal Analysis' (1995) MLJI at 45.

[134] *In re a Ward of Court* [1996] 2 IR 79, per Lynch J.

Although she was not fully in PVS and had some minimal cognitive ability to recognise strangers and track people with her eyes, much of this was considered to be reflex from the brain stem, and the judge was of the opinion that 'if such minimal cognition as she has includes an inkling of her catastrophic condition, then I am satisfied that that would be a terrible torment to her and her situation would be worse than if she were fully PVS.'

[12.70] The ward's family requested that the gastrostomy tube used for feeding the woman be withdrawn but the hospital and healthcare professionals responsible for her care refused, as it was felt that such action would violate their philosophy and code of ethics. In 1995 the ward's mother, in her capacity as committee of the ward, obtained High Court consent for withdrawal of the feeding tube, Lynch J concluding that the courts should approach such cases from the standpoint of 'a prudent, good and loving parent in deciding what course should be adopted.'[135] He also said that while the best interests of the ward was 'the acid test', account had to be taken of what the ward's own wishes would have been had she been granted a momentary lucid period. Following the granting of the order allowing the tube to be withdrawn, the case was appealed to the Supreme Court.

[12.71] As a preliminary issue, the Supreme Court explained the Court's jurisdiction to consent to withdrawal on behalf of the ward, as coming within the ancient *parens patriae* power of the Lord Chancellor of Ireland over those of unsound mind.[136] This power had been transferred to the High Court by various Acts of the English Parliament and the Oireachtas.[137] By a four-to-one majority the Supreme Court held that the High Court was justified in giving consent to withdrawal of the feeding tube on the grounds that this was in the best interests of the ward, it was lawful and in pursuance of the ward's Constitutional rights to life, privacy, self-determination and bodily integrity.[138] In doing so, the Court did not use the 'prudent parent test' applied by Lynch J but came to the same conclusion nonetheless. Egan J, dissenting, decided that the inevitable result of removing the tube would be to kill the ward, which in view of the Constitution's protection of life, would require strong justification not present in this case.

[12.72] All of the majority judgments base their decision on the best interests of the ward, although each one's interpretation of what is meant by that test is slightly different.[139] Hamilton CJ was of the view that the trial judge had decided the matter appropriately, taking into account the ward's condition and its duration, the intrusiveness of the treatment and its futility, the wishes of the ward's mother and the medical

---

[135] *In re a Ward of Court* [1995] 2 ILRM 401 at 419. See criticism of this test in Hanafin, 'D(en)ying Narratives: Death, Identity and the Body Politic' (2000) 20 Legal Studies No 3, 393 at 402–403.

[136] For further discussion, see Tomkin and McAuley, '*Re a Ward of Court*: Legal Analysis' (1995) MLJI 45 at 46–47.

[137] Lunacy (Ireland) Act 1901, s 4; Government of Ireland Act 1920; Courts of Justice Act 1924, s 19(1); Courts of Justice Act 1936, s 9(1); and Courts (Supplemental) Provisions Act 1961, s 9(1).

[138] See similar decision in Germany in *OLG Frankfurt, a M,* a decision from 15.7.1998 – 20 W 224/98, NJW 1998, 2749, discussed in Aziz, 'The Role of Care Assistants in the Withdrawal of Hydration and Nutrition in Germany' (1999) 7 Med L Rev 307–326.

[139] For a general commentary, see Feenan, 'Death, Dying and The Law' (1996) ILT 90–94.

evidence. Blayney J seemed to deviate slightly from the language of best interests, saying that the question was whether it was for the 'benefit' of the ward that her life be prolonged. However, as he approved of the High Court decision, which was grounded on best interests, this may have been what he intended. Denham J adopted a broader notion of best interests test in suggesting that, amongst 15 factors to be taken into account, any wishes expressed by the ward prior to her incapacity should be considered.[140] Indeed, Denham J is alone in making reference to what the ward's own wishes might have been prior to her loss of capacity although this is just one of fifteen factors to be considered by the court. Judges O'Flaherty and Egan specifically referred to the substituted judgment test with O'Flaherty J stating that it was impossible to adapt the idea of a 'substituted judgment' to the circumstances of this case as the ward had never expressed any views on the matter. He acknowledged, however, that the test might be relevant 'where the person has had the foresight to provide for future eventualities'.

[12.73] It is crucial to the decision that in the context of the right to life some of the judges recognise that the right to life is not absolute and necessarily implies the right to die a natural death. Hamilton CJ stated:

> As the process of dying is part, and an ultimate inevitable consequence, of life, the right to life necessarily implies the right to have nature take its course and to die a natural death and, unless the individual concerned so wishes, not to have life artificially maintained by the provision of nourishment by abnormal artificial means, which have no curative effect and which are intended merely to prolong life.[141]

He went on to explain that this does not give a right to terminate one's own life or to have death accelerated. It is confined to the natural process of dying. Loss of mental capacity does not result in the diminution of that person's constitutional rights and in this case the ward's right to life necessarily implies a right to die a natural death. The cause of death would not be the withdrawal of food and nutrition, but the original injuries she sustained during the operation.

[12.74] O'Flaherty J concurred, saying that the present case was not about euthanasia, which involved the termination of life by a positive act.[142] This case concerned 'the withdrawal of invasive treatment in order to allow nature to take its course'.[143] He was of the opinion that advances in medical technology now resulted in the rendering a patient a prisoner in a ward from which there may be no release for many years without any

---

[140] The use of best interests has been criticised by Hanafin, who says that as the patient was unconscious and no longer capable of having interests, this was a 'fictional strategy'. 'D(en)ying Narratives: Death, Identity and the Body Politic' (2000) 20 Legal Studies No 3, 393.

[141] *In re a Ward of Court* [1995] 2 ILRM 401 at 426.

[142] Iglesias argues to the contrary: 'The intent in the deprivation of nourishment is to bring about death, which means to kill. I cannot interpret this but as euthanasia. The issue of whether this mode of death may be chosen by the person themselves, or by their legal representatives, does not alter the facts, nor the fundamental moral and legal question of the euthanasia intent manifested in those facts. And whether intentions to bring about the death of a patient are carried out in what is done (action), or in what is omitted (omission), does not make them less euthanasia intents.' 'Ethics, Brain-Death, and the Medical Concept of the Human Being' (1995) MLJI 51–57 at 57.

[143] *In re a Ward of Court* [1995] 2 ILRM 401 at 432.

enjoyment or quality of life, indeed without any life in the proper meaning of the word. He found it impossible to use the substituted judgment test in the circumstances, as the ward had never expressed her wishes on this matter before her injuries, therefore it was necessary to use the best-interests test to decide the matter.[144] On this basis he was satisfied that the trial judge had made the correct decision and that nature should take its course.[145]

[12.75] Denham J also took the view that the right to life under the Constitution is not absolute, no more than life itself is an absolute. She was of the opinion that the sanctity of life was an intrinsically important part of our society, not from a religious perspective, but in terms of the respect granted to all persons' right to life under the Constitution. Respecting death also gives respect to life – life need not be preserved at all costs, as this would not be sanctifying life. 'To care for the dying, to love and cherish them, and to free them from suffering rather than simply to postpone death, is to have fundamental respect for the sanctity of life and its end.'[146] Although the State has an interest in the protection of life in the common good, the State also recognised that respect for the life of an individual also entailed respecting the right to refuse medical treatment for religious or other reasons.

[12.76] Egan J, dissenting, took the view that the right to life is the highest in the hierarchy of rights in the Constitution. It would require a strong and cogent reason to justify the taking of a life, which was, in his view, what was proposed to be done by the removal of a feeding tube. He was concerned about the slippery slope on which the courts might be embarking by accepting the High Court's decision. This was not a case of full PVS, the ward had some minimal cognitive function and Egan J was concerned at the drawing of the line between PVS and cases of minimal consciousness:

> If slightly more cognitive function existed, would a right to withdraw sustenance still be claimed to be permissible? Where would the line be drawn? Cognition in a human being is something which is either present or absent and should, in my opinion, be so recognised and treated. Any effort to measure its value would be dangerous.[147]

He was of the view that, notwithstanding the horrendous situation faced by the ward's family, any sympathy for their plight did not justify making the orders sought.

[12.77] In relation to the specific application of the best interests test Hamilton J described as 'the proper test' Lynch J's enunciation of the issue in terms of whether it

---

[144] For arguments as to why the best interests test is inapplicable to patients in PVS, see Harmon, 'Falling Off the Vine: Legal Fictions and the Doctrine of Substituted Judgment' (1990) 110 Yale LJ 1; Minnow, *Making All the Difference: Inclusion, Exclusion and American Law* (Cornell Univ Press 1990) at 325.

[145] Brock is of the view that the use of such language as 'letting nature take its course' and 'stopping prolonging the dying process', is part of the court's way of shifting responsibility from the doctor who stops the life support to the fatal disease itself. There is an unease in the courts with equating treatment withdrawal and killing. By distinguishing between the two, the courts are attempting to distance themselves from death's violent nature, and ultimately serve to confuse the issue. See Brock, *Life and Death: Philosophical Essays in Biomedical Ethics* (Cambridge University Press, 1993) p 211.

[146] *In re a Ward of Court* [1995] 2 ILRM 401 at 459.

[147] *In re a Ward of Court* [1995] 2 ILRM 401 at 437.

was in the ward's best interests 'that her life should be prolonged by continuance of the particular medical treatment which she was receiving'. The Supreme Court upheld Lynch J's application of the best interests test as the most suitable to decisions of 'a prudent, good and loving parent'. In considering the best interests of the ward, the court balanced the benefits and burdens of continued treatment. The burdens were characterised as burdens upon the enjoyment of specific constitutional rights. These rights included the right to life which is expressly guaranteed in art.40.3 of the Irish Constitution and the unenumerated rights including the right to privacy and bodily integrity which flow from the Christian and democratic nature of the State. Doubt has however been cast upon the appropriateness of the application of the best interests test to such a situation as occurred in the Ward of Court case. 'There is a fear that the best interests as identified by the court may not necessarily be the best interests of the patient, but may merely coincide with the best interests of the patient as perceived by third parties such as the medical profession and the judiciary.'[148] Keane argues that another problem with the best interests test is that if it is uncritically adopted to determine whether the ward's life should be allowed to continue, not only in terms of her medical welfare, but in terms of whether it is for her benefit to continue to exist, the court establishes 'a criterion with ominous implications for other patients with serious disabilities'.[149]

[12.78] The right to privacy was also seen as contributing significantly to the Supreme Court's decision, although the Court did not elaborate on the exact meaning of the right. Hamilton CJ and O'Flaherty J both mentioned privacy as one of the constitutional rights relevant in this case, and both made the point that such rights were not diminished by the ward's incapacity. In her more detailed judgment, Denham J said that part of the right to privacy is the giving or refusing of consent to medical treatment. 'Merely because medical treatment becomes necessary to sustain life does not mean that the right to privacy is lost, neither is the right lost by a person becoming insentient.' In such cases the exercise of the right may take place through a different process, but the right exists nonetheless. Part of this right is also concerned with the right to die naturally, with dignity and with minimum suffering.

[12.79] Following the judgment of the Supreme Court in this case, the medical and nursing professions continued to follow their previous stance on this issue. The Irish Medical Council and the Irish Nursing Board both issued statements to the effect that it was not ethical for a doctor or nurse to withdraw artificial hydration or nutrition from a patient who is not dying, the argument here being that the ward could have lived for many more years in her condition and was not facing imminent death.[150] The result of this was that the ward could not have her feeding tubes withdrawn at the facility where

---

[148] Keane, 'Withdrawal of Life Support for Patients in PVS' (2011) Medico-Legal Journal of Ireland 17(2) 83–92.

[149] Byrne and Binchy, *Annual Review of Irish Law 1995* (Round Hall, 1997), p 156 at 178, quoted by Keane, 'Withdrawal of Life Support for Patients in PVS' (2011) Medico-Legal Journal of Ireland 17(2) 83–92.

[150] Irish Medical Council, 'Statement of the Council after Their Statutory Meeting on 4 August 1995' (The Medical Council, 1995) and Irish Nursing Board 'Guidance of the Irish Nursing Board of 18 August 1995 (The Nursing Board 1995). See (1995) MLJI p 60.

she had lived and was taken home by her family and cared for by volunteer nurses until she died.

[12.80] The Medical Council's current Guide to Professional Conduct and Ethics (8th edn) does not deal with the issue of withdrawal of artificial nutrition and hydration directly but states as follows:

> 45.1 Food and drink are basic needs of human beings. All patients are entitled to appropriate food and drink and to assistance from healthcare staff if they need help to eat or drink.
>
> 45.2 If a patient is unable to take sufficient food or drink orally, you should consider giving nutrition and/or hydration by subcutaneous, intravenous or enteral feeding routes. You should assess whether doing this will be of overall benefit to the patient, taking into account the patient's views, if known, and balancing the benefits, burdens and risks of each form of treatment. You should be sensitive to the emotional impact on the patient and their family of not providing nutrition and/or hydration. If you decide that providing artificial nutrition or hydration through medical intervention will not be of overall benefit to the patient, you must make sure the patient is kept as comfortable as possible and their symptoms addressed. Where possible, you should tell the patient and/or those close to them of your decision and the reasons for it.[151]

[12.81] In a more recent and difficult case, *PP v HSE*,[152] the High Court had to consider whether treatment should be withdrawn from a 26 year old pregnant woman who was also the mother of two young children. The tragic circumstances of this case were that the woman, NP, was admitted to hospital with headaches and nausea. She sustained a fall while in hospital and was found to be unresponsive. She was transferred to a specialist hospital but her condition was such that her family was advised that she had suffered brain stem death and should not be resuscitated in the event of cardiac arrest. At that time she was 15 weeks pregnant. She was then transferred back to the original hospital where she had first been admitted. At the time of the court hearing, NP was in the intensive care unit of that hospital where she was supported by mechanical ventilation and fed by a nasogastric tube. She was also maintained on high doses of medications for a number of conditions including pneumonia, fungal infections, high blood pressure and fluid build-up. The plaintiff, who was the woman's father, was informed that it was intended to maintain these measures for the duration of the pregnancy and he believed that this was unreasonable and that treatment should be discontinued.

[12.82] The medical evidence before the court was to the effect that NP's situation would rapidly deteriorate and become unsustainable. The unborn child was in a very abnormal environment and it would not be possible to maintain the pregnancy until viability at 32 weeks. The court took the view that on the extraordinary facts of the case continuing treatment of the woman 'would cause distress to the unborn child in circumstances where it has no genuine prospect of being born alive.' This would be a 'distressing exercise in futility for the unborn child.'

---

[151] Medical Council, Guide to Professional Conduct and Ethics (8th edn, 2016) available at www.medicalcouncil.ie.

[152] *PP v Health Service Executive* [2014] IEHC 622.

[12.83] In relation to the obligation on the State to vindicate the right to life of the unborn under art 40.3.3° of the Constitution, the court had to consider how far the Court should go in terms of trying to vindicate that right in the circumstances of this case. The court referred to *In Re a Ward of Court (No 2)*[153] in which the High Court held that the right to life ranked first in the hierarchy of personal rights although it might nevertheless be subject to certain qualifications. 'Thus although the State has an interest in preserving life, this interest is not absolute in the sense that life must be preserved and prolonged at all costs no matter what the circumstances.' The Court stated that the question was whether even if the artificial measures sustaining the mother were to be continued, there was a realistic prospect of the child being born alive.

[12.84] The court referred to *SR (a ward of court)*[154] in which an order was made allowing the hospital to discontinue treatment of a six year old child who had suffered catastrophic brain damage from a near drowning incident when just under two years of age. In that case the court said that the determination of what was in the best interests of the child required a balancing exercise to be undertaken involving the pain and suffering of the child, the longevity and quality of life the child could expect, the pain and suffering of the proposed treatment, and the views of the child's parents and doctors. Kearns P stated that the 'proper test' was to ask 'what the ward would choose if he were in a position to make a sound judgment.'[155] The court also stated that the presumption in favour of the sanctity of life was not irrebuttable and can be deviated from in exceptional circumstances. Kearns P concluded that the medical evidence was that further invasive treatment of the child was not in his best interests, would involve unnecessary pain and discomfort and would be futile.

[12.85] The court in PP stated that the principles outlined in *SR* were also appropriate for application here and that the facts were even stronger here. 'This unfortunate unborn has suffered the dreadful fate of being present in the womb of a mother who has died, and in which the environment is neither safe nor stable, and which is failing at an alarming rate.' The court held that the somatic support being provided to the mother was being maintained 'at hugely destructive cost' to both her remains and to the feelings of her family. The unborn child was facing into 'a perfect storm' from which it had no realistic prospect of emerging alive. 'It has nothing but distress and death in prospect.' The court concluded that 'to maintain and continue the present somatic support for the mother would deprive her of dignity in death and subject her father, her partner and her young children to unimaginable distress in a futile exercise which commenced only because of fears held by treating medical specialists of potential legal consequences. It therefore authorised at the discretion of the medical team the withdrawal of support being provided for NP.

[12.86] One of the interesting issues that arose in this tragic case was the question of what rights are engaged by a deceased woman in such circumstances. It might be argued

---

[153] *In Re a Ward of Court (No 2)* [1996] 2 IR 79.

[154] *SR (a ward of court)* [2012] 1 IR 305.

[155] For discussion of this case and a critique of the use of 'substituted judgment' in such cases see Somers, "Deciding obliquely and by a side wind': Substituted judgment and end-of-life decisions for minors'. (2013) 19(1) MLJI 11–17.

that the dead have no interests and no rights[156] but the court stated that it was 'unimpressed with any suggestion that considerations of the dignity of the mother are not engaged once she has passed away.' The court said the mother's right to retain dignity in death was a 'hallmark of civilised societies from the dawn of time' and was a deeply ingrained part of our humanity. However, when the woman who dies is pregnant at the time of her death, the rights of the child who is living and whose interests are 'not necessarily inimical' to those of the woman, must prevail over the feelings of grief and respect for a mother who is no longer living.

[12.87] It was not necessary for the court to carry out a balancing exercise between the mother and the unborn child because NP was dead and the interests of the child were not contrary to those of the mother in this case. Therefore the only interests the court had to consider were those of the unborn child.[157] As the medical evidence was clear and unequivocal in stating that the child had no realistic prospect of being born alive, the mother's treatment could be discontinued on grounds of futility. If the facts had been different and there was indeed some prospect of survival for the foetus, the court's decision might have been different. The court would then have had to consider whether the prospect of survival was reasonable in the circumstances bearing in mind the obligation in art 40.3.3° to vindicate the right to life of the unborn 'as far as practicable'. The court expressly stated that its focus was on survival and not on whether the child might be born with significant disability.

[12.88] It has been suggested that this case demonstrates an unintended consequence of the protection of the unborn under the Irish Constitution.[158] Mulligan argues that although international best practice supports the maintenance of support in a brain dead pregnant woman in limited circumstances, this case establishes that in Irish clinical practice the management of such cases will be dominated by the requirements of art 40.3.3° of the Constitution. She speculates as follows:

> If there is a possibility that the foetus will survive, the maintenance of foetal life will trump other concerns. It seems that Irish doctors are not entitled to consider factors such as the views of the next of kin, the previously expressed views of the dead woman, or the likelihood of the foetus being born with a serious disability. As a result, they are deprived of the capacity to make this most difficult of decisions using their best clinical and ethical judgement.[159]

[12.89] Since the introduction of the Assisted Decision-Making (Capacity) Act 2015, whether these factors may be considered in an appropriate case will depend on the facts,

---

[156] *Airedale NHS Trust v Bland* [1993] AC 789. Lord Keith said to a person such as Tony Bland, it must be a 'matter of complete indifference' whether he lives or dies.

[157] There is a suggestion that this case establishes that the welfare and interests of the unborn child may justify invasive treatment of pregnant women. See de Londras, 'Constitutionalising fetal rights: a salutary tale from Ireland' (2015) 22(2) Michigan Journal of Gender and Law; Enright, 'PP v HSE: Practicability, Dignity and the best interests of the unborn child' 26 Dec 2014. Available at www.humanrights.ie.

[158] Mulligan, 'Maternal brain death and legal protection of the foetus in Ireland' (2015) Med law Intl 1–14.

[159] Mulligan, 'Maternal brain death and legal protection of the foetus in Ireland' (2015) Med law Intl 1–14 at 14.

the prospect of survival of the foetus, and the existence of an advance directive or assisted decision-making representative. The Act stipulates in s 87(6)(a) that where a directive-maker lacks capacity and is pregnant, but her advance directive does not specifically state whether or not she intended a specific refusal of treatment set out in the directive to apply if she were pregnant, and the refusal of treatment would have a deleterious effect on the unborn, there is a presumption that treatment shall be provided or continued. Section 87(6)(b) provides that where a directive-maker lacks capacity and is pregnant, and her advance directive specifically states that her specific refusal of treatment set out in the directive is to apply even if she were pregnant, and the refusal of treatment would have a deleterious effect on the unborn, then an application must be made to the High Court to determine whether the refusal of treatment should apply. The Court will consider the potential impact of the refusal of treatment on the unborn, the invasiveness, duration and risk of harm to the woman if the treatment were to be given, and any other relevant matters.

ASSISTED SUICIDE

[12.90] Nature is not kind to some people. Some people are afflicted with devastating illnesses that cause pain, disability, discomfort and dependence for years before death. For them, life may become unbearable and death brings with it the promise of release and peace. Some people in this position want nothing more than to have a peaceful death in the arms of their family. But sometimes such a death is impossible without the assistance of a third party – a life partner, a family member, or a medical practitioner.[160] At common law, a person who committed suicide was regarded as a self-murderer.[161] Consequently, anyone who instigated or aided another to commit suicide was guilty of murder as an accomplice. In Ireland the Criminal Law (Suicide) Act 1993 was enacted to decriminalise suicide but provides for the criminalisation of assisted suicide in s 2, subs (2): 'A person who aids, abets, counsels or procures the suicide of another, or an attempt by another to commit suicide, shall be guilty of an offence and shall be liable on conviction on indictment to imprisonment for a term not exceeding fourteen years.' A prosecution under this section may only be instigated with the consent of the Director of Public Prosecutions. Similar measures exist in the UK,[162] Canada,[163] Australia,[164] New Zealand[165] and in most US states.[166]

---

[160] Madden, 'Is there a right to a good death?' (2013) 19, 2 MLJI 60–68 at 62.

[161] For a discussion of the history of suicide and its prohibition, see Trowell, *The Unfinished Debate on Euthanasia* (SCM Press, 1973) 1–11. See also McLean, *Assisted Dying: Reflections on the need for law reform* (Routledge-Cavendish 2007).

[162] Suicide Act 1961, s 2(1).

[163] Criminal Code 1985, s 241.

[164] ACT Crimes (Amendment) Ordinance (No 2) 1990 s 17(1) and (2), NSW Crimes Act 1900 s 31 C (1) and (2), NT Criminal Code 1983 s 168, Qld Criminal Code 1995 s 108, SA. Criminal Law Consolidation Act 1935 s 13(a)(5), Tas Criminal Code 1924 s 163, Vic Crimes Act 1958 s 6B(2), WA Criminal Code 1913 s 228.

[165] Crimes Act 1961 s 179.

[166] See New York Task Force on Life and the Law, *When Death Is Sought: Assisted Suicide and Euthanasia in the Medical Context* (1994); Smith, 'What About Legalised Assisted Suicide?' (1993) 8 Issues in Law and Med 505.

[12.91] In England similar provisions are contained in the Suicide Act 1961. These provisions were interpreted in *Attorney General v Able*[167] where the question for the Court was whether a booklet distributed by the Voluntary Euthanasia Society, called 'A Guide to Self-Deliverance' contravened the Act. The booklet was designed to reduce the incidence of unsuccessful suicides, to discourage hasty and ill-conceived suicides and to overcome people's fear of dying. It also contained information about various methods of suicide. The Court held that for supply of the booklet to amount to an offence under s 2(1) of the Act, it had to be proved that the supplier, whilst intending the booklet to be used by a person actually contemplating suicide and with the object of assisting or otherwise encouraging him, supplied the booklet to such a person who then read it and, except in the case of an attempted offence, was assisted or encouraged by reading it to commit or to attempt to commit suicide. Whilst there might be circumstances in which supply of the booklet would undoubtedly amount to an offence, without proof of the necessary intent it could not be said in advance that any particular supply would be an offence. Accordingly, the Court held that it was for a jury to decide in each case whether the necessary facts had been proved. The Court was particularly concerned about the danger of usurping the jurisdiction of the criminal courts. While recognising the advantages of the application of the law being clear in relation to future conduct, it would only be proper to grant a declaration if it was clearly established that there was no risk of the Court treating conduct as criminal which was not clearly in contravention of the criminal law.

[12.92] Although there is considerable support for the right of competent adults to make autonomous healthcare decisions, even where their refusal of treatment will lead to death, concern is commonly expressed when the person expresses a wish or intent to die and seeks assistance in order to do so, usually due to physical impairment which prevents the person being able to take his own life. Some studies show a link between depression and interest in hastened death in patients who are seriously ill, leading to concern over the vulnerability of such patients who actively request assisted suicide, also referred to as assisted dying:[168]

> Depression is a concern in requests for euthanasia or physician-assisted suicide because it is potentially reversible and may affect the patients' competency, particular in the relative weighting they give to positive and negative aspects of their situation and possible future outcomes. Depressed patients can be viewed as a vulnerable population in this context as their request for death may be part of their illness, with the correct response being treatment rather than assistance in dying.[169]

[12.93] In some instances partners, parents or children seek to assist a loved one who requests their help in dying, as they do not have the physical capacity to end their own lives due to disease or disability. The legal position is that a person who intentionally kills another may be prosecuted for murder even though they were motivated by a desire to end the other person's suffering or to give effect to the person's clear wishes. For some people, so-called 'mercy killing' occupies the lower end of the murder spectrum but this

---

[167] *Attorney General v Able* [1984] 1 All ER 277.

[168] Levene and Parker, 'Prevalence of Depression in Granted and Refused Requests for Euthanasia and Assisted Suicide: A Systematic Review' (2011) J Med Ethics 37: 205–211.

[169] Levene and Parker at 205.

does not mean that the courts are willing or able to allow mercy killings to be treated any differently from other murders.[170] Whether the Director of Public Prosecutions would initiate such a criminal charge, or indeed whether a jury would convict a person in such circumstances is open to question and must depend on the facts of the individual case.[171]

Physician-assisted suicide

[12.94] The question also arises as to whether doctors should respect the autonomy of those who want to accelerate their own death. Gawande argues that society already recognises a form of assisted suicide by allowing people to refuse food or water or medications or treatments.

> We accelerate a person's demise every time we remove someone from an artificial respirator or artificial feeding...Cardiologists now accept that patients have the right to have their doctors turn off their pacemaker – the artificial pacing of their heart – it they want it. We also recognise the necessity of allowing doses of narcotics and sedatives that reduce pain and discomfort even if they may knowingly speed death. All proponents seek is the ability for suffering people to obtain a prescription for the same kind of medications, only this time to let them hasten the timing of their death. We are running up against the difficulty of maintaining a coherent philosophical distinction between giving people the right to stop external or artificial processes that prolong their lives and giving them the right to stop the natural, internal processes that do so.[172]

[12.95] In some cases a patient may request the assistance of their doctor to provide medication, set up an intravenous drip, or other means to enable the patient to take their own life. As discussed above, Irish law currently provides that any person, including a doctor, who actively assists a patient to commit suicide, will incur criminal liability.[173] A successful prosecution would have to show that the doctor intentionally assisted or encouraged the commission of the act in question or that he was at least ready to assist, if required to do so. In *R v Cox*,[174] Dr Cox had given a 70 year old terminally ill patient a

---

[170] See comprehensive discussion of mercy killing by Huxtable, *Euthanasia, Ethics and The Law: From Conflict to Compromise* (Routledge-Cavendish, 2007) 34–84.

[171] In the first prosecution for assisted suicide in Ireland, *DPP v O'Rorke* in 2015, the defendant was charged with assisting the suicide of her close friend who suffered from multiple sclerosis, by making arrangements for her to travel to Dignitas in Zurich, a plan that was thwarted when the travel agent alerted police. The judge directed the jury to find Ms O'Rorke not guilty on two charges due to lack of evidence and she was acquitted by the jury on a third charge. See media reports on www.thejournal.ie 'Gail O'Rorke cleared on two charges of assisting the suicide of her friend' 24 April 2015.

[172] Gawande, *Being Mortal. Illness, Medicine, and What Matters in the End* (Profile Books 2014) at 243–244

[173] Most famously, Dr Jack Kevorkian (widely known as Dr Death) performed, on his own admission, 130 assisted suicides and led a crusade against state laws that prohibited his activities. In November 1998 he recorded one such incident whereby he administered a lethal injection to one of his patients, following which he was charged and convicted of second-degree murder and delivery of a controlled substance. In April 1999 he was sentenced to 10–25 years on the murder charge, and 3–7 on the other charge. He served 8 years in prison and was later paroled in 2007 on the basis that he would not offer suicide advice to any other person.

[174] *R v Cox* (1992) 12 BMLR 38.

dose of potassium chloride that was guaranteed to kill her. She had rheumatoid arthritis, gastric ulcers, gangrene and body sores. She was in extreme pain which was not well managed. There was evidence that she had repeatedly asked Dr Cox and others to kill her. Dr Cox could not be charged with murder as the patient's body had been cremated and therefore it was impossible to prove the cause of her death. He was however charged and convicted of attempted murder and given a suspended sentence. Dr Cox was not struck off the medical register following a hearing by the General Medical Council and returned to practise.[175]

[12.96] In *R v Chard*,[176] the defendant was prosecuted for providing the deceased person with paracetamol pills at her request, which she used to commit suicide. The defendant said that it had been the deceased's wish to have the option of taking her own life. The judge directed the jury to find the defendant not guilty, as there was no evidence to support the charge of assisting the suicide. He said that providing the deceased with an option of taking her own life was not sufficient to warrant a conviction. An argument could be made, along the lines of this case that a doctor who provides medication merely provides the patient with the option of committing suicide, rather than directly assists in the commission of the suicide itself. However, given the stigma attached to such conduct, it is more likely that it would be held to be, at the very least, counselling or procuring suicide. It would most likely be irrelevant that the patient was suffering from a terminal disease, and that death was imminent in any event. The doctor could also face disciplinary proceedings before the Medical Council due to the provisions of the Guide to Professional Conduct and Ethics, which currently provides that doctors must not take part in the deliberate killing of a patient.[177]

[12.97] The distinction between voluntary euthanasia and assisted suicide is based on the level of participation of the person providing the assistance. Thus, if death occurs as a result of an overt deliberate act of the doctor at the request of the patient, this is voluntary euthanasia. If the doctor participates in the events leading up to the suicide, such as by providing the medication by which the patient's death will occur but the patient does the final act himself, this is assisted suicide.[178] Euthanasia is discussed further later.

[12.98] Where a doctor complies with a patient's refusal of treatment, resulting in the patient's death, it is possible that an allegation of assisted suicide could be made if the refusal of treatment by the patient was treated as suicide. In older cases such as *John F Kennedy Memorial Hospital v Heston*,[179] the courts drew an analogy between refusals of treatment and suicide, thereby justifying the Court's decision to override the former. 'If the state may interrupt one mode of self-destruction, it may with equal authority interfere with the other…the state's interest in sustaining life in such circumstances is

---

[175] Jackson, *Medical law: Text, Cases and Materials* (3rd edn, 2013) 877.

[176] *R v Chard,* The Times, 23 September 1993.

[177] Medical Council, *Guide to Professional Conduct and Ethics* (8th edn, 2016), para 46.9 Available at www.medicalcouncil.ie.

[178] For comprehensive discussion, see Otlowski, *Voluntary Euthanasia and the Common Law* (OUP, 1997) at 61.

[179] *John F Kennedy Memorial Hospital v Heston* 58 NJ 576 (1971).

hardly distinguishable from its interest in the case of suicide.'[180] More recent cases have distinguished between the two as the right to self-determination has taken a stronger foothold. Refusal of treatment is now generally interpreted by the courts as being aimed at the avoidance of unwanted treatment, pain or the violation of religious principles, rather than at causing one's own death.[181] It is also the case that in many refusals of treatment, the courts have taken the view that it is the underlying disease not the withdrawal of life-support that causes the patient's death.

[12.99] Freeman questions the consistency of the law in allowing a person to refuse medical treatment with the consequence that the patient will die, but not allowing a person to have assistance in committing suicide. He says that there are different forms of suicide and different refusals of treatment. Some refusals of treatment are suicidal as opposed to a cry for help. Others demonstrate not so much an intention to put an end to life, as a decision that treatment is no longer worthwhile because it is just putting off the inevitable, or causes more pain than the patient is prepared to endure. The law appears to allow a doctor to withdraw treatment in response to such a refusal but would not require a doctor to respect a request to withhold or withdraw treatment where the patient's intention was suicidal. 'Since the doctor cannot always be certain into which category the patient falls, it may be that the only safe advice to offer him or her is to treat.'[182]

[12.100] In *Bouvia v Superior Court*,[183] the patient was a 28-year-old quadriplegic woman who required permanent hospitalisation, but who was likely to live for a further 20 years. She had expressed the wish to commit suicide and had unsuccessfully sought court permission to starve herself to death. She then applied to the Court for an injunction ordering that the doctors remove the naso-gastric tube with which she was being fed. The California Court of Appeal upheld her claim that she had an absolute right to refuse life-saving treatment, and rejected arguments that the state had an interest here in the prevention of suicide and the preservation of life. The Court held that her refusal of treatment was a decision to let nature take its course, rather than a wish to end her life, thus evading the suicide issue.[184] In any event, the Court was of the view that her motivation was irrelevant, as she had an absolute right to refuse treatment.[185]

[12.101] The doctors and hospital in this case had argued that Ms Bouvia should not be allowed to refuse medical treatment whilst in their care, as it would be tantamount to suicide and that they could accordingly be liable for assisted suicide. The Court held that the patient was not committing suicide but letting nature take its course and therefore no criminal liability attached to the doctors or hospital. The Court held that to establish liability for assisted suicide there must be some affirmative act such as providing a gun, poison, knife or other instrumentality by which a person could inflict upon themselves

---

[180] *John F Kennedy Memorial Hospital v Heston* 58 NJ 576 (1971) pp 581–2.

[181] Otlowski, *Voluntary Euthanasia and the Common Law* (OUP, 1997) at 66.

[182] Freeman, 'Denying Death its Dominion: Thoughts on the Diane Pretty Case' (2002) Med L Rev 10: 245–270 at 248.

[183] *Bouvia v Superior Court* 225 Cal. Reptr 297 (1986).

[184] See also *B v A NHS Hospital Trust* [2002] EWHC 429.

[185] Fisher, 'The Suicide Trap: *Bouvia v Superior Court* and the Right to Refuse Medical Treatment' (1987) 21 Loy L Rev 219, 237.

an immediate and fatal injury. This was 'far different from the mere presence of a doctor during the exercise of a patient's constitutional rights':[186]

> On this reasoning, a doctor's compliance with the refusal of treatment by a patient, who has decision-making capacity, would not attract criminal liability for assisting suicide. However, it may be wondered to what extent this reasoning has been influenced by policy considerations and in particular, the natural reluctance of the courts to impose criminal liability on doctors.[187]

[12.102] Two decisions of the US Supreme Court in 1997 dealt with the Constitutional position of state laws which prevented doctors from prescribing medication to hasten death. The Court held that laws which made it a crime to assist a suicide did not violate individual rights guaranteed under the US Constitution. The cases, *Washington v Glucksberg*[188] and *Vacco v Quill*,[189] were brought by terminally ill patients and doctors involved in the care of the terminally ill. The patients were in the final stages of their illnesses and wanted their doctors' help in ending their lives. The doctors testified that, in certain circumstances, it would be consistent with good medical practice to prescribe drugs in order to hasten the death of a mentally competent terminally ill patient. The laws in Washington and New York prohibited them from providing such assistance.

[12.103] In *Glucksberg* it was argued that the due process clause of the Constitution entitled the plaintiffs to a protected liberty interest and that any state law which infringed this fundamental Constitutional right had to be subject to strict scrutiny. The due process clause of the Fourteenth Amendment had been held to protect certain liberties against state interference such as the right to marry, the right to marital privacy, to use contraception and to abortion. However, it was recognised by the Court that to expand the boundaries of the clause would be dangerous, as it would substitute the subjective beliefs of the judiciary for the considered will of the democratic process.[190] Rehnquist CJ, giving the unanimous opinion of the Court, rejected the argument that this case was about the 'right to die' and described it rather as a right to assistance in committing suicide. He concluded that this right did not have any place in American legal tradition, and he distinguished assisted suicide from refusals of medical treatment on the basis of the doctrine of informed consent and the fact that forced medical treatment was a battery. Accordingly, the Court held that the state law prohibiting physician-assisted suicide did not violate the due process clause of the Constitution.

[12.104] In *Quill* it was argued that the New York law prohibiting physician-assisted suicide violated the equal protection clause of the Constitution on the basis that the statute discriminated against terminally ill patients who were not on life support and could not have assistance in dying, as opposed to those patients on life support who had an absolute right to refuse such treatment and thus end their lives. The Court held that there were a number of differences between the two situations: First, in the case of the

---

[186] *Bouvia v Superior Court* 225 Ca Rptr 297 at 306.

[187] Otlowski, *Voluntary Euthanasia and the Common Law* (OUP, 1997) at 78.

[188] *Washington v Glucksberg* 521 US 702 (1997).

[189] *Vacco v Quill* 117 S Ct 2293 (1997).

[190] See Carolan, 'US Supreme Court Rules: No Constitutional Right to Physician Assisted Suicide' (1997) MLJI 43 at 47; and Carolan, 'US Supreme Court Confronts 'Right to Die' (1998) Medico-Legal Journal Vol 66 Part 2, 65–69.

withdrawal of life-sustaining treatment death was caused by the illness, while in assisted suicide death was caused by the lethal dose of medication. Second, the withdrawal of life support or the administration of high doses of pain relieving medication which might hasten death, was not synonymous with a desire to end life. The patient might want to live, but not with the pain which he suffered. In assisted suicide, the clear intent is to bring about death. The right to decline medical treatment is not based on a right to die, but on a protection of bodily integrity and freedom from non-consensual touching. Accordingly, the New York law protected valid and important public interests and bore a rational relation to the legitimate end pursued by the state.

[12.105] It is perhaps significant that, despite the Court's ruling in these cases, it also expressly acknowledged that the question of physician-assisted suicide will not go away.[191] As Rehnquist CJ said in *Glucksberg:* 'Throughout the nation, Americans are engaged in an earnest and profound debate about the morality, legality, and practicality of physician-assisted suicide. Our holding permits this debate to continue, as it should in a democratic society.' This prophecy has certainly come true with many jurisdictions around the world continuing to grapple with this difficult issue.

[12.106] There are currently four US states that have introduced legislation allowing physician-assisted suicide, namely Oregon, Washington, California and Vermont. In Oregon, the Death with Dignity Act was introduced in 1997 to legalise physician-assisted suicide. It does not legalise assistance provided by any other party nor does it legalise euthanasia, even where performed by a doctor. The Oregon Health Plan provides for the cost to be borne by the state for low-income people. The Act requires that the patient be an adult who has capacity to make decisions regarding healthcare, and have an illness that is expected to lead to death within six months. The patient must make one written and two oral requests (at least 15 days apart) to his physician. The patient's primary physician and a consultant are required to confirm the diagnosis of terminal illness and the prognosis, determine that the patient is capable, and refer the patient for counselling if it is felt that the patient's judgment is impaired by depression or other psychiatric or psychological disorder. All feasible alternatives must be made known to the patient and all prescriptions for lethal medications must be reported to the Oregon Health Division. Those who adhere to the requirements of the Act are protected from criminal prosecution.

[12.107] Contrary to fears that had been expressed that, if physician-assisted suicide were legalised, it would be forced upon terminally ill patients who were poor, uneducated or uninsured, no obvious abuses of the law or unintended consequences appear to have occurred so far.[192] Battin also suggests that no evidence exists to support those fears.[193] However, Finlay and George dispute these findings on the basis that Battin's research focused on vulnerability based on race, gender or other socioeconomic status and did not refer to emotional vulnerability, personality type or the prevalence of

---

[191] For detailed analysis of these cases, see Pratt, 'Too Many Physicians: Physician-Assisted Suicide After *Glucksberg/Quill*' (1999) 9 Alb LJ Sci and Tech 161.

[192] Fraser and Walters, 'Death – Whose Decision? Physician-Assisted Dying and the Terminally Ill' (2002) West J Med 176:120–123.

[193] Battin et al, 'Legal Physician-Assisted Dying in Oregon and the Netherlands: Evidence Concerning the Impact on Patients in 'Vulnerable' Groups' J Med Ethics 2007; 33:591–7.

depression.[194] The decision to request and use a prescription for lethal medication is most commonly associated with concern about loss of autonomy and dignity, dependency and loss of control of bodily functions, rather than with fear of intractable pain.[195] In Oregon and Washington, the vast majority of patients using the law were white, well-educated, insured, dying of cancer and receiving hospice care. The legislation is not highly utilised in practice – from 1997 to 2015, a total of 1,545 people have had prescriptions written and 991 patients have died from ingesting medications prescribed under the Act.[196] During 2015, the rate of deaths under the Act was 38.6 per 10,000 total deaths.

[12.108] Many other states in the US have put forward bills to legalise some form of assisted suicide.[197] The most recent bill to receive approval was in California when in September 2015, the California State legislature approved a bill that will allow physician- assisted suicide for terminally ill people. The End-Of-Life Options Act, which came into effect in June 2016, is modelled on the law in Oregon but will expire after ten years unless re-approved. The Act differs from that in Oregon by requiring doctors to consult in private with the patient, in an attempt to ensure that there is no possibility of coercion in the patient's choice.

[12.109] Even though other states have not introduced legislation permitting physician-assisted suicide, nonetheless they may have judicial decisions that effectively prevent prosecution in such cases. For example in Montana, the Supreme Court ruled in 2009 that doctors prescribing life-ending medication to patients with terminal illnesses who have requested it and who do the final act themselves, are not subject to homicide statutes.[198] The Court said that although the state's Constitution did not guarantee a right to physician-assisted suicide, there was nothing in case law or statute in Montana indicating that doctor-assisted death is contrary to public policy. The Court said that 'each stage of the physician-patient interaction is private, civil and compassionate ... The physician and terminally ill patient work together to create a means by which the patient can be in control of his own mortality. The patient's subsequent private decision whether to take the medicine does not breach public peace or endanger others.'

---

[194] It is feared that suicidal ideation or depression will lead people to make erroneous choices motivated by factors which in some cases might be ameliorated. Opponents of assisted suicide therefore argue that depression may make the person incompetent to make such a decision, and also if the person was treated for depression, they might change their mind. However, depression may or may not amount to a negation of competence, as most people who know they will die in the coming months feel some degree of sadness and even depression but this does not negate their competence to make a will or refuse medical treatment. See discussion by McLean, *Assisted Dying: Reflections on the Need for Law Reform* (Routledge-Cavendish, 2007), pp 39–41.

[195] Magnusson, *Angels of Death: Exploring the Euthanasia Underground* (Yale University Press, 2002) at p 90.

[196] Detailed official statistics available at www.public.health.oregon.gov/ ProviderPartnerResources/ EvaluationResearch/DeathwithDignityAct/Documents/year18.pdf.

[197] For useful graphical representation of the complex US position see https:// www.deathwithdignity.org/take-action/.

[198] *Baxter v Montana* MT DA 09–0051, 2009 MT 449.

[12.110] Some jurisdictions impose requirements on assisted suicide based on the suffering of the patient, in other words, the patient must have had a terminal illness.[199] This would not include patients who are paralysed but not terminally ill. In Europe, countries such as Belgium,[200] Luxembourg[201] and the Netherlands[202] state that the patient must be in constant and unbearable suffering which cannot be alleviated. This is discussed further later.

'Right to die' cases in the UK

[12.111] In the absence of legislation facilitating the provision of assistance in dying there have been cases brought in a number of jurisdictions which are referred to as the 'right-to-die' cases. To look firstly at the position under English law, it had been speculated that when the ECHR was incorporated into English law, there would be a flood of litigation on issues such as assisted suicide. The Human Rights Act 1998 came into force in the UK in October 2000 and was considered in the context of an application for assisted suicide in the case of *R (On the application of Pretty) v DPP*.[203] Diane Pretty, a 42-year-old married woman, was diagnosed with motor neurone disease, which is a progressive neuro-degenerative disease of the central nervous system. The disease causes muscle weakness, difficulty in swallowing and speaking. Death usually occurs as a result of weakness in the breathing muscles, leading to respiratory failure and pneumonia. Pretty's condition had deteriorated rapidly since the diagnosis; she no longer had any movement in her arms or legs and was fed by a tube. 'Essentially she is paralysed from the neck downwards. She has virtually no decipherable speech. The disorder is now at an advanced stage and the prognosis, in particular in relation to her life expectancy, is very poor. Her intellect, however, and her capacity to make decisions are unimpaired.'

[12.112] Ms Pretty sought to be able to control the time and method of her death but, because of the nature of her illness, was unable to take her own life, an action which would not have constituted a criminal offence. She wanted her husband to be able to carry out some of the steps leading to her death, although she stated that the last acts directly leading to her death would be carried out by herself. She sought an undertaking from the Director of Public Prosecutions (DPP) that her husband would not be prosecuted if he provided such assistance. The DPP refused to give such an undertaking on the basis that it would be improper for him to decline to prosecute in advance of any breach of the criminal law. Pretty sought judicial review of that decision.

[12.113] The Court of Appeal agreed with the DPP that it was not within his power to give an undertaking regarding future criminal conduct. The Court recognised the

---

[199] Oregon Death with Dignity Act, s 1.01(12); Washington Death with Dignity Act, RCW 70.245.010(13).

[200] Act on Euthanasia, May 28, 2002, s 3(1).

[201] Loi du Mars 2009 sur l'euthanasie et l'assistance au suicide, article 1.

[202] Termination of Life on Request and Assisted Suicide (Review Procedures) Act 2001, s 2(1)(b).

[203] *R (On the application of Pretty) v DPP* [2001] UKHL 61, (2002) 35 EHRR 1, (2002) 66 BMLR 147. See English et al, 'Human Rights and Assisted Suicide' (2002) Journal of Medical Ethics 28(1): 53; Tur, 'Legislative Technique and Human Rights: the Sad Case of Assisted Suicide' (2003) Crim L Rev 3.

conflict that arose here between the right to life and the right to decide what happens to one's own body. The Court was of the view that 'English law curtails a person's right to bodily autonomy in the interest of protecting that person's life even against her own wishes. Thus, deliberate killing, even with consent and in the most pitiable of circumstances, is murder.' Tuckey LJ went on to say that the person's own wishes are not determinative of what can or must be done and that the crucial distinction was between 'killing and letting die'. English law puts helping someone to take their own life on the wrong side of the line because, as Hoffmann LJ said in *Bland,* 'the sanctity of life entails its inviolability by an outsider.'[204] The question for the Court was whether this position was in breach of that person's human rights under the ECHR. In this regard, Pretty based her argument on five articles: art 2 (right to life), art 3 (prohibition of torture and cruel and degrading treatment), art 8 (right to respect for private life), art 9 (right to freedom of thought, conscience and religion) and art 14 (prohibition of discrimination).

[12.114] Article 2 of the ECHR provides that everyone's right to life shall be protected by law and has been interpreted as requiring the State to take adequate measures to safeguard lives from attack. However, it does not require the State to prohibit suicide or force treatment on those who refuse it. Nor does it require the State to prohibit passive euthanasia. The Court concluded that art 2 might permit the State to allow assisted suicide, but could not oblige the State to do so. If the contrary were the case, people attempting suicide could not be saved by medical intervention for fear that they would have a claim for wrongful life, and that outcome was contrary to public policy. Article 3 provides that no one shall be subjected to torture or to inhuman or degrading treatment or punishment. This is an unqualified right which permits of no derogation. As with art 2, the State is obliged not only to refrain from such treatment itself, but also to take reasonable steps to ensure that people are not subjected to such treatment by others.[205] It was argued before the Court that art 3 confers the right to die with dignity. By permitting Pretty to receive the necessary help by which to end her suffering, the State would be protecting her from the degrading effects of her disease. Tuckey LJ did not accept this interpretation of the article. He held that the right to human dignity enshrined in the article was not the right to die with dignity, but the right to live with as much dignity as possible, until life reaches its natural end.[206] 'This may well mean not taking futile and undignified steps to prolong life beyond its natural death…But that is very different from allowing people to take active steps to bring life to a premature end.'

[12.115] This decision was appealed to the House of Lords which rejected the argument that Pretty's desire to end her life engaged her right under art 8 or any other Convention right. She then appealed to the European Court of Human Rights on the basis that the decision of the DPP not to grant immunity from prosecution to the applicant's husband if he assisted her in committing suicide, was contrary to Pretty's rights under arts 2, 3, 8,

---

[204] *Airedale NHS Trust v Bland* [1993] AC 789 at 831.

[205] *Costello-Roberts v UK* (1995) 19 EHRR 112; *A v UK* (1998) 27 EHRR 611; *Z v UK* E Ct HR 29392/95, 10 May 2001.

[206] He referred here to *D v UK* (1997) 42 BMLR 149, (1997) 24 EHRR 423, where it was held that deporting a person dying of AIDS to a country where he will receive no treatment or proper care amounts to inhuman or degrading treatment. This was the right to live with dignity until natural death.

9 and 14 of the Convention.[207] The Court was not persuaded by her argument that the right to life enshrined in art 2 of the Convention also inferred a negative right to end that life. 'Article 2 cannot, without a distortion of language, be interpreted as conferring the diametrically opposite right, namely a right to die; nor can it create a right to self-determination in the sense of conferring on an individual the entitlement to choose death rather than life.' Article 3 was described by the Court as imposing a primarily negative obligation on states to refrain from inflicting serious harm on persons within their jurisdictions, although the article was flexible enough to address other situations that might arise. In this case the State had not inflicted any ill-treatment on Pretty, nor had there been any complaint regarding the medical care that she was receiving. In that sense the case was distinguishable from *D v UK* where the State's act in removing the applicant to a jurisdiction where he would not have received appropriate medical treatment was impugned. Pretty's argument was that by refusing to grant immunity to her husband, the State was failing to protect her from the inevitable suffering she would endure at the end of her illness, and that this constituted inhuman treatment. The Court was of the opinion that this would place a new meaning on the word 'treatment', which was not in accordance with the fundamental objectives of the Convention. An obligation to sanction steps intended to terminate life could therefore not be derived from art 3.

[12.116] The European Court of Human Rights diverged from the House of Lords decision in relation to art 8, holding that Pretty's desire to end her life *was* engaged under that article. However, it went on to hold that the infringement of her rights under art 8 was justified under art 8(2) as a necessary and proportionate restriction which was in the public interest. The nature of that interest was 'to safeguard life by protecting the weak and vulnerable and especially those who are not in a condition to take informed decisions against acts intended to end life or to assist in ending life.'[208] The nature of the blanket ban was not disproportionate to the need to protect vulnerable citizens as the DPP had a discretion not to prosecute where this would clearly be inappropriate. While expressing sympathy for Pretty's situation, the Court similarly dismissed arguments under arts 9 and 14 of the Convention.

[12.117] The Court's ruling in relation to immunity from prosecution has been criticised on the basis that the legislative provisions in relation to assisted suicide were drafted in such wide terms due to the impossibility of crafting words that would fit only those cases deemed appropriate for prosecution. However, a blanket ban also exposes morally undeserving individuals to prosecution, depending on the view taken by the DPP. Tur says that the legislative technique adopted by the legislation 'privileges justice over certainty because in the absence of any published criteria or policy, the citizen cannot know in advance whether or not morally conscientious and excusable assisted suicide will or will not be prosecuted.[209] Thus, a couple who seeks non-criminal assisted suicide must implement their choice in order to find out whether they are at risk of prosecution.

---

[207] *Pretty v the United Kingdom*, (2002) 35 EHRR 1, Application no 2346/02, Strasbourg 29 April 2002.

[208] *Pretty v the United Kingdom*, (2002) 35 EHRR 1 at para 74.

[209] Tur, 'Legislative Technique and Human Rights: the Sad Case of Assisted Suicide' (2003) Crim L Rev 3 at 10.

'There is a peculiar cruelty or inhumanity in the law saying to them that because they respect the law so much they must endure their sad plight.'[210]

[12.118] The issue of immunity from prosecution was again the subject of judicial ruling in *R (on the application of Debbie Purdy) v DPP*[211] in which Mrs Purdy, who suffered from multiple sclerosis, was concerned about the legal position of her husband if he helped her to travel to another jurisdiction where she could lawfully be assisted to die.[212] She said that the provisions of the Suicide Act engaged her rights under art 8 of the ECHR and that the State's permitted derogation under art 8(2) 'in accordance with the law' could not apply in the absence of a specific public policy as to when the DPP would or would not prosecute in such circumstances. She was essentially seeking not an immunity from prosecution for her husband but for guidance as to the factors the DPP would take into account when deciding whether to prosecute. Her argument was that the DPP was exercising his discretion in deciding whether to prosecute and that citizens were entitled to know in an open and transparent way what factors would be considered in the exercise of that discretion. Purdy said that unless she was able to weigh up the likelihood of her husband's prosecution in advance she might have to go unaided to Switzerland in advance of when she would like. The Court of Appeal, although expressing sympathy for Purdy's plight, was of the view that it was bound by the decision in *Pretty* and did not accept the argument that the DPP's refusal to guarantee immunity to her husband breached standards of foreseeability in the law.

[12.119] Purdy then appealed to the House of Lords which reached a different conclusion. Departing from its earlier decision in *Pretty,* and following the decision of the European Court of Human Rights, the Court found that Purdy's rights under art 8 of the ECHR were engaged by the DPP's refusal to give more specific guidance on how he exercised his discretion. Giving the main judgment for the court, Lord Hope expressed his preference for the European Court of Human Rights approach in *Pretty* which recognised that the right to private life and self-determination encompassed the right not to be 'forced to linger on in old age or in states of advanced physical or mental decrepitude which conflict with strongly held ideas of self and personal identity.'[213] In relation to the issue of whether the interference with the art 8 right was in accordance with law as necessary in a democratic society, the Court held that the principle of legality required rules to be sufficiently precise, accessible and foreseeable to those affected by them. The court therefore directed the DPP to formulate an offence-specific policy identifying the factors to be considered in deciding whether or not to prosecute.

---

[210] Tur, 'Legislative Technique and Human Rights: the Sad Case of Assisted Suicide' (2003) Crim L Rev 3 at 11.

[211] *R (on the application of Debbie Purdy) v DPP* [2009] UKHL 45.

[212] See analysis by Greasley, 'The Right to Die and the Right to Help: *R (on the application of Debbie Purdy) v DPP* [2009] and its legacy' in Herring and Wall (eds) *Landmark Cases in Medical Law* (Hart Publishing, 2015) 271–294.

[213] Quoted by Greasley, 'The Right to Die and the Right to Help: *R (on the application of Debbie Purdy) v DPP* [2009] and its legacy' in Herring and Wall (eds) *Landmark Cases in Medical Law* (Hart Publishing, 2015) 271–294 at 276.

[12.120] Shortly after the ruling in *Purdy*, the DPP issued an interim policy for prosecutors, which was finalised in 2010 after public consultation.[214] Some of the factors that might result in prosecution include where the victim was under 18 years or lacked mental capacity, the victim had not reached a 'voluntary, clear, settled and informed decision to commit suicide', or had not unequivocally communicated his decision, the suspect was not wholly motivated by compassion or had pressurised the victim to commit suicide, or the suspect was a healthcare professional or carer or person in authority and the victim was in his or her care. Factors against prosecution include where the 'the actions of the suspect, although sufficient to come within the definition of the offence, were of only minor encouragement or assistance', the suspect had sought to dissuade the victim from this course of action, and had reported the suicide to the police and fully assisted them in their enquiries.[215]

[12.121] Since 2010 the DPP has published a number of accounts of cases in which the policy has been applied. For example, in a case in 2010, the suspect's acts of booking a hotel room in Switzerland for his parents and accompanying them there were described as of minor assistance.[216] Providing medication, setting up a drip or crushing or dissolving tablets for the patient is likely to make prosecution more likely than simply making travel arrangements.[217] Similar guidance is available from the DPP in Northern Ireland[218] and to some extent in Scotland.[219]

[12.122] It is not required under the guidelines in England that the victim must be terminally ill but one of the factors mitigating against prosecution is that the suspect was motivated by compassion, which might mean relief of the victim's suffering. Jackson also notes that the involvement of healthcare professionals is more likely to result in their prosecution even though they are unlikely to be motivated other than by compassion.[220] She says this might make it more likely that doctors may be nervous about giving patients their medical records to take with them to Dignitas in case this is seen as providing assistance. However, the General Medical Council has stated that simply providing a patient who wishes to have an assisted death with a copy of their notes would not be sufficient to challenge a doctor's fitness to practise.[221] The

---

[214] See discussion by Lewis, 'Informal Legal Change on Assisted Suicide: The Policy for Prosecutors' (2011) Legal Studies Vol 31 No 1 p 119–134.

[215] See http://www.cps.gov.uk/publications/prosecution/assisted_suicide_policy.html.

[216] See DPP decision on prosecution: the death of Sir Edward and Lady Downes (2010) available at www.cps.gov.uk.

[217] Lewis, 'Informal Legal Change on Assisted Suicide: The Policy for Prosecutors' (2011) Legal Studies Vol 31 No 1, at 121.

[218] See News Release 'PPS Publishes Policy on Assisted Suicide' (25 February 2010), available at http://www.ppsni.gov.uk.

[219] Unlike England and Wales, Scotland has no statutory crime of assisting suicide. The Crown Office and Procurator Fiscal Service has published a Prosecution Code which sets out the factors that would be considered in relation to a decision whether or not to prosecute a crime. Available at www.copfs.gov.uk. This was unsuccessfully challenged in the *Petition of Gordon Ross (AP) for Judicial review* [2015] CSOH 123

[220] Jackson, *Medical law: Text, Cases and Materials* (3rd edn, 2014) at 888.

[221] General Medical Council 'Guidance for the investigation committee and case examiners when considering allegations about a doctor's involvement in encouraging or assisting suicide' (2012) www.gmc-uk.org.

preference for non-healthcare professional assisters is questionable from a practical perspective as the involvement of doctors is less likely to result in botched suicide attempts and more screening for depression or other mental health issues.[222]

> Botched suicides assisted by amateurs and ill considered decisions to die by some of the most vulnerable people in society are the likely outcomes of the assisted dying policy of the DPP... It is a hard truth to face, but it takes expertise to achieve a humane assisted death. By ruling out medical involvement, the DPP policy ensures that no such expertise will accumulate.[223]

[12.123] Seale also makes the point that the preference for amateur assisters also puts those who have no family and friends in a difficult position. Such a person might reasonably turn to a third party such as a doctor or solicitor for assistance in such circumstances. This was argued in *R (Martin) v Director of Public Prosecutions*[224] where Mr Martin said the DPP's policy was defective unless it enabled him and those who might be prepared to assist him to know as a matter of probability whether a particular course of conduct might result in their prosecution. The court disagreed and held that the DPP had done what had been asked of him by the court in *Purdy* and that the DPP could not be expected to specify in advance which particular cases would not result in prosecution as each case must be determined on its facts.

[12.124] In the most recent case on assisted suicide in England, *Nicklinson v Ministry of Justice*,[225] Tony Nicklinson was totally paralysed but retained his cognitive functions and was able to communicate by blinking his eyes and using computer software. He sought a declaration that it would not be unlawful for his doctor to terminate his life on grounds of necessity. The High Court and Court of Appeal refused his application firstly on the basis that any change in the law was a matter for Parliament, secondly that euthanasia was similar to murder and there was no defence of necessity available; and thirdly although art 8 of the ECHR was engaged in these matters there was a wide margin of appreciation given to member states which was not violated by a blanket ban on assisted death. Mr Nicklinson died a week after the court's decision but the family was given leave to appeal to the Supreme Court. Mr Nicklinson's case was joined by Mr Lamb, who argued that the law should be changed to allow him to receive assistance in dying, and Mr Martin (both of whom suffered from severe paralysis) who argued that the DPP's policy should be clearer. The latter point was rejected by the Supreme Court on the basis that the most the court could do is require the DPP to indicate the relevant factors to be taken into account, the Court could not go further and dictate what needed to be in the policy.[226]

---

[222] See discussion by Lewis, 'Informal legal change on assisted suicide: the policy for prosecutors' (2011) 31 Legal Studies 119–34.

[223] Seale, 'Do it properly or not at all' (2010) 340 British Medical Journal 1719.

[224] *R (Martin) v Director of Public Prosecutions* [2012] EWHC 2381 (Admin).

[225] *Nicklinson v Ministry of Justice* [2012] HRLR 16, (2012) 124 BMLR 191.

[226] O'Sullivan argues that the Prosecutorial Policy has (effectively) amended s 2 of the Suicide Act 1961 by making compassion/motive a definitional element of the offence. See O'Sullivan, '*Mens rea*, motive and assisted suicide: does the DPP's Policy go too far?' (2015) Legal Studies, 35: 96–113.

[12.125] The Court was unanimous in holding that the prohibition of assisted suicide does interfere with art 8 rights. However, the majority rejected the appeal on the grounds that it was for Parliament to decide whether the current law was incompatible with those rights. Four of the judges were of the view that the court lacked the authority to make such a decision which was a matter for Parliament. The other five judges accepted that the court had the competence to make such a declaration of incompatibility but three of these judges thought it would be inappropriate for the court to make such a declaration without giving Parliament the opportunity to consider and amend the law. Only Lady Hale and Lord Kerr were prepared to make a declaration of incompatibility in this case.

> This remarkable 'non-decision' is as clear a message as it is possible for a court to send a legislature that circumstances must change'... The institutions of the state are failing their citizens in not grasping the moral nettle on this issue. They are coming perilously close to an abrogation of constitutional responsibility.'[227]

[12.126] Lady Hale queried whether it is 'reasonably necessary to prohibit everyone who might want to end their own lives in order to protect those whom we regard as vulnerable to undue pressure to do so?' She perceived the universal ban on assisting suicide as forcing people such as the plaintiffs to stay alive 'not for the sake of protecting themselves, but for the sake of protecting other people' and concluded that it would be entirely possible for the legal system to devise a process for identifying those few people who should fall within a well-defined exception. She also took the view that the universal prohibition is a disproportionate interference with art 8 as 'it goes much further than is necessary to fulfil its stated aim of protecting the vulnerable' and 'fails to strike a fair balance between the rights of those who have freely chosen to commit suicide but are unable to do so without some assistance and the interests of the community as a whole.'

[12.127] The *Purdy* and *Nicklinson* decisions appear to mirror modern public debate about assisted dying. 'That debate is no longer, in the main, a contest between those who embrace an absolute principle of the sanctity of human life and those who do not, but instead a debate about how the interests some might have in a controlled death are to be balanced with the possible negative effects of relaxing the prohibition on assisted dying.'[228] Greasley points out that in neither the court cases nor the surrounding public debates has the basic moral permissibility of helping someone like Debbie Purdy or Tony Nicklinson to die come under serious scrutiny. Instead the arguments are about whether it is possible to provide codified exceptions to the ban on assisted suicide without risking abuse of vulnerable people who are not in a position to make informed decisions. This, in reality, is the nub of the problem.

[12.128] In other developments in the UK, the Falconer Commission on Assisted Dying[229] found that the current legal status of assisted dying is 'inadequate and incoherent' and that there is a strong case for providing the choice of assisted dying for

---

[227] Laurie, Harmon and Porter, *Law and Medical Ethics* (10th edn, 2016) para 18.61.

[228] Greasley, 'The Right to Die and the Right to Help: *R (on the application of Debbie Purdy) v DPP* [2009] and its legacy' in Herring and Wall (eds) *Landmark Cases in Medical Law* (Hart Publishing 2015) 271–294 at 289–90.

[229] www.commissiononassisteddying.co.uk/.

terminally ill people.[230] 'Even with skilled end of life care, the Commission finds that a comparatively small number of people who are terminally ill experience a degree of suffering towards the end of their life that they consider can only be relieved either by ending their own life, or by the knowledge that they can end their life at a time of their own choosing.'[231] Assisted dying bills have been presented to Parliament both in England and Scotland in recent years. The English Bill required a judge in the family division of the High Court to confirm that a terminally ill patient with less than six months to live has reached a voluntary, clear, settled and informed decision to control the time and manner of their death. Both Bills were defeated in Parliamentary votes.[232]

Assisted dying in Europe

[12.129] An issue that has been highlighted in the debate about assisted dying relates to death tourism, where people who seek assistance with dying choose to travel, sometimes with their partners or families, to other jurisdictions to avail of such services there. EU citizens are legally entitled to travel abroad to seek access to healthcare services that are unavailable in their own states and this form of tourism has sometimes caught public attention where spouses, parents or children of severely disabled individuals explain their desire to assist their family member to travel, commonly to Switzerland, to avail of assisted suicide procedures available in that country. Similar situations have been highlighted in England and elsewhere where the national laws prohibit assistance with dying.

[12.130] In *A Local Authority v Z*[233] a Local Authority in England applied for an injunction to prevent a man from taking his wife to Switzerland for assisted suicide. She suffered from an incurable condition called cerebellar ataxia, which meant she was unable to look after herself. Hedley J refused the application on the grounds that Mrs Z had been found to be competent and therefore entitled to make her own decisions. Any criminality in the proposed behaviour could be investigated by the appropriate authorities and acted upon as appropriate. This case did not expand on the lawfulness or otherwise of assisted suicide, as the hearing concentrated on the legitimacy of injunctive relief in the circumstances of the case.

[12.131] The majority of European countries impose criminal liability on any form of assistance to suicide. In *Koch v Germany*[234] in 2012 the applicant was the widower of a woman who had been almost completely paralysed and in need of constant care since 2002. She wished to put an end to her life, which she perceived as undignified and requested from the Federal Institute for Drugs and Medical Devices to be provided with a lethal dose of a substance to enable her to do this. The Institute turned this request

---

[230] The findings of the Commission were tainted somewhat by criticism that 9 of the 12 members had publicly stated their commitment to a change in the law before the commission was convened and that therefore the commission was predisposed to this outcome.

[231] Available at www.demos.co.uk.

[232] For further details about the English Assisted Dying Bill see http://services.parliament.uk/bills/2015-16/assisteddyingno2.html and for details of the Scottish Bill see http://www.parliament.scot/parliamentarybusiness/Bills/69604.aspx.

[233] *A Local Authority v Z* [2005] 1 FLR 740.

[234] *Koch v Germany* (2012) 56 EHRR 195.

down, arguing inter alia that art 8 of the ECHR, on which the wife of the applicant had relied, did not encompass a right to assisted suicide. She lodged an appeal against the decision but before the appeal was heard she went to Switzerland where she committed suicide with the help of the Dignitas organisation. Her widower pursued the appeal but the Administrative Court (and also the Constitutional Court) held the action was inadmissible as his rights had not been violated by the refusal to provide the relevant substance.

[12.132] On appeal to the European Court of Human Rights, it was held that since the applicant and his wife had been married for a long time, had had a very close personal relationship and the Applicant had accompanied her over the entire period of her suffering, the applicant had been affected personally by the refusal of the Federal Institute for Drugs and Medical Devices to provide the requested substance. Accordingly the German court's failure to conduct a judicial review of that decision was an unjustifiable infringement of the applicant's rights under art 8. The European Court briefly dealt with the question of whether art 8 of the ECHR granted a right to receive assistance for a suicide in certain cases. As in prior decisions, it pointed out that contracting states of the European Convention on Human Rights enjoy a wide margin of appreciation in this area. The decision whether to grant a right to an assisted suicide is largely up to the member states. Therefore, refusing to grant it does not amount to an infringement of the European Convention on Human Rights.

[12.133] In *Haas v Switzerland*[235] a 57 year old Swiss citizen who suffered from a bipolar disorder for 20 years wished to commit suicide. He attempted to obtain a lethal substance that was only available on medical prescription but was not able to obtain a prescription. Mr Haas filed applications with the domestic authorities to obtain permission to acquire the substance without prescription, but they all rejected his applications. He filed an application with the European Court of Human Rights, complaining of a violation of his right to respect for his private life. He argued that, due to the domestic courts' decisions, his right to decide the moment and the manner of his death had not been respected.

[12.134] The Court acknowledged that the right of an individual to decide how and when to end his life, provided that said individual was in a position to make up his own mind in that respect and to take the appropriate action, was one aspect of the right to respect for private life. However, the dispute here was whether or not under art 8 the State had a positive obligation to enable him to obtain, without a prescription, a substance enabling him to end his life without pain and without risk of failure. Although the Court recognised that Mr Haas might have wished to commit suicide safely, with dignity and without excessive pain, it was nevertheless of the opinion that the requirement under Swiss law for a medical prescription in order to obtain sodium pentobarbital had a legitimate aim, namely to protect people from taking hasty decisions and to prevent abuse. That was all the more true in a country such as Switzerland, which readily allowed assisted suicide.

[12.135] The Court considered that the risk of abuse inherent in a system which facilitated assisted suicide could not be underestimated. The Court agreed with the

---

[235] *Haas v Switzerland* (2001) 53 EHRR 33.

Swiss Government's argument that the restriction on access to the relevant substance was intended to protect health and public safety and to prevent crime. It also shared the view of the Federal Court that the right to life obliged States to put in place an appropriate procedure to ensure that a decision to end one's life did in fact reflect the free will of the party concerned. The Court considered that the need for a prescription, issued on the basis of a full psychiatric report, constituted a means of fulfilling that requirement. There was accordingly no violation of art 8.

[12.136] In *Gross v Switzerland*[236] the applicant did not have a terminal illness but for many years had expressed the wish to end her life as she was becoming increasingly frail with the passage of time and was unwilling to continue suffering the decline of her physical and mental faculties. She wished to be provided with access to an appropriate substance by which she could end her life but was unable to access a prescription from doctors as she did not have a terminal illness as required under relevant guidelines. The case primarily raised the question whether the State had failed to provide sufficient guidelines defining whether medical practitioners were authorised to issue a medical prescription to a person in the applicant's condition and, if so, under what circumstances.

[12.137] The Court acknowledged that there may be difficulties in finding the necessary political consensus on such controversial questions with a profound ethical and moral impact. However, these difficulties were inherent in any democratic process and could not absolve the authorities from fulfilling their task therein. The Court noted that:

> Without in any way negating the principle of the sanctity of life protected under the Convention, the Court has considered that, in an era of growing medical sophistication combined with longer life expectancies, many people are concerned that they should not be forced to linger on in old age or in states of advanced physical or mental decrepitude which conflict with strongly held ideas of self and personal identity.

The Court concluded that Swiss law, while providing the possibility of obtaining a lethal dose of sodium pentobarbital on medical prescription, did not provide sufficient guidelines ensuring clarity as to the extent of this right. Therefore there had been a violation under art 8.

Case law in other jurisdictions

[12.138] In the landmark Canadian case of *Carter v Canada*,[237] T, a patient with a fatal neurodegenerative condition, challenged the constitutionality of the Criminal Code provisions that made it illegal to aid or abet a person to commit suicide. The Supreme Court of Canada declared that the relevant provisions were incompatible with s 7 of the Canadian Charter of Rights and Freedoms[238] and are of no force or effect to the extent that they prohibit physician-assisted death for a competent adult person who clearly

---

[236] *Gross v Switzerland* [2013] ECHR 580. See Black, 'Existential suffering and the extent of the right to physician-assisted suicide in Switzerland: Gross v Switzerland [2013] ECHR 67810/ 10' (2014) Medical Law Review, Vol 22, No 1, pp 109–118.

[237] *Carter v Canada* [2015] 1 SCR 331.

[238] Section 7 provides 'Everyone has the right to life, liberty and security of the person and the right not to be deprived thereof except in accordance with the principles of fundamental justice.'

consents to the termination of life and has a grievous and irremediable medical condition (including an illness, disease or disability) that causes enduring suffering that is intolerable to the individual in the circumstances of his or her condition. The Court held:

> The right to life is engaged where the law or state action imposes death or an increased risk of death on a person, either directly or indirectly. Here, the prohibition deprives some individuals of life, as it has the effect of forcing some individuals to take their own lives prematurely, for fear that they would be incapable of doing so when they reached the point where suffering was intolerable. The rights to liberty and security of the person, which deal with concerns about autonomy and quality of life, are also engaged. An individual's response to a grievous and irremediable medical condition is a matter critical to their dignity and autonomy. The prohibition denies people in this situation the right to make decisions concerning their bodily integrity and medical care and thus trenches on their liberty. And by leaving them to endure intolerable suffering, it impinges on their security of the person.

[12.139] The Court accepted the object of the prohibition which was described in *Rodriguez v British Columbia (Attorney General)*[239] as 'the protection of the vulnerable who might be induced in moments of weakness to commit suicide.' However, the Court found that the prohibition was over-broad as its object was not, broadly, to preserve life whatever the circumstances, but more specifically to protect vulnerable persons from being induced to commit suicide at a time of weakness. Since a total ban on assisted suicide clearly helps achieve this object, individuals' rights are not deprived arbitrarily. However, the prohibition also catches people outside the class of protected persons. It follows that the limitation on their rights is in at least some cases not connected to the objective and that the prohibition is thus overbroad.

[12.140] The court was satisfied that a system with properly designed and administered safeguards offered a less restrictive means of reaching the government's objective. The Court suspended its declaration of invalidity for one year in order to give Parliament time to develop an appropriate regulatory regime. The relevant Bill, which is referred to as C-14, was passed in June 2016. The Bill creates exemptions from the offences of culpable homicide, of aiding suicide and of administering a noxious thing, in order to permit medical practitioners and nurse practitioners to provide medical assistance in dying and to permit pharmacists and other persons to assist in the process; specifies the eligibility criteria and the safeguards that must be respected before medical assistance in dying may be provided to a person; requires that medical practitioners and nurse practitioners who receive requests for, and pharmacists who dispense substances in connection with the provision of, medical assistance in dying provide information for the purpose of permitting the monitoring of medical assistance in dying, and authorize the Minister of Health to make regulations respecting that information; and creates new offences for failing to comply with the safeguards, for forging or destroying documents related to medical assistance in dying, for failing to provide the required information and for contravening the regulations. It provides for reviews to take place within 180 days of the Bill coming into effect to study the legal and ethical issues relating to requests by mature minors for medical assistance in dying, to advance requests and to requests where mental illness is the *sole* underlying medical condition. It also provides

---

[239] *Rodriguez v British Columbia (Attorney General)* [1993] 3 SCR 519.

for a parliamentary review of its provisions and of the state of palliative care in Canada to commence five years after commencement.

[12.141] One of the most contentious aspects of the Bill during the parliamentary debates was whether it should be limited to those with terminal illnesses. The Bill as passed will allow assisted dying only for consenting adults who have a grievous and irremediable medical condition. To be considered as having a grievous and irremediable medical condition, the person must meet all of the following conditions. The person must

- have a serious illness, disease or disability
- be in an advanced state of decline that cannot be reversed
- be suffering unbearably from the illness, disease, disability or state of decline; and,
- be at a point where natural death has become reasonably foreseeable, which takes into account all medical circumstances

It is therefore not necessary to have a fatal or terminal condition to be eligible for medical assistance in dying.[240]

[12.142] The issue of assisted suicide has also been explored in the South African case of *Stransham Ford v Minister of Justice and Correctional Service* in 2015[241] in which the court held that the Canadian Charter of Rights is very similar to the South African Bill of Rights and therefore the reasoning of the Canadian Supreme Court in Carter case was 'not only enlightening but very persuasive'. In this case a lawyer with advanced terminal cancer sought an order enabling him to lawfully receive assistance from a doctor to end his life. In his view, assisted dying was the only way that he would be released from his eventual unbearable suffering and for him to prevent the imminent intolerable and undignified suffering that was to occur in the future.[242]

[12.143] Fabricius J agreed with the contention that 'it is a fundamental human right to be able to die with dignity' and that although there were palliative care options open to the applicant, 'a decision of a person on how to cease to live was in many instances a decision very important to their own sense of dignity and personal integrity, and that was consistent with their lifelong values and that reflected their life's experience.' He quoted from *S v Makwanyane*[243] in which O'Reagan J discussed the notion that the right to life must be a life that is worth living:

> The right to life is, in one sense, antecedent to all other rights in the Constitution. Without life in the sense of existence, it would not be possible to exercise rights or to be the bearer of them. But the right to life was included in the Constitution not simply to enshrine the right to existence. It is not life as mere organic matter that the Constitution cherishes, but the right to human life: the right to share in the experience of humanity. This concept of human life is at centre of our constitutional values. The Constitution seeks to establish a

---

[240] For more details see www.canada.ca/health.

[241] *Stransham Ford v Minister of Justice and Correctional Service* [2015] 3 All SA 109 (GP) (4 May 2015).

[242] The applicant is reported to have died peacefully a few hours before the judgment was delivered.

[243] *S v Makwanyane* [1995] ZACC 3, 1995 (3) SA 391 (CC).

society where the individual value of each member of the community is recognised and treasured. The right to life is central to such a society. The right to life, thus understood, incorporates the right to dignity. So the rights to dignity and to life are intertwined. The right to life is more than existence, it is a right to be treated as a human being with dignity: without dignity, human life is substantially diminished. Without life, there cannot be dignity.'

[12.144] Fabricius J held that the Applicant was a mentally competent adult who had freely and voluntarily, and without undue influence requested the Court to authorize that he be assisted in an act of suicide. He held that the Applicant was entitled to be assisted by a qualified medical doctor, who is willing to do so, to end his life, either by administration of a lethal agent or by providing the Applicant with the necessary lethal agent to administer himself. No doctor was obliged to accede to the applicant's request but any doctor that did so would not be subject to prosecution. The learned judge also held that the common law crimes of murder or culpable homicide in the context of assisted suicide by medical practitioners, insofar as they provide for an absolute prohibition, unjustifiably limit the Applicant's constitutional rights to human dignity, and freedom to bodily and psychological integrity and to that extent were declared to be overbroad and in conflict with the Bill of Rights. This case is currently under appeal to the Supreme Court of Appeal.

[12.145] The inconsistencies in the current legal framework of many jurisdictions were also recognised in the recent report of the Legal and Social Issues Committee of the Parliament of Victoria, Australia:

> On the one hand, doctors, on a patient's request, can withdraw life sustaining treatment with death the certain outcome, while they can also deliver lethal doses of morphine and other drugs, as long as the intent is to relieve pain. On the other hand, a loving husband who assists his frail, suffering and near death wife to die could be guilty of murder, while a person near death and in unacceptable pain, cannot receive help to end their own suffering.[244]

In recommending an assisted dying framework, the Committee sought to 'strike an appropriate balance between respecting the end of life choices of Victorians while recommending a sufficiently robust eligibility framework for competent adults that protects against abuse.'

[12.146] It might therefore be said that with legislative developments in the United States, case law in Canada and South Africa, as well as some of the judges' comments in the English case of *Nicklinson*, there appears to be an inexorable movement towards greater recognition of the need to strike a more appropriate balance between a right to assistance in dying as an aspect of respect for the individual's right to life (of which dying with dignity is a part) and the State's interest in protecting the principle of the sanctity of life and potentially vulnerable members of society.

---

[244] Legislative Council, Legal and Social Issues Committee, Parliament of Victoria, *Inquiry into end of life choices* (June 2016) xvi.

Irish case law

[12.147] The case of *Fleming v Ireland*[245] in 2013 was the first Irish case to deal with assisted dying. The appellant Marie Fleming was 59 years of age and suffering from multiple sclerosis since 1989. At the time of the hearing she was unable to control an electric wheelchair, had no bladder control, and required assistance to eat and drink, and to be washed, dressed and repositioned in her wheelchair. The appellant also frequently experienced choking episodes which were frightening, distressing and exhausting for her. She had severe pain in her head, eyes, temples, neck, back, arms, hands, hips, and legs. The appellant reported taking maximum doses of analgesia as a result of which she suffered side effects such as dry mouth, heart palpitations, drowsiness and nausea. Ms Fleming had no underlying mental illness that might be likely to affect her decision-making capacity.

[12.148] While the appellant considered travelling to Switzerland to avail of the facility offered by Dignitas to end her own life five years previously, she postponed the decision because of the wishes of her partner and the location of the clinic. The appellant claimed that she would now end her life if she were able to do so and regrets not doing so before she lost the use of her arms. The appellant stated that she was living with little or no dignity and she was horrified at the thought of enduring months without being able to communicate, in pain and isolation, with full consciousness or being heavily sedated to the point of being barely conscious. Her wish and her request to the Court were for assistance in having a peaceful dignified death in the arms of her partner and with her children in attendance. There were several methods of suicide contemplated by the appellant all of which would require assistance in advance by another person, most likely her partner. She was not prepared to progress this plan if it exposed him to the risk of criminal prosecution. She was therefore challenging the constitutionality of s 2(2) of the Criminal Law (Suicide) Act 1993, as well as an order declaring that this provision is incompatible with the obligations of the State under the European Convention on Human Rights.

[12.149] In the High Court[246] Kearns P giving judgment for the court, observed that there are 'profound and different moral, ethical, philosophical and religious views on the question of end-of-life decisions such as the issue in controversy here.' He went on to acknowledge that inasmuch as Ms Fleming was advancing 'a conscientious and considered decision to seek the assistance of others to take active steps to end her own life in the face of a terminal illness which has ravaged her body and rendered her life one of almost complete misery', the court considered that 'such a decision is *in principle* engaged by the right to personal autonomy which lies at the core of the protection of the person by Article 40.3.2°.' However he went on to say that the court had chosen the words 'in principle' advisedly, because it considers that there are here powerful countervailing considerations which fully justify the Oireachtas in enacting legislation such as the 1993 Act which makes the assistance of suicide a criminal offence:

> The Court believes there is a real and defining difference between a competent adult patient making the decision not to continue medical treatment on the one hand – even if

---

[245] *Fleming v Ireland* [2013] IEHC 2, [2013] IESC 19.
[246] *Fleming v Ireland* [2013] IEHC 2.

death is the natural, imminent and foreseeable consequence of that decision - and the taking of *active steps* by *another* to bring about the end of that life of the other. The former generally involves the passive acceptance of the natural process of dying, a fate that will ultimately confront us all, whereas the latter involves the *active* ending of the life of *another* – a totally different matter.[247]

[12.150] While the court accepted the right of a competent adult not to be compelled to accept medical treatment even if this hastened the person's death, the taking of active steps by a third party to bring about death was 'an entirely different matter, even if this is desired and wished for by an otherwise competent adult who sincerely and conscientiously desires this outcome.' Kearns P went on to say:

> *If* this Court could be satisfied that it would be possible to tailor-make a solution which would address the needs of Ms. Fleming *alone* without any *possible* implications for third parties or society at large, there might be a good deal to be said in favour of her case. But this Court cannot be so satisfied.[248]

The court noted that it may be possible for the Oireachtas to conceive of a solution to the acute personal and ethical dilemmas presented by this and other similar cases which would provide for extensive safeguards of the kind said to be found in the regulatory regime prevailing in jurisdictions such as Switzerland, the Netherlands and certain US states such as Washington and Oregon which have liberalised the law in this area. These safeguards might include 'a requirement that the patient is terminally ill; that he or she is facing intolerable pain; that the patient has been examined by a range of physicians over a period of time and has been appropriately counselled; that steps are taken to ensure that the patient is competent and not suffering from depression; that the patient has a settled will to bring about his or her end in this fashion and that the proposed course of action is reported to the appropriate authorities.'

[12.151] Kearns P went on say however that even if legislation were to be introduced with such safeguards as outlined, serious concerns would remain. For example, there might be an incorrect diagnosis of the patient, and it is impossible to predict with accuracy the duration and course of a terminal illness. The level of pain a person is prepared to accept will also vary from person to person and is difficult to objectively assess. Also, Kearns P noted that expert witnesses had powerfully expressed to the Court their concerns in relation to potentially vulnerable people who might put themselves under pressure to seek assisted suicide in order not to be a burden to their families. Their evidence was that relaxing the ban on assisted suicide would bring about a paradigm shift with unforeseeable (and perhaps uncontrollable) changes in attitude and behaviour to assisted suicide, matters which struck the Court as 'compelling and deeply worrying':

> If this Court were to unravel a thread of this law by even the most limited constitutional adjudication in her favour, it would – or, at least, might – open a Pandora's Box which thereafter would be impossible to close. In particular, by acting in a manner designed to respect her conscientious claims and to relieve her acute suffering and distress, this Court might thereby place the lives of others at risk. The Court is well aware that such is not the intention of Ms. Fleming and we are fully conscious that those who urge such change profoundly disclaim any such intention. But such might well be the unintended *effect* of

---

[247] *Fleming v Ireland* [2013] IEHC 2 para 53.
[248] *Fleming v Ireland* [2013] IEHC 2 para 55.

such a change, specifically because of the inability of even the most rigorous system of legislative checks and balances to ensure, in particular, that the aged, the disabled, the poor, the unwanted, the rejected, the lonely, the impulsive, the financially compromised and the emotionally vulnerable would not disguise their own personal preferences and elect to hasten death so as to avoid a sense of being a burden on family and society. The safeguards built into any liberalised system would, furthermore, be vulnerable to laxity and complacency and might well prove difficult or even impossible to police adequately.

[12.152] Ms Fleming argued that she was discriminated against by virtue of her disability in that she was prevented from taking her own life, an action that had been decriminalised by the Suicide Act 1993. In rejecting this claim, the Court acknowledged that inasmuch as the 1993 Act failed to make separate provision for persons in the plaintiff's position, the precept of equality in art 40.1 is here engaged. But the Court considered that this differential treatment was amply justified by the range of factors bearing on the necessity to safeguard the lives of others. The court again stressed the 'profound difference between the law permitting an adult to take their own life on the one hand and sanctioning another to assist that person to that end on the other. This is true even if the very disability under which the plaintiff labours is the very reason she needs the assistance of others to accomplish this task.'

[12.153] Ms Fleming argued that the Suicide Act 1993 was incompatible with her rights under the European Convention on Human Rights (ECHR). However, the court held that although her art 8 rights were engaged by the provisions, the interference with such rights was justified under art 8(2) as the ban on assisted suicide was 'rationally connected to legitimate state interests pressing in a democratic society, namely, the protection of the right to life, especially of the vulnerable. The prohibition is a proportionate measure designed to promote those interests and the objective it serves cannot be achieved in any less intrusive fashion.'[249]

[12.154] An argument was also put to the court that Ms Fleming and her partner were unaware of the principles or guidelines or policies that may be adopted or followed by the office of the Director of Public Prosecutions (DPP) in deciding, in particular cases, whether to prosecute or consent to the prosecution of a person who assists someone in Ms Fleming's position in procuring her own death. It was argued that the court should follow the principle set out in the English case of *R (Purdy) v DPP*[250] in which the House of Lords ruled that the lack of a published policy of the (UK) DPP in relation to prosecutions under equivalent provisions of UK law rendered the relevant law insufficiently clear, accessible and precise to permit a person potentially affected by it to know the degree to which it would affect his or her actions and that this amounted to an unjustified intrusion into the private life of a person such as Mrs Purdy. As a result the existing law and code of prosecution failed to meet the requirements for clarity imposed in respect of any such intrusion, by art 8(2) of the schedule to the Human Rights Act 1998 (UK), that is art 8(2) of the European Convention on Human Rights. The House of Lords ruled that the DPP should adopt and publish an offence specific policy identifying the facts and circumstances that would be taken into account in deciding whether or not

---

[249] *Fleming v Ireland* [2013] IEHC 2 para 124.
[250] *R (Purdy) v DPP* [2010] 1 AC 345 discussed above at para **[12.118]**.

to prosecute such an offence. Lawyers for Ms Fleming in this case argued that there existed no good reason for any different form of direction or order in the Irish courts.

[12.155] Kearns P stated that the decision in the *Purdy* case has limited relevance in this jurisdiction as there is no express power conferred on the DPP in Ireland to do what was ordered in the United Kingdom. 'On the contrary, it would amount to forcing her into adopting a role which would in effect override statutory measures laid down by the Oireachtas.' The Court held that the DPP exercises a discretion *ex post facto* in relation to the facts of any incidents brought to her notice. 'Guidelines for prosecutors do not and cannot provide for offence specific criteria referable to the decision to prosecute.' However, Kearns P went on to say that 'the very fact that UK guidelines on assisted suicide now exist must surely inform any exercise of discretion by the Director in this jurisdiction. Without being compelled in an impermissible way under our law to issue offence-specific guidelines, the Director in this jurisdiction is nonetheless in as good a position as the Director in the UK as an incidental beneficiary of what happened in that jurisdiction.' The DPP would therefore have extensive material to provide guidance whether or not to prosecute in a given case.

[12.156] Somewhat unusually perhaps the judgment of the court concluded with a statement that might be interpreted as indicating the Court's preference for how the DPP might deal with a case of assisted suicide along the facts as presented by Ms Fleming:

> The Court feels sure that the Director, in this of all cases, would exercise her discretion in a humane and sensitive fashion, while it would stress that, of course, she must retain the full ambit of that discretion to decide whether to prosecute or not.

This approach has been described as the court trying to have it both ways.[251] On the one hand that court held that the DPP is precluded from issuing guidelines as this would amount to altering existing law by indicating in advance who might and might not be prosecuted for a particular offence. On the other hand, the court held that the DPP is free to exercise discretion after the event not to prosecute and should take into account guidelines made in another jurisdiction when exercising such discretion. 'The decision suggests that the DPP cannot legally do what is done in England – but also that in truth, we expect her to deal with cases in exactly the same way, based on the very guidelines that she is not entitled to issue.'

[12.157] On appeal to the Supreme Court, Denham CJ giving judgment for the court stated 'There is no explicit right to commit suicide, or to determine the time of one's death, in the Constitution.'[252] Therefore any such right would have to be found as part of another expressed right or in an unenumerated right. Denham CJ referred to *In Re a Ward (withholding medical treatment) (No 2)*[253] where Hamilton CJ stated:[254]

> As the process of dying is part, and an ultimate inevitable consequence, of life, the right to life necessarily implies the right to have nature take its course and to die a natural death and, unless the individual concerned so wishes, not to have life artificially maintained by the provision of nourishment by abnormal artificial means, which have no curative effect

---

[251] O'Mahony, 'DPP needs clear protocols after assisted suicide ruling,' (2013) Irish Times Jan 15
[252] *Fleming v Ireland* [2013] IESC 19 para 99.
[253] *Ward (withholding medical treatment) (No 2)* [1996] 2 IR 79.
[254] *Ward (withholding medical treatment) (No 2)* [1996] 2 IR 79 at 124.

and which is intended merely to prolong life. This right, as so defined, does not include the right to have life terminated or death accelerated and is confined to the natural process of dying. No person has the right to terminate or to have terminated his or her life or to accelerate or have accelerated his or her life.

Denham CJ said 'That case decided that the right to life extended to a right to die a natural death or let nature take its course. While at the extremity of any principle distinctions may be fine, nevertheless a competent patient who refuses treatment is making a decision as to how to live the reminder of his or her life even when death results. That case did not decide, therefore, that there was a right to terminate life or a right to have it terminated.'

[12.158] Denham CJ said that the State has a positive obligation to protect life. However the precise extent of the State's obligation in any given circumstance is a matter which may require careful analysis and, at least in some cases, a careful balancing of other constitutional considerations. While the State is required to seek to discourage suicide generally and to adopt measures designed to that end, 'it does not, however, necessarily follow that the State has an obligation to use all of the means at its disposal to seek to prevent a person in a position such as that of the appellant from bringing her own life to an end'. She indicated that perhaps this was a matter for the legislature to decide, bearing in mind the balance to be struck and the practical application of any such measures that might be adopted:

> Nothing in this judgment should be taken as necessarily implying that it would not be open to the State, in the event that the Oireachtas were satisfied that measures with appropriate safeguards could be introduced, to legislate to deal with a case such as that of the appellant. If such legislation was introduced it would be for the courts to determine whether the balancing by the Oireachtas of any legitimate concerns was within the boundaries of what was constitutionally permissible.[255]

[12.159] Denham CJ said while it was possible to construct a libertarian argument that the State is not entitled to interfere with the decisions made by a person in respect of his or her own life up to and including a decision to terminate it, it was not possible 'to discern support for such a theory in the provisions of the Constitution, without imposing upon it a philosophy and values not detectable from it.' Since there was no right to commit suicide under the Constitution, the Appellant was not being treated unequally nor was she discriminated against by the failure to allow her assistance in committing suicide which she was unable to do unaided due to the level of her disability.

[12.160] In relation to the appellant's arguments that the provisions of the Suicide Act were incompatible with the ECHR, Denham CJ reiterated the principles adopted by the ECtHR in *Pretty v United Kingdom*[256] and *Haas v Switzerland*,[257] discussed earlier. She went on to say that States are entitled to regulate activities which are detrimental to the life and safety of persons and that the ECtHR had held that it was primarily for the States to assess the risk and likely incidence of abuse if the general prohibition on assisted suicides were relaxed, or if exceptions were to be made. She pointed out that in Ireland the complex issue of assisted suicide has been assessed, and the legislature has

---

[255] *Fleming v Ireland* [2013] IESC 19 at para 108.
[256] *Pretty v United Kingdom* (Appl No 2346/02).
[257] *Haas v Switzerland* (Appl No 31322/07).

legislated on it in s 2(2) of the 1993 Act. Therefore the arguments on the basis of incompatibility were dismissed.

[12.161] Although the protection of personal autonomy was recognised by the High and Supreme Courts in Fleming as a core constitutional value, there is no further guidance or explanation of how autonomy is to be interpreted in this context or what weight is to be given to it.[258] Campbell argues that this is significant insofar as autonomy is said to be a *right* protected by the Constitution. 'Autonomy appears almost parenthetically in Irish jurisprudence, loosely interpreted as a general capacity for self-rule or self-determination: the ability to govern oneself and make one's own choices without undue interference.' She says Marie Fleming's actions were those of a competent, rational individual with a clear and settled desire to end a life which she found incompatible with her sense of what life should be:

> It is difficult to see how the interests of the vulnerable can be served by condemning someone in Ms Fleming's situation to live a life so entirely at odds with her own purposes. This complex, tragic case and others similar to it highlight the value of autonomy and underscore the point that 'to respect autonomy only when it is cost-free or not socially disruptive is to fail to take it seriously.'[259]

EUTHANASIA

[12.162] The word 'euthanasia' comes from the Greek expression for a good death but in modern usage, it is usually taken to mean a situation in which a doctor kills a patient at the patient's request. As discussed above, while it is generally accepted in most jurisdictions, including Ireland, that doctors must respect their patient's decisions to be allowed to die, killing a patient, even with the patient's consent or at their request, is regarded as morally and legally different.[260] Euthanasia is different from assisted suicide in that in the former it is the doctor's actions that bring about the death of the patient, whereas in the latter the patient takes the final steps to commit suicide themselves, albeit with the assistance of the doctor who has prescribed the necessary medication to enable the patient to do so.

[12.163] The most common distinction drawn between killing and allowing someone to die is based on the difference between acts and omissions resulting in death. A person kills if he does something that causes another to die who otherwise would not have died. A person allows someone to die if he has the ability and opportunity to prevent someone from dying, but does not act to prevent the death. Rachels describes the distinction between acts and omissions as follows:

---

[258] See discussion by Campbell, 'The limits of autonomy: an exploration of the role of autonomy in the debate about assisted suicide' in Donnelly and Murray (eds) *Ethical and legal debates in Irish healthcare, Confronting Complexities* (Manchester Univ Press 2016) 55–70.

[259] Campbell, at 66 quoting from Gaylin and Jennings, *The Perversion of Autonomy: Coercion and Constraints in a Liberal Society* (Georgetown Univ Press 2003) at 45.

[260] Otlowski argues that this alleged distinction reveals an element of self-deception which may assist doctors in justifying their conduct in permitting patients to die. Otlowski, *Voluntary Euthanasia and the Common Law* (OUP, 1997) at 192.

In the first, Smith stands to gain a large inheritance if anything should happen to his six-year old cousin. One evening, while the child is taking his bath, Smith sneaks into the bathroom and drowns the child, and then arranges things so that it will look like an accident. In the second, Jones also stands to gain if anything happens to his six-year old cousin. Like Smith, Jones sneaks in planning to drown the child in his bath. However, just as he enters the bathroom Jones sees the child slip and hit his head, and fall face down in the water. Jones is delighted; he stands by, ready to push the child's head back under if it is necessary, but it is not necessary. With only a little thrashing about, the child drowns all by himself, 'accidentally,' as Jones watches and does nothing.[261]

[12.164] The question for the law is whether in the foregoing example Smith, who kills, is more culpable than Jones, who allows the child to die. If, as Rachels argues, there is no moral difference between the two, then the fact that one is killing and the other is allowing the child to die, is not a morally important difference. When it comes to medical decision-making at the end of life, the same kind of reasoning may apply. According to this argument, if, for example, a doctor satisfies his patient's request to switch off the ventilator, he kills his patient just in the same way as if the patient's son, impatient for his inheritance, went into the room and unplugged the machine. When the doctor removes the ventilator he performs an action that causes the patient to die, when otherwise they would have continued to live, in other words, he kills. The intention and effect are the same in both scenarios, although clearly the motivation is different. In the case of the doctor, his actions would probably be held to be justifiable, whereas in the case of the son, they would not.

[12.165] 'One can kill or allow to die with or without the victim's consent, with a good or bad motive and in or not a social role that authorises such action; these factors determine whether what was done was morally justified, not whether it is a case of killing or allowing to die.'[262] The term 'active euthanasia' is sometimes used to refer to the deliberate killing of a patient at her request, whereas the term 'passive euthanasia' describes the withholding or withdrawal of life-prolonging medical treatment. Otlowski neatly summarises the legal position as follows:

> A doctor may lawfully perform passive euthanasia at the request of a competent patient: that is, he or she may, at the patient's request, deliberately withhold or withdraw treatment with the intention of facilitating the patient's death. This conclusion, in turn, highlights the law's starkly differential treatment of active and passive euthanasia. A doctor who performs active euthanasia will potentially face criminal liability for murder even in circumstances where the acts causing death were performed at the patient's request. Yet, a doctor who withholds or withdraws treatment at the request of a competent patient, intending that the patient's death will result, will not be criminally liable for the patient's death. Thus, even though the object and end result of active and passive euthanasia are the same, the legal consequences are vastly different.[263]

[12.166] One may consider the example of the patient with a potentially lethal disease that is prevented from causing the patient's death by the intervention of the doctor's application of life-sustaining treatment. When the treatment is withdrawn, even though

---

[261] Rachels, 'Active and Passive Euthanasia' (1975) New Eng J of Med 292/2, 78–80.

[262] Brock, *Life and Death: Philosophical Essays in Biomedical Ethics* (Cambridge University Press, 1993) p 238.

[263] Otlowski, *Voluntary Euthanasia and the Common Law* (OUP, 1997) at 55.

this involves action by the doctor, the patient is allowed to die, and the doctor's actions are justifiable, because the disease proceeds to kill the patient. However, this would mean that the impatient son in the example above also simply allows his mother to die.[264] Similarly, with the decision not to place the patient on life support in the first place, for example, in the case of a patient who is dying of cancer and who suffers respiratory failure: doing nothing in those circumstances may be acceptable. However, doing nothing is not always justifiable, as where a doctor deliberately lets a patient die who was suffering from a routinely curable disease. In such a case, the doctor's actions are the same, in that he allows the disease to kill the patient, but in the latter case he would be prosecuted.

[12.167] Gillon argues against the *necessary* moral equivalence of killing and letting die though he does acknowledge that there are cases in which they are equivalent.[265] He claims that there is a strong universal prohibition on killing but a much more ambivalent attitude to letting die, and that this arises from the assumption that all of us owe a strong duty to all others not to kill each other, but that we may or may not, depending on the circumstances, owe a duty to each other to preserve each other's lives. Consequentialist arguments may be brought to bear on why the distinction between the two should be maintained, ranging from the public perception of the higher culpability of someone who kills, the costs of keeping people alive as opposed to killing them, the 'harm' inflicted on the patient in killing as opposed to letting die and the respect accorded to the patient's autonomy in each case. By contrast, Otlowski argues from the perspective of patient autonomy, that it is an unjustifiable infringement of liberty to deny active voluntary euthanasia to those who choose it.[266] Harris argues similarly, that it is a form of tyranny, an attempt to control the life of a person who has his own autonomous view about how life should go, and that this constitutes an ultimate denial of respect for persons.[267]

The doctrine of double effect

[12.168] In the treatment of certain illnesses, such as cancer, it sometimes becomes necessary to administer large doses of pain killing drugs to ease the patient's suffering. These drugs may carry higher risks of causing respiratory depression and hastening the

---

[264] For a detailed philosophical perspective on this issue, see Quinn, 'Actions, Intentions and Consequences: The Doctrine of Doing and Allowing' (1989) The Philosophical Review, Vol XCVIII, No 3.

[265] Gillon, 'Euthanasia, Withholding Life-Prolonging Treatment, and Moral Differences Between Killing and Letting Die' (1988) Journal of Medical Ethics, 14:115–117.

[266] It seems ironical that a competent patient who is terminally ill cannot lawfully request medication to induce death, yet an incompetent patient in PVS who has not expressed a wish to die, may have nutrition and hydration withdrawn in his best interests. Otlowski, *Voluntary Euthanasia and the Common Law* (OUP, 1997). Also see Sloss, 'The Right to Choose How to Die: A Constitutional Analysis of State Laws Prohibiting Physician-Assisted Suicide' (1996) 48 Stanford L Rev 937: 'Of course the law must limit the extent to which physicians may act to hasten a patient's death, but should the law define those limits to permit involuntary physician-assisted euthanasia of incompetent, non-terminal patients ... while prohibiting voluntary physician-assisted euthanasia for competent, terminally ill patients ...?'

[267] Harris, 'Euthanasia and the Value of Life' in Keown, (ed) *Euthanasia Examined: Ethical, Clinical and Legal Perspectives* (Cambridge University Press, 1995) 6 at 19.

patient's death.[268] Most would agree that not to administer such drugs would result in unacceptable pain for the dying patient, and therefore the actions of the doctor are justified on the basis of his intention to relieve suffering as opposed to bring on the patient's death.[269] The doctrine of double effect is invoked here to substantiate the argument.[270] The doctrine distinguishes between the consequences a person intends and those that are unintended but foreseen.[271] It holds that an action with a bad consequence, such as the patient's death, is justifiable if that consequence is not intended and is necessary to achieve a proportionately good effect, here, the relief of the patient's pain.[272]

[12.169] There are cases in which the distinction between foresight and intention are blurred, but in relation to pain control it seems clear that the death of the patient is an unintended but foreseen side-effect and therefore morally permissible.[273] The doctor must clearly have reached the conclusion that death is an acceptable outcome for this patient in the circumstances as, for example, if the doctor gave an otherwise healthy patient with a mild headache a lethal injection, this would be a deliberate act causing death, and would be morally prohibited.[274] 'She could not claim that her intention was

---

[268] The World Health Organisation (WHO) states, 'If shortening of life results from the use of adequate doses of an analgesic drug, this is not the same as intentionally terminating life by overdose'. WHO *Cancer Pain Relief and Palliative Care* (Geneva: 1990).

[269] See comments by Devlin J in *R v Adams* (8 April 1957), where he noted that the doctrine of double effect permits doctors to relieve pain, even if this incidentally shortens life by hours or even longer. See Palmer, 'Dr Adams' Trial for Murder' (1957) Crim L Rev 365. Also see comments by Lord Goff in *Airedale NHS Trust v Bland* [1993] AC 789 where he said that it was an established rule that a doctor caring for a patient who was dying from cancer could 'lawfully administer pain-killing drugs despite the fact that he knows that an incidental effect of that application will be to abbreviate the patient's life.'

[270] The doctrine of double effect is thought to have originated with some Roman Catholic theologians such as Thomas Aquinas but has now become part of general moral philosophical doctrine. The doctrine has four conditions. First, the action itself must not be inherently wrong. Secondly, the intention must be solely to produce the good effect. Thirdly, the good effect must not be achieved through the means of the bad effect. Fourthly, there must be a favourable balance between the good and the bad effects of the action. The doctrine may be applied in the area of self-defence where the desired end is to avoid harm, all other effects being unintended, and has traditionally been used in arguments on abortion where the woman's life is endangered by continuation of the pregnancy. See Dunstan, 'Double Effect' in Dunstan, Dunstan and Wellbourn (eds) *Dictionary of Medical Ethics* (2nd edn, Darton, Longman and Todd Ltd, 1981) p 145; Price, 'Euthanasia, Pain Relief and Double Effect' (1997) 17(2) Legal Studies 323–342.

[271] Quill, Lo and Brock, 'Palliative Options of Last Resort: A Comparison of Voluntarily Stopping Eating and Drinking, Terminal Sedation, Physician-Assisted Suicide, and Voluntary Active Euthanasia' (1997) 278 JAMA 2099; and Meisel, Snyder and Quill, 'Seven Legal Barriers to End-of-Life Care' (2000) 284 JAMA 2495.

[272] Bole, 'Double Effect: Theoretical Function and Bioethical Implications' (1991) Journal of Medicine and Philosophy, Vol 16: 467–585.

[273] In the same way as surgery is lawful even though there is a chance of death. See Emanuel, 'Why Now?' in Emanuel (ed) *Regulating How We Die: Ethical, Medical and Legal Issues Surrounding Physician Assisted Suicide* (Harvard University Press, 1998).

[274] Jackson, *Medical Law: Text, cases and* materials (3rd edn, 2013) p 894. See also Brock, *Life and Death: Philosophical Essays in Biomedical Ethics* (Cambridge University Press, 1993), at 239.

merely to relieve pain and that the patient's death was a foreseen but unintended side effect. Instead, while death may not be the *principal* purpose of a doctor who administers a potentially lethal dose of opioids, she must have decided that the patient's interest in pain relief now outweighs her interest in continued life.'[275]

[12.170] As an alternative to pain relieving drugs that shorten life, terminal sedation of a patient may be performed[276] to induce a state of decreased consciousness and take away the patient's perception of distressing symptoms. These sedating drugs may be used intermittently or continuously until death, and the depth of the sedation can vary from a lowered state of consciousness to unconsciousness before withdrawal of a ventilator, or to relieve pain where other options have failed.[277] Proponents of terminal sedation who nonetheless seek to distinguish it from euthanasia or assisted suicide say that the intention of the doctor here is to sedate, not to kill, in order to relieve pain. However, this has been criticised as a smokescreen[278] and a fig-leaf for euthanasia.[279]

[12.171] One of the issues in the debate about the ethical acceptability of terminal sedation centres on whether it shortens the patient's life. When the patient's life expectancy is short, for example two weeks, when sedation is started, continuous deep sedation is thought to have no or limited effect on life shortening and thus is said not to be the moral equivalent of euthanasia. When it is used for patients with a longer life expectancy with the intention to hasten death at the patient's request, it is argued that this practice is the moral equivalent of euthanasia in that the act of inducing unconsciousness in such patients crosses the line between making the patient's suffering tolerable and terminating the patient's conscious existence.

[12.172] In the context of whether terminal sedation can be justified under the doctrine of double effect, it may be argued that terminal sedation satisfies the requirement that the treatment is beneficial to the patient, and that the doctor does not intend death but the relief of the patient's pain. However, it is also the case that the sedation may precede the withdrawal of nutrition and hydration from the patient, a procedure that is not a method of relieving pain. While the withdrawal of nutrition and hydration may satisfy the doctrine of double effect in that the death is not intended, merely foreseen, it may be argued that it does not satisfy the other prerequisites of the doctrine, namely that the nature of the act must be morally good, such as the relief of pain, and that the bad effect (death) is not a means of achieving the good effect (relief of pain). If the patient does not die from the underlying disease or the medication, he will die from starvation or dehydration.[280] Accordingly, withdrawing food and water from a terminally sedated

---

275 Jackson, *Medical Law: Text, cases and* materials (3rd edn, 2013) p 894.

276 There seems to be disagreement as to whether this is a common, widely accepted practice or an exceptional event. See Williams, 'The Principle of Double Effect and Terminal Sedation' (2001) 9 Med L Rev 41–53 at 48–49.

277 Williams, 'The Principle of Double Effect and Terminal Sedation' (2001) 9 Med L Rev 41–53. See also Rietjens et al, 'Continuous Deep Sedation for Patients Nearing Death in the Netherlands: Descriptive Study' (2008) BMJ Vol 336 No 7648.

278 Clarke, 'What is the Doctrine of Double Effect?' (1997) 93 Nursing Times 15.

279 Truog, Berde et al, 'Barbituates in the Care of the Terminally Ill' (1991) 327 New Eng J of Med 1678 at 1680.

280 Williams, 'The Principle of Double Effect and Terminal Sedation' (2001) 9 Med L Rev, p 52.

patient cannot be justified under the principle of double effect. 'It appears, therefore, that any justification for terminal sedation will have to rely on the admittedly 'morally and intellectually dubious distinction between acts and omissions'[281] and the notion of the patient's best interests.'[282]

[12.173] Some palliative care specialists are opposed to the legalisation of assisted dying and claim that with advances in medical treatments and medicinal products, pain can be relieved in almost all cases. However, it is argued that 'we should not permit the legitimate esteem in which they are held to blind us to the paternalism inherent in their approach'.[283] Apart from pain, there are also other symptoms that can accompany death which are more difficult to treat and may be as terrible for the patient to bear, such as nausea, vomiting, shortness of breath, inability to handle secretions, nightmares and episodic delirium. Given the distress that these symptoms may cause, the view that the undoubted expertise of palliative care specialists has removed the need for consideration of assisted dying may be challenged. 'Even if it were possible to alleviate all of these – and the hospice doctors do not claim that it is – there are still many people who do not want to go on to the bitter end and do not see why that should be required of them.'[284]

[12.174] Terminal sedation was recognised in the US Supreme Court decision *Washington v Glucksberg*[285] as one of the situations in which doctors are already involved in making decisions that hasten the death of terminally ill patients. The American Medical Association decided in 2008 that doctors can offer palliative sedation when symptoms, such as pain, shortness of breath, dyspnea, nausea and vomiting, cannot be diminished through all other means of palliation. It does not accept such sedation to combat emotional distress some terminally ill patients experience at the end of life, and it must never be used to intentionally cause a patient's death.[286] Such measures are also supported by other professional organisations in the US such as the American Academy of Hospice and Palliative Medicine and the American Academy of Pain Medicine. The enactment in the Netherlands of the Termination of Life on Request and Assisted Suicide (Review Procedures) Act in 2002 was followed by a small decrease in rates of euthanasia and an increased application in use of deep sedation, especially for patients with cancer, pulmonary diseases and diseases of the nervous system.[287]

---

[281] Per Mustill J in *Airedale NHS Trust v Bland* [1993] 1 All ER 821 at 399.

[282] Williams, 'The Principle of Double Effect and Terminal Sedation' (2001) 9 Med L Rev, p 53.

[283] McLean, *Assisted Dying: Reflections on the Need for Law Reform* (Routledge-Cavendish, 2007) at 46.

[284] Davies, 'The Case for Legalising Voluntary Euthanasia,' Thomasma and Kushner (eds) *Birth to Death: Science And Bioethics* (Cambridge University Press, 1996) 83–85 at 88, cited by McLean, *Assisted Dying: Reflections on the Need for Law Reform* (Routledge-Cavendish, 2007) at 47.

[285] *Washington v Glucksberg* 521 US 702 (1997) at 805, per Stevens J.

[286] See www.ama-assn.org.

[287] Euthanasia dropped from 2.6% of all deaths in 2001 to 1.7% in 2005; deep sedation increased from 5.6% to 7.1% in the same period. Rietjens et al, 'Continuous Deep Sedation for Patients Nearing Death in the Netherlands: Descriptive Study' (2008) BMJ Vol 336 No 7648.

CONCLUSION

[12.175] We know that in the past death came sooner, often as a result of acute infection, childbirth, accident, or due to the progression of an untreated disease. In modern times death comes later, may be postponed and managed in intensive medical settings, and often follows one kind of medical decision or another. With medical technology we gain greater control over how and when we die but with greater control comes greater responsibility for the range of complex decisions medical technology makes available.[288] 'While legal challenges in relation to assisted suicide and euthanasia might capture the public imagination, clarity and understanding are also needed in relation to more routine but also complex and contested decisions and interventions such as starting, stopping and descalating treatment, sedation and pain management and the provision of nutrition and hydration.'[289]

[12.176] The value of autonomy has been discussed in various contexts throughout this book but it is perhaps particularly relevant, and maybe more difficult to protect, in the dying process. In an essay on autonomy in 1986 Dworkin wrote:

> The value of autonomy...lies in the scheme of responsibility it creates: autonomy makes each of us responsible for shaping his own life according to some coherent and distinctive sense of character, conviction, and interest. It allows us to lead our own lives rather than be led along them, so that each of us can be, to the extent such a scheme of rights can make this possible, what he has made himself.[290]

Although autonomy has a clear appeal in respecting the views of the individual in relation to how he or she wants their life to be, simple reliance on autonomy perhaps provides an inadequate foundation for the ethical importance of patient-centred dying.[291] It offers solutions where there is a contest between individual choice and the principle of sanctity of life but Donnelly claims it runs into difficulties in relation to people who may be confused, distressed, disturbed and vulnerable. She suggests the concept of dignity might present a better fit by not being reliant on capacity or rationality and because it requires that individual perspectives of what is or is not dignified must be taken into account. 'Thus, respect for dignity has a subjective element and respecting the views of the dying person is an essential part of respecting his or her dignity.'[292]

[12.177] In arguing for the prioritisation of a patient-centred approach to end-of-life care Donnelly claims that 'the legal framework for end-of-life care in Ireland is fragmented, uncertain and incomplete.'[293] Although the case law discussed in this

---

[288] McCarthy, *Submission to Joint Committee on Health and Children* 24 October 2013.

[289] McCarthy, *Submission to Joint Committee on Health and Children* 24 October 2013.

[290] Dworkin, 'Autonomy and the Demented Self' (1986) Milbank Quarterly 64, supp 2: 4–16

[291] Donnelly, 'Patient-centred dying: the role of law' in Donnelly and Murray (eds) *Ethical and Legal Debates in Irish Healthcare, Confronting Complexities* (Manchester University Press 2015) 222–235 at 224

[292] Donnelly, 'Patient-centred dying: the role of law' in Donnelly and Murray (eds) *Ethical and Legal Debates in Irish Healthcare, Confronting Complexities* (Manchester University Press 2015) 222–235 at 225.

[293] Donnelly, 'Patient-centred dying: the role of law' in Donnelly and Murray (eds) *Ethical and Legal Debates in Irish Healthcare, Confronting Complexities* (Manchester University Press 2015) 222–235 at 225.

chapter clarifies some issues such as the fact that end-of-life care must respect constitutional rights to autonomy, dignity and bodily integrity (whether the person has capacity or not), artificial nutrition and hydration is not legally distinct from other medical treatment and a diagnosis of PVS is not required for it to be discontinued, advance decisions are to be respected if they meet certain criteria, and there is no constitutional right to assisted suicide, beyond this decisions are made in a legal vacuum.[294]

---

[294] Donnelly, 'Patient-centred dying: the role of law' in Donnelly and Murray (eds) *Ethical and Legal Debates in Irish Healthcare, Confronting Complexities* (Manchester University Press 2015) 222–235 at 225.

Chapter 13

Property in the Human Body

INTRODUCTION

[13.01] The centrality of autonomy to discussions of medical law and ethics has been emphasised throughout this book. Respect for autonomy entails the acknowledgement and acceptance that the patient has the right to control what happens to his own body. In many instances, respect for autonomy is demonstrated through the concept of informed consent and/or refusal of treatment as discussed in chapter 10. However, another way in which respect for the right of the individual to control his own body might be demonstrated is through a property framework which would give individuals decision-making control but may also raise complex questions regarding the limits of ownership and commercialisation of body parts and tissue:

> Property, through the bundle of rights that it confers, is a powerful control device which also carries with it a particular message – one of the potential for commerce and trade; of market advantage and disadvantage. To recognise a 'quasi-property' claim is to support a normatively strong connection to that item and, accordingly, to establish a strong, justiciable legal interest; by the same token, 'full' property rights will only be recognised where there is little or no prospect of exploitation or other harm, which can include the 'harm' of disrespect for the dignity of the human organism.[1]

[13.02] At common law the issue of property rights in the human body arose only in relation to dead bodies but with developments in medical science in more recent years, judicial attention has turned to ownership of human tissue taken from living persons for diagnostic or research purposes and rights to control the use of and access to such tissue. This has received attention in the context of control and ownership of reproductive material and also in relation to biobanking, which offers huge potential benefits to public health but also raises complex issues in relation to respect for the rights of those whose tissue is stored for research purposes. These issues will be discussed below.

OWNERSHIP OF DEAD BODIES

[13.03] It is commonly assumed that our bodies are ours. This is understandable. Our bodies are our way of interacting with the world and with others. It is by our bodies (or at least parts of them) that we are identifiable to other people. To many people their bodies define who they are and enable them to be who they are.'[2] However, although from the perspective of autonomy we may speak of the right to control what happens to

---

[1]   Laurie, Porter and Harmon, *Law and Medical Ethics* (10th edn, OUP, 2016) at 14.04.

[2]   Herring and Chau, 'Interconnected, inhabited and insecure: why bodies should not be property.' J Med Ethics 2014; 40:39–43.

'our own bodies', this is a 'highly individualistic way of conceiving of the body'.[3] From a legal perspective, the common law traditionally took the view that corpses and their parts are not capable of being owned, although those charged with their disposal have certain powers and responsibilities in respect of them. The exact origins of this position are unclear but it is often attributed to Coke, who wrote in 1644 that 'the burial of the cadaver (that is, *caro data vermibus*[4]) is *nullis in bonis*[5] and belongs to Ecclesiastical cognizance'.[6] Cases dating from the 17th and 18th centuries provide further authority for the principle that there is no property in a dead body.[7] For example, in *Hayne's case* the defendant was charged with stealing the sheets that bound four bodies, and upon conviction, he was whipped for petty larceny. At this time, grave robbing was punishable as a theft of coffins and burial shrouds rather than theft of the bodies themselves. When it became known that corpses could also have value for medical research and training purposes, graves began to be robbed for that purpose also in an activity known as 'burking', so-called after its infamous originators Burke and Hare.[8] However, academic commentators dispute the exact provenance of the rule, with some claiming that it has been based on a misunderstanding of the older cases.[9]

[13.04] Regardless of its exact origins, by the 19th century the principle was entrenched in English law and is cited in cases such as *R v Lynn*,[10] *R v Sharpe*,[11] *Foster v Dodd*,[12] *R v Price*[13] and *Williams v Williams*.[14] These cases posed difficulties for the courts, as the 'no property' rule meant that since there was no property, there could be no prosecution for theft and so the cases were decided on the basis of offences against public health and

---

[3]   Herring and Chau, 'Interconnected, inhabited and insecure: why bodies should not be property.' (2014) J Med Ethics; 40:39–43.

[4]   Translated as 'flesh given to worms'.

[5]   Translated as 'belonging to nobody'.

[6]   3 Co Inst 203.

[7]   For example *Hayne's case* [1614] 12 Co Rep 113 and *Handyside's case* [1749] 2 East PC 652.

[8]   For detailed discussion, see Rodgers, 'Human Bodies, Inhuman Uses: Public Reactions and Legislative Responses to the Scandals of Bodysnatching' (2003) Vol 12(2) Nottingham Law Journal 1–17.

[9]   For example, it has been argued that the ruling in *Hayne's case* was not that the corpse was not property but that the corpse could not own property. See Mason and Laurie, 'Consent or Property? Dealing with the Body and its Parts in the Shadow of Bristol and Alder Hey' (2001) 64(5) MLR 710 at 714. Also Magnusson, 'The Recognition of Proprietary Rights in Human Tissue in Common Law Jurisdictions' (1992) 18 Melbourne University Law Review 601 at 603.

[10]   *R v Lynn* [1788] 2 TR 394. This was the first reported conviction for disinterment of a corpse without authority. The defendant was charged with entering a burial ground and taking a coffin out of the earth, from which he took a dead body and carried it away for the purpose of dissecting it. It was argued that the offence was limited to stealing the shroud and trespass in disturbing the soil but the Court held that 'common decency required that the practice should be put a stop to' and that 'the offence was cognizable in a criminal court as being highly indecent and contra bonos mores: at the bare idea alone of which nature revolted.'

[11]   *R v Sharpe* [1857]169 ER 959.

[12]   *Foster v Dodd* [1866] LQ 1 QB 475, (1867) LR 3 QB 67.

[13]   *R v Price* [1884] 12 QBD 247.

[14]   *Williams v Williams* All ER 840.

decency.[15] It may thus be argued that property rights do not appear to provide any procedural advantage to claimants in the post-mortem context, and that cases dealing with interferences with dead bodies can be perfectly well decided and remedied without the fictional and unnecessary appeal to the right to property in the body of the deceased.[16] In any event legislation was later introduced in many jurisdictions, including Ireland,[17] to regulate access to the non-owned corpse in order to enable medical schools to obtain and retain corpses donated for education and training purposes.

[13.05] A more modern example of the application of this 'no property' rule can be seen in *Dobson v North Tyneside Health Authority*[18] in which a deceased woman's next of kin brought an action for medical negligence against the defendant for failing to diagnose tumours in the deceased's brain at a time when early diagnosis might have saved her life or at least lessened her pain with radiotherapy. The family required release to them of the brain of the deceased in order to have an independent post-mortem examination carried out, which they claimed would substantiate the allegation of negligence. However, the brain had been already disposed of by the hospital following the post-mortem examination and inquest, as was standard practice at that time. The family brought an action for conversion (a tort which protects against interference with possessory and ownership interests in personal property) in respect of the disposal of the brain on the basis that the defendant owed a duty to preserve it. The action failed on the grounds that the hospital did not owe a duty to preserve body parts indefinitely and the family was unable to show actual possession of the brain at the time it was disposed of. The Court of Appeal confirmed the principle that there was no legal right to possession of the deceased's brain because the plaintiff administratrix, who had the legal duty to dispose of the body, had not been appointed until after the burial of the remainder of the deceased's body.

[13.06] Despite the acceptance of the 'no property' rule, the courts also recognised the need to carve out exceptions to it in certain circumstances. One of these exceptions relates to the situation where the person in possession of a body applies 'work and skill' to it in such a way as to transform it into something else that may be regarded as property. For example, in the landmark Australian case of *Doodeward v Spence*[19] the facts concerned an action for conversion and detinue of the body of a two-headed foetus which had been delivered stillborn to a woman 40 years earlier and preserved by the doctor as a medical specimen. It was sold to the plaintiff's father as part of the doctor's estate after his death and later passed into the possession of the plaintiff who exhibited it for profit. The defendant, who was the Inspector of Police, seized it and prosecuted him for indecent exhibition of a corpse, to which Doodeward pleaded guilty. At the conclusion of the case the police officer returned the glass container to the plaintiff but

---

[15] See Matthews, 'The Man of Property' (1995) 3 Med L Rev 251.

[16] Sperling, *Posthumous Interests: Legal and Ethical Perspectives* (Cambridge University Press, 2008) at 142.

[17] Anatomy Act 1832, repealed by Medical Practitioners Act 2007, s 106.

[18] *Dobson v North Tyneside Health Authority* [1996] 4 All ER 474.

[19] *Doodeward v Spence* [1908] 6 CLR 406. See discussion by Skene, '*Doodeward v Spence* (1908)' in Herring and Wall, *Landmark Cases in Medical Law* (Hart Publishing, 2015) 11–20.

retained the foetus at a university museum. Doodeward took a private action to recover it.

[13.07] At first instance the matter was dismissed but Doodeward successfully appealed to the High Court. The three-judge court unanimously held that immediately after death, a corpse could not be the subject of property. However, they expressed different views as to whether there could *ever* be property in a dead body. In a widely cited extract Griffith CJ said that:

> When a person has by the lawful exercise of work or skill so dealt with a human body or part of a human body in his lawful possession that it has acquired some attributes differentiating it from a mere corpse awaiting burial, he acquires a right to retain possession of it, at least as against any person not entitled to have it delivered to him for the purposes of burial.[20]

In the present case the doctor initially acquired the foetus lawfully and applied some work and skill to it by virtue of which it had acquired a pecuniary value. Therefore an action could lie for an interference with the plaintiff's right of possession.

[13.08] Barton J focused on whether there was a duty to bury the foetus and held that a right to possession existed because neither the doctor nor anyone else had a duty to bury the foetus. 'In effect the person in possession could lawfully retain possession unless someone else could prove a better right to possession.'[21] He agreed with Griffith CJ that the doctor was entitled to lawful possession which the law would enforce by ordering that the foetus be returned. Higgins J considered the 'work or skill' argument and seemed to accept it but he said that in the present case, there had been no change in the character of the foetus by virtue of skill or labour applied to it. On balance, therefore, the plaintiff was held to be entitled to the return of the body. The decision of the court means therefore that if property rights arise in circumstances where 'work and skill' has been applied, then those property rights accrue to the person who has done the work. Although this case was decided more than a century ago, Skene explains that the principles it establishes have remained central in Australian law on the acquisition of proprietary interests in human bodily material. 'Until Parliament intervenes, State judges are bound by the 'no property' principle that was established in *Doodeward* and they must adapt it so that it can be applied fairly in modern situations that could not have been envisaged when *Doodeward* was decided.'[22]

[13.09] In further illustration of the 'work and skill' exception, the facts of *R v Kelly and Lindsay*[23] are also of interest. This case involved the prosecution of a sculptor and technician in respect of body parts stolen by the technician from the Royal College of Surgeons to enable the sculptor to use the body parts as moulds for his craft. The accused men argued that theft could not have taken place, as there were no property rights attached to the objects that had been taken. Although the Court did not recognise full ownership, they did identify a proprietary interest in the body parts. The Court held that the common law rule that body parts do not constitute property is subject to an

---

[20] *Doodeward v Spence* [1908] 6 CLR at 414.

[21] Skene '*Doodeward v Spence* (1908)' in Herring and Wall, *Landmark Cases in Medical Law* (Hart Publishing, 2015) 11–20 at 15.

[22] Skene '*Doodeward v Spence* (1908)' in Herring and Wall, *Landmark Cases in Medical Law* (Hart Publishing, 2015) 11–20 at 11.

[23] *R v Kelly and Lindsay* [1998] 3 All ER 741.

exception where those parts have acquired different attributes by virtue of the application of skill, such as dissection or preservation techniques, for exhibition or teaching purposes. In this case work had been done on the body parts by the College to enable them to be used for teaching purposes and this enabled the court to consider them as specimens owned by the College. As a result, the defendants were capable of being convicted of theft of the specimens.

[13.10] Following this case it was thought that this may, in fact, avoid the perceived necessity for change to the general rule, as the exceptions may allow for solutions to be found to the particular problems posed by the rule, in particular in relation to transplantation procedures.[24] However, it was also argued that the 'work and skill' exception was an example of forcing the law.[25] In future cases it was thought that the exception may be extended to include body parts with a use or significance beyond their mere existence, even without the acquisition of different attributes.[26] Examples of this might include organs or body parts intended for use in transplantation, or the extraction of DNA as exhibits in a trial. This is discussed further later in relation to reproductive material.

[13.11] In recent years, it has been argued that property law should apply to grant rights to the relatives of deceased persons in circumstances where the deceased's organs were retained following post-mortem examination. Following a number of high-profile official inquiries into post-mortem practices and organ retention in the UK,[27] claims were brought by bereaved parents in respect of post-mortem examinations carried out on the bodies of their deceased children. In *AB v Leeds Teaching Hospital NHS Trust*[28] parents sued the hospital for psychiatric injury sustained on learning that organs had been retained without the parents' knowledge. A claim was also made for wrongful interference with the body, which was a previously unrecognised form of legal action. Gage J followed the previous line of authority in confirming the 'no property in a human body' rule but held that parts of a body may acquire the character of property if skill and work were applied to it. In the circumstances of this case, the Court held that the post mortems had been lawfully carried out and the pathologist had applied work and skill in dissecting and 'fixing' the organ in order to produce blocks and slides for microscopic examination. This gave the pathologists possessory rights to the retained samples. Gage J held that there was no tort of wrongful interference with a body or conversion but he also held that a doctor is obliged to pass on any instructions received from parents to the

---

24 Grubb, 'I, Me, Mine: Bodies, Parts and Property' (1998) 3 Medical Law International 299–317 at 308.

25 White, 'The law relating to dealing with dead bodies' (2000) 4 Med Law International 145; Atherton, 'Who owns your body?' (2003) 77 Australian Law Journal 178.

26 This was mentioned by the court in *R v Kelly and Lindsay R v Kelly and Lindsay* [1998] 3 All ER 741 at 750.

27 Bristol Royal Infirmary Inquiry, *Interim Report: Removal and Retention of Human Material* (May 2000); *Report of the Royal Liverpool Children's Hospital (Alder Hey) Inquiry*, House of Commons (Jan 2001) (Redfern Report); Advice from the Chief Medical Officer, *The removal, retention and use of human organs and tissue from post-mortem examination* (London: Dept of Health 2001).

28 *AB v Leeds Teaching Hospital NHS Trust* [2004] 2 FLR 365.

pathologist. The pathologist is bound to adhere to any such lawful instruction within his duty of care.

[13.12] The UK Human Tissue Act 2004 now covers the storage, use and, for deceased persons, removal of organs and tissue. It established a Human Tissue Authority, which provides guidance about the Act, ensures best practice and licenses organisations that store human tissue for research.[29] The removal, storage and use of tissue from living individuals as part of their diagnosis or treatment does not fall within the scope of the Act and is covered by the usual ethical rules on consent to treatment. Consent is the central tenet of the legislation, and carrying out certain activities (referred to as scheduled purposes) without the necessary consent is a criminal offence. A person may give consent for their tissue to be used for research after their death and if there is no record of the deceased person's wishes, consent for research can be obtained from someone nominated by them to act on his or her behalf; or, if no one has been nominated, from a person in a 'qualifying relationship' – such as a partner, relative or friend.

[13.13] In a similar case to *AB* in Scotland, *Stevens v Yorkhill NHS Trust and another*,[30] the pursuer (plaintiff) claimed that it was never explained to her that the post mortem which she authorised to be carried out on her daughter would involve removal and retention of organs. She argued that there was a duty of care owed to inform her and seek her separate authorisation to the organ retention. She also argued that Scots law provided that wrongful interference with a corpse was actionable as an affront to human dignity. The Court found authority for the claim in the ancient *action injuriarum* which allowed the pursuer to recover damages for *solatium* (which is injury to feelings rather than psychiatric injury). The Court followed Gage J in relation to the acknowledgement of a duty of care owed to inform the mother about organ retention. The Court did not discuss issues relating to property rights.

[13.14] In Ireland in 2000 a controversy arose surrounding the retention of organs following post-mortem examinations without the knowledge or consent of the families of the deceased. This mirrored similar controversies in England, Scotland and Northern Ireland and gave rise to a public outcry regarding the breach of trust and lack of communication on the part of hospitals and medical staff to the families of deceased persons. The Madden Report on Post Mortem Practice and Procedure (2006), which was established to examine paediatric post-mortem practices, concluded that:

> [P]ost-mortem examinations were carried out in Ireland according to best professional and international standards and that no intentional disrespect was shown to the child's body. The root causes of this controversy have been a lack of communication with parents as to why organs were retained, the difference in perspective as to their symbolic significance, and the legislative vacuum on the role of consent in postmortem practice.[31]

---

[29] See http://www.hta.gov.uk/.

[30] *Stevens v Yorkhill NHS Trust and another* [2007] SCLR 606. See also *Report of the Independent Review Group on the Retention of Organs at Post-Mortem* (Jan 2001) (McLean Report).

[31] The Madden Report on Post Mortem Practice and Procedure (2006), at para 7.1. Available at www.health.gov.ie/publications-research/.

[13.15] The Report discussed the legal position in relation to property rights in the human body and acknowledged the lack of a legislative framework or judicial authority to support the recognition of such rights on the part of the parents of the deceased child. It acknowledged that one of the options for the recognition of the authority of parents in relation to the bodies of their deceased children was the property model:

> This argument would follow the line of thought sometimes expressed by bereaved parents to the effect that their children's bodies 'belong' to them, and that any removal or retention of organs was akin to 'stealing' what rightfully belongs to the parents. Other families find the language of ownership insensitive and abhorrent, as they prefer to identify with a sense of continuing parenthood, and see the child as a continuing member of the family.[32]

[13.16] The Report acknowledges that common law has rejected a property approach to the human body and that although many commentators have argued that the foundation of this principle rests on flimsy evidence from misreported cases, the principle of 'no property in the human body' has long stood the test of time and is likely to be accepted by the Irish courts. The differing views expressed by the English courts, discussed above, indicate the lack of clarity that exists in relation to whether or not the pathologist's act of fixing the organ transforms it into an item of property. It is similarly unclear whether or not the 'work and skill' exception would be applied in these circumstances in Irish courts, but, as with the 'no property' rule itself, it is likely to be followed unless affected by legislative change. The interpretation of the rule in the context of pathology practice and organ retention remains undecided. The Report recommended that the best resolution of this issue for bereaved parents was to enact clear and unambiguous legislation to ensure that organ retention practices could not happen again in the future without the knowledge and authorisation of the parents. The Government accepted the recommendations of the Report and undertook to introduce human tissue legislation to deal with post-mortem practice. Proposals for a Human Tissue Bill were published for consultation in 2009 but have not yet been enacted.

[13.17] Cases arising out of organ retention practices were also brought by bereaved parents in Ireland for personal injuries, anxiety, distress and annoyance, loss and damage, misrepresentation, breach of contract, negligence, breach of duty, breach of bailment, conversion, detinue and trespass to the person. However, the issue of property rights in respect of the retained organs was not discussed in the judgments. In *O'Connor & Tormey v Lenihan*[33] the plaintiffs had two children who had died in 1996 and 1998. They first learned in 2000 that organs removed following post-mortem examinations carried out on their children had been retained. They sought damages for personal injuries arising from the distress suffered at the time they received this information and their subsequent retrieval and burial of the retained organs. Although very sympathetic to the plaintiffs' distress, Peart J held that no expert evidence of psychiatric illness or injury had been adduced by them to substantiate a personal injuries claim. For that reason, the claims were dismissed.

[13.18] In a case of broadly similar facts, *Devlin v the National Maternity Hospital*,[34] the Supreme Court upheld the judgment of the High Court that the accepted practice of the

---

[32] The Madden Report on Post Mortem Practice and Procedure (2006) at para 12.1.

[33] *O'Connor & Tormey v Lenihan* [2005] IEHC 176.

[34] *Devlin v the National Maternity Hospital* [2007] IESC 50.

1980s was that when there had been consent to the post mortem, it was implicit that the pathologist had permission to remove or retain organs:

> This practice, and implicit acceptance, stemmed from Victorian times. Probably with the best of motives parents were not 'troubled' with the grim reality of a post-mortem and the need to retain organs and samples of tissue. This practice was exercised with a complete lack of understanding as to the rights of parents in relation to their children, and the retention of organs indefinitely and without consultation. The position of parents, their rights, and family rights, and the dignity of the child, are now acknowledged. However, this case stems from a time when a paternalistic attitude to parents was endemic in hospitals. In this case the parents did not consent to the removal of their child's organs at post-mortem, and the court is required to consider the consequences.

[13.19] The plaintiff claimed that on learning about the retention of her child's organs she suffered shock and post-traumatic stress, a psychiatric illness. The Court held that grief and sorrow are not a basis on which to award damages and that the test for nervous shock had not been satisfied, specifically in relation to the requirement that the nervous shock sustained by a plaintiff must be by reason of actual or apprehended physical injury to the plaintiff or a person other than the plaintiff. In upholding the High Court's dismissal of the action, Denham J said:

> The hospital's practice in relation to post-mortems of children in the 1980s was rooted in times long past. Probably with the best of motives, the policies were paternalistic and inappropriate. While it may have been thought kind not to trouble or disturb the parents, the decision to be made as to a post-mortem and their child's body is theirs to make…This was a misunderstanding, by the medical profession, of the rights of the parents. While parents may choose not to receive full information at the time, they must be given that choice when they are requested to authorise a post-mortem of a child. In the tragic and stressful situation of the death of a child parents may not wish to receive all the information at that time, but they are entitled to receive it specifically in relation to their child then, or later, or to receive it generally from printed information.

There are no cases in Ireland which clarify whether human bodies or their parts might be considered to be the subject of property rights and therefore the matter remains in this jurisdiction.

Ownership of Tissue from Living Bodies

[13.20] In relation to the removal of tissue from a living person the common law generally took the position, similar to that which applied to dead bodies, that such tissue had been abandoned by its original 'owner' or was '*res nullius*', ie belonging to no one.[35] This principle was developed at a time when the tissue was removed because it was diseased and therefore of no value to anyone. In more modern times, the courts appear to have become more willing to consider deviating from the common law rule, for example in the prosecution of cases involving theft of urine or blood in the context of driving under the influence of prohibited substances. In *R v Welsh*[36] the judge made passing reference to the tipping out of a urine sample as a 'technical property offence'.

---

[35] McHale, 'Waste, Ownership and Bodily Products' (2000) 8(2) Health Care Analysis 123–35.
[36] *R v Welsh* [1974] RTR 478.

In *R v Rothery*[37] the defendant was charged with the theft of the container in which a blood sample was stored but it is not clear whether the container and the blood were regarded as one entity.

[13.21] Why does it matter whether we own our bodies or not? A large part of the concern that arises in relation to the concept of ownership of the body is that commodification transforms us into objects of property-holding, rather than active human subjects and that this is inconsistent with respect for human dignity.[38] Dickenson argues that the distinction between persons and things is as much a philosophical question as a legal one, and that it draws its origins from Kant who said:

> Man cannot dispose over himself because he is not a thing; he is not his own property; to say that he is would be self-contradictory; for insofar as he is a person he is a Subject in whom the ownership of things can be vested, and if he were his own property he would be a thing over which he could have ownership. But a person cannot be a property and so cannot be a thing which can be owned, for it is impossible to be a person and a thing, the proprietor and the property.[39]

Dickenson says that human tissue and human genetic material, however, fall between two stools, containing elements of both person and thing, subject and object, and that perhaps societal discomfort with commodification is based on the realisation that recent developments take us closer to the object end of the spectrum. According to Kantian philosophy, this radically undermines our humanity. The extent to which such discomfort may influence the legal framework around human tissue remains to be seen.[40] Herring and Chau say that 'it is understandable that we like to think of our bodies as human and as something over which we have control. Hence lawyers reach for the comforting notions of property, bodily integrity and privacy. These conjure up an image of the body as contained, under control and ours.'[41]

> In fact our bodies are 'leaky', mutable, occupied and used by a host of non-human organisms. Our true sense of self and identity is not found in our bounded, owned body, but in the breaking, mixing and interaction of our bodies with others and with the wider environment. We need a statute that does not emphasise control but rather acknowledges our leakiness; does not emphasise individualist concerns, but acknowledges the communal nature of our bodies; does not emphasise a right to profit, but rather the common good.[42]

---

[37] *R v Rothery* [1976] RTR 550.
[38] Dickenson, *Property in the Body: Feminist Perspectives* (Cambridge University Press, 2007) at p 4.
[39] Kant, *Lectures on Ethics* (Indianapolis, Bobbs-Merrill) 1963, p 4, cited in Dickenson *Property in the Body: Feminist Perspectives* (Cambridge University Press, 2007) at 5.
[40] See further Matthews, 'Whose Body? People As Property' (1983) Current Legal Problems 193 at 208; Mortimer, 'Property Rights in Body Parts: The Relevance of Moore's Case in Australia', (1993) 19 Monash University Law Review 217 at 245; Herring and Chau, 'My Body, Your Body, Our Bodies' Med Law Review 15, Spring 2007, pp 34–61.
[41] Herring and Chau, 'Interconnected, inhabited and insecure: why bodies should not be property.' (2014) J Med Ethics 40:39–43.
[42] Herring and Chau, 'Interconnected, inhabited and insecure: why bodies should not be property.' (2014) J Med Ethics 40:39–43.

[13.22] In an important US case called *Moore v Regents of California*,[43] the plaintiff was receiving treatment for hairy cell leukemia at the University of California Medical Centre. As a result of Moore's condition it was necessary to remove his spleen. His treating physician, Dr Golde, recognised the potential commercial advantage of Moore's cells due to their unique qualities. He was subsequently encouraged to return to the medical centre for ongoing treatment where blood, serum, skin, bone marrow and semen were harvested from him and used for research purposes without his knowledge or consent. Throughout the period of time that Moore was under Dr Golde's care, Dr Golde and his colleagues were actively involved in a number of activities which were concealed from Moore. Specifically, the defendants were conducting research on Moore's cells and planned to benefit financially and competitively by exploiting the cells and their exclusive access to the cells by virtue of Golde's ongoing doctor-patient relationship with Moore. Golde established a cell-line from Moore's T-cells which he patented and later sold to a drug company for €15 million.[44]

[13.23] When Moore discovered the truth he took an action against the researchers, the university and the drug company for conversion, in effect claiming a proprietary interest in each of the products that might be created from his cells or the patented cell-line. He also alleged breach of fiduciary duty and lack of informed consent as he had not been told about the use of his cells. Although the Supreme Court upheld the claims in relation to failure to obtain informed consent, the Court stated that what Moore was asking it to do in relation to the conversion action was 'to impose a tort duty on scientists to investigate the consensual pedigree of each human cell sample used in research.' The Court rejected Moore's claim for conversion on the grounds that there was no reported judicial decision to support his contention that he had retained an ownership interest in his cells following their removal, and Californian statute law also drastically limited the right of a patient to exercise control over excised cells.

[13.24] The Court rejected the argument that the unusual circumstances of Moore's claim should be used as a basis to extend the theory of conversion. It said:

> There are three reasons why it is inappropriate to impose liability for conversion based upon the allegations of Moore's complaint. First, a fair balancing of the relevant policy considerations counsels against extending the tort. Second, problems in this area are better suited to legislative resolution. Third, the tort of conversion is not necessary to protect patients' rights. For these reasons, we conclude that the use of excised human cells in medical research does not amount to a conversion.

The Court went on to say that the extension of conversion law into this area would hinder research by restricting access to the necessary raw materials and that the exchange of scientific materials would be compromised if each cell sample were to

---

[43] *Moore v Regents of California* [1990] 271 Cal Reptr 146 (Cal Sup Ct). For discussion see Dickens, 'Living Tissue and Organ Donors and Property Law: More on Moore' (1992) 8 Journal of Contemporary Health Law and Policy 73; Alta Charo, 'Body of Research – Ownership and Use of Human Tissue' (2006) NEJM Vol 355 No 15: 1517–1519; Creagh, 'Property in the Living Body' (2001) Bar Review 209.

[44] It has been estimated that the therapies developed from the patented cell-line are worth in excess of $3 billion. Merz, 'Biotechnology: Spleen-rights', The Economist, 11 August 1990, 30.

become the potential subject matter of a lawsuit. In other words, the court did not say that the removed cells were not property per se, but rather that the patient retains no ownership interest in a body part that has been removed.[45]

[13.25] Mosk J filed a powerful dissent from the majority opinion and said the fact that a patent had been granted in respect of the cell-line did not necessarily prohibit recognition of Moore's rights to share in the commercial exploitation of the cell-line derived from his own body tissue. He said that this was an unfair result which was not compelled by the law of patents. He went on to say 'a patent is not a license to defraud', and suggested that a better approach might be to recognise Golde and Moore as joint inventors in order to ensure that each contributor is fairly compensated. Mosk J also opposed the policy considerations which found favour with the majority and argued that these were outweighed by two contrary considerations. The first consideration is that 'our society acknowledges a profound ethical imperative to respect the human body as the physical and temporal expression of the unique human persona':

> Research with human cells that results in significant economic gain for the researcher and no gain for the patient offends the traditional mores of our society in a manner impossible to quantify. Such research tends to treat the human body as a commodity – a means to a profitable end. The dignity and sanctity with which we regard the human whole, body as well as mind and soul, are absent when we allow researchers to further their own interests without the patient's participation by using a patient's cells as the basis for a marketable product.[46]

[13.26] The second consideration was that of equity. 'Our society values fundamental fairness in dealing between its members, and condemns the unjust enrichment of any member at the expense of another. This is particularly true when, as here, the parties are not in equal bargaining positions.' Mosk J said that the university's denial of Moore's claim to a share in the proceeds of the cell-line was 'inequitable and immoral':

> The person who furnishes the tissue should be justly compensated...If biotechnologists fail to make provision for a just sharing of profits with the person whose gift made it possible, the public's sense of justice will be offended and no one will be the winner.[47]

[13.27] In relation to the issue of non-disclosure, the Court also took the view that a doctor who intends to treat a patient in whom he has either a research interest or an economic interest is under a fiduciary duty to disclose such interest to the patient before treatment and that Golde's failure to do so in this case gave rise to a cause of action. Mosk J also agreed with this decision but was of the view that a nondisclosure action was an inadequate remedy for three reasons. Firstly, he said the majority's reasoning was that the threat of litigation for non-disclosure would have a prophylactic effect and would give physician-researchers the incentive to disclose any conflicts of interest before treatment, thereby protecting patients' rights to make an informed choice. Mosk J was of the view that this remedy was illusory, as it fell within the realms of an action for medical negligence, which would therefore require the patient to prove a causal

---

45 This was pointed out by Broussard J in his dissent in *Moore*.
46 Quoting from Danforth 'Cells, Sales and Royalties: The Patient's Right to a Portion of the Profits' (1985) 6 Yale Law and Policy Review 179 at 190.
47 Quoting Murray, 'Who Owns the Body? On the Ethics of Using Human Tissue for Commercial Purposes' (1986) IRB: A Review of Human Subjects Research 5.

connection between the non-disclosure and an injury sustained by the patient. The patient would have to prove that if he had been fully informed, he would have refused consent to the relevant procedure, and that any reasonable person would have done likewise. Mosk J said that few judges would believe that disclosure of the possibility of research would dissuade a reasonably prudent person from consenting to the treatment and that therefore the threat of such litigation is 'largely a paper tiger'.

[13.28] Secondly, Mosk J said that the nondisclosure action was inadequate because it fails to solve half of the problem in that it gives the patient only the right to refuse consent, it does not allow him to give consent on the basis that he can share in the proceeds despite sound reasons for recognising the patient's right to participate in such benefits. Thirdly, he said that the non-disclosure action failed to reach a major class of potential defendants, namely researchers who fall outside of the doctor-patient relationship. In this case, the imposition of a duty of disclosure could only be placed on Dr Golde by virtue of the doctor-patient relationship he had with Moore. No such duty could be imposed on the other researchers involved in these activities, as they were not doctors and they did not have a fiduciary relationship with Moore. Yet some of these parties may well have participated more in, and profited more from, such exploitation than the doctor involved. Thus, the true exploiters may escape liability.

[13.29] The main significance of the *Moore* case is in denying the ownership claim of a patient in respect of cells taken from his body and used by doctors and researchers to invent a cell-line which they patented. The case protects the concept of ownership of tissue in the hands of the researchers, but not the person from whom it emanated. It is important and necessary to recognise the value, time and skill brought by researchers to turn material into a patentable product. However:

> It is entirely reasonable to hold that some financial reward should be given to the source of the valuable sample while, at the same time, accepting that the majority of the spoils should return to those who have done the work in creating a patentable invention. It is *not* reasonable to exclude completely from the equation the one person who can make everything possible.[48]

[13.30] Similar circumstances arose in *Greenberg v Miami Children's Hospital Research Institute Inc* in 2003[49] in which a law suit was brought by parents of children with a rare and incurable genetic disorder called Canavan disease against researchers who patented a test for the disease using samples donated by the families. The families were concerned that by patenting the test, the researchers could limit access to information and research about the disease as well as the test itself, whereas the families wanted to ensure that information and testing were freely available. They therefore claimed a property interest in their samples and the genetic information contained in them. A preliminary ruling rejected the property claim argued by the families but suggested that an argument on grounds of unjust enrichment might be successful.

---

[48] Laurie, Harmon and Porter, *Law and Medical Ethics* (10th edn, 2016) at 14.19, emphasis in original.

[49] *Greenberg v Miami Children's Hospital Research Institute Inc* 264 F Supp 2d 1064 (SS Fla 2003).

[13.31] Under Florida law, the elements of a claim for unjust enrichment are (1) that the plaintiff conferred a benefit on the defendant, who had knowledge of the benefit; (2) the defendant voluntarily accepted and retained the benefit; and (3) under the circumstances it would be inequitable for the defendant to retain the benefit without paying for it. It was not contested that the families conferred a benefit on the researchers, including, among other things, blood and tissue samples and soliciting financial contributions. However, the defendants contended that the plaintiffs had not suffered any detriment, and that no plaintiff had been denied access to Canavan testing. Furthermore, the plaintiffs received what they sought – the successful isolation of the Canavan gene and the development of a screening test. The plaintiffs argued, however, that when the defendants applied the benefits for unauthorised purposes, they suffered a detriment. Had they known that the defendants intended to commercialise their genetic material through patenting and restrictive licensing, the families would not have provided their samples to the researchers under those terms.

[13.32] The Court held that the families had alleged more than just a donor-donee relationship and that the facts painted 'a picture of a continuing research collaboration that involved Plaintiffs also investing time and significant resources in the race to isolate the Canavan gene'. Therefore, the Court held that the families had sufficiently established the requisite elements of an unjust enrichment claim and refused to dismiss the claim on that ground. The case was ultimately settled on the basis that the plaintiffs agreed not to further challenge Miami Children's Hospital's ownership and licensing of the Canavan gene patent; the hospital would continue to license and collect royalty fees for clinical testing for the Canavan gene mutation; and there would be licence-free use of the Canavan gene in research to cure Canavan disease.[50]

[13.33] A further case arose in 2006 in *Washington University v Catalona*.[51] Professor William Catalona, a surgeon and researcher employed at Washington University in St Louis, Missouri, collected thousands of research samples from excised cancerous tissues of his patients and stored them in a biobank operated by the university and used strictly for research purposes. Patients were asked to sign consent forms which stated that they did not assert any ownership rights in respect of any products arising from the research and that the donations were a gift to research at Washington University. In 2003 Catalona left the university to work elsewhere and wrote to the research participants inviting them to sign an authorisation form which would allow their samples to be released from the biobank into his custody. The university brought an action to clarify the ownership of these samples.

[13.34] In Missouri, where this case occurred, property ownership is determined by proof of exclusive possession and control of the property. The Court concluded that the university had been in exclusive possession of the samples and bore all legal and compliance risks in relation to them, as well as having control over them. The Court also considered whether the samples constituted a gift from the research participants or a

---

[50] See discussion by Bovenberg, 'Inalienably yours? The new case for an inalienable property right in human biological material: empowerment of sample donors or a recipe for a tragic anti-commons?' (2004) 1:4 SCRIPT-ed 591.

[51] *Washington University v Catalona* 490 F 3d 667 (2007), *Catalona v Washington University* 128 S Ct 1122, 169 L Ed 949 (2008).

bailment, which is a contractual obligation to retain possession of property on the expectation that the property will be returned to the owner in the future. It was held that the informed consent forms signed by the participants constituted clear and convincing evidence that they intended to make a gift to the university and that this intention could not later be revoked following a change of heart by the participants. The Court held that it was not a bailment, as the research participants did not have any expectation of having the samples returned to them at a future date even if they declined to participate further in the research. The Court followed the principle established in *Moore* that a research participant does not retain any ownership rights in the samples after the donation of the biological materials. It stated 'if left unregulated and to the whims of research participants, these highly-prized biological materials would become nothing more than chattel going to the highest bidder.'[52]

[13.35] It has been argued that a consent model is not necessarily the solution to these sorts of dilemmas as the only right that a consent requirement gives is to consent or refuse. There may be people who are willing to participate in research but who have concerns about some of the uses of their material so they will not be satisfied with such a limited range of options.

> A property right would offer an opportunity for an element of continuing control over samples after surrender and would allow for a legally recognised voice in how they are used. The same is not true once an initial consent has been obtained, for so long as the requisite information is disclosed at the time the sample is provided, the sample source's 'rights' have been exhausted.[53]

[13.36] Legislative intervention has taken place in the UK in relation to some practical aspects of body parts to allow the individual concerned to exercise some control over the use of his body parts. The Human Tissue Act 2004 makes consent the fundamental principle underpinning the lawful storage and use of body parts, organs and tissue from the living or the deceased for specified health-related purposes and public display. Consent is not required for the research use of 'existing holdings' (human tissue already in storage for a scheduled purpose when the Act came into force), or for the use of residual tissue from living individuals for research on an anonymous basis where the research has been approved by a research ethics committee. In relation to the sale of bodies or body parts, under s 32 of the Act, it is an offence to engage in commercial dealings in 'controlled material', ie material which consists of or includes human cells which is – or is intended to be – removed from a human body for the purpose of transplantation. The Act is silent on the sale of bodies, body parts or tissue for other purposes and such sales are therefore outside the remit of the Human Tissue Authority.[54] The Act does not apply to gametes, which are dealt with by the Human Fertilisation and Embryology Act 2008.

[13.37] Other international documents dealing with prohibition of commercialisation of the human body include the Council of Europe's Convention for the Protection of Human Rights and Dignity of the Human Being with Regard to the Application of

---

[52] *Washington University v Catalona* 490 F 3d 667 (2007), *Catalona v Washington University* 128 S Ct 1122, 169 L Ed 949 (2008) at 1002.

[53] Laurie, Harmon and Porter, *Law and Medical Ethics* (10th edn, 2016) at 14.24.

[54] https://www.hta.gov.uk/policies/sale-bodies-body-parts-and-tissue.

Biology and Medicine: Convention on Human Rights and Biomedicine. Article 21 of the Convention, headed 'Prohibition of financial gain,' states: 'The human body and its parts shall not, as such, give rise to financial gain.' Article 22, under the heading 'Disposal of a removed part of the human body,' dictates that:

> When in the course of an intervention any part of a human body is removed, it may be stored and used for a purpose other than that for which it was removed, only if this is done in conformity with appropriate information and consent procedures.

Ireland is not a signatory to this Convention. Other important documents also reaffirm that the human body and its parts, including blood, should not give rise to financial gain. For example some declarations by the United Nations Educational, Scientific and Cultural Organization, particularly the Universal Declaration on the Human Genome and Human Rights, the International Declaration on Human Genetic Data, and the Universal Declaration on Bioethics and Human Rights, repeat the principle of non-commercialization and the prohibition of the use of the human body for profit.

[13.38] For the European Union, the key reference document for the biotechnology sector is Directive 98/44.[55] According to European Union legislation, the following are patentable, provided they satisfy the requisites of novelty and originality and are susceptible to industrial application: biological material which is isolated from its natural environment or produced by means of a technical process, even if it previously occurred in nature;[56] any technical process by means of which biological material is produced, processed, or used, even if it previously occurred in nature; any new application of biological material or of a process already patented; and inventions relating to an element isolated from the human body or otherwise produced by means of a technical process, even if its structure is identical to that of a natural element, provided that its function and industrial use are disclosed in the patent application.[57] 'All commercial rights or patents apply to the results of research and not to the samples collected, for which no rights of ownership are typically legally recognized.'[58]

[13.39] In the Irish context, the law is currently silent on these issues and therefore the legal status of human tissue is uncertain. Good clinical practice normally dictates over-collection of tissue at surgery so as to ensure sufficient material for sampling and diagnosis. This tissue is commonly archived and may be made available, subject to

---

[55] European Parliament, Council of the European Union. Directive 98/44/EC of the European Parliament and of the Council of July 6, 1998 on the legal protection of biotechnological inventions. Official Journal of the European Communities. 1998; L213:13–21.

[56] This does not apply to inventions whose commercial exploitation would be contrary to public order and morality, in particular patents may not be granted for uses of human embryos for industrial or commercial purposes – *Brüstle v Greenpeace* C-34/10. See discussion by Harmon, Laurie and Courtney 'Dignity, Plurality and Patentability: the unfinished story of *Brüstle v Greenpeace*' (2012) 38 European Law Rev 92; Pila, 'Intellectual property rights and detached human body parts' (2014) J Med Ethics 40:27–32. See also discussion in Laurie, Harmon and Porter, *Law and medical ethics* (10th edn, OUP 2016) paras 14.57–14.64.

[57] Petrini, 'Ethical and legal considerations regarding the ownership and commercial use of human biological materials and their derivatives', (2012) J Blood Med. 3: 87–96.

[58] Petrini, 'Ethical and legal considerations regarding the ownership and commercial use of human biological materials and their derivatives', (2012) J Blood Med. 3: 87–96.

research ethics approval and usually strictly on an anonymous basis for research, medical training, audit of laboratory procedures and scholarship. The large scale collection of such tissue, either archival samples or tissue specifically donated by patients or donors for research purposes, is referred to as biobanking, which is considered in more detail in the next section. Whether such tissue would be regarded as personal property in Ireland is a moot question, the answer to which may depend on the context in which the issue arises. Were the facts of *Moore* to come before a court in this jurisdiction, 'the court would undoubtedly be cognisant not only of patients' rights to autonomy, privacy and dignity, but also the substantial public interest in the activities of treatment, archiving, research and teaching.'[59] The application of patent law to advances in biotechnology and human genetics may also create further ambiguities and legal problems.[60]

OWNERSHIP OF REPRODUCTIVE MATERIAL

[13.40] The question arises as to whether there are fundamentally different and distinct issues applicable to reproductive material (semen and ova) which render it necessary to apply a different framework entirely and whether a property analysis is appropriate in this context. It is generally considered ethically unacceptable that semen or ova taken from a man or woman could be used for any purpose other than that for which it was donated. The reason for this is that with a donation of gametes there is a donation of genetic information which is readily usable to produce a new individual. Although we generally do not worry about the natural loss of semen and ova, we are very anxious about their storage and subsequent use. The reason for this seems to come within the issue of privacy and bodily integrity as 'once down the drain the information they contain, in practical terms, is not usable: it will never find genetic expression: it will never mix with another germ cell's information to produce a new individual: we can forget about it.'[61] However, if not 'down the drain', it may be used to fertilise an egg, and may develop into a new individual who will forever have a genetic connection with the semen donor.

---

[59] Madden, 'Legal Status of Archived Human Tissue'. (2004) MLJI 10(2): 76.

[60] See Sheikh, 'Owning' Life: New Frontiers in Patent Law, Genetics and Biotechnology?' (1999) MLJI 23; Mills, 'Biotechnology and the Ethical Moral Concerns of European Patent Law' (2000) Eurowatch 46.

[61] Jansen, 'Semen and Ova as Property' (1985) 11 Journal of Medical Ethics 123. Jansen considers the reasons why so much emotion is expended in relation to the use of stored gametes in comparison to situations in which gametes are lost every day naturally without any controversy. He examines the quantitative arguments in relation to the number of eggs a woman might release during her lifetime and the opportunities for those to become babies through sexual reproduction. He concludes that there is not the time for more than about 15 or 20 of the 7 million eggs with which a woman is born (of which only about 300,000 are left by the time of fertilisation due to the process of atresia in which eggs degenerate and are lost naturally) to become babies (69 if multiple ovulations are included). The other 299,000 are destined for oblivion. The comparison for males is 'even more spectacular' as only an infinitesimal fraction of the semenatozoa which he may have produced during his lifetime are likely to fertilise an egg. Jansen argues that no one cares about these semen and eggs that are wasted, as long as they are wasted in nature.

[13.41] Therefore, it is the potential of the ova or semen to become a new, unique individual which makes it different from donations of other body parts.[62] 'The germ cells differ from other human tissues that can be donated because they carry readily utilisable genetic information.'[63] It is this fact that makes gametes the subject of so much concern and emotional debate, that is, their ability to find genetic expression in a new living human being. By comparison, the donation of a kidney, while it may indeed be life-saving, does not have the potential to *create* a new existence carrying forward the genetic inheritance of the donor. This valuable and important potential is rightly a matter of personal responsibility for the donor of the gametes. Jansen argues that it should also be considered his property to deal with as he wishes. 'This potential should always remain the responsibility, the provenance, the dominion, perhaps the property, of the donor.'[64]

[13.42] If the person from whom the gametes are taken is alive, then following the common law cases in respect of which theft actions were successful in relation to urine and blood, it could be argued that semen could similarly be the subject matter of a prosecution for theft[65] and, in that sense at least, could be regarded as 'property'.[66] However, the case of *Moore v University of California*[67] indicates an unwillingness on the part of the courts to consider, at least in the context of donation of biological

---

[62] Jansen claims that the courts of common law countries have held that once organs or tissues are separated from a person, the person has little or no right of ownership over those separated parts. 'Human body parts in law appear simply to be incapable of being owned.' He asks whether this lack of dominion over body parts could be applicable to frozen semen. However, he acknowledges that the idea that semen stored on behalf of a man, who might, for example, be undergoing chemotherapy treatment for cancer, might be used for any purpose other than the purpose for which it was stored, that is to impregnate the man's wife in the future, would be unthinkable. Jansen, 'Semen and Ova as Property' (1985) 11 Journal of Medical Ethics 123.

[63] Jansen, 'Semen and Ova as Property' (1985) 11 Journal of Medical Ethics 123 at 124.

[64] Jansen, 'Semen and Ova as Property' (1985) 11 Journal of Medical Ethics 123 at 125.

[65] In England, a case was settled out of court in early 2000 involving a claim by an Austrian businessman that a fertility clinic used his semen without his consent. He sued the clinic for unauthorised use of his semen after learning that his former girlfriend had given birth to a daughter using his frozen semen without telling him. He sued for breach of contract and breach of duty rather than for theft of his semen but the case opens up previously unexplored possibilities in the context of property rights in gametes. See brief description of the case in British Medical Journal (2000) 320: 464.

[66] See also 'birth control fraud' cases where it has been alleged that women have 'stolen' semen in order to become pregnant. These cases have usually come about through consensual sexual intercourse where the man has been deceived as to the contraceptive protection taken by the woman. His genetic parentage thus gives rise to liability for maintenance of the child, irrespective of his lack of knowledge or consent to such paternity. Claims have been brought in this context for breach of contract, deceit and trespass to the person. More interestingly here, claims have also been brought for conversion (where a person deliberately deals with the property of another in such a way as to be an unjustifiable denial of that person's rights to the property). See further Madden, 'Recent Developments in Assisted Human Reproduction: Legal and Ethical Issues' (2001) MLJI Vol 7 No 2 53–61; Sheldon, 'Semen Bandits, Birth Control Fraud and the Battle of the Sexes' (2001) 21 Legal Studies 460–480.

[67] *Moore v Regents of California* [1990] 271 Cal Reptr 146 (Cal Sup Ct).

material for research purposes, that the individual from whom the material is derived could have a property right in the material once it has left the body.

[13.43] In relation to the ownership of body parts or genetic material of a person who is now deceased, the common law rule is that there is no such right of ownership. However, as discussed earlier, there is an exception in relation to situations in which work or skill has been employed on the parts/material, in which case there would be a right of possession in the person who had applied the skill. This would enable him to exclude others from possession of the parts. It is unclear to what extent preservation (particularly relevant in the context of gametes) without application of any other specific skill would satisfy this test. The exception was developed to reward the creator of a new 'thing' for his efforts, so that mere storage/freezing of gametes (without application of any other specific skill which might change its characteristics) might not necessarily entitle the clinic to legal possession.

[13.44] However, in *R v Kelly and Lindsay*[68] the preservation of body parts by the Royal College of Surgeons was sufficient to accord property rights to the College so by analogy, preservation of gametes might similarly be seen as the application of work and skill to enable the clinic, not the individuals from whom the material was derived, to gain ownership of the gametes. Different policy provisions undoubtedly apply in this context however. Given the potential use of the gametes to create a child, it is unthinkable that a clinic would be granted ownership rights in relation to semen and eggs that could enable the clinic to use these gametes to create a child without the knowledge and consent of the persons from whom they were taken.

[13.45] Gamete providers are commonly given decision-making authority in relation to what may be done with the gametes, ie storage for future use, donation for research or to another couple, or destruction after expiry of a fixed time period. There is an argument that decision-making authority implies a property right or interest in the person from whom they were derived. It is argued that a property interest in gametes must exist, regardless of whether an action for conversion will lie - the term 'property' merely designates the locus of dispositional control over the object or matter in question. The scope of that control is a separate matter and will depend upon what bundle of dispositional rights exist with regard to that object.[69] This argument is based on the right of a person to decide what is to be done with stored semen and, logically, this must be the person who made the deposit of the semen. This right implies a property right or ownership in the semen, which means the semen donor has the right to decide what happens to it. However, it is argued that this conclusion is drawn from a circuitous

---

[68] *R v Kelly and Lindsay* [1998] 3 All ER 741.

[69] Robertson, 'Posthumous Reproduction' (1994) 69 Ind LJ 1027 at 1038. This article follows Robertson's general proposition in favour of procreative liberty, as discussed in his book, *Children of Choice: Freedom and the New Reproductive Technologies* (Princeton University Press, 1994). He admits that no right can be absolute but that the right to reproduce should only be interfered with in instances when the State can show such great harm resulting from the exercise of the right, that the fundamental interest in having children is justifiably limited.

process of deriving ownership from dispositional control and then dispositional control from ownership:[70]

> Parents have the right to control virtually every aspect of their children's lives, from the medical care they will receive to where they will live to the kind of education they get. Yet parents do not own their children, and children are not property. Doctors and hospitals often rely on family members to make decisions about what should be done with incompetent patients, including whether the patients should be kept on life-support, yet these surrogate decision-makers do not own their incompetent relatives, and incompetent patients are not property. These are situations in which individuals have dispositional authority, but not a property interest.

[13.46] The counter-argument may be simply put thus – since the abolition of slavery, people cannot be bought or sold and therefore cannot be regarded as property. Property is essentially something which can be bought and sold in a market, therefore simply having decision-making authority over something is not sufficient to regard it as property:

> Whether semen is property depends on what we think may permissibly be done with it. If there is a strong moral, legal, or policy argument against allowing individuals to store semen for the purpose of posthumous reproduction, then semen should not be considered property for that purpose. In the absence of a compelling argument against posthumous reproduction, individual autonomy should prevail, and semen is correctly regarded as property that can be bequeathed by will.[71]

[13.47] A number of cases have arisen in relation to ownership of gametes in the context of surviving spouses seeking the right to access semen stored prior to their husband's

---

[70] Steinbock, 'Semen as Property' (1995) 6(2) Stanford Law and Policy Review 57 at 60. Steinbock's arguments are based on the premise that individual autonomy should prevail in instances of posthumous reproduction unless there are convincing arguments to the contrary. She considers in detail the *Hecht* and *Davis* cases and concludes that these cases represent judicial decisions 'to eschew a categorical approach to the ownership issues raised by disputes over bodily parts and gametes.' p 60. See also Tober, 'Semen as Gift, Semen as Goods: Reproductive Workers and the Market in Altruism' (2001) 7 Body and Society 137–60.

[71] Steinbock, at 66. She argues that it is relevant to consider the quality of life of the child who may be born as a result of posthumous conception and whether it is a serious disadvantage to a child to be born without a father. She discusses Robertson's premise that it is always better for a child to be born than not to be born but she says that this justification for posthumous reproduction is to confuse two very different situations. One is whether existing lives are worth living due to serious handicaps and whether stopping treatment on such a child can be justified. The other situation is whether or not to bring a child into existence at all in circumstances in which it is likely to have a substandard life. She states, 'Refraining from procreating is not the moral equivalent of killing. Causing the death of an existing child deprives that child of its life, a life that may well be of value to the child, despite its limits, burdens, and difficulties. By contrast, no one is harmed by not being brought into existence. The child who is never conceived is not frustrated or miserable or unhappy. To be sure, if one is not conceived, one is deprived of the opportunity to exist. But this is not a harm to *anyone*. It is not as if there are potential children waiting in the wings, so to speak, longing for the chance to be born. The decision not to procreate makes no one worse off, and so the decision not to procreate does not require a justification. A responsible decision to procreate, however, requires thoughtful consideration of the welfare of the children one brings into the world.' At 63.

death. In the earliest of these reported cases in 1984, *Paraplaix v CECOS*,[72] the widow of a man who had died from cancer requested the release of her husband's frozen semen to her.[73] Her husband had not made any specific disposition of the semen in the event of his death. The deceased's widow and parents argued that the semen formed part of the movable property of the deceased's estate and was therefore capable of being inherited. As they were the natural heirs of the deceased, they became the owners of the semen and CECOS[74] was a bailee obliged to deliver the semen to them. CECOS argued firstly on privity of contract grounds, that it was obligated only to the deceased donor himself in contract, and secondly that semen, being an indivisible part of the body in the same way as a limb or organ, was not inheritable.

[13.48] The deceased's widow was ultimately successful although not on the property argument.[75] The Court seemed to have been more influenced by privacy arguments and procreational autonomy. It held that Mr Paraplaix's intent to preserve his opportunity to procreate, by entering into an agreement with CECOS for semen preservation, obligated CECOS to return the semen to the person for whom it was intended – namely, his wife. It defined semen as 'the seed of life; it is connected to the fundamental liberty of a person to conceive or not to conceive.' As such it should not be the subject of legal rules or contracts but should be governed by 'the intent of the man from whom it emanates.' The Court was satisfied, despite the absence of any clear statement left on the matter by the man in question, that his intent was to make his wife the mother of a common child either before or after his death.[76] The Court found this evidence from the unusual

---

[72] *Paraplaix v CECOS*, Trib.gr.inst. Creteil, 16–17 Sept 1984, Gazette du Palais (2e sem.) 560. For further discussion, see Jones, 'Artificial Procreation, Societal Reconceptions: Legal Insight from France' [1988] 36 Am J of Comparative Law 525–545. Also Shapiro and Sonnenblick, 'The Widow and the Semen: The Law of Post-Mortem Insemination' (1986–7) 1 J Law and Health 229; Kerr, 'Post-Mortem Semen Procurement: Is it Legal?' (1999) 3 DePaul J Health Care 39.

[73] Posthumous conception is now prohibited in France by legislation which provides that assisted conception may only take place where the man and woman are both alive. Law 94–654 of 29 July 1994, art 8. Where one partner dies, the other partner may be asked to consent to donating stored embryos to another couple. The position in other European countries is varied. For example, the Spanish legislation permits posthumous conception where the woman's partner has expressly consented to such conception to take place within six months of his death. If a child is born, the deceased man is considered the child's legal father. Posthumous conception is prohibited in Sweden (Regulations and General Recommendations No 35 of 30 November 1989, rubric 4), Denmark (Law No 460 of 10 June 1997, ss 15(2), (3) and 19), Germany (Law of 13 December 1990, s 4(1)(3), and Switzerland (Federal Law of 18 December 1998, art 3(4)). Other countries, such as Norway, Austria, and Belgium do not have any specific measures dealing with posthumous conception.

[74] Centre d'Étude et de Conservation du Semene – a French federation of 20 semen banks.

[75] The Court specifically rejected the applicability of the Civil Code by finding that semen does not constitute a 'thing in commerce but secretion containing the seed of life destined for human procreation.' *Paraplaix v CECOS*, Trib.gr.inst. Creteil, 16–17 Sept 1984, Gazette du Palais (2e sem) at 562.

[76] It may be argued that the Court, in investigating and deciding on the basis of the deceased's intent, was using the substituted judgment standard as used in the law of medical treatment decision-making for the incompetent patient. In this way, the Court examined the deceased's expressed intentions in order to pursue the decision which he would have made had he survived.

circumstances of the marriage (the couple married two days before Mr Paraplaix died from cancer) and the testimony of his surviving widow and parents to that effect. Although the Court did not discuss the specific source of the 'right to give life' or procreative liberty, the effect of its decision was to expand the right of procreative autonomy:[77]

> The case expands the procreative rights of both semen donors and unmarried, non-medically sterile women…In effect, the decision authorised a 'single' heterosexual woman to become inseminated through the services of CECOS. Presented with the choice between maintaining one's procreative means in a repository subject to state control or returning the same to an individual with whom the donor had been intimately related, the court chose the private sphere.[78]

[13.49] In the United States a different approach was taken in *Hecht v Superior Court of Los Angeles County*, where a legal dispute began as a result of a bequest by William Kane of 15 vials of his semen to his long-time companion, Deborah Hecht, for the purpose of conceiving a child after his death. Kane had expressly authorised the semen bank to release the semen to his executor. He had bequeathed the semen to Hecht in his will and appointed her his executor. One month later he committed suicide. Kane's two adult children from a previous marriage wished to have the semen destroyed 'to prevent the birth of a fatherless child, disruption of their existing family, and additional emotional, psychological and financial stress.' They characterised the desire to father children after one's death as 'egotistic and irresponsible.' Hecht argued that the destruction of the semen bequeathed to her would violate her Constitutional rights to privacy and liberty in procreation. At first instance, the Court ordered the semen destroyed. However, the Californian Court of Appeal overturned this order and held that at the time of his death:

> [Kane] had an interest, in the nature of ownership, to the extent that he had decision-making authority as to the use of his semen within the scope of policy set by law. Thus, the decedent had an interest in his semen which falls within the broad definition of property … as anything that may be subject of ownership and includes real and personal property and any interest therein.[79]

[13.50] Further, the Court held that there were no legislative provisions existing in California which could justify infringement of this authority. Therefore Kane had the right to bequeath the right to the semen by will. However, the Court limited its decision by concluding that because of the unique nature of semen as property, the ownership interest may be affected by factual circumstances and public policy. The Court was unable to decide, due to genuine issues of material fact as to Kane's testamentary capacity, what Kane's intention was in relation to the semen and adjourned the case until this, and other issues, were adjudicated.[80]

---

[77] Jones, 'Artificial Procreation, Societal Reconceptions: Legal Insight from France' (1988) 36 Am J of Comparative Law 525–545 at 530.

[78] Jones, at 539–540.

[79] *Hecht v Superior Court of Los Angeles County* 20 Cal Reptr 2d 275 at 281.

[80] In March 1994 a probate judge in Los Angeles ruled, on the facts, that Hecht was entitled to at least 3 of the 15 vials of semen left by Kane under an agreement signed by the parties after his death.

[13.51] This case demonstrates a willingness to consider semen as property in some sense – to the extent at least that it may be considered part of the deceased's estate.[81] The case was lauded by some as respecting the right of a man to do what he wishes with his semen while others warned of 'semen bank orphans'[82] (in other words, semen left in a semen bank without any decision as to its future use or any person competent to make such decisions), and it was opposed by others as the pursuit of immortality by storage of gametes for use decades after one's death.[83]

[13.52] In the UK, the issue of control and disposition of gametes is determined by the provisions of the Human Fertilisation and Embryology Authority Acts 1990–2008. In *R v Human Fertilisation and Embryology Authority (ex parte Blood)*[84] Stephen Blood was admitted to hospital with meningitis and while he was in a coma, his wife, Diane, asked doctors to remove semen from him so that it might be stored for future use. Mr Blood subsequently died and Mrs Blood sought access to the semen in order to conceive a child.[85] The Human Fertilisation and Embryology Authority took the view that the storage was unlawful and that the intended use of the semen would be illegal. This was based on the wording of the 1990 Act (repeated in the 2008 Act) which in Schedule 3 makes written consent to the posthumous use of semen mandatory.[86] The case was brought by way of judicial review of the Authority's decision to refuse to deliver up the semen to Mrs Blood for use in the UK and, alternatively, its refusal of a request to allow Mrs Blood to export the semen to another European country for treatment there.

[13.53] The Court of Appeal considered three issues – the storage and use of the semen in the UK, the export of semen (including EU law), and the decision of the Human

---

[81] Atherton, 'En Ventre sa Frigidaire: Posthumous Children in the Succession Context' (1999) 19(2) Legal Studies 139–164, at 152.

[82] This is also referred to by Steinbock, who argues that, on the fact of *Hecht*, it *must* be detrimental to a child to learn that its parent committed suicide before its conception. The assurance given in Kane's letter to his children, and expressly extended to any children yet to be conceived, that he loved them in his dreams, might not be enough to alleviate their feelings of rejection and abandonment. However, she says that this is different from the situation in which, say, the widow of a man who died of natural causes wants to conceive a child through use of his semen, as the child in this case should not feel rejected by its father. Steinbock, 'Semen as Property' (1995) 6(2) Stanford Law and Policy Review, 57 at 64.

[83] See generally Cannold, 'Who owns a dead man's semen?' (2004) 30 J Med Ethics 386.

[84] *R v Human Fertilisation and Embryology Authority (ex parte Blood)* [1997] EWCA Civ 4003.

[85] Morgan and Lee, 'In the Name of the Father? Ex parte Blood: Dealing with Novelty and Anomaly' (1997) Modern Law Review 841–856 at 841.

[86] The relevant provisions of the 1990 Act are as follows. Section 4(1) provides:

No person shall – (a) store any gametes, or (b) in the course of providing treatment services for any woman, use the semen of any man unless the services are being provided for the woman and the man together … except in pursuance of a licence.

It is also provided that certain conditions must be complied with by the licence holder under the terms of the Act. Those conditions, which were directly relevant to Mrs Blood, were set out in Schedule 3 of the Act which, inter alia, sets out the conditions in relation to the storage of gametes. Paragraph 8(1) states 'A person's gametes must not be kept in storage unless there is an effective consent by that person to their storage and they are stored in accordance with that consent.' Paragraph 1 requires that any consent given in pursuance of the Acts must be written.

Fertilisation and Embryology Authority (HFEA). In relation to storage and use in the United Kingdom, the Court held that the Act was clear that no storage of gametes could lawfully take place without written consent. Therefore, the storage of Mr Blood's semen was prohibited in the absence of written consent and the Authority had no discretion to authorise treatment in the UK. In relation to the export issue, the Court was of the opinion that it was unrealistic of the Authority to argue that its refusal of permission to export the semen was not withholding the provision of fertilisation treatment in another European State under arts 59 and 60 of the EC Treaty:

> From a functional point of view the ability to provide those services is not only substantially impeded but made impossible ... However, the fact that there is interference with the freedom to provide services does not mean that art 59 is infringed. It means no more than that ... the interference has to be justified in accordance with the well-established principles if it is not to contravene art 59. Those principles are ... that the decision must be non-discriminatory, it must be justified by some imperative requirement in the general interest, it must be suitable for securing the attainments of the objects which it pursues and it must not go beyond what is necessary to attain that objective...[87]

[13.54] The decision of the HFEA in this case, according to the Court, was made without due consideration having been taken of the cross-border rights to which Mrs Blood was entitled to under EC law. If the Authority had taken into account that Mrs Blood was entitled to receive treatment in another Member State unless there was some good reason why she should not be allowed to receive that treatment, and if the Authority had also taken into account the fact that this case did not set a precedent (it being made clear by the Court that the taking of semen in these circumstances was technically an offence), their decision may well have been different. The Court therefore allowed the appeal and remitted the matter to the HFEA, which subsequently permitted Mrs Blood's application to export the semen to Belgium. The Court did not consider the issue of the best interests of Mr Blood, stating only that:

> The question of the lawfulness of the storage is quite separate from the lawfulness of the taking of the semen from Mr Blood as he lay unconscious. The Act does not deal with this and the propriety of the treatment involved in taking the semen in this case is governed by common law principles relating to the patient's consent to the electro-ejaculation which have not been argued before us. It is therefore not necessary to make any comment about this.[88]

[13.55] The Human Fertilisation and Embryology Act 2008 therefore gives dispositional control to gamete providers, although it does not specify the issue of ownership. By requiring the gamete providers to give an effective written consent to the use to which the gametes may be put '...an aspect of a "property" interest in a "thing" is present – dispositional control – but it is difficult to see a set of "rights" over embryos that come close to anything other than a quasi-property interest in embryos and semen'.[89]

---

[87] *R v Human Fertilisation and Embryology Authority, ex p Blood* [1997] EWCA Civ 4003.

[88] *R v Human Fertilisation and Embryology Authority, ex p Blood* [1997] EWCA Civ 4003, at para 29.

[89] Grubb, 'I, Me, Mine: Bodies, Parts and Property' (1998) 3 Medical Law International 299–317 at 304.

[13.56] The issue of ownership of gametes was considered in the landmark case[90] of *Yearworth v North Bristol NHS Trust* in 2009.[91] The facts of the case were that six men were diagnosed with cancer for which they received chemotherapy treatment at a hospital in Bristol for which the defendant was responsible. The men accepted the advice of doctors at the hospital that they should undergo chemotherapy but that the treatment might damage their fertility. They were invited to produce semen samples prior to the start of the treatment on the basis that the hospital, which had a fertility unit licensed by the HFEA, would freeze their samples for their possible future use. The men all agreed to do so.

[13.57] The men signed consent forms for the storage and use of their semen in accordance with the Human Fertilisation and Embryology Act.[92] They were informed that their semen would be stored in liquid nitrogen and that the hospital would look after the samples with all possible care. The semen provided by the men was duly stored by the hospital but in June 2003 the amount of liquid nitrogen in the tanks in which the samples were stored fell below the requisite level and the men's semen thawed and perished irretrievably. The men were told about the loss of their semen and five of them alleged that they suffered consequent psychiatric injury, namely a mild or moderate depressive disorder. Three of the five men subsequently recovered their natural fertility so their claims were limited to the period during which they believed their fertility had been irretrievably lost, the fourth man's semen count was too low to have given rise to paternity in any event, the fifth man had died in the intervening period, and the sixth man alleged continuing mental distress in that it was unclear whether his fertility potential would recover in the future. The men claimed for compensation for the psychiatric injury and distress caused by the breach of duty.

[13.58] The Court took the view that damage to, and consequential loss of, the semen did not constitute 'personal injury'. Lord Judge CJ said:

> [I]t would be a fiction to hold that damage to a substance generated by a person's body, inflicted after its removal for storage purposes, constituted a bodily or 'personal injury' to him....We must deal in realities. To do otherwise would generate paradoxes, and yield ramifications, productive of substantial uncertainty, expensive debate and nice distinctions in an area of law which should be simple and the principles clear.[93]

[13.59] The men also claimed compensation in respect of the damage or loss of their property, ie their semen. Therefore the Court had to consider the novel claim that the men had legal ownership or possession of the semen at the time when the loss occurred.

---

90   A similar argument to that in *Yearworth* was made in *L v Human Fertilisation and Embryology Authority, Secretary of State for Health* [2008] EWHC 2149 in which a woman sought to store and use her deceased husband's semen despite the lack of written consent from him. The woman argued that the common law recognised the acquisition of property rights in biological materials in some circumstances. Although this argument was rejected by the court, the point was made that the common law does not stand still.

91   *Yearworth and others v North Bristol NHS Trust* [2009] EWCA Civ 37.

92   The events in this case took place under the provisions of the Human Fertilisation and Embryology Act 1990 but the amendments introduced by the 2008 Act would not have altered the outcome even if they had been in force at the time.

93   *Yearworth and others v North Bristol NHS Trust* [2009] EWCA Civ 37, para 23.

The Court of Appeal held that the question of whether something is capable of being owned cannot be decided in a vacuum and must be reached in context. Lord Judge CJ said 'the concept of ownership is no more than a convenient global description of different collections of rights held by persons over physical and other things.' He reflected upon the historical position in relation to the human corpse as well as the common law rule that a living human body is incapable of being owned. He discussed the case law above, both in the UK and US, as well as the Human Tissue Act 2004 and the Human Fertilisation and Embryology Act 2008. The latter imposes limitations on the ability of the gamete provider to deal with their gametes as they might wish by obliging licensed clinics to comply with the provisions of the Act in respect of storage and use of gametes. Thus, it was argued on behalf of the Trust that since the men could only have requested, as opposed to *directed*, the Trust to deal with their semen in a particular way, within the scheme of the Act, this equated to a denial of the men's ownership of the semen.

[13.60] Although the court could have upheld the men's claim by reference to the exception to the 'no property' rule set out in the *Doodeward* and *Kelly* cases discussed above, namely on the basis of the 'work and skill' applied in the freezing of the semen which conferred on it a substantially different attribute, ie the arrest of swift perishability. However, the Court declined to take this approach, as it was of the view that the 'no property' rule itself did not have a solid foundation and the distinctions drawn on the basis of the 'work and skill' exception were not entirely logical. Alternatively the court could have declined to address the issue on the basis that it was a matter to be dealt with by Parliament. Instead, the Court took a broader approach and held re-examined the law in this area.

[13.61] The Court held that the men did have ownership of the semen for the purposes of their claims in tort.[94] They had a right to possession which would found a claim in bailment (this is an obligation arising from taking possession of someone else's goods and it involves the assumption of responsibility for their safekeeping and return) if the semen they had deposited for their later use was negligently destroyed. The Court took the view that the men had deposited their semen on the basis that they retained control of it. The provisions of the Act in prioritising the requirement for consent from gamete providers preserved the right of the men to direct that the semen *not* be used in a certain way and therefore 'their negative control over its use remains absolute'. Although their rights to the use of the gametes had been restricted by the Act, this did not derogate from their ownership. The Court drew an analogy with statutes which limit a person's ability to use his land, such as building regulations and tenancy law, without eliminating his ownership of the land. Although the licence holder, namely the clinic, has duties under the Act which may conflict with the wishes of the men, for example in relation to continued storage past the expiration of the maximum statutory storage period, the Court held that 'no person, whether human or corporate, other than each man has any *rights* in relation to the semen which he has produced.'[95]

---

[94] See discussion by Skene, '*Jonathan Yearworth and others v North Bristol NHS Trust* [2009]' in Herring and Wall, *Landmark Cases in Medical Law* (Hart Publishing, 2015) 295–306.

[95] *Yearworth and others v North Bristol NHS Trust* [2009] EWCA Civ 37, para 45(f)(v).

[13.62] The court also referred to *Washington University v Catalona* discussed earlier,[96] and accepted the proposition that where the donors of tissue abandon that tissue, researchers may gain a proprietary interest in it to the exclusion of the donor. However, in this case the men had not 'abandoned' the semen in the way one might describe other products of the body such as hair clippings left on the barber's floor. In depositing the semen with the clinic, all parties intended that the semen would be available for the men to use later. By agreeing to take possession of the semen on behalf of the men, the clinic had assumed the responsibility of safe keeping. The court held that the liability under bailment of the semen was unique in these circumstances and the men were entitled to compensation for any psychiatric injury or distress reasonably foreseeable as a consequence of the breach of duty and breach of promise.

[13.63] This case is significant because it is the first major departure from previous judicial reasoning on the issue of property in the body and separated body parts.[97] Up to this point 'the approach of the courts when considering proprietary interests in human bodily material has been pragmatic and piecemeal', and due to the legal impact of the early case law, 'later judges have been constrained by these decisions.'[98] Although the Court was emphatic to point out that its decision was context-specific and should therefore be confined to the facts of the case, the decision is 'an important turning point in medical jurisprudence' and that it 'signals a sea change in judicial attitude towards patients' rights.'[99] It is also noteworthy because 'it is the first time that a case involving human tissue has been considered under the law of bailment.'[100] Quigley is of the view that this is particularly beneficial in cases such as this, where damages for psychiatric injury and mental distress are notoriously difficult to recover in tort so this ruling creates another option for plaintiffs. It is unclear whether the reasoning in this case would apply to cases involving other forms of tissue, as great emphasis was placed in this case on the mental distress suffered by the men due to the implication of the loss of the semen for their future chances of fatherhood. Cases involving other forms of tissue are unlikely to attract the same level of damages.

[13.64] Although the court did not discuss the property rights issue in *Warren v Care Fertility (Northampton) Ltd*[101] it is nonetheless useful to note the attitude of the courts to

---

96 Para **[13.33]**.

97 Similar decisions have been made in Australian courts since *Yearworth*. See *Bazley v Wesley Monash IVF* [2010] QSC 118 in which the court held that the co-executors of the estate of a man who had stored semen sample shortly before his death had sufficient proprietary interests in the semen to legally demand its return from the laboratory where it was held. The New South Wales Supreme Court similarly found that the widow of a recently deceased man had a right to possession of his semen in *Jocelyn Edwards; Re the estate of the late Mark Edwards* [2011] NSWSC 478. See also *Re H, AE (no 3)* [2013] SASC 196 and commentary by Skene, Proprietary Interests In Human Bodily Material: *Yearworth*, Recent Australian Cases on Stored Semen and their Implications (2012) Med Law Review 1–19.

98 Skene, 'The current approach of the courts' (2014) J Med Ethics 40(1) 10–13.

99 Laurie, Harmon and Porter, *Law and Medical Ethics* (10th edn, OUP, 2016) para 14.30. See also Harmon and Laurie, '*Yearworth v North Bristol NHS Trust*: property, principles, precedents and paradigms' (2010) 69 Cam LJ 476; Rostill, 'The ownership that wasn't meant to be: *Yearworth* and property rights in human tissue' (2014) 40 J Med Ethics 14.

100 Quigley, 'Property: The Future of Human Tissue?' (2009) 17 Medical Law Review 457 at 464.

101 *Warren v Care Fertility (Northampton) Ltd* [2014] EWHC 602.

applications for access to reproductive material outside of the statutory provisions. In this case the plaintiff sought a declaration that it was lawful for her late husband's semen, which had been taken prior to his unsuccessful treatment for cancer, to be stored beyond the statutory period for her use. In granting the declaration the court held that the plaintiff's husband had not been given certain information prior to the storage of his semen. Given that there was no conflict between the rights of the deceased and those of the plaintiff, the court agreed to take a purposive approach to the interpretation of the Act. As the Act allowed the storage and use of semen by a named person subject to the consent of the deceased gamete-provider, which had been provided in this case, the court was prepared to grant the declaration in keeping with his wishes.

[13.65] In the absence of legislation or judicial interpretation of common or indeed constitutional law principles in Ireland, the law in relation to property rights in bodies, living or dead, body parts or biological material, remains unclear. If the government chooses to regulate then it also matters how we regulate because 'as we have seen there is potential for harm and confusion, the chilling of research or the undermining of medical treatment if we do not regulate with an eye to the many and varied interests held in tissue.'[102] If it is left to the courts, on the one hand the courts may choose to broadly adopt the common law 'no property' principle acknowledging the exceptions that have been accepted in England and other jurisdictions. On the other hand the courts might be prepared to recognise the modern commercial value of the human body, its parts and tissue and attempt to fashion a solution that would balance the interests of researchers, commercial enterprises and funding agencies against the autonomy and privacy rights of tissue providers who seek to control and perhaps share in the commercial application of their tissue. In the end:

> Governments may set up regulatory authorities as the significance of each scientific advance becomes apparent but they are relatively powerless in the face of global pressures. What does seem clear is that, so far as the domestic scene is concerned, our courts must appreciate that this is a field in which technology and societal attitudes are advancing and being fashioned rapidly – and the common law must keep pace and accelerate as is necessary.[103]

BIOBANKING

[13.66] Medical progress is based on research and the human body and its tissue are indispensable for that purpose.[104] The use of tissue in research is not new but the modern focus on genetic characteristics and the large-scale nature of such research which may extend across many generations and groups of individuals has changed the design of such research and the legal and ethical issues it raises. 'As a consequence of the developments in human tissue research, the status of the human tissue has changed from a *res derelicta* into a substance which has personal (informational) value; because of the

---

[102] Goold, 'Why does it matter how we regulate the use of human body parts?' (2014) J Med Ethics 40:3–9.

[103] Laurie, Harmon and Porter, *Law and Medical Ethics* (10th edn, OUP) 2016 para.14.65.

[104] See discussion in Nuffield Council of Bioethics Report (2011) *Human Bodies: Donation for Medicine and Research*. Available at www.nuffieldbioethics.org.

commercial prospects the research offers, human tissue has also become a commodity.'[105]

[13.67] Tissue collections, sometimes called biobanks, are assembled for use in patient-care and research activities.[106] Human biobanks and genetic research databases are structured resources that can be used for the purpose of genetic research which include: (a) human biological materials and/or information generated from the analysis of same; and (b) extensive associated information.[107] They have a high impact potential for public health and medicine, as new drug discovery and the development of so-called personalised medicine depend on the study of large collections of epidemiological, clinical and biological samples and information from large numbers of patients and healthy persons.[108] These databases may be disease-specific or unspecified collections of tissue that is donated or left over after surgery (population-based biobanks) and they may be established on a commercial basis or in the public sector. When combined with personal information about the donor/patient, they create a valuable virtual database as a source for research.

[13.68] The practice of biobanking raises profound ethical and legal questions about the circumstances under which such banks are established and how the benefits of the banks are harnessed.[109] The scope of variations between biobanks is growing and there are fundamental questions about how best to govern and regulate them given the differences between the characteristics of collections. Policymakers and lawmakers have struggled with these issues, and existing regulatory frameworks have come under sustained criticism:[110]

> Without any specifically tailored, comprehensive provision for biobanks, a highly complex, confusing, inconsistent, uncoordinated, duplicative yet incomplete governance patchwork has evolved. It is characterized by an excessive number of legal, ethical, and other guidance instruments; an array of competing regulatory authorities and actors, whose roles, remits, and responsibilities often are unclear; a *de facto* over-dependence on

---

[105] Roscam-Abbing, 'Human Tissue Research, Individual Rights and Bio-Banks' in Gunning and Holm (eds) *Ethics, Law and Society, Vol II* (Ashgate, 2006) 7–16, at 7.

[106] Biobanks used in patient care include umbilical cord blood banks, which comprise collections of umbilical cord blood retained after delivery of a child to enable storage of stem cells for possible autologous transfusion (transfusion to the same donor) in the future. Such collections may also be used for unrelated transfusion, subject to matching with the recipient. For further details and discussion see European Group on Ethics in Science and New Technologies to the European Commission, Opinion No 19 Ethical Aspects of Umbilical Cord Blood Banking (2004).

[107] OECD 2009. Guidelines for Human Biobanks and Genetic Research Databases (00 2009 3B 1 P) no 89497. For more detail on trends in biobanking in Europe, see Schulte in den Baumen et al, 'Data Protection and Sample Management in Biobanking – A Legal Dichotomy' (2010) Genomics, Society and Policy Vol 6 No 1 pp 33–46.

[108] Zika et al, *Pharmacogenetics and Pharmacogenomics: State-of-the-Art and Potential Socio-Economic Impact in the EU* (2006) Euro Commission DG JRC/IPTS, EUR 22214.

[109] Andrews, 'Harnessing the Benefits of Biobanks' (Spring 2005) Journal of Law, Medicine & Ethics 22–30 at 23.

[110] Gibbons, 'Regulating Biobanks: A Twelve-Point Typological Tool' (2009) Med Law Rev 17, pp 313–346.

informal systems, self-regulation, and 'soft' regulatory techniques; and a worrying legitimacy deficit.[111]

[13.69] In addition to these important concerns about regulation and governance, there are also other issues that relate perhaps more personally to the person from whom the tissue is taken. Unlike other forms of medical research discussed in Chapter 14, the focus of concern here is not the physical integrity of the research participant, but rather on the control he has over his biological material. The concept of battery protects living people from physical interventions, but there is no overriding legal concept to govern the relationship between the tissue source and the biobank.[112] Questions which arise here include what type of information should the tissue source be given about the purposes to which the tissue will be put; what form of consent is appropriate; what should be done with genetic information obtained from a biobank; under what circumstances is commercialisation of samples and information in biobanks acceptable; how can people protect themselves from the unauthorised use of or commercialisation of their tissue samples; and how should the benefits of biobanking be shared?[113]

[13.70] Confidentiality and data protection principles also apply here due to the informational value of human tissue, and therefore safeguards must be built into the biobank relating to the quality of data, data security and other protections, which will be discussed below. A great variability exists in the identification of the samples used, depending on the source of the material and the purpose of the research. In some studies where individuals just serve as the sources of the samples, identifying them is not necessary. For other studies in which extensive information on diagnosis, family history and demographics is crucial, the ability to identify the source of the sample is essential.[114]

Consent

[13.71] The doctrine and meaning of informed consent in healthcare has been discussed in Chapter 10. In relation to research it is also a fundamental prerequisite that research should not be undertaken without the subject/participant's consent. 'The research goals of advancing scientific understanding and curing diseases are laudable, but research is not a matter of conscription. People can refuse to participate in research, even if it

---

[111] Gibbons, at 314 quoting from Kaye and Gibbons, 'Mapping the Regulatory Space for Genetic Databases and Biobanks in England and Wales' (2008) 9 Med Law Intl 111 at 126.

[112] See discussion of an altruism based system in Nuffield Council of Bioethics Report (2011) *Human Bodies: Donation for Medicine and Research*. See critique of this approach by Devaney, 'Rewards and incentives for the provision of human tissue for research' (2014) J Med Ethics 40:48–50. Devaney argues that a fair system for incentivising and rewarding the provision of human tissue in research should be developed.

[113] Derived from Andrews, 'Harnessing the Benefits of Biobanks' (Spring 2005) Journal of Law, Medicine & Ethics 22–30 at 24.

[114] Godard et al, 'Data Storage and DNA Banking for Biomedical Research: Informed Consent, Confidentiality, Quality Issues, Ownership, Return Of Benefits. A Professional Perspective' (2003) Eur J of Hum Gen 11, Suppl 2, S88–S122.

involves no risk to them and enormous potential benefit to the community.'[115] In recent years there have been calls for the reconceptualisation of participation in health research as a moral obligation. For example, Harris argues that seriously debilitating diseases give rise to important needs and since medical research is necessary to relieve those needs in many circumstances, people are morally obliged to act as research subjects.[116] Similarly, Rhodes says that research participation is a moral obligation for reasons of justice, beneficence and self-development: because we all benefit significantly from modern medicine, we are all required to do our part in advancing the state of medical knowledge.[117] However, if research participation is considered as a duty, then it may not make sense to seek informed consent at all since the freedom to decline to participate is restricted by the blameworthiness that would attach to such an action. People may thus choose to participate in research to avoid blame rather than based on their understanding of the risks and benefits of participation. Despite these arguments in favour of a moral duty to participate in research, informed consent currently remains the gold standard.

[13.72] In seeking informed consent to donate tissue to a biobank, it is generally agreed that the following information should be provided to donors:[118]

- the voluntary nature of participation;
- the type of consent used (specific or general);
- the circumstances of sampling, including risks of the procedure;
- the purposes, nature, extent and duration of the proposed use of the tissue;
- the possibility of transfer of samples and data to third parties;
- the possibility of communication of research results to the donor;
- information on the possible consequences of the communication of results for the donor and his family;
- storage and security/protection of personal data;
- the identifiability or anonymity of the samples and/or data;
- the right to withdraw at any time, and the consequences of withdrawal;
- any commercialisation prospects for the proposed research, and;
- any payments for donors or other form of benefit sharing.

[13.73] One of the most interesting issues in relation to informed consent in this context is the question of whether consent may be given in advance for future unspecified research uses to which the samples may be put, variously known as general, broad or blanket consent. Some argue that individuals cannot consent to a variety of uses which are not known at the point at which consent is given, as this cannot be accurately

---

[115] Andrews, 'Harnessing the Benefits of Biobanks' (Spring 2005) Journal of Law, Medicine & Ethics 22–30 at 24.

[116] Harris, 'Scientific Research is a Moral Duty' (2005) Journal of Medical Ethics 31, No 4,242–48.

[117] Rhodes, 'Rethinking Research Ethics' (2005) Am J Of Bioethics 5, No 1; Rhodes, 'In Defense of the Duty to Participate in Biomedical Research' (2008) Am J Of Bioethics 8, No 10 : 37–38. See also Schaefer et al, 'The Obligation to Participate in Biomedical Research' (2009) JAMA 302, 67–72; and Rennie, 'Viewing Research Participation as a Moral Obligation: In Whose Interests?' (2011) Hastings Centre Report 41, No 2: 40–47.

[118] Watson, Kay and Smith, 'Integrating Biobanks: Addressing the Practical and Ethical Issues to Deliver a Valuable Tool for Cancer Research' (2010) Nature Reviews Cancer, Vol 10: 646–651.

described as informed consent.[119] For example, Árnason says that 'There is no such thing as 'general informed consent.' The more general the consent is, the less informed it becomes. It is misleading to use the notion of informed consent for participation in research that is unforeseen and has not been specified in a research protocol.'[120]

[13.74] There may be two options in relation to informed consent in this context. The first option is to obtain informed consent from participants before their healthcare information is placed in the database. But at this point no specific research plans exist, so it is impossible to explain any of the ingredients of informed consent to the prospective participants. There are no specific objectives to be explained, no determinate risks or benefits to be assessed. Informed consent for research before entering the database would, therefore, be 'empty and senseless'. The only specific ingredient that would be possible to explain is the right to withdraw information from the database at any time. The second option would be to obtain informed consent from individual participants for each particular research after entering the database. But because of the heavy emphasis on coding and privacy this would be extremely complicated and cumbersome. Not only would it jeopardise individual privacy but also, according to many scientists, it would severely limit the research possibilities that the database is intended to provide.[121]

[13.75] The classical ethical approach would insist that where it is impossible to specify in advance all future uses of the samples, it is necessary to get fresh consent for each use as it arises. Although laudable in its strict adherence to the ethical values enshrined in the doctrine of informed consent, this approach is perceived as problematic in practical terms, as the individual tissue source may have died in the intervening period, or may be uncontactable. Re-contacting donors some time after the initial donation also runs the risk of insufficient positive responses, which may undermine the value of the research.[122] From the perspective of researchers, 'the cry is widely heard that informed consent documents have become almost unintelligible, that individuals' fears are unfounded, their desires for control unwarranted, and that research is being dramatically slowed and even brought to a halt'.[123]

[13.76] To overcome these difficulties, it has been proposed that a general or broad form of consent might be used which acknowledges that the samples might be put to other, unspecified uses in the future and dispenses with the requirement for further consent from the tissue source. This may be referred to as the 'right to take a risk', which allows

---

[119] See Annas, 'Rules for Research on Human Genetic Variation – Lessons from Iceland' (2000) NEJM 342: 1830–33; Chadwick and Berg, 'Solidarity and Equity: New Ethical Frameworks for Genetic Databases' (2001) Nature Reviews Genetics, 2:318–21; O'Neill, 'Informed Consent and Genetic Information' (2001) Studies in History and Philosophy of Biological and Biomedical Sciences 32(4): 689–704.

[120] Árnason, 'Coding and Consent: Moral Challenges of the Database Project in Iceland' (2004) Bioethics, Vol 18 No 1.

[121] Árnason, 'Coding and Consent: Moral Challenges of the Database Project in Iceland' (2004) Bioethics, Vol 18 No 1.

[122] Roscam-Abbing, 'Human Tissue Research, Individual Rights and Bio-Banks' in Gunning and Holm (eds) *Ethics, Law and Society, Vol II* (Ashgate, 2006) 7–16, at 13.

[123] Wright Clayton, 'Informed Consent and Biobanks' (2005) Journal of Law, Medicine and Ethics, Spring 15.

donors to waive further information and consent as long as they are fully informed at the time of initial consent about the incomplete degree of information to be provided to them in the future.[124] Opponents of general consent argue that the impracticality of re-contacting donors does not justify departure from important ethical principles and that it 'implies an erosion of the informed consent requirement that is neither necessary, nor proportional, and therefore not legally justified.'[125] Studies of patients and tissue donors vary in relation to the preference shown for general or specific consent with common influencing factors including sponsorship by industry, public data sharing, the range of options given for the control of data, and the degree of positive experience of the healthcare system and perception of the biobank.[126]

[13.77] One solution to the difficulty of re-contacting donors for fresh consent is to allow for a waiver of consent if the samples are anonymised and the research receives ethical approval from a research ethics committee, both of which are thought to provide sufficient safeguards against any potential harm to tissue donors. For example, under the UK Human Tissue Act 2004, tissue from living patients, for example biopsy or blood samples, can ordinarily be used for research only with the person's consent. However, consent is not required for research on tissue from living patients if the samples are anonymised (or coded to make sure patient or participant information is not identifiable) and the project has recognised ethics committee approval; or if the tissue samples were obtained before 1 September 2006 (when the Human Tissue Act came into force).

[13.78] Another solution is not to 'stubbornly insist' on informed consent in circumstances in which it clearly does not fit, as in relation to biobanks where full information regarding future research projects cannot be given, but rather to find another way in which individuals may express their willingness to participate. This might be called 'permission' or 'authorisation' in order to avoid confusion with the traditional model of informed consent.[127] Authorisation might be said to be in the spirit of informed consent, but it is far more general and open and should, therefore, not be confused with it. Authorisation does not imply consent to any particular research project but implies that an individual permits in writing that healthcare data will be processed from his medical records and moved in a coded form into the database. The authorisation also implies that the individual has been informed about, and that he claims to have understood at least the following: what information about him will be placed into the database; how privacy will be secured; how the information will be connected to other data; who will have access to the information; in what context the

---

[124] Discussed in Schulte in den Baumen et al, 'Data Protection and Sample Management in Biobanking – A Legal Dichotomy' (2010) Genomics, Society and Policy Vol 6 No 1 pp 33–46 at 39. The authors acknowledge that the 'right to take a risk' is a highly individualistic approach and is not yet a widely accepted concept in the biobanking community or among data protection experts.

[125] Roscam-Abbing, 'Human Tissue Research, Individual Rights and Bio-Banks' in Gunning and Holm (eds) *Ethics, Law and Society, Vol II* (Ashgate, 2006) 7–16, at 13.

[126] D'Abramo, Schildmann and Vollmann, 'Research participants' perceptions and views on consent for biobank research: a review of empirical data and ethical analysis', BMC Medical Ethics (2015) 16:60.

[127] Árnason, 'Coding and Consent: Moral Challenges of the Database Project in Iceland' (2004) Bioethics, Vol 18 No 1.

information will be used and for what purposes;[128] how consent for genetic research will be obtained; what are the foreseeable risks and benefits of participation; how research on the data will be regulated; and that the individual has the right to withdraw the healthcare data at any time.[129]

International regulation and guidelines

[13.79] The establishment of population-based genetic databases is extensively covered in European and international regulations.[130] For example, in 2003 the World Health Organisation (WHO) stated that archived material removed in the course of medical care should be capable of being used for research once anonymised and subject to strong ethical justification to deviate from traditional consent requirements.[131] The Human Genome Organisation (HUGO),[132] the Council for International Organisations of Medical Sciences (CIOMS)[133] and UNESCO[134] have recommended that human biological samples may be used for research in either anonymised or coded form without re-consent, provided certain conditions have been met. These include notification of such a policy to patients, no objection by patients, approval by an ethics committee, minimal risk, potential significant benefits and the impracticability of obtaining consent in the circumstances.[135] In relation to samples specifically collected for research use, the question arises as to whether the samples may be used for further research for which consent was not initially obtained.[136] Although it is commonly accepted that future uses should be specifically disclosed to the donor at the outset if possible, in recent years there has also been discussion of a concept of general or broad

---

[128] For example, in Iceland these purposes are stated in the Act on a Health Sector Database No 139/1998, art 10: 'Data recorded or acquired by processing on the health-sector database may be used to develop new or improved methods of achieving better health, prediction, diagnosis and treatment of disease, to seek the most economic ways of operating health services, and for making reports in the health sector.'

[129] Árnason, 'Coding and Consent: Moral Challenges of the Database Project in Iceland' (2004) Bioethics, Vol 18 No 1, at 45.

[130] For example, Council of Europe (1997) Convention for the Protection of Human Rights and Dignity of the Human Being with regard to the Application of Biology and Medicine: Convention on Human Rights and Biomedicine, Oviedo, 4. IV.1997; European Group on Ethics (EGE) in Science and New Technologies to the European Commission (1998) Ethical Aspects of Human Tissue Banking; World Medical Association (2002) Declaration on Ethical Considerations regarding Health Databases.

[131] WHO (European Partnership on Patients Rights and Citizens Empowerment) (2003) Genetic Databases – Assessing the Benefits and the Impact on Human Rights and Patient Rights, Geneva. Section 4.4.

[132] Human Genome Organisation (1998) Statement on DNA Sampling: Control and Access, para 6.1 – referring to general consent as 'blanket consent'.

[133] CIOMS (2002) International Ethical Guidelines for Biomedical Research Involving Human Subjects, Geneva, Guideline 4.

[134] UNESCO (2003) International Declaration on Human Genetic Data, Geneva, arts 16 & 17.

[135] See discussion by Knoppers, 'Biobanking: International Norms' (2005) Journal of Law, Medicine and Ethics, Spring 7.

[136] Recommendation Rec (2006) 4 of the Committee of Ministers to member states on research on biological materials of human origin.

consent (also called authorisation) which is particularly suited to large-scale longitudinal studies or research databases. Although not universally accepted yet, 'eventually it may constitute an acceptable exception for certain types of biobanking research provided it is justified both scientifically and ethically and certain criteria are met.'[137]

[13.80] Some European jurisdictions permit general or broad consent for unspecified future research use, for example Germany,[138] Sweden,[139] Iceland and Estonia.[140] General consent is seen as acceptable in these jurisdictions if two conditions are met, namely research ethics review and the right of the participant to withdraw at any time.[141] This is a relaxation of the classical research ethics position in relation to biobanks and a less strict standard of consent.[142] The first condition does not appear to pose significant problems, at least if research ethics committees apply consistent standards. Research ethics review is familiar to researchers working in biomedical research although some may argue that it slows the progress of their research and imposes an unnecessary bureaucracy on them. The second condition is perhaps more difficult as the withdrawal of samples in any significant number from the database conflicts with the scientific imperative of maintaining the statistical integrity of the population based databases, particularly given the ambition to use them as the vehicle for longitudinal studies. All biobanks incorporate the right of tissue sources to withdraw their samples but the interpretation of the right varies. For example, in Iceland the samples will not be withdrawn or destroyed but will be noted on a coded list of persons who have opted out so their data will not be used by biobanks.[143]

[13.81] The UK Biobank offers a set of graded options for withdrawal, ranging from complete withdrawal to discontinued participation and no further contact requested,[144]

---

[137] Knoppers, 'Biobanking: International Norms' (2005) Journal of Law, Medicine and Ethics, Spring 7, at 9.

[138] Nationaler Ethikrat (2004) *Biobanken fur die Forschung* Berlin, Germany.

[139] Biobanks Act 2003.

[140] Kaye et al, 'Population Genetic Databases: A Comparative Analysis of the Law in Iceland, Sweden, Estonia and the UK', TRAMES 8:15–33.

[141] Roscam-Abbing says that this is incompatible with the right to private life under the ECHR, which, in the medical context, implies the obligation to provide sufficient information to allow the donor to make a well-founded decision. Roscam-Abbing, 'Human Tissue Research, Individual Rights and Bio-Banks' in Gunning and Holm (eds) *Ethics, Law and Society, Vol II* (Ashgate, 2006) 7–16, at 13.

[142] Elger and Caplan, 'Consent and Anonymisation in Research Involving Biobanks' (2006) EMBO Reports Vol 7 No 7 1–6 at 3.

[143] Regulations issued by the Icelandic Ministry of Health and Social Security on the Keeping and Utilisation of Biological Samples in Biobanks No 134/2001. This is described by some ethicists as a somewhat diluted version of withdrawal.

[144] www.ukbiobank.ac.uk. For further discussion of guidance available in the UK, see Medical Research Council, Human Tissue and Biological Samples for Use in Research, Operational and Ethical Guidelines 2001; House of Lords Select Committee on Science and Technology, Human Genetic Databases: Challenges and Opportunities 2001; Human Genetics Commission, Inside Information: Balancing Interests in the Use of Personal Genetic Data 2002. For details about the Scottish biobank, Generation Scotland, see http://www.generationscotland.org/.

which attempts to balance the interest of the donor in the removal of the data with the interest of the scientist in some form of continued access to the data if possible. In Estonia, donors have the right to have their data deleted from the database on request, with any violation of this right being punishable as a criminal offence.[145] The German Ethics Council says that donors must have the right to withdraw their consent at any time and that this right cannot be waived. However, there should be provision for donors to allow samples and data to continue to be used if their identity cannot be disclosed.[146]

[13.82] The Council of Europe's Committee of Ministers recommended in 2006 that information and consent or authorisation to obtain biological materials for research should be as specific as possible with regard to any foreseen research uses and the choices available in that respect.[147] It provides that residual biological materials removed from persons for purposes other than research, should only be made available for research activities with appropriate consent or authorisation. Article 22 provides that if the proposed use of identifiable biological material is not within the scope of prior consent given by the person, reasonable efforts should be made to obtain fresh consent. However, if this is not possible with reasonable efforts, the material can be used for research subject to independent evaluation that the research addresses an important scientific interest; the aims of the research could not reasonably be achieved using biological materials for which consent can be obtained; and there is no evidence that the person concerned expressly objected to such research use. Unlinked anonymised samples may be used for research, provided such use does not violate any restrictions placed by the person concerned.

[13.83] A new set of recommendations to the Council of Europe member states on the removal, storage and use of biological materials for research purposes was adopted by the Committee of Ministers in May 2016 to take into account 'new developments in the field of biobanking, such as the increasingly diverse origin of biological materials stored in collections, the difficulty to guarantee non-identifiability of such samples, the increasing amount of research involving materials coming from different collections, and the importance of research on biomaterials removed from persons not able to consent.'[148] Article 10 provides that prior to consent to or authorisation for the storage of biological materials for future research, the person concerned should be provided with comprehensible information that is as precise as possible with regard to:

- the nature of any envisaged research use and the possible choices that he or she could exercise;

- the conditions applicable to the storage of the materials, including access and possible transfer policies; and

- any relevant conditions governing the use of the materials, including re-contact and feedback.

---

[145] Human Genes Research Act 2000.

[146] Nationaler Ethikrat, *Biobanks for Research OPINION* (2004).

[147] Recommendation Rec (2006) 4 of the Committee of Ministers to member states on research on biological materials of human origin.

[148] Recommendation CM/Rec (2016) 6 of the Committee of Ministers to member States on research on biological materials of human origin (Adopted by the Committee of Ministers on 11 May 2016).

The person concerned should also be informed of the rights and safeguards provided for by law, and specifically of his or her right to refuse consent or authorisation and to withdraw consent or authorisation at any time. Prior to the removal of biological materials for storage for future research, the person concerned should be provided with additional information specific to the intervention carried out to remove the materials.

[13.84] Article 11 provides that biological materials should only be removed for storage for future research with the prior, free, express and documented consent of the person concerned that is: (i) specific to the intervention carried out to remove the materials; and (ii) as precise as possible with regard to the envisaged research use. Biological materials previously removed for another purpose should only be stored for future research with the consent of the person concerned, as provided for by law. Whenever possible, consent should be requested before biological materials are removed. Biological materials previously removed for another purpose and already non-identifiable may be stored for future research subject to authorisation provided for by law. There are also provisions in relation to persons unable to give consent, governance of collections, the giving of feedback to individuals in relation to the material they provided and access and oversight.

[13.85] In relation to the use of biological materials in research, art 21 provides that this is only permissible if the research is within the scope of the consent or authorisation given by the person concerned. If the proposed use of identifiable biological materials in a research project is not within the scope of prior consent or authorisation, if any, given by the person concerned, consent or authorisation to the proposed use should be sought and, to this end, reasonable efforts should be made to contact the person concerned. The wish of the person concerned not to be contacted should be observed. Where the attempt to contact the person concerned proves unsuccessful, these biological materials should only be used in the research project subject to an independent evaluation of the fulfilment of the following conditions:

  i.   evidence is provided that reasonable efforts have been made to contact the person concerned;
  ii.   the research addresses an important scientific interest and is in accordance with the principle of proportionality;
  iii. the aims of the research could not reasonably be achieved using biological materials for which consent or authorisation can be obtained; and
  iv.   there is no evidence that the person concerned has expressly opposed such research use.

Any use of biological materials in an identifiable form should be justified in advance in the research protocol. Non-identifiable biological materials may be used in a research project provided that such use does not violate any restrictions defined by the person concerned before the materials have been rendered non-identifiable and subject to authorisation provided for by law.

[13.86] In the United States the prevailing opinion for some time was in favour of the classical standard of informed consent. In dealing with the difficulties of obtaining consent for future unspecified uses, multi-layered consent was seen as the most acceptable means of ensuring that participants were informed of the relevant information and choices. This form of consent allowed for different choices to be presented on a detailed form, enabling participants to choose to limit their consent to use for research into a specific disease or a specific research project if they wished. This was seen by some as imposing a burden on research.[149] The National Bioethics Advisory Committee proposed a strategy of waivers in which informed consent would not be necessary where the research involved no more than minimal risk, it would not adversely affect the rights or welfare of the subjects, the research could not practicably be carried out without the waiver, and whenever appropriate, the subjects would be provided with additional information following their participation. It was also recommended that, despite the granting of the waiver, consent should be sought unless it was impracticable to locate the subjects in question.[150]

[13.87] The US Office for Human Research Participation (OHRP)[151] has adopted a different solution. It takes the view that research on unidentifiable specimens should not be described as research involving human subjects and therefore it is not necessary to obtain informed consent or research ethics review. This is based on the interpretation of 'research involving human subjects' as involving an interaction with a living person. The OHRP considers private information or specimens not to be individually identifiable when they cannot be linked to specific individuals by the investigator(s) either directly or indirectly through coding systems.[152] To come within this definition, the following conditions must be met: the private information or specimens were not collected specifically for the currently proposed research project through an interaction or intervention with living individuals; and the investigator(s) cannot readily ascertain the identity of the individual(s) to whom the coded private information or specimens pertain because, for example, the investigators and the holder of the key enter into an agreement prohibiting the release of the key to the investigators under any circumstances, until the individuals are deceased; there are IRB-approved written policies and operating procedures for a repository or data management centre that prohibit the release of the key to the investigators under any circumstances, until the individuals are deceased; or there are other legal requirements prohibiting the release of the key to the investigators, until the individuals are deceased. The advantage of this approach is clearly that it facilitates research by avoiding the requirement for informed consent and ethics review simply by entering into an agreement prohibiting the researchers accessing the code by which the tissue sources might be identified.

[13.88] There is no legislation currently in place in Ireland dealing with the use of human tissue for research although there are biobanks in existence in this jurisdiction operating under their own codes of governance.[153] The Tissue and Cells Regulations

---

[149] Elger and Caplan, 'Consent and Anonymisation in Research Involving Biobanks' (2006) EMBO Reports Vol 7 No 7 1–6 at 3

[150] NBAC (1999) *Research Involving Human Biological Materials: Ethical Issues and Policy Guidance,* Vol 1, Rockville MD, USA.

[151] OHRP is part of the Office of the Assistant Secretary for Health (OASH) in the Office of the Secretary (OS), US Department of Health and Human Services. It provides clarification and guidance, develops educational programmes and materials, maintains regulatory oversight, and provides advice on ethical and regulatory issues in biomedical and behavioural research.

[152] Guidance on Research Using Coded Private Information or Specimens (2008) See http://www.hhs.gov/ohrp/policy/cdebiol.html.

[153] See for example Biobank Ireland http://www.biobankireland.com/governance/.

(2006) apply only where the tissues and cells are used for human application, not research.[154] The former Irish Council for Bioethics published an opinion on the storage and use of human biological material in 2005 in which it recommended a form of layered consent which would provide participants with options relating to future unspecified use of their biological material.[155] It recommended that these options might include refusal of such future use; limitation of future use for research related to the condition for which the sample was originally collected; request for further contact and fresh consent for any future use; or permission for future use without the requirement for fresh consent but subject to approval by a research ethics committee. Proposals for human tissue legislation were published by the Department of Health in 2009 but have not yet been enacted.

Data protection

[13.89] EC Directive 95/46/EC provides for the protection of individuals with regard to the processing of personal data and in relation to the free movement of such data. It was transposed into national law in Ireland by the Data Protection Act 2003. Its objective is to secure the free flow of personal data within the internal market while ensuring a high level of protection for citizens. Health data have a special position in the Directive but the protections offered therein are not absolute and may be overridden by considerations of the public interest where required.

[13.90] Biobanks were not commonplace at the time when the Data Protection Directive was drawn up and thus are not explicitly mentioned in the Directive. However, art 8 provides that the general prohibition on processing of sensitive data (which includes health data) does not apply where the data subject has given his explicit consent to the processing (para 2 (a)); where the processing is required for the purpose of preventive medicine, medical diagnosis, the provision of care or treatment or the management of healthcare services (para 3); or where Member States have, for reasons of substantial public interest, laid down additional exemptions by national law or by decision of the supervisory authority subject to the provision of suitable safeguards (para 4). Recital 34 to the Directive which relates to art 8(4) provides that public health is a legitimate ground for Member States to derogate from the prohibition on the processing of sensitive data. These appear to be the only legal basis for biobanks in the Directive.[156] However, art 8(4) is not harmonising, as it enables rather than obliges Member States to lay down exemptions for reasons of public interest:[157]

> While the Directive enables Member States to set up regulations which enable biobanks to achieve their goals, there is no harmonized legal situation in Europe. Member States are

---

[154] European Communities (Quality and Safety of Human Tissues and Cells) Regulations 2006 (SI 158/2006). The Irish Medicines Board is designated as the competent authority for the implementation of this legislation.

[155] Available at www.health.gov.ie.

[156] See Schulte in den Baumen et al, 'Data Protection and Sample Management in Biobanking – A Legal Dichotomy' (2010) Genomics, Society and Policy Vol 6 No 1 pp 33–46 at 38.

[157] Article 8(4) of the Directive 95/46/EC provides that: 'Subject to the provision of suitable safeguards, Member States *may*, for reasons of substantial public interest, lay down exemptions in addition to those laid down in para 2...' (emphasis added).

not obliged to use art 8(4) for biobanking purposes and if they do, they still have discretion how and to what extent they use it. The Directive also empowers Member States to define divergent safeguards which may force biobanking networks and multi-centre research studies using biobanks to follow a 'gold standard' (in this case the strictest regulatory environment) approach whenever they want to transfer data.[158]

[13.91] It is unclear whether biological samples themselves constitute data for the purposes of the Directive. Under art 2(a) of the Directive, personal data is 'any *information* relating to an identified or identifiable natural person' (emphasis added). Therefore, biological material may not be seen as data, as it is not information itself. 'Like a hard drive, it contains data but another technical step is required to extract the data'.[159] The Directive applies if data are extracted from biological material in a way which could identify a person. As the Art 29 Data Protection Working Party stated in 2007:

> Human tissue samples (like a blood sample) are themselves sources out of which biometric data are extracted, but they are not biometric data themselves (as for instance a pattern for fingerprints is biometric data, but the finger itself is not). Therefore the extraction of information from the samples is collection of personal data, to which the rules of the Directive apply. The collection, storage and use of tissue samples themselves may be subject to separate sets of rules.[160]

Therefore, a biobank may not encounter data protection issues if it stores and transfers information to a third party without any collection of secondary processing of personal information. However, the separation of data and samples seems artificial to most researchers and there is a growing tendency to apply the legal framework of data protection to both samples and data.[161]

[13.92] In *S and Marper v the UK*,[162] the applicants complained under art 8 of the ECHR that authorities in the UK continued to retain their fingerprints, biological samples and DNA profiles after criminal proceedings against them had ended with an acquittal or been discontinued. The Court held that all three categories of personal information constituted personal data within the meaning of the Data Protection Directive. It considered that the systematic retention of such material was sufficiently intrusive to constitute interference with the right to respect for private life. An individual's concern about the possible future use of private information is legitimate and the Court could not discount the possibility that in the future the private-life interests bound up with genetic information may be adversely affected in novel or unanticipated ways. Although interference with private life may be justified 'where necessary in a democratic society', the margin of appreciation to be accorded to States in this regard must be narrower where the right at stake is crucial to the individual's enjoyment of intimate or key rights. The blanket and indiscriminate nature of the retention in this case of persons suspected but not convicted of criminal offences failed to strike a fair balance between the

---

[158] See Schulte in den Baumen et al, 'Data Protection and Sample Management in Biobanking – A Legal Dichotomy' (2010) Genomics, Society and Policy Vol 6 No 1 pp 33–46 at 38.

[159] See Schulte in den Baumen at 40.

[160] http://ec.europa.eu/justice/policies/privacy/docs/wpdocs/2007/wp136_en.pdf. See also Solbakk, Holm, and Hofmann (eds) *The Ethics of Research Biobanking* (2009 Springer) p 291.

[161] *Marper v the UK* ECtHR Appl Nos 30562/04 and 30566/04.

[162] *Marper v the UK* 30562/04 [2008] ECHR 1581.

competing public and private interests involved, and thus the State had overstepped any acceptable margin of appreciation in this regard. The Court therefore held that there had been a violation of art 8 of the ECHR.

[13.93] It appears that there is no competence for the EU to govern the exchange of biological samples themselves, as this falls under the field of property law in many Member States.[163] Thus problems arise under data protection when samples are shipped routinely amongst EU Member States and beyond. It is argued this arises from the fact that public health is not harmonised in the Data Protection Directive as well as the perception that data protection principles are interpreted differently in Member States and their ethics committees.[164]

[13.94] As a result of the differences in interpretation of the Directive across the member states, it was agreed to introduce a new data protection regulation. The EU General Data Protection Regulation (GDPR) was published in May 2016.[165] Following a two-year implementation period, the GDPR will be applied across the EU from 25 May 2018. The GDPR will replace the existing EU Data Protection Directive 95/45/EC, adopting a more harmonised approach to data protection across the EU. It is aimed generally at 'enhancing data protection rights of individuals and improving business opportunities in the digital single market.' As a regulation, the GDPR will be directly applicable in the member states, without the need for any implementing legislation. The GDPR continues to treat health data[166] as sensitive personal data, similar to the position currently under the Directive. But the GDPR now specifically lists genetic data[167] and biometric data[168] as sensitive personal data and Recital 53 permits Member States to introduce further conditions around the processing of biometric, genetic, or health data. Recital 35 provides that personal data concerning health includes 'information derived

---

[163] For example, in Germany the donor retains property rights even after the biological material is permanently extracted from the body. See Schulte in den Baumen et al, 'Data Protection and Sample Management in Biobanking – A Legal Dichotomy' (2010) Genomics, Society and Policy Vol 6 No 1 pp 33–46 at 40. See also De Faria, 'Ownership Rights in Research Biobanks: Do We Need a New Kind of "Biological Property"?' (2009) in Solbakk et al (eds) *The Ethics of Research Biobanking,* (Springer, 2009) 263–276.

[164] See Schulte in den Baumen et al, 'Data Protection and Sample Management in Biobanking – A Legal Dichotomy' (2010) Genomics, Society and Policy Vol 6 No 1 pp 33–46 at 44.

[165] Regulation (EU) 2016/679 of the European Parliament and of the Council of 27 April 2016 on the protection of natural persons with regard to the processing of personal data and on the free movement of such data, and repealing Directive 95/46/EC (General Data Protection Regulation).

[166] Defined by art 4(15) of the Regulation as personal data related to the physical or mental health of a natural person, including the provision of healthcare services, which reveal information about his or her health status.

[167] Defined by art 4(13) of the Regulation as personal data relating to the inherited or acquired genetic characteristics of a natural person which give unique information about the physiology or the health of that natural person and which result, in particular, from an analysis of a biological sample from the natural person in question.

[168] Defined by art 4(14) of the Regulation as personal data resulting from specific technical processing relating to the physical, physiological or behavioural characteristics of a natural person, which allow or confirm the unique identification of that natural person, such as facial images or dactyloscopic data.

from the testing or examination of a body part or bodily substance, including from genetic data and biological samples'.

[13.95] Of particular relevance in the context of research is Recital 26 of the Regulation which defines personal data as including data which have undergone pseudonymisation, which could be attributed to a natural person by the use of additional information. This is important in research where data is commonly coded or linked-anonymised and therefore a code exists which could link the data with an individual. To determine whether a natural person is identifiable, the Regulation says that account should be taken of all the means reasonably likely to be used, such as singling out, either by the controller or by another person to identify the natural person directly or indirectly. To ascertain whether means are reasonably likely to be used to identify the natural person, account should be taken of all objective factors, such as the costs of and the amount of time required for identification, taking into consideration the available technology at the time of the processing and technological developments.

[13.96] The Regulation states that the principles of data protection will therefore not apply to anonymous information, namely information which does not relate to an identified or identifiable natural person or to personal data rendered anonymous in such a manner that the data subject is not or no longer identifiable. This would apply, for example, where data is rendered fully anonymous by the destruction of any code by which the data could be linked back to the individual. This Regulation does not therefore concern the processing of such anonymous information. Nor does it apply to the personal data of deceased persons.

[13.97] Recital 33 of the Regulation states that it is often not possible to fully identify the purpose of personal data processing for scientific research purposes at the time of data collection. Therefore, data subjects should be allowed to give their consent to certain areas of scientific research in keeping with recognised ethical standards for scientific research. Data subjects should have the opportunity to give their consent only to certain areas of research or parts of research projects to the extent allowed by the intended purpose.

Chapter 14

Medical Research

INTRODUCTION

[14.01] Progress in medicine cannot occur without research and although sometimes new treatments and techniques can be tested on animals, it is not possible to know with certainty how humans will respond to treatments unless research is carried out with human participants. Until relatively recent times the advances made by medical science, many of which relied heavily on experiments carried out on human beings, were generally accepted as an unqualified and unquestioned good due to the potential benefit to be gained for society.[1] There are numerous historical examples of researchers all across the world who used humans for research without their knowledge or consent with resulting death, disease and injury in many cases. The legacy of unethical experimentation has cast a long shadow over research, which can result in a poor public understanding of the objectives and methodologies employed in biomedical research:

> The term 'research' has a negative meaning to many people; there is an image of a self-serving scientist indulging, in secrecy, in some dubious project, using misappropriated blood or tissue or organs, for personal advancement or gratification. On the other hand, everyone wants to see medicine advance and conquer all the illnesses of mankind and many people feel a duty to help in some way in this advance.[2]

[14.02] In the past, doctors advanced medical care by trying out new therapies on their patients and, in line with prevailing wisdom at that time, little information was sought by or given to patients, as they trusted that their doctors would do the right thing for them. However, 'it was not until the unthinkable happened that it was realised that some doctors could betray that trust.'[3] Contemporary research ethics really began as a consequence of disclosure of the unethical experimentation carried out during World War II. As a result of the atrocities carried out during this time, particularly in concentration camps in Germany, which were disclosed during the Nuremberg Trials, measures were adopted to ensure that such horrors could not happen again. International standards for research were developed and have been regularly updated since then to

---

[1] Brazier cites the example of the development of the smallpox vaccine in 'Exploitation and Enrichment: The Paradox of Medical Experimentation' (2008) 34 Journal of Medical Ethics 180–83, in which she describes how the non-therapeutic experiment carried out on an eight-year-old boy has saved the lives of millions of people but would not be sanctioned by a modern research ethics committee.

[2] Ó Briain, 'Advancing Medical Knowledge While Protecting Human Research Subjects' (2000) Medico-Legal Journal of Ireland 79.

[3] Ó Briain, 'Advancing Medical Knowledge While Protecting Human Research Subjects' (2000) Medico-Legal Journal of Ireland 79.

ensure that a proper balance is struck between the protection of the individual research participant[4] and the interests of the common good in finding effective treatments and cures for human diseases. These are discussed in more detail below. Before turning to the specific ethical and legal issues that arise in research, it is important to describe what medical research is, and to set out some relevant distinctions.

[14.03] Medical research involves the study of human diseases and conditions including the detection, cause, prevention, treatment and rehabilitation of persons affected, the design of methods, drugs and devices to diagnose, support and maintain the affected person, and the scientific investigation required to understand the underlying biological processes which affect disease and well-being. This chapter will focus largely on clinical trials which involve investigational medicinal products. Such trials might, for example, test the administration of a new drug to compare it with an existing drug that is already available on the market. Due to the important safety and efficacy concerns that arise in such studies, clinical trials are heavily regulated to ensure the safety of the research participants. Other kinds of clinical research such as research into behavioural treatments or radiology are not as heavily regulated but are guided by non-binding ethical documents such as the Declaration of Helsinki, the CIOMS guidelines and others.[5]

Difference between research and clinical audit

[14.04] One of the grey areas in medicine in this context is the difference between research and clinical audit, as there are certain similarities between the two activities but they involve significantly different ethical and legal frameworks. Both research and clinical audit start with a question, both expect the answer to change or influence clinical practice, both require formal data collection on patients, and both depend on using an appropriate method and design to reach sound conclusions. However, by comparison with research, clinical audit is a clinically-led quality improvement process that seeks to improve patient care and outcomes through systematic review of care against explicit criteria, and acts to improve care when standards are not met.

[14.05] The audit process involves the selection of aspects of the structure, processes and outcomes of care which are then systematically evaluated against explicit criteria. If required, improvements should be implemented at an individual, team or organisation level and then the care re-evaluated to confirm improvements.[6] The distinction drawn between audit and research simply put is that research investigates what should be done

---

4   The term 'research subject' is commonly used in texts on this topic but in recent years, the term 'participant' has been considered preferable, as it better symbolises the voluntary and informed nature of the involvement of those who choose to be part of medical research. Therefore, the term 'research participant' will be used in this chapter, except where quoting from other sources.

5   Wade argues that since these kinds of trials also pose risks to the health of subjects and should also be governed by law. Wade, 'Children in clinical trials in Ireland: addressing the gaps in the legal framework.' In Donnelly and Murray (eds) *Ethical and Legal debates in Irish Healthcare* (Manchester University Press 2016) at 164.

6   Commission on Patient Safety and Quality, *Building a Culture of Patient Safety* (2008) at para 7.3.1. Available at www.health.gov.ie.

and why some treatments work better than others, whereas audit investigates whether best practice is being followed, and if not, why not.[7] While not all doctors are actively involved in research activities, all are now expected to participate in clinical audit activities in order to maintain their professional competence and ensure that their practice is in line with national norms.[8]

Research and innovative therapy

[14.06] Another important distinction exists between innovative treatment and research. In general, doctors should only give their patients treatment that has been tested and found to be effective in humans. However, in circumstances where all other possible treatments have been ineffective and the patient's condition is very serious, a doctor may want to give a patient a new treatment which has not yet been tested. The doctor's goal in this instance is not to carry out research on the patient but to provide care for the patient, however it may not be clear as to whether the proposed treatment is safe or effective. Where a doctor departs significantly from standard practice, this innovative approach does not necessarily constitute research. The Declaration of Helsinki, discussed in more detail later, states that in the treatment of a patient, where proven interventions do not exist or have been ineffective, the physician, after seeking expert advice, with informed consent from the patient or a legally authorised representative, may use an unproven intervention if in the physician's judgment it offers hope of saving life, re-establishing health or alleviating suffering.[9]

[14.07] The difficulty in drawing a sharp distinction between therapy and research can be seen in *Simms v Simms*[10] which concerned an 18-year-old boy and a 16-year-old girl who had variant Creutzfeldt-Jakob disease (the human form of BSE). This is a rare, fatal and incurable neurodegenerative disease which the Court said had transformed two 'normal energetic teenagers into helpless invalids' within a year of the first symptoms being diagnosed. Both were confined to wheelchairs; some, very limited communication and recognition of family members was possible. Both lacked capacity to consent and without treatment both were bound to die of the condition. The parents of these young people applied for a declaration that the proposed treatment, which had never been tested in humans, would be in the best interests of their children. This was recognised by all to be their 'last chance'.

[14.08] Expert witnesses agreed that there could be no certainty as to whether the proposed treatment would have any significant beneficial effect in the case of either patient. As scientists, the experts were, therefore, unwilling to recommend its use. However, from the individualised perspective of clinical care, by contrast, there remained a chance that therapy might benefit the particular patients. As clinicians, the experts would therefore be willing to try it out.[11]

---

[7] Wade, 'Ethics, Audit and Research: All Shades of Grey' (2005) BMJ 330: 468.

[8] Maintenance of professional competence is now mandatory in Ireland under the Medical Practitioners Act 2007. This includes participation in clinical audit.

[9] World Medical Association, Declaration of Helsinki: Ethical Principles for Medical Research Involving Human Subjects (7th version 2013), http://www.wma.net/

[10] *Simms v Simms* [2002] EWHC 2734.

[11] Harrington, 'Deciding Best Interests: Medical Progress, Clinical Judgment and the "Good Family"'. www.eureca.manchester.ac.uk/newsletters/cases/Biomedical-case-study-1.pdf

What is applied in *Simms*, therefore, is a fairly weak version of the *Bolam*[12] test: one which permits treatment in the absence of negative opinion, rather than on foot of positive endorsements. To search for affirmative support for every type of novel therapy would run counter to the public interest in medical progress.[13]

[14.09] In granting the declaration Dame Butler-Sloss P accepted that it was untried treatment and that the legal test for ordinary medical treatment is that it must be accepted as proper by a responsible body of medical opinion. However, she said that 'if one waited for this test to be satisfied to its fullest extent, no innovative work such as the use of penicillin or performing heart transplant surgery would ever be attempted'. She held that 'where there is no alternative treatment available and the disease is progressive and fatal, it seems to me to be reasonable to consider experimental treatment with unknown benefits and risks, but without significant risks of increased suffering to the patient, in cases where there is some chance of benefit to the patient.' The Court therefore decided that it would be lawful to administer the experimental therapy on the basis that it would be in their best interests having regard to their dire prognosis without therapy and the lack of available alternatives.

Therapeutic v non-therapeutic research

[14.10] Another distinction exists, at least in theory, between therapeutic and non-therapeutic research. Therapeutic research offers some potential benefit to the patient-participants and may be regarded as a combination of therapy and research. The goal of therapy is benefit for an individual patient and therefore this must always take precedence in clinical research. Risk of harm or injury is an inevitable factor in any therapy and the patient-participant must be informed of these risks. However, even though risks are included in the research protocol, the protocol for clinical research should never involve a therapy which of itself offers less than standard treatment. Even if a double-blind protocol is employed,[14] the patients in the control group, the group that does not receive the drug or therapy being evaluated, should at least receive a drug or therapy which meets the norms for standard treatment. The danger with labelling research as 'therapeutic' is that it enables researchers to apply a lower level of protection for research participants than would otherwise apply.[15] Therefore it has been argued that a high standard, such as a 'probable' or 'reasonably foreseeable' benefit, must be met before an experiment should be classified as therapeutic.[16] However the purpose of research is to answer the question as to whether the treatment will be effective, so it is

---

[12] Referring to *Bolam v Friern Hospital Management Committee* [1957] 2 All ER 118 where the court held that doctors can escape liability for negligence by proving that they acted in accordance with the practice of a responsible body of relevant professional opinion.

[13] Harrington, 'Deciding Best Interests: Medical Progress, Clinical Judgment and the 'Good Family'. http://www.eureca.manchester.ac.uk/newsletters/cases/Biomedical-case-study-1.pdf

[14] See para **[14.16]**.

[15] Levine, 'International codes of research ethics: Current controversies and the future' (2002) 35 Indiana Law Review 361.

[16] Verdun-Jones and Weisstub, 'Drawing the distinction between therapeutic research and non-therapeutic experimentation: clearing a way through the definitional thicket' in Weisstub (ed) *Research on Human Subjects: Ethics, Law and Social Policy* (Elsevier Science: Oxford 1998).

difficult to describe a trial as therapeutic if it is unknown in advance whether it will actually provide any medical benefit for the patient.

[14.11] Non-therapeutic research aims at obtaining knowledge which will be utilised for the health of people in the future rather than the individual participants themselves. Ethical principles allow people to accept a risk of harm even where there is no benefit to themselves, as this is an expression of altruism and a commitment to communitarian welfare. However it is important that the participant should be clearly informed that the research protocol is non-therapeutic so that there is no potential for confusion in relation to individual benefit. There is a danger in this context that either participants may misunderstand this or that researchers might exaggerate the likelihood of a direct benefit to participants in order to be able to enrol participants who lack capacity and avoid the more restrictive rules that govern non-therapeutic research, referred to as 'benefit creep.'[17]

Phases of the research process

[14.12] Research is different from experimentation in that it implies 'a predetermined protocol with a clearly defined end-point. Experimentation involves a more speculative, ad hoc approach to an individual subject.'[18] Medical research takes place over a period of time in a number of different phases. The first step in the process towards licensing new medicines for human use involves animal testing.[19] If animal tests show that there is a reasonable likelihood that the new drug will work and that it is unlikely to have unacceptable side-effects, then the phase involving human participants will commence. When the research is concerned with testing and development of a medicinal drug or treatment for safety and efficacy, it is referred to as a clinical trial.

[14.13] Phase I of the clinical trial will usually involve a small number of healthy volunteers who are given the drug to test its toxicity. Phase I trials are usually non-therapeutic in the sense that the recipients are normally healthy adult volunteers who are not expected to get any clinical benefit from the drug. There are potential risks involved for any such volunteers, as this will be the first application of the drug in humans.[20] Phase II will involve the use of the drug in patients suffering from the condition which

---

17 Noah, 'Informed Consent and the Elusive Dichotomy between Standard and Experimental Therapy' (2002) 28 American Journal of Law and Medicine 361.

18 Laurie, Harmon and Porter, *Law and Medical Ethics* (10th edn, 2016) para 19.07.

19 For discussion of the ethics of animal testing see Nuffield Council on Bioethics *The Ethics of Research Involving Animals*. Available at www.nuffieldbioethics.org; Ryder, 'Painism; some moral rules for the civilised experimenter' (1999) 8 Cambridge Quarterly of Healthcare Ethics 35–42; Quigley, 'Non-human primates; the appropriate subjects of biomedical research?' (2007) 33 Journal of Medical Ethics 655–8.

20 This was seen in England in 2006 when eight men volunteered to take part in a Phase I trial of a drug thought to help in the treatment of arthritis, leukaemia and other conditions. The drug had been tested in primates and it was expected that the dose would be well tolerated in humans but this turned out not to be the case. Six of the men suffered multiple organ failure; the other two had been given a placebo or dummy drug. See findings of an investigation into the incident by Duff *The Expert Group on Phase One Clinical Trials: Final Report* (2006), available at www.dh.gov.uk/.

the drug aims to treat in order to evaluate its effectiveness and any side-effects. Phase III involves monitoring a larger group of participants who take the drug for a longer period of time under supervision. After this phase, the drug may then be licensed for clinical application but will continue to be monitored in the general population – this may be called Phase IV even though strictly speaking it is no longer research.[21]

Randomised controlled trials (RCTs)

[14.14] In certain clinical trials, participants are randomised or enrolled by chance into various groups within the trial. A researcher might want to evaluate the efficacy of a particular drug when compared with an existing one and in order to ensure that he is not biased to influence the outcome, participants are assigned to different 'arms' of the study to receive either the new drug or the existing treatment. It is usual to also include a placebo arm in the trial, in which participants receive a look-alike drug that has no active ingredient, commonly referred to as a 'sugar pill'. Studies have shown improvement in the condition of some participants after receiving a sugar pill, a phenomenon referred to as 'the placebo effect'.[22]

[14.15] Where there is no known treatment for the particular condition, it is reasonable to include the use of a placebo in the design of the trial as the participant is no worse off taking the placebo than not taking part in the trial at all. However, where there is a treatment already in existence and the researcher wants to study the safety and efficacy of a new drug, a placebo arm is more difficult to justify as the participants receiving the placebo are receiving no treatment at all whereas if they had not agreed to participate in the trial they would at least have received the current treatment. The Declaration of Helsinki deals with this by stating that 'the benefits, risks, burdens and effectiveness of a new intervention must be tested against those of the best current proven intervention' except that the use of placebo is acceptable where no current proven intervention exists.[23] The Declaration allows for a further limited exception where 'for compelling and scientifically sound methodological reasons the use of placebo is necessary to determine the efficacy or safety of an intervention and the patients who receive placebo or no treatment will not be subject to any risk of serious or irreversible harm'.[24] It cautions that extreme care must be taken to avoid abuse of this option.[25]

---

[21] Jackson, *Medical Law: Text, cases and materials* (3rd edn, OUP, 2013) 454.

[22] For a useful history and explanation of the placebo effect, see Evans, *Placebo, Mind Over Matter in Modern Medicine* (OUP, 2004) Ch 1.

[23] World Medical Association, Declaration of Helsinki: Ethical Principles for Medical Research involving human subjects (7th version 2013) www.wma.net. para 33.

[24] World Medical Association, Declaration of Helsinki: Ethical Principles for Medical Research involving human subjects (7th version 2013) www.wma.net. para 33.

[25] The concept of the placebo has also been extended into research into new surgical techniques, referred to as 'sham surgeries', where for example some participants receive surgical implants and others do not. Those who do not receive the implant nonetheless receive anaesthesia, preparation for surgery including incisions where relevant, and surgical after care. See discussion of the use of fetal brain implants for patients with Parkinsons disease in Dekkers and Boer, 'Sham neurosurgery in patients with Parkinson's disease: is it morally acceptable?' (2001) 27 J Med Ethics 151.

[14.16] Some drug trials are 'double-blinded' which means the assignment of participants to the various arms of the trial will be done without the knowledge of either researcher or participants. This may pose ethical problems for researchers who are also the treating doctors of the research participants, as they, as doctors, are obliged to treat in the patient's best interests.[26] Therefore, if a doctor believes that a particular drug is the optimum treatment for his patient's condition, then by enrolling a patient in a research study in which the patient may be randomised to receive a placebo, this may be said to conflict with his ethical duties.[27] However, such a trial is deemed to be ethical as long as the doctor has what is referred to as 'equipoise'. This is a state of uncertainty or scientific disagreement about the best way to treat a particular condition due to competing information on the topic.[28] The research is thus justified, as it will help to clarify which, if any, treatment is more effective for the condition. Once it becomes clear that one treatment is performing better, then equipoise is lost and the trial should be halted, as there is no longer any justification for continuing research on human participants, and also it would be in the best interests of all participants to receive the effective treatment, not only those who were randomised into this particular group. The principle of equipoise has been criticised on the basis that it would not allow rational individuals to consent to participate in trials that were socially valuable but did not satisfy the requirements of this principle. This attitude has been described by some commentators as paternalistic interference, in other words, a restriction of a person's liberty on grounds that the restriction will protect or promote the person's welfare.[29]

[14.17] A further ethical challenge in RCTs is in relation to obtaining informed consent as the participants are not told which arm of the trial they have been randomised to, as this might distort the results of the trial. Therefore it may be argued that they cannot be fully informed. However, it may be counter-argued that so long as the participants are fully informed about and understand the nature of the RCT and understand that they may be randomised to any of the arms of the trial, this is thought to be sufficient.[30] Informed consent to research is discussed in more detail below.

INTERNATIONAL CODES AND GUIDANCE

[14.18] The development of international codes on research practice and ethics has been directly shaped by historical events such as the 'research' carried on in concentration camps in Germany during World War II. During this time, researchers exposed human

---

[26] Laurie, Harmon and Porter, *Law and Medical Ethics* (10th edn, 2016) 19.31.

[27] Jackson, *Medical Law: Text, Cases and Materials* (3rd edn, OUP, 2013) at 456.

[28] See further London, 'Equipoise and International Human Subjects Research' (2001) 15 Bioethics 312–32.

[29] See further Edwards, Kirchin and Huxtable, 'Research Ethics and Paternalism', (2004) Journal of Medical Ethics 88–91: and Gerrard and Dawson, 'What is the Role of the Research Ethics Committee? Paternalism, Inducements and Harm in Research Ethics' (2005) Journal of Medical Ethics 419–23.

[30] Problems may arise due to participants' misunderstanding of the nature of RCTs even where they have signed informed consent forms. See Edwards, Lilford and Hewison, 'The ethics of randomised control trials from the perspective of patients, the public, and healthcare professionals' (1998) 317 BMJ 1209.

participants to extreme cold, low-pressure chambers, malaria, typhus and unproved therapies in order to gain information which might prove useful for the treatment of German soldiers and members of the air force.[31] The people used for these experiments were prisoners in the camps who were weak and vulnerable. They suffered horrific injuries and death as part of these experiments and many were deliberately killed in order to obtain biological specimens.[32]

[14.19] In 1947 criminal trials against some of the doctors responsible for these atrocities began in Nuremberg.[33] The doctors argued in their defence that their research was no different from the studies being conducted elsewhere in the world and that there were no internationally agreed standards in place against which they should be measured.[34] They also argued that although initially opposed to these lethal experiments, they became convinced that it made no sense not to risk the lives of a few in order to potentially save the lives of many. One of the best known doctors on trial, Gerhard Rose, illustrated this argument by reference to their attempts to find a vaccine for typhus which had the capacity to save the lives of thousands of people.[35] He argued that it was inconsistent of the Allies to fail to acknowledge this point, as they too knowingly risked the lives of soldiers in the war, on the grounds that the sacrifice of a few was necessary to save the lives of many in the war effort. Most of the doctors were convicted despite their protests.[36]

[14.20] At the conclusion of the Nuremberg Trials, the Court drew up a set of principles to identify permissible medical experiments, which became known as the Nuremberg Code.[37] These principles stressed that the voluntary consent of the human participants is absolutely essential; the experiment should be such as to yield fruitful results for the good of society; it should be designed and based on the results of animal experimentation and a knowledge of the natural history of the disease or other problem; it should be conducted in such a way as to avoid all unnecessary suffering; no experiment should be conducted where it is likely that death or disabling injury will occur; and the degree of risk to be taken should never exceed that determined by the humanitarian importance of the problem to be solved by the experiment. Although the

---

[31] In some instances the object of the experiments was not to find out how to rescue or cure but how to destroy and kill. See Taylor, *Opening Statement of the Prosecution,* 9 December 1946, (US Government Printing Office, 1949).

[32] For discussion of the historical background to regulation of research see Coleman, Menikoff, Goldner and Dubler, *The Ethics and Regulation of Research with Human Subjects* (Lexis Nexis, 2005) Ch 1.

[33] Trials of War Criminals before the Nuremberg Military Tribunals, United States v Karl Brandt (US Gov Printing Office, Wash DC 1949). 16 out of 29 doctors were found guilty, seven were hanged.

[34] Murphy, *Case Studies in Biomedical Research Ethics* (2004) Mass. Inst. of Technology at 2.

[35] Caplan, 'How did medicine go so wrong?' in Caplan (ed) *When medicine went mad: bioethics and the holocaust* (Human Press: Totowa NJ 1992) 53–92.

[36] For detailed discussion, see Weindling, 'The Ethical Legacy of Nazi Medical War Crimes: Origins, Human Experiments, and International Justice' In Burley and Harris (eds) *A Companion to Genethics* (Blackwell Publishing, 2004) Ch 5.

[37] *Trials of War Criminals Before the Nuremberg Military Tribunals Under Control Council Law No10,* Vol 2, 181–2. (US Government Printing Office, 1949).

publication of the Code was symbolically very significant, its impact on the medical profession was limited, as it was assumed to be related to the atrocities carried out in the Nazi concentration camps with very little resonance for the conduct of 'ordinary' research.[38] Thus, the application of the Code to atomic, biological and chemical warfare military research was treated as a state secret in the US and released only in 1975 when the code was declassified. In the 1950s and 1960s the US had additionally begun to put in place a system of research regulation but it was sporadic and not popular with many doctors, who resisted the formalisation of codes which they felt would interfere with the doctor-patient relationship.

[14.21] There were other scandals too in other countries such as Japan and the United States during and after World War II. For example, between 1930 and 1945, Japan conducted extensive trials on biological warfare in China in which it is estimated that over 3,000 people died from deliberate exposure to anthrax, cholera and typhoid as well as being dehydrated, frozen or given transfusions of animal blood. After the war, the United States gave immunity from prosecution to the Japanese researchers in return for sharing of information about their experiments.[39]

[14.22] One of the most infamous examples of unethical research is the Tuskegee Syphilis study, the memory of which still influences healthcare debates in the US today.[40] This study began in 1932 when the public health service enrolled African-American men in Alabama in a study of the natural history of syphilis. About half of the men had syphilis at the time of enrolment, although they were not told of this fact. Other men contracted syphilis during the course of the study. There was concern at that time that the disease behaved differently according to race as well as the efficacy and safety of certain treatments. The men, who were generally poor and uneducated, were studied at various points during their lives and post-mortem examinations were carried out on them after death to provide definitive data. During the course of the study, effective treatments became available for syphilis but these were not provided to the men, whose names were circulated to doctors in the area to ensure that they did not receive treatment. The study ran from 1932 until 1972 when public attention was drawn to it by the media, and the study was stopped.[41] A $10 million out-of-court settlement was reached in 1974 and the US government promised to give lifetime medical benefits and burial services to all living participants.[42] A formal apology was given by the US President, Bill Clinton, in 1997 to seven participants still living at that time.[43]

---

38 Jackson, *Medical Law, Text, cases and materials* (3rd edn, OUP, 2013) 464.

39 Harris, *Factories of Death: Japanese Biological Warfare 1932–45 and the American Cover-Up* (Routledge, 1994).

40 Many people believe that a major impact of the Tuskegee experiments is a legacy of mistrust within the African American community towards the medical profession and public health authorities. For example, participation by African Americans in clinical AIDS trials has been disproportionately small in comparison to the number of African-Americans who have been infected with HIV. Clark, 'A Legacy of Mistrust: African-Americans, the Medical Profession, and AIDS'. 65 Linacre Quarterly 66 (1998), quoted in Coleman et al, *The Ethics and Regulation of Research with Human Subjects* (Lexis Nexis 2005) at 44.

41 Reverby, 'Normal exposure' and inoculation syphilis: a PHS 'Tuskegee' doctor in Guatemala 1946–48' (2011) 23 Journal of Policy History 6–28.

42 www.cdc.gov/tuskegee/timeline.htm.

43 Jones, *Bad Blood: The Tuskegee Syphilis Experiment* (Free Press, 1993); Reverby, *Tuskegee's Truths: Rethinking the Tuskegee Syphilis Study* (University of North Carolina Press, 2000).

[14.23] A further and final example relates to an article published in 1966 by Beecher who exposed the myth that unethical experimentation was not carried out in a country such as the US.[44] He showed that many studies published in reputable scientific journals at that time were unethical, which shocked many within the research community and led to further calls for tighter regulation. These studies included, for example, one which was designed to learn about the functional anatomy of the urinary tract where doctors inserted catheters into the bladders of healthy newborns, injected radio-opaque dye and performed multiple x-rays to follow the track of the dye. In a second example, doctors suspected that liver injury might result from the administration of an antibiotic so they administered the drug to children in a children's centre including so-called 'mental defectives or juvenile delinquents' who had no disease other than acne. The researchers halted the trial prematurely due to high incidences of significant liver dysfunction. These examples and others led to a demand for international consensus on research ethics standards and governance, which are discussed below.

[14.24] The publication by the US Department of Health, Education and Welfare of the Belmont Report (entitled Ethical Principles and Guidelines for the Protection of Human Subjects of Research) in 1978 is an important historical document in the field of medical research ethics.[45] The Report identified three main concepts by which to evaluate the ethics of research: respect for persons, beneficence and justice. The first principle, respect for persons, incorporates at least two ethical convictions: firstly, that individuals should be treated as autonomous agents, and secondly that persons with diminished autonomy are entitled to protection. The second principle, beneficence, means that persons are treated in an ethical manner not only by respecting their decisions and protecting them from harm, but also by making efforts to secure their well-being. Two general rules have been formulated as complementary expressions of beneficent actions in this sense: firstly, do no harm and secondly, maximise possible benefits and minimise possible harms. The third principle, justice, means that equals ought to be treated equally. In the specific context of research, the selection of research participants should be scrutinised in order to determine whether some classes (eg welfare patients, particular racial and ethnic minorities, or persons confined to institutions) are being systematically selected simply because of their easy availability, their compromised position, or their manipulability, rather than for reasons directly related to the problem being studied. Finally, whenever research supported by public funds leads to the development of therapeutic devices and procedures, justice demands both that these not provide advantages only to those who can afford them and that such research should not unduly involve persons from groups unlikely to be among the beneficiaries of subsequent applications of the research. This report has been very influential in the development of research ethics in the United States and elsewhere, and it provides the moral framework for understanding regulations in the United States on the use of humans in experimental research.[46]

---

[44] Beecher, 'Ethics and Clinical Research' (1966) 274 NEJM 1354–60. See also example of cancer immunity study cited by Katz et al in *Experimentation with Human Beings: The Authority of the Investigator, Subject, Professions and State in the Human Experimentations Process* (Russell Sage Foundation, 1972) p 9–65.

[45] The Belmont Report, Ethical Principles and Guidelines for the Protection of Human Subjects of Research (1978), available at www.ohsr.od.nih.gov/guidelines/belmont.html.

[46] For details of the research regulatory system in the US see www.hhs.gov/ohrp/.

[14.25] In 1964 the World Medical Association adopted the Declaration of Helsinki, which has been updated on a number of occasions since that time,[47] and remains one of the leading reference points in the evaluation of the ethics of research studies. The principles in the Declaration focus on the primacy of the well-being, privacy, autonomy and dignity of human research participants and stress the necessity for studies to be submitted for consideration to an independent research ethics committee prior to commencement. Other international research guidelines include the CIOMS guidelines in 1982, updated most recently in 2002, published by the World Health Organisation (WHO) and the Council for International Organisations of Medical Sciences.[48] These guidelines focus in particular on the application of the Declaration of Helsinki to research carried out in developing countries where different socio-economic, political and cultural factors may otherwise make it easier and cheaper to conduct research without observing restrictive regulations applicable elsewhere. The principle underlying these guidelines is that the research should leave low-resource countries or communities better off than previously or at least no worse off. 'It should be responsive to their health needs and priorities in that any product developed is made reasonably available to them, and as far as possible leave the population in a better position to obtain effective healthcare and protect its own health.' The participants selected for participation should be the least vulnerable necessary to accomplish the purposes of the research.

[14.26] Further guidance is provided by the International Conference on Harmonisation of Technical Requirements for Registration of Pharmaceuticals for Human Use (ICH) in which the regulatory authorities in Europe, the United States and Japan are participants.[49] The purpose of these guidelines is to strive towards greater harmonisation of regulations in order to reduce duplication in trials of new medicinal products. To do this, there must be mutual acceptance of data generated during clinical trials in these regions which have been conducted following ICH guidelines such as the Guidelines for Good Clinical Practice (GCP).

[14.27] The Council of Europe Convention on Human Rights and Biomedicine (1997)[50] was an attempt at international cooperation to harmonise legal standards on the application of human rights in relation to the development of new biomedical technologies.[51] It provides that research on persons may be carried out only if:

- there is no alternative of comparable effectiveness to research on humans
- the risks which may be incurred by that person are not disproportionate to the potential benefits of the research
- the research project has been approved by the competent body after independent examination of its scientific merit, including assessment of the

---

[47] The Declaration of Helsinki (7th version 2013) www.wma.net.

[48] International Ethical Guidelines for Biomedical Research Involving Human Subjects. Available at www.cioms.ch/.

[49] www.ich.org/products/guidelines.html.

[50] Convention for the Protection of Human Rights and Dignity of the Human Being with regard to the Application of Biology and Medicine: Convention on Human Rights and Biomedicine 1997, art 16.

[51] Ireland has not signed or ratified this Convention.

importance of the aim of the research, and multidisciplinary review of its ethical acceptability

- the persons undergoing research have been informed of their rights and the safeguards prescribed by law for their protection
- the necessary consent as provided for under art 5 has been given expressly, specifically and is documented. Such consent may be freely withdrawn at any time.

[14.28] Principles which are common to many of these international documents include the following:

- The research proposal must be scientifically valid;
- The risks must be proportionate to the benefits;
- It must be approved by an ethics committee;
- If competent, the research participants must give informed consent;
- If incompetent, there must be sufficient protections in place;
- The research must be halted if there is a risk of injury or death;
- The research must be stopped if equipoise is lost;
- The participants must be free to withdraw;
- The participants should have access to information about the research after it has been concluded;
- Research findings should be disseminated, and;
- Any participants injured as a result of the trial should be compensated.[52]

PARTICIPATION IN RESEARCH

[14.29] It has been argued that all citizens who use health services have a duty to participate in research which is undertaken at improving the safety, quality and success of medical interventions. Harris argues that participation in research should be regarded as the equivalent of jury service and taxation, in other words activities that are necessary in the public good.[53]

> We all benefit from the existence of the social practice of medical research. Many of us would not be here if infant mortality had not been brought under control, or antibiotics had not been invented. Most of us will continue to benefit from these and other medical advances. Since we accept these benefits, we have an obligation in justice to contribute to the social practice which produces them.

Caplan argues similarly but goes further in arguing that it might even be appropriate for a hospital to refuse to treat those who are unwilling to take part in research. He is of the view that individuals should be bound by the rules of 'fair play' to participate in research if they wish to accept the benefits of medical research in their own treatment. Thus, '[M]edical institutions which clearly and forthrightly identify themselves to patients as research institutions would be within their rights to exclude persons who refuse to participate in any form of research.'[54]

---

[52] Jackson, *Medical Law: Text, Cases and Materials* (3rd edn, OUP, 2013) at 466–467.
[53] Harris, 'Scientific research is a moral duty' (2005) 31 J of Med Ethics 242–248.
[54] Caplan, 'Is there an obligation to participate in biomedical research?' in Spicker et al (eds) *The use of human beings in research* (Kluwer, 1988) 229–248.

[14.30] Irrespective of whether there is an ethical obligation to participate in research, there is no such legal duty on citizens to do so, and voluntary informed consent is now regarded as the gold standard for participation. In the past, researchers commonly conscripted poor, elderly, mentally incapacitated persons and prisoners to their studies, as a result of which they suffered horrific injuries and loss of life. For example, in one study Japanese researchers distributed sweets laced with anthrax to children in China, exposing Chinese civilians to bio weapons and killing people to study the dying process.[55] As a result of these kinds of abuses, modern regulations put in place to protect participants require that the selection of research participants should be scrutinised in order to determine whether some classes of participants are systematically selected simply due to their easy availability, their compromised position or their manipulability. Research participants may be healthy volunteers, patients, adults with capacity, adults without capacity, or children. Each of these groups of participants is treated somewhat differently in terms of regulatory and consent requirements to ensure that their particular interests and rights are protected.

Healthy volunteers

[14.31] There are clear advantages to using healthy adults as volunteers as there are no complicating existing medical conditions to deal with and there are usually no issues regarding their decision-making capacity. However, as this group of participants does not have the medical condition being studied, their participation in the research will not confer any potential benefit on them and is therefore of a non-therapeutic nature. These participants are sometimes recruited as 'controls' in a trial, meaning that they are recruited to resemble the experimental group, (for example, they are in the same age range) but they do not receive the experimental treatment. Changes are then measured in both the treatment group and this group, to compare the effect of the new drug, medical device, procedure, or prevention. The ethical justification for their participation is based on the view that individuals with capacity can exercise their right to exercise altruism and solidarity by participating in research which may confer benefit on society. Because participation will not confer any benefit on such participants and may carry a risk of harm, it is necessary to ensure that their consent to participate is voluntary and informed. In light of this requirement it is important to consider how participants might be recruited and compensated for their participation.

Payments and other inducements

[14.32] Healthy volunteers are usually recruited through local media advertising, newsletters and posters in public buildings, social media and other formats. Although many people are willing to become involved through general interest or solidarity with a family member who has the disease being studied, another motivating factor in some cases is when payments or other benefits are used as an inducement.[56] This arguably not only affects the ethical justification of altruism but may also be seen as problematic as 'those most susceptible to inducement may be the least able to assess the aims and

---

[55] Murphy, *Case Studies in Biomedical Research Ethics* (2004) Mass Inst of Technology at 92.

[56] See discussion of ethical issues in Nuffield Council on Bioethics, Human Bodies: donation for medicine and research (2011) chapter 4. Available at www.nuffieldbioethics.org.

technical information relating to the research and to decide on whether or not the risk is worth taking.'[57] McNeill argues that financial inducement to participate in research should not be allowed to add to the risks already presented to relatively poor people who already have higher risks of poor health and adverse life events. Studies show that financial inducements increase people's willingness to participate in research regardless of the level of risk posed[58] as well as incentivising poorer people to misrepresent certain medical conditions they may have, such as depression, in order to be accepted on to the trial. This may further raise the risks of their participation as well as potentially skewing the research results.

[14.33] Others argue that payments are not necessarily coercive as people have a choice whether to accept them or not. Those participants who accept such payments do so because it is worthwhile to them in the same way as payment for other work. 'Many people would not work if they were not paid; in that sense wages are inducements. Few people think that, as a result, it is wrong to offer wages. Those that do have concerns about the existing wage system usually object that wages are too *low*, not that they are too high, or that they are offered at all.'[59] On this basis payment offers a reasonable compensation for the time and discomfort of participation without negativing the voluntariness of the decision. It may thus be argued that rather than trying to maintain a low level of payment so as not to run the risk of being a coercive offer, researchers should instead be seen as employing the participants which would also enable them to benefit from other employment conditions and regulation of health and safety.[60] Savulescu claims that payment of research participants is not a major ethical issue. 'The major ethical issues related to projects involving risk and payment are those two bread-and-butter issues of the research ethics review: evaluation of harm and informed consent.'[61] He argues that the ethics committee should therefore focus on the risk of harm and its disclosure to participants rather than whether or not participants are paid.

[14.34] An example of where payment was used as an incentive to recruit healthy volunteers took place in the UK in 2006 when a phase I trial of a drug for arthritis, leukaemia and multiple sclerosis was commenced with eight male healthy adult volunteers (known as the TGN1412 trial). The recruitment of the men through advertisement offered payment of £2,000 for the participants' time, access to free food, digital television, pool table, video games, and internet. Earlier toxicology studies had not shown any adverse effects in monkeys[62] and it was expected to be safe in humans. The six volunteers who received the active drug suffered life-threatening organ failure,

---

[57] McNeill, 'Paying people to participate in research: why not?' (1997) 11 Bioethics 391–6.

[58] Bentley and Thacker, 'The influence of risk and monetary payment on the research participation decision making process' (2004) 30 Journal of Medical Ethics 293–8.

[59] Wilkinson and Moore, 'Inducement in research' (1997) 11 Bioethics 373–89.

[60] Lemmens and Elliott, 'Justice for the professional guinea pig' (2001) 1 American Journal of Bioethics 51–3.

[61] Savulescu, 'The Fiction of 'Undue Inducement': Why Researchers Should Be Allowed to Pay Participants Any Amount of Money for Any Reasonable Research Project', Am J of Bioethics Vol 1, Issue 2, February 2001, pp 1g–3g.

[62] The monkeys had in fact been given a dose 500 times higher than the dose given to the volunteers, but had not suffered adverse effects.

the other two had received a placebo.[63] A report into the trial found that the pre-clinical development studies that were performed with TGN1412 did not predict a safe dose for use in humans, even though relevant regulatory requirements had been met and the Expert Group made detailed recommendations about dosage in 'first-in-man' studies of this kind. The Report did not discuss the issue of inducements but it is interesting that as a result of (or despite) the extensive media publicity surrounding this clinical trial, including the high fees involved and its effect on the volunteers, there was a reported increase in inquiries from members of the public about participation in clinical trials.[64]

[14.35] Other inducements might also be offered depending on the perceived needs and interests of the cohort of participant to be recruited. For example, the Tuskegee Syphilis study mentioned above[65] offered poor black male participants otherwise unattainable benefits in terms of medical care and survivors insurance. They were enticed and enrolled in the study with incentives including medical examinations, transportation to and from the clinics, meals on examination days, free treatment for minor ailments and guarantees that provisions would be made after their deaths in terms of burial stipends paid to their survivors.

[14.36] In terms of regulation of financial inducements, the language used in international guidance documents is somewhat vague as it is recognised that some level of recompense is acceptable in order to recruit participants to lengthy and burdensome trials. However, the guidance commonly refers to the balance that needs to be struck to ensure that the payments should not be so large as to exert undue influence or present a coercive offer to potential participants. For example, art 12 of the Additional Protocol to the Council of Europe's Convention on Human Rights and Biomedicine[66] provides that ethics committees which review research protocols must be satisfied that no undue influence, including that of a financial nature, will be exerted on persons, particularly dependent or vulnerable persons, to participate in research. Article 28(1)(h) of the EU Clinical Trials Regulation 2014,[67] discussed in more detail later, also states that a clinical trial may be conducted only where 'no undue influence, including that of a financial nature, is exerted on subjects to participate in the clinical trial'.

Prisoners

[14.37] The involvement of prisoners in medical research is ethically difficult due to the historical connotations arising from research carried out during the 1930s and 1940s as well as the fact that participants in this group are limited in their choices due to their

---

[63] For further details see The Expert Group on Phase One Clinical Trials: Final report (2006). Available at www.dh.gov.uk.

[64] Ferguson, 'Clinical trials and healthy volunteers' (2008) 16 Medical Law Review 23–51.

[65] Para **[14.22]**.

[66] Convention for the protection of Human Rights and Dignity of the Human Being with regard to the Application of Biology and Medicine (Oviedo 1997). Additional Protocol on Biomedical Research (2005).

[67] Regulation (EU) No 536/2014 of the European Parliament and of the Council of 16 April 2014 on clinical trials on medicinal products for human use, and repealing Directive 2001/20/EC.

imprisonment and other social circumstances and may have impaired capacity in terms of the voluntariness of their participation.[68] The Helsinki Declaration states that 'when seeking informed consent for participation in a research study the physician should be particularly cautious if the potential subject is in a dependent relationship with the physician or may consent under duress. In such situations consent should be sought by an appropriately qualified individual who is completely independent of this relationship.'[69]

[14.38] In the US, federal regulations prohibit such persons being offered advantages such as food, and quality of living conditions in return for their participation if they would be such as to affect the person's ability to weigh up the risks involved.[70] It is important not to ban research on this group entirely, however, as very valuable findings may arise from both medical and behavioural research carried out in these settings such as the effect of imprisonment, the social and psychological circumstances of people within this group, alcohol and drug problems and so on. In the European context, the Additional Protocol to the Convention on Human Rights and Biomedicine on Biomedical Research (2005) states that 'where the law allows research on persons deprived of liberty, such persons may participate in a research project in which the results do not have the potential to produce direct benefit to their health only if the following conditions are met: (a) research of comparable effectiveness cannot be carried out without the participation of persons deprived of liberty; (b) the research has the aim of contributing to the ultimate attainment of results capable of conferring benefit to persons deprived of liberty, and (c) the research entails only minimal risk and minimal burden.'[71]

Patients

[14.39] In Phase II and III trials the study drug is studied in patients with the relevant medical condition in order to assess its effectiveness. The Declaration of Helsinki justifies the participation of patients only if the physician has good reason to believe that participation will not adversely affect the health of the patients.[72] One of the difficulties here is that patients who enrol as participants in clinical trials often mistakenly perceive them as potentially therapeutic even when they have been specifically told that this is not the case. This phenomenon is called 'therapeutic misconception' and is an understandable emotional response based on hope that the trial will prove to be their best chance at recovery from their disease. The terminology used in research ethics guidelines, participant information sheets and consent forms often causes further

---

[68]   See Charles, Rid et al 'Prisoners as research participants: current practice and attitudes in the UK' (2014) J Med Ethics Online.

[69]   Declaration of Helsinki para 27.

[70]   45 CFR 46.306.

[71]   See Elger and Spaulding, 'Research on prisoners – a comparison between the IOM committee recommendations (2006) and European regulations' (2010) 24 Bioethics 1.

[72]   Declaration of Helsinki (7th version 2013) para 14.

confusion by blurring the line between research and treatment, obscuring the purposes of the research and exaggerating the potential benefits to participants.[73]

[14.40] The dual role of doctors as researchers may also lead to misunderstanding as patients and families may make trial participation decisions based in part on interactions with their doctors. Patients generally find it difficult to recognise and to know how to respond when their doctor has switched hats and is acting primarily as a researcher rather than as a treating doctor focused exclusively on patient benefit.[74] It is common for patients to express their gratitude to their medical team by agreeing to participate in research, particularly if they have an ongoing relationship with the team.[75] It is also difficult for patients to believe that their doctor would knowingly harm them or use them as a means to his own end. This poses a challenge for doctors, who may have divided loyalties in attempting to function both as doctor and researcher. A doctor's primary obligation is to safeguard his patient's health, whereas as researcher there are additional objectives involved, including the accumulation of knowledge, career advancement and perhaps financial gain.

[14.41] As a result of this potential confusion, Annas argues that doctors should not be permitted to play both roles:

> It is unlikely that it will ever be possible…for patients not to indulge in self-deception by imagining that research is really treatment and that they are patients, not research subjects. We cannot separate the subject into two persons. But we can assure that the subject-patient always has a physician whose only obligation is to look out for the best interests of the patient. Thus, we can (and should) prohibit physicians from performing more than minimal risk on their patients, and as a corollary, only permit physician-researchers to recruit the patients of other physicians for their research protocols. In this way, at least the 'doubling' of physician and researcher can be physically (and perhaps psychologically) eliminated. [76]

It may be argued that the law should go further in regulating this relationship by increasing accountability through tighter supervision of situations where this dual-role is at play and by penalising those who breach their patient's trust.

Older people

[14.42] One of the pre-requisites for participation in research is informed consent. Consent presupposes that the participant has decision-making capacity and is given relevant information in a way that is comprehensible to him or her. The stereotypical

---

[73] King argues that the consent form should be much less ambiguous and when no benefit for the patient is expected, should simply state 'you will not benefit'. See King, 'Defining and describing benefit appropriately in clinical trials' (2000) 28 Journal of Law, Medicine and Ethics (2000) 332 at 334.

[74] See generally Charuvastra and Marder, 'Unconscious emotional reasoning and the therapeutic misconception' (2008) 34 Journal of Medical Ethics 193–7; Oberman and Frader, 'Dying Children and Medical Research: Access to Clinical Trials as Benefit and Burden' (2003) Am J of Law, Med & Ethics 29:301–317.

[75] Ingelfinger, 'Informed (but uneducated) consent' (1972) 287 NEJM 466.

[76] Annas, 'Questing for Grails: Duplicity, Betrayal and Self-Deception in Postmodern Medical Research' (1996) 12 J Contemp L & Policy 297 at 322.

research participant is a young healthy male volunteer, and in general, older people are less frequently invited to participate.[77] Two reasons are usually given for the exclusion of older people, one ethical and one physiological. The ethical reason is that there may be a difficulty in obtaining consent from older people due to incapacity and therefore it may be unethical to expose this group to risk. However, it should not be assumed that this is the case, as age is not a pre-determinant of incapacity and all persons should be presumed to have capacity unless the contrary is established.[78]

[14.43] A second reason relates to the physiology of the older person, as it is thought that they metabolise drugs differently and their participation may therefore distort the research findings. 'The fact that they respond differently to drugs and may manifest adverse reactions at lower doses, does increase the risk that older participants will be injured during drug testing.'[79] Therefore, researchers who recruit younger participants can be more confident that if an adverse reaction is experienced, this is more likely to be as a result of the drug rather than any other medical condition. However, the very fact that they may have different physiological responses to medication means that it is necessary in some cases to include older people in clinical trials in order to test the safety and efficacy of drugs across a broad age spectrum in the community.

Women

[14.44] The second group sometimes excluded from participation in clinical trials is women, even where the disease being studied affects both males and females. The non-participation of women in clinical trials was traditionally justified on the basis that women may also metabolise drugs differently and their participation may distort the research findings. However, as with older people, if this is a drug that will be used in the general population, it is necessary to ensure that women are included at the research stage since they may be prescribed these drugs in the future. Therefore, a pharmaceutical company that fails to involve certain groups such as women in a trial for a drug which will ultimately be marketed for those groups may be negligent in not having tested the drugs for safety and efficacy prior to licensing.

> The relative neglect of women's health needs raises issues of justice, as well as calling into question the scientifically dubious practice of marketing drugs and procedures which have been inadequately tested for their impact on women. Since the choice and definition of problems for research is influenced by the under-representation of women at all stages of the research process, research on conditions specific to females receives low priority, funding and prestige.[80]

[14.45] A further reason for the traditional exclusion of women from trials is that the drug may have unknown effects on the female reproductive organs, or on any future children. For this reason, women of child-bearing years are commonly excluded to avoid

---

[77] Ferguson, 'Selecting Participants When Testing New Drugs: The Implications of Age and Gender Discrimination' (2002) Medico-Legal Journal Vol 70 Part 3, 130–134.

[78] See discussion in chapter 9.

[79] Ferguson, 'Selecting Participants When Testing New Drugs: The Implications of Age and Gender Discrimination' (2002) Medico-Legal Journal Vol 70 Part 3, 130–134 at 131.

[80] Fox, 'Research bodies: Feminist perspectives on clinical research' in Sheldon and Thomson (eds) *Feminist perspectives on Health Care Law* (Cavendish 1998) 115–34.

the occurrence of such a risk as the research sponsors try to avoid incurring legal liability to the woman or any children born with a disability as a consequence of the study drug. However, the same principle applies here in relation to the need to study the safety of certain drugs, for example drugs for treating depression, during pregnancy, but this is an issue that is commonly neglected.

> Pregnant women need safe and effective treatment with adequate pharmacokinetic details to identify the appropriate therapeutic dose across each of the trimesters of pregnancy and to quantify the risks of exposure of the fetus. Reticence to treat pregnant womens' health needs because of concern about lack of evidence of safety for the fetus has its own risks, as is often seen in undertreated or untreated asthma, depression, diabetes, and cancer.[81]

[14.46] In the US, federal regulations allow clinical research involving pregnant women as long as earlier studies have been carried out on animals and non-pregnant women, any risks to the foetus are minimal and are as a result of procedures carried out which offer some benefit to the woman or foetus, and other conditions are complied with.[82] In the EU until 2016 most clinical trials in which women of childbearing age were included required that effective contraception must be used. For this reason, the only data available to evaluate reproductive risk when a new medicinal product is approved for marketing was from non-clinical studies. However, although these non-clinical studies can be useful to predict human risk, the extent of prediction needs to be taken with caution in the absence of clinical trials on this group. Consequently, many medicinal products are subject to contraindications or special warnings because they have not been sufficiently studied during pregnancy or studies in animals have revealed adverse effects on the foetus.[83] The International Ethical Guidelines for Clinical Research of the Council for International Organizations of Medical Sciences (CIOMS) adopted the presumption that pregnant women should be eligible for participation in clinical research and goes on to say that 'Research should be performed only if relevant to the particular health needs of a pregnant women or her fetus, or to the health needs of pregnant women in general.'[84]

[14.47] The EU Clinical Trial Regulation 2014[85] (which came into effect in May 2016) now adopts a minimal risk standard to clinical trials and provides that a clinical trial on pregnant or breastfeeding women may be conducted only where the following conditions are met:

---

[81] Foulkes et al, 'Clinical Research Enrolling Pregnant Women: A Workshop Summary' J Womens Health (2011) Oct; 20(10): 1429 1432.

[82] 45 Code of Federal Regulation (CFR) 46.204.

[83] Committee For Medicinal Products For Human Use (Chmp) 2005 Guideline On The Exposure To Medicinal Products During Pregnancy: Need For Post-Authorisation Data www.ema.europa.eu.

[84] Council for International Organizations of Medical Sciences (CIOMS) International ethical guidelines for biomedical research involving human subjects. 2002. www.cioms.ch.

[85] Regulation (EU) No 536/2014 of the European Parliament and of the Council of 16 April 2014 on clinical trials on medicinal products for human use, and repealing Directive 2001/20/EC, art 33.

(a)   the clinical trial has the potential to produce a direct benefit for the pregnant or breastfeeding woman concerned, or her embryo, foetus or child after birth, outweighing the risks and burdens involved; or

(b)   if such clinical trial has no direct benefit for the pregnant or breastfeeding woman concerned, or her embryo, foetus or child after birth, it can be conducted only if:

   (i)   a clinical trial of comparable effectiveness cannot be carried out on women who are not pregnant or breastfeeding;

   (ii)   the clinical trial contributes to the attainment of results capable of benefitting pregnant or breastfeeding women or other women in relation to reproduction or other embryos, foetuses or children; and

   (iii)   the clinical trial poses a minimal risk to, and imposes a minimal burden on, the pregnant or breastfeeding woman concerned, her embryo, foetus or child after birth;

(c)   where research is undertaken on breastfeeding women, particular care is taken to avoid any adverse impact on the health of the child; and

(d)   no incentives or financial inducements are given to the subject except for compensation for expenses and loss of earnings directly related to the participation in the clinical trial.

Children and minors

[14.48] In the same way that it is necessary to carry out research with older people and pregnant women, it is also crucially important to do research with children. Children respond differently to drugs and it is impossible to know whether adult-tested drugs will be safe and effective for use with children and in what doses. Children are not miniature versions of adults and thus it is not safe to reduce the adult dosage of a drug by guessing the proportionate weight of the child relative to the adult. 'In addition, certain diseases and conditions, such as the complications associated with prematurity, affect only children, thereby necessitating research with them.'[86] As with adults, research with children potentially involves both therapeutic and non-therapeutic components and therefore research will necessarily involve sick children as well as those who can act as healthy controls.

[14.49] There has been considerable debate about the acceptability of children as research participants in biomedical and behavioural research. Since the publication of the Nuremberg Code and the first Declaration of Helsinki, ethicists have argued that children must not be subjected to medical experimentation. There was a long-running debate in the 1970s in the US between renowned ethicists Ramsay and McCormick on this issue.[87] Ramsay was of the view that, consistent with the Nuremberg Code, children who had not yet achieved some level of intellectual sophistication and emotional

---

[86] Wade, 'Children in clinical trials in Ireland: addressing the gaps in the legal framework' in Donnelly and Murray (eds) *Ethical and legal debates in Irish healthcare* (Manchester University Press 2016)163–176 at 163.

[87] Cited by Oberman and Frader, 'Dying Children and Medical Research: Access to Clinical Trials as Benefit and Burden' (2003) Am J of Law, Med & Ethics 29:301–317.

maturity could not make autonomous decisions about whether or not to participate in research. This precluded their participation unless the research held out a prospect of providing individual benefit.[88] By contrast, McCormick argued that the wholesale exclusion of children resulted in disadvantage to the entire paediatric population and that if there were no realistic risks, children *should* participate because their participation would benefit others.[89]

[14.50] The key issues in the debate about children's participation have not fundamentally changed since the 1970s but are perhaps particularly exacerbated in relation to clinical trials. 'There is a growing consensus that to exclude children from clinical research disadvantages them as a group and is therefore unethical.' Such exclusion would mean that children would continue to experience the impacts of diseases which might have become curable if research were carried out.'[90] There are a number of difficulties that arise in this context notwithstanding the importance of carrying out such research in the interests of all children, namely the capacity of the child to assent to their own participation and how their best interests should be protected, particularly in non-therapeutic clinical trials.

[14.51] As discussed in Chapter 11, when the patient is a young child who does not have the legal capacity to make such decisions, a parent or legal guardian must give consent on his behalf. Good communication between parents or guardians and the medical profession is vital if meaningful collaboration is to take place in making such decisions. However, this does not detract from the value and importance of respecting the autonomy of the child and ensuring that they participate as much as possible in decision-making about their own health. Guidelines on treatment of children generally provide that the child's wishes should be taken into account and, as the child grows towards maturity, given more weight accordingly. In order to participate meaningfully in decision-making, children should be given the necessary information in a way that they can understand so that they can fully comprehend the consequences of their decision. This applies equally in the research context.

[14.52] Article 12 of the United Nations Convention of the Rights of the Child[91] (UNCRC) requires that 'the child who is capable of forming his or her own views [be accorded] the right to express those views freely in all matters affecting the child, the views of the child being given due weight in accordance with the age and maturity of the child.' In 2009, the United Nations Committee on the Rights of the Child stated that '[C]hildren, including young children, should be included in decision-making processes, in a manner consistent with their evolving capacities.'[92] Many professional organisations

---

[88] Ramsay, *The Patient as Person: Explorations in Medical Ethics* (Yale University Press, 1970) 1–58.

[89] McCormick, 'Proxy Consent in Experimental Situations' (1974) 18 Perspectives Biol & Med 2.

[90] Wade, 'Children in clinical trials in Ireland: addressing the gaps in the legal framework' in Donnelly and Murray (eds) *Ethical and legal debates in Irish healthcare* (Manchester University Press 2016) 163–176 at 166.

[91] General Assembly Resolution 44/25, November 1989, art 12.

[92] Committee on the Rights of the Child, General Comment No 12 *The Right of the Child to Be Heard* (2009) UN Doc CRC/C/GC/12, para 100.

have thus recommended that decision-making involving the healthcare of older children and adolescents should include, to the greatest possible degree, the assent of the patient, as well as the participation of the parents and doctors. Participation by the child in medical research raises the same issues about the extent to which the autonomy of the child is respected in enabling the child to make his own decision while at the same time ensuring that the risks of the research do not outweigh any potential harms to the child. These issues have been discussed more fully in the context of medical treatment decisions in Chapter 11.

[14.53] It is often argued that a decision about a child's competence to participate in decision-making should not depend on an arbitrary age limit but rather on an evaluation of the child's ability to understand the nature and purpose of the research and the implications of their decision.[93] This can be influenced by the way in which information is presented to children, and if it is presented in a way that children can understand, such as using age-appropriate language, illustrations and props, then many children will be competent. While development varies across individual children, existing data suggests that most children develop this ability by approximately age 14 as it is at this age that most children begin to understand that there are moral reasons to help others, even when doing so is not required.[94] However, from a practical and legal perspective, it may be simpler to have a straightforward cut-off point for consent and therefore legislation in many countries provides for consent from parents where the child is under that cut-off point. This usually ranges from 14–16 years of age.

[14.54] In circumstances where the child is below the relevant legal age for consent, it is nonetheless regarded as best practice in keeping with art 12 of the UNCRC to also involve the child in the decision-making process as much as possible and seek their assent to participation. For children under the age of legal maturity, it is important that healthcare professionals do not merely pay lip-service to the notion of respecting the child's need for information, but that the child is listened to and provided with sufficient information in a form that is suitable for the child's age to enable him to share the responsibility for the decision-making. This means that the child will not be the only decision-maker but will share this power and responsibility with adults. Difficulties may, of course, arise where there are different views expressed by the child and his parents in this context and ultimately a decision may be made by the adults in the child's best interests to which the child objects. However, if the child's views are to be overruled, the reasons for this should be explained to the child in language that he can understand and efforts should be made to act in a way that most closely accords with the child's wishes where possible.[95]

[14.55] In relation to the provision of information about research, researchers must discuss the purpose of the research, whether there are any direct benefits for the child,

---

93 Medical Research Council Ethics Guide: Medical Research Involving Children (2004).

94 Wendler, 'Assent in Paediatric Research: Theoretical and Practical Considerations' (2006) Journal of Medical Ethics 32: 229–234.

95 Donnelly and Kilkelly, 'Child-Friendly Healthcare: Delivering on the Right to Be Heard' (Winter 2011) Med L Rev, 19, pp 27–54 at 31–32.

the difference between treatment and research, the meaning of research terms used,[96] the nature of each procedure, how long it will continue, the potential harms, the name of the responsible doctor and how children can withdraw from the project.[97] Consent must also be given freely and without any pressure from the researchers or doctors.

Legal provisions in relation to minors

[14.56] The European Communities (Clinical Trials on Medicinal Products for Human Use) Regulations 2004[98] were introduced in Ireland to give effect to Directive 2001/20/EC of the European Parliament, known as the Clinical Trials Directive. The Directive has now been repealed by the 2014 Clinical Trial Regulation.[99] As this is a Regulation rather than a Directive it does not require transposition into national law and takes effect automatically. The Directive provision will however still apply three years from the date of entry into force of the Regulation (28 May 2016) to clinical trials applications submitted before the date of entry into force, and clinical trials applications submitted within one year after the entry into application if the trial sponsor opted for the old system. Therefore it is necessary to examine both sets of provisions.

[14.57] The 2001 Directive, as transposed by the 2004 Regulations in Ireland, provides that a minor is a person under the age of 16 years. By comparison, the 2014 Regulations define a minor as 'a subject who is, according to the law of the Member State concerned, under the age of legal competence to give informed consent'. Therefore under current law in Ireland, for the purposes of participation in clinical trials, anyone over the age of 16 years can consent on his/her own behalf. For all other research that is not governed by the Clinical Trials Regulation, the person must be over the age of 18 years in order to provide consent.[100]

[14.58] Under both the 2001 Directive and the 2014 Regulations, the requirement for informed consent includes the following conditions: every person with parental responsibility for the minor must have had an interview with the investigator, or another member of the investigating team, in which he or she has been given the opportunity to

---

[96] In consent documents, different words are sometimes used to describe the same thing eg 'research project', 'research study', 'research experiment' and 'medical study'. These are considered by researchers as semantically equivalent but parents may rate the risks differently depending on their perception of the description used. See Cico et al, 'Informed Consent Language and Parents' Willingness to Enrol Their Children in Research' (2011) IRB: Ethics & Human Research, Vol 33, No 2.

[97] Royal College of Paediatrics and Child Health: Ethics Advisory Committee: Guidelines for the Ethical Conduct of Medical Research Involving Children (2000). See also van der Pal, Sozanska, Madden, Kosmeda, Debinska, Danielewicz, Boznanski and Detmar. 'Opinions of Children about Participation in Medical Genetic Research' (2011) Public Health Genomics 14 (4–5): 271–278.

[98] SI 190/2004.

[99] Regulation (EU) No 536/2014 of the European Parliament and of the Council of 16 April 2014 on clinical trials on medicinal products for human use, and repealing Directive 2001/20/EC.

[100] Section 23 of the Non-Fatal Offences Against the Person Act 1997 provides a defence to a medical practitioner who accepts the consent of a person aged 16 years to medical, surgical or dental treatment without seeking the consent of the parents. This does not include medical research.

understand the nature, objectives, risks and inconveniences of the trial and the conditions under which it is to be conducted; that person's consent has been given in consultation with the registered medical practitioner who has been treating the minor; the minor has received information according to his or her capacity of understanding, from staff with experience with minors, regarding the trial, its risks and its benefits[101]; and the explicit wish of a minor who is capable of forming an opinion and assessing the information referred to in the previous paragraph to refuse participation in, or to be withdrawn from, the clinical trial at any time is considered by the investigator.

[14.59] Under the 2001 Directive, no incentives or financial inducements may be given to the minor or to a person with parental responsibility for that minor, except provision for compensation in the event of injury or loss. By comparison, art 32 of the new 2014 Clinical Trials Regulation provides that no incentives or financial inducements are given to the subject or his or her legally designated representative except for compensation for expenses and loss of earnings directly related to the participation in the clinical trial. This means that some form of compensation to minors is now permitted albeit that it is limited to expenses and loss of earnings.

[14.60] Under the 2001 Directive, the clinical trial must relate directly to a clinical condition from which the minor suffers or is of such a nature that it can only be carried out on minors, and some direct benefit for the group of patients involved in the clinical trial is to be obtained from that trial. This seems to mean that where the trial is of a non-therapeutic nature, children cannot participate as they will not derive any 'direct benefit' from the research.[102] By contrast the Royal College of Paediatrics adopts a 'minimal risk' standard in relation to research involving children so that non-therapeutic research is not considered unethical or illegal. The College guidelines state that parents may consent to the participation of their children where the risks are sufficiently small to mean that the research can be reasonably said not to go against the child's interests.[103]

[14.61] An important difference between the 2001 Directive and the 2014 Regulation in this context is that, unlike the Directive, the Regulation explicitly addresses the levels of risk and burden minors (and incompetent subjects) may be exposed to in the context of non-therapeutic research. The Regulation adopts a 'minimal risk' threshold in art 32, subs (g) of which provides that a clinical trial can only involve minors where there are scientific grounds for expecting that participation in the clinical trial will produce: (i) a direct benefit for the minor concerned outweighing the risks and burdens involved; or (ii) some benefit for the population represented by the minor concerned and such a clinical trial will pose only minimal risk to, and will impose minimal burden on, the minor concerned in comparison with the standard treatment of the minor's condition. 'This means that clinical trials with IMPs (investigational medicinal products) can be conducted on individual children even if there is no prospect of direct benefit to them. It is sufficient that there is a benefit to the population they represent, ie children in the

---

[101] Article 29 of the 2014 Regulation sets out the requirements for informed consent. See para [14.82] below.

[102] Cave, 'Seen but not heard? Children in clinical trials' (2010) Medical Law Review 18(1):1.

[103] Royal College of Paediatrics, 'Child health: Ethics Advisory Committee guidelines for the ethical conduct of medical research involving children' (2000) 82 Archives of Disease in Childhood 177–182.

same age category.[104] However, these trials may only proceed if the trial contains minimal risk and minimal burden in comparison with the standard treatment of the minor's condition.

[14.62] A difficulty arises in relation to the last phrase of subs (g) 'in comparison with the standard treatment' as it is not clear how research ethics committees will interpret this provision. Westra argues that the only interpretation that has been publicly brought forward so far implies that research ethics committees must compare the research risks and burdens with the risks and burdens the subjects are exposed to when being treated for their condition. As long as the research risks and burdens do not exceed that level, they can be regarded as minimal for the subjects at stake. Thus, the added phrasing sets a so-called relative standard for the concepts of minimal risk and minimal burden: the meaning of 'minimal' depends on the severity of the standard treatment.[105] Where the trial is expected to yield a benefit for the child, then the comparison to standard treatment in order to determine acceptable risk levels is appropriate. However, Wade argues that 'in determining acceptable risk levels for trial which *do not* offer the prospect of direct benefit to the child, this phrase is inappropriate.' Westra agrees that this interpretation is problematic because it means that research ethics committees may make exceptions to the minimal risk and burden requirement. 'They may approve non-therapeutic research with risks and burdens far exceeding the level usually regarded as minimal. This is because the standard treatments of many conditions are quite risky and burdensome.' She believes that 'exposing incompetent research subjects to more than minimal risks and burdens purely for research purposes may occasionally be acceptable, but should always be regarded as a last resort.'

Neonatal research

[14.63] The neonatal period refers to the first four weeks of a child's life. In clinical trials carried out in this early stage of life, researchers aim to discover which treatment is most effective for premature infants who have breathing difficulties, seizures and other difficulties shortly after birth. Therefore, there are clearly sound and important scientific and ethical justifications for carrying out such research. Research on premature infants is in principle similar to research on children of any age prior to maturity in that the locus of decision-making is with their parents or guardians. However, the context in which such research is carried out raises practical and ethical difficulties in relation to informed consent, as the parents may be distressed following a premature and unexpected delivery of the baby, the mother may be physically exhausted and in post-partum pain, and the fact that the baby is in neonatal intensive care is likely to be a source of extreme anxiety for both parents. In an English report arising out of complaints by parents of babies who had been enrolled into such a trial, it was acknowledged that there was general recognition and acceptance in society of the need for, and therefore the need to take part in, research of good quality if there are to be

---

[104] Wade, 'Children in clinical trials in Ireland: addressing the gaps in the legal framework.' In Donnelly and Murray (eds) *Ethical and Legal Debates in Irish Healthcare* (Manchester University Press 2016) at 167.

[105] Westra, 'Ambiguous articles in new EU Regulation may lead to exploitation of vulnerable research subjects.' (2016) J Med Ethics 42:189–191.

advances in medical practice. 'What was totally unacceptable to those interviewed was the apparent lack of adequate explanation, of choice and of consequent properly elicited and recorded consent, and of involvement in later decision making'.[106]

[14.64] Therapeutic research on this category of patients may be justified on the basis that the research has the potential to benefit the child. Therefore, if valid informed consent can be obtained from the parents of the newborn child then, providing the other conditions in relation to minimal risk are satisfied, the research may proceed. However, despite the presence of their signature on a consent form, this will not be sufficient if the parents later complain that their consent was not freely given due to undue influence or pressure from the doctor, particularly where he has a dual role as researcher as well as the person responsible for the treatment of their child.[107] In the face of such an allegation the doctor would have to show that he had adequately explained the gravity of the situation and had taken reasonable steps to ensure that the parent(s) did not overestimate the possible benefits to the child nor underestimated the risks. In light of this it would be best practice, where possible, to have an independent person present during the consent process to provide advice and support to distressed parents, as well as giving information in comprehensible language with as much time as possible in the circumstances for the parents to consider their decision. Details on the consent process involved in such research should be carefully scrutinised by the relevant research ethics committee prior to granting approval for the research.[108]

[14.65] If consent cannot be obtained due, for example, to the absence of the father and the temporary incapacity of the mother due to her medical condition after birth, the situation is very difficult. In an emergency situation where the research drug must be given within a short time after delivery, the mother may be unconscious and the researchers will have to establish that it is in the best interests of the child to be enrolled in the trial.[109] 'But if participation in the trial exposes the child to foreseeable risks which are high or out of proportion to the potential benefits, or participation in the trial deprives the child of the opportunity of receiving alternative treatment which would have been of benefit to her, then inclusion in the trial will be unlawful.'[110] If the mother is not unconscious she may nonetheless be so exhausted, shocked or distressed in the circumstances that this may be thought to preclude her ability to understand the necessary medical information to enable her to make a decision as to whether to consent to her child's participation in the trial. However, the doctor must be extremely cautious in such circumstances before deciding that the mother's psychological condition

---

[106] In addition to research governance failings, there were also allegations that some of the consent forms purportedly signed by the parents were not valid. Report of a Review of the Research Framework in North Staffordshire Hospital NHS Trust, available at http://www.publications.doh.gov.uk/pdfs/northstaffsexec.pdf

[107] See discussion above at para **[14.40]**.

[108] Plomer, 'Participation of Children in Clinical Trials: UK, European and International Legal Perspectives on Consent' (2000) Med Law I Vol 5, 1–24 at 15.

[109] Emergency research and the possibility of a waiver of consent are considered later at para **[14.85]**.

[110] Plomer, 'Participation of Children in Clinical Trials: UK, European and International Legal Perspectives on Consent' (2000) Med Law I Vol 5, 1–24 at 13.

precludes her capacity to give consent.[111] Plomer describes the potential legal liability that might arise in such circumstances:

> Clinicians who proceed to include a new born baby in a clinical trial in an emergency without the parent(s)' consent on the basis that the parents' mental distress or shock impaired their legal capacity, without independent evidence to support their judgment, are undoubtedly leaving themselves open to an action in battery. If the child has not suffered and even benefitted from inclusion in the trial, liability will still arise in battery if the research procedures involved any form of physical intervention or examination of the child's body, as the tort does not require proof of damage but protects instead the physical integrity of the individual's body: the essence of the tort of battery is the 'unpermitted contact'.[112]

Foetal research

[14.66] It is important to carry out research on foetuses and the uterine environment in order to better understand some common diseases affecting children, causes of miscarriage, neurological disabilities and so on. Foetuses may become available for research in Ireland as a result of miscarriage.[113] The distress experienced by a woman who suffers a miscarriage makes it difficult to anticipate how she might be approached in such circumstances to give consent. This issue was briefly addressed in the Report of the Working Group on Post Mortem Practice in 2006,[114] which considered the application of the recommendations of the Madden Report on Post Mortem Practice and Procedure to children who died before birth. Although the focus of the report was to look at the area of post-mortem examinations, the possibility of seeking consent from the parents for the use of the foetal remains for teaching and research purposes was also considered. The Report explains that there is no specific statutory regulation of examination of foetal remains in Ireland. It is therefore unclear whether the foetus would come within the definition of a 'person', as it has not achieved independent existence after birth.

[14.67] In *McGeehan v National Maternity Hospital, Stanley and Rafter*[115] the question arose as to whether the plaintiff was entitled to take an action as a dependant under the Civil Liability Act 1961 on behalf of her child who was stillborn in the National Maternity Hospital in 1991. Section 48(1) of that Act provides that where the death of a person is caused by a wrongful act such that that person, if he had survived, would have been entitled to take an action, then the dependants can bring an action. Section 58 provides that the law relating to wrongs applies to an unborn child for his protection in the same way as if the child were born, provided the child is subsequently born alive. Kearns J held that the only interpretation of the Act is that 'no such wrongful action is deemed in law to take place where the child is not born alive'. However, he also stressed

---

[111] Plomer, 'Participation of Children in Clinical Trials: UK, European and International Legal Perspectives on Consent' (2000) Med Law I Vol 5, 1–24 at 13.

[112] Plomer at 14.

[113] In jurisdictions where abortion is permissible, the aborted foetuses may also be available for research purposes with the consent of the woman.

[114] Report of Working Group into Post-Mortem Practice and Procedure (2006) available at www.health.gov.ie

[115] *McGeehan v National Maternity Hospital, Stanley and Rafter* (21 April 2004) HC, Kearns J.

that he was not deciding the issue 'on the basis that the child was not a person and in any way was to be regarded in any way less than any other citizen, whether born alive or, tragically in this case, as a still birth.'

[14.68] Small amounts of human tissue[116] are removed from the body of a deceased person (including children and foetuses) during post-mortem examination to enable pathologists to conduct a microscopic examination[117] in order to ascertain the exact cause of death. The Report of the Working Group recommends that provided a valid authorisation is given by the family of the deceased, these blocks and slides may be retained and subsequently used for legitimate educational and research purposes by the hospital.[118] These recommendations have not yet been given statutory effect and in the current absence of human tissue legislation in Ireland, it remains a matter of good practice for hospitals to ensure that any research use of foetal remains is subject to consent or authorisation from the parent(s).[119]

Research involving adults lacking capacity to give consent

[14.69] In the same way as it is necessary to conduct paediatric research in order to provide benefit to children, it is also important to carry out research to ensure the future well-being of incapacitated adults while at the same time ensuring that their rights are not infringed:

> Not only is research necessary to help identify, understand and manage the unique diseases and conditions which affect people with mental illness, intellectual disability, age-related illness and critical conditions, it is also necessary to address the atypical effects of standard therapies on their bodies. The poor evidence base, the frequency of negative outcomes and the lack of specific therapies suggest that this research should be regarded as a public health priority. To deny incapacitated adults the benefits of medical research through unduly cautious research regulation is irresponsible; not kind nor caring. It condemns the population of incapacitated adults to poor quality care.[120]

[14.70] The Clinical Trials Directive 2001[121] makes specific provision for research involving adults who are incapable of giving informed consent. Article 5 provides that such persons may be included in a trial only if the research meets the general requirements for research participation amongst the general population, as well as nine

---

[116] Small pieces of tissue are embedded in paraffin wax and stored in boxes.

[117] Shavings of tissue blocks are mounted on glass slides. The glass slides are then stained and placed on the microscope for examination.

[118] Report of the Working Group on Post Mortem Practice (2006) p 12. Available at www.health.gov.ie.

[119] The Health Service Executive has published Standards and Recommended Practices for Post Mortem Examination Services which are available at www.hse.ie.

[120] Liddell et al, 'Medical Research Involving Incapacitated Adults: Implications of the EU Clinical Trials Directive 2001/20/EC' (Autumn 2006) Med Law Review 14, pp 367–417 at 370.

[121] Directive 2001/20/EC of the European Parliament and of the Council of 4 April 2001 on the approximation of the laws, regulations and administrative provisions of the Member States relating to the implementation of good clinical practice in the conduct of clinical trials on medicinal products for human use.

further specific requirements listed below. The general requirements refer to an assessment that the benefits of the proposed trial outweigh the risks; the necessity to give the participant the opportunity to understand the objectives, risks and inconveniences of the trial; the rights of the participants to physical and mental integrity and privacy; the requirement for written consent; the right to withdraw from the trial at any time; and the provision of insurance to cover the liability of the researcher and sponsor of the trial.

[14.71] The additional requirements prescribed by art 5 are follows:

(a)   the informed consent of the legal representative has been obtained; consent must represent the subject's presumed will and may be revoked at any time, without detriment to the subject;

(b)   the person not able to give informed legal consent has received information according to his/her capacity of understanding regarding the trial, the risks and the benefits;

(c)   the explicit wish of a subject who is capable of forming an opinion and assessing this information to refuse participation in, or to be withdrawn from, the clinical trial at any time is considered by the investigator or where appropriate the principal investigator;

(d)   no incentives or financial inducements are given except compensation;

(e)   such research is essential to validate data obtained in clinical trials on persons able to give informed consent or by other research methods and relates directly to a life-threatening or debilitating clinical condition from which the incapacitated adult concerned suffers;

(f)   clinical trials have been designed to minimise pain, discomfort, fear and any other foreseeable risk in relation to the disease and developmental stage; both the risk threshold and the degree of distress shall be specially defined and constantly monitored;

(g)   the Ethics Committee, with expertise in the relevant disease and the patient population concerned or after taking advice in clinical, ethical and psychosocial questions in the field of the relevant disease and patient population concerned, has endorsed the protocol;

(h)   the interests of the patient always prevail over those of science and society; and

(i)   there are grounds for expecting that administering the medicinal product to be tested will produce a benefit to the patient outweighing the risks or produce no risk at all.

[14.72] Some of these requirements have been criticised on the basis that the wording is unclear, ill-advised or unduly restrictive. Article 5 also fails to recognise any exceptions to the requirement for prior consent, which causes severe problems for research into emergency and critical care. It does not define who should be recognised as a legal representative, with the result that Member States have highly disparate definitions with some states such as Austria and Germany imposing a requirement that such a person must be appointed by a judge, whereas in the Netherlands a life companion may act as proxy. In Ireland a person who by virtue of their family relationship with the subject is suitable, available and willing to act may be considered the legal representative. If no such person exists, a person other than a person connected with the conduct of the trial, who is a solicitor nominated by the relevant healthcare provider may act as legal representative.[122] Although some pluralism is perhaps justified, it makes international trials cumbersome and unwieldy as well as enabling some member states to define legal representatives in an overly broad way irrespective of whether they are appropriately qualified or subject to potential conflicts of interest.[123] It would have been preferable to define legal representatives on the basis of their personal relationship with the participant so that they may anticipate the way in which the participant may experience the research, and be ready to revoke consent in circumstances where the burdens of the trial become too great.

[14.73] The 2014 Clinical Trials Regulation[124] has changed this by providing that a legally designated representative is 'a natural or legal person, authority or body which, according to the law of the Member State concerned, is empowered to give informed consent on behalf of a subject who is an incapacitated subject or a minor'. Therefore a family member may only give consent if the law of the relevant Member State gives the family member such authority.[125] The Regulation states that a clinical trial may only be conducted with incapacitated persons where:

(a) the informed consent of their legally designated representative has been obtained;

(b) the incapacitated subjects have received the information referred to in art 29(2) in a way that is adequate in view of their capacity to understand it;

(c) the explicit wish of an incapacitated subject who is capable of forming an opinion and assessing the information referred to in art 29(2) to refuse participation in, or to withdraw from, the clinical trial at any time, is respected by the investigator;

(d) no incentives or financial inducements are given to the subjects or their legally designated representatives, except for compensation for expenses and loss of earnings directly related to the participation in the clinical trial;

(e) the clinical trial is essential with respect to incapacitated subjects and data of comparable validity cannot be obtained in clinical trials on persons able to give informed consent, or by other research methods;

(f) the clinical trial relates directly to a medical condition from which the subject suffers;

(g) there are scientific grounds for expecting that participation in the clinical trial will produce

    (i) a direct benefit to the incapacitated subject outweighing the risks and burdens involved; or

---

[122] European Communities (Clinical Trials on Medicinal Products for Human Use) Regulations 2004 (SI 190/2004), Sch 1 s 2.

[123] Liddell et al, 'Medical Research Involving Incapacitated Adults: Implications of the EU Clinical Trials Directive 2001/20/EC' (Autumn 2006) Med Law Review 14, pp 367–417 at 397.

[124] Regulation (EU) No 536/2014 of the European Parliament and of the Council of 16 April 2014 on clinical trials on medicinal products for human use, and repealing Directive 2001/20/EC, Recital 20.

[125] See discussion of Assisted Decision-Making (Capacity) Act 2015 in Chapter 9.

(ii) some benefit for the population represented by the incapacitated subject concerned when the clinical trial relates directly to the life-threatening or debilitating medical condition from which the subject suffers and such trial will pose only minimal risk to, and will impose minimal burden on, the incapacitated subject concerned in comparison with the standard treatment of the incapacitated subject's condition.

[14.74] The main differences between the 2001 Directive and the 2014 Regulation in this context are:

- In relation to informed consent, the Directive stated that the consent given by the legal representative represents the presumed will of the subject and could be revoked at any time without detriment to the subject. This has been removed from the text of the 2014 Regulation.

- In relation to the provision of information to the subject, the wording of (b) has been changed by the 2014 Regulation to ensure that the subject themselves has received information in a way that is adequate in view of their capacity to understand it. This is more person-centred than the wording of the Directive as it places an obligation on the researcher to give the research subject information in a manner that is tailored to the person's capacity.

- The right of the subject to withdraw from participation in the trial has also been strengthened by the 2014 Regulation. Whereas under the Directive such a wish to withdraw had to be considered by the researcher, it now must be respected by the researcher under the Regulation. The requirement for the subject's wishes to be respected is thus more decisive than under the Directive.[126]

- The provisions in relation to financial inducements have been made more explicit under the 2014 Regulation by a specific prohibition on inducements being paid not only to the subject but also to the legally designated representative, and also clarifying that the prohibition does not apply to compensation for expenses or loss of earnings related to participation in the trial.

- The justification for the participation of incapacitated persons under the Directive was that such research was essential to validate data obtained in clinical trials on persons able to give informed consent or by other research methods and relates directly to a life-threatening or debilitating clinical condition from which the incapacitated adult concerned suffers. The 2014 Regulation reframes the emphasis by stating that the clinical trial must be essential with respect to incapacitated subjects and data of comparable validity cannot be obtained in clinical trials on persons able to give informed consent, or by other research methods and the clinical trial relates directly to a medical condition from which the subject suffers.

- The 2014 Regulation also states that there must be scientific grounds for expecting that participation in the clinical trial will produce a direct benefit to

---

[126] This may still raise issues in respect of incapacitated persons who are used to being treated without consent as they may not understand the difference between treatment and research and may not believe that their wishes not to take part will be respected. See Jackson, *Medical Law, Text, Cases and materials* (3rd edn, 2013) 486.

the incapacitated subject outweighing the risks and burdens involved, or some benefit for the population represented by the incapacitated subject concerned when the clinical trial relates directly to the life-threatening or debilitating medical condition from which the subject suffers. This is broader than the Directive's provisions which imposed a requirement that the research produce a benefit to the subject which outweighed the risks or no risk at all. Rather than requiring that the research incur no risks for the subject, which was considered to be very restrictive as it would be almost impossible to justify any non-therapeutic procedures at all, the Regulation adopts a minimal risk threshold similar to the provisions in relation to research involving minors. This risk is to be assessed relative to the standard treatment of the incapacitated subject's condition.

INFORMED CONSENT

[14.75] It has been stated that 'the duty imposed upon those engaged in medical research…to those who offer themselves as subjects for experimentation… is at least as great as, if not greater than, the duty owed by the ordinary physician or surgeon to his patient.'[127] In *Halushka v University of Saskatchewan*[128] the court held that there can be no exceptions to the ordinary requirements of disclosure in the case of research as there may well be in ordinary medical practice. 'The subject of medical experimentation is entitled to a full and frank disclosure of all the facts, probabilities and opinions which a reasonable man might be expected to consider before giving his consent.'

[14.76] The theory, history and principles of informed consent have been discussed in Chapter 10 in the context of medical treatment. The importance of respecting self-determination is recognised in both ethics and law in most jurisdictions and is now regarded as an essential prerequisite for research with human beings.[129] This was not always the case as prior to the 20th century people were used for research without their knowledge and contrary to their wishes in many cases. In modern times it is widely recognised and enshrined in law as well as in ethical guidance documents that participants must be given the opportunity to choose whether to participate based on appropriate information as well as an assessment of their capacity to comprehend the information and make a decision.

[14.77] The kind of information commonly required to be given to potential participants includes the nature of the research, its purposes, risks and benefits, alternatives to participation, who will carry out the research, and whether participants can later change their mind. The amount of information can be overwhelming, and the Belmont Report also rightly points out the importance of ensuring that the research participants understand the data presented to them.

---

[127] *Halushka v University of Saskatchewan* 52 WW R 608 (Sask 1965).

[128] *Halushka v University of Saskatchewan* 52 WW R 608 (Sask 1965).

[129] However, in some cultures autonomy is not valued in the same way as in Western countries so, for example, husbands may give consent for the involvement of their wives, or the tribal elders may give consent on behalf of those living in their community.

Researchers have a moral responsibility to adapt information so that it is understandable by potential research participants. It should be presented in an organised way in languages…that are understood by potential subjects. The need to ensure comprehension of the study becomes more important as the study's degree of risk increases.[130]

[14.78] The way in which information is presented forms a crucial part of ensuring comprehension, as researchers commonly use a technical vocabulary that acts as a barrier to understanding for those unfamiliar with such terms. However, there is a danger too in over-simplifying information if watered-down, non-technical language is used. The way in which the information is framed may reflect a bias on the part of the researcher which may lead potential participants to focus on the potential benefits without reflecting carefully on the risks. When poorly conducted, the informed consent process may be little more than 'an empty ritual, a piece of paper put in front of a person for a quick signature'.[131] Equally, if the consent process is too lengthy and complicated there is a risk that potential participants may not give close enough attention to their involvement. Therefore, it is difficult for researchers to know what standards of disclosure should be used in this regard and many researchers express frustration with the current informed consent process and find it a confusing area of law.[132]

[14.79] Research is, of course, different from medical treatment in that it is not always possible to know in advance what the potential risks and benefits will be. Thus, some argue that consent can never be fully informed in the same way as perhaps consent to medical treatment can be:

> Despite the extensive laboratory testing of a new drug, the fact remains that a clinical trial is an experiment. The information most useful to a potential volunteer – what will happen? – is unknown. Even the known 'facts' such as toxicology reports and statistics from animal testing are merely interpretations of data. A statistician can easily manipulate such data to imply the desired results. Those with experience in financial accounting may testify to the manipulability of numerical data. [133]

[14.80] In the design of information sheets and consent forms, researchers, doctors and research ethics committees discuss at length how to effectively communicate the risks of participation. As mentioned above, although the readability of these documents must be set at a level that enables participants of all reading abilities to access the information, it is also the case that if the document is overly simple it may not be specific enough to communicate the particular risks and it may necessarily be too long and onerous to expect a layperson to read. Ziker says that 'efficiency demands the standardisation of informed consent documents. However, to effectively communicate health risks, we must resist standardisation and consider the subjective, individual needs of the volunteer. The informed consent document should serve merely as a starting point for the communication.'[134] Further study is required to scrutinise the gap between the ethical

---

[130] Murphy, *Case Studies in Biomedical Research Ethics* (2004) Mass Inst of Technology at 54.
[131] Murphy, *Case Studies in Biomedical Research Ethics* (2004) Mass Inst of Technology at 57.
[132] Dodds-Smith, 'Clinical Research' in Dyer (ed) *Doctors, Patients and the Law* (Blackwell Publishing, 1992) 140 at 155.
[133] Ziker, 'Reviving Informed Consent: Using Risk Perception in Clinical Trials' (2003) Duke L & Tech Rev 15.
[134] Ziker, 'Reviving Informed Consent: Using Risk Perception in Clinical Trials' (2003) Duke L & Tech Rev 15.

ideal of informed consent to research and the reality of the communication between researchers and participants in order to inform the further development of effective policies and informed consent processes in this context.

[14.81] In terms of legal regulation and ethical guidance on informed consent,[135] art 5 of the Council of Europe Convention on Human Rights and Biomedicine[136] states the general principle that 'an intervention in the health field may only be carried out after the person concerned has given free and informed consent to it. This person shall beforehand be given appropriate information as to the purpose and nature of the intervention as well as on its consequences and risks.' The Clinical Trials Directive 2001,[137] as transposed in Ireland by the Clinical Trials Regulations 2004,[138] is more specific in its provisions. It requires that consent be given freely after that person is informed of the nature, significance, implications and risks of the trial, is evidenced in writing, dated and signed, or otherwise marked, by that subject (or recorded in writing in the presence of two witnesses if the subject is unable to mark his or her consent).[139] Part 3 requires that the subject has had an interview with the investigator, or another member of the investigating team, in which he or she has been given the opportunity to understand the nature, objectives, risks and inconveniences of the trial and the conditions under which it is to be conducted, the subject has been informed of his or her right to withdraw at any time without any detriment, and has been given a contact point through which to obtain further information.

[14.82] The Clinical Trials Regulation 2014[140] (which came into effect in May 2016) defines informed consent as 'a subject's free and voluntary expression of his or her willingness to participate in a particular clinical trial, after having been informed of all aspects of the clinical trial that are relevant to the subject's decision to participate.'[141] Article 29 sets out the requirements for a valid informed consent by the subject or his or her legally designated representative. It imposes similar requirements as were imposed by the 2001 Directive in relation to consent being written, dated and signed. It also stipulates that adequate time shall be given for the subject or his or her legally designated representative to consider his or her decision to participate in the clinical trial.

[14.83] Article 29(2) states that information given to the subject or, where the subject is not able to give informed consent, his or her legally designated representative for the purposes of obtaining his or her informed consent shall:

---

[135] See guidance provided by the HSE National Consent Policy, Part 3 available at www.hse.ie.

[136] Convention for the Protection of Human Rights and Dignity of the Human Being with regard to the Application of Biology and Medicine: Convention on Human Rights and Biomedicine, Oviedo 1997.

[137] Directive 2001/20/EC of the European Parliament and of the Council of 4 April 2001 on the approximation of the laws, regulations and administrative provisions of the Member States relating to the implementation of good clinical practice in the conduct of clinical trials on medicinal products for human use.

[138] European Communities (Clinical Trials on Medicinal Products for Human Use) Regulations, 2004 (SI 190/2004).

[139] Paragraph 3 of Part 1 of Schedule 1.

[140] Regulation (EU) No 536/2014 of the European Parliament and of the Council of 16 April 2014 on clinical trials on medicinal products for human use, and repealing Directive 2001/20/EC.

[141] Recital 21.

(a)   enable the subject or his or her legally designated representative to understand:

    (i)   the nature, objectives, benefits, implications, risks and inconveniences of the clinical trial;

    (ii)   the subject's rights and guarantees regarding his or her protection, in particular his or her right to refuse to participate and the right to withdraw from the clinical trial at any time without any resulting detriment and without having to provide any justification;

    (iii)   the conditions under which the clinical trial is to be conducted, including the expected duration of the subject's participation in the clinical trial; and

    (iv)   the possible treatment alternatives, including the follow-up measures if the participation of the subject in the clinical trial is discontinued.

The information shall

(b)   be kept comprehensive, concise, clear, relevant, and understandable to a layperson;

(c)   be provided in a prior interview with a member of the investigating team who is appropriately qualified according to the law of the Member State concerned;

(d)   include information about the applicable damage compensation system referred to in art 76(1); and

(e)   include the EU trial number and information about the availability of the clinical trial results.

[14.84] This information shall be prepared in writing and be available to the subject or, where the subject is not able to give informed consent, his or her legally designated representative. In the interview referred to in point (c) above, special attention shall be paid to the information needs of specific patient populations and of individual subjects, as well as to the methods used to give the information. In the interview it shall also be verified that the subject has understood the information. This is a welcome advance on the requirement in the 2001 Directive that the subject must have been given 'the opportunity to understand' what they were consenting to, as there is now an obligation on the researcher to inquire whether the subject has understood the information given and the nature of their participation. The Regulation also states that national laws may require both the signature of the incapacitated person *and* the signature of his or her legally designated representative on the informed consent form. Similar provisions exist in relation to minors.

EMERGENCY RESEARCH

[14.85] Although it is widely accepted that the consent of the participant is necessary for participation in research, this is usually not possible in emergency research. Such research is very valuable and important in seeking new and more effective treatments for brain trauma, stroke, heart attack and other sudden incapacitating conditions where patients are rushed to hospital for emergency treatment. Typically, treatment for these conditions must commence within hours, preferably as soon as possible. It is often impossible to seek consent within such a tight time frame because the patient is unconscious or unaccompanied. It is necessary to consider how best we should balance the values involved in emergency research, including the crucial need for research to test promising treatments for patients in an emergency setting as weighed against the need to protect individuals from exploitation and harm in the event that the new therapies turn out to be harmful, and respect for autonomy which entails seeking consent from persons prior to their participation in research.[142]

[14.86] Although medical treatment may be given to a person in such circumstances in order to save their life or prevent serious injury, this does not apply to research in the same way. Some argue that research in these circumstances is ethically unsound and should simply not take place at all but this would inhibit very valuable research and would be contrary to public health. It may be argued that unless participation in research offers the patient the best chance of saving their life or avoiding serious injury, it may not be ethically justifiable to enrol them in a trial without their consent.[143] However, Brody argues that even when individual autonomy cannot be respected because consent cannot be obtained, the research can still be conducted ethically, as long as other values are sufficiently protected, namely great social need, potential for direct benefit to the participants, and protection of individuals from exploitation and harm.[144]

[14.87] The Council of Europe Convention on Human Rights and Biomedicine (1997),[145] provides that consent to treatment may be dispensed with only when because of an emergency situation the appropriate consent cannot be obtained (art 8).[146] The purpose of this article is to allow the doctor to act immediately in an emergency without having to wait until the patient or his representative gives consent. This applies to situations such as where the patient is in a coma following an accident and it is necessary to treat in order to protect the patient's life and/or health. Treatments without consent are limited to those which cannot be delayed. However, the Convention does not explicitly refer to medical research in this context and therefore art 8 does not extend to the participation of patients in emergency research, particularly since the exception given in the article is expressly limited to circumstances where treatment is necessary for 'the benefit of the health of the individual concerned'.

[14.88] Articles 16 and 17 of the Convention refer to the need to obtain specific consent in writing in advance of a clinical trial and there is no mention of an exception for emergency research in either of these two articles. It has been argued that if the benefit in question was intended by the writers of the Convention to extend to the potential, hypothetical benefits of research rather than the proven benefits of a given treatment then arguably art 8 would have been drafted differently. 'In particular, one would have expected the expression "potential benefit" to have been expressly used to indicate that the emergency provisions contained in art 8 extend to the conduct of research consistently with arts 16 and 17 which regulate the conduct of research and refer to the hypothesised benefits of research as "potential".'[147]

---

[142] Brody, 'In Case of Emergency: No Need for Consent' (1997) 27 Hastings Centre Rep at 7.

[143] Jackson, *Medical Law: Text, Cases and Materials* (OUP, 2010) at 479.

[144] Brody, 'In Case of Emergency: No Need for Consent' (1997) 27 Hastings Centre Rep at 7.

[145] Available at www.coe.int.

[146] Ireland is not currently a signatory to the Oviedo Convention.

[147] Plomer, 'Participation of Children in Clinical Trials: UK, European and International Legal Perspectives on Consent' (2000) Med Law I Vol 5, 1–24 at 17.

[14.89] In 1996 the European Union adopted guidelines for good clinical practice through the International Conference on Harmonisation of Technical Requirements for Registration of Pharmaceuticals for Human Use (ICH). The objective of the guidelines is to provide a unified standard for the EU, Japan and the US to facilitate the mutual acceptance of clinical data by the regulatory authorities in these jurisdictions. The guidelines are more extensive than the Convention in respect of certain matters such as informed consent, as they require the disclosure of information to the participant in relation to reasonably foreseeable risks and benefits, alternative procedures, rights to compensation in the event of trial-related injury, confidentiality of records and the right to withdraw from the trial at any time. In relation to emergency research the Guidelines allow such research to proceed in the absence of prior consent in the following circumstances:

- the situation is an emergency;
- prior consent of the subject is not possible;
- the subject's legally acceptable representative is not available;
- measures to protect the rights, safety and well-being of the subject have been described in the protocol and/or elsewhere;
- the relevant ethics committee has approved the measures and protocol, and;
- the subject or his/her legally acceptable representative should be informed about the trial as soon as possible and consent to continue should be requested.

[14.90] There appears to be greater flexibility in the ICH guidelines in this context in that they do not require that the intervention is for the immediate benefit of the individual participant. Therefore, emergency research is not restricted to therapeutic research only and may include non-therapeutic research. 'Such a possibility, however, will undoubtedly give rise to legitimate concerns that the interests of highly vulnerable patients run the danger of being sacrificed in the interest of science. The requirement that the research receive prior approval from an independent research board is undoubtedly an important control. But the requirement that the protocol should contain a description of measures to protect the rights, safety and well-being of the human subject seems too unspecific and weak to import any meaningful limits.'[148]

[14.91] In Ireland the European Communities (Clinical Trials on Medicinal Products for Human Use) Regulations 2004[149] did not make any provision for an exception to the requirement for consent in cases of emergency research. The regulations provide that research on adults lacking capacity to give informed consent is only allowed if, inter alia: consent is given by the person's legal representative, the trial relates to a life-threatening or debilitating condition from which the person suffers, it has been approved by a relevant ethics committee and there are grounds for expecting that it will produce a benefit to the patient outweighing the risks or produce no risk at all. This means that, in principle, if no legal representative has previously been appointed in relation to the patient (which, for example, would commonly apply in circumstances involving

---

[148] Plomer, 'Participation of Children in Clinical Trials: UK, European and International Legal Perspectives on Consent' (2000) Med Law I Vol 5, 1–24 at 20.

[149] SI 190/2004 implementing the European Clinical Trials Directive 2001/20/EC, amended subsequently by SI 878/2004 (charges), SI 374/2006 (investigators brochure and other changes) and most recently in 2009 (SI 1/2009) to add advanced therapy medicinal products.

otherwise healthy adults who have sustained injuries in a road traffic accident), the patient cannot be enrolled in the trial.

[14.92] In the UK, regulations were introduced in 2006 to allow such trials to proceed notwithstanding the absence of consent from a legal representative provided that it is necessary to act as a matter of urgency, it is not practicable to obtain consent from a legal representative, the procedure has been approved by an ethics committee and steps must be taken to seek consent either from the patient himself after recovery of capacity or from a legal representative as soon as practicable after the initial emergency has passed.[150]

[14.93] The responses of Member States to the problems raised by emergency research have been diverse. Some countries adopted a waiver system which allows the research to proceed in the absence of proxy consent if treatment and associated research must commence as a matter of urgency. In most instances, however, it was not a complete waiver but rather a deferral of consent until the patient or his legal representative could be informed and their consent sought to continued participation. The period of time during which consent is waived is usually capped until such time as the emergency circumstances have passed, and as a further protection, notice must be posted at the clinical trial sites notifying the public that such trials are being conducted on patients who are unable to consent.[151]

[14.94] In the United States the Food and Drug Administration (FDA) and the Department of Health and Human Services issued regulations that provide a waiver of informed consent requirements for emergency research under certain conditions.[152] The regulations allow a waiver when the potential subject is in a life-threatening situation, where consent of the subject or a surrogate cannot be obtained, and available treatments are unproven or unsatisfactory. Additional protections for participants are provided by the requirement to publicly disclose the proposed research and consult with the community from which the patients may be drawn. However, Carnahan argues that although in principle a waiver represents a justifiable exception to the requirement of informed consent due to the importance of advancing medical research in emergency care, the wording of this waiver is fraught with ambiguities and may be unethical, as it is not drawn sufficiently narrowly to assure respect for individual autonomy and fails to provide clear guidelines to aid the researcher in complying with the waiver's requirements.[153]

[14.95] The 2014 Clinical Trials Regulation[154] now deals with clinical trials in emergency situations in art 35 which provides that informed consent to participate in a

---

[150] Medicines for Human Use (Clinical Trials) (Amendment No 2) Regulations 2006.

[151] Discussed by Liddell *et al*, 'Medical Research Involving Incapacitated Adults: Implications of the EU Clinical Trials Directive 2001/20/EC' (Autumn 2006) Med Law Review 14, pp 367–417 at 404.

[152] 21 CFR 50.24 (1999).

[153] Carnahan, 'Promoting Medical Research Without Sacrificing Patient Autonomy: Legal and Ethical Issues Raised by the Waiver of Informed Consent for Emergency Research' (1999) 52 Okla L Rev 565.

[154] Regulation (EU) No 536/2014 of the European Parliament and of the Council of 16 April 2014 on clinical trials on medicinal products for human use, and repealing Directive 2001/20/EC.

clinical trial may be obtained, and information on the clinical trial may be given, after the decision to include the subject in the clinical trial, provided that this decision is taken at the time of the first intervention on the subject, in accordance with the protocol for that clinical trial and that all of the following conditions are fulfilled:

(a) due to the urgency of the situation, caused by a sudden life-threatening or other sudden serious medical condition, the subject is unable to provide prior informed consent and to receive prior information on the clinical trial;

(b) there are scientific grounds to expect that participation of the subject in the clinical trial will have the potential to produce a direct clinically relevant benefit for the subject resulting in a measurable health-related improvement alleviating the suffering and/or improving the health of the subject, or in the diagnosis of its condition;

(c) it is not possible within the therapeutic window to supply all prior information to and obtain prior informed consent from his or her legally designated representative;

(d) the investigator certifies that he or she is not aware of any objections to participate in the clinical trial previously expressed by the subject;

(e) the clinical trial relates directly to the subject's medical condition because of which it is not possible within the therapeutic window to obtain prior informed consent from the subject or from his or her legally designated representative and to supply prior information, and the clinical trial is of such a nature that it may be conducted exclusively in emergency situations;

(f) the clinical trial poses a minimal risk to, and imposes a minimal burden on, the subject in comparison with the standard treatment of the subject's condition.

[14.96] Following such an intervention, informed consent in accordance with art 29[155] must be sought to continue the participation of the subject in the clinical trial, and information on the clinical trial shall be given, in accordance with the following requirements:

(a) regarding incapacitated subjects and minors, the informed consent shall be sought by the investigator from his or her legally designated representative without undue delay and the information referred to in art 29(2) shall be given as soon as possible to the subject and to his or her legally designated representative;

(b) regarding other subjects, the informed consent shall be sought by the investigator without undue delay from the subject or his or her legally designated representative, whichever is sooner and the information referred to in art 29(2) shall be given as soon as possible to the subject or his or her legally designated representative, whichever is sooner.

For the purposes of point (b), where informed consent has been obtained from the legally designated representative, informed consent to continue the participation in the clinical trial shall be obtained from the subject as soon as he or she is capable of giving informed consent.

---

[155] See para **[14.82]** above.

GENETIC RESEARCH

[14.97] There are two broad categories of research involving human genetics – (i) research designed to learn about the genome, including studies exploring the relationship between genes and persona characteristics or susceptibility to disease, and (ii) research designed to change the genome, which involves inserting 'normal' genes into individuals who have undesirable mutations.[156] Genetic research can be very complex and sometimes suffers from a negative public perception.[157] In a national study carried out in Ireland in 2005, while those surveyed were generally positive about genetic research, there were some reservations regarding the ethics of such research.[158] O'Neill states that public trust in medicine and science has faltered despite reported successes in this field, increased efforts to respect personal rights, stronger regulations and consideration of environmental concerns than was previously the case.[159]

[14.98] Some genetic research is performed by recruiting individuals to donate tissue samples, including blood, saliva, and other bodily fluids, and/or to provide information about their family medical history. In other cases, researchers use pre-existing tissue samples that were originally obtained for other purposes such as medical or surgical treatment, which was stored as part of the person's medical records.[160] Biological material donated for research purposes can also be stored as part of a bio bank. In many cases research can be carried out on samples in conjunction with associated clinical information in relation to the donor of the sample, for example research to identify a marker for a particular disease. In such cases the researchers would need to know the diagnosis of the donor in order to see if a relationship exists between a specific marker and the disease. However they would not need to access the identity of the donor. However, in other cases researchers may need to know the identity of the donor in order to link longitudinal clinical data obtained from the donor over a number of years with genetic markers in the sample to see how diseases develop over time. Issues relating to

---

[156] Coleman et al, *The ethics and regulation of research with human subjects* (Lexis Nexis 2005) at 697.

[157] See Medical Research Council's Report in the UK – Public Perceptions of the Collection of Human Biological Samples (2000), which showed a wide variation in knowledge and understanding of the goals of genetic research, and a negative association with this type of research where understanding was lacking. Available at www.mrc.ac.uk.

[158] For instance, consistent with generally positive attitudes to medical research, over 70% agreed that 'new genetic developments will result in cures for many diseases'. In relation to the ethical question 'Is research on human genetics tampering with nature?', results indicated some concern among the Irish public. A significant proportion (42%) felt that it was tampering with nature. Participants also appeared to be well informed (ie less than 10% reported they had never heard of any of the listed forms of genetic research). Highest approval levels were reported for stem cell research using adult human tissue (49%) and for cloning human cells to combat disease (42%). Cousins, McGee, Ring, Conroy, Kay, Croke, and Tomkin, *Public Perceptions of Biomedical Research: A Survey of the General Population in Ireland* (Health Research Board: 2005). Psychology Reports. Paper 8.

[159] O'Neill *Autonomy and Trust in Bioethics* (Cambridge University Press, 2002) p 11.

[160] The issue of property rights in biological material used for research purposes was discussed in *Moore v Regents of the University of California* 51 Cal 3d 120, 271 Cal Rptr 146, 793 P 2d 479, cert denied 499 US 936 (1991). See Ch 13 at para **[13.22]**.

consent, anonymisation and data protection are clearly of crucial importance here in reassuring donors that their rights and interests are protected. These issues have been considered in Chapter 13 in the context of bio banks.[161]

[14.99] Genetic research is also actively pursued by pharmaceutical companies in order to investigate the genetics of drugs responsiveness so as to improve the benefit/risk profiles of medicines in the patient populations for whom their products are prescribed. Pharmacogenetics involves the study of DNA variations and their influence on individual differences in drug responses. Research is also ongoing to investigate the effect of polymorphisms[162] in candidate genes known to play a role in a drug's mechanism of action. Research into the genetics of disease characteristics will also help to understand disease susceptibility and biological pathways in order to produce therapies that are better targeted to the disease.[163] Although investment by such companies in research has produced significant advances in medicine, there is also an associated danger involved in the injection of a profit motive into the system by which new medicines are developed and tested in humans. In particular, there is a concern that doctors who act as researchers acquire financial interests in the drug research they conduct on humans which conflict with their responsibility to protect human participants from unnecessary risk.[164] These issues are considered below.

[14.100] The tragic death of Jesse Gelsinger in 1999 during a gene therapy trial shook the field of clinical research in a similar way to the Tuskegee experiments described above.[165] Gelsinger suffered from a rare metabolic disorder that prevents the body from breaking down ammonia. Many people with this disorder die at a young age, but Gelsinger had a mild version and led a fairly normal life through medicine and a special diet. Since a single-gene defect is responsible for OTCD, researchers considered it a prime candidate for gene therapy, a still-experimental treatment that attempts to replace defective genes with normal ones. When he was 18 years old, Gelsinger enrolled in a clinical trial at the University of Pennsylvania as an altruistic measure. He knew he would not benefit from the study himself, but wanted to help those with more severe cases. However, shortly after the researchers injected Gelsinger with the replacement genes his ammonia levels skyrocketed. Within a few days, he suffered brain damage and organ failure, and was in a coma. His family removed him from life support and he died. A Food and Drug Administration (FDA) investigation concluded that the scientists involved in the trial, including the lead researcher, Dr James M Wilson (University of Pennsylvania), broke several rules of conduct:

- inclusion of Gelsinger as a substitute for another volunteer who dropped out, despite Gelsinger having high ammonia levels that should have led to his exclusion from the trial;

---

[161] Para **[13.66]**.

[162] The presence of genetic variations within a population.

[163] Renegar et al, 'Returning Genetic Research Results to Individuals: Points to Consider' (2006) Bioethics Vol 20, No 1, pp 24–36.

[164] Gatter, 'Financial Conflicts of Interest in Human Subjects Research; Domestic and International Issues' in Iltis, Johnson and Hinze (eds) *Legal Perspectives in Bioethics* (Routledge, 2008) 29.

[165] Para **[14.22]**.

- failure by the university to report that two patients had experienced serious side effects from the gene therapy, and;
- failure to disclose, in the informed-consent documentation, the deaths of monkeys given a similar treatment.

[14.101] The investigation also found that James Wilson did not disclose to the Gelsingers that he was conducting the clinical trial with a private company in which he had a stake, and stood to make a substantial profit if the trial was successful. The FDA sanctioned the researchers and Gelsinger's family sued Wilson and others involved in the study, leading to an out-of-court settlement. It was thought that the revelations, government sanctions and civil lawsuit would lead to widespread reform. However, many argue that this has not come to pass and that things have moved in the opposite direction. More than ever, clinical trials are the lifeblood of the pharmaceutical and biotechnology industries. Their profitability depends upon developing new drugs, which in turn depends upon continued testing on human subjects. Companies can lose substantial sums of money each day that a new drug's approval is held up and demand for quick, easy and plentiful access to human test subjects has therefore become insatiable as companies seek to swiftly move drugs from 'bench to trench'. This situation has led to a number of emerging and proposed research practices which cause concern, including the recruitment of participants from low educational and socio-economic backgrounds and the proliferation of the conduct of clinical trials in the developing world where research ethics governance may not be highly valued.[166] The issue of conflict of interest is discussed further later.

FEEDBACK OF RESEARCH RESULTS TO PARTICIPANTS

[14.102] An important issue on which there is still some disagreement internationally is whether and what research data should be fed back to individual research participants. Although this applies to all forms of medical research, it is perhaps particularly evident in debates about genetic research. Part of the challenge here is that it is argued that genetic research data is not 'information' for the participant-as-patient. Researchers argue that they should not be under an obligation to report individual findings to participants as the data has not been confirmed in a clinical setting and its release may be open to misinterpretation by the participant who may suffer harm in the form of anxiety and distress, as a result. However, there is increasing ethical literature stressing the importance of respect for patient autonomy and the requirement to do more than treat participants as a means to an end. Some commentators call for a routine disclosure of research results referring to individual participants, while others restrict the obligation to the communication of general results referring to the sample of participants.[167]

---

[166] Obasogie, 'Ten Years Later: Jesse Gelsinger's Death and Human Subjects Protection' Bioethics Forum. Available at www.geneticsandsociety.org.

[167] See Kollek and Petersen, 'Disclosure of Individual Research Results in Clinico-Genomic Trials: Challenges, Classification and Criteria for Decision-Making' (2011) J Med Ethics 37:271–275; Knoppers et al, 'The Emergence of an Ethical Duty to Disclose Genetic Research Results: International Perspectives' (2006) Eur J Hum Genet;14:1170–8; (contd.../)

[14.103] There are different types of individual data that may be sought by participants. Apart from identifying information possibly held by researchers (even if coded to respect participants' privacy), genetic mutations may also have been identified amongst the samples which might have clinical relevance for the individuals concerned. These may, for example, relate to the development of cancer or other diseases and could indicate a need for the individual to follow up with further clinical tests. Research participants are sometimes invited to indicate on their consent form whether they wish to receive information from the research. If the participants have given their consent to receive such information, the question arises as to what information should be fed back and on what basis. If clinical benefit to the participant is to be used as the benchmark for disclosure, then care must be taken to ensure that the quality standards used for detection of the genetic markers are of high clinical validity and consistency. There is no consensus on what constitutes clinical utility in this context and it is likely that the assessment of the clinical utility of genetic data varies widely. It is therefore argued that clinical utility is not sufficient as a criterion to determine whether and in what circumstances individual research results should be disclosed.[168] However, although researchers may argue against disclosure in terms of cost, time and their lack of clinical expertise, Kollek and Petersen argue that taking patient autonomy into account points to the opposite conclusion. They say that the fact that clinical utility cannot be defined in the context of research points instead to a duty to report all individual research findings, irrespective of their character and clinical utility.

[14.104] In addition to feeding back research results to the individual participants, other issues arise in relation to disclosure to genetic relatives of the participants, as the information may have relevance for them also.[169] The potential conflict that may arise where the individual does not consent to wider disclosure of genetic information is considered in Chapter 8. This also points to the need for appropriate counselling of participants both in relation to the significance of the findings for themselves, but also the potential significance for other relatives. There is a danger that the offer of disclosure of genetic data may raise unrealistic expectations or fears and therefore any information disclosed should be made as clear and specific as possible. It may be preferable for the participant to choose a doctor to whom the information may be given and who may be better able to communicate the significance of the findings for the individual, though some may argue that this is a paternalistic approach.

[14.105] There is also an issue here in relation to what is referred to as 'incidental findings'. This relates to information about the subject that is learned during the course of the study that does not directly relate to the research. For example, in a research study

---

[167] (\...contd) Ravitsky and Wilfond, 'Disclosing Individual Genetic Results to Research Participants' (2006) Am J Bioeth; 6:8–17; Murphy J et al, 'Public Expectations for Return of Results from Large-Cohort Genetic Research' (2008) Am J Bioeth; 8:36–43; Renegar G et al, 'Returning Genetic Research Results to Individuals: Points to Consider' (2006) Bioethics Vol 20 No 1 pp 24–36.

[168] Kollek and Petersen, 'Disclosure of Individual Research Results in Clinico-Genomic Trials: Challenges, Classification and Criteria for Decision-Making' (2011) J Med Ethics 37:271–275 at 272.

[169] See Symposium on 'Should we offer Genomic Research Results to a Participant's Family, Including after the Participant's death?' (2015) Journal of Law, Medicine and Ethics, Vol 43.3.

on genetic markers for a particular disease, it may be necessary to analyse samples from a number of generations of the same family. During the study the researchers may discover information about the family that is not related to the disease being studied, such as the fact that one of the subjects has a serious medical condition that he or she is unaware of, or that an individual's parents are not who he or she thought they were. The question arises as to what should be done with this information.

[14.106] It may be argued that researchers should confine their disclosure to data that is relevant to the research itself as they do not have a clinical relationship with the participant and do not therefore have the duty of care a physician would have to his patient. Other arguments against disclosure are that it would be too time consuming and costly to contact research participants, and that disclosure would therefore inhibit important research. The return of individual results to participants would also require that biobanks retain links to identifying information, which implies the risk of breaching confidentiality. It is also argued that participants also risk being harmed by being informed about and acting on incidental findings whose quality, accuracy, clinical utility, or even origin is uncertain.[170] 'It is further important to consider that giving participants information about incidental findings blurs the distinction between research and healthcare, a confusion that resembles the therapeutic misconception. The therapeutic misconception is held by individuals who believe that they receive care when they function as research participants.'

[14.107] Arguments in favour of disclosure include the duty of beneficence, in other words, that if the researcher has information that could be of clinical benefit to the participant through giving him or her the opportunity to seek further clinical tests and early treatment, the researcher has an ethical duty to provide such information to the participant. It is also argued that it is in keeping with respect for autonomy and the right to self-determination of participants to provide important information in time so that they can change their lives and therefore be more autonomous. There is also an argument in favour of disclosure on grounds of reciprocity, in other words that participants are providing a valuable and important service to society by their participation in research and deserve reciprocal benefits of being informed of matters that are of direct clinical benefit to them.[171]

[14.108] It is also important to note in this context the right not to know one's genetic characteristics as stated in art 5(c) of the Universal Declaration on the Human Genome and Human Rights 1997 which provides that 'the right of each individual to decide whether or not to be informed of the results of genetic examination and the resulting consequences should be respected.' Therefore researchers must take care to ensure before giving information to participants that this is information they have indicated they wish to know. A clearly worded consent form which anticipates such incidental findings and communicates the research team's policy on such findings is therefore very important in this regard.

---

[170] Viberg et al, 'Incidental findings: the time is not yet ripe for a policy for biobanks', (2014) European Journal of Human Genetics 22, 437–441.

[171] Viberg et al, 'Incidental findings: the time is not yet ripe for a policy for biobanks', (2014) European Journal of Human Genetics 22, 437–441.

[14.109] It is also important to draw a distinction between an incidentally discovered disease and an incidentally discovered increased genetic *risk* for disease of unclear predictive value. Bio bank research and rapidly increasing studies in genomics continue to identify many genes and biomarkers associated with risk of disease. 'Genetic testing for monogenic disorders are well established in health services, but little is yet known of the best way to handle complex risk information associated with multifactorial disorders in which the predictive importance of individual elements – genetic, epigenetic, or environmental – will differ for different individuals. The value of being informed about an incidentally discovered genetic risk (be it inherited or caused by a virus) is therefore much more difficult to ascertain than that for an incidentally discovered pathogenic condition revealed, for example, in a brain imaging study.'[172]

[14.110] It might be concluded conclude that 'If results can enhance treatment, if they concern a material risk, if they have clinical utility, if they are life-saving – then they should be disclosed. It may seem that no one could object to these proposals, as they condition disclosure to what clearly would be beneficial for the participant.'[173] However it remains open to question whether these conditions of analytical validity, clinical significance, and actionability imply the same straightforward beneficence to the disclosure of complex genetic risk information of unclear predictive value. Between genes and multifactorial diseases like diabetes, cardiovascular disease, and dementia, they explain that there are complex processes involving both genes and environment. The disease depends not only on deviation in several, rather than single, genes but also on interaction with environmental factors such as diet, exercise, and smoking. The information given to participants will be an expression of a risk that is dependent not only on various environmental factors but also on the penetrance of the disease (ie how likely it is that a particular genetic defect will be expressed and actually lead to symptoms). The meaning of the risk information also depends on the level of accuracy of the analytical test.[174]

[14.111] Viberg et al believe that participant's responses to offers of genetic risk information are relevant only if they understand what that information really is and how it differs from information about disease or immediate disease risk that can be obtained from imaging studies or other tests.[175] There is no generally agreed policy on this issue and the approach usually taken is that it is a matter for the researchers to formulate and state their policy in relation to incidental findings in their research documentation for ethical approval and to communicate this policy clearly to participants so that they know what information they can reasonably expect to receive.

---

[172] Viberg et al, 'Incidental findings: the time is not yet ripe for a policy for biobanks', (2014) European Journal of Human Genetics 22, 437–441.

[173] Viberg et al, 'Incidental findings: the time is not yet ripe for a policy for biobanks', (2014) European Journal of Human Genetics 22, 437–441.

[174] Viberg et al, 'Incidental findings: the time is not yet ripe for a policy for biobanks', (2014) European Journal of Human Genetics 22, 437–441.

[175] See also Knoppers, 'Paediatric research and the communication of not-so incidental findings,' (2012) Paediatrics & Child Health, Vol 17 Issue 4, p 190–192.

CONFLICT OF INTEREST

[14.112] A number of research 'scandals' in the late 1990s in the US raised issues regarding researchers' and institutional conflicts of interest, the most troubling of which results from a financial interest held by the researcher and/or his institution in the outcome of the clinical trial.[176] The existence of conflicts of interest and their non-disclosure to research participants has led to concerns about the validity of the informed consent process which is a prerequisite for the ethical conduct of clinical trials. The most notable illustration of this problem is that of Jesse Gelsinger, referred to above, where it was alleged that the financial interests of the researcher caused him to take unreasonable risks with Jesse Gelsinger's life that had not been disclosed to Gelsinger, and caused the university's research ethics board to approve both the trial and the fact that a conflict of interest existed.[177]

[14.113] Financial conflicts of interest may take a number of different forms.[178] Firstly, researchers and research institutions have an interest in obtaining grants from drug companies to conduct future research, as they depend on such grants to help fund substantial portions of their operating expenses. They must compete for these grants with other researchers and institutions and thus offer to conduct the trial in such a way as to encourage the sponsor to choose their particular institution. Secondly, many researchers and institutions have an ownership interest in the material being tested and often establish start-up or spin-off companies to patent their intellectual discoveries. Thirdly, they may own shares in the drug company that is sponsoring the clinical trial. Fourthly, they may have a consulting position within the drug company, arising from the company's desire to benefit from the knowledge of academic expertise. Fifthly, they often receive fees for each participant recruited to the trial.[179]

[14.114] Financial interests such as those mentioned above may also be supplemented by interests in academic success and promotion, publication interests and other important indirect or non-financial interests. Such financial interests are said to create conflicts because they raise the possibility that researchers will conduct clinical trials other than with strict scientific objectivity and may not prioritise the safety and well-being of the human participants in the trials they conduct. This may be evidenced by researchers not observing strict adherence to recruitment criteria, deviating from research protocols, failing to report negative findings of research, failing to inform

---

[176] Further details of these research scandals are provided by Goldner, 'Regulating Conflicts of Interest in Research: The Paper Tiger Needs Real Teeth', 53 St Louis U LJ 1211 (2009) at 1229–1231.

[177] *Gelsinger v Trustees of the University of Pennsylvania* (Phila Cnty Ct of CP 2000).

[178] Gatter, 'Financial Conflicts of Interest in Human Subjects Research; Domestic and International Issues' in Iltis, Johnson and Hinze (eds) *Legal Perspectives in Bioethics* (Routledge, 2008) at 31.

[179] €27m was paid in Ireland in 2015, according to figures compiled by member companies and published on the IPHA's transferofvalue.ie website. Of this, €6.8m related to fees paid to healthcare professionals.

participants of risks and failing to transfer participants from experimental to standard treatment when their condition has deteriorated.[180]

[14.115] There is also evidence that the involvement of the pharmaceutical industry in research distorts the results.[181] It has been argued that there is a statistically significant relationship between positive findings in studies funded by for-profit entities versus those funded by not-for-profit sources, between industry sponsorship and pro-industry conclusions and between author conflicts of interest and the greater likelihood of reporting a drug to be superior to placebo.[182] Goldner claims that 'Industry funding may result in study designs that are more likely to lead to favourable results, such as utilizing protocols that involve placebos or other poor comparators, doses that are inappropriate, carefully constituted experimental populations, inappropriate surrogate endpoints, trials whose lengths are sufficiently short so as to be unlikely to show side effects, and definitions that are unlikely to show activity or not likely to show side effects.'

[14.116] Bekelman et al also found a 'significant association between industry sponsorship and pro-industry conclusions' in biomedical research, and Lexchin et al showed that studies sponsored by pharmaceutical companies were four times more likely to have outcomes favouring the sponsors' products than studies funded by other sources.[183] Bradley says that 'while there is no evidence that industry funding produces studies of lower methodological quality, it may be that, by setting the research agenda, determining the trial design and suppressing or delaying unfavourable findings, the industry subtly influences the impression of drug therapies under research.'[184] Marcia Angell, former editor of the influential New England Journal of Medicine, states that '[I]t is simply no longer possible to believe much of the clinical research that is published, or to rely on the judgment of trusted physicians or authoritative medical guidelines.' She says that the medical profession needs to wean itself almost entirely from its pervasive dependence on industry money, that conflicts of interest 'corrupt the

---

[180] Gatter, 'Financial Conflicts of Interest in Human Subjects Research; Domestic and International Issues' in Iltis, Johnson and Hinze (eds) *Legal Perspectives in Bioethics* (Routledge, 2008), at 34.

[181] Lexchin and O'Donovan state that there is a significant body of empirical sociological evidence of 'corporate bias' in the science of drug testing, bias that has resulted in the pharmaceutical industry being decisive in shaping regulatory policy. Furthermore, they say that recent systematic reviews have shown strong evidence of 'sponsorship bias' in the production of knowledge about pharmaceuticals, evidence that pharmaceutical industry funding of clinical trials significantly enhances the chances of pro-industry results. Lexchin and O'Donovan, 'Prohibiting or 'Managing' Conflict of Interest? A Review of Policies and Procedures in Three European Drug Regulation Agencies', (2009) Social Science & Medicine 1–5.

[182] Goldner, 'Regulating Conflicts of Interest in Research: The Paper Tiger Needs Real Teeth' 53 St. Louis U LJ 1211 (2009) at 1219.

[183] Bekelman, Li and Gross, 'Scope and Impact of Financial Conflicts of Interest in Biomedical Research: A Systematic Review', Journal of the American Medical Association, Vol 289 (2003) pp 454–465; Lexchin et al 'Pharmaceutical Industry Sponsorship and Research Outcome and Quality: Systematic Review', British Medical Journal Vol 326 (2003) pp 1167–1170.

[184] Bradley, 'The Medical Profession and the Pharmaceutical Industry: Entwined, Entangled or Ensnared?' in O'Donovan and Glavanis-Grantham (eds) *Power, Politics and Pharmaceuticals: Drug Regulation in Ireland in the Global Context* (Cork University Press, 2008) 117–134.

medical profession, not in a criminal sense, but in the sense of undermining the impartiality that is essential both to medical research and clinical practice'. She argues that:

> There is clearly also a need for the medical profession to wean itself from industry money almost entirely. Although industry–academic collaboration can make important scientific contributions, it is usually in carrying out basic research, not clinical trials, and even here, it is arguable whether it necessitates the personal enrichment of investigators. Members of medical school faculties who conduct clinical trials should not accept any payments from drug companies except research support, and that support should have no strings attached, including control by drug companies over the design, interpretation, and publication of research results.[185]

[14.117] The challenge in this area is to identify policies that will promote greater accountability among research institutions and healthcare professionals in relation to their oversight of conflicts of interest. This may, for example, take the form of regulators imposing an absolute prohibition on certain types of conflicts as well as permitting other forms subject to disclosure (for example by way of a public register) and close monitoring.[186] Goldner argues that in order to be effective, an abolitionist position should be enforced with vigour and with meaningful and appropriately severe sanctions for serious violations that would have a significant deterrent effect.[187] He believes that such a policy is unlikely in the United States at least and that a more appropriate response would be to develop new federal conflict of interest committee regulations which would require that institutions develop conflict of interest committees to provide an ethical analysis of the effect of a conflict on research and the appropriate way to remedy it when necessary. A majority of members without institutional ties would be preferable on such a committee.

[14.118] Goldner's proposals for reform include recommendations that such regulations should also establish requirements for disclosure of all financial conflicts of interest of any amount to the conflict of interest committee, provide a non-exclusive list of potential management techniques, grant the conflict of interest committee the authority to prohibit research from commencing or continuing until conflict of interest concerns are resolved and require that serious or continuing violations are reported to appropriate governmental agencies. Violations of such regulations, that is the failure of an institution to deal with conflict of interest concerns appropriately and in accordance with the federal guidelines, should result in suspension of federal funding of research for some or all projects at the institution. Researchers who fail to report conflicts or who otherwise violate conflicts of interest regulations should be subject to a range of sanctions, including limitations on participation in research projects, debarment from receiving federal funding and other penalties. He suggests that regulations should also require

---

[185] Angell, 'Drug Companies & Doctors: A Story of Corruption' (January 15, 2009) *New York Review of Books*, www.nybooks.com.

[186] See useful discussion of this issue in the US context by Goldner, 'Dealing with Conflicts of Interest in Biomedical Research: IRB Oversight as the Next Best Solution to the Abolitionist Approach' (2000) 28(4) Journal of Law, Med & Ethics 379–404.

[187] Goldner, 'Regulating Conflicts of Interest in Research: The Paper Tiger Needs Real Teeth' 53 St. Louis U LJ 1211 (2009) at 1246–1249.

public disclosure of investigator conflicts of interest, both via a publicly accessible website, and also in informed consent documents provided to participants. Institutions should also be required to mandate training of all investigators in both the ethical norms that underlie appropriate conflict of interest reporting and management prior to the submission of any research protocols for institutional approval.

[14.119] At the EU level, the European Research Council (ERC) which supports and funds pan-European research published a Scientific Misconduct Strategy in 2012[188] which takes the view that host institutions of the ERC applicants and grant holders have the primary responsibility for the detection of scientific misconduct and for the investigation, and adjudication of any breaches of research integrity that may arise. In addition all concerns about potential scientific misconduct or suspected breaches of research integrity concerning an ERC applicant or project will be addressed by the ERC within the applicable legal and procedural framework. The 2014 Clinical Trial Regulation also provides that in the application dossier presented for authorisation in respect of a clinical trial 'any conditions, such as economic interests and institutional affiliations, that might influence the impartiality of the investigators shall be presented'.[189]

[14.120] There are also guidelines in place in Ireland on this issue from the Medical Council as well as the Irish Pharmaceutical Healthcare Association, which represents the pharmaceutical industry in Ireland and which has published a Code of Practice in compliance with advertising regulations for medicinal products.[190] The Medical Council states in the 8th edition of the Guide to Professional Conduct and Ethics (2016)[191] as follows:

> 25.6 If you are paid, directly or indirectly, by pharmaceutical, medical device or other commercial companies or organisations to conduct medical research, you must make sure that such payment does not influence your study design or interpretation of research data.
>
> 25.7 If you are paid, directly or indirectly, from pharmaceutical, medical device or other commercial companies or organisations in connection with medical research, you must address any potential conflict of interest and disclose the payment in any publication of research results.[192]

---

[188] www.erc.europa.eu/.

[189] Regulation (EU) No 536/2014 of the European Parliament and of the Council of 16 April 2014 on clinical trials on medicinal products for human use, and repealing Directive 2001/20/EC Annex 1 para 66.

[190] See www.ipha.ie/alist/codes-of-practice.aspx. See also www.transferofvalue.ie/ for details of payments made by pharmaceutical companies.

[191] Medical Council, Guide to Professional Conduct and Ethics (8th edn, 2016) available at www.medicalcouncil.ie/.

[192] Further guidance on conflicts of interest is also provided in para 62 of the Medical Council's Guide (2016).

LEGAL REGULATION OF CLINICAL TRIALS IN IRELAND

[14.121] The European Directive on Clinical Trials 2001[193] was transposed into Irish law by the European Communities (Clinical Trials on Medicinal Products for Human Use) Regulations 2004.[194] These regulations replaced the controls previously applicable to the conduct of clinical trials on medicinal products for human use under the Control of Clinical Trials Acts 1987 and 1990. Therefore, they did not impact on any other activities traditionally carried out by ethics committees, such as trials not involving medicines. Issues dealt with in the regulations include procedures for obtaining a favourable ethics committee opinion; procedures for obtaining authorisation for the conduct of clinical trials from the Health Products Regulatory Authority; controls that apply to the manufacture, supply and importation of investigational medicinal products; obligations for the reporting of adverse events; obligations for compliance with standards of good clinical practice (GCP) and good manufacturing practice (GMP).

[14.122] Currently all interventional clinical trials must be authorised by the Health Products Regulatory Authority (HPRA)[195] following review of detailed medical and scientific data which will include data relating to laboratory and animal testing and tests for toxicity. The researchers must also obtain a positive opinion from a recognised Research Ethics Committee,[196] which can reject a clinical trial on ethical grounds. Research ethics committees (RECs) therefore play a very important role in the regulation and governance of clinical research. The role of the REC is to provide independent advice on the extent to which a research proposal complies with recognised ethical standards. The REC must be satisfied about the scientific quality of the research proposal and of its conformity with national law. In addition to their role in the protection of participants, RECs also specifically help to ensure that research is soundly based and trustworthy, and consequently that medical interventions and treatments prescribed to patients have been assessed adequately.[197] Once authorisation has been received from the HPRA and the Ethics Committee, a clinical trial can then be carried out by the pharmaceutical company or commissioned to medical/academic institutions, as well as specialist clinical research companies.

[14.123] The legal framework for clinical trials has now been replaced by the Clinical Trials Regulation 2014[198] which became applicable on 28 May 2016. Since this is a Regulation rather than a Directive, it is directly binding in Member States without the need for transposing legislation. The 2001 Directive has been repealed by the new

---

[193] Directive 2001/20/EC of the European Parliament on the approximation of laws relating to the implementation of good clinical practice in the conduct of clinical trials on medicinal products for human use. (OJ L121 01.05.2001 p. 34–44).

[194] SI 190/2004, which came into force on 1 May 2004.

[195] Formerly known as the Irish Medicines Board.

[196] Twelve RECs were recognised by the Department of Health as the supervisory authority under Reg 7 of the European Communities (Clinical Trials on Medicinal Products for Human Use) Regulations 2004.

[197] Council of Europe Steering Group on Bioethics 'Guide for Research Ethics Committee Members' (2010) available at www.coe.int.

[198] Regulation (EU) No 536/2014 of the European Parliament and of the Council of 16 April 2014 on clinical trials on medicinal products for human use, and repealing Directive 2001/20/EC.

Regulation except that it will still apply for three years from 28 May 2016 to clinical trials applications submitted before the entry into application (28 May 2016) and clinical trials applications submitted within one year after the entry into application if the sponsor opted for old system.

[14.124] The Clinical Trials Regulation aims to create an environment that is more favourable and efficient for conducting clinical trials, with the highest standards of patient safety, for all EU Member States. Under the 2001 Directive there was an attempt to harmonise legal requirements in Member States to enable multi-jurisdictional trials to be conducted more easily but this was not successful as Member States transposed the Directive in differing terms in their own jurisdictions. The need to comply with different regulations in different states made it difficult to perform a given clinical trial in several Member States and was seen as putting the EU at a competitive disadvantage in relation to research and clinical trials. In order to encourage and facilitate such research it was recognised that the administrative burdens of compliance with different legal requirements in different Member States would have to be addressed. This has been achieved by the agreement of the Member States to introduce the new measures by way of Regulation which has automatic legal effect in exactly the same terms in all Member States. 'Divergences of approach among different Member States will be therefore kept to a minimum.'[199]

[14.125] Part of the process is therefore designed to simplify the procedures for the submission of an application dossier for the authorisation of a clinical trial. Under the new Regulation, the multiple submission of largely identical information should be avoided and replaced by the submission of one application dossier to all the Member States concerned through a single submission portal.[200] This streamlined application procedure via a single entry point, known as an EU portal, for all clinical trials conducted in Europe, should help to make EU research more efficient, productive and ultimately more competitive. Registration via the portal will be a prerequisite for the assessment of any application.

[14.126] On submission of an application dossier to the EU portal for authorisation of a clinical trial, the sponsor[201] will propose one of the Member States concerned as the reporting Member State. The application dossier must contain, inter alia, details about the conduct of the clinical trial, including the scientific context and arrangements taken; identification of the sponsor, investigators, potential subjects, subjects, and clinical trial sites; details of the investigational medicinal products and, where necessary, the auxiliary medicinal products, in particular their properties, labelling, manufacturing and control; and measures to protect subjects. Within 10 days from the submission of the application dossier, the reporting Member State must validate the application and notify the sponsor, through the EU portal, whether the clinical trial applied for falls within the scope of the Regulation and whether the application dossier is complete. The timeline of

---

[199] Regulation (EU) No 536/2014 of the European Parliament and of the Council of 16 April 2014 on clinical trials on medicinal products for human use, and repealing Directive 2001/20/EC Recital 5.

[200] Article 5.

[201] Defined as an individual, company, institution or organisation which takes responsibility for the initiation, for the management and for setting up the financing of the clinical trial.

10 days is significant as art 5 provides that where the reporting Member State has not notified the sponsor within the period of 10 days, the clinical trial applied for shall, by default, be deemed to fall within the scope of the Regulation and the application dossier shall be considered complete.

[14.127] Article 3 of the Regulation states that a clinical trial may be conducted only if: (a) the rights, safety, dignity and well-being of subjects are protected and prevail over all other interests; and (b) it is designed to generate reliable and robust data. Article 4 provides that a clinical trial shall be subject to scientific and ethical review which must be performed by an ethics committee in accordance with the law of the Member State concerned. Therefore the Regulation takes the position that it should be left to the Member State concerned to determine the appropriate body or bodies to be involved in the assessment of the application to conduct a clinical trial and to organise the involvement of ethics committees within the timelines for the authorisation of that clinical trial as set out in this Regulation.

[14.128] In relation to the composition of the body with responsibility for the assessment of the clinical trial application dossier, art 9 provides that Member States must ensure that the persons validating and assessing the application do not have conflicts of interest, are independent of the sponsor, of the clinical trial site and the investigators involved and of persons financing the clinical trial, as well as free of any other undue influence. Member States must also ensure that the assessment is done jointly by a reasonable number of persons who collectively have the necessary qualifications and experience and at least one layperson shall participate in the assessment. Special consideration must be given to the assessment of clinical trials which involve subjects who are minors, incapacitated persons, pregnant and breastfeeding women, people in emergency situations, or other identified specific population groups, such as elderly people or people suffering from rare and ultra-rare diseases. The body carrying out the assessment should avail of specific expertise in the relevant subject area such as paediatrics, and consider relevant advice on clinical, ethical and psychosocial questions in the field of the relevant disease and the patient population concerned

[14.129] Articles 6 and 7 set out in more detail what the assessing body will consider in its assessment of the application dossier. It will consider the anticipated therapeutic and public health benefits taking account of the following (not an exhaustive list):

- the characteristics of and knowledge about the investigational medicinal products;
- the relevance of the clinical trial, including whether the groups of subjects participating in the clinical trial represent the population to be treated, or if not, the explanation and justification for this;
- the current state of scientific knowledge;
- whether the clinical trial has been recommended or imposed by regulatory authorities in charge of the assessment and authorisation of the placing on the market of medicinal products;
- the reliability and robustness of the data generated in the clinical trial, taking account of statistical approaches, design of the clinical trial and methodology, including sample size and randomisation, comparator and endpoints;

- The risks and inconveniences for the subject, taking account of the characteristics of and knowledge about the investigational medicinal products and the auxiliary medicinal products; the characteristics of the intervention compared to normal clinical practice; the safety measures, including provisions for risk minimisation measures, monitoring, safety reporting, and the safety plan; the risk to subject health posed by the medical condition for which the investigational medicinal product is being investigated;

- Compliance with the requirements concerning the manufacturing and import of investigational medicinal products and auxiliary medicinal products;

- Compliance with the labelling requirements;

- The completeness and adequateness of the investigator's brochure;

- Compliance with the requirements for informed consent set out in this Regulation;

- Compliance of the arrangements for rewarding or compensating subjects with the requirements set out in this Regulation and investigators;

- Compliance of the arrangements for recruitment of subjects with the requirements set out in this Regulation;

- Compliance with Directive 95/46/EC (Data Protection Directive);

- Compliance with the applicable rules for the collection, storage and future use of biological samples of the subject.

Following assessment, each Member State concerned shall notify the sponsor through the EU portal as to whether the clinical trial is authorised, whether it is authorised subject to conditions, or whether authorisation is refused. Many of the other provisions of the Regulation have been discussed earlier in this Chapter.

[14.130] For health research that does not come within the Clinical Trials Regulation, Part 3 of the proposed Health Information and Patient Safety Bill[202] in Ireland provides for a voluntary, national, streamlined research ethics approval structure. The Bill proposes a single point of contact via the Health Information and Quality Authority (HIQA) and single ethical approval for national or regional health research. Health research is defined broadly as 'human health research' but does not cover otherwise governed health research such as clinical trials.

[14.131] The Bill sets out provisions in relation to the approval and membership of research ethics committees, the factors to be taken into consideration by a research ethics committee before granting ethics approval, and it also sets out the relationship between these provisions and the Data Protection Acts, including the provision of an avenue for researchers to apply for a data protection consent exemption in certain limited and restricted circumstances. It is not clear at the time of writing when this Bill will be enacted and therefore further discussion of its proposed provisions will be postponed until future editions of this book.

---

[202] Available at www.health.gov.ie.

Index

737

50748242

* 5 0 7 4 8 2 4 2 *